PROBATION, PAROLE,

and COMMUNITY CORRECTIONS

PROBATION, PAROLE, and COMMUNITY CORRECTIONS

Second Edition

Edited by
Robert M. Carter
Leslie T. Wilkins

JOHN WILEY & SONS, INC.

New York / London / Sydney / Toronto

Library of Congress Cataloging in Publication Data:

Carter, Robert Melvin, 1929-   comp.
  Probation, parole, and community corrections.

  Edition for 1970 published under title: Probation
and parole.
  Includes bibliographical references and index.
  1. Probation—Addresses, essays, lectures.
2. Parole—Addresses, essays, lectures.
3. Community-based corrections—Addresses, essays,
lectures.   I. Wilkins, Leslie T., joint comp.
II. Title.

HV9278.C28 1976   364.6'3   75-44332
ISBN 0-471-13845-2
ISBN 0-471-13846-0 pbk.

Printed in the United States of America

10 9 8 7 6 5 4 3 2

Preface

The first edition of this anthology was published in 1970, 6 years ago; yet, of the 52 selections in the current edition, 35 did not appear in 1970—indeed, they could not have been included because they had not yet appeared in print. And even among the few selections that appear in both editions, a significant proportion deal with matters of history or relate to statements by official bodies with regard to policy or correctional ethics.

The fact that it has been considered necessary at this time to prepare a complete revision of this anthology may, of course, indicate several possibilities. It could be that little of classical or timeless significance is ever written in this area and that most materials concerning probation and parole are ephemeral and perhaps trivial. On the other hand, it could signify that there has been so much rapid and significant change in probation and parole that these recent upheavals could be represented only by constructing a very different anthology.

Although there has been and still is much trivia in the annals and journals of corrections, the particular area of parole has undergone extraordinary change in the last 6 years. These have been changes not only of procedure but also of substance, including philosophy and ethical concerns. There have, of course, been rumblings of change in many other parts of the criminal justice system, but it is in parole decisionmaking that revisionist or revolutionary thinking has had the most important impact on practice.

There can be little doubt that the American Society of Friends (Quakers) has had tremendous impact on the design of penal systems over the last 2 centuries. The Pennsylvania system was modeled upon their philosophies of reform through penitence. Another major landmark in penal policy must now be recognized, again originating from the Quaker movement. In 1971, *A Report on Crime and Punishment* prepared for the American Friends Service Committee was published wherein they modify, to the point of reversal, the earlier perspective. They note, "(T)he horror that is the American prison system grew out of an eighteenth-century reform by Pennsylvania Quakers and others against the cruelty and futility of capital and corporal punishment. This two-hundred-year-old experiment has failed." There is no doubt that the influence of the penitentiary model ranged far beyond the shores of the United States for the Quakers sold their ideas well. The buyers quickly became convinced of the value of the product. Offenders could be "treated," and the way to solve the problem of crime was by reformation of the criminals. Of course the means for obtaining the reformation of the offender have been interpreted differently at different times and places. However, the essential idea of the modification of the "personality" of the individual has remained central, whether through the medium of the provision of work skills, behavioral modification, group therapy, religious conversion, or other methods, not excluding the use in recent times of chemicals and surgical procedures.

The layman's current view of the treatment of offenders fits very closely to the professional view of the recent past; offenders are to receive "treatment" that will reduce the probability that they will commit further crimes. The current professional view of "treatment," as it is now provided, is that it has been given a fair trial and has failed all reasonable tests. The search for alternative philosophical bases for the disposition of offenders has perhaps been one of the major reasons for the rapidity of change in the thinking and procedures of probation and parole.

Disillusionment with the prison and other forms of incarceration has led to the search for community-based alternatives; these newer forms of corrections still seem, in general, to be based on the belief that offenders can be reformed, provided they are given "support," "help," "guidance," or "supervision." There is also the idea that the public can be protected because the offender can be watched—surveillance is part of the package. Because of the importance of this form of "treatment," this edition includes a new section (Section V) covering community-based corrections.

The connection between the basic idea of treatment and the concept and practice of probation and parole is self-evident. However, the difficulty of reconciling the demand for *equity* in dispositions with individualized treatment in each case has, at last, come to be recognized. The major change in policy of the United States Board of Parole and the Adult Authority of the State of California, for example, derives directly from a decision of principle to opt for the concept of *equity* as the dominant value determining parole decison-making policy. With the emphasis on equity, the indeterminate sentence and the uncertainty on the part of the offender as to the period of time he will be detained in incarceration has been challenged. It seems that equity and indeterminacy (the central underpinning of any treatment model) are correctional oil and water. Furthermore if detention is to be rational, it would seem reasonable to suggest that the offender himself is entitled to know the information used to arrive at the decision and how it is used in his particular case to mean a specific period of incarceration.

Notes on significant research, court decisions, and the other stimulations for the changes that have taken place, both in practice and in the contents of this anthology, are contained in the introduction to each of the 8 sections of this edition. It should not be inferred that we see special merit in those selections that appear in both editions—they are not necessarily timeless or especially significant. Rather they represent a particular concern that we consider to be deserving of coverage and recognition; it is certainly possible that other materials address the same issues as well or better. We would stress that the inclusion or exclusion of any particular selection should not be interpreted as support for the concept that what has been or is being done in probation, parole, or community corrections is the best that might be done. The views of the two editors differ in many respects and we have attempted to be as objective as possible in our search of and selection from the literature; we know that we have included certain perspectives with which we both disagree. We do not claim that our anthology is devoid of deficiencies and defects—for those we are responsible.

We express our deep appreciation to the authors and the publishers of the selections in this volume for their kind permission to reprint. It is clear that the developments that have taken place in probation, parole, and community-based corrections have resulted, in large measure, from those whose writings appear in this anthology.

The purpose of this edition is the same as that of the first edition—to provide both the student and the practitioner with convenient access to some of the most significant literature in the field. By compilation into one volume of the important contributions of official bodies, administrators, learned societies, and practitioners, as well as researchers and teachers, the reader may be able to appreciate more fully the heritage and tradition of probation, parole, and community corrections and the scope of current thinking in these fields. The extent of what remains to be done should be as obvious from this volume as that which has been and is being accomplished.

Robert M. Carter

LOS ANGELES, 1975

Leslie T. Wilkins

ALBANY, 1975

Contents

ix

PROBATION, PAROLE,

and COMMUNITY CORRECTIONS

CONTROVERSY
OVER
REHABILITATION

Not long ago there was almost universal agreement among both academic criminologists and practitioners in the field that offenders not only should, but also could, be rehabilitated. Today a very large proportion of those who could claim to be experts take the view that offenders are not being rehabilitated; many take the view that they cannot be rehabilitated, while others think that attempts at rehabilitation are undesirable on ethical grounds. Perhaps the more sophisticated viewpoint is that represented by the last class of opinions. This group does not deny that it might possibly become feasible to change behaviors of offenders, but it is argued that any measures that could be effective would be so intrusive that it would not be morally acceptable to use them. A variation of this belief is that it is more dehumanizing to treat a person as "sick" than to treat him as "wicked." Therefore a policy for the treatment of offenders that refers to the moral concept of "just deserts" has been put forward. In simple terms, the suggestion is that the "punishment should fit the crime."

Of course the various theories, viewpoints, and ethical arguments are not as simple as characterized briefly above. The flavor of this debate and various viewpoints are reflected in selections presented in this section. For each general perspective there are many variants upon which books could be, and indeed already have been, written. If we are accused of giving undue emphasis to the emerging antitreatment/rehabilitation schools of thought, it is because there has been more literature published in the last 100 years that takes the treatment/rehabilitation approach, and this traditional viewpoint is being challenged as a failure.

Perhaps the most influential document published since the first edition of this anthology is the report of the Society of Friends Service Committee from which we have abstracted a summary. The whole report is quite short (some 179 pages) and since there can be no doubt about the importance of this work, we recommend, to the student who is not immediately convinced by the abstracts, that the full work be read. We are reminded of the importance of the Society of Friends in the development of prisons and prison reform over the last 200 years. It is surprising to find the present report putting forward views that conflict so strongly and directly with those that were historically argued. If the Friends Committee, with so much investment in the rehabilitative model, has changed its viewpoint, we must view this changed perspective even more seriously.

The Society of Friends document, research results summarized for us in the article by Robert Martinson, and the views expressed by Norval Morris and Gordon Hawkins strongly suggest that no kind of treatment of offenders has any better outcome than any other. Some may take the view that anything done is equally effective; others, that everything is equally ineffective or equally damaging. Treatments that amount to almost no intervention in the life of the offender and treatments that are most intrusive have been compared; when allowance is made for the exposure to risk and the initial probability of success or failure, no significant differences are found. It should be noted, however, that nowhere has it been deemed possible to experiment with a placebo. Thus although we may reasonably infer that all treatments are equal, because all treatments do nothing ($T_1 = T_2 = T_3 \ldots = 0$), we cannot prove the last term, but we can point to the different magnitudes and the widely different costs of the treatments.

The treatment (or punishment) of the offender is not, of course, the sole purpose of the criminal justice machinery. It is also believed that what is done to one offender is supposed to have an effect on the behavior of the remainder of society. We present one perspective on this aspect of criminal justice with the paper by Norval Morris and Frank Zimring.

While it is true that more and more people are taking the view that the problem of crime cannot be simplified to the problem of the criminal, no one takes the view that nothing should be done to the proven offender. Even if it is true that dealing with offenders will not stop crime, we are not going to stop dealing with offenders. If we cannot give a treatment that reduces the probability of further offenses (by, say, therapy, trade training, behavior modification, or even physical surgery), at least we can keep the offender off the streets; we can isolate or insulate him from "normal" people. If the system cannot deliver reconditioned human beings, the system must identify for society those who are likely to be troublesome. Society may relax its demands on the system to remodel if it can demand prediction—"if you cannot modify behavior to be acceptable, tell us who is not going to behave acceptably."

It is not difficult to believe in the feasibility of efficient prediction of the probability of dangerous criminal behavior. Even in business, prediction works —life actuarial tables, accident insurance, and the like are clear examples; surely such methods seem as though they could be used. The article by Leslie Wilkins, however, indicates why these different kinds of prediction cannot be compared. While everyone dies at some time, few persons commit violent crimes—the experience base is very different. There can be no predictive statements, no matter upon what basis they are made, which do not have two kinds of error. There are those who are incorrectly predicted as failures who would succeed, and there are those who are incorrectly predicted as successes who would fail. The ratio of false positives to false negatives varies with the proportion of the population to be classified, as well as the power of the prediction instrument. These technical considerations cannot be separated from ethical issues—no prediction can be completely and always correct and there is the value to be attributed to the "trade-off."

Some might take the view that while it is theoretically interesting to speculate on the ethical factors involved in various predictive systems, the methods of prediction are so poorly developed in the field of criminal justice that it is better to take such actions as would be ethical on the assumption that we cannot predict at all. However, there are occasions where ethical and logical constraints require us to use whatever predictive ability we have in order to assist those concerned with making rational decisions. Suppose, for example, that a person has been advised by a medical practitioner to have a particular operation. The operation is explained, but to give his informed consent, the patient wants to know whether his chances of survival are greater after than before and the exact probability as to whether he may not survive the operation. These predictions cannot be totally accurate, but what better basis has the layman for his decision than the best estimation in probability terms that the expert can give him? Can the medical practitioner refuse to give an estimate of probabilities because he cannot estimate them with complete accuracy? Are we in a position that is not morally comparable? We shall return to the issues of prediction again in Section VIII.

The idea of treatment and the hope of rehabilitation has come to be accepted by laymen at the time that it is beginning to be rejected by experts. The students who enter the field of criminal justice will normally enter as laymen with beliefs in rehabilitation and the hope that they can help offenders. The evidence is that they might well be able to help offenders, but that they have no real grounds for expecting "pay-off" in terms of reduced crime. If they consider it wrong to provide help for persons who are not going to be grateful to them for what they have done and show this gratitude by modification of their behavior, they might consider a different profession.

The major issue in the debate about rehabilitation in this editorial viewpoint is not whether treatment can be made to work (a question of efficiency), but rather a matter of learning how to measure costs and of determining the relative payoffs for society on the one hand and the individual on the other. When this is done, the ethics of the balance between society and the individual will determine the choices to be made.

1

Crime and Criminal Justice at the Turn of the Century

LESLIE T. WILKINS

We are focusing our attention today on the turn of the century—the year 2000. Does this seem a long way off? Does 1986 seem to be half way there, or considerably less than half way? In some respects, we can say that 1986 is half way towards the year 2000, because we can do the simple arithmetic involved. But in terms of the character, quality and types of events, we would do well to assume that a difference of any number of years in the more distant future is greater than a similar difference at more proximate dates. The ten years from 1990 to 2000 may be expected to see more significant changes than the ten years from 1980 to 1990. This is the inference which must be drawn from the best data we have, as interpreted by the great majority of experts in all fields.[1]

SOURCE. *Annals of the American Academy of Political and Social Science,* **408,** July 1973, pp. 13–26. Reprinted with permission of the editor, *Annals of the American Academy of Political and Social Science.*

[1] On this most futurists agree. Some of the features of accelerating change are discussed by Margaret Mead. See, for example, Margaret Mead, "The Future: Prefigurative Cultures and Unknown Children," in A. Toffler, ed., *The Futurists* (New York: Random House, 1972).

NON-LINEAR TIME

What is the significance of this non-linear idea of time upon our concepts of justice, crime, police, the courts and the other services or procedures concerned with social control through law? Clearly, the legal process has tended, and still tends, to be reactive rather than proactive. Situations first arise, and then procedures are worked out or adapted to cope with the changed situations or changed perspectives. We are all familiar with the Blue Laws; with the divergence between the current legal view of the use of certain stimulants and contemporary social philosophy and medical opinion; with the differential difficulties in legalizing acts currently illegal, as distinct from the difficulties in making additional acts illegal. Laws are easier to make than to un-make. Thus, an increasing residue of inappropriate legislation tends to remain on the statute books. New legislation could, perhaps, be made in advance of a problem, but it would be difficult, or impossible, to remove legislation—to legalize acts—before the climate of opinion was past ready.

Legislation, by reason of its very nature, has difficulties in coping with projections and probabilities; future events, no matter how probable, do not provide a strong argument. Legislation must, by this token, and indeed almost by definition, always be out-of-date![2] If the rate of change is itself changing—and there seems to be considerable agreement that this is so—then it follows that we must postulate that legislation will become more and more irrelevant to current situations, as we project the time base for "current" further and further towards 2000. If the disparity between law and the needs of contemporary social control is mismatched, then that degree of mismatching will tend to increase as we move towards the next century.

CAN THE RULE OF LAW SURVIVE TO 2000?

If this argument is considered to be reasonable, then we might assess some of the probable consequences for law and social control. We may, indeed, ask whether our present concepts of the nature of law and the legal processes can survive much further into the future. If we wish to continue to have a form of social control through law, then considering new forms of legal philosophies at this time might be essential. We may be able, by means of the legal process, to deal with consequences of some events after they have taken place, but can we postulate the feasibility of reconstructing a legal system once it has broken down? Legal controls may be delayed in dealing with external problems; it may be both feasible and reasonable for law to be reactive rather than proactive about matters

---

[2] Most authorities would argue that this was not only a correct assessment, but that it was a necessary and appropriate feature of law. Barbara Wooton, *Crime and the Criminal Law* (London: Stevens and Sons, 1963) has some interesting comments on the problems of crime preventive methods and law.

external to itself; but could law possibly be reactive to its own failure to operate? This latter form of failure is a different kind of breakdown—the breakdown of the machinery, the thing itself, rather than the things or events to which it reacts. The prospects are none too bright.

Can we see any traces of a new philosophy of law and social control which could begin to accommodate change—and change at an ever increasing rate? Guides to the future may usually be found in the present. Much of the future is in the pipeline today; a product must be on the drawing board before it can be on the production line, and on the production line before it can be on the market. What, then, of the changing state of law and social control as it now appears?

Current Projections and Planning

In the current trends, I find little upon which to base hopes of the survival of law as a viable social control mechanism. One thing is clear: the majority of the current planning in the criminal justice system, which is not regressive, seeks solutions by means of more-of-the-same.[3] The idea of more-of-the-same makes projections—using mathematical formulations—extremely easy. Demographers could simply forecast the future populations, if it were given that the birth and death rates would remain constant. Indeed, such projections are trivial, even as projections. If we are a little more sophisticated, we can assume that the rate-of-change of the rate-of-change will remain the same—that the sort of changes which are now currently going on indicate the kinds of changes which may be expected in the future. This basis might give a more useful set of projections. If we make such kinds of projections with regard to our criminal justice processes, there is only one outcome, namely, the total breakdown of the system. This breakdown must take place before the year 2000.

Such an outcome is a distinct possibility. It is, in my view, much more than a possibility; it has the appearance of a certainty, if we assume that the idea of more-of-the-same continues to be invoked as the solution of present and projected problems of crime and social control. What may change this perspective? Perhaps the best known way of ensuring that we do not go down an undesirable road is that we become aware of the contingencies of this course of action, or inaction, and divert the existing trends by the conscious planning and developing of appropriate strategies. In a complex society, such planning calls for the use of all the techniques of modern analysis. It may be that our present techniques are not adequate; but as yet we do not know this because we have not attempted to apply them in the area of criminal justice. Research is too expensive; we cannot bother about long term problems; instant solutions are required to today's problems—preferably by using yesterday's methods.

---

[3] Many critics of current criminal policy have put forward this viewpoint. Perhaps the best evidence in support of this and other similar claims is to be found in the supporting statements made by any criminal justice agency, which accompany requests for budget increases.

Making Projections Invalid

These projections may be invalidated if those concerned see the disaster when its first manifestations appear and then change course, in any direction other than ahead. If we are fortunate—and we may have some slight degree of luck—the breakdown will be somewhat localized, not too widespread, in the first instance. From the local breakdowns we may be able to learn of the consequences of the courses of action to which we are committed. The events at Attica, the Tombs and other dramatic incidents illustrate this kind of breakdown.[4] And it is possible to learn from events like Attica. We can adjust to these kinds of events like a blind man steered by trippings. As I see it, the road toward 2000 which the field of criminal justice seems likely to take is of this form. There will be serious, dramatic and violent breakdowns in our attempts to implement the more-of-the-same of current law and order practices. We will be steered by the resulting dramatic events, quite probably, into random responses and diversionary tactics, rather than into the development of a strategy based on projections, planning and attempts to foresee the consequences of probable events before they occur.

Having thus established my position as a prophet of gloom, it is hardly necessary for me to reveal myself as a critic of the present system. Indeed, the basis for gloom about the future is essentially derived from a critical appraisal of the present. We are inventing the future now.

THE DYNAMIC CONCEPT OF CRIME

I must now state one theoretical position. I cannot discuss crime in the future without saying something about the dynamics of crime—or more particularly, what we mean when we use that word.

Crime, sin and deviation from normal behavior have been the concern of mankind from earliest times. If people are to live together in groups, it is essential that they be able to make predictions of each other's probable behavior. It is easy to think that if everybody obeyed the law, and if the law were of sufficient coverage and specificity, then we would be able to predict behavior and to have an ordered society. But in the social world of man there seems to be little connection between law and order—despite the conjunction of recent times into one word "law'n'order" which means something different from either law or order! Despite centuries of concern regarding individual actions regarded as intolerable, the behaviors which have been prohibited at different times and in different places fail to reveal many common features. Almost any crime has at some time and in some connection been lauded as a virtue.[5] In history, a very

---

[4] T. Platt, *The Politics of Riot Commissions* (New York: Collier Books, 1971) provides ample evidence of local breakdowns in social control and the means employed to deal with the situations.

[5] Kai T. Erikson, *Wayward Puritans: A Study in the Sociology of Deviance* (New York: John Wiley, 1966).

considerable number of methods for stating the prohibitions and for mediating the controls can be found: kings, priests, doctors (medicine men!) and, occasionally, some persons rather akin to academics. Some common feature might be found in functional terms, if not in terms of the particular acts or events. It appears that for a society to function as a social organization, there is a need for some of its members to be treated as outcasts, criminals or heretics. The pretext upon which the exclusion is made does not seem to matter; it is the act of exclusion which is significant. As Kai Erikson has suggested, and I agree, this rejection process provides a boundary defining function for society. The proportion of the population rejected has varied over time and varies within extremely wide limits today between jurisdictions. Clearly, the majority of the population is usually included rather than excluded; but there have been exceptions.[6]

The proportion of the population defined by a society as representing its outcasts is dependent upon its machinery of government. This is almost self-evident, since we may, operationally, define law as that which legislators legislate; these laws describe the kinds of persons who may be incarcerated or otherwise separated from society. If there is any moral basis for law, it must be accepted that that morality is mediated through the political system. We are currently seeing a growing awareness of the close interconnectedness between the political system and the legal system; the moral underpinnings for this are in doubt. The more certainly and the more widely the legal system is thought to be associated with the political system, the more legal concepts and procedures will be questioned, especially by those who do not favor the party in power.

CRIME, POLITICS AND MORALS

It is difficult to postulate a system of law which is not supported, to a greater or lesser degree, by some ethical premises. It is difficult to consider the probable future states of a criminal justice system without making somewhat detailed assumptions about the likely political structure. The connection—both logical and operational—between law, morals and politics may take different forms, but the tripartite connections are essential. Where can we look for some indication of the probable nature of moral value systems in the future?

It is likely that, even today, the moral climate of a nation or state and the values subscribed to by the majority of the population are more accurately reflected in the political structure, rather than in the religious protestations. For an indication of the prevailing ideas of what may be right or wrong, we would be advised to consider the speeches and actions of politicians, rather than to analyze

---

[6] Although it is difficult to compare data regarding the disposal of offenders in different countries, the differences in the proportions of the population who are, at any time, incarcerated in penal institutions varies widely. A comment on this issue is given in Nils Christie, "Changes in Penal Values," *Scandinavian Studies in Criminology* (Oslo, Norway: Scandinavian University Books, 1968), vol. 2.

the homilies of the priests. And politics is, of course, about power, rather than about morals. There is a further complication, or a fourth dimension; namely, that of technology or knowledge—the moral, the political and the epistemological systems interact in the process of law. The prominence of any of these as compared with the others varies from time to time, and each may have some elements of conflict with the others.

In the area of law, crime and social control, we have, then, the intersections of several dimensions. At the conceptual level—as distinct from the operational level—two major considerations appear in any attempt to project into the future: namely, the technological and the moral future states. Projecting technological developments accurately is generally thought to be simpler; and indeed, there have been some quite remarkable forecasts. Where serious forecasts have been made, with the use of sophisticated methods of analysis, and have subsequently been disproved, the projected date for the technological development has often been found to be the inaccurate factor. The developments took place before the expected time.[7] On the other hand, projecting likely future moral standards seems to be much more difficult. We cannot quantify moral positions; we cannot use envelope curves or other numerical analyses of trends. In the current symposium, we do not have a presentation dealing with projections with respect either to moral value systems or to political trends.

Moral Values and Crime

Although discussing morals is completely outside my particular field of expertise, it is essential that I make some statements in this area. I may be completely wrong about these issues; but in order to make my analysis hold together, I must make some suggestions with regard to the present connection between the fields of criminology and moral philosophy and then set forth some guesses about the future.

There is little doubt that several aspects of crime and illegal behavior in the United States, and in many other countries, are related to the Judaic–Christian ethic and, particularly, to that aspect which has been termed the White Anglo-Saxon Protestant ethic. I would accept Eric Trist's listing of "four corner-stones of our traditional morality: achievement, self-control, independence, and endurance of distress (grin and bear it!)."[8] Of course, some of these values are shared by cultures which are not dominated by the American way of life. However, we must also acknowledge that economic forces, in addition to moral or religious forces, have tended to spread these kinds of values widely in all developed and developing countries. Linked with this package of values is the political doctrine of democracy as practiced at present. I must confess as an amateur in this area,

---

[7] Erich Jantsch, "Technological Forecasting in Perspective," Publication of the Organization for Economic Co-operation and Development no. 21, 931 (Paris: 1967), especially pp. 42–44.

[8] Eric Trist, "Urban North America" (Paper presented at the World Congress on Mental Health, Edinburgh, England, 1969).

that I am surprised that the commentators take too little account of the impact of Greek and Roman culture on value systems. I wish only to stress one point: namely, that it is impossible to discuss the future of crime, how it is defined and what may be done about it, without paying considerable attention to the probable changes of moral standards and value systems. If there are doubts about this thesis, perhaps one supporting note might be made. Almost all authorities agree that child-rearing practices are related to the probability of criminal behavior later in life; certainly, it must be agreed that concepts of moral values are learned in childhood. Even if modified or unlearned at a later stage, usually a foundation of moral concepts is set in the home.

As already stated, it is difficult to deal with projections in these terms because we lack any reasonable metric. It is a useful strategy when faced with a problem which cannot be solved to see whether it can be made more complex. In operational research circles, it is recognized that a factor which cannot be measured in absolute terms can often be graded in comparative terms. For example, it would be absurd for me to ask, "How happy are you today?" but, to ask, "Are you happier today than yesterday?" would be somewhat more reasonable. Similarly, it is sometimes possible to obtain a crude measure of an interaction between two factors without being able to assess either singly.[9] In order to attempt to use this strategy, I want to demonstrate that our system of knowledge interacts with our system of morals. I shall then consider some of the interactions which I think I observe in relation to value systems and then try to formulate some conjectures regarding moral values for the future.

The Interaction between Morals and Knowledge

A fair presentation of the relationship between our system of knowledge, technology and morals would become a rather lengthy discussion of semantics and the relationship between linguistic glossaries, technology, metaphors and values.[10] However, for our present purposes an example may suffice. One may recall the discussion of the moral issues of abortion. The question as to when life begins relates to aspects of knowledge of the gestation processes, and this is turned into a consideration of a moral nature. I am not arguing for the relevance of this approach, but noting its existence. It might appear that a detailed consideration of almost any issue of morals is related in contemporary thought to technology and the assumed state of knowledge. It is unlikely that a connection between moral and knowledge dimensions will cease in the near future. We will, I suspect, continue to relate our beliefs to our knowledge and to discuss moral issues in the

---

[9] Stafford Beer, "The Law and the Profits: The Sixth Frank Newsam Memorial Lecture" (Paper presented at the Police College in Bramshill, England, Oct. 29, 1970). He notes, "[Sir Charles] Goodeve proposed that we should try to produce an eudemonic measure . . . [the complexity] of each of the two conditions is too great for analysis, the only thing left to measure is the difference between them . . . [a] difference *in potential*."

[10] Donald Schon, *Displacement of Concepts* (London: Tavistock Publications, 1959).

light of technology. I would go so far as to predict that a closer association between knowledge systems and moral values will characterize the future.

FUTURE VALUE CONFLICTS

As in other areas, I would expect conflicting approaches to develop. Cults which may be characterized by an anti-scientific set of rituals may also be expected to gain strength. Attempts, by various means and for a variety of probable ends, to separate the consideration of ethical and belief issues from the field of knowledge, may be expected to find many supporters. Those who find the connection between moral values and knowledge inconvenient may try to find support for their moral claims by bizarre beliefs or in counter-knowledge. Odd, long forgotten and often inconsequential phrases culled from once revered texts will be rediscovered and used to serve as the basis for an image for a new faith. Beliefs, practices and moral standards which could not find support in more rational or scientific concepts may, thus, claim antiquity, revelation or insight. It is then possible to separate beliefs from knowledge and yet to furnish an attractive product. The Bible will continue to be popular as a source of materials for those who find it desirable to separate belief systems from knowledge systems. Other ancient books, as well as rites, rituals and taboos will also become attractive sources. We may expect to see a preference for Eastern or African cultures, rather than Western or even Near Eastern. This class of organization will regard the scientific method and changing technology as irrelevant.

Another class of ritual system may also gain considerable support. Rather than regarding the world of technology as irrelevant, these groups will have a distinctive anti-scientific appeal. Some may claim to have knowledge beyond that offered by scientific explanation. The proponents of this class of rituals hope to capitalize upon the prestige of science while attempting to undermine the basic principles of the scientific method. They can do this by discussing with special confidence those areas of knowledge which scientists consider to be characterized by the greatest degree of uncertainty.

A third class of ritual organization, which will probably attract less support than the other two, may be categorized as pseudo-scientific. The most legitimate of these may be little more, or less, than play groups for working scientists. These organizations, although possessing certain of the qualities of the other groups, may lead to scientific speculation and provide a link with artists, poets and musicians to produce art forms and develop the creative imagination of their participants.

A Seller's Market for Rituals

The origins of the new ritual groups will differ. Some may be invented by well-intentioned persons disturbed by the state of affairs or by society's problems as they perceive them. Many will have a good economic basis in their origin; the leaders will be disguised businessmen providing a product for a market. The important point is, of course, not whether there is or is not an economic base for the ritual pedlars, but that a demand will exist for their product. I think we are due for an extensive sellers market for these products. The world—and the United States in particular—is likely to be in such a state and individual persons so emotionally set, that the new cult producers can expect a great boom. One ingredient will be necessary for a new ritual cult to prosper: the cult must be uncoupled from contemporary problems; put another way, the keynote of success will be social irresponsibility. The emphasis will be on experiential and not upon intellectual content. Belief systems which do not impact upon collective behavior, except in terms of rituals, seem strongly favored. For this reason, a falling market will characterize the older religious organizations which have adapted to contemporary society. The rituals of organized religions will be unable to take care of moral issues, for, at a social level, they will be far too complex and difficult. Thus, the majority of these institutions which in the past have led in setting moral values now seem likely to take a policy of inaction, leaving their individual adherents to take up any personal moral position they might desire. Putting this into commercial terms: the packaging of moral concepts and religious-type observances as the same product will be seen to be poor marketing policy. The Church has carried out some very important market surveys already—commissioning a very respectable, but definitely commercial, research organization to do this work.

It appears most probable that the very organizations which in the past have provided moral directions will be superseded by groups which primarily provide a variety of social contexts in which like-minded persons get together. Such groups will offer a "cop out" at the socio-moral level which will usually be both politically and culturally acceptable. There is, certainly, no indication that these groups are likely to develop into bodies where the focus for their appeal would be the consideration of the problematic social control in terms of moral objectives.

The New Moral Philosophers

It is, accordingly, difficult to guess the source of the development of the moral concepts of the twenty-first century. Certainly, we may hope that a small group of painters, poets, novelists, playrights and, perhaps, musicians will have an impact beyond their proportions.[11] We might also hope for the return of the role of the medieval court jester! The majority of the populace will drop out of involvement in moral issues—they will not be around even to chant the "Amen"; they will express their moral values, if at all, only through the ballot box. That is, if the ballot box can survive.

---

[11] There is little doubt that Charles Dickens, through the medium of his novels, had a very considerable impact upon prison reform. The television "investigative reporter" has had a very considerable impact, where this medium is widely used. Among contemporary authors, the novelist, Arthur Hailey, has highlighted current problems of social control and technology, in his novels, *Airport, Wheels* and *Hotel.*

But there will be moral values to guide policy in the next decade or two, derived mainly from the idea that the survival of the human race is an essential good. Values will be preached more by intellectuals, especially scientists, than by theologians. New and different kinds of conflicts will involve the new moralists, whether technologists or non-scientists.

The Doctrine of Survival and Self-interest

The emphasis upon the essential good—that is, the survival of the human race—will lead to conflict with values which see the advantage in short term and local or national goals. There will be no conflict between science and religions, as in the nineteenth century. Religious and related kinds of groups will, in certain areas, form loose associations with the values expressed by certain of the new moralists. Other religious and ritual groups will tend to ally themselves with political and reactionary forces, hence, with power rather than academic or intellectual leadership. In the main, we can expect only coalitions of convenience between multifarious pressure groups.

The main value of the late twentieth and early twenty-first century, as I see it, is that of enlightened self-interest; this is, I believe, an optimistic viewpoint. If we cannot achieve this as a value, there is little chance for survival. By main value in this sense, I refer to the dominant value which might characterize those in power. There will be other values and more moral positions taken by quite large minorities, and these secondary values will inform the basic idea of enlightened self-interest. At this level of the value system, I would again agree with Trist[12] who defines the values of the future as: "self-actualisation, self-expression, interdependence and a capacity for joy."

SOLUTION OR RESOLUTION?

In the light of these projections regarding the nature of the value system of the future and the rise of the new moralists, we may now state certain contingencies regarding the nature of crime and what the society of the turn of the century might do about it. There seem to be a number of consequences arising from these projections which will have an impact upon crime, how it is defined and the action taken to deal with it. However, criminology takes a position which lies uneasily between morals and technology, mediated by the concepts of law. The impact of technology on crime will be as significant as the impact of changing values. Value systems emphasize the human actors in the situation, event or act which is defined as criminal; technology tends to emphasize the circumstances surrounding the event and the techniques available to those who commit crimes, as well as to those who attempt to prevent them.

Until most recently society has attempted to deal with those events which

---

[12] Trist, "Urban North America."

were defined as criminal by seeking to deal with the person who committed the act. We even refer to a crime as being "solved" when we have found someone who can be blamed for committing it; this is an odd use of the term "solved." I know of no teacher who would regard a problem as solved when a student was able to point out some situation which could be blamed. Further, the emphasis on the person who is seen as the criminal—the one who can be blamed—has led us to ignore the other concomitants of the crime: the victim particularly, the situation and often many more factors.[13] A change in any one element of a complex set can result in a different outcome; perhaps, an outcome which may be more desirable. We may find greater success in attempting to deal with crime rather than with criminals. Making crime more difficult may not prevent the professional; however, he who becomes a criminal begins his career as a non-professional. If the first crime, committed by any kind of criminal can be delayed —the first crime which a criminal commits taking place at a later age—we shall have reduced the volume of crime and also the probability of a criminal career as the probability of a serious and lengthy criminal career is most highly cor-related with the age at first offense. To delay the first criminal act—not prevent it—may be an expected result of making crime more difficult. Making crimes more difficult, although not preventing them, does not address the criminal in any way; it is a matter of technology and management.

There has been little development of technology which makes crime more difficult; techniques have been concerned with the various aspects of the finding of guilt and the allocating of blame. Fingerprints, voiceprints, lie-detectors and the like help only in pinning the blame the more certainly upon the person who has already been suspected. Even the modus operandi index is used to identify persons who may have committed the crime, rather than for purposes of prevent-ing further crimes of a similar nature. There will be a growing interest in systems for preventing crime or for making crimes more difficult. As a by-product, how-ever, many of these methods will produce rather unpleasant conditions for those who are protected.

Law'n'Order

It is not possible for us to do things about probable crimes without affecting ourselves. The controller is not independent of the controlled. There is a penalty which we must pay in terms of our own freedom for every restriction we can invent to deal with the criminal. It seems likely that the idea of adding more powers of control—the law'n'order syndrome—will continue to grow for some years yet, but before the turn of the century, a reversal will take place. The prisons have claimed that they could reform and rehabilitate offenders; there is no evi-dence of that despite the large sums society pays for the incarceration of offenders. The judges have claimed that they have dispensed justice; there is no evidence that sentencing practices are equitable, let alone just. All concerned with the criminal

[13] R. Jeffrey, *Crime Control through Environmental Design* (London: Sage, 1971).

justice system have claimed to be able to perform those miracles society orders; not a claim has been supported. More police, we are told, will lead to less crime; we cannot establish the marginal efficiency of one more—or even less—policeman. This game is almost up. Society is beginning to note that prisons cannot save souls and is suggesting—at present somewhat mildly—the possibility of saving some money and—while we may not know exactly what justice is, while we are trying to find out—at least having equity in the disposition of offenders.

The money which is being fed into the criminal justice machinery at the present time by state and national agencies is going to act exactly like a hormone weed-killer: stimulating an unbalanced growth spurt such that the plant dies. The forces of law'n'order are now in the growth spurt stage, the unhealthy growth spurt which is prognostic of disaster. As knowledge increases, it will become even more apparent that the current view of crime control does a disservice to society, by ignoring all but a few elements in the handling of any antisocial event. An increased ability to deal with complex issues will enable the large number of decision processes, situations, personality factors and many more of the elements of any crime to be considered, without the excessive simplification which characterizes our present tactics.

The fear of crime—and indeed many other kinds of fears—is the main trigger for action, while at the same time, an inefficient motivator. There is a necessity to deal with the dramatic event which generates maximum fear—the mass murderer or kidnapper—without reference to the fact that such events are extremely rare. We move as frightened children away from the sound of one big bang and then from another. The development of information systems will enable a more reasoned use of data to inform policy which eventually will seep through to our bureaucratic structure. We have been told that we should do something about social ills, because they give rise to crime. Hopefully, we shall learn that this is a poor, fear based policy. We should deal with social ills—such as, child neglect, poverty, unemployment, overcrowding and the like—because these are evils in their own right.

HOW THE PRESENT MAY AFFECT THE FUTURE

Like the hip bone to the thigh bone, the past is connected to the future by the sinews of the present. But the lessons of the present will take a long time to be learned in the field of criminal justice. The feedback of information about the effects of decisions which might guide policy is almost entirely lacking. The data which do exist are most unreliable. There is no efficient way for the system to learn by its mistakes; indeed, there is a very strong tendency to deny that mistakes are made. Where the processes are so illadjusted to learning, the probability of adaptation to change seems remote. Yet, the pressures of crime and public reactions to it are likely always to be strong and to grow stronger. Thus, something will have to be done; what will be done, more often than not, will be reactionary. The past times were better: there were fewer problems then; if we cannot return to yesterday's problems, we can return to yesterday's solutions—and our politicians will!

It is also possible to persuade the public that the problems which are troubling them are yesterday's problems; thus, they welcome outdated remedies for the wrong problems. What does threaten us today? Is it street crime? How dangerous is it to carry out desired activities? Who are the enemies of society? What kinds of crime will characterize the future, and how should we be preparing our social defense? It is possible to put the threats and fears of contemporary society into perspective, but only with considerable difficulty.

Let us consider an example which may indicate what I mean. Suppose that the parents of a son or daughter between the ages of ten and fourteen received a message that their child was dangerously ill in a hospital. The informant, after being asked quickly what happened, says that he does not have any idea, but the parent is to come at once. On the way one would be trying to think what could have happened. What would be the guesses in such a situation? Would the greatest fear be that the cause of the trouble was a crime or a car accident? (How should I write that last word; with or without quotation marks: an "accident" or an accident?) In any event, what would be a reasonable strategy of social action? If car accidents cause, say, ten times more damage than do events which we now call crime, would it not be reasonable to devote ten times the amount of money we spend on crime to attempt to reduce accidents? If this would not be seen as a rational strategy—and it apparently is not so regarded—what are the reasons for this?

Keeping Crime Visible

There seems to be a need to keep crime visible—to personalize it in terms of the criminal. The criminal is somebody whom we can fear and, hence, hate. Conversely, we are grateful when some white knight slays the dragon, but this dragon has to be visible. Making roads safer does not have the symbolic appeal of bringing a villain to justice. In England, they are very defensive about the idea of parliamentary government; every Fifth of November children burn in effigy a certain Guy Fawkes, who once, in the seventeenth century, attempted to destroy the government. While the cellars of the House of Commons are being searched for the physical form of Guy Fawkes, we cannot be as concerned with what might be going on in the committee rooms upstairs. While we attempt to detect the gunpowder treason and plot,[14] we will have less concern for the gentlemanly ploys and strategies which subvert the very nature of the democratic process: the one villain can be identified, the collective villains can hide. There is little chance but that the public will continue to be persuaded more by symbols of harm which they can see, than by discussions of harms which are invisible.

[14] The children's rhyme—somewhat akin to some Christmas jingles—runs thus: "Be pleased to remember/The Fifth of November/The gun-powder treason and plot/ . . . Penny for the Guy, Mister?"

Our ideas of property must, and will, change; only if this happens can we hope to protect our concepts of human dignity. Private companies now hold much more information about individuals than do official bodies. What are their rights to this property? To what extent does the disturbance of the coating on a computer tape represent a property? The tape exists in the same form, whether it contains no information or very different forms of information. How can juries deal with these kinds of evidence? What constitutes the theft of information? We are working towards some concepts to deal with these issues, but largely concepts which were current generations ago.

Our physiological reactions to threats are still the same as they were in cave-dwelling days—the level of adrenalin rises when we hear a sudden loud noise. But, sounds are no longer prognostic of the same threats as those for which additional adrenalin flow was useful. The things or conditions which are most threatening to us today are invisible, although some may be seen by the use of a microscope. Perhaps the most serious kinds of threats to the continuance of the human race cannot be foreseen by the use of any current or probable aids. These events which could destroy us can only be inferred by means of sophisticated statistical analysis. One such threat is the possibility of error in our defense systems; another is, of course, the ecological balance problem. A single offender may make a decision to commit a crime against us and be held responsible, in much the same way as in the past. But, who makes the decisions of the large corporate enterprises? Applications of current legal philosophies can, in these kinds of cases, be extremely dysfunctional.[15] How can we develop and put into effect a rational view of collective responsibility and collective guilt? The Nuremberg Trials did not provide a very satisfactory doctrine for these issues. Perhaps, we should not even try developing collective guilt, but rather seek some other ethical basis for our protection.

CONCLUSION

What is probable and what is desirable are different things. If what is probable is not seen as desirable, we can do something about it—if, but only if, we are aware of the probability. There is a strong tendency to believe that what is desirable is the more probable; while there may be no direct reason why this should be so, there is little doubt that possible developments which are seen as desirable tend

---

[15] When railway workers, airport controllers, or others work by the rules, the system breaks down. This breakdown is not due to a failure of law or a failure of those concerned to abide by the law; it arises because the workers are following closely the rule of law. The point is that laws are not necessarily made to facilitate the working of systems, but to exculpate those in high positions in such systems. The laws specify who—at a lower level than the lawmakers—may be blamed if anything goes wrong. A classical analysis of such cases is given by J. Bensman and I. Gerver, "Crime and Punishment in the Factory: A Functional Analysis," in L. Rosenberg, I. Gerver, and F. H. Howston, eds., *Mass Society in Crisis* (New York: Macmillan, 1964).

to gain in their levels of probability.[16] We are inventing the future now; we must make that process a conscious and rational one. We must accept the idea that the idea of relevance must be future oriented.

Present day values, expressed in terms of immediate relevance, may pave the way towards disaster. Higher levels of abstraction may be more relevant than more concrete considerations. Research investigations which are focused on contemporary problems may have dangerously little pay-off. Research takes time; times change, and they are changing very fast. Thus, we have an interesting paradox: making research more relevant can result in findings that are irrelevant. Research on today's problems—unless, by chance, those problems have an element of generality—would seem to be poor strategy. In the immediate future—and perhaps for at least the next six or seven years—most research expenditure in the social field, and particularly in crime related areas, will be influenced by short term political considerations. In present times there is no sign of any degree of detachment of research funding from local and national governmental interests. Too strong pressure to be relevant—the relevance being determined by specific, local, immediate or bureaucratic considerations—will direct research away from findings which have a high degree of generality; thus, millions of dollars will be wasted.

---

[16] See, for example, F. W. Irwin, "Stated Expectations as Functions of Probability and Desirability of Outcomes," *Journal of Personality* 21 (1953), pp. 329–335, and R. W. Marks, "The Effect of Probability, Desirability and Privilege on the Stated Expectations of Children," *Journal of Personality* 19 (1951), pp. 332–351.

2
Struggle for Justice

AMERICAN FRIENDS SERVICE COMMITTEE

The promise of parole and probation has been grounded not only by a chronic inability to generate the political support required for their implementation but, much more fundamentally, by an inability of these institutions to produce significant results even when their stipulated ideal conditions have been met; they have typically degenerated into stylized ritual at best or, more commonly, function as an auxiliary policing device for the increased surveillance of suspect groups (usually poor or black). There is neither consensus among the experts nor validation by research of any categories of diagosis for criminal behavior. There is no reliable device for classifying individuals for "treatment" purposes and no significant evidence that any one form of "treatment" is superior to any other. The legacy of a century of reform effort is an increasingly repressive penal system and overcrowded courts dispensing assembly line justice.

Reforms currently proposed follow traditional lines: more and better trained personnel at higher salaries, more programs both in and out of institutions, more money for courts and corrections all along the line. The premise of such an approach is that the programs are on the right track but have never been given a fair trial, that the blame for past failure is public and legislative inaction.

Our problems, however, go much deeper than stingy budgets, hostile public opinion, or lack of manpower. We have grave doubts that the successful implementation of the kinds of reform proposed would serve legitimate public interest or alleviate the major abuses of our present programs. This concern arises

SOURCE. Excerpts from *Struggle for Justice: A Report on Crime and Punishment in America,* New York: Hill and Wang, 1971. Reprinted with permission of the publisher and the American Friends Service Committee.

from compelling evidence that the individualized treatment model, the ideal toward which reformers have been urging us for at least a century, is theoretically faulty, systematically discriminatory in administration, and inconsistent with some of our most basic concepts of justice.

At the outset, therefore, let us set down our rationalization for the existence of any system of criminal justice. In some cases—though we differ on which—most of us accept the necessity of restraining someone against his will and depriving him of his liberty. Most of us will do this, moreover, not only when the person to be restrained appears to others as an immediate and obvious "danger" (itself a dangerously ambiguous concept), but also in general, that is, we accept the premise that at least some basic rules are necessary to organized society, mutual respect, and personal safety, and that these rules may require some sort of enforcement.

If it is conceded that in some circumstances we might employ coercion against an individual to achieve some compelling social goal, it confuses analysis and obscures the moral nature of our act to pretend that we are not employing punishment.

Exclusively moral considerations might lead to the conclusion that punishment for offenses against society should be imposed according to the moral responsibility of the offender; thus, under the ordinances of Manu in ancient Hindu administration, the high-caste Brahman who violated the law was subject to much more severe penalties than the lower-caste Sudra, who was not supposed to enjoy the Brahman's fine perception of the difference between right and wrong.

The emergence of treatment-oriented discretionary individualization and the undermining of the legitimacy of retribution provided a natural means out of this embarrassing dilemma. To punish the little man more severely for his little acts, which might appear as open hypocrisy by retributive standards, is no longer a problem if society can be persuaded that "treatment" is not "punishment" and if the criteria for the extent of state intervention are all the social and psychological, but not the moral, deficiencies of the offender.

THE FALLACY OF THE INDIVIDUALIZED TREATMENT MODEL

The utilitarians perceived crime as a natural phenomenon flowing directly from humanity's self-seeking nature. Since human beings are motivated to maximize pleasure and minimize pain, they can be expected to transgress when they see it is to their advantage to do so. To insure public safety, punishment for a criminal act needed only to offer sufficiently more pain than the transgression was worth, thereby deterring the offender from further crime and warning other potential offenders.

The Quakers in Pennsylvania differed largely by placing increased emphasis on reformation. They developed a solitary confinement system that, by holding the convict in total isolation and thus quarantining him from other prisoners, was supposed to encourage his meditation, reflection, and penitence. Though the expensiveness of this system never allowed it to be given a thorough trial, an attempt was made to perpetuate the isolation of convicts through such devices as the Auburn (silent) system.

The individualized treatment model, the outcome of this historical process, has for nearly a century been the ideological spring from which almost all actual and proposed reform in criminal justice has been derived. It would be hard to exaggerate the power of this idea or the extent of its influence. In recent years it has been the conceptual foundation of such widely divergent approaches to criminal justice as the President's Crime Commission Report, the British "Why Prison?—A Quaker View of Imprisonment and Some Alternatives," and the American Law Institute's Model Penal Code. Like other conceptions that become so entrenched that they slip imperceptibly into dogma, the treatment model has been assumed rather than analyzed, preached rather than evaluated.

The underlying rationale of this treatment model is deceptively simple. It rejects inherited concepts of criminal punishment as the payment of a debt owed to society, a debt proportioned to the magnitude of the offender's wrong. Instead it would save the offender through constructive measures of reformation, protect society by keeping the offender locked up until that reformation is accomplished, and reduce the crime rate not only by using cure-or-detention to eliminate recidivism, but hopefully also by the identification of potential criminals in advance so that they can be rendered harmless by preventive treatment. Thus, the dispassionate behavioral expert displaces judge and theologian. The particular criminal act becomes irrelevant except insofar as it has diagnostic significance in classifying and treating the actor's particular criminal typology. Carried to an extreme, the sentence for all crimes would be the same: an indeterminate commitment to imprisonment, probation, or parole, which ever was dictated at any particular time by the treatment program. Any sentence would be the time required to bring about rehabilitation, a period which might be a few weeks or a lifetime.

At every level—from prosecutor to parole-board member—the concept of individualization has been used to justify secret procedures, unreviewable decision making, and an unwillingness to formulate anything other than the most general rules or policy. Whatever else may be credited to a century of individualized-treatment reform effort, there has been a steady expansion of the scope of the criminal justice system and a consolidation of the state's absolute power over the lives of those caught in the net.

The discretionary power granted to prosecutors, judges, and administrators in an individualized treatment system is unique in the legal system, awesome in scope and by its nature uncontrollable.

DETERRENCE

The frequent criticism that our high rate of recidivism proves that punishment does not deter is wide of the mark and results from a confusion of general prevention with efforts to rehabilitate individual offenders. The theory of general prevention is not concerned with the effects of punishment upon the subsequent career of someone who has been punished. It concentrates instead upon the efficacy of the threat of punishment upon those who are disposed to or tempted by crime.

The claim is that without the general deterrent threat of punishment society would relapse into chaos, barbarism, and anarchy. Implicit in this view is the notion that fear of punishment is the only significant deterrent of criminal behavior. While we do not know the size of the marginal class that exists on the borderline of criminality and is kept in check only by the fear of punishment, we are convinced that at least for serious crime the immediate effect of general prevention for the largest part of the population is negligible.

Justice Holmes giving a very different policy implication, said that while the law could not ignore the public's insistence on revenge, neither should the law encourage it. Thus, a major protection that punitive criminal law provides society is its defense of social order against private revenge, blood feuds, or lynch law —in other words, against the "law-abiding."

PAROLE

The terminating program in the rehabilitative routine is parole. In many ways it epitomizes the treatment–punishment mixture. Theoretically the parole agent aids the parolee's transition back into the community by mixing the two functions help and surveillance. On the one hand he enforces (with considerable leniency) special rules of conduct—the conditions of parole. In this way he protects the parolee from slipping back into harmful behavior patterns and likewise helps the community by keeping the parolee out of trouble. On the other hand he "works with the parolee," giving him counseling, moral support, and some concrete help, such as aid in securing employment and residence.

In practice there is a serious flaw in this helping–surveillance relationship. The parole agent is in theory required to enforce very restrictive rules of conduct, so restrictive that the parolee's life chances would be seriously reduced if he were forced to live by them. For instance, one of the rules in California is that the parolee must not "associate" with other ex-convicts or persons with bad reputations. For a person who lives among other working and lower-class persons, which is the case of most parolees, not associating with ex-convicts or persons with "bad reputations" is clearly unrealistic. Furthermore, the California parolee may not leave the county of residence, drive a car, or change jobs without his agent's permission. And he may not drink "to excess." In actuality, the agent, in order to prevent having to "violate" the majority of his case load and in order to increase the life chances of the parolee, enforces a much more lenient set of informal rules. The problem with this is that the formal rules still exist and are invoked when some outside attention is directed toward a particular parolee. When this occurs, the parolee is often held to answer for behavior that the parole agent had known about and had explicitly condoned.

Moreover, the agent is not in a good position to help the parolee. He is not a professional therapist (if this would help) and has few resources to supply concrete help, such as a job, which the parolee often needs desperately. At best, parole is an obstacle the ex-convict has to contend with among the many other obstacles in his path. At worst, it is a trap that when sprung intensifies his feelings of injustice toward the hypocritical, unpredictable rehabilitative system.

NOTES ON THE ELIMINATION OF DISCRETION

Our recommendations on the reduction or elimination of discretion in the criminal justice apparatus are tied to the present situation in our society, to discrimination, corruption, and the abuse of power. We are not legal philosophers working out rules for millennia to come. Today the evils of discretion far outweigh conceivable benefits, but this might not always be true. In today's world, however, we recommend the following to give the reader some idea of how a nondiscretionary criminal justice system would work.

Vagueness of laws as a source of discretion is to be eliminated. A person is to know in advance what the charge will be. Many laws are to be eliminated, such as those applying to crimes without victims. Some criminal matters are to be removed to tort law, in cases where the community has little interest and the matter can be put on a quantitative basis involving compensation for damage incurred by the victim.

Police discretion obviously can never be wholly eliminated. It is to be controlled via guidelines from the community or from the police department. These are to be public. Other limitations include measures for community accountability by police, easier false arrest suits, applicability of the law to police as well as to citizens.

Money bail is eliminated. Everyone awaiting trial is released except those few for whom there is heavy evidence that they will commit violent crime before trial; detention of these persons is not to be allowed to interfere with their preparation of a trial defense. Failure to bring the case to trial within a specified period of time results in dismissal of the case. Plea-bargaining is abolished. Even guilty pleas go to trial. All charges bearing penalties are brought to court, with the provision that all felony cases are to be tried. The investigatory agencies of the state—crime labs, investigators—are at the disposal of both sides in the adversary process.

The facts are determined in a trial-like proceeding. The defendant, if found guilty, has access to a wide range of community services. Here is where the community gets its chance to show its concern for the individual. However it cannot coerce the individual into accepting such signs of concern and no penalty will be attached to failure to make use of such services.

If after a predetermined number of chances this community process fails to prevent law violations by one who has used these services, the offender is to be delivered to the punitive agency of the state. From this point on, all offenders in a broad class—such as type of crime, but not according to the unique characteristics of the individual—are to be treated alike.

Whatever sanction or short sentence is imposed is to be fixed by law. There is to be no discretion in setting sentences, no indeterminate sentences, and unsupervised street release is to replace parole.

The elimination of most discretion will shift many practices—such as sentencing and the supervision of street probation—out of the hands of administrative agencies and into a realm where the constitutional protections of due process and equal application of the law will apply.

Here we will suggest that the law should deal only with a narrow aspect of the individual, that is, his criminal act or acts.

The whole person is not the concern of the law. Whenever the law considers the whole person it is more likely that it considers factors irrelevant to the purpose of delivering punishment. The other factors, by and large, have been and will certainly continue to be characteristics related to influence, power, wealth, and class. They will not be factors related to the needs or the treatment potentialities of the defendant.

A necessary corollary of our principle of punishing for the act is that specific punishment be assigned to the act. All persons found guilty of the same criminal act under the same circumstances are dealt with uniformly.

Two exceptions to this corollary exist, which do not damage the general principle. The first is that society may want to assign more intense punishments to repetitions of the same criminal act or class of criminal acts, such as crimes of theft, crimes involving assaults on persons, or for felonies in general. For many crimes there might be no jail term for first offenses. These qualifications can be clearly spelled out in the definition of the act and the punishment, and do not allow our old nemesis, the misuse of discretionary power, to slip back into the administration of the law.

3
Rehabilitation: Rhetoric and Reality

NORVAL MORRIS AND GORDON HAWKINS

The American correctional system handles about 1.3 million offenders on an average day; it has 2.5 million admissions in the course of a year; its annual budget is over a billion dollars, of which well over half goes to feed, clothe, and guard adult criminals in prisons and jails. The facilities, programs, and personnel of the correctional systems are badly overtaxed. Moreover, assuming that present trends in courts and convictions continue, the system will in the future, unless policies are radically changed, have to face even more extreme pressures.

Imprisonment remains the core of the system, and, as Hans Mattick pointed out, "the genius of American penology lies in the fact that we have demonstrated that eighteenth and nineteenth century methods can be forced to work in the middle of the twentieth century."

There are 25 prisons in the United States over a hundred years old. Sixty-one prisons opened before 1900 are still in use. Inside these fortress structures only a small fraction of those confined are exposed to any kind of correctional service other than restraint. As for the local jails which handle those awaiting trial and misdemeanants, these were described by a task force of the President's Crime Commission as "generally the most inadequate in every way. . . . Not only are the great majority of these facilities old but many do not even meet the minimum standards in sanitation, living space, and segregation of different ages and types

SOURCE. *Federal Probation,* XXXIV, December 1970, pp. 9–17. Reprinted with permission of the authors and *Federal Probation.*

of offenders that have obtained generally in the rest of corrections for several decades."

Our program thus addresses an antique, overloaded, neglected, expensive, cruel, and inefficient "correctional" system. Hence, our edicts:

1. The money bail system shall be abolished. All but the small number of offenders who present high risk of flight or criminal acts prior to trial shall be granted pretrial release upon such conditions and restrictions as the court may think necessary and with stringent penalties for failure to appear.

2. Unless cause to the contrary can be shown, the treatment of offenders shall be community-based.

3. For a felony no term of imprisonment of less than 1 year shall be imposed by the courts.

4. All correctional authorities shall develop community treatment programs for offenders, providing special intensive treatment as an alternative to institutionalization.

5. All correctional authorities shall make an immediate start on prison plans designed to reduce the size of penal institutions, develop modern industrial programs, and expand work release, graduated release, and furloughs for prisoners.

6. All state and federal laws restricting the sale of prison-made products shall be repealed.

7. All local jails and other correctional facilities including probation and parole services shall be integrated within unitary state correctional systems.

8. All correctional authorities shall recruit additional probation and parole officers as needed for an average ratio of 35 offenders per officer.

9. Parole and probation services shall be made available in all jurisdictions for felons, juveniles, and such adult misdemeanants as need or can profit from them.

10. Every release from a penal institution for felons and for such categories of misdemeanants as the correctional authorities see fit shall be on parole for a fixed period of between 1 and 5 years.

THE CUSTODIAL FUNCTION: BAIL

A primary function of the jail remains, as it has always been, the custody of persons pending trial; so that the bulk of the jail population is made up of unconvicted defendants. A large proportion of these, from 40 to 60 percent, will later be released without being convicted. In addition to those found not guilty and released, there are large numbers who on conviction are given shorter terms than they have already served while awaiting trial or are placed on probation rather than imprisoned. The majority of the persons thus detained are there because they cannot pay bail.

Justice and economy demand that there should be a substantial increase in the proportion of accused persons released pending trial. Quite apart from the costs in terms of human suffering and the wastage of human resources involved in needless pretrial detention, the cost in terms of money is enormous. We must reduce pretrial detention to the minimum by abolishing money bail and releasing all defendants save the few for whom detention is essential in the interests of the community.

It has been argued against our plan for the abolition of money bail that it would be improper to empower magistrates and judges to jail only defendants they believe to be dangerous on the ground that reliable methods for predicting dangerousness have not been developed. But judges at present commonly set high money bail as a means of keeping in jail persons they fear will commit crimes if released before trial, although the only recognized constitutional purpose of the bail system is ensuring appearance at trial. Further, judges are no better qualified to predict nonappearance than to predict dangerousness, although the whole bail system postulates their ability to do so. Research which has already begun on identifying the factors relevant to the risk of flight before trial should be continued and intensified, and further research is certainly necessary to discover the factors bearing on the likelihood of persons' committing various offenses while released pending trial. This does not mean, however, that we can afford to preserve the present largely ineffective, highly inequitable, and almost criminally wasteful bail and detention system until those researches have been completed.

THE CORRECTIONAL FUNCTION

There is a marked tendency for some of the experts in the field of corrections to declare flatly that imprisonment has failed. Others have been more cautiously agnostic and have said merely that we know nothing about the effectiveness of imprisonment. It is necessary therefore, first of all, to say something about this prevailing pessimism or skepticism, to consider how far it is rationally justified or to what extent it may be due to the demise of exaggerated hopes and the frustration of ideals. One source of disaffection is easy to identify. The President's Commission Task Force Report on Corrections states: "The ultimate goal of corrections under any theory is to make the community safer by reducing the incidence of crime." But at a time when the incidence of crime does not appear to have been reduced—rather the reverse—and the community certainly doesn't feel safer, this "ultimate goal" seems to be receding rather than coming closer. So, not surprisingly, some persons have assumed that all our correctional programs have failed.

About this two things need to be said. In the first place the incidence of crime is not simply a function of penal practice. There is no evidence that the volume or rate of crime is so related to penal policy that it is dependent upon and varies with changes in correctional programs and practices. But there is considerable evidence that the amount and rates of crime are related to such factors as the density and size of the population; the age, sex, and race composition of the population; the strength and efficiency of the police force; and many other factors outside and beyond the control of penal administration. To attribute an increase in crime to penal policy is therefore like holding an umbrella responsible for the rainfall. Nevertheless the principal function of the prison is the treatment of convicted offenders, the declared purpose of that treatment being to prevent the offender from offending again. And this means that in one respect, at least, it is possible to talk meaningfully about the effectiveness of imprisonment. For the effectiveness of the prison system as a crime control agency in relation to the offenders who have been processed through it is, to a degree, measurable.

Here, too, it is frequently and quite confidently asserted that we have failed. "Between 60 percent and 70 percent of the men who leave prison come back for new crimes," says John Bartlow Martin. Where what Daniel Glaser in *The Effectiveness of a Prison and Parole System* (1964) calls "the legend that two-thirds return to prison" originated is not known. Possibly it started in this methodologically confused way. Most prison populations include about two-thirds who have been in prison before. It is easy but wrong to conclude that prisons therefore have a 60- to 70-percent failure rate. The prison is a sample grossly skewed by recidivists. Much lower failure rates can produce a prison population where two-thirds are ex-prisoners; prison is in large part a collection of its own failures.

The kind of rigorous studies necessary to determine the extent to which released prisoners in the United States return to prison have not been done. Those studies which have attempted to follow releasees suggest on the contrary that about two-thirds do *not* return. One of the principal conclusions of Glaser's study is that "in the first two to five years after their release, only about a third of all the men released from an entire prison system are returned to prison." In view of the fact that many studies have shown that a 3-year followup accounts for about 90 percent of the probable future returns to prison, Glaser's findings suggest that it is unwise to dismiss prisons as complete failures.

On the other hand, neither can one say that their effectiveness has been demonstrated. The two-thirds "success" rate, a figure which incidentally also holds for the English prison system, no doubt masks a great deal of "spontaneous remission" in cases where the experience of imprisonment was irrelevant to later lawful behavior and conceivably more rigorous followup studies would uncover a good deal more postrelease criminality than the rather crude methods so far employed.

However that may be, it leads us to consider a deeper source of disquiet and cynicism—the fact that there is some evidence to support what Nigel Walker calls "the hypothesis of the interchangeability of penal measures." This is the hypothesis that of the offenders who do not repeat their offenses after a given type of sentence all but a very few would have refrained similarly after most other kinds of sentence—in other words, that for most offenders penal measures are interchangeable. There is no reason, however, why these findings should be regarded as depressing or should give rise to cynicism.

The similarity between the reconviction rates of offenders despite differences in their sentences is not really very surprising. "Treatment" in penal institutions generally consists of little more than variations in the conditions of custody, and probation rarely involves more than cursory supervision. It would be surprising if either proved a significant influence on conduct.

It is, of course, understandable that anyone committed to belief in the superiority of a particular penal method should feel some chagrin. But for an objective observer there are positive inferences to be drawn for social policy which, to a large extent, counterbalances any negative implications. For the interchangeability hypothesis indicates that one of the major penological problems of our time —overcrowding, shortages of adequate staff and equipment, and all the social and economic costs of maintaining penal institutions—can be drastically reduced without any increase in reconviction rates simply by sentencing fewer offenders to imprisonment.

COMMUNITY TREATMENT

In the light of our phenomenal ignorance, what rational strategy is possible? The first point to note is that our ignorance is not total. Three propositions advanced by Leslie Wilkins in a survey he did in 1967 for the Council of Europe entitled "The Effectiveness of Punishment and Other Measures of Treatment" are directly relevant to policy making in this field:

1. Humanitarian systems of treatment (e.g., probation) are no less effective in reducing the probability of recidivism than severe forms of punishment.

2. Money (if not souls) can be saved by revised treatment systems. The cheaper systems are more often than not also more humanitarian.

3. Much money is wasted in many countries by the provision of unnecessary security precautions.

One of the most striking pieces of evidence which would support those propositions is an impressive attempt at controlled experimentation in the correctional field: the California Youth Authority's Community Treatment Project, now in its eighth year. The saving in public money is certainly substantial. The cost of the California Community Treatment Project per youth is less than half the average cost of institutionalizing an offender. Moreover, the program is now handling a group larger than the population of one of the new juvenile institutions that the California Youth Authority is building. An investment of some $6- to $8-million is thus obviated. At the same time the program offers not merely "equal protection to the public" but also, at less than half the price, much more effective protection than the traditional methods.

It is true that there are always likely to be offenders who because of the nature of their offenses (e.g., gross cruelty, violence, or sexual molestation) will have to be imprisoned if only because the community would not accept their release. And in some cases involving multiple offenses or serious, persistent recidivism institutionalization may offer the only effective protection for society. But, as the President's Crime Commission reported, "for the large bulk of offenders . . . institutional commitments can cause more problems than they solve."

Our edict dealing with the development of community treatment programs also reflects our judgment that, in regard to the general deterrence question, it is better in the present state of knowledge for the penal system to concentrate on the task of making the community safer by preventing the actual offender's return to crime upon his release than to pursue the problematic preclusion of offenses by others. This does not mean that the general preventive aspect of penal policy is to be disregarded. But over a wide area it is likely that the shame, hardship, and stigma involved in arrest, public trial, and conviction are the principal elements in both individual and general deterrence rather than the nature of the sentence or the disposition of offenders. We must not habitually and thoughtlessly override the immediate object of preventing the offender from repeating his offense by assumptions of the efficacy of punishments on deterring potential imitators.

INSTITUTIONAL TREATMENT

We have argued that one of the principal practical implications of our discussion is that the enormously expensive and clumsy machinery of imprisonment is today relied on excessively and that its use could be drastically curtailed with great advantage in terms of financial, social, and human costs. This is not a revolutionary theory. Indeed today it would be widely accepted as a truism of sound sentencing practice that a prison sentence should be imposed only when no alternative punishment is reasonably appropriate. This approach to sentencing has received a most interesting formulation in the sentencing provisions of the American Law Institute's Model Penal Code. The code specifically directs the court not to impose a sentence of imprisonment unless it is of the view that such a sentence is necessary for the protection of the public. The code further provides that for a felony no term of imprisonment of less than 1 year shall be imposed by the court. This is, of course, not a technique for increasing the duration of prison sentences, though it may in occasional cases have that effect; the theory is that if a court does not think the crime or the criminal merit or require a prison sentence of at least a year's duration then punishment other than imprisonment should be imposed. In England—and the story is substantially the same in most countries—only about 1 in every 30 of those convicted by the criminal courts is sentenced to prison; if only indictable offenses are considered, less than 1 in every 5 so convicted is imprisoned. As the excellent sentencing handbook prepared by the Home Office for the use of the courts puts it: "Imprisonment is thus increasingly coming to be regarded as the sentence to be imposed only where other methods of treatment have failed or are considered inappropriate."

Nevertheless the fact remains that although the prison or penitentiary as we know it will almost certainly have followed the death penalty, banishment, and transportation into desuetude before the end of the century, institutional confinement in some form will remain necessary for some offenders. The kinds of diversification and modification in the prison system which will develop cannot be planned in detail or predicted with certainty. In a dynamic situation it is unwise to attempt to impose final lines of development, but some forms of innovation and variation are already in evidence. Moreover, change is essential. Worldwide experience with all "total institutions," prisons and mental hospitals alike, reveals their adverse effects on the later behavior of their inmates. For some time, therefore, experimental development has been taking place, tending toward the eventual elimination of prison in the form we now know it.

That form is, in outline: a walled institution where adult criminals in large numbers are held for protracted periods, with economically meaningless and insufficient employment, with vocational training or education for a few, with rare contacts with the outside world, in cellular conditions varying from the decent to those which a zoo would not tolerate, the purposes being to lead the prisoners to eschew crime in the future and to deter others of like mind from running the risk of sharing their incarceration. It is confidently predicted that before the end of this century prison in that form will become extinct, though the word may live on to cover quite different social organizations.

This is not, of course, advocacy of a general "gaol delivery." Prison, the basic sanction of criminal justice, must be preserved until its alternatives and its modifications are demonstrably of greater social utility. In our present ignorance of the effectiveness of our armory of punishments against criminals and of their educative and deterrent effects on the community, experimentation cannot be precipitate, and penal reforms within the walls remain an important aim. What is suggested is that the variations and modifications of prison are already at a stage where their recognition as such is necessary. We deal here with a few aspects of that experimentation which merit further development.

The open institution plays an increasingly important part in the prison systems of the world, for long-term and short-term prisoners, for the unconvicted and the convicted, for the duration of confinement, and as a release measure. Its role must be expanded. Likewise, though it would be unwise to turn our prisons into mental hospitals, there is a proportion of prisoners for whom effective treatment can be given only in an institution which in its routine, purposes, and techniques is closer to a mental hospital than to a prison. Hence institutions like Patuxent in Maryland, Grendon Underwood in England, and Herstedvester in Denmark are the shape of the future for, say, 10 percent of prisoners now in our security institutions.

One aspect of the work in the Danish institution, Herstedvester, leads helpfully to a further variation or mutation on prison. The period that criminals actually spend in Herstedvester has been steadily reduced over the years until now the norm is less than 2 years. At a rough estimate, the norm of "time in" for similar criminals in England and Australia would be 4 years, and in America 7 years. The period and intensity of supervision is, however, much greater after the prisoner leaves Herstedvester than is the aftercare supervision following imprisonment in most other countries, and there is a much higher likelihood of the criminal's return to Herstedvester for misbehavior or difficulty in social adaption short of crime. If necessary, those paroled from Herstedvester are helped and supported in the community, supervised and controlled, for many years; the period in the institution is merely a part of the overall correctional effort, institutional and in the community, and in duration it is often the lesser part.

A similar idea is to be seen also in the reorganization of the Swedish correctional system,[1] with the administrative consolidation of probation, prison, and aftercare services, regionalization, flexibility of release and transfer procedures, and a deliberate plan to make the prison term merely a part of the correctional plan and to reduce the period of imprisonment. Such plans are creating, in effect, a new short-term imprisonment, with surveillance and support in the community thereafter, instead of the former protracted prison sentences.

No matter how modified, prison remains expulsion from the group. It is a banishment. And it is a strange and inefficient banishment since there is normally a return; a new and meaningful life is not possible in the place to which the criminal is banished, and life there tends to sever his cultural roots and to cripple him socially and sometimes psychologically for his return.

Other modifications of the prison are also taking place, however, and these have as their purpose the reduction of the degree and duration of banishment, the diminution of the social isolation of prison, and the preservation of the familial and social ties which are so important to a law-abiding life. Some of these modifications are home leave, working out, day leave, furloughs to find employment, unrestricted correspondence, frequent visits by family and approved friends, and halfway hostels as release procedures.

There is a conflict inherent in our prison purposes. As a deterrent punishment we impose social isolation and at the same time we aspire to influence the prisoner to reformation; yet experience, and such evidence as we have, leads inexorably to the view that in the preservation and strengthening of the prisoner's familial ties, and the preservation and creation of other social links with the community, lies our best hope for his avoiding crime on release. We must, in our own interests, preserve and nourish his family and community relationships.

Letters to and from family and friends have been treated as rare privileges; the advanced correctional administrators of the world now regard letters as necessities of rehabilitation, and pathetic arguments about the administrative problems of censoring so many letters are quickly met. Likewise, visits are moving from rare privileges to essential and reasonably frequent therapeutic opportunities.

Some countries develop systems of home leave, allowing all but a few prisoners regular home leave after part of their sentence has been served. Such systems start as a release procedure but work their way back into the prison regime; they start as a privilege allowed to the younger prisoners and develop into a wise rehabilitative process applicable to most prisoners. Home leave must be used in our penal system, not for reasons of sentimentality but because it better protects

---

[1] See "Lessons from the Adult Correctional System of Sweden," *Federal Probation,* December 1966.

the community and maximizes the chances of reform by preserving the prisoner's familial and desirable community relationships. When allied with some indefiniteness in the duration of the sentence, the regular testing of fitness for release by a home-leave program is obviously sound community protection.

Similar pressures lie behind "day leave" in the Scandinavian systems and behind "working out" as it develops in several regions of the world. Part-time imprisonment thus stands both as an alternative to prison and as a modification of prison.

Yet even when reduction of the social isolation is achieved there are a number of features of the prison system which demand urgent attention; the problem of providing effective prison industries is one of them. In the vast majority of correctional institutions penal work programs are small and inefficient and involve repetitive drudgery with outdated equipment. The President's Crime Commission found that idleness was the "prevailing characteristic of most American prisons and jails." A number of state and federal laws restricting the sale of prison-made products have helped to ensure the continuance of this situation.

Such legislation represents a pernicious perversion of public policy. It is based on the unacceptable premise that when a person is convicted of a crime and sent to prison he ceases to be a citizen. The threat to organized labor or business interests in the community by prison industry is minuscule. The extent of the demoralization entailed in keeping prisoners in a state of workless, infantile dependency is incalculable. The development of prison industries can provide not only for the habilitation of inmates to constructive and rewarding employment but also provides opportunities for training in vocational skills. That effective prison industries can be developed has been demonstrated by the success of Federal Prison Industries, Inc. A better model for state systems possibly, because of the scale of operations, might be the Swedish work program where the penal administration slogan is: "First build a factory, then add a prison to it." Soon in this country we must experiment with the full wages prison, since the logic behind it is compelling.

Another respect in which American prisons are deficient and indeed represent dangerous anachronisms is in their size. Forty years ago the American Prison Association warned that no prison should contain more than 1,200 inmates. Today not only do some 45 American penal institutions contain more than that number but there are also a number of prisons such as the State Prison of Southern Michigan at Jackson, San Quentin in California, and the Ohio Penitentiary at Columbus which hold more than three times that number. Yet even 1,200 inmates would be regarded as far too many by most penologists today. The British Howard League for Penal Reform has stated that 150 is the optimum size and the energetic and imaginative Swedish director general of prisons, Torsten Eriksson, regards 60 inmates as the maximum desirable population for a penal institution! Be that as it may, our institutions are grossly too large. There is little point in arguing the merits of this; few will disagree. It is the question of ignorance and tradition masquerading as political and social priorities. With small institutions, much else that we all seek to achieve in our correctional work is possible; with the mega-institution, little is possible. Discussing the number of staff and prisoners with a warden of a small jail, one of the authors asked, "What is your inmate-staff ratio?" and received the comforting reply, "Some like it, some don't."

PAROLE AND PROBATION

Although, as we have said, four-fifths of the correctional budget is spent and nine-tenths of correctional employees work in penal institutions, only one-third of all offenders are confined in them; the remaining two-thirds are under supervision in the community. We have already indicated that, for the great majority of those confined, special community programs must be developed as alternatives to institutionalization. It remains to deal with the two-thirds of offenders already being supervised outside the walls on parole or probation.

More than 60 percent of adult felons in the Nation as a whole are released on parole before the expiration of the maximum terms of their sentences. But there are sharp variations in the extent of parole use in different states, from one in which only 9 percent of prisoners are paroled to some where virtually all are. Most juveniles are released on parole but supervision is commonly inadequate. Most misdemeanants are not paroled. Nearly two-thirds of the local jails have no parole procedures, and those that do release only 8 percent of inmates in this way. Slightly more than half of all offenders sentenced to correctional treatment are placed on probation. Yet there are still many jurisdictions which lack any probation facilities for misdemeanant offenders. Of 250 counties studied by the President's Crime Commission Survey of Corrections one-third provided no probation service at all. Many small juvenile courts rely almost entirely on suspended sentences in lieu of probation supervision.

Various studies have attempted to measure the success of parole and probation. As far as parole is concerned, authoritative estimates indicate that among adult offenders 55 to 65 percent of those released are not subsequently returned to prison. And only about one-third of those that are returned have been convicted of new felonies; the remainder are returned for other parole violations. Success rates for probation are generally considerably higher than for parole.

Yet these successes in both parole and probation have been achieved by services for the most part grossly understaffed, almost always underpaid, and too often undertrained. The best estimate available from current research indicates that an average of 35 cases per officer is about the highest ratio likely to permit effective supervision and assistance in either service. Of course, no caseload standard can be applied to all types of offenders. The optimum overall caseload of 35 is based on a determination of what an average caseload would be when different types of offenders were given the appropriate kinds and degrees of supervision. Up to 20 persons in a caseload of 35 could receive close intensive supervision; if none required such supervision, the caseload could be larger.

Current average caseloads vastly exceed the optimum level. Over 76 percent of all misdemeanants and 67 percent of all felons on probation are in caseloads of 100 or more. Less than 4 percent of the probation officers in the Nation carry caseloads of 40 or fewer. Adults released on parole are supervised in caseloads averaging 68; and over 22 percent of adult parolees are being supervised in caseloads of more than 80. The average caseload for juveniles is about 64.

It is clear that there is considerable need for additional probation and parole officers. It must be remembered that offenders are kept under such supervision at much less cost than in institutions. The national survey of corrections done for the President's Crime Commission found, for example, that to keep a juvenile offender on probation costs only one-tenth of the amount required to keep him in a state training school. Similar 1-to-10 cost ratios prevail in regard to both felons and misdemeanants. It is true that this difference arises in part because expenditures for probation and parole are currently inadequate but, as the President's Crime Commission points out, probation and parole expenditures "can clearly be increased several fold and still remain less expensive than institutional programs." When one takes into account also capital costs (up to and beyond $20,000 per bed in a correctional institution), the cost of welfare assistance for prisoners' families, and the loss in production and taxable income involved in imprisonment, the 1-to-10 ratio is clearly a considerable underestimate of the real cost differential. In these circumstances the failure to provide adequate probation and parole facilities for misdemeanants, who make up more than two-thirds of the nearly 2 million commitments to all correctional facilities and programs in a year, is extremely costly as well as unsound penal practice.

INTEGRATED AND REGIONAL STATE CORRECTIONAL SYSTEMS

One of the currently contentious issues in the organization of corrections in the federal system is whether the federal probation and parole services should be joined with the Federal Bureau of Prisons and the Federal Parole Board in a single department administratively responsible to the Department of Justice. Unification and regionalization at the federal level, and in a country the size of the United States, raise problems of great complexity, with political and jurisprudential penumbrae which at present we would prefer to avoid; let us therefore suggest only some of the advantages of a unified and regionalized structure for a state as distinct from a federal correctional system.

Such an integrated, regional correctional system is, of course, not unknown in this country. The Wisconsin system is so organized. The advantage of unifying institutional and extra institutional processes into some coherent single administrative structure of probation, prison, and parole, flows essentially from the fact that the connnection between institutional and noninstitutional correctional processes is growing closer and requires overall planning. The prison is now rarely thought to provide an independent, self-contained correctional process. All who hope to rehabilitate offenders see the process as involving a gradual release procedure and an effective aftercare program linked in a single plan. And effective probation is coming to be seen as requiring some institutional support in an appreciable proportion of cases. The probation hostel may be necessary for some cases; institutional control of leisure in community treatment centers may be needed for others.

And so prison, probation, and parole grow closer together and structurally intertwine. The prison may be required as a base from which the prisoner goes out to work; a halfway house may be used as a release procedure; and aftercare will always be closely linked with the prison program and should provide the last stage in the execution of the prisoner's rehabilitative plan. It is hard to provide such continuous institutional and postinstitutional correctional processes, and such institutional and contemporaneously noninstitutional processes (halfway house, working out, community treatment center, probation hostel) unless there is the closest of ties between those responsible for the various services.

Continuity of treatment plan and execution is necessary to the release procedure; it also proves necessary when we apply more effective control mechanisms in our aftercare processes, for this reason: At present when a prisoner on parole breaks a condition of his release, the choice facing the correctional authorities is too limited. He can be warned, or he can be taken back into custody. Just as we are developing "halfway-out" houses as release procedures so should we develop "halfway-in" houses to provide for those released prisoners who require a period of closer control, than can be given when they are relatively free on parole but who do not need to be sent back to prison. This group may not be large, but it is appreciable, and again there is a happy confluence between better rehabilitative processes and less cost.

Another advantage of unification of correctional service should be mentioned. It has long seemed to us that the prison warden, to be entirely effective in his job, should not only be informed concerning probation and parole work but also should have had a period of active involvement in casework in the community. Likewise, the senior probation or parole officer should have had institutional experience if he is to be most effective. Within the correctional system, no one should reach a high position without a variety of work experiences both inside and outside the walls. Thus the theme of continuity of treatment would be maintained by the very structure of the services involved.

So much for the value of unification in a state system. Regionalization needs little justification. It carries forward the theme of avoiding enterprises too large for any single man to have reasonably close and detailed acquaintance with their workings. And there is also the advantage of linking the correctional system, in each of the regions, close to the needs, opportunities, and social attitudes of the particular social group in which the offender lived and will live; regional differences require appropriate differences in correctional systems. Finally and obviously, regionalization greatly facilitates maintaining closer ties between the prisoner and his family, by visits and furloughs, than is possible where correctional administration is not regionalized.

SENTENCING

To Blackstone the judicial function of sentencing the convicted criminal presented no trace of intellectual challenge, the judge acting merely as a channel through which the law expressed its predetermined and impartial decision. We expect more from our criminal sanctions than we did in Blackstone's day, but we have neither developed techniques nor fashioned principles to meet our expectations. Over 20 years ago Mr. Justice Frankfurter said that "the inadequacy of our traditional methods for determining the appropriate treatment for offenders, once wrongdoing is established, can no longer be disregarded." But in the intervening years there has been little change, although about half the states are now undertaking projects to revise their penal laws and sentencing codes.

Insofar as the work of the correctional system is largely determined by the court's sentence, it is necessary to say something about sentencing policies and procedures. In this we are broadly in agreement with the approach taken by the American Law Institute in its Model Penal Code; and this agreement is reflected in several of the edicts in this chapter.

We are not here concerned to deal with the precise number of punishment categories required or the penalties to be attached to each category. The important points are that there should be what Herbert Wechsler calls "discipline in legislative use of penal sanctions."

The code embodies statutory criteria and separate sentencing provisions to discriminate between offenders requiring lengthy imprisonment and others. Thus courts are allowed to impose extended terms of imprisonment—beyond the ordinary maximum—in cases where the defendant is a persistent offender, a professional criminal, a dangerous, mentally abnormal person, or a multiple offender whose criminality is particularly extensive. The provision of statutory criteria of this kind to guide courts in the exercise of their discretion is an important move in the direction of rational sentencing policy.

No less important are the code's provisions regarding statutory standards governing the granting of probation. In almost every jurisdiction of America legislatures have restricted the power of the courts to grant probation. These arbitrary denials of discretion to the courts, like mandatory prison sentences, are met with evasion in many cases but they represent an improper obstruction to the course of justice. At the same time, the statutory provisions authorizing the use of probation are commonly couched in such vague and general terms that, as the President's Crime Commission puts it, "each judge is left virtually unrestrained in applying his own theories of probation to individual cases."

The Model Penal Code directs the court to suspend sentences or grant probation unless it finds that imprisonment is necessary for the protection of the public because (a) there is undue risk that during the period of a suspended sentence or probation the defendant will commit another crime; or (b) the defendant is in need of correctional treatment that can be provided most effectively by his commitment to an institution; or (c) a lesser sentence will depreciate the seriousness of the defendant's crime. These standards too are general but they clearly accord a priority to dispositions which avoid institutionalization. And at the same time, the code provides a lengthy list of grounds which "shall be accorded weight in favor of withholding sentence of imprisonment."

We are also in agreement with the provision of the Model Penal Code regarding parole. Our edict to the effect that every release be upon parole for a fixed period of between 1 and 5 years is derived from the code. It is based on the theory that parole should be seen as an essential part of every institutional sentence and not as an act of benign clemency on the part of the authorities. The parole period is a period of supervised conditional release required for community protection which starts when parole release occurs. At present the period of parole is measured by the length of the unexpired portion of the prison sentence, which is dangerously irrational. It means that those who are the worst risks and therefore are held longest in institutions have the shortest period under supervision, whereas the best risks, released early, have the longest terms under supervision.

Another respect in which sentencing practices are deficient at present relates to the imposition of fines. An inordinate number of offenders are imprisoned for failure to pay fines. For some states as many as 60 percent of jail inmates have been imprisoned for default in payment of fines. Sentences which offer the choice of paying a fine or going to prison are discriminatory in that those unable to pay are punished more severely. A substantial reduction in needless imprisonment can be achieved by allowing time to pay fines and by the use of civil attachment and execution for the collection of unpaid fines. In England the number of committals in default of payment of fines was reduced from 85,000 in 1910 to less than 3,000 in 1947 by these methods; and today less than 1 percent of fines lead to imprisonment for default.

CONCLUSION

The program outlined here will provide both cheaper and more effective social protection. At the same time it will, in the main, be less afflictive and involve less disruption of family life and less suffering on the part of innocent dependents. No doubt those who still subscribe to the curious notion that by hurting, humiliating, and harassing offenders we can somehow morally improve them will see this as a defect in our approach. But until some evidence is adduced in support of this idea we are not disposed to take it seriously.

4

Viewpoint
on Rehabilitation

ROBERT MARTINSON

The idea that a primary goal of criminal justice is to "rehabilitate" criminal offenders has been so ingrained in the public mind over the last century that it still takes the form of an unexamined assumption. Consider the very name we give to our post-adjudicatory system—"corrections." This name implies a program and a purpose, and it even embodies an implicit promise to the criminal offender. It avoids or downgrades such major functions of punishment as the deterrence of incipient offenders and the temporary incapacitation of those apprehended and sent to prison.

There are recent indications that "rehabilitation" (I prefer the term "correctional treatment") is about to lose its privileged status as an unthinking axiom of public policy. The National Commission on Standards and Goals had a number of critical things to say about "treatment" and the assumptions of the "medical model." Inmate spokesmen and ex-offender organizations have become increasingly ambivalent, if not openly hostile, toward newer forms of "behavioral modification." Attorney General Saxbe has apparently called rehabilitation a "myth," thus setting the stage for a national debate in which unfortunate terms like "bleeding hearts" may provide more heat than clarity.

SOURCE. *Criminal Justice Newsletter,* National Council on Crime and Delinquency, 5(21), November 18, 1974, pp.4–5. Reprinted with permission of the author and the National Council on Crime and Delinquency.

Recently, in New York State, Mr. Peter Preiser, Commissioner of Correctional Services, was accused of "stock bureaucratic defensiveness" by the *New York Times.* The *Times* had previously noted with satisfaction that Mr. Preiser had supported a college program for inmates, but on this occasion Mr. Preiser had defended himself against a state auditor's report by insisting that there is no evidence that correctional programs (treatment) have a substantial or even measurable effect on recidivism rates.

If rehabilitation of criminal offenders is to become an hypothesis subject to debate and not an article of faith, both the proponents and the opponents of particular methods—vocational training, education, psychotherapy, group counseling, or whatever—will need to carefully reexamine the available scientific evidence about the success or failure that we have met when we have tried to rehabilitate offenders with various treatments and in various institutional and noninstitutional settings. The field of penology has produced a voluminous research literature on this subject but until recently there has been no comprehensive and systematic review of this literature.

THE SURVEY

A massive New York State survey was initiated in 1966 by the Governor's Special Committee on Criminal Offenders to fill this unmet need. My colleagues and I were hired by the committee to undertake a comprehensive survey of what was known about rehabilitation.

First, we undertook a six-month search of the literature for any available reports on attempts at rehabilitation published in the English language from 1945 through 1967. We then picked from that literature all those studies whose design and execution met the conventional standards of social science research. We excluded studies only for methodological reasons; for example, the study presented insufficient data, used unreliable resources, used samples that were undescribed or too small, or provided no true comparability between treated and untreated groups. Using these standards, we drew from the total number of studies 231 acceptable ones that we not only analyzed ourselves, but summarized in detail so that a reader would be able to compare our results with his independent conclusions.

The survey was formally completed in 1970 and reedited for final publication in 1972. It was released to its coauthors in 1973 after being subpoenaed as evidence in a case before the Bronx Supreme Court, and will be published by Praeger in 1975, under the title, *The Effectiveness of Correctional Treatment.*

Persuaded that the general conclusions of the survey should be made available to policy-makers and the public in a non-technical format, I recently published a brief summary of the findings in relation to recidivism, the phenomenon that reflects how well our present treatment programs are performing the task of rehabilitation.

THE FINDINGS: NO DECISIVE IMPACT

I made the following rather bald summary of our findings: *With few and isolated exceptions, the rehabilitative efforts that have been reported so far have had no appreciable effect on recidivism.* Those who wish to examine the detailed evidence and analysis upon which this conclusion is based are referred to the much more complex and detailed analysis in the original volume.

Nowhere in this volume is it asserted that rehabilitation is a "myth." That is a conclusion I have come to, however, based on the evidence made available by this volume. Others may conclude that all the evidence is not in or may renew their faith in forced state treatment in other ways. What the volume does do is to lay out before the reader the best available social scientific evidence that bears on the question.

The survey was limited to the rehabilitation methods generally in use during the period from 1945 through 1967, including small caseloads on probation or parole, intensive supervision in specialized caseloads, early releases from confinement, variation in sentence length and degree of custody, casework and individual counseling, psychotherapy, group therapies of various kinds, so-called "milieu therapy," halfway houses, pre-release guidance centers, tranquilizing drugs, plastic surgery, and other factors. Methods not evaluated included work release, methadone maintenance, recent forms of so-called "behavior modification," and what have come to be called diversion methods.

THE DANGERS OF MISINTERPRETATION

Once a piece of scientific work enters the maelstrom of practical politics there is a danger that tentative conclusions will become dogma or that findings that are limited will be overgeneralized. *The Effectiveness of Correctional Treatment* is a highly techincal volume meant to contribute toward a knowledge base for criminal justice in the hope that decisions can be guided by evidence. In presenting its essential findings to a wide variety of audiences in recent years, I have noted the following persistent misinterpretations:

Question. Isn't research that shows "no effect" a waste of time and money?

Answer. On the contrary. If the research meets the minimum scientific standards, and shows that a "treatment" has no effect on recidivism, this calls the treatment into question and it may be abandoned or modified.

Question. Isn't this evaluation research so pragmatic and atheoretical that any conclusions are hazardous?

Answer. Perhaps so, but this is the best body of evidence currently available on the effectiveness of correction treatment, and the conclusions derive not from a few selected studies but from the cumulative evidence of over two hundred studies involving tens of thousands of subjects.

Question. Doesn't this study conclusively prove that our criminal justice system is a failure?

Answer. No. Only that the weight of the evidence is that the *addition* of treatment elements ("programs" of the kind evaluated) to the system has no appreciable effect in changing offenders into non-offenders. The system may still deter *potential* offenders or temporarily incapacitate those who are incarcerated. These, and many other aspects of criminal justice remain to be evaluated.

Question. Doesn't the survey show that probation and parole are ineffective and should be abandoned?

Answer. Not in the least! Indeed, it indicates that those placed on probation *do no worse* than those imprisoned and may do slightly better. It does indicate that *small caseloads* on probation do no better than standard caseloads, and that probation *supervision* (as currently practiced) is not an effective "treatment," i.e., does not substantially improve the behavior of those supervised over what would be expected.

Question. Wouldn't treatment work if it were accomplished in the community rather than in the prison?

Answer. A large number of these treatment programs took place outside of prison, and the burden of the evidence is not encouraging. Also, in figuring the relative costs of probation and confinement, we must include the possible cost to the public of having a larger number of potential offenders at large, and not rest our case simply on a comparison of recidivism rates.

Question. Does the survey recommend that we abolish or reduce programs such as vocational training, prison education, counseling, or group therapy that are found to be ineffective?

Answer. If the sole justification for a "program" is that it will reduce recidivism among those who receive it, then the survey will provide evidence as to whether this is achieved, and may therefore call many such programs into question. My own position is that we should cease demanding from our criminal justice networks what they are unable to accomplish, thus freeing them to justify their activities in a proper way. For example, if a prison needs facilities to reduce inmate idleness, a law library, weightlifting equipment, or a television set might accomplish this somewhat better than an additional counselor or psychiatrist. After all, do we vary the food or clothing or visits given to inmates on the grounds of rehabilitation or on the grounds that we believe in a minimum standard of human decency in criminal justice?

Question. If rehabilitation is ultimately shown to be a "myth," must we then "get tough" with offenders?

Answer. Why must we reel from pillar to post in our reactions, substituting rhetoric for the search for more effective policies? We have spent 3.2 billion dollars since the Safe Streets Act and only now has Congress insisted that this effort be evaluated. I am now involved in research on deterrence through the Crime Control and Offender Career project. Preliminary findings indicate that deterrence "works," but we do not know within what limits or with what costs.

After all, there are various ways of "getting tough," and our planning agencies need to know whether we need milder and more certain penalties or more severe penalties for those we now convict and incarcerate. In addition, almost nothing is known about crime prevention other than deterrence. Knowledge that we have had over-inflated expectations about "treatment" should lead one to demand evidence of the effectiveness of these alternate proposals. Otherwise we may simply go galloping down another blind alley.

5

Deterrence and Corrections

NORVAL MORRIS AND FRANK ZIMRING

It is fashionable to bewail our ignorance of effective correctional processes—fashionable but perverse. We know a lot better than we do. In particular, we know how to avoid many of the socially injurious consequences of our penal sanctions for inmates and, through them, for the community to which they return. The mega-institution and the protracted prison sentences which characterize American corrections are outmoded and inept. But we are trapped by inertia, irresponsibility, ignorance, and cost: the four horsemen of political inaction. Headway is made in some states and in some agencies, but the over-all picture is bleak.

The remedies lie deep in social attitudes and social organization, but also in the acquisition of knowledge of the effects of correctional changes on social and political phenomena. We must increase our capacity to avoid inflicting social injury by our penal sanctions, and we must also learn how to reform such criminals as are responsive without jeopardizing other legitimate aims of punishment. We must discover the extent to which ameliorative and re-educational correctional methods can be pursued without interfering with the other purposes of our criminal-justice system. Is there a conflict between reformation and deterrence? Are the hard-nosed right in their view that the "bleeding-heart" treaters will, even if they lead a few criminals to conformity, nevertheless increase the

SOURCE. *Annals of the American Academy of Political and Social Science,* **381**, January 1969, pp. 137–146. Reprinted with permission of the authors and the editor, *Annals of the American Academy of Political and Social Science.*

impact of crime on society by reducing the extent to which threatened punishments coerce men from crime?

No one theory explains the different punitive measure in our criminal-law system. Prevention, reformation, deterrence, retribution, expiation, the Kantian argument that punishment is an end in itself—all these mingle in wild semantic and dialectic confusion in most discussions of the purposes of punishment. It may be that the Freudians are right and that our rationalizations for punishment conceal deep needs for vengeance and for the reinforcement of the group superego by the suffering inflicted on the criminal taboo-breaker; but certainly, within these rationalizations, deterrence and reformation hold primacy of place. Both are seen as means to the ends of increasing and preserving the welfare of society; to many, they are also seen as conflicting and competing means. Whether they conflict, in fact, will be known only when we better understand our capacity to influence human behavior by threats and by retraining programs, and understand the proper limits and roles of each. We are in the prehistory of such studies. Even the conceptual framework for the acquisition of knowledge of the consequences of threats on human behavior has not been devised.

Legislators, when defining penal sanctions, think and act predominantly in terms of deterring prospective offenders—and properly so. Correctional officers in their work think and act predominantly in terms of rehabilitating offenders committed to their custody. Deterrence concerns the correctional officer in an institution only with regard to disciplinary offenses, and then his reliance on deterrent processes is strong indeed. The mixes of deterrence and reform are thus different at different levels of the criminal-justice system.

Our dedication to corrections must not lead us to repudiate deterrence. Our criminal-law system has deterrence as its primary and essential postulate. And there are many examples of the threat of punishment under the criminal law clearly influencing human behavior. Honest reader, consider your income tax return, and what it would be like were you assured that it could not be checked. If we have misjudged you, consider the impact on your neighbor's tax return! On the other hand, there are many areas where variations in the severity of the penal sanction seem to be irrelevant to the incidence of the behavior threatened— capital punishment as distinguished from protracted imprisonment for homicide; the gross increase in sanctions for narcotics offenses; and, generally, variations in minima and maxima of terms of imprisonment for a wide diversity of criminal offenses. Here, as elsewhere, the compelling lesson is that it is foolish in the extreme to offer general propositions about crime and criminals. We must address the diversity of our purposes and the varieties of human behavior we seek to influence.

It is at the sentencing level that the balance between reform and deterrence becomes most difficult. Will a lenient sentence on this offender attenuate the assumed twin general deterrent effects of the sentence on those who are like-minded and on society at large? Hardly, if it is not reported to them, as is the rule. So the question must be raised at a more subtle level: Will a settled course of such leniency have these effects? Here the issue becomes real. And even-handed justice requires a settled course, as distinct from capriciousness, in sentencing. But the question is not easy to answer because we know little of the boundaries and operations of deterrent processes. The polar deterrence argument becomes a bore; a modest beginning on the search for more knowledge becomes a compelling need. We have endured a surfeit of unsubstantiated speculation, continuing, quite literally, since man first laboriously chipped out his penal codes on tablets of stone or scrawled them on chewed and pounded bark. It is time we did better. To do so, it may be wise first to get our terms clear, then to assess what we now know, and then to suggest a strategy for our search.

DISTINCTIONS

Criminal sanctions function both in the macrocosm of society and in the microcosm of criminals within society. In society as a whole, it would be safe to say that the existence of formal prohibitions and punishments imposed by society influences every individual's superego, and, to a certain extent, conditions his behavior. It is likely that his behavior is more largely influenced by formal and informal sanctions standing outside the criminal law, but it would be hard to deny that there is a relationship between the precepts of the criminal-justice system and the values supported by less formal social sanctions, or to deny that the former may influence the latter. Further, for some people and for some crimes, the existence of punishment and, perhaps, a particular level of punishment, prevents them, as potential offenders, from becoming actual offenders, thus having a generally deterrent effect. Secondly, in its relation to criminals who are apprehended and subjected to sanctions, it becomes the function of punishment to reform where possible, to deter where possible from future crimes, with threats added to the experience of punishment, and, generally, to work on the offending criminal with the aim of rendering society safe from his depredation (in effect, of removing him from the microcosm into the macrocosm).

"Deterrence" is thus used in at least two senses: to refer to the influence of threatened sanctions on an individual who has been convicted of crime and punished—"special deterrence"—and also, in a wider sense, to refer to its operation on the rest of society—"general deterrence."

Further, the concept of "general deterrence" is itself used in at least two senses: first, as describing the effect of the threat of punishment as directly influencing the behavior of those within the macrocosm of society, and, second, and in a less precise way, as, by its very proclamation and existence, educating and habituating men to avoid that which is prohibited, not by the threat of the imposition of a sanction on them, but by the very strength and formality of this method of enunciating a behavioral precept. European criminologists use the phrase "general prevention," as distinct from "general deterrence," to cover this last concept, but there are difficulties here, too. The idea of general prevention too easily embraces a whole host of socially ameliorative processes such as the improvement of education, the elimination of slums, a negative income tax, and many other social processes which many of us would regard as preventive of crime, as well as physical barriers to crime.

It is rarely wise to quibble about definitions; clarity as distinct from agreement is the touchstone. But at the present level of the literature and research in this field, it seems necessary to make at least the above distinction between "special" and "general" deterrence, to recognize that the concept of "general deterrence" includes both the threat element and the educative—habituative element, and to appreciate the necessity for their separate analysis.

This attempt to clarify terms solves no problems, but it may make their solution possible. Yet, more carefully defined concepts than "special deterrence" and "general deterrence" (in its two aspects of coercion to virtue through threat and persuasion to virtue by consolidation of social values) are necessary. Let us now mention two of these: the channeling effects of threats and the concept of "marginal deterrence."

It is insufficient to ask: Did the threatened punishment operate or not operate? It may well have had *channeling* effects that are not measurable in terms of the threat succeeding or not succeeding in absolute terms. Consider a typical example. Traveling at sixty miles an hour, you approach a fifty-miles-an-hour speed-limit sign, and reduce your speed to forty-nine miles an hour. The general deterrent threat has operated absolutely in your case. But the car behind glides by, its driver having seen the sign, and reduced his speed from seventy to fifty-five miles an hour. The threat has had an influence on his behavior, a channeling effect. The car behind him, which you had both passed when it was traveling at forty-five miles an hour, now increases its speed to fifty miles an hour. The general deterrent threat has had a quite different channeling effect on the behavior of the driver of that third car. These channeling effects of threats on behavior must be borne in mind throughout studies in this field.

The second further concept that we must now mention is of even more importance: it is the concept of marginal deterrence. The question—do criminal sanctions deter?—although frequently asked, is not particularly helpful. We impose criminal sanctions for a wide diversity of purposes, and many criminal prohibitions would exist even if we were confident of the absence of deterrent efficacy of the sanctions attached to them. The issue is rarely: Does a given sanction deter? It is usually: Would a more severe penalty attached to that criminal prohibition more effectively deter? In the capital punishment debate, the real issue is not whether the death penalty is a deterrent to homicide or attempted homicide, but whether it is a more effective deterrent that the alternative sanction of protracted imprisonment which would be applied. Hence the key question in deterrence research is whether variations in the severity of threatened sanctions will affect a given crime rate. It is only to the extent that we must increase punishment to achieve a larger deterrent effect, imposing a punishment more severe than would otherwise be imposed, that any conflict can arise between deterrence and the other purposes of punishment. Hence the central importance of the concept of marginal deterrence and of research into marginal deterrence.

SPECIAL DETERRENCE

Let us first consider existing knowledge in special deterrence and then turn to what we know and how we may learn more about general deterrence. There are very few empirical studies in special deterrence. The reason for this is, of course, the prodigious difficulty of isolating the threat effect—either of a repetition, or a more severe dose, of the medicine—from the many other effects of the criminal sanction.

Corporal punishment in a variety of brutal forms has been applied by most criminal-justice systems at some stage in their evolution and then abandoned by virtually all. Its purposes were both general and special deterrence. It is interesting that the argument for special deterrence was abandoned earlier than the argument for general deterrence in relation to corporal punishment. It required no very precise measuring instruments to appreciate that when a person had been flogged for a crime of violence, if he later committed a crime of violence, he tended to do so with greater vigor and brutality than he had earlier demonstrated. But, again, one must resist the temptation to extrapolate such findings beyond their proper base. On the order of 70 percent of first-timers in prison all over the world do not return. A proponent of special deterrence could strenuously contend that this is a consequence of the special deterrent effect of the imprisonment, and not of any reformative process that might have been applied to the offender while he was incarcerated. Again, we face a situation where knowledge rather than speculation is required.

Nearly twenty years ago, the elder of us conducted a small empirical study in special deterrence. He studied the question whether the length of the periods of imprisonment imposed on 302 confirmed recidivists had any effect on the duration of their subsequent periods of freedom. The entire group were failures, in the sense that they were studied while they were in the convict prisons of England; all had lengthy criminal records. The group had a total of 2,720 periods of imprisonment and 2,720 subsequent periods of freedom prior to their last period of incarceration. It emerged that the length of each period of penal confinement had no measurable effect on the subsequent interval between discharge and reconviction. It is true, however, that a finding that the length of time which an individual spends in prison appears to have no influence on the length of time he spends out of prison does not completely confute the argument that special deterrence is operative on the individuals covered by the study. Criminals tend to get longer prison sentences as their careers in crime get longer and their status as criminals becomes more confirmed. Since those individuals are more confirmed criminals when they are serving long sentences than they are at the stage in life when they are serving short sentences or receiving probation, it may be plausible to suppose that, even in the absence of any effect owing to threat and punishment, the periods of time that they would spend out of prison after longer prison sentences would be shorter than the periods of time that they have spent out of prison earlier in their careers when their commitment to crime was not so manifest. Thus, finding that the periods of time seemed to be the same is not a total rebuttal of the argument that long sentences in prison make future criminal threats more frightening to criminals and deter them from future criminal activity for some period of time. It should also be noted that it is more likely that the police will pick up an individual with a long criminal record as a suspect, and it is more likely that the police will have an accurate idea of what kind of crime an individual is apt to commit, if he has a long record of prior convictions. To the extent that detection has any bearing on how long a period an individual spends out of jail, this would mean that criminals would spend less time out of jail during the later stages of criminal careers because they would be caught more quickly. These are the ways in which a special deterrent effect might possibly be concealed in an habitual criminal study. It still is true, however, that the apparent lack of relationship between the severity in the punishment that we impose in habitual criminal situations and the results which we seem to obtain is a substantial disappointment for those who would argue for a unitary, effective universe of special deterrence. And, of course, that experiment painfully established what all correctional workers already well know—that longer sentences of imprisonment have an injurious effect on a man's capacity to live without crime in the community, even if he wants to. Hence, one cannot tell whether the result is due to the deleterious effect of long-term imprisonment overcoming the possibly special deterrent effects of the more protracted sentences, or whether the more protracted sentences had no special deterrent effect at all. We cannot, by such simple techniques, reach confident conclusions about special deterrence.

Special legislation concerning habitual criminals is pervasive, and there are provisions in most criminal-justice systems increasing punishments for recidivists; both have special deterrence as their primary purpose. They may include the purpose of lengthy warehousing of the dangerous person, until either his danger passes or the years diminish his capacity to injure the community, but special deterrence is also involved. It is well established by many follow-up studies that the lengthier the offender's correctional record, and the longer and more frequent the penal sentences that have been imposed on him, the more likely he is to relapse into crime. One would be wrong to allege that this disproves the special deterrent effects of such punishment. Again, we are lost among too many variables.

It has proved possible to demonstrate that reducing the number of prison terms imposed on defined categories of offenders and substituting noninstitutional treatment measures on them has not increased their recidivist rates. This would seem to indicate that, certainly for first offenders—or perhaps one should more carefully speak of them as those for the first time convicted—reducing the severity of the sentence that would otherwise have been imposed does not reduce the special deterrent effects of the criminal law. The key question here is marginal deterrence, and none seems to obtain at these intervals.

For our part, though we are in favor of experimentation in special deterrence, we do not regard it as of equal importance to research in general deterrence. It seems to us that the general sentencing pattern which is emerging in this country does not place great stress on special deterrence; much more emphasis is placed on general deterrence. Diverse views of the moral gravity of the offense are of predominant importance and they are expressed in terms of a relationship between the assumptions of general deterrence and estimates of the capacity and the likely will of the offender to avoid crime in the future. Within correctional systems themselves, the emphasis shifts to rehabilitative purposes, and here the length of the sentence which has been imposed for purposes of general deterrence may have an inhibiting effect on correctional possibilities; but, again, special deterrence is not much considered except when the correctional officer faces a disciplinary problem within a prison: then, special and general deterrent purposes can be heard resoundingly to dominate decisions.

GENERAL DETERRENCE

A first task for the student of deterrence is to assess in the criminological literature what we now know of deterrence. The capital punishment controversy has produced the most reliable information on the general deterrent effect of a criminal sanction. It now seems established and accepted that the existence or nonexistence of capital punishment as a sanction alternative to protracted imprisonment for convicted murderers makes no difference to the homicide rate or to the attempted-homicide rate. Suppose this is true; there is a temptation to extrapolate such a proposition to other crime and to deny the operation of marginal general deterrence in them. This temptation should be resisted, for it is easy to demonstrate contrary situations for other crimes where increased sanctions (maintaining stable reporting, detection, arrest, and conviction rates) lead to reduced incidence of the proscribed behavior. For example, parking offenses can, indeed, be reduced by an increased severity in sanctions if one is determined about the matter. And, to take a current example, experience in the United Kingdom leads compellingly to the view that the use of the breathalyzer and a more extensive application of criminal sanctions to drunken driving can by the general deterrent process substantially reduce the mortality and morbidity rates from drunken driving. There is, of course, a trap in this example, because what emerges is that, in the recent United Kingdom breathalyzer program, the size of the punishment has remained constant; all that has varied, and varied substantially, is the definition of the crime and the method of detecting the offense and prosecuting it to a conviction. It is, of course, truistic that the variables of detection rate and conviction rate will interrelate with the severity of the sanctions, and that we must bear these relationships in mind whenever we are seeking to assess the consequences of various deterrent strategies in the criminal-justice system.

The criminological literature, apart from that dealing with capital punishment and drunken driving and certain studies of parking offenses and of bad-check laws, does not provide a great deal of insight into our problem. There are, happily, several other disciplines, farther advanced than we are, capable of guiding our search. Philosophers have long speculated about these problems; more recently, other disciplines, particularly psychology and psychiatry, have begun to contribute the chips of knowledge which will make up the mosaic of general deterrence. Kurt Lewin and his followers working on field theory, those studying the concept of cognitive dissonance, the educational psychologists, and those interested in animal behavior (only somewhat disparate fields)—all have contributions to make to our manipulation of criminal sanctions for general deterrent purposes. And the psychiatrists, both those of Freudian orientation and their collectivist colleagues more interested in conditioning, have knowledge relevant to our task. Indeed, one of the problems in this search for understanding of this basic postulate of the criminal law—that its sanctions deter—is the collation of information from such a disparity of disciplines that the capacity of any one man to draw it together is strained. Happily, there are methods of handling even this difficulty and of achieving interdisciplinary collaboration on the acquisition of that fundamental knowledge of penal sanctions which Hammurabi really needed but did not have before he leapt to the codifying exercise which has sustained his name and inspired his equally unsure successors.

We have many lessons to learn from research in related fields, but one emerges compellingly: deterrence is not a unitary phenomenon. The critical intellectual work involved in structuring an investigation of deterrence is a search for major variations in threat situations which account for the substantial observed variations in the effects of threats on behavior. Let us list just a few of these variables: the nature of the behavior subject to a threat, differences in the perceived credibility of the threat, differences in the magnitude and kind of consequences threatened, variations in the personal structure of the threatened audience, the social orientation of the threatened audience, the form in which threats are communicated, and the nature of the agency which is issuing the threat. Experience indicates that the collection, collation, and evaluation of deterrence-related material is a substantial undertaking. The literature of potential importance in this area is vast, and it is neither organized nor indexed in a manner which makes its identification and retrieval for our purposes an easy task. We have been involved in this work for three years, and the task continues to stretch before us.

We seek knowledge of the marginal deterrent effects of criminal sanctions in channeling human behavior by the threat of punishment. The literature does not take us any distance. Empirical research is a necessary means, and its methodology is not obvious. For the time being, we put aside the educative and habituative effects of criminal sanctions, which are sometimes included under the rubric of general deterrence, and concentrate on general deterrence by threat of criminal sanction, in the hope of ultimately moving to a cost-benefit analysis of different criminal-deterrence strategies. Such an inquiry into marginal general deterrence involves the counting of acts which are *not* committed or which were differently committed. At first blush, this seems an impossible task; but it must be remembered that whenever reliable information is available concerning the rate of crime, it speaks both to the number of types of acts committed in the population over a period of time and to the number of acts not committed. If research is designed so that accurate information is available about the rate of commission of a particular act after a new deterrent strategy is introduced, and if the likely rate in the absence of a deterrent strategy or with the application of an alternative strategy is known, then we have a base-line capable of providing information about the number of acts not committed, or differently committed, as a result of the introduction of that particular strategy. Jurisdictions frequently modify their penal sanctions, and it might be thought that historical or retrospective studies of the consequences of these modifications would guide our search. The problem is, of course, that useful comparisons of a rate of crime before and after the changes in punishment policy depend, in each case, on the assumption that any changes noted in the rate of a particular threatened behavior can be attributed to a specific shift in a facet of punishment policy, and to that change exclusively. The world rarely holds still for the researcher in this way. Moreover, social conditions which cause nonexperimental changes in penal sanctions may be expected to cause other changes in social conditions which will also affect movements in the crime rate. A particular danger associated with the retrospective study of changes in the levels of punishment is that increases in penalties are frequently associated with increased levels of enforcement and with extended publicity campaigns about the evils of the behavior being punished. Also, they are often introduced in response to abnormally high rates of criminal behavior of the type which is now to be more severely punished. Hence, quite apart from the increased severity of the sanction being imposed, the rate for that type of crime may be expected to "regress" to more typical historical levels. Difficulties in drawing firm conclusions from such retrospective or historical studies have been explored in detail in the literature on capital punishment.

The comparative study is the next obvious method of searching out data on the marginal deterrent effects of punishment. Comparison can be made between crime rates in areas with more severe penalties for a given type of prohibited behavior, and crime rates in areas with less severe penalties for that behavior. Such comparative exercises would be reliable if we could find a set of comparison areas with a different punishment policy towards a particular criminal act, yet so similar to each other in every other way that the differences observed between the two crime rates could reasonably be attributed to the differences in punishment policy. Again, our observations are confounded by a myriad of variables. This is not to say that such comparative studies may not be valuable, for they have proved to be valuable in relation to capital punishment; it is merely to say that they run the substantial risk of attributing differential results to false causes, and that this risk must be guarded against.

Survey research is a third method of studying the marginal effects of general deterrence. Threats can hardly operate on those who do not know about them; further, it is possible to test the relationship between knowledge and attitudes to behavior, and to make tentative assumptions about the effects of such attitudes on behavior itself. Hence, reliable information about public knowledge of, and attitudes and responses to, elements of a threat and punishment system is a valuable addition to our store of knowledge about deterrent processes. Survey research may be directed at representative samples of the population as a whole or at samples of distinct subpopulations whose responses to punishment policy can be assumed to be different from that of the general population, and whose involvement in criminal activities is extensive enough to make distinct subgroup responses of particular significance in relation to effective criminal-regulation.

Historical, comparative, and survey methods can all throw light on our central question; but the incisive beam is likely to come only from the field experiment. Here, as elsewhere in criminology, the field experiment which is designed deliberately to test the consequences of increased or reduced severity of a punishment for a given type of human behavior has substantial political obstacles to its acceptance and implementation. Nevertheless, only field experiments provide sufficient opportunity for the independent variation of a single component in the deterrence strategy—say, the increase in the maximum punishment that the court may impose—and, thus, for a detailed evaluation of the relationship of that component to the rest of the threat and enforcement system. Not only are field experiments politically unpopular, but they are also extremely expensive. Further, there are serious ethical and legal problems in their implementation, though it is our view that such obstacles are not at all insuperable, particularly if the variation in punishment imposed in the experiment is downward rather than toward more severity.

It is not always necessary to require the experimental manipulations of legislative prescription of penalties to achieve field experiments. Legislatures are hesitant to collaborate, and the hypotheses that we have concerning the marginal general deterrent effects of sanctions are probably at an insufficient level of soundness to warrant large-scale experimentations. Opportunities for smaller experiments—soundings in deterrence—exist which will begin to provide the history of knowledge on which the serious experimental studies of deterrence will be based in the future. It may be of interest if we mention a few of such empirical soundings in deterrence in which the Center for Studies in Criminal Justice has been involved. It will take some time before we can write up their conclusions; they are listed now in order to suggest the tactics of research rather than the conclusions of research.

We found a group of traffic offenders in a large city being quite differently punished depending on which court they were, by chance, taken to. We are pursuing a study of the effects of different punishments on these two groups. We are studying the effects on driving behavior of compulsory attendance at driving school as a court sanction. We are studying the efficacy of different threats and different educative techniques on false fire alarms from fire-alarm boxes proximate to Chicago public schools. A study of the deterrent effects of differential threats governing insufficient-fund checks of large and small amounts has been undertaken. Of particular interest in the light of general theoretical doubts about the applicability of criminal sanctions to negligent behavior, we are pursuing a study of losses of industrial keys subject to different fines in a large automobile plant. In all these situations, we have found research opportunities in nature or have attempted to create them with methodological gambles of a high magnitude. They are experiments in methods of inquiry.

The broad aim of our efforts is to contribute toward the development of a general theory of deterrence in criminal law. The need here is great; our ignorance not only seriously impedes effective social control, but, of particular importance to the person interested in correctional work, it also impedes the acceptance of more effective and more humane treatment methods.

6

Directions
for Corrections

LESLIE T. WILKINS

I was more than usually reluctant to prepare this paper. Among the subject areas upon which this Society receives discourses, the area I have to discuss must be the most primitive, and indeed, hardly a fit topic for such an august body. Nonetheless, unscientific and totally unsatisfactory as is the present state of knowledge in the area of concern, there is little doubt as to its importance in contemporary society. Much money is being spent on crime control, but the basis for what is done is seldom more than unsupported belief. Penology has a level of knowledge which might place it as some kind of applied mythology!

BELIEFS VERSUS DATA

The subject matter of penology lies somewhere between religion, morals, and politics, and is buffeted by changing technology and the state of knowledge. Perhaps this is why, if you ask the average man-in-the-street (or on the Clapham omnibus for that matter!), what ought to be done about thieves and robbers, drug addicts and sexual deviants, it is expected that whatever views he may express will be asserted with considerable conviction and certitude. On the other hand, if you were to ask a person who has been associated with an academic study of

Source. *Proceedings of the American Philosophical Society,* **118,** (3), June 1974, pp. 235–247. Reprinted with persmission of the American Philosophical Society.

these problems there will be far less conviction and certainty expressed. Furthermore, the layman will seldom differentiate between the two quite different questions: what ought to be done, and what kinds of treatment might be meted out to offenders such that they were least likely to commit any further crimes. Questions of values and questions of efficiency are all too often confused.[1]

PERSONS, THINGS, AND SITUATIONS

Acts which are defined as crimes are, of course, assumed to be undesirable to the majority of the population. There are also other kinds of events which have similarly undesirable consequences. However, the fact that an act is considered to be a crime focuses attention on the offender as the cause almost to the exclusion of other elements in the crime situation—the opportunities, the physical environment, the victim or, indeed, the law itself. The belief that crime can be solved by dealing only with one element in the complex of forces and situations is indicated in the language which is used. A crime is said to be solved when a person has been identified who performed the act. When somebody can be blamed, there is little else which seems to be regarded as necessary—all television dramas of the who-done-it variety end there. The idea of crime control through environmental planning; the study of victimless crimes; the analysis of opportunity and target hardening and all other methods which are not totally offender-related are quite new.[2] It is still a heresy to suggest that some crime problems can be generated and exacerbated by what is done (with the best of all possible intentions) to reduce the problem. The modification of economic theory to consider illegal transactions has not yet had much attention and it is not surprising that few successes can be quoted in the development of macro-control methods of crime prevention.

While I shall deal with certain aspects of penology (which is concerned with the ways in which offenders are dealt with), this should not be taken to indicate that it is my view that the major impact upon the dysfunctional behavior which we designate as crime, can be best controlled by inventing further forms of punishment, treatments, or conditionings. Rather than seek to deal with social ills because they are believed to be causes of crime, I would recommend that we should deal with them because they are social ills. Rather than expect that a more than marginal change in the incidence and prevalence of crime might be related to action concerning offenders, I would expect more profit to arise from research investment in the study of victims, the environment in which crimes take place, the decision processes of criminal justice personnel, and the economics of the illicit market place. In short, the excessive emphasis in the past upon the offender has not paid off and if we are to deal realistically with crime it is necessary to study less romantic and dramatic elements—to emphasize *things* and *situations* in relation to *decisions*.

[1] John Hogarth, *Sentencing as a Human Process* (Toronto, 1971); see also reviews in *Osgood Law Journal* 10, 1 (1972): pp. 269–272.

[2] C. Ray Jeffery, *Crime Prevention through Environmental Planning* (Beverley Hills, 1971).

If a different perspective is taken in regard to the balance of elements in crime control, the offender (who is usually poor and will always be with us) may fit into the picture in a somewhat different way. There are outstanding problems in relation to rational and ethical action with regard to offenders. Even if he ceases to be the chief focus of our attack upon crime, the offender has to be dealt with, if only because he is *there.*

SOCIAL CONTROL AND MORALS: SOCIO-CULTURAL NORMS FOR PUNISHMENT

The problem of crime is larger than the problem of the offender. In order to establish a setting for the consideration of penology in contemporary society it seems necessary first to note some of the more general socio-cultural factors which may underlie differences in approach and give an indication of the background to some problems.

It is interesting to note that it is possible for persons from almost any country to be tourists in other countries throughout the world without running into difficulties with the criminal law; this despite the fact that, in law, a person who is visiting a different country is assumed to have agreed to abide by the laws of that country. We might, from this observation, assume that the moral values and norms supported by the law and for breach of which penalties will be incurred, are of considerable similarity in almost all countries of the world. This is indeed the case. The imposition of laws by colonial powers was complained of by many countries which have recently gained independence. National commissions, set up in these countries to work out a law more suited to the culture and new national identity have failed to produce criminal codes differing in any significant degree; and such differences have related to religious practices or victimless crimes. There are certainly few differences in the norms supported by the criminal law among the countries of the Western world.

Despite this similarity of the expected forms of behavior on the part of citizens and residents of the countries of, for example, the European Common Market, the extent of punishment seems to vary widely. There are no satisfactory international statistics which would enable comparisons in any degree of detail. However, there is one figure which seems to be highly comparable and which has a high degree of expected accuracy. Persons who are in prison in any country are counted; counted very frequently! Persons who have lost their liberty because of accusation of criminal behavior may represent various categories of persons, but all are clearly defined by the appropriate authorities in the country as being unworthy of being at liberty within that culture. The proportion of the populations of countries (*a*) at liberty and (*b*) incarcerated, would seem to provide one reasonable measure. The incarceration rate in the early 1970's in Holland is about twenty-five per hundred thousand; in England and Wales about one hundred per hundred thousand; while in Norway it is about fifty per hundred thousand.[3] Both

---

[3] Nils Christie, *Changes in Penal Values, in Scandinavian Studies in Criminology* (Oslo, 1968), pp.

Canada and the United States (national) have rates above 200 per hundred thousand. The range of difference in the incarceration rate between countries at the present time is far greater than the range of variation which can be found within any country for which data exist over the last hundred years. For England and Wales, for example, it is necessary to go back as far as 1852 to find an incarceration rate as high as that which now applies in that country. Between the two world wars the incarceration rate dropped to around the same figure as now characterizes Holland, namely, less than thirty per hundred thousand. Other countries show less variation over the last fifty years. Thus we may conclude that differences in incarceration (the proportion of the society which is defined as outcast) varies more between countries than within countries. As one crude measure of the effectiveness of the action taken to deal with criminals, it might be expected that the countries with high incarceration rates would show less crime—particularly as they have followed the same policy for many years. Exact tests cannot be made, but it is evident that there is no correlation in the expected direction. If a correlation exists, it indicates that the countries with lower incarceration rates over long periods of time have less crime today than those which have consistently practiced a more punitive policy.[4]

THE STAGE ARMY OF PRISONERS

The main component of the variation in the incarceration rates in different countries is the mean time for each offender, rather than the number of offenders. Lack of data regarding releases from prison on parole and by other procedures makes it impossible to determine precisely the average period of incarceration for similar crimes in different countries, since the length of sentence does not always provide a base. However, most countries seem to have developed a loose general tariff of penalties and to have established implicit conventions regarding the disposal of offenders for crimes of varying levels of seriousness and frequency. Within countries where analyses have been made of the increase in the incarceration rates, the major proportion of the increase has been found to be due to the increase in the going rate for certain offenses.[5]

It may be suggested that criminal sanctions possess some characteristics in common with money—they may become devalued. The application of this factor to the specific sanction of the fine is self-evident. Thus for the punishment to be constant in proportion to the deprivation of goods, the sum of money must be

---

161–172; see also, Leslie T. Wilkins, *Social Deviance* (London, 1964), pp. 162–166.

[4] No causal relationship is, of course, presumed. However, there is some ground for postulating that penal measures suffer from devaluation. It has also been suggested that the probability of detection, rather than the penalty if found guilty, has the major preventive impact.

[5] Analyses have been presented from time to time demonstrating this fact in the annual publication *Criminal Statistics of England and Wales* (London, H.M.S.O.).

increased. Christie[6] (1968: p. 165) raises an analogous point. "When daily existence is characterized by greater security against need, more leisure, and fewer
limitations on self-development, then a lesser deprivation of these benefits will
compensate for the same crime." While this may be a reasonable inference regarding changing penal values within a society it is difficult to fit this explanation to
the differences between countries, because according to this the United States,
having the highest standard of living should show a lesser punitive index than
other Western countries. A different form of devaluation might be a better analogue. Punitive values may be related to prior values in the same country or
jurisdiction—there is a going rate for burglary of, say, (x). This value (x), because it does not seem to deter or correct offenders is subsequently raised to
$(x + d)$; and gradually the $(x + d)$ value becomes the going rate for the same
crime. This means that the same stage army of prisoners goes around and around,
spending longer on the inside than before. Except for the members of this circulat-
ing brigade of outcasts the changing punitive values are of only symbolic importance.

The Prison Commissioners' Reports for England and Wales have shown for
many decades the proportion of offenders who, once received into prison, were
later again returned to prisons.[7] Although the data may be somewhat unreliable,
an almost identical proportion has been shown for the last fifty years.

LEARNING ABOUT EFFECTIVENESS OF PENAL MEASURES

Various authorities in societies have been punishing other members of society
from time immemorial. It would seem reasonable to suppose that something was
learned during that period. On consideration, however, it will be realized that
learning can only take place if there is, in the system, some form of feedback.
Could anybody ever learn to play darts if between them and the target was a
screen, over which the darts were lobbed? Yes, perhaps, if there was somebody
on the other side who reported what each dart achieved. Decision-makers in the
criminal justice procedures are, as it were, lobbing darts (offenders who are found
guilty) over a screen where they are out of sight. Few, if any, decision-makers
obtain information as to the outcome of their decisions to incarcerate, fine, place
on probation, or discharge. Decisions are made as though rightness or wrongness
has nothing to do with what happens as the result of the decision; indeed this view
is often explicitly argued—the quality of the very process of coming to a decision
provides sufficient justification for the belief that the decision is right.   ·

It will be noted that I have spoken of punishment. This is not a fashionable
word. It has become customary to speak of penal measures as "the treatment of
offenders." Prisons, we are told, should be called "correctional institutions," and

---

[6] Nils Christie, *op. cit.,* fn. 3, pp. 165.
[7] Commissioners of Prisons, *Annual Reports,* England and Wales (London, H.M.S.O.).

we even have special places called "medical facilities." In short, the public has been sold a medical model for the treatment of offenders.

It is difficult to see how an analogy with medical procedures could become so generally accepted within a framework of justification of decisions (whether implicit or explicit) which is independent of considerations of outcomes. The term "treatment of offenders" is usually taken to suggest far more than a euphemism for punishment. Indeed to make this suggestion would be found offensive to almost any official in the field.

The medical analogue[8] in the field of penology has many ramifications. Indeed the majority of the questions of procedures and moral implications derive from this model. It is certainly assumed, even on the part of most of the general public, that offenders are not sent to prison merely to be punished. It will be obvious that the questions which may be asked about punishment differ from those which might be asked about treatment. Punishment requires a moral justification; treatment, while not being without moral constraints, requires an assessment of effectiveness. Punishment may be justified with respect to past events alone, while treatment must take into account probable future states. (Will the patient live?)

At this point, let us take the present rhetoric about penology on its own merits. What can be said of the effectiveness of penal measures? For practitioners in the field, measures of effectiveness present difficulties. Methods which are seen as moral necessities are also, by that token alone, seen as effective. What is good, must be right. It is obviously better to give prison inmates trade training than to leave them idle or engaged on mundane tasks of no later value to them. This may be correct in a moral sense—it is more humanitarian, and hence, better, but it does not follow that fewer crimes will be committed later by those who have had the trade training. Logic is not enough to prove effectiveness; hard data are required.

In recent years there have been a number of research studies and attempts to assess the effectiveness of correctional procedures. A summary of these studies may be useful.[9]

THE PRESENT STATE OF KNOWLEDGE

It must first be noted that the low level of sophistication of research, the lack of rigor of the analysis and the imprecision of the language used in the field of penology are seldom equaled in any area of serious study. Bailey was able to show that the greater the degree of rigor in the research methods which were used in different studies to evaluate penal treatment, the less was the likelihood that the studies would claim successful outcomes.[10]

---

[8] By medical model is meant the analogy with clinical medicine—preventive or social medicine and epidemiological research are different models and are not discussed.

[9] Leslie T. Wilkins, *Evaluation of Penal Measures* (New York, 1969), pp. 109–113.

[10] Walter C. Bailey, "Correctional Treatment: An Analysis of One Hundred Correctional Outcome Studies," *Jour. Criminal Law, Criminology and Police Science* **57**, 2 (1966): pp. 153–160.

It is difficult to claim any degree of generality for the findings of research carried out in a specific geographic location or with respect to any particular class of offender. Some results do seem to be supported when the research is replicated in other jurisdictions, but other findings do not seem so robust. It is often difficult to decide whether the limitations of the findings are or are not due to the limitations of the data or the research models. It should also be noted that money for research investigations into penal matters usually comes from the same source as the money to support the programs to be assessed. In order to be persuaded to put up money for reforms or training programs in prisons, legislators must, it seems, be told that the new idea will work better than the old. The tendency to assume that enlightened treatment (group therapy psychiatric counseling, trade training, work release, or any current fashion in social work) must necessarily result in fewer reconvictions for the offenders concerned, coupled perhaps with the fear that rigorous testing might prove this faith unfounded, has had serious impacts upon research designs and the publication of research results. There are problems arising from incompetence, unbridled enthusiasm, economy, misunderstanding, and many other factors, not excluding plain political suppression and distortion of results, which make the interpretation of the present state of knowledge in this field extremely hazardous.

In attempting a summary of the position at this time it is inevitable that personal prejudice will obtrude to some degree; some would accept results which I would regard as too uncertain to list, while others might include more among the unsatisfactory proof category. Nonetheless, with an intention to be fair, the following is my list of truth claims.

a) Humanitarian methods of treatment (*e.g.* probation or fines) are *no less* effective in reducing the probability of an offender to recidivate. This statement seems to hold for developed countries of the Western world. (Note: no claim is made as to the deterrent effect upon others who are not offenders.)

b) Because humanitarian methods usually involve less intervention in the personal life of the offender, they are usually cheaper than methods which require more stringent supervision. Until more is known about saving souls it would seem to be good policy to save money.

c) In particular, money may be saved in the reduction of unnecessary expenditure on the provision of security devices. Very few incarcerated persons require maximum security.

d) Harsh penalties are supported by the beliefs of many experienced persons, but there is, to date, no research which has shown any support for these forms of belief.

e) Studies of deterrence to others seem to indicate that for trivial offenses there may be some relation to severity of the penalty. This is not an invariable result, as there have also been studies which have shown an increase in the crime (e.g. using slugs in parking meters), following upon publicity regarding some heavy exemplary penalties. For more serious crimes there is evidence that neither the penalties which actually exist in law, nor the beliefs about the penalties which would follow from a criminal act (and these differ), have any impact upon the probability of committing the act.

f) It is generally believed that when an object is defined (or labeled), this fact does not change the thing so defined. There is, however, strong evidence to show that the very fact of labeling people can influence their subsequent behavior. A large body of theory named, appropriately enough, "labeling theory" has been developed and the general findings are supported by research in many countries.

g) It is possible to predict with reasonable accuracy the non-specific recidivism of offenders who are found guilty on one or more occasions. Correlations between 0.40 and 0.50 are expected. Estimates of such probabilities by statistical methods exceed in efficiency clinical judgments of similar probabilities for similar groups.[11]

h) The case-load size of a probation officer is not associated with the probability of his cases to commit further crimes.

In summary and in one simple phrase, it is not unreasonable to say that research findings tend to show that the less it is found necessary to interfere with the personal autonomy of the offender, the better are his chances for going straight in the future. This is true after making all corrections possible for the different risks involved, by use of matching designs or mathematical modeling. Furthermore it is known that the levels of perceived necessity of interference with the personal autonomy of offenders varies within extremely wide limits. So far it has been impossible to carry out research into treatment of offenders where a control group was given only a placebo. Thus while there is evidence that very little is as good as much, there is no evidence as to what might happen if nothing at all were done. We might suppose, however, that the impact would be greater upon the general citizenry than upon the offender population!

CONSEQUENCES OF MEDICAL MODEL

At the present time, no known correctional methods support the use of the medical model. Differential treatment effects have not been isolated, despite apparently wide differences in the treatment actually given. Bloodletting and leeching were characteristic of medical practice in the past but today methods which do not improve the prognosis for recovery would not be acceptable to medical ethics. If correctional procedures cannot show treatment effects then the medical analogue seems to break down on this point.[12]

There are many other unsatisfactory elements in the medical model of treatment of offenders, not only in terms of inadequate representation (mapping) which the model affords, but in the concomitant perspectives on problems and

[11] Paul E. Meehl, *Clinical vs. Statistical Prediction* (Minneapolis, 1954).

[12] The medical analogue breaks down in other ways too, although there are some specific cases where it might seem to apply. For a more detailed discussion of the inadequacy of the medical model see, Leslie T. Wilkins, *Evaluation of Penal Measures* (New York, 1969), pp. 18–20.

policies. However, until quite recently, the most prevalent humanistic and modern view in penology was concerned with the medical model and hence sought to demonstrate the effectiveness of treatment through the establishment of diagnoses. Indeed reception and classification prisons came to be called "Diagnostic Centers"—again rather more than a mere euphemism.[13] Medical analogies are quite widely accepted by the courts and in institutions and among informed members of the general public. Of course, some cases which appear in court do represent medical problems, but these, rather than tending to add support to the model, actually stress the inappropriateness of legal concepts in relation to physical or mental dysfunction.

In the early days the offender was to be rehabilitated by inculcation of habits of industry, and trade training was the reformers' demand. Later came more concern for the psyche, and group therapy and related measures became the vogue. Most recently, of course, token economies and other such procedures which derive from theories of operant conditioning are the most fashionable. The psychiatric, conditioning or other medical analogies have much in common with the nineteenth-century sin-and-wickedness model. Each of these conceptual frameworks denies that the offender is, by his act, commenting not only upon himself but also upon society. All we have to do to solve the problem of crime is to solve the problem of the offender—get him out of his laziness, help him solve his personality problems, cure him of his madness, help (or make) him adjust to our society because our society is obviously good!

BADNESS OR MADNESS, OR MERELY BEHAVIOR?

A small group of realists are now taking the view that crime cannot be simplified into either badness or madness; that the problem of crime is the problem of human behavior. Taking note of the research and evaluation of the treatment model they claim that, if this model was ever likely to work at all, this fact should have been evident before now. They claim, and I think correctly, that more punitive measures can be and are applied in the form of treatment than would be the case if we were more honest and discussed punishment in clear terms. Most of this group would claim that probation and parole supervision are not therapy but are intrusive and onerous restrictions on reasonable personal autonomy. Moreover, the terms on which parole is granted are such as to ensure that any person who, for any reason, is wanted for return to prison can be so dealt with without further access to the courts or counsel.

A tract which strongly represents these views, entitled *Struggle for Justice,*[14] was recently published by a group of Quakers. It is interesting that it is the Quakers who are again becoming heavily involved in the debate about penology.

---

[13] Jessica Mitford, *Kind and Usual Punishment* (New York, 1973).

[14] American Friends Service Committee Report, *Struggle for Justice* (New York, 1971).

QUANTIFICATION OF MORAL VALUES

The treatment concept or medical analogy provides an escape from important questions. It is difficult to say how much time in incarceration is sufficient on moral grounds to repay a crime of some specific level of seriousness. Such decisions invoke a kind of moral calculus and require also some basis in equity. When a judge could play the role of god or act without challenge on behalf of the king, this was not important. A personal view substituted for a more generally acceptable moral standard. With increased communications and a wider interest in the criminal outcasts, questions began to be asked. Furthermore, some people, even such as newspaper men, began making comparisons between the sentence lengths meted out in different jurisdictions and in different parts of the same jurisdiction; they also went so far as to suggest that there should, perhaps, be less variation.

But the claim for equity has no meaning if we can use the treatment argument. Treatment is not punishment and hence comparisons are invalid. Thus, by this model, the length of time of incarceration is not expected to be a function of the crime, but rather is to be determined by a need for treatment on the part of the individual offender. It would be wrong to release a person before he is cured; and how long this will take cannot be stated in advance. The kind of treatment indicated is not a matter for public debate, but for experts in private consultation with the patient and other experts.

To treat every person as a unique individual may seem a very pleasant and moral code of behavior. Indeed it is, but only under certain conditions. (I shall return to this as the issue of personal autonomy.) In making decisions which affect others, the treating of each person *decided about* as a unique individual, means that there can arise no question of equity, since equity implies some basis for comparison. Thus in the name of treatment, good works and attention to the needs of the offender, a jargon developed which sounded humanistic, modern, and scientific to some, and soft and pampering of criminals to others. In fact it was neither, becoming only an excuse for the exercise of individual judgment or professionalism on the part of those in a position to make the decisions. Many decisions had a profound effect upon the offender but could not be challenged in court nor subject to appeal, and many were made in closed chambers. Moreover, the offender who might wish to modify his behavior so as to obtain an early release could not obtain any clear idea as to what action on his part might help or prejudice his case. If he was seen as sick, perhaps he should play sick at least at first, since to claim that he was not sick would perhaps be construed as a further symptom of his troubles![15]

---

[15] Gene Kassebaum *et al., Prison Treatment and Parole Survival* (New York, 1971), p. 5.

DECISION ERRORS

Producer versus Consumer Risk

In any decision there are always two ways of being wrong. A decision is incorrect if we reject the hypothesis when it is in fact true, and also (although not necessarily equally) wrong if we accept the hypothesis when it is in fact false. Since in almost every case of a decision there are some future consequences, a trade-off between types of error will almost always exist, although not always clearly in consumer-producer terms. If it is insisted that every guilty person must be punished (or treated), then it must follow that this involves a much higher risk that the innocent will also be incorrectly punished than would be the case where we were prepared to allow that some guilty might go free.

In the criminal justice procedures there seems to have developed a somewhat peculiar argument with a view to avoiding this issue. It seems to be held that errors in decisions are of no consequence so long as the individual concerned was honest and tried his best (intent) to make the right decision. The criterion of a decision seems to be determined, on this theory, by the quality of the processes involved in making it, and is in no way related to the possible kinds of outcomes. This, I would assert, is neither a moral nor a rational point of view; it tacitly implies a belief in perfection (or the pursuit of perfection) as a goal and as the ultimate criterion of moral value; it does not seek to come to terms with uncertainty and the probability of error; it is so obviously unrealistic that it is immoral.

It seems that we must behave as though, no matter what decisions are made, no matter how experienced the decision-makers, no matter how effective the methods upon which reliance is placed, some decisions will be made incorrectly. To start from the opposite postulate is to claim a form of divinity.

That error is an integral part of any decision or measurement appears to be a difficult concept for some persons to accept. Even if they give verbal accord with the concept of the generality of error, they do not usually accept the consequences which follow in terms of the strategies which should be employed. It has been claimed by one learned judge that, although some of his decisions might, at a later date, be proved to be wrong, they were nonetheless quite correct at the time they were made![16] The business world is more realistic. In quality control, for example, it is recognized that there is a consumer risk and a producer risk, and that these must be weighed in terms of inspection policy. No business could ignore the consumer risk, since to do so would soon result in bankruptcy; conversely, no business could seek to produce a perfect product at all times, reducing the consumer's risk to zero, since to do so it would need to spend far too much on inspection and in rejection of defective batches of the product, and would thus cease to be competitive.

---

[16] Personal communication: speaker may be assumed to wish to remain anonymous.

In the field of crime there are many kinds of issues where the consumer-producer-risk model would be useful. It may be, for example, that in some areas fear of crime may lead to such heavy policing that it becomes replaced by the fear of the police. But this kind of consideration is beyond the range of the topic of today's paper. We are examining issues concerned with the disposition of offenders after the finding of guilt by a court.

Past and Future

If the disposition of the offender is made only in terms of his offense—a single event which has taken place in the past and which is known in some detail—the nature and qualities of errors in decisions are not closely analogous with the consumer-producer model. However, it is difficult to assume that decisions regarding disposition of offenders are made on any such simple terms. Indeed, if they were, the wisdom of such a basis for decision might be questioned.

The implications for the two classes of error in the disposition of offenders are most clearly seen in the application of the medical analogy, where the probable future criminality of the offender is given consideration. No matter how high the correlation between observations and the predicted outcome, some persons predicted as recidivists will not, in fact, be found guilty of further crimes, while others who will be predicted as successful, will in fact be subsequently found guilty of some further offenses.[17] These are two kinds of error. The problem is now how to eliminate these errors, although we may attempt to reduce them, but since we cannot expect ever to achieve a correlation of 1.0, we must consider the relative weight of the two kinds of error. Is a false positive as bad as a false negative? If not, what is the ratio which can be regarded as morally acceptable? It is surprising that despite the considerable concern in the legal and criminological literature for decisions such as sentencing or the granting of parole and the like, the emphasis is on getting the decision right, rather than upon moral aspects of the accommodation of error, uncertainty, and probability. The issue of uncertainty becomes the more apparent when use is made of actuarial tables to facilitate decisions.

As has been noted earlier, actuarial methods, applied to predictions of recidivism, are superior to subjective assessments.[18] Actuarial predictions are, of course, given in terms of probabilities and expressed numerically, and not in terms of "probable cause" or "beyond reasonable doubt." It is, for example, possible to identify a class of offenders who have a probability of 0.90 of committing another offense. Such tables of probabilities have been criticized by criminal justice practitioners as inaccurate—they point out that among the 90 percent risk category, for every 100 offenders there will be ten who will be incorrectly classified as recidivists. The objection has some point if all the cases in the 90 percent category

---

[17] Leslie T. Wilkins, *Evaluation of Penal Measures* (New York, 1969), pp. 125–130.
[18] See fn. 10.

are treated as failures, since this is treating a 90 percent category as though it were a 100 percent category, and, as we have noted, such a category cannot exist. The problem is not with the estimation of risk categories, but with the difficulty of accommodating the concept of risk at all in legal or moral decisions.

To some extent the dilemma may be avoided by failing to take note of any probable future states. A court may take the view that it should act with respect to the past and only to the past. If a person has committed a violent act, the court may be justified in punishing him accordingly. If, however, the court assumes that past violent acts provide information about future such acts, the position is changed. There is then the question of error to be resolved. There may be a small amount of information about the likelihood of future criminal acts encoded in the past acts, but it is a very small amount. It is difficult to say when a decision is, in fact, based only on past behavior. The average citizen (as well as the businessman and the courts) tends to make implicit predictions on the basis of observations of, and from knowledge about, past events. People tend to believe that persons who have committed violent acts *are* dangerous persons—a continuous state is inferred from discrete events. In this respect most people are mostly wrong. There are a few cases in which they may be right, and these are too often better remembered than are the others.

Proneness to Violence

A recently completed study utilized a very large variety of psychological tests which were expected to be predictive of violent acts and supplemented these with a number of other items of data. A base sample of just over 4,000 young men was available from one of the major institutions in California. This represents the most comprehensive attempt to obtain prediction tables for violence-proneness carried out to date. The authors (Wenk and Emrich)[19] claim that their results "strongly suggest that a useful violence index could be constructed. . . . " At some remote future date, perhaps, but the results would seem to require an adjustment of moral trade-off. Let their data speak for themselves.

Those individuals who have the top 260 scores were classified as violent-prone, and the remainder of the sample as not violent-prone. On the first step with variable one (history of violence), twenty-eight individuals were correctly classified as violent-prone as they were also found to be in the violent subsample (true positivies). These hits stand against 256 individuals who were misclassified. According to the prediction index, twenty-four persons were classified as non-violent (false negatives); and 232 persons were classified by the index as violent-prone and turned out to be non-violent (false positives).

[19] Ernst A. Wenk and Robert L. Emrich, "Assaultive Youth: An Exploratory Study of the Assaultive Experience and Assaultive Potential of California Youth Authority Wards," *Jour. Research in Crime and Delinquency* **9**, 2 (1972): pp. 171–196.

Moral Trade-off

Thus, in order to pick up about half of the persons who were violent, approximately nine out of ten persons would be inappropriately treated as though they would also be violent offenders. It would be noted that the best predictor from the very large battery of items proved to be the previous incident of violence. The authors tried to improve on this by adding information but found that, "On the second step with variables one and two, twenty-one persons were correctly classified as violent-prone . . . " and the prediction deteriorated at each further step.

The implications of the two kinds of error in decision-making are made very clear in these data. How many persons who are suspected (wrongly) of being dangerous is it reasonable to incarcerate (i.e. treat as dangerous), in order to be right about some others? Is it reasonable, for example, to incarcerate as probably dangerous, one hundred persons of whom ten may be correctly assigned to the dangerous category? (This represents the level possible with the present state of knowledge.) If ninety wrong for ten right is too high a price, then would fifty for ten be morally acceptable? If not fifty, then what other number? If we act at all, there has to be some number. The only way to ensure that we do not incarcerate any person incorrectly is to incarcerate none, and conversely, if we wish to incarcerate all potentially dangerous persons, we must incarcerate all persons, since everybody has some risk of committing a violent act. Immediately we invoke the future risk of crime, or as soon as we make inferences about the state of the person as the justification for our action, we must attend to the problem of the trade-off of errors.[20]

It may be suggested that a person who has once committed a violent act (or, perhaps, some other criminal act) has by that token forfeited his right to the same trade-off level as the person who has not committed such an act. However, the same constraints apply. The basic division is: (*a*) to deal with the person in terms of an idea of just deserts in respect of the past act or acts which we call criminal, or (*b*) to consider the moral aspects of the trade-off of false positives as against harms which might be saved to unknown victims. A mixed strategy would require a model of a form rather like that shown in Table 1.

There is difficulty even in establishing a hierarchy in the first column. It is necessary to decide whether two non-violent crimes proven are equal to, greater or less than one violent crime in terms of the impact upon the tolerated ratio of false positives to true positives in the category concerned. Further, it might be considered that the seriousness of the crimes should be taken into account, and perhaps also the interval between any two crimes. Would a similar diminution

---

[20] It will be noted that the concept of a state is central to the medical model. The justification of an inference that a state exists in relation to a crime must depend upon information about factors and situations *other than* the crime itself. A question then arises as to whether the legal process is qualified to make inferences in regard to matters which are not specifically within the ambit of law, but which relate to medicine or physical conditions.

Table 1

Classification of Person	Level of False Positive Regarded as Morally Acceptable			
(1) No proved offenses*	none tolerated			
(2) One prior, non-violent proved offense	some slight reduction in the value of (p)*			
(3) One prior violent proved offense**	p-value less than above (? by how much?)			
(4) Two prior non-violent proved offenses	lower p-value than line (2) or line (3) or both			
(5) Two prior violent	?	?	?	?
....			(see below)	
.... &c				

* p = estimated probability.
** By "proved offenses" is meant cases which have been through the "due process of criminal justice"—not arrests.

of the p-value for false positives be acceptable as a moral basis if of two crimes one crime were more serious than another. Clearly whatever may be decided could be fitted to some kind of linear function which expresses moral acceptability in terms of the seriousness of the offense(s) and the probability of false positives. But judicial decisions are not usually discussed in such terms.

FROM TREATMENT—TOWARDS EQUITY

An Application of a Model

Much of the information with regard to the impact of prison upon offenders derives from research into parole decisions. Case history data are obtained on follow-up of parolees during supervision in the community and provide a basis from which to assess the effectiveness of treatment, training, and other penal measures.

Decisions by parole boards have many similarities with judicial decisions in sentencing.[21] However, it must be noted that parole decisions can apply only to persons who have been sentenced to prison, whereas the courts decide whether prison is, in their view, necessary in each case. Thus parole decisions represent a selected sample of decisions and may be considered to relate to the more serious cases.[22]

[21] The dichotomy between incarceration and liberty is beginning to be eroded by new correctional procedures such as weekend incarceration and halfway houses. However, the major decision in any individual case must be whether the offender may be left in liberty (or nearly so), or must be placed in captivity (or nearly so). Such decisions are not available to the parole boards, who can consider

Recently, the United States (Federal) Parole Board gave permission for, and indeed cooperated with research workers in, a study of their decision-making.[23] Files were made freely available, and these and other data were supplemented by frank discussions between the research workers and the Board chairman and members. Prior to the research the Board had insisted that it did not have a policy, except that each case was decided on its merits and that each petitioner was treated as a unique individual.[24] Certain critics had seen this as resulting in arbitrary and capricious decisions. Research revealed that the Board was not capricious, and that a policy did, in fact, exist. There was a strong tendency for the amount of time offenders were held in incarceration to be a function of two factors, namely, (*a*) the seriousness of the offense for which the person was found guilty;[25] (*b*) the probability (subjective and/or objective) that further offense(s) might be committed if the offender were released on parole.[26] (A "salient factor score" is obtained for each case.)

These factors are almost independent of each other; indeed some of the most serious crimes tend to be associated with a much lower than average probability to commit further crimes. Another consideration, not completely independent, was the behavior of the offender while in prison.[27] However, a two-dimensional model was considered to be adequate as a first approximation. The results of

---

for release only after incarceration. There are also legislative constraints upon the range of decisions which both parole boards and judges can make. No research study in any parallel to the Federal Parole Board project has been made in respect of judicial sentencing and legislative intent in fixing ranges for penalties for crimes. One fact may be inferred with some safety—legislators in fixing minimum penalties are not concerned with the medical analogue for the treatment of offenders.

[22] Department of Justice, Law Enforcement Assistance Administration, Parole Decision-making Project Reports (twelve reports in series). To be published shortly.

[23] The research was funded by the Department of Justice, Law Enforcement Assistance Administration, and carried out by a research team under the auspices of the National Council on Crime and Delinquency and the School of Criminal Justice, State University of New York at Albany.

[24] This is, of course, the medical model.

[25] The assessment of the seriousness of the offense is subjective, but is still capable of being systematized. The Board ranked offenses and established a seven-point category scale for seriousness. Studies have shown that there is a very high degree of consensus between persons of quite different social, ethnic, and economic backgrounds in regard to the assessment of the ranking for seriousness of crimes.

[26] The original prediction score was derived by the use of statistical analysis of prior case material. The probability was found to be associated with facts about the commitment offense, such as whether there were co-defendants and the type (not seriousness) of crime; previous criminal career; prior treatment; employment; education. Only one item was future oriented, namely whether the parolee would reside with his wife and/or children after release. The main weight was found to be required to be placed upon the prior criminal record—this was the most predictive datum. It must be stressed that the items which were given weight in the probability assessment *were not* subjective, identified, or assessed by the research workers, but were derived from analysis of partial data.

[27] Behavior in prison is not found to be related to the probability of subsequent criminal activity. Nonetheless it is regarded as reasonable to give some weight to behavior which may have been particularly bad or particularly good. The identification of any such behaviors by the interviewing officer would be a valid reason for him to argue for a departure from the time set by the guidelines.

mapping the model (seriousness *x* risk) on to the Board's previous case decisions were communicated to the Board. A conclusion was reached that the model could be used to provide guidelines for future decisions. These guidelines are in the form of a matrix of time of imprisonment graduated in two-dimensions in a consistent pattern. The least serious and lowest risk cases are to be detained the least time, and there are progressive increments in time detained in incarceration in each dimension.

The model expressed in guidelines enables the Board to review its policy as such, determining issues in terms of principles rather than on a case-by-case basis. The guidelines also enable deviations from the pattern to be identified and considered specifically. Every six months the Board is provided with data showing how decisions have been made in comparison with the model. Reasons given by decision-makers for departures from the guideline times are also considered. There is, thus, a review procedure and a form of quality control of the decision process. A base line is now determined and any changes can be consciously made and the impact of changes assessed. There is, of course, no intention that the guidelines should make change less easy or probable, but only that changes shall be recognized as such and assessed in terms of policy. If the pattern of decision-making is deviating from policy, either the policy can be changed or the decision can be brought more into line. It will be noted that there is a trade-off issue in the parole decision model which is similar to that posed in the more general case. The two-dimensional guidelines for decisions provide a gradient in terms of the time an offender is detained in prison. Should, it may be asked, the gradient be similar for each of the dimensions—or are increments in seriousness (least to most) more important than increments in risk category (least to most). There are also different possibilities for assessing the gradients. However, if the least serious set of cases (say, lowest tenth percentile) defines the low point for time detained, and the most serious set (say, ninetieth percentile) defines the high point, then there may be said to be an average time gradient over all risk groups. Similarly, the lowest risk group, summed over all levels of seriousness, and the highest risk group also summed over all levels of seriousness, may provide a basis for calculating the average time gradient for risk category. We may then ask whether seriousness is more important than risk, or whether both are regarded as equally significant—in this case the same average gradient should presumably apply to each factor.

On this model the Federal Parole Board tends to give more weight to the seriousness dimension than to that of risk. This does not seem unreasonable. Perhaps the most important consideration arising from the research and its application is that the gradients can now be identified, studied, compared over time (and eventually, perhaps between jurisdictions), and form the basis for informed criticism leading to further modification of policy in the light of this and other kinds of information. The model, even with the analysis of gradients, does not give any indication of what is the right period for incarceration, nor, of course, whether any incarceration is right. Perhaps all times are too long, or too short. Perhaps the gradients in each direction should be steeper or less steep. The model does not define the boundaries, but can ensure that the variations between decisions are not erratic. The model can be claimed to help with questions of equity if not of justice. It is, specifically, not concerned with treatment in terms of the medical analogue.

There may appear to be some inconsistency in the use of the second dimension of risk in a model which focuses upon equity. If a future perspective is taken, then the issue of false positives can surely arise. However, in this particular case the dimension of risk may be seen in two ways. It is true that items from the case files (additional to the information about the kind of crime accounted for by the seriousness dimension) do in actual fact prove to be predictive of future criminality.[28] But these items relate, in the main, to features of the past criminal career. It seems equally as reasonable to defend the additional penalty (more time to be served) for high risk persons (low salient factor score) as it is to seek to defend the decisions on predictive grounds. We have, then, at least at the moment and in this specific case, a situation where an unsatisfactory model and a more satisfactory one lead to similar courses of action. The seriousness of the commitment crime, plus prior criminal record and style of life of the offender are reasonable grounds for considering the penalty (for those who see imprisonment as a penalty), while at the same time those who believe in treatment tend to agree that it takes more time to treat a person who has committed a serious crime and who also had a long record of offenses. Perhaps agreement as to what is to be done, which derives from such basically different propositions, provides one further indication of our lack of knowledge in this field.

THE NEW DIRECTIONS?

It is necessary, as a matter of considerable urgency, that we unscramble the technological, medical, scientific, and moral questions in relation to dysfunctional behavior; when this is done we may find appropriate problem-solving methods for each kind of issue.

Something like prisons will be needed for a long time. They are needed for the separation from society of persons who cannot be expected to function safely in freedom. Prisons also provide a means of punishment which does not have the unpleasantness of other punishments like flogging and death. Society will continue to demand forms of punishment. It is not unreasonable for persons who have suffered from some crime to demand that the offender "get out of here." When "out of here" did not mean into some other similar society (such as the next state!), and when transport was slow, there were several variations of the general theme of "out of here." Few areas of the world can today employ such methods. The prison has to suffice.

According to any reasonable definition of treatment, no prison provides treat-

---

[28] Those who would take the more optimistic view of the ability of those-who-would-do-good to make others better, tend to criticize prediction tables because they do not show any significant weight

ment.[29] Then if treatment is indicated in any case, which may first be discovered through the criminal justice process, the diversion of that case from the penal system is required. Not only have the correctional services failed to demonstrate that they provide treatment, it would indeed be inappropriate for them to do so. The legal system is concerned with matters of guilt, human rights, and the concept of responsibility—in short, moral, not medical and not technological questions.

It would seem to follow that no offender should be detained in prison for one day longer than is justified in terms of his offense and his prior record of crimes merely because he is seen to be in need of, or to be under treatment. The prison exists to serve the community, not the prisoner.

The prison is there because society demands it, and because society pays for it. Prison is a kind of factory where the product is punishment, and we buy its products through taxation. We are also paying for offenders to be kept away from us and decent people like us, at least for a period of time. This purchase of relief may have some value in reduced risk, but again there is the question of the moral value of the trade-off to be resolved. If any taxpayer thinks that correctional services are helping offenders to rehabilitation or reintegration into society, the evidence is all against him.

It may be argued that we should continue to hide our heads in the treatment sands, because, if prisons come to be seen for what they are—places for isolation and punishment—then they might degenerate further and become even less acceptable on moral grounds. The opposite case can also be made with equal plausibility since the treatment perspective, as we have noted, provides an excuse for many inequitable measures and even abuses of power. Perhaps a more honest descriptive language would lead to more effective and more humanitarian procedures. Or, perhaps, an honest language is morally desirable in its own terms?

The methods whereby prisons are operated need not involve very different procedures from those currently in fashion. There is no reason why persons who are incarcerated (for purposes of isolation, punishment or both) should not be: (*a*) treated humanely; (*b*) taught trades; (*c*) provided with socially useful activities in their captivity; (*d*) adequately rewarded for work done; (*e*) given group therapy or other treatment (medical or psychiatric) if they volunteer for it; (*f*) provided with similar protections as those given to persons on the outside in so far as is feasible; (*g*) permitted to spend their time in captivity in as dignified a manner as is possible. The prisoner is still to be seen as a person while the society within which he is permitted to move is constrained.

---

to factors which relate to the time in the institutions or to different situations when the offender is released. The failure of prediction methods to show any such weights is not due to the fact that such items have been left out of the analyses; many such items are put into the equations but the methods whereby the tables are obtained (multiple regression and/or discriminant function analysis) clearly indicate that any weighting of these factors would be inappropriate and would reduce the predictive power. This is a further proof that treatment effects cannot be recognized by analyses of past records.

[29] Many books have been published on this point. Among the more recent and more powerful is that by Jessica Mitford (fn. 13 above).

There are many things which can now be done to humanize prisons. All these should be done, not because it is good for the prisoners, but because it is good for society and the prison staffs. If prison officers are to keep a special kind of isolation-society in operation they need every incentive and means to maintain their dignity, humanity and sense of humor.

SUMMARY AND CONCLUSION

There is a similarity to my prescription for the outside society and the inside (prison) society. Outside the prison system I would argue for consideration of those elements in the crime which extend beyond the persons and actions of the offenders (e.g. the victims, situations and environments, and the law itself), while within the prison and penal system I would similarly argue that we must take a broader perspective to include the institutional structure, the decision processes, the custodial personnel, and even the architecture as well as the inmate himself. To get the criminal's behavior into perspective we must see it in relation to the environment in which the act is embedded—whether this is the constrained society of the prison or the larger free society. This is the systems theoretic approach. The treatment model cannot do this; moreover, like other treatments penal treatments are liable to serious side-effects.

Emphasis upon the guilty offender, to the exclusion of other considerations, can almost certainly lead us to underestimate the impact of crime-control measures upon the liberties of all. The most subtle form of emphasis upon the offender is that which persuades us that we are doing all this for his own good—because it is all treatment! To defend society, it is necessary to defend the criminal.

If we are going to deal with social dysfunctional which we call crime, we must deal with it as a social problem and not as sickness nor as separate unconnected events which are due to individual wickedness. We must seek to remove the field of crime from the level of political slogans where a "war on crime" can quickly become a "war on criminals," and, moreover, where "criminals" may be none too clearly defined.

Is it possible to make the general public concerned about dangerous situations or criminogenic states without reduction of these to the form of the dangerous person? The prisons belong to the taxpayers. What is done in prisons and in the courts is done with taxpayers' money. Do those who pay for it have a clear idea of what they want from the penal system? Do they even know what they are getting? Is there adequate accountability by the penal system to the community? To ask the questions is to answer them.

I think, nonetheless, that we shall move rapidly towards a new approach to crime. My grounds for this are that expenditures on criminal justice have more than doubled in the last four years.[30] Anybody can see that, by following a policy

---

[30] The National Advisory Commission suggests that the annual cost of an effective criminal justice system will reach between $20 and $30 billion in 1983. Even this estimate presumes that the rate of

of more-of-the-same (a linear trend projection will suffice), we shall soon be bankrupt; not because of crime, but because of what we are doing about it.

A projection of bankruptcy, it may be thought, is a great incentive to change the order of business. My fear, however, is that in criminal justice, the data are so bad, the philosophies so muddled, the symbolism so powerful, the language so dishonest, and slogans so useful and easy, that rational projection does not apply. Perhaps the public will not buy a new model for criminal justice until they crash the present one. Unfortunately there are not many alternative models on the drawing boards. But even if there were, no simulation methods for testing them have been developed. Research has been directed towards patching up those holes in the system which have disturbed administrators, and in the course of this has often made still further holes. Radical analysis and propositions of alternatives, together with fundamental research, have not attracted supporting funds.

Only those who have made a serious study of the problem of crime acknowledge that they do not have sufficient information. Everybody else, and especially politicians, knows exactly what should be done. In criminal-justice matters, the degree of confidence with which views are expressed tends to be inversely proportional to the quality of knowledge.

---

increase in expenditure which has characterized in the last few years will diminish. In fact the expenditure doubled in four years from 1968 to 1972; there certainly was not any doubling in the efficiency nor a comparable reduction in recorded crime or the fear of crime.

PROBATION

Probation, according to the American Correctional Association, may be defined as a sentence, as an organization, or as a process. "As a sentence, probation represents a judicial disposition which establishes the defendant's legal status under which his freedom in the community is continued, subject to supervision by a probation organization and subject to conditions imposed by the court. As an organization, probation is a service agency designed to assist the court and to execute certain services in the administration of criminal justice. As a process, probation involves the presentence investigation for the court and the supervision of persons in the community."

This section introduces probation by describing its historical development. For both general aspects and those relating specifically to the United States, we rely on source materials from the United Nations.

Perhaps the most authoritative documents published in the field of criminal justice are the various reports of the President's Commission on Law Enforcement and Administration of Justice in 1967 and the 1973 reports of the National Advisory Commission on Criminal Justice Standards and Goals. We have selected materials prepared by each of these Commissions.

Our first selection is from the 1967 report of the President's Commission. Although this document is in some respects out-of-date, it is precisely on this account that it has interest; furthermore, it is difficult to find as significant and useful a summary. It will be interesting to see how the projected figures for the use of probation in 1975 compare with the actual data that will become available almost concurrently, with publication of this anthology.

The optimism that characterized the 1967 report is hardly tempered in the

1973 Standards and Goals report. Rehabilitation claims are made quite strongly
—probation is as good as any other correctional disposition, if not better, and it
is cheaper. Yet the Commission argues that probation had not been adequately
financed, staffed, or equipped—Standards and Goals still make the standard
claims. These statements may be true, but today there would be less hope of their
acceptance without much stronger supporting data.

Probation, insofar as the term serves to indicate what probation officers do,
is much more than the supervision of offenders. Probation officers provide important services to courts. The Standards and Goals abstract provides details of these
activities and information on the administration of probation service. It might be
noted that, under the subheading "Overemphasis on Casework," this report
shows some significant dissatisfaction with the "medical model" for the treatment
of offenders, regarding it more as inadequate than inappropriate.

The American Bar Association prepared standards for probation which, in
1970, were approved by the House of Delegates of the American Bar Association.
These standards form the latter part of the article by Dr. Herbert S. Miller. Dr.
Miller addresses the issue of sentencing in relation to the granting of probation;
it is particularly interesting to note that he suggests that the sentencing decision
be considered in two parts. Recent research about sentencing has shown that the
courts do proceed this way and that the sentencing decision is a bifurcated
process. The implications for the application of the philosophy of "just deserts"
(see Section I), are, it seems, important. If, according to "just deserts," the
disposition of the offender should reflect the seriousness of the crime, then a scale
of dispositions in terms of their severity would seem to be required. By this means,
the seriousness of the offense could be matched with the severity of the disposition. If, however, probation is considered first, it would appear to be given priority
and hence be unlikely to "scale" with the other forms of disposition by the courts.
It is interesting to try to consider a crime that is "just sufficiently" serious to
justify incarceration and an almost exactly similar crime that would justify release
on probation. Is there such a cross-over point? Is there a band of overlap where
characteristics of the offender, rather than of the offense, should be given the
critical weight? Since it has not been possible to identify with certainty a type of
offender for whom probation is indicated, should the award of probation be
constrained only by the type of offense? If so, what is the nature of the justification? Alternatively, if the nature of the offender, rather than of the offense, is the
critical consideration, how is this to be justified in terms of equal justice for all?

Legally the responsibility for the disposition of offenders found guilty is fixed
upon the court. Nonetheless as the article by Professor Eugene H. Czajkoski
indicates, this is an uncertain description of facts; Professor Czajkoski goes so far
as to say that "to even the most casual observer of the court, it is evident that
the judge's role in sentencing has shrunk almost to that of a mere announcer."
It is clear from Czajkoski's descriptions that the probation officer is not only a
supervisor of cases, but also an essential part of the means and function of
sentencing.

One of the main ways in which the probation officer influences the sentencing decision is through the content of the presentence report. In the real world in which the probation officer functions there are hundreds of items of information that might be noted in the report. He must select information out of the situation that comprises the offender's background, current status, and the elements of the crime, and other areas that he considered relevant. His beliefs about the causes of crime may well influence this selection as may other attitudes or beliefs of his own, or those he attributes to the members of the court to whom he will report. Robert M. Carter shows that there is a strong tendency for the selection of information items to cluster around a very few issues. However, there is also considerable variation between probation officers in regard to the items they consider of importance, and a strong interest in psychiatric and psychological explanations is clearly evident.

There are several formats for presentence reports. Two examples are given in this section—a "short form" and the normal report form as used by the Federal Courts. The items of information required are somewhat similar in all jurisdictions; some require more detail than others, but the core of items is common.

This section concludes with a report of a research study that examines the relationship between the disposition of the offender by the court and the probation officer's recommendation in the case. Over ten years there was 96–97 percent agreement in the California Superior Courts between a probation officer's recommendation for probation and the court disposition of probation. Where the officer's recommendation was against probation, there was somewhat less agreement with the courts determination, and there was more variability over time. It seems clear that either probation officers are extremely adept at anticipating the decisions of the judges they serve, or that probation officers have considerable power to influence the kind of disposition an offender receives. Or, perhaps by chance, probation officers are rather like judges in the ways in which they relate to offenders and to information about them. There is some evidence that each possible explanation is partially true.

7

The Legal Origins
of Probation

UNITED NATIONS

The origin, development, and fate of specific methods for the treatment of offenders can be properly understood only against the wider background of contemporary cultural, social, and economic forces. Insofar as crime is defined as socially undesirable behavior subject to legal sanctions, the primary and constant object of criminal policy is the elimination or reduction of crime. The use or avoidance of specific methods, however, has varied very widely in both time and space, and these variations have tended to correspond with variations in social and political structure, in levels of knowledge, and in cultural values.[1]

Probation is an essentially modern method for the treatment of offenders and

SOURCE. *Probation and Related Measures,* United Nations, Department of Social Affairs, New York (Sales No.: 1951. IV. 2), E/CN/.5/230, 1951, pp. 15–26.

[1] *Cf.* Thorsten Sellin, "Foreword." to George Rusche and Otto Kirchheimer *Punishment and Social Structure* (1939), p. vi: "Fundamentally . . . the aim of all punishment is the protection of those social values which the dominant social group of a State regard as good for 'society'. . . . The means to secure the protection of 'society' have varied greatly because the law-enforcing powers of different societies have chosen those means which they believed to be at a given time most likely to secure obedience to their law. These beliefs are in turn dependent on tradition, the level of knowledge, and the nature of social economic institutions and conditions. The sanguinary punishment and tortures of old are no evidence of bloodthirstiness or sadism on the part of those who used them. They rather testify to the fact that those who designed them could conceive of no better, that is, more efficient, way of securing protection for the social values which they treasured. The character of punishments, then, is inextricably associated with and dependent on the cultural values of the State that employs them."

as such, it is rooted in the broader social and cultural trends of the modern era. In the history of criminal policy, the development of probation and related measures constitutes an integral part of the more general movement away from the traditional punitive and repressive approach, and towards the substitution of humanitarian and utilitarian consideration for considerations of general deterrence and retribution. This modern trend coincides with attempts to prevent crime by the improvement of social conditions and by the development of social services. It is characterized, furthermore, by the recognition of the social rehabilitation of the individual offender as a main object of criminal policy, and the rational selection and development of effective means to this end.

The origin of probation was not the result of a deliberate creative, legislative, or judicial act, but rather the result of gradual growth, and almost unconscious modification of existing legal practices.

THE ORIGINS OF PROBATION AND ENGLISH COMMON LAW

Several attempts have been made to trace back the legal origins of probation to mediaeval and early modern European law. The precedents found in this period of legal history, however, generally relate to the suspension of punishment subject to good behavior rather than to probation as such, that is, a *combination* of the conditional suspension of punishment and the personal supervision of the released offender during a trial period. There can be little doubt that there has not been any continuous process of historical development linking early Continental instances of the use of the conditional suspension of punishment with contemporary probation. Probation as it is known today has been derived from the practical extension of the English common law, and an analysis of the legal origins of probation must therefore be principally concerned with England and America.

In England and the United States of America probation developed out of various methods for the conditional suspension of punishment. Generally speaking, the court practices in question were inaugurated, or adopted from previously existing practices, as attempts to avoid the mechanical application of the harsh and cruel precepts of a rigorous, repressive criminal law. Among these Anglo-American judicial expedients which have been mentioned as direct precursors of probation, are the so-called benefits of clergy, the judicial reprieve, the release of an offender on his own recognizance, provisional release on bail, the provisional "filing" of a case, and other legal devices for the suspension of either the imposition or the execution of sentence. With a view to a full understanding of the legal origins of probation, it is necessary to review briefly the nature of these practices.

The Benefit of Clergy

The so-called benefit of clergy was a special plea of devious origin by virtue of which certain categories of offenders could, after conviction, but before judgment, claim exemption from, or mitigation of, punishment. In practice it was primarily a device to avoid capital punishment. The importance of this plea in the criminal proceedings of the eighteenth and early nineteenth century is beyond any doubt: "According to the common practice in England of working out modern improvements through antiquated forms, this exemption was made the means of modifying the severity of the criminal law." It is, however, extremely doubtful whether this device had any direct influence on the later development of the suspension of sentence or of any other immediate precursor of probation.

The Judicial Reprieve

The judicial reprieve was a temporary suspension by the court of either the imposition or the execution of a sentence. It was used for specific purposes such as to permit a convicted person to apply for a pardon, or under circumstances such as where the judge was not satisfied with the verdict or where the evidence was suspicious. Although this measure involved only a temporary stay of imposition or execution of sentence, it did lead, in some cases, to an abandonment of prosecution. It does not appear, however, that in England this device "was ever extended to embrace what is now termed an indefinite suspension of sentence, particularly in cases which presented no peculiar reasons, arising out of the lack of or limitations on procedure, for withholding execution of sentence." On the other hand, "there is, no doubt, more than a modicum of good reason in tracing the later pretensions of American courts to a power of indefinite suspension of sentence back to this early practice of reprieve in English courts."

The Recognizance

The recognizance is a legal device deeply embedded in English law. It originated as a measure of preventive justice, and as such it "consists in obliging those persons, whom there is a probable ground to suspect of future misbehavior, to stipulate with and to give full assurance to the public, that such offence as is apprehended shall not happen. . . . " This "assurance to the public" is given by entering into a recognizance or bond (with or without sureties) creating a debt to the State which becomes enforceable, however, only when the specified conditions are not observed. The recognizance is entered into for a specified period of time.

At an early date the use of the principle of the recognizance (or binding-over) was also extended to actual offenders arraigned before the criminal courts. The device came to be used both to ensure the appearance of an offender before the court at a future date when called upon, and as a disposition (or part thereof) in the case of convicted offenders. With the passing of time, the recognizance came to be used almost exclusively with reference to criminal proceedings rather than as a measure of preventive justice. It should be noted, however, that the recognizance, when used in connection with persons arraigned before criminal courts, does not lose its character as a measure of preventive justice but is actually designed to ensure the future law behavior of the offender or, as Blackstone said, "must be understood rather as a caution against the repetition of the offence, than [as] any immediate pain or punishment."

For centuries the courts of England on occasion bound over and released minor offenders on their own recognizance, *with or without sureties*. Similarly, instances of this practice can be found in the records of the American colonies. During the first half of the nineteenth century this device was adopted with increasing frequency particularly in the case of youthful and petty offenders, the imprisonment of whom did not appear to be warranted. The practice seems to have been common in New England (particularly Massachusetts) at the time, and was to be found also in other jurisdictions of the United States of America.

The device of binding-over was used extensively and imaginatively by Judge Peter Oxenbridge Thacher during his term of office (1823–1843) in the Municipal Court of Boston, and the practices developed by him were of particular significance in the later development of probation in Massachusetts. The earliest recorded case in this connection is the case of *Commonwealth v. Chase* (1830). In Judge Thacher's opinion we find in this case a clear statement of the nature of the practice of binding-over as employed by him:

The indictment against Jerusha Chase was found at the January term of this court, 1830. She pleaded guilty to the same, and sentence would have been pronounced at that time, but upon the application of her friends, and with the consent of the attorney of the commonwealth, she was permitted, upon her recognizance for her appearance in this court whenever she should be called for, to go at large. It has sometimes been practised in this court, in cases of peculiar interest, and in the hope that the party would avoid the commission of any offense afterwards, to discharge him on a recognizance of this description. The effect is, that no sentence will ever be pronounced against him, if he shall behave himself well afterwards, and avoid any further violation of the law.

In 1836, the State of Massachusetts, as part of a general revision of its statutory law, gave legislative recognition to the practice of release upon recognizance, *with sureties*, at any stage of the proceedings, in so far as it applied to petty offenders in the lower courts. In the report of the commissioners charged with the revision of the statutory law of the State, the commissioners formulated the theoretical basis of this alteration in the law relating to the punishment of petty offenders, as follows:

This alteration consists in the discretionary power proposed to be given to the courts and magistrates, before whom this class of offenders may be brought, to discharge them, if they have any friends who will give satisfactory security for their future good behavior, for a reasonable time. When such sureties can be obtained, it can hardly fail to operate as a powerful check upon the conduct of the party, who is thus put upon his good behavior. And if his character and habits are such that no one will consent to be sponsor for him, it must forcibly impress on his mind the value of a good character, while it deprives him of all ground of just complaint of the severity of the law, or the magistrate.

It is significant to compare this formulation of the theory underlying the use of release on recognizance with a British formulation of the second half of the nineteenth century. In a book published in 1877, Edward William Cox, Recorder of Portsmouth, specifically described the release of offenders on their own recognizance, with sureties, as a "substitute for punishment," and he noted that, while the conduct of the released offenders was proper, no further action was taken. In particular, he was strongly motivated by the desire to avoid the demoralizing and contaminating influence of short terms of imprisonment, especially in the case of first and juvenile offenders. As for the *rationale* of the use of the recognizances, with sureties, he says, "The suspension only of the judgment, the knowledge that if he [the offender] offends he may yet be punished—the hold which his bail thus has upon him, to a great extent guarantee that if there is in him an inclination to redeem himself he will return to a life of honesty."

Provisional Release on Bail

It has been noted in the preceding paragraphs that the device of releasing an offender on his own recognizance (binding-over) may be used *with or without sureties.* Conversely, the device of sureties (or bail) may be employed either with or without simultaneously binding over the defendant on his own recognizance. The significance of the device of sureties, when combined with the recognizance, as a precursor of probation, has already been discussed; it remains to be pointed out, however, that both in English and in the United States of America the device of bail as such (that is, when not used in conjunction with the recognizance) has similarly been of major historical significance in the evolution of probation, namely, as a device for the provisional suspension of punishment in relation to rudimentary probation practices.

Binding-Over, Bail and the Origins of Probation

It has been noted above, that the recognizance is essentially a preventive rather than a punitive measure of dealing with actual or potential offenders. In the early nineteenth century the increased use of this device was motivated, no doubt, to a considerable extent by considerations of mercy and in this respect the device was one of measures employed to reduce the hardships involved in the mechanical application of a rigorous criminal law. The rehabilitative object of the measure—i.e., the prevention of crime by the restoration of the offender as a law-abiding member of society—was, however, always present. Nevertheless, during this era the device came to be applied with an increasing realization of its rehabilitative potentialities, and came to be accompanied by increasingly effective safeguards and aids in the form of the personal supervision of, and assistance to, the released offender during the trial period. It should further be noted that the recognizance has always contained the germs of supervision—it involves the conditional suspension of punishment, and some vigilance is required to ascertain whether the conditions concerned are being complied with.

It is clear that the provisional release of offenders in the charge of sureties similarly contained the germs of probationary supervision (irrespective of whether this device was combined with the recognizance or not). In view of their financial interest in the conduct of the provisionally released offender, sureties are bound to try to ensure the good behavior of the offender through personal supervision, assistance or influence. The deliberate use, by the courts, of the salutory influence of sureties on offenders released conditionally, either on their own recognizance or on bail, indeed seems to have been in a very real sense the first, rudimentary stage in the development of probation.

The Provisional "Filing" of Cases

The practice of provisionally "filing" a case seems to have been peculiar to Massachusetts. This device consisted of the suspension of the imposition of sentence when, "after verdict of guilty in a criminal case . . . the Court is satisfied that, by reason of extenuating circumstances, or of the pendency of a question of law in a like case before a higher court, or other sufficient reason, public justice does not require an immediate sentence. . . . " The use of this procedure was subject to the consent of the defendant and of the prosecuting attorney, and the suspension was made subject to such conditions as the court in its discretion might impose. The order that a case be laid on file was not equivalent to a final judgment, but left it within the power of the court to take action on the case at any time, upon motion of either party.

CONCLUSION: THE SUSPENSION OF SENTENCE AT COMMON LAW

By way of summary, it may be noted that there existed, during the nineteenth century and earlier, several legal devices which enabled the English and the American courts to suspend either the imposition of sentence (recognizance to keep the peace or to be of good behavior and to appear for judgment when called upon, provisional release on bail, the provisional "filing of a case," and the judicial reprieve) or the execution of sentence (also the judicial reprieve). That these devices existed, and allowed *at least* for the *temporary* suspension of sentence for *specific purposes,* is beyond any doubt. The question whether the English and American courts possess, at common law, an inherent power to suspend sentence *indefinitely* is, however, more problematic.

In analyzing the question of an inherent judicial power to suspend sentence *indefinitely,* it is necessary to distinguish clearly between the use of the special devices of the recognizance and bail, on the one hand, and other devices used for the provisional suspension of punishment, on the other hand. Prior to statutory provisions to this effect, the courts both in English and in the United States of America *did,* in fact, engage in the suspension of the imposition of sentence when releasing offenders on their own recognizances, and took no further action with regard to the infliction of punishment if the condition of good behavior was complied with. Similarly, this procedure was followed, prior to statutory authorization, in at least two of the other countries of the Bristish Commonwealth, viz., New Zealand and Canada. Both in England and in certain jurisdictions of the United States of America (notably Massachusetts), the conditional suspension of the imposition of sentence, with the ultimate release of the offender from all punishment in case of good behavior, was practised (without statutory authorization) also in relation to the provisional release of offenders on bail.

For all practical purposes it may be said that—beyond the relatively circumscribed practice of suspending the imposition of a sentence by means of releasing an offender on a recognizance and/or bail—the English courts *did not* assume the existence of an inherent common law power to suspend sentence indefinitely. In the United States of America, however, a variety of practices developed, with a tendency to extend the suspension of sentence beyond the employment of the recognizance and/or bail. In particular, this involved the suspension of the imposition or of the execution of sentence on the basis of the common law precedent of the judicial reprieve. With the increasing use of the conditional suspension of punishment, with or without some sort of probationary supervision, courts in different jurisdictions adopted contradictory points of view on the question of the existence, at common law, of an inherent judicial power of indefinite suspension of sentence. While some held that the courts had such a power, others rejected this view arguing either that the conditions justifying the recognition of such a power in England did not obtain in the United States, or that the indefinite suspension of sentence by the court constituted an encroachment on the executive prerogative of pardon and reprieve, and thus infringes upon the doctrine of the separation of powers.

The United States Supreme Court finally expressed itself on the issue in question in the so-called *Killits case.* In his opinion in this case, the late Chief Justice White decided that English common law did not give the Federal courts the power to suspend sentence indefinitely:

> It is true that, owing to the want of power in common law courts to grant new trials and to the absence of a right to review convictions in a higher court, it is we think, to be conceded: (*a*) that both suspensions of sentence and suspensions of the enforcement of sentence, temporary in character, were often resorted to on grounds of error or miscarriage of justice which under our system would be corrected either by new trials or by the exercise of the power to review; (*b*) that not infrequently, where the suspension either of the imposition of a sentence or of its execution was made for the purpose of enabling a pardon to be sought or bestowed, by a failure to further proceed in the criminal cause in the future, although no pardon had been sought or obtained, the punishment fixed by law was escaped. But neither of these conditions serves to convert the mere exercise of a judicial discretion to temporarily suspend for the accomplishment of a purpose contemplated by law into the existence of an arbitrary judicial power to permanently refuse to enforce the law.

With reference to the decision in the Killits case, the *Attorney General's Survey* concludes as follows:

> For practical purposes it may be said that this decision served to explode the erroneous belief that had grown up in some States. . . . It may be concluded, therefore, that there

is no historical warrant in the English common law for the claim that American courts have an inherent power to suspend sentence indefinitely. Where this power has been asserted, it has been based on a misconception of English authorities or recognized because it tempered the criminal law with mercy and had grown as a local practice.

It should be noted that Court's decision in the Killits case did not seek to invalidate the practice of releasing offenders on their own recognizances but referred to "the fact that common law courts possessed the power by recognizances to secure good behavior, that is, to enforce the law. . . . " This fact did not, however, afford support for "the proposition that those courts possessed the arbitrary discretion to permanently decline to enforce the law."

From the point of view of the development of probation as a distinct method for the treatment of offenders, the extent to which the judicial devices in which it had its historical origins, were, in fact, extra-legal and not warranted by the English common law, is of small significance. The important point is that these devices developed, and could in fact only develop, in a system of common law jurisdiction which is flexible enough to allow for the gradual adjustment of existing practices to new needs and new objectives. In England this process of adjustment was more conservative and it is probable that the courts stayed within their common law powers; in any case, the legality of the devices used for the conditional suspension of punishment, in relation to early pre-statutory probation practices, was never challenged in England, in Canada or in New Zealand. In the United States of America, the courts overstepped their common law powers, and the resulting diversity and confusion of principles and authorities necessitated the authoritative revision of the legal bases of the practices that have developed. Nevertheless, the definitive explosion of the doctrine of an inherent judicial power to suspend sentence indefinitely came when probation was already a well established part of the administration of criminal justice, and when public opinion had already been fully prepared for this new method for the treatment of offenders. Consequently, the final rejection by the Supreme Court of the doctrine of a common law judicial power of indefinite suspension of sentence actually served as a stimulus for the enactment of statutes expressly authorizing the suspension of sentence and probation.

8

The Origin of Probation in the United States

UNITED NATIONS

The state of Massachusetts shares with England the honor of having given the probation system to the world. During the first half of the nineteenth century, Massachusetts judges sought diligently and in a variety of ways to render the administration of justice more humane, and a favorable judicial climate was thus established for the development of rudimentary "probation" practices.

The first bold step taken beyond the initial rudimentary probation practices (consisting of release on recognizances with sureties) was taken in Boston in 1841. On a day in August of that year a local cobbler, John Augustus, attended the police court in that city, and decided to stand bail for a man charged with being a common drunkard. The court permitted this, and the defendant was ordered to appear for sentence in three weeks, at which time the defendant was brought back showing convincing signs of reform. Instead of the usual penalty—imprisonment in the House of Correction—the judge imposed a nominal fine of one cent and ordered the defendant to pay costs.

Encouraged by his first experience, Augustus proceeded to stand bail for more offenders, and to undertake the task of supervising and guiding their behavior during the period pending judgment. All the early cases handled by him were adult males charged with common drunkenness, but he gradually extended the scope of his activities to include women (at first also common drunkards) and

SOURCE. *Probation and Related Measures,* United Nations, Department of Social Affairs, New York (Sales No.: 1951.IV.2), E/CN/.5/230, 1951, pp. 29–42.

children, and ultimately persons charged with a wide variety of offences. He also extended his activity to include work in the municipal court. Subsequently Augustus continued his labors for eighteen years until his death in 1859. During this period he "bailed on probation" almost 2,000 persons and achieved a very high proportion of successes.

During this period of his activities in the courts of Boston, John Augustus developed several of the features that later became characteristic of the probation system.

As regards the selection of probationers, he confined his effort "mainly to those who were indicted for their first offence, and whose hearts were not wholly depraved, but gave promise of better things. . . . " He did not assume the responsibility for an offender "merely at the solicitation of the unfortunate, or without due investigation into the merits of their cases and a scrupulous examination into the history and character of each individual." "Great care was observed . . . to ascertain whether the prisoners were promising subjects for probation, and to this end it was necessary to take into consideration the previous character of the person, his age and the influences by which he would in future be likely to be surrounded, and although these points were rigidly adhered to, still they were the circumstances which usually determined my action."

When Augustus undertook the responsibility for offenders, he agreed to "note their general conduct," and to "see that they were sent to school or supplied with some honest employment." In addition, he very often provided, or arranged for, accommodation.

He agreed also to make an impartial report to the court, whenever required to. In addition he maintained a careful register of all cases handled.

After the death of John Augustus, his work was continued by Rufus R. Cook, Chaplain to the county gaol and representative of the Boston Children's Aid Society, and other less well-known pioneer "probation officers" whose work was largely voluntary. These men "seem to have carried out the essential features of probation—investigation of defendant before release, the regular reports and home visits. . . . However, their work was of the 'rescue' sort. . . . It is evident that the investigations were necessarily meagre, that probation periods were very short (only a few weeks at the start), and that records, plans of treatment and close supervision were not much in evidence."

By a law of 1869, the State of Massachusetts provided for the appointment of a state agent of the Board of State Charities to investigate cases of children tried before the courts, to attend such trials and to receive children for placement if the court so ordered. The state agents appointed under this new measure (with the assistance of voluntary organizations) exercised supervision over the behavior of deliquent children placed on probation under the existing common law practice.

Probation came to be regulated by statute for the first time in 1878, when Massachusetts passed a law providing for the appointment of a paid probation officer for the courts of criminal jurisdiction in the city of Boston. It is of no mean significance that this pioneer statute on probation specifically contrasts probation with punishment by directing that "such persons as may reasonably be expected to be reformed without punishment" should be selected to be put on probation. Of equal significance is the fact that the statute does not restrict the application of probation to any particular class of offenders (first offenders, young offenders, etc.) or to any particular class of offences, but postulates the likelihood of the individual offender's being reformed without punishment, as the only criterion for the selection of offenders to be released on probation.

The Massachusetts statute of 1878 was designed to deal with the appointment and duties of a probation officer rather than with the legal issues involved in probation. It provided for the annual appointment, by the Mayor of Boston, of a "suitable person" either from the ranks of the police force of the city or "from the citizens at large." The incumbent of the position was to be "under the general control" of the chief of police of the city.

The statute prescribed the duties of the probation officer as including court attendance, this investigation of the cases of persons charged with or convicted of crimes or misdemeanors, the making of recommendations to the courts with regard to the advisability of using probation, the submission of periodical reports to the chief of police, visiting probationers, and the rendering of "such assistance and encouragement [to probationers] as will tend to prevent their again offending."

The statute further gave to the probation officer the power to re-arrest a probationer, without further warrant but with the approval of the chief of police; in such a case the court might "proceed to sentence or make such other disposition of the case as may be authorized by law."

In accordance with the provisions of the statute of 1878, the Mayor of Boston appointed Captain E. H. Savage, formerly Chief of Police, as first statutory probation officer. Generally speaking, the previously existing common law practice of probation remained unaltered, the only significant innovation being the official nature of the new arrangements for the exercise of probationary supervision. The practice of probation under this new arrangement is described as follows, in contemporary records:

[The probation officer] obtains information from the police and in other ways regarding those who have been arrested, and when their cases are called for trial, he takes on probation by authority of the courts those who may reasonably be expected to reform without punishment.

The term of probation ranges from three months to one year, under such conditions as seen best suited to the case. The officer becomes bondsman in a certain sum for the faithful performance of these conditions and for the prisoner's appearance at court from time to time until the case is finally disposed of. The time of continuance for appearance usually ranges from six to twelve weeks.

The correctional authorities in Massachusetts soon showed that they were aware of the importance of the new arrangements provided for by the statute of 1878. In their annual report published in 1800, the Prison Commissioners made reference to the "very important experiment" that was being tried in the city of

Boston, and recommended that legislative provision be made for the extension of the system to other cities.

By a statute of 1880 the right to appoint probation officers was extended to all cities and towns in Massachusetts. In contrast with the statute of 1878 relating to Boston, the statute of 1880 was merely permissive and only a few towns or cities in the state exercised the option of appointing probation officers. Probation was established on a state-wide basis in Massachusetts in 1891, when an act was passed transferring the power of appointment of probation officers from the municipal authorities to the courts, and making such appointment mandatory instead of permissive. Each police district and each municipal court was required to appoint a probation officer, and the probation system was thereby firmly established throughout the lower courts of the state. It was extended to the superior courts by an act of 1898 which authorized the latter to appoint their own probation officers.

It should be noted that the Massachusetts statutes of 1878 to 1898 were designed to supplement, not supplant, the existing common law system of probation. The essential legal features of the common law system—the suspension of the imposition of sentence, "bailing on probation," and the return of the probationer to the court, to be discharged or disposed of otherwise, at the end of the probation period—were taken for granted. The statutes in question dealt primarily with the appointment, remuneration, control and duties of probation officers, and thus enabled the courts to use probation more freely and more effectively. In fact, the introduction of statutory provisions in relation to probation should be seen as an integral part of a continuous process of growth and development, applying both to the probation system in Massachusetts as such and to its acceptance by public opinion. Only this circumstance made it possible for the first probation statute in the world to be passed practically without public discussion or controversy.

9
Probation

PRESIDENT'S COMMISSION ON LAW ENFORCEMENT
AND ADMINISTRATION OF JUSTICE

Slightly more than half of the offenders sentenced to correctional treatment in 1965 were placed on probation—supervision in the community subject to the authority of the court. Table 1 sets forth data from the National Survey of Corrections and the Federal corrections system on the number of persons under probation on an average day in 1965 and the number in institutions or on parole. Also shown are estimates of what these populations are likely to be in 1975. As the table indicates; probation is the correctional treatment used for most offenders today and is likely to be used increasingly in the future.[1]

The estimates for probation shown in the above table project a growth in the number of adults on probation almost 2½ times greater than the growth in institutional and parole populations. The projected growth in juvenile probation is also substantial. As Chapter 4 of this report shows, there are rapidly developing very promising intensive community supervision and residential programs, which

SOURCE. *Task Force Report Corrections.* The President's Commission on Law Enforcement and Administration of Justice, Washington D.C., U.S. Government Printing Office, 1967, pp. 27–37.

[1] These projections are drawn from the special study completed by R. Christensen, of the Commission's Task Force on Science and Technology. The projections, together with the 1965 data supplied by the National Survey of Corrections and special tabulations provided by the Federal Bureau of Prisons and the Administrative Office of the U.S. Courts indicate the following: The number of adults in jails and prisons and on parole in 1965 was 475,042; for 1975 it is projected as 560,000. There were 459,140 adults on probation in 1965: for 1975 the number is projected as 693,000. The population of juvenile training schools and parole programs in 1965 was 123,256; for 1975 it is projected as 210,000. The number of juveniles on probation in 1965 was 224,948, and for 1975 the number is projected as 378,000.

Table 1   *Number of Offenders on Probation, and on Parole or in Institutions, 1965;
Projections for 1975*

Location of Offender	1965		1975	
	Number	Percent	Number	Percent
Probation	684,088	53	1,071,000	58
Parole or institution	598,298	47	770,000	42
Total	1,282,386	100	1,841,000	100

SOURCES. 1965 data from National Survey of Corrections and special tabulations provided
by the Federal Bureau of Prisons and the Administrative Office of the U.S. Courts; 1975 projections by R. Christensen, of the Commission's Task Force on Science and Technology.

could further shift the number of juveniles destined for institutions to community-
based treatment. Thus, the projections for juvenile probation might actually be
low.

The best data available indicate that probation offers one of the most significant prospects for effective programs in corrections. It is also clear that at least
two components are needed to make it operate well. The first is a system that
facilitates effective decision-making as to who should receive probation; the second is the existence of good community programs to which offenders can be
assigned. Probation services now available in most jurisdictions fall far short of
meeting either of these needs.

PRESENT SERVICES AND NEEDS

Current probation practices have their origin in the quasi-probationary measures of an earlier day. The beginnings of probation are usually traced to Boston,
where in 1841 a bootmaker bailed a number of defendants in the lower court on
a volunteer basis. In 1897, Missouri passed legislation that made it possible to
suspend execution of sentence for young and for petty offenders. This statute did
not make provision for the supervision of probationers. However, Vermont established such a plan on a county basis in 1898, and Rhode Island established a
State-administered system in 1899.[2]

After the turn of the century, the spread of probation was accelerated by the
juvenile court movement. Thirty-seven States and the District of Columbia had
a children's court act by 1910. Forty of them had also introduced probation for
juveniles. By 1925, probation for juveniles was available in every State, but this
did not happen in the case of adult probation until 1956.

[2] Paul W. Tappan, "Crime, Justice, and Correction" (New York: McGraw-Hill Book Co., 1960),
pp. 546–549.

Table 2   *Number of Felons and Juveniles on Probation, 1965, and Annual Costs of Services for Each Group*

Type of Probation	Number on Probation	Annual Costs
Felony	257,755	$37,937,808
Juvenile	224,948	75,019,441
Total	482,703	112,957,249

SOURCES. National Survey of Corrections and special tabulations provided by the Federal Bureau of Prisons and the Administrative Office of the U.S. Courts.

Within States, probation coverage is still often spotty. Services for juveniles, for example, are available in every county in only 31 States. In one State, a National Survey staff observer noted, only two counties have probation services. A child placed on probation in the other counties is presumed to be adjusting satisfactorily until he is brought back to court with a new charge.

Table 2 shows the number of delinquents and adult felons on probation at the end of 1965 and the annual costs of these services. It is quickly apparent in terms of the number of persons served and of total operating costs that the juvenile system has relatively greater resources than the adult. Cost comparisons, however, require qualification. The juvenile total includes the cost of many foster homes and some private and public institutional costs. Furthermore, juvenile probation in some jurisdictions has a substantial responsibility for orphaned or other non-delinquent dependent children.

Probation in the United States is administered by hundreds of independent agencies operating under a different law in each State and under widely varying philosophies, often within the same State. They serve juvenile, misdemeanant, and felony offenders. In one city, a single State or local agency might be responsible for handling all three kinds of probation cases; in another, three separate agencies may be operating, each responsible for a different type of probationer. All of these probation programs must contend with similar issues.

ADVANTAGES OF PROBATION

There are many offenders for whom incarceration is the appropriate sanction —either because of their dangerousness or the seriousness of their offense, or both. But in the vast majority of cases where such a sanction is not obviously essential, there has been growing disenchantment with relying heavily on institutions to achieve correctional goals. The growing emphasis on community treatment is supported by several kinds of considerations.

The correctional strategy that presently seems to hold the greatest promise, based on social science theory and limited research, is that of reintegrating the offender into the community. A key element in this strategy is to deal with problems in their social context, which means in the interaction of the offender and the community. It also means avoiding as much as possible the isolating and labelling effects of commitment to an institution. There is little doubt that the goals of reintegration are furthered much more readily by working with an offender in the community than by incarcerating him.

These justifications seem to be borne out by the record of probation services themselves. Probation services have been characteristically poorly staffed and often poorly administered. Despite that, the success of those placed on probation, as measured by not having probation revoked, has been surprisingly high. One summary analysis of outcomes observed in 11 probation studies indicates a success rate of from 60 to 90 percent.[3] A survey of probation effectiveness in such States as Massachusetts and New York and a variety of foreign countries provides similar results with a success rate at about 75 percent.[4] An exhaustive study was undertaken in California when 11,638 adult probationers granted probation during the period 1956–1958 were followed up after 7 years. Of this group, almost 72 percent were successful in terms of not having their probation revoked.[5]

These findings were not obtained under controlled conditions, nor were they supported by data that distinguished among the types of offenders who succeeded or the types of service that were rendered. Nevertheless, all of the success rates are relatively high. They are the product of a variety of kinds of probation administered at different times and places. Even when interpreted skeptically, they are powerful evidence that a substantial number of persons can be placed on probation and have a relatively high rate of success.

Two controlled experiments, one in Utah and one in California, in which the relative effectiveness of institutionalization and community supervision under special conditions with small caseloads and specifically designed treatment programs, were directly tested with randomly selected groups. In both instances the special community treatment was clearly superior in terms of reducing recidivism.

Perhaps the best known effort to determine the extent to which probation services could be used was a demonstration project conducted in Saginaw, Mich., over a 3-year period.[6] Here, trained probation officers with relatively low caseloads were assigned to an adult criminal court that had used probation a little more than the 50 percent average for the State. With full services available, including complete social histories for the use of the court at the time of sentenc-

[3] Ralph W. England, Jr., "What is Responsible for Satisfactory Probation and Post-Probation Outcome?" Journal of Criminal Law, Criminology, and Police Science, 47:667—676 (March-April 1957).

[4] Max Grünhüt, "Penal Reform" (New York: The Clarendon Press, 1948), pp. 60–82.

[5] George F. Davis, "A Study of Adult Probation Violation Rates by Means of the Cohort Approach," Journal of Criminal Law, Criminology, and Police Science, 55:70–85 (March 1964).

[6] "The Saginaw Probation Demonstration Project," Michigan Crime and Delinquency Council of the National Council on Crime and Delinquency (New York: The Council, 1963).

ing, judges imposed prison sentences for only about 20 percent of all of the defendants who appeared before them. There is some evidence that the revocation rate for those granted probation was lower than in the prior 3-year period. Although these findings require more rigorous testing, they lend weight to the view that a high percentage of offenders can be supervised in the community and succeed.

Offenders can be kept under probation supervision at much less cost than in institutions. The National Survey found, for example, that the average State spends about $3,400 a year (excluding capital costs) to keep a youth in a State training school, while it costs only about one-tenth amount to keep him on probation.

Objections might be raised as to the validity of such comparisons, since expenditures for probation services are now much too meager. However, with the 1-to-10 cost ratios prevailing, probation expenditures can clearly be increased several fold and still remain less expensive than institutional programs. This is especially true when construction costs, which now run up to and beyond $20,000 per bed in a correctional institution, are included. The differential becomes even greater if the cost of welfare assistance for the families of the incarcerated and the loss in taxable income are considered.

PROBATION SUPERVISION

There is an extremely wide variation among States in both the laws permitting probation and the way in which probation is practiced. Probation agencies range from those that depend on the ingenuity of a single probation officer to large multidivisional programs offering clinical, diagnostic, detention, foster care, and local institutional programs.

Badly undermanned in general by staff who are too often undertrained and almost always poorly paid, probation agencies only occasionally mount the type of imaginative programs that fulfill their potential for rehabilitation. The extent to which probation is used varies widely from jurisdiction to jurisdiction, paralleling to a large extent the adequacy of staffing ratios.

The Standard Caseload

The administrative problem that has probably plagued probation officials most has been the achievement of a manageable workload for probation officers. Whenever probation programs are subject to criticism, the oversized caseload is usually identified as the obstacle to successful operation. Efforts to reduce caseloads have been the source of a continuing struggle between probation administrators and local and State budget authorities. Some apparently simple but quite important issues are involved.

Over the past decade, a number of efforts have been made to improve the effectiveness of probation and parole supervision by simply reducing the size of an officer's caseloads. Caseloads have been reduced under experimental conditions from 75 to 30 and to 15.[7] It appears from these studies that the simple expedient of reducing caseloads will not of itself assure a reduction in recidivism. Those experiments with reduced caseloads have shown that to reduce recidivism requires classification of offenders with differential treatment for each class.[8]

The concept of an "average caseload" is administratively convenient when calculating broad estimates of the resources necessary to effect some improvement in staffing ratios. However, this useful idea usually becomes translated into the "standard caseload" that each officer should carry. Differences in individual probationers' needs require different amounts of time and energy from a probation officer. The typical probation caseload is usually a random mixture of cases requiring varying amounts of service and surveillance but usually treated as if all the cases were much the same. Clearly, the value of differential treatment requires that probation manpower ratios vary directly with the kind and amount of services to be performed.

Further work is needed to specify with greater accuracy the levels of service required for various kinds of cases. But enough experience is already available to implement a broad, if somewhat rough, system of differential treatment such as is already being used in various forms by a number of agencies.

Planning for Differential Treatment

Differing caseload sizes are only one aspect of the need for differential treatment adapted to the type and circumstances of the offender. Another major requirement for using a differential treatment system is an adequate case analysis and planning procedure. Probably no deficiency is more universally apparent in current programs than the nearly complete lack of careful planning by probation officers, their supervisors, and clinical program consultants, including the active participation of offenders themselves. A common observation of probation officers who have moved from routine to intensive experimental programs is that, for the first time, they are provided an opportunity to develop systematically a plan that is carefully tailored for the offender.

---

[7] California Department of Corrections, Division of Adult Parole, "Special Intensive Parole Unit, 15–Man Caseload Study" (Sacramento: The Department, November 1956) and "Special Intensive Parole Unit, 30–Man Caseload Study" (Sacramento: The Department, December 1958). See also Bertram M. Johnson, "An Analysis of Predictions of Parole Performance and of Judgments of Supervision in the Parole Research Project," California Youth Authority Research Report No. 32 (Sacramento: The Authority, December 1962).

[8] See Stuart Adams, "Effectiveness of Interview Therapy With Older Youth Authority Wards, An Interim Evaluation of the PICO Project," Research Report No. 20 (Sacramento: California Youth Authority, January 1961); Joan Havel and Elaine Sulka, "Special Intensive Parole Unit, Phase 3" (Sacremento: California Youth Authority, March 1962); Walter Burkhart and Arthur Sathmary, "Narcotic Treatment Control Project, Phases 1 and 2," California Department of Corrections, Division of Research, Publication No. 19 (Sacramento: The Department, May 1963); M. Q. Warren et al., "Community Treatment Project, 5th Progress Report," California Youth Authority, Division of Research (Sacramento: The Authority, August 1966).

Such planning must determine the kind and intensity of supervision needed by the probationer. For some, assignment to relatively high caseloads for nominal supervision may well be indicated.[9] Other probationers will require assignment to specialized caseloads with varying intensity and kinds of supervision. Programs may range from assistance in dealing with important social agencies such as schools, to group counseling or family counseling. Alcoholics, addicts, and those with mental or physical problems may require special treatment.

In planning, the ability to place an offender in the community where he is most likely to succeed is an important factor. Of significant assistance in providing this capacity has been the Interstate Compact for the Supervision of Probationers and Parolees. Under the leadership of the Council of State Governments, this program has developed to the point where today thousands of probationers and parolees are able to return and be supervised by agencies in their home States, after being adjudicated criminal or delinquent elsewhere. All States are members of the compact for adults. Several have yet to ratify a similar compact for juveniles, and this failure creates a needless gap in services.

Another important part of probation planning is determination of the period during which various kinds of probation supervision are required. Studies of both probation and parole outcome reveal consistently that most difficulties with offenders occur within the first 1 or 2 years under supervision. For those who avoid difficulty through this period, the probability is exceedingly good that they will no longer be involved in criminal activity. Some offenders require extended periods of probation; for them, reduced supervision may be feasible during the latter portion of their probation terms. However, for the vast majority of offenders, inflexible and lengthy probation terms result in unnecessary restraints and costs.

Manpower Needs

More manpower is needed for probation services than is now available. Data as to exact size of the manpower gap based on careful experimentation with differential treatment must await further studies. However, sufficient data are available now to give a fair approximation of the numbers of officers needed.

Using as a desirable caseload average for juveniles and adult felons the level of 35 an approximate picture of the need for probation officers can be gained. Table 3 shows the size of caseloads in which probationers are currently supervised. With fewer than 4 percent of the probation officers in the Nation carrying caseloads of 40 or less, it is obvious that the gap between optimal and actual levels of staffing is great.

[9] Joseph D. Lohman, Albert Wahl, and Robert M. Carter, "The Ideal Supervision Caseload: A Preliminary Evaluation," The San Francisco Project Research Report No. 9 (Berkeley: University of California School of Criminology, February 1966). For a study of differential caseload levels, see "California Department of Corrections Parole Work Unit Program, Report Submitted to Joint Legislative Budget Committee" (Sacramento: The Department, December 1966).

Table 3   *Percentage Distribution of Probationers, by Size of Caseload in Which Supervised, 1965*

Caseload Size	Juvenile Probation	Felony Probation
	(Percent)	(Percent)
Under 40	3.7	0.8
41–60	19.7	5.0
61–80	49.2	14.1
81–100	16.7	13.1
Over 100	10.7	67.0

SOURCE. National Survey of Corrections.

In 1965 there were 6,336 juvenile probation officers and 2,940 probation officers supervising offenders convicted of felonies.[10] These officers are responsible for both presentence investigations and supervision. Providing enough officers to conduct needed presentence investigations and also reduce average caseloads to 1 officer for each 35 offenders would immediately require an additional 5,300 officers and supervisiors for juveniles and 8,500 for felons.

PROBATION AND REINTEGRATION

Probation was introduced initially as a humanitarian measure. The early pioneers simply wished to keep first offenders and minor recidivists from undergoing the corrupting effects of jail. They were volunteers—ministers and others— whose philosophy was that the offender was a deprived, perhaps uneducated person who needed help in adjusting to his environment.

During and after World War I, however, a marked change occurred in this orientation. As probation services continued to expand, there was increasing demand for professionally educated people, especially trained social workers, to serve as probation officers. The training of social workers, in turn, was profoundly influenced by the introduction of psychiatric, expecially psychoanalytic, theory, and was primarily concerned with the individual and his emotional problems and deficiencies.

The emphasis was on seeing the offender as a disturbed person for whom some degree of psychotherapy was indicated. The professional probation caseworker, therefore, came to be valued for his ability to offer such individually oriented therapy.

More recent theories of reintegration are now influencing the training of probation officers and place greater emphasis on developing the offender's effective participation in the major social institutions of the school, business, and the church, among others, which offer access to successful, nondelinquent careers.

[10] Estimate derived from the National Survey of Corrections and data supplied by the Federal Bureau of Prisons and the Administrative Office of the U.S. Courts.

Experience with programs that have attempted rehabilitation in isolation from these institutions indicates that generally such efforts have only a marginal bearing on an offender's success or failure.[11]

This point of view does not deny the importance of increasing individual capacity, but it does make clear that correctional techniques are nearsighted when they fail to take into account and make needed changes in an offender's social and cultural milieu. Successful adjustment on his part will often require some kind of personal reformation, but it will also usually require conditions within the community that will encourage his reintegration into nondelinquent activities and institutions.

This type of approach has several implications. One of these is the location of probation offices. Characteristically, most are now located in a county courthouse or in a juvenile hall. Probationers are expected to report to these places for counseling and then are visited occasionally in their homes or on their jobs. The kind of approach discussed here would indicate that many probation offices should be relocated, particularly into the centers of high crime and delinquency and close to the community resources that are needed for an effective program.

For those offenders who need minimum supervision, probation officers need to have immediate access to channels to which these persons can be diverted. For others, probation officers need to be close to and interacting with major social influences in the offenders' lives. Centers situated in areas of caseload density, for example, could provide an opportunity for frequent, possibly daily participation of probationers in organized programs calculated to contribute to their socialization.

Neighborhood-based probation services could well be housed with other community services such as welfare, employment, and health agencies. Already some experimentation in this direction indicates that probation services can be brought more directly into the social as well as the psychological life of the probationer.

The reintegration procedures through which the offender is geared into the school or the job are not clearly defined or established. The problems are much easier to describe than the solutions. However, an approach can be defined and some specific correctional strategies discussed for dealing with the major social institutions—the family, the school, and employment.

The Family

Few would challenge the all-important role of the family as the universal social institution that nurtures, protects, and shapes the individual from infancy to independence. Thy dysfunctional, inadequate, or broken family emerges as a principal source of delinquency. Particularly in the case of the preadolescent or

[11] See H. G. Meyer, E. F. Borgatta, and W. C. Jones, "The Girls at Vocational High" (New York: Russell Sage Foundation, 1965), pp. 180, 205—217; and Evelyn S. Guttman, "Effects of Psychiatric Treatment on Boys at Two Training Schools," Research Report No. 36 (Sacramento: California Youth Authority, 1963).

early adolescent delinquent the effort to strengthen the family function is of prime importance.

Two major approaches shape the methods of family therapy. One is the use of the family as a field for corrective intervention on behalf of one or more of its members. Personality difficulties of these members are addressed with the family as the milieu from which the individuals emerge, but the focus is on the individual rather than the family as a whole.

The other approach sees the whole family as the target for treatment. This is the essentially reintegrative type of family therapy. Its objectives are the rehabilitation of the entire family as a healthy functioning unit. There is heavy concentration on instilling healthy child-rearing practices in cases where the children are young, on developing in adolescents the ability to cope with their present situation and those in which they may eventually find themselves, and on making complementary the dual roles of husband-and-wife and father-and-mother. An effort is made to strengthen family ties generally, and to help the family (including the delinquent or pre-delinquent) become effective in the community.

The Youth Development Project, conducted at a psychiatric outpatient clinic connected with the University of Texas Medical Branch, involves a team of therapists who engage in an intensive diagnostic-treatment effort lasting 2 or 3 days, during which the entire family of a delinquent are patients at the clinic. Described as multiple impact therapy, the treatment seeks to give insight and direction to the family that is motivated to seek help with its problems. Probation officers participate in these programs and later maintain contacts with the family in an effort to encourage and renew the self-reformation effort. The technique is particularly appropriate to those sparsely populated regions where treatment resources are scarce.

Other forms of family therapy have been used with the families of delinquents in large cities, often from lower socio-economic groups. Nathaniel Ackerman, of New York City, a pioneer in family therapy, has worked with families of delinquents using an approach which combines analysis, group therapy, and family education. Virginia Satir, of a group in Palo Alto, Calif., which has developed "conjoint family therapy," has coached a variety of workers in correctional institutions and community-based programs in methods of family therapy.

At Wyltwick School for delinquent boys in New York, an experiment has been carried on for some time with families of delinquents from slum areas. At first, the family is interviewed together, using joint therapists. Then the parents talk with one therapist and the children with another. Often in these second sessions "the lid comes off" and the parents and children express their true feelings about each other and what is wrong with the family situation. Delinquent acts may be revealed as rooted in complete misunderstanding by the children or the parents. Reassembled once more, the family may be able to clear up some of these misunderstandings and jointly find a way to deal with the roots of delinquency.

The experiment is now being evaluated. Charles H. King, superintendent of the school, believes that the vast majority of families of delinquents can profit from family therapy, although some families will gain more from it than others and retain their gains better.

The School

Among social institutions, the school clearly is second only to the family in its universal impact. It encompasses all youth, including those most prone to law violation. Chapter 3 of the Commission's General Report examines the operation of the school, particularly the slum school, in relation to delinquency. The inability of poorly financed, overcrowded, and inadequately staffed schools to meet the needs of delinquency-prone populations is described in some detail. The linkage between a child's failure in school and his involvement in delinquency is clearly drawn.

The inability or disinclination of many school systems to cope with the problems of the potential delinquent is intensified where the identified offender is concerned. Once the delinquent label has been officially affixed, all the problems of the marginal youth become more acute; the school's anticipation of trouble tends to be realized, and the level of tolerance of deviant behavior is lowered. Behavioral difficulty and failure to achieve in school frequently lead to truancy, then to dropping out or to expulsion. Once the delinquent youth's ties with the schools are severed, the probability of further delinquency is substantially increased.

The general problems of education for disadvantaged youth have great relevance to corrections, but the solutions obviously lie well beyond the capacity of correctional agencies to undertake. Large-scale programs, now underway, stimulated by Federal legislation in 1965, attempt to create substantial educational opportunities for the disadvantaged. Identified delinquents will benefit directly from these programs. Educational programs for delinquents in institutions are being assisted by Federal grants from the Office of Education.

Educational programs for offenders in the community are of several kinds. The first group is directed toward increasing the competence of offenders to participate more effectively in school programs through special classes for the educationally retarded and the use of programed learning techniques. The availability of funds for probation officers to purchase such services when needed would be particularly useful here.

Other programs directed toward offenders include those which simultaneously affect their motivations, behavior, and education skills. A particularly interesting attempt in this direction is the Collegefield project carried on in conjunction with the Newark State Teachers College, New Jersey. Delinquents assigned by a juvenile court participate in group counseling sessions for half of the day and then are taught by teachers experienced in the public school system. In this setting, youngsters are enabled not only to upgrade their academic skills but also to learn the kind of behavior required to participate in school. Moreover, the group experience increases motivation as peers define success in school as important to status in the group. When youths complete this program, they are moved into regular classroom situations.

Another major category of programs for offenders are those which direct their effort toward the school system itself. Some juvenile courts, for example, make a probation officer responsible for encouraging a specific school to develop intensive programs to attract and hold youths with deficiencies and to develop a greater tolerance on the part of administrators and teachers toward them.

A program which focuses on the school and the offender at the same time is carried out as part of the California Community Treatment project. Experienced and certificated tutors assist marginal students to meet the demands of the educational system. In addition to educational coaching, the tutor counsels the youth concerning his personal behavior in school. He invests considerable time in communication with school counselors and other officials in order to interpret the youngster's needs and problems, to secure development of specialized, low-stress school programs—in short, to increasing the tolerance level of the school system. Program supervisors credit this special program with maintaining a substantially larger proportion of the delinquent population in school and with assuring some educational achievement for the youth who has been suspended or expelled.

Employment

The kind of job a person holds determines, to a large extent, the kind of life he leads. This is true not merely because work and income are directly related, but also because employment is a major factor in an individual's position in the eyes of others and indeed of himself. Work is therefore directly related to the goals of corrections. Glaser concludes in his extensive study, "The Effectiveness of a Prison and Parole System," that "unemployment may be among the principal causal factors in recidivism of adult male offenders."[12] It is difficult for probationers, and often to a greater extent for parolees, to find jobs. They are frequently poor, uneducated, and members of a minority group. They may have personal disabilities—behavior disorders, mental retardation, poor physical health, overwhelming family problems. And they have in any case the stigma of a criminal record to overcome.

A recent study of Federal releasees shows that, during the first month after release, only about 1 out of every 4 releasees was employed at least 80 percent of the time, and 3 out of 10 were unable to secure jobs. After 3 months, only about 4 out of 10 had worked at least 80 percent of the time, and nearly 2 out of 10 still had not been able to find work of any kind.[13]

VOCATIONAL TRAINING AND PLACEMENT PROGRAMS. The problem can be alleviated somewhat by improving the employment skills of offenders and by having more job-placement programs in correctional agencies. Offenders typically lack information about the local labor market as a whole, especially if they have

---

[12] Daniel Glaser, "The Effectiveness of a Prison and Parole System"(Indianapolis: Bobbs-Merrill, 1964), p. 329.
[13] Ibid., p. 328.

not had very much work experience. Several Federal antipoverty agencies have established programs specifically aimed at improving employment opportunities for offenders and have included offenders in other programs. The Department of Labor has initiated several special projects for offenders, including a parole employment evaluation center in New York City under the auspices of the New York Division of Parole that provides intensive and continuing vocational counseling services and makes special provision for bonding when indicated.

The 1965 amendments to the Vocational Rehabilitation Act also opened significant vocational opportunities to offenders. By previous definition, the handicapped were persons with physical and mental conditions which created obstacles to employment. The amendments revised this definition in such a way as to cover offenders by interpreting physical and mental to include behavioral disorders characterized by deviant social behavior or impaired ability to carry out normal relationships with family and community which may result from vocational, education, cultural, social, and environmental factors. A number of research and demonstration programs in correctional institutions and community programs have been funded under these provisions. The most far-reaching of the demonstration programs was inaugurated in November 1965 to serve Federal offenders. This is a series of eight projects in which State vocational rehabilitation agencies provide intensive service to offenders at Federal probation offices and correctional institutions.[14] Programs such as this offer distinct promise for the future and merit active support.

The offender, like any other citizen, may take advantage of the placement service offered by the local public employment service. In some States, the U.S. Employment Service has undertaken special cooperative arrangements with correctional agencies. Some employment offices report a significant number of referrals and placements of offenders; others achieve minimal results. One significant factor appears to be whether there is an especially interested placement officer who is willing to devote extra time, provide some special counseling, and persist even though initial referral or placement of an individual offender does not effect permanent employment. The other important ingredient is the close support of probation or parole staffs in seeing that offenders keep their appointments and follow through when referrals are made.

In most states, parole and probation officers must help find employment for offenders. Many experience severe difficulty in discharging this task. Some correctional personnel, however, have exhibited special interest and skill in the employment field and have found work for a siginificant portion of their caseloads. Their performance indicates that, with the appropriate commitment of correctional manpower and training, the unemployment problem of offenders could be better controlled. In larger probation and parole agencies, special staff could profitably be provided for job placement.

RESPONSE OF THE COMMUNITY.   A survey conducted in 1966 by the Min-

---

[14] Richard A. Grant, "Vocational Rehabilitation Involvement in the Field of Corrections" (paper presented at the Midwest Institute on Correctional Manpower and Training, Topeka, Kans., Mar. 28, 1966).

nesota Division of Adult Corrections gives an idea of employer policies on hiring offenders. Among 983 firms, it found that almost 40 percent indicated at least a general reluctance to hire offenders for any position. Another 28 percent would hire them for specific jobs only. Perhaps these attitudes toward offenders are similar to those expressed by the average citizen. In any case, they represent a substantial barrier to employment and a challenge to correctional agencies. Where negative attitudes have existed, agencies have shown that they can be diminished by good communication between correctional personnel and employers. It is clearly the responsibility of all correctional agencies to seek out that kind of communication as a basis for more specific efforts.

Some unions have been hostile toward providing opportunities for offenders, and others have been indifferent to requests for assistance. However, where union and correction officials have attempted to discuss the problem of the employment of offenders and work toward solutions, the results have been gratifying. In Connecticut, New York, Ohio, and Washington unions have been found sympathetic to the employment of offenders, and some have taken positive steps to help. For example, at the Federal penitentiary in Danbury, Conn., the International Ladies Garment Workers Union has established a program to train sewing machine repairmen on machines furnished by several local companies and provides a card to graduates of the program which helps them to find employment on release.

Business has also set up training programs at Danbury. The Dictograph Corporation trains microsoldering technicians in the penitenitary and employs them when they are in work-release or parole status. In several prisons IBM trains key punch operator, programers, and systems analysts, hiring some itself and referring others to jobs elsewhere.

Training programs offered either directly by unions or by employers with union approval have been a useful method of developing positive relationships between corrections and employment. The creation of trade advisory boards and other liasion groups has also helped to improve the employment climate.

RESTRICTIVE POLICIES AND PROCEDURES. General attitudes toward offenders have in some cases been formalized into policies that do not allow for special circumstances and require specific changes in laws or rules. Among these are bonding and licensing. Bonding against theft by employees is common practice in larger retail and service businesses, usually through blanket bonds covering all employees.

Both employer and offender often assume that all bonding automatically excludes individuals with criminal records, and some employers probably use bonding requirements as an excuse to turn away applicants with records. In some cases, bonding requirements do automatically bar offenders, and in others offenders have difficulty in satisfying the bonding company of their reliability. Letters received from 12 correctional administrators in answer to the Commission's inquiries agreed that bonding is a problem for the offender, particulary in clerical, sales, and commercial occupations.

Some experimental programs to overcome bonding problems are now under-way. The Labor Department has funded a bonding demonstration project under the Manpower Development and Training Act that will contract with a bonding company to provide bonds for 1,700 individuals in New York, Washington, Chicago, Los Angeles, and other cities. Programs similar to these are also being funded by the Department of Health, Education, and Welfare. An interesting variation is offender participation in the development and operation of such programs. In one project, persons bonded will become members of a corporation, Trustworthy, Inc., and will participate in recruiting and screening prospective candidates for bonding. Efforts of this type need extensive expansion and support, and individual employers and insurers must be encouraged to eliminate flat restrictions on bonding for offenders.

The same need for elimination of blanket or irrational restrictions on offenders exists with respect to regulatory and licensing laws relating to employment and other activities. In the employment field, a survey by Spector in 1950 for the Council of State Governments found that most States regulate entry to over 75 different occupations, ranging from law and medicine to barbering and undertak-ing.[15] Conviction may well be relevant in some cases to the protection of the public through such regulation. It is relevant to the offense they have committed to revoke the license of a lawyer convicted of embezzling the funds of clients or a teamster convicted of vehicular homicide. But it is hard to see why, on the other hand, a man convicted of larceny should not be permitted to cut hair or run a restaurant.

Nonetheless, licensing laws and authorities usually do not confine restrictions to situations in which there is a rational connection between an offense and the practice of an occupation. Licenses are in many cases primarily revenue measures or else products of pressure by unions or trade associations to limit access to an occupation. In other instances they may indeed serve the purpose of protecting the public through the establishment of standards of competency and honesty, but they may rely on excessively broad prohibitions to do so. Licensing authorities may interpret a general requirement such as "good moral character" as a flat proscription against all offenders. A general overhaul of all State and local licens-ing and employment regulations to eliminate such irrational barriers would do much to help in the reintegration of offenders as useful citizens.

GOVERNMENT AGENCIES. Local and Federal Government agencies have traditionally barred offenders from employment. In doing so, they have raised serious questions about their commitment to the rehabilitative efforts of other public agencies and have set a conspicuously poor example for private employers.

Recently, the Federal Government has significantly modified its position. The Civil Service Commission, on August 15, 1966, announced a new Federal employ-ment policy regarding the hiring of former offenders. The Commission and the

---

[15] Sidney Spector and William Frederick, "A Study of State Legislation Licensing the Practice of Professions" (Chicago: Council of State Governments, 1952), pp. 1–8.

employing agencies will accept applications from persons who have records of criminal convictions and will consider for employment those adjudged to be good risks.

A number of State governments have made outstanding gains in employing offenders. Local governments are reexamining their policies. In January 1966, the city of New York ended its 50-year-old policy of automatically rejecting persons as employees who had been convicted of crimes and began to hire such persons, including parolees. The new standard is based on individual evaluation of the applicant. According to the city, its experience has been very good.

While these are encouraging steps, much more needs to be done. Every level of government should revise its policies to provide the offender a reasonable opportunity for appropriate employment.

RESTRICTIONS AND CONDITIONS ON PROBATION

The use of probation is influenced importantly by requirements imposed by statute or sentencing courts. The basic structure of sentencing laws is discussed in Chapter 5 of the Commission's General Report and the report of the Task Force on Administration of Criminal Justice. The most important types of legal restrictions and conditions on probation use are touched on here.

Statutory Restrictions

The use of probation in juvenile cases is rarely restricted by statute. Whatever restraints courts may labor under in this area are usually only the result of custom or the pressure of community feeling about certain offenses. This is not the case in probation for adults.

Only 15 States have no statutory restrictions on who may be granted probation in felony cases. In the remaining 35 States, probation is limited by such factors as type of offense, prior convictions, or whether the defendant was armed at the time of offense. The type of offense is the most commonly used device for restricting probation; offenders guilty of rape and murder are the most widely excluded from probation consideration. Beyond these two there is little consistency between States.

The report of the Task Force on Administration of Justice advocates the general reduction of the various outright prohibitions and restrictions on probation and, in their stead, the provision of statutory standards to guide courts in using their discretion in decision-making. The sense of this approach is that probation legislation cannot take into account all possible extenuating circumstances surrounding the commission of an offense or the circumstances of particular offenders.

The key to differential treatment of various offenders lies in the ability of decision-makers, in this case the sentencing judge, to base their decision on a full appraisal of the offender, his personal and social characteristics, and the available types of programs which are best suited to those characteristics. Inflexible restrictions based on narrow criteria defeat the goals of differential treatment by restricting the options from which a judge may choose.

Probation Conditions

This is another area where patterns typically vary between juvenile and adult systems. A number of juvenile courts follow the common adult practice of spelling out probation conditions in detail and of routinely imposing a standard set when granting probation. A more usual practice in juvenile courts is simply to require the cooperation of the probationer with the probation officer. In effect this leaves the imposition of restrictions to the discretion of the probation officer responsible for the supervision of the case.

Delegating rulemaking power to a probation officer invites possible abuse of that discretion. Additionally, a number of correctional officials will argue that a difficult role conflict is created when the probation officer is given the task of being simultaneously rulemaker, enforcer, and helper. If a violation of a rule can serve as the basis for a revocation of probation, it needs to be clearly defined to the probationer. Best practice would require that such rules and conditions imposed be carefully reviewed by the court.

Differential treatment requires that rules be tailored to the needs of the case and of the individual offender. The procedure followed in a number of courts is to have the probation officer who submits a presentence report make recommendations about the conditions which seem indicated in a specific case. They therefore can be discussed with the prospective probationer and his counsel as well as the probation officer. Such a procedure is superior on several counts and could well be emulated by all courts.

Other issues related to probation and parole conditions are discussed in connection with parole. Two points, however, are peculiar to probation. The first of these is the practice in some courts of routinely imposing a jail term as a "condition" to probation prior to the start of the probation period. The argument usually advanced for this practice is that it gives the offender a taste of incarceration that tends to deter him from further criminal activities.

Correctional personnel have generally sought to discourage commitments to jail as a condition of probation, questioning whether it in fact operates as a deterrent and pointing out that a jail term may complicate reintegration by causing an offender to lose his job and otherwise disrupting his community ties.

The question of the deterrent effect of such a condition requires research and experimentation that has yet to be undertaken. It seems clear, however, that the indiscriminate use of incarceration in a class of cases that presumably includes many offenders not likely to repeat their acts and amendable to other corrective methods is unwise. Whether or not to use short-term detention as a deterrent should be carefully determined in each individual instance, and until more knowledge is available as to its effectiveness in accomplishing these purposes it should be used extremely sparingly.

Financial reimbursement to victims is another condition used quite frequently in probation. It is not uncommon for a large probation agency to supervise the collection of millions of dollars in restitution for crime victims each year. Restitution can serve a very constructive purpose and of course it represents practical help for the victim. The central problem is to make certain that the rate of such payments is related to the ability of the offender to pay so that it does not prevent an offender from successfully reestablishing himself in the community, or so that it does not automatically destine him for a jail term for failure to meet the conditions of probation. An installment plan is a partial remedy for the problem. In many cases only partial restitution may be possible. Perhaps the best approach is for the probation officer to include in his presentence report an analysis of the financial situation of the defendant, an estimate of a full amount of restitution for the victim, and a recommended plan for payment.

ADMINISTRATION AND ORGANIZATION

Let us emphasize the need to develop organizational coherence in corrections. Nowhere is this more needed than in probation services. In the main, as shown in Table 4, adult probation services are State functions while juvenile probation services are local functions, though there are within these generalizations a very wide variety of administrative patterns.

In 32 States, juvenile courts administer probation services. Elsewhere, juvenile services are operated by State correctional agencies in five States, by the State welfare department in seven, and by other State or local agencies in the remainder. In 30 States, adult probation is combined with with parole services. In the other such services are administered by a separate State board or agency or are under local jurisdiction. This diversity is largely the result of historical accident. Since juvenile probation services were developed in juvenile courts, they were administered locally. Services for adults, in the majority of States, were grafted onto existing state-wide parole supervision services.

There are two major questions in regard to organization and administration. The first is the desirability of direct administration of local probation services by a judge, and the second is the relative merits of State and local administration.

Local Administration of Probation by Courts

Some city and county probation systems are administered directly by a judge and others by relatively independent probation agencies. When probation is administered immediately by a judge, there frequently exists the kind of shared knowledge of function and communication about program content that is found nowhere else in the correctional apparatus. The judge in these jurisdictions is probably as well informed about correctional alternatives as any decision-maker in corrections. This is particularly true of the juvenile system. Moreover some juvenile court judges have, by virtue of their position, succeeded in developing

Table 4　*Administration of Juvenile and Adult Probation, by Type of Agency, 50 States and Puerto Rico, 1965.*

Type of Agency	Number of Jurisdictions	
	Juvenile	Adult
State:		
Corrections	5	12
Other agencies	11	25
Local:		
Courts	32	13
Other agencies	3	1
Total	51	51

SOURCE. National Survey of Corrections,

considerable attention and official support for juvenile probation services. This has also happened to a much lesser extent in adult services.

In most major cities, however, the probation department is a complex organization requiring continuous and intensive administrative attention by professional, full-time managers. This is particularly true of local juvenile probation departments, which often operate detention homes, psychiatric clinics, and foster homes, as well as carrying out supervision functions. To manage so widely dispersed an operation requires specialized expertise and close control which are almost impossible for a judge whose career investment is not in administration. Moreover, organizational effectiveness and continuity of policy are apt to be seriously impaired in an agency subject to detailed administrative direction by both a judge and a chief probation officer.

Various procedures have been adopted by city and county probation agencies to give greater autonomy to probation staffs. One of the most common is to provide that a chief probation officer is hired by a committee of judges and is responsible to them in broad policy matters. Detailed administration is left in his hands. Other systems involve the use of citizen groups or city or county officials in the appointment of probation staffs.

A consideration frequently voiced against shifting probation services away from direct judicial administration is that a judge may more fully trust the information and services provided by staff under his immediate control. However, probation administrators in city, county, and State jurisdictions where probation services are provided to the courts by independent agencies contend that this is not a significant problem. They point out that, in many localities and States where such systems exist, close and very satisfactory working relationships develop between sentencing judges and probation staffs.

State vs. Local Administration

The second major organizational issue is that of State as against local administration. Table 4 showed that in the juvenile field 16 States have centralized State administration for probation services, while in the adult field 37 States are so organized. Other States continue to locate probation departments at the couty level. In this group are 9 of the most densely populated States.

A number of reasons are advanced for probation being a local function. First, local programs can typically develop better support from local citizenry and agencies. Once the offender is adjudged criminal or delinquent, and turned over to a State agency, there is a tendency to withdraw local services. Agencies at the same jurisdictional level tend to be united by a variety of administrative and traditional ties that do not extend to other levels. Employees of local jurisdictions usually have greater identification and ties with their communities, hence greater access to local resources.

Secondly, smaller operations tend to be more flexible and less bound by bureaucratic rigidity. Given aggressive leadership and community support, they may indeed outstrip the larger, more cumbersome State service. Finally, combining all local probation services in several large States, such as New York, Illinois, or California, could result in very large State operations. It would place a tremendous burden on administration. If it were weak, ineffectual, or politically determined, serious damage could result. While all of these risks prevail at lower levels of government—indeed they probably occur more frequently—the impact of any single poor leader is less widely spread.

On the other hand, State administration has some clear advantages. First there exists a greater probability that the same level of services will be extended to all areas and all clients. Uniform and equitable policies will be applied in recommendations for institutional and out-of-home placement. Wide variations in policy are manifest where administration is local. Some economies in detention and diagnostic-services are possible if they are operated regionally rather than locally.

Another major advantage in the State's operation of probation services is the possibility of combining them with parole services and also better coordinating them with institution programs. Presently 30 of the 50 States combine felony probation and parole services for adults while 13 do so wholly or in part for juveniles.

The advantages of such combined services are several. A single agency is able to offer a continuity of service. Thus, the youngster placed on probation who fails and is sent to a training school can be handled by the same community agency when later released on parole. Information about the youth is readily available to the agency and important contacts with families and other significant persons can be maintained and further developed.

Combined services provide economies in the distribution of services. A single officer in a sparsely populated area of a State can service both probation and parole cases in the area. Similarly, the officer in an urban area can mobilize community resources in a given area of a city for both types of cases.

Additionally, there is a tendency for a local agency to "solve" a problem case, or one that requires a substantial investment of services or money, by commitment to the State institution. This would be minimized if a single agency operated both programs.

The greatest resistance to combining probation and parole services generally stems from the fact that this inevitably means that probation services would become part of a State system and move away from local control. The opposite alternative—parole supervision services being administered by a series of local agencies—is clearly undesirable. Virtually every correctional authority contends that parole services must be centrally administered and coordinated with the institutional system, particularly in view of the increasing need to coordinate such services with various institutional and part-way programs.

A final argument for State administration of probation services is the historical fact that State agencies have generally been in the forefront of developing innovative programs, demonstration projects, and correctional research. Extensive research and demonstration are almost nonexistent at the local level.

State Responsibilities to Local Programs

Even without State administration, various State services can nonetheless be used to bolster local programs significantly. As in the case of intake and detention services, a central agency concerned with probation administration is needed at the State level. It could provide centralized statewide statistics on such matters as probation recommendations and adjudicative dispositions; frequency of use of jails and State institutions; the number of successful completions and revocations of probation; and the use of residential centers and homes.

Information on outcomes of various treatment efforts needs to be maintained at a central information center. Such a center could also provide assistance in the design and operation of demonstration and research projects at the local level and provide date-processing capability that only the larger operations can develop. Through these devices all jurisdictions could be assisted in program experimentation and innovation.

A most important service for the State agency is the provision of assistance to local services in staff training and recruitment. The State agency could do much to bring together the academic community and the world of practice. The "career day" program, where social science faculty and students are invited to observe correctional programs and participate in discussions with practitioners, is an example.

Training is another area in which vigorous State agency efforts might develop not only the knowledge and talent of local staff but some uniform levels of program adequacy and policy consistency as well. Traveling teams, local or regional institutes, seminars based at universities and colleges, training conferences for administrators and supervisors are all media that can be used by a State agency to assure statewide dissemination of current correctional theory and practice concepts.

Standard setting is commonly considered an appropriate State agency function. Normally, this would consist of establishing some objective norms for staff qualifications, possibly for staff salary level, and some outlines of the kind of information to be contained in various reports. Standards of treatment or practice are more difficult to define, although some norms concerning fair procedures could be developed with reasonable clarity. Standard setting should be done jointly by State agencies and local agencies, both public and private. Statewide consultation services are vital to the implementation of those standards.

Perhaps the most effective way of improving local services is by direct State subsidy for all or part of the cost of local probation services. Such subsidies now are used quite effectively in many States. Some of the most effective State subsidies include salaries; cost of local camps, institutions, foster homes, group homes, and halfway house operations; and cost of special clinical, diagnostic, and consultation services. Logic would dictate that the State subsidy be invested in a manner calculated to effect the greatest improvement for the tax dollars spent. That is, it should not be simply a device for transferring a portion of a local correctional budget upward to the State level, but rather should depend upon measurable improvement and performance.

A variant of the subsidy is the provision of specific services by the State agency. Noninstitutional placements in State-operated group homes and residential centers, clinical diagnosis, and consultation are examples.

Probation services under optimal conditions would be administered at the State level. If they are located there, they require sound financial support and backing. If they are to continue to be administered at the local level, it is clear that staff training and program content can be assured only if the State government provides undergirding services and vigorous leadership in making sure that local programs are effective.

10
Probation: National Standards and Goals

NATIONAL ADVISORY COMMISSION ON CRIMINAL
JUSTICE STANDARDS AND GOALS

Extensive use of institutions has been giving way to expanded use of community-based programs during the past decade. This is true not only in corrections, but also in services for the mentally ill, the aging, and dependent and neglected children.

The movement away from institutionalization has occurred not only because institutions are very costly, but also because they have debilitating effects on inmates, who have great difficulty in reintegrating themselves into the community. Therefore, it is essential that alternatives to institutionalization be expanded in use and enhanced in resources. The most promising process by which this can be accomplished in corrections—probation—is now being used more as a disposition. Even greater use can be projected for the future.

Broad use of probation does not increase risk to the community. Any risk increased by allowing offenders to remain in the community will be more than offset by increased safety due to offenders' increased respect for society and their maintenance of favorable community ties. Results of probation are as good, if not better, than those of incarceration.[1] With increased concern about crime, reduc-

---

SOURCE. *Corrections,* National Advisory Commission on Criminal Justice Standards and Goals, Washington, D.C., U.S. Government Printing Office, 1973, pp. 311–340.

[1] See National Council on Crime and Delinquency, *Policies and Background Information* (Hackensack, N.J.: NCCD, 1972), pp. 14–15.

tion of recidivism, and allocation of limited tax dollars, more attention should be given to probation, as a system and as a sentencing disposition.

Although probation is viewed as the brightest hope for corrections, its full potential cannot be reached unless consideration is given to two major factors. The first is the development of a system for determining which offenders should receive a sentence of probation. The second is the development of a system that enables offenders to receive the support and services they need so that ultimately they can live independently in a socially acceptable way.

Currently, probation has failed to realize either of these. Probation is not adequately structured, financed, staffed, or equipped with necessary resources. A major shift of money and manpower to community-based corrections is necessary if probation is to be adopted nationally as the preferred disposition, as this Commission recommends. The shift will require strengthening the position of probation in the framework of government, defining goals and objectives for the probation system, and developing an organization that can meet the goals and objectives. In this chapter, consideration will be given to what must be done if probation is to fulfill its potential as a system and as a disposition.

DEFINITIONS

In corrections, the word "probation" is used in four ways. It can refer to a disposition, a status, a system or subsystem, and a process.

Probation as a court disposition was first used as a suspension of sentence. Under probation, a convicted offender's freedom in the community was continued, subject to supervision and certain conditions established by the court. A shift now is occurring, and probation is being used increasingly as a sentence in itself. The American Bar Association Project on Standards for Criminal Justice defines probation as:

A sentence not involving confinement which imposes conditions and retains authority in the sentencing court to modify the conditions of sentence or to re-sentence the offender if he violates the conditions. Such a sentence should not involve or require suspension of the imposition or execution of any other sentence. . . .

A sentence to probation should be treated as a final judgment for purposes of appeal and similar procedural purposes.[2]

Probation as a status reflects the position of an offender sentenced to probation. For the offender, probation status has implications different from the status of either free citizen or confined offender.

Probation is a subsystem of corrections, itself a subsystem of the criminal and juvenile justice system. Unless otherwise specified, "probation" will be used throughout this chapter to refer to the probation subsystem. When used in this

---

[2] American Bar Association Project on Standards for Criminal Justice, *Standards Relating to Probation* (New York: Institute of Judicial Administration, 1970), p. 9.

context, probation refers to the agency or organization that administers the probation process for juveniles and adults.

The probation process refers to the set of functions, activities, and services that characterize the system's transactions with the courts, the offender, and the community. The process includes preparation of reports for the court, supervision of probationers, and obtaining of providing services for them.

The terms written report or "report" will be used to denote both presentence investigation reports and social studies prepared for the courts. The term "presentence investigation report" is used for those dealing with adults and "social study" for those dealing with juveniles.

"Intake" refers to the process of screening cases prior to court appearance, in order to take or recommend a course of action. It involves discretion to resolve a matter informally, to arrange court-based diversion services, or to proceed with a court hearing. It also may include investigative or assessment activities and pretrial release or detention decisions.

EVOLUTION OF PROBATION

Probation's origins go back to English common law and the efforts to alleviate the severity of criminal sanctions. The earliest probation device appears to have been "benefit of clergy," which was used originally to release clergymen from criminal court on the theory that only church courts had jurisdiction over their personnel. Later, "benefit of the clergy" was extended to include anyone who could read.

Judicial reprieve, another device used in the Middle Ages, was the precedent for the practice of suspension of sentence, which was brought to America from England. Recognizance practice also was developed in England, apparently in the 14th century, involving release with some type of surety or bail to assure good behavior.

John Augustus, a Boston shoemaker, is recognized as the father of probation in this country. As a volunteer, he asked the court to release certain offenders he thought he could assist. Practices he began using in 1841 have stood the test of time: investigation and screening, interviewing, supervision of those released, and services such as employment, relief, and education. His efforts were so successful that legislation formally establishing probation and providing for paid staff was enacted in Massachusetts in 1878. By 1900, six States had enacted probation legislation; four dealt with adult probation and two related only to children.

Probation as a disposition and a system is essentially a development of the 20th century. The first directory of probation officers in the United States, published in 1907, identified 795 probation officers, mostly serving juvenile courts. Some were volunteers, some welfare workers, some attached to courts, and some employed part-time. By 1937 more than 3,800 persons were identified as probation officers, of whom 80 percent worked full-time and the rest had additional duties, such as sheriff, welfare worker, minister, attendance officer, or attorney.

In 1947, the directories began to include both probation and parole. In 1970, nearly 25,000 persons were identified as probation and parole personnel, and only 2 percent had other duties such as county welfare worker or sheriff.

As probation use increased, growing interest in its effectiveness developed. One demonstration of its effectiveness was the Saginaw Project conducted in Michigan between 1957 and 1962. The project, staffed by trained workers with manageable workloads, had three objectives. First, probation should be used for 70 to 75 percent of convicted offenders. Second, there should be no increased risk to community safety. Third, actual tax dollar savings should be achieved by reduced construction and maintenance of institutions. All objectives were accomplished.[3]

Followup studies of probation elsewhere indicated that failure rates of persons on probation were relatively low.[4] Although many of these studies were not conducted under controlled conditions, with definitive information about variables such as service rendered and matched groups of offenders, the gross evidence cannot be discounted.

GOVERNMENTAL FRAMEWORK OF PROBATION

The position of probation in the government framework varies among the States. The continuing controversy over the most appropriate placement of probation centers on two main issues: whether it should be a part of the judicial or executive branch of government; and whether it should be administered by State or local government.

In all States, corrections components and subsystems, except probation and some juvenile detention facilities, operate within the executive branch. Probation is found in the executive branch in some States, in the judicial in others, and under mixed arrangements elsewhere.

State governments operate most subsystems of corrections. The exceptions are probation, jails, and some juvenile detention facilities. Juvenile probation usually developed in juvenile courts and thus became a local function. As adult probation services developed, they generally were combined with existing statewide parole services or into a unified corrections department that also included parole and institutions. The exceptions were in major cities that had already created probation organizations for the adult courts and States in which probation responsibilities were divided.

Variations in the way probation has been organized and placed within the government framework have created differences between States as well as within States. Ohio provides an example of the complicated arrangements that have

---

[3] National Probation and Parole Association, Michigan Council, *The Saginaw Probation Demonstration Project* (New York: National Council on Crime and Delinquency, 1963).

[4] See Robert L. Smith. *A Quiet Revolution* (Washington: U.S. Department of Health, Education, and Welfare, 1972).

developed. There, juvenile probation is a local function in the judicial branch, but the State aid program is in the executive branch. Adult probation can be either a State or local function. A State agency in the executive branch can provide probation service to local courts, or they may establish their own. Where local probation exists, the control may be shared by both branches in an arrangement under which the county commissioners and judges of the court of common pleas must concur on appointments.

In New York State the State Division of Probation is in the executive branch as are all local probation agencies except those in New York City, which are in the judicial branch.

Such variations appear to have arisen as emphasis was given to one or the other of the two traditional functions of probation officers: to provide presentence reports and other services for the courts; and to supervise and provide services for probationers. These are different tasks with different objectives.

Variations occur within probation itself. There may be one agency for all offenders or separate agencies for juveniles and adults. Adult probation may be divided into one agency for felons and another for misdemeanants.

The question of where probation should be placed in the framework of government becomes more critical as its use expands and staff numbers increase. It is time to take a serious look at where probation could function most effectively, rather than using chance and history to support the status quo.

Judicial vs. Executive Branch

In the debate over the appropriate governmental branch for the probation system, those who favor the judicial branch give the following rationale.

1. Probation would be more responsive to court direction. Throughout the probation process, the court could provide guidance to probation workers and take corrective action when policies were not followed or proved ineffective.

2. This arrangement would provide the judiciary with an automatic feedback mechanism on effectiveness of dispositions through reports filed by probation staff. Judges, it is urged, may place more trust in reports from their own staff than in those from an outside agency.

3. Courts have a greater awareness of needed resources and may become advocates for their staffs in obtaining better services.

4. Increased use of pretrial diversion may be furthered by placing probation in the judicial branch. Courts have not been inclined to transfer authority and therefore may set more stringent limitations on the discretion of nonjudicial personnel to release or divert than on judicial staff.

The arguments for keeping probation in the judicial branch, which center around the direct relationship between the courts and probation, are not persuasive. Subsystems of the criminal justice system in the executive branch are able to work effectively with the courts.

Those who oppose placement of probation within the judiciary argue that:

1. Under this arrangement judges frequently become the administrators of

probation in their jurisdictions—a role for which they usually are ill-equipped. The current trend toward use of court administrators reflects the belief that judges cannot be expected to have the time, orientation, or training to perform two such distinct roles.

2. When probation is within the judicial system, the staff is likely to give priority to services for the courts rather than to services to probationers.

3. Probation staff may be assigned functions that serve legal processes of the court and are unrelated to probation, such as issuing summonses, serving subpenas, and running errands for judges.

4. Courts, particularly the criminal courts, are adjudicatory and regulatory rather than service-oriented bodies. Therefore, as long as probation remains part of the court setting, it will be subservient to the court and will not develop an identity of its own.

Another class of arguments supports placement of probation in the executive branch of government, rather than merely opposing placement in the judicial branch.

1. All other subsystems for carrying out court dispositions of offenders are in the executive branch. Closer coordination and functional integration with other corrections personnel could be achieved by a common organizational placement, particularly as community-based corrections programs increase. Furthermore, job mobility would be enhanced if related functions are administratively tied.

2. The executive branch contains the allied human service agencies including social and rehabilitation services, medical services, employment services, education, and housing. Where probation also is in the executive branch, opportunities are increased for coordination, cooperative endeavors, and comprehensive planning.

3. Decisions involving resource allocations and establishment of priorities are made by the executive branch. It initiates requests to the legislative bodies, either local or State, for appropriation of funds, and by so doing sets priorities for allocating limited tax dollars. When probation is included in the total corrections system, more rational decisions about the best distribution of resources can be made.

4. Probation administrators are in position to negotiate and present their case more strongly, if they are in the executive branch. When probation is part of the court system the judge, not the probation administrator, is responsible for presenting the budget request and acting as negotiator. The latter is not a role traditionally undertaken by the judiciary.

On balance, the arguments for placement of probation in the executive branch of government are more persuasive. Such placement would facilitate a more rational allocation of probation staff services, increase interaction and administrative coordination with corrections and allied human services, increase access to the budget process and establishment of priorities, and remove the courts from an inappropriate role.

For these reasons, this report calls for inclusion of probation departments within unified State correctional systems. (See Chapter 16, Statutory Framework of Corrections.) Moreover the chapters which deal with intake services (Chapter 8 for juveniles and Chapter 9 for adults) recommend that staff performing services for the courts (as against services to pretrial releasees as probationers) should be under the administrative control of the courts.

This is, in the Commission's view, the proper long-range objective. It would do away with the current duality of roles for probation staff. However, in view of the current variety of local arrangements, it may for the present be appropriate for personnel carrying out services to the courts to be employed by the probation division of a unified State Corrections system but detailed to perform court services. It would be essential in such an arrangement that probation staff take direction from the court and the court administration in establishment of policies, procedures, and performance standards for carrying out their tasks and that the probation division be responsive to the needs of the courts. Where such an arrangement appears to be desirable, written agreements setting out and defining the relationship between the court and the corrections system should be developed and agreed to by both.

State vs. Local Administration

Few States in which probation is a local function have provided any leadership or supervision for probation agencies. Tremendous variations are likely to exist within a State in terms of number of staff employed in counties of similar size, qualifications of personnel employed, and relative emphasis on services to courts and probationers. County probation agencies often are small and lack resources for staff training and development, research and program planning, and, more basically, services to the probationers.

STATE EFFORTS TO SET STANDARDS.   Attempts to bring about some degree of uniformity have been limited. In a few States where probation is a local function, standards are set by the State in either the judicial or executive branch. For example, in New Jersey the judicial branch is responsible for setting standards for its local probation systems, while in California the responsibility is placed in the executive branch.

The degree to which local probation systems comply with State standards is dependent upon the rewards and sanctions used. As a reward for meeting specified standards, the State may provide either revenue or manpower. Michigan assigns State-paid probation officers to work alongside local probation officers. The more common practice, however, is direct payment by the State to local governments for part of the costs of probation services. New York State reimburses local communities up to 50 percent of the operating costs for probation programs, provided that local communities meet State staffing standards. This subsidy has nearly doubled in the last 6 years and has resulted in an increase of probation staff in the State from 1,527 in 1965 to 1,956 in 1972.[5]

---

[5] Information supplied by the New York State Division of Probation.

The States of California and Washington use a different approach in providing revenue to local jurisdictions. These States attempt to resolve a problem that is inherent when probation is a local function; namely, that financing probation is a local responsibility. However, when juveniles or adults are sent to correctional institutions, these are usually administered and financed by the State. A consequence often is the shifting of financial responsibility from the local government to the State government by sentences of incarceration rather than probation.

California and Washington have developed probation subsidy programs in which counties are reimbursed in proportion to the number of individuals that remain in the community rather than being sent to State institutions. The subsidy program in California was developed as a result of a study that indicated that some individuals eligible for commitment to State correctional institutions could safely be retained on probation and that with good probation supervision, they could make a satisfactory adjustment. It was estimated that at least 25 percent of the new admissions to State correctional institutions could remain in the community with good probation supervision.

The California Probation Subsidy Program was instituted in 1966 by the State's youth authority. The youth authority was authorized to pay up to $4,000 to each county for every adult and juvenile offender not committed to a State correctional institution. The counties were required to demonstrate a commitment to improved probation services, including employment of additional probation workers and reduction of caseloads. In addition, each county had to demonstrate innovative approaches to probation, such as intensive care probation units for dealing with hard-core adult and juvenile offenders.

California estimates that, even with expanded probation services, the cost of probation runs little more than one-tenth of the cost of incarceration, approximately $600 per person annually for probation, compared to $5,000 annually for institutionalization. In all, the program has resulted in substantial savings to taxpayers. In the six years between 1966 and 1972, California canceled planned construction, closed existing institutions, and abandoned new institutions that had been constructed. Almost $186 million was saved in these ways, while probation subsidy expenditures came to about $60 million. Furthermore, although there has been a general decrease in commitments to State institutions throughout the United States, the decrease is sharper in those counties in California that participate in the subsidy program. The decrease in those counties almost doubles that of Caifornia counties not participating in the subsidy program.[6]

The State of Washington has had a similar experience with the probation subsidy program begun in January, 1970. Its purpose was to reduce the number of commitments to institutions from county juvenile courts. In the 2 years the program has been in operation, there has been a marked reduction in the number of children and youth sent to State institutions. To illustrate, in 1971, the State received 55 percent fewer commitments than expected.[7]

---

[6] Smith. *A Quiet Revolution,* gives the background of and experience under California's probation subsidy plan.

[7] Information supplied by the Washington State Department of Social and Health Services.

ADVANTAGES OF STATE ADMINISTRATION. Even in those instances where the State provides financial incentives to local jurisdictions, as in California, participation of counties is discretionary. Uniformity in probation can be achieved only when there is a State-administered probation system, which also has a number of other distinct advantages.

A State-administered system can more easily organize around the needs of a particular locality or region without having to consider local political impediments. It also can recommend new programs and implement them without requiring additional approval by local political bodies.

A State-administered system provides greater assurance that goals and objectives can be met and that uniform policies and procedures can be developed. Also, more efficiency in the disposition of resources is assured because all staff members are State employees and a larger agency can make more flexible use of manpower, funds, and other resources.

When it is simply not possible for a State to administer a probation system, the State, through a designated agency in the executive branch, should be responsible for developing standards for local probation systems that provide for a minimum acceptable level of functioning. State standards have a greater chance of being implemented if the State indicates a willingness to share the costs with local governments when standards are met and maintained.

In addition to setting standards for local jurisdictions, the State agency should be responsible for establishing policies, defining statewide goals, providing staff training, assisting in fiscal planning and implementation, collecting statistics and data to monitor the operations of local probation agencies, and enforcing change when necessary. Through these means, a state-supervised program can bring about some degree of uniformity in operations throughout the State, but not to the same degree as a State-administered program.

PROBATION ADMINISTRATION

The complexities of administering a probation system have been reflected in several studies. A poll conducted for the Joint Commission on Correctional Manpower and Training indicated that administrators felt the need for more training, especially in public administration.[8] Another study revealed support for two different types of education for administrators. One group advocated social work education, apparently representing a concern for substantive practice matters. The others advocated public administration because of a concern about managerial responsibilities.[9]

---

[8] Joint Commission on Correctional Manpower and Training, *Corrections 1968: A Climate for Change* (Washington: JCCMT, 1968), p. 30.

[9] Herman Piven and Abraham Alcabes, *The Crisis of Qualified Manpower for Criminal Justice: An Analytic Assessment with Guidelines for New Policy* (Washington: Government Printing Office, 1969), vol. 1.

Need for Administrators to Formulate Goals

The administrator is expected to formulate goals and basic policies that give direction and meaning to the agency. If these goals are not formulated specifically, they are made by default, for staff will create their own framework. Should policies and goals not be developed quickly or well enough, persons outside the agency may determine policies, with or without consideration of long-range goals.

Unfortunately, clearly defined objectives for probation systems rarely are set forth. The probation administrator has contributed to variations in philosophy, policy, and practice. Often staff members of the same agency have different perceptions, with top management having one view, middle management another, and line personnel reflecting some of each.

Probation staff members bring to the organization their own backgrounds and the beliefs they acquired before becoming employees. These in turn are modified by other staff members, judges, law enforcement officials, personnel of other parts of the correctional system, probationers, complainants and witnesses, lawyers, and the news media.

If an administrator has failed to define goals and policies for his organization, dysfunction within the organization must follow. Some dysfunctioning is rooted both in tradition and rapid growth.

Training for Probation Work

Since the 1920's there has been an emphasis on social work education as a prerequisite for entering probation. The preferred educational standard was a master's degree in social work. This emphasis was paralleled by the concept of professionalism. To achieve professionalism, staff members had to be provided opportunities to increase their knowledge and skills. Such a thrust created a staff expectation that they would have opportunity to use the increased knowledge and skills. However, as probation systems grow in size, agencies tend to develop the characteristics of a bureaucracy that increase constraints on staff behavior which result in frustration.

New graduates of schools of social work have been reluctant to enter probation. Newer staff members sent by probation agencies to graduate schools of social work often leave the agency as soon as they fulfill any commitment made to secure the education. Such workers are likely to express their reason for leaving as frustration over the lack of opportunity for using their knowledge and skills.

Dysfunctions in Probation Operation

Training emphasis has been at a staff level, and this too can contribute to dysfunction. More emphasis has been placed on training probation officers than on equipping executives and middle-level managers with skills to administer effectively. Organizational change must begin with the executives and middle management if probation officers are to have an opportunity to use increased knowledge and skills acquired through training.

Another dysfunction may result from the change from one-to-one casework emphasis of the probation officer to the group emphasis needed for an administrator. Many staff members are promoted from the ranks of probation officer to supervisor and administrator. If effective organizations are to be developed, supervisors and administrators should meet and work with staff on a group basis. If the supervisors and administrators do not have the skills to do this effectively, they will revert to the pattern of one-to-one relationship.

Another form of dysfunction may stem from promotion of a probation officer to a supervisory or administrative position. Ideally a supervisor should receive training that enables him to create a supportive atmosphere for the probation officer, both inside and outside the agency. The probation officer who has been promoted but given no training for his new role has a natural tendency to see himself as doing his job well by concentrating on internal matters. Support and supervision of staff may consist of nothing more than shuffling papers, reporting statistics, and giving basic training to probation officers.

SERVICES TO PROBATIONERS

The Current Service System

Many problems have prevented development of a system for providing probationers with needed resources. For one thing, the goal of service delivery to probationers has not been delineated clearly and given the priority required. Services to probationers have not been separated from services to the court. Generally, both services are provided by the same staff members, who place more emphasis on services to the court than to probationers.

Because the goal for service delivery to probationers has not been defined clearly, service needs have not been identified on a systematic and sustained basis. Priorities based on need, resources, and constraints have not been set. Measurable objectives and ways of achieving them for various target groups have not been specified. Moreover, monitoring and evaluation of services have been almost nonexistent.

Another problem is the lack of differentiation between services that should be provided by probation and those that should be delivered by such agencies as mental health, employment, housing, education, and private welfare agencies. Because of community attitudes toward offenders, social agencies other than probation are likely to be unenthusiastic about providing services to the legally identified offender. Probation offices usually lack sufficient influence and funds to procure services from other resources and therefore try to expand their own role and services. This leads to two results, both undesirable: identical services are duplicated by probation and one or more other public service agencies, and probation suffers from stretching already tight resources.

Some probation systems have assumed responsibility for handling matters unrelated to probation such as placement of neglected children in foster homes and operation of shelter facilities, both of which are the responsibilities of the child welfare or other public agencies. Probation also has attempted to deal directly with such problems as alcoholism, drug addiction, and mental illness, which ought to be handled through community mental health and other specialized programs.

These efforts to expand probation's role have not been successful because there is not enough money to provide even the traditional basic probation services.

Overemphasis on Casework

One result of the influence of social work on probation has been an overemphasis on casework. Development of child guidance clinics in the 1920's and 1930's influenced particularly the juvenile courts and their probation staff.

The terms "diagnosis" and "treatment" began to appear in social work literature and not long after in corrections literature. Those terms come from the medical field and imply illness. A further implication is that a good probation practitioner will understand the cause and be able to remedy it, just as the medical practitioner does. Essentially, the medical approach overlooked any connection between crime and such factors as poverty, unemployment, poor housing, poor health, and lack of education.

A review of the literature of the 1930's, 1940's, and 1950's indicates that the casework method became equated with social work, and in turn, casework for probation became equated with a therapeutic relationship with a probationer. A study manual published by the National Probation and Parole Association in 1942 reflects this equation in the table of contents. The titles of three of the chapters are: "Social Casework," "Case Study and Diagnosis," and "Casework as a Means of Treatment."[10]

The literature discussed the development of social work skills in interviewing, creating therapeutic relationships with clients, counseling, providing insight, and modifying behavior. When practitioners began to view themselves as therapists, one consequence was the practice of having offenders come to the office rather than workers going into the homes and the communities.

Although the literature refers to probation officers working with employers, schools, families, and others in the probationer's life, the chief concern is the relationship between probation officer and probationer. Indeed, if probation staff members see casework as their model, it may well be asked how much contact and what kind of contact they should have with persons other than probationers.

Recently a much broader view of social work practice has been developed, a view that social workers in corrections have taken an active role in developing. After a 3-year study of social work curriculum sponsored by the Council on Social

---

[10] Helen D. Pigeon, *Probation and Parole in Theory and Practice* (New York: National Probation and Parole Association, 1942).

Work Education in the 1950's, the report of the project on "Education for Social Workers in the Correctional Field" said:

> The social task in corrections seems to call for social workers rather than for caseworkers or group workers. All social workers in corrections work with individuals, groups and communities, with less emphasis on the use of one method than is characteristic of many social work jobs.[11]

A task force organized in 1963 by the National Association of Social Workers to study the field of social work practice in corrections suggested that the offender's needs and the service system's social goals should determine methodology. The task force stated that social workers should have an array of professional skills—based on knowledge, understanding, attitudes, and values required for professional use of the skills—from which they could draw on appropriate occasions to meet the offender's needs and the goals of the probation system.[12]

When casework was applied to probation, a blurring of roles occurred between the probation officer and the probation agency. When each probation officer is assigned a certain number of cases, it is implied that he has full responsibility for all individuals concerned. He is expected to handle all the problems that the offenders in his caseload present and to have all the necessary knowledge and skills. The role of the agency in this arrangement is unclear.

No one person can possess all the skills needed to deal with the variety of complicated human problems presented by probationers. This situation is complicated by the diversity of qualifications required by jurisdictions throughout the country for appointment to the position of probation officer. The requirements range from high school or less to graduate degrees. Requirements for prior experience may be nonexistent or extensive.

Furthermore, few criteria exist as to what is acceptable performance. This deficiency makes it necessary for individual probation officers to set their own standards and gives them a great deal of latitude in working with probationers. Therefore it is difficult to assess the degree to which any probation officer has been successful in positively influencing a probationer.

The expectation that probation officers must know what their probationers are doing is traditional. If a probationer is arrested, the first question likely to be asked is when the probation officer last saw his client. The probation officer is expected to account for what is known, or more specifically for what is not known, about the probationer's activities. One consequence is that a probation officer quickly learns that he must protect himself. The system demands accountability when probationers get into the public view through alleged violations or new crimes. Probation staff members recognize that a high level of visibility exists, that they are answerable for their decisions, and that, if the matter comes to the attention of the court, the decisions will have to be justified.

---

[11] Elliot Studt, *Education for Social Workers in the Correctional Field* (New York: Council on Social Work Education, 1959), p. 50.

[12] G. W. Carter, *Fields of Practice: Report of a Workshop* (New York: National Association of Social Workers, 1963).

THE CASELOAD STANDARD.   One impact of the casework model has been a standard ratio of probationers to staff. The figure of 50 cases per probation officer first appeared in the literature in 1917. It was the consensus of a group of probation administrators and was never validated. The recommendation later was modified to include investigations.

The caseload standard provides an excuse for officers with large caseloads to explain why they cannot supervise probationers effectively. It also is a valuable reference point at budget time. Probation agencies have been known to attempt to increase their staff and reduce the size of the caseload without making any effort to define what needs to be done and what tasks must be performed. Caseload reduction has become an end unto itself.

When caseloads alone have been reduced, results have been disappointing. In some cases, an increase in probation violations resulted, undoubtedly due to increased surveillance or overreaction of well-meaning probation officers. Some gains were made when staff members were given special training in case management, but this appears to be the exception. The comment has been made that with caseload reduction, probation agencies have been unable to teach staff what to do with the additional time available.

The San Francisco Project described in a subsequent section challenged the assumption of a caseload standard. Four levels of workloads were established: (1) ideal (50 cases); (2) intensive (25, i.e., half the ideal); (3) normal (100, twice the ideal); and (4) minimum supervision (with a ceiling of 250 cases). Persons in minimum supervision caseloads were required only to submit a monthly written report; no contacts occurred except when requested by the probationer. It was found that offenders in minimum caseloads performed as well as those under normal supervision. The minimum and ideal caseloads had almost identical violation rates. In the intensive caseloads, the violation rate did not decline, but technical violations increased.

The study indicated that the number of contacts between probationer and staff appeared to have little relationship to success or failure on probation. The conclusion was that the concept of a caseload is meaningless without some type of classification and matching of offender type, service to be offered, and staff.[13]

But the caseload standard remained unchanged until the President's Commission on Law Enforcement and Administration of Justice (the Crime Commission) recommended in 1967 a significant but sometimes overlooked change by virtue of the phrase "on the basis of average ratio of 35 offenders per officer."[14] The change was to a ratio for staffing, not a formula for a caseload.

Agencies are now considering workloads, not caseloads, to determine staff requirements. Specific tasks are identified, measured for time required to accomplish the task, and translated into numbers of staff members needed.

THE DECISIONMAKING FRAMEWORK.   The framework for making deci-

---

[13] James Robison et al., *The San Francisco Project,* Research Report No. 14 (Berkeley: University of California School of Criminology, 1969).

[14] President's Commission on Law Enforcement and Administration of Justice, *The Challenge of Crime in a Free Society* (Washington: Government Printing Office, 1967), p. 169.

sions about probationers varies widely from agency to agency and within a single agency. Some decisions about a case, such as recommendations for probation revocation or termination, may be made only by the head of the probation agency, while other decisions about the same case may be made by any of a number of staff workers. Consequently, many probational personnel may not know who can make what decisions and under what circumstances. Part of the difficulty may come from statutes that define the responsibilities of a probation officer more explicitly than those of an agency. In addition, probation administrators often do not establish a clear decisionmaking framework.

The decisionmaking patterns vary not only for staff but for the offender placed on probation. If the system views its task as surveillance of the probationer, he has low status in any decisionmaking. The decisions are made for and about him, but not with him. If the system is oriented toward service, using the social work model, his role in decisions still is likely to be circumvented. This occurs despite the social work concept that the client has the right to be involved in what is happening to him, that is, self-determination.

This paradox exists because the probationer has an assigned status restricting his behavior. Probation conditions, essentially negative in nature although often expressed in a positive fashion, are imposed on him. The probationer may have to obtain permission to purchase a car, to move, to change a job, and this necessity restricts his choices of action. The probationer, therefore, has the task of adapting to an assigned status while seeking to perform the normal roles of a self-sufficient individual in the community: working, being a parent or a family member, paying taxes, obeying the law, meeting financial obligations, etc. Technical violations of probation conditions can result in revocation and commitment to a correctional institution.

If the client consults a noncorrectional social agency, he has the right to explain his problems and to terminate the relationship with that agency if he chooses. A probation client legally is required to appear but not legally required to ask for help. He may or may not be ready to receive help. He may be encouraged by staff to use resources of other community agencies, but the decision rests with him.

He may, however, be required to utilize some services offered by probation, such as psychiatric examination or testing. He may have some goals, but they are accepted by probation staff only if they are consistent with the conditions of probation or with the notions of the probation system, which usually means the probation officer. In short, the probationer's right to participate in decisionmaking has been limited by probation conditions and the role assigned him by the probation staff or the system.

Although probation staff members may be receptive to the social work concept of self-determination, they are aware that they occupy a position of authority. The very words "probation officer" signify authority, indicating an assigned role of power over another individual.

Furthermore, probation staff members may not be aware of or sensitive to what it means to be a probationer. A study on the interaction between parole staff and parolees indicated that most staff were relatively unaware of the difficulties of being a parolee. Staff and parolees saw the difficulties of parolees differently. Significantly, the parolees seemed more aware than the staff of what the staff could do and consequently to whom they could turn for expert information and advice when needed.[15]

For the most part, the probation system has tended to view offenders as a homogeneous group. The assumption has been that all require the same kind of service; namely, treatment on a one-to-one basis. Confusion exists about the form of treatment to be used and what it is supposed to accomplish. Discussion with most probation staff members reveals their difficulty in explaining what they do to "treat" a probationer and why. They speak of a relationship with each probationer as an end in itself and the sole means of providing services to individuals. Probation staff members also perceive the periodic contact they must make to account for the probationer's presence in the community as helping, treating, or rehabilitating the probationer.

Probationers are a heterogeneous group. The needs of juveniles differ from those of adults; girls and women have different needs than boys and men. There may be some common needs but one means, casework, will not meet them all. For example, casework is not a satisfactory technique for the probationer who has a drug problem. The problem of a probationer may not be interpersonal but one that should be met through specific help such as a job, employment training, or education. Reducing caseloads alone to improve supervision does not necessarily result in better probation services. Research in the past decade provides evidence that other approaches are needed.

The emphasis should be on classification of offenders and development of appropriate service programs, which usually are labeled "treatment." The impetus for this shift has been slowed by lack of research and the ideology of the caseload standard. A recent monograph from the Center for Studies of Crime and Delinquency at the National Institute of Mental Health, provides a good summary of the various models that have been or are being tested.[16] These include specialized supervision programs, guided group interaction programs, and delinquent peer group programs, as well as out-of-home placement and residential treatment. The monograph also covers specialized units in probation and parole, such as the California Community Treatment Project and the Community Delinquency Control Project of the California Youth Authority.

Classification of probationers is only one approach to typology. Another is identification and classification of the probationer's needs. To date, this has not been done systematically by any probation agency; what have been identified as basic needs usually are derived from anecdotal reports concerning individual offenders.

---

[15] Elliot Studt, *People in the Parole Action System: Their Tasks and Dilemmas* (Los Angeles: University of California Institute of Government and Public Affairs, 1971).

[16] Eleanor Harlow, J. Robert Weber, and Leslie T. Wilkins, *Community-Based Correctional Programs: Models and Practices* (Washington: Government Printing Office, 1971).

A third approach to the typology question involves the question, "Who is to be changed?" To date the primary target for change has been the probationer. A suggestion has been made that the typological approach might be applied to families and to the community.[17]

Future Directions for Service Delivery

To implement an effective system for delivering services to all probationers, it will be necessary to:

1. Develop a goal-oriented service delivery system.

2. Identify service needs of probationers systematically and periodically, and specify measurable objectives based on priorities and needs assessment.

3. Differentiate between those services that the probation system should provide and those that should be provided by other resources.

4. Organize the system to deliver services, including purchase of services for probationers, and organize the staff around workloads.

5. Move probation staff from courthouses to residential areas and develop service centers for probationers.

6. Redefine the role of probation officer from caseworker to community resource manager.

7. Provide services to misdemeanants.

DEVELOPING GOALS. The probation services system should be goal-oriented, directed toward removing or reducing individual and social barriers that result in recidivism among probationers. To achieve this goal, the probation system should provide a range of services directly and obtain others from existing social institutions or resources. The goal should be to help persons move from supervised care in their own communities to independent living.

The probation system must help create a climate that will enable the probationer to move successfully through transitions from one status to another. The first is from the status of an individual charged with committing an offense to that of a probationer living in the community but not completely independent. The final transition occurs when probation is terminated and the probationer moves from supervised care to an independent life. The goal should be to maintain in the community all persons who, with support, can perform there acceptably and to select for some type of confinement only those who, on the basis of evidence, cannot complete probationer status successfully, even with optimal support.

With this goal in mind, the practice of commitment to an insitution for the intitial period of probation (variously known as shock probation, split sentence, etc.), as the Federal and some State statutes permit, should be discontinued. This type of sentence defeats the purpose of probation, which is the earliest possible reintegration of the offender into the community. Short-term commitment sub-

---

[17] Seymour Rubenfeld, *Typological Approaches and Delinquency Control: A Status Report* (Rockville, Md.: National Institute of Mental Health, Center for Study of Crime and Delinquency, 1967), pp. 21–25.

jects the probationer to the destructive effects of institutionalization, disrupts his life in the community, and stigmatizes him for having been in jail. Further, it may add to his confusion as to his status.

IDENTIFYING NEEDS OF PROBATIONERS.   To plan for services, a probation system must initiate and maintain as assessment of needs of its target group, the probationers. This assessment must be ongoing because needs change. An inventory of needs should be developed by involving probationers rather than relying solely on probation staff to identify what it believes probationers' problems to be. More specifically, needs assessment requires:

● Knowledge of the target group in terms of such factors as age, race, education, employment, family status, availability of transportation.
● Identification of what services the offender most wants and needs to remove individual and social barriers.
● Identification of services available and conditions under which they can be obtained.
● Determination of which needed and wanted services do not exist or are inadequate.

From an assessment of needs, problem areas can be highlighted and priorities determined. This process makes it possible to specify how the various needs identified are to be met; whether directly through the probation system or through other social institutions; for what number or percentage of the target group; in what period of time; and for what purpose. Specifying objectives provides a means for evaluating whether the system was able to accomplish what it set out to achieve. If an objective is not met, the basis for pinpointing possible reasons is provided.

DIFFERENTIATING INTERNAL AND EXTERNAL SERVICES.   Direct probation services should be defined clearly and differentiated from services that should be met by other social institutions. Generally the kinds of services to be provided to probationers directly through the probation system should:

● Relate to the reasons the offender was brought into the probation system.
● Help him adjust to his status as a probationer.
● Provide information and facilitate referrals to needed community resources.
● Help create conditions permitting readjustment and reintegration into the community as an independent individual through full utilization of all available resources.

In addition, probation must account to the court for the presence and actions of the probationer.

Other needs of probationers related to employment, training, housing, health, etc. are the responsibility of other social institutions and should be provided by them. Therefore, most services needed by probationers should be located outside the system itself. These services should be available to probationers just as they are to all citizens, but some social institutions have created artifical barriers that deny ready access by persons identified as offenders.

Employment is an example. Some probation agencies have created positions of job developers and employment finders. Probation systems should not attempt to duplicate services already created by law and supposedly available to all persons. The responsibility of the system and its staff should be to enable the probationer to cut through the barriers and receive assistance from social insitutions that may be all too ready to exclude him.

The probation system has a responsibility to assure that probationers receive whatever services they need. To mobilize needed resources for helping probationers, the probation system must have funds to purchase services from an individual vendor, such as a person to provide foster care for a probationer or a psychiatrist to provide treatment, or from agencies or social institutions, such as marital counseling, methadone maintenance, education, and training. The potential for purchasing services for groups has been largely untapped. For example, juvenile probationers with reading difficulties may need diagnostic testing and remedial help. If these cannot be provided through local schools, the probation agency may have to locate a resource and purchase the needed testing and remedial help.

For older probationers who are unemployed or underemployed, probation staff may interest a university or college in developing special programs. These might include courses to provide remedial education or vocational training, depending upon the identified need of a given group of probationers.

Many other kinds of services may be purchased. Regardless of the service purchased, it is essential that provision be made for monitoring and evaluation of the services to insure that they are, in fact, being provided and that they meet the specified objective.

ORGANIZING THE SYSTEM TO DELIVER SERVICES.   To meet the needs of the increased number of individuals that will be placed on probation within the next decade, the probation service system must be organized differently than it has been. With the recognition that needs continually change, that the probation system itself will not be able to meet all the needs of the probationers, that many of the needs can be met through existing community resources, that new resources will have to be developed, and that some services will have to be purchased, the system should be organized to accomplish the following work activities:

● Needs assessment—ongoing assessment of probationers' needs and existing community resources.

● Community planning and development—establishing close working relationships with public and private social and economic groups as well as community groups to interpret needs; identifying needs for which community resources do not exist; and, in concert with appropriate groups, developing new resources.

● Purchase of services—entering into agreements and monitoring and evaluating services purchased.

● Direct services—receiving and assessing probationers; obtaining and providing information, referral, and followup; counseling; and supervising.

Differentiating work activities permits staff assignments to be organized around a workload rather than a caseload. Tasks directed toward achieving specific objectives should be identified and assigned to staff to be carried out in a specified time. This activity should be coordinated by a manager who makes an assessment of the staff members best able to carry out given tasks. Thus, the manager should know the capacities and capabilities of his workers and their specific areas of competence. He also should be able to help his subordinates work together as a team rather than as individuals.

A trend in modern organizational theory is to use teams of staff members with different backgrounds and responsibilities. Teams of individuals from varying disciplines and with differing skills may be assembled for a given task and project and disbanded when the project is completed. The leadership within the team may change, with a junior person serving as the team leader if there is particular need for his knowledge and skills.

In examining the various functions within the probation service delivery system it becomes apparent that there is a range of jobs requiring different kinds of knowledge and skills. Paraprofessionals and those in other "new career" occupations can provide services complementary to those of the probation officer. The potential for assigning a group of probationers to a team of probation officers, paraprofessionals, and other new careerists, headed by a team leader who does not function in the traditional social work supervisory role, is worth testing.

LOCATION OF SERVICES.   Probation services should be readily accessible to probationers. Therefore they should be based in that part of the community where offenders reside and near other community services. Staff serving probationers should be removed from courthouses and separated from staff providing services to the courts.

Services to probationers in rural areas may have to be organized on a regional rather than the traditional county basis. Service centers should be located in the more populated areas, with mobile units used for outlying districts. In such areas, where transportation is a problem, it is important that probation and other community services be in the same physical location.

Services to offenders should be provided in the evening hours and on weekends without the usual rigid adherence to the recognized work week. The problems of offenders cannot be met by conventional office hours. Arrangements should be made to have a night telephone answering service available to probationers.

PROBATION OFFICERS AS COMMUNITY RESOURCE MANAGERS.   The responsibility for being the sole treatment agent that has traditionally been assigned to the probation officer no longer meets the needs of the criminal justice system, the probation system, or the offender. While some probation officers still will have to carry out counseling duties, most probation officers can meet the goals of the probation services system more effectively in the role of community resource manager. This means that the probation officer will have primary responsibility for meshing a probationer's identified needs with a range of available services and for supervising the delivery of those services.

To carry out his responsibilities as a community resource manager, the probation officer must perform several functions. In helping a probationer obtain needed services, the probation officer will have to assess the situation, know available resources, contact the appropriate resource, assist the probationer to obtain the services, and follow up on the case. When the probationer encounters difficulty in obtaining a service he needs, the probation officer will have to explore the reasons for the difficulty and take appropriate steps to see that the service is delivered. The probation officer also will have to monitor and evaluate the services to which the probationer is referred.

The probation officer will have a key role in the delivery of services to probationers. The change in responsibility will enable him to have greater impact on probationers. As community resource manager, he will utilize a range of resources rather than be the sole provider of services—his role until now and one impossible to fulfill.

SERVICES TO MISDEMEANANTS.   The group that comprises the largest portion of the offender population and for which the least service is available are misdemeanants. Misdemeanants usually are given short jail sentences, fines, or suspended sentences. Even in jurisdictions with means to provide services to misdemeanants, probation is used in a relatively small percentage of cases. The rationale usually given is that misdemeanants are not dangerous to the community. But they are a major factor in the national crime problem: they tend to be repeaters; they tend to present serious behavior problems; as a group, they account for a large expenditure of public funds for arrest, trial, and confinement with little or no benefit to the community or the offender. The offense has been the determining factor rather than the offender.

If probation services continue to be provided as they now are, it will not be feasible to meet the varied needs of misdemeanants, many of whom come from disadvantaged groups and lack opportunities for training and jobs. However, with a probation service system that draws upon a range of resources to meet probationers' needs, as described in this chapter, it will be possible to provide services to misdemeanants. Misdemeanants should be placed on probation long enough to allow for effective intervention, as indicated in Chapter 5 Sentencing.

SERVICES TO COURTS

The services of probation to the courts traditionally have taken the form of reports. Originally, the probation officer submitted orally to the judge information used for screening candidates for probation. With the expansion of probation, the process became formalized, and written reports were prepared. The report became a record available to any probation officer handling the same case, but the agency limited outside access, thus establishing the confidentiality concept.

The initial purpose of investigation and report was to provide information to the court. However, other uses were proposed and adopted. A written report could assist the probation officer to whom a probationer was assigned, the institution to which he might be sent, the paroling or aftercare agency when the person was considered for release from an institution, and researchers.

Consistent efforts have been made through the years to improve the reports. Both private and public agencies have published documents setting forth what the contents should be. The National Council on Crime and Delinquency, originally organized as the National Probation Association, was the first private agency to do so. The American Correctional Association has focused on standards for the presentence report. The American Bar Association Project in 1970 also published presentence report standards. The U.S. Children's Bureau was the first Federal agency to publish standards for social studies. The Probation Division of the Administrative Office of the United States Courts has published material on presentence reports for the Federal probation staff that has influenced probation personnel nationwide. Many State agencies also have published standards.

The efforts and products of the various organizations have been influenced by people who shared the same education and sometimes had overlapping memberships or roles in both private and public sectors. Social work was the common background for many of the individuals who had key parts in determining what information was to be included in the written report. Their frame of reference was a social work model that involved strong emphasis on the person's life history.

Several criticisms have been made about the usual process of investigation and report. The literature emphasized the need to verify; this has been carried to extremes; e.g., staff members would attempt to verify the education of a 45-year-old defendant. Another criticism has been that investigations and reports became equated, so that the report contained almost all information secured in the process of investigation. Critics would ask, for example, why reports had to contain information about the defendant's deceased grandparents, including where they were born, where they had lived, and what work they had done.

Publications recommending what the contents of reports should be sometimes called for information not needed by the judge. The U.S. Courts Probation Division lists two categories of data—essential and optional. According to this publication essential data should appear in all reports while documenting optional data would depend on the requirements of a specific case. Under "health" the following is listed as essential data:

> Identifying information (height, weight, complexion, eyes, hair, scars, tattoos, posture, physical proportions, tone of voice, manner of speech).
> Defendant's general physical condition and health problems based on defendant's estimate of his health, medical reports, probation officer's observations.
> Use of narcotics, barbiturates, marijuana.
> Social implications of defendant's physical health (home, community, employment, association.)[18]

The last three items presumably are of value to the judge, but it is doubtful that the court requires the identifying information of the first item.

Essential and Nonessential Information

If the decisions to be made can be specified, the information required can be determined. The information actually required is what a person *needs to know.*

[18] Administrative Office of the U.S. Courts, Division of Probation, *The Presentence Investigation Report* (Washington: AOUSC, 1965), p. 17.

Nonetheless other information invariably is obtained that is *nice to know*. This distinction was raised in the decision game played in the course of the San Francisco Project carried out by the United States Probation Office, Northern District of California and the School of Criminology, University of California at Berkeley.[19]

The project staff selected cases previously referred for presentence reports. The contents of the reports were analyzed and classified under 24 subject headings commonly used by the probation staff. The information for each heading was reproduced on a file card. The cards were then arranged with the captions visible so that all 24 titles could be shown at the same time to the probation staff. By selecting a caption and turning the card, the probation staff could read the information on that particular subject. They were allowed to select any cards they wished for making disposition recommendation on that particular case, and in any order.

The results upset some of the assumptions. Some probation officers used only one card in making recommendations. The most cards used by any probation officer was 14. The average number of cards used to make a recommendation for disposition was 4.7. Significantly, only one card—the offense—was used in every case.

The study indicated that probation officers are using fewer pieces of information recommending disposition than was previously assumed. The offense and prior record are two key factors. Attitude, employment history, and marital history are factors of moderate importance. It would appear that most data traditionally collected and presented in written reports actually are not used by staff to develop recommendations for disposition.

Articles in correctional publications emphasize the diagnostic aspect in making good investigations and written reports, with the apparent implication that probation workers operate from a different theoretical basis than that used by a judge. One study examined presentence reports in an effort to discern differences and similarities in the theoretical frameworks underlying the operation of the probation officer and the court. The analysis revealed no differences. The findings suggest that the work of a probation officer in preparing presentence reports is not based on diagnostically oriented casework.[20]

In 1970, 66 judges of courts with misdemeanant jurisdiction and 65 judges of courts with felony jurisdiction in New York City responded to a questionnaire asking them to list information they deemed (1) essential, (2) desirable but not essential, and (3) of little or no value for presentence reports. Sixteen different items, under captions generally used by probation staff and judges, were given on the questionnaire. Only 10 items were listed by 55 percent or more of the judges with felony jurisdiction, while the judges in the other courts selected only eight items. The topics rated highest were: offense, drug use or involvement, employ-

[19] Robison et al., *The San Francisco Project.*

[20] Yona Cohn, "The Presentence Investigation in Court: A Correlation between the Probation Officer's Reporting and the Court Decision," unpublished doctoral thesis, Columbia University School of Social Work, 1969.

ment history, prior record, and mitigating circumstances. The result was a recommendation that presentence reports should focus on those items, limited in number, deemed essential by the judges.[21]

A study asking probation officers to rank the most important information used in selecting recommendations for juvenile cases indicated that information about an offense was first, family data second, and previous delinquency problems third. The same group of officers, when asked what they thought the court would consider most important, ranked present offense first, previous delinquency second, and the child's attitude toward the offense third. In both rankings the least important of those aspects questioned were child's interests, activities, and religion.[22]

In a study about criteria for probation officers' recommendations on juveniles, an analysis was made of the data contained in the reports.[23] The items most often recorded were objective, such as age, sex, religion, race, the delinquent act, family composition, school and church attendance, and economic situation. Missing were such subjective items as personalities of the child and parents as well as personal relationships within the family. Yet, according to the literature, that subjective material supposedly is the most important in understanding a child and his pathology and in developing a treatment plan.

The evidence suggests that written reports should contain only that information relative and pertinent to the decision being made by the judge. Thus, probation agencies should first ask the judges to identify that information needed by the court. The evidence indicates judges want to know the "here and now" of the offender, not a detailed life history.

The American Bar Association project calls for two categories of written report. The first is a short-form report used for disposition or for screening to select those cases requiring additional information. The second category is a more complete investigation. The latter report, if properly used, would be prepared in only a limited number of cases. The ABA recommendation should be adopted. The use of the two reports has been discussed in Chapter 5 of this report.

Although correctional institutions and paroling authorities may challenge the brevity of reports, those agencies have the responsibility to identify their actual informational needs. When that is done, the informational requirements of institutions and parole can be met. Probation staff, or the investigating officers who may be assigned this responsibility in the future, can always collect more information than will be included in a report designed for a judge. A supplemental report might be made for the correctional institutions and the paroling authorities.

[21] Data from unpublished report on the study results.

[22] Seymour Z. Gross, "The Pre-Hearing Juvenile Report: Probation Officer's Conception," *Journal of Research in Crime and Delinquency,* 4 (1967), 212–217.

[23] Yona Cohn, "Criteria for the Probation Officer's Recommendations to the Juvenile Court Judge," *Crime and Delinquency,* 9 (1963), 262–275.

Responsibility for Written Reports

At present probation officers do the investigation and prepare the written report. The judge may hold the probation officer accountable for the report's contents. Good administrative practice dictates that staff and judges understand that the agency, and not the individual officer, is accountable for the written report.

Good administration would use other staff to collect basically factual information and thus free probation officers to use their skills more appropriately. For example, other employees could collect prior police and court records, employment records, and school records. The probation officer's time could thus be used for interviewing defendant, family, police officer, complaining witness, and those persons significant in the defendant's current situation.

Prepleading Investigations

In some criminal justice systems the investigation and written report are completed before an adult defendant pleads or is found guilty or before a juvenile has the first hearing. The practice for juveniles undoubtedly developed from the concept of a "preliminary investigation before the filing of a petition," the language contained in some statutes. This practice raises legal questions: a child is questioned about his acts, supposedly delinquent, before the court even has determined the allegations to be proved. The problem becomes complicated when the child or his family are questioned by intake staff, even though the allegations have been denied.

The practice in the adult courts has developed through the requirement that a defendant indicate beforehand whether he will plead guilty. There is considerable doubt about the desirability of making an investigation that includes questioning the defendant about the offense for which he has not yet been found guilty. The argument is that this practice enables probation to have the report available more readily after the plea is entered.

While there may be some strong reasons for conducting prepleading investigations, especially when it increases the possibilities for diversion, the practice should be governed by the safeguards presented in Chapter 5 of this report.

Confidentiality

Influenced by the practice followed by doctors and lawyers, probation systems and staffs began operating on a principle of confidentiality. The purpose was to assure offenders and others that information given to probation staff would not be released indiscriminately and, accordingly, that probation staff might be trusted. However, the relationship in probation is different from that between a doctor or lawyer and his client, where the information is privileged. A probation officer receives information only because he is an employee of an organization.

Thus the information belongs properly to the agency itself, not to the staff member.

Confidentiality of written reports has been a subject of debate for years and has been tested from time to time in the courts. The conflict is intensified by variations among States. For juveniles, there is often a provision protecting records or placing responsibility on the judge to decide whether counsel for a child can see the social study. In some States, the law provides the judge with the option of disclosing the presentence report in whole or in part.

Many probation staff argue that disclosure will "dry up" sources of information who fear retaliation if the defendants learn the sources of information. It is also argued that disclosure could damage the offender, his family, and the potential relationship with the probation officer; and, as a result, probation staff might produce superficial reports.

Those advocating disclosure believe the defendant has the right to be aware of any and all information being used to decide his disposition. The point is also made that the offender has the right to refute damaging information or to clarify inaccuracies or misstatements.

The arguments have been examined by the ABA project, the American Law Institute in drafting its Model Code, and the National Council on Crime and Delinquency in its Model Sentencing Act. All recommend disclosure.

The question has come before the court in various States as well as before the Federal courts. No decision ever has been rendered establishing any constitutional right for an offender to have access to the written report. Significantly, however, the Supreme Court of New Jersey in its decision, *State* v. *Kunz,* 55 N.J. 128, 259 A.2d 895 (1969), has mandated disclosure of the presentence report. The issue of disclosure is discussed in Standard 5.16 of Chapter 5 of this report.

Cases Requiring Reports

The written report is used according to statutes which generally establish one of three categories:

1. The judge can decide whether or not to have a report.
2. There must be a report in certain kinds of cases regardless of the disposition.
3. Probation as a disposition can be used only if a written report is used.

Requiring a written report before a disposition of probation can be used may not be as valuable as requiring a written report before an individual can be sent to a correctional facility. Rumney and Murphy, in a followup study in 1948 of the first thousand juveniles and adults placed on probation in Essex County, New Jersey in 1937, found that:

Our studies failed to disclose any significant difference with respect to outcome as between those who were released on probation following investigation by a probation officer and those who were released on probation by the court without preliminary investigation.[24]

If the principle is adopted that probation should be used as disposition of first choice and a correctional facility only as last choice, it becomes essential that a written report be required whenever a court contemplates a disposition involving commitment to an institution. That is, institutionalization should be justified.

Other potentials for the written report still are untapped. Greater use should be made of dispositional alternatives such as fines. Information relevant to the defendant's potential for paying a fine could be provided in the written report. Research should be used to identify reporting elements that would allow more differentiation among offenders as to appropriateness of various dispositions.

Juvenile Intake

The process of screening cases at the juvenile level and effecting adjustments without formal court intervention appeared almost as soon as the juvenile court was created. This process commonly is called "intake." It appeared in different forms as juvenile courts were created in different communities. Essentially it involved discretion to look into a matter and resolve it informally.

Many factors led to the practice of adjusting juvenile cases. Some matters were too trivial to warrant action other than a warning not to repeat the act. Parents sometimes came with their child to the court seeking advice or direction rather than any disciplinary action by the court. In some situations, because favorable home conditions existed, the odds were favorable that results of informal adjustment would be as good as or better than formal court action.

The process called "intake" has been practiced in different ways by various courts resulting in a variety of procedures. In some places, it was limited to screening out cases. In other places, the process was expanded to "unofficial probation," which meant interaction among a child, family, and probation officer with all the ingredients of probation as a disposition by the court except formal court action.

The first edition of the Standard Juvenile Court Act, published in 1926 by the National Probation Association, provided a procedure for a preliminary inquiry and investigation before the filing of a petition. The comment was made that the court had an inherent right to exercise discretion before accepting official jurisdiction, and that the practice of screening had grown so widespread that it should be recognized in law.

Screening of cases at intake continued, and use of "unofficial probation" became so common that it was formally recognized by the U.S. Department of Health, Education, and Welfare in reporting national juvenile court statistics. The

---

[24] Jay Rumney and Joseph D. Murphy, *Probation and Social Adjustment* (New Brunswick, N.J.: Rutgers University Press, 1952), p. 252.

term continued until challenged by the Advisory Council of Judges of the National Probation and Parole Association in 1954. The judges, representing a cross-section of courts throughout the country, declared that granting probation was a judicial function and should not be confused with a nonjudicial service rendered for a limited period of time. The phrase "nonjudicial service" was used 3 years later by the U.S. Department of Health, Education, and Welfare in reporting juvenile court statistics. The term "informal service" also is used. (See Chapter 8, Juvenile Intake and Detention.)

"Standards for Specialized Courts dealing with Children," a 1954 publication from the Children's Bureau, offered ideas to rectify some abuses that had developed. The publication indicated that referral of a child or family to a social agency should be voluntary, attendance at any conference in an effort to adjust a matter should be voluntary, and conditions should not be imposed on any of the parties.

Guides for Juvenile Court Judges, published in 1957 by the National Council on Crime and Delinquency, presented guidelines for a screening process and, for the first time, criteria for selecting cases for diversion or judicial handling. The book provided that in all cases handled nonjudicially, voluntary acceptance by all parties was essential, the allegation of delinquency or neglect should not be disputed, and the parent or child must be aware of his right to a court hearing. The time during which the matter might be handled nonjudicially was limited; no nonjudicial service should extend beyond 3 months without review by court.

Guidelines have since been made statutory in several States. Although the intake or screening process may be carried out in a juvenile court because of the judge's decision to do so, the preferable pattern is for a statutory provision or a rule providing for the nonjudicial service. This is particularly true when the statute or rule includes the provision that no report from staff at intake can be made available to the judge until after a hearing has been held to determine the validity of the allegations of the petition.

Criteria for selecting cases to be handled nonjudicially—that is, without the filing of a petition—are:
- There is need for a relatively short period of service.
- The matter is not an emergency, and the offense has not had serious repercussions in the community.
- All parties cooperate and a disposition involving change of custody is not in question.

Criteria for selecting cases to be handled judicially, with filing of petition and formal court hearing, are:
- Either party indicates a desire to appear before the court.
- There is a dispute about the allegations of the petition.
- A serious threat to others is involved.

Decision-making at the point of intake is extremely important. Two basic decisions must be made, and both involve a considerable amount of discretion. The first decision is relatively simple: does the matter fall within the jurisdiction of the court? For example, if the allegation is delinquency, is the child within the age range for that particular State? If there is jurisdiction, the second question is whether official intervention and the authority of the court are required.

These key decisions require that competent staff be assigned to intake work. The staff must be skillful interviewers, have a broad knowledge of resources available, and be able to make decisions quickly.

Intake screening requires continuing staff training. The criteria staff must use are subjective. That subjectivity permits a latitude that tends to widen unless the staff engages in a continuing process of examining how and why they make decisions at intake.

Adult Pretrial Services

Probation staff have provided services prior to hearings in juvenile matters for some time, but they have been reluctant to do so at the pretrial stage for adults. The contrast is sharpest in the area of detention, both prehearing and pretrial.

The premise usually is expressed in law that a child is to be released to parents unless there is substantial probability the child will not appear in court or would commit, before the time of the court hearing, an act that would be a crime if done by an adult. Probation staff members assess a child's potential and may be authorized by a judge or by statute to screen children away from detention. Many children therefore are not detained.

The opposite prevails for the adult. When arrested, the adult literally has to prove to the court he should be released. Proof usually is provided in the form of bail or bond. The number of people annually passing through the jails of this country is estimated at no less than one million and as high as four and a half million. The distinguishing feature about the jail inmate is that he is poor and cannot afford bail. Many studies have indicated that at least half of the inmates awaiting trial in jails are there only because they do not have enough money to post bail.[25]

As presently constituted, the jails in this country have been described as a menace to the society they allegedly are serving. Jailing people awaiting trial because they cannot afford bail is ineffective, inhumane, and perhaps unconstitutional. To those sent to jail, the experience is psychologically and sociologically devastating and at the same time provides opportunities to acquire an education in crime.

Various strategies for decreasing the jail population have been advanced, including: decriminalization of such offenses as drunkenness and vagrancy; diversion just after a defendant's arrest; greater use of summons by the police rather than arrest; bail reform; and release on recognizance (ROR). The Vera Institute of Justice, in its Manhattan Bail Bond Project in 1961 to 1964, focused attention

---

[25] See, for example, Caleb Foote, "Compelling Appearance in Court: Administration of Bail in Philadelphia," *University of Pennsylvania Law Review,* 102 (1954), 1031; Alfred Kamin, "Bail Administration in Illinois," *Illinois Bar Journal,* 53 (1965), 674; Charles O'Reilly and John Flanagan, *Men in Detention: A Study of Criteria for the Release on Recognizance of Persons in Detention* (Chicago: Citizens' Committee for Employment, 1967).

on the judge's need for information at the time of arraignment. The courts long have had the authority to release individuals on recognizance. The Vera study indicated that when information about the defendant was provided to the judge, the possibilities of ROR increased. Information was collected and was withheld from the court in some cases and not in others to determine the outcome. Four times as many individuals were released on recognizance when the information was provided.[26]

The Manhattan Bail Bond Project proved that information could be secured easily and given to the judge at arraignment or shortly thereafter. The results of that project had national impact. The project was replicated throughout the country, usually under the sponsorship of private groups. Only a small number of probation agencies have undertaken this type of pretrial service.

The ABA project has recognized that adults are jailed unnecessarily pending trail and proposed that release on recognizance be considered in every case. Their standards include provision for investigation for that purpose. The quickest way to expand ROR programs may be for probation personnel to collect information for the judge for pretrial decisions. Probably the largest publicly administered release on recognizance program is that conducted by probation in New York City.

Staff other than probation officers should be employed for ROR programs. In New York City the position of investigator, not probation officer, is used. The rationale for using an investigator is that only a limited amount of information is collected and discretion in using the information is quite limited.

As the defendant has not been tried, information about the crime must be excluded from any ROR investigation. Information as to the defendant's stability in the community is sought, including length of residence, employment, family, prior record, and references.

ROR programs could and should be expanded to include supervised release, in which the offender is accountable to an agency while he is awaiting hearing or trial. It would be more economical to supervise many defendants in the community who now are jailed awaiting trial: certainly it would be less damaging.

MANPOWER FOR PROBATION

The Commission's general positions on manpower for corrections are discussed in Chapter 14 of this report. Only those manpower issues which have special force for probation are considered here.

The recommended shift of emphasis in sentencing to probation will require, among other things, a considerable expansion in the size of probation staffs. Hence it is essential to take careful account of ways in which the manpower base may be expanded and how staff may most effectively be utilized.

---

[26] Charles Ares and Herbert Sturz, "Bail and the Indigent Accused," *National Probation and Parole Association Journal,* 86 (1962) 12–20.

Education for Probation Work

Since the turn of the century, social work education has been specified by hiring agencies as the preferred training for probation. By 1967, the President's Commission on Law Enforcement and Administration of Justice identified the master's degree in social work as the preferred educational qualification.

In the course of a 3-year study, the Joint Commission on Correctional Manpower and Training found that the preferred standard was not being met in most agencies. Moreover, the evidence indicated that graduate schools of social work could not turn out sufficient M.S.W.'s to meet the demand. Joint Commission studies indicated that persons with bachelor's degrees can do and are doing probation officers' jobs effectively. It therefore recommended the undergraduate degree as the standard educational requirement for entry-level professional work in probation.[27]

New Careers in Probation

Probation and other subsystems of corrections will need many more personnel than are likely to come to them from colleges and universities. And there are other good reasons why persons with less than college education should be employed for work in probation.

Allied human services which have faced similar needs for more workers have come to realize that many tasks traditionally assigned to professionals can perfectly well be handled by people with less than a college education, even some who have not graduated from high school. Moreover, these people often have a better understanding of the client's problems than professionals do. Hence progressive agencies, particularly those in education and health, have made concerted efforts to recruit people with less than a professional education and to set up career lines by which these paraprofessionals may advance.

Probation has lagged behind in this movement. But the shift from a caseload model to one based on offender classification should encourage the introduction of new career lines into the probation system. This would follow the Joint Commission recommendation that agencies set up career ladders that will give persons with less than a college education a chance to advance to the journeyman level (probation officer) through combined work-study programs.

It has been amply demonstrated that paraprofessionals can be used in probation. The National Institute of Mental Health funded a program for the Federal Probation Office in Chicago, to employ paraprofessionals in both full-time and part-time capacities. The results were so promising that Congress has appropriated funds to include paraprofessionals as a regular part of the staff in fiscal 1973.

---

[27] Joint Commission on Correctional Manpower and Training, *A Time to Act* (Washington: JCCMT, 1969), p. 30.

A recent study identified four groups of tasks that can be carried out by staff other than probation officers. The tasks are related to:

● Direct service—for example, explain to the individual and family the purpose of probation.

● Escort—such as accompanying probationer to an agency.

● Data gathering—collect information, such as school progress reports, from outside sources and disseminate it to probation staff. ·

● Agency and personnel development—such as taking part in staff meetings for training and research activities.[28]

Other tasks could be assigned; for example, accounting for the presence of the probationer in the community.

New Careers for ROR Reports

If probation is to provide the information judges need at arraignment to consider possible release on recognizance of adult defendants awaiting trial, new career opportunities should be introduced. For example, a separate group of staff members—none of whom need be probation officers—could be trained to interview, investigate, and report to the judge on ROR investigations.

Use of Volunteers

Probation began through the efforts of a volunteer. More than a century later probation is turning once again to the volunteer for assistance. Many people are ready and willing to volunteer if asked and provided the opportunity.

In addition to serving as probation officers, volunteers can perform many other tasks that would extend the scope of current services to probationers. Many volunteers have special skills that are extremely helpful to probationers. And the very fact that they are volunteers creates a sense of personal equality very different from the superior/inferior attitude that usually characterizes the relationships of probation officers and probationers.

Volunteers can provide direct service to one probationer, to selected small groups of probationers, and to individuals or groups outside probation. Tutoring a child is an example; offering advice on buying a car or borrowing money is another. Serving as receptionists in a probation service center and speaking before professional organizations are still other examples.

For specific programs involving the use of volunteers the reader is referred to Chapter 7 in this report entitled "Corrections and the Community." The reader should also consult the "Citizen Action" chapter in the Commission's Report on Community Crime Prevention.

---

[28] New York State Division of Probation, *The Paraprofessional Demonstration Project in Probation,* New York City: 1971.

A Choice of Tracks for a Career

At present, the only way to advance in a probation agency in terms of salary and status is to be promoted to an administrative or supervisory job. A more intelligent manpower policy would permit those employees who are doing a service job they like and are probably best qualified for, to continue in service to probationers, with the knowledge that they will receive salary raises in line with their performance there.

Employees should have the choice of two tracks in their career—direct services to probationers, or administration. Both tracks should offer the reality of advancement in terms of money, status, and job satisfaction.

Individuals desiring to go into administration should be able to do so on the basis that they are interested in management and have acquired the knowledge and skills necessary to carry out management responsibilities. The fact that they have remained in a certain position (usually probation officer) for a specified period should not automatically qualify them for management positions. Nor should movement into management positions be restricted only to those in probation officer titles. Such a restriction limits recruitment of many competent individuals and screens out staff members in other titles. The system should not depend solely on promotion from within. For the most effective utilization of manpower, individuals with necessary education and background should be able to enter the system at the level for which they are qualifed, in services delivery or management.

State Responsibility

The State should be responsible for manpower planning and utilization, including staff development. Efforts to resolve manpower problems have been piecemeal, and the States have provided little leadership. Probation agencies have tried to solve the problem through such devices as increasing wages, reducing workloads, and providing more training. These devices, however, do not get at the root of the problem: designing a range of jobs directed toward meeting agency goals through a more effective services delivery system that also provides workers with a sense of accomplishment and opportunities for career development.

Standard 10.1

Organization of Probation

Each State with locally or judicially administered probation should take action, in implementing Standard 16.4, Unifying Correctional Programs, to place probation organizationally in the executive branch of State government. The State correctional agency should be given responsibility for:

1. Establishing statewide goals, policies, and priorities that can be translated into measurable objectives by those delivering services.

2. Program planning and development of innovative service strategies.

3. Staff development and training.

4. Planning for manpower needs and recruitment.

5. Collecting statistics, monitoring services, and conducting research and evaluation.

6. Offering consultation to courts, legislative bodies, and local executives.

7. Coordinating the activities of separate systems for delivery of services to the courts and to probationers until separate staffs to perform services to the courts are established within the courts system.

During the period when probation is being placed under direct State operation, the State correctional agency should be given authority to supervise local probation and to operate regional units in rural areas where population does not justify creation or continuation of local probation. In addition to the responsibilities previously listed, the State correctional agency should be given responsibility for:

1. Establishing standards relating to personnel, services to courts, services to probationers, and records to be maintained, including format of reports to courts, statistics, and fiscal controls.

2. Consultation to local probation agencies, including evaluation of services with recommendations for improvement; assisting local systems to develop uniform record and statistical reporting procedures conforming to State standards; and aiding in local staff development efforts.

3. Assistance in evaluating the number and types of staff needed in each jurisdiction.

4. Financial assistance through reimbursement or subsidy to those probation agencies meeting standards set forth in this chapter.

Standard 10.2
Services to Probationers

Each probation system should develop by 1975 a goal-oriented service delivery system that seeks to remove or reduce barriers confronting probationers. The needs of probationers should be identified, priorities established, and resources allocated based on established goals of the probation system. (See Standards 5.14 and 5.15 and the narrative of Chapter 16 for probation's services to the courts.)

1. Services provided directly should be limited to activities defined as belonging distinctly to probation. Other needed services should be procured from other agencies that have primary responsibility for them. It is essential that funds be provided for purchase of services.

2. The staff delivering services to probationers in urban areas should be separate and distinct from the staff delivering services to the courts, although they may be part of the same agency. The staff delivering services to probationers should be located in the communities where probationers live and in service centers with access to programs of allied human services.

3. The probation system should be organized to deliver to probationers a range of services by a range of staff. Various modules should be used for organizing staff and probationers into workloads or task groups, not caseloads. The modules should include staff teams related to groups of probationers and differentiated programs based on offender typologies.

4. The primary function of the probation officer should be that of community resource manager for probationers.

Standard 10.3
Misdemeanant Probation

Each State should develop additional probation manpower and resources to assure that the courts may use probation for persons convicted of misdemeanors in all cases for which this disposition may be appropriate. All standards of this report that apply to probation are intended to cover both misdemeanant and felony probation. Other than the possible length of probation terms, there should be no distinction between misdemeanant and felony probation as to organization, manpower, or services.

Standard 10.4
Probation Manpower

Each State immediately should develop a comprehensive manpower development and training program to recruit, screen, utilize, train, educate, and evaluate a full range of probation personnel, including volunteers, women, and ex-offenders. The program should range from entry level to top level positions and should include the following:

1. Provision should be made for effective utilization of a range of manpower on a full- or part-time basis by using a systems approach to identify service objectives and by specifying job tasks and range of personnel necessary to meet the objectives. Jobs should be reexamined periodically to insure that organizational objectives are being met.

2. In addition to probation officers, there should be new career lines in probation, all built into career ladders.

3. Advancement (salary and status) should be along two tracks: service delivery and administration.

4. Educational qualification for probation officers should be graduation from an accredited 4-year college.

Standard 10.5

Probation in Release on Recognizance Programs

Each probation office serving a community or metropolitan area of more than 100,000 persons that does not already have an effective release on recognizance program should immediately develop, in cooperation with the court, additional staff and procedures to investigate arrested adult defendants for possible release on recognizance (ROR) while awaiting trial, to avoid unnecessary use of detention in jail.

1. The staff used in the ROR investigations should not be probation officers but persons trained in interviewing, investigation techniques, and report preparation.

2. The staff should collect information relating to defendant's residence, past and present; employment status; financial condition; prior record if any; and family, relatives, or others, particularly those living in the immediate area who may assist him in attending court at the proper time.

3. Where appropriate, staff making the investigation should recommend to the court any conditions that should be imposed on the defendant if released on recognizance.

4. The probation agency should provide pretrial intervention services to persons released on recognizance.

11
The American Bar Association Looks at Probation

HERBERT S. MILLER[1]

In 1963 the American Bar Association began considering the formulation of standards covering the entire spectrum of the administration of criminal justice. In 1964 funds were obtained to finance the studies. A 16-member Special Committee on Standards for the Administration of Criminal Justice was made responsible for the overall supervision and coordination of the project. To conduct the studies and provide tentative drafts for Special Committee and ABA consideration, seven advisory committees were appointed: Police Function; Pre-Trial Proceedings; Prosecution and Defense Functions; Criminal Trial; Sentencing and Review; Fair Trial and Free Press; and Judges Function.[2] Fifteen reports have been issued.[3]

Source. *Federal Probation,* XXXIV, December 1970, pp. 3–9. Reprinted with permission of the author and *Federal Probation.*

[1] Mr. Miller is also Reporter for the American Bar Association's Committee on Sentencing and Review (Standards Relating to Probation).

[2] For a more detailed description of Committee operations see Bratton, *Standards for the Administration of Criminal Justice,* 10 Nat. Resource J. 127 (1970).

[3] For information about copies of these reports write the *American Bar Association,* 1155 East 60th Street, Chicago, Ill. 60637. Copies cost $2 for individual volumes or $1 per volume for 10 or more copies.

With the exception of the *Standards Relating to Probation,*[4] *Electronic Surveillance* (Tentative Draft, June 1968), and *Police Function* (in process), the Standards are directed primarily to lawyers and judges. This basic thrust is reflected in the membership of the Special Committee, the advisory committees, and the reporters conducting the research.[5]

BACKGROUND OF THE PROBATION STANDARDS

The membership of the Advisory Committee on Sentencing and Review, which was responsible for the report on probation, is a faithful mirror of membership generally on all advisory committees, being made up of judges, prosecutors and defense attorneys, and several law professors.[6] It will be noted that only James V. Bennett (a lawyer) had operational experience in corrections.

Discussions on probation began after the Committee completed its report on standards relating to *Appellate Review of Sentences* (Approved Draft, February 1968) and had largely completed its work on *Sentencing Alternatives and Procedures* (Approved Draft, August 1968). The Committee believed that probation was sufficiently important to warrant separate consideration.[7]

Using the report on Sentencing Alternatives as a starting point, Part I, General Principles, breaks new ground in approaching probation as a sentence just like any other sentence. Part II, The Presentence Report, affirms the purpose of the presentence report—primarily for the use of the judge—and delineates materials which could be included therein. Part III, Conditions of Probation, outlines how conditions of probation should be prescribed and modified, and contains guidelines as to the kinds of conditions which may be imposed. In Part IV, Termination, the standards recommend early termination and a method by which collateral effects of a criminal record can be mitigated. In Part V, Revocation of Probation and Other Sanctions, emphasis is placed on alternatives to

---

[4] American Bar Association Project on Standards for Criminal Justice, Standards Relating to Probation, 110 pp. (Approved Draft, August 1970).

[5] The only reporter who is not a lawyer is Herman Goldstein, (Advisory Committee on the Police Function), professor of police science at the University of Wisconsin, formerly administrative assistant to O. W. Wilson, former chief of Chicago Police.

[6] Hon. Simon E. Sobeloff, Chairman, United States Circuit Judge, Fourth Circuit (Chief Judge, 1958-64); James V. Bennett, Director, United States Bureau of Prisons, 1937-64; C. Clyde Ferguson, Jr., Professor of Law, Rutgers University Law School; Richard E. Gerstein, State Attorney, Eleventh Judicial Circuit of Florida, since 1957; Jack P. F. Gremillion, Attorney General of Louisiana, since 1956; Hon. Florence M. Kelley, Administrative Judge Family Court, City of New York; Hon. Theodore B. Knudson, Chief Judge, District Court of Minnesota (Minneapolis); Hon. Edwin M. Stanley, Chief Judge of the United States District Court for the Middle District of North Carolina; William F. Walsh, practicing lawyer; Herbert Wechsler, Professor of Law, Columbia University Law School; Hon. Luther W. Youngdahl, United States District Court Judge for the District of Columbia.

[7] In the *Standards Relating to Sentencing Alternatives and Procedures* the Committee discussed sentences not involving confinement and in a general way procedures for revocation or modification of such a sentence. (§§ 2.3, 5.5, and 6.4). In addition, Part IV covers the presentence report, including the time of its preparation, disclosure, and additional services (of a diagnostic nature).

revocation, which is to be invoked as a last resort. Counsel is recommended for the probationer in all revocation cases and proceedings based solely upon the alleged commission of another crime prior to its disposition are discouraged.

Part VI represents a departure from other reports released by the Special Committee on Standards for Criminal Justice. It not only discusses the role of probation officers, but also examines problems in administering probation departments and recommends standards covering personnel and the services they perform.[8]

Because the terrain was unfamiliar, special efforts were made to contact professionals in the field:

(1) Members of the Committee used their wide contacts in the criminal justice system to get reactions on matters before the Committee.

(2) The reporter contacted a number of probation departments to obtain reactions and research reports. He also met with a group of professionals for a detailed review of proposed standards and commentary.[9]

THRUST OF THE STANDARDS

Section 1.3, Criteria for Granting Probation, states that probation should be the sentence unless certain negative findings are made by the court. This supports the Committee view that probation should be the starting point in judicial reasoning about a specific sentence.

Another feature of section 1.3 is the requirement that in arriving at a sentence the court consider available institutional and community resources, as well as the crime and the background of the offender. In addition Section 2.3 (ii) (G) and (I) calls for the presentence report to include information about the community

[8] The hesitancy in exploring administrative and personnel aspects of probation was offset by the feeling that probation is an adjunct to the judicial function and because a substantial number of probation departments are locally administered. For instance, many large states have locally administered probation services (California, Illinois, Indiana, Massachusetts, New Jersey, New York, Ohio, Pennsylvania, and Texas). In others with state administered probation systems the larger metropolitan counties may still be locally administered (e.g., Hennepin County in Minnesota and Milwaukee County in Wisconsin).

[9] Present for this review were F. Lovell Bixby, former Consultant on Probation, Administrative Office of New Jersey Courts, and former Commissioner of the New Jersey Department of Corrections; Paul W. Keye, Commissioner of Corrections, Minnesota, formerly Director of Court Services for the Hennepin County District Court, Minnesota; Richard A. Chappell, former Chairman of the United States Board of Parole and former Chief of the Federal Probation Service; Robert L. Carter, Division of Research, Washington State Department of Corrections, formerly Research Criminologist at the University of California, Berkeley, and former United States probation officer in the Northern District of California; Robert L. Smith, Deputy Chief, Division of Corrections, Department of Youth Authority, former probation and parole officer in California, and Project Director for the Board of Corrections *Probation Study* (1964); Vincent O'Leary, professor at the School of Criminal Justice. New York State University, Albany, formerly Assistant Director (Corrections) of the President's Commission of Law Enforcement and Justice, John A. Wallace, Director of the New York City Probation Department, separately examined the material.

to which the offender would return and describe relevant services available to him. The thrusts of these standards is to give the court data on factors directly related to the community needs of the potential probationer and the services that could serve those needs. In part it reflects the expansion of community services now being made available to disadvantaged persons, some of whom may have criminal records.[10]

Section 6.2(i), Supervision of Probationers, further stresses the importance of community services and facilities, relating them directly to the supervisory role of probation departments. It recommends that where feasible, branch probation offices should be located in the community; that helping services should be obtained from community facilities in appropriate cases; and that where necessary, probation personnel should actively intervene with such facilities on behalf of their probationers. This standard is the result of findings that many offenders have difficulty in effectively coping with some conditions of probation. They may be intimidated by the central probation office located in an official governmental building. Similarly, they, as disadvantaged persons, may feel inadequate when dealing with a particular community service available. They may, therefore, require direct aid from the probation department in obtaining assistance which could enhance the chance of successful probation.

What these standards emphasize is the probation officer's role in relation to the community in which his probationers live and the diverse services that may be available. It may require a renewed effort on the part of probation departments to reach out into the community as they have never done before.

Conditions of probation are discussed systematically, perhaps for the first time, in Part III and Section 5.1 of the Standards. Several important points emerge. First, the sentencing court must conscientiously impose the conditions as they relate to the circumstances of each case and not in a routine fashion. Second, while the probation officer must have flexibility in interpreting conditions, in no circumstances should court-imposed conditions be so loose that in fact the probation officer decides what conditions are pertinent and applicable. Third, conditions should be subject to modification in appropriate cases, and the probationer should feel free to request a clarification or change. Finally, enforced compliance or modification of conditions is preferred to revocation, which should be used as a last resort.

Perhaps of most interest to probation officers is the material contained in Part VI, Probation Department Administration, Services and Personnel. The first issue for the Committee was the administrative structure of probation departments and their relationship to other criminal justice agencies (Section 6.1). The Committee was cognizant of the debate on whether probation departments

---

[10] The President's Commission of Law Enforcement and Administration of Justice had this to say about the typical offender in the United States: "The offender . . . is likely to be a member of the lowest social and economic groups in the country, poorly educated and perhaps unemployed, unmarried, reared in a broken home, and to have a prior criminal record." *The Challenge of Crime in a Free Society* 44 (1967).

should be part of a comprehensive corrections department or should be locally supervised by the courts. A perusal of studies on the subject convinced the Committee that adequate probation services could be provided under diverse structures, but that the state must set standards and provide methods and means through which these standards could be enforced. The commentary offers examples of ways in which some states have formulated and implemented standards.[11]

Section 6.4, Appointment of Probation Personnel, of the Standards recommends that in local systems judges should appoint the chief probation officer. The standard also explicitly states that the chief probation officer should make all appointments of probation personnel in accordance with the merit system and provide for tenure and removal only after a hearing before an appropriate body. This standard recognizes a key role for judges in setting broad policies but also recognizes that the chief probation officer must be the chief administrator with responsibility for staffing the department.

Section 6.5, Qualifications for Probation Officers and Other Personnel, makes one key departure from accepted standards. The usual standard requires a bachelor's degree and a year of graduate study, or as a substitute 1 year of paid full-time casework experience under professional supervision in a recognized social agency.[12] Section 6.5 would authorize part-time or summer work to be considered and expands the kind of employment which would fulfill the work requirement to include not only casework but counselling, community or group work in a recognized social, community, correctional, or juvenile agency dealing with offenders or disadvantaged persons. The Committee felt that many community programs sponsored by federal and state governments and foundations indicate that disadvantaged persons may need a wide variety of community-oriented services which can effectively be offered by persons with diverse backgrounds.

Section 6.5 also recommends that the staff include persons who may lack professional qualifications but have backgrounds similar to those of the probationers themselves. This standard stems, in part, from Committee findings that substantial research and experimentation have begun to recognize that the conventional social work background does not always equip probation officers to relate to the offender group. Moreover, much of the research and experimentation indicated that those with similar backgrounds, operating under professional supervision, might provide the kind of communication now missing, and might even excel in certain semiprofessional tasks.

Section 6.6 makes clear that enhanced educational opportunities for nonprofessionals and professionals alike are essential for probation departments to effectively function in the rapidly changing world in which we live.

The above discussion emphasizes the approach found in almost all of the

---

[11] See *Standards Relating to Probation* 77–79 (Approved Draft, August 1970).

[12] See the Correctional Standards selected by the Special Committee on Correctional Standards for the President's Commission on Law Enforcement and Administration of Justice in *Task Force Report: Corrections* 207 (1967).

standards which have been published, that of delineating roles played by the participants in a rapidly changing criminal justice process. In some instances the standards codify roles which have been established by custom, practice, and law and in others point up new directions concerning roles being played or to be played in the future.

IMPLEMENTING THE STANDARDS

The *Standards Relating to Probation* may or may not become binding upon probation systems or departments. Nevertheless, their dissemination (about 12,000 copies of the Standards have been published and distributed) and the inclusion of the standards in their entirety in this publication assures widespread knowledge of their content. Through the American Bar Association and its Sections on Judicial Administration and Criminal Law efforts are being made to gain wide understanding of the standards and their implementation.[13]

The judiciary may play several important roles in achieving implementation of these standards. First, the appellate courts may cite them in appropriate cases.[14] Second, judges may play an active role in obtaining community backing for better probation services.

Judges should take the lead in explaining and interpreting the purpose of probation, the success that it does and can enjoy, and its lower costs, both social and financial. Judges should also encourage their probation departments to undertake programs to inform the community about the nature and objectives of probation. . . . Judges and their probation personnel should make themselves available to speak before citizen groups and professional, business, labor and other organizations to explain the attributes and needs of probation services. (*Standards Relating to Probation.* 74)

I submit that in the hands of probation personnel these standards provide a previously unavailable weapon in the struggle to achieve adequate probation services. I encourage you to use them.

STANDARDS RELATING TO PROBATION*

PART I. GENERAL PRINCIPLES

1.1   Nature of sentence to probation.
   (a)   The legislature should authorize the sentencing court in every case to

---

[13] Some states have begun revising their rules of criminal procedure in light of the standards adopted by the American Bar Association.

[14] As of late 1969, many standards had been cited in 94 federal and state appellate courts. See Kirshen, *Appellate Court Implementation of the Standards for the Administration of Criminal Justice,* 8 Am. Crim. L.Q. 105 (1970).

   * Approved by the House of Delegates of the American Bar Association, August 1970.

impose a sentence of probation. Exceptions to this principle are not favored and, if made, should be limited to the most serious offenses.

(b)   In this report the term "probation" means a sentence not involving confinement which imposes conditions and retains authority in the sentencing court to modify the conditions of the sentence or to resentence the offender if he violates the conditions. Such a sentence should not involve or require suspension of the imposition or the execution of any other sentence.

(c)   Upon a sentence to probation, the court should not be required to attach a condition of supervision by the probation department if in its judgment supervision is not appropriate for the particular case.

(d)   The court should specify at the time of sentencing the length of any term during which the defendant is to be supervised and during which the court will retain power to revoke the sentence for the violation of specified conditions. Neither supervision nor the power to revoke should be permitted to extend beyond a legislatively fixed time, which should in no event exceed two years for a misdemeanor or five years for a felony.

(e)   A sentence to probation should be treated as a final judgment for purposes of appeal and similar procedural purposes.

(f)   Upon revocation of probation the court should have available the same sentencing alternatives that were available at the time of initial sentencing. The court should not foreclose any of these alternatives before revocation.

1.2   Desirability of probation.

Probation is a desirable disposition in appropriate cases because:

(i)   it maximizes the liberty of the individual while at the same time vindicating the authority of the law and effectively protecting the public from further violations of law;

(ii)   it affirmatively promotes the rehabilitation of the offender by continuing normal community contacts;

(iii)   it avoids the negative and frequently stultifying effects of confinement which often severely and unnecessarily complicate the reintegration of the offender into the community;

(iv)   it greatly reduces the financial costs to the public treasury of an effective correctional system;

(v)   it minimizes the impact of the conviction upon innocent dependents of the offender.

1.3   Criteria for granting probation.

(a)   The probation decision should not turn upon generalizations about types of offenses or the existence of a prior criminal record, but should be rooted in the facts and circumstances of each case. The court should consider the nature and circumstances of the crime, the history and character of the offender, and available institutional and community resources. Probation should be the sentence unless the sentencing court finds that:

(i)   confinement is necessary to protect the public from further criminal activity by the offender; or

(ii)   the offender is in need of correctional treatment which can most effectively be provided if he is confined; or

(iii)   it would unduly depreciate the seriousness of the offense if a sentence of probation were imposed.

(b)   Whether the defendant pleads guilty, pleads not guilty or intends to appeal is not relevant to the issue of whether probation is an appropriate sentence.

PART II. THE PRESENTENCE REPORT

2.1   *Availability and use.*

(a)   All courts trying criminal cases should be supplied with the resources and supporting staff to permit a presentence investigation and a written report of its results in every case.

(b)   The court should explicitly be authorized by statute to call for such an investigation and report in every case. The statute should also provide that such an investigation and report should be made in every case where incarceration for one year or more is a possible disposition, where the defendant is less than [21] years old, or where the defendant is a first offender, unless, the court specifically orders to the contrary in a particular case.

2.2   *Purpose of report.*

The primary purpose of the presentence report is to provide the sentencing court with succinct and precise information upon which to base a rational sentencing decision. Potential use of the report by other agencies in the correctional process should be recognized as a factor in determining the content and length of the report, but should be subordinated to its primary purpose. Where the presentence investigation discloses information useful to other correctional agencies, methods should be developed to assure that this data is made available for their use.

2.3   *Content, scope and length of report.*

Presentence reports should be flexible in format, reflecting differences in the background of different offenders and making the best use of available resources and probation department capabilities. Each probation department should develop gradations of reports between:

(i)   a short-form report for primary use in screening offenders in order to assist in a determination of when additional and more complete information is desirable. Short-form reports could also be useful in courts which do not have adequate probation services;

(ii)   a full report, which normally should contain the following items:

(A)   a complete description of the offense and the circumstances surrounding it, not limited to aspects developed for the record as part of the determination of guilt;

(B)   a full description of any prior criminal record of the offender;

(C)   a description of the educational background of the offender;

(D)   a description of the employment background of the offender, including any military record and including his present employment status and capabilities;

(E)   the social history of the offender, including family relationships, marital status, interests and activities, residence history, and religious affiliations;

(F)   the offender's medical history and, if desirable, a psychological or psychiatric report;

(G)   information about environments to which the offender might return or to which he could be sent should probation be granted;

(H)   supplementary reports from clinics, institutions and other social agencies with which the offender has been involved;

(I)   information about special resources which might be available to assist the offender, such as treatment centers, residential facilities, vocational training services, special educational facilities, rehabilitative programs of various institutions to which the offender might be committed, special programs in the probation department, and other similar programs which are particularly relevant to the offender's situation;

(J)   a summary of the most significant aspects of the report, including specific recommendations as to the sentence if the sentencing court has so requested.

A special effort should be made in the preparation of presentence reports not to burden the court with irrelevant and unconnected details.

2.4   When prepared.

(a)   Except as authorized in subsection (b), the presentence investigation should not be initiated until there has been an adjudication of guilt.

(b)   It is appropriate to commence the presentence investigation prior to an adjudication of guilt only if:

(i)   the defendant, with the advice of counsel if he so desires, has consented to such action; and

(ii)   adequate precautions are taken to assure that nothing disclosed by the presentence investigation comes to the attention of the prosecution, the court, or the jury prior to an adjudication of guilt. The court should be authorized, however, to examine the report prior to the entry of a plea on request of the defense and prosecution.

2.5   Availability of report; challenge of its contents.

Standards dealing with the disclosure of the presentence report and the resolution of controversy as to its accuracy are developed in the separate report of this Advisory Committee on Sentencing Alternatives and Procedures.

PART III. CONDITIONS OF PROBATION

3.1   Imposition and implementation of conditions.

(a)   All conditions of probation should be prescribed by the sentencing court and presented to the probationer in writing. Their purpose and scope and the possible consequence of any violations should be explained to him by the sentencing court or at an early conference with a probation officer.

(b)   Probation officers must have authority to implement judicially prescribed conditions; but the conditions should be sufficiently precise so that probation officers do not in fact establish them.

(c)   The probationer should have the right to apply to the sentencing court for a clarification or change of conditions.

3.2   Nature and determination of conditions.

(a)   It should be a condition of every sentence to probation that the probationer lead a law-abiding life during the period of his probation. No other conditions should be required by statute; but the sentencing court should be authorized to prescribe additional conditions to fit the circumstances of each case. Development of standard conditions as a guide to sentencing courts is appropriate so long as such conditions are not routinely imposed.

(b)   Conditions imposed by the court should be designed to assist the probationer in leading a law-abiding life. They should be reasonably related to his rehabilitation and not unduly restrictive of his liberty or incompatible with his freedom of religion. They should not be so vague or ambiguous as to give no real guidance.

(c)   Conditions may appropriately deal with matters such as the following:

   (i)   cooperating with a program of supervision;

   (ii)   meeting family responsibilities;

   (iii)   maintaining steady employment or engaging or refraining from engaging in a specific employment or occupation;

   (iv)   pursuing prescribed educational or vocational training;

   (v)   undergoing available medical or psychiatric treatment;

   (vi)   maintaining residence in a prescribed area or in a special facility established for or available to persons on probation;

   (vii)   refraining from consorting with certain types of people or frequenting certain types of places;

   (viii)   making restitution of the fruits of the crime or reparation for loss or damage caused thereby.

(d)   Conditions requiring payment of fines, restitution, reparation, or family support should not go beyond the probationer's ability to pay.

(e)   The performance bond now authorized in some jurisdictions should not be employed as a condition of probation.

(f)   Probationers should not be required to pay the costs of probation.

3.3   Modification and termination of conditions.

Conditions should be subject to modification or termination by the court. All changes in conditions should be presented to the probationer in the manner prescribed in section 3.1 of this Report. Where the proposed modifications would result in a form of confinement as a condition of continued probation, the probationer should be afforded the procedural rights set forth in Part V of this Report.

PART IV. TERMINATION

4.1   Satisfactory completion of probation term.

It should be provided that probation automatically terminates upon the successful completion of the term set by the court at the time of sentencing. It is nevertheless desirable that the fact of termination be recorded in an order of the court, a copy of which should be furnished to the probationer.

4.2   Early termination.

The sentencing court should have the authority to terminate probation at any time. Such authority should be exercised prior to the term fixed in the original sentence if it appears that the offender has made a good adjustment and that further supervision or enforced compliance with other conditions is no longer necessary.

4.3   Criminal record.

Every jurisdiction should have a method by which the collateral effects of a criminal record can be avoided or mitigated following the successful completion of a term on probation and during its service.

PART V. REVOCATION OF PROBATION AND OTHER SANCTIONS

5.1   Grounds for and alternatives to probation revocation.

(a)   Violation of a condition is both necessary and a sufficient ground for the revocation of probation. Revocation followed by imprisonment should not be the disposition, however, unless the court finds on the basis of the original offense and the intervening conduct of the offender that:

(i)   confinement is necessary to protect the public from further criminal activity by the offender; or

(ii)   the offender is in need of correctional treatment which can most effectively be provided if he is confined; or

(iii)   it would unduly depreciate the seriousness of the violation if probation were not revoked.

(b)   It would be appropriate for standards to be formulated as a guide to probation departments and courts in processing the violation of conditions. In any event, the following intermediate steps should be considered in every case as possible alternatives to revocation:

(i)   a review of the conditions, followed by changes where necessary or desirable;

(ii)   a formal or informal conference with the probationer to reemphasize the necessity of compliance with the conditions;

(iii)   a formal or informal warning that further violations could result in revocation.

5.2   Arrest of probationers.

(a)   Formal arrests of probationers for the alleged violation of conditions of their probation should be preceded by the issuance of an arrest warrant based upon probable cause that a violation has occurred. Arrests without a warrant should be permitted only when the violation involves the commission of another crime and when the normal standards for arrests without a warrant have otherwise been met.

(b)   Probation officers should not be authorized to arrest probationers.

5.3   Proceedings following commission of another crime.

A revocation proceeding based solely upon commission of another crime ordinarily should not be initiated prior to the disposition of that charge. However, upon a showing of probable cause that another crime has been committed by the probationer, the probation court should have discretionary authority to detain the probationer without bail pending a determination of the new criminal charge.

5.4   Nature of revocation proceedings.

(a)   The court should not revoke probation without an open court proceeding attended by the following incidents:

(i)   a prior written notice of the alleged violation;

(ii)   representation by retained or appointed counsel; and

(iii)   where the violation is contested, establishment of the violation by the government by a preponderance of the evidence.

Sentence should be imposed following a revocation according to the same procedures as are applicable to original sentencing proceedings.

(b)   The government is entitled to be represented by counsel in a contested revocation proceeding.

(c)   As in the case of all other proceedings in open court, a record of the revocation proceeding should be made and preserved in such a manner that it can be transcribed as needed.

(d)   An order revoking probation should be appealable after the offender has been resentenced.

PART VI. PROBATION DEPARTMENT ADMINISTRATION, SERVICES AND PERSONNEL

6.1   Legislative responsibility; administrative structure.

(a)   Legislative bodies should appropriate sufficient funds so that all trial courts administering criminal justice will have adequate probation services and personnel in order to implement properly the standards developed in this Report.

(b)   It is appropriate for probation services to be administered at either the state or local level, but in no event should control be vested in an agency having prosecutorial functions.

6.2   Establishing minimum standards.

Minimum standards for probation services should be formulated and enforced by an appropriate state agency and should be applicable to all probation departments within the state. In addition to the standards recommended in this report, the following general principles are important in developing minimum standards:

(i)   Supervision of probationers.

There should be a sufficiently low average caseload to provide adequate supervision for probationers and to encourage the development of variable caseloads for different types of offenders and assignment techniques which will maximize the benefit of offered supervision. In appropriate cases, supervision should be supplemented by group counseling and therapy programs. Where feasible, branch probation offices should be located in the community in which probationers live so as to meet more effectively the demands of supervision. To complement supervision, helping services should be obtained from community facilities in appropriate cases and, where necessary, probation personnel should actively intervene with such facilities on behalf of their probationers;

(ii)   Research and statistics.

Accurate and uniform records and statistics should be available as a foundation for research into sentencing criteria and probation department programs. Continuous research and evaluation, involving a cooperative effort among operations and research personnel, should be an integral part of probation departments;

(iii)   Working conditions.

To help achieve the standards recommended in this Report, probation personnel should have adequate office space, clerical assistance and conference facilities.

6.3   Collateral services.

In appropriate cases, probation departments should be prepared to provide additional services which may be foreign to the traditional conceptions of providing presentence reports and supervising convicted offenders. Examples of such additional services include the preparation of reports to assist courts in making pretrial release decisions and assistance to prosecutors in diverting selected charged individuals to appropriate noncriminal alternatives.

6.4   Appointment of probation personnel.

(a)   Responsibility for appointing chief probation officers in local probation departments should reside solely in the chief judge of the court or an appropriate judicial body. Consideration should be given to the creation of an agency or committee to advise in recruiting and screening chief probation officers. Such a committee should consist of representatives of government, the judiciary, the bar, and the community.

(b)   Chief probation officers should make all appointments of probation personnel in accordance with a merit system. After a probationary period, tenure should be granted and removal permitted only after a hearing conducted by a civil service commission or other career service organization.

6.5   Qualifications for probation officers; other personnel.

(a)   The educational and occupational requirements for probation officers should be possession of a bachelor's degree supplemented by:

(i)   a year of graduate study in social work, corrections, counseling, law, criminology, psychology, sociology, or related fields; or

(ii)   a year of full-time casework, counseling, community or group work experience in a recognized social, community, correctional or juvenile agency dealing with offenders or disadvantaged persons, or its equivalent as determined by the hiring agency.

(b)   A significant number of probation officers in a department should have graduate degrees in one of the subjects enumerated in this section.

(c)   While the core of any probation department should be professionally educated and trained personnel, it is desirable that the staff include individuals who may lack such professional qualifications but have backgrounds similar to those of the probationers themselves. In addition, in appropriate cases citizen volunteers should be used to assist probation officers.

6.6   Education and training.

(a)   Fellowships for graduate study should be made available to probation officers and college graduates interested in probation. In addition, probation officer trainee programs combining work and education should be established for high school graduates and college students.

(b)   In-service education and training programs should be jointly planned and developed by appropriate state agencies, universities, and local probation departments. In state and larger local probation departments, implementation of these programs should be made a full-time responsibility.

6.7   Salaries of probation personnel.

(a)   Entry salaries should be competitive with entry salaries offered in related fields such as welfare, education, and community action programs.

(b)   Salaries should be structured so that promotion to an administrative or supervisory job is not the only means of obtaining a higher salary. Merit pay increases should be available for outstanding job performance, advanced academic achievement, or completion of special in-service training.

12
Exposing the Quasi-Judicial Role of the Probation Officer

EUGENE H. CZAJKOSKI

As judges appear to be shedding more and more of their judicial functions, the role of the probation officer is undergoing sympathetic change. While there is a distinction to be made between the judicial tasks of a judge and the judge's administrative tasks, the distinction often becomes blurred in the actual operation of the court. Constitutionally, the judge may delegate his administrative powers but he may not delegate his judicial powers. Under the circumstance where judicial powers and administrative powers are becoming increasingly confused, the probation officer seems to find himself more and more in a quasi-judicial position.

Unquestionably, there is a difference between administrative decision-making and adjudication. Administrative decision-making depends on free, extensive and informal discussions with many interests and informed individuals or groups. Adjudication requires formalized procedures, the building of a record, and the presentation and cross-examination of evidence. In adjudication, the final judgment is based on the record alone. The aforementioned difference is well known and this discussion of the probation officer's quasi-judicial role does not rest on

SOURCE. *Federal Probation*, XXXVII, September 1973, pp. 9–13. Reprinted with permission of the author and *Federal Probation*.

an analysis between judicial process and administrative process. It rests rather on the analysis of judicial effect. Questions are raised as to the propriety of the probation officer's achieving judicial effect without judicial process.

The case for the quasi-judicial role of the probation officer is made along five lines of functional analysis.

PLEA BARGAINING AND THE ABDICATION OF THE JUDGE FROM SENTENCING

It wasn't too long ago that plea bargaining was curtained off in the courtroom. To insure a valid guilty plea, one which could not later be upset on appeal, judges engaged in a litany with the defendant wherein the question was asked, "Did anyone make you any promises?"[1] Promises made to induce a guilty plea were, in effect, denied in open court. Everyone involved, including the judge, knew about the plea bargaining and the promises made but all, especially the defendant, (lest his deal be upset) denied the negotiated promises in open court. All seemed to have benefited from the charade except that it was unseemly for the court to participate in subterfuge and, certainly, the recipient of justice was often left with a quizzical notion of the basic honesty of the court. Now that plea bargaining is openly acknowledged and has the imprimatur of the United States Supreme Court,[2] the air in the courtroom is a little clearer. Another result is that the pace of plea bargaining, with its newfound legal respectability, has been stepped up.

To even the most casual observer of the court, it is evident that the judge's role in sentencing has shrunk almost to that of a mere announcer. Not unwillingly, it seems, the judge has abdicated a major portion of his sentencing role. It is the prosecutor, the chief plea bargainer, who in reality determines sentence.

Some very large prosecution offices have gone so far as to produce handbooks to guide assistant district attorneys in fixing sentence through bargaining. Completely ignoring the generally accepted correctional philosophy that sentencing should be in accord with the individual characteristics of the offender, the guidelines used by prosecutors are usually based on the crime committed. The prosecutor's influence in sentencing is drawing us further back toward classical concepts of penology (sentencing in accordance with the crime) even while lawyers in other contexts, such as through the Model Penal Code of the American Law Institute and the Model Sentencing Act of the National Council on Crime and Delinquency, espouse sentencing in accordance with the characteristics of the individual offender. It is doubtful that prosecutors are moved by one or the other

---

[1] An example of the detailed questioning pursued by a judge prior to accepting a guilty plea can be found in: Frank J. Remington, *et al., Criminal Justice Administration.* New York: The Bobbs-Merrill Co., 1969, p. 567.

[2] In *Brady* v. *U.S.,* 397 US 742 (1970), the Supreme Court held that plea inducements were generally compatible with the goals of the criminal justice system.

of the two philosophical stands. It is more likely that they are motivated by production goals and by bureaucratic standards of efficiency and self-interest.

By permitting plea bargaining, judges have left themselves little to do other than to certify conditions previously agreed to by defendant, prosecutor, and police. Largely relieved of their sentencing role, many judges also appear to be also giving up their role of interpreting the law for trial juries.[3] Many juries find themselves having to decide on the requirements of law as well as decide on facts to be fitted to law. The fitting is less likely to be done by judges these days.

The abdication of sentencing responsibility to the plea bargaining system leaves the probation officer in an even more peculiar position than it leaves the judge. Theoretically, the probation officer is supposed to make sentencing recommendations to the judge on the basis of his professional estimate of the rehabilitation potential of the defendant. Whether or not a defendant is sentenced to probation probably depends more now on his success in plea bargaining than on his promise of reformation. How does the probation officer fit into this new scheme of extensive plea bargaining? What point is there in conducting an elaborate social investigation by way of evaluating rehabilitation potential? In answer to the first question, Professor Blumberg points out that the probation officer serves to "cool the mark" in the production-oriented and confidence game-like system of expeditiously moving defendants through the court by means of plea bargaining.[4] The probation officer can assure the defendant of how wise it was for him to plead guilty and of how much benefit there is to be derived from the correctional efforts arising out of the sentence. In answer to the second question, social investigations of defendants (presentence reports) are becoming shorter, more factual, and less analytical.

Like the judge's role, the probation officer's role in sentencing is diminishing. If it has become the judicial role of the judge to simply certify the plea bargaining process, then the probation officer's role is quasi-judicial in that he does the same thing. It is admittedly a peculiar argument, but where the probation officer does a perfunctory presentence report and aims his recommendation toward what he already knows will be the plea bargaining sentence, then he is indeed playing out a de-facto judicial role.

It has long been argued that the probation officer's role in sentencing has been a quasi-judicial one, especially where the judge more-or-less automatically imposes the sentence recommended by the probation officer. Various empirical studies have shown a very high correlation between probation officer recommendation and disposition made by the judge. Carter and Wilkins have pointed out that judges have followed probation officer recommendations in better than 95 percent of the cases.[5] Among the factors which might explain the high level of

---

[3] This phenomenon has been reported to the writer by a number of practicing trial lawyers, and it would appear to warrant some empirical investigation before a trend can be agreed upon.

[4] Abraham Blumberg, *Criminal Justice.* Chicago: Quadrangle Books, 1967.

[5] Robert M. Carter and Leslie T. Wilkins, "Some Factors in Sentencing Policy," *Journal of Criminal Law, Criminology and Police Science,* 58, No. 4 (1967), pp. 503–514.

agreement between recommendations and dispositions, it was postulated that probation officers make their recommendations in anticipation of what the judge desires (second guessing the judge). Nowadays it is more likely that the prosecutor has found a way to communicate the plea bargaining agreement to the probation officer and the probation officer responds with an appropriate recommendation (or no recommendation) in his presentence report.

Insofar as it firmly determines sentence, the plea bargaining process clearly undermines the professional role of the probation officer. It is now probably more appropriate for the probation officer to counsel the prosecutor on rehabilitation potential than the judge. The prosecutor might want to use the probation officer's professional estimate in the plea bargaining. As a matter of fact, probation officers frequently conduct "prepleading investigations" which are used by both judge and prosecutor to decide plea matters.

INTAKE PROCEDURES

Intake service by probation officers in adult courts is practically unknown. At the juvenile court level, however, it is considered good practice to have some form of intake apparatus.

When serving as a functionary in a juvenile court's intake unit the probation officer is asked to decide which cases are appropriate for formal judicial processing. This kind of decision is obviously a judicial one somewhat akin to those made by the judges or magistrates at preliminary hearings. Except for supervision within an administrative hierarchy, the probation officer in intake functions quite independently in his quasi-judicial decision-making. Despite the fact that the intake process does not meet the ordinary requirements for adjudication, there have been few complaints from defendants subjected to the process. Clearly, inasmuch as intake offers the defendant an opportunity for leniency and perhaps a chance for being saved from legal stigmatization, there is little inclination on the part of defendants to challenge the procedure. Indeed, very many of them consent to an informal probation supervision which is carried out in nearly the same way as adjudicated probation. Behavior required of the defendant is almost the same in both cases and there is a "penalty" for failure under both formal and informal supervision. Under informal probation supervision, the penalty becomes referral to the court for formal judicial processing, the threat of conviction and the likelihood of incarceration.

In terms of controlling input to the court the intake probation officer is very much like the prosecutor. The pattern for both the probation officer and prosecutor usurping judicial prerogatives begins to emerge.[6]

---

[6] The efforts of defense lawyers to find a role in the intake process is explained in: Margaret K. Rosenheim and Daniel L. Skoler, "The Lawyer's Role at Intake and Detention Stages of Juvenile Court Proceedings," *Crime and Delinquency,* 11, No. 2 (1965), pp. 167–174.

SETTING THE CONDITIONS OF PROBATION

The granting of probation always involves conditions either by specification or by implication. It is usually the court that sets conditions of probation and it has frequently been held in case law that the court may not delegate its power and responsibility to impose conditions. It has also been frequently held that the court may not delegate the setting of conditions to the probation department. It is hard to find an intrinsic legal reason why a probation department cannot be given the responsibility for imposing conditions of probation. In the legal cases which have denied probation departments such authority, there has usually been the background of statutes requiring the courts to set conditions. Where statutes do not specifically state that the court must set the conditions of probation, it appears that the setting of conditions may be left to the probation department. In any case, it is common for the judge to impose a "blanket" condition such as "heed the advice of the probation officer" which in effect gives the probation officer condition-setting power.

Oral or unrecorded conditions have been generally held to be invalid and in order for a defendant to be bound by conditions, they must be definite, clearly stated, and effectively communicated to the defendant. Unfortunately, conditions of probation are notoriously vague and poorly communicated to the defendant. Typical conditions of probation include such ambiguous requirements as: Avoid undesirable associates; stay away from disreputable places; and do not keep late hours. Such conditions are obviously very difficult for the defendant to conscientiously manage. What is "undesirable"? What is "disreputable"? Standards for adhering to such conditions are seldom adequately set down and the enforcement of those conditions, where it is done at all, is left to the personal, and frequently capricious, judgment of the probation officer. The indefinite conditions become a vehicle for maintaining the moral status quo as interpreted by the probation officer. According to surveys made by Arluke, conditions seem slow to change.[7] While a few jurisdictions are turning to brief, streamlined sets of conditions, for the most part, particularly in the juvenile courts, conditions of probation remain moralistic, negativistic, and vague.

Apart from conditions of probation serving as a means for controlling nonlegally proscribed behavior, in other words, behavior which is morally undesirable but not unlawful, conditions of probation intrude upon or become substitutes for certain formal judicial processes. Many conditions of probation involve monetary obligations. Some are the kind that any citizen may have, e.g., support of depend-

---

[7] Nat R. Arluke, "A Summary of Parole Rules—Thirteen Years Later," *Crime and Delinquency*, 15 No. 2 (1969), pp. 267-274. Although Arluke surveyed parole conditions (dealing with about 50 parole jurisdictions is easier than trying to deal with literally hundreds of probation jurisdictions), his findings are relevant to probation conditions. Probation conditions and parole conditions are very similar and both are frequently administered in unison by a single agency having combined probation and parole functions. For a specific analysis of conditions of probation and for demonstration of their similarity to conditions of parole also see: Judah Best and Paul I. Birzan, "Conditions of Probation: An Analysis," *Georgetown Law Journal*, 51 (1963), pp. 809-836.

ents; and others arise out of criminal conviction, such as fines or restitution. Because of the existence of such monetary conditions of probation, the probationer is deprived of the usual judicial safeguards and is placed in the administrative or quasi-judicial hands of the probation officer.

Consider, for instance, the matter of supporting dependents. Defendants who are on probation as a result of criminal conviction are seldom brought into civil or family court on the issue of supporting dependents. Dependents wishing support from the probationer need only go to the probation officer to obtain satisfaction. The probation officer, using the condition of probation, can compel support payments in amounts determined by the probation officer himself, through his own administrative investigation. Without a court hearing on the question of support payments, the order of the probation officer in enforcing the conditions of probation has significant judicial effect. Were he not on probation for a criminal case, the defendant might easily seek an adjudication process in the appropriate court on the question of support. Instead he is forced to submit to the judicial effect brought about by the probation officer enforcing a standard condition of probation. The defendant makes his case before the probation officer and not before the court which is specially set up to adjudicate the question of family support.

A similar usurpation of civil court process occurs when a restitution condition is imposed on a criminal court probationer. It is usually left to the probation officer to determine the appropriate restitution payment. Too often, victims, particularly corporate victims, seek to gain through restitution conditions that which they would have great difficulty in gaining in civil court. Civil courts are comparatively careful in restoring exactly what has been lost. Relying on adversary proceedings, they analyze and evaluate the loss in fair detail. Civil courts may hold jury trials on matters of restitution. When the criminal court probation officer is given the responsibility of settling the matter of restitution, he does not have the same resources for hearing evidence on the loss as do the civil courts. He usually accepts the victim's flat statement as to what the loss is. The probationer, since he is not arguing the matter in a genuine court setting, can do little to rebut the victim's claim. Victims frequently do far better in gaining restitution through the criminal court probation officer than through a civil court. Because he is operating on the basis of a criminal conviction having occurred, the probation officer is bound to presume in favor of the victim in terms of both the quality and quantity of the restitution claim. Since the criminal court judge rarely conducts a full-dress hearing on the question of restitution, preferring to assign resolution of the matter to the probation officer, the judicial effect of the probation officer's determination of restitution is significant indeed.

PROBATION VIOLATION PROCEDURES

The traditional view of probation has been that it is a privilege rather than a right and as such the probation status does not invoke ordinary due process.

While this view has experienced considerable erosion in recent years, the revocation of probation remains highly discretionary. In some jurisdictions, probation violation hearings closely approach the characteristics of a trial. Still a hearing is not a trial and the courts generally retain substantial discretion in revocation of probation proceedings.[8]

While it is the judge who actually revokes probation, it is the probation officer who initiates the revocation action and largely controls it. In a very high proportion of cases, the judge's revocation action is in accord with the probation officer's recommendation. The hegemony of the probation officer in probation violation proceedings is well known and requires little unfolding here. It plainly casts the probation officer in a quasi-judicial role.

In the case of so-called technical violations, the judicial role of the probation officer becomes amplified. Technical violations are those which are somehow covered by the conditions of probation but which are not specified in criminal statutes. Failure to report to the probation officer or failure to avoid undesirable persons might be a type of technical violation. Oftentimes probation officers proceed on the basis of technical violation when new criminal offenses are suspected but cannot be easily proved. Police and prosecutors regularly call upon the probation officer to invoke some technical violation against a probationer who they believe has committed a new crime. It is patently easier to put a defendant behind bars as a result of a probation violation hearing than it is to send him to prison as a result of a full-fledged trial. In consenting to proceed on the basis of a technical violation when the real issue is a new criminal offense, the probation officer is playing a judicial role. In effect, he is deciding that there is sufficient basis to conclude that the defendant is guilty of the new offense and thus deserves to have the technical violation placed against him. Given the vague and all-encompassing nature of conditions of probation, it is not difficult for the probation officer to muster a technical violation as needed. Many probationers are in a steady state of probation violation as a result of conditions relating to keeping "decent hours," abstaining from alcohol, and various prohibitions relating to sexual activity. These violations usually go unenforced by the probation officer until such time as he is given reason to believe that a new criminal offense has occurred. Invoking the technical violation thus becomes the result of the probation officer's making the adjudication that a crime has been committed. The probationer has a hearing on the technical violation but is denied a trial on the suspected crime which triggered the technical violation.

PUNISHMENT BY THE PROBATION OFFICER

The legislator sets punishment, the judge imposes it, and the administrator executes it. Under our constitutional scheme, it is the judge who decides when

[8] For a very thorough review of legal practices in probation revocation see: Ronald B. Sklar, "Law and Practice in Probation and Parole Revocation Hearings," *Journal of Criminal Law, Criminology and Police Science,* 55 (1964), pp. 175–198.

a particular individual is to have legal punishment. While probation is a sentence, it is ideologically not a punishment. Nevertheless, implicit in probation supervision are numerous opportunities for punishment. With his awesome authority over the probationer, the probation officer may in various ways restrict his liberty. It is easily argued that restriction of liberty amounts to punishment. The probation officer, in the name of rehabilitation and under the banner of standard conditions of probation, can demand that the probationer not live in or frequent certain areas, that he not engage in certain employment, and that he refrain from a number of interpersonal associations.

Sometimes probation-officer-decided punishments are more direct than denial of freedom. In some jurisdictions, a probationer may not receive a driver's license without the specific approval of the probation officer. From place to place, various occupational licenses are subject to the approval by the probation officer. If one chooses not to regard the probation officer's withholding of license approval as punishment and therefore not in the nature of a judicial action, it is at least still possible to conceive of the probation officer's approval role in licensing as being quasi-judicial.

In sum, the probation officer's role is multi-faceted. Many of the facets are not easily recognized and may be dysfunctional to our concepts of justice and due process. It is difficult to say whether the probation officer's quasi-judicial role is increasing. It is very closely tied to the judge, but the judge seems to be giving up more and more of his own judicial role. If the probation officer ties in more with the prosecutor, then the probation officer's quasi-judicial function may paradoxically increase because of the judicial aggrandizement of the prosecutor's office through plea bargaining and other arrangements.

13

The Presentence
Investigation Report

ADMINISTRATIVE OFFICE
OF THE UNITED STATES COURTS

ITS FUNCTIONS AND OBJECTIVES

The presentence investigation report is a basic working document in judicial
and correctional administration. It performs five functions: (1) to aid the court
in determining the appropriate sentence, (2) to assist Bureau of Prisons institutions in their classification and treatment programs and also in their release
planning, (3) to furnish the Board of Parole with information pertinent to its
consideration of parole, (4) to aid the probation officer in his rehabilitative efforts
during probation and parole supervision,[1] and (5) to serve as a source of pertinent
information for systematic research.

The primary objective of the presentence report is to focus light on the
character and personality of the defendant, to offer insight into his problems and
needs, to help understand the world in which he lives, to learn about his relationships with people, and to discover those salient factors that underlie his specific

SOURCE. *The Presentence Investigation Report,* Division of Probation, Administrative Office of the
United States Courts, Washington, D.C., U.S. Government Printing Office, pp. 1–21. (Editorial
Adaptations.)
[1] The Federal probation officer also supervises persons released from Federal correctional institutions and the U.S. Disciplinary Barracks.

offense and his conduct in general. It is not the purpose of the report to demonstrate the guilt or the innocence of the defendant.

Authorities in the judicial and correctional fields assert that a presentence investigation should be made in every case. With the aid of a presentence report the court may avoid committing a defendant to an institution who merits probation instead, or may avoid granting probation when confinement is appropriate.

Probation cannot succeed unless care is exercised in selecting those who are to receive its benefits. The presentence report is an essential aid in this selective process.

The probation officer has the important task of gathering information about the defendant; evaluating, assimilating, and interpreting the data; and presenting them in a logically organized, readable, objective report. Each defendant should be investigated without any preconception or prejudgment on the probation officer's part as to the outcome of the defendant's case.

The probation officer must be completely objective and impartial in conducting the investigation and in writing the presentence report. He not only reports the tangible facts in the case, but also such subjective elements as the defendant's attitudes, feelings, and emotional reactions. He presents them so as to give to the court an accurate, unbiased, and complete picture of the defendant and his prospects for becoming a law-abiding, responsible citizen. Every effort must be made to check the accuracy of information which is likely to be damaging to the defendant or to have a definite bearing on the welfare of the family and the safety of the community.

OUTLINE, CONTENTS, AND FORMAT OF THE REPORT—

Identifying Information

The following identifying information is requested on Probation Form No. 2, the first page of all presentence reports.

Date.   Give the date the presentence report is typed.

Name.   Enter the name of the defendant as shown on the court record. Also insert the true name, if different, and any aliases.

Address.   Give the present home address.

Legal Residence.   Give the legal residence (county and State) if different from the present home address. Otherwise insert "Same."

Age and Date of Birth.   Give the age on last birthday and the date of birth. Use the symbol "ver." when verified by an official source.

Sex.

Race.   Race is determined by ancestry; e.g., white, Negro, American Indian. It should not be confused with national origin.

Citizenship.   Give name of country. Citizenship refers to the country of which the defendant is a subject or citizen.

Education.   Give highest grade achieved.

Marital Status.   Single, married, widow, widower, divorced, legally separated, common law.

PROBATION FORM **2**
FEB 65

UNITED STATES DISTRICT COURT

Eastern District of Michigan

PRESENTENCE REPORT

NAME John Jones

ADDRESS 1234 Beach Street
Detroit, Michigan 48201

LEGAL RESIDENCE Same

AGE 38 DATE OF BIRTH 8–25–26
(ver.)

SEX Male RACE White

CITIZENSHIP United States

EDUCATION High School

MARITAL STATUS Married

DEPENDENTS Four (wife and three
children)

SOC. SEC. NO. 000–11–2222

FBI NO. 678910

DATE October 14, 1964

DOCKET NO. 56971

OFFENSE Possession of
Distilled Spirits
26 U.S.C. 5686(b)

PENALTY $5,000 or 1 year,
or both

PLEA Guilty, 2–14–64

VERDICT

CUSTODY Personal Bond

ASST. U.S. ATTY. James E. Carver

DEFENSE COUNSEL

Thomas Flanigan
781 Cadillac Tower
(Court Appointed)

DETAINERS OR CHARGES PENDING: None

CODEFENDANTS *(Disposition)* Case of Robert Allen pending

DISPOSITION

DATE

SENTENCING JUDGE

Dependents. List those entirely dependent on the defendant for support; e.g., "Three (wife and two children)."

Social Security No.

FBI No.

Docket No.

Offense. Give a brief statement, including statutory citation; e.g., "Theft of Mail (18 U.S.C. 1708)."

Penalty.   Insert statutory penalty for the specific offense. This should be obtained from the U.S. attorney in each instance. The probation officer should not attempt to state the penalty on the basis of his knowledge.

Plea.   Nature and date.

Verdict.   Date.

Custody.   Give status (summons, personal or surety bond, recognizance, jail) and period in jail.

Assistant U.S. Attorney.   Give name of the assistant U.S. attorney handling the case.

Defense Counsel.   Give name and address. When appointed by court, this should be indicated.

Detainers or Charges Pending.   Give the name and address of the office issuing the detainer or preferring the charge. Also give the dates action was taken.

Codefendants.   Enter the names of codefendants, if any, and status of their respective cases. If there are no codefendants, insert "None."

The following information, below the double rule on form 2, is inserted after the final disposition of the case:

Disposition.   Sentence imposed by the court.

Date.   Date of sentence.

Sentencing Judge.

Presentence Report Outline

The presentence report outline adopted by the Judicial Conference Committee on the Administration of the Probation System on February 11, 1965, consists of the following marginal headings and the respective subheadings:

OFFENSE
    Official version
    Statement of codefendants
    Statement of witnesses, complainants, and victims
DEFENDANT'S VERSION OF OFFENSE
PRIOR RECORD
FAMILY HISTORY
    Defendant
    Parents and siblings
MARITAL HISTORY
HOME AND NEIGHBORHOOD
EDUCATION
RELIGION
INTERESTS AND LEISURE-TIME ACTIVITIES
HEALTH
    Physical
    Mental and emotional
EMPLOYMENT
MILITARY SERVICE

FINANCIAL CONDITION
    Assets
    Financial obligations
EVALUATIVE SUMMARY
RECOMMENDATION

In each presentence report the probation officer should follow the title and exact sequence of these headings.

The suggested contents for the marginal headings are given starting on this page. The items listed under *Essential Data* are those which should appear in *all* presentence reports. Those listed under *Optional Data* will appear in many reports, depending on their significance in the particular case. Each probation officer will determine which of the optional data are essential for the respective defendants under study and how each is to be treated.

In writing the report the probation officer need not follow the sequence of the *essential* and *optional* items. This may prove awkward, hinder readability, disrupt the trend of thought, and obstruct the logical development of the subject matter in question. He will have to shape the general content of the report according to the requirements of each case.

Offense

OFFICIAL VERSION
    Essential Data:
        Nature and date of plea or verdict.
        Brief summary of indictment or information, including number of counts, period covered, and nature, date(s), and place(s) of offense.
        Extent of property or monetary loss.
        Extent of defendant's profit from crime.
        Aggravating and extenuating circumstances.
        Nature and status of other pending charges.
        Days held in jail.
        Reasons for inability to divert (juvenile cases).
    Optional Data:
        Date and place of arrest.
        Circumstances leading to arrest.
        Statement of arresting officers.
        Attitude of defendant toward arresting officers.
        Degree of cooperation.
        Where detained prior to trial or sentence.
        Amount of bond.
        Extent to which offense follows patterns of previous offenses.
        Relation of offense to organized crime or racket.
        Amount of loss recovered.
        Has full or partial restitution been made.
        Other violations involved in addition to those charged.

STATEMENT OF CODEFENDANTS

Essential Data:

Extent of their participation in offense.

Present status of their case.

Optional Data:

Attitude toward offense.

Attitude toward defendant.

Their statement of defendant's participation in offense.

Relative culpability of defendant in relation to codefendants and coconspirators.

Statement of Witnesses, Complainants, and Victims (Optional.)

Defendant's Version of Offense

Essential Data:

Summary of account of offense and arrest as given by defendant if different from official version.

Discrepancies between defendant's version and official version.

Extent to which defendant admits guilt.

Defendant's attitude toward offense (e.g., remorseful, rationalizes, minimizes, experiences anxiety, etc.)

Defendant's explanation of why he became involved in the offense.

Extent to which offense was impulsive or premeditated.

Environmental and situational factors contributing to offense, including stressing situations, experiences, or relationships.

Optional Data:

Defendant's feelings from time of offense until his arrest.

Defendant's reactions after arrest (e.g., defiant, relieved, indifferent, etc.).

Defendant's attitude toward the probation officer and his degree of cooperation.

Defendant's attitudes toward prior convictions and commitments if they contribute to an understanding of the present offense.

Prior Record

Essential Data:

Clearance with FBI, social service exchange and police departments and sheriffs' offices in respective localities where defendant lived.

Juvenile court history.

List of previous convictions (date, place, offense, and disposition).

List of arrests subsequent to present offense (date, place, offense and disposition).

Military arrests and courts martial (date, place, offense, and disposition) not covered in *Military Service.*

Institutional history (dates, report of adjustment, present release status, etc.).

Previous probation and parole history (dates, adjustment, outcome).

Detainers presently lodged against defendant.

Optional Data:

Defendant's explanation why he was involved in previous offenses.

Codefendants in previous offenses.

Family History

DEFENDANT

Essential Data:

Date, place of birth, race.

Early developmental influences (physical and emotional) that may have a significant bearing on defendant's present personality and behavior.

Attitudes of the father and the mother toward the defendant in his formative years, including discipline, affection, rejection, etc.

By whom was defendant reared, if other than his parents.

Age left home; reasons for leaving; history of truancy from home.

Relationship of defendant with parents and siblings, including attitudes towards one another.

Extent of family solidarity (family cohesiveness).

Relatives with whom defendant is especially close.

Optional Data:

Naturalization status (country of birth and place and date of entry into United States).

Order of birth among siblings.

PARENTS AND SIBLINGS

Essential Data:

(All information optional.)

Optional Data:

Parents (name, age, address, citizenship, naturalization status, education, marital status, health, religion, economic status, general reputation). If deceased, also give age at death and cause.

Siblings (same as parents, above).

History of emotional disorders, diseases, and criminal behavior in the family.

Attitude of parents and siblings toward defendant's offense.

Marital History

Essential Data:

Present marriage, including common law (date, place, name and age of spouse at time of marriage).

Attitude of defendant toward spouse and children and their's toward him.

Home atmosphere.

Previous marriage(s) (date, place, name of previous spouse, and outcome; if divorced, give reasons).

Children, including those from previous marriage(s) (name, age, school, custody, support).

Optional Data:

Significant elements in spouse's background.

History of courtship and reason for marriage.

Problems in the marriage (religion, sex, economics, etc.).

Attitude of spouse (and older children) toward offense.

Attitude of defendant and spouse toward divorce, separation, remarriage.

Contacts with domestic relations court.

Juvenile court record of children.

Social agencies interested in family.

Divorce data (including grounds, court, date of final decree, special conditions, and to whom granted).

Home and Neighborhood

Essential Data:

Description of home (owned or rented, type, size, occupants, adequacy, and general living conditions).

Type of neighborhood, including any desirable or undesirable influences in the community.

Attitude of defendant and family toward home and neighborhood.

Optional Data:

Date moved to present residence and number of different residences in past 10 years.

How long has defendant lived in present type of neighborhood.

What race, nationality, and culture predominate.

Prior home and neighborhood experiences which have had a substantial influence on the defendant's behavior.

Education

Essential Data:

Highest grade achieved.

Age left school and reason for leaving.

Results of psychological tests (IQ, aptitude, achievement, etc.), specify test and date.

Optional Data:

Last school attended (dates, name, address).

Previous school attended covering 5-year period (dates, name, address).

School adjustment as evidenced by conduct, scholastic standing, truancy, leadership, reliability, courtesy, likes and dislikes, special abilities and disabilities, grades repeated, and relationships with pupils and teacher.

Business and trade training (type, school, dates,).

Defendant's attitude toward further education and training.

Ability to read and write English.

Religion

Essential Data:

Religious affiliation and frequency of church attendance.

Optional Data:

Church membership (name, address, pastor).

Member of what church organizations.

What has religious experience meant to defendant in the past and at present.

What are defendant's moral values.

What is the pastor's impression of the defendant.

Interest and Leisure-Time Activities

Essential Data:

Defendant's interests and leisure-time activities (including sports, hobbies, creative work, organizations, reading).

What are his talents and accomplishments.

Optional Data:

Who are his associates; what is their reputation.

Extent to which he engages in activities alone.

Extent to which he includes his family.

Extent to which his leisure-time pursuits reflect maturity.

Health

PHYSICAL

Essential Data:

Identifying information (height, weight, complexion, eyes, hair, scars, tattoos, posture, physical proportions, tone of voice, manner of speech).

Defendant's general physical condition and health problems based on defendant's estimate of his health, medical reports, probation officer's observations.

Use of narcotics, barbiturates, marihuana.

Social implications of defendant's physical health (home, community, employment, associations).

Optional Data:

History of serious diseases, including venereal disease, tuberculosis, diabetes (nature, date, effects).

History of major surgery and serious injuries (nature, date, effects).

Hospital treatment (hospital, dates, nature, outcome).

Last medical examination (date, place, pertinent findings).

Current medical treatment (prescribed medicine and dosage).

Use of alcohol.

Allergies (especially penicillin).

MENTAL AND EMOTIONAL

Essential Data:

Probation officer's assessment of defendant's operating level of intelligence as demonstrated in social and occupational functions.

Personality characteristics as given by family members and as observed by probation officer.

Attitude of defendant about himself and how he feels others feel about him (parents, siblings, spouse, children, associates).

Social adjustment in general.

Social implications of mental and emotional health (home, community, employment, associations).

Optional Data:

IQ (support with test scores).

Findings of psychological and psychiatric examinations (tests, date, by whom given).

Emotional instability as evidenced by fears, hostilities, obsessions, compulsions, depressions, peculiar ideas, dislikes, sex deviation (include any history of psychiatric treatment).

Defendant's awareness of emotional problems and what he has done about them.

Employment

Essential Data:

Employment history for past 10 years (dates, nature of work, earnings, reasons for leaving).

Employer's evaluation of defendant (immediate supervisor, where possible), including attendance, capabilities, reliability, adjustment, honesty, reputation, personality, attitude toward work, and relationships with coworkers and supervisors.

Occupational skills, interests, and ambitions.

Optional Data:

If unemployable, explain.

Means of subsistence during unemployment, including relief and unemployment compensation.

Military Service

Essential Data:

Branch of service, serial number, and dates of each period of military service.

Highest grade or rank achieved and grade or rank at separation.

Type and date of discharge(s).

Attitude toward military experience.

Optional Data:

Inducted or enlisted.

Special training received.

Foreign service, combat experience, decorations and citations.

Disciplinary action not covered in *Prior Record*.

Veteran's claim number.

Selective Service status (local board, classification, registration number).

Financial Condition

ASSETS

Essential Data:

Statement of financial assets.

General standard of living.

Optional Data:

Net worth statement.

Property (type, location, value, equity).

Insurance (type, amount, company).

Checking and saving account (bank, amount).
Stocks and bonds (type, value).
Personal property (car, furniture, appliances).
Income from pensions, rentals, boarders.
Family income.
Available resources through relatives and friends.

FINANCIAL OBLIGATIONS

Essential Data:
Statement of financial obligations.
Optional Data:
Current obligations, including balance due and monthly payment (home mortgage, rent, utilities, medical, personal property, home repairs, charge accounts, loans, fines, restitution).
Money management and existing financial delinquencies.
Credit rating.

Evaluative Summary

Essential Data:
Highlights of body of the report.
Analysis of factors contributing to present offense and prior convictions (motivations and circumstances).
Defendant's attitude toward offense.
Evaluation of the defendant's personality, problems and needs, and potential for growth.
Optional Data:
Reputation in the community.

COMMENT.   Writing the evaluative summary is perhaps the most difficult and painstaking task in the entire presentence report. It has a significant bearing on the future course of the defendant's life. It is here that the probation officer calls into play his analytical ability, his diagnostic skills, and his understanding of human behavior. It is here that he brings into focus the kind of person before the court, the basic factors that brought him into trouble, and what special helps the defendant needs to resolve his difficulties.

The opening paragraph of the evaluative summary should give a concise restatement of the pertinent highlights in the body of the report. There should follow in separate paragraphs those factors which contributed in some measure to the defendant's difficulty and also an evaluation of his personality.

Recommendation

Essential Data:
Recommendation.
Basis for recommendation.

Optional Data:
   Suggested plan, including role of parents, spouse, pastor, further education, future
      employment.
   Sentencing alternatives.

COMMENT.   Some judges ask for the probation officer's recommendation
regarding probation or commitment. Where recommendations are requested,
they should be a part of the presentence report. If the judge does not wish to have
the recommendations included as a part of the report, they may be given on a
separate sheet which may be detached if the presentence report is later sent to
an institution.

If it is recommended that the defendant be placed on probation, the proposed
plans for residence, employment, education, and medical and psychiatric treatment, if pertinent, should be given. The part to be played in the social adjustment
of the defendant by the parental and immediate family, the pastor, close friends,
and others in the community should also be shown. If commitment is recommended, the probation officer should indicate what special problems and needs
should receive the attention of the institutional staff.

Where the judge asks for sentencing alternatives, they may be included in this
part of the report.

14

The Selective Presentence Investigation Report

ADMINISTRATIVE OFFICER
OF THE UNITED STATES COURTS

In February 1965 the Probation Division of the Administrative Office issued Publication No. 103, *The Presentence Investigation Report.* This was a definitive standard to be followed in preparation of a presentence investigation report for the U.S. District Courts. The publication prescribes practice and technique for U.S. probation officers to use as a guide in investigating defendants and reporting their findings and recommendations to the courts.

Following publication the probation system subjected the new format to extensive trial. The Probation Division launched a series of training programs to familiarize officers with the new method.

In June 1967 the probation system took the final step in adopting the publication as the standard to be followed by all probation officers throughout the country. Memorandum No. 509, issued by the Chief of Probation, specified that presentence investigation reports must cover all areas identified by the first 14 marginal headings of the approved outline contained in Publication 103. In the

SOURCE. *Federal Probation,* XXXVIII, December 1974, pp. 47–54. Reprinted with permission of *Federal Probation.*

ensuing years the probation system has developed an investigative capacity of high standards in the correctional field.

As experience with the new report developed, however, a new need emerged. Presentence investigation reports became longer. The continuing workload on U.S. district judges has forced them to ask for relief from whatever quarter available. The recognition has emerged that there are criminal cases in which the court may safely sentence the defendant without the information available in all 14 marginal headings of the presentence investigation report.

In August 1972 the Judicial Conference Committee on the Administration of the Probation System agreed that there was need for a format for a shorter presentence investigation report that would be acceptable not only to the courts but also to probation officers, the Bureau of Prisons, and Board of Parole.

To address the problem of what kind of shorter report should be available as standard, the Committee on the Administration of the Probation System authorized a committee to receive and review recomendations. The Committee on the Presentence Format, consisting of representatives from the Federal Bureau of Prisons, U.S. Board of Parole, Probation Division, and various field offices met and considered the changes outlined in *The Selective Presentence Investigation Report* (Publication No. 104). This monograph, reprinted here in its entirety, was approved unanimously by the Committee on the Administration of the Probation System and is recommended to all probation officers as a supplement to *The Presentence Investigation Report*. It should serve all probation officers as a guide in conducting presentence investigations and in writing reports.

PRESENTENCE INVESTIGATION REPORT

Purpose of Presentence Investigation Report

The presentence investigation report is a basic working document in judicial and correctional administration. It performs five functions: (1) To aid the court in determining the appropriate sentence, (2) to aid the probation officer in his rehabilitative efforts during probation and parole supervision,[1] (3) to assist Bureau of Prisons institutions in their classification and treatment programs and also in their release planning, (4) to furnish the Board of Parole with information pertinent to its consideration of parole, and (5) to serve as a source of information for systematic research.

The objectives of the presentence report are to focus light on the character and personality of the defendant, to offer insight into his problems and needs, to help understand the world in which he lives, to learn about his relationships with people and to discover those salient factors that underlie his specific offense and his conduct in general and to suggest alternatives in the rehabilitation process.

Most authorities in the judicial and correctional fields assert that a presen-

---

[1] The Federal probation officer also supervises persons released from Federal correctional institutions and the U.S. Disciplinary Barracks.

tence investigation should be made in every case. With the aid of a presentence report the court may decide to commit a defendant to an institution or may grant probation. The presentence report is an essential aid in the selection process.

The Presentence Investigation Report outline adopted by the Judicial Conference Committee on the Administration of the Probation System on February 11, 1965, consists of the following marginal headings and the respective subheadings:

OFFENSE
    Official version
    Statement of codefendants
    Statement of witnesses, complainants, and victims
DEFENDANT'S VERSION OF OFFENSE
PRIOR RECORD
FAMILY HISTORY
    Defendant
    Parents and siblings
MARITAL HISTORY
HOME AND NEIGHBORHOOD
EDUCATION
RELIGION
INTERESTS AND LEISURE-TIME ACTIVITIES
HEALTH
    Physical
    Mental and emotional
EMPLOYMENT
MILITARY SERVICE
FINANCIAL CONDITION
    Assets
    Financial obligations
EVALUATIVE SUMMARY
RECOMMENDATION

Interest in a shorter form of reporting results from the search for a more flexible alternative that will continue to meet the needs of all agencies. What is proposed here is to complement the present presentence report, not replace it. The new format is to be used where the issues are clear and disposition may be made on less comprehensive information. If the offense is aggravated or the issues complicated the comprehensive presentence format is to be used.

The Development of the Presentence Investigation

The proper administration of justice requires diligence and care in selecting appropriate sentences for convicted offenders. Appropriate sentences seek to assist offenders to become responsible, self-respecting persons while maintaining public confidence in the system and function of law.

The presentence investigation report makes a major contribution in the selection of appropriate sentences. In modern society the presentence investigation report is a formal substitute for the greater understanding of individual offenders which judges had through informal circumstances when the national population was distributed throughout smaller communities.

The development of presentence investigation reports has been influenced by the "case method" approach used in the search for the cause of criminal behavior. That approach assumes that if knowledge can be acquired of all the facts about an offender the cause of his criminality can be discovered and a course of corrections determined. Although the "case method" approach to criminality has not resulted in any integrated theory of crime or corrections, the method continues to have an influence in presentence investigation reporting. In some presentence investigation reports there is a tendency to provide exhaustive historical accounts of an offender's life, perhaps from anxiety that some single pertinent factor, however insignificant it might appear at the time, might be excluded and lost to the future. To provide balance for any compulsiveness that has resulted from the "case method" influences, there is need for guidelines which encourage greater selectivity in report preparation.

A short precise report, fully read and considered is more effective and functional than a comprehensive report not considered or used. The effectiveness of a presentence investigation is directly related to the proficiency with which the findings are communicated, *and the extent to which the report is relied upon.*

Due to the nature of the judicial process it is not possible to develop reports with such precision as to eliminate the accumulation of information which will not be used. To do so would require the anticipation of judgments before they are made, and even if such were allowed by the judiciary, it would be a dangerous direction to take. Experience leads to the conclusion, however, that guidelines can be established that allow greater efficiency in the development of purposeful information and reduce the amount of information reported and not used.

The greater the consequences of a judgment, the more a court wants comprehensive understanding of all factors in arriving at a decision. For example, if an individual has committed a violent or potentially violent offense, any consideration for release on probation requires more comprehensive knowledge of the individual than for a situational first offender, who has committed a nonviolent offense. Guidelines should assure that comprehensive reports are available when needed, but that comprehensive reports be held to a minimum when such detail does not serve a real purpose.

Interest in the development of shorter presentence reports derives from two considerations: (1) The importance of expediting accountability if confidence in the administration of justice is to be maintained, and (2) significant increases in presentence demands upon the probation system. Expediting the processing of justice is perhaps the most urgent contemporary need to strengthen the effectiveness of the criminal law. In seeking solutions, however, care should be exercised to keep all aspects of the problem in perspective.

Time lapses between the commission of offenses and the identification of alleged offenders, and between the identification of alleged offenders and indictment and determination of guilt, exceed the lapses between determination of guilt and actual sentencing. The time between determination of guilt and sentencing during which presentence investigations are conducted is probably the most standardized in the administration of justice. Delays in sentencing are frequently the result of matters not related to the investigation, such as the accommodation of counsel schedules and delays pending the trial of codefendants. The time between the finding of guilt and sentencing can also be skewed if calculations include the few defendants who disappear and remain in a fugitive status for lengthy periods of time.

United States probation offices have been very successful in attaining high standards in the completion of presentence investigation reports for district courts. Experience suggests that high quality professional reports contribute significantly to the confidence held by many in the processing of criminal justice in the United States district courts. United States attorneys, defense counsel, offenders, and members of offenders' families all have an opportunity to be aware of the quality of presentence reports made available to the United States district courts. Although the reports are rarely accessible to the press, members of the press are aware that United States district judges are well-informed about offenders and offenses prior to making judgments. If confidence in the administration of justice by the United States district courts is to be held by the general public, it is essential that the public know that court decisions are well-informed and well considered. Probation is a valid and vital concept. In the absence of discriminating selection procedures, however, probation can easily become a mere form of leniency. For the sake of confidence it is essential that the public realize that discriminating selections are made in the use of probation.

If strengthening public confidence in the system of law is a primary goal in expediting the administration of justice, it is essential that quality not be sacrificed in the process. To sacrifice quality in presentence investigations in order to expedite the processes of justice would be much like "robbing Peter to pay Paul."

During the past few years United States probation offices across the country have experimented in the use of shortened presentence investigation reports. Generally "fill-in" forms and "check-lists" have met with dissatisfaction from judges and probation officers alike. A variety of approaches to the problem have been made, however, and the recommendations which follow concerning the development of *Selective Presentence Investigation Reports* derive from experiences of probation offices across the country as well as an evaluation of the "short-form presentence report," by the Office of Probation for the Courts of New York City.

Several related professions have shown renewed interest in shorter style reports. In the field of psychological testing, for example, the traditional report was an elaborate recitation of the tests used, the responses, and conclusions that could be drawn. The current mode is to a much shorter report, one to three pages in length, reporting only the significant findings and giving a diagnostic opinion.

A shortened report saves time in dictating, typing, and reading. It is conceivable that there will also be a saving in the investigative effort. In dictating the report, the probation officer should include all information that the court "needs to know" and exclude what is "nice to know." The emphasis is on providing the essentials necessary to arrive at a sentencing decision or a decision regarding the ultimate release of the offender if he should be confined. Other considerations are secondary. A thorough investigation will be required although shortcuts will suggest themselves as it becomes certain that the selective format will suffice. It is in the dictation that the probation officer must delete extraneous material. Only the elemental facts are to be presented.

RECOMMENDATIONS FOR SELECTIVE PRESENTENCE INVESTIGATION REPORTS

(1) Terms such as "short-form," "abbreviated," "miniform," or "limited," should be avoided in referring to any presentence investigation reports completed for United States district courts, United States magistrates, the Federal Bureau of Prisons, and the United States Board of Parole. It is not intended that the courts or the other units of the correctional system be provided with a report that is less than adequate, nor shall a selective report be regarded as a shortcut in the judicial process.

(2) These guidelines shall be adopted for the discriminating use of presentence investigation reports which are less comprehensive than those adhering to the format outlined in Publication No. 103, *The Presentence Investigation Report.*

(3) These less comprehensive reports shall be identified as *Selective Presentence Investigation Reports.*

GUIDELINES FOR THE USE OF SELECTIVE PRESENTENCE INVESTIGATION REPORTS

There are circumstances concerning Federal offenders under which selective presentence investigation reports, completed in accordance with discriminating criteria, will be adequate for all purposes for which the report is to be used. Following are guidelines for the use of *Selective Presentence Investigation Reports.*

Selection

Unless the court directs otherwise, the probation officer, following an initial interview with the offender, shall determine whether a comprehensive report or a selective report is to be completed in accordance with the following criteria.

Unless for good reason the probation officer determines otherwise, *Selective Presentence Investigation Reports* will be completed for the following categories:

(1) All misdemeanor defendants with less than three prior convictions, unless weapons or violence have been involved.

(2) Defendants in immigration law violations involving illegal entry or reentry, or transporting aliens.

(3) Miscellaneous Federal Regulatory Statutes: Agriculture and Conserva-

tion Acts, Fair Labor Standards Acts, Food and Drug Acts, Migratory Bird Laws, and Motor Carrier Act violations.

(4) Defendants involved in fraud occurring against lending and credit institutions, Veterans Administration, Railroad Retirement Act, and Social Security Act where the aggregate loss is less than $1,000.

(5) Embezzlement of bank or postal funds, public moneys or property, lending credit, and insurance institutions, by officers of a carrier in interstate commerce and embezzlement by officers of labor organizations, or federally insured financial institutions when the aggregate loss is less than $1,000.

(6) Income tax fraud including evasion and failure to file when the taxes evaded total less than $1,000.

(7) Defendants involved in violations of Internal Revenue Liquor laws (except those of a highly commercial nature).

(8) Theft, including larceny and theft from post offices and federally insured banks; mail theft, theft of United States property, and thefts occurring on government reservations, etc., when the aggregate loss is less than $1,000.

(9) Forgery, including postal forgery and forgery of obligations and securities of the United States when the total loss is less than $1,000.

(10) Selective Service Act violations.

(11) Prison escape (walkaway only, or failure to return from furlough).

(12) In a limited number of other felony cases where recent classification material is available from institution, a selective presentence report may be sufficient.

Unless the probation officer determines that a selective report will be adequate, the comprehensive report will be completed for all defendants not described by the above categories, including:

(1) All felony offenders not listed above.

(2) All offenders revealing tendencies toward violence in current offense, prior record, or personal history.

(3) All offenders believed to be operating in connection with organized crime.

(4) All misdemeanor offenders having three or more prior convictions.

(5) Any offender believed likely to be committed for study to the Bureau of Prisons (18 U.S.C. 4208(b) or 5010(e), 4252, or 5034).

Format

The following categories of information will comprise the core, or essential factors to be included in a *Selective Presentence Investigation Report.*

FACE SHEET.   To be identical with the face sheet used for the standard comprehensive report.

OFFENSE—OFFICIAL VERSION

DEFENDANT'S VERSION OF OFFENSE

PRIOR RECORD

PERSONAL HISTORY

EVALUATIVE SUMMARY

RECOMMENDATION

When it is pertinent to the selection of sentence or in the subsequent correctional process additional information will be included in the report under one or more of the following topical categories:

PERSONAL AND FAMILY HISTORY
   Parents, brothers, sisters
HOME AND NEIGHBORHOOD
EDUCATION
RELIGION
INTERESTS AND LEISURE-TIME ACTIVITIES
HEALTH
   Physical
   Mental and emotional
EMPLOYMENT
MILITARY SERVICE
FINANCIAL CONDITION
   Assets
   Financial Obligations

Information reported under the core and selected topical headings should be in a narrative form. Elemental facts are best expressed in short sentences. Long involved explanations should be avoided, and whenever possible to do so with accuracy, information should be summarized rather than reported in detail. For example,

> *Employment.*—The defendant has been employed steadily as a machinist, working for three different firms during the past 10 years. He has held his current job with Apex Machine Shop for 3½ years and now earns $6.85 per hour. He is considered to be a reliable, honest employee.

The Selective Presentence Report is not to be interpreted as restrictive. If the investigation develops additional information the officer may include further categories of information or prepare a more lengthy report as outlined in Publication No. 103. For those offense categories included in the Selective Report Guidelines the probation officer shall commence with the assumption that a selective report will be prepared. A change to preparing a report as outlined in Publication No. 103 is made only as circumstances dictate during the investigation.

Probation Officer's Part in the Investigation

The guide for the conduct of a presentence investigation is contained in Publication 103, *The Presentence Investigation Report.* Publication 104 provides an alternative report format in appropriate instances. The fundamentals of careful investigation and verification are spelled out in Publication 103 and these are to be followed by all officers investigating defendants before the Federal courts. In this regard probation officers must pay scrupulous attention to standards for verification of information. Every effort must be made to check the accuracy of information which is likely to be damaging to the defendant or to bear on the welfare of the family and the safety of the community.

The recent trend toward disclosure of the presentence report to the defendant and both counsel acts as a healthy check on the accuracy of its contents. Disclosure does not, however, relieve the probation officer of the burden to check the facts carefully, sift available data, and reject information that will not stand tests of validity.

OUTLINE, CONTENTS, AND FORMAT OF THE REPORT

Face Sheet

The current face sheet, Probation Form 2, will be used for all presentence reports. In addition to its normal use, for selective reports the face sheet may provide information in capsule form if doing so eliminates material from the body of the report. For example, there may be an additional typed entry: "Religion _____ (faith) _____ (attends)." The face sheet may contain reference to alcohol or drug involvement. The "Custody" category may inform as to whether bond was made, by whom, and the amount.

In general the face sheet will be filled out in accordance with the instructions of Publication 103. Information contained on the face sheet need not be repeated in the body of the report.

Offense: Official Version

The official version of the offense may be obtained from the office of the U.S. attorney. The report should contain information on codefendants, if any, the relative culpability of the defendant, and whether the codefendant has been apprehended and the disposition made in his case.

In those instances in which an adequate concise report delineating the defendant's relative culpability is available from the investigating officer the "Official Version" may simply refer the reader to that report as an attachment. In that event details of the offense need not be provided in the text.

Defendant's Version of Offense

A summary of the defendant's version of the offense should be provided. Whatever the defendant says about the offense and his part in it is necessary to understand him.

Prior Record

The prior criminal record shall be provided in detail, except that multiple prior arrests of a minor nature may be summarized, e.g., "From 1968 to 1972 Mr.

Jones was arrested a total of 10 times for drunkenness and minor traffic violations. The drunk arrests were resolved by referral to the county rehabilitation center, the traffic violations resulted in forfeiture of bail ranging from $25 to $50."

Although the FBI record has a fairly complete coverage of arrests and convictions the probation officer shall clear with local identification bureaus, police departments, and sheriffs' offices in those communities where the defendant has resided. Where the FBI fingerprint record does not give the disposition of a case, the probation officer shall obtain the missing information from the law enforcement office which filed the print or the court in which the case was tried.

Personal History

This topical heading is a composite of several headings used in the comprehensive report. The probation officer shall provide a history of the development and social relationships of the defendant. This section should include a reference to educational attainment, any drug or alcohol history, and employment stability. However, extraneous detail about the family is to be avoided. The officer shall bear in mind that detailed information about the family is more pertinent in understanding juvenile and youth offenders than it is in the case of the older offender. In many instances it is sufficient to provide a summary that informs the court that the family history has been explored and found to be unremarkable.

No presentence investigation is complete unless the spouse, if any, has been interviewed. The report shall carry the essential details of the marriage, date, number of children, and a synopsis of the relationship.

Evaluative Summary

The opening paragraph of the evaluative summary gives a concise restatement of the pertinent highlights in the body of the report. The attitude of the defendant toward his offense is significant in determining whether he should be considered for probation. Writing the evaluative summary is the most demanding task in the preparation of the report. It is here that the probation officer focuses on those factors, social and personal, the result in this defendant's presence before the court and the special assistance that will be required in this person's situation.

Recommendation

If it is recommended that the defendant be placed on probation, the proposed plans for residence, employment, education, and medical and psychiatric treatment, if relevant, should be given. The part to be played in the social adjustment of the defendant by the parental and immediate family, close friends, and other resources in the community should also be shown. If commitment is recommended, the probation officer shall indicate what special problems and needs should receive the attention of the institutional staff. Where the judge asks for sentencing alternatives, they may be included.

APPENDIX

The selective presentence investigation report on the following pages is presented to illustrate the outline, format, and style recommended in writing a selective presentence report. Names and dates in the report have been altered to protect the identity of the defendant.

Offense: Official Version.—Official sources reveal that during the course of routine observations on December 4, 1973, within the Postal Office Center, Long Island, New York, postal inspectors observed the defendant paying particular attention to various packages. Since the defendant was seen to mishandle and tamper with several parcels, test parcels were prepared for his handling on December 5, 1973. The defendant was observed to mishandle one of the test parcels by tossing it to one side into a canvas tub. He then placed his jacket into the tub and leaned over the tub for a period of time. At this time the defendant left the area and went to the men's room. While he was gone the inspectors examined the mail tub and found that the test parcel had been riffled and that the contents, a watch, was missing.

The defendant returned to his work area and picked up his jacket. He then left the building. The defendant was stopped by the inspectors across the street from the post office. He was questioned about his activities and on his person he had the wristwatch from the test parcel. He was taken to the postal inspector's office where he admitted the offense.

Defendant's Version of Offense.—The defendant admits that he riffled the package in question and took the watch. He states that he intended to sell the watch at a later date. He admits that he has been drinking too much lately and needed extra cash for "drinking money." He exhibits remorse and is concerned about the possibility of incarceration and the effect that it would have on his family.

PRIOR RECORD

Date	Offense	Place	Disposition
5-7-66 (age 26)	Possession of Policy Slips	Manhattan CR. CT. N.Y., N.Y.	$25.00 Fine 7-11-66
3-21-72 (age 32)	Intoxication	Manhattan CR. CT. N.Y., N.Y.	4-17-72 Nolle

Personal History.—The defendant was born in New York City on February 8, 1940, the oldest of three children, He attended the public school, completed the 10th grade and left school to go to work. He was rated as an average student and was active in sports, especially basketball and baseball.

The defendant's father, John, died of a heart attack in 1968, at the age of 53 years. He had an elementary school education and worked as a construction laborer most of his life.

The defendant's mother, Mary Smith Jones, is 55 years of age and is employed as a seamstress. She had an elementary school education and married defendant's father when she was 20 years of age. Three sons were issue of the marriage. She presently resides in New York City, and is in good health.

Defendant's brother, Paul, age 32 years, completed 2½ years of high school. He is employed as a bus driver and resides with his wife and two children in New York City.

Defendant's brother, Lawrence, age 30 years, completed three semesters of college. He is employed as a New York City firefighter. He resides with his wife and one child in Dutch Point, Long Island.

The defendant after leaving high school worked as a delivery boy for a retail supermarket chain, then served 2 years in the U.S. Army as an infantryman (ASN 123 456 78). He received an honorable discharge and attained the rank of corporal serving from 2-10-58 to 2-1-60. After service he held a number of jobs of the laboring type.

The defendant was employed as a truck driver for the City of New York when he married Ann Sweeny on 6-15-63. Two children were issue of this marriage, John, age 8, and Mary, age 6. The family has resided at the same address (which is a four-room apartment) since their marriage.

The defendant has been in good health all of his life but he admits he has been drinking to excess the past 18 months which has resulted in some domestic strife. The wife stated that she loved her husband and will stand by him. She is amenable to a referral for family counseling.

Defendant has worked for the Postal Service since 12-1-65 and resigned on 12-5-73 as a result of the present arrest. His work ratings by his supervisors were always "excellent."

Evaluative Summary.—The defendant is a 33-year-old male who entered a plea of guilty to mail theft. While an employee of the U.S. Postal Service he rifled and stole a watch from a test package. He admitted that he planned on selling the watch to finance his drinking which has become a problem resulting in domestic strife.

Defendant is a married man with two children with no prior serious record. He completed 10 years of schooling, had an honorable military record, and has a good work history. He expresses remorse for his present offense and is concerned over the loss of his job and the shame to his family.

Recommendation.—It is respectfully recommended that the defendant be admitted to probation. If placed on probation the defendant expresses willingness to seek counseling for his domestic problems. He will require increased motivation if there is to be a significant change in his drinking pattern.

Respectfully submitted,

Donald M. Fredericks
U.S. Probation Officer

PROBATION FORM **2**
FEB 65

UNITED STATES DISTRICT COURT

Central District of New York

PRESENTENCE REPORT

NAME   John Jones

DATE   January 4, 1974

ADDRESS
 1234 Astoria Blvd.
 New York City

DOCKET NO.   74—103

OFFENSE   Theft of Mail by Postal
 Employee (18 U.S.C.
 Sec. 1709) 2 cts.

LEGAL RESIDENCE
 Same

AGE 33   DATE OF BIRTH 2—8—40
 New York City

PENALTY   Ct. 2 — 5 years and/or
 $2,000 fine

SEX Male   ACE Caucasian

CITIZENSHIP   U.S. (Birth)

PLEA   Guilty on 12—16—73 to Ct. 2
 Ct. 1 pending

EDUCATION 10th grade

VERDICT

MARITAL STATUS Married

CUSTODY   Released on own
 recognizance. No time in
 custody.

DEPENDENTS   Three
 (wife and 2 children)

ASST. U.S. ATTY
 Samuel Hayman

SOC. SEC. NO. 112—03—9559

FBI NO. 256 1126

DEFENSE COUNSEL   Thomas Lincoln
 Federal Public
 Defender

DETAINERS OR CHARGES PENDING:
 None

Drug/Alcohol Involvement:
 Attributes offense to
 need for drinking money

CODEFENDANTS *(Disposition)*
 None

DISPOSITION

DATE

SENTENCING JUDGE

15

The Presentence Report and the Decision-Making Process

ROBERT M. CARTER

The decision-making process is perhaps the most important—and least under-stood—single dimension of the correctional system. The decisions made by pro-bation officers, parole officers, institutional officials, paroling authorities, administrators, and others not only determine the specific course of action for a given offender, but also have long-range implications for the direction of the correctional process.

A great variety of decisions are made in every phase of the correctional system. For example, at the judiciary level a decision is made whether to release a defendant on bail or on his own recognizance. If the former, a decision must be made on the amount of bail. The prosecuting agency must resolve the number and they types of charges to be brought against a defendant. The probation officer, in writing a presentence report, must make a recommendation for disposition. At the institutional level, further decisions select the facility and program for the inmate. The paroling authority must determine whether to grant parole, the duration of the parole, and any special provisions for this conditional liberty.

SOURCE. *Journal of Research in Crime and Delinquency,* **4,** July 1967, pp. 203–211. Reprinted with the permission of the National Council on Crime and Delinquency. Copyright, 1967, National Council on Crime and Delinquency.

When supervising in the field, probation and parole officers must elect a course of action which includes the location and time of contacts with the offender and other persons, purpose of the contacts, amount of time to be devoted to specific cases, and so on.

Such decision-making should be related to the currently accepted generalizations about crime and the correctional process. If decisions have no explicit basis, they not only tend to be sporadic, confusing, and even disruptive, but may be antithetic to an agency's stated objectives. Wilkins has given us an exhaustive examination of the action-theory relationship.[1]

This study explores the decision-making process at the probation officer level and focuses on the presentence report and the data utilized in recommendations for probation or imprisonment. Certain demographic characteristics of the offender population—prior record, current offense, and data relating to stability —are important in determining the recommendation.[2] However, the order in which probation officers seek such information and the point in their information-gathering activity when decisions are made regarding the recommendation have not been determined. The following questions need clarification and are explored below:

1. At the presentence level, what is the order in which probation officers gather information?

2. At what point in the collection of data is a decision made relating to the recommendation?

3. Once a decision has been made, may any additional data received change that decision?

4. Do officers develop a style for collecting information and making decisions? How consistent is this style from case to case?

THE RESEARCH METHOD

The method utilized in investigating these questions about the decision-making process is a modification of the "decision-game" developed by Wilkins.[3] Five cases, all previously referred for presentence reports, were selected from the files of the United States Probation Office, Northern District of California. The cases were subjected to content analysis and the materials then classified under twenty-four subject headings. The terms of classification were those commonly used in the Probation Office. Each item of information was then reproduced on a file card with a title printed on the lower edge describing the nature of the information on the card. The cards were then arranged and placed in a binder so only the

[1] Leslie T. Wilkins, *Social Deviance: Social Policy, Action, and Research* (Englewood Cliffs, N.J.: Prentice-Hall, 1965).

[2] Joseph D. Lohman, Albert Wahl, and Robert M. Carter, "Presentence Report Recommendations and Demographic Data," *The San Francisco Project, A Study of Federal Probation and Parole,* Research Report No. 5, February 1966, School of Criminology, University of California.

[3] Wilkins, *op. cit. supra* note 1, pp. 294–304.

lower edge showing the classification title was visible and all twenty-four titles were visible at the same time. The content of any card could be identified by the title and could be read by turning the card. Each card was numbered for reference purposes.

The twenty-four cards contained the following categories of information:

Offense (description)
Plea
Confinement Status (custody or community)
Status of Legal Representation (appointed or retained attorney)
Defendant's Statement concerning Offense
Age
Place of Birth
Race
Education
Religion
Employment History
Marital Status
Residence Data
Military History
Psychological/Psychiatric Data
Drug Usage Data
Alcoholic Involvement History
Homosexuality
Prior Criminal Record
Family History
Leisure-Time Activities and Interests
Medical History
Attitude of Defendant
Family Criminality

The U.S. Probation Officers participating in this "decision-game" were asked to utilize the information on the cards in making a recommendation as to disposition of the case. The data contained most of the information which had been available to the probation officers who had made the original recommendation in these five cases. This meant the probation officer could conduct his presentence investigation and make a recommendation by direct reference to the cards rather than going into the field to collect information.

The participants were allowed to "gather" information or "conduct" the presentence investigation any way they desired; that is, they could first determine the defendant's age by turning the "age" card or the nature of the offense by turning the "offense" card. After the probation officer selected each card, he was asked whether he could make a recommendation as to disposition and, if so, the nature of his recommendation. If unable to make a decision, the probation officer was asked to select another card (gather more information), then another, until he could make a recommendation.

The order in which the cards were chosen and the recommendation decided upon were recorded on separate sheets. Once the officer made a recommendation for a case, he was asked to select not less than three additional cards to ascertain the "correctness" of his decision. He could change his recommendation at any time. However, following any change, he was again asked to select not less than three additional cards. The officers were requested to make their recommendations using as little information as possible, yet at the same time be sure their decisions were "correct." In short, the officers were able to select as much information as they needed to make a recommendation in which they were confident.

Fourteen United States Probation Officers in the Northern District of California participated in this "decision-game," resulting in seventy recommendations. One decision was excluded because a probation officer recognized the case as one for which he had written the presentence report. Thus, sixty-nine decisions were available for review.

FACTORS IN DECISION-MAKING

In this study the decision-making process consisted of three primary components: gathering information preparatory to making a decision; arriving at the decision or the selection of alternatives; and, finally, gathering additional information to confirm, modify, or reject the original decision.

A frequency distribution of the total number of cards selected, both those used in the information-gathering phase (before the decision) as well as those used to confirm, modify, or reject the decision, appears in Table 1.

The data may be rearranged to provide a frequency distribution of the cards selected before the decision was made (Table 2).

A frequency distribution of the first three choices of the cards selected before the decision (Table 3) shows more clearly the value and importance of certain types of information.

Table 1 presents the frequency distribution of the total number of cards selected and reveals that information-gathering, -confirming, -modifying, and -rejecting are accomplished with relatively small amounts of information. The average number of cards selected for the sixty-nine decisions was 7.8 per case. This included the three cards required to confirm, modify, or reject the decision. Two types of information were selected in each case: offense description and prior record. Six other cards were selected in more than half the cases: psychological and psychiatric data, the defendant's statement, the defendant's attitude, employment history, family history, and age. Fourteen cards either were not selected at all or were selected in less than a fourth of the cases.

Table 2 deals only with the cards selected or information gathered before the decision and indicates that one card or item of information—the current offense —was selected in *all* cases. The prior criminal record card was selected in about four-fifths of the cases (81.2 percent). The card containing psychological and

Table 1   *Frequency Distribution of Card-Items Selected By Probation Officers for Presentence Recommendations in Sixty-Nine Cases*

Item on Information Card	Number of Times Card Was Selected	% of Times Card Was Selected
Offense	69	100.0
Prior Record	69	100.0
Psychological/Psychiatric	55	79.7
Defendant's Statement	48	69.6
Defendant's Attitude	43	62.3
Employment History	42	60.9
Age	37	53.6
Family History	36	52.2
Marital Status	29	42.0
Medical History	20	29.0
Education	15	21.7
Military History	12	17.4
Alcoholic Involvement	11	15.9
Homosexuality	11	15.9
Drug Usage	9	13.0
Interests and Activities	9	13.0
Family Criminality	8	11.6
Plea	5	7.2
Confinement Status	5	7.2
Residence Data	3	4.3
Religion	3	4.3
Legal Representation	0	0.0
Place of Birth	0	0.0
Race	0	0.0

psychiatric data was the only other card selected in more than half the cases (52.2 percent). The average number of cards selected prior to making a decision was 4.7. Seventeen cards either were not selected at all or were selected in less than a fourth of the cases. Some recommendations were made with the information on a single card. The most information required by any one officer to make a decision necessitated selection of thirteen cards.

Tables 1, 2, and 3 clearly indicate that the information gathered during the presentence investigation is of varying importance in making a recommendation. The tables further indicate the "essential" quality of some information, most notably data relating to the offender's current and past criminal behavior. Other information, such as data relating to the defendant's attitude, statement of the offense, psychological and psychiatric evaluations, age, employment history, and family background, is of moderate importance. The balance of the information collected is seemingly of minor significance in making a decision.

Table 2   *Frequency Distribution of Card-Items Selected before Presentence Decision in Sixty-Nine Cases*

Item on Information Card	Number of Times Card Was Selected	% of Times Card Was Selected
Offense	69	100.0
Prior Record	56	81.2
Psychological/Pyschiatric	36	52.2
Defendant's Statement	31	44.9
Age	24	34.8
Family History	23	33.3
Defendant's Attitude	19	27.5
Employment History	16	23.2
Marital Status	11	15.9
Military History	8	11.6
Homosexuality	5	7.2
Alcoholic Involvement	5	7.2
Drug Usage	5	7.2
Plea	5	7.2
Medical History	5	7.2
Education	4	5.8
Confinement Status	1	1.4
Residence Data	1	1.4
Family Criminality	1	1.4
Interests and Activities	1	1.4
Legal Representation	0	0.0
Place of Birth	0	0.0
Race	0	0.0
Religion	0	0.0

A fourth frequency distribution (Table 4) presents data on the cards selected after making the decision, the information gathered to confirm, modify, or reject the original decision.

VARIATION AND RECOMMENDATIONS

Because of the limited number of decisions examined, it is difficult to evaluate the full significance of Table 4, particularly as it relates to the data of the previous tables. The general impression provided by the data is that certain kinds of information are used uniformly to arrive at the point of decision, while other types of information are used generally to "confirm, modify, or reject" the decision. Additional data are needed before further analysis of this phase can be made.

Are presentence decisions changed upon the receipt of additional information? The current data indicate that the probation officer is not likely to change his original conclusion, limited as his information may be at that point. Of the sixty-nine initial decisions, sixty-five (94.2 percent) remained unchanged upon the

Table 3   *Frequency Distribution of the First Three Card Items ᵃ Selected before Presentence Decision in Sixty-Nine Cases*

Item on Information Card	Number of Times Card Was Selected	% of Times Card Was Selected
Offense	67	97.1
Prior Record	47	68.1
Defendant's Statement	22	31.9
Family History	18	26.1
Psychological/Psychiatric	15	21.7
Plea	5	7.2
Defendant's Attitude	2	2.9
Alcoholic Involvement	2	2.9
Employment History	1	1.4
Marital Status	1	1.4

ᵃSome decisions were reached with information from less than three cards. In this case only the cards selected before the decision are included in this table.

receipt of additional information. Only one was reversed (changing a prison recommendation to a probation recommendation) and three were modified (from recommendations for confinement to recommendations for observation and study under appropriate federal statutes).

A brief examination of the "decision-making" of the probation officers indicates that each officer develops his own style. Four of the fourteen officers followed identical patterns of card selection for each of the five cases; the remainder were quite consistent in their choices of information in each of the five cases, although some minor variations were apparent. None of the officers selected information at random; instead they followed a common basic pattern that was still somehow unique to the individual. For example, one officer never utilized employment information in making a decision but always used that information to confirm his decision. Another officer always studied the type of plea entered by the defendant prior to making his decision, yet no other officer selected that card at any time, either before or after the decision.

The final recommendations made by the officers in these cases showed considerable divergence. In Case 1, all fourteen officers ultimately recommended probation, although the number of cards selected prior to making the decision ranged from two to five. In Case 2, eight officers recommended imprisonment; one, a "split sentence" (jail followed by probation); one, probation; and four that the defendant be committed for a period of observation and study. The number of cards selected in reaching these recommendations was three to eleven. In Case 3, all fourteen officers recommended imprisonment and the number of cards selected was one to thirteen. In Case 4, five officers recommended imprisonment; two, probation; four, a "split sentence"; and two, county-jail commitment. The number of cards was two to ten. In Case 5, seven officers recommended probation,

Table 4   *Frequency Distribution of Card-Items Selected Following Presentence Decision in Sixty-Nine Cases*

Item on Information Card	Number of Times Card Was Selected	% of Times Card Was Selected
Employment History	26	37.7
Defendant's Attitude	24	34.8
Psychological/Psychiatric	19	27.5
Marital Status	18	26.1
Defendant's Statement	17	24.6
Medical History	15	21.7
Family History	13	18.8
Prior Record	13	18.8
Age	13	18.8
Education	11	15.9
Interests and Activities	8	11.6
Family Criminality	7	10.1
Alcoholic Involvement	6	8.7
Homosexuality	6	8.7
Drug Usage	4	5.8
Confinement Status	4	5.8
Military History	4	5.8
Religion	3	4.3
Residence	2	2.9
Offense	0	0.0
Plea	0	0.0
Legal Representation	0	0.0
Place of Birth	0	0.0
Race	0	0.0

three, probation with psychiatric treatment as a condition; three, commitment for observation and study; and one, imprisonment. The number of cards selected was four to twelve.

Cases 1 and 3, where the probation officers agreed on the recommendation, were selected by the writer as cases likely to result in consistent recommendations; one for probation; the other for imprisonment. The three other cases, which resulted in considerable divergence of recommendations, were chosen as cases where clear and uniform recommendations were not likely to emerge. However, all five were chosen as typical of those coming to the attention of the U.S. Probation Officer.

The variation observed in the recommendations made by the probation officers in the five cases takes on increased significance when we consider the final disposition of cases in the district court. Agreement between recommendation of officers and dispositions in court has been shown to be 96 percent for recommendations of probation and 88 percent for recommendations of imprisonment.[4]

While the divergence in recommendations may appear distressing, there is a countervailing force in the operational situation; namely, the development of more uniform recommendations through the informal process of discussing cases in the office, at coffee breaks, at lunch, and so forth, and the formal process of case conferences between the officers and supervisory personnel. In addition, if the chief probation officer disagrees with the recommendation of a probation officer, he may append his own recommendation to the presentence report. Inasmuch as all presentence reports and recommendations are reviewed by the chief probation officer, the tendency toward uniformity is reinforced and formalized. However, these processes are still relatively inexplicit and unofficial aspects in the decision-making process.

IMPLICATIONS

This inquiry into decision-making by probation officers, and, more specifically, decision-making as it relates to the presentence report recommendation, utilized the "decision-game" device developed by Wilkins. In general terms, this has been found to be a satisfactory instrument for simulating the presentence report investigation, although there are obvious limitations to any substitute for analysis of an actual investigation. The "decision-game" technique appears to have far greater application for correctional research than has been utilized to date.

The data suggest probation officers make decisions relating to presentence report recommendations with relatively small amounts of information. The current study reflects an average of 4.7 items of information utilized prior to the decision, and a range of one to thirteen items employed in making the decision. The receipt of additional information after the recommendation has little effect upon the recommendation, although the additional data may result in some modification in a few cases.

The probation officers, as a group, employ similar methods and techniques in their information gathering activities before making a decision. Even though these officers develop a specific and unique method of style, the individual variations are not significant. Attempts to isolate and identify these differences according to the personal characteristics (academic background, years of experience, etc.) of the probation officers were unsuccessful. Further study may establish significant relationships between method of decision-making and the background of the individual officer.

Since most of the data collected in the presentence report investigation is not employed in the development of a recommendation, further research may uncover what information is required and used to make decisions elsewhere in the

[4] Robert M. Carter, "It Is Respectfully Recommended . . . ", *Federal Probation*, June 1966, pp. 38-42.

correctional process. The data not employed in effecting the presentence report recommendation may be of some significance in decision-making by institution and paroling authorities or by the district courts, although such usage appears limited in application as well as relevance.

Although the "research" decisions of probation officers for three of the five cases manifested substantial differences, a greater uniformity actually exists by virtue of both formal and informal processes within the Probation Office. These informal processes and their influence in effecting uniformity also warrant further investigation.

Previous research has identified demographic characteristics which differentiated between offenders recommended for probation and for imprisonment.[5] The data most significant for this differentiation (prior criminality, current offense, and stability factors) are the items of information the probation officers most often collect early in the presentence investigation and use for presentence report recommendations.

This finding raises several questions: How much presentence investigation time is utilized to gather information of very minor significance in making a recommendation? More positively, how long does it take (or how much effort is required) to gather the "essential" information, information on the current offense, prior record, and so on? Do probation officers, after "deciding" on a recommendation early in the presentence investigation, seek further information which justifies the decision, rather than information which might lead to modification or rejection of that recommendation?

Although the current inquiry into decision-making is limited in scope, it clearly indicates the need for additional research into the decision-making process and its relationship to the total correctional process.

[5] Lohman, Wahl, and Carter, *supra* note 2.

16
Some Factors in Sentencing Policy

ROBERT M. CARTER, LESLIE T. WILKINS

The probation officer as a member of the court staff has two major functions to fulfill. The first is to conduct an investigation of an offender which culminates in a presentence or probation report. This report is frequently accompanied by a recommendation to the court as to the selection of an appropriate sentence. The second function is to provide supervision for offenders placed on probation or some other form of conditional liberty. Despite the recent focus of correctional interest and attention, and a considerable volume of literature, the terms and conditions of these functions remain relatively vague. It is proposed to examine here a segment of one of these, namely the presentence report recommendation and its relationship to the court disposition. Our purpose is not so much to provide data, but to make explicit some questions about presentence report recommendations and their relation to court dispositions.

Even though corrections is a relatively new field in the United States, some of its components have already become so institutionalized that they form a cornerstone for the development of a correctional folklore or mythology. In essence, it appears that the increasing problem of crime and delinquency is being addressed by the application of principles and practices which have not been substantially modified, or even questioned, since their inception. Yet, the correc-

SOURCE. *Journal of Criminal Law, Criminology and Police Science,* **58** (4), 1967, pp. 503-514. Reprinted with special permission from the *Journal of Criminal Law, Criminology and Police Science.* Copyright © by the Northwestern School of Law, Volume **58** (4).

tional systems must change if for no other reason than that of the increasing number of offenders processed. Tradition would have it that the changes be in the direction of increased probation and parole staff, prison personnel, new institutions, and related services. If these be the sole nature of the changes—more of what already exists—there will be a reliance upon a view of the past without a realistic vision of the future.

CASE LOAD SIZE

The fifty-unit workload as the standard for probation and parole supervision is an example of one of the myths. Where did this number come from? On what empirical data is it based? Is it an appropriate limitation of case load size? If it is not appropriate, what should be the workload for corrections? A search of the literature dates the fifty-unit concept back to at least 1922, when Charles L. Chute, then President of the National Probation Association, observed: "To this end fifty cases is as many as any probation officer ought to carry."[1] The fifty-unit concept found its way in the prestigious academic literature when Sutherland[2] in 1934, and Tannenbaum[3] in 1938, suggested that fifty cases "is generally regarded as the maximum number" and "the best practice would limit the caseload of a probation officer to fifty cases." The concept of fifty entered the professional literature when the American Prison Association in 1946 indicated that a probation officer "should not have more than fifty cases under continuous supervision."[4] An almost identical statement appears in the 1954 revision of the Manual of Correctional Standards.[5] Not until 1966, (while still suggesting a fifty-unit workload) did the American Correctional Association indicate that "where methods of classification for case loads have been developed through research, varying standards of workloads may prevail."[6]

The institutionalization of the fifty-unit concept is now firmly entrenched. Budgets for operating agencies, testimony before legislative bodies, standards of practice, and projections for future operational needs all center about this number. There is no evidence of any empirical justification for fifty, nor for that matter, any other number.

The following discussion relates mainly to the federal probation system, and we are indebted to the Administrative Office of the United States Courts for furnishing pertinent data. Information has also been drawn from the San Francisco Project, a study of the federal probation system, supported by the National Institute of Mental Health.[7] It should be noted that these data cover different

---

[1] Chute, *Probation and Suspended Sentence*, 12 J. Crim. L. & C. 562 (1922).

[2] Sutherland, *Principles of Criminology*, 359, (1934).

[3] Tannenbaum, *Crime and the Community*, 462 (1938).

[4] *Manual of Suggested Standards for a State Correctional System* (Am. Pris. Assn.) 13 (1946).

[5] *Manual of Correctional Standards* (Am. Corr. Assn.) 43 (1954).

[6] *Ibid.* 109 (1966).

[7] See Lohman, Wahl & Carter, *A Non-Technical Description of the San Francisco Project*, The San Francisco Project Series (April 1965).

populations over different periods of time, and are not to be seen as interesting in themselves, but as throwing light on the presentence report recommendation and court disposition.

RECOMMENDATIONS AND DISPOSITIONS

The Relationship

The presentence report is a document basic to the functioning of both judicial and correctional administrations. The contents of the report, including the recommendation, assist the court in making a judgment consistent with its dual responsibilities to society and the defendant. Within the federal system the report aids the institutions within the Bureau of Prisons in determining classification and treatment programs and also in planning for subsequent release. The report provides information to the Board of Parole, furnishing information believed to be pertinent to its deliberations. Furthermore, the report contributes to the probation officer's rehabilitative efforts while an offender is under his supervision.[8]

In February, 1965, with the publication of a 39-page monograph entitled *The Presentence Investigation Report*, a standard outline and format was adopted for the preparation of presentence reports in the federal courts.[9] The final paragraph headings of the report are "Evaluative Summary" and "Recommendation." The importance of these paragraphs is recognized by the American Correctional Association which includes among its standards for the preparation of presentence reports a "recommendation for or against probation, or for other disposition according to court policy."[10]

The fact that there is a substantial number of sentencing alternatives available to federal judges also means that an equal number of possible recommendations may be considered by the probation officer. The selection ranges, of course, from probation with or without a fine or restitution, and/or jail sentence, and imprisonment under various statutes which determine parole eligibility, to other dispositions which include commitment for observation and study and continuances for community observation.

Because of this variety of available disposals, the relationship between a recommendation and a disposition may be more simply considered from one of two directions. The first method would be to contrast recommendations for probation made by the probation officers with actual court dispositions resulting in probation. The second would be from an opposite direction, viewing recommendations against probation (or for imprisonment) with actual court dispositions for probation.

---

[8] The federal probation officer supervises persons released on parole or mandatory release from federal correctional institutions or the United States Disciplinary Barracks.

[9] *The Presentence Investigation Report* (Adm. Off. U.S. Cts.) (1965).

[10] *Manual of Correctional Standards* (Am. Corr. Assn.) 521 (2d ed. 1959).

Data developed during the San Francisco Project contrast recommendations and dispositions for 500 consecutive cases processed through the United States District Court in the Northern District of California between September 1964 and August 1965.[11] These data indicate that:

> . . . there is a close relationship between the recommendation of probation and the actual granting of probation. Probation was recommended in 227 cases and was granted in 212 of those cases. If the 7 cases of "observation and study" are not included, probation was granted, when recommended, 212 of the 220 cases or in 96 percent of the cases. In only 2 of the 227 cases was there a substantial difference between the probation officer's recommendation and the court's disposition of the cases. In these instances, prison sentences were ordered where probation had been recommended.[12]

These data closely parallel the California data. The percentages of probation officer recommendations for probation followed by California Superior Courts, for the years cited, are shown in Table 1.

Data on the federal system, arranged by the ten judicial circuits, indicate the relationship, shown in Table 2, between probation officer recommendations for probation and such dispositions in court for Fiscal Year 1964.

The patterns in these first two tables exhibit almost total agreement between a probation officer's recommendation for probation and an actual disposition of probation. However, this trend appears less stable when viewed from the opposite perspective—the relationship between recommendations against probation (or for imprisonment) and court dispositions of probation. California data reveal, in Table, 3 the percentages of "against probation" recommendations and probation dispositions in court.

Table 1   *Percentage of Probation Officer Recommendations for Probation Followed by California Superior Courts (%)*

1959	95.6
1960	96.4
1961	96.0
1962	96.5
1963	97.2
1964	97.3
1965	96.7

Source. State of California, Department of Justice. *Delinquency and Probation in California*, 1964, p. 168; and *Crime and Delinquency in California*, 1965, pp. 98–99.

[11] Carter, *It is Respectfully Recommended* . . . , 30 Fed. Prob. 2 (1966).
[12] *Ibid.* 41.

Table 2   *Percentage of Probation Officer Recommendations for Probation Followed by Ten Judicial Circuits, Fiscal Year 1964(%)*

First Circuit	99.4
Second Circuit	96.0
Third Circuit	93.2
Fourth Circuit	93.3
Fifth Circuit	95.2
Sixth Circuit	93.9
Seventh Circuit	89.9
Eighth Circuit	95.0
Ninth Circuit	93.5
Tenth Circuit	97.8
Overall	94.1

SOURCE. Data furnished by the Administrative Office of the United States Courts.

It is noteworthy that California authorities indicate the "superior court judges are more lenient than probation officers as to who should be granted probation."[13] This pattern has already been observed by one of the authors,[14] and by others,[15] in respect to the federal probation officer. Further confirmation of this pattern is found throughout the federal system as indicated by a review, in Table 4, of "against probation" recommendations and probation dispositions according to the ten judicial circuits for Fiscal Year 1964.

Table 3   *Percentage of Probation Officer Recommendations Against Probation not Followed by California Superior Courts (%)*

1959	13.5
1960	12.8
1961	14.8
1962	17.4
1963	21.6
1964	21.1
1965	19.9

SOURCE. State of California, Department of Justice, *Delinquency and Probation in California*, 1964, p. 168, and *Crime and Delinquency in California*, 1965, pp. 98–99.

[13] *Deliquency and Probation in California, 1964* (Calif. Dept. of Justice) 166 (1964)
[14] Carter, *supra* note 11.
[15] Lohman, Wahl & Carter, *San Francisco Project* series (Report No. 2) 8 (Berkeley: June 1965).

Table 4   *Percentage of Probation Officer Recommenda-tions Against Probation Not Followed by Ten Judical Cir-cuits. Fiscal Year 1964(%)*

First Circuit	7.3
Second Circuit	9.5
Third Circuit	27.4
Fourth Circuit	31.8
Fifth Circuit	11.5
Sixth Circuit	19.3
Seventh Circuit	15.9
Eight Circuit	16.5
Ninth Circuit	23.3
Tenth Circuit	9.2
Overall	19.7

SOURCE. Data furnished by the Administrative Office of the United States Courts.

As already indicated, the probation officer has a wide latitude in his choice of a recommendation. Table 5 presents data on the specific recommendations of probation officers in the Northern District of California between September 1964 and February 1967, and shows the wide variety of possible recommendations.

Table 6 presents overall data on the relationship between recommendations and dispositions of 1,232 cases processed through the District Court in Northern California. The reader will note that of 601 cases recommended for probation, 15 were ordered imprisoned; of 334 cases recommended for imprisonment, 31 were placed on probation.

These data seem to support certain generalizations about the nature of the relationship between probation officer recommendations and court dispositions. We have seen that there is a very strong relationship between recommendations *for probation* and court dispositions of probation, an average agreement of about ninety-five percent. It has also been observed that the strength of the relationship diminishes slightly when recommendations *against probation* (or for imprison-ment) are contrasted with court dispositions of probation. Thus, it may be con-cluded that where disagreements exist between recommendations and dis-positions, they occur when the officer recommends imprisonment. In a sense, if this relationship measures "punitiveness" then it may be concluded that the probation officer is more punitive than the judge.

OUTCOME OF SUPERVISION ACCORDING TO THE RECOMMENDATION

Very limited data are available on the outcome of supervision, i.e., the viola-tion rate, according to recommendations of probation officers. The 1964 cohort

Table 5   *Probation Officers' Recommendations as to Sentence Northern District of California, September 1964 to February 1967*

Recommendation	Total	Percent of Total
All Cases	1,232	100.0
No recommendation	67	5.4
Mandatory sentence (Under certain narcotic law violations)	45	3.6
Probation	601	48.9
Regular	(284)	(23.1)
With Fine and/or Restitution	(197)	(16.0)
Split Sentence (Imprisonment up to Six Months Followed by Probation)	(49)	(4.0)
Under Youth Corrections Act	(71)	(5.8)
Fine only	38	3.1
Jail only	35	2.8
Imprisonment	334	27.1
Parole Eligibility After 1/3 Sentence	(234)	(19.0)
Parole Eligibility At Any Time	(64)	(5.2)
Under Youth Corrections Act	(36)	(2.9)
Observation and study	51	4.2
Adult	(39)	(3.2)
Youth	(12)	(1.0)
Continuance for 90 days observation	16	1.3
Deferred prosecution	3	.2
Commitment under federal juvenile delinquency act	2	.2
Other recommendations	40	3.3

SOURCE. Unpublished San Francisco Project data.

study of Davis[16] examined the violation status of 11,638 adult defendants granted probation in California Superior Courts between 1956 and 1958. Davis showed that 27.1 percent of the defendants recommended for and placed on probation were "revoked," while 36.7 percent of the defendants placed on probation against the recommendation of the probation officer were revoked. Davis concluded that the "difference in revocation rates was very significant and indicates that the two groups were not alike in their tendency to recidivism."

It is questionable that this single explanation for the ten percent differential in revocation rates occurs simply because of differences in the two groups. There

[16] Davis, *A Study of Adult Probation Violation Rates by Means of the Cohort Approach*, 55 J. CRIM L., C. & P. S. 70 (1964).

Table 6 *Probation Officers' Recommendation and Subsequent Court Dispositions, Northern District of California, September 1964 to February 1967*

Recommendation	Total	Disposition								
		Mandatory	Probation	Fine Only	Jail Only	Imprisonment	Observation and Study	Continuances	Deferred Prosecution	Other
All Cases	1,232	45	671	30	27	337	73	18	2	29
No Recommendation	67	—	44	2	2	14	1	—	—	4
Mandatory	45	45	—	—	—	—	—	—	—	—
Probation	601	—	551	5	3	15	17	2	—	8
Fine Only	38	—	14	22	—	1	—	—	—	1
Jail Only	35	—	5	1	19	8	2	—	—	—
Imprisonment	334	—	31	—	2	281	13	5	—	2
Observation and Study	51	—	3	—	—	9	38	1	—	—
Continuances	16	—	6	—	—	—	—	10	—	—
Deferred Prosecution	3	—	—	—	—	—	—	—	2	1
Federal Juvenile Delinquency Act	2	—	1	—	—	—	—	—	—	1
Other	40	—	16	—	1	9	2	—	—	12

SOURCE. Unpublished San Francisco Project data.

are two other possible explanations for this. One explanation may be that subtle differences exist in the supervision provided by a probation officer who may feel "resentful" in having an individual placed on probation against his recommendation. The second possibility is that the defendant's attitude toward a probation officer who recommended that he be imprisoned instead of placed on probation may affect the outcome of supervision. While there are no measures of these two negative factors, it is possible that they account for a large portion of the observed differential. There are other interesting studies which support the hypothesis of self-fulfilling prophecies.

Another way of viewing Davis' data is to emphasize that 63.3 percent of those who received an unfavoable probation recommendation but were placed on probation completed their probation without revocation. Thus, to deny probation to all those with negative recommendations from probation officers would suggest that approximately two out of every three defendants with such recommendations would be denied the opportunity to complete probation successfully. Davis inquired as to the number of defendants who, denied probation on unfavorable recommendations, would have succeeded on probation if given the opportunity. There are, at this time, no data to answer this question.[17]

Other data are available from the Administrative Office of the United States Courts which indicate that despite considerable variation in the use of probation, the overall violation rates, or the rates broken down by "major," "minor," or "technical" are almost identical. Table 7 of the Administrative Office report is reproduced here to show probation violation rates for 1965, according to the actual percentage of persons placed on probation by the 88 U.S. District Courts, arranged by quartiles.

The data in Table 7 reveal that approximately 19 percent of those placed under probation supervision violate the terms of this conditional liberty, regardless of the percentage of the offender population on probation.

FACTORS AFFECTING THE AGREEMENT BETWEEN RECOMMENDATIONS AND DISPOSITIONS

Reverting to the possible explanations for the high degree of agreement between probation officer recommendations and court dispositions, it is possible that four factors, operating independently, but more probably simultaneously, account for this relationship:

1. The court, having such high regard for the professional qualities and competence of its probation staff, "follows" the probation recommendation—a recommendation made by the person (probation officer) who best knows the defendant by reason of the presentence investigation;

2. There are many offenders who are "obviously" probation or prison cases;

[17] Wilkins, *A Small Comparative Study of the Results of Probation*, 8 *British J. Crimino. 201* (1958).

Table 7 *(Table A 18 of the Administrative Office of the U.S. Courts covering 88 United States District Courts) Comparison of the Use of Probation in District Courts, by Type of Violation, Fiscal Year 1965 (Excludes violators of immigration laws, wagering tax laws and violators of Federal regulatory acts)*

Item	88 District Courts	Quartile Groups of Courts			
		First 22 District Courts	Second 22 District Courts	Third 22 District Courts	Fourth 22 District Courts
Average					
Actual percent placed on probation	49.0	65.9	53.8	47.2	36.9
Total removed	11,259	2,263	2,759	3,678	2,559
No violations	9,157	1,843	2,267	2,973	2,074
Violated probation	2,102	420	492	705	485
Technical violation	344	78	85	106	75
Minor violation	577	111	120	216	130
Major violation	1,181	231	287	383	280
Percent					
Violated Probation	18.7	18.5	17.8	19.2	18.9
Technical violation	3.1	3.4	3.1	2.9	2.9
Minor violation	5.1	4.9	4.3	5.9	5.1
Major violation	10.5	10.2	10.4	10.4	10.9

SOURCE. Administrative Office of the United States Courts, *Persons Under the Supervision of the Federal Probation System.* (Washington, D.C.: 1965), p. 33.

3. Probation officers write their reports and make recommendations anticipating the recommendation the court desires to receive. (In this situation, the probation officer is quite accurately "second-guessing" the court disposition);

4. Probation officers in making their recommendations place great emphasis on the same factors as does the court in selecting a sentencing alternative.

Data from the San Francisco Project confirm the fact that probation officers and judges apply approximately equal significance to similar factors.[18] Examination of 500 probation officer recommendations according to the major categories of recommendations for probation and recommendations for imprisonment (or against probation), produced data on the legal and demographic characteristics of the offender population which had an important effect upon the recommendation selected. In general terms, the proportion of recommendations for probation increased with the number of years of education, average monthly income, higher occupational levels, residence, marital and employment stability, participation in church activities, and a good military record. Recommendations for imprisonment (or against probation) increased proportionately when offenders exhibited such characteristics as homosexuality, alcoholic involvement, the use of weapons or violence in the commission of the offense, the existence of family criminality, and drug usage. Age (in the range examined) did not significantly distinguish between the two recommendations, and racial and religious affiliation differences were absent. The female, however, was more likely to be recommended for probation than the male offender.

Certain offense categories (e.g. embezzlement, theft from interstate shipments or theft of government property, and false statement) usually produced recommendations for probation, while other offense categories (e.g. bank robbery, the interstate transportation of stolen motor vehicles [Dyer Act], and National Defense law violation) usually resulted in recommendations for imprisonment. Offenders who entered a plea of guilty, retained their own attorneys, or who were released to the community on bail, bond, or personal recognizance while the presentence investigation was being conducted, had significantly greater chances of being recommended for probation. It is recognized, of course, that a recommendation for or against probation is generally based upon some combination of characteristics—some obvious, others subtle—rather than upon any single characteristic or piece of information.

It is apparent that not all factors are of equal significance in determining the probation officer's recommendation. Accordingly, statistical computations produced a general ranking of the significance or importance of various factors.[19]

A further examination of the 500 cases was made, reviewing the selection of the sentencing alternative by the court. Again, statistical computations were

[18] See Lohman, Wahl & Carter, *San Francisco Project* series (Reports 4 and 5) (Berkeley: December 1965, February 1966).

[19] *Ibid.*

completed and a second rank order of the significant or important factors was produced.

These two sets of data—one relating to the recommendation, the other to the disposition—are summarized in Table 8. The rankings were based on probability

Table 8   *Rank of Demographic Factors Utilized by Probation Officers for Recommendations and District Court Judges for Sentencing Alternatives. According to Probability and Contingency Coefficient Values (500 Federal Offenders, Northern District of California September 1964 to August 1965).*

Demographic Factors	Probation Officers' Ranking	District Court Judges' Ranking
Prior Record	1	3
Confinement Status	2	2
Number of Arrests	3	4
Offense	4	1
Longest Employment	5	5
Occupation	6	8
Number of Months Employed	7	6
Income	8	10
Longest Residence	9	7
Military History	10	9
Number of Residence Changes	11	17
Distance to Offense	12	14
Number of Aliases	13	24
Marital Status	14	11
Legal Representation	15	13
Weapons and Violence	16	15
Family Criminality	17	21
Plea	18	18
Education	19	12
Church Attendance	20	16
Narcotics Usage	21	23
Sex	22	19
Alcoholic Involvement	23	25
Crime Partners	24	20
Homosexuality	25	26
Race	26	28
Age	27	22
Religion	28	27

SOURCE. Joseph D. Lohman, Albert Wahl and Robert M. Carter. *San Francisco Project* series, Report 5, (Berkeley: February 1966), p. 68.

Spearman's p = .90

and contigency coefficient values. A correlation was computed and a significant value of .90 was obtained. These data indicate that there is considerable agreement between probation officers and judges as to the significance of certain factors and characteristics for decisions relating to probation or imprisonment recommendations and dispositions.

Another possible explanation of the close agreement between recommendations and dispositions is certainly that some cases are clearly probation or imprisonment cases. However, there are no "hard" data to identify which cases are "clearly" probation or prison cases. An actual, but extreme example of an "imprisonment case" is the bank robber who, armed with an automatic pistol and with an accomplice waiting in a stolen automobile, robbed a bank of $35,000, pistol-whipped a teller, and in the flight from the scene, engaged in a gun battle with pursuing police. It is doubted that probation officers or judges would be inclined to see probation as a suitable disposition for such a case, regardless of any other factors involved. An example of the "probation case" is the young married offender, who, unemployed prior to the Christmas season, made a false statement to the Post Office for employment, concealing a prior misdemeanor arrest. In general terms, this type of offender would normally be seen as a suitable candidate for probation.

From observation and conversations with judges and probation officers during the past years, it appears that judges do indeed have a high regard for their probation staff and value their professional judgment as to the disposition of a case. It is suspected that this is especially true in the federal system in which probation officers are appointed by the court and serve at its pleasure. This esteem for probation officers and their services by the court may also contribute to the high agreement between recommendations and dispositions, even though there are no statistical data to support this.

The fourth potential explanation for the close agreement between recommendations and dispositons—probation officers anticipating the recommendation the court desires—is now to be discussed.

VARIATION AMONG PROBATION OFFICERS AND PROBATION OFFICES

Disparities in sentencing have been of considerable interest in recent years and attempts to reduce these frequently observed differentials have normally been focused on judges. For example, sentencing institutes for judges have been developed at the federal and state level, as well as training programs for newly appointed or elected judges. That attention should be directed toward judges—for they impose the sentences—is certainly normal and, on the surface, a logical approach to resolving disparities. However, this pattern ignores one of the facts of community life—in this case the judicial community and its social system—that many persons play a part in the functioning of the community. Included in the judicial community are probation officers, prosecutors, defense attorneys, perhaps to a lesser extent the law enforcement agencies, and other judges on the same bench.

It seems to have been generally assumed that the judges are solely responsible for the disparities and that the remainder of the judicial community plays only a minor role which remains constant, neither supporting nor contributing to the disparities. Although we do not have complete data upon which a judicial "community-effect" can be shown to be a basis for disparities, there are data available which demonstrate the supporting role of at least one member, namely the probation officer.

If we assume that probation officers are "constant" and that judges are "variable," we would expect to find significant differences in the relationship between officer recommendations and court dispositions as we move toward extremes in the use of probation or imprisonment. We would not, in the federal system for example, expect to find the more than 94 percent agreement between recommendations and dispositions spread uniformly throughout the system, for some courts use probation frequently, others infrequently. In Fiscal Year 1965, individual federal courts had a range of probation usage in excess of fifty percent, with one court using probation for 23.8 percent of its cases, another for 75.7 percent of its cases. The percentage of defendants on probation in Fiscal Year 1965 by the ten judicial circuits is shown in Table 9.

Thus, on a circuit-wide basis, there is a high of 63.8 percent in the usage of probation ranging to a low of 43.7 percent, an overall spread of twenty percent, and as noted above, the variation is even more marked among individual courts. Six of the eighty-eight district courts used probation in excess of seventy percent

Table 9   *Percentage Use of Probation in Ten Federal Judicial Circuits (%)*

First Circuit	53.0
Second Circuit	45.2
Third Circuit	63.8
Fourth Circuit	60.8
Fifth Circuit	44.8
Sixth Circuit	44.3
Seventh Circuit	44.4
Eighth Circuit	49.9
Ninth Circuit	49.0
Tenth Circuit	43.7
Overall	49.0

SOURCE. Administrative Office of the United States Courts. *Persons Under the Supervision of the Federal Probation System, Fiscal Year 1965*, pp. 103–105.

for their defendants; twelve courts used probation for less than forty percent of their defendants.

Despite the variation among courts, individually or circuit wide, the relationship between probation officer recommendations and court dispositions is generally quite constant, whether there is high, moderate, or low usage of probation. This may be seen more precisely in Table 10 which provides data for Fiscal Year 1964 on sixteen selected federal courts: the five with the highest usage of probation, the five with the lowest use of probation, and the six courts which were within one percent of the national average for use of probation.

It will be seen, for example, that in District *A*, probation was recommended for approximately three of each four defendants (147–55); in District *H*, the recommendations are about equal (152–149), while in District *N*, probation is recommended for about one defendant in three (148–310). However, the "agreement" rate between probation recommendations and dispositions in District *A* is 97.3 percent, in District *H*, 95.4 percent, and in District *N*, 93.7 percent.

These data indicate clearly that the recommendation-disposition relationship does not vary greatly from court to court, and that disparities in sentencing are supported, at least in terms of recommendations, by the probation officer member of the judicial "influence group". To be sure, there may be differences in the Districts which justify high or low use of probation, but thus far these have not been demonstrated. These data raise some interesting and important questions regarding the utility of sentencing institutes for judges, by themselves, as the solution to disparities, and suggest that probation officers, and perhaps prosecuting and defense attorneys, be included in such institutes.

The data in Table 10 have indicated that there is considerable variation in officer recommendations for or against probation in different Districts, but that rate of agreement between recommendations and dispositions is relatively constant between Districts. Accordingly, we would expect to find a common frame of mind, or "influence group set", among officers in a single District which leads to the agreement in that District, regardless of the frequency of probation or imprisonment dispositions. Thus, where probation is used frequently, we would expect the officers in that court to be sympathetic to such usage and we would anticipate that little variation would exist among officers. If this is the case, we would not expect to find much significant variation among probation officers in a single District. We would not expect to find large differences among colleagues appointed by the same court, operating in a similar fashion as regards court and office policies and directives, appointed under uniform standards, paid identical salaries, and theoretically sharing similar views of the correctional process.

Let us return to our data on the 1,232 recommendations made by the probation officers in the Northern District of California as shown in Table 5. By restricting ourselves to a probation-imprisonment, dichotomy, we observe that probation was recommended 64.3 percent of the time (601 of 935 cases) and that imprisonment was recommended 35.7 percent (334 of 935 cases). The recommendations of 19 probation officers in Northern California for probation or imprison-

Table 10 Use of Probation and Recommendations for and Against Probation by Selected United States District Fiscal Year 1964

	Percentage Use of Probation	Recommended for Probation			Recommended Against Probation			Recommendations Given by Probation Officers: Percent of Total Cases
		Number of Defendants	Number Granted Probation	Percentage Granted Probation	Number of Defendants	Number Granted Probation	Percentage Granted Probation	
A	78.3	147	143	97.3	55	20	36.4	73.2
B	71.4	144	137	95.1	90	31	34.4	88.0
C	70.7	27	26	96.3	7	0	—	82.9
D	70.4	20	19	95.0	11	2	18.2	43.7
E	70.2	125	125	100.0	28	1	3.6	77.3
F	50.8	106	100	94.3	112	17	15.2	89.3
G	50.0	16	16	100.0	17	1	5.9	82.5
H	50.0	152	145	95.4	149	19	12.8	80.9
I	50.0	14	13	92.9	9	0	—	60.5
J	49.7	12	12	100.0	36	6	16.7	15.4
K	49.6	29	28	96.6	36	0	—	47.4
L	36.8	28	28	100.0	19	0	—	13.6
M	36.5	61	61	100.0	117	14	12.0	73.0
N	35.6	158	148	93.7	310	21	6.8	87.8
O	28.5	92	82	89.1	74	25	33.8	35.1
P	26.3	44	38	86.4	174	24	13.8	90.8
Total for all District courts	50.2	6868	6463	94.1	7691	1518	19.7	63.1

Source. Data furnished by the Administrative Office of the United States Courts.

ment are presented in Table 11. (Officers who made less than 15 recommendations are excluded.)

The percentage of recommendations for probation is almost 50 percent—from a low of 40.0 to a high of 88.9 percent. Three officers recommended probation for less than 50 percent of their cases; three officers between 50 and 60 percent, six between 60 and 70 percent, five between 70 and 80 percent, and two in excess of 80 percent.

While this individual variation may be attributed, in part, to the geographic basis for assignment of cases or to other administrative reasons, it is statistically significant and suggests that probation officers, even in the same District do not view the correctional process from identical perspectives.

What accounts for this variation among officers? In part, administrative and geographic considerations may be an explanation. There may be differences in probation-suitability among persons from metropolitan areas, (e.g., San Francisco-Oakland) and less developed or rural areas such as the northern coast or

Table 11 *Individual Probation Officer Recommendations for Probation and Imprisonment Northern District of California, September 1964 to February 1967*

Probation Officer	Number of Recommendations	Number of Probation Recommendations	Number of Prison Recommendations	Percentage of Probation Recommendations
1	55	40	15	72.7
2	39	25	14	64.1
3	46	21	25	45.7
4	57	35	22	61.4
5	16	14	2	87.5
6	20	13	7	65.0
7	55	22	33	40.0
8	38	22	16	57.9
9	22	17	5	77.3
10	58	46	12	79.3
11	59	32	27	54.2
12	57	35	22	61.4
13	54	42	12	77.8
14	36	17	19	47.2
15	56	34	22	60.7
16	46	31	15	67.4
17	60	43	17	71.7
18	18	16	2	88.9
19	42	24	18	57.1

SOURCE. Unpublished San Francisco Project data.

central valleys of California. But it is equally possible that these variations are due to personal characteristics, including academic training, age, and vocational background. Some general, but not conclusive observations can be made based on the probation officers in Northern California. For example, probation officers with graduate training or graduate degrees in social work or social welfare recommended probation for 56.3 percent of their cases; officers with graduate work or graduate degrees in criminology in 69.6 percent of their cases, and officers with graduate work or graduate degrees in sociology in 67.7 percent of their cases. Officers with the longest service recommended probation for 54.0 percent of their cases, while the "newer" officers recommended probation for 68.4 percent. Three hypotheses are suggested by these and other data:

1. Some of the variation in probation officer recommendations is a product of the individual background of the officer and includes vocational experience and academic training.

2. The differences or variations tend to diminish with the period of employment; that is, officers with different backgrounds are far more dissimilar upon entering the probation service than after exposure to the agency.

3. With an increase in the period of service (i.e., more experience) there is a decrease in recommendations for probation. This may represent a more "realistic" or less "optimistic" view of the benefits of probation treatment for a greater number of offenders, than was the view held by the officer earlier in his professional career.

"SECOND-GUESSING" OR "FOLLOWING"

There is, in our search for variation, the possibility that the probation officer attempts to second-guess the court by making recommendations which are anticipated to be those desired by the court. If this were the case, one measure of this factor would be that different judges receive different rates or percentages of probation or imprisonment recommendations. Thus, properly "second-guessing" a punitive judge would require a larger proportion of imprisonment recommendations; second-guessing a "lenient" judge would require more probation recommendations. Returning to the data on the 1,232 cases in the Northern District of California, and again restricting ourselves to a probation-imprisonment dichotomy, we find some, but not significant variation in the percentage of probation recommendations to individual judges. These data are in Table 12. Since none of these judges has a reputation of being punitive or lenient, we can only surmise that in this District, there is little if any second-guessing.

A review of Table 12 will also indicate that individual judges are equally receptive to recommendations for probation; the relationship between recommendations for probation and such dispositions being 97.2 percent over-all and constant between judges.

It appears that judges "follow" probation officer recommendations; there is no other ready explanation of the individual officer variation in probation recom-

Table 12 *Recommendations for and Against Probation According to United States District Court Judges Northern District of California September 1964 to February 1967*

Judge	Number of Cases Disposed of in Court	Number of Recommendations for Probation	Number of Recommendations Against Probation	Percentage of Cases Recommended for Probation	Number of Cases Granted Probation	Number of Cases Denied Probation	Percentage Agreement Between Probation Recommendations and Dispositions
Total	831	527	304	63.4	512	278	97.2
1	64	40	24	62.5	38	23	95.0
2	58	30	28	51.7	29	23	96.7
3	160	103	57	64.4	99	53	96.1
4	156	114	42	73.1	111	38	97.4
5	88	57	31	64.8	57	30	100.0
6	100	58	42	58.0	56	36	96.6
7	60	39	21	65.0	38	18	97.4
8	73	46	27	63.0	44	26	95.7
9	72	40	32	55.6	40	31	100.0

SOURCE: Unpublished San Francisco Project data.

mendations and the high overall relationship between recommendations and dispositions. This also tends to confirm the observation that probation officers contribute to the problems of disparities in sentencing. From these data, all four previously suggested explanations of the close agreement between recommendation and disposition (probation officers and judges giving approximately equal weight to similar factors, the "following" of recommendations by the court, the presence of "obvious" probation or imprisonment cases, and some "second-guessing") appear appropriate.

SUMMARY

In this paper, some of the dangers of continued reliance on tradition and the development of a body of correctional folklore have been pointed out. It has been determined that the relationship between recommendations for and dispositions of probation are high and that the relationship diminishes when viewed from the recommendations against and the subsequent grant of probation perspective. Limited data on the outcome of supervision by recommendation and by percentage use of probation are provided. We have inquired into the reasons for the close agreement between recommendation and disposition and suggest that four factors, in varying degrees, account for it. We have observed that the overall relationship between recommendation and disposition does not vary from District Court to District Court, but rather remains relatively constant, regardless of the percentage use of probation. We suggest that disparities in sentencing are supported by the probation officer and it appears that these differences, in part, are a reflection of the officer's individual academic training and experience. Length of service brings about a trend toward conformity with colleagues and the development of a more conservative perspective toward the use of probation.

There are other segments of the presentence report process to which questions should be addressed. These include operational and administrative considerations, the decision-making processes of probation officers, and an examination of the nature and impact of the social system of correctional agencies. Within the operational considerations would be inquiries as to the role of subprofessionals in presentence investigations, the rearrangement of the standard presentence format to provide a developmental sketch instead of the current segmented report, a determination as to the appropriateness of "confidential" presentence reports, the collection of presentence data in a fashion which allows computer analysis, and the separation of the investigation and supervision functions. Although some examination has been made of the decision-making process,[20] we need additional information about the sequence of data collection, the relative importance of certain kinds of data, and the eventual use of the data for decision-

---

[20] *Ibid.*

making within the correctional system. We find almost a complete void in knowledge on the social systems of correctional agencies, although available data indicate that the system itself has a profound influence on job behavior, beliefs, values, and the definition and achievement of correctional goals. Indeed, we know more about the social systems of the offenders with whom we deal than about the systems of the agencies which provide correctional services.

There are vast gaps in our knowledge about the entire correctional process, but these gaps may be closed by imaginative, innovative, and creative research and operational designs and programs. This requires a willingness to subject our current traditional, correctional models to scrutiny and a willingness to set aside those features, cherished though they may be, which are inefficient and ineffective.

PAROLE

This section begins with the official viewpoint (insofar as there can be any such thing) with regard to parole and draws upon the 1967 President's Commission Reports and the 1973 National Standards and Goals. The history of parole is described in the first selection and some data with respect to the frequency of the use of parole and on recidivism are given.

It is interesting to note that the President's Commission report states that " . . . actually prisoners serve as much time in confinement in jurisdictions where parole is widely used as in those where it is not. No consistent or significant relationship exists between the proportion of prisoners released on parole in a State and the average time served for felonies before release." It would seem, therefore, that where parole is used extensively, the amount of surveillance offenders receive is greater than in cases where it is used less. The situation may have changed since 1967, but this seems doubtful. One major change from the situation described in the Commission report relates to the interest taken by the courts in the parole-decision process. (See paper by Professor Donald Newman later in this Section for an update on this issue. The "New Criminologists" will find much in this paper to feed their criticism of the parole decision-making and supervision processes.)

The National Commission on Standards and Goals realistically comments that parole seems to be without any specific goals. It notes, " . . . the objectives of parole systems vary widely. Without clearly stated and understood objectives, the administrator cannot make the most basic decisions . . . " The report quotes from the National Parole Institute paper of 1966, *Selection for Parole*. The information considered by parole board members to be the most important in parole decisions had estimates of the likelihood of recidivism and the concept of "just deserts" ranked fourth with less than half of the sample nominating these items. Yet no boards used "prediction tables." Perhaps part of the reason is indicated in the next item in the Section.

The Chairman of the United States Board of Parole and others authored an article "Making Paroling Policy Explicit," setting out the policy guidelines developed by a research team working with the Board of Parole. The basis for the parole decision is made explicit; it can, for example, be noted from an inspection of the guidelines that more weight is given by the Board to the seriousness of the instant offense (the offense for which the parole applicant was committed to prison on the particular occasion), than is given to a prediction score (salient factors). It appears that the concept of equity, rather than the probability of recidivism, is the major determinant of the parole decision. It may be of interest to consider this result in the light of other materials presented in this Section, including the statements in the two governmental reports.

The use of guidelines by the United States Board of Parole and the fact that these are known to all who wish to know them has, of course, raised some interesting issues before the courts. The guidelines are associated with considerable administrative changes from the previous procedures, including appeals and regional structures.

The granting of parole is a risk-taking decision for the Parole Board. If the Board continues to detain an offender, there is little risk; if they release and the parolee commits another crime, they are subject to criticism. The only information feedback that Boards receive is when they make the "liberal" decision—the risk-taking decision to release. If they detain a man who would have been successful, it can always be believed that his eventual success was due to his being detained longer. The article by Dr. Norman Holt reviews a large number of research studies carried out in California. Surprisingly, perhaps, he shows that the risky decision is usually the best. For example, his data support his forthright statement, " . . . if returning technical violators to prison is supposed to be a way to prevent new felonies it sure doesn't work that way in California."

Paul Takagi's manuscript, "The Parole Violator as an Organization Reject," reveals the problems of decision making and highlights not only the variations between parole officers but also between parole offices. Without being made explicit, a kind of "policy of the office" seems to develop in relation to recommendations regarding parolees. There is a variance between and within both parole officers and offices, while perceptions of the opinions of supervisors also seem to have some influence on the decisions made. This finding indicates the utility of decision research using simulation methods.

In his article "The Legal Model for Parole," Professor Donald Newman discusses the important and difficult issue of the concept of parole as privilege or right and the implications in practice of the interpretation in law of this difference. He reviews some of the major questions about the parole decision and the freedom of action available to parole boards. At the end of the article, Professor Newman looks towards the probable future of parole, both as a means of release from prisons and as a process of supervision. He sees many decisions with regard to the surveillance of ex-inmates on parole being first made by parole boards and only later, when challenged, reviewed by the appellate courts.

As an attempt to balance the generally "just deserts" and "equity" emphasis which may be noted in our selections, we have included an extract from a report by Dr. Eliot Studt. Dr. Studt believes that the probability of recidivism could be influenced by more effective assistance provided through the medium of parole aftercare. She claims, however, that parole officers "manage their cases with relative efficiency through the correctional procedures. They (parole agents) are not equipped by the structure with the means to deal with many of the conditions affecting parolee success or failure. . . . " She believes that provision of economic support during reentry, perhaps achieved through sheltered employment, the provision of emergency service on a 24-hour-a-day basis, the involvement of the parolees in the work of parole service, such as by service on advisory boards and as co-workers in community organization, together with the restoration of civil rights would work towards the better reintegration of the ex-inmate into society. She sees these changes in the role of parole agents and parolees as requiring a reduction in or abolition of the surveillance function in parole. According to her model, parole casework would become a completely helping profession. It would seem that if this were to become the case, parole would cease to be a requirement of release from prison, and the consultation of the parolee with his parole agent would become voluntary. If this were not so, the question of enforcement of "treatment" would arise; the parole agent would stipulate the kinds of "treatment" which were "needed" and hence also "required." Failure to accept the required treatment unless it were completely voluntary would have to be sanctioned. It would be easy to be back at a punitive (sanctioning) system where the concept of "treatment" was again the only criteria.

It seems fairly clear—to some of us it seems established—that the "treatment" concept and the concept of "just deserts" and "equity" cannot mix. Furthermore, a treatment system backed by a punishment system presents serious ethical problems. Dr. Studt's article and the consequences which may be inferred to arise from her postulates might be compared with the abstract from *Struggle for Justice* in our first Section. There is much material for debate; many problems call for attempts at resolution. The current atmosphere of self-examination, court decisions, as well as external criticisms of the parole philosophy and administrative machinery from liberal and conservative spokesmen alike will most likely change the environment of parole.

17
Parole and Aftercare

THE PRESIDENT'S COMMISSION ON LAW ENFORCEMENT
AND ADMINISTRATION OF JUSTICE

The test of the success of institutional corrections programs comes when offenders are released to the community. Whatever rehabilitation they have received, whatever deterrent effect their experience with incarceration has had, must upon release withstand the difficulties of readjustment to life in society and reintegration into employment, family, school, and the rest of community life. This is the time when most of the problems from which offenders were temporarily removed must be faced again and new problems arising from their status as ex-offenders must be confronted.

Many offenders are released outright into the community upon completion of their sentences, but a growing number—now more than 60 percent of adult felons for the Nation as a whole—are released on parole prior to the expiration of the maximum term of their sentences. Parole supervision, which in general resembles probation in methods and purposes, is the basic way—and one of the oldest— of trying to continue in the community the correctional program begun in the institution and help offenders make the difficult adjustment to release without jeopardy to the community. Furloughs, halfway houses, and similar programs are important supplements to effective parole programs, as are prerelease guidance and other social services discussed later in this chapter.

Parole is generally granted by an administrative board or agency on the basis of such factors as an offender's prior history, his readiness for release, and his need for supervision and assistance in the community prior to the expiration of his

SOURCE. *Task Force Report: Corrections* The President's Commission on Law Enforcement and Administration of Justice, Washington, D.C., U.S. Government Printing Office, 1967, pp. 60–71.

sentence. The Federal system and those of a few States have a mandatory supervision procedure for offenders not released on parole. Under such a procedure, when an inmate is released for good behavior before serving his maximum term, he is supervised in the community for a period equivalent to his "good time credit."

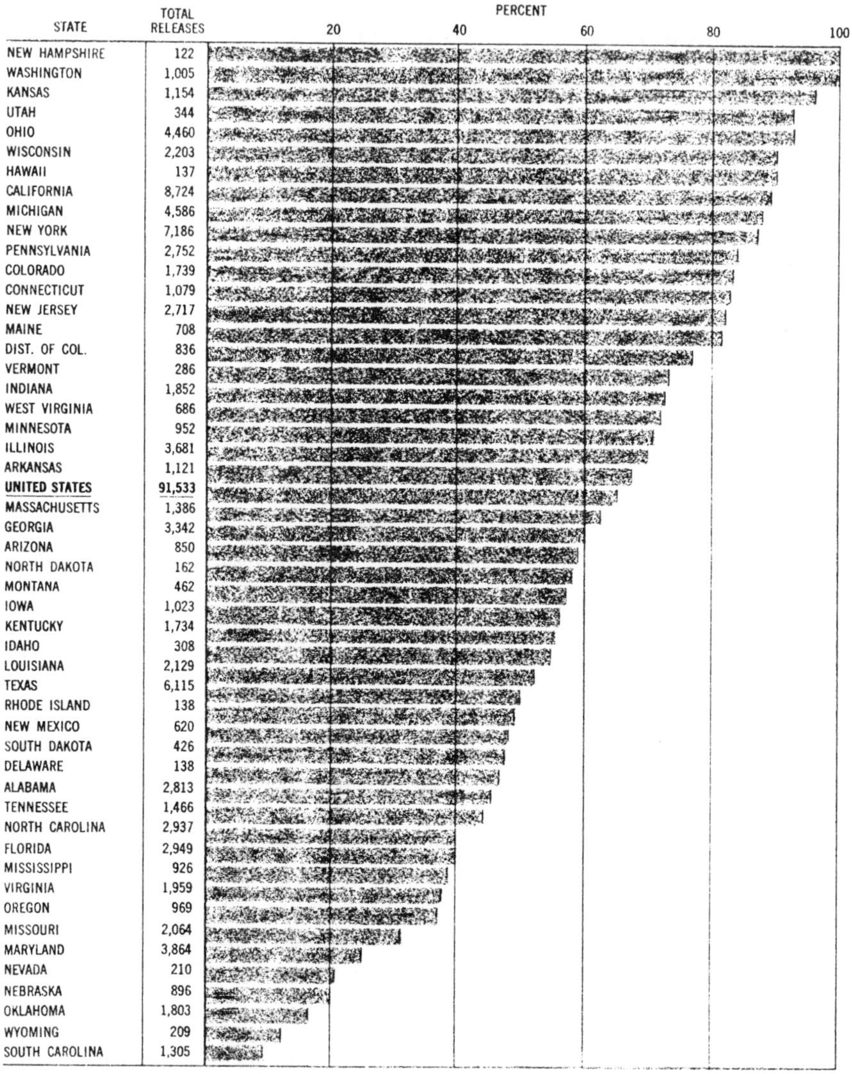

STATE	TOTAL RELEASES	PERCENT
NEW HAMPSHIRE	122	
WASHINGTON	1,005	
KANSAS	1,154	
UTAH	344	
OHIO	4,460	
WISCONSIN	2,203	
HAWAII	137	
CALIFORNIA	8,724	
MICHIGAN	4,586	
NEW YORK	7,186	
PENNSYLVANIA	2,752	
COLORADO	1,739	
CONNECTICUT	1,079	
NEW JERSEY	2,717	
MAINE	708	
DIST. OF COL.	836	
VERMONT	286	
INDIANA	1,852	
WEST VIRGINIA	686	
MINNESOTA	952	
ILLINOIS	3,681	
ARKANSAS	1,121	
UNITED STATES	91,533	
MASSACHUSETTS	1,386	
GEORGIA	3,342	
ARIZONA	850	
NORTH DAKOTA	162	
MONTANA	462	
IOWA	1,023	
KENTUCKY	1,734	
IDAHO	308	
LOUISIANA	2,129	
TEXAS	6,115	
RHODE ISLAND	138	
NEW MEXICO	620	
SOUTH DAKOTA	426	
DELAWARE	138	
ALABAMA	2,813	
TENNESSEE	1,466	
NORTH CAROLINA	2,937	
FLORIDA	2,949	
MISSISSIPPI	926	
VIRGINIA	1,959	
OREGON	969	
MISSOURI	2,064	
MARYLAND	3,864	
NEVADA	210	
NEBRASKA	896	
OKLAHOMA	1,803	
WYOMING	209	
SOUTH CAROLINA	1,305	

Figure 1 *Inmates released on parole as percentage of all persons released from state prisons, 1964.*

Table 1 shows the average number of offenders under parole supervision in 1965 and the yearly cost of operations. Data include the small number of offenders released under mandatory supervision but do not include the very limited number of persons on parole from misdemeanant institutions.

HISTORY AND PRESENT EXTENT OF PAROLE.

Parole has had a long history. Its early traces appeared in the United States in the 19th century. The first official recognition came in 1876 at New York's Elmira Reformatory. Parole for juveniles, sometimes referred to as "aftercare," can be traced back to the houses of refuge for children established in the latter half of the 19th century. Juvenile parole developed for many years as part of the general child welfare field, but recently, while still retaining a close involvement with child welfare programs, has assumed a more distinct status.

The growth of parole services has been continuous, though uneven, the adult field expanding more rapidly than the juvenile. There remain, however, significant gaps in its use. The one of probably most general importance is its infrequent use for misdemeanants sentenced to jail. The National Survey of Correction found that most misdemeanants are released from local institutions and jails without parole. Information available from a sample of 212 local jails indicates that 131 of them (62 percent) have no parole procedure; in the 81 jails that nominally have parole, only 8 percent of the inmates are released through this procedure. Thus, 92 percent are simply turned loose at the expiration of their sentence.

In the juvenile field, the administrative fragmentation of parole programs makes it difficult to develop precise statistical data on the extent to which parole is used as a method of release. The National Survey found that, although most youngsters are released under parole status from training schools, supervision programs for them often are inadequate.

Table 1 *Average Number of Persons on Parole from State and Federal Correctional Institutions, 1965, by Type of Institution from Which Released, and Annual Costs of Supervision*

Type of Institution	Number on Parole[a]	Annual Costs of Supervision
Prisons	112,142	$35,314,047
Training schools	60,483	18,593,975
Total	172,625	53,908,022

[a]Includes a small number of persons released under mandatory supervision.

Source. National Survey of Corrections and special tabulations provided by the Federal Bureau of Prisons and the Administrative Office of the U.S. Courts.

More exact data can be obtained about the use of parole for adult offenders released from prisons. Figure 1, adapted from the National Prisoner Statistics of the Federal Bureau of Prisons, discloses sharp variations in the extent of parole use among individual States, from one in which only 9 percent of prisoners were released on parole to others where virtually all were. These reflect in large part differences in sentencing practices as well as parole policies.

THEORY AND PURPOSE

While parole has on occasion been attacked as "leniency," it is basically a means of public protection, or at least has a potential to serve this purpose if properly used. Actually prisoners serve as much time in confinement in jurisdictions where parole is widely used as in those where it is not. No consistent or significant relationship exists between the proportion of prisoners who are released on parole in a State and the average time served for felonies before release. The most recent tabulation of median time served for felonies before first release, which was made in 1960, showed that the five States with the longest median time served were Hawaii, Pennsylvania, Illinois, New York, and Indiana. The percentages released by parole in these States in the same year were 99, 89, 47, 87, and 88 respectively. The five States with the shortest median time served for felonies before first release were New Hampshire, Maine, South Dakota, Montana, and Vermont, with percentages of release by parole of 98, 92, 49, 90, and 5 respectively.[1]

Arguments couched in terms of "leniency" deflect attention from a more important problem. The fact is that large numbers of offenders do return to the community from confinement each year. The task is to improve parole programs so that they may contribute to the reintegration of these offenders. The best current estimates indicate that, among adult offenders, 35 to 45 percent of those released on parole are subsequently returned to prison.[2] The large majority of this group are returned for violations of parole regulations; only about one-third of those returned have been convicted of new felonies. Violation rates are higher for juveniles. However, because additional kinds of violations are applicable to them, such as truancy and incorrigibility, precise comparison with adult rates is difficult.

Ideally, the parole process should begin when an offender is first received in an institution. Information should be gathered on his entire background, and skilled staff should plan an institutional program of training and treatment. A continuous evaluation should be made of the offender's progress on the program. At the same time, trained staff should be working in the community with the offender's family and employer to develop a release plan.

---

[1] U.S. Department of Justice, Federal Bureau of Prisons, "National Prisoner Statistics: Characteristics of State Prisoners, 1960" (Washington: The Bureau, n.d.), table R. 1. p. 67.

[2] Daniel Glaser and Vincent O'Leary, "Personal Characteristics and Parole Outcome," National Parole Institutes. Office of Juvenile Delinquency and Youth Development, U.S. Department of Health, Education, and Welfare (Washington: U.S. Government Printing Office, 1966).

Information about the offender, his progress in the institution, and community readiness to receive him would, under such ideal conditions, be brought together periodically and analyzed by expert staff for presentation to a releasing authority whose members were qualified by training and experience. After thoughtful review, including a hearing with the offender present, the releasing authority would decide when and where to release him. On release, he would be under the supervision of a trained parole officer able to work closely with him and the community institutions around him. If there were a violation of parole, a careful investigation would be made and the reasons behind the violation evaluated. A report would be submitted to the releasing authority which, on the basis of careful review of all the evidence and a hearing with the offender, would decide whether to revoke his parole.

Unfortunately, there are wide discrepancies between this description of what parole purports to be and the actual situation in most jurisdictions. One purpose of this chapter is to explore the nature and implication of those discrepancies.

LEGAL FRAMEWORK

The legal framework within which parole decisions are made varies widely from one jurisdiction to another. The general structure of sentencing laws is discussed in Chapter 5 of the Commissions's General Report and in the volume on the administration of justice, and it will not be detailed here.

Parole for Adults

Basically, the parole decision for adult offenders may depend on statutes enacted by the legislature, on the sentence imposed by the court, or on the determination of correctional authorities or an independent parole board. For certain offenses some statutes require that various amounts of time must be served before parole can be considered, or they prohibit parole entirely. The basic trouble with such restrictions is that they allow no consideration of individual circumstances. Consistently, correctional authorities have found that they interfere with effective decision-making; at times they cause unnecessary confinement; and at times they result in substantial inequities.

If minimum sentences are to be imposed, clearly the law needs to provide that they can be neither excessively long nor set so close to the maximum as to make discretion in granting parole illusory. In a few States, indeterminate sentencing is authorized, permitting consideration for parole at any time, without service of a minimum term. "Good time" or other credits earned by conduct during imprisonment may reduce the time that must be served in some jurisdictions prior to eligibility for parole.

Under any such variant, eligibility for parole does not, of course, mean that parole will in all cases be granted. In some, offenders may be released outright at the end of their term. The requirement of mandatory supervision in force in the Federal system and several States is one attempt to deal with this problem.

In general, mandatory supervision laws require that any prisoner released prior to the expiration of his term by reason of having earned good time or other credits during imprisonment, must be released to a parole officer subject to parole supervision and conditions. Since virtually all prisoners earn good time credits, which may amount to a substantial fraction of their term of sentence, such a provision insures supervision for a period on release unless it is explicitly waived by a parole authority as being unnecessary. The limitation of mandatory supervision to the period of good time credit is one means of insuring that supervision does not become a mere extension of sentence, but obviously it is a rule-of-thumb standard that may bear no relation to the need for supervision.

Parole for Juveniles

With respect to juveniles, a number of legal issues are involved in commitment and subsequent release. Those which most directly affect parole practice are restrictions as to when a juvenile can be released. Of these the most important are: (1) stipulated periods of time a youth is required to stay in a training school; and (2) the requirement of approval from a committing judge before release can be authorized.

The National Survey found that three States stipulate by law a minimum period of confinement before parole can be considered for a youngster. One State has a 12-month minimum, another 18 months, and a third varying minimums. In many other States, minimum terms are established by administrative action. Such requirements ignore the facts of the individual case and can require unnecessary and damaging stays in institutions. While the usefulness of minimum sentences is debated extensively in the adult field, no authoritative body advocates their use for juveniles.

More widespread, and in some respects more difficult to change, is the procedure found in nine States, under which committing judges must become officially involved before juveniles can be released on parole. The problem with this approach is that a judge must be aware of a child's behavior in an institution after commitment by the court as well as current factors in the community situation. Since it is difficult at best to provide both kinds of information to a judge, he is apt to have to act on the basis of incomplete knowledge. Furthermore, such control by the court unnecessarily complicates programing for youngsters while they are in institutions. Judicial control over release has been eliminated by the vast majority of States and should be eliminated in the remainder.

THE DECISIONAL PROCESS

In the main, releasing authorities must depend on others for information about persons being considered for release. The size and quality of the staff who compile and analyze this information is therefore crucial. They must be able to develop and assemble vital information and present it in such a way as to establish its relevance to the decision.

Far too typically, overworked institutional caseworkers must attempt to gather information on a prisoner from brief interviews with him, meager institutional records, and letters to community officials. This information is often fitted into a highly stereotyped format. Frequently, the sameness of reporting style and jargon makes it very difficult for board members to understand the individual aspects of a given case and assess them wisely. This can lead to decisions which are arbitrary and unfair as well as undesirable from a correctional standpoint.

A significant increase in the number of institutional caseworkers responsible for compiling and analyzing information and great improvement in the quality of their work are required. The ratio recommended by the U.S. Children's Bureau for this kind of staff for young offenders in juvenile training schools is 1 to 30. The National Survey shows that it was 1 to 53 in 1965. For adults prisons, the American Correctional Association recommends a ratio of 1 to 150. This appears to be quite minimal when compared to juvenile standards, but it would be a great improvement over the actual 1965 ratio of 1 to 253.

Not only must caseworkers be of sufficient number and quality, but they must also have access to channels of essential information. Close coordination is needed with parole field staff to obtain information about the offender's background, attitudes of his parents, conditions in the community, and the availability of a job. Other vital channels exist within the institution itself. Caseworkers often have far less contact with offenders than do group supervisors, vocational teachers, and others. These individuals are valuable sources of information and should be consulted in preparing reports. Methods need to be devised to use them more fully.

Another type of staff in acutely short supply is clinical personnel. Psychiatrists and psychologists are badly needed for better assessment of cases such as those involving sex offenders and various types of violent offenders. Their skills are important, for example, in helping to decide whether a violent crime was an expression of persistent emotional disturbance likely to be manifested in further violence.

The National Survey showed that in the juvenile field there were the equivalent of only 46 full-time psychiatrists serving 220 juvenile institutions across the United States. More than half of these were in 5 states; one State had 10 of the 46. Not only were these psychiatrists responsible for diagnostic work, but most were carrying treatment responsibilites as well.

Use of Statistical Aids

The data presented to releasing authorities are of many kinds. Assuming that the information is accurate, parole officials must still face the problem of evaluating its meaning. One method, by far the most common, is for the decision-maker to depend basically on his own judgment of the circumstances in an individual case.

Another way of approaching a parole decision is through the use of statistical analyses of the performance of offenders paroled in past years to determine the violation rates for various classifications. Violation rates are related to age, offense, education, work history, prior record, and other factors. The categories are then combined to produce a "probability-of-violation score" for an offender according to his characteristics.

A series of efforts have been made in recent years to develop such procedures.[3] Experiments have also been undertaken to compare the case method and the statistical method. Psychiatrists, psychologists, sociologists, and prison officials have been asked to classify large numbers of cases on the basis of probable success on parole. When statistical prediction methods have been applied to the same group of cases, they have proved better able to determine the probabilities of parole violation for groups of inmates.[4]

Despite the utility of statistical techniques and the potential for increased usefulness with the advance of computer technology, no serious authority has proposed the substitution of the statistical for the case method. Factors unassociated with risk must be considered. Moreover, any individual case may present considerations which are too detailed for statistical analysis or which must be weighed from the standpoint of fairness.[5] Nonetheless, statistical analysis is useful as a general means for educating parole authorities in the significance of various factors in assessment of cases, as a way of evaluating the effectiveness of various treatment alternatives upon parole, and as a check for individual case dispositions. Much further work is needed to develop statistical analysis, particularly to predict the likelihood of violent crimes, as opposed to other offenses, and as a means for determining the optimum time for release.

National Reporting System

Closely related to the development of such research within each parole agency is the need for a national system of sharing parole statistics. At present, it is very difficult to assess the significance of different rates of revocation, since gross figures do not permit any comparisons among programs in different jurisdictions.

Some data are now available from pilot attempts to develop a national parole reporting system that would permit comparisons. Under a grant awarded by the National Institute of Mental Health to the National Parole Institutes[6] in 1966,

---

[3] See Norman Johnson, Leonard Savitz, and Marvin E. Wolfgang, "The Sociology of Punishment and Correction" (New York: John Wiley and Sons, 1962), pp. 249–309.

[4] Don Gottfredson, "Comparing and Combining Subjective and Objective Parole Predictions," California Department of Corrections Research Newsletter, 3: 11–17 (Sept.–Dec. 1961). See also Hermann Mannheim and Leslie T. Wilkins, "Prediction Methods in Relation to Borstal Training" (London: Her Majesty's Stationery Office, 1955).

[5] Norman S. Hayner, "Way Do Parole Boards Lag in the Use of Prediction Scores?" Pacific Sociological Review, 1: 73–78 (Fall 1958).

[6] The National Parole Institutes are cosponsored by the Interstate Compact Administrators Association for the Council of State Governments, the U.S. Board of Parole, the Association of Paroling Authorities, and the National Council on Crime and Delinquency.

30 States were experimenting with the development of common definitions and methods for reporting. Only as such definitions are developed can meaningful comparisons be made. And only when these comparisons are made can answers be found to such questions as these: How do the results of parole compare from one agency to another? What are the results of different parole programs for different kinds of offenders? What is the result of releasing certain kinds of offenders earlier or later?

Parole Hearings

Releasing authorities can also achieve more rational decision-making by improving their hearing procedures. Improvements must promote both fairness and regularity, as well as effective correctional treatment. In several States there are no hearings at all for adult offenders; decisions are made by parole authorities solely on the basis of written reports. In juvenile programs, hearings are even less common, with reliance again on written reports and also on staff conferences at which the offender may not be present.

Procedures for parole hearings are extremely diverse. In many States, especially those with numerous institutions, the parole board is divided into subcommittees, each of which conducts hearings. In some States, one or more board members conduct hearings and report back to the rest of the board. In still other States, boards conduct all hearings *en banc.*

Policies with regard to hearings on revocation of parole are even more varied. About half the States grant hearings as a matter of "grace," rather than regarding them as a normal function of the parole board. Again, some States have no hearings at all on revocation questions. Often, when hearings are held, they occur some time after a parolee's freedom has been terminated and he has been returned to prison.

Authorities on parole procedures regard well-conducted hearings as vital to effective decision-making, in terms of expanding the information available to the board as well as for their effect on offenders. Hearings commonly give parole boards an opportunity to identify important points on which information is needed in making their decision. For example, a board may well find from interviewing an inmate that he has several contacts in the community not mentioned in any official report, which later investigation by staff may reveal to have considerable bearing on the place to which he might subsequently be paroled.

The other aim of a hearing is to create conditions which enhance the treatment goals for an inmate. This does not mean that the hearing should take on the character of a counseling session. The simple opportunity of being given what he perceives to be a fair hearing can be important in creating those conditions. Board members also can often influence the behavior of inmates by encouraging their participation in institutional programs and other self-improvement efforts or by frankly discussing with them, at appropriate times, the probable consequences of failure to participate in programs or of misconduct.

Well-conducted hearings further the trend for parole boards to increase the involvement of inmates in the decisions which affect them and to confront them more directly with the information upon which a decision is being made. Earlier concepts concerning the treatment of offenders placed most emphasis upon the need to resolve their emotional problems. A more recent refinement of this view stresses the need for the offenders to be helped to confront and deal with "here and now" issues as a means of strengthening their problem-solving abilities.

An illustration of the trend toward "confrontation" is the way in which inmates are notified of parole decisions. Typically, parole decisions have been to tell inmates if parole was granted or denied. They have had little opportunity to discover the reasons for the decisions and discuss them with parole board members. An increasing number of parole boards have adopted the practice of calling inmates back after a hearing to discuss the decision on their cases. Institution staff and board members in these States—for example, Minnesota and Iowa—report it to be an improvement over prior methods.

Board members are most helpful when they demonstrate a genuine interest in the welfare of an inmate, an ability to withstand manipulation or deception, and a willingness to discuss candidly with an inmate the realities of his case. It is important, however, that board members avoid trying to use the hearing for extensive problem-solving with inmates or as a substitute for work which should be done by staff.

ORGANIZATION OF PAROLE AUTHORITIES

The administrative organization of parole authorities is another factor that aids or impedes decision-making. Again, there are wide variations in practice among jurisdictions and also a historical separation between the juvenile and adult fields that persists to this day.

Existing Patterns of Organization

In the adult field, every State has an identifiable and separate parole authority, although in four States the power of these authorities is limited to recommending a disposition to the Governor. A sense of the growth of parole in this country can be obtained by a review of the Wickersham Report of 1931 which indicated that 20 States had no parole boards at all. By 1939, the Attorney General's Survey of Release Procedures indicated there were still 16 States in which the Governor was the paroling authority.

In 41 States today the parole board is an independent agency; in 7 States, it is a unit within a larger department of the State; and in 2 States, it is the same body that regulates correctional institutions. In no jurisdiction in the adult field is the final power to grant or deny parole given to the staff directly involved in the operation of a correctional institution.

The situation in the juvenile field is quite different. The great majority of releasing decisions directly involve the staff of training schools. This is the case in 34 of the 50 States and Puerto Rico. In the other 17 jurisdictions, boards and agencies are used that, to varying degrees, are independent of the training school itself. Table 2 illustrates the variety of releasing authorities used in those 17 States.

Independence and Integration

The two dominant patterns of the juvenile and adult fields—the juvenile centering parole decision-making primarily in the institutions and the adult centering it in autonomous groups—symbolize two points of view about parole decision-making. The basic argument for placing release decisions in the hands of institutional staff is that they are most intimately familiar with the offender and are responsible for developing programs for him; thus they are most sensitive to the optimum time for release. It is also argued that autonomous boards tend to be unconcerned or insensitive about the problems of institutional programs and the aims of their staffs, that their tendency to be preoccupied with issues apart from the rehabilitative aspects of an individual's treatment leads them to make inappropriate case decisions. Such autonomous groups are often viewed by institutional personnel as unnecessarily complicating decision-making and infringing on the "professional judgment" of competent staff.

Division of labor between institutional staff and autonomous releasing authorities is complicated by the growing use of partial release programs, for work, study or the like. The result may be anomalous as when, for example, an institution decides that an inmate should be allowed to go into the community on a work-release basis and he does well there, but a parole board subsequently decides that he should not be paroled. This can occur because a parole board usually takes into consideration various factors which are less emphasized by institutional officials, such as the disposition of co-defendants' cases or his probable behavior

Table 2 *Types of Parole Authorities for Juveniles, Other than Training School Staffs, 17 States. 1965*

Paroling Authority	Number of Jurisdictions
Youth authorities	4
Training school board	3
Institutions board	2
Department of Corrections	2
Department of Public Welfare	2
Parole board	2
Board of control	1
Ex-officio board	1

SOURCE. National Survey of Corrections.

in an environment other than the town adjoining the institution, where leisure time will be much less structured.

A major argument against giving the parole-decision power to institutional staff is that they tend to place undue emphasis upon the adjustment of offenders to institutional life. There is a temptation to set release policies to fit the needs of the institution, to control population size and even as a means for getting rid of problem cases even though longer control may be desirable. The opposite, but equally unfortunate, temptation is to use unwarranted extensions of confinement as penalties for petty rule violations. Finally, decision-making by institutional staff lends itself to such informal procedures and is so lacking in visibility as to raise questions concerning its capability to maintain fairness or even the appearance of fairness.

There have been a number of attempts to devise organizational means for promoting closer coordination between the staffs of institutional programs and releasing authorities. At one extreme is the integration of the releasing authority within a centralized correctional agency, with the parole board appointed by that agency. Wisconsin and Michigan have had such a system for some years, and Ohio has recently adopted a variant of it for its adult system.

Another way of promoting integration between releasing authorities and correctional systems can be found in the youth authority structures in Illinois, Massachusetts, Ohio, California, and Minnesota. Here the power of release is given to the board that has general control over the entire correctional system, both in institutions and in the community. No serious efforts in recent years have been made to extend such patterns to the adult area.

A third method, used in Alaska, Tennessee, and Maine, is to have the director of corrections serve as chairman of the paroling authority, with the members appointed by the Governor. This system may produce better coordination, but the director of corrections usually has so many other responsibilities that he cannot adequately carry parole board duties. To meet this problem, Minnesota has the parole board chairman appointed by and serving at the pleasure of the director of corrections, with other members appointed by the Governor. Other States have used coordinating committees, on which parole board members sit with institutional officials, or they housed both agencies in the same State department, giving each a great deal of autonomy.

In juvenile parole, where only a few totally independent parole boards exist and there have been no significant efforts to establish more, the main issue is whether there should be a central correctional authority with release power, or whether this decision should rest entirely with the institutions. The view of most leading juvenile authorities is that there should be a decision-making body within a central correctional agency of the State that controls all releases to the community and returns to institutions. Institutional recommendations and opinions should, in their view, weigh heavily, but final decisions should rest with the central body.

The principal advantages cited for this system are that it would meet the need in large multi-institution programs for maintenance of consistency in policies among institutions or among field offices which make revocation decisions and would minimize policy conflicts that can arise between releasing authorities and institutions. Properly developed, it also could provide procedural safeguards against capricious or irresponsible decisions.

Such an independent decision-making group within a parent agency seems to be the most effective solution to the problem of coordination within juvenile agencies. It is the one to which the juvenile field is apparently moving and is the alternative to which the adult field also seems to be heading.

Parole Board Personnel

Sound organizational structure is important, but it cannot substitute for qualified personnel. Increasing the competence of parole decision-makers clearly deserves high priority for the development of effective correctional programs.

In the juvenile field, staff responsible for the paroling functions are in most States persons drawn from central juvenile agencies or juvenile institutions. Thus, the quality of parole personnel is generally related to the level of training and experience required of staffs in the juvenile programs of specific jurisdictions. Improving personnel quality for juvenile parole decision-making can be undertaken generally in a straightforward way.

For boards dealing with adult offenders the problem is more complicated. For example, the National Survey revealed that in four States, in 1965, membership on the parole board was automatically given to those who held certain public offices. In one of these States, the board consisted of the Governor, the Secretary of State, the State Auditor, the State Treasurer, and the Superintendent of Public Instruction. Clearly, such ex-officio parole board members have neither the time nor the kind of training needed to participate effectively in correctional decision-making. Correctional authorities have uniformly advocated the elimination of ex-officio members from parole boards.

A more pervasive problem in the adult field is the part-time parole board. At present, 25 States have such part-time boards; 23 States have full-time boards; and 3 jurisdictions have a combination of the two. Part-time parole boards are usually found in smaller States; of the 21 jurisdictions with the smallest population, 19 have part-time parole boards. Among the 10 largest States, only Illinois has a part-time parole board.

Usually the part-time member can give only a limited amount of time to the job and almost inevitably part-time parole board members also have business or professional concerns outside the parole field which demand their attention and energy. Even a relatively small correctional system requires a considerable investment in time and energy if careful study and frequent review are to be given to all parole cases and if prompt and considered action is to be taken in parole revocation. It would appear that a full-time releasing authority should be the objective of every jurisdiction. Even in smaller correctional systems there is enough work generally to occupy the full-time attention of board members. An alternative to the complete replacement of the part-time parole board members in States with very small populations is to supplement them with parole examiners, a concept discussed in more detail in a subsequent section.

Appointment of Board Members

One of the most critical issues in obtaining qualified parole board members is the method of their appointment. Table 3 shows the methods by which adult parole board members were appointed in 1965. As indicated there, parole board members in 39 States were appointed by Governors.

In many jurisdictions, highly competent individuals have been appointed to parole boards and some have gained experience through service for many years. But in 1965 parole board members in 44 jurisdictions in the United States were serving terms of 6 years or less. It is not unusual to have new parole board members appointed whenever there is a change in a State administration. On some occasions, this system has resulted in the appointment of board members largely on the basis of political affiliations without regard to qualification for making parole decisions.

To avoid this situation, Michigan and Wisconsin have adopted a "merit system" for appointment of parole board members. Appointees are required to have a college degree in one of the behavioral sciences and also experience in correctional work. Some have previously held important positions in correctional institutions or in field supervision.

Other steps can be taken to help insure the appointment of parole board members with requisite education and training. Maine, California, and New Jersey outline some qualification requirements in their laws. Florida requires that appointees pass an examination in penology and criminal justice, administered by experts in these fields. The system of making appointments from a list of candidates nominated by committees of qualified persons, as used in the appointment of judges in some jurisdictions, could be adapted to the parole setting.

Qualifications and Training of Members

The nature of the decisions to be made in parole requires persons who have broad academic backgrounds, especially in the behavioral sciences, and who are

Table 3.   *Method of Appointment to Adult Parole Boards, 50 States and Puerto Rico, 1965*

Appointing Officer or Agency	Number of Jurisdictions
Governor	39
State officials	4
Corrections agency	4
Ex-officio	4

SOURCE. National Survey of Corrections.

aware of how parole operates within the context of a total correctional process. It is vital that board members know the kinds of individuals with whom they are dealing and the many institutional and community variables relating to their decisions. The rise of statistical aids to decision-making and increased responsibilities to meet due process requirements make it even more essential that board members be sufficiently well trained to make discriminating judgments about such matters.

The number of persons with the requisite skills is presently quite limited. Training programs designed especially for parole board members are badly needed. An effort in this direction was the National Parole Institute's training programs. Supported by a grant from the Office of Juvenile Delinquency between 1962 and 1965, the institutes provided a series of week-long intensive training programs for parole decision-makers and developed useful publications and guides. Programs of this type need to be expanded and maintained on a regular basis.

Use of Professional Examiners

Another device to aid in improving parole decision-making is the use of professional parole examiners to conduct hearings and interviews for the parole board, which delegates to them the power to make certain kinds of decisions within the policies fixed by the board. Under this system, a parole board can concern itself with broad policy questions, directly pass on a limited number of specific cases, and act as an appellate body on the decisions of its examiners.

California now has examiners in both its adult and youth authorities. The U.S. Board of Parole has recently appointed an examiner. The decision-making responsibility given to these persons varies according to the system. Experience thus far indicates that the use of such officers could be greatly expanded.

The major argument for this approach is that it permits the development of a corps of professional examiners who have the background and skills necessary to perform the complex tasks involved. At the same time, it frees the parole board to carry out functions that should not be delegated. Another argument for this system is that professional examiners with tenure, training, and experience in the correctional field would be able to bridge more effectively the gap between parole boards and institutions.

The use of examiners would also reduce the need for constantly increasing the size of parole boards to meet increasing workload. One State now has a parole board of 10 members; in others, 7-member boards are not uncommon. With examiners a parole board would perhaps need no more than five members. As noted, in those States where part-time boards were still retained, the professional hearing examiner would be particularly useful.

One objection to use of examiners is that inmates wish to confront decision-making authorities directly. However, the limited experience to date indicates that this need not be a serious problem if examiners are given prestige and authority.

SUPERVISION OF PAROLEES

Among the principal sorts of limitations on the parole decision-maker are the resources available for community supervision: number of staff, their training and organization, and the community resources at hand for effective programing. Releasing authorities face one sort of question in considering parole for an offender who will be supervised in a small caseload by a trained parole officer working intensively with the offender and community agencies. The questions are very different in considering release to a parole officer who is so overburdened that he can give no more than token supervision.

Some Major Supervision Issues

Originally, parole involved a "ticket of leave" system under which a released prisoner reported regularly to police officials. Emphasis was almost entirely on controlling the offender to make certain that he conformed to the conditions of his release. Increasingly, as parole agencies developed their own staff, the tasks of control were supplemented by efforts to provide assistance to parolees. At first such assistance was direct and tangible in form, such as obtaining housing and money for the parolee. Later, more stress was placed on referral to other agencies and counseling of various kinds. Most recently, as in the case of probation, emphasis has been placed also on use of the parole officer to mediate between offenders and community institutions and to stimulate and organize needed services.

Again as with probation, control and assistance constitute the main themes of parole supervision. In fact, several research projects have been able to classify parole officers on the basis of their relative concern about the two.[7] These differences in emphasis are associated with different behavior on the part of officers.

Experiments indicate that certain offenders perform more successfully with parole officers who use certain styles of supervision than with others.[8] This has led to the development of specialized caseloads in which offenders with designated problems or characteristics are supervised by officers with special aptitude for managing them. In the adult field, 10 States now report the use of caseloads of this kind. The majority are for narcotic offenders; others are for alcoholics, mental defectives, or violent offenders. The State of New York has even developed specialized caseloads for "gifted offenders."

Research is needed to develop two kinds of information: (1) an effective classification system through which to describe the various types of offenders who

---

[7] Daniel Glaser, "The Effectiveness of a Prison and Parole System" (Indianapolis: Bobbs-Merrill Co., 1964), pp. 429–442.

[8] Stuart Adams, "Interaction between Individual Interview Therapy and Treatment Amenability in Order Youth Authority Wards," in "Inquiries Concerning Kinds of Treatment for Kinds of Delinquents," Monograph No. 2 (Sacramento: California Board of Corrections, 1961), pp. 27–44.

require different styles of supervision and the types of parole officers who can provide them; and (2) a set of treatment theories and practices which can be applied successfully to the different types of parolees.

The Transition to the Community

The time when an offender re-enters the community presents special problems and needs. Statistical data clearly demonstrate the critical problems of prerelease preparation. Table 4 shows the months on parole completed by those who were declared violators during 1964 in the State of Washington where because of its sentencing system virtually every parolee has a number of years remaining on his sentence when he is paroled. The pattern of violation which is shown is common to all jurisdictions. Violations on parole tend to occur relatively soon after release from an institution, nearly half of them within the first 6 months after offenders are released, and over 60 percent within the first year.

Obviously, prerelease and immediate postrelease programing should receive a very high priority among efforts to strengthen parole services. Theoretically, as noted above, preparation for release—the ultimate goal of correctional institution programs should begin on the first day of admission. In reality, concern about release, as measured in specific programs efforts, usually begins during the last days of confinement.

The Federal system and several States, however, have prerelease classes in penitentiaries. Michigan and Colorado, among others, have separate facilities to which inmates are assigned for a period of time before release. Although such programs are a step forward, they suffer from being located far from the community where the released offender must make his adjustment. Location of prerelease centers in the heart of the community would overcome some of these

Table 4 *Months Completed on Parole by Parole Violators, State of Washington, 1964*

Months on Parole	Violators	
	Number	Percent
6 or less	476	43
7–12	208	19
13–18	93	8
Over 18	328	30
Total	1,105	100

SOURCE. "Post-Institutional Behavior of Inmates Released from Washington State Adult Correctional Institutions," Washington Department of Institutions Research Review, 19:56 (April 1965).

obstacles, permitting inmates to go into the community, deal with real problems, and return each day to receive some help in coping with their problems. Parole staff would be given invaluable opportunities to observe progress under the actual stresses of community life. Existing half-way house programs in a number of cities provide models for such centers.

The role of the parole officer is also crucial in preparing for the return of an offender. The officer should be in contact with the offender's family prior to release and make arrangements when necessary with schools, mental health services, potential employers, and other community resources. Prerelease visits by parole agents to offenders in institutions are very useful in providing continuity of treatment upon release, although distance makes such visits difficult in some jurisdictions.

Employment as a Condition for Release

Over the years, parole systems have been plagued by large numbers of inmates who have been granted parole but have no jobs to go to on release. Stable and meaningful employment has been consistently stressed by correctional authorities as critical to the successful reintegration of offenders into the community.

Many releasing authorities therefore require the offender to have a job as a condition of release. Thus a number of inmates have been held in prisons pending the development of employment, a situation highly demoralizing to the inmates and their families. Moreover, the inmate who is required to find a job before release may well secure one which is temporary or unattractive as permanent employment.

Several States have adopted modified requirements that provide for release without employment for certain inmates under stipulated conditions. An example is a New York plan called "release on reasonable assurance." Under this procedure, selected parolees can be released without a prearranged job if they have a stable home situation, a marketable employment skill or evidence of clear community interest in helping them to find work.

Research has found that inmates released under these circumstances have no higher violation rates than those who were required to find a job before release.[9] Inmates who are allowed to find jobs after release must, of course, be able to be able to do so quickly and to hold the jobs they find. Success in this depends heavily on the ability of the parole agency and allied community resources to generate employment opportunities.

General Control Concerns

The major frame of reference around which a parole officer exercises control is the rules and conditions established by the paroling authority. Such rules for

---

[9] John M. Stanton, "Is It Safe to Parole Inmates Without Jobs?" *Crime and Delinquency,* 12: 147–150 (April 1966).

adults generally forbid unauthorized association with persons having a criminal record and seek to control behavior in such areas as drinking, employment, and mobility. Parolees usually must secure permission to change their residence, to travel to another area, to marry or to buy a car. With juveniles there is must less uniformity, and in some jurisdictions few specific conditions are used.

The strictness with which parole rules are enforced varies greatly from jurisdiction to jurisdiction, depending in part on the training of the parole officer but chiefly on the formal and informal policies of the parole system. Enforcement involves many unofficial understandings. Extremely detailed rules are often overlooked by parole officers, particularly if they have reason to feel confident about a parolee. On the other hand, where conditions are relatively broad, researchers have demonstrated that both officers and parolees understand that certain rules operate although they are never explicitly set out in the parole agreement.[10]

A key problem in both situations is how to enhance a parole officer's ability to use discretion and at the same time provide checks against its abuse. It is important to recognize that parole rules are not an end in themselves. They are meant to be tools of supervision that assist an officer to work with an offender to prevent further crime. Overly stringent rules that are strictly and universally enforced are self-defeating. Conditions that are rarely enforced make parole supervision almost meaningless.

Rules of parole seem to be best when they are relatively few, simple, and specifically tailored to the individual case. But no matter how well rules are chosen, the final test lies in how well they are applied and sanctioned. This involves great skill and sensitive judgment on the part of the parole officer. Training, rigorous personnel screening methods, and effective staff supervision are critically needed if that level of skill and judgment is to be developed and maintained.

Specific Law Enforcement Duties

A number of parole laws provide that officers can order a parolee to be taken into confinement, usually pending an investigation about commission of a new offense. Clearly, this is a power that can be badly abused, and on occasion it has been. There have been instances in which parolees have been confined for extended periods of time on alleged parole violations or simply as punishment for misconduct. Consequently the parole officer's power to detain the parolee has been increasingly surrounded with procedural safeguards in many parole systems.

A more general question that has troubled parole authorities, especially those in the adult field, is the method by which essentially law enforcement functions should be carried out when serious violations of parole conditions are suspected. The predominant opinion in the parole field is that supervision staff should not assume the role of police officers. A recent survey of parole board members, for

---

[10] Glaser, "The Effectiveness of a Prison and Parole System," fn. 7 suprà, p. 428.

example, showed that only 27 percent of them believed that parole officers should be asked to arrest parole violators and only 13 percent believed that parole officers should be allowed to carry weapons.[11] The task of a parole officer is generally seen as developing close working relationships with police departments rather than performing law enforcement functions directly. But this does not mean that parole officers can neglect responsibility for control and surveillance.

Programs to effect liaison with police departments have been developed in the States of New York and California. There, certain parole officers, designated as investigators, are specially trained and assigned to units responsible for liaison with police departments. They cooperate in police intelligence efforts, and they relieve parole officers of some surveillance responsibilities. Most often they undertake investigations in cases at the request of a parole officer who suspects that a parolee is involved in criminal activities. They also initiate inquiries on the basis of information from other contacts, often the police.

These efforts to achieve effective police relationships need careful study. Some observers question the practice, contending that it is not an appropriate activity for a parole agency or that it could better be handled by each parole agent in his own district. Advocates of this system contend that it creates much closer cooperation with police agencies, defines the role of the regular parole officer more clearly, and relieves him of tasks for which he has little training.

Staff Needs

The National Survey found that in 1965 there were about 2,100 parole officers and administrative staff responsible for adult parole services in the United States and another 1,400 assigned to parole for juveniles. Table 5 shows the estimated size of caseloads in which parolees were being supervised in 1965.

One fact stands out: There are simply not enough parole officers available to carry out the tasks assigned to them. The Survey shows that adults released on parole are supervised in caseloads averaging 68. Not only is the parole officer responsible for those 68 cases, but in 30 States he will probably be conducting presentence investigations in probation cases. In virtually all States, he will be investigating release plans and developing future employment for offenders still in prison. It should be noted, too, that over 22 percent of adult parolees were being supervised in caseloads of more than 80 in 1965.

In the juvenile field, a number of States have well-developed aftercare programs, but in many others such services are nonexistent or depend upon extension of help by local probation officers or welfare departments. The average caseload for juveniles is about 64. This average does not include those juveniles released on parole in 10 States where the Survey found it impossible to estimate the

---

[11] "Description of Backgrounds and Some Attitudes of Parole Authority Members of the United States," National Parole Institutes (New York: National Council on Crime and Delinquency, August 1963, mimeo.).

Table 5   *Percentage Distribution of Parolees, by Size of Caseload in Which Supervised, 1965*

Caseload Size	Juvenile Parole (Percent)	Adult Parole (Percent)
Under 50	28.2	7.9
51–60	4.7	25.4
61–70	48.8	20.7
71–80	5.7	23.2
Over 80	12.6	22.8

SOURCE. National Survey of Corrections.

adequacy of aftercare services because the parole cases were so mingled with others such as welfare clients or were handled on such an informal basis that virtually no organized data were available. As in the case of adults, this caseload average does not include the heavy time commitments that juvenile aftercare workers must make to contacting parents and others in the community in preparing for release of juveniles.

As with probation, there is no single caseload standard which can be applied to all parolees. Different cases require different kinds of supervision. Some need intensive contact, while others can be managed in larger caseloads. The most complete data available as to the optimum average caseload was developed from a series of studies made in California during the last decade. Recently the State's adult parole system has sought to determine what an average caseload would be when different types of parolees were matched with appropriate kinds and degrees of supervision. At present, the results from this particular study indicate that caseloads should average around 37, although the average has been dropping the longer the study has run.[12]

The best estimate available from current research seems to be that caseloads should generally average 35 per officer. At that level, some offenders who needed it could be closely supervised in caseloads of 20 or lower, and others could be handled adequately in caseloads as high as 75 or even more. Such a caseload average would permit intensive supervision of those offenders who appear to have a potential for violence, as well as those with special treatment needs. It would enable the officer to have significant face-to-face contacts with offenders and to deal with emerging problems before they led to failure and perhaps to further offenses. With such a reasonable workload, the officer would have time to contact employers, families, schools, and law enforcement agencies as well as the parolees themselves.

[12] See "California Department of Corrections Parole Work Unit Program, Report Submitted to Joint Legislative Budget Committee" (Sacramento: The Department, Dec. 1966).

Field Staff Administration

In 34 States, the agency that administers the State training schools and camps also provides parole supervision services for juveniles released from those institutions. In the remaining 16 States, these services are provided through a variety of sources. Some of those States provide virtually no services at all. In five States, local probation departments are given responsibility for aftercare programs, though they have no official relationship to the agency administering the training schools. In other States, training schools make special arrangements with local agencies to provide aftercare supervision, sometimes on a case-by-case basis.

Although there is some disagreement, the dominant view among standard setting agencies such as the U.S. Children's Bureau is that parole supervision in the juvenile field should not be the responsibility of an institution but should be administered by an agency with responsibility for both the institution and the field staff. There is no significant support for an independent parole board controlling the field staff that serves juvenile offenders.

The existence of independent parole boards in the adult field, however, has meant that controversy has centered on whether parole officers should report to the independent parole board or to a central department of corrections which also operates correctional institutions. The National Survey covering the 50 states and Puerto Rico showed that 31 jurisdictions have field parole staff reporting through an executive to the parole board responsible for the release of offenders. The other 20 jurisdictions have field staff reporting through an executive to a State department of correction or similar agency.

The arguments for placing parole supervision services under an independent parole board can be summarized as follows:

1. The paroling authority is in the best position to promote parole and gain public acceptance for it. Since it is held responsible for parole failures, it should be responsible for supervision services.

2. Paroling authorities in direct control of administration are in the best position to evaluate the effectiveness of parole services.

3. Supervision by the paroling authority properly divorces the parolee from the correctional institutions.

4. An autonomous paroling authority in charge of its own services can best present its own budget request to the legislature.

Among the arguments for including both parole supervision and institutions in a single department of corrections, with the parole authority having responsibility and authority only for case decisions, are these:

1. The correctional process is a continuum. All staff, institutional and parole, should be under a single administration rather than being divided, with resultant competition for public funds and friction in policies.

2. A consolidated correctional department has the advantage of consistent administration, including staff selection, in-service training, and supervision.

3. Boards are ineffective in performing administrative functions. Their major focus should be on case decisions, not on day-by-day field operations.

4. The growing number of programs part way between institutions and parole can best be handled by a single centralized administration.

Local factors are quite important in deciding on the best course to follow. If the management of a State prison system is stagnant and the parole board is active and effective, obviously parole supervision should stay with the parole board. On the other hand, where there is at least equal capacity and motivation on the part of the parole board and the department of corrections, the value of integrating institutional and field programs seems to be an overriding reason for one responsible administration covering all correctional programs. The trend in recent years has been in this direction.

18
Parole: National Standards and Goals

NATIONAL ADVISORY COMMISSION
ON CRIMINAL JUSTICE STANDARDS AND GOALS

Almost every offender who enters a correctional institution is eventually released. The only relevant questions are: When? Under what conditions?

Most offenders released from a correctional institution re-enter the community on parole. In 1970, the latest year for which complete data are available, almost 83,000 felons left prison; 72 percent of them were released by parole. Nineteen percent were released by discharge and 9 percent by other forms of conditional release.[1] Parole is the predominant mode of release for prison inmates today, and it is likely to become even more so. This trend can be highlighted by comparing the figures for 1970 stated above with those from 1966, when 88,000 felons left prison; 61 percent were released by parole, 34 percent by discharge, and 5 percent by other forms of conditional release.[2]

A 1965 study by the President's Commission on Law Enforcement and Administration of Justice (the Crime Commission) showed that slightly more than

SOURCE. *Corrections,* National Advisory Commission on Criminal Justice Standards and Goals, Washington, D.C., U.S. Government Printing Office, 1973, pp. 389–436.

[1] *National Prisoner Statistics: Prisoners in State and Federal Institutions for Adult Felons, 1970* (Washington: Federal Bureau of Prisons, 1970), p. 43.

[2] *National Prisoner Statistics: Prisoners in State and Federal Institutions for Adult Felons, 1966* (Washington: Federal Bureau of Prisons, 1968), p. 43.

112,000 offenders were then under parole supervision. By 1975, the Commission estimated, this number would be more thán 142,000.[3]

These figures include only those offenders sentenced to State prisons. They do not include youth committed to juvenile institutions, virtually all of whom are released under some form of supervision at the rate of about 60,000 a year.

None of these figures include persons sentenced to jail, workhouses, and local institutions. More than one million persons were released from such facilities in 1965, according to the Crime Commission. It is in these facilities that some of the most significant gaps in parole services exist.

The National Survey of Corrections made for the Crime Commission found that almost all misdemeanants were released from local institutions and jails without parole. Of a sample of 212 local jails, the survey found 62 percent had no parole programs at all. In the 81 jails that offered parole, only 8 percent of the inmates actually were released through this procedure.[4] There is little reason to believe the situation has changed radically since 1965, although efforts have been made in several jurisdictions to extend parole services to jail populations. The need for parole services is acute at the misdemeanant level.

Parole has been attacked as leniency, but its proponents argue that it is both humanitarian and designed to protect the public. They advance these arguments on two grounds. First, virtually everyone convicted and sent to a correctional institution will return to the community. He can be turned loose by discharge with no continuing responsibility on his part or the State's, or he can be released under supervision at what appears to be an optimal time and be assisted in reintegration into the community. From this perspective, parole is simply a form of graduated return to the community, a sensible release procedure.

A second major argument is that the sentencing judge cannot anticipate what new information may be available to a parole board or what circumstances might arise to indicate the optimum release date. Unlike the judge, a paroling agency has the advantage of being able to observe the offender's behavior. Furthermore, decisions on release made at the time of sentencing may be more angry than rational. Greater objectivity in appraising the offender may be achieved by a parole board when the passions that may have been aroused by an individual's offense have cooled.

Available evidence supports the view that parole does not lead necessarily to a lessening of the amount of time inmates actually serve in prison. In fact, one major criticism of present parole laws is that their administration tends to result in more severe penalties in a criminal justice system that already imposes extensive State control.

---

[3] President's Commission on Law Enforcement and Administration of Justice, *Task Force Report: Corrections* (Washington: Government Printing Office, 1967), pp. 6–8. Publication referred to hereinafter by title.

[4] *Task Force Report: Corrections,* p. 61.

Inmates released on parole in the United States in 1964, the last time national data of this kind were available, actually served slightly *more* time than those released through unconditional discharge (Table 1). The table does not show the additional time served by offenders returned to prison as parole violators, a hazard to which those discharged unconditionally are not subject. In the major proportion of parole revocation cases, violation of parole rules rather than new felony offenses cause the offender's return to prison to serve more of his sentence. Thus arguments are made that the sentencing structures supporting extensive parole use should be severely modified because of their capacity to inflict additional and unwarranted "punishment."

DEFINITION AND HISTORY

The classic definition of parole was provided in the Attorney General's Survey of Release Procedures in 1939 as "release of an offender from a penal or correctional institution, after he has served a portion of his sentence, under the continued custody of the state and under conditions that permit his reincarceration in the event of misbehavior."[5] Though some jurisdictions impose limitations on parole use, offenders generally can be released on parole and repeatedly returned to confinement for parole violation until the term of their original commitment has expired.

Yet to many, parole is still seen as "leniency" for offenders. Others contend that, in well-operated systems, different types of offenders should serve differing periods of time, and the more dangerous and violence-prone should serve more time. This is seen as a proper use of sentencing and parole flexibility. To actually understand parole and to make it a more effective instrument of public policy requires sophisticated knowledge of all its processes, procedures, and objectives. Understanding is obscured by the use of such value-laden terms as leniency, harshness, punishment, or coddling. All of them oversimplify what is a complex administrative, legal, and political issue.

Table 1. *Number and Types of Releases in 1964 and Median Time Served*

Type of release	Number	Median time served
Discharge	22,883	20.1 months
Parole	42,538	21.1 months

SOURCE. *National Prisoner Statistics, State Prisoners: Admissions and Releases, 1964* (Washington: Federal Bureau of Prisons, 1967.)

[5] *Attorney General's Survey of Release Procedures* (Washington: Government Printing Office, 1939), vol. IV, p. 4.

Parole resembles probation in a number of respects. In both, information about an offender is gathered and presented to a decisionmaking authority with power to release him to community supervision under specific conditions. If he violates those conditions, the offender may be placed in, or returned to, a correctional institution. Parole, however, differs from probation in a significant way. Parole implies that the offender has been incarcerated in a correctional institution before he is released, while probation is granted by a judge in lieu of any kind of confinement.

Recent development of informal institutions (half-way houses, etc.) used by both courts and parole boards make the distinction between probation and parole increasingly difficult to sustain. To add further confusion, some jurisdictions use the term "bench parole" to refer to a form of minimally supervised probation.

Parole and probation also differ significantly in terms of who makes the decision. Parole is almost always an administrative decision; the granting of probation, a court function.

The power to determine when an offender may be released from an institution, to fix the conditions of his supervision, and to order parole revocation almost always passes from the court to an agency within the executive branch. In the case of adults this agency is usually a parole board; in the case of juveniles, an institutional official. As a condition of probation, a sentencing judge may require an offender to spend some time in an institution before he is released under community supervision, as in the "split sentence" in Federal jurisdictions. In this situation, authority to fix conditions and powers of revocation and discharge continue with the court after the offender is released from confinement. Therefore, the case almost always is classified as probation.

Parole also needs to be distinguished from one other kind of release. In a number of jurisdictions—New York, Wisconsin, the Federal system—adult offenders are automatically released under supervision when they have served a portion of their sentence and have earned a specified amount of time off for good behavior. Legislation specifies the calculation "good time," and the parole authority exercises no discretion in the matter. The procedure is called "mandatory" or "conditional" release and is used to provide supervision for those offenders who have been denied parole, are ineligible for it, or have previously refused it. Although released automatically, such offenders may be returned to serve the remainder of their terms if they violate any of the release conditions. The advantage of mandatory release is that supervision is provided for those not paroled. Its main disadvantages are that time under supervision usually is short, and inmates are released simply because they have earned time off for good behavior, with little regard for their readiness to return to the community.

The beginning of parole in the United States generally is identified with the Elmira Reformatory in New York, which opened in 1876. In the Elmira system, sentences were indeterminate, dependent on "marks" earned by good behavior. Release was for a six-month parole term, during which the parolee had to report regularly to a volunteer guardian or sponsor.

Elmira drew wide attention by its new approach to imprisonment, which was markedly different from the tradition of incarceration for a term fixed at the time of sentence. The designation of certain institutions for youthful felons as "refor-matories," and the accompanying practice of permitting indeterminate sentences and parole, spread rapidly through the United States in the last quarter of the 19th century and the beginning of the 20th. This sentencing system, including its provisions for parole, soon was extended to prisoners of all ages. By 1922, parole laws had been passed by 45 States, and in 1945 Mississippi became the last State to develop parole legislation.

This does not imply, however, that neither parole laws or practices have developed uniformly. States still vary widely in the proportion of inmates released under parole supervision. In 1968, for example, the National Prisoner Statistics of the Federal Bureau of Prisons showed that among offenders released in the States of Washington, New Hampshire, and California, more than 95 percent were released under parole supervision. During the same period, less than 10 percent of inmates released in Oklahoma were released on parole. In Nebraska the comparable figure was 20 percent. Nationwide, releases to parole supervision were approximately 60 percent of all releases.

The history of parole for juvenile offenders is different from that for adults. For juveniles, parole usually is traced to the houses of refuge for children in the latter part of the 19th century. From these settings, children were released to work for several years in private homes. Total control of the child was vested in the family to whom he was released. It was the family's responsibility to deter-mine when he had earned his freedom.

The child protection programs developed later assumed many of these activi-ties. Although in recent years juvenile programs have become more correctional, they have continued to be involved closely with child welfare activities.[6] In many States, juvenile aftercare services are the responsibility of the welfare department or a similar agency containing a broad range of services. In these settings, delin-quency is seen as merely a symptom of a young person's need for State services. Labels such as "delinquent," "dependent," or "neglected" are de-emphasized. The general thrust is to treat these children within the context of child welfare.

Juvenile parole authorities usually are more than willing to distinguish their services from those for adults. Juvenile officials typically use the term "aftercare" as a synonym for parole, but in many ways the difference is more than semantic. The problems presented by the young releasee are different from those of the adult offender. School attendance and vocational training programs are much more likely to be a central feature of programs for juveniles, while employment is the major concern for adult offenders.[7] The two concerns might be cursorily equated. But no one may be legally required to work, while school attendance is compul-sory for juveniles. In fact, chronic truancy is a juvenile "crime."

Juvenile and adult parole services usually are not organized similarly. The National Survey of Corrections showed that in 1965 parole boards decided on the

---

[6] See Anthony Platt, "The Rise of the Child-Saving Movement: A Study of Social Policy and Correctional Reform," *Annals of the American Academy of Political and Social Sciences,* 381:21 (January 1969).

[7] See William Arnold, *Juveniles on Parole* (Random House, 1970).

release of juveniles in only two States, although such boards released adults almost everywhere in the country.

SENTENCING STRUCTURES

Any parole system and set of standards designed to improve its functioning can be understood and evaluated only in terms of the structure in which it exists. All parole systems, no matter how autonomous, are part of a larger process—not only of corrections generally, but also of a complex sentencing structure involving trial courts and legislative mandates. The structure and functions of parole systems and their relative importance in the jurisdiction's total criminal justice picture all depend largely on the sources of sentencing authority and limits on sentencing alternatives and lengths.[8] In most jurisdictions, for most offense categories, the sentences that can be imposed and the proportion of sentences actually served are determined by a balance of decisionmaking powers among legislatures, trial courts, and parole authorities. As noted in Chapter 5 of the Commission report, there is no sentencing structure common to all jurisdictions. The relative importance and power of parole determinations vary markedly from one jurisdiction to another and within jurisdictions from one offense category to another.

Variations in Structure

Throughout the history of American criminal justice, there have been various models of "ideal" sentencing structures proposed in different jurisdictions. Some have been tried, all have been debated, most have been modified. But there is still no uniform sentencing structure. The Model Penal Code of the American Law Institute, the Model Sentencing Act proposed by the National Council on Crime and Delinquency, suggestions of the Crime Commission, and the American Bar Association's Minimum Standards for Sentencing are recent attempts to propose sentencing structures suitable for all offenders in all jurisdictions. Because there have been no common standards for sentencing structures and processes, establishing standards for parole functions is extremely complex.

It might be possible to reach agreement on matters such as structure and composition of parole boards, appropriate workloads, staff training and development, and proper procedures for granting and revoking. But it must be remembered that the meaning and importance of the paroling function vary from one postconviction system to another. For example, in jurisdictions where legislatures set long maximum terms that trial judges cannot modify, where good-time laws are stringent, or where pardon is almost unheard of, parole becomes not only an important method of release but virtually the *only* method. Furthermore, where sentences are long, it may mean that parolees must be supervised for decades.

---

[8] See Chapter 5 of this report. See also Daniel Glaser, Fred Cohen, and Vincent O'Leary, *The Sentencing and Parole Process* (Washington: U.S. Department of Health, Education, and Welfare, 1966).

The situation is different in systems that have relatively short legislative limits on sentences, with judges empowered to fix upper terms less than statutory maxima, and with liberal good-time allowances or frequent use of pardon. In such cases parole determinations may play a relatively minor part in overall release processes. In short-sentence jurisdictions, parolees terminate supervision fairly quickly. In jurisdictions in which minimum sentences are not required by either legislation or court determination, parole authorities have wide discretion to release inmates at any time.

Variations also exist among jurisdictions in regard to institutionalized juvenile delinquents, but they are not nearly as disparate as in the case of adults. The extent of control by the State over juvenile offenders generally is fixed by age rather than by offense. In most jurisdictions juvenile commitments do not have fixed minimum terms, so that release authorities have wide discretion.

But laws relating to juveniles are by no means uniform in all jurisdictions. For example, the National Survey of Corrections reported that in five States juveniles can be paroled from State training schools only with the committing judge's approval. In three States, the time a juvenile must serve before release is fixed in advance by the court. In effect, these are minimum sentences.

The sentencing system finally adopted is crucial to the parole function because it fixes the amount and the character of discretion a parole system can exercise. Seeking to eliminate the abuses that lurk in discretion, some persons would eliminate any form of discretionary release after sentencing by the trial judge.[9] However, most authorities hold that discetion is inevitable; the task is to limit and control it. From this view, many more problems arise when the entire releasing decision is placed in the hands of the trial judge or made dependent on a system of totally fixed sentences set by the legislature than if the decision is shared with a parole authority.[10]

On the other hand, most parole officials do not want the amount of power implicitly delegated by completely indeterminate sentencing. They feel that the awesome task of determining sentence limits should be left to judicial and legislative branches.

Sentencing Consistent With Parole Objectives

The sentencing system that seems most consistent with parole objectives has the following characteristics:

1. Sentence limits set by legislation, with the sentencing judge having discretion to fix the maximum sentence, up to legislative limits.

2. No minimum sentences, either by mandate or by judicial sentencing authority.

---

[9] See *Struggle for Justice: A Report on Crime and Punishment in America,* Prepared for the American Friends Service Committee (Hill and Wang, 1971), ch. 8.

[10] See American Bar Association Project on Minimum Standards for Criminal Justice, *Sentencing Alternatives and Procedures* (Institute for Judicial Administration, 1967), Sec. 3, pp. 129–199.

3. Comparatively short sentences for most offenses, with a legislative maximum not to exceed five years for most offenders.

4. Mandatory release with supervision for offenders ineligible for parole, so that they are not held in an institution until their absolute discharge date.

5. All parole conditions set by the paroling authority, but with opportunity for a sentencing judge to suggest special conditions.

6. Legislative prohibition of offenders' accumulating consecutive sentences if it interferes with minimum parole eligibility.

7. Legislative provisions for alternatives to reimprisonment upon parole revocation.

8. No offenses for which parole is denied by legislation.

In general, the intent of such a system is to give to the legislature and sentencing judges the authority to set outer limits of sentence but not to restrict parole authorities by setting minimum terms. At the same time, the sentencing structure provides supervised release for those offenders whom parole authorities cannot conscientiously release under regular parole criteria. The sentencing structure may provide for extended terms for dangerous offenders, though parole eligibility requirements should remain roughly the same in these cases.

A system of this kind would give parole authorities discretion over the release of offenders whom trial courts decided need incarceration. Yet it would be a limited discretion. Parolees would not be under supervision for excessive time periods nor, if parole were denied, would they be incarcerated for unnecessarily long terms.

PURPOSES OF PAROLE

The objectives of parole systems vary widely. Without clearly stated and understood objectives, the administrator cannot make the most basic decisions regarding effective resource allocation. Even a casual attempt to clarify the purposes of parole will reveal that objectives frequently are in conflict. One of the parole administrator's chief tasks is to minimize this conflict.

A Basic Purpose: Reduction of Recidivism

Few things about parole evoke consensus, but there is some agreement that one objective and measure of success is reduction of recidivism. Even this consensus quickly becomes less firm when two specific functions are examined: (1) provision of supervision and control to reduce the likelihood of criminal acts while the offender is serving his sentence in the community (the "surveillance" function), and (2) provision of assistance and services to the parolee, so that noncriminal behavior becomes possible (the "helping" function).[11]

---

[11] American Correctional Association, *Manual of Correctional Standards* (Washington: ACA, 1966), p. 114.

To the extent that these concerns can be integrated, conflicts are minimized, but in the day-to-day activity of parole administration they frequently clash. Decisions constantly must be made between the relative risk of a law violation at the present time and the probable long-term gain if a parolee is allowed freedom and opportunity to develop a legally approved life style. Resources are needed to clarify the choices and risks involved. Key requirements for this kind of assistance are development of clear definitions of recidivism and creation of information systems that make data available about the probabilities of various types of parole outcome associated with alternative decisions. (These requirements are discussed in some detail in Chapter 15 of the Commission Report.)

Varied Concerns of Parole Boards

Reducing the risk of further criminality is not the sole concern. In fact, it actually may be secondary in some instances. A wider variety of concerns was expressed in a questionnaire completed by nearly half the parole board members in the United States in 1965, who were asked to indicate what they considered the five most important factors to be weighed in deciding on parole. Table 2 shows the items selected by at least 20 percent of those responding as being among the five most important considerations. The first three items selected as being the most important were related to the risk of violation. However, the next four related to three other concerns: equitable punishment, impact on the system, and reactions of persons outside the correctional organization.

A number of other studies have noted the same phenonemon.[12] Most parole board members consider risk a paramount concern, but other factors assume such importance in certain cases that risk becomes secondary. A well-known inmate convicted and sentenced for violation of a public trust may be denied parole repeatedly because of strong public feelings, even though he might be an excellent risk. In another type of case, an offender convicted of a relatively minor crime may be paroled even though a poor risk, because in the opinion of the board he has simply served enough time for the offense committed. To some analysts these other-than-risk considerations are viewed simply as contingencies that arise from time to time; to others they involve objectives central to parole decisionmaking. In either case, considerations other than risk assessment figure prominently in parole decisionmaking and must be accounted for in any discussion of objectives. To judge from questionnaires returned by parole board members and from studies in the field, there seem to be at least three core sets of concern other than reducing recidivism,[13] which significantly and regularly impinge upon most parole decisionmakers.

---

[12] See Robert Dawson, *Sentencing: The Decision as to Type, Length, and Conditions of Sentence* (Little, Brown, 1969).

[13] Keith Hawkins, "Parole Selection: The American Experience," unpublished doctoral dissertation, Cambridge University, 1971.

Table 2. *Items Considered by Parole Board Members to be Most Important in Parole Decisions*

Item	Percent Including Item as One of Five Most Important
1. My estimate of the chances that the prisoner would or would not commit a serious crime if paroled.	92.8
2. My judgment that the prisoner would benefit from further experience in the institution program or, at any rate, would become a better risk if confined longer.	87.1
3. My judgment that the prisoner would become a worse risk if confined longer.	71.9
4. My judgment that the prisoner had already been punished enough to "pay" for his crime.	43.2
5. The probability that the prisoner would be a misdemeanant and a burden to his parole supervisors, even if he did not commit any serious offenses on parole.	35.3
6. My feelings about how my decision in this case would affect the feelings or welfare of the prisoner's relatives or dependents.	33.8
7. What I thought the reaction of the judge might be if the prisoner were granted parole.	20.9

SOURCE. National Parole Institutes, *Selection for Parole* (New York: National Council on Crime and Delinquency, 1966).

Fairness and Propriety

Parole programs are part of larger systems of criminal justice. They are governed by concepts of propriety and modes of conduct arising from American culture and law. Especially in recent years, parole systems have been expected to conform with practices that enhance the ideals of fairness and reflect hallmarks of American justice such as procedural regularity, precedent, and proof.

Most recently these issues have been reflected in increased sensitivity to inmates' or revokees' rights to counsel, the right of a hearing on parole grant and revocation, and disclosure of information used in decisionmaking. Reflecting this emphasis, some parole board members may even refuse to consider at a parole violation hearing evidence that might have been secured by questionable search procedure. Comparable issues also arise in establishing conditions for parole supervision, which are expected to meet the tests of relevance, reasonableness, and fairness.

Appropriate Sanctions and Public Expectations

Though it seldom is stated openly, parole boards often are concerned with supporting a system of appropriate and equitable sanctions. This concern is reflected in several ways, depending upon a jurisdiction's sentencing system. One of the most common is through decisions seeking to equalize penalties for offenders who have similar backgrounds and have committed the same offense but who have received different sentences.

Alternatively, decisions to grant or deny parole, particularly in well-known cases, often may hinge on the question, "Has this person served enough time for the act he committed?" Considerable differences in these matters exist from one system to another, as well as among individuals in the same system. Such concerns usually are less apparent in, and perhaps less relevant to, juvenile agencies. However, in many parole systems, maintaining an appropriate system of sanctions directly or indirectly underlies most decisionmaking. How significant these considerations are depends on the kind of sentencing framework in which the parole system is operating.

In addition to issues of equity, parole decisionmakers sometimes respond to actual or anticipated public attitudes. Such concerns for public acceptance of parole generally, and case decisions specifically, govern the kinds of risks that are acceptable and the actions considered feasible by parole decisionmakers. This public reaction issue is particularly acute in cases affecting society's core beliefs. Criteria having little to do with the question of risk may be used by parole officials in dealing with certain cases, particularly those involving crimes seen as "heinous." The concern is more for meeting general social norms and responding according to public expectations.

Maintenance of the Justice System

A third set of concerns that influences parole decisionmaking relates to support of other criminal justice operations. Parole boards play a crucial role as a kind of system regulator, influencing other parts of the justice system, from police to prisons. For example, in some systems where a parole board has extensive control over the amount of time a large proportion of inmates will serve, institutional populations can change dramatically depending on board policy. Not only do parole board decisions influence institutional size, but they also reinforce behavior that can have profound effects on the kinds of programs sustained. Inmates are more likely to participate in a program the parole board explicitly values than in one to which the board pays no attention.

Institutional staff members have an obvious stake in the programs in which inmates are involved. Hence they too are affected by parole decisions. Various parole officials are sensitive to the correctional impact of their decisions and some take this factor into account in their decisions.[14] In some instances, boards will

---

[14] Keith Hawkins, "Some Consequences of a Parole System for Prison Management," in D. F. West, ed., *The Future of Parole* (London: Gerald Duckworth, 1972).

be reminded forcefully of their effect on inmates and institutions. For example, it is not uncommon during times of high prison tension (as after riots), when parole policy is under attack by inmates and sympathizers, for boards to become more "liberal." In such instances, the degree of risk acceptable for parole, conditioned by pressures within the institutions, shifts perceptibly. Parole boards directly affect parole supervision staff by the kind of offenders they release and revoke, and by the policies surrounding these actions.

System maintenance and other basic concerns cited clearly influence parole decisionmaking. However, questions of risk, fairness, public expectation, and system maintenance are not the only considerations affecting parole authorities. Of great importance as well are the beliefs they hold concerning the sources of criminality, strategies for changing offenders, and the nature of the relationship between the correctional system and the offender.

ORGANIZATION OF PAROLING AUTHORITIES

Most persons concerned with parole decisionmaking for juveniles are full-time institutional personnel. On a few juvenile jurisdictions have noninstitutional personnel determining parole releases.

Different circumstances prevail in the adult area. For example, adult boards tend to carry many more direct State-level administrative responsibilities than do releasing authorities for juveniles. Table 3 shows that in 1965, 14 adult parole boards supervised probation services for the courts of the State. Few parole decisionmaking groups for juvenile offenders had a similar responsibility. The table also shows the historical link in many States between parole and the clemency or pardon authority of the governor. Many boards carried out advisory functions for the governor in executive clemency matters and in one State, Alabama, the board granting paroles also had the power to pardon.

Although there is considerable variety in the organizational settings in which parole decisionmakers work, at least two dominant organizational strains can be identified—the institutional model, which largely predominates in the juvenile field, and the independent model, the most common in the adult field. Considerable controversy has arisen around these two models.[15]

The Institutional Model

In general, the institutional model perceives parole as being bound closely to institutional programs. It places the release decision with the correctional facility's staff. Parole is simply one more of a series of decisions affecting the offender. The persons most familiar with the case make the releasing decision; and this makes it possible to develop a rational and consistent set of decisions that affect the inmate. The Crime Commission reported that 34 of 50 States used this form of organization in the juvenile field.

[15] *Task Force Report: Corrections,* pp. 65–66.

Table 3   *Responsibilities of Adult Paroling Agencies Other Than Parole, 1965*

Additional Responsibility	Number of Boards
Holds clemency hearings	28
Commutes sentences	24
Appoints parole supervision staff	24
Administers parole service	20
Paroles from local institutions	19
Grants or withholds "good time"	17
Supervises probation services	14
Grants pardons, restorations, and remissions	1
Fixes maximum sentence after 6 months	1
May discharge prior to sentence expiration	1
Sets standards for "good time"	1
Acts as advisory board on pardons	1
None	5

SOURCE. National Council on Crime and Delinquency, *Correction in the United States* (New York: NCCD, 1967), p. 215.

The major arguments raised against the institutional model is that too often institutional considerations, rather than individual or community needs, influence the decisions. Overcrowding in the institution, desire to be rid of a problem case or to enforce relatively petty rules, or other concerns of institution management easily become the basis of decisionmaking. Institutional decisionmaking also lends itself to such informal procedures and lack of visibility as to raise questions about its capacity for fairness or, what may be as important, the appearance of fairness.

The Independent Authority

In the adult field, a good deal of reform was associated with removing parole decisionmaking from institutional control to an independent authority. Undoubtedly much of the basis for this reform came from the view that paroling authorities were being swayed too easily by institutional considerations or were not being objective enough.[16] The change was so complete that today no adult parole releasing authority is controlled directly by the operating staff of a penal institution.

Whatever its merits in fostering objectivity, the independent parole board also has been criticized on several counts. First, the claim is made that such boards

[16] *Attorney General's Survey of Release Procedures* (1939), vol. IV, p. 49.

tend to be insensitive to institutional programs and fail to give them the support they require. Second, independent boards are accused of basing their decisions on inappropriate considerations, such as the feelings of a local police chief. Third, their remoteness from the institutional program gives independent boards little appreciation of the dynamics in a given case; their work tends to be cursory, with the result that too often persons who should be paroled are not, and those who should not be paroled are released. Fourth, the argument is made that independent systems tend to place on parole boards persons who have little training or experience in corrections.

Lack of knowledge about corrections, combined with the distance of the parole board from institutional programs, builds unnecessary conflicts into the system. The rapid growth of partway release programs and halfway houses has increased the probability of those conflicts. In short, critics of the independent model assert that important decisions are being made concerning the correctional system, its programs, and the offenders in it by persons far removed from the system who have little appreciation of its true nature.

The Consolidation Model

While these arguments and their rebuttals continue, an alternate system has gained considerable support in recent years, tending to cut the ground away from both major models. This system is linked with a general move toward consolidation of all types of correctional services into distinctive departments of corrections that subsume both institution and field programs. The consolidation model, emerging from the drive toward centralized administration, typically results in parole decisions being made by a central decisionmaking authority organizationally situated in an overall department of corrections but possessing independent powers. The director of corrections may serve on such a releasing authority, or he may designate a staff member to do so. In the youth field, the centralized board may have policy responsibilities for institutions as well as parole decisionmaking.

Proponents of the consolidation model argue that there is increased concern for the whole correctional system in departments where parole releasing authority is part of a centralized system. They claim that sensitivity to institutional programs seems more pronounced in consolidated systems than in completely autonomous ones. They also contend that removal of parole decisionmaking from the immediate control of specific correctional institutions tends to give greater weight to a broader set of considerations, a number of which are outside direct institutional concerns.

Although variations in organizational or administrative arrangements may be required to meet special circumstances, certain general organizational requirements seem clear. Among the most essential requisites is that the organizational structure of parole authorities should foster close coordination between parole decisionmakers and the increasingly complex set of programs throughout the correctional network. Yet sufficient autonomy should be preserved to permit parole boards to act as a check on the system.

The trend in this country clearly is in the direction of consolidation. More than 60 percent of the State parole boards responsible for release of adult offenders now function in common administrative structures with other agencies for offenders.[17] This trend enhances integration of correctional operations. If parole boards are to function as useful and sophisticated decisionmaking units that balance a wide set of concerns, they also must achieve and maintain some degree of autonomy from the systems with which they interface. This issue involves appointment and tenure methods, as well as the tasks and functions for which parole authorities take responsibility.

Articulation of Criteria for Decisions

Articulation of criteria for making decisions and development of basic policies is one of the chief tasks that parole decisionmakers need to undertake. While discretion is a necessary feature of parole board operations, the central issue is how to contain and control it appropriately. Few parole boards have articulated their decision criteria in much detail or in writing, even though research has shown that criteria exist. Parole board members tend to display, with slight variations, a consistent response to case situations of which they may be only marginally aware.[18]

Articulating the basis of decision systems is crucial to improving parole decisions, because criteria must be specified before they can be validated. For example, 75 percent of 150 board members queried in 1965 by the National Probation and Parole Institute asserted that rapists generally were poor parole risks. Research data have shown such an assumption to be wrong.

Articulation of criteria is crucial to staff and inmates alike. The notion of an inmate's participation in a program of change depends on an open information system. His sense of just treatment is extricably bound with it. As one parole board member put it:

> It is an essential element of justice that the role and processes for measuring parole readiness be made known to the inmate. This knowledge can greatly facilitate the earnest inmate toward his own rehabilitation. It is just as important for an inmate to know the rules and basis of the judgment upon which he will be granted or denied parole as it was important for him to know the basis of the charge against him and the evidence upon which he was convicted. One can imagine nothing more cruel, inhuman, and frustrating than serving a prison term without knowledge of what will be measured and the rules determin-

---

[17] National Probation and Parole Institutes, *The Organization of Parole Systems for Felony Offenders in the United States.* 2d ed. (Hackensack, N.J.: National Council on Crime and Delinquency, 1972). Unless otherwise stated, factual data on State parole systems given in this chapter are from this publication.

[18] Don Gottfredson and Kelly Ballard, "Differences in Parole Decisions Associated with Decision Makers," *Journal of Research in Crime and Delinquency,* **3** (1966), 112.

ing whether one is ready for release. . . . Justice can never be a product of unreasoned judgment.[19]

And without valid information on the basis of parole decisions, correctional staffs hardly can be expected to deal realistically with offenders or to shape meaningful programs with them.

In most parole systems, board members are so heavily committed to case-by-case decisions that these additional tasks, and those to be suggested subsequently, will require a substantial alteration in work style. Smaller States will need to shift from part-time to full-time parole boards. Other States will require additional personnel at the parole decisionmaking level.

Parole

Need for Appeal Procedures

Besides the pressure for clearly articulated policies, there is also is a rapidly developing demand for mechanisms by which correctional, and specifically parole, decisions can be appealed. The upsurge of cases being considered by the courts documents this need.[20] The courts can and will test at least certain aspects of parole decisions. Yet if parole authorities are to develop correctional policy consistent with correctional needs and judicial standards, they need to establish self-regulation systems, including internal appeal procedures.[21]

Where the volume of cases warrants it, a parole board should concentrate its major attention on policy development and appeals. The bulk of case-by-case decisionmaking should be done by hearing examiners responsible to the board and familiar with its policies and knowledgeable as to correctional programs.

Hearing examiners should have statutory power to grant, deny, or revoke parole, subject to parole board rules and policies. In cases of offenders serving long sentences, those involved in cases of high public interest, or others designated by the parole board, two or more parole members personally should conduct the hearings and make decisions. Hearing examiners operating in teams of two should handle the large part of day-to-day interviewing and decisionmaking for the board. Inmates and parolees should be entitled to appeal decisions to the parole board, which could hear cases in panels or en banc. As action is taken on these cases and the system of appeals refined, the board should further articulate its policies against which unwarranted uses of discretion could be checked.

Instead of spending his time routinely traveling from institution to institution hearing every type of case, the board member should be deciding appeals and hearing cases of special concern. He should be developing written policies and using monitoring systems by which decision outcomes could be observed and

---

[19] Everette M. Porter, "Criteria for Parole Selection" in *Proceedings of the American Correctional Association* (New York: ACA, 1958) p. 227.

[20] For examples of this growth in interest by the courts, see Comment, "The Parole System," *Pennsylvania Law Review,* **120** (1971), 282.

[21] Edward Kimball and Donald Newman, "Judicial Intervention in Correctional Decisions: Threat and Response," *Crime and Delinquency,* **14** (1968), 1.

strategies for improvement developed. The use of the board for all types of appeals from correctional decisions (loss of good time, denial of privileges) also should be considered.

In smaller systems, many of these activities would have to be carried out by the same persons. However, procedures can and should be developed to assure attention to each separate function—policy development, hearings, and appeals. Only a few of these crucial activities now are carried out by the average parole board. They are critically needed, and the kind of system described here would greatly facilitate their attainment. Parts of such a system have been used successfully by the California and Federal parole boards and other governmental agencies.

An advisory group, broadly representative of the community and specifically including ex-offenders, should be established to assist the parole board by reviewing policies and helping shape and implement improvement strategies developed. This kind of link to the public is critically needed if sensible policies are to be developed and support for their adoption achieved.

PAROLE AUTHORITY PERSONNEL

The most recent data available on members of juvenile parole releasing authorities indicate that by far the largest number are full-time staff of juvenile correctional institutions.[22] In several States, such as California and Minnesota, youth commissions parole juveniles. In others, such as Wisconsin and Illinois, the same board is responsible for release of both juveniles and adults.[23] The issues of appointment, qualifications, and training raise precisely the same questions for juvenile release authority members as they do for board members responsible for adult release.

In 41 States, adult parole board members are appointed by the governor. In seven jurisdictions, they are appointed in whole or in part by the department of corrections.

A similar problem exists with any part-time member of a paroling authority. In 18 States, parole board members responsible for the parole of adult males are part-time employees. In six others only the chairman is a full-time employee. Part-time board members tend to be located in the smallest States, but there are exceptions. Tennessee and South Carolina, for example, with part-time boards, have larger populations than several other smaller States that have full-time boards. If parole services were extended to local jails and one board was made responsible for jails, training schools for delinquents, and adult prisons, a full-time board would be needed in virtually every State.

For larger States, the relevant question is, What is the optimum size of the parole decisionmaking authority? Almost half of parole boards for adult offenders consist of three members; 18 jurisdictions have five members; six have seven

---

[22] National Council on Crime and Delinquency, *Correction in the United States* (New York: NCCD, 1967), p. 104.
[23] *Correction in the United States,* p. 86.

members; and one parole board, New York's, consists of 12 members. Some parole authorities argue that boards could grow indefinitely. But with a shift in emphasis toward policy articulation and appeals, it would seem prudent to hold the size to a manageable level. Few, if any, State boards should exceed five members. As the workload expands beyond the capacity of these members, hearing examiners should be appointed. The largest States might need 20 hearing examiners or more.

Qualifications of Board Members

Two dilemmas that are common to most appointive public offices are also seen in deciding on the best method of selecting parole board members: first, how to secure appointees with expertise and willingness to challenge the system when necessary rather than merely preserving it; second, how to select parole board members who will be responsive to public concern, as expressed through elected officials, without making politics rather than competence the basis for appointment.

Parole decisionmakers too frequently have shown the negative possibilities of both dilemmas. In many instances they have become so coopted by a correctional system that there is no independent check against abuses of public or offender interests. Too many times appointments have been governed by patronage considerations, a dangerous criterion when human freedom is at stake and the most difficult moral, legal, and scientific issues are involved.

If parole authorities are to have the competence required for their tasks, specific statutory qualifications for board members must be developed. In 24 States there are no statutory requirements for parole members responsible for the release of adult offenders. In one State generalized references to character are made. In another 21 only the broadest references to experience or training are enunciated.

According to the findings of the first National Parole Conference in 1939, board members "should be selected on the basis of their integrity and competence to deal with human and social problems, without reference to political affiliations."[24] More recently the standards proposed by the American Correctional Association required that parole board members should "command respect and public confidence," be "appointed without reference to creed, color or political affiliation," possess "academic training which has qualified the board member for professional practice in a field such as criminology, education, psychiatry, psychology, law, social work and sociology," and "have intimate knowledge of common situations and problems confronting offenders."[25]

No single professional group or discipline can be recommended as ideal for all parole board members. A variety of goals are to be served by parole board members, and a variety of skills are required. Knowledge of at least three basic

[24] *Proceedings, National Parole Conference, 1939* (Leavenworth, Kan.: Federal Prison Industries, Inc., 1970), p. 113.

[25] American Correctional Association, *Manual of Correctional Standards,* p. 119.

fields should be represented on a parole board: the law, the behavioral sciences, and corrections. Furthermore, as a board assumes responsibility for policy articulation, monitoring and review, the tasks involved require persons who are able to use a wide range of decisionmaking tools, such as statistical materials, reports from professional personnel, and a variety of other technical information. In general, persons with sophisticated training and experience are required. In this context, the standards suggested by the American Correctional Association should be statutorily required for each jurisdiction.

Hearing examiners require less specialized education and training. More critical in these roles are persons with educational and experiential qualifications that allow them to understand programs, to relate to people, and to make sound and reasonable decisions. These roles should offer particular opportunities for ex-offenders and for those persons most sensitive to the implications of offenders' lifestyles.

Making the Appointment

A critical question concerns who should make the actual appointment to the parole board. Two basic choices are the governor or the head of the department of corrections. Appointment by the governor provides the board increased autonomy and greater responsiveness to public influence. But it increases the likelihood of lack of coordination with the corrections agency, oversensitivity to public reactions, and appointment of unqualified personnel. Selection by the director of corrections, who is himself selected on the basis of professional qualifications, is more likely to secure appointment of knowledgeable persons, protection from political influence, and some shielding from an undue concern for public criticism. The major disadvantage is the possible appointment of a "rubber stamp" decisionmaking body.

Some type of device must be employed if competent board personnel are to be selected. Each State should require by law that nominees for parole board positions first be screened by a committee broadly representative of the community. Representatives of groups such as the State bar and mental health associations should be included, as well as representatives of various ethnic and socioeconomic groups. The law should require that appointments be made only from the approved list of nominees.

Terms of Office, Salary

A number of other suggestions to improve parole board appointments have been made and should be adopted. One of these is to provide parole board members with substantial terms of office, as long as 12 years, during which they cannot be removed except for good cause.[26]

---

[26] Phillip E. Johnson, *Federal Parole Procedures* (Washington: Administrative Conference of the United States, 1972).

A matter of particular importance in attracting well-qualified persons to parole positions is the compensation. According to the most recent data available, the median salary for full-time parole board members is $19,000 a year. This is not a salary which in 1972 can attract the type of personnel needed for parole decisionmaking posts. The salary for such positions should be equivalent to that of a judge of a court of general jurisdiction.

Training for Board Members

Improvement in the performance of parole members depends heavily on the availability of a training program. The National Probation and Parole Institutes have undertaken to provide biennial training sessions for new members. But much more needs to be done in this area. Ongoing training is needed by both new and experienced board members.

An effective ongoing program should inform board members of recent legal decisions and advances in technology and acquaint them with current correctional practices and trends. Because of the relatively small number of parole board members in each State, such a program would have to be national in scope. An exchange program of parole board members and hearing officers also should receive support. Recent experiments carried out by the National Probation and Parole Institutes, in which parole board members had the opportunity to visit other States, proved to be valuable experience for participants.

THE PAROLE GRANT HEARING

The parole hearing is a critical moment for inmates. At this point they are legally "eligible" for release, their case is studied, they are interviewed, and the decision is made. In all States except Texas, Georgia, and Hawaii, adult felony offenders are present at hearings at the time of parole consideration. Four States screen files and grant interviews only to eligible inmates who seem to merit parole consideration. All other States hear every offender at least once, even those unlikely to be released. Many parole authorities see an inmate several times during the course of his sentence. In fact, a number of States provide for at least annual review of each case, no matter how remote release may be.

Formal hearing procedures are much less common with juveniles. More often, primary emphasis is placed on written reports or staff conferences at which the youth may or may not be present.

Procedures followed at parole hearings for adult offenders are extremely diverse. In some States, each parole applicant is heard by the full parole board. In others, especially those with many correctional institutions, boards are split into smaller working panels, each of which conducts hearings. In several jurisdictions, a single parole board member may conduct a hearing unless the case is regarded as unusually important, when a larger subcommittee or the entire board conducts the hearing. In the Federal system and in California, the parole boards appoint "hearing officers" to assist in some hearings. The number of cases considered in a single day by boards or panels for adult offenders ranges from 15 to 60.

Information Base

Information available to the parole board at the time of a hearing typically is prepared by institutional staff. It is usually based on reports on the offender's adjustment to prison life. Some parole boards request special investigations of release plans for all inmates, while others prefer to wait until they make a tentative decision that parole is indicated. A few States have reports prepared by professional clinical personnel. Since these professionals are scarce, most reports prepared for parole boards are written by caseworkers who actually have relatively little opportunity to observe inmates.

Glaser has suggested use of revised reporting systems, wherein staff members who have the most contact with inmates would be involved most directly in providing data for the board's decisions.[27] With the increasing stress on reintegration, most parole board members need a great deal more information about community services available to released offenders, as well as on feasible programs that might be undertaken. This lack is not solely an information gap; unfortunately, the basic problem is that community resources are meager.

Right to a Hearing

In most jurisdictions the offender has no statutory rights in the parole consideration process, except in some instances the right to a personal appearance before the parole board. Yet at these hearings, the traditional stance has been that the inmate and his record must make an affirmative case for parole. The Model Penal Code represents a turn-around in the traditional assumption that the burden of proof (however evaluated) rests on the inmate. It proposes that an inmate is to be released on parole when he is first eligible unless one of the following four conditions exists:

1. There is a substantial indication that he will not conform to conditions of parole.

2. His release at that time would depreciate the seriousness of the crime or promote disrespect for the law.

3. His release would have substantially adverse effects on institutional discipline.

4. His continued correctional treatment, medical care, or vocational or other training in the institution will substantially enhance his capacity to lead a law-abiding life when released at a later date.[28]

---

[27] Daniel Glaser, *The Effectiveness of a Prison and Parole System* (Bobbs-Merrill, 1964), ch. 9.

[28] American Law Institute, *Model Penal Code,* (Philadelphia: ALI, 1962).

Recently the National Commission on Reform of Federal Criminal Laws substantially endorsed the presumption and the four considerations of the Model Penal Code. It offered in addition the proviso that, once an inmate has served the longer of five years or two-thirds of his sentence, he should be paroled unless the board is "of the opinion that his release should be deferred because there is a high likelihood that he would engage in further criminal conduct."[29]

Procedural Guidelines

In the past few years there has been a noticeable increase in complexity of procedural requirements for parole hearings. Of those jurisdictions holding personal interviews, for example, 21 now permit the "assistance" of attorneys in behalf of the inmate. Seventeen allow the inmate to be represented at the hearing by persons other than counsel whom he feels will help him present his case for granting parole. A verbatim record of proceedings is made in 11 jurisdictions.

Development of guidelines for desirable parole hearings should attend to several concerns simultaneously. First, such hearings should provide parole authorities with as much relevant and reliable information about each case as possible. Second, the hearing process itself should carry the hallmark of fairness. Not only should it be a fair determination in substance, but to the extent possible it also should be perceived by the inmate as fair. Third, as far as practicable the hearing should enhance the prospects for an inmate's successful completion of his parole.

To these ends the hearing can make a number of contributions. The manner in which the inmate is interviewed and notified of decisions affecting him can support or undermine respect for the system of justice. Any opportunity for the offender's active participation in decisions can greatly affect his commitment to the plans made. In the final analysis, *his* commitment is the crucial factor in whether or not these plans will be carried out.

In keeping with the reintegration emphasis, a modern corrections system should embrace a wide variety of alternative programs, not only for institutions, but also for release or partway release. Except in rare cases it will probably be too cumbersome for a parole board to approve specific actions in detail. With community corrections, halfway houses, prerelease centers, split sentences, and similar developments, the line between parole and prison already is becoming blurred. It therefore appears necessary that the parole board increasingly test the appropriateness of programs and match individuals with them by criteria fixed in advance, rather than try to make clinical decisions on an individual's readiness for release.

---

[29] National Commission on Reform of Federal Criminal Laws, *Final Report* (Washington: Government Printing Office, 1971), p. 300.

The Automatic First Hearing

A number of practical steps for parole hearings flow from these changes in overall correctional processing. Every inmate should routinely be seen by a parole authority during the first year of incarceration. This review should be automatic and no application by the inmate should be required. Such a hearing might result in consideration of early parole. More often, it would be devoted to a review of the particular objectives and programs developed by the inmate and staff. Any program involving release for long periods should involve the parole board hearing staff.

The important element of this first, automatic hearing is that the board approves program objectives and program categories for offenders rather than attempting to make detailed clinical judgments about each case. The objective of the hearing, however, should not be to coerce the inmate to subject himself to specific institutional treatment programs. The traditional ineffectiveness of such programs does not make participation a good basis for a parole decision.

A particularly critical determination during this initial interview is scheduling another interview or hearing, if one is necessary before the inmate's release. It should be increasingly common to approve an inmate's program, including a full-time parole release date, as far as a year in advance without requiring another hearing or further interviews by the parole board. If the objectives of the program are met, administration of the parole board's plan would be left to the offender and institutional and field staffs. Should substantial variations occur or important new information develop, the board could be notified and a new hearing scheduled. On the other hand, not all release dates can be predetermined at an initial interview. Additional hearings may be required either because of the length of the inmate's sentence or by the circumstances of a particular case. In such instances, a new hearing date would be fixed after the initial interview. In no case should more than a year transpire between hearings.

Under this plan, the parole board would function more to monitor the decisions of others than to make detailed judgments in individual cases. The plan should also reduce the number of individual release hearings conducted by board representatives. This is particularly important since there is a practical limit on the number that can be conducted in a day. An effective hearing requires close attention of board representatives, institutional staff, offenders, and other persons involved in tailoring programs and releases to individual cases. It also requires careful recording of plans and decisions. With a system of this kind, no more than 20 cases should be heard in a day.

Prompt Decision and Notification

If this system is to work, it requires involvement of at least two representatives of the parole authority who are empowered to grant parole in all but the most exceptional cases. A current problem in a number of parole jurisdictions is that only a single representative of the parole authority actually hears offenders' cases. He is not able to take final action on any case until he returns to a central point where other board officials can join him in making a decision. Hence there is often inordinate delay, while the inmate and others involved must simply mark time. Not only does such delayed decisionmaking lower morale, but also available parole resources may deteriorate and no longer be open to the inmate when the parole finally is granted. The job that was waiting is lost; the chance to participate in vocational education programs is gone.

Delay in making parole decisions should be eliminated. The key lies in sufficient decisionmaking power being allocated at the point of hearing. In almost all cases two examiners can perform the necessary hearing functions if they can agree.

Allied to prompt decisionmaking is the manner in which an inmate is notified of determinations affecting him. About half of the State jurisdictions now inform inmates of the decision and the reasons for it as soon as it is made, at the hearing itself. This practice is relatively new. Formerly, the almost universal practice was to send word of release or deferral to the inmate through a board representative or an institutional official. Such officials have no way of clarifying the meaning of the decision or its implications to the inmate. This task can and should be done only by parole decisionmakers, not by others trying to represent them. Parole authorities should explain the reasons for their decisions directly to the inmate and answer any questions he has.

Written Decisions

Also critical in this respect is the necessity for parole decisionmakers to spell out in writing the reasons for their decision and to specify the behavioral objectives they have in mind. Currently only about 12 parole boards dealing with adult offenders document the reasons for their decisions. It should be a universal practice. It is important for future hearing representatives to have available the reasoning of prior hearing officials.

Likewise, it is important for institutional officials to have the written parole opinion to assist them in shaping future programs for offenders denied parole. It also is important for board self-evaluation; research should be able to measure the relationship between reasons for actions and subsequent events and decisions. Board documents provide a basis for checking the reasons for decisions against the criteria used. This is particularly crucial in a two-tiered system of decision and review in which appeals can be made.

Due Process Requirements

Provisions for sharing the bases of decisions with offenders, making a written record of proceedings, requiring written reasons for decisions, and allowing a two-tiered appeal process not only are good administrative practice but also are consistent with legal requirements of procedural due process. They may come to be viewed as legally necessary. So far, however, courts have been restrained in requiring elaborate procedural safeguards during parole consideration. For example, The Federal Second Circuit Court of Appeals in the recent case of *Menechino* v. *Oswald,* 430 F. 2d 403 (2d Cir.1970), in referring to the parole board's function said:

> It must make the broad determination of whether rehabilitation of the prisoner and the interest of society generally would best be served by permitting him to serve his sentence beyond the confines of the prison walls rather than by being continued in physical confinement. In making that determination, the Board is not restricted by rules of evidence or procedures developed for the purpose of determining legal or factual issues.

However, the Supreme Court, in a recent case involving parole revocation hearings, laid down strict procedural requirements to safeguard due process. (See subsequent section on revocation.) It may well be that such requirements will be deemed necessary for the grant hearing as well.

Trends in court decisions are difficult to predict. Certainly in the last few years appellate courts have ordered changes in parole proceedings, particularly those surrounding revocation. There is sound basis in correctional terms alone for elements in the parole hearing that embrace some characteristics of administrative hearings occurring at other points in the criminal justice process. The value of information disclosure, for example, does not rest simply upon legal precedent. Parole boards have as much stake in the accuracy of records as other criminal justice officials. Evidence indicates that decisions are much more likely to be documented carefully and fully when information is disclosed and when those whose interests are at stake have a chance to examine and test it. Rather than resulting in an adversary battle, disclosure more often than not provides information not contained in the report. This is an important addition for decisionmakers.

Information sharing underlies much of the emphasis in modern corrections that is moving toward an open, reality-testing base. From this perspective, it is expected that offenders will be given available evidence and facts. In the average parole file little material is so sensitive that it cannot be reviewed with the inmate. Of course, if there is a need to treat with caution professional material such as certain types of psychiatric reports, it can be held back.

The suggested procedures of the American Bar Association for disclosure of presentence investigation material seem eminently suitable for the parole hearing stage. Materials could be withdrawn when deemed necessary, with a notation made of this fact in the file. In case of appeal, the full parole board would be notified as to what material had been withheld from the inmate and could take this into consideration.

Representation

The issue of inmate representation by lawyers or other spokesmen causes difficulty for many parole board members because it seems to create an unnecessarily adversarial system out of essentially a "clinical" decision process. However, several arguments for representation can be advanced. The offender's representative has the freedom to pursue information, develop resources, and raise questions that are difficult for an inmate in a helpless position. To the extent that the information base can be enlarged by representatives and issues sharpened and tested more directly, there is likely to be improvement in the whole process of parole board decisionmaking. Equally important, however, is the impression of fairness given to the inmate who is represented. Indeed in many cases it is more than simply a feeling of fairness. It is clear that, in too many situations, the lack of ability to communicate well, to participate fully in the hearing, and to have a sense of full and careful consideration, is extremely detrimental.

Representation also can contribute to opening the correctional system, particularly the parole process, to public scrutiny. It is important that more people become personally involved in the correctional process, since the reintegration movement rests on the involvement of community resources and representatives. Involvement of persons from the outside also provides opportunity for remedy of any abuses in parole processes.

Ultimately the credibility of a parole system will rest on its openness to public scrutiny. For these reasons, a system of providing, or at least allowing, representation for the offender at parole hearings should be sponsored by parole officials. Because of the diversity in parole eligibility and program administration among parole systems, the precise interviews with inmates at which representation is appropriate or feasible will vary. But the principle of allowing representation when crucial decisions regarding the offender's freedom are made should guide the board in fixing policies. Lawyers are only one possible kind of representative; citizen volunteers also could serve as offender representatives.

The idea of representation at hearings may be annoying to parole officials. Implementation may increase costs. On balance, these inconveniences seem a small price for the prospective gains. Assuming representation, the board should be able to prevent abuses in the conduct of hearings. It is crucial for parole boards to develop appropriate policies for information disclosure, forms and methods of representation, and procedural rules to be followed at the hearings.

Model for the Parole Grant Hearing

The hearing examiner model can be easily adapted to parole systems from administrative law. Hearing examiners play a central role in an administrative agency's treatment of controversy. Matters are scheduled before the examiner who conducts a full hearing and then prepares a report which contains findings of fact, conclusions of law, and recommended order. This report, the transcript, and the evidence introduced constitute the exclusive basis for decision. The hearing examiner makes the initial decision which, unless appealed to the full Board or Commission, becomes the decision of the agency.

A party dissatisfied with the recommendations or findings of the hearing examiner can appeal his decision to the full agency board which, being charged with the responsibility for decision, may overturn the findings of the examiner.

The full board does not hear the matter de novo, but on briefs and arguments. The final order of the board can then be appealed to court by a dissatisfied party. Court review would determine whether there is substantial evidence on the record as a whole to support the agency decision, or whether it is erroneous as a matter of law.

Adaptation of the administrative law model for use of hearing examiners in parole grant hearings is represented in Figure 1.

When a parole grant hearing is scheduled, a hearing examiner should conduct a full personal hearing with the inmate, his representative, and appropriate institutional staff members. Contents of any written reports supplied to the hearing examiner should be openly disclosed and become a part of the record, except that the parole board may establish guidelines under which certain sensitive information could be withheld from the inmate with notation of this fact included in the record.

A verbatim transcript of the proceedings should be made. The hearing examiner should make his decision on the basis of criteria and policies established by the parole board and specify his findings in writing. He should personally inform the inmate of his decision and provide him a copy of the full report. The hearing examiner's report, with the transcript and evidence, should constitute the exclusive record.

If the decision of the hearing examiner is not appealed by the inmate or the

Figure 1   *Hearing Examiner Model*

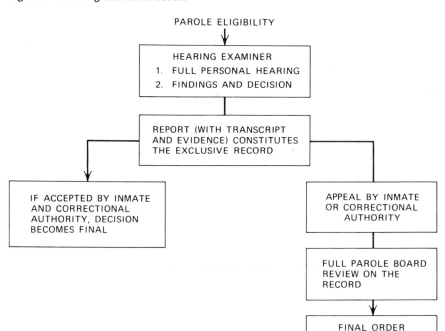

correctional authority within five days after the hearing, the decision of the hearing examiner should be final. If the decision is not accepted by the inmate or the correctional authority, appeal should be made to the parole board. The full parole board should review the case on the record to see if there is substantial evidence to support the finding or if it is erroneous as a matter of law. The order of the parole board should be final.

REVOCATION HEARINGS

Until the late 1960's, procedures in many jurisdictions for the return of parole violators to prison were so informal that the term "hearing" would be a misnomer. In many instances revocation involved no more than the parole board's pro forma approval of the request of the parole officer or his field staff supervisor. In many jurisdictions the revocation decision represented almost unfettered discretion of parole authorities. In addition to minimal procedural formality, the grounds for revocation also were non-specific, involving such assessments as "generally poor attitude" or allegations of "failure to cooperate," rather than specific breaches of conditions or commission of new offenses.

This was particularly true in revocation of the aftercare of juveniles, where the decision to revoke was viewed primarily as a casework determination. Ostensibly, it did not involve a breach of conditions but was simply an action for the youth's welfare.

This general stance of casual and quick return of both adults and juveniles rested primarily on the "privilege" or "grace" doctrine of the parole grant. To many parole officials, revocation did not warrant much concern with due process, procedural regularity, or matters of proof, hearing, and review.

In 1964 a study of parole board revocations showed that there was no hearing at all in at least seven States. In those States providing a hearing, the alleged violator frequently was returned to prison directly from the field on allegation of the field agent or on a warrant issued by the board. An actual hearing or review of this return by the parole board did not take place until weeks, sometimes months, after the parolee had been returned to the institution.[30] In most cases, then, revocation was a fait accompli by the time the board's representative next visited the institution to review the revocation order and officially declare the parolee a violator.

In a small minority of cases, board members canceled the warrant of field complaint and permitted the prisoner again to resume parole. However, since the parolee had been moved to the institution, employment and family relationships already were disturbed. In effect a canceled revocation order meant that the parolee once again had to be transported to his local community and begin readjustment process all over again. Counsel rarely was permitted to represent

[30] Ronald Sklar, "Law and Practice in Probation and Parole Revocation Hearings," *Journal of Criminal Law and Criminology,* 55 (1964), 75.

the alleged violator at such hearings. Any witnesses to the alleged violation almost always were seen outside the hearing at the parole board offices, rarely subject to confrontation or cross-examination by the parolee. While at the time of the survey some States allowed parolees to have "assistance" of lawyers, no jurisdiction assigned counsel to indigent parolees.

Intervention by Appellate Courts

Since the 1960's there has been considerable appellate court intervention in the parole process generally and in revocation procedures specifically. This new vigor is consistent with a general distinction in administrative law between granting a privilege (as in parole) and taking it away once it has been given (as in revocation). Courts generally have held that initial granting or denial of a privilege can be done much more casually and with fewer procedural safeguards than taking away a privilege once granted.

Development of court-imposed requirements for procedural due process in parole revocation has been somewhat erratic. One of the important leading cases in the Federal jurisdiction was *Hyser* v. *Reed,* decided in the D.C. Circuit in 1963 (318 2d 225, 235). The decision in this case generally supported the common position that revocation was strictly a discretionary withdrawal of a privilege not requiring adversarial hearings at which inmates are represented by counsel and so forth. This part of the decision was consistent with both the law and the general sentiment of most parole authorities at the time. What *Hyser* did do, however, was to deal with the venue question of where the revocation hearing should take place.

The court supported the U.S. Parole Board practice of conducting a fact-finding hearing on the site of the alleged offense or violation of condition, with review at the institution only if the first hearing determined the offender should be returned. This decision was sensible, particularly in those cases involving a mistake or failure to find any infraction. If in fact the parolee did not commit the alleged infraction he could continue his parole uninterrupted.

Subsequent to the *Hyser* decision, however, courts in some Federal and State jurisdictions reversed the first part of the decision; namely, the lack of any right, constitutional or otherwise, for due process to be applied at revocation proceedings. Most courts that departed from *Hyser* in this regard did so on the basis of the Supreme Court decision in a case involving "deferred sentencing" or probation revocation. In *Mempa* v. *Rhay,* 389 U.S. 128(1967), the Supreme Court held in 1967 that a State probationer had a right to a hearing and to counsel upon allegation of violations of probation. A number of courts interpreted the principle of *Mempa* to apply to parole as well.

The extension of *Mempa* procedural requirements to parole revocation was fairly common in both State jurisdictions and in various Federal circuits. In almost all cases, conformity with *Mempa* requirements meant a reversal of former legal positions and a major change in administrative practices. For example, the New York Court of Appeals, resting its decision on the *Mempa* case, reversed its former position and required the New York Parole Board to permit inmates to be represented by counsel at revocation hearings, *People ex rel.* v. *Warden Green-haven,* 318 NYS 2d, 449 (1971). The rationale most often used as a basis for the requirement of procedural due process at parole revocation was expressed in another Federal Circuit Court case, *Murray* v. *Page,* 429 F. 2d 1359 (10th Cir. 1970):

> Therefore, while a prisoner does not have a constitutional right to parole, once paroled he cannot be deprived of his freedom by means inconsistent with due process. The minimal right of the parolee to be informed of the charges and the nature of the evidence against him and to appear to be heard at the revocation hearing is inviolate. Statutory deprivation of this right is manifestly inconsistent with due process and is unconstitutional; nor can such right be lost by the subjective determination of the executive that the case for revocation is "clear."

By and large parole officials have resisted attempts by courts, or others, to introduce procedural due process requirements into parole revocation and at other stages of parole. Resistance has rested not simply on encroachment of authority but also on the possible negative effects of stringent procedural requirements on parole generally and on administrative costs. Some parole officials argue that elaborate revocation hearings would create demands on the parole board's time grossly incommensurate with personnel and budget. Other opponents of procedural elaborateness have argued its negative effects on the purpose and use of revocation.

Resistance to increased procedural requirements in revocation apparently is diminishing, whether by persuasion or court order. As of 1972, 37 jurisdictions allow counsel for adult inmates at the time of parole revocation. Nineteen permit disclosure of the record to the offender or his lawyer. Thirty-two States provide for the right to hear witnesses. In some places due process procedures have been extended even to the operation of juvenile aftercare revocation. For example, in Illinois a juvenile parolee is notified in writing of the alleged parole violation and of the fact that he has a right to a hearing.

The State of Washington has developed perhaps the most elaborate system for handling adult parolees accused of violation. It affords them the following rights and procedures: the right to a hearing before parole board members in the community where the violation allegedly occurred; the right to cross-examine witnesses; the right to subpoena witnesses; the right to assistance of counsel, including lawyers provided at State expense for indigent parolees; and the right to access to all pertinent records.

Supreme Court Decision

The Supreme Court on June 29, 1972 dealt with several crucial issues relating to parole revocation in the case of *Morrissey* v. *Brewer,* 408 U.S. 471 (1972). Two parolees appealed an appellate court's decision on the ground that their paroles were revoked without a hearing and that they were thereby deprived of due process. The appellate court, in affirming the district court's denial of relief, had reasoned that parole is only "a correctional device authorizing service of sentence outside a penitentiary" and concluded that a parolee, who is thus still "in custody," is not entitled to a full adversary hearing, as would be mandated in a criminal proceeding.

In reversing the Court of Appeals decision, the Supreme Court held that:

> . . . the liberty of a parolee, although indeterminate, includes many of the core values of unqualified liberty and its termination inflicts a "grievous loss" on the parolee and often on others. It is hardly useful any longer to try to deal with this problem in terms of whether the parolee's liberty is a "right" or a "privilege." By whatever name, the liberty is valuable and must be seen as within the protection of the Fourteenth Amendment. Its termination calls for some orderly process, however informal.

In considering the question of the nature of the process that is due, the Court delineated two important stages in the typical process of parole revocation: the arrest of the parolee and preliminary hearing; and the revocation hearing.

While the Court stated it had no intention of creating an inflexible structure for parole revocation procedures, making a distinction between a preliminary and a revocation hearing was an important decision, since many of the jurisdictions that do grant hearings grant only one. The Court also laid out a number of important points or steps for each of the above two stages which will undoubtedly apply to future parole actions.

In regard to the arrest of the parolee and a preliminary hearing, the Court indicated that due process would seem to require some minimal prompt inquiry at or reasonably near the place of the alleged parole violation or arrest. Such an inquiry, which the Court likened to a preliminary hearing, must be conducted to determine whether there is probable cause or reasonable grounds to believe that the arrested parolee has committed acts that would constitute a violation of parole conditions. It specified that the hearing should be conducted by someone not directly involved in the case.

In interpreting the rights of the parolee in this process, the Court held that the parolee should be given notice of when and why the hearing will take place, and the nature of the alleged violation(s). At the hearing, the parolee may appear and speak in his own behalf. He may bring letters, documents, or individuals who can give relevant information to the hearing officer. On request of the parolee, persons who have given adverse information on which parole revocation is to be based are made available for questioning in his presence unless the hearing officer determines that the informant would be subjected to risk of harm if his identity were disclosed.

The Court also specified that the hearing officer should have the duty of making a summary or digest of what transpires at the hearing and of the substance of evidence introduced. On the basis of the information before him, the officer should determine whether there is probable cause to hold the parolee for the final decision of the parole board on revocation.

The Court said there must also be an opportunity for a hearing, if it is desired by the parolee, prior to the final decision on revocation by the parole authority. This hearing must be the basis for more than determining probable cause; it must lead to a final evaluation of any contested relevant facts as determined to warrant revocation. The parolee must have an opportunity to be heard and to show, if he can, that he did not violate the conditions, or, if he did, that circumstances in mitigation suggest the violation does not warrant revocation. The revocation hearing must be tendered within a reasonable time after the parolee is taken into custody.

The minimum requirements of due process for such a revocation hearing, as set by the Court, include (a) written notice of the claimed violations of parole; (b) disclosure to the parolee of evidence against him; (c) opportunity to be heard in person and to present witnesses and documentary evidence; (d) the right to confront and cross-examine adverse witnesses (unless the hearing officer specifically finds good cause for not allowing confrontation); (e) a "neutral and detached" hearing body such as a traditional parole board, members of which need not be judicial officers or lawyers; and (f) a written statement by the factfinders as to the evidence relied on and reasons for revoking parole.

Issues Still Unresolved

The Court left several questions unresolved. The extent to which evidence obtained by a parole officer in an unauthorized search can be used at a revocation hearing was not considered. Nor did it reach or decide the question whether the parolee is entitled to the assistance of retained counsel or to appointed counsel if the parolee is indigent.

While the Court did address certain features of the parole revocation process prior to a formal revocation hearing, it did not specify requirements for the process by which offenders are taken and held in custody. Present law and practice in many jurisdictions empower individual parole officers to cause the arrest of parolees for an alleged violation and to hold them in custody for extensive periods.

It is a power that needs careful control because it is easy to abuse, especially in those cases in which the arrest does not lead to a hearing, in which there is no review, and in which the parolee simply is held for a while in jail and then released back to parole status. This is a practice called "jail therapy" by which the parole officer "punishes" the parolee briefly (if he is a drunk, for example, he may be held in "protective custody" over New Year's Eve), then releases him back to community status. While this short-term confinement may not be undesirable in all cases, the lack of administrative control over its use is.

The use of all arrest and hold powers should be carefully narrowed. Parole field agents should be able to arrest and hold only when a warrant has been secured from a representative of the parole board on sufficient evidence. The warrant or similar document requiring parole commissioner approval of administrative arrest should be universally used. At present, only about half the State jurisdictions require such a warrant; in the remainder the parole agent can pick up an alleged violator on his own initiative and have him detained by signing a "hold" order. Initial two-step review of administrative arrest should be established, with appropriate provisions for emergency situations but with no application to law enforcement officer arrests for new offenses.

It must be remembered that taking no action and returning the parolee to the institution are not the only two courses open. The work of the California community treatment programs shows that the availability of alternative measures— short-term confinement or special restrictions—can be extremely useful in dealing with parolees instead of causing them a long-term return to an institution. Likewise, the Model Penal Code suggests that jurisdictions develop alternatives to the no action vs. full revocation dilemma. Such alternative modes need to be developed and formalized and used much more extensively.

ORGANIZATION OF FIELD SERVICES

Transfer of Adult Parole to Correctional Departments

One of the clearest trends in parole organization in the last few years is consolidation of formerly autonomous agencies or functionally related units into expanding departments of corrections. Some of these departments have been made part of still larger units of State government, such as human resources agencies, which embrace a wide range of programs and services. One clear indication of this trend is the number of States that have shifted administrative responsibility for parole officers from independent parole departments to centralized correctional agencies.

Most recently the States of Oregon, New York, and Georgia have made such transfers. A number of smaller States still have parole supervision staffs responsible to an independent parole board. Practically every large State now has adult parole field staff reporting to the same administrative authority as the personnel of the State penal institutions. Today, the majority of parole officers at the State level work for unified departments of correction.

The emergence of strong and autonomous correctional agencies represents an important step toward removal of a major block to needed correctional reform —fragmented and poorly coordinated programs and services. It is important that such consolidations continue, particularly among the services available for misdemeanants, where the more serious program gaps now exist. How quickly and effectively consolidation will take place depends largely on development of coordinated corrections units in large urbanized regions or absorption of these facilities and services into State programs.

Juvenile Parole Organization

The problems in parole services for juvenile delinquents had some of the same characteristics. The National Survey of Corrections found tremendous shortcomings in juvenile aftercare programs. In some States young persons released from training schools were supervised by institutional staff. In others they were made the responsibility of local child welfare workers, who simply included these youngsters in their caseloads of dependent or neglected children. In some States no organized program of juvenile parole supervision existed. Whether distinct juvenile correctional agencies should exist or whether such services should be carried out as a regular part of welfare services has been a matter of controversy for years.[31]

The events of the last years have virtually ended that argument. Distinct divisions and departments of juvenile correctional services are emerging. There is less agreement about whether such departments should be combined with agencies serving adult offenders. Yet it is widely agreed that separate program units should be maintained, even if adult and juvenile programs are combined in a single agency. Statewide juvenile correctional services embracing both institutions and field aftercare represent an established trend that should be supported.

Consolidation is not simply a matter of administrative efficiency; it facilitates important parole objectives as well. From the reintegration perspective, the task of parole staff is to intervene between the offender and his world and, if needed, to work with him to find satisfying and legal modes of behavior.

Confinement is minimized and made to serve as much as possible the goal of dealing with problems in the community. Prerelease activities and community-based correctional facilities, through which offenders can participate increasingly in community life, are central. To be effective, both of these programs require extensive involvement of field staff. It is no longer sufficient to wait for the "transfer" of a case from an institution to a parole staff. The system now must work in such a way that heavy expenditures of field staff energy in the community and with the offender are made for many months prior to his "release" on parole. This requires a close interrelationship between institution and field staffs.

Linking Institutional and Field Staffs

The lack of continuity and consistency of services between institutional and field services has been a severe problem to many jurisdictions. It often is further complicated by what could be described as rural vs. urban perspective. Institutions generally are located miles from population centers. The manpower they tend to recruit is drawn largely from small town and rural areas. The result is that institutional staff may have little understanding of city and especially ghetto life. In contrast, most field workers live in or near the large population centers in which most offenders reside, and more field workers than institutional workers are from minority groups. This cultural difference contributes to feelings of mistrust, hostility, and incredulity that handicap communication between institutional and field staffs.

---

[31] See, for example, State of New York, Governor's Special Committee on Criminal Offenders, *Preliminary Report* (1968), pp. 61–66.

A number of steps are needed to overcome this communication breakdown. An ongoing series of joint training sessions involving field workers and institutional counselors can be helpful in achieving mutual understanding. Promotions from institutional services to field services and vice versa also can have some effect in building communication channels.

Most important is that institution and field staff be under common administrative direction. It is not enough that they be simply linked administratively at the top; linking must be at the program level as well. This can be done in several ways. One is to provide that both institutional and field services be regionalized and placed under common administrators in each area. Obviously, in States where there are only one or two institutions, problems are compounded for the whole community-based thrust. But even here some program consolidations are possible by devices such as placing all institutional programming responsibilities under full control of the head of parole field services for the last months of the inmate's confinement.

The stress on linking institutional and community supervision also has implications for systems that combine probation and parole services in a common administrative unit. Although this combination is infrequent among juvenile services, in 38 States the same State agency carries responsibility for the supervision of adult parolees and probationers. Having these services in a single agency has great economic advantages and provides an even quality of service to all areas of a State. There also are significant advantages in being able to influence staff toward more consistent programs for offenders. Tying staff to locally based institutional resources can work well for both probationers and parolees. However, in urban areas where case volume is sufficient, specialized staff who work with specific institutions are needed. Such tasks demand considerable time and require field staff to become intimately familiar with institutional personnel and participate actively in their programs.

Caseload vs. Team Assignments

The caseload—the assignment of individual offenders to individual officers—is the almost universal device for organizing the work of parole officers. This concept is being modified importantly in a number of offices through development of team supervision. A group of parole officers, sometimes augmented with volunteers and paraprofessionals, takes collective responsibility for a parolee group as large as their combined former caseloads. The group's resources are used differentially, depending upon individual case needs. Decisions are group decisions and generally involve parolees, including the parolee affected by the decision. Tasks are assigned by group assessment of workers' skills and parolees' objectives and perceptions.

Under the reintegration model, for example, various groups or organizations such as employers, schools, or welfare agencies may become someone's "caseload" and the major targets of his activities. Community representatives are dealt with directly, are directly involved, and help to shape programs. The parole office, instead of being located in a State office building, shifts to the community. The staff becomes expert in knowing both the formal and informal power structure of the community in which it operates and works closely with police, schools, employers, and probation officers. Such functions have a significant impact on the kind of manpower and training required for field staff. For example, there is a heavy involvement of volunteers as tutors and job finders that requires a staff able to use and work with such personnel.

The emphasis in a traditional parole agency is directed toward the proper administration of the specific caseload assigned to each individual officer. It is an administrative style familiar to most large bureaucracies. Front-line workers have responsibility for specific and clearly defined tasks and are checked by their supervisors to see that those tasks are carried out. The supervisors are under the command of middle managers who in turn report to someone above them.

Although the rhetoric of the organization is couched in such phrases as "helping the offender" and "developing a positive relationship," organizational controls tend to be attached to activities designed largely to foster the surveillance work of the agency or protect it from outside criticism. Parole officer performance most often is judged by the number of contacts that have been made with parolees, often with little regard for the quality of events that transpired during these contacts. Complete and prompt reports showing compliance with agency policies, such as written travel permits for parolees, are valued highly and require a major investment of parole officer time.

The result of this kind of administration is a rigid chain of command that is regimented, standardized, and predictable and that allocates power to persons on the basis of their position in the hierarchy. The parolee, being the lowest, is the least powerful.

Flexibility in Organizational Structure

A correctional policy that assumes parolees are capable of making a major contribution toward setting their own objectives and sees the parole agency's main task as helping the parolee realistically test and attain those objectives also must place a premium on developing an organizational structure that promotes flexibility. This means that managers must learn how to administer a decentralized organization that must adhere to broad policies and yet allow for a high degree of individual autonomy.

The dilemmas that arise when a manager tries this style of administration are many. Their resolution requires a sophisticated knowledge of administration and organizational techniques. One of the highest priorities for effective development of community-based services lies in providing managers with precisely this kind of skill.

Nelson and Lovell summarize the issues well:

The correctional field must develop more collaborative, less hierarchical administrative regimes in order to implement its reintegration programs. The hierarchical format was developed to achieve the goal of production and orderly task performance. When individual change is the prime purpose of the organization, this format is inappropriate for people cannot be *ordered* to change strongly patterned attitudes and behavior. Nor is change apt to come about through the ritual performance of a series of tasks. . . . Power must be shared rather than hoarded. Communication must be open rather than restricted. Thus the managers of reintegration programs will need the skills of cooptation, communication, and collaboration.[32]

Resistance to reintegration-style programs can be widespread. Take for example a job function that has been interpreted traditionally as one of surveillance, head-counting, and maintenance of order. Management says the job is best accomplished by a new set of techniques—including relaxed, open and free communication, and decisionmaking involving parolees. Staff members should perceive themselves less as policemen than as counselors. It is highly likely in such a case that some staff will resist the changes.

Persons who see themselves as professionals also can be major obstacles to change. The trend toward a reintegration model and away from a rehabilitation model has been frustrating to several traditional professional groups who perceive their "expertise" as being challenged or, at worst, rejected. Meetings are held to organize opposition to "nonprofessional practices" and to changes that are "untested" and that have strayed from the "tried and true." It is not surprising that administrators sometimes capitulate. But "let's not rock the boat" or "let's wait till next year" are the cliches of timid leadership that lead to stagnant bureaucracies. It takes great skill and perseverance to change on agency. There is no substitute for intelligence, skill, and above all, courage.

COMMUNITY SERVICES FOR PAROLEES

A significant number of parolees can do very well without much official supervision, according to repeatedly validated research.[33] Many offenders can be handled in relatively large caseloads simply by maintaining minimum contact with them and attending to their needs as they arise. Most of these parolees probably should be released from any form of supervision at all. Outright discharge from the institution would be an appropriate disposition and should be used much more frequently than it is. Failing that, minimum supervision can and should be employed for a significant group.

For those parolees requiring more intensive help, the emphasis in recent years, and one worthy of support, has been toward effecting as many needed services as possible through community resources available to the general population. To

[32] Elmer K. Nelson and Catherine H. Lovell, *Developing Correctional Administrators* (Washington: Joint Commission on Correctional Manpower and Training, 1969), p. 14.

[33] See Joseph D. Lohman, Albert Wahl, and Robert Carter, *The San Francisco Project: The Minimum Supervision Caseload,* Research Report No. 8 (Berkeley: University of California, 1966).

the extent that offenders can gain access to these opportunities on the same basis as other citizens, the additional blocks that arise when parolees attempt to move into the mainstream of community life are reduced.

Moreover, more resources usually are available to programs designed to deal with a broad public spectrum. For example, vocational training programs operated by correctional agencies cannot begin to offer the range of services offered by government agencies to economically deprived groups in general. Skills developed in programs for these groups are usually much more marketable. Job placement is also more likely to be operating effectively.

Finally, using such services allows flexibility and speed in adapting to needs. It avoids creation of additional specialized bureaucracies on State payrolls that respond more readily to their own survival needs than to changing needs of offenders. Provision of funds to parole agencies to purchase resources in the community represents an important new approach to the problems of securing needed services.

From this perspective, a major task of parole officers is to make certain that opportunities in community services and programs actually exist for parolees and to prepare and support parolees as they undertake these programs. Offenders often are locked out of services for which they apparently qualify according to the criteria established by the agency, not because of any official policy barring them but because of covert resistance to dealing with persons thought to be troublesome. Mental health agencies deny assistance to offenders on grounds that such persons cannot benefit from their programs. Public employment offices often are reluctant to refer to an employer a person viewed as unreliable. Public housing resources may be restricted because of biases against persons with records.

Considering these reactions and the discrimination that too often exists against minority group members, who constitute a significant portion of the offender population in many areas of the country, the need for a parole staff that is willing and able to play the role of broker or resource manager for parolees is clear. This need involves more than skills at persuasion or aggressive argument. It also requires a knowledge of the sources of power in a community and the ability to enlist those sources in changing agency behavior.[34]

Undoubtedly, the trend toward creating new ways of delivering services to meet human needs—mental health, family counseling, physical rehabilitation, employment, and financial assistance—will modify the parole officer's tasks in several important respects. Human service centers designed to deliver a wide range of programs will develop.[35] Part of the task of parole staff will be to support such efforts and play an appropriate role in a coordinated human-services delivery

---

[34] John M. Martin and Gerald M. Shattuck, "Community Intervention and the Correctional Mandate," consultant paper prepared for the President's Commission on Law Enforcement and Administration of Justice, 1966.

[35] U.S. Department of Health, Education, and Welfare, Community Service Administration, *Toward a Comprehensive Service Delivery System through Building the Community Service Center* (1970).

system. Increasingly, the parole officer's unique responsibility will be to make certain that offenders obtain the benefit of available resources, to counsel parolees about the conditions of their parole, and to help them meet those conditions.

Financial Assistance

Perhaps the most common problem immediately confronting offenders released from adult correctional institutions is the need for money for the most basic needs—shelter, food, and transportation. Most States provide new releasees with transportation, some clothes, and modest gate money totaling perhaps $50. Inmates fortunate enough to have been assigned to programs in which money can be earned in prison frequently are much better off financially than those who were not. Those who have participated in work-release programs usually will have saved a portion of their salary for the time of their release.

Data that show parole failure rates clearly related to the amount of money an offender has during the first months of release can be explained in a number of ways.[36] Nevertheless, it is a consistent finding and, in the day-by-day existence of parolees, lack of funds is a critical problem.

A number of solutions to this problem have been tried over the years, the most common being a loan fund arrangement. Although there are several difficulties in administering such a fund, it is a practical necessity in every parole system until arrangements for sufficient "gate money" or other subvention can be provided.

The most practical and direct way to meet the problem is to provide offenders with opportunities to earn funds while they are incarcerated. For those who are unemployed, funds should be provided, much in the manner of unemployment compensation, when they are first released until they are gainfully employed. The State of Washington recently has adopted precisely such legislation. It should be adopted in every jurisdiction.

Employment

Closely related to the problem of finances is that of getting and holding a decent job. While it is difficult to demonstrate experimentally a precise relationship between unemployment and recidivism, the gross picture does show a fairly consistent link between unemployment and crime.[37] Hence every parole system should maintain its own measures of unemployment rates among its populations.

For the offender already on the street, the most critical skill required of a parole officer is directing him to a wide variety of services available in the community. A prime resource is the State employment service. Almost everywhere such services have commitments at the policy level to extend special assistance in the placement of parolees.

However, the test of these programs is found in the day-by-day working relationships between local employment personnel and parole officers. How well

---

[36] Glaser, *The Effectiveness of a Prison and Parole System,* pp. 333–348.
[37] Glaser, *The Effectiveness of a Prison and Parole System,* ch. 14.

they cooperate is colored by the attitudes of local employment department staff but more importantly by the skill of the parole staff in maintaining relationships. A wide variety of other programs exist; for example, those sponsored by the Office of Economic Opportunity, the Office of Vocational Rehabilitation, and the large number sponsored by the Department of Labor. The key issue in using these programs is good communication at the local operational level.

The most acute employment problems are those associated with persons about to be released on parole. It is a time of great strain on the parolee. The difficulty of finding employment often is an additional source of anxiety because the most common reason why offenders are held beyond the date fixed for their release is that they have no job to go to.

Many States have developed systems of "reasonable assurance," under which a definite job is not required before an inmate is released, provided some means can be found to sustain him until one can be found. This generally is a far better practice than holding him until a job is promised. Parolees find it much easier to get a job if they can personally interview employers. Research consistently has shown offenders do as well, if not better, if they can find their own job.[38]

Partial release programs in the community go a long way toward eliminating many of these problems. While the offender still is confined, he has the chance to make contacts in the community, be interviewed by employers, work directly with a parole officer, or actually begin an employment program through work release. In terms of a broad correctional strategy aimed at coping with employment problems, prerelease programs are of pivotal importance.

Another activity that has grown in recent years, under sponsorship of both private and public sources, is job training programs in institutions that are connected to specific job possibilities on the outside. The Office of Vocational Rehabilitation has programs in a number of institutions. The Department of Labor has made numerous efforts in this area. Such programs need to be supported because of the large-scale resources and expertise they represent and the network of relationships they possess in the free community.

Residential Facilities

Another major need of many newly released offenders is a place to live. For some, the small, community-based residential facility is extremely useful in a time of crisis.

Young persons particularly need to have a place to go when events begin to overwhelm them. Such centers also can be useful for dealing with offenders who may have violated their parole and require some control for a short period, but for whom return to an institution is unnecessary.

To the extent that such facilities can be obtained on a contract basis, the flexibility and, most probably, the program quality increase. For young offenders especially, bed space in small group facilities can be secured through many private

---

[38] John M. Stanton, "Is It Safe to Parole Inmates Without a Job?" *Crime and Delinquency,* 12 (1966), 149.

sources. This is less true for adults, and development of State operated centers may be required.

Differential Handling

Making all programs work requires a wide variety of resources, differential programming for offenders, and a staff representing a diversity of backgrounds and skills. Some offenders may be better handled by specialized teams. Drug users of certain types may be dealt with by staff who have considerable familiarity with the drug culture and close connections with various community drug treatment programs. Other offenders may require intensive supervision by officers skilled at maintaining close controls and surveillance over their charges. While the latter may be assigned to a specialized caseload, assignments to specialized treatment caseloads in general should involve a great deal of self-selection by the offender. Arbitrary assignments to "treatment" groups easily can result in the offender's subversion of program objectives. An ongoing program of assessment and evaluation by staff and parolees is needed to make certain that offenders are receiving the kind of program most appropriate for them.

MEASURES OF CONTROL

There is an increasing tendency to minimize use of coercive measures and find ways by which offenders' goals and aspirations can be made congruent, if not identical, with agency goals. These trends can be seen in the shifting emphasis of parole rules, the clearest manifestation of the coercive power of parole.

Until the 1950's parole rules heavily emphasized conformity to community values and lifestyles with little or no relationship to the reason why a person originally committed a crime. One State's rules, only recently amended, give the flavor of such conditions. They provided in part that:

> The person paroled shall in all respects conduct himself honestly, avoid evil associations, obey the law, and abstain from gambling and the use of intoxicating liquors. He shall not visit pool halls, or places of bad repute, and shall avoid the company and association of vicious people and shall at least once each Sunday attend some religious service or institution of moral training.

In the 1950's many rules of this type were replaced by more specific conditions such as requiring the parolee to obtain permission to purchase a car. Until the late 1960's almost every State had a long list of parole conditions.[39] As "tools of the parole officer," these conditions gave reason to expect that violations would occur often although official action would not be taken unless the parole officer felt the case warranted it. Problems of differential enforcement were bound to

---

[39] Nat Arluke, "A Summary of Parole Rules," *Journal of the National Probation and Parole Association,* 218 (January 1956), 2–9.

occur, and did. A great deal of ambiguity developed for both parolees and parole officers as to which rules really were to be enforced and which ignored. Studies have demonstrated that officers tend to develop their own norms of behavior that should result in return to prison. These norms among parole officers became very powerful forces in shaping revocation policies.[40]

The recent trend has been toward reducing rules and making them more relevant to the facts in a specific parole case. Part of this move undoubtedly has been stimulated by the interest of the courts in parole conditions. Conditions have been struck down by the courts as unreasonable, impossible of performance, or unfair. Additional principles constantly are being developed, as when a Federal court recently restrained the State of California from prohibiting a parolee from making public speeches *Hyland* v. *Procunier,* 311 F. Supp 749, 750 (N.D. Calif. 1970).

Several States have reduced the number of parole conditions considerably. In 1969, 45 jurisdictions prohibited contact with undesirable associates; today 35 do so. Ten States removed the requirement of permission to marry or file for divorce. Oregon, as a specific example, has removed nine discernible general conditions, including the requirement of permission to change residence or employment, to operate a motor vehicle, or to marry; the proscription of liquor or narcotics and contacts with undesirables; and dictates that the parolee maintain employment, support his dependents, and incur no debts. Idaho has removed seven such rules from its agreement of release.

Perhaps the most substantial change in procedure occurred in the State of Washington, where the standard parole conditions imposed on all inmates were reduced to four. They required the parolee to (1) obey all laws, (2) secure the permission of a parole office before leaving the State, (3) report to the officer, and (4) obey any written instructions issued by him. The State parole board imposes additional conditions in individual cases as seems appropriate. Conditions also may be added during the course of parole on the parole officer's application.

The advantage of this system is that both the parolee and parole officer know which conditions are to be enforced, although obviously violations of the remaining rules are judged individually and may not result in a return to prison. The other advantage is that much unnecessary anxiety is avoided over rules that rarely, if ever, would result in a return to prison. More such candor should be encouraged in parole supervision practice.

The removal of unnecessary rules also helps to shape the activity of the parole officer more positively. When unclear or unnecessary rules exist, the effect is twofold: a great deal of busy work by a parole officer; and a corruption of his relationship with the parolee. The thrust of the reintegration approach is toward an open problem-solving relationship between the parole officer and the parolee in which the parolee's objectives are clarified and tested against the limits under which both he and the parole officer must live. The fewer the limits required by

---

[40] James Robinson and Paul Takagi, "The Parole Violator as an Organization Reject" in Robert Carter and Leslie Wilkins, eds., *Probation and Parole: Selected Readings* (Wiley, 1970).

the parole system, the greater the opportunity of locating alternative behavior styles that are satisfying and meet the tests of legality. This is not to say that rules should not be enforced, but that there should be as much honesty in the enforcement process as possible.

Some parolees do require fairly intensive and directive supervision. In such cases, parole officers with the skill and aptitude for this kind of case should be assigned. Some intensive supervision caseloads (12 to 20 parolees) can be differentiated as caseloads for surveillance rather than for counseling and support. The parolee may not be in a position to see the relevance of any services offered, but he can respond positively to the knowledge that his daily whereabouts and activities are under careful scrutiny. In the eyes of the parolee, the efficacy of intensive surveillance caseloads resides in the credibility of the counselor and those he recruits to assist.

The need for high surveillance and intensive supervision for some offenders raises directly the question of the extent to which parole officers should assume police functions, such as arresting parolees, and the associated question as to whether they should be armed. A 1963 survey of parole authority members in the United States revealed that only 27 percent believed that parole officers should be asked to arrest parole violators. Only 13 percent believed that parole officers should be allowed to carry weapons.[41] In general, most parole officers accept the proposition that arrests by parole officers may be necessary on occasion but strong liaison with police departments should be depended on in the majority of instances when arrests are needed.

Guns are antithetical to the character of a parole officer's job. Much concern among some parole officers as to the need to be armed arises from their anxiety in working in areas of cities in which they feel alienated and estranged. This anxiety can be allayed by assigning to such districts persons who live in them. The RODEO project in Los Angeles, where probation officers are assigned two community assistants drawn from the neighborhood, is an excellent example. Because of their intimate knowledge of the community, such workers are able to keep well informed of the activities of their charges without the necessity of using tactics normally associated with police agencies.

MANPOWER

Problems of manpower for corrections as a whole are discussed in Chapter 14 of the Commission report. Here the discussion will be limited to special manpower problems of parole systems.

---

[41] National Parole Institutes, *Description of Backgrounds and Some Attitudes of Parole Authority Members of the United States* (New York: National Council on Crime and Delinquency, 1963).

Recruitment and Personnel Practices

Nothing indicates more starkly the relatively low priority that parole programs have received in governmental services than parole officers' salaries. The National Survey of Corrections indicated that in 1965 the median starting parole officer salary in the United States was approximately $6,000 a year. Although the studies of the Joint Commission on Correctional Manpower and Training three years later showed this salary base had risen, most of the gain could be accounted for by a national upswing in salary levels. It did not represent a substantial gain compared to other positions in government and industry.

The essence of an effective parole service lies in the caliber of person it recruits. Until salaries are made attractive enough to recruit and hold competent personnel, parole programs will be sorely handicapped. Almost half of the State agencies responsible for parole services surveyed by the Joint Commission reported serious difficulties in recruiting new officers.[42]

Though merit system procedures have significantly dampened political patronage influences in staff selection and promotion, they have brought a series of built-in restrictions. These must be overcome if a reintegration style for parole agencies is to be effected. The great difficulties attached to removing incompetent employees and the lack of opportunities for lateral entry are two examples. The most acute problems are those surrounding the criteria for staff selection and promotion. The issue bears most specifically on the employment and advancement of minority group members. For example, in 1969, while blacks made up 12 percent of the general population, only 8 percent of correctional employees were black, and they held only 3 percent of all top and middle level administrative positions.[43]

Some reforms are beginning, but merit systems are traditionally suspicious of new job titles and slow to establish them. When a new program is initiated, existing job titles frequently do not fit. The red tape and delays encountered in hiring staff often seriously damage programs. A sense of the frustration felt by administrators who are trying to modernize their programs is captured in the statement of one State parole system head, who asserts that merit systems can be and frequently are the single largest obstacle to program development in community-based corrections.

Manpower Requirements

The problems of trying to determine staffing needed to carry out an effective parole supervision program is complicated tremendously by lack of agreement on objectives and knowledge of how to reach them. Within any correctional policy,

---

[42] Joint Commission on Correctional Manpower and Training, *A Time to Act,* Washington: (JCCMT, 1969), p. 13.

[43] *A Time to Act,* p. 14.

a number of alternative styles are needed, ranging from no treatment at all to a variety of specific and carefully controlled programs. Perhaps the most discouraging experiments in parole supervision were those that sought to test the thesis that reducing caseloads to provide more intensive services would reduce recidivism.

The project that broke most completely from this notion was the Community Treatment Project of the California Youth Authority. The program involved classification of offenders by an elaborate measure of interpersonal maturity or "I-level" and use of treatment techniques specifically designed for each "I-level" type. Treatments ranged from firm, controlling programs for manipulative youths to supportive and relatively permissive approaches for those assigned to a category that included neurotic and anxious youngsters. With certain exclusions, offenders were assigned randomly to 10-man caseloads in the community, each of which was designed to carry out treatments consistent with a particular classification, or to a term in a training school followed by regular parole supervision.[44]

The results of the project were impressive. After 24 months, those assigned to special caseloads had a violation level of 39 percent. Those assigned to a regular program had a 61 percent failure rate. Of interest also was the variation in success rates among "I-level" types. Some researchers argue that some of the research results should be attributed to differences in official reaction to the behavior of those in special caseloads as opposed to those in regular ones,[45] rather than improvements in the offenders. Yet results in the context of other research efforts described by Stuart Adams make the argument for a differential treatment approach fairly strong.[46]

The Work Unit Parole program in effect in the California Department of Corrections since 1964 divides parolees into several classifications (based in part on their prior record and actuarial expectancy of parole success). It requires certain activities from the parole officer for each classification of parolee and thereby is able to control the work demands placed on an individual officer.

In this system the ratio of officers to parolees is approximately 1 to 35.[47] Two facts about the program should be noted.

1. The ratio of 1 to 35 does not express a caseload. Officers are assigned to a variety of tasks that are quantifiable. These task-related workloads are the basis for staff allocation.

2. The workload ratios for a specific agency would depend on the kinds of offenders they have to supervise and the administrative requirements of that agency.

The important point is that the concept of a caseload as a measure of workload is outmoded, especially in an era stressing a variety of skills and team supervision. The task is to spell out the goals to be accomplished and the activities associated

[44] Marguerite Q. Warren, "The Case for Differential Treatment of Delinquents," *Annals of the American Academy of Political and Social Science*, 381 (1969), 46.

[45] Paul Lerman, "Evaluating the Outcomes of Institutions for Delinquents," *Social Work*, 13 (1968), 3.

[46] Stuart Adams, "Some Findings from Correctional Caseload Research," *Federal Probation*, 31 (1967), 148.

[47] California Department of Corrections, *Work Unit Program, 1971* (Sacramento, 1971).

with their attainment, and to assign staff on that basis. Research information must continuously inform the judgment by which these allocations are made.

Education and Training Needs

Both the Correction Task Force in 1967 and the Joint Commission in 1969 agreed that a baccalaureate degree should be the basic education requirement for a parole officer, and persons with graduate study might be used for specialized functions. Both also stressed the need to create opportunities for greater use of persons with less than college-level study. Many tasks carried out by a parole officer can be executed just as easily by persons with much less training, and many skills needed in a parole agency are possessed by those with limited education. As observed earlier, persons drawn from the areas to be served are good examples of staff with needed specialized skills. Ex-offenders also are an example of a manpower resource needed in parole agencies. A growing number of agencies have found such persons to be an immensely useful addition to their staffs.[48]

Ways of recruiting, training, and supervising these relatively untapped sources of manpower for parole and other elements of corrections are discussed in Chapter 14 of the Commission report.

STATISTICAL ASSISTANCE

Proper organization, selection, and training of personnel are necessary for improved parole services, but in themselves they are insufficient. The crucial task of making the "right" decision remains for whoever must make it, whatever his position in the organization. Although the typical parole board member deals with a variety of concerns in decisionmaking, his basic objective is to lessen as much as possible the risk that an offender will commit another crime. This criterion remains paramount, but it is so variably interpreted and measured that severe handicaps impede its attainment.

To begin with, the measures of recidivism currently used in individual jurisdictions vary so much that useful comparisons across sytems, and indeed within systems, are virtually impossible. In one jurisdiction, only those parolees who return to prison are counted as failures, no matter what may have transpired among those parolees not returned. In another, everyone who has been charged with a violation as measured by the number of parole board warrants issued is treated as a failure.

The length of time under parole supervision confounds other comparisons. Thus recidivism variously includes the rest of the parolee's life, the span of the parole period only, or the time immediately following discharge.

The computational methods used in developing success or failure ratios also can do more to confuse than to assist understanding. In one State, recidivism is measured by the proportion of offenders returned to prison compared with the

[48] Vincent O'Leary, "Some Directions for Citizen Involvement in Corrections," *Annals of the American Academy of Political and Social Science*, 381 (1969), 99.

number released in the same period. In another, a much lower rate is shown for exactly the same number of failures because it is arrived at by computing the number of persons returned to prison in a given period compared with the total number of persons supervised during the same period. Until uniform measures are developed, vitally needed comparisons are not possible. Nor will meaningful participation in policy decisions be possible for agencies and persons outside the parole system.

Uniform Parole Reports System

A major effect to help solve the problem of uniform measures of recidivism was development of the National Uniform Parole Reports System, a cooperative effort sponsored by the National Parole Institutes. This program enlisted the voluntary cooperation of all State and Federal parole authorities having responsibility for felony offenders in developing some common terms to describe parolees —their age, sex, and prior record—and some common definitions to describe parole performance. Parole agencies for the last several years have been sending this information routinely to the Uniform Parole Report Center, where it is compiled. The results are fed back to the contributing States. Comparisons across the States thus are beginning to be possible. This effort represents a long step in developing a common language among parole systems.

Although this national system has made great strides, many additional steps need to be taken to develop its capacity fully. The Uniform Parole Report System needs to tie into a larger network that includes data from correctional institutions, so that information collected on the offender can be linked to parole outcome and crucially needed comparative data on discharged offenders can be obtained.

Important also is the need to tie in, on a national basis, to crime record data systems so that followup studies extending beyond parole periods can be carried out. The Uniform Parole Report System should have access to national criminal history information so that the experiences of parolees who have been classified according to a set of reliable factors can be checked. Attempts to use the usual criminal identification record alone to describe the results of parolee performance inevitably suffer from such gross inadequacies as to be almost completely useless. The careful definitions built into the Uniform Parole Report System should be combined with access to criminal data. This would enable tracing of subsequent parolee histories and could be a powerful tool for policy development and research

A comparable system for releases from juvenile institutions also is needed. Information on misdemeanants released on parole is almost nonexistent. Development of statewide statistical services in corrections is the key for such misdemeanant record-keeping.

Uses and Limitations of Statistics in Parole

Thus far the stress on statistical development has been on its utility as a national reporting system. But equally needed is a basic statistical system in each parole jurisdiction to help it address a variety of concerns in sufficient detail for practical day-to-day decisionmaking. There are a number of ways such data can be used.

Since the 1920's a number of researchers have concerned themselves with developing statistical techniques for increasing the precision of recidivism probability forecasting, as noted in Chapter 15 of the Commission report. Although the methods may vary in detail, the basic aim of the studies has been to identify factors that can be shown to be related statistically to parole outcome and, by combining them, to ascertain recidivism probability for certain parolee classes. These statements usually have been labeled "parole predictions."

Typically, the probability statements produced by statistical techniques are more accurate in estimating the likely outcome of parole than are traditional case methods. There has been relatively little use of these devices in the parole field, although some experimentation has been carried on in several jurisdictions.

A major source of resistance to the use of prediction methods is found in the nature of the parole decision itself.[49] Parole board members argue, for example, that simply knowing the narrow probability of success or failures is not nearly as helpful as knowing what type of risk would be involved. For example, they are more likely to tolerate higher risks if an offender is likely to commit a forgery than if he is prone to commit a crime against a person. Most prediction systems depend largely on prior events, such as criminal age and criminal record. This does not help a parole board that must deal with the offender as he is today within the realities of the decisions and time constraints available to them.

Technology is capable of dealing with a number of the additional concerns of parole authorities and probably will continue to make statistical information increasingly valuable. Currently a major research project is under way with the U.S. Parole Board seeking ways in which statistical material can assist the parole board member in his decisionmaking. Significant help lies in this direction, and each jurisdiction should be made fully aware of the possibility of using statistical information in parole decisionmaking.

With computer technology and the possibility it offers of instant feedback, the usefulness of this kind of system should increase. It seems doubtful, however, that statistical methods in the foreseeable future can substitute entirely for the judgments of parole board members and examiners. The impact and the variety of elements other than the estimation of risks are profound. The intricacies that arise in the individual case make total dependence on any statistical system highly risky at best.

Statistical predictions can be helpful in giving guidelines to parole board members as to general categories into which particular inmates fit, how other inmates similarly situated were treated earlier, and what the trends are in broad decisions. This information is important for parole decisionmakers. But most experts are convinced that the optimum system is one in which both statistical

---

[49] Norman S. Hayner, "Why Do Parole Board Members Lag in the Use of Prediction Scores?" *Pacific Sociological Review,* (Fall 1958), 73.

and individual case methods are used in making decisions about individuals.
Daniel Glaser sums up the issue as follows:

I know of no instance where an established academic criminologist, judge or correctional administrator has advocated the replacement of case studies and subjective evaluation by statistical tables for sentencing, parole or other major decisions on the fate of an offender. The many reasons for insisting upon case data may be grouped into two categories. First of all, these officials must make moral decisions for the state as a whole in determining what risks would justify withholding from or granting freedom to a man. . . . Secondly, there always is some information on a case too special to be readily taken into account by any conceivable table in estimating what risks are involved in a specific official action. Thirdly, there are many types of predicitions besides the overall prospect of violations which judges and parole board members must consider. These include the type of violation, and the consequences of certain types of violations for community treatment of other parolees.[50]

---

[50] *The Effectiveness of a Prison and Parole System,* p. 304.

Standard 12.1

Organization of Paroling Authorities

Each State that has not already done so should, by 1975, establish parole decisionmaking bodies for adult and juvenile offenders that are independent of correctional institutions. These boards may be administratively part of an overall statewide correctional services agency, but they should be autonomous in their decisionmaking authority and separate from field services. The board responsible for the parole of adult offenders should have jurisdiction over both felons and misdemeanants.

1. The boards should be specifically responsible for articulating and fixing policy, for acting on appeals by correctional authorities or inmates on decisions made by hearing examiners, and for issuing and signing warrants to arrest and hold alleged parole violators.

2. The boards of larger States should have a staff of full-time hearing examiners appointed under civil service regulations.

3. The boards of smaller States may assume responsibility for all functions; but should establish clearly defined procedures for policy development, hearings, and appeals.

4. Hearing examiners should be empowered to hear and make initial decisions in parole grant and revocation cases under the specific policies of the parole board. The report of the hearing examiner containing a transcript of the hearing and the evidence should constitute the exclusive record. The decision of the hearing examiner should be final unless appealed to the parole board within 5 days by the correctional authority or the offender. In the case of an appeal, the parole board should review the case on the basis of whether there is substantial

evidence in the report to support the finding or whether the finding was erroneous as a matter of law.

5. Both board members and hearing examiners should have close understanding of correctional institutions and be fully aware of the nature of their programs and activities of offenders.

6. The parole board should develop a citizen committee, broadly representative of the community and including ex-offenders, to advise the board on the development of policies.

Standard 12.2

Parole Authority Personnel

Each State should specify by statute, by 1975, the qualifications and conditions of appointment of parole board members.

1. Parole boards for adult and juvenile offenders should consist of full-time members.

2. Members should possess academic training in fields such as criminilogy, education, psychology, psychiatry, law, social work, or sociology.

3. Members should have a high degree of skill in comprehending legal issues and statistical information and an ability to develop and promulgate policy.

4. Members should be appointed by the governor for six-year terms from a panel of nominees selected by an advisory group broadly representative of the community. Besides being representative of relevant professional organizations, the advisory group should include all important ethnic and socio-economic groups.

5. Parole boards in the small States should consist of no less than three full-time members. In most States, they should not exceed five members.

6. Parole board members should be compensated at a rate equal to that of a judge of a court of general jurisdiction.

7. Hearing examiners should have backgrounds similar to that of members but need not be as specialized. Their education and experiential qualifications should allow them to understand programs, to relate to people, and to make sound and reasonable decisions.

8. Parole board members should participate in continuing training on a national basis. The exchange of parole board members and hearing examiners between States for training purposes should be supported and encouraged.

Standard 12.3

The Parole Grant Hearing

Each parole jurisdiction immediately should develop policies for parole release hearings that include opportunities for personal and adequate participation by the inmates concerned; procedural guidelines to insure proper, fair, and thorough consideration of every case; prompt decisions and personal notification of decisions to inmates; and provision for accurate records of deliberations and conclusions.

A proper parole grant process should have the following characteristics:

1. Hearings should be scheduled with inmates within one year after they are received in an institution. Inmates should appear personally at hearings.

2. At these hearings, decisions should be directed toward the quality and pertinence of program objectives agreed upon by the inmate and the institution staff.

3. Board representatives should monitor and approve programs that can have the effect of releasing the inmate without further board hearings.

4. Each jurisdiction should have a statutory requirement, patterned after the Model Penal Code, under which offenders must be released on parole when first eligible unless certain specific conditions exist.

5. When a release date is not agreed upon, a further hearing date within one year should be set.

6. A parole board member or hearing examiner should hold no more than 20 hearings in any full day.

7. One examiner or member should conduct hearings. His findings should be final unless appealed to the full parole board by the correctional authority or the inmate within 5 days.

8. Inmates should be notified of any decision directly and personally by the board member or representative before he leaves the institution.

9. The person hearing the case should specify in detail and in writing the reasons for his decision, whether to grant parole or to deny or defer it.

10. Parole procedures should permit disclosure of information on which the hearing examiner bases his decisions. Sensitive information may be withheld, but in such cases nondisclosure should be noted in the record so that subsequent reviewers will know what information was not available to the offender.

11. Parole procedures should permit representation of offenders under appropriate conditions, if required. Such representation should conform generally to Standard 2.2 on Access to Legal Services.

Standard 12.4
Revocation Hearings

Each parole jurisdiction immediately should develop and implement a system of revocation procedures to permit the prompt confinement of parolees exhibiting behavior that poses a serious threat to others. At the same time, it should provide careful controls, methods of fact-finding, and possible alternatives to keep as many offenders as possible in the community. Return to the institution should be used as a last resort, even when a factual basis for revocation can be demonstrated.

1. Warrants to arrest and hold alleged parole violators should be issued and signed by parole board members. Tight control should be developed over the process of issuing such warrants. They should never be issued unless there is sufficient evidence of probable serious violation. In some instances, there may be a need to detain alleged parole violators. In general, however, detention is not required and is to be discouraged. Any parolee who is detained should be granted a prompt preliminary hearing. Administrative arrest and detention should never be used simply to permit investigation of possible violations.

2. Parolees alleged to have committed a new crime but without other violations of conditions sufficient to require parole revocation should be eligible for bail or other release pending the outcome of the new charges, as determined by the court.

3. A preliminary hearing conducted by an individual not previously directly involved in the case should be held promptly on all alleged parole violations, including convictions of new crimes, in or near the community in which the violation occurred unless waived by the parolee after due notification of his rights. The purpose should be to determine whether there is probable cause or reasonable

grounds to believe that the arrested parolee has committed acts that would constitute a violation of parole conditions and a determination of the value question of whether the case should be carried further, even if probable cause exists. The parolee should be given notice that the hearing will take place and of what parole violations have been alleged. He should have the right to present evidence, to confront and cross-examine witnesses, and to be represented by counsel.

The person who conducts the hearing should make a summary of what transpired at the hearing and the information he used to determine whether probable cause existed to hold the parolee for the final decision of the parole board on revocation. If the evidence is insufficient to support a further hearing, or if it is otherwise determined that revocation would not be desirable, the offender should be released to the community immediately.

4. At parole revocation hearings, the parolee should have written notice of the alleged infractions of his rules or conditions; access to official records regarding his case; the right to be represented by counsel, including the right to appointed counsel if he is indigent; the opportunity to be heard in person; the right to subpoena witnesses in his own behalf; and the right to cross-examine witnesses or otherwise to challenge allegations or evidence held by the State. Hearing examiners should be empowered to hear and decide parole revocation cases under policies established by the parole board. Parole should not be revoked unless there is substantial evidence of a violation of one of the conditions of parole. The hearing examiner should provide a written statement of findings, the reasons for the decision, and the evidence relied upon.

5. Each jurisdiction should develop alternatives to parole revocation, such as warnings, short-time local confinement, special conditions of future parole, variations in intensity of supervision or surveillance, fines, and referral to other community resources. Such alternative measures should be utilized as often as is practicable.

6. If return to a correctional institution is warranted, the offender should be scheduled for subsequent appearances for parole considerations when appropriate. There should be no automatic prohibition against reparole of a parole violator.

Standard 12.5

Organization of Field Services

Each State should provide, by 1978, for the consolidation of institutional and parole field services in departments or divisions of correctional services. Such consolidations should occur as closely as possible to operational levels.

1. Juvenile and adult correctional services may be part of the same parent agency but should be maintained as autonomous program units within it.

2. Regional administration should be established so that institutional and field services are jointly managed and coordinated at the program level.

3. Joint training programs for institutional and field staffs should be undertaken, and transfers of personnel between the two programs should be encouraged.

4. Parole services should be delivered, wherever practical, under a team system in which a variety of persons including parolees, parole managers, and community representatives participate.

5. Teams should be located, whenever practical, in the neighborhoods where parolees reside. Specific team members should be assigned to specific community groups and institutions designated by the team as especially significant.

6. Organizational and administrative practices should be altered to provide greatly increased autonomy and decisionmaking power to the parole teams.

Standard 12.6

Community Services for Parolees

Each State should begin immediately to develop a diverse range of programs to meet the needs of parolees. These services should be drawn to the greatest extent possible from community programs available to all citizens, with parole staff providing linkage between services and the parolees needing or desiring them.

1. Stringent review procedures should be adopted, so that parolees not requiring supervision are released from supervision immediately and those requiring minimal attention are placed in minimum supervision caseloads.

2. Parole officers should be selected and trained to fulfill the role of community resource manager.

3. Parole staff should participate fully in developing coordinated delivery systems of human services.

4. Funds should be made available for parolees without interest charge. Parole staff should have authority to waive repayment to fit the individual case.

5. State funds should be available to offenders, so that some mechanism similar to unemployment benefits may be available to inmates at the time of their release, in order to tide them over until they find a job.

6. All States should use, as much as possible, a requirement that offenders have a visible means of support, rather than a promise of a specific job, before authorizing their release on parole.

7. Parole and State employment staffs should develop effective communication systems at the local level. Joint meetings and training sessions should be undertaken.

8. Each parole agency should have one or more persons attached to the central office to act as liasion with major program agencies, such as the Office of Economic Opportunity, Office of Vocational Rehabilitation, and Department of Labor.

9. Institutional vocational training tied directly to specific subsequent job placements should be supported.

10. Parole boards should encourage institutions to maintain effective quality control over programs.

11. Small community-based group homes should be available to parole staff for prerelease programs, for crises, and as a substitute to recommitment to an institution in appropriately reviewed cases of parole violation.

12. Funds should be made available to parole staffs to purchase needed community resources for parolees.

13. Special caseloads should be established for offenders with specific types of problems, such as drug abuse.

Standard 12.7
Measures of Control

Each State should take immediate action to reduce parole rules to an absolute minimum, retaining only those critical in the individual case, and to provide for effective means of enforcing the conditions established.

1. After considering suggestions from correctional staff and preferences of the individual, parole boards should establish in each case the specific parole conditions appropriate for the individual offender.

2. Parole staff should be able to request the board to amend rules to fit the needs of each case and should be empowered to require the parolee to obey any such rule when put in writing, pending the final action of the parole board.

3. Special caseloads for intensive supervision should be established and staffed by personnel of suitable skill and temperament. Careful review procedures should be established to determine which offenders should be assigned or removed from such caseloads.

4. Parole officers should develop close liaison with police agencies, so that any formal arrests necessary can be made by police. Parole officers, therefore, would not need to be armed.

Standard 12.8

Manpower for Parole

By 1975, each State should develop a comprehensive manpower and training program which would make it possible to recruit persons with a wide variety of skills, including significant numbers of minority group members and volunteers, and use them effectively in parole programs.

Among the elements of State manpower and training programs for corrections that are prescribed in Chapter 14 of the Commission report, the following apply with special force to parole.

1. A functional workload system linking specific tasks to different categories of parolees should be instituted by each State and should form the basis of allocating manpower resources.

2. The bachelor's degree should constitute the requisite educational level for the beginning parole officer.

3. Provisions should be made for the employment of parole personnel having less than a college degree to work with parole officers on a team basis, carrying out the tasks appropriate to their individual skills.

4. Career ladders that offer opportunities for advancement of persons with less than college degrees should be provided.

5. Recruitment efforts should be designed to produce a staff roughly proportional in ethnic background to the offender population being served.

6. Ex-offenders should receive high priority consideration for employment in parole agencies.

7. Use of volunteers should be extended substantially.

8. Training programs designed to deal with the organizational issues and the kinds of personnel required by the program should be established in each parole agency.

19
Making Paroling Policy Explicit

DON M. GOTTFREDSON, PETER B. HOFFMAN, MAURICE H. SIGLER, AND LESLIE T. WILKINS

Are parole boards using the right determinants for parole selection? The best answer they can offer at this time, without assurance, is: "Possibly." Ostensibly, at least, they consider the prisoner's offense, prior record, educational and employment history, military record, drug or alcohol problems, institutional discipline, and other matters. But they have not articulated the weight that should be given to each. Should a good military record, for example, outweigh a poor alcohol history, or vice versa? They might argue that every case is unique, but, if this is totally true, they cannot hope ever to establish generally applicable criteria.

UNIQUENESS AND EQUITY

By "equity" or "fairness" we mean that *similar* persons are dealt with in *similar ways* in *similar* situations. Fairness thus implies the idea of similarity and of comparisons. Obviously, if every person or every case were unique, there would be no grounds for comparison and, hence, no way to provide for fairness. Will an individual, then, see his treatment as fair if he sees himself as similar, in all

SOURCE. *Crime and Delinquency,* **21,** January 1975, pp. 34–44. Reprinted with permission of the authors and the National Council on Crime and Delinquency.

significant ways, to another person who received exactly similar treatment? Not quite, since, if only one other person were required for comparison, it would not be unreasonable to maintain that *both* were treated unfairly. However, as the sample of similar persons increases, similar treatment among that sample becomes more likely to be regarded as fair. The idea of fairness thus becomes closely related to statistical concepts of similarity and sample size.

A complaint that a parole board is "unfair" implies that similar persons convicted of similar crimes are receiving dissimilar treatment. The factor taken into consideration in the reference sample of persons and characteristics may vary in some degree from one critic to another. Some critics will look with particular care at race (unfairness related to racial characteristics is defined as "racism" because "race" is not seen as a reasonable or morally acceptable justification of differences in treatment); others will look with particular care at the type of offense; some will look at both types of offenses and race. However, the scale and scope of comparison upon which critics may rely are not likely to be wider than the scale and scope of factors the board might consider. If the board uses a parole selection model built upon common elements of comparison (fairness criteria), it can respond precisely to criticisms. If it sustains a balance with respect to crime seriousness, probability of reconviction, and behavior in the institutional setting and ignores race, it is not likely to be accused of racial bias.

If the board has before it, in each case in which a decision is made, a chart indicating the balance among the most important factors that arise in any discussion of "fairness," it can, if it wishes to do so, still depart from the calculated figure, but, in so doing, it would be making a value judgment of further factors not included in the model. If the decision makes these further factors explicit, a sound case for it will have been established. Though the general policy of the board would not be defended by such a model, clearly the decisions *within* the model would be "fair." If attention were diverted from individual cases to questions of general principles of parole, the understanding and control of the system would, we suggest, be greatly increased. Attention could then be more thoroughly devoted to humanitarian considerations because the routine comparative work (even though highly complex) could be delegated to "models" of "fairness."

REASONS FOR DENIAL: IMPORTANCE OF WEIGHTS

To ascertain whether a parole board is using the *right* selective features, we must first find out what the *primary* ones are and what weights are given to them in practice. This requires some sort of measurement. Merely saying that certain factors are important in granting or denying parole oversimplifies the issue. Parole selection is not simply as yes-or-no decision; the question of *when* an inmate should be paroled is more complex than *whether* he should be. The trend toward abolition of minimum sentences imposes greater responsibility on a parole board, which must decide how much time, within the limits set by statute and the sentencing judge, the offender should serve before release.

Thus we have a starting point—the weights being given to the offense and to the offender's characteristics. Examining how these weights are applied in practice will provide a measure of unwritten or *implicit* policy and thus put the parole board in a good position to formulate *explicit* policy.

The National Advisory Commission on Criminal Justice Standards and Goals states:

> The major task of the parole board is articulation of criteria for making decisions and development of basic policies. This task is to be separated from the specific function of deciding individual parole grant and revocation cases, which may be performed either by the board in smaller state or by a hearing examiner.[1]

The issue of explicit general policy and its relation to discretion in parole selection has been considered by a number of authors.[2] A principal method suggested for controlling discretion is the stipulation that reasons for denial of parole be given in writing. While this is a start in the right direction, it cannot, by itself, resolve the matter of equity. True, the inmate may have a right to know the basis for his continued deprivation of liberty and he may be aided thereby in taking corrective action to increase the likelihood of rehabilitative gains and the probability of being granted parole at a later review. Similarly, the paroling authority may profit from the exercise by learning to state more explicitly what often are vague impressions. But these expected gains do not address the issue of fairness entirely. Providing reasons for parole denial identifies the *criteria* used *but not the weights* given to them.

For example, the Model Penal Code lists four primary reasons for denying a prisoner release on parole:

(*a*) There is substantial risk that he will not conform to the conditions of parole; or

(*b*) his release at that time would depreciate the seriousness of his crime or promote disrespect for law; or

(*c*) his release would have a substantially adverse effect on institutional discipline; or

(*d*) his continued correctional treatment, medical care, or vocational or other training in the institution will substantially enhance his capacity to lead a law abiding life when released at a later date.[3]

If parole selection were truly an either-or (parole/no parole) decision—as it may be in jurisdictions with long minimum sentences—such reasons might suffice. However, when minimum sentences are short or are not given (following the present sentencing trend), parole selection is, in reality; more of a deferred sentencing decision—a decision on *when* to release—than a parole/no parole decision. Merely giving reasons for denial does not suffice because they relate only

---

[1] National Advisory Commission on Criminal Justice Standards and Goals, *Report of the Task Force on Corrections: Summary Report on Corrections*—Working Draft (Austin, Texas: Office of the Governor, Criminal Justice Council, 1972), p. 39.

[2] K. C. Davis, *Discretionary Justice* (Baton Rouge: Louisiana State University Press, 1969); F. L. Bixby, "A New Role for Parole Boards," *Federal Probation,* June 1970, pp. 24-28; F. Remington et al., *Criminal Justice Administration* (Indianapolis: Bobbs-Merrill, 1969).

[3] American Law Institute, *Model Penal Code* (May 4, 1962), § 305.9.

to the fact of the denial; they include no criteria on the length of the consequent "continuance" or "set off." Thus a parole board considering a bank robber may give him a continuance of three years for reasons *a* and *b* quoted above and in a similar case of another bank robber give a continuance of five years for the same reasons. Without explicit guidelines that cover not only the criteria used but also the weights to be given them, a parole board will not be more likely to arrive at equitable decisions than it is when it gives no reasons at all, and observers will not have much more opportunity to challenge these decisions.

PRIMARY CRITERIA

One phase of the Parole Decision-making Project conducted by the NCCD Research Center was identification of weights given to various criteria in the parole decision. It became apparent early in the project that, as other research endeavors had shown, parole board members place little value on the mere presentation of the prediction device known as an "experience table."[4] A study of criteria used in making parole *decisions* (as distinguished from criteria used in predicting parole *outcome*), in which board members completed a set of subjective rating scales for a sample of actual decisions over a six-month period, showed that the primary concerns were severity of offense, parole prognosis, and institutional behavior and that a parole board's decisions could be predicted fairly accurately by knowledge of its ratings on these three factors.[5]

From this knowledge, the development of an explicit indicant of parole selection was possible. For initial decisions a chart was constructed with one axis reflecting offense severity and the other reflecting parole prognosis (risk). The intersection of these axes gives the expected decision (in months to be served before the review hearing). In the examples presented in Figure 1, the expected decision in high severity/good prognosis cases (such as armed robbery, first offender) is 20 months to be served before review consideration; in low severity/poor prognosis cases, the expected decision is 14 months to be served before review consideration. At review considerations, cases with "adequate" or "very good" institutional adjustment (discipline and program progress ratings were highly correlated) were generally released; those with ratings of "below average" or "poor" were likely to be "set off" for another hearing.

As an aid in actual case decision-making, this type of chart could be used in the following manner. After scoring the case on severity and prognosis, the parole board member or hearing examiner would check the table to see the expected decision. In practice, a range (e.g., 20 to 24 months) would be appropriate to allow for some variation within broad severity or risk categories. Should he wish to

---

[4] See P. Hoffman and H. Goldstein, *Do Experience Tables Matter?* Parole Decisionmaking Project, Report No. 4; and P. Hoffman et al., *The Operational Use of an Experience Table*, Parole Decision-making Project, Report No. 7 (Davis, Calif.: NCCD Research Center, June 1973).

[5] P. Hoffman, *Paroling Policy Feedback*, Parole Decision-making Project, Report No. 8 (Davis, Calif.: NCCD Research Center, June 1973).

Figure 1   *Time to Be Served Before Review (in Months)*

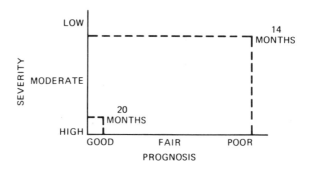

make a decision outside the expected range, he would be obligated to specify the factors which make that particular case unique (such as unusually good or poor institutional adjustment, credit for time spent on a sentence of another jurisdiction, etc.). At the review hearing, the decision to parole or continue would be based primarily on institutional performance.

GUIDELINES: CONSTRUCTION AND USE

The United States Board of Parole showed considerable interest in implementing this model. Very likely, one reason was that the Board, under heavy criticism for several years, was attempting at that time to move ahead on its own proposal for change, which included regionalization, a plan that called for delegating the routine decision-making power (parole grants and revocations) to an expanded staff of hearing examiners, with the Board performing a policy-setting and appellate function. Obviously, decision guidelines of the type developed could enable the Board to exercise control more effectively over the decisions of the expanded and decentralized staff.

The result was that the Parole Decision-making Project staff was requested to formulate parole selection policy guidelines in as objective a format as possible. The staff replied that the Board itself might rank-order offense types by severity and then, for each risk classification (the determination of which could be aided by a statistical predictive device), decide on an explicit policy. However, the Board expressed doubt about undertaking the task without having more familiarity with this type of device. The Project staff, therefore, was requested to provide two sets of policy guidelines—one set for adult offenders, the other for youth—based on the Project's coded material reflecting parole board policy during the preceding two years.[6] These guidelines were to be tested for six months, after which the board would make any modifications deemed necessary. A plan

---

[6] For a description of sampling and coding procedures, see Susan M. Singer and D. M. Gottfredson, *Development of a Data Base for Parole Decision-making,* Parole Decision-making Project, Report No. 1 (Davis, Calif.: NCCD Research Center, June 1973).

to facilitate periodic consideration of guideline modifications was also requested.

The study cited above[7] yielded a set of guidelines based on subjective ratings. The new requirement was a table based on more objective measures. Thus, for the parole prognosis axis, an eleven-factor predictive (salient factor) score (see Appendix A) that had been worked out by the Project was substituted for the subjective ratings. These "experience table" scores were combined to form four classes of risk: very good (9–11), good (6–8), fair (4–5), and poor (0–3).[8]

For the severity scale, a different procedure was necessary. The median time served was calculated for each offense in each category of offense ratings coded by the Project.[9] Offense ratings with similar median times served were combined to produce six severity level classifications.[10]

The median time served for each severity/risk level was then tabulated (separately for youth and adult cases) for the large sample of final decisions (parole/mandatory release/expiration) coded by the Project. "Smoothing," based on agreement by two Project staff members after visual inspection, increased the consistency of these medians, although no attempt was made to force uniform or linear increments. Each median was then bracketed ($\pm$ x months) to provide a "discretion range"—the guideline table. Table 1 displays the original adult guidelines. The size of the appropriate range was determined after informal discussions with several board members and hearing examiners and, while arbitrary, is to some extent proportional to the size of the median. Since not all offenses were included in this listing, instructions were prepared which explained that an unlisted offenses's appropriate severity level could be determined by comparing that offense with others of similar severity that were listed. In addition, because not all offense ratings (e.g., vehicle theft) were specific enough to cover the scale of severity possible (e.g., theft of one vehicle for personal use up through large-scale theft for resale), the instructions indicated that the offense ratings listed were to used only as a guide and that the hearing panel's determination of the severity category should be supported by the description of the offense in the hearing summary. In other words, the severity rating is a subjective determination guided by objective indicants.

In October 1972 the United States Board of Parole launched a pilot project to test the feasibility of regionalization. Comprised of five institutions in the Northeast, making up about one-fifth of the Board's total workload, the project had a number of innovative features, including opportunity for the prisoner to be represented by an advocate, written reasons for parole denial, a two-stage administrative appeal process, and the use of decision guidelines.

---

[7] See text *supra* at note 5.

[8] This was one of the Project's first predictive measures and was based on a relatively small sample. As soon as a more powerful device is formed, it can be readily substituted; similarly, if a different combination of score categories is desired, the guidelines can be changed accordingly.

[9] For coding definitions and procedures, see D. M. Gottfredson and Susan M. Singer, *Coding Manual*, Parole Decision-making Project, Report No. 2 (Davis, Calif.: NCCD Research Center, June 1973).

[10] Some offense ratings had been excluded because of lack of specificity.

Table 1 *Average Total Time (including jail time) Served before Release, U.S. Board of Parole, Pilot Regionalization Project, Guidelines for Decision-making, Adult Cases*

Offense Categories*	Salient Factor Score (Probability of Favorable Parole Outcome)			
	9–11 (Very High)	6–8 (High)	4–5 (Fair)	0–3 (Low)
A-Low Severity[a]	6–10 months	8–12 months	10–14 months	12–16 months
B-Low/Moderate Severity[b]	8–12 ″	12–16 ″	16–20 ″	20–25 ″
C-Moderate Severity[c]	12–16 ″	16–20 ″	20–24 ″	24–30 ″
D-High Severity[d]	16–20 ″	20–26 ″	26–32 ″	32–38 ″
E-Very High Severity[e]	26–36 ″	36–45 ″	45–55 ″	55–65 ″
F-Highest Severity[f]	Information not available because of limited number of cases.			

*NOTES: (1) If an offense can be classified in more than one category, the most serious applicable category is to be used. If an offense involved two or more separate offenses, the severity level may be increased. (2) If an offense is not listed above, the proper category may be obtained by comparing the offense with similar offenses listed. (3) If a continuance is to be recommended, subtract one month to allow for provision of release program.

a. Minor theft; walkaway (escape without use of force); immigration law; alchohol law.

b. Possess marijuana; possess heavy narcotics, less than $50; theft, unplanned; forgery or counterfeiting, less than $50; burglary, daytime.

c. Vehicle theft; forgery or counterfeiting, more than $500; sale of marijuana; planned theft; possess heavy narcotics, more than $50; escape; Mann Act, no force; Selective Service.

d. Sell heavy narcotics; burglary, weapon or nighttime; violence, "spur of the moment"; sexual act, force.

e. Armed robbery; criminal act, weapon; sexual act, force and injury; assault, serious bodily harm; Mann Act, force.

f. Willful homicide; kidnapping; armed robbery, weapon fired or serious injury.

For all initial hearings, the examiners were instructed to complete an evaluation form that included a severity rating scale and the salient factor score. Should they make a recommendation outside the guideline table, they were instructed to specify the case factors which compelled them to do so. The format of the hearing summary was designed so that the last section begins with the following standardized statement, the blanks to be filled in with the appropriate phrase or number:

The hearing panel considers this to be a [ ] offense severity case with a salient factor score of [ ]. The subject has been in custody for a total of [ ] months.

A decision to [   ] is recommended. (Indicate reasons if the decision is outside the guidelines.)

For review hearings, completion of the evaluation form was required before any continuance was recommended for reasons other than institutional discipline or failure to complete specific institutional programs, so that the guidelines would not be exceeded by arbitrary continuances. If a parole grant was recommended, completion of the form was not necessary. At early review hearings (requested by institutional staff when, in their judgment, an inmate has shown exceptional institutional progress meriting earlier parole consideration) the guidelines are consulted also to see whether the exceptional progress justifies the advanced parole date recommended.

Statistical tabulations for the first four months (October 1972 through January 1973) show the numbers and percentages of panel recommendations within and outside the guidelines (Table 2). Of all initial decision recommendations (adult and youth) 63 per cent were within the decision guidelines. About one-third of panel recommendations outside the guidelines were for continuances of one, two, or three months under the guideline specification, partly because of a desire to allow more than the thirty-day release preparation period built into the guideline table. With continuing use of guidelines, release at review consideration (given good institutional adjustment) will occur more frequently, uncertainty in release program planning will be lessened, and the need for the lengthy post-decision release planning periods will be reduced.

During the course of this study, the project case summaries were examined to identify recurring explanations for decisions outside the guidelines, and a list of examples of such cases was prepared as a guideline supplement (see Appendix B). The list does not, in itself, justify a deviation from the guidelines in an individual case; it is merely a reminder that the deviation can be considered.

GUIDELINE MODIFICATION

Since usage of the guidelines may induce rigidity—just as the absence of guidelines produces disparity—the Board adopted two basic procedures for modifying and updating them.

First, the Board may modify any guideline category at any time. For example,

Table 2 *538 Initial Decision Recommendations, Pilot Project Guideline Usage, October 1972 to January 1973[a]*

Site	Number and Percentage of Recommendations				
	Within[b] Decision Guideline	1–3 Months Longer	1–3 Months Shorter	4 or more Months Longer	4 or more Months Shorter
Adult Institutions	266 (64.6%)	20 (4.9%)	59 (14.3%)	26 (6.3%)	41(10.0%)
Youth Institutions	73 (57.9%)	11 (8.7%)	10 (7.9%)	21 (16.7%)	11 (8.7%)
All Institutions	339 (63.0%)	31 (5.8%)	69 (12.8%)	47 (8.7%)	52 (9.7%)

a. In the first four months of operation the panels failed to complete the evaluation form in only three cases out of 541 hearings.

b. Includes cases in which a decision within the guidelines was precluded by the minimum or maximum term.

after three months of guideline usage it decided to place three additional offenses on the guideline chart—Selective Service violation (determined by vote of the Board to be an offense of moderate severity), violation of the Mann Act with force (very high severity), violation of the Mann Act without force for commercial purposes (moderate severity).[11]

Second, at six-month intervals the Board will be given feedback from the decision-making of the previous six months and will examine each category to see whether the median time to be served has changed significantly. For example, the adult guidelines for the high severity/fair risk category show 26–32 months (see Appendix C), a median of 29 months $\pm$ 3. If after six months the median within this category is found to have statistically shifted—e.g., to 31 months— a new guideline of 28–34 months may be created.

At these policy meetings feedback will be provided the Board concerning the percentage of decisions falling outside each guideline category and the reasons given for these decisions. This will serve two purposes: The reasons for the deviations from the guidelines may be examined to certify their appropriateness, and the percentages of decisions within and outside the guidelines (and their distribution) for each category can be evaluated to determine whether the width for the category is appropriate. That is, too high a percentage of decisions outside the guideline range without adequate explanation may indicate either that a wider range is necessary or that the hearing panels are inappropriately exceeding their discretionary limits. On the other hand, a very high percentage of decisions within the guidelines may indicate excessive rigidity. The guidelines themselves cannot provide answers to these questions of policy.

IMPLICATIONS AND LIMITATIONS

By articulating the weights given to the major criteria under consideration, explicit decision guidelines permit assessment of the rationality and appropriateness of parole board policy. In individual cases they structure and control discretion—thus strengthening equity (fairness)—without eliminating it.

The decision guidelines method has implications not only for original parole selection decisions but also for decisions on parole violation and reparole. It appears equally applicable to judicial sentencing, in which similar problems of disparity arise.

The guidelines concept, the scales used, the procedures for applying them in individual cases, and the procedures to be used in their modification—all of these need to be refined; at present, they are admittedly crude. They appear, nevertheless, to be useful.

---

[11] The first set of guidelines used offense descriptions prepared in another context for use in a decision game. After the first six months, revised guidelines were prepared specifically for federal offenders; they are shown as Appendices C and D.

APPENDIX A

SALIENT FACTOR SCORE

_____ A.   Commitment offense did not involve auto theft.

_____ B.   Subject had one or more codefendants (whether brought to trial with subject or not).

_____ C.   Subject has no prior (adult or juvenile) incarcerations.

_____ D.   Subject has no other prior sentences (adult or juvenile)—i.e., probation, fine, suspended sentence.

_____ E.   Subject has not served more than 18 consecutive months during any prior incarceration (adult or juvenile).

_____ F.   Subject has completed the 12th grade or received G.E.D.

_____ G.   Subject has never had probation or parole revoked (or been committed for a new offense while on probation or parole).

_____ H.   Subject was 18 years old or older at first conviction (adult or juvenile).

_____ I.   Subject was 18 years old or older at first commitment (adult or juvenile).

_____ J.   Subject was employed, or a full-time student, for a total of at least six months during the last two years in the community.

_____ K.   Subject plans to reside with his wife and/or children after release.

_____ Total number of correct statements = favorable factors = score

APPENDIX B

GUIDELINE USAGE—AUXILIARY EXAMPLES

The following are recurrent situations in which a decision outside the guidelines might be considered.

Decisions Longer than Indicated by the Guidelines

1. The subject was committed for a probation violation which involved a new serious offense.

2. More time is necessary to complete a special institutional program (e.g., one-year drug abuse program).

3. The instant offense was actually a series of separate offenses (e.g., a series of bank robberies).

4. The salient factor score appears substantially inconsistent with clinical judgment (e.g., a high salient factor score for a person with a severe history of narcotic addiction).

5. A very high severity offense rating is normally indicated and there were additional aggravating circumstances (e.g., a bank robbery in which a person was injured or a weapon was fired).

6. Extremely poor institutional conduct (e.g., serious or repeated disciplinary infractions).

Decisions Shorter than Indicated by the Guidelines

1. Substantial medical problems.

2. Subject faces a substantial additional state-commitment sentence.

3. Subject has been in continuous custody on a separate charge for a substantial period of time.

4. The salient factor score appears substantially inconsistent with clinical judgment (e.g., a low salient factor score for a first offender).

5. Deportation-only cases.

6. Extremely good institutional program progress.

APPENDIX C

GUIDELINES FOR DECISION-MAKING, ADULT CASES (REVISED APRIL 1973) AVERAGE TOTAL TIME (INCLUDING JAIL TIME) SERVED BEFORE RELEASE

Offense Categories*	Salient Factor Score (Probability of Favorable Parole Outcome)			
	9–11 (Very High)	6–8 (High)	4–5 (Fair)	0–3 (Low)
A-Low Severity[a]	6–10 months	8–12 months	10–14 months	12–16 months
B-Low/Moderate Severity[b]	8–12 "	12–16 "	16–20 "	20–25 "
C-Moderate Severity[c]	12–16 "	16–20 "	20–24 "	24–30 "
D-High Severity[d]	16–20 "	20–26 "	26–32 "	32–38 "
E-Very High Severity[e]	26–36 "	36–45 "	45–55 "	55–65 "
F-Greatest Severity[f]	Information not available because of limited number of cases.			

*NOTES: (1) If an offense can be classified in more than one category, the most serious applicable category is to be used. If an offense involved two or more separate offenses, the severity level may be increased. (2) If an offense is not listed above, the proper category may be obtained by comparing the offense with similar offenses listed. (3) If a continuance is to be recommended, subtract one month to allow for provision of release program.

a. Immigration law; walkaway (escape without use of force); minor theft (includes larceny and simple possession of stolen property less than $1,000).

b. Alcohol law; Selective Service; Mann Act (no force, commercial purposes); theft from mail; forgery/fraud (less than $1,000); possession of marijuana (less than $500); passing/possession of counterfeit currency (less than $1,000).

c. Simple theft of motor vehicle (not multiple theft or for resale); theft, forgery/fraud ($1,-000–$20,000); possession of marijuana ($500 or over); possession of other "soft drugs" (less than $5,000); sale of marijuana (less than $5,000); sale of other "soft drugs" (less than $500); possession of "heavy narcotics" (by addict, less than $500); receiving stolen property with intent to resell (less than $20,000); embezzlement (less than $20,000); passing/possession of counterfeit currency ($1,000–$20,000); interstate transportation of stolen/forged securities (less than $20,000).

d. Theft, forgery/fraud (over $20,000); sale of marijuana ($5,000 or more); sale of other "soft drugs" ($500–$5,000); sale of "heavy narcotics" to support own habit; receiving stolen property ($20,000 or over); passing/possession of counterfeit currency (more than $20,000); counterfeiting; interstate transportation of stolen/forged securities ($20,000 or more); possession of "heavy narcotics" (by addict, $500 or more); sexual act (fear, no injury); burglary (bank or post office); robbery (no weapon or injury); organized vehicle theft.

e. Extortion; assault (serious injury); Mann Act (force); armed robbery; sexual act (force, injury); sale of "soft drugs" (other than marijuana—more than $5,000); possession of "heavy narcotics" (nonaddict); sale of "heavy narcotics" for profit.

f. Aggravated armed robbery (or other felony)—weapon fired or serious injury during offense; kidnapping; willful homicide.

APPENDIX D

GUIDELINES FOR DECISION-MAKING, YOUTH CASES (REVISED APRIL 1973) AVERAGE TOTAL TIME (INCLUDING JAIL TIME) SERVED BEFORE RELEASE

Offense Categories*	Salient Factor Score (Probability of Favorable Parole Outcome)			
	9–11 (Very High)	6–8 (High)	4–5 (Fair)	0–3 (Low)
A-Low Severity[a]	6–10 months	8–12 months	10–14 months	12–16 months
B-Low/Moderate Severity[b]	8–12 "	12–16 "	16–20 "	20–25 "
C-Moderate Severity[c]	9–13 "	13–17 "	17–21 "	21–26 "
D-High Severity[d]	12–16 "	16–20 "	20–24 "	24–28 "
E-Very High Severity[e]	20–27 "	27–32 "	32–36 "	36–42 "
F-Greatest Severity[f]	Information not available because of limited number of cases.			

*NOTES: (1) If an offense can be classified in more than one category, the most serious applicable category is to be used. If an offense involved two or more separate offenses, the severity level may be increased. (2) If an offense is not listed above, the proper category may be obtained by comparing the offense with similar offenses listed. (3) If a continuance is to be recommended, subtract one month to allow for provision of release program.

a. Immigration law; walkaway (escape without use of force); minor theft (includes larceny and simple possession of stolen property less than $1,000).

b. Alcohol law; Selective Service; Mann Act (no force, commercial purposes); theft from mail; forgery/fraud (less than $1,000); possession of marijuana (less than $500); passing/possession of counterfeit currency (less than $1,000).

c. Simple theft of motor vehicle (not multiple theft or for resale); theft, forgery/fraud ($1,000–$20,000); possession of marijuana ($500 or over); possession of other "soft drugs" (less than $500); possession of "heavy narcotics" (by addict, less than $500); receiving stolen property with intent to resell (less than $20,000); embezzlement (less than $20,000); passing/possession of counterfeit currency ($1,000–$20,000); interstate transportation of stolen/forged securities (less than $20,000).

d. Theft, forgery/fraud (over $20,000); sale of marijuana ($5,000 or more); sale of other "soft drugs" ($500–5,000); sale of "heavy narcotics" to support own habit; receiving stolen property ($20,000 or over); passing/possession of counterfeit currency (more than $20,000); counterfeiting; interstate transportation of stolen/forged securities ($20,000 or more); possession of "heavy narcotics" (by addict, $500 or more); sexual act (fear, no injury); burglary (bank or post office); robbery (no weapon or injury); organized vehicle theft.

e. Extortion; assault (serious injury); Mann Act (force); armed robbery; sexual act (force, injury); sale of "soft drugs" (other than marijuana—more than $5,000); possession of "heavy narcotics" (nonaddict); sale of "heavy narcotics" for profit.

f. Aggravated armed robbery (or other felony)—weapon fired or serious injury during offense; kidnapping; willful homicide.

20
Rational Risk Taking: Some Alternatives to Traditional Correctional Problems

NORMAN HOLT

Most of you here today are familiar with the growing number of studies questioning the value of traditional correctional programs. I assume that all of us share at least some of that skepticism since if we were content with our present programs we wouldn't be at this conference. The bulk of these studies are well summarized in Jim Robison and Gerald Smith's article entitled "The Effectiveness of Correctional Programs," and in Kassebaum, Ward and Wilner's book *Prison Treatment and Parole Survival*. This body of evidence prompted Dr. Bennett, head of Research for the California Department of Corrections, to publish an article recently advocating that we concentrate on changing correctional systems rather than changing offenders. My remarks are basically an elaboration of that point of view.

SOURCE. *Proceedings: Second National Workshop on Corrections and Parole Administration,* American Correctional Association, March 1974, pp. 35–48. Reprinted with permission of the author and the American Correctional Association.

What I'll try to do is outline three different "systems change" type programs which have strong research foundations, inmate support, proven effectiveness, and that will save you lots of money. Before getting there, however, we need to deal briefly with the related issue of length of incarceration and parole outcome. It's not only a crucial issue to what I'll present later but also involves some unpublished literature with which you may be less familiar.

TIME SERVED AND PAROLE OUTCOME

Even if we grant that one is not much better than another or even that few show significant advantages over having no programs or doing nothing at all, it's still possible that the act of intervention itself may have some value. More specifically, it can be argued that longer incarceration has a sobering and deterrent effect on the offenders. The counter position, of course, is the "prisonization" argument which holds that institutions are schools of crime and the longer inmates are kept the more criminal they become.

Until recently the evidence on either side has been less than conclusive. Several reports were done by commissions which examined existing evidence. Emphasis is usually placed on comparing sentences and recidivism of different states and the same state over time. One such effort in 1967, sponsored by the Youth and Adult Corrections Agency and entitled *Organization of State Correctional Services in the Control and Treatment of Crime and Delinquency*, concluded that "We are putting too many people into correctional institutions and keeping them too long." (p. 153) This study also pointed out "that California is one of the dubious leaders in the national averages of number of persons committed to prison and the length of time they serve in prison." (p. 160)

The same point was made recently by the *Correctional System Study* (also referred to as the Keldgord Report), which concluded, "In summary, the best solution (and there is almost no second best) calls as a first step for the drastic reduction of prison terms back towards what is elsewhere more customary. It is evident that long prison terms have not made California any more 'crime free.' This change is urgently needed." (p. 57, part 3) The study goes on to recommend that the average time in California prisons be reduced to 24 months or less from its current all time high of 36 months. And again a report examining existing evidence entitled *Crime and Penalties in California*, conducted by the Assembly Office of Research, reached the conclusion that "There is no evidence that severe penalties effectively deter crime. There is no evidence that prisons rehabilitated most offenders. There is evidence that larger numbers of offenders can be effectively supervised in the community at insignificant risk and considerable savings in public expense." (p. iv)

Original research on the issue in California dates back to 1959. During that year the prisons became seriously over-crowded and to reduce this pressure about 20 percent of those with parole dates (700 inmates) were given early releases averaging about a 5-month reduction. The same problem arose again in 1962 and the same solution was applied. Parole outcome data on these early releases was then compared to those who stayed their full term by Paul Mueller. The early releasees were specially selected to represent a low risk group so that few people were surprised when the early releases did better on parole. Mueller concluded, with appropriate caution, that "Despite a few statistically significant differences within sub-groups, it is probably best to interpret these findings generally as indicating no essential effects on parole outcomes from granting advanced releases." The advantage of this study was that it compared long and short sentences in the same jurisdiction over the same time period. The disadvantage, of course, was that the two groups had different profiles.

A more controlled analysis was done in 1969 (Jaman and Dickover). This involved matching pairs of offenders by crime, race, age, commitment record, narcotic history, type of parole supervision and Base Expectancy level (predicted parole success). The major difference was that one of each pair was selected for having served less than the average months in prison while the other had served more than the average. Two years after being paroled those who served the shorter sentences were found to have done significantly better. Unfortunately, an analysis of 35 variables not controlled for showed the two groups were not entirely comparable on all items, but at least you could reasonably conclude that shorter terms were not associated with higher recidivism for this sample.

In 1970 the legislature commissioned a major study of this issue by Public Systems Incorporated. Data cards on 8,000 parolees were supplied by the Department of Corrections. After an intensive analysis of time served and parole outcome the study concluded "Length of time served by California prisoners has no relationship on their performances after release." (p. 23)

These studies, comparing early and late releases, involve a serious problem, however, that compromises their conclusiveness; conscious decisions are made by parole boards that some offenders will serve more time than others. Thus, any differences favoring earlier releases can always be explained as good decision-making. Conversely, similar outcomes can be interpreted as reflecting the optimum readiness for release. And even comparison of parolees with similar backgrounds doesn't destroy the argument since it can still be maintained that these decisions also rely on subjective material which can't be codified.

It seemed that the only way to finally resolve this issue was through a controlled experiment. With this in mind the Adult Authority agreed to participate in an experiment in which early releases would be granted to a group of inmates selected at random. The procedure was to create a study sample of over 1,300 inmates who had been granted parole dates six months in the future. Using a random table of numbers half the men were selected to be released 6 months early while the others (the control group) were paroled at the normal time. The important point is that the early releases were not selected by any criteria, subjective or otherwise.

The parole performance of both groups was evaluated one year after release (Berecochea, Jaman, and Jones). As had been expected the performance of the early releases was not significantly better or worse than the control group. (See Table 1) This should put the issue to rest.

We've reached the point then when we can say with some confidence and degree of certainty, both that programs don't rehabilitate nor do longer sentences deter the offender.

Where does that leave us? I think it leaves us in the enviable position where the most rational correctional policy is not only the most humane but the cheapest, and that policy is to get people out of our correctional systems as soon as possible and keep them out. The three California projects I'll discuss today had this as their goal. None of these were directed toward changing the offender in any basic way. Their purpose was rather to change the way the system processed offenders. The first sought to keep from returning parolees to prison. The second was developed to get inmates to parole sooner, and the third was directed towards getting men off parole where supervision couldn't be justified.

These projects are described as examples of "Rational Risk Taking" and some explanation of this term is in order. "Rational" is used here in the technical sense to describe a process by which a goal is stated, alternative courses of action are evaluated with existing data, the most promising one is selected and the chosen course of action is systematically evaluated. I mean this to compare with other types of risk taking not to imply that there is some magical way to run a correctional system without any risk. Every course of action involves risks. The choice is really between continuing to take the old risks, with which we are comfortable, or to take some new ones. And secondly, whether we select the new or old risks, should we rationalize the risk taking process.

In 1965 the Parole Division in California began a conscious effort to reduce the number of parolees returned to prison for violating technical conditions of parole. Parole agents were encouraged to find alternative ways of dealing with the parolee in the community and asked to recommend a return to prison only as a last resort.

These efforts were demonstrating some success when, in 1969, the parole board began giving its full support to the idea. The other two options open to the board were to return the parolee to prison as a regular violator (with an average stay of 18 months) or a short term return (averaging about 4½ months).

The extent of this effort can be seen in comparison with an early year. During 1968 1,371 parolees were returned to prison as technical violators. By 1970 the number had dropped to 1,023, while only 794 were returned in 1971. This dramatic change resulted both from higher recommendation rates and more parole board concurrence. Parole agents were only recommending 55% of the violators for community disposition in fiscal year 1968–69, compared to over 70% by 1971. These later recommendations were accepted 72% of the time by the board compared to 60% during the 1968–69 period. What this amounted to was about a 50% increase in community based dispositions in three years.

Naturally there was an ongoing concern with this effort to keep parolees in the community. We wanted to make sure that the public wasn't being subjected to an undue amount of crimes by parolees.

With this in mind a sample consisting of all violators in Los Angeles County for two months was studied in terms of their subsequent parole behavior (Miller and Downer, 1972). There were 99 parolees who had violated the conditions of parole but were continued on parole anyway. Their performance for the following 12 months was then analyzed. The results (See Table 2) surprised everyone. The parole violators who remained in the community got into only about as much trouble as we expect for new men coming out of the institutions. They were no more likely to be arrested (45.4% compared to 46.6%) during the next 12 months and not much more likely to be returned to prison (13.1% compared to 9.7%).[1] Even at this the comparison was probably the wrong one to make. In California most minor violations are handled informally by the parole agent. Thus the study group included only those who had demonstrated difficulty in adjusting, unlike new releases. A fairer comparison of outcome would probably have been with parolees returned to short term institutional programs. This would be the board's second option for these cases. Comparable figures for releases from these programs show that 37% of the addicts, 22% of the non-addicts returned to prison within 12 months. In either case, however, the results are strong enough to speak for themselves.

Needless to say this data seriously challenges the traditional idea that parolees having problems are doomed to eventual failure or that small problems necessarily predict major difficulties to come and, therefore, it's best to get the parolee off the street. In addition, our statewide data on parolees involved in new felonies would seem to further question the credibility of that idea. At the same time the number of technical violators being returned to prison was being reduced the percentage of parolees committing new felonies and being returned to prison was going down. Those men released in 1967 (thus exposed to parole in 1967–68) had a one year new felony return rate of 7.1%. Releasees in 1970 (doing parole in 1970–71) improved on that with only 4.9% being returned with new felony convictions. Comparable figures for these same years for technical violators returned to prison were 11.8%, 9.7%, 7.0%, and finally 4.8% for the 1970 releases.

Another relevant comparison was made possible by the fact that the women's parole system didn't participate in these efforts. Their one year return rates for 1967–70 releases were for technical violations 20.6%, 17.8%, 18.1%, and 21.2%; with new felony rates of 2.5%, 2.6%, 3.1%, and finally 4.8% for those experiencing parole in 1970–71. In contrast to the men's system the technical rates for women remained stable while the new felony rates doubled.

If returning technical violators to prison is supposed to be a way of preventing new felonies, it sure doesn't work that way in California.

One final comment on this project. There was an unanticipated side benefit that we discovered later. The Parole Division had a chronic problem of parolees absconding. Of those being released from prison we could count on better than one out of ten being gone and their whereabouts unknown before the seventh month of parole. This would amount to 600 or 700 men each year. The rate began dropping from 11.8% in 1968 to 9.2% and then 7.8%, and finally down to 6.2% in 1971. We became aware of this as reports started coming in from parole offices.

---

[1] A detailed analysis showed first term non-addicts to be the best risk group.

With the high continue on parole rates parolees were saying they thought they would get a fairer shake when their problems were reviewed, with a good chance of keeping their parole and were staying in town to see what would happen.

OPTIMUM RELEASE PROGRAM

The releasing policy of the California Parole Board until 1970 was to grant a specific date of parole about seven months in advance. Provisions were also made to reconsider special hardship cases for earlier release where the situation warranted. This was broadened to include situations where an employer had an urgent need for the man's services and could not hold the job open until the scheduled parole date. The rigidity in this system made it difficult to secure firm job offers before release and most inmates chose to simply wait and spend their first few weeks on parole looking for employment. By the time work was found the parolee had used up his resources, borrowed against his first pay check and was getting started with two strikes against him. Jobs offered at the time parole was granted had a habit of vanishing before his parole date arrived and since the inmate was going to be released on a given date, regardless of what he did, there was no motivation to prepare himself for parole. This lack of motivation came through loud and clear when we evaluated the effects of pre-release classes (Holt and Renteria). The last few months in prison were "dead time" in the worst sense of the word.

When we began giving inmates 3-day pre-release furloughs[2] we found not only were many more securing employment but so many more were qualifying for early release consideration that the procedures began to break down. In the Los Angeles area alone the number of requests processed per month went from an average of 7 per month in 1968 to 24 in 1969 and up to 60 per month in 1970. Since the board found itself agreeing with the parole agents' recommendations 90% of the time anyway, they decided to delegate advancement authority to the Parole Divison.

The Optimum Release Program gave the parole agent the flexibility to release up to 60 days early any inmate coming to his caseload who had been able to put together his best possible parole program for that particular time. This involved finding a decent job, a place to live, and taking care of other details. The inmate can now control his date of release through his own efforts. If he doesn't want to make the effort he stays until his original release date. Rather than having a man with a good program sit around two more months, the agent advances him to parole.

Needless to say the inmates' interest in planning their parole programs picked up considerably. The problem quickly changes from trying to motivate inmates to attend pre-release functions to guarding the doors to keep those not yet eligible from sneaking in.

---

[2] For an evaluation of this program see N. Holt, "Temporary Prison Release."

Our evaluation of these procedures in terms of parole performance doesn't suggest any miracles. Initial employment seems to be better; 73% actually worked for some time on the job they were released to compared to only 57% of those advanced under the old system. It may have some effect in reducing problems during the first 90 days. For those advanced by parole agents 6% had serious problems compared to 15% of those advanced by the board. When those inmates released early are compared with the others they show better results but they are a better risk group to start with.

Those advanced who failed within 6 months tended to be a poor risk group whose plans were not all that sound. For the most part they involved low paying jobs which didn't last. Only about 200 parolees were studied in detail, however, so we probably shouldn't conclude any more than that they are doing at least as well as they did before.

The major benefit to the correctional system, of course, is getting rid of those pre-release cases who were simply doing "dead time." The rates have been fairly stable with about half the releases being advanced for an average of 45 days early. California paroled about 9,000 men in 1971 with 45% being advanced 1½ months each. The savings involved about 6,700 man months, thus reducing the need for over 500 prison beds.

ONE YEAR PAROLE DISCHARGES

The third project was an outgrowth of the two previously described. The push (from 1969 to 1971) to keep parolees in the community had saved about 700 prison beds while early releases under the Optimum Release Program accounted for another 500. In addition, added efforts were being made to grant more parole dates. In 1968, 6,177 inmates were granted parole. The figure climbed to 6,691 the following year and was up to 7,078 in 1970. Beds were also being saved by fewer new inmates from the courts and fewer parolees returning with new felony convictions.

Much of these "bed savings" began showing up as an increased workload for the Parole Division. The number of male felons on parole increased from 10,764 in 1968 to 13,943 at the end of 1970. During the first half of 1971 the increase accelerated to over one new caseload per week.

Within a year or two this new influx of parolees would have become eligible for discharge and the population would have stabilized. In the meantime, however, the Parole Division faced a critical growth problem.

A few years earlier the legislature had passed a law allowing for the review and discharge of parolees who had been on parole for 24 continuous months. These procedures generated considerable savings without an increase in danger to the community (Robison, Robison, Kingsnorth, and Inman). We wondered if we couldn't discharge some parolees even sooner. With this in mind we began looking through our data for a target population, possibly an offense group, higher Base Expectancy levels, or first termers. The original thinking was to look at some groups for possible discharge after 18 instead of 24 months, thus requiring an examination of the last six months on parole. We found, however, that we only had good data at 6, 12, and 24 months, forcing us to think more ambitiously in terms of 12 month discharges.

The procedure was to divide the sample along background variables hoping to find something associated with unusually good parole performance in the second year. First came the bad news; when we took into consideration (controlled for) performance during the first year no variable examined could discriminate or predict second year outcome. Then came the good news; the thing we were controlling for—first year performance—was an excellent predictor by itself. Regardless of background characteristics, parolees who do well the first year were very unlikely to have trouble in the second 12 months (see Table 3). The key factor in subsequent success proved to be doing the first year on parole without an arrest. Less than 3% of this group were returned with new felonies the second year and only 15% had more than a minor arrest.

At the time it was hard to foresee the importance of the role the "arrest free" variable was to play. Parolees have little control over their background characteristics. If the man was originally committed for robbery there is nothing he can do about that fact. There are things he can do, however, to effect his likelihood of being arrested. Every parolee then, was coming out of prison equal and with a fresh start towards discharge. Parole agents began playing heavily on this fact in their initial contacts, telling the man that his parole term was up to him.

Equally important was the clear, unambiguous nature of the "arrest free" criteria. Earlier procedures relied on criteria such as "demonstrated rehabilitation." The varied interpretaion of this caused endless disagreements, both within the Parole Division and with the parole board. For example, the rate of discharge recommendations for those eligible for two year consideration initially varied from 96% to 29% between parole offices (Robison, et al., p. 30). This made it very difficult for the parolee to know what he had to do for a discharge and impossible for his parole agent to make any promises. By contrast, everyone understood what not being arrested meant.

The criteria also made it possible to shift the burden of proof from justifying the discharge to justifying continued supervision of the eligibles. This was important because what we were asking the agents to do was to give up their best cases and take on new parolees in their place. Some reluctance was naturally anticipated. To reinforce this change a requirement was made that if the agent didn't recommend discharge he not only had to document the parolee's problems but to show how continued supervision would solve that problem.

The new procedures began in July of 1971. During the first three months over 1,000 parolees were discharged. Parole agents recommended discharge for 94% of the eligible cases reviewed while the parole board was concurring with 87% of these recommendations. By the first quarter of 1972 the rates were even higher with 98% recommended for discharge, with 89% board acceptance. In other words, if the parolee was arrest free he was virtually assured of an early discharge. During the first 12 months about 2,300 cases were removed from supervision in this way.

The subsequent evaluations involved a six month and one year follow-up study (Jaman, Bennett, and Berecochea). A sample of 349 was selected from the first group to be discharged at 12 months. A control group of 632 men was then selected from the year before the new procedure. Both groups were arrest free from their first 12 months on parole but the second group, of course, had remained under parole supervision during the subsequent six months. The arrest records (CII reports) of each group was then tabulated in terms of the six months period.

The men discharged actually did better than the earlier group who were kept under parole supervision (See Table 4). Eighty-six percent were still arrest free six months later compared to 78% of the earlier sample. Only 1% of the discharges had unfavorable outcomes compared to 6.3% of those supervised.

For the 12 months comparision a different contol group was selected. Since parolees in general had been doing better each year some small bias could be introduced in comparing the discharges with parolees from the year before. For the second study a sample of 413 was selected whose 12 months period coincided with the early discharges and who were themselves discharges but after 24 rather than 12 months on parole. In other words, they had been paroled a year earlier. Again, neither group had been arrested during the first year and the difference was the comparison group spent twice as long under supervision. Thus, what was being compared was the value of the additional year of supervision.

Both groups did almost identically well after discharge. About 1% were reconvicted and returned to prison with about ¾ remaining arrest free for the next 12 months. Ninety-seven percent of the early discharges were considered favorable outcomes compared to 95% of the two year discharges. It seems clear that the additional year of supervision had no value in terms of the parolees' later performance nor any value to public protection during the extra 12 months they were under supervision.

The first years benefit to the system was eliminating the need for 46 additional parole agents at an average cost of $20,000 each, or about one million dollars saved. This procedure has obvious implications for probation departments as well as other parole systems.

The potential savings of the three projects is hard to estimate but with prison cost of about $4,000 per bed the savings of 1,300 beds could run as high as another 4 or 5 million dollars. All the projects were done with existing resources. No new buildings were built and no new positions were required. The project development phase required some extra administrative time and a great deal of research effort, but researchers are notoriously under-worked anyway and no one seems to mind.

What I've tried to do today is to present three "systems change" projects selected as examples of a methodology I describe as "Rational Risk Taking." This selection by no means exhausts the list of projects which have used this method with profit. And the entire list merely scratches the surface of possibilities. I hope that when this conference is over that each of you will examine your own correctional systems and ask yourself this question, "Are we taking rational risks or are we taking that other kind?"

Table 1 *One Year Parole Outcome of Inmates Released Six Months Early Compared to a Control Group Released at the Normal Time*

Study Group	Mean BE Score	Mean Months Served	Base	Number Rel'd	Parole Outcome Within First Year						
					Not Returned to Prison				Returned to Prison		
					Total	Favorable	Misc. Unfav.	Pending	Total	Board Ord.	Crt. Comt.
Experimentals	39.8	31.5	No.	494	426	326	63	37	68	38	30
			Pct.	100.0	86.2	66.0	12.8	7.5	13.8	7.7	6.1
Controls	40.8	37.9	No.	515	452	362	60	30	63	38	25
			Pct.	100.0	87.8	70.3	11.7	5.8	12.2	7.4	4.9
Total	40.3	34.8	No.	1,009	878	688	123	67	131	76	55
			Pct.	100.0	87.0	68.2	12.2	6.6	13.0	7.5	5.5

Components of Chi-square Due to Differences in Parole Outcome Categories	Degrees of Freedom	Chi-Square	Probability
A. Favorable, Unfavorable, Pending	2	1.919	$P > 0.05$
B. Board vs. Court Returns to Prison	1	0.264	$P > 0.05$
C. Returned vs. No Return to Prison	1	0.524	$P > 0.05$
D. Total	4	2.707	$P > 0.05$

Differences in Mean BE Scores and Mean Months Served	Degrees of Freedom	t-Test	Probability
E. Difference in BE Scores	1,007	1.24	$P > 0.05$
F. Difference in Months Served	1,007	4.29	$P < 0.05$
G. Deviation of Observed Difference in Months Served from Expected Difference of Six Months	1,007	0.25	$P > 0.05$

SOURCE. Berecochea, John E., Dorothy R. Jaman, and Welton A. Jones, "Time Served in Prison and Parole Outcome: An Experimental Study," Research Division, Department of Corrections, State of California, Research Report No. 49, October 1973.

Table 2 *Performance of Parolees 12 Months After Being Continued on Parole Compared to First Year Parole Outcome For All New Parolees (in percentages)*

	No Arrests	Minor Problems	Returned To Prison	Total Number
Violators Continued on Parole	45.4%	41.5%	13.1%	(99)
All Releases to Parole for 1970	46.6%	43.7%	9.7%	(6,858)

*Miller and Downer, p. 5.

Table 3 *Two Year Parole Outcome for Inmates Paroled in 1967 By the Type of Difficulty During the First Year (in percentages)*

Parole Status At 24 Months	Arrest Free at 12 Months		Other Favorable At 12 Months		Other Unfavorable Or Pending At 12 Months	
	First Termers	Multiple Termers	First Termers	Multiple Termers	First Termers	Multiple Termers
Favorable	85%	85%	56%	51%	14%	9%
Other Unfavorable Or Pending	8	7	20	25	51	54
Technical Violation (TFT)	5	5	18	17	18	21
New Felony Conviction (WNC)	2	3	6	7	17	16
Total	100%	100%	100%	100%	100	100
Total Number	(1593)	(834)	(841)	(634)	(418)	(329)

SOURCE. Jaman, Dorothy R., Lawrence A. Bennett, and John E. Berecochea, "One Year After Early Discharge From Parole: Policy, Practice, and Outcome," Research Division, Department of Corrections, State of California, Research Report No. 51 (forthcoming).

Table 4 *Performance Six Months Later for Parolees Discharged at One Year Compared to a Similar Group Under Parole Supervision*

Before the One Year Discharge Policy (in percentages)

	Total Number	Arrest Free	Other Favorable	Pending	Miscellaneous Unfavorable
One Year Discharged Group	(379)	85.8%	8.3%	5.0%	1.0%
Similar Group Under Supervision In 1969	(632)	77.7%	13.8%	2.2%	6.3%

Table 5 *Performance One Year Later for Parolees Discharged at 12 Months Compared to a Similar Group Discharged During the Same Period*

After 24 Months of Supervision (in percentages)

	Total Number	Arrest Free	Other Favorable	Pending, Miscellaneous Unfavorable	Recommitted To Prison
One Year Discharge Group	(341)	72.7%	24.0%	2.4%	0.9 %
Similar Group Discharged After Two Years	(413)	74.1%	20.6%	4.3%	1.0%

Source. Jaman, Dorothy R., Lawrence A. Bennett, and John E. Berecochea, "One Year After Early Discharge From Parole: Policy, Practice, and Outcome," Research Division, Department of Corrections, State of California, Research Report No. 51 (forthcoming).

Bibliography

Bennett, Lawrence A., "Should We Change the Offender or the System?" *Crime and Delinquency,* Vol. 19, No. 3, July 1973, pp. 332–342.

Berecochea, John E., Dorothy R. Jaman, and Welton A. Jones, "Time Served in Prison and Parole Outcome: An Experimental Study," Research Division, Department of Corrections, State of California, Research Report No. 49, October 1973.

Holt, Norman, "Temporary Prison Release, California's Prerelease Furlough Program," *Crime and Delinquency,* October 1971, pp. 414–430.

Holt, Norman and Rudy Renteria, "Prerelease Program Evaluation: Some Implications of Negative Findings," *Federal Probation,* June 1969, pp. 40–45.

Jaman, Dorothy R., Lawrence A. Bennett, and John E. Berecochea, "One Year After Early Discharge from Parole: Policy, Practice, and Outcome," Research Division, Department of Corrections, State of California, Research Report No. 51 (forthcoming).

Jaman, Dorothy R., Robert M. Dickover, and Lawrence A. Bennett, "Parole Outcome as a Function of Time Served," *British Journal of Criminology,* January 1972.

Kassebaum, Gene G., David A. Ward, and Daniel M. Wilner, *Prison Treatment and Parole Survival,* New York: John Wiley, 1971

Keldgord, Robert E., Robert O. Norris, and Patricia A. Hagen, "Correctional System Study," Board of Corrections, Human Relations Agency, State of California, July 1971.

Kolodney, Steve E., Paul L. Patterson, Douglas Daetz, and Robert L. Marx, "A Study of the Characteristics and Recidivism Experience of California Prisoners." Public Systems Incorporated, February 15, 1970.

Lamson, Robin, Carol Crowther, Betty Spacy, and Veronica Crump, "Crime and Penalties in California." Prepared by The Assembly Office of Research for the Assembly Committee on Criminal Procedure, March 1968.

Miller, D.E. and Carol Downer, "Parole Decision Making and Its Consequences: A One Year Follow-Up of Region III Parole Violators Continued on Parole." Los Angeles Research Unit, Department of Corrections, State of California, Administrative Report, May 18, 1972 (mimeographed).

Mueller, Paul F.C., "Advanced Release to Parole." Research Division, Department of Corrections, Youth and Adult Corrections Agency, State of California, Research Report No. 20, 1965.

Robison, James and Gerald Smith, "The Effectiveness of Correctional Programs," *Crime and Delinquency,* Vol. 17, No. 1, January, 1971.

Robison, James O., Margo N. Robison, Rodney Kingsnorth, and Nelson G. Inman, "By the Standard of His Rehabilitation; Information, Decision, and Outcome in Terminations From Parole: The Implementation of Penal Code Section 2943," Research Division, Department of Corrections, State of California, Research Report No. 39, January 1971.

Youth and Adult Corrections Agency, "The Organization of State Correctional Services in the Control and Treatment of Crime and Delinquency," State of California, May 10, 1967.

21

The Parole Violator as an Organizational Reject

JAMES ROBISON AND PAUL T. TAKAGI

INTRODUCTION

Correctional Objectives

Correctional systems, comprising prisons and parole, are given responsibility for protecting society through the control of identified offenders. The means available for control are both external (through confinement and surveillance) and internal (through rehabilitation). Rehabilitation is expected to lessen the likelihood of return to criminal pursuits, and recidivism rates are supposed to measure whether this has been accomplished. One of the stated objectives of a correctional system, and the one to which most attention is usually directed, is to "minimize" recidivism. Parole provides a setting in which a modicum of external control exists and one in which treatment processes may be extended, but it is primarily the testing ground for the entire system.

Any separate program or operation within the correctional system, regardless of its immediate and specific aim, is likely to be initially justified on the basis of its presumed relevance to the lowering of recidivism, and the operation will be evaluated on the basis of its effect on the parole revocation rate. Specific criteria

SOURCE. Unpublished manuscript prepared at the School of Criminology, University of California, Berkeley, 1968. Reprinted with permission of the authors.

347

are sometimes developed with reference to particular programs, and the evaluation is made in accordance with these (for example, measured grade improvement of inmates exposed to academic instruction, postrelease job attainment of those who receive vocational training, or changes in psychological test performances of inmates or parolees in group counseling); but the question which almost always takes precedence is: what percent of offenders in the program violated parole, as compared to the same type offenders who did not receive it? An unequivocal answer is usually unobtainable, because few programs have operated under an adequately controlled research design. In those programs where adequacy has been approached (that is, those controlling for "expected" performance through the employment of randomized assignment, actuarial risk classification, cohort follow-up), statistically significant and positive outcome findings have been rare, and the percent differences disappointingly slight when measured against the expenditures invested to obtain them.[1] It becomes important to examine just what is being measured by the parole revocation criterion.

The Criterion of Effectiveness

Confinement (or reconfinement) is usually viewed as an undesirable but necessary step taken in response to certain damages or dangers suffered by the community. When a recidivism rate rises, persons who accept these rates as a fairly direct index of parolee performances are quick to assume that the rise reflects a deterioration in the quality of offenders passing through the system. Other persons, stressing the indirect quality of the link between offender behavior and official dispositions, assume instead that the rise may reflect merely a change in policy or in the techniques of counting:

> The evaluation of prison programs aimed at changing behavior must ask the question: Do formal parole dispositions reflect only parolee behavior, or are there other sources of variance of parole violation rates, stemming from the parole decision itself?[2]

There is considerable evidence which indicates that these dispositions are a function of the decision-maker—evidence usually in the form of statistical disparity in decision practice which may not be plausibly attributed to client differences. These sources of variance, once isolated, are more easily subject to control than those stemming from client behavior; consequently, they promise an economical opportunity for dramatic shifts in recidivism rates and reduction in public costs.

---

[1] Within the California Department of Corrections: the Pilot Intensive Counseling Organization, the Intensive Treatment Project, the Special Intensive Parole Unit, the Increased Correctional Effectiveness Project, the Narcotic Treatment and Control Project, and the Parole Work Unit Program.

[2] Robert Martinson, Gene Kassenbaum and David Ward, "A Critique of Research in Parole," *Federal Probation,* Vol. **28.** No. 3, (September, 1964).

PAROLE OUTCOME IN CALIFORNIA

In California, statewide trends over the period 1960–1965 showed an increasing proportion of unfavorable outcomes for parolees. This resulted primarily from a rise in the number of those who were returned to prison to finish term, particularly those returned on technical violations. Meanwhile, there was an almost constant rate for parole violators returned with a new prison commitment. Thus, the increased violation rate was almost wholly a function of the behavior of decision-makers within the state correctional agency, thereby attesting to the position that the exercise of administrative discretion of the sort involved in the technical return can have a significant impact upon the apparent effects of a program.

The awareness of the possibilities for choice among policy options as well as variability in the interpretation of fixed policies is critical to the understanding of outcome statistics. It follows that since decision-making behavior is of such consequence, recidivism rates and public cost can be reduced (or increased) by changing parole agent behavior (decision criteria) without any expectation that it would mediate change in parolee behavior; or by changing agents (training) for the purpose of mediating parolee behavior change (treatment gain).

Statistics on parole dispositions over a number of years revealed that some parole offices in the state produced lower violation rates than others. With the introduction of a control for differences among offices in terms of their actuarial risk of return to prison for parolees, statistically significant deviations from the actuarially "expected" performance still remained for a number of the offices. Among the empirical findings, in addition to performance differences among offices for the same period, were differences within offices over time[3] and differences among individual agents.[4]

In addition, documentation that the paroling board—the official administrative decision-making body—closely followed the original report recommendation was obtained when Robison determined that nearly 80 percent of the recommendations of parole agents against revocation and over 90 percent of their recommendations for revocation were accepted by the Adult Authority.

PILOT STUDIES

Since it was evident that parolee dispositions (violation rates) were not direct indices of parolee behavior and that these measures were influenced by variables within communities and the correctional agency, pilot studies aimed at some

[3] Dorothy Jaman and P. Mueller, "Evaluation of Parole Outcome by Parole Districts of Release, 1957–1960 Releases," Research Report No. 21, Measurement Development Section, Research Division, California Department of Corrections, 1965.

[4] J. Robison, "Progress Notes: Toward the Proposed Study of Parole Operations," San Francisco Research Unit, 1965, unpublished.

specification of the operant variables in these dispositions were undertaken by Robison, Gaines, and Takagi.

Community Factors

Robison and Gaines[5] rank-ordered parole offices on the basis of the direction and magnitude of difference between expected and observed performances of parolees released to them. Noting that the "unfavorable outcome" criterion was a composite—in that if any of several alternative "most serious dispositions" (that is, jail sentence of 90 or more days, prison return WNC [with new commitment], prison return TFT [to finish term]) was accorded a parolee, the parolee's outcome was classified as unfavorable—the investigators rank-ordered offices on each of the separate outcome components and compared these rankings. Their findings were:

1. A strong inverse relationship (Spearman's rho $= -.754, p <.01$) existed across offices between the incidence of long jail sentences and of prison returns to finish term.

2. Across offices, neither long jail sentences nor prison returns to finish term were significantly related to prison returns with new commitment (rho: long jail versus return WNC $= +.121$; rho return TFT versus return WNC $= -.166$; rho necessary for significance at $p <.05 = .455$, at $p <.01 = .644$, one-tailed tests).

3. A direct and significant relationship was found across parole offices between expected-observed performance differences and the TFT rate; districts with a high observed-versus-expected outcome difference had a higher incidence of prison returns to finish term (rho $= .634, p < .05$). Offices with higher incidences of long jail outcome fared better than those with low in terms of expected-versus-observed differences, but not significantly so (rho $= -.249$).

Robison and Gaines interpreted these findings as suggestive that long jail sentences and technical returns to prison were true alternatives and raised the question, "How much discretion exists within the parole district office regarding the choice between these alternatives?" They speculated that the prison return TFT might, in part, be a response to a deficit in available jail facilities within the geographic area covered by a parole office, and constructed a jail capacity index (daily jail population versus total county population) on which parole districts were compared. They found a positive (rho $= .567, p <.05$) relationship between the incidence of long jail sentences accorded parolees and the index of jail capacity for the districts' area of supervision; an inverse (rho $= -.497, p < .05$) relationship was found to exist between prison returns TFT and the local county jail capacity.

Robison and Gaines concluded that since parole units which appeared to be doing more poorly than expected in terms of unfavorable disposition were those

[5] J. Robison and Helen Gaines, "On the Evaluation of Parole Outcome by District of Release," Supplement to the Jaman-Mueller Study of 1957–1960 Releases, unpublished.

with a higher utilization of technical prison return, and that since such districts tended to cover geographic areas with a relative deficit in county jail capacity, support was provided for the hypothesis that parole districts' performances as ordinarily evaluated (obtained-versus-expected with B.E. control for parolee risk level) were partially constrained or facilitated by local community factors external to the state correctional agency. Thus, a variable within the community was linked to "unsuccessful" offender outcomes.

Parole Agent and Office Factors

While Robison and Gaines looked beyond the correctional agency for factors connected with violation rates, Takagi looked for variables within the agency. He undertook a pilot study of two parole district offices—one which historically had a low rate of technical parole violation, and another with a high rate.[6] Identical sets of stimuli (nine actual parolee case histories in which behavior had occurred which prompted a consideration of violation) were submitted to the agents in both offices with a request to make recommendations on these cases to either continue the subject on parole or return him to prison. The findings of this study were:

1. A difference in "violation rate" existed between the two offices on the standardized task, and this difference corresponded to their actual histories of performance.

2. No agent among the fourteen in the experiment produced sets of recommendations which agreed, above a level expected by chance, with the actual case recommendations. (Responses ranged from 9 out of 9 "return to prison" recommendations by one agent, to 9 out of 9 "continue on parole" recommendations by another agent.)

3. Questionnaire responses to items about parole practice indicated differing orientations among agents in the two offices, and these orientations tended to be associated with the differences in parole outcome.

The present paper is concerned with the problem of variation in agent recommendations across district offices and regional areas. The study is a replication of Takagi's pilot study expanded to include all the units in a state parole agency.

PROCEDURE

All members of a state parole agency were the subjects. These included 260 caseload-carrying agents, 38 unit office supervisors, 5 regional administrators, and 15 additional members from regional and headquarters staff, including the chief of the parole agency. Data collection was completed within a six-week period in late 1965.

Two sets of data were collected from the subjects. The first set consisted of

---

[6] P. Takagi, B. Granlund, and J. Robison, *Uniformity in Decision-Making,* San Francisco Parole Research Unit, 1964.

responses to a questionnaire with the usual demographic items, career plan items, professional versus administrative conflict items, and an assortment of items on actual parole operations in the areas of prerelease, supervision, and case decision-making. The second set consisted of responses to ten actual parolee case histories already processed by the parole agency and the parole board. The case histories were abstracted and summarized. In each case an emergency (or incident) had occurred and the subjects were requested to make a decision on what they would do if they were handling the cases, that is, recommend "return to prison" or "continue on parole." Thus, data were obtained from subjects who were all members of the same organization, were governed by the same rules and regulations, had the same parole board in mind in arriving at their case recommendations, and responded to a constant set of stimuli (case histories).

For the ten cases selected for the study, about two-thirds of the agents' recommendations were "return to prison" and one-third "continue on parole." Recommendation patterns for individual cases ranged in severity from one case which 90 percent of the agents chose to "continue on parole" to another which 93 percent chose to "return to prison."

The Respondents' Recommendation Distribution

The subjects had been asked to provide a recommendation of either "return to prison" or "continue on parole" for each of the ten cases presented to them. An individual subject could conceivably have decided to "return" as few as zero or as many as ten of the cases. Table 1 presents the distribution of recommendations for all 318 subjects (supervisors and administrators included).

About half the subjects (49 percent) decided to return either six or seven of the cases. The range among the 318 was from one agent who chose to continue all but one case on parole to five agents who chose to return all ten to prison. Subjects who continued the same *number* of cases on parole were not often in agreement about *which* of the cases they would continue. For example, the most frequent number of "continue" recommendations was three cases (seven returns), produced by 88 subjects; these 88 arrived at three "continues" in over twenty different ways, and every one of the ten cases appeared in at least one of these combinations of three.

Variability in the response of different individuals to a common stimulus is, of course, to be expected. Nevertheless, it is striking that parole agents, given materials based on and very similar to the originals prepared by parole agents, and called upon to arrive at recommendations from the types of information they routinely use in preparing their own violation reports, vary in their responses to the extent that they do. The actual "legal" decision-makers for the correctional agency—the members of the Adult Authority—rely most heavily upon violation reports of this sort (and the parole agent recommendations accompanying them) in arriving at the final disposition on actual cases. The variability among agents on case recommendations, as documented above, offers some support for an assertion often heard from parolees: "Whether or not you make it on parole all depends on which agent you happen to get."

Table 1 *Number of "Return" Recommendations on Ten Cases (N = 318) Return Recommendations.*

	Zero	One	Two	Three	Four	Five
Number of respondents	0	1	2	7	26	36
Percent of respondents	0.0	0.3	0.6	2.2	8.2	11.3
	Six	Seven	Eight	Nine	Ten	Total
Number of respondents	67	88	53	33	5	318
Percent of respondents	21.1	27.6	16.7	10.4	1.6	100.0

Position in the Administrative Hierarchy

The respondents were classified by their position in the organization hierarchy, and the percent of total recommendations which were to "continue" was obtained for each class (Table 2).

The lowest status members in the agency hierarchy (Parole Agents I) tended to recommend to continue least often (or conversely, to be most likely to recommend return to prison); at each step up in organizational rank there was an increase in the proportion of recommendations to continue. Given identical case stimuli, caseload-carrying agents (PA I—full caseload; PA II—half caseload) produce an average of 3.27 "continues" (33 percent) for the ten cases, while those in full supervisory or administrative positions average 4.07 (41 percent). In Table 3, respondents are cross-classified on the basis of whether they carry actual caseloads and whether the number of "continue" recommendations they offered was above the median for all subjects.

Table 2 *Percent "Continue" Recommendations by Position in the Parole Agency*

Number of Subjects	Position in Agency	Percent "Continue" Recommendations
20	Administrators and HQ staff	45.0
38	Unit supervisors (PA III)	38.4
33	Assistant supervisors (PA II)	34.8
227	Parole agents (PA I)	32.4
318	All subjects	34.2

Table 3   *Comparison of "Continue" Recommendations by Position in the Agency*

Position	"Continue" Recommendations				Total
	Three or Fewer		Four or More		
Supervisory, administrative	19	(33%)	39	(67%)	58
Line, caseload-carrying	160	(62%)	100	(38%)	260
All subjects	179		139		318

$$X^2 \,(1 \text{ d.f.}) = 14.81, p < .001 \text{ (two-tailed)}$$

Thus, for the cases used as stimuli in the present study, a statistically significant difference exists between the recommendations of caseload-carrying agents and those in supervisory or administrative positions, with the former class being more "conservative" in their judgments of appropriate case dispositions.

Geographic Region

At the time these data were collected, the state was divided into five parole regions, with a separate regional administrator for each area. Each region contained from six to ten parole unit offices. The regional administrator was the final level of review within the parole division on violation reports prepared by the parole agent for submission to the parole board, and the administrator or his representative was the person in attendance before the parole board when the case was presented for disposition. The agent's written recommendation was appended to the report, and the agent's unit supervisor, as well as the regional administrator, might add his own written agreement with or dissent from the agent's recommendation.

The case recommendation data were examined to determine whether there were differences in recommendation pattern among the five geographic regions (Table 4).

Table 4   *Number of "Continue" Recommendations by Parole Region (Parole Agents and Unit Supervisors)*

Region	Total Subjects	"Continued" above Median		Average "Continued"
III	52	25	(48.1%)	3.52
IV	72	33	(45.8%)	3.68
II	64	29	(45.3%)	3.48
V	63	22	(34.9%)	3.78
I	47	16	(34.0%)	3.13
State	298	125	(41.9%)	3.34

Though regions varied from one in which 34 percent of the subjects recommended that four or more cases be continued to another with 48 percent, the differences among regions were not found to be statistically significant (X^2, 4 d.f., = 4.03, $p < .50$, two-tailed).

The Parole Unit Office

A typical parole unit office is staffed by a unit supervisor, an assistant supervisor, and six parole agents. In the data which follow, no distinction has been made between the parole agents and the assistant supervisors, who also carry a partial caseload. Thirty-eight offices were represented in the study. The case recommendations for the two most extreme offices are presented in Table 5.

The average number of cases continued ranged from 1.62 in office X to 4.62 in office O. In office X, where the supervisor continued only one of the ten cases, there were only two agents who continued as many as three; in office O, the supervisor continued six cases, and only one agent there continued as few as three. It has long been generally believed in this agency that the unit supervisor sets the tone of the office. Further attention will be paid to the matter of correspondence between the recommendations of supervisors and their agents at a later point in this report. First, however, the case recommendation data will be examined against the parole agents' career backgrounds in terms of educational specialty and prior work experience.

Parole Agent Background, Education

Over three-fourths of the caseload-carrying parole agents in the study were college graduates, and over 90 percent had at least 90 units of college training. In Table 6, for each group of agents indicating a particular area of study, the number and percent of agents responding with more than the median number of recommendations to continue are shown.

Among those representing the more clearly defined educational specialties,

Table 5   *Number of "Continue" Recommendations in Two Extreme Unit Offices*[a]

Number of Subjects	Number of Cases "Continued"							
	Zero	One	Two	Three	Four	Five	Six	Seven
5		X						
4		X			O			
3		X			O		O	
2		X		X	O		O	
1		XS	X	XO	O		OS	

[a]X, agent in office X; O, agent in office O; and S, office supervisor.

Table 6 *Broad Area of Study by Number and Percent of Subjects Above Median on "Continue" Recommendations*

Broad Area of Study	Number of Subjects	Number of "Continues" above Median	
Social work	18	13	(72.2%)
Sociology	50	20	(40.0%)
Psychology	51	19	(37.3%)
Criminology	31	9	(29.0%)
Law, other social sciences	30	13	(43.3%)
Education, humanities	21	6	(28.6%)
Several, other, no response	59	20	(33.9%)
Total	260	100	(38.5%)

agents who had majored in Social Work (a fairly small group, numbering 18) appear markedly oriented to continuation, with over 70 percent continuing four or more of the sample cases; agents with a background in Criminology seemed slightly return-prone, with less than 30 percent offering as many as four continues. Many of the agents selected more than one alternative on the area of study questions, while some specified a different major from any listed, and a few failed to respond. These subjects (several, other, no response) were removed and the median test was applied for the remaining and more clearly defined academic groups. Statistically, a trend association is demonstrated between education background and orientation to case decision-making (X^2, 5 d.f., = 10.80, $p < .10$, two-tailed).

Parole Agent Background, Prior Work Experience

Parole agents were asked what kind of work they had been doing immediately prior to becoming a parole agent, and their responses were classified into the categories shown in Table 7.

Table 7 *Prior Work Experience by Number and Percent of Subjects Above Median on "Continue" Recommendations*

Number of Subjects	Prior Work Experience	"Continues" above Median	
39	Social casework, welfare	19	(48.7%)
52	Probation, juvenile hall	23	(44.2%)
28	Law enforcement	9	(32.1%)
34	State corrections: counselor	10	(29.4%)
51	State corrections: officer	14	(27.4%)
56	Other, no response	25	(44.6%)
260	Total	100	(38.5%)

Agents who entered parole service from some other position within the state correctional system and those who came from law enforcement jobs (police, deputy sheriff) appear somewhat more conservative in their recommendations than agents from the remaining groups. Former correctional counselors appear no more lenient than former correctional officers. However, when the large "other, no response" category (which contained former businessmen, students, military men, etc.) was removed and the median test was applied, no statistically significant association was demonstrated between prior work experience and case recommendations (X^2, 4 d.f., $= 6.58$, $p < .20$, two-tailed).

A Parole Agent Value

In carrying out the task of case supervision, the parole agent is regulated, to a large extent, by minimum contact requirements specified by the parole agency. Similarly, the parole agent manual specifies many conditions under which the preparation and submission of a report is required. Nevertheless, the type of recommendation to be made on a violation report (for example, return to prison, continue on parole) is always to be decided on the basis of the agent's professional judgment. These judgments are, of course, tempered by what the agent feels is expected of him. The agents were asked to respond to the question, "If a parole agent wishes to continue working with a case, do you feel he should be permitted to do so even though a 'return' is called for according to policy?" Table 8 presents the relationship between answers to this question and the number of respondents scoring above the median in "continue" responses.

The median test was applied to the data in Table 8, and a weak association was found to exist between agents' beliefs about whether they should be permitted to continue working with cases despite contrary policy, and their performance on the case recommendation task ($X^2 = 2.54$, $p < .10$, one-tailed). The responses of all agents in each office to the "value" item were averaged to provide an index for comparison against a similarly obtained office index on the case recommendations task. The median test was applied to determine if there was an association

Table 8 *Parole Agent Value and "Continue" Recommendations*

"Should Agent Be Permitted to Continue when Policy Calls for Return?"	Number of Subjects	"Continues" above Median	
"Agree" or "strongly agree"	120	52	(43.3%)
"Disagree" or "strongly disagree"	134	44	(32.8%)
Total	254[a]	96	

[a]Six subjects failed to reply.

between the two measures on an office-by-office basis. The finding was not statistically significant ($X^2 = .95$, $p < .25$, one-tailed).

Agent Perception of the Unit Supervisor

In actual cases of parolee violations, the unit supervisor has the right to dissent from the recommendations of his parole agents, but is not empowered to alter or overrule their recommendations. However, since the supervisor ordinarily has more experience in the organization than his subordinates have and, since he is also in a position of authority over them in regard to many administrative aspects of parole, it is plausible that parole agents orient themselves toward the unit supervisor in their approach to the professional task of determining appropriate case recommendations.

An item on the study questionnaire addressed to parole agents' perception of their supervisors asked, "Does your supervisor favor recommending continuance or reinstatement of marginal parolees?" Agreement on this item was compared to agreement on the agent "value" item discussed in the previous section. In Table 9, responses of individual agents are compared in terms of their agreement or disagreement (by agent), and unit offices are compared on an index of agreement (by office).

From Table 9, it is evident that responses to the two questionnaire items are not closely associated—whether the comparison is made on the basis of individual agents or of unit offices, nearly half (45%) of the sample is incongruent (that is, agent values right to continue but believes supervisor disfavors "continue" on marginal cases, or vice-versa). In a statistical test, a trend-level association was found on the agent-by-agent data (by agent: X^2, 3 d.f., $= 2.39$, $p < .10$, one-tailed; by office: X^2, 3 d.f., $p < .40$, one-tailed). This is a rather weak indication that agents' orientations coincide with, or are tempered by, the orientation of the supervisor.

In the previous section, findings indicated a low-level association between agents valuing the right to continue cases despite policy and their performances on the case recommendation task. In the preceding paragraph, the association between this value and agents' beliefs about their supervisors' orientations is also

Table 9   *Parole Agent Value and Belief About Unit Supervisor Regarding "Continue"*

	By Agent (Agree-versus-Disagree)		By Office (Above-versus-Below Median Agreement)	
Both in favor	60	(24%)	10	(26%)
Agent in favor	60	(24%)	9	(24%)
Supervisor in favor	53	(21%)	8	(21%)
Neither in favor	81	(31%)	11	(29%)
Total	254 Agents	(100%)	38 Offices	(100%)

shown to be slight. The data were next examined to determine whether a correspondence existed between agents' beliefs about their supervisors and their own performance on the case recommendation task (Table 10).

The association between parole agents' beliefs about whether their supervisor favors continuation and their own performance on case recommendations is found to be highly significant statistically on the agent-by-agent comparison (X^2, 1 d.f., $= 9.43, p < .005$, one-tailed), as well as on office-by-office comparison (X^2, 1 d.f., $= 3.16, p < .05$, one-tailed). Thus, while a supervisor's influence over his agents' *value orientation* appeared slight, his influence over their *performance* is quite evident.

The considerable variability found across parole unit offices on the case recommendation task (see section on The Parole Unit Office) warrants the inference that the unit office be considered the most important organizational influence on decision-making. The findings in the present section strongly suggest that the unit supervisor's orientation has a powerful impact on the case recommendations of his subordinates. Whether this impact is associated with informal but direct coercive influence by the supervisor, or is a spontaneous outcome of the parole agents' respect for him, unit offices where agents are above the median in believing that the supervisor favors "continue" are more than twice as likely to be above the median for offices on test cases continued by these subordinates (67 percent vs. 30 percent for the remaining offices). This is an association that could only be produced if there were some consistency in belief among the agents within the separate offices. However, since both measures are based on responses from subordinates, there is no guarantee that the belief about the unit supervisor is valid. As a check, the supervisor's own responses to the case recommendation task were compared for each office against his agents' belief about him. Across the 38 districts, a statistically significant association was found to exist (X^2, 1 d.f., $= 4.45, p < .025$, one-tailed) when the median test was applied.

Agents' and Supervisor's Value, Belief, and Performance

In the preceding section, responses to two questionnaire items—one dealing with parole agents' values about their right to continue cases and another directed at whether they believed their supervisor to be in favor of continuing cases—were

Table 10 *Agent "Continue" Recommendations and Beliefs About Unit Supervisor*

Agent Belief	Above Median, by Agent			Above Median, by Office		
	Total	Number	Percent	Total	Number	Percent
Supervisor "favors" continue	113	55	48.7	18	12	66.7
Supervisor "disfavors" continue	141	41	29.1	20	6	30.0
Total	254 Agents			38 Offices		

each found to have some correspondence with their performance on test case recommendations. It was also noted that the tendency to answer both these items in the same direction (Table 9) was not strong. In Table 11, agents have been classified into three categories on the basis of congruence or disparity between value and belief, and these types examined against the case recommendation responses.

A large difference exists between the two congruent types ("neither favors continue" and "both favor continue") on the case recommendation task; with the type of agents who believe "both favor continue" more than twice as likely to provide an above-median number of "continue" recommendations. Within the disparate type (one in favor, other against), which falls between the others on case recommendation responses, are to be found two subtypes—one with the agent favoring and his supervisor seen as opposed and the other with the supervisor favoring and the agent opposed—32 percent of the former subtype and 42 percent of the latter gave an above-median number of "continue" recommendations. The median test, applied to the data in Table 11, shows the recommendation difference among the three agent types to be statistically significant (X^2, 2 d.f., $= 11.54$, $p < .005$, one-tailed). The difference between the two disparate subtypes is not significant (X^2, 1 d.f., $= .79$, $p < .50$, two-tailed).

Given the findings presented earlier—the correspondence of the agent's belief about the unit supervisor with both his own and the supervisor's performance on the case recommendation task—one would, of course, expect there to be a correspondence between agents and supervisory on case recommendations. In Table 12 unit supervisors have been separated into those who made four or more "continue" recommendations on the ten test cases, and those who made three or fewer. The recommendation performance of agents under each of the types of supervisor is presented.

It was noted earlier that the supervisors were generally more likely than were subordinates to continue the test cases. In this study two out of three supervisors gave four or more "continues," compared to two out of five subordinates. Despite this general difference, the data in Table 12 reveal a statistically significant

Table 11 *Agent "Continue" Recommendations Versus Value and Belief About Supervisor*

	Number of Cases "Continued"					
	Three or Less		*Four or More*		*Total*	
Neither favors "continue"	59	(73%)	22	(27%)	81	(100%)
One in favor, other against	72	(64%)	41	(36%)	113	(100%)
Both favor "continue"	27	(45%)	33	(55%)	60	(100%)
Total	158		96		254	

Table 12   *"Continue" Recommendations of Supervisors and Their Subordinates*

The Supervisor Continued	The Subordinate "Continued"				Total	
	Three or Less		Four or More			
Three or more cases (N = 25 supervisors)	103	(57%)	77	(43%)	180	(69%)
Three or less cases (N = 13 supervisors)	57	(71%)	23	(29%)	80	(31%)
Total (N = 38 supervisors)	160 Agents	(62%)	100 Agents	(38%)	260	(100%)

association between supervisor and subordinate performances (X^2, 1 d.f., = 4.03, $p < .025$, one-tailed).

Discussion of Findings on Hypothetical Performance

The situation prepared by the investigators is, of course, an artificial one; responses to questionnaire items and judgments about what one would do with a case based simply on knowledge from a report do not have any necessary bearing on what happens in real life. While the test cases selected appear to cover a wide range on a "continue-likelihood" scale from one which 90 percent of agents say they would retain on parole to one which 93 percent say they would return, there is at this time little knowledge about just how representative the test case parolees are of those to be found in the actual parole population. It seems likely, however, that the ten cases are not typical but are, for the most part, "marginal" types. Probably the majority of actual violators are more "clear-cut," in that parole agents would have less difficulty agreeing with one another about whether "continue" or "return" was the appropriate disposition. The investigators did believe, and some evidence from the pilot study offered support for such a belief, that even though they were working with "artificial" data which might exaggerate real differences, these data correspond to the actual state of affairs. Additional findings relevant to this issue are contained in the next section of this report.

RESULTS: ACTUAL PERFORMANCE

The Outcome Criteria

For the purpose of documenting whether the measures applied in the current investigation bore any relationships to what was actually happening in parolee violation and recidivism, the data were compared with that available on all parolees released from prison to California supervision in 1965—the year in which the "hypothetical" data were collected. Each parolee was followed for one year subsequent to his release from prison, and the most serious disposition which he received during that period was recorded. Since the hypothetical data were collected in late September 1965, this meant that some of the parolees were released ten months prior to, and would be followed two months subsequent to, the time of questionnaire administration, while others would not yet be released for two months and were consequently followed to a point fourteen months after the agents were studied. Most of the parolees were between these extremes and therefore more closely anchored in time to the hypothetical data.

Material was available on 7301 parolees, classified by the parole unit office to which they were released.[7] Two indicators of parole performance at one year were selected for examination. The first indicator, and the one most obviously relevant to the hypothetical data, was return-to-prison-to-finish-term—an administrative disposition within the authority of the parole board which can occur subsequent to a law infraction or technical violation. These prison-returns are to be distinguished from returns-to-prison with new commitment—a court action taken subsequent to a felony conviction occurring during parole. The second indicator selected, favorable parole outcome, is accorded to a parolee who, throughout one year subsequent to release, has had no difficulty or only minor difficulty (for example, suspended jail sentences, jail sentence under 90 days, misdemeanor probation).

Two types of comparison were employed for each of the criteria. The first involved asking the question: How many of the parole offices which are above the median for offices on this criterion (for example, percent of releases with favorable parole outcome at one year exposure) are also above the median on another measure (for example, "continue" recommendation measure obtained from hypothetical data)? The second type asked the question: What percent of the parolees released to offices above the median on a given measure received a particular disposition (for example, technical return to prison) in their first year on parole?

While the two outcome criteria, technical prison return and favorable outcome, are mutually exclusive in regard to any given parolee, there is no necessary inverse relationship between these two measures in terms of parole office performance. One might expect that unit offices with a higher technical return rate would consequently have a lower overall rate of favorable out-comes. It has, however, been argued that an office can, through judiciously invoking a technical return, offset some other unfavorable outcome, thereby nullifying any decrease in (and conceivably increasing) its favorable outcome rate. (See section entitled Pilot Studies: Community Factors, for findings related to this topic.) On the 1965 outcome data, a comparison was made of office performance on these two criteria

[7] Dorothy R. Jaman, "Parole Outcome for Six Years of Felon Releases to California Parole," Staff report, CDC Research Division Measurement Unit, October 1967.

(median test) and no significant association was found (X^2, 1 d.f., = 2.64, $p <$ 20, two-tailed).

Hypothetical Recommendations and Actual Outcome

The parole unit offices were divided into those above and those at or below the median on "continue" recommendations offered by parole agents in the test situation, and two types of determination were then made for these districts from the actual 1965 outcome data: (1) the offices' locations above or below the median on the actual outcome, and (2) the number of parolees in these offices who received the criterion disposition. The findings for the second type of comparison appear in Table 13 for both technical prison return and favorable outcome.

The more continue-oriented offices, as measured by parole agents' recommendations on ten case stimuli, had a significantly higher proportion of favorable parolee outcome for cases released in the same year (X^2, 1 d.f., = 5.51, $p < .01$, one-tailed), and a significantly lower proportion of parolees returned to prison to finish term (X^2, 1 d.f., = 7.92, $p < .005$, one-tailed). Thus, agent behavior in an artificial test-taking situation is found to be associated with actual recidivism rates, lending support to the hypothesis that formal parole violations are a function of decision-maker judgment as well as an index of parolee performance.

In regard to the magnitude of differences between high and low continue-oriented offices, some points of reference may be helpful. Offices above the median on "continue" recommendations for test cases show a 2.6 percent lower technical return rate and a 2.4 percent higher favorable outcome rate than offices at or below the median. The difference, though statistically significant, appears negligible in size. Had the lower group of offices performed at the same rate as the higher, there would have been 82 fewer technical returns to prison and 92 more favorable outcomes. Another perspective regarding the size of the obtained difference is provided by an answer to the question: Considering only the actual outcome rates, just how great is the difference between the performances of those offices above the median on these rates as compared with offices at or below the median? The answers are 6.4 percent for technical prison returns (12.4% versus 18.8%), and

Table 13 *Hypothetical Recommendations and Actual Outcome*

Office Performance on Test Cases	Parole Outcome at One Year, 1965 Releases		
	Number Released	Technical Returns	Favorable Outcomes
Above median continued (18 offices)	3810	525 (13.8%)	2482 (65.1%)
At or below median continued (20 offices)	3491	564 (16.2%)	2181 (62.5%)
Total	7301	1089 (14.9%)	4663 (63.9%)

6.9 percent for favorable outcome (68.1% versus 61.2%). Thus, the differences obtained by classifying offices on the case recommendation task should be viewed against the maximum difference attainable under these conditions (that is, 2.6% obtained versus 6.4% limit for technical return and 2.4% obtained versus 6.9% limit on favorable outcome). One may legitimately wonder whether, since the limiting differences are so small, there is really any point in paying so much attention to performance variation among parole offices. Several considerations are relevant to this question. First, as has been earlier acknowledged, since the majority of decisions about continuing cases on parole or returning them to prison probably pose little uncertainty, variability in case recommendation can be expected to occur only on cases which are more or less marginal. However, the problem of defining marginality has not been solved. Second, the differences in percent have been presented using all outcomes as a base, rather than the criterion outcome (that is, technical return). Thus, suppose that the low-continue offices had performed at the same level as high-continue offices on the technical return rate and returned 82 fewer parolees (482 rather than 564). Viewed against this base, 15 percent of the cases considered were marginal ones who would have been continued rather than returned. Third, a median split provides a conservative index of the differences among offices. For the one year outcomes on 1965 prison releases, individual parole office technical-return rates ranged from 9.3 percent to 28.7 percent, and favorable-outcome rates ranged from 54.5 percent to 73.3 percent.

Agent Value and Belief, and Actual Parole Outcome

In earlier pages of this report, two questionnaire items were described, compared with one another, checked against hypothetical case recommendations, and finally combined to provide three basic types:

1. Agent values "continue" and believes supervisor favors it.
2. Disparity between agent value and belief about supervisor regarding "continue."
3. Agent does not value "continue" or believe supervisor favors it.

For the purpose of testing these questionnaire responses against actual parole performance, the 38 parole offices were cross-classified in the three types with a reliance upon whether the office was above or below the median on each of the two measures. This procedure generated nine type 1 offices, eight type 3 offices, and twenty-one type 2 offices. Within type 2 (the disparate class) there were ten offices of the agents favor–supervisor disfavors subtype, and eleven of the reverse subtype. In Table 14, actual parole performance is examined in terms of technical return and favorable outcome rates across the three basic office types.

Statistically significant differences were found to exist among office types on each of the outcome criteria (technical return, X^2, 2 d.f., $= 10.4$, $p < .005$, one-tailed; favorable outcome, X^2, 2 d.f., $= 4.75$, $p < .05$, one-tailed). Unit parole

Table 14   *Actual Parole Performance versus Agent Value and Belief About Supervisor*

Office Type	Parole Outcome at One Year, 1965 Releases				
	Number of Releases	Technical Returns		Favorable Outcomes	
1. Both agents and supervisor favor "continue"	2146	278	(13.0%)	1399	(65.2%)
2. Disparity between agents and supervisor regarding "continue"	3587	553	(15.4%)	2296	(64.0%)
3. Neither agents nor supervisor favor "continue"	1568	258	(16.5%)	968	(61.7%)
Total	7301	1089	(14.9%)	4663	(63.9%)

offices, classified in terms of whether the agents value and believe their supervisor to favor continuation of cases on parole, provide actual parole outcomes in correspondence with their orientation. Within type 2, the two office subtypes produce identical technical return rates (15.4 percent) while a 64.8 percent favorable outcome rate exists for the supervisor favors–agents disfavor subtype, as compared to 63.1 percent for the reverse subtype.

SUMMARY AND CONCLUSIONS

In 1967, there were 7584 adult male felons admitted to California state prisons. One out of four of these men (1867) were administrative readmissions —cases returned to prison by the parole board for infractions or faulty adjustment on parole. An additional 11 percent of the admissions (847) were also parole violators, but these were judicial re-admissions—cases returned by the courts on a new felony commitment. With 25 percent of prison intake in the hands of parole board members, it is important to examine the process by which parole revocation occurs.

The revocation decision is, in part, a penalty and, in part, a prediction. One problem is to decide whether the immediate act or the chronic adjustment which precipitated the violation report warrants, in itself, imposing the punishment of further incarceration. The other problem is an attempt to foresee whether, if the man were continued under parole supervision, future incidents of a still more serious nature would be likely to occur. In weighing this risk, limited-term protection can be purchased by reimprisonment, which postpones the opportunity for new violations to occur, but may increase the likelihood of their eventual occurrence by interruption in the process of offender-readjustment to the community. Maintenance of an offender in a prison is over three times as costly as maintaining him on parole ($50/mo. versus $166/mo. for the California Department of Corrections), but the cost to society of new crimes can also be great. Under conditions of potentially great loss and uncertainty about the likelihood of its occurrence, one is tempted toward cautious solutions and conservative decisions. In buying insurance for awhile against a few, it is probable that many parolees who pose no serious threat are also reincarcerated; in the absence of sufficient information, there is a dilemma for decision-makers as to where the balance is to be struck.

The present study has demonstrated marked inconsistencies in judgment among parole agents about the appropriate case disposition to be made after a parolee incident. The decision task with which the agents were presented might be considered artificial and unfair, and designed to promote uncertainty and lack of reliability; however, the task is a good simulation of the real decision task with which the parole board is routinely faced. It is true that the parole board members have more information available at the decision point (i.e., a case history of the subject's past prison experience and earlier social adjustment), but it is unlikely that this older source of information has much separate impact on the decisions, given the fact that a high correspondence exists between those decisions and the parole agent's recommendation on the violation report. It is accepted that uncertainty may have been increased because of the types of case on which judgments were to be made (they may be atypical, and more "marginal" than the everyday distribution of violators) and that the findings consequently exaggerate the level of disagreement that might be routinely expected. *Regardless of the extent to which this is so, findings from that "artificial" situation have been shown to correspond with differences on actual revocation rates produced by the same parole agents—*suggesting that the marginal case is commonly confronted in real practice.

Parole agents appear to be quite susceptible to influence about the type of case recommendation they will make, even though recommendations are to be based on their professional judgment. There are tendencies toward agreement among agents within a given office, but large differences in recommendation patterns between offices. While there is some indication that the agent's personal background (his educational specialty and prior types of job) has a bearing on these judgments, and that his current value orientation is involved, the most definite correlate shown in the present study was the agent's assessment of his supervisor's orientation. Further indication of this willingness (or at least capability) to provide expected parolee performances was yielded by the definite fall in the actual revocation rate subsequent to the present study. That fall is attributable to increased pressure upon agents to recommend continued parole supervision for many types of violator—a pressure originating from headquarters and transmitted through the unit supervisors. Whether these pressures are formally or informally exerted, the response to them can markedly shift the overall *rate* of revocation; it does not necessarily follow that *variability* in judgment of recommendation among parole agents will be reduced. In the two years subsequent to the 1965 study on which this report is based, considerable attention was directed by the agency to the matter of the case decisions—reports by agents were subjected to closer scrutiny at each level of review, and training sessions for agents were focused upon case reporting and recommendation. This emphasis might be expected to increase the reliability of judgment. However, when the ten test cases from the 1965 study were readministered in late 1967 and early 1968, variability in the recommendation-pattern was still quite evident.

The average number of cases continued was considerably higher than before —4.87 for new agents who had not been present for the earlier study, and 4.97 for experienced agents undergoing re-test; the average in 1965 had been 3.27. Seventy-one percent of the new agents, and 78 percent of the experienced ones continued four or more of the ten cases, compared to only 38 percent in 1965. Despite this marked shift in the central tendency—or overall "revocation rate" —on these cases, the range of response was still high.

One of the main difficulties facing correctional administrators in their attempts to improve effectiveness of operations has resulted from the failure to systematically record and analyze the material on which decisions at critical choice points are made. Ordinarily, when such efforts are made, the energy is misspent by a concentration of attention on output (the number of dipositions of a given sort by parole board members) with almost no attention devoted to the extent of its correlation with input (parole agent recommendations) or to the substance of that input (reported information characteristics which may have little reliability or actual relevance). Though a substantial proportion of parole agent work time is devoted to the preparation of narrative reports for the parole board, little opportunity is provided for obtaining a cumulative systematic knowledge base, since translation of the narrative form into a code structure which will permit analysis is a laborious and seldom-attempted process.

Correctional experience, then, has been recorded in fragments, separated into case folders, stuffed into filing cabinets, and eventually burned. That is the past. Will the future be different?

22
Legal Model for Parole: Future Developments

DONALD J. NEWMAN

INTRODUCTION

From a legal perspective, parole is and has been something of an anomaly. Although it often exists within and derives from a common framework of welfare law, the parole board rarely has been treated as an administrative agency nor its decisions correlated with and controlled by forms of procedural regularity often required in administrative law practice. It was not long ago that Kenneth Culp Davis in his administrative law text devoted only a paragraph to parole, saying, in effect, that while a parole board looks and acts like an administrative agency, it is not an administrative agency. Legislatures, delegating broad discretionary authority to parole boards and courts exercising a firm "hands off" policy in regard to both the grant and revocation of parole, supported this position.

It may be, however, that the situation is changing. Certainly the "hands off" doctrine has been breached at many points in correctional processing from deferred sentencing as in *Mempa v. Rhay* to the treatment of prison inmates. The *Zeitgeist* of civil rights, wars on poverty and violence, emerging demands for due process in welfare decisions, all have found sympathetic listeners at both appellate courts and in legislatures. Kenneth Davis, with many others, has reexamined

SOURCE. *Proceedings of the One Hundreth Annual Congress of Corrections,* American Correctional Association, 1971, pp. 294–307. Reprinted with permission of the author and the American Correctional Association.

discretionary decisions in the context of a necessity for increased visibility and effective controls. The long-range impact of all this may indeed be an increased judicialization of the parole process, from grant to revocation.

If there is in fact such a trend toward challenge and proof in parole as well as other correctional decisions, it cannot really be assessed, nor accurately predicted, unless the entire process is examined not as it is, but as it is becoming. Parole as we have known it—including its purposes as well as its goals—is no more static than the legal context in which it exists. As correctional philosophies and concerns change their focus, so must parole become modified to meet new demands and to fulfill new purposes. Parole exists as part of a larger correctional endeavor, taking its functions and its rationale from the overall ideology. If, as many claim and as signs and portents show, corrections is moving from a rehabilitative to a reintegrationist focus, then parole in the future may have various new characteristics and purposes.

ASSUMPTIONS OF PAROLE

When parole was first adopted, as even today, there were some basic assumptions—some explicit, others implicit—about its use. Parole was viewed (and to a large extent still is) as a privilege earned by prisoners and not as a right. Paroling authorities were expected to be cautious and careful in their release decisions, returning to the community only good risk prisoners at the time in their sentences when they were best ready for reentry into society. The parole board was seen as having a double sort of role, in part acting as a court of leniency that could lessen excessively harsh sentences and partly as a board of persons with clinical expertise who could decide when repentant or rehabilitated offenders could safely be returned to the outside world.

In the past, as now, parole involves more than simply a premaximum release decision. One condition that has always been assumed is that the paroled inmate would return to the community only under supervision of a trained field agent who would exert his efforts to help the prisoner readjust and who perhaps would continue the therapeutic endeavors begun in prison. The assumption was and is that parole is not simply release from incarceration, not really a major change in status, but an extension of a sentence of incarceration served in the community by the grace of God and the parole board under close surveillance, supervision, and guidance.

Whether these assumptions about parole systems were ever really operational is a moot point. It is probable that in the past, as today, the total parole process is much more complex than commonly believed and that all or most of the assumptions are only partly met.

THE DECISIONS OF PAROLE

A parole system in full operation involves a set of interlocking decisions that roughly fall into three major categories: (1) who shall be released from prison and when; (2) the conditions, rules and nature of community supervision; and (3) revocation policies and procedures. By and large, the first decision (release) is made by a parole board which may be created and structured in various ways in different jurisdictions. Whatever the appointment procedures and structure, in virtually all instances parole boards have separate and distinct authority from institutional staff. In fact, in many instances parole boards are not only separate and distinct from the prison but from the profession of correctional administration. The basic assumption underlying the independent structure of the board is that it should be neutral from daily correctional concerns, much as a judge is neutral from (but obviously related to) the activities of police and prosecutors.

In some cases there is an assumption that the board members have a certain degree of expertise indicated by training or experience, for making their decisions. This certainly was a popular expectation some years ago when the completely indeterminate sentence as the basis for sentencing systems was popular. In fact, the whole concept of the completely indeterminate sentence rested on the assumption that persons sentenced to prison would be examined by a board of "experts" who would have the skills as well as the total discretion to decide when, if ever, to release prisoners from the one-day-to-life sentences they were serving. With the exception of laws directed to certain offense or offender categories, today the completely indeterminate sentence idea is rarely in use and has few supporters among professionals in correctional administration. In part, I suppose, this is because there are in fact no "experts" really skillful or confident enough to claim or exercise such limitless discretion. In any event, most paroling authorities today operate within outside controls of minimum or maximum sentences (or both) fixed by legislation and by courts.

The nature of the release decision is in itself interesting. It is commonly believed that parole boards act to release good risk prisoners back to the community. In operation, however, this is by no means always the case. As a parole board member once said to me, "There are no good risk men in prison. Parole is really a decision of *when* to release bad risk persons." This is not to say that paroling authorities have been unconcerned with risk. Quite the contrary. Risk of new crimes tends to be an important, although not an exclusive factor in determining not only when to release persons, but when to hold some prisoners to maximum term or to mandatory release date.

If risk of recidivism (either by a new crime or a violation of supervision rules) were the *only* concern of parole boards, the task would perhaps be easier. Over the years it has been proposed that parole boards could be replaced by computers or that prison authorities could make release decisions without the necessity of going through a hearing before an "outside" parole board. But in the past, as today, the fact is that computer prediction is not much better, if at all, than board selection in terms of risk. Furthermore, the board relates its decisions to other concerns, such as internal prison control and morale, community sentiment, and the political implications of their decisions. Any computer would tell you that Alger Hiss would be a good risk on release, and yet no paroling authority that I know of would release such a prisoner the first time he became eligible. Beyond this, however, (and let me recognize that considerations other than risk are, in each instance, highly disputatious) it is a characteristic of our justice system that even the least among us has a right to his day in court. By and large, this doesn't only mean appearance in formal trial and appellate courts. Most of us who are judged (and who isn't?) want to be judged by other persons, not by machines. It is consistent with our democratic ideology that in a decision as important as parole a prisoner be given the *right to appear* before other men, to state his case and to answer whatever questions may be put to him. At other points in the criminal justice process one could argue, I suppose, that computers could set bail, or determine charges or perhaps replace the jury or the judge. Somehow, I would guess, this would be reprehensible to us and I suspect the same thing is true of the parole decision.

In terms of prison personnel making the release decision, one could argue in similar vein that the police could initiate prosecution, conduct the trial and sentence offenders, thereby achieving maximum efficiency by avoiding the slow, costly, and admittedly often pro-forma appearances before the prosecutor, magistrate, judge, and jury. As with machine decision-making, it seems to me that decisions made within a single agency about the lives and freedom of people is somehow repugnant to our ideology. Though a man's keeper should have his say, it seems inappropriate, somehow, to be both jailer and paroling authority, and a form of fundamental fairness requires both the warden and the prisoner to state their cases before a neutral decision-making body.

The second aspect of the parole complex relates to the rules and conditions of supervision and to surveillance and supervision as an experience not only for the prisoner coming out of an institution but for his field agent as well. In theory, the parole agent is viewed as an extension of the authority of the prison. By custom, rationale, and recruitment, he is more often viewed (and more often views himself) as closer to the treatment than the custodial aspect of imprisonment. In practice he has the dual role of law enforcement authority and guidance counselor to the released prisoner.

Almost universally, parolees are held to higher standards of morality and have their movements and decisions much more restricted than citizens not under sentence. The nature and the range of appropriate rules and conditions of parole (as well as the question of whether there are *inappropriate* rules and conditions, and, if so, how these can be effectively challenged) is an important and not fully-agreed upon part of the paroling process. The skills required to be a field agent (whether achieved by education or experience, or both) while not completely defined, rest on an assumption that the parole officer will not only keep an eye on his charges, but will assist them in both community adjustment and in solving personal problems. An assumption underlying this assumption is that the field agent will be given a relatively small and manageable caseload. Obviously, the most highly trained and skilled field agent can at any one time work effectively with only a limited number of the very difficult problem persons who commonly are in and released from prison.

The philosophy of parole which views the released person as still having inmate status would allow for easy and quick return to prison without any necessity to base revocation on objective evidence or to adhere to "due process" requirements in the sense of testing the decision in an adversary hearing before either a court or an administrative board. In fact, the ease and skillful use of revocation to prevent further crimes is often given as a precondition for liberal paroling practices. Today, however, there is some evidence that this underlying principle of the parolee's status as that of inmate-on-the-streets is being challenged so that the ease and informality of revocation may be disappearing, increasingly being subject to court or even legislative intervention.

CONTROLS ON PAROLING DECISIONS

Paroling decisions, from release to revocation, are not, of course, made in a vacuum but exist within the particular sentencing structure of a given jurisdiction. Controls on the authority of parole boards and even field agents sometimes come from the legislature. In a few jurisdictions, for example, certain offenses are defined as non-paroleable. Therefore an individual sentenced for such a crime must serve his maximum time (or his maximum less time off for good behavior) in prison. However, today in most jurisdictions and for most crimes, there are fixed maximum sentences. No matter how much the paroling authority may desire to retain a man in prison, he cannot be held beyond the statutory maximum of his sentence. (Although, see for example, The Model Penal Code provision for "Separate Parole Terms" which makes length of parole a function of time served rather than time remaining under the maximum. In effect, this would allow certain persons to be under sentence, though not always in prison, beyond the statutory limits for their crimes.) In some jurisdictions, legislatures also fix minimum sentences for certain crimes, either as specific minima or minima calculated as a proportion of the maximum. While there is some variation in the use of good time laws (i.e. in some states good time comes off the maximum, in others, it reduces the minimum), in general the paroling authority has no discretion to release the prisoner, or even to see him, until he has served the minimum time fixed by statute or set within permissible limits by the sentencing judge. In most states today, legislatures use their authority to set *outer* limits to sentences but give to the trial court judge considerable discretion to fix sentences within these boundaries. Legislation in many jurisdictions allows judges to set maximum terms less than the statutory maxima or to fix minimum terms, or both. In this way, courts exert control on parole boards just as do legislatures by providing perimeters for the parole decision.

Sentencing structures are formal and largely structural controls on the parole system, but there are other controls currently emerging or already operative in some jurisdictions. For example, the Model Penal Code has proposed it to be an appropriate legislative task not only to set the minimum and maximum sentencing limits, thereby curtailing some parole discretion, but to express themselves in regard to the criteria that may appropriately be considered by the parole board in making their release decision, in setting conditions of community supervision, and in initiating and carrying through revocation decisions. This is generally not operative in most jurisdictions, but given the prestige of the drafters of the Model Penal Code and the care with which it was constructed, it may well foretell an important trend.

In addition to the possibility of legislatively fixed criteria guidelines, there is today an apparent increase in trial and appellate court intervention in parole and revocation decisions. Generally, a distinction is being drawn between the initial release decision, where courts have followed with some consistency the "hands-off" doctrine, and revocation decisions which courts are increasingly viewing as a somewhat different matter from the decision of whether or not to initially release a prisoner. This is consistent with the dichotomy in administrative law between the granting of a privilege, such as a license, and taking it away. The concept commonly used is "vestment," meaning that once a person has been given a certain status, such as that of parolee, it cannot be removed without following more formal proceedings whether before a court or before some kind of in-house review panel, where matters of evidence and challenge become not only important, but necessary.

There is another more subtle but very important control on the parole decision, namely, that of the information system which feeds material to parole boards to assist them in making release or revocation decisions. Obviously a decision is only as fair or accurate as the information on which it is based. Just as in the sentencing determination where judges of practical necessity rely on the presentence investigation report, so parole boards rely on correctional files (of which the presentence report is often an integral part), evaluation of custodial and treatment personnel, and comments and judgments of parole field agents. In actual practice, personal confrontation with the inmate being considered for parole (or being considered for revocation) plays a relatively minor part in the decision. The fact is that a person's official record, including recommendations and comments of various personnel who deal with him, is of major importance in parole decision-making. Now, in any record about any person, whether for the purposes of parole or to establish a credit rating, there is no such thing as the "whole truth" or "all the facts." Written information—particularly information based on opinion, including clinical diagnoses—is necessarily selective and to some extent slanted. This is not to say that information given to parole authorities is deliberately distorted, inaccurate, or necessarily insufficient. It is to say, however, that the way a case is presented, that is, the kind of information included and the kind of information excluded, almost invariably determines the decision of the board or for that matter of any other decision maker. While correctional authorities and field agents may have no direct say in any given decision by the parole board, they do have control over the information flow. It is in this sense that the type and form of information presented to paroling authorities can be viewed as a form of control over their decisions.

CURRENT TRENDS AFFECTING PAROLE

The parole system as we know it may be due to some dramatic changes if certain trends in criminal justice in general and sentencing continue. Some of these trends having particular relevance to the paroling function include the following:

1. *Shorter Sentences.* In general, throughout the nation, sentences to incarceration are becoming shorter. Complete indeterminate sentences, with natural life as the maximum, have virtually disappeared except for certain crimes. The National Council on Crime and Delinquency, in its Model Sentencing Act, has proposed a five-year maximum for all felonies except for "atrocious crimes." Within the past decade almost half of the states have revised (or are revising) their criminal codes (including sentencing provisions) so that today it is possible in these states to give shorter sentences than was true in the past. In practice this seems to be the case. At the same time, there is increasing pressure to do away with minimum sentences or (with no pun intended) to minimize the minimum. As codes get revised it becomes increasingly impossible for punitive judges to give sentences such as 14½ to 15 years and in many jurisdictions legislation now prevents judges from piling consecutive sentences on a particular offender. In any case, it appears that in the future paroling authorities will be dealing with a shorter time span but at the same time will be less likely to have their hands tied by long minimum sentences.

2. *The Reintegration Model of Corrections.* Among professionals and laymen alike there is currently a good deal of disillusionment with the use of imprisonment as a means of treating criminal offenders. Few judges whom I know sentence a person to prison actually believing that it will help him. Few persons in correctional administration really believe that effective rehabilitation can take place in a situation of total repression, degradation, and control. In the past decade or so the major rationale for imprisonment has rested on a theory of rehabilitation which sees the cause of crime as lying within certain traits—character disorders —of persons who are sent to institutions. These traits—psychological and attitudinal for the most part—are to be somehow modified by counseling, group therapy, or psychotherapy while the person is incarcerated. This whole theory of rehabilitation as it applies to criminal offenders and to prisons is in current dispute. Emerging to replace it is a model of reintegration in which primary emphasis is on community treatment by providing aid and assistance at all levels of the entire life organization of persons under sentence in the community. In the reintegration model, imprisonment is seen as useful for diagnosis or cooling-off, if it is useful at all, but not for treatment. The stance is that if incarceration must be used—for whatever reason—diagnosis or to escape community wrath—the person should be returned to the community as rapidly as possible and helped to make his adjustment on the street. To the extent that this approach begins to dominate correctional thinking, of course, it will accelerate the trend toward shorter sentences and may well call for new functions for parole authorities. A

great deal of action will be moved from the state level to the local community.

3. *Increasing Use of Mandatory Release.* Many jurisdictions are increasingly using mandatory release (sometimes known as "parole of right") in addition to parole and maximum discharge. Mandatory release is related to good time laws so that an individual who successfully serves given periods of time in prison can earn a release date shorter than the maximum imposed by legislation or by the court. At this date, assuming he has earned all his good time, he *must* be released. Increasingly, this "mandatory release" is accompanied, mandatorily, by community supervision. Except for the release decision itself, mandatory release looks exactly like parole. Mandatory release has a number of advantages not only for the inmate but for the paroling authority as well. There are certain inmates whom the parole board would like to see under supervision in the community and yet who, because of record or prognosis, are persons for whom the board would hesitate to grant parole. According to standard criteria of risk and other variables, the mandatory release person may not be paroleable yet, in a system with fairly liberal good time laws (so that mandatory release dates come reasonably early), paroling authorities can avoid the parole decision and yet know that the individual will go on the street under supervision. The elaboration of mandatory release requirements and programs may well be a trend to move the parole position away from the absolute dichotomy of either paroling a person or holding him to his maximum term.

4. *Court Intervention in a Parole Grant and Revocation.* It is important to stress that however much paroling authorities may oppose such intervention, the trend appears to be clear. The whole spirit of the time, involving such matters as the emergence of civil rights movements, the war on poverty, the emergence of welfare rights laws and the like, makes it highly improbable that the correctional system will escape the kinds of procedural controls that have been imposed upon other administrative agencies by higher courts.

5. *Better Research.* The state of research, in criminal justice generally and in corrections (including parole) particularly, is changing. Practically every major university today has some kind of program in criminal justice administration and in turn these programs have research components. This represents a major change away from criminology—where the focus was largely on the etiology of criminal behavior—to essentially operational research. Collectively, sophisticated attention is being paid to such things as decision-making and the consequences of decisions in police departments, prosecutor's offices, courts and correctional agencies. Until now, a good deal of research in parole has been largely in-house, that is, it has been what is known as "gate-keeping" research. By and large it involved no more than simple summary data on the number of cases considered, the type of decisions made, and the outcome in terms of revocation. Now, however, much more sophisticated questions and techniques are being developed and much more elaborate studies are being undertaken. For example, until recently, parole success or failure was measured by recidivism rates where recidivism was treated as more or less an absolute. While anyone sophisticated in the ways of parole and revocation knew that recidivism was not absolute but was in fact a

decision or a series of decisions, it has never really been looked at in this way. For the first time, studies are being done of parole agent's discretion in initiating or not initiating revocation (even when new crimes are involved), in the use of the revocation on the old sentence as a bargain with the prosecutor to avoid prosecution for a new crime, and the use (and perhaps misuse) of violations of rules and conditions as the basis for revocation. Some sophisticated questions are being put that may have important consequences for paroling decisions and their evaluation. For example, one can ask, "What is recidivism?" Eliminating rule infraction as the basis for revocation for the moment (although recognizing that these may be used in lieu of prosecution), recidivism generally has been tabulated as commission of a new crime. However, one can ask whether a person is considered a recidivist (even by parole standards) only if he commits a crime similar to the one for which he was originally convicted. Or is new crime recidivism based on any crime? For example, if a person is paroled after serving part of a sentence for murder and if he steals a car, is he a recidivist? Or, put the other way, suppose a person sentenced for stealing a car while on parole commits a homicide, is he a recidivist? The *sophisticated* question is whether unrelated crime among a population of parolees is any higher than among a population of nonparolees with the same socioeconomic characteristics. These, and numberless other questions, are potential research bases in the system, although the kinds of research that deal with them are just emerging.

6. *Extension of Parole Services.* In the classic tradition, when the term "parole" is used it is generally taken to mean the discretionary release of adult felons from prisons. Various forms of parole have been used with juveniles and youthful offenders (generally called "aftercare") released from state training schools. By and large, however, parole in any shape or form has not been used widely with minor criminal offenders incarcerated in jails. This is clearly enunciated as a major problem in the reports of the President's Crime Commission. However, the situation appears to be changing and it is likely that misdemeanant parole will assume major importance in the future. New York, for example, has expanded its parole board and its services to include misdemeanant parole within its ambit. If one simply looks at the relative numbers of persons held in jail in comparison to those held in prison and, if as seems to be likely, jailing will play a more important part in future correctional developments than imprisonment, then it is clear that the implications of misdemeanant parole are indeed major. If it does come about that jail parole becomes more widely used as an integral part of the parole system, it will, of course, call for a reexamination of procedures, policies, criteria and skills of paroling authorities, boards and field agents alike.

7. *Release Other Than On Parole.* It may be that paroling authorities will have an important role to play in the various so-called partial release decisions that are now made in a number of correctional systems. For example, work release from prisons (sometimes called "daytime parole") is becoming common. With this program there is a question of how persons are (or should be) selected for work release, including whether the decision should be left to the correctional authorities or should be lodged with "neutral outsiders" such as the parole board.

Likewise, furloughs are being increasingly used (or proposed) with adult prisoners. Again, there is a question of how furlough decisions are made, how criteria for its use are arrived at, and questions about the nature of supervision, if any, while the person is home on leave. The same applies to the various other alternatives to total imprisonment that are now emerging in what is generally known as "community corrections." Halfway houses (whether halfway in or halfway out) are currently fashionable, posing an interesting question of the extent to which parole and paroling authorities have, or might have, important functions in these programs.

THE FUTURE OF PAROLE

Given these correctional trends (and the other general cultural trends of population composition, density, and changes in political and social philosophy) one can put a number of questions about the future of parole as both a concept and an operational reality in our society. It seems to me that parole as it is known as a form of discretionary release of prisoners from maximum security adult institutions will not continue undisturbed over the next few years. At the same time it seems to me that parole will remain not only an important but a *critical* part of correctional administration. Trends and pressures, however, will force some major changes in the use of parole and in the assumptions under which the system now operates. In my opinion some of the major implications for the future of parole systems will include the following:

1. *Reversal of Basic Assumptions.* All signs seem to point in the direction that incarceration in prisons, particularly maximum security prisons, will be reserved primarily for dangerous persons. If so, this means that a large number of inmates (and offense categories) now found in prisons will be handled in community treatment facilities. No longer will maximum security prisons be used to house offenders convicted of nonsupport, alcoholic check writing, and other minor felonies. It seems to me that prisons increasingly will be used primarily to incapacitate rather than to rehabilitate those offenders whose criminal conduct indicates a high degree of dangerousness. (Dangerousness, by and large, is taken to mean a high risk of committing crimes of personal violence rather than crimes against property even if chronic and repetitive.) If this is so, it will mean that the decision of the parole board shifts from one of whom to let out of prison to one of whom to retain. In the future, persons convicted of felonies may touch base in prison for a short time and then be returned to the community. If they cannot initially make probation, then, at most, a short diagnostic sentence would be imposed consistent with the reintegration philosophy that seems to be emerging in American correctional administration. This means that for most persons who are received at a prison, parole will become relatively *automatic unless there is negative evidence* that the person should not be released. This is a marked reversal of common assumption and practice. Today, generally speaking, an affirmative case must be made by the prisoner (and his record must support it) in order for

him to gain the "Privilege" of community supervision. The basic assumption is that an offender *will be held* in prison *unless* he can make a case for release. The other way of phrasing the assumption, the reverse, (as it is done in the Model Penal Code), is that the person *will be paroled unless* there is negative evidence to indicate that he is dangerous and should be held for purposes of incapacitation. If indeed this does come about—that is, if it becomes the operational reality of parole—then there must be some rethinking about the criteria for the decision, about the skills of paroling authorities, about the consequences of nonrelease (instead of the consequences of release) and in short, an entire reevaluation of the concept of parole and reorganization of paroling facilities in the correctional structure.

2. *Increased Procedural Regularity.* If the paroling focus shifts to selecting those who should be held for purposes of incapacitation rather than rehabilitation (including the possibility of extended terms of certain dangerous persons—extended, that is, beyond the statutory maximum) then the issue of deprivation of liberty becomes much sharper and perhaps more important in the parole process. Assuming this trend, there is no doubt that within our constitutional framework, and guided by the recent and current activities of appellate courts, there will be much firmer insistence on formalization of parole and revocation hearings. The consequences will be that the parole board, in letting men out or putting them back, will be required to act much like a court of law in their processing.

3. *More Accurate Feedback.* If research really does get better and more sophisticated, there is no doubt that there will be a steady accumulation of more accurate and meaningful information about parole, revocation and other correctional decisions as well. If such research (involving hard data gathering and feedback) should come about, it is well to remember that it is likely to be a two-edged sword: on the one hand it will subject parole and revocation decisions to careful scrutiny by outsiders and at the same time it will provide valuable information about the whys, wherefores, and consequences of decisions which are too often made blindly.

4. *Different Information.* By and large the type of information now contained in correctional files is either routine and demographic or psychotherapeutically oriented. In general, the information contained in correctional files (which follow the medical model of "diagnosis" and "prognosis" reports) has been *trait-oriented* and *family-centered.* The predominant operational theory is that a person becomes criminal because of certain characteristics or traits (emotions, values, attitudes) with the corresponding task of corrections to be the modification of these traits. In correctional files there is commonly very little information about the offender's environment so, for example, a correctional file on a person coming from a metropolitan ghetto may look almost exactly like the file of an offender coming from a small village. Except by inference—work record, school behavior —one doesn't get very much flavor about the way a person's life is organized with the possible exception of his relationships in his immediate family. Many correctional files I have seen have almost no information about peers, about neighborhoods, or about other conditions or characteristics of the life which the person

leads or has led. Yet, for years such factors have dominated criminological theory and it would seem that they would be particularly relevant to paroling authorities. It seems to me that the future holds promise not only of better and more accurate information, but also of information which is more useful and relevant to the kinds of decisions necessarily made by paroling authorities, such as the likelihood of successful community adjustment, of committing new crimes, of "making it" on the outside.

5. *New Techniques in Treatment and Supervision.* As most of you know, pharmacology has worked a major revolution in the world of mental hospitals. Thorazine has liberated thousands of formerly hopeless cases. It may well be that pharmacology and chemistry will provide some helpful aids to community supervision, at least in certain cases of inmates who otherwise would have to remain incarcerated.

Likewise there are some recent developments in electronic tracking of probationers and parolees (associated primarily with Dr. Ralph Schwitzgebel of Harvard) by means of which the almost total surveillance and control system of the prison can be carried into the street. Whether such techniques are proper in a democratic society (even with prisoners), whether, even if proper in a Constitutional sense such devices should be used, are moot questions. The answers, however, must initially be made by parole authorities, although eventually they may be made by the Supreme Court. Whatever the ultimate decision, there is no doubt that electronic surveillance and conditioning techniques can be used at the present time in order to keep parolees under surveillance and possibly deter antisocial trends in their behavior while on parole. The technological revolution has affected all institutions in our society (including drive-in churches) and its implication for parole decision-making (whether by the board or by the field agent) are sure to be felt. The force of these developments, the direction they take, and their long-range consequences for parole, of course, are not known. What is certain is that persons currently involved in parole will have a lot to say about the future in regard to these matters.

SUMMARY

Looking ahead one can fairly ask the question of whether parole will remain an important part of correctional development. It is my opinion, of course, that parole is indeed important and necessary and that its importance will not decrease. Furthermore, it is likely that even with shortened sentences and the focus on community treatment, parole activities will increase. However, it is equally likely that they will be significantly different activities (perhaps it would be better to call them "parole-like" activities). Decisions will have to be made about misdemeanants, about persons on partial release, about dangerous persons, and in so doing parole agencies will be confronted with the possible necessity of developing new skills, new techniques, and new technologies, each of which can be very helpful and each of which can be quite potentially dangerous to parole within the democratic ideology. All institutions and organizations in our society are undergoing changes, and very rapid changes at that. It is highly likely that parole will remain an integral part of our correctional system (as long as we have a correctional system) but that it will look much different ten years from now than it does today. In the interim, it may require the recruitment or training of persons with new skills and, perhaps more important, with new perspectives, to participate in all capacities within a responsible paroling authority.

23

New Directions in Parole Service

ELIOT STUDT

Many factors contribute to the inability of parole agencies to provide parolees with services that are fully relevant and effective for their reintegration into the community. Among these factors are the lack of adequate resources, the relatively low level of public support for services to parolees, and the apathy of the community in providing opportunities to parolees. Of particular importance is the parole agency's double assignment, to serve parolee needs while protecting the community from their behavior.

ORGANIZATIONAL FACTORS

However, the findings of the Parole Action Study suggest that two additional organizational factors tend to inhibit the development of an improved service technology for parole. These concern the lack of administrative information about the critical problems that affect all, or large subgroupings, within the

SOURCE. Elliot Studt, Chapter X, *Surveillance and Service in Parole: A Report of the Parole Action Study,* pp. 193–204, Institute of Government and Public Affairs, University of California at Los Angeles, 1972 and the National Institute of Law Enforcement and Criminal Justice, U.S. Department of Justice, May, 1973. Copies of the full report, which includes the supporting data for the conclusions reported in this excerpt, may be obtained from the Institute for Social Science Research, UCLA, or from the National Technical Information Service, U.S. Department of Commerce, Springfield, Virginia 22151.

parolee population; and the inherent limitations of the principal service mechanism—the agent with his caseload—for achieving technological development.

1. *Administrative information about parolee tasks and problems.* When planning for services at any level of the agency—from agent caseload to the total population of the state—the responsible official needs to know the problems experienced by the clients in his caseload, as well as the relative volume of the different kinds of problems. Only with such knowledge can he assign priorities and provide the range of means required for the different kinds of indicated services. A careful examination of all the accounting procedures used by the agents in California revealed that few procedural means are available for channelling information about the actual needs of the parolees to upper decision makers.

The primary source of information about parolee problems in most parole organizations—as well as in other service agencies—is the process of referring "problem cases" from the agents upward to superior officials, who then classify these cases as representing typical parolee problems. Because these cases are problems for the agent, they tend to be a better index of those situations which the agents find difficult to manage within normal organizational patterns than of the problems that harrass sizable groups among the parolees, including those parolees who do not appear as "problem cases."

The parole agency is not alone among service agencies in assuming that the employed officials are the most competent persons to identify the client problems that should be addressed by service programs. But this pattern for defining client needs directs administrative attention to solving the problems the employees experience in performing their own tasks. Such information is useful for certain aspects of program analysis and planning. It does not, however, include information from those best able to report it, the clients, either about their priority needs or about the agency processes that interfere with effective service. Lacking that important corrective in service planning, an assessment of the services by those who are expected to benefit, the parole agency is inevitably handicapped in allocating its available resources to service programs with the greatest payoff for parolee welfare.

2. *The inadequacy of the agent's position for technological development.* All the Study's observations of agents at work suggest that they are already doing much that could be expected of them in the way of service, given the organization of their jobs and their lack of tools for giving practical assistance. It is true that few are master caseworkers; but most agents are kindly persons who evidence common sense and ingenuity in coping. What they can do, given their position and resources, is give advice and occasional referrals, and manage their cases with relative efficiency through the correctional procedures. They are not equipped by the structure with the means to deal with many of the conditions affecting parolee success or failure; as a consequence, agents often do not hear from the parolees about the problems they are facing. Parolees quickly learn which requests are worth bringing to the agents' attention. When parolees told the Study's interviewers about problematic situations, they were almost always asked, "Have you

discussed this with your agent?" And the common response was "What's the use? He couldn't do anything about it anyway."

The previous chapters have documented the structural factors that limit the agent's ability to respond effectively to the parolee's real service needs. He operates alone as the agency in action with his caseload and has limited means to draw on the resources of other personnel when team operation is needed. He cannot possibly develop the entire range of specialized technological competence that may be needed. He often lacks the resources required when the parolee's problems concern practical matters, such as economic need, lack of transportation, or access to normal opportunity systems in the community. His caseload frequently evidences in concentrated form all the social problems common to most persons in a disadvantaged neighborhood. And his contacts with each parolee are structured by the requirements of surveillance rather than by patterns designed to facilitate the discovery and servicing of client needs.

Basic to both these organizational factors is the continuing agency perception of parolees as "nonpersons," wards who are to be done to and for while their behavior is controlled, who are not even qualified to report accurately about what their needs actually are. As a result parole service operations continue to be, except in occasional instances, those of the wise guardian who "knows what is best" for the ward and acts on that formulation, while he lacks an important part of the information he needs in order to decide "what is best." This is a critical disadvantage for the development of a parole service technology of real power, since adequate definition of the problem is an essential first step in effective problem solving.

The Parole Action Study explicitly undertook a "census" of parolee tasks, and of the problems faced in performing those tasks, as these were defined by the parolees out of their own experiences. Here we summarize what the parolees said about their critical problems as one contribution to the planning for services in parole.

THE PAROLEES REPORT

From the many kinds of information the Study's researchers gathered in interviews with more than 350 parolees, the following list of critical issues, of top priority for the parolees, has been summarized. It is not exhaustive and many important practical problems are not mentioned. The list does, however, suggest the directions in which parole service technology should move if it is to provide more supportive conditions for the work of the parolees on their survival tasks.

1. *Economic support during reentry.* Two kinds of financial provisions are needed by most parolees during the reentry period: a basic income, something like unemployment compensation, paid on a weekly basis until the first paycheck is received, to cover maintenance costs during the period of job-hunting; and a lump sum, determined on a case-need basis, to cover "foundation" needs, such as union fees, a car and car insurance, an adequate wardrobe, a timepiece, initial costs in

renting an apartment, and so forth. The parolee's family, when it is available, usually carries the burden of these costs, along with the additional burden of providing emotional support during a difficult period. Many families are drained beyond the limits of their financial capacity by the costs of supporting a noncontributing member; and few have enough funds to provide in full for the minimal reestablishment costs.

2. *Status clearance services.* Few parolees have adequate bonafides at the time of release to permit them to perform such normal economic operations as cashing checks. In addition, many are burdened with serious economic and legal liabilities, incurred before their commitment to prison, which interfere with their ability to perform the tasks of reentry. Many of these legal and economic entanglements require the help of technical experts, such as lawyers and accountants, for resolution; yet most parolees lack the "know how" or finances to secure the appropriate assistance. A relevant program of service to parolees might well include systematic provisions for regularizing the civil status of the parolee.

3. *Emergency service.* Because the parole office is open for only 40 hours a week, and agents are often absent from the office in the field, many parolee emergencies are not dealt with at the time when help could be effective. The parole conditions cover the parolee's life on a 24-hour, seven-day-a-week, basis; and for parolees personal emergencies are no respecters of office hours. At the same time, nothing is more disrupting than an emergency—whether it is an arrest, the death of an out-of-state family member, a car accident, or an eviction from home— either for his success on parole or for his stable adjustment in the community. It seems only reasonable, when the parole agency expects parolees to act under guidance and with permission, that its representatives should be available to assist the parolee when he has to make critical decisions, or is under special duress, in situations with implications for parole success.

4. *Support for parolee employment.* In seeking employment, many parolees have handicaps that have nothing to do with the fact that they are on parole: ethnicity, age, lack of skills, or inadequate education. It is therefore of the greatest importance that, insofar as possible, they not be denied employment on the basis of their record alone. Certain important steps are being taken to open additional employment opportunities to persons with criminal records, but additional changes in state and local policies are needed if the employment market is to be freely open to parolees with appropriate skills. A service program for parolees could usefully take leadership in influencing policy changes in the following areas: civil service employment; trades governed by state licensing boards; companies that subject employees to security checks in order to qualify for government work; and the personnel policies of large-scale enterprises.

5. *Protective arrangements with law enforcement.* Since the agency acts in a position of guardian toward the parolee, it would seem particularly important that it be prepared to act with law enforcement to ensure that its wards are not discriminated against in situations, such as an arrest, that are critical for parole success. Provision of this sort of assistance requiring working policies, established district by district with local police officials, providing that the parole agency will

be involved whenever a parolee is arrested and desires the assistance of an agent. The timing of agency involvement in parolee encounters with law enforcement is critical, since what happens before a parolee is actually booked often determines in large measure the seriousness of the charge and the possibility of release on bail or on own recognizance, as well as the parolee's ability to keep his job or to communicate with his family members and legal adviser. Positive services to parolees, when they are involved with the police or in jail, should be an essential part of a parole service program.

6. *Parolee rights in decision making.* Nothing contributes more directly to the parolee's sense that he is a "nonperson" in the eyes of the agency than his inability to participate in his own behalf during the decision processes connected with preparing a violation report to the Board. Fundamental to the giving of any service are the rules guaranteeing fairness and respect of persons that govern relationships between the agency and its clients; and such rules are abrogated when any person whose personal liberty is in jeopardy is denied full information and an opportunity to act with others in his own defense. Although the parole agency does not control all aspects of revocation decision making, it can design administrative provisions that support fair and rational procedures during its own part in the decision making process. Guarantees of the parolee's rights to complain, and to contest agency decisions, are fundamental to effective parole service.

7. *Reduction of surveillance activities.* All the Study's data suggest that surveillance activities, while consuming much of the agents' time, produce little in the way of protection of the community from criminal behavior. At the same time, parolees report that many surveillance activities actively introduce insecurities into their performance of social survival tasks. A positive program of service in parole would therefore do well to examine the agent's work assignments with the goal of eliminating all surveillance activities that cannot be specifically justified by the facts of the individual case, while freeing agent time for the provision of expert services as they are requested by parolees.

8. *Restoration of civil rights.* The community's unwillingness to accept the parolee as a reintegrated and normally contributing member is most explicitly implemented by his loss of most civil rights during the period of his sentence and the permanent loss of certain civil rights once he has been convicted. The "civil death" provisions in our criminal laws stem from the early days of the common law when they were used to permit the confiscation of offenders' property by the crown; there is no parallel modern rationale for adding the loss of civil rights to the punishment of imprisonment. Nevertheless, modern parolees still suffer the degradation of legal nonpersonhood at the same time that they are asked to perform the responsibilities of normal citizens. A service program for parolees that seeks to restore parolees to self-respect and social adequacy should consider seriously the legal handicaps under which they now operate, and should take measures to reduce the degree to which punishment by imprisonment automatically results in the loss of the rights guaranteed to all other persons by the Constitution.

We noted in the introduction to this report from the parolees that the list is not exhaustive. However, if the parole agency took the first steps necessary to deal with those issues that do appear on the list, it would find itself grappling with many of the system conditions which now most seriously interfere with the parolees' own efforts to reestablish themselves as contributing community members. In the resulting program, those parolees who need additional, individualized help, over and above the support of favorable conditions, could easily be identified; and help could be provided on an individual or group basis as appropriate to the type and volume of the needs so discovered.

IMPLICATIONS FOR AGENCY CHANGE

It is clearly not appropriate for researchers to attempt to describe the service program that might evolve as the parole agency undertook to secure more generally supportive conditions for parolee reintegration into the community. An adequate resolution of any one of the issues outlined above could conceivably lead to important changes in the parole program as it now stands, as well as in the structure of interagency relationships within which the agency must operate. No person outside that structure can prescribe just how such changes should, or could, be made. However, the findings of the Parole Action Study do warrant certain suggestions as to first steps leading to the technological development of parole services. These suggestions are offered with considerable understanding—gained from experience in attempting to institute organizational change—of the difficulties attending any such enterprise.

1. *An ongoing needs-census.* Finding means for identifying on a regular basis both the top priority problems of the general parolee population, as well as the special problems of subgroups, would seem an essential first step in developing a parole problem-solving technology with an array of different kinds of strategies. The parolees themselves should be formally involved in the process of need-identification, in order to correct for the inevitable tendency of service workers to define as client needs what are actually the problems of the workers; and to make sure that problems that are normally not brought to the attention of agents, and that require more highly organized strategies than the agent is able to implement by himself, are properly reported.

2. *Organization by caseloads.* Serious consideration should be given to the implications of the present organization of agent work by caseloads for effective problem solving in parole. The caseload pattern was designed specifically for surveillance as it has been traditionally conceived. As the primary service mechanism it is extremely limited. It relies primarily on a counseling strategy, which is useful for individualizing parolees and for dealing with personal factors, but has minimal capacity to influence the conditions which may exacerbate the personal difficulties beyond the possibility of resolution. A revision of the organizational patterns for service would not necessarily eliminate the value of ongoing relationships between individual parolees and agents, when such are necessary for specific tasks, since it is possible to combine a modified form of caseload assign-

ment for certain purposes with specialized assignments and team operations in different problem-solving strategies. A change in this direction would greatly increase the flexibility with which agency resources are made available in response to need, as well as the ease with which strategies other than individual counseling could be implemented.

3. *The involvement of administration in service.* Many of the system problems experienced by parolees can be addressed only through strategies involving persons in positions of higher authority in the agency. Such problems usually concern the policies of agencies and governmental units outside the control of the parole authority, and often affect classes of parolees that cut across agent, district, or regional caseloads. The strategies for tackling such problems imply the use of a variety of community organization, public relations, interagency planning, and legal techniques, all of which necessarily involve upper policy makers in the action. Both parolees and agents can become valuable members of teams responsible for information-gathering and for certain kinds of action in strategies that are led by administrative officials. The use of teams that cut across hierarchical levels, in which each participant performs according to his competence, is a primary, and often the most effective, means to achieve participant management. It also permits the development of much more sophisticated and powerful strategies, since it relates upper administrative personnel more closely and accurately to service needs, and adds their skills to the pool of human resources available for service action.

4. *New roles for parolees.* Each of the organizational changes suggested above depends in large measure on the explicit recognition of parolees as active partners in the work of parole, capable of contributing to agency problem solving wherever its actions impinge directly on their experiences. The suggestions, therefore, imply the development of various new formal roles for parolees in the agency, not simply as "aides" to individual agents, but as *consumers* who use the voluntary request for service as a vote on service relevance and effectiveness, as *members of advisory boards* to administrators at various levels, as *co-workers* in various community organization endeavors, and as *organizers* of their own resources in behalf of general services to parolees. Raising the status of the parolee vis-à-vis the agency would do much both to raise the status of the parolee in the community and to diminish the intensity of the role conflict now experienced by the parolee as he attempts to be both the adequate "man in the community" and the dependent "parolee in the agency."

How far any parole agency will be permitted to go in elevating the parolee's status within the agency and the community remains problematical. The caseload mechanism is valued by many criminal justice officials as a primary tool of surveillance, and therefore as necessary for the protection of the public from parolees. Community members expect the agent to spread stigma by alerting those who deal with parolees of possible danger to themselves. When a parolee is arrested the police expect the agent to act as a supportive law enforcement officer, rather than as an advocate in behalf of the parolee. And many of the system conditions, which from the parolee's point of view are handicaps to reintegration, are seen by the public as properly a continuation of the punishment the parolee earned when he committed his offense. It may be that one agency cannot organize itself for effective action both as a protector of the public against parolees and as a service agency in their behalf. But that formulation of the issue cannot be fully supported until parole agencies with strong service orientations push the development of a service technology capable of tackling system barriers to reintegration as far as the community will permit.

All the findings of the Parole Action Study indicate that it is both foolish and wasteful for the community to open prison doors with one hand and maintain barriers to normal integration with the other. The consequence of such a policy is to establish the parole agency as a "holding" enterprise, responsible for overseeing an enclave of disenfranchised and handicapped persons within the community. It seems clear that, if parole agencies are to fulfill their claims to rehabilitating parolees through service, they must confront the community with the question "rehabilitation for what?", spelling out explicitly the community's share in the task of restoring parolees to normal contributing membership in the community.

An essential first step is to restore parolees to the status of "men in the agency" and, with their help, to formulate in specific terms the necessary conditions for their operation as "men in the community." Once it is clear what community and agency provisions are essential to support the transition of parolees from inmates in prison to established normals in the community, a service program can be designed that has some chance of becoming both relevant and effective for reintegration.

SUPERVISION

The ultimate test of probation and parole is found in the community to which convicted offenders are released under some form of conditional freedom. Although supervision by the probation or parole officer is the operational component of probation and parole best known, most visible and of greatest interest to the public, accurate evaluation of the effect of supervision remains a very elusive factor in terms of analysis and review.

Defendents are normally placed on probation either by having the imposition of sentence suspended by the court or by having a specific sentence imposed and its execution suspended. In the latter case, a sentence (for example, 5 years imprisonment or 6 months in the county jail) is imposed on the defendent, but its execution is suspended and he is conditionally released on probation. If a violation of probation occurs, the sentence originally imposed may be ordered or a lesser sentence may be given, but more severe sanctions than those originally ordered cannot be applied. In the sentencing situation in which a specific sentence was not ordered, a violation of probation may result in any sentence being given which might have been imposed at the time of the original sentencing; thus, all of the sentencing options available to the court when probation was ordered are still available if probation is violated. This sentencing distinction, although significant in the violation of probation, is of lesser importance in terms of the supervision process.

Although philosophically and operationally similar to probation supervision, parole supervision has some unique features closely related to the characteristics and experiences of the parolee population. Not the least of these is the rather obvious fact that the parolee has been absent from the community for an extended period of time ranging from perhaps as little as one year through two or three decades of confinement. During that time frame, there has been change—not only in the inmate/parolee, but everywhere. The offender released from an institution finds that nothing is the same as when he entered the institution—not family or personal relationships, not the community, not society. Adjustment to these changes is difficult and it appears that the longer the period of confinement, the more difficult the adjustment to the free world. The granting of probation and parole attaches conditions to the continued freedom of the probationer and parolee and these conditions are generally the standards against which that freedom and definitions of successful and unsuccessful probation and parole are measured.

Although supervision has both assistance and control elements, there are numerous other variables that influence the supervision process. These include caseload size, types of probation and parole officers, offenders, treatments, and the social systems within probation and parole agencies to include varying administrative styles. Also significant are the law-enforcement, judicial, and correctional decisionmakers and their decisions, which determine input and outgo in probation and parole, the administrative organization of caseloads, the community itself, and cost and political considerations. These many factors make supervision exceedingly complex and the writings in this section should demonstrate the complexity of supervision practice.

This section begins with the editors conceptually examining the caseloads into which probationers and parolees are normally grouped for supervision by the probation and parole agency. We follow with an article by Carl B. Klockars, who examines four elements in a theory of probation supervision, including the working philosophy of the officer, the organizational context in which the officer finds himself, the legal and logical definitions of revocation of probation, and the psychological approach of the probationer. In a third article, former parole officer, Richard Dembo, examines the relationships between orientation and activities of the parole officer on three dimensions—the parole officer's conception of the parolee, his view of the purpose of parole, and his belief in the method of rule or condition enforcement.

The Conditions of Probation utilized in the United States Courts are provided and attorneys Carl H. Imlay and Charles R. Glasheen offer considerable insight into the conditions and revocation of probation, focusing upon "undesirable conditions"—those that either may be difficult to enforce, may not have any relationship to the rehabilitation process, may violate constitutional rights, or have been arbitrarily imposed for punitive reasons. Eugene C. Dicerbo, a longtime chief probation officer in the Federal system, deals with the difficult question of when probation (and implicitly, parole) should be revoked.

The Certificate of Parole utilized by the United States Board of Parole is presented and Nat R. Arluke, a parole administrator with years of experience in New Jersey, summarizes the wide variety of parole rules utilized in the United States. Finally, Ralph C. Brendes provides an overview of the important interstate probation and parole compact.

24
Caseloads: Some Conceptual Models

ROBERT M. CARTER AND LESLIE T. WILKINS

There may be some doubt that crime and delinquency are rapidly increasing in the United States. There can, however, be no doubt that crime and delinquency are outgrowing our present capacity to deal effectively with them. This situation will undoubtedly continue as long as the mounting problems of crime and delinquency are addressed by conventional models utilizing the principles and traditions of the past.

In corrections, we try to cope with the problem by taking additional measures, but tend to focus on providing traditional services to the increased numbers of offenders processed through the systems. It seems probable that changes in corrections are likely to have a "more-of-the-same" quality—increased probation and parole staff and prison personnel, more bastille-like institutions, and expanded, but essentially similar programs.

We cannot continue, however, to employ additional personnel indefinitely, build new institutions, or recreate established programs. The trend in corrections has been quite consistent—to create more of what already exists and to depend upon past experience[1] without much attempted innovation. In the main, our

SOURCE. Unpublished manuscript prepared at the School of Criminology, University of California, Berkeley, 1968.

[1] For an example of tradition in corrections see Carter, Robert M. and Takagi, Paul T. *"Persistent Problems and Challenges in Correctional Supervision,"* Criminologica, November-December, 1967, **Vol 5,** Number 3.

current and planned correction procedures are determined neither by imaginative and creative thinking supported by the utilization of available technology nor by other new knowledge in the social and behavioral sciences.

CASELOAD SIZE

The purpose of this paper is to examine the area of caseloads in correctional supervision. A review of recent relevant research points to the futility and frustration engendered by continued "numbers-research," that is, the "proper" ratio of presentence investigations to cases under supervision or "optimal" caseload size. We propose that explicit models for caseload supervision can provide a new perspective for viewing caseload management.

A brief summary of four research studies—three relating to parole in California and one to probation and parole in the Federal system (each, in part "numbers-oriented") provides a background against which the necessity for the construction of caseload models becomes apparent.[2]

BACKGROUND SUMMARY

The Special Intensive Parole Unit (SIPU) studies by the California Department of Corrections began in 1953. Phase I of SIPU, involving 4300 men established experimental caseloads of 15 parolees and control caseloads of 90. The 15-men caseloads were supervised intensively for the first three months following release and were then reassigned to regular 90-man caseloads. A review of the California data did not show significantly better parole adjustment for those in smaller caseloads.

Phase II of SIPU commenced in 1956 and involved some 6200 parolees. The experimental caseloads were increased to 30 and length of stay in these caseloads was increased to six months before reassignment. At the end of Phase II, significant difference in outcome were again absent.

Phase III of SIPU was undertaken in 1957. It had 35- and 72-unit caseloads and involved some 3700 parolees. The first findings of Phase III reflected somewhat better performance of the 35-man caseloads, particularly for certain types of offenders, namely, the medium-risk category. One of the important findings which emerged was that the effect of caseload size was not a simple function of number but of the interaction of several factors, including types of parolees and possibly types of agents.

Phase IV of SIPU, beginning in 1959, had several components, including a study of high-risk category parolees and an agent-parolee interaction study. The latter project made use of a research design which placed agents and parolees

---

[2] For a recent review of caseload research, see S. Adams, "Some Findings From Correctional Caseload Research," *Federal Probation,* December, 1967.

together in patterns which had both logical and empirical justification. Thus, "low-maturity" parolees[3] were matched with external-approach (control orientated) parole agents, and "high-maturity" cases were supervised by internal-approach (casework oriented) agents. Caseload sizes were reduced to 15 and 30 for the experimental group caseloads as compared with 70 for the control group caseloads. Phase IV findings indicated that the only recorded variable which made a difference in parole outcome was the amount of time the agent devoted to supervision. Further, the 15-man caseloads performed no better than the 30-man caseloads.

A 1959 variant of the SIPU studies involved narcotics offenders in the Narcotics Treatment and Control Project (NTCP). Here 30-man caseloads were compared with 70-man caseloads. The results of two initial phases of the project were inconclusive with respect to caseload size. A two-year third phase of the NTCP research involved 15- and 45-man experimental caseloads in tests against 70-man caseloads. No differences were found between 15- and 45-man caseloads, which tends to confirm the findings of Phase IV of SIPU, although the experimental group performed better than the control group in the 70-man caseloads.

In 1965, the California Department of Corrections moved into a parole work unit program based upon estimates of the needs of parolees and the time required for parole officers to provide appropriate services. Here, emphasis was was shifted from *number of cases* to *amount of time* required to meet parolee needs. A three-fold classification system was developed along the traditional lines of maximum, medium, and minimum supervision. Maximum cases were allotted about 5 units of time, medium 3 units, and minimum about 1 unit. Parole officers were to supervise 120 time-units of work, that is, caseloads of about 25 maximum risk cases, 40 medium risk cases, 120 minimum risk cases, or some combination thereof. Some 6000 parolees were involved in the work unit program; 6000 other parolees were supervised in 72-man caseloads. During the first six months of the programs, work unit parolees did no better than conventionally supervised parolees, but in the second six months, the work unit parolees performed better in several categories, some of which may be equated directly with cost-savings.

The San Francisco Project, a study of federal probation and parole, began in 1964 under a National Institute of Mental Health grant to the University of California. Four types of caseloads, with probationers and institution releasees randomly assigned to each, provided varying intensities of supervision ranging from minimum to intensive, and varying caseload sizes from 25 to 100. Preliminary data from this study indicate that the offenders assigned to varying size caseloads have violation rates well within those which would be expected of federal offenders under normal levels of supervision. These data are of particular significance when it is observed that the outcomes of supervision (violation rates) among the four types of caseloads are almost identical despite enormous variation in attention given the cases as measured by the number of contacts by probation and parole officers.

[3] *Ibid.*

In summary, the various experimentation on caseload size and performance of adult offenders on probation or parole has produced results which are far from encouraging. It appears certain that mere manipulation of caseload size is irrelevant to success or failure under correctional supervision—that is, the "numbers game"—be the number 15, 25, 30, 45, 50, 70, 90 or 100—is not significant in contrast to the nature of the supervision experience, the classification of offenders, officers, and types of treatment, and the social systems of the correctional agency.

THE NEED FOR MODELS AND SIMPLE EXAMPLES

The data which have been presented thus far suggest the need to create, make explicit, and examine various models for correctional supervision. As far as we know, supervision models have not previously been constructed, and the simple examples which will be presented should be taken to represent no more than a stimulation to complex analyses.

The initial problem in our model construction is the portrayal of the offender population. Since there is variation among offenders, whether the characteristic examined is height or weight, education, or prior criminal record, the distribution may be seen as taking the form of a curve. On some characteristics, this curve might be statistically "normal," on other characteristics, it may be skewed to the left or right. For our purposes, let us envision the offender population as comprising a normal curve as shown on Chart 1. The possibility of its shape being skewed left or right is indicated by the broken-line curves labeled "A" and "B."

Since the conventional method of assigning offenders to caseloads is motivated in part by administrative desires to maintain "balanced" caseloads, and as a result case 1 is assigned to officer A, case 2 to officer B, 3 to C, 4 to A, 5 to B, 6 to C, and so on, we find that each officer receives for supervision, offenders who comprise a caseload that is a miniature reproduction of the total offender curve, *whatever its real shape*. This conventional model is illustrated in Chart 2.

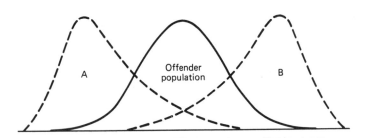

Chart 1   *Offender distribution curve.*

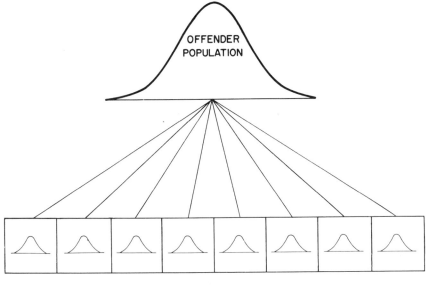

Chart 2   *Conventional supervision model.*

The conventional model illustrated is not, of course, found in most field operations, for probation and parole agencies normally consider the extent of the geographic area to be covered by their agents. In general terms, caseload sizes are equated with geography: the principle applied is that as the supervision area increases, caseload size decreases. Thus, the probation or parole officer working in a densely populated metropolitan area will have a smaller geographic area and a larger number of cases than his rural or suburban counterpart who has a greater area to cover.

Chart 3 illustrates the conventional supervision model with geographical considerations. It is to be noted that the supervising officers again receive offenders who comprise a miniature reproduction of the total offender curve. It is, of course, possible that significant differences exist—or that separate curves exist—for urban, suburban, and rural offenders.

Another model encountered in probation and parole supervision includes the single-factor specialized caseloads. Based upon a single factor or characteristic, such as sex, age, high violence-potential, or drug use, certain offenders are removed from the general population for placement in specialized caseloads. Thus, female offenders, or drug addicts are grouped into single caseloads for supervision purposes and, on occasion, a distinct treatment or approach is utilized for these caseloads. In the main, however, it appears that there is simply an organization of some caseloads around a simple characteristic. The single-factor specialized caseloads are illustrated in Chart 4.

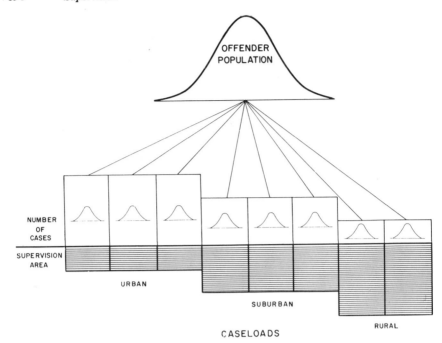

Chart 3   *Conventional supervision model with geographic considerations.*

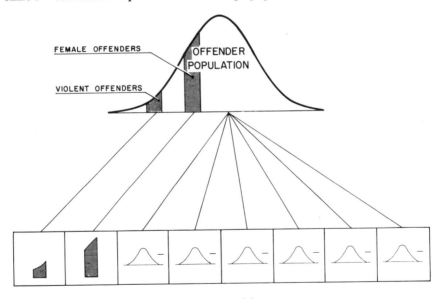

Chart 4   *Single-factor specialized caseloads.*

It is important to note, however, that the removal of a group of offenders from the general offender population on the basis of a single factor *does not* actually remove a portion of the curve as illustrated in Chart 4. Rather, there is an isolation of a grouping of offenders, who themselves constitute a separate curve, probably skewed right or left depending upon the characteristic measured. Female offenders, for example, are not a distinct and separate portion of the total offender curve, but rather comprise a cross-section of the total offender curve as portrayed in Chart 5. One of the dilemmas for treatment posed by these single factor classification caseloads is that the caseloads are not made homogeneous simply because all offenders assigned to them share a single characteristic such as sex or history of drug use.

Let us briefly examine the supervision model which serves as the basis for the numbers game. Chart 6 illustrates the arrangement of caseloads for a probation or parole agency providing supervision for 700 offenders. These caseloads are arranged in two different fashions—70 and 100 offenders per caseload. If the conventional method of assigning offenders is utilized so that caseloads are balanced, the only difference between the 70 and 100 offender caseloads is number. Each caseload receives a miniature distribution of the total offender population: there is no classification by treatment needs, types of offenders, types of probation

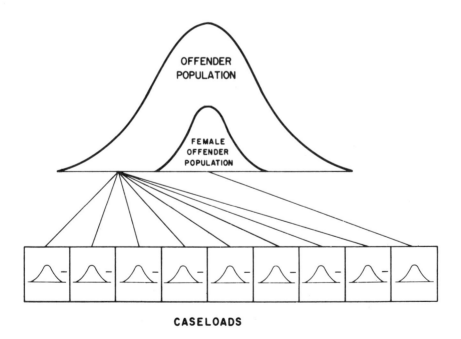

CASELOADS

Chart 5   *Single-factor specialized caseloads.*

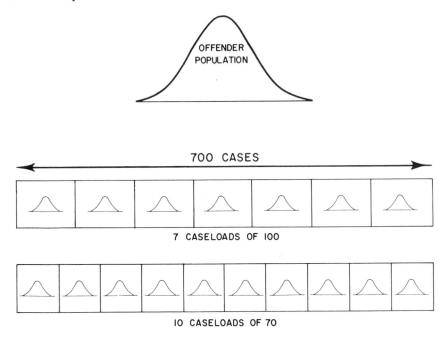

Chart 6   *The "number game" supervision model.*

or parole officers, or any other consideration. This may well explain some of the difficulty, indeed futility, of attempting to produce changes in the outcome of supervision by mere manipulation of caseload size.

SLIGHTLY COMPLEX MODELS

We have seen the development of multi-factor classification tables for offenders. Often called expectancy or actuarial devices, these tables are created from various combinations of factors and predict, to a greater of lesser extent, success or failure under probation and parole supervision. In a sense, these experience tables attempt to make more explicit the "experienced opinions" of probation and parole officers, administrators, and others charged with decision-making functions in the correctional process. It should be noted that these various tables are geared toward predicting the outcome of supervision—in terms of success or failure and only infrequently for determining the needs of the offenders during the period of supervision.

Chart 7 reflects a model curve for an offender population distributed along a numerical scale from 0 to 100 based upon any combination of factors. In this

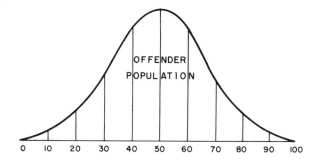

Chart 7   *Multifactor classification curve.*

model, the offenders toward the "0" end of the curve are considered low-success potential, those toward the "100" end, are high-success potential.

This model of the offender population can serve as a basis for the development of caseload management principles, even thought it does not concern itself with types of officers or treatments, or considerations of the offender population other than those specifically measured. A multi-factor classification of offenders and their distribution along a normal or some other shaped curve can be meaningfully utilized only if we are willing to move away from what might be called a "horizontal" organization for caseload management, both for the offender distribution and for caseloads. The supervision process may be more meaningful if we constructed and operated from "vertical" models and multi-factor classification.

The "vertical" model requires that the offender distribution curve, arranged by some multi-factor classification, and the organization of caseloads, be "turned on end" as shown in Chart 8. Assuming a total offender population of 1000 with 15 probation and parole officers for supervision, this model is based upon the view that not all offenders need equal amounts or intensities of supervision and the need for the creation of varying size caseloads which allow for varying intensities or types of supervision. The high-success potential or low-need offenders are grouped into larger caseloads; the low-success potential or high-need offenders are grouped into smaller caseloads. The high-low need and high-low success potential elements are estimated by the multi-factor classification.

In Chart 8, twenty-five percent of the high-success potential/low-need offenders have been grouped into a large caseload of 250. Ten percent of the low-success potential/high-need offenders have been grouped into small caseloads of 25. The remaining offenders have been grouped into two other size caseloads on the same potential and need criteria. These numbers are for illustrative purposes only; the operational organization of such caseloads would be administratively determined, in part by the number of offenders to be supervised, officers available for supervision, and the type of the offender distribution curve.

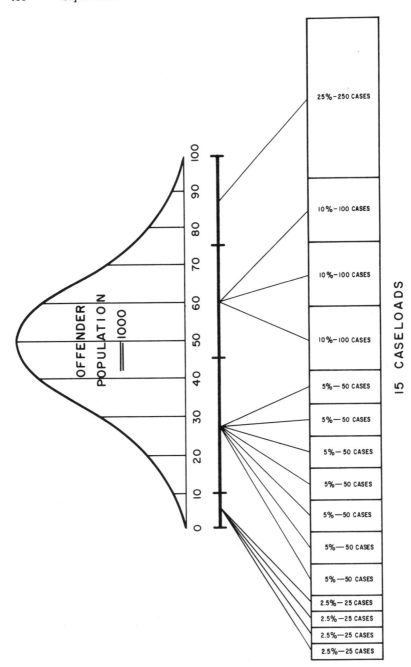

Chart 8   *Multifactor classification and vertical caseloads.*

We are now in a position to compare the conventional model with a "vertical model," in both instances using a 1000 offender population and 15 probation or parole officers. This is shown in Chart 9.

A number of problems emerge from the suggested "vertical" model of supervision as a replacement for the conventional "horizontal" models. The most important relates, of course, to the effectiveness of the suggested model as measured by a number of variables including, but not limited to, outcome of supervision and cost. There variables are directly involved with two basic premises of corrections—the protection of society and the best interests of the offender. We must inquire as to the appropriate maximum and minimum size of caseloads, and to types of probation and parole officers who provide supervision, and there must be concern for the types and nature of the supervision experience. The factors utilized for classification must be examined to determine their appropriateness and perhaps to distinguish classification for the purposes of treatment and classification for the predicted outcome of supervision.

In summary, we have proposed another way of viewing caseload management and probation and parole supervision. Whether the "vertical" model is indeed a better conceptualization of supervision remains to be tested.

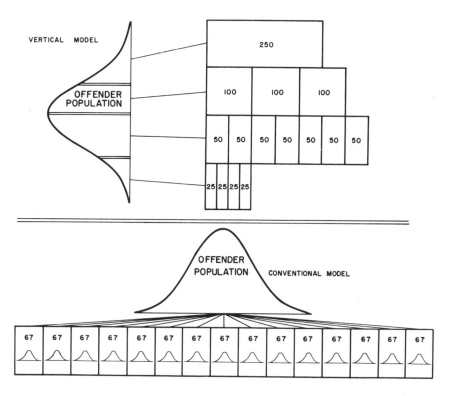

Chart 9 *Conventional versus vertical model: 1000 cases—15 officers.*

25

A Theory of Probation Supervision

CARL B. KLOCKARS, JR.

As the literature of probation demonstrates, a thoroughly eclectic discipline possesses an almost infinite capacity to generate the most diverse forms of theory. Probabation students' published attentions to supervision include everything from after-dinner speeches to decision models. Speeches tell the reader a good deal about the speaker and decision models tell a good deal about the officer, but neither seems to capture what probation supervision is.[1] Decision models cannot be considered inappropriate since knowledge of decision-making is certainly of legitimate scientific concern. The speeches, as well as the dozens of articles which discuss the question of what probation supervision "ought to be," can be sympathetically interpreted as teaching theories. One cannot object to the treatment of probation problems at this level either. The vast majority of improvements in probation services has resulted, not from the scientific demonstrations of efficiency, but rather through the efforts of moral men from Augustus through Charles Chute and Rufus Cook to those who wish to enter the field with "oughts" today.

SOURCE. Reprinted with special permission of (the author and) the *Journal of Criminal Law, Criminology and Police Science,* **63** (4), pp. 550–557. Copyright © 1972 by Northwestern University School of Law.
[1] Because what passes for probation supervision theory is so diverse, we shall not attempt any history of such efforts here. The best article on the subject is Lewis Diana's highly critical *What is Probation?,* 51 Crim.L.C. & P.S. 189 (1960). It has received little attention and less rebuttal. A slightly watered-down version of it appears in Probation and Parole 39–56 (R. Carter & L. Wilkins eds. 1970).

Our intention is to provide a description and analysis of the standard form of probation supervision.[2] To do so four elements must be considered. The first is the working philosophy of the officer—the way he sees his job and duties. The second is the organizational context in which the officer finds himself. The third is the legal and logical definition of revocation, and the fourth is the psychological approach of the probationer. It is our observation that each of these four components responds to movement in the other. As a result, any theory of probation supervision must not only cite each of these components but also specify the nature and mechanics of their interaction.

WORKING PHILOSOPHY OF THE PROBATION OFFICER

The first and broadest component of the theory of probation supervision is the role which the officer sets for himself and the logic and rationale he develops to explain what he does or what he ought to do. So pervasive is this component of probation supervision, it gives particular warp and depth to all other components. Our observations yield a typology of probation officer[3] which falls roughly between the thesis, "Probation is not Casework,"[4] and the antithesis, "Probation is Casework."[5]

The Law Enforcers[6]

At the probation-is-not-casework pole we find officers who stress the legal authority and enforcement aspects of their role. Of prime importance to such officers are (a.) the court order ("His only job is to help the offender comply with the order of the court.");[7] (b.) authority ("I will fully execute that authority but only that authority delegated to me by the court.");[8] (c.) decision-making power

[2] The theory of probation supervision presented here was developed during two years of partici-pant observation research in a large metropolitan probation office. Nearly one hundred officers supervised more than seven thousand probationers and parolees. The theory is a revised and expanded section of a restricted circulation monograph which the author composed for the department: Make Believe Bureaucracy: A Case Study in Probation (Mimeo., 1970). All investigations were made with the full knowledge and consent of the department administration.

[3] The typology we present is naturally a compromise with reality. We do not pretend that it captures all of what any officer is. Nevertheless certain characteristics of officer behavior and rationale can be separated and rendered meaningful for the ends intended here.

[4] Blake, *Probation is not Casework,* 12 Fed.Probation 54 (June 1948).

[5] Meeker, *Probation is Casework,* 12 Fed.Probation 51 (June 1948).

[6] The terminology here is based in part upon titles and descriptions suggested for police officers in R. Taft & R. England, Criminology 321 (1964). Our categories are also similar to those suggested by Ohlin, Pivin & Pappenfort, *Major Dilemmas of the Social Worker in Probation and Parole,* 2 National Probation & Parole Assoc. J. 211 (1956).

[7] Hardman, *The Function of the Probation Officer,* 24 Fed.Probation 4 (Sept. 1960). Hardman adds that he will "defend this definition before the parole board, the supreme court, or the angels in heaven."

[8] Ibid. at 7.

("Once I have made a decision, I will steadfastly resist all client efforts to alter my decision by threats, tantrums, seduction, illness, etc.");[9] (d.) officer responsibility for public safety ("It is the criterion of safety for society that will determine for the parole officer whether the level of adjustment achieved is acceptable or whether he is so dangerous to society that he must be removed from its midst and returned to prison.");[10] and often (e.) police work ("What it simmers down to is police work. We're the policemen back of the agencies.").[11]

While these characteristics are found in the officer at this pole of our typology, we must add that the philosophies and rationales which cause certain officers to gravitate to this pole are all too easily relegated to a "junior G-man"[12] model. One may find officers at this pole with examined philosophies which dictate that firmness, authority, and rule abidance are essentials of social life and ought to be enforced during the probation period. What will concern us however is that their behavior is unshakably law- and rule-enforcing.

The Time Servers

For the purposes of our typology, time-serving officers are nearly the functional equivalent of the law enforcers. They comprise that category of probation officers who find no law-enforcing or casework vocation in probation. Instead, they see their jobs as having certain requirements to be fulfilled until retirement. They have little aspiration to improve their skills; they are not likely to attend seminars or training institutes, nor do they belong to professional associations. Their conduct on the job is rule-abiding and their job responsibilities are met minimally but methodically. Rules and regulations are upheld but unexamined. They don't make the rules; they just work there.

The Therapeutic Agent

At the other pole of officer role conception is the officer who considers himself a therapeutic agent. Here, the officer's role is emphasized in the administration of a form of treatment[13] artfully "introducing the probationer to a better way of

---

[9] Ibid.

[10] G. Giardini, The Parole Process 265 (1959).

[11] Officer opinion cited in Diana, supra note 1, at 199.

[12] An epithet common among officers studied by P. Takagi, Evaluation Systems and Adaptations in a Formal Organization: A Case Study of a Parole Agency 116 (unpublished Ph.D. dissertation at Stanford University, 1967). Social casework has only recently discovered the meaning of "authority" which sociology has classically held for it. As a turning point, one might suggest Fink's *Authority in the Correctional Process,* 25 Fed.Probation 34 (Sept. 1961). See also D. Dressler, Practice and Theory of Probation and Parole 170 (1969) for a recent attempt to redefine authority in such a way as to make it palatable to those who had learned it as a synonym for "authoritarianism."

[13] I have chosen to reproduce the rhetoric of the therapeutic agent to dramatize both the inseparability of form and content and the tenacious grasp on a sophmoric identity which such an acrobatic rhetoric represents. A leading social casework theorist expresses this exactly as she shares with us some insights into "process":

life"[14] by the "motivation of patterns of behavior which are constructive,"[15] by "giving support and guidance to those who are unable to solve their problems by themselves,"[16] and by "providing an opportunity to work through his ambivalent feelings."[17] This is accomplished through the use of knowledge of the offender history "analyzed in terms of psychological, physiological, and social factors,"[18] "day-by-day analyses of recorded interviews (which) develop the kind of skill needed in the evaluation of the individual considered for probation,"[19] and the loan of the officer's "own ego to the client's in the perception and appraisal of reality."[20] Charles Shireman has attempted to summarize this working philosophy as follows:

1. We take conscious pains in our every contact with the offender to demonstrate our concern about him and our respect for him as a human being.
2. We seize every opportunity to help the offender come to understand the nature of the shared, problem-solving, helping process by actually experiencing it.
3. We recognize, bring into the open, and deal directly with the offender's negative attitudes toward us as the representatives of social authority.
4. We "partialize" the total life problem confronting the offender.
5. We help the individual perceive the degree to which his behavior has and will result in his own unhappiness.[21]

We find further that officers of the therapeutic agent type are likely to belong to professional associations, actively campaign for recognition of the professional status of probation officers, display various diplomas and certificates testifying to their skills, and speak in the argot of social casework wherever possible.

The Synthetic Officer

The fourth and final officer type in our classification is distinguished by his recognition of both the treatment and law enforcement components of the proba-

---

In short, working from a process base the social worker conceives all phenomena as unique within classes or categories, as characterized by continuous change and direction toward an end, as embodying potential for such change which itself shifts in the course of time. He uses a process, a professional social work process, to affect processes, that is, the life process of an individual, group, or community, in order that the processes affected may have the best possible chance for self-realization in relation to a purpose which has brought worker and clientele together. R. Smalley, Theory for Social Work Practice 130 (1967).

[14] Glover, *Probation: The Art of Introducing the Probationer to a Better Way of Life,* 15 Fed.Probation 8 (Sept. 1951).

[15] Gronewald, *Casework in Probation,* 39 Prison J. 45 (Oct. 1959).

[16] Ibid.

[17] Ibid.

[18] Ibid. at 43.

[19] Ibid.

[20] Ibid. at 45.

[21] Shireman, *Casework in Probation and Parole: Some Considerations in Diagnosis and Treatment,* 27 Fed.Probation 51 (June 1963).

tion officer's role. His attempts at supervision reflect his desire to satisfy the arguments of both the therapeutic and law-enforcing agents. Thus, he sets for himself the active task of combining the paternal, authoritarian and judgmental with the therapeutic. In so doing, he may unknowingly solve what is alleged to be the classical dilemma of corrections. The most common way of phrasing this dilemma is that, for therapeutic purposes, the probation officer must require the probationer to "tell all" but must also recognize that revelation of the wrong sort may result in revocation.[22] Clearly, a central issue of probation supervision is the treatment-control dilemma and its resolution in the revocation decision.

REVOCATION AND THE LOGIC OF TREATMENT

Straightforward confrontation with the question of revocation should define a strategy of supervision, clarify it, and set its boundaries. For the law enforcer and time server the logic is simple—revocation should be recommended whenever the rules of probation are violated. The simplicity and directness of this answer are not available for those with a faith in probation as treatment.

Extensions of the logic of treatment demand not only that probation itself be a treating process but also that the officer be provided with therapeutic alternatives. Such a portrait of corrections is painted when probation is treatment under supervision in society, when parole is more restricted training for social adjustment, and when prison is genuinely rehabilitative treatment which prepares the prisoner for reentry into society. When added to this portrait of corrections, such conceptions as the halfway house suggest an even smoother curve.

This, of course, is not the case. Probation cannot operate on the assumption of the rehabilitative nature of the prison. Instead it must operate on the assumption of the destructive nature of prisons, and, if it wishes to consider itself a treatment agency, probation must do so with the simultaneous recognition of nontherapeutic alternatives. In short, revocation must be viewed as the boundary of treatment and the beginning of its compromise.

Arguments to the contrary assert that penal institutions need not be treatment facilities *in se* but may be considered so *per se.* In a variation on a behaviorist theme revocation becomes a sanction, probation and parole become rewards, and the entire correctional process emerges as an extended shaping mechanism. This argument, however, is unconvincing. Few institutions, if any, have been able to demonstrate that their inmates profited from their stay there. On the other hand, modern penology has shown that institutionalization has a high probability of damaging the inmate and returning him to society in worse condition than when he entered. Even if the institutional experience itself is harmless, the loss of employment, separation from family, and label of convict are most likely to be harmful.

Recognition of the boundaries and compromise of treatment at revocation forces those who believe in treatment to adopt a single, consistent rationale for

[22] See Ohlin, Pivin & Pappenfort, supra note 6, at 211-25.

revocation. That rationale is that the probationer is dangerous to himself or others. Considering the nature of penal institutions, no other rationale is consistent with a faith in treatment.

Such a conception of revocation bears double-edged consequences for probation. While this conception is predicated upon a faith in probation as treatment, those who hold such a faith must advocate probation even when, in treatment, it is not successful. A treatment strategy of probation with the conception of revocation we have suggested must also provide the officer with both power to guide and control the probationer during treatment and definitions of desired conduct which direct and inform him. In addition, this power can only be acquired from revocation as a threat which will usually remain unfulfilled.

Probably much probation work is conducted by threats of revocation. Our observations confirm that threats are regularly used and carried out by time servers and law enforcers. However, as a strategy for the therapeutic or synthetic officers, threats seem to dissolve quickly because with the single "clear-and-present-danger" exception they are not carried out. Nevertheless, for the majority of probationers who do not seem to break the rules of probation anyway the simple threat-of-revocation strategy probably works as well as any other.

The central problem which remains is the resolution of genuine treatment and control in an effective supervision strategy. Our observations suggest that such a resolution does exist. This resolution is removed from the boundaries of revocation. It gains its strength from the definition of the officer-probationer-department triad. It is slow to degenerate and operates on the medium of exchange.[23]

A THEORY OF PROBATION SUPERVISION

The strategy of exchange is only implicitly understood by officers who employ it. Nevertheless, it seems to be applied by all officers of the synthetic type. We know of no other form of supervision in which the synthetic officers' aspirations can be satisfied. Let us first present diagrammatically the parties involved in probation supervision:

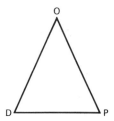

Figure 1   *Supervision triad.*

[23] The notation used in our theory is roughly appropriated from F. Heider, *The Psychology of Interpersonal Relations* (1958).

wherein O represents the officer; P, the probationer; and D, the department. Let us now look sequentially at the way in which the bonds of the triad are completed.

The Initial Interview

The first meeting between the probationer and the officer serves to define the components of their relationship. It defines not only the restrictions which will be placed upon the probationer, but also suggests the medium of exchange through which exceptions may be sought. The initial interview regularly includes an explanation of the rules and regulations by which the probationer is expected to live. These may range from requirements such as seeking permission to marry or obtain a pilot's license, to technical violations such as using alcohol or frequenting places of probable criminal association.[24] In the department which we studied, many of these rules may be printed and distributed to the probationer. Here, the probation officer functions as an officer of the court. Our triadic diagram is now rendered as:

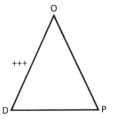

Figure 2 *Supervision triad.*

indicating the officer's responsibility to the department and its regulations.

The second substantive component of the initial interview is an extension of aid, assistance, and guidance by the officer to the probationer. Statements and assurances such as "I am here to help you," "Your problems and difficulties are my responsibilities as well," and offers of referral for employment, family, medical, or psychological counselling characterize this component. While our observations reveal a wide variation in the style of such offers, all are intended to show interest and give assistance. Consequently, we may now complete the officer-probationer bond in our diagram as:

---

[24] Arluke, *A Summary of Parole Rules: Thirteen Years Later,* 15 Crime & Delinquency 267 (1969).

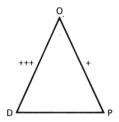

Figure 3   *Supervision triad.*

if the officer is able to convince the probationer of the sincerity of his interest.

At this point we have not yet completed the bond between the department and the probationer. It is the most critical bond in the triad because its completion resolves the treatment-control dilemma. As we have suggested above, the problem of the synthetic officer is that he bears two compelling but patently inconsistent roles, one or both of which are denied by other officer types. Such a problem is authentic and our initial observations and interviews in the department were bent upon articulating it. Remarkably, in our search for the classical dilemma of corrections, logically expressed in the role of the probation officer, we found no evidence of its existence. Watching, participating in, and discussing case relationships suggested to us that for probation it was a logical reality but a sociological fiction. The synthetic officer is able to dispose of it by including a managed reality of the "department" in the case relationship. In order to clarify this last statement, we report the responses of two synthetic officers to the question, "How can you tell a probationer that he should bring his problems to you and tell you honestly about the difficulties he is having when he knows that if you find out too much you can lock him up?"

Officer One: "I tell my probationers that I'm here to help them, to get them a job, and whatever else I can do. But I tell them too that I have a job to do and a family to support and that if they get too far off the track, I can't afford to put my job on the line for them. I'm going to have to violate them."

Officer Two (A Narcotics Specialist): "From the beginning I tell them what the rules are. They know, though, that more than anything else I require that they be honest with me. And they know too that if they're honest with me, (and I can tell if they're not), I won't screw them."

In each of these statements the controlling element of the officer's role is transferred to the department. In the first, the officer claims that his evaluation and position are at stake. In the second, the officer further separates himself as the mediator between departmental rules and the probationer. We may observe that "screwing the probationer" means reporting information which would be negatively judged by departmental standards. Because the department is designated as a distinct participant in the case relationship, one which bears the sanctioning and authoritative responsibility, we can now complete our triadic diagram of the initial phase of probation supervision:

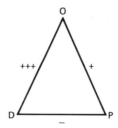

Figure 4 *Supervision triad.*

THE ORGANIZATION CONTEXT AND THE RULES OF PROBATION

Before we extend our theory to include the development of the relationship which our diagram signifies, it is appropriate to ask to what extent "the department" corresponds to the benevolent-but-unyielding-despot role ascribed to it. To free us, at least in part, from the real differences between departments, we can observe that no single philosophical position exists to which the field of probation is committed. Consequently, value positions are not closed and substantive evaluation is not logically possible.[25]

Since the illogic of evaluations has been of little concern to more sophisticated fields of study than probation, an examination of the rules of probation and the officer's discretion with respect to their application is more compelling. We shall consider three aspects of the rules of probation in their organizational context. First, probation rules are generally silly. If they were taken seriously, very few probationers would complete their terms without violation. Among prohibitions are liquor usage, gambling, indebtedness, and association or correspondence with "undesirables." Among permissions necessary from the officer are marriage, change of employment, and travel out of the community. Among requirements are curfews, treatment for venereal disease, and church attendance.[26] Arluke's evaluation of them is worth repeating:

Some parole conditions are moralistic, most are impractical, others impinge on human rights, and all reflect obsolete criminological conceptions. On the whole they project a percept of a man that does not exist.[27]

---

[25] This is in part the thrust of P. Takagi, supra note 12, whose research attempted the exploration of evaluative discrepancies suggested by Scott, *Organizational Evaluation and Authority,* 1967 Admin.Sci.Q. 93. The problem of evaluation of the probation officer's performance is elegantly assumed under Herbert Simon's observation more than a quarter of a century ago:

There is one important difference between permitting a subordinate discretion over a value premise and permitting him discretion over a factual premise. The latter can always be evaluated as correct or incorrect in an objective, empirical sense. . . . To a value premise . . . the terms correct and incorrect do not apply. Simon, *Decision Making and Organizational Authority,* 4 Pub.Admin.Rev. 18 (1944).

[26] Arluke, supra note 24, at 265.

[27] Ibid. at 269.

Secondly, because of the nature of the rules, strict administration of them is tempered both by the officer's access to information of violations and by an attitude of reasonableness toward vigorous enforcement. Beyond this, however, at least two authors in professional publications suggest that probation rules are to be thought of only as flexible guidelines.[28] A final point in reference to rule violation and departmental hegemony is that the vast majority of information about a probationer's conduct can only be provided by the officer. Thus, even if rules were practical and even if they were stipulated as inflexible and indiscriminate, the officer would still have the option of providing (albeit at his own risk) the information upon which they could be applied. This third aspect of the character of probation rules in their organizational context is salient even under present conditions. It is possible for an officer to "screw" his probationer.

The implication of these observations is that the "department," as the genuine bearer of the authority and control components of the officer role, is to no small extent a fiction. The rules, their application, and their dismissal are largely a matter of the discretion of the officer, who, with very little personal risk, may conceal or permit their violation.

EXCHANGE STRATEGY AND THE DEVELOPMENT OF SUPERVISION

The fictional nature of the rules of probation in their organizational setting, combined with the synthetic officer's artificial manipulation of "the department," introduce properties to the case relationship which not only increase the officer's control but also suggest patterns of case development. If we adopt a market analogy, the probationer can be considered a consumer who wishes to purchase the completion of his term. In the triadic relationship which the synthetic officer structures, the probationer is provided with two currencies. The first is compliance with the rules of his probation. In following such rules he purchases his completion by demonstrating what is thought to be satisfactory social maturity. If he can complete his term without violation, he will have little need to draw upon the second currency which is available to him.

This second currency may be called rapport. It consists of appeals for aid, assistance, or understanding combined with the confession of problems. For those probationers who are helped by probation, it is the stuff of which counselling is made. Honest counselling is possible in this case because, analogically, the department and officer are different sellers. What cannot be purchased from the department with rule compliance can be purchased from the officer with rapport.

The analogy of two sellers which the probationer perceives, however, is only an illusion. He is dealing with a near-perfect monopoly. The officer controls the definitions and resulting permissions. He is able to dramatize his own separation

---

[28] Dicerbo, *When Should Probation be Revoked?*, 30 Fed.Probation 11 (June 1966); D. Dressler, *supra* note 12, at 254.

from his departmental superego by techniques ranging from forceful restatement ("These are the rules. I didn't make 'em; you didn't make 'em, but we both have to live with 'em.") to revelation of his own jeopardy ("My supervisor is on my neck over what I'm letting you get away with."). While maintaining the separation, he may also grant exception ("I'm going to go out on a limb for you.") or express charity ("You were right to tell me the truth. We can work on it together and keep what happened between ourselves.").

Practically, the officer who holds such a monopoly has two advantages. First, he is capable of creating "false bottoms" on the availability of pardons for violations. The criteria for satisfactory conduct can be set at virtually any level. The officer's defnitions are perceived as those of the department. Secondly, the officer is able to adjust those false bottoms, while giving the impression of following departmental policy.[29]

In terms of our original diagrams, the serial development of probation supervision structured in the manner suggested, can be signified as shown in Figure 5. The exchange of signs from the O–D bond to the O–P bond represent the primary process exchange of permission for rapport as the case relationship develops. This exchange is predicated upon the recognition of some difficulty in abiding by the defined rules. In the absence of this difficulty, probation is essentially perfunctory and there are no structural reasons for the supervision relationship to develop beyond Stage I. Other roles may develop based upon personal attraction, interests, or mutual experience, but from the reference of an officer and a probationer they are incalculable. Consider, for example, the officer who learns about jazz from a musician probationer.

While the transfer of signs represents the primary process of exchange, that is not all it represents. In addition, the officer adds to the bargain an apparent

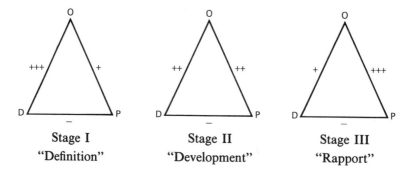

Stage I	Stage II	Stage III
"Definition"	"Development"	"Rapport"

Figure 5   *The development of probation supervision. Stage I, "Definition"; Stage II, "Development"; Stage III, "Rapport."*

---

[29] A complication intrudes here when the decision to revoke probation is genuinely considered. It is that a consideration of the judge's criteria for granting a revocation must be made by the officer. If the judge refuses to grant revocation when requested by the officer, the officer not only loses face but also destroys any chance of regaining rapport.

change in his fidelity to the department. He can no longer be simply an agent. In light of the investment which he makes for rapport with the probationer, he cannot maintain for the probationer's eyes the same strength of attachment to his officer position. He may, of course, still hold it, but, in effect, he says that the job and the rules are secondary and the man is what really matters.

Consequently, we have represented the bond between the officer and the department as minimal in the final stage. In some cases, where an apparent team of officer and probationer develops against department rules, this minimally positive bond is indeed an overstatement.

DISCUSSION

Several theoretical analyses of structurally similar positions give formal credence to the conception we have developed here. Perhaps the broadest of these is Simmel's analysis of the respective characteristics of the dyad and triad. Critical is Simmel's observation that:

The dyad represents both the first social synthesis and unification and the first separation and antithesis. The appearance of the third party indicates transition, conciliation and abandonment of absolute contrast. . . . [30]

According to Simmel, the triad offers the advantage of non-partisanship and mediation roles. This is the intent and result of the inclusion of "the department" in the case relationship. Simmel claims further that the triad transforms the nature of conflict from its invariably personal quality in the dyad. He observes:

A third mediating social element deprives conflicting claims of their affective qualities because it neutrally formulates and presents these claims to the two parties involved. Thus the circle that is fatal to all reconciliation is avoided: the vehemence of the one no longer provokes that of the other. . . . [31]

In the triadically-structured case relationship the officer need never come into direct personal conflict with his probationer. He can claim to be only the objective reader of departmental regulations. Furthermore, the quality of the officer's affective responses can only be interpreted as partisan to the probationer's interests.

One can find similarly structured analyses of specific occupations. The most famous is the foreman. Variously called a "marginal man of industry,"[32] "the man in the middle,"[33] and a "master and victim of doubletalk,"[34] his position is located between worker and management. He owes allegiance to both but can fully

---

[30] G. Simmel, *The Sociology of Georg Simmel,* 145 (K. Wolff, transl. & ed. 1964).

[31] Ibid. at 147.

[32] Wray, *Marginal Men of Industry: The Foreman,* 46 Am.J.Sociology 298 (1949).

[33] Gardner & Whyte, *The Man in the Middle: Position and Problems of the Foreman,* 1945 J. Applied Anthropology 1.

[34] Roethlisberger, *The Foreman: Master and Victim of Doubletalk,* 23 Harv.Bus.Rev. 283 (1945).

maintain the identity of neither. Effective foremanship depends upon the foreman's ability to manipulate a situation structurally similar to that of the synthetic officer. The difference between the positions is the privilege, which the officer enjoys, of defining his own criteria of conduct, while the foreman's criteria are dictated and evaluated by others.

Goffman cites baseball umpire Babe Pinelli's vision of his task as the product of the rules of the game, the player's enthusiasm and the benevolent impartiality with which they must be reconciled. Pinelli states:

It is easy for any umpire to thumb a man out of the game. It is often a much more difficult job to keep him in the game—to understand and anticipate his claim so that a nasty rhubarb cannot develop.[35]

In contrast, however, the umpire's rules are closely supervised and his performance is both public and evaluable.

A closer parallel to the triadic case relationship and its place in a manipulatable rule structure is the drama staged regularly in many large automobile sales agencies. The plot begins with the customer's decision on a car about which to negotiate a price. The customer is then led to a room where he waits, while the salesman leaves to "find out what he can do." He invariably returns with an offer, the generosity of which he punctuates in many ways. If the customer cannot be convinced, this exit and consultation with a higher authority may be repeated. Various *leitmotifs* intervene as the climax approaches. The climax occurs when the source of authority or an available substitute appears. His performance either closes the deal or terminates the negotiations. The customer never comes into direct conflict with the salesman, nor is the salesman's performance anything but accommodating.

While the similarities to the case supervision pattern we have sketched are clear in this last example, we do not wish to suggest that the intent of the case supervision drama is as crassly motivated nor as interpersonally impoverished. There is a difference, which ought not be minimized, between an artificial performance designed to increase commissions and a crescive drama based upon a genuine interest in the welfare of a client. Whether or not that drama can survive its disenchantment, remains a central problem of the social psychology of probation.

---

[35] E. Goffman, *The Presentation of Self in Everyday Life,* 98 (1959).

26
Orientation and Activities of the Parole Officer

RICHARD DEMBO

There are two major approaches for understanding the role of the parole officer:

(1) development of an attitude profile of the parole officer, and
(2) inferring parole officer attributes and activities from their underlying philosophies of the parole process.

The attitude profile approach can be traced to Ohlin, Piven and Pappenfort (1956), who formulated three probation and parole officer orientations: punitive, protective, and welfare officers. Pownall (1963) and Glaser (1964) further refine this classification by conceiving four types of parole officers (welfare, paternal, passive, and punitive) as products of two basic factors of their jobs: assistance (material, counseling, mediation) and control (surveillance, restriction, punishment).

The second approach to understand the role of the parole officer derives from Rowan's (1956) formulation that outlines dimensions of treatment and surveillance philosophies which appear to underlie the parole supervision process and

SOURCE. Reprinted from *Criminology* 10 (2), August 1972, pp. 193–215 by permission of the Publisher, Sage Publications, Inc. (and the author).

relate these to the officer's background, his attitudes, and job activity attributes. Rowan considered differences between the two philosophies on three key dimensions: (1) use of rules and regulations, (2) amount of caseload work, and (3) evaluation of parolee traits. This formulation implies a series of officer attributes related to these philosophies.

I chose to study the orientation-activity approach of Rowan. This approach was considered superior to the attitude-profile method of assessing the role of the parole officer for two reasons. First, by suggesting these three dimensions of social-psychological orientation: (1) the conception of the parolee, (2) the view of parole purpose, and (3) the belief in method of rule enforcement, Rowan includes both the Pownall and Glaser formulations, and enables us to develop a more complete profile of the parole officer. Second, though the Pownall and Glaser typologies are clear in the delineation of officer roles on the two dichotomized control and assistance dimensions, officer orientations are related to other attributes and values that the typology does not make clear. Here I will try to develop a measure of parole officer orientations and relate these to their background-attitude characteristics and their job activities.

THE THREE DIMENSIONS OF PAROLE OFFICER ORIENTATION

The three dimensions of officer orientation are conceived to lie on a continuum from high to low. Further, my first hypothesis is that these three dimensions are interrelated. If this is true, a single measure of officer orientation with the three dimensions can be formed. The dimensions of this overall measure are discussed below.

Dimension 1: Conception of the Parolee

The first dimension represents the divergent ways that parole officers see their clients. One way refers to the conceived rehabilitation potential of the client, the other to the degree he is categorized as a "type," or viewed as an individual. I shall argue that viewing the parolee as essentially *anti-social,* a type (the stigmatizing position), and as an *individual* in a positive sense (the affirmative position) is derivative of an officer's evaluations of the parolee's background.

As Goffman (1963) and Szasz (1963) observed, stigmatization of those with "bad moral" records or those failing to fulfill certain "contractual obligations" provides a way of eliminating from concern those who are seen as denying the social order or as representing failures in the motivational assumptions upon which the social system works. To label a person a criminal implies social undesirability, and this can be used to segregate further those so considered. In addition, such stigmatization overlooks the social problems that produced the bad moral records. With this point of view, stigmatization is selective perception, which punishes failure to meet the moral mark set as the societal norm. This negative view of the parolee as an individual reflects, as Kitsuse (1962) observed, a *"retros-*

pective reinterpretation of the deviant's behavior and social origins in the light" of his present parole status.

A positive, personal conception of the parolee shows him as a person with ability to make a useful contribution to society. Research with such an affirmative approach has been discouraged by normative sanctions implicit in present laws and mores. Currently we lack an appropriate language to develop more fully this conceptual model. For the most part, those who conceive of the parolee or offender in a positive manner are suspected of secretly envying his deviance, or else are considered misguided. However, this orientation is sufficient to view the parolee as one who violated the law due to inadequate socialization to normative expectations, or as acting out internal conflicts. Basically social psychiatric in orientation, this approach stresses a focus on treatment in the development of a positive self-image and help in "proper" living.

Dimension 2: View of Parole Purpose

This dimension takes into account the distinction between police and social work approaches to deviant behavior. As applied to parole work, this view, on the one hand, has the parole officer at work to prevent postincarceration deterioration of parolees with adverse consequences for community stability and safety. On the other hand, the officer is conceived as a treatment worker who, by trying to rehabilitate the parolee, makes concern for community safety unnecessary.

Corresponding to the idea of the parole officer as a keeper of social order is a control orientation to his work, which involves the use of surveillance, restriction, and punishment techniques to effect parolee compliance with existing laws and community norms implicit in parole rules and regulations (see Pownall, 1963; Glaser, 1964).[1] In exerting control measures for compliance, this type of officer engages in self-fulfilling prophecy activity (see Merton, 1957) by continually reinforcing his primary concern for community safety, relating to parolees in the assumption that they are a threat to it.

Treatment orientation to the parolee uses material help, referrals to specialists for aid, counseling, and mediation techniques in an attempt to reintegrate the client in the community. This focuses on the social and emotional disabilities that hinder parolee commitment to law-abiding community participation. Treatment-oriented officers may variously attribute parolee disabilities to psychological, social, or cultural factors, or combinations of these. Of key significance, however, is the belief that appropriate techniques can be applied to effect change in the particular area(s) of parolee disability that prevent acceptable social participation in community life.

Dimension 3: Belief in Method of Rule Enforcement

The *use of parole rules to deter crime* and *literal enforcement* of their intent imply a punitive orientation toward the parolee. Extracting from Erikson (1962), this officer-type plays boundary maintainer by continually exerting negative sanctions to keep the parolee aware of his probationary status in the community. A parolee seen as a threat to strongly held values will be subject to repressive actions; or, according to Becker (1963), enforcers enforce rules in selective ways, depending on underlying evaluations of their clientele. Further, the regular application of rules in a repressive manner enables this type of enforcer to show continued justification for this orientation, punishing those regarded as unwilling or unable to support the values which he "protects."

Restitutive rule enforcement involves *use of rules as a constructive aid* and their *"interpretive"* enforcement. Here there is concern with enhancing the parolee's readjustment to community life by providing a manner of rule enforcement tapered to his needs and providing him with a general framework of objectives and expectations upon which he can base his actions. From this point of view, crime is seen as a manifestation of energies and drives that are capable of redirection. To this end, creative use of parole rules and regulations are needed, since they direct parolee orientation toward community involvement.

Convergence of the Three Dimensions

Just as the various subdimensions within the above dimensions are related to one another, so, too, is there a convergence of association *among* them. The intercorrelation of the orientation dimensions is based on their relationship to punishment and reintegrative views toward deviance.

The punishment orientation to deviant behavior, implicit in the stigmatizing approach to the parolee, relates to stringent rule enforcement. This is so, since fear of his return to crime necessitates strong controlling measures to constrain the parolee to minimal conformity to the parole contract. This perspective gives rise to concern for the consequences of parolee infraction of established norms, focusing on community protection against parolee deterioration. Essentially, the punishment orientation to deviant behavior involves, as Kitsuse (1962) and Erikson (1962) show, an act of social judgment by a defining agent, representative of existing norms. The agent then acts in such a manner as to both support his orientations and elicit behavior from parolees which is taken to validate his position.

Alternatively, the reintegrative-oriented officer conceives of the individual as a key player in the social adjustment process. He orients his restitutive application of parole rules toward the parolee's rehabilitation by assisting him in overcoming the particular disabilities that prevent his reintegration into the community. His rehabilitation orientation assumes a positive evaluation of the parolee's potential for good citizenship. This positive evaluation takes into consideration problem areas for treatment, whose amelioration is believed crucial to conforming behavior. Here, again, a parole officer's orientation and action support his positive attitude, eliciting parolee responses that appear to confirm his position.

I now come to my first hypothesis, that the three parole officer orientation dimensions are positively related to each other, such that the stigmatizing (dimension 1), community protection (dimension 2), and repressive (dimension 3) orientations go together, as do the affirmative (dimension 1), offender rehabilitation (dimension 2), and restitutive (dimension 3) orientations. The former group of orientations will be called the punishment view of deviance; the latter is the reintegrative view of deviance. These hypothesized relationships are depicted in Table 1.

CHARACTERISTICS OF PUNISHMENT- AND REINTEGRATIVE-ORIENTED PAROLE OFFICERS

Since there are few systematic studies of the parole officer from which to generate sound hypotheses, the background, attitude, and other activity attributes of punishment and reintegrative-oriented officers are stated in null-hypothesis form.

My personal experience as a parole oficer and the speculation underlying the derivation of the punishment and reintegrative orientations provides a series of related job activites and decision-actions, reflective of the differences in the main concerns of officers holding each of the orientations. The punishment-oriented officer abides by his law enforcement responsibilities and provides few client-centered services. Clients are viewed in a stigmatized manner as those from whom the community is to be protected, and as objects which make this type of officer's enforcement objectives easy or difficult to achieve. Reintegrative-oriented officers believe in the ability of people to help others if enough effort is made. To this end, services are provided to clients and efforts directed to reestablish and keep the offender in the community. The following job activities and decision-actions were studied: (1) excess hours worked, (2) ratio of absconder visits made, (3) number of motor vehicle license referrals, (4) rate of clients declared in technical violation,

Table 1 *Parole Officer Orientation*

Dimension	Punishment-Orientation	Reintegrative-Orientation
1. Conception of the Parolee	**Stigmatizing**	**Affirmative**
a. Conceived rehabilitation potential	Essentially antisocial	Capable of positive response
b. Degree categorized as type	Type	Individual personality
2. View of Parole Purpose	**Community Protection**	**Offender Rehabilitation**
	Control-oriented	Treatment-oriented
3. Belief in Method of Rule Enforcement	**Repressive**	**Restitutive**
a. Type of rule use	To deter return to crime	Constructive aid
b. Method of rule enforcement	Literal rule enforcement	Interpretive rule enforcement

and (5) percentage of technically violated clients recommended for return to prison.

PROCEDURE

All parole officers with four or more years' employment in the New York State Division of Parole, the last two years being in continuous caseload supervision, were selected to be interviewed. Criteria for the purposive sample assisted in the selection of officers believed to have passed the mechanical stage of job performance and developed a style of supervision. Selection of this sample assured that parole officers who supervised parolees during the 21-month period for which I was to gather job activity and decision-action data would be interviewed.[2] Ninety-four of the 98 officers were interviewed in the ten division district offices to which they were assigned throughout the state. The median age was 44.9 years; 93.6% of the officers had over five years of service, 43.6% over eleven years, and 23.4% had over seventeen years; 93.6% were college graduates, and 26.6% held advanced degrees.

Two data sources were used: officer interviews and review of agency records for job activity and decision-action information. An officer interview schedule was designed which included twenty rating-scale items to probe locations on the three orientation dimensions.

Rating scales were devised. Following a conceptualization of each orientation dimension, a series of orientation postures on issues implicit to the dimension or subdimension probed was evolved. Each scale combined polar postures on the issue described. These position possibilities, or definitions of the orientation dimension or subdimension, were, then, formulated into the rating scale sets. Additional interview questions included a seventeen-item ranking question probing job dissatisfactions, the Eysenck-Nagel survey of opinion question set exploring liberal-conservative attitudes, (see Nagel, 1963), a question probing types of cases preferred to supervise, and a question set probing control attitudes. Traditional items were used to determine officer background characteristics and part-time employment.

Rates of overtime hours, ratio of absconder visits, number of motor vehicle license referrals, rate of clients declared in technical violation of parole, and the percentage of recommendation of return to prison for these technically violated clients were obtained from the Buffalo, Albany, and Bronx field offices selected for closer study. Selection of these three offices was based on their geographical location, making them fairly representative of the range of community contexts in which the division works. Easy access resulted in the inclusion of New York office (metropolitan New York City minus Bronx) warrant data.

Since caseload sizes were found to vary from office to office and due to the unique relationship patterns relating to officer work styles in each office, job activity and decision-action measures were obtained separately for each office. Officers were coded as punishment or reintegrative-oriented depending upon their location above or below the median on each dimension, according to the hypotheses.[3]

RESULTS

Correlation analyses of officer orientations proceeded through three stages: (1) interitem correlation analysis of rating scale items within each orientation dimension subdimension, (2) analysis of subdimension relationships, and (3) relationships of the three orientation dimensions.

Intradimension/Subdimension Item Relationships

Item relationships were examined by means of Pearson's correlation coefficients, as were the relationships of the other orientation subdimensions and dimensions, and officer background, attitude, other activity, job activity, and decision-action attributes. An item (or in the case of more than two item correlation possibilities,average item) correlation level of .10 was selected as that minimally acceptable for an item to be included for subsequent analyses.[4] As a result of this analysis, eighteen of the twenty items were retained for further study.

Subdimension Relationships

Having obtained sufficient interitem relationships to continue the analyses, a second analysis was performed exploring the relationships of the subdimensions of the conception of the parolee and belief in method of rule enforcement orientation dimensions. In this analysis, score totals of each repective subdimension, derived by summing the scores of each component item-set, were run against each other.

The resulting correlations of the conceptions of the parolee and belief in method of rule enforcement subdimensions (.21 and .28 respectively) were higher than an r of .1701 needed for correlations to be considered significant at the .05 one-tailed test level for an n of 94.

Relationships of the Three Officer Orientation Dimensions

In this analysis phase, correlations among the total scores for the three orientation dimensions were studied. The results in Table 2 support the orientation dimension relationships postulated in hypothesis 1. A further statistical analysis found the dimensions to be separate or independant of one another.

According to the findings, the officer who views the parolee in an affirmative manner sees rehabilitation as the purpose of parole and supports restitutive rule enforcement measures. Conversely, a stigmatizing conception of the parolee relates to a community protection view of parole purpose and the belief in repressive rule enforcement. An overall score of parole officer orientations (hereafter called

Table 2 *Intercorrelations (r) of the Three Parole Officer Orientation Dimensions (n = 94)*

	1	2	3
1. Conception of the parolee	–		
2. View of parole purpose	.41	–	
3. Belief in method of rule enforcement	.37	.38	–

Note: r needed if significant at the one-tailed test .05 level: .1701.

Table 3 *Correlations (r) Between Reintegrative Scores and Parole Officer Characteristics*

Hypothesis	n	r	r Needed if Significant at .05 Level, Two-Tailed Test	Result
Background				
H-2 Ethnic affiliation is unrelated to reintegrative score	94	.0717	±.2006	Cannot reject null-hypothesis
H-3 Location of early life is unrelated to reintegrative score	94	−.0971	±.2006	Cannot reject null-hypothesis
H-4 Place of longest residence is unrelated to reintegrative score	94	.2462	±.2006	Reject null-hypothesis
H-5 Educational background is unrelated to reintegrative score	94	−.1533	±.2006	Cannot reject null-hypothesis
H-6 Employment background is unrelated to reintegrative score	94	.0303	±.2006	Cannot reject null-hypothesis
H-7 Father's occupation is unrelated to reintegrative score	94	−.0514	±.2006	Cannot reject null-hypothesis
Attitudinal				
H-8 Liberalism-conservatism is unrelated to reintegrative score	94	.4257	±.2006	Reject null-hypothesis
H-9 Cases preferred to supervise are unrelated to reintegrative score	89	.2546	±.2102	Reject null-hypothesis
H-10 Job dissatisfactions are unrelated to reintegrative score	57	.3923	±.2606	Reject null-hypothesis
H-11 Control attitudes are unrelated to reintegrative score	94	.2409	±.2006	Reject null-hypothesis

Table 3 *(continued)*

		One-Tailed Test		
Other Activities				
H-12 Type of part-time employment is unrelated to reintegrative score	21	.4643	$\pm$.4309	Reject null-hypothesis
Job Performance				
Job Activities				
H-13 High reinregrative score is positively related to excess hours worked	24	−.0249	.3405	Not verified
H-14 High reintegrative score is positively related to low ratio of absconder visits made	24	.3065	.3405	Not verified
Decision-Actions				
H-15 High reintegrative score is positively related to large number of motor vehicle license referrals	24	−.2784	.3503	Not verified
H-16 High reintegrative score is positively related to low rate of clients declared in technical parole violation	52	.4026	.2301	Verified
H-17 High reintegrative score is positively related to low percentage rate of recommending technical violator's return to prison	22	.2677	.3601	Not verified

Note: Hypotheses numbers referred to in the text are given in the above table. Thus, H-14 is the hypothesis that punishment-oriented officers make a high ratio of absconder visits, and reintegrative-oriented officers make a low ratio of these visits.

the reintegrative score) was, therefore, derived by summing the total scores for dimensions 1, 2 and 3. The higher the score, the greater the reintegrative orientation; the lower the score, the greater the punishment orientation.

Relationship of Parole Officer Orientations to Background, Attitude, other Activity, and Job Performance Characteristics

The hypotheses exploring the relationship of punishment and reintegrative orientations to background, attitude, other activities, and job behavior are given in Table 3. For each hypothesis, the overall reintegrative score was correlated with the appropriate measure. Correlations and the sample sizes on which they are based are also given in this table. Null-hypotheses concerning background, titude, and other activity attributes were rejected if the correlation between the overall reintegrative score and the appropriate measure was greater in absolute value than a correlation needed to be significantly greater than zero at the .05 level for a two-tailed test of the given n. Table 3 hypotheses examining job performance were considered verified if: (1) the relationship was in the predicted direction, and (2) significant at the .05 level for a one-tailed test. Job behavior hypotheses were stated in terms of the reintegrative orientation.[5]

The results in Table 3 establish a significant relationship between officer orientations and their place of longest residence (H-4), liberal-conservative attitudes (H-8), cases preferred to supervise (H-9), job dissatisfactions (H-10), control attitudes (H-11), part-time employment (H-12), and rate of technical violation warrant issuance (H-16). I would have expected one of the sixteen hypotheses to be confirmed on a chance basis alone. The seven of the sixteen hypotheses actually confirmed could not under the assumption of the random process model be explained on a chance basis.

THE RELATIONSHIP OF AGE AND LENGTH OF TIME SUPERVISING PAROLEES

The following analysis was conducted to test the possibility that the relationships between reintegrative scores and previously determined parole officer attributes could be explained on the basis of age and number of years supervising parolees. Correlations were obtained among age, reintegrative scores, and the seven officer attributes; correlations were gathered among years of supervising parolees, reintegrative scores, and the seven officer attributes. These relationships are shown in Table 4. Since I had no specific hypotheses relating these factors to

Table 4   *Correlations (r) Among Age, Length of Time Supervising Parolees, Reintegrative Scores, and Confirmed Parole Officer Characteristics*

	Age	Years Supervising Parolees	n
Reintegrative score	.2821	.0421 ($+$.2006)	94
Place of longest residence	.2201	.1845 ($+$.2006)	94
Liberalism	$-$.0016	$-$.2672 ($+$.2006)	94
Cases prefer supervising	$-$.0380	$-$.0963 ($+$.2006)	94
Job dissatisfaction areas	$-$.2118	$-$.4357 ($+$.2606)	57
Control	$-$.1044	$-$.1592 ($+$.2006)	94
Social work p/t job	.2267	$-$.0278 ($+$.4309)	21
Rate of technical violation warrants	.3625	.1932 ($+$.2708)	52

Note: Correlation levels needed for significance at the two-tailed test .05 level noted in parentheses.

reintegrative scores and officer attributes, a .05 significance level for a two-tailed test for the specific n is used.

Table 4 shows the following relationships:

(a) *Age:* Positively related to reintegrative scores (.2821), place of longest residence (.2201), and to issuance of technical violation warrants (.3625).

(b) *Years of supervising parolees:* Related to conservative attitudes (−.2672) and job dissatisfactions due to difficult cases, political aspects, constant crises situations or long hours (−.4357).

Since age is related to reintegrative scores, place of longest residence, and rate of technical violation warrant issuance, the question arises whether age might explain the relationship between reintegrative scores and these two officer attributes. This was tested by partial correlation analyses probing the relationship between reintegrative scores, places of longest residence, and technical violation warrant issuance rate, controlling for age.

The first partial correlation analysis reduced the original relationship between reintegrative scores and place of longest residence from .2462 to .2102, or .0360. The second analysis reduced the relationship between reintegrative scores and rate of technical violation warrant issuance from .4026 to .3569, or .0457. The resulting correlations in both instances were still significant at the .05 level. Accordingly, age cannot account for reintegrative scores or the previously confirmed parole officer characteristics.

Similarly, since the number of years supervising parolees is unrelated to reintegrative scores, it cannot be used to explain the relationship of reintegrative scores to the seven confirmed officer attributes. The relationship of increasing years supervising parolees with conservative attitudes and job dissatisfactions for reasons of difficult cases, political aspects, constant crises situations, or long hours suggests a tendency toward cynicism among officers with long periods of service unrewarded by advancement. This shifting of job dissatisfaction from problems of client care to those of the system in which he works is supported by increasing conservative attitudes, which serve to reduce the force of agency treatment objectives by questioning their value. Why, for example, should one rehabilitate the offender, when the general decline of ethical standards of conduct, collectivism, and social disorganization are believed present?

DISCUSSION OF THE FINDINGS

Two Parole Officer Groups

The results presented in Table 3 show the existence of two parole officer groups, originally uncovered by Reed and King (1966) in their study of North Carolina probation officers: (1) an urban liberal, probationer-oriented group favoring unofficial actions short of revocation and (2) a rural-conservative group, with a preference for officer-oriented, or social-order rationalizations favoring revocation.

Apparently, the experience of living in the cosmoplitan, urban culture sensitizes officer awareness and fosters reintegrative concern for the antisocial products of indigenous slums. And, conversely, prolonged life experience in the predominantly white, Protestant, rural culture does not stimulate concern and involvement in antisocial persons, making it conducive to punishment orientations. In addition to confirming the results of Reed and King's work, my study went further in conceptualizing the basis for officer decision-making and in extending the list of parole officer characteristics.

The Relationship Between Parole Officer Orientations and Background Attributes

Of the six officer background factors explored in this study (place of longest residence, subject area interest, early life location, father's occupation, employment background, and ethnic affiliation), only place of longest residence was found significantly related to officer orientations (Table 3). These results suggest that cultural life experience is most critical in determining officer views of deviance.

The Relationship Between Officer Orientations and Attitudes

The results presented in Table 3 show that parole officers who have high reintegrative scores are liberal, prefer to supervise difficult cases or have no supervision preferences, are dissatisfied with job factors limiting direct client contact of failures, and have low control attitudes, and, conversely, officers with low reintegrative scores tend to be conservative, prefer to supervise low-risk cases, are dissatisfied with the political factors, long hours, difficult cases, and constant crises situations encountered in their work, and possess high control attitudes.

The Relationship Between Officer Orientations and Other Activities

The results in Table 3 indicate that officers with high reintegrative scores (if they hold part-time employment) tend to hold social-work-type jobs, whereas officers with low reintegrative scores have nonclient-oriented, part-time employment. This finding indicates that officer orientations are related to their outside activities and shows that these orientations are important in understanding these activities.

The Relationship Between Officer Orientations, Job Activities, and Decision-actions

The near zero correlation between reintegrative scores and excess hours worked indicates that officer orientations are not related to the tendency to work overtime. Administrative pressures to work the required 37½-hour week appear mostly responsible for the fact that H-13 was not verified. This belief in working the standard work week derived from two main sources: a belief that caseload needs be placed on a priority basis and fulfilled accordingly, and as a result of a successful lawsuit against the division in the 1950s by officers demanding compensation for numerous overtime hours worked in performance of their duties. One consequence of this legal action was greater agency concern for overtime work, and encouragement of line supervisors to limit its occurrence by officers under their charge.

Though not significantly correlated, the relationship between high reintegrative scores and low ratio of absconder visits made, and, conversely, between low reintegrative scores and high ratio of absconder visits made, is in the predicted direction and high. This shows that officer orientations are reflected in his tendency to peform absconder work.

Technically, attempts should be made to locate and apprehend absconders, since, if arrested on a new charge, the parolee could claim that his obligation to the division no longer binds if few efforts were made to find him. However, leads are not always available on absconders. Given this situation of uncertainty, the results suggest that officer orientations are related to the emphasis he places on absconder work. An officer with high reintegrative scores will tend to devote little effort to locating absconders, perhaps preferring to spend more effort in working with active cases, whereas officers with low reintegrative (or punishment-oriented) scores will tend to place absconder work on a higher level of work priority.

The high negative correlation between reintegrative scores and number of motor vehicle license referrals made, shown in Table 3, was unanticipated and difficult to understand. It is true that most requests for a motor vehicle license come from the parolee, and the processing of the request by the parole officer involves considerable time and effort. Accordingly, officers with large, active caseloads may place license requests on a low work priority.

Further, in large metropolitan areas, with adequate means of transportation, the needs for a license are limited to employment reasons, whereas in rural areas (such as those covered by the Albany and Buffalo field offices) a license may be more of a personal necessity for parolees residing in outlying areas with poor public transportation.

While officer work pressures and client necessity for a driver's license may explain why frequency of license referrals is not related to officer orientations, they do not help to understand why referral rates are negatively correlated to reintegrative scores. Presently, I cannot offer reasons to account for this unexpected result of my study.

The significant relationship between high reintegrative scores and low technical violation rates, and, conversely, between low reintegrative scores and high technical violation rates (H-16, Table 3), supports the argument that parole officer technical violation activity is related to their orientations. The reasons for this relationship seem clear.

Naturally, no one knows the parole officer's caseload as well as he. Through regular home visits, visits to the parolee's place of employment and client office reports, the officer gains the most complete current adjustment information on his charges. When the senior parole officer is approached and requested to issue a technical violation warrant (only senior and higher parole officials can effect formal warrant issuance), the parole officer must bring the case up to date. In his decision to issue a warrant, the senior parole officer must, because of his limited understanding of the case, rely chiefly on the parole officer's accounting and presentation of the client's case. While, in some instances, the parole officer has previously discussed a particular parolee's behavior with his senior, this may often not occur, expecially in the case of the older, more experienced officers who are permitted greater freedom in governing their caseloads. The relationship between officer orientations and rate of technical violation warrant issuance exists, then, since the officer can relatively easily effect such action to a degree consistent with his presuppositions.

The finding that officer orientations are related to recommendations of return to prison of those technically violated (H-17, Table 3; such that officers with high reintegrative scores tend to recommend return to prison for a small percentage of cases technically violated, officers with low reintegrative scores tend to recommend a large percentage of technical violation cases returned), while not statistically significant, is in the direction predicted, and fairly high. While the officer does not have final say about whether a parolee is returned to prison or restored to the community (final authority resting with the parole commissioners), the finding indicates that his case recommendations tend to be consistent with his orientations.

SUMMARY

The determined relationships between parole officer orientations (H-1), and their background (H-4), attitudes (H-8, H-9, H-10, and H-11), part-time work (H-12), and technical violation warrant issuance rate (H-16), shows that an officer's view of deviance provides a basis for understanding his attitudes and activities.

The findings point to the critical need for interaction studies of parole officers and clients. For, just as the data show that parole officers' orientations are related to their job behavior, so, too, parolee orientations may affect casework outcomes. The results of such a study will permit more prediction and influence in parole outcome than is now possible for the many clients presently being processed without deep impact and meaningful transformation being made in their lives.

NOTES

1. Pownall (1963) and Glaser (1964) see the control and assistance dimensions as complementary elements of the parole officer's job. However, the speculation underlying the orientations of Pownall and Glaser is that they are antithetical. The treatment officer

regard control measures as self-defeating for his purpose of developing trust, and the control-oriented officer would react, arguing that giving the parolees assistance is wasteful, if not coddling.

2. Limited data on motor vehicle license referrals and overtime hours worked restricted my period of coverage on these dimensions from 7/1/67 to 6/30/68 and from 1/19/67 to 7/5/67, respectively.

3. The data were coded as follows: (1) nonminority affiliation, rural location of early life and place of longest residence, law, business, or physical science educational background, law, industry, or finance previous employment, white-collar father's occupation, low violation risk cases preferred to supervise (adult vehicle/property offenders or murder/manslaughter offenders), work-oriented job dissatisfactions (difficult cases, political aspects, constant crises situations, long hours) and nonclient-oriented part-time employment were coded 0; (2) minority affiliation, urban location of early life and place of longest residence, social science, education, or social work educational background, social work previous employment, blue-collar or service worker father's occupation, desire to work with problem cases or no supervision preference (alcoholic, sex, drug offender, multiple age-crime types or no preference), client-oriented job dissatisfactions (failures and factors preventing direct contact and service to clients—e.g., paperwork, heavy caseloads, lack of community support/resources for treatment or interagency cooperation, administrative difficulties) and social work part-time employment were coded 1. Scorings on the Eysenck-Nagel opinion survey and Guttman scorings on the control attitude question set were directly punched for computer analysis. White and Protestant officers were classified as nonminority-affiliated; others were placed in the minority category. Educational background was indexed by categorizing the last 6 points or 2 semesters part-time subject area in which courses were at least begun prior to assuming the position of parole officer.

4. The .10 average correlation was used as the acceptance level as it was statistically significant at the .10 level.

5. Since the sample was not a probability sample, the use of the statistical model, strictly speaking, did not apply. However, it was used for heuristic purposes as a basis of comparison of my results to assist in examining the hypotheses.

REFERENCES

BECKER, H. S. (1963) *Outsiders: Studies in the Sociology of Deviance.* New York: Free Press.
ERIKSON, K. T. (1962) "Notes on the sociology of deviance." Social Problems 9 (Spring): 307–314.
GLASER, D. (1964) *The Effectiveness of a Prison and Parole System.* Indianpolis, Ind.: Bobbs-Merrill.
GOFFMAN, E. (1963) *Stigma.* Englewood Cliffs, N.J.: Prentice-Hall.
KITSUSE, J. I. (1962) "Societal reaction to deviant behavior: problems of theory and method." Social Problems 9 (Winter): 247–256.
MERTON, R. K. (1957) "The self-fulfilling prophecy," pp. 421–436 in *Social Theory and Social Structure.* New York: Free Press.
NAGEL, S.S. (1963) "Off-the-bench judicial attitudes," pp. 29–53 in G. Schubert (ed.), *Judicial Decision-Making.* New York: Free Press.

OHLIN, L. E., H. PIVEN, and D. M. PAPPENFORT, (1956) "Major dilemmas of the social worker in probation and parole." National Probation and Parole J. 11 (July): 211–225.

POWNALL, G. A. (1963) "An analysis of the role of the parole officer." Ph.D. dissertation. University of Illinois.

REED, J. P. and C. E. KING, (1966) "Factors in the decision-making of North Carolina probation officers." J. of Research in Crime and Delinquency 3 (July): 120–128.

ROWAN, J. R. (1956) "Let's define surveillance and treatment in parole." Proceedings of Amer. Correctional Assn: 117–120.

SZASZ, T. S. (1963) *Law, Liberty, and Psychiatry.* New York: Macmillan.

27
Conditions of Probation

ADMINISTRATIVE OFFICE, UNITED STATES COURTS

PROBATION FORM No. 7
(February 1964)

Conditions of Probation

•

UNITED STATES DISTRICT COURT
FOR THE

_____

To _____   Docket No. _____

Address _____

In accordance with authority conferred by the United States Probation Law, you have been placed on probation this date, _____ , for a period of _____ by the Hon. _____ United States District Judge, sitting in and for this District Court at

CONDITIONS OF PROBATION

It is the order of the Court that you shall comply with the following conditions of probation:

(1) You shall refrain from violation of any law (federal, state, and local). You shall get in touch immediately with your probation officer if arrested or questioned by a law-enforcement officer.
(2) You shall associate only with law-abiding persons and maintain reasonable hours.
(3) You shall work regularly at a lawful occupation and support your legal dependents, if any, to the best of your ability. When out of work you shall notify your probation officer at once. You shall consult him prior to job changes.
(4) You shall not leave the judicial district without permission of the probation officer.
(5) You shall notify your probation officer immediately of any change in your place of residence.
(6) You shall follow the probation officer's instructions and advice.
(7) You shall report to the probation officer as directed.

The special conditions ordered by the Court are as follows:

I understand that the Court may change the conditions of probation, reduce or extend the period of probation, and at any time during the probation period or within the maximum probation period of 5 years permitted by law, may issue a warrant and revoke probation for a violation occurring during the probation period.

I have read or had read to me the above conditions of probation. I fully understand them and I will abide by them.

(Signed)_____   _____
                    Probationer   Date

You will report as follows:

_____   _____
        U. S. Probation Officer   Date

SOURCE. United States Courts; reprinted with special permission.

28

See What Conditions
Your Conditions are In

CARL H. IMLAY AND CHARLES R. GLASHEEN

This is a particularly appropriate point in time to scrutinize our standards relating to probation. We have emerged from a period of national preoccupation with "the problem of crime in the streets" with its intensive focus on the problems of apprehending and trying offenders.

In a more reflective mood, we are now perhaps better prepared for a reassessment of the programs we prescribe for probationers. We already have an excellent blueprint outlined in the *Standards Relating to Probation* of the American Bar Association, recommended by its Advisory Committee on Sentencing and Review and approved by the ABA's House of Delegates in August 1970. The humanitarian approach of the chairman of that committee, Circuit Judge Simon E. Sobeloff, is eloquently reflected in the text of the draft of those standards.

A consideration prompting reexamination of the "condition of our conditions" is the right of paid counsel given by Congress to the indigent probationer faced with revocation of probation. As of February 11, 1971, every such person can ask to be represented at his revocacation hearing pursuant to the new statute (Public Law 91–447) amending the Criminal Justice Act to so provide (18 U.S.C. 3006A). While no statutory change affects in any way the judge's role in originally setting conditions for probation, or in revoking probation, the presence of paid attorneys at revocation hearings may have a certain catalyst effect in time. Part

SOURCE. *Federal Probation*, XXXV, June 1971, pp. 3–11. Reprinted with permission of the authors and *Federal Probation*.

of their role at the hearing will be to attack the conditions charged as violated. They will urge that a condition was vaguely worded, that it failed adequately to inform the probationer of restrictions applicable in a given situation, or that it constituted an impermissible intrusion into his private life. This kind of adversarial testing at the revocation stage may encourage greater precision in the original drafting of probation conditions.

We do not here suggest that the federal courts do not have broad authority in setting probation conditions. This power comes in part from the Federal Probation Act itself,[1] in part from the notion that probation is granted as an act of "judicial grace,"[2] and in part from the idea that the defendant "consents" to the term.[3] In some instances probation conditions have been upheld which are said to "restrict (the probationer's) constitutional rights."[4] However, in spite of these broad powers, probation orders are subject to some limitations. For example, the order must not be capricious nor impose impossible conditions.[5] If the condition imposes restrictions on the probationer in respect to activities which otherwise would be a matter of constitutional right, the restrictions should have a clearcut relationship to the probationer's program of rehabilitation.[6]

STANDARD CONDITIONS

The ABA Standards refer to probation as "an affirmative correctional tool."[7] In this spirit we would expect that each of the conditions of probation would be of benefit to the probationer and relevant to his rehabilitation program; consequently each condition should be tested to see whether it performs that function.[8] There are several conditions which are routinely applied, as it is believed that they are helpful to the defendant's rehabilitation. Perhaps the most fundamental of these conditions is that the probationer shall not violate any law.[9] (Although failure to support one's legal dependents would be a violation of the law in most jurisdictions and thus implicit in this condition, it is often set out expressly.) The idea that the probationer shall not leave the jurisdiction without permission is also considered fundamental.[10] In most instances the probationer is required to be employed and in some cases the type of his employment is restricted.[11] Of necessity the probation order usually contains a condition relating to the probationer's reporting to a probation officer. In the hope of preventing further offenses of the same type, other conditions are often imposed. For example, some courts have restricted those with whom the probationer may associate,[12] prohibited a telephone in defendant's home,[13] restricted the use of an automobile,[14] prohibited the defendant from employing women,[15] and have ordered the probationer to stay away from a particular woman.[16] While these special restrictions might not be relevant in preventing recidivism in probationers generally, they may be helpful in an individual case. For example, a restriction against having a telephone in his home may be highly relevant to the rehabilitation program of a bookmaker. It may have no discernible relationship to the program for a tax-evading businessman.

It is for this reason that the ABA Standards[17] recommend that the sentencing court be authorized to prescribe conditions to fit the circumstances of each case.

UNDESIRABLE CONDITIONS

Essentially we are concerned in this article with certain conditions which have been imposed (or at least their imposition has been suggested) and which, for one reason or another, are undesirable; for example, the condition (1) may be difficult to enforce, (2) it may not have any relation to the probationer's rehabilitation, (3) it may violate the probationer's constitutional rights, or (4) it may have been arbitrarily imposed for punitive reasons. In some cases a condition may be undesirable for all four of the above reasons.

In order to place the problem in actual context, it may be useful to consider certain questionable conditions of probation imposed by some courts across the country today, as for example:

Must attend church.
Cannot marry without permission of the supervising officer.
Cannot smoke.
Total abstention from alcohol.
Cannot frequent places where liquor is served or sold.
Must not grow a beard or long hair or wear clothing not in conformance with the customs of the community.
Require the wife to report when the probationer is unable to do so.
Submit to search and seizure at the discretion of the probation officer, including home as well as person.
Pursue medical or psychiatric treatment.
Unrealistic fines and restitution.
Refrain from driving a car, especially where a car is needed in work or in the home.
Requirement as to how earnings are to be spent.
Refrain from associating with *any* person who has been convicted at one time or another.
Requirement to pursue employment which is contrary to probationer's interests.
Requirement to contribute to a charitable cause.
Requirement to do charitable work.
Cannot become pregnant during probation.
Unrealistic restrictions on travel (e.g., a weekend trip from Chicago to Milwaukee to visit family members).
Restrictions on dates.
Be at home at unrealistic evening hours.
Unrealistic reporting requirements (e.g., an invalid, a person living a considerable distance from the office, or during hours of probationer's employment).
Requirement to attend school when past the compulsory attendance age.
Requirement to live in a special place of noninstitutional residence.

Of the above list an example of an unconstitutional condition is that the probationer attend church. The first amendment implications of such a condition are discussed hereinafter. Some conditions are so invasive of the probationer's private life or marital relationships as to be constitutionally suspect (e.g., making a probationer's wife report, a ban on a probationer becoming pregnant). Some conditions which might be valid if more narrowly described are so broadly stated as to be prone to constitutional attack (e.g., a condition that probationer submit to unlimited search of his home at the sole discretion of the probation officer, as discussed *infra*).

The rest of the list falls into several categories. Some of the conditions may be patently arbitrary (e.g., cannot smoke). Some would be arbitrary in certain situations as, for example, an absolute ban on frequenting places where liquor is served or sold in an area where most hotels and restaurants serve liquor in some form. Some other conditions are arbitrary only because they are unreasonably and overstrictly phrased. For example, a requirement that a probationer be at home by nine o'clock every evening may be arbitrary, though a requirement that he be home by midnight may not.

Several are pertinent only to certain specific probation situations and would be arbitrary in other situations. Consider, for example, a condition that the probationer refrain from driving a vehicle during the period of probation. Where a person has evidenced a pattern of criminal behavior involving past illegal use of an automobile and would not otherwise be dependent for his livelihood on the use of an automobile, reasonable restrictions on the use of vehicles may well be permissible. Where, however, a probationer's illegal behavior had no causal relation to the use of an automobile, or he is dependent on driving to retain his job (e.g., a truckdriver, cabbie, etc.), an absolute ban on driving would bear the hallmark of arbitrariness.

We do not attempt in the following portions of this article to discuss whether these conditions would have any merit in particular instances from the point of view of the correctional specialist. We only undertake to discuss the application of legal tests to some of these conditions, and to identify possible bases of future attack.

CONDITIONS MUST BE CLEAR AND DEFINITE

One cardinal thesis of the law is that everyone must be fairly informed of its application. One Roman emperor, Caligula, will always be known for his departure from this role, and for that one fact alone. Caligula posted the ordinances of Rome so high on the walls that no citizen could read them, and thus had to act at his peril.

It should be stated at the outset that for any condition to be effective, or indeed beyond constitutional attack, it must clearly and definitely set forth a standard of conduct which the probationer can follow.[18] Would it be proper, for example, to impose a condition requiring that the probationer dress according to "community standards"? In addition to the obvious practical problem which such a condition presents, its enforcement might invoke constitutional attack. The authorities are uniform in holding that statutory law to be valid, must be definite and clear. The United States Supreme Court has held that "a statute which . . . requires the doing of an act in terms so vague that men of common intelligence must necessarily guess at the meaning and differ as to its application, violates the first essential of due process of law."[19] This rule of definiteness applies to court orders.[20] A condition which is vague and indefinite subjects the well intentioned probationer to revocation if he fails accurately to guess what the court, or his probation officer, consider as violative of the vague condition. It is suggested that a condition requiring that the defendant dress according to an undefined, if not subjective standard, is so vague as to be of little value. Even if we try to define in specifics the far-out attire of hippies, we become mired in semantics. Further, such a condition is vulnerable to attack as a violation of the probationer's constitutional rights. One proposition seems clear. A dress standard expressed in general terms not only fails to relate in logic to a program of rehabilitation (is social maladjustment correlated with any mode of dress?) but may be constitutionally "void for vagueness." Probation conditions in short should not be so vague or ambiguous as to give no real guidance.[21] As Shakespeare phrased it (*Hamlet,* Act 1, Sc. 1), "How absolute the knave is! We must speak by the card or equivocation will undo us."

CONDITIONS WHICH VIOLATE PROBATIONERS' RIGHTS TO EXPRESSION

As indicated above, the imposition of a particular condition may raise a question as to what constitutional rights a defendant has while on probation. We have already considered the question of whether a condition concerning hair or clothing style may be invalid for vagueness. An additional question is presented, i.e., whether an individual has a constitutional right to present a certain appearance, and if so, whether this right is applicable in the probation setting.

There may be today among the middle aged exemplars of our American conscience, a tendency to regard long hair and strange clothes as suspect, and the youths who affect these modes as being equally suspect.

From these overt life styles, the shocked middle aged observers deduce a syndrome of antisocial conduct such as rioting, pot-smoking, and sex. The simplistic solution is to order the strange looking kid to cut his hair and assume a "clean cut" appearance, which unlike the experience of Samson, will perfect a happy transition. In short, the abracadabra of the judge will do the trick. Not being behavioral scientists, the authors will not further dissect the premises underlying this syllogism. We can, however, point out some areas of possible legal objection which could be urged by some zealous lawyer in some courtroom somewhere.

Recent discussions of the United States Supreme Court and of some other federal courts have indicated that an individual's right to a particular hair style or mode of dress is constitutionally protected. These decisions are based on two separate theories.

First, it has been held that clothing or appearance may constitute a form of expression in the public school situation. The Supreme Court recently held in *Tinker* v. *Des Moines School Board* that the wearing of a black arm band to express dissatisfaction with the United States involvement in the Vietnam War is a form of expression, and thus constitutionally protected.[22] We might reasonably expect that this theory will be urged to protect other unusual clothing or hair styles when worn for the purpose of protest.[23] Conceivably a probationer might urge that his first amendment rights of speech and petition would, in similar circumstances, be curtailed by the overbroad language of a probation order.

The second theory used to support a constitutional right to appearance in the school setting is found in *Breen* v. *Kahl,* where the United States District Court for the Western District of Wisconsin, in dictum, said that a statute prescribing hair or clothing style "would clearly fail under the 14th Amendment."[24] The district court in an opinion affirmed by the Seventh Circuit noted that the right of an individual to present himself to the world in the manner of his choice is a highly protected freedom, and if restricted, the state must bear a "substantial burden of justification."

Neither of these cases deals with the rights of a probationer. The *Breen* case specifically notes that it does not deal with the imposition of stringent standards of personal appearance in penal institutions. The court was of the opinion that appearance standards in prisons are for the purpose "of discipline or deliberate degradation of inmates."

The reasoning of *Breen* does not really bear on the power of a court to impose clothing or hair style restrictions on probationers, who as a class enjoying conditional liberty, cannot be precisely analogized either to public school students, or to prisoners. A probationer subject to revocation for such reasons, may, however, ultimately urge a constitutional right to present whatever physical appearance he desires to the public. At that point, if it be first determined that such a right exists in any probationer, it would seem necessary that there be some demonstrable showing that in the circumstances *of that case* there is some relationship between the required physical appearance and the probationer's rehabilitation.

THE PROBATIONER'S CONSTITUTIONAL PROTECTION AGAINST SELF-INCRIMINATION

Probation conditions may raise questions of violations of the probationer's rights under the fifth amendment guarantee against self-incrimination.

Courts have, in some cases, imposed conditions of probation which require that the defendant reveal all of the details about the crime of which he has been convicted. In one such case in the District of Massachusetts the defendant was convicted of tax evasion because he had deducted bribes paid to get work.[25] The federal court in Boston granted probation when the defendant agreed to testify before the grand jury. When he later refused to testify, the Government asked that his probation be revoked. The district court upheld the principle that the probation order can include a condition that the person testify as to the facts of the case for which probation is granted, noting the broad powers set out in the probation statute. In addition, the court ruled that once a person is convicted of a crime, he no longer has a privilege against self-incrimination as to that crime.[26]

Other areas of self-incrimination may present different problems. Suppose, for example, that a court imposes as a condition of probation that the defendant shall turn over a copy of his income tax form to his probation officer. There seems to be little doubt that as a general proposition one's tax form can be used against him in a criminal action without violating the fifth amendment. In *United States* v. *Sullivan,* the Supreme Court held that the appropriate time to object to self-incrimination by a tax return is on the return itself.[27] Several years later the *Sullivan* case was cited by the United States Court of Appeals in *Stillman* v. *United States.*[28] In that case, the defendant's tax form was introduced into evidence against him in a trial for violation of the Price Control Act. The defendant objected to its admission saying that it violated the fifth amendment privilege against self-incrimination. The court rejected this saying that the tax forms were public records and their admission did not violate the defendant's fifth amendment rights.

In 1968, however, the Supreme Court handed down a series of opinions, of which *Marchetti* v. *United States* is representative.[29] In that case, the Supreme Court held that the federal statute requiring gamblers to register and pay a tax was violative of the defendant's fifth amendment right against self-incrimination. The court does note that unlike the income tax return in *Sullivan,* every portion of registering has the direct consequence of incriminating the gambler. Presumably, *Marchetti* would not affect the validity of a probation condition that the probationer turn over to the probation office a copy of the same tax return he filed with the Internal Revenue Service. The incrimination question might however be presented if the probationer is also ordered to furnish additional followup details of his business transactions, based on information derived from his tax return or inspection of his books. While we may probably assume the validity of routine investigation of this sort, suppose the probationer comes under suspicion of violating the terms of his probation (sometimes by the commission of another crime), and further investigation is for the very purpose of establishing that fact? Can he at some point refuse interrogation by taking the privilege? At what point? Or, on the other hand, is he a quasi-prisoner whose liberty is validly conditioned on full disclosure and his cooperation to the extent of revealing all information necessary to police the conditions of probation? Hasn't he, by accepting probation, validly waived the privilege? These broad questions probably have no categorical solutions, and will not until related to the facts of some specific future case.

CONDITIONS WHICH RESTRICT THE PROBATIONER'S RIGHT OF ASSOCIATION

It is quite common for courts to impose a condition restricting the probationer's right of association. The right of association is the natural right of a person to select his friends and associates and join legitimate organizations. Such a condition raises the question of whether the defendant's first amendment right of freedom of association has been violated.

The most common condition of this type prohibits the probationer from associating with persons who have previously been convicted of a crime or who are presently engaged in some unlawful undertaking. No cases have been discovered concerning the constitutionality of this condition. From a practical point of view it would seem to be helpful in preventing further criminal action, especially where a person is believed to be presently involved in crime. There could well be situations, however, where the condition would be intolerable, as where the person with the record has some special relationship (e.g., his uncle) or affiliation (e.g., his employer) with the probationer. Therefore, the court may be well advised to allow the probation officer to make exceptions where he feels it is reasonable to do so.

In at least one case, a sentencing court has limited a defendant's right of association with individuals who do not necessarily have a criminal background. In that case the defendant was convicted of unauthorized wearing of a military uniform.[30] One condition of probation was that the defendant was not to associate with members of the Students for a Democratic Society (S.D.S.). On appeal, the defendant complained that this condition violated his first amendment right of expression and assembly. The reviewing court noted that the trial court had broad discretion in setting conditions. It further noted that if the defendant did not like the conditions, he could reject them and go to prison. If the defendant "chose to enjoy the benefits of probation; he must also endure its restrictions." This case would appear to permit the trial court to restrict the defendant's association in any reasonable manner.

CONDITIONS INVOLVING CRUEL AND UNUSUAL PUNISHMENT

The Eighth Amendment's prohibition against cruel and unusual punishment might conceivably provide a basis of attack on conditions imposed on probationers in some situations. At the present time, however, its relevance is in doubt. The only case considering whether a probation condition was cruel and unusual involved a defendant who was convicted of a violation of the Selective Service Act.[31] On appeal to the Ninth Circuit the defendant objected to a probation condition which required that he give a pint of blood. The opinion-writing member of the court rejected the defendant's argument, which was apparently based on the eighth amendment, saying that:

The conditions of probation are not punitive in character and the question of whether or not the terms are cruel and unusual and thus violative of the Constitution of the United States does not arise for the reason that the Constitution applies only to punishment.

The other two members of the court concurred in the opinion but held that the requirement of giving a pint of blood invaded "the physical person in an unwarranted manner and (is) void on its face." The concurring opinion (which on the point of giving blood was a majority) did not reach or consider the argument that the eighth amendment applied.[32]

CONDITIONS REQUIRING THAT THE PROBATIONER SUBMIT TO SEARCH

Courts granting probation frequently attempt to fashion the conditions in such a manner that future crimes of the same nature are discouraged. In certain instances this may include a condition that the probationer submit to a search of either his person, home, or business without the formalities of a search warrant. The question is thus raised whether this condition violates the defendant's fourth amendment rights.

A decision of the U.S. District Court for the Southern District of New York dealing with the search of a parolee, provides some background to this problem.[33] In that case the court noted that if the defendant is imprisoned, substantially all of his fourth amendment rights will be lost. Consequently, there is little reason to object to searches without warrants where the defendant is out of prison. The court also suggests that close surveillance is necessary because of the high rate of recidivism and to retain public support of the parole or probation system. For a general discussion see White, The Fourth Amendment Rights of Parolees and Probationers.[34]

There are at least two cases where a sentencing court has imposed a condition requiring that the probationer submit to a search without a warrant. In one District of Columbia case, the defendant was convicted of selling obscene articles.[35] The court suspended sentence placing the defendant on probation, and required that he "allow police to search any premises he operates or manages without a search warrant." The reviewing court (the District of Columbia Court of Appeals) upheld the rationale of this condition, noting that the trial court had broad discretion in setting probation conditions, and rejected,

... appellants' contention that a condition can never be imposed which would restrict their constitutional rights, because the alternative is imprisonment in jail which certainly restricts their rights. The choice is theirs to either serve a jail sentence or accept the condition.

A similar condition was imposed in a North Carolina decision.[36] In this case, the defendant was convicted of manufacturing liquor and agreed to "permit any lawful officer to search his premises without a search warrant." The police later searched the defendant's home without a warrant, and discovered whiskey on which the tax had not been paid. This evidence was suppressed by the trial court for the purpose of a second conviction, but allowed for the purpose of revoking the defendant's probation.

Although the North Carolina case seems internally inconsistent, it appears that a court may require as a condition of probation the consent by the probationer to future searches. The fourth amendment bans only "unreasonable searches and seizures," and it has long been the law that a person may, by his consent, waive his right to absolute privacy of his person and property. On the theory that, by accepting the conditions of probation, the probationer waives the full spectrum of rights on which he might otherwise insist, the search condition is valid within bounds of reason. The exercise of any search would have to be constrained, and limited to the immediate and apparent needs of enforcing probation. It is suggested that the probationer would be protected against arbitrary or oppressive actions.[37] Such a search could become "unreasonable" if made too often, at an unreasonable hour, if unreasonably prolonged, or if done in some other oppressive manner.

CONDITIONS WHICH AFFECT THE PROBATIONER'S RIGHT TO RELIGIOUS FREEDOM

On occasion courts have imposed probation conditions which relate to the probationer's religious habits. Thus courts have required that as a condition of probation the defendant must agree to attend church on a regular basis. The question may be raised whether this violates the probationer's first amendment right to freedom of religion.

In dealing with the right to freedom of religious belief and religious expression (albeit, outside the context of probation), it seems clear that one has a right not only to believe as he pleases, but also to disbelieve if he so chooses. The United States Supreme Court has held that the Federal Government cannot:

. . . force or influence a person to go to or to remain away from church against his will. . . . No person can be punished for entertaining or professing religious beliefs or disbeliefs [or] for church attendance or nonattendance.[38]

These first amendment prohibitions directed against the sovereign itself, are not the subject of waiver.

It appears that the right to disbelieve or to refrain from attending church is an absolute one protecting even a probationer. It was so held in a 1946 *Virginia* case where the defendant, a juvenile delinquent, was placed on probation on the condition that he "attend Sunday school and church each Sunday hereafter for a period of one year."[39] The reviewing court held that this condition violates the freedom of religion clause of the United States Constitution. The court noted that "no civil authority has the right to require anyone to accept or reject any religious belief or to contribute any support thereto. The growth of religion is not made dependent on force or alliance with the state."[40]

One troublesome aspect of the problem might arise if a court conditioned probation on the probationer's forbearance from some activity otherwise prescribed by a religious sect. Legal historians remember the confrontation between law enforcement and the early Mormons practicing plural marriage. In the last decade the emergent Black Muslim religious sect has presented the challenging question of how the categorical imperative of the first amendment can be squared with the imperatives of law enforcement. Muslims have been alleged to be an activist group whose religious exercise in institutions has at times been on a collision course with rules of internal discipline.[41] Although the question of the exercise of the Muslim religion by probationers has not been squarely raised in litigation, the right of the Muslims to practice their religion in prison has been the subject of various cases in the Fourth Circuit.[42] At least with respect to certain specific practices, enjoyed by all other religions, their right to unrestrained religious freedom in the prison setting has been upheld.[43] It has however been suggested that the rights of prisoners generally to unrestrained and unquestioned religious freedom is not without any limit. Activities which would, for example, threaten the safety or health of others, or create another breach of the peace, might be restrained regardless of whether they were given a religious imprimatur by some religious group. As Justice Murphy put the problem in one case:[44]

> We cannot conceive that cursing a public officer is the exercise of religion in any sense of the term. But even if the activities of the appellant which preceded the incident could be viewed as religious in character, and therefore entitled to the protection of the Fourteenth Amendment, they would not cloak him with immunity from the legal consequences for concomitant acts committed in violation of a valid criminal statute.

But limitations on religious activities as well as on speech and assembly in the prison setting, have been said to be dependent on a showing of "clear and present danger,"[45] if they constrain first amendment rights.

Applying these principles to the probation setting (where institution discipline is not a factor), we would speculate that a court would be impelled to look for circumstances of a most unusual sort to justify a condition which limits religious practice or religious association. It would seem that the condition would have to curb some antisocial conduct constituting a "clear and present danger" to the state to justify any invasion of the free atmosphere of religious thought and expression.

OTHER CONDITIONS OF PROBATION

There are a number of conditions which though not unconstitutional have been critized for numerous reasons. One such condition is the "split sentence" where probation is provided to follow a fixed term of detention of up to 6 months on the same count, or where, in a mixed sentence, probation is made to follow a term of imprisonment on another count.[46] Another probation variant is commingling periods of jail confinement with periods of release.[47] Such conditions have been described as being at odds with the fundamental philosophy of probation.[48] The purposes of probation have been stated to be: to promote rehabilitation of the offender by continuing normal community contact, to avoid the negative effects of confinement, and to minimize the impact of the conviction upon innocent dependents of the offender.[49] The American Bar Association defines probation as to exclude confinement.[50] Nevertheless the courts as a matter of law have generally sustained the practice of combining probation with incarceration. The Court of Appeals for the Seventh Circuit, while upholding the trial court's right to impose such a condition, noted that:

> The prevailing opinion among criminologists and probation officers, as well as others who have studied the question, is that mixed sentences should not be imposed. Undesirable as the practice may be, we think it was within the power of the (court).[51]

Our discussion of short-term incarceration prior to probation does not include the use of halfway facilities as a condition of probation. Use of this rehabilitative procedure avoids many of the negative effects of imprisonment, while providing the substantial guidance which some probationers need. Congress has recently amended the federal probation laws allowing courts to require as a condition of probation that the probationer "reside or participate in the program of a residential community treatment center, or both, for all or part of the period of probation."[52]

Residence or participation in a Center program is to be considered for persons with clearly definable needs which can be met by the services offered by the Center. These services include close supervision, employment counseling and placement, individual and group counseling, and in some instances, out-patient psychiatric services.

This kind of program is, of course, remedial in nature and not at all akin to the mixing of probation with short-term incarceration.

A District of Columbia decision presents a case where a condition, while not unconstitutional, was beyond the scope of the probation statute.[53] In that case the trial court required that the defendant write an essay satisfactory to the judge. The Court of Appeals held that there was no basis in law for requiring such a condition.

A Michigan case presents another example of this type of undesirable condition.[54] There the defendant was convicted of a violation of the liquor law and as a condition of probation, was required to leave the state of Michigan for a period of 5 years. The Supreme Court of Michigan ruled that banishment could tend to incite dissension, invoke retribution, and disturb the fundamental equality of political rights among the several states. Such a method of punishment was not merely unauthorized by statute, but was held contrary to public policy.

We might anticipate other similar attacks on various of the questionable conditions listed *supra,* some of which might be considered potently arbitrary or unreasonable, or contrary to public policy. One example is a condition that the probationer marry a girl he has made pregnant. A condition that the probationer should not marry without permission might well be asserted to contravene public policy, as might a condition imposed on a married probationer that he have his wife report when he is unable to do so. Others listed might be attacked as arbitrary; or at least, provide a highly vulnerable basis for revocation proceedings in the event of noncompliance.

WHAT CONDITIONS OF PROBATION ARE DESIRABLE?

The standard seven conditions of the Federal Probation System set forth in Probation Form No. 7, "Conditions of Probation," contain the boilerplate conditions, and need not be further expounded upon here. The conditions, of course, can be and should be supplemented by special conditions appropriate in an individual case. The establishment of a tailored program of rehabilitation should be undertaken with all of the foresight and precision that goes into drafting an important contract. In fact, a probation order *is* an important social contract, the subject matter of which is the acquistion of conditional liberty in return for obedience to prescribed norms of behavior.

It would be presumptious to recommend lists of individual conditions appropriate only in limited instances. The American Bar Association's *Standards Relating to Probation*[55] suggests that the sentencing judge should be enabled "to prescribe additional conditions to fit the circumstances of each case." The standards do contain the caveat that the conditions should be reasonably related to his rehabilitation, and should not be so vague or ambiguous as to give no real guidance.

The Standards also specify (§ 3.1 (b)) that probation officers "must have authority to implement judicially prescribed conditions; but the conditions should be sufficiently precise so that probation officers do not in fact establish them." To give the probation officer the power to create certain reasonable exceptions (as, for example, exceptions to travel restrictions in emergencies or in other exigent circumstances) seems a wise delegation to meet unforeseen situations that may develop during the period of probation supervision.

Another situation which will necessitate an additional condition in federal probation orders emerges from Public Law 91–492, creating Federal Community Treatment Centers. As pointed out in a memorandum of February 12, 1971, sent to all federal probation officers and federal judges by Mr. Merrill Smith, chief of the Division of Probation of the Administrative Office, when residence or participation in a center is ordered by the court at the time of judgment, a special condition should be incorporated in the order that the probationer shall reside in, or where applicable, participate in the center program, until discharged by the center director.

Another condition appropriate in certain cases is restitution of the fruits of the crime or reparation for loss or damage caused thereby. This condition has the desirable effect of stressing primarily that a tort has been committed against other warm-bodied human beings, which tort can to some extent be expiated in a visible way (rather than stressing the wrong against that amorphous entity—the state —personified in street jargon as "the Man," "the Fuzz," "the Establishment," etc.). Restitution provides a catharsis or purgation of guilt which the penitent may feel only when forced with the concrete evidence of his wrong-doing.

Restitution and fines should never be so burdensome as to impose a hardship on the probationer and his family. Like any other probation condition, this one should be tempered to his particular abilities and needs.

CONCLUSION

We believe it can be fairly stated that probation is the ultimate test of our wisdom in dealing with the offender and is certainly increasing in social importance. The pending federal criminal caseload was up 18 percent in 1970 over 1969,[56] and in 1970 the cost of imprisonment was 1,000 percent more expensive than probation or parole.[57] The pressure on existing federal penal and correctional institutions is a matter of such universal knowledge it hardly needs belaboring. It follows, at least in the short haul, that the number of federal probationers has nowhere to go but up.

Probation, however, is a highly individualized matter and does not lend itself to wholesaling techniques (if it did we could readily sentence by computer). The first point of departure in planning a probation program for the individual is the role of the judge in framing a probation order. Our point is that it should be carefully drawn to maximize liberty while effectively protecting the public from further violations of law. Three words describe the basic necessities of a probation order; "relevancy," "clarity," and "legality." A fourth might be "foresight" since the conditions of probation will serve as the probationer's *modus vivendi* during the supervision period. The order is not a waybill for a trip to oblivion, but the court's prescription for a successful cure. It should, therefore, be crafted with the needs of a particular individual in mind, which means more than adopting the preprinted conditions on a form. This is the challenge put to the judge and to the probation officer.

REFERENCES

1. 18 U.S.C. §3651 *et seq.*
2. *Escoe* v. *Zerbst*, 295 U.S. 490 (1935)
3. *United States* v. *Smith,* 414 F.2d 630 (5th Cir. 1969), rev'd, on other grounds, 90 S. Ct. 1555.
4. *Huffman* v. *United States,* 259 A.2d 342 (D.C. Ct. App. 1969).
5. *Sweeney* v. *United States,* 343 F.2d 10 (7th Cir. 1965); Re *Bine,* 306 P.2d 445 (Sup. Ct. Calif. 1957)
6. Comment, *Judicial Review of Probation Conditions,* 67 Colum. Law Rev. 181 (1967); *cf. Butler* v. *D.C.,* 346 F.2d 798 (D.C. Cir. 1965).
7. American Bar Association, *Standards Relating to Proabation,* Approved Draft, p.1.
8. American Bar Association, *Standards Relating to Probation,* Comment, 67 Colum. Law Rev., *supra* note 6, *Butler* v. *D.C., supra,* note 6.
9. *Dillingham* v. *United States,* 76 F.2d 35 (5th Cir. 1935).
10. *Ibid.*
11. *Whaley* v. *United States,* 324 F.2d 356 (9th Cir. 1963) *cert. denied,* 376 U.S. 911; *Barnhill* v. *U.S.,* 279 F.2d 105 (5th Cir. 1960); Re *Osslo,* 334 P.2d 1 (Sup. Ct. Col. 1958).
12. *United States* v. *Smith, supra* note 3.
13. *People* v. *Stanley,* 327 P.2d 973 (Dist. Ct. of App. Calif. 1958).
14. *State* v. *Smith,* 233 N.C. 68, SE.E.2d 495 (1950).
15. *State* v. *Rogers,* 221 N.C. 462, 20 S.E. 2d 297 (1942).

16. *Willis* v. *U.S.*, 250 A. 2d 569 (D.C. App. 1969).

17. American Bar Association, *Standards Relating to Probation*, §3.2(a).

18. See for example, *Cramp.* v. *Orange Co.*, 368 U.S. 278 (1961); 16 Am. Jur.2d, *Constitutional Law* §552.

19. *Cramp.* v. *Orange, supra*, note 18.

20. Am. Jur.2d, *Constitutional Law* §552.

21. American Bar Association, *Standards Relating to Probation*, §3.2(b).

22. *Tinker* v. *Des Moines School Brd.*, 393 U.S. 503 (1969); *see generally*, Denno, *Mary Beth Tinker Takes the Constitution to School*, 38 Fordham, L.R. 35 (Oct. '69).

23. See *Breen* v. *Kahl, infra*, note 24.

24. *Breen* v. *Kahl, 296 F. Supp. 702 (W.D. Wisc. 1969), aff'd 419 F.2d 1034 (C.A. 7, 1969), cert denied*, 398 U.S. 937.

25. *United States* v. *Worchester*, 190 F. Supp. 548 (Mass. 1960).

26. *Ibid.; see also Worchester* v. *C.I.R.*, 370 F.2d 713, 716 (C.A.I., 1966); *United States* v. *Qualls*, 182 F. Supp. 213 (N.D. Ill. 1960); *Kaplan* v. *U.S.*, 234 F.2d 345 (8th Cir., 1956).

27. *United States* v. *Sullivan*, 274 U.S. 259 (1927).

28. *Stillman* v. *United States*, 177 F.2d 607 (9th Cir. 1949).

29. *Marchetti* v. *United States*, 390 U.S. 39 (1968).

30. *United States* v. *Smith,* 414 F.2d 630 (5th Cir. 1969), rev'd on other grounds 90 S. Ct. 1555.

31. *Springer* v. *United States*, 148 F.2d 411 (9th Cir. 1945).

32. *See generally*, comment *Judicial Review of Probation*, 67 Colum. Law Rev. 181 at 206 (1967).

33. *United States* v. *Follette*, 282 F. Supp. 10 (S.D. N.Y. 1968).

34. White, *The Fourth Amendment Rights of Parolees and Probationers*, 31 Univ. of Pittsburgh Law Rev. 167 (1969).

35. *Huffman* v. *United States*, 259 A.2d 342 (D.C. Ct. of App. 1969).

36. *State* v. *White, 264 N.C. 600, 142 S.E. 2d 153 (1965).*

37. *United States* v. *Follette, supra,* note 33; White, *The Fourth Amendment Rights of Parolees and Probationers, supra,* note 34.

38. *McCallom* v. *Brd. of Education*, 333 U.S. 203 (1948).

39. *Jones* v. *Commonwealth*, 185 V. 335, 38 S.E. 2d 444 (1946).

40. *Ibid.*, at 448.

41. Frankino, *The Manacles and the Messenger*, 14 Catholic Univ. Law Rev. 30 (1965).

42. For example, *Sewell* v. *Peglow*, 291 F.2d 196 (4th Cir. 1961); and 304 F.2d 670 (1962).

43. *Sewell* v. *Peglow, supra; Fulwood* v. *Clemmer*, 206 F. Supp. 370 (D.C. 1962); *Childs* v. *Peglow*, 321 F.2d 487 (4th Cir. 1963).

44. *Chaplinsky* v. *New Hampshire*, 315 U.S. 568. 571.

45. See *Fulwood* v. *Clemmer, supra; The Manacles and the Messenger, supra,* at pp. 53–58.

46. See 18 U.S.C. 3651 (second par.).

47. *Petersen* v. *Dunbar* 355 F.2d 800 (9th Cir. 1966); *United States* v. *Murphy* 217 F.2d 247 (7th Cir. 1954).

48. Scudder, *"In Opposition to Probation with a Jail Sentence,"* Fed. Probation (June 1959), pp. 12–17; and compare: Hartshorne, *The 1958 Federal "Split Sentence Law." Ibid.* at pp. 9–12.

49. American Bar Association, *Standards Relating to Probation,* §1.2.

50. *Ibid.*, at §1.1.

51. *United States* v. *Murphy, supra,* note 47.

52. P.L. 91–492 (Oct. 22, 1970).

53. *Butler* v. *D.C.,* 346 F.2d 798 44 (D.C. Cir. 1965).

54. *People* v. *Baum,* 231 N.W. 95, 251 Mich. 187 (1930).

55. ·*Ibid.,* at §3.2.

56. Annual Report of the Director of the Administrative Office (1970) at p. I–5.

57. *Ibid.,* at p. IV–10.

29

When Should Probation be Revoked?

EUGENE C. DICERBO

Just as disparities in sentence have been of concern to judges and probation officers, so are the disparities in the revocation of probation. The criteria for revoking probation are not uniform in district courts throughout the country and, at times, not even among judges in the same district court.

Some judges and probation officers insist that convictions for new offenses should be the only basis for revocation. Others believe that infractions of the conditions of probation other than the commitment of a new offense should also be justification for revocation, particularly where such violations are committed by an indifferent probationer who is unwilling to cooperate with the probation office and the court. And other judges contend that the circumstances of the violation, the general attitude and outlook of the probationer, his adjustment with his family, in the community, and on the job, and his efforts to comply with the conditions should also be considered by the probation officer before recommending revocation and the court before revoking probation.

It is the purpose of this article to focus attention on the question of when and when not to revoke probation and to offer some guidelines which will help the probation officer in making recommendations to the court where there are alleged violations.

Source. *Federal Probation*, XXX, June 1966, pp. 11-17. Reprinted with permission of the author and *Federal Probation*.

I have long been of the opinion that it should not be necessary for the probation officer to bring each probation violator to court. The court should have sufficient confidence in his probation staff to allow it to decide when any single infraction or series of infractions should be brought to the court's attention.

What, then, are some of the criteria for determining whether to bring a case to court on a revocation hearing and to recommend for or against revocation?

MINOR VIOLATIONS

Let us begin with a discussion of the more or less minor infractions of the conditions of probation. Suppose a probationer, who otherwise has been cooperative, does not keep an appointment or two. Is this sufficient grounds to bring him to the court as a violator? Hardly.

Consider the probationer who on two or three occasions overlooked sending or bringing in his monthly supervision report. Should he be brought to court as a violator? Hardly.

If a young probationer persists in staying out late hours despite the admonition of his parents, does this constitute a valid reason for reporting him as a violator considering the fact that he does not get into trouble? I have had but few cases where a compromise could not be reached—where the parents, the probationer, and probation officer could not arrive at an understanding as to what hours the probationer should maintain.

What is to be done with a probationer who, now and then, receives a traffic ticket for illegal parking, for driving 5 or 10 miles over the speed limit, for failing to come to a complete stop at a stop sign? It is my contention that these infractions seldom fall within the criteria for revoking probation.

What should be done with a probationer who purchases an automobile or motorcycle contrary to the instructions of the probation officer? The probation officer may be concerned about serious consequences that may result if the probationer has a car or motorcycle. Instead of bringing the probationer to court, would it not be better to ask the probationer to sell the vehicle? Should he not comply, then revocation proceedings might be instituted. If liability insurance is the concern, he should be asked either to obtain the insurance or to sell the vehicle.

Should a probationer be brought to court when he, contrary to the instructions of the probation officer, marries? It is doubtful whether any court would revoke probation in such a case. Some courts would even regard this as an unreasonable and unwarranted restriction.

Is a probationer who quits his job without first clearing with his probation officer in violation of probation? Should not the probation officer determine the circumstances for his leaving the job, especially if it was on short notice? Were there interpersonal relationships and problems on the job which made it unpleasant or even unbearable?

What if the probationer refuses to take a job suggested by the probation officer? Should the officer not first learn the probationer's reasons for not doing so? They may be quite valid and understandable.

What if a probationer refuses to attend group counseling sessions? Is this to be considered in violation of his probation? He may have good reasons for not participating in group meetings.

FELONIES AND MISDEMEANORS

We now come to violations which involve convictions for a new felony or misdemeanor.

A probationer is convicted of a minor offense such as "disorderly conduct" or "assault and battery" in a fist fight with no serious injury resulting. Is his probation to be revoked? It is my feeling that the matter should be brought to the court's attention. But in his report the probation officer may recommend that probation not be revoked if the probationer's probation adjustment has been satisfactory.

Take the case of a probationer with no prior criminal record and an excellent probation adjustment who was convicted and committed for a minor offense for which he served a 30-day jail sentence. The offense and the jail sentence did not come to light until some time after his release from jail. Meanwhile, the probationer returned to his place of employment and continued to work regularly. The officer is faced with the decision whether to institute revocation proceedings or notify the court of the offense and recommend that probation continue. True, the welfare of the community takes precedence over the welfare of the individual. But this man posed no threat to society and, moreover, was highly respected by the members of his community. Would society benefit more from additional punishment or more from his rehabilitation which was interrupted by the short period of incarceration?

Let us assume that the same person was committed on a felony conviction and for a longer period. What consideration, if any, should be given to the absence of a prior criminal record and an excellent adjustment up to the time of the new offense? At first glance this might appear to be a clear-cut violation of probation. A closer examination into the facts might reveal a more complex situation because of the presence of mitigating factors and extenuating circumstances. Perhaps the probationer should receive the benefit of the doubt if he manifests redeeming characteristics, if the details of the offense indicate nothing heinous, if he became involved unwittingly, or if the period of incarceration is of such length that there would be little gained by additional confinement.

There is the question whether a conviction is necessary before any court action can be taken in a revocation proceeding. The following case illustrates the question in point.

Amassing a record of nine arrests, all for illicit liquor and all pending in local court during active supervision, a bootlegger was referred to the court for violation of probation because there was continuation of a pattern disclosed in the presentence report. He had no visible means of support and was, in effect, making a mockery of probation. At a hearing before the court he maintained he was being harrassed by the local police and that he was innocent of all of the charges. In deferring action the judge elected to wait for a conviction on the alleged offenses. The probation officer fulfilled his obligation by calling the alleged violation to the court's attention.

Cases pending in local and even in federal courts present a problem when the 5-year maximum probation period is soon to terminate. Should the probationer be brought before the court despite the fact that disposition has not been made of the pending case? In view of the possibility of an acquittal, it would seem unfair to declare a probationer a violator. Perhaps the wisest course would be to permit probation to terminate on the assumption that if convicted the probationer will be punished adequately for the new offense. Another possibility is to have a warrant issued and execution deferred until the outcome of the pending case.

REALISTIC CONDITIONS OF PROBATION

The degree to which probation conditions are violated is directly related to the extent to which the conditions are realistic. Unrealistic conditions invite violations. Whether sanctions are to be imposed for violating a condition of probation would depend to a large extent on whether they are reasonable and enforceable. A comprehensive presentence investigation report will assist the court in deciding what special conditions of probation should be imposed in a given case: If the court, for example, contemplates assessing a fine, the presentence report will inform the judge of the financial status of the defendant. Too often a fine or restitution places a burden on the defendant, adding to the financial problems that got him into difficulty in the first instance. Nothing is gained by imposing a fine or restitution that he obviously cannot live up to and which actually cannot be enforced.

Other unrealistic conditions of probation which may be difficult to enforce are regular attendance at church, abstaining completely from alcoholic beverages, association with persons with arrest records, leaving the boundaries proscribed by the court or the probation officer. When such conditions are established, the probationer who does not comply may believe he is getting by with something; or he may have a sense of guilt for circumventing the conditions without disclosing the violation to his probation officer. Neither reaction is good.

Conditions of probation should be established by the court primarily to assist the probationer to become a law-abiding, self-respecting person. Conditions of probation should not be imposed as a punitive device. Nor should rigid compliance be expected in every instance. There should be flexibility in the application of the conditions, depending on the merits of the individual case.

What shall be the position of the probation officer when the court imposes conditions that are unrealistic and almost impossible to enforce? The probation officer is charged with the responsibility of seeing to it that the probationer complies with all conditions. Where he finds the conditions are unreasonable and he is losing control of the situation, he should notify the court that the conditions are difficult to enforce and also offer suggestions for modification of the conditions.

It is important that the probation officer make certain that the probationer fully comprehends each condition of probation and what is expected of him. It is not sufficient merely to have him indicate by his signature of the "Conditions of Probation" form that he understands each condition.

FINES AND RESTITUTION

Where the court orders payment of a fine or restitution at a fixed rate within a prescribed time, should the court be notified when an otherwise cooperative probationer falls behind a payment or two? It would seem that this condition is akin to the requirement that monthly supervision reports be submitted by a certain date each month. The probation office should have the responsibility for determining whether it is necessary to bring a probationer to court when a specified amount is not paid by a certain date.

In evaluating the financial situation of a probationer, the probation officer is confronted with two considerations: Was the probationer in a position to make payment of even nominal amounts, manifesting good faith, or was he unable to make payments because of inadequate earnings, illness, or other valid reason? Deliberate failure to make payments, on the other hand, is tantamount to flouting the order of the court.

Recently, two brothers on probation were brought before the court for failure to make regular payment on a sizeable fine. One was delinquent in the amount of several hundred dollars; the other had failed to meet a deadline date but later paid the fine in full. Expressing the opinion that these men had deliberately defied his order and that there were no mitigating circumstances, the court revoked probation and imposed a prison sentence. In an appeal, the decision of the District Court was upheld by the Circuit Court of Appeals.

By no means academic, these questions are based on actual cases. When they arise, they require the careful examination of every probation officer. They also vividly portray the need for a common denominator for determining what type of action the officer should take when a probationer jeopardizes his status. Careful consideration is especially required where a balance remains as the 5-year maximum period of supervision draws to a close. Although I do not generally subscribe to the policy that a jail sentence should be imposed for nonpayment of fine or restitution, I do believe that the attitude of the probationer and his reasons for failure to comply demand careful scrutiny. The following court decision covers this very point:

Where one convicted of tax offenses was granted probation on condition that he pay fines within a specified time, bare nonpayment of fines was not conclusive of disobedience of probation terms and did not subject him to imprisonment as of course; his probation was not beyond redemption if in reality he was too poor to pay, not to blame for it, and sincere in his try. . . . Even though accused accepted probation when sentenced, two years later when he defaulted in payment of his fines and his probation was revoked he could deny commensurate fairness of fines.[1]

Judges often have remarked that they do not deem it wise to have their orders ignored or to leave defendants with the impression that the court does not always mean what it says. Therefore, where a balance remains on a fine or restitution the court should be so apprised. If a justification exists, probation may be allowed to terminate with restitution remaining as a moral obligation and the fine either remitted or left as a money judgment to be confessed at some future date if circumstances so warrant.

Where conditions of probation are unfulfilled as the expiration date of probation approaches, the action taken by probation officers may vary. In some districts the court allows the probation officer to determine whether probation should be allowed to terminate without fulfillment of the conditions imposed. In our court, when it appears a condition of probation will not be met, the matter is brought to the court in advance of the expiration date, often with a plan or suggestion for a course of action—for example, extension of the period of probation. In this respect, it would be helpful if each court would let its probation officers know what types of unfulfilled conditions should be brought to its attention.

IS THE VIOLATION DELIBERATE?

When a probationer violates the conditions of his probation, the probation officer must determine whether the violation is deliberate, whether the violation is the result of an unrealistic condition, whether the probationer is the victim of a generally poor social adjustment. We are dealing with persons who are "socially wrong" or "socially sick." We are dealing with patterns of behavior that have been firmly established over many years. Some of these patterns are acceptable to the cultural group of which the probationer is a part, but are not necessarily acceptable to the larger society. For many of our probationers general adjustment to school is not good, school truancy is high, trade training and industrial skills are lacking, there are marital breakdowns, there are poor adjustments to military service, and social and moral values are in conflict with society in general. Life, for them, is filled with maladjustments of one kind or another. In many instances violations of probation may be symptoms of a poor social adjustment, but a poor social adjustment should not necessarily be regarded as a violation of probation.

In determining whether to recommend revocation, the probation officer must keep in mind the attitude and outlook of the probationer. Certainly a person who is penitent and who has done his best to live up to the conditions of his probation should be placed in a different category than one who is indifferent, or even

[1] *U.S.* v. *Taylor,* 4th Cir. 1963, 321 F.2d 339.

arrogant, and whose only regret is that he was caught. And it is especially important at this time for the probation officer to help the probationer appreciate the advantages that will accrue when he meets his financial and moral obligations and measures up to the trust the court has placed in him.

The probation officer should avoid setting limits for his probationers based on his own standards of living and moral and social values. The standards of conduct he establishes must not only be realistic, but also meaningful and acceptable to the probationer.

REVOCATION SHOULD SERVE A CONSTRUCTIVE PURPOSE

When it becomes necessary to revoke probation a constructive purpose should be served. A plan should be formulated that is in the best interests of the probationer, his family and the community. Little is gained where the court disposition is for the sake of punishment only.

It may be that the probationer has demonstrated that he is not a law-abiding, responsible person, and even poses a threat to society. He may need the kind of discipline and training he will get in an institution. If employment has been his problem, he may obtain in the institution the kind of training needed to find a job.

Assuming the probationer is not in the need of descipline or training and does not impose a threat to the free community, should probation be revoked? This would depend on a number of factors, including his attitude, his home and community adjustment, his adjustment on the job, and the nature of his probation violation. Imprisonment should be imposed only as a last resort.

The argument that commitment for violation of probation serves as a deterrent is not without merit. Several years ago an epidemic of theft and forgery of government checks in the form of income tax refunds spread through a section of our district. Despite the fact that these checks had been issued in rather small amounts, the practice became more than a nuisance because restitution was not made in a majority of the cases. As more and more jail terms were imposed for violation of probation, not only did restitution payments increase in the active probation cases, but thefts also diminished to the point that they were no longer widespread.

Thus far our discussion has centered for the most part around the probationer and the officer. In restitution cases that eventually result in violation of probation, what consideration should be given to the aggrieved party? When a probationer is sentenced to imprisonment for failure to make restitution, the victim suffers the entire loss. If the probationer is not a menace to the community, perhaps a recommendation can be made that probation be allowed to continue if for no other reason than to satisfy the losses suffered by the victim. This problem will be resolved, in part, when we have legislation providing compensation to victims of crime.

There is also the possibility that the probationer believes he is getting away with something and that the court does not mean what it says. What has to be resolved, then, is the question: Does rigid compliance and swift justice make for better probation or a fuller appreciation of probation on the part of the public?

VIOLATION HEARING AND REPORT

It is the general practice of courts to require a violation report in connection with a revocation hearing. In it are presented the facts surrounding the alleged violation. Included in the report should be a summary of the probationer's conduct while on probation, and his general attitude and outlook. The report should indicate whether the violation is incidental or a part of a general pattern. The probationer is required by law to be present at the revocation hearing.[2]

It is not necessary that the violation hearing be conducted as a trial. With respect to specifications of charges or a trial upon charges, it is not formal.[3]

The law further stipulates that "As speedily as possible after arrest the probationer shall be taken before the court for the district having jurisdiction over him.[4]

With the recent decisions of the Supreme Court that a defendant be represented by the counsel at every step of due process, it would seem that the probationer's attorney should be present at the hearing. The United States attorney should also be part of the proceeding to make whatever comments or recommendations are indicated.

If, after listening to all parties concerned, the court decides to revoke probation, it might be limited with respect to the sentence it can impose. In the event imposition of sentence was suspended originally, the court is empowered to impose any sentence within the limits prescribed by the penalty provisions of the statute involved.[5]

If a definite sentence was imposed originally and the execution of the sentence was suspended, the court may not exceed the original sentence.[6]

There are occasions where a probationer is serving a state or local sentence which continues beyond the expiration date of the period of probation imposed by the United States district court. To allow the probation to terminate or to seek a warrant for violation of probation is a question that, at times, is difficult to decide.

If returning the probationer to court in the distant future will not serve a constructive purpose, perhaps the ends of justice can be met by permitting probation to expire or, better yet, by the court entering an order terminating probation. To impose additional imprisonment after a lengthy period of incarceration is tantamount to adding salt to the wound.

---

[2] 18 U.S.C. 3653. See also *Escoe* v. *Zerbst,* 295 U.S. 490.

[3] *Manning* v. *U.S.* 5th Cir. 1947, 161 F.2d 827, Cert. den. 322 U.S. 792; 68 S.Ct. 102. *Bernal-Zaguetta* v. *U.S.* 9th Cir. 1955, 225 F.2d 64; *U.S.* v. *Hollien,* D.C. Mich. 1952, 105 F. Supp. 987.

[4] 18 U.S.C. 3653

[5] *Scalis* v. *U.S.* 1st Cir. 1932, 62 F.2d 220; *Gillespie* v. *Hunter,* 10th Cir. 1948, 170 F.2d 546; *Roberts* v. *U.S.* 320 U.S. 264, 64 S.Ct. 113.

[6] *Roberts* v. *U.S.* 320 U.S. 264, 64 S.Ct. 113.

In such cases, careful scrutiny of the presentence report and an evaluation of the probationer's conduct while under supervision can help determine the proper course of action. If a person poses a threat to society, a warrant is in order. The court will then have at the time of the probationer's release a report of his attitude toward authority, his adjustment in prison, and also the presentence report.

What shall be done about the probationer who absconds? After all possible efforts have been made to locate the probationer, a warrant should be requested. In fugitive status a probationer may possibly become involved in other infractions of the law in order to avoid apprehension.

Some years ago we supervised a 35-year-old unmarried male whose background was favorable and whose adjustment was most satisfactory. Suddenly he moved and quit his job to accept another without notifying the probation officer. Members of his family were asked where he lived and where he was employed. They did not know. The family saw him occasionally, reporting that he was well and was working regularly. Each time the probation officer's message was relayed to him, asking that he get in touch with his officer.

Convinced that he had not absconded, the probation officer continued to make inquiries until there came to his attention the name and address of an acquaintance of the probationer who might know his address. In writing to the acquaintance it was explained that unless the probationer was heard from within 10 days, there would be no alternative but to refer the matter to the court for appropriate action. It had been 9 months since the last monthly supervision report had been received. Within a few days all nine reports, properly executed, were received in the mail. When the probationer was interviewed later he explained that he was frightened when he entered into a clandestine relationship with a woman who was separated from her husband. At our insistence the affair was terminated and the probationer successfully completed the balance of his period of supervision.

No doubt this was an extreme case and 9 months was an unreasonably long time. Nevertheless, it illustrates the need for exercising patience and understanding lest the officer fall victim to a hasty and faulty decision.

In general, it is my belief that after all possible leads to locate an absconder have been exhausted, the probation officer has valid reason for petitioning the court for a warrant.

SUMMARY OF GUIDELINES FOR REVOCATION

1. Conditions of probation should be realistic and purposive and geared to help the probationer develop into a law-abiding, self-respecting person. They must be flexible in their application. Each case should be judged on its own merits —on the basis of the problems, needs, and capacity of the individual offender. Unrealistic conditions which cannot be enforced invite violations.

2. The probation officer should make certain that the probationer fully understands the limitations placed upon him in the general and special conditions

imposed by the court. Merely signing the "Conditions of Probation" form does not mean he has correctly interpreted each condition.

3. Violations of the conditions of probation do not necessarily reflect a poor probation adjustment. The conditions imposed may have been unrealistic. Perhaps too much was expected in requiring some probationers to live up to certain conditions. The customs, feelings, attitudes, habit patterns, and moral and social values of the cultural group of which a probationer is a part should be considered in assessing his noncompliance with the conditions. Probationers differ in their ability to comply or conform. It is entirely possible we are imposing a standard of conduct which is realistic for us but not for the probationer.

4. In offenses where a fine and/or restitution are being considered by the court, the probation officer should explain in detail the defendant's financial obligations and resources in order that the fine or restitution imposed will be commensurate with the defendant's ability to pay. In too many instances an automatic fine or restitution is imposed without knowledge of the financial burden it places on the probationer and his family.

5. While I do not advocate revocation of probation merely for failure to keep appointments, to submit monthly reports, to observe a curfew, to remain within the district, I do believe that a generally unfavorable attitude and deliberate noncompliance with the conditions of probation and the instructions of the probation officer are grounds for revocation.

6. Although I believe that all convictions for new offenses should be brought to the court's attention, it does not follow that probation should be automatically revoked. No violation should result in automatic revocation. It may be more beneficial to society, and also to the probationer and his family, to have him continue on probation than to sentence him to imprisonment.

7. Where a probationer is arrested on a new charge and is held in jail, I do not believe he should be regarded as a violator until he has been convicted. There is always the possibility of an acquittal. And we must keep in mind that in some local jurisdictions considerable time elapses between arrest and trial.

8. Lest the probation officer be guilty of usurping the power of the court, all unfulfilled conditions of probation—for example, not paying a fine or restitution in full by the terminal date—should be brought to the court's attention in advance of the termination date. Recommendations for a course of action should be included in the report.

9. To assist the court at the revocation hearing, the probation officer should prepare a formal report containing details of the alleged violation, factors underlying the violation, the probationer's attitude toward the violation, a summary of his conduct during supervision, and his general attitude and outlook.

10. The probationer should be present at the revocation hearing. It would seem that the United States attorney and also counsel for the probationer should be present. But it must be remembered that the revocation hearing is not a new trial.

11. Where it is necessary to revoke probation, imprisonment should serve a constructive purpose and not be used merely for punishment's sake. In certain

cases, particularly where an indifferent probationer deliberately fails to comply with the conditions of probation, it may be necessary to revoke probation so that the public—and other probationers, too—will have a fuller appreciation for probation, and realize that the primary purpose of probation is the protection of the public, that the court means what it says, and that the conditions of probation are not to be flouted.

30

Certificate of Parole

UNITED STATES PAROLE BOARD

Parole Form H-8
(Rev. Jan. 1967)
(Formerly Parole Form 17)

The United States Board of Parole
Washington, D.C. 20537

Certificate of Parole

Know all Men by these Presents:

It having been made to appear to the United States Board of Parole that

...., Register No. ...., a prisoner in

the ....,
is eligible to be PAROLED, and that there is a reasonable probability that he WILL REMAIN AT
LIBERTY WITHOUT VIOLATING THE LAWS, and it being the opinion of the said United States Board of
Parole that the release of this person is not incompatible with the welfare of society, it is ORDERED by the

said United States Board of Parole that he be PAROLED on ...., 19......,

and that he remain within the limits of...until

...., 19.......; or in the event of a committed fine or a committed fine and costs, until
the same have been paid or he has been discharged under the provisions of Section 3569, Title 18, U.S. Code, or
until other action may be taken by the said United States Board of Parole.

Given under the hands and the seal of the United States Board of Parole

this .... day of ...., nineteen hundred and ....

UNITED STATES BOARD OF PAROLE,

By ....
Parole/Youth Division Executive.

[SEAL]

ADVISER ....

PROBATION OFFICER ....

This CERTIFICATE OF PAROLE will become effective on the date of release shown on the reverse
side. If the parolee's continuance on parole becomes incompatible with the welfare of society, or if he fails
to comply with any of the conditions listed on the reverse side, he may be retaken on a warrant issued by a
Member of the Board of Parole, and reimprisoned pending a hearing to determine if the parole should be
revoked.

SOURCE. United States Board of Parole; reprinted with special permission.

CONDITIONS OF PAROLE

1. You shall go directly to the district shown on this CERTIFICATE OF PAROLE (unless released to the custody of other authorities). Within three days after your arrival, you shall report to your parole adviser if you have one, and to the United States Probation Officer whose name appears on this Certificate.

2. If you are released to the custody of other authorities, and after your release from physical custody of such authorities, you are unable to report to the United States Probation Officer to whom you are assigned within three days, you shall report instead to the nearest United States Probation Officer.

3. You shall not leave the limits fixed by this CERTIFICATE OF PAROLE without written permission from the probation officer.

4. You shall notify your probation officer immediately of any change in your place of residence.

5. You shall make a complete and truthful written report (on a form provided for that purpose) to your probation officer between the first and third day of each month, and on the final day of parole. You shall also report to your probation officer at other times as he directs.

6. If in any emergency you are unable to get in touch with your parole adviser, or your probation officer or his office, you shall communicate with the United States Board of Parole, Department of Justice, Washington, D.C. 20537.

7. You shall not violate any law. You shall get in touch immediately with your probation officer or his office if you are arrested or questioned by a law-enforcement officer.

8. You shall not enter into any agreement to act as an "informer" or special agent for any law-enforcement agency.

9. You shall work regularly unless excused by your probation officer, and support your legal dependents, if any, to the best of your ability. You shall report immediately to your probation officer any changes in employment.

10. You shall not drink alcoholic beverages to excess. You shall not purchase, possess, use, or administer marihuana or narcotic or other habit-forming or dangerous drugs, unless prescribed or advised by a physician. You shall not frequent places where such drugs are illegally sold, dispensed, used or given away.

11. You shall not associate with persons who have a criminal record unless you have permission of your probation officer. Nor shall you associate with persons engaged in criminal activity.

12. You shall not have firearms (or other dangerous weapons) in your possession without the written permission of your probation officer, following prior approval of the United States Board of Parole.

I have read, or had read to me, the foregoing conditions of parole. I fully understand them and know that if I violate any of them, I may be recommitted. I also understand that special conditions may be added or modifications of any condition may be made by the Board of Parole at any time.

....
(Name)

....
(Register No.)

WITNESSED ....

....
(Title)

....
(Date)

UNITED STATES BOARD OF PAROLE:

The above-named person was released on the ....day of ...., 19......., with a total of...........................days remaining to be served.

....
(Warden or Superintendent)

31
A Summary of Parole Rules

NAT R. ARLUKE

In 1956 a summary was published of the conditions of parole then existing in each of the forty-eight States.[1] The general conclusions reached at that time were that in many states the conditions were entirely too numerous to be of much real value, that some of the statements listed as conditions were actually interpretations of policy or were included in the penal statutes of the state, that many of the regulations were unrealistic and unenforceable, and that the basic rules were not uniform throughout the states.

How, if at all, have parole rules changed since 1956?

Currently, as was the case thirteen years ago, no single parole regulation is common to all the states.

In the states that have added regulations, marked increases occur in the categories of motor vehicle registration and license restrictions; narcotics usage; support of delinquents; the purchase and possession of weapons and the use of hunting licenses; limitations on out-of-state, county, or community travel; compulsory agreements to waive extradition; limitations on indebtedness; and approval of marriage and divorce.

SOURCE. *Crime and Delinquency,* **15,** April 1969, pp. 267–274. Reprinted with the permission of the author and the National Council on Crime and Delinquency. Copyright, 1969, National Council on Crime and Delinquency.

[1] Nat R. Arluke, "A Summary of Parole Rules," *NPPA Journal,* January 1956, pp. 6-13.

Some states–notably California, Colorado, Mississippi, and Missouri—have decreased the number of conditions; most have increased them.

Conditions of parole are authorized by law and, once adopted, should have the full impact of the law. However, in many cases, their impact is greater than that of the law: although a violation of a parole condition is not universally an offense requiring court appearance, trial, conviction, and sentence, the parolee's loss of freedom probably will be much more expeditious than a return resulting from the trial process.

Practically all the rules of parole can be justified in one way or another, including the prohibition of liquor, undesirable associates, and changing employment or living quarters. Yet many arguments can be made in each case indicating the inconsistency and unworkableness of the rules. If they are to serve as positive guides in the development of acceptable behavior patterns, they must be administered in a manner that will finally permit the parolee, on release from parole supervision, to lead the life of a normal citizen.

The rules must be reasonable, practical, and with the intent of the law, and they should not require behavior that is illegal, immoral, or impossible. Redundancies, impracticability of application, multiplicity of regulations, and lack of uniformity are among the serious defects that continue to exist in most states.

The courts have become more concerned with the rights of prisoners, probationers, and parolees. There is every indication that technical violations of parole may have to be considered in an adversary-type hearing on the site of the alleged revocation, with witnesses and attorneys present. The current tendency in some states to increase the number of rules and regulations may be related to the fact that obtaining a revocation will depend on proof in court that the regulations in question have been violated.

Conditions of parole, like those of probation, can be extremely broad because the grant is a privilege; yet, to be effective they must be tailored to the needs of the parolee. But they must not be disproportionate to his needs and must not impose undue hardships.[2]

Violation of parole conditions—there are about fifty different ones throughout the country—is frequently the basis of the adverse public image of parole systems and correction. The public might better understand and parolees might better comply with the conditions if they were simplified and standardized. Standardization will become increasingly more important as we become an even more mobile nation. There is no adequate reason for us to delay in developing a model code of conduct and requirements applicable on local, state, and federal levels.[3]

Some parole conditions are moralistic, most are impractical, others impinge on human rights, and all reflect obsolete criminological conceptions. On the whole they project a percept of a man who does not exist. Nevertheless, prisoners

---

[2] Weigard v. Kentucky, 397 S.W.2d 180 (1968), which struck down banishment as a condition of probation.

[3] "A Plea for a Stronger, More Active American Correctional Association," Harry C. Tinsley, *American Journal of Correction,* September-October 1964, pp. 6-10.

are required to sign the agreement, obviously with many reservations, before being paroled. The most tangible result is the growing number of violations of the conditions imposed.[4]

Conditions should be regarded as aids to successful adjustment rather than as punitive restrictions. Today, courts and paroling authorities are retreating from long lists of specific prohibitions and restrictions. At one time, conditions were predominantly couched in negative terms, and many such prohibitions are still in use: the parolee is required to be in at certain hours and is forbidden to touch intoxicating liquor or to frequent places where it is sold, to own a car, to get married, to leave town, and to particpate in a variety of similar activities. The current trend is to frame conditions in positive terms: the parolee is expected to support his dependents, is encouraged to work steadily, is expected to live a law-abiding life and to confer with his parole officer on all basic decisions, etc. A long list of prohibitions was, I believe, characteristic of the era when probation and parole officers were generally untrained, the service was new, and the list was deemed capable of controlling behavior. Courts and paroling authorities have since discovered that improved selection of parole officers makes it possible to place more discretion in their hands and that casework services are more effective than mechanical rules.[5]

Conditions of parole should be realistic and flexible. Each case should be judged separately, taking into consideration the problems, needs, and capacity of the individual offender. Conditions that cannot be enforced invite violations.

The parole officer should make certain that his client fully understands the limitations placed upon him by the general and special conditions imposed by the court. Merely signing the "Conditions of Parole" form does not mean he has correctly interpreted each condition.[6]

FREQUENCY OF PAROLE RULES

A comparison of the chart with the results published in 1956 shows the following developments:

1. *Liquor usage.*—Oddly, three states (Florida, Idaho, Michigan) have moved from "allowed but not to excess" to "prohibited." To counter-balance this, three states that had prohibited the use of liquor (Kansas, Louisiana, Mississippi) have discarded this regulation. Missouri, Virginia, and West Virginia previously were the only states with no liquor regulation; West Virginia now prohibits usage. Hawaii and Alaska have both included liquor usage as "prohibited."

2. *Change of employment or living quarters.*—Five states (Arizona, Okla-

---

[4] Manuel Lopez-Rey, "Release and Provisional Release of Sentenced Prisoners," *British Journal of Criminology,* July 1966, pp. 236-68.

[5] Ben S. Meeker, "Probation and Parole Officers at Work," *NPPA Journal,* April 1957, pp. 99–110.

[6] Eugene C. DiCerbo, "When Should Probation Be Revoked?" *Federal Probation,* June 1966, pp. 11–17.

homa, Vermont, West Virginia, and Wyoming) have no regulation in this regard now and did not have any thirteen years ago. One state (Mississippi) has dropped the regulation, while four states (Alabama, California, Montana, and New Mexico) have added it.

3. *Undesirable associations or correspondence.*—Five states (Iowa, Montana, New Mexico, West Virginia, and Wyoming) had no such regulation but have now included it. Virginia did not have it then and has not included it now, while Wisconsin has dropped the rule. One state (South Dakota) has moved from "prohibited" to "must have permission," while two states (Colorado and New Hampshire) have done the opposite.

4. *Filing written reports.*—Six states (Delaware, New Jersey, New York, North Carolina, Rhode Island, and West Virginia) did not require this previously and still do not. Four states (Maryland, Alabama, Colorado, and Utah) that did not require it before do so now, while four others (Indiana, Mississippi, South Dakota, and Wisconsin) so specifying have eliminated it.

5. *Marriage approval.*—Six states (Arizona, Georgia, Louisiana, Mississippi, South Carolina, and Virginia) that did not have this requirement still do not have it. Nine states previously without it have added it, and four states (Delaware, New Hampshire, New Jersey, and New Mexico) have included divorce approval in their regulations. Hawaii and Alaska include this regulation.

6. *Out-of-state travel.*—Six states (Alaska, Arizona, California, Florida, North Dakota, and Virginia) do not mention this regulation; seven states (including Hawaii) have added it; and four states (Louisiana, Mississippi, Tennessee, and Washington) have deleted it.

7. *First arrival report.*—Eleven states (including Hawaii) do not have this condition. Six states (Alaska, Kansas, Montana, Nevada, North Dakota, and Wyoming) that did not have it before have added it, and four states that did have it (Mississippi, Missouri, New Mexico, and Tennessee) have eliminated it.

8. *Motor vehicle registration and license.*—Eight states (including Hawaii) did not and still do not have this regulation. Twelve states that did not have it have now added it. One state (South Carolina) did have it but has deleted it.

9. *Narcotics usage.*—Eleven states have no parole condition specifically restricting the use of narcotics. Ten states have added regulations and five states that restricted usage (Kansas, Louisiana, Mississippi, New York, and Washington) have expunged the rule.

10. *Participation in anti-narcotics program.*—Three states (California, Illinois, and Texas) require in certain cases that the parolee participate in an anti-narcotics program.

11. *Support dependents.*—Twelve states do not mention this condition. Ten states previously without it have since added it. Two states (California and Wisconsin) have withdrawn it.

12. *Possession, sale, or use of weapons; obtaining hunting license.*—Seven states did not and still do not specify any regulations. Sixteen (including Alaska and Hawaii) that did not mention it now do so. One state (Missouri) has eliminated the rule.

13. *Out-of-county or community travel.*—Sixteen states do not have any restriction in this regard. Nine states that did not have it have added it. Five states (Arkansas, Georgia, Idaho, Iowa, and South Carolina) have deleted it. Kansas has limited travel without approval to a radius of fifty miles, while Mississippi has limited it to "a specified area."

14. *Agree to waive extradition.*—Fourteen states (including Hawaii) do not have this requirement. Seventeen states (including Alaska) that did not have it have now added it. Two states previously having it (Kentucky and Missouri) have withdrawn it.

15. *Indebtedness.*—Twenty-six states do not have any regulation in this regard. Thirteen states have added the condition: no state that had it has eliminated it.

16. *Curfew.*—Forty states do not have any curfew regulations. Three states did have it but deleted it (Colorado, Nevada, and New York). Five states (Illinois, Maine, Michigan, New Hampshire, and North Dakota) have continued the regulation and five states have added it (Hawaii, Minnesota, South Dakota, Tennessee, and Utah).

17. *Civil Rights; Suffrage.*—Forty-two states did not and still do not have any regulations in this area. Four states that had restrictions (Alabama, California, Colorado, and Maine) have removed them. One state (Nevada) has added restrictions.

18. *Gambling.*—Four states (Arizona, Florida, Nebraska, and South Dakota) have a regulation prohibiting gambling. One state (Iowa) that did prohibit it deleted the rule. The rest of the states did not and still do not have any restriction.

19. *Airplane license.*—Of the three states requiring approval, Pennsylvania did so previously; Iowa and Ohio have added it and also require approval for powerboat licenses. Two states (California and Maine) have withdrawn the requirement.

20. *Report if arrested.*—Two states previously having this regulation have kept it (Maine and New Jersey). Colorado, which did have it, has discontinued it, while four states that did not have it (Delaware, New Mexico, New York, and North Carolina) have added it.

21. *Treatment for venereal disease.*—Two states that had this requirement (Florida and Pennsylvania) continue it, while Alabama, which did not have it, has now included it.

22. *May receive credit if returned as a violator.*—Of the four states that permitted credit for the time served on parole, New Jersey still does, while Colorado, New York, and Ohio have eliminated the rule. Five states (Hawaii, New Mexico, North Carolina, Pennsylvania, and Rhode Island) have added it.

23. *Criminal registration.*—Three states (Alabama, New Mexico, and Pennsylvania) require registration.

24. *Church attendance.*—This condition is advised or recommended in Alabama, Florida, and North Carolina; is compulsory in Nebraska; and has been removed in Kansas.

25. *Permit home and job visits by parole officer.*—This condition is a require-

Comparison of parole regulations

	Federal Parole	Alabama	Alaska	Arizona	Arkansas	California	Colorado	Connecticut	Delaware	Florida	Georgia	Hawaii	Idaho	Illinois	Indiana	Iowa	Kansas	Kentucky	Louisiana
1. Liquor usage	4	2	2	2	2	2	2	2	2	2	2	2	2	2	2	2		2	
2. Change of employment or living quarters	1	1	1		1	1	1	1	1	1	1	1	1	1	1	1	1	1	1
3. Undesirable associations or correspondence	1	2	2	2	2	2	2	2	2	2	2	2	2	2	2	2	2	2	2
4. Filing written reports	3	3	3	3	3	3	3	3		3	3	3	3	3		3	3	3	3
5. Approval of marriage (or of divorce*)		1	1		1	1	1	1	1*	1		1	1	1	1	1	1	1	
6. Out-of-state travel		1			1		1	1	1		1	1	1	1	1	1	1	1	
7. First arrival report	3	3	3		3	3	3	3		3	3		3	3	3	3	3	3	3
8. Motor vehicle registration and license			1		1	1	1	1	1	1			1	1	1	1	1	1	
9. Narcotics usage	2	2			2	2	2	2	1	2	2	2	2	2	2	2		2	
10. Participation in anti-narcotics program					3									3					
11. Support dependents	3	3	3				3	3	3	3	3	3		3			3	3	3
12. Weapons; hunting license	1		1		2	2	2	2	1	1	2	2	2	2	2	1	1	1	
13. Out-of-county or community travel (limited to specific area*)	1					1	1		1					1	1		a	1	1
14. Waiver of extradition		3	3		3	3	3	3	3	3	3	1	3	3		3			
15. Indebtedness		1			1	1		1			1	1				1			
16. Curfew													b	c					
17. Civil rights; suffrage														2					
18. Gambling				2					2										

Key: 1. Must have permission. 2. Prohibited. 3. Compulsory. 4. Allowed but not to excess.
a. 50 miles b. 11:00 p.m. c. 10:30 p.m.

Maine	Maryland	Massachusetts	Michigan	Minnesota	Mississippi	Missouri	Montana	Nebraska	Nevada	New Hampshire	New Jersey	New Mexico	New York	North Carolina	North Dakota	Ohio	Oklahoma	Oregon	Pennsylvania	Rhode Island	South Carolina	North Carolina	Tennessee	Texas	Utah	Vermont	Virginia	Washington	West Virginia	Wisconsin	Wyoming
2	2	2	2	2			2	2	2	2	4	2	2	2	2	2	2	2	2	2	2	2	2	2	2	2	2	2	2	2	2
1	1	1	1	1		1	1	1	1	1	1	1	1	1	1	1	1		1	1	1	1	1	1	1	1	1	1	1		1
2	2	2	1	1	2	2	2	2	2	2	2	2	2	2	2	2	2	2	2	2	2	1	2	2	2	2		2	2		2
3	3	3	3	3		3	3	3	3	3		3			3	3	3	3	3			3		3	3	3	3	3	3		3
1	1	1	1	1		1	1	1	1	1*	1*	1*	1	1	1	1	1	1	1	1		1	1	1	1	1		1	1	1	1
1	1	1	1	1		1	1	1	1	1	1	1	1	1		1	1	1	1	1	1	1	1		1	1	1		1	1	1
3	3		3	3		3	3	3	3	3		3		3	3	3	3	3	3	3			3				3				3
1	1	1	1	1		1	1	1	1	1	1	1	1	1	1	1		1	1	1		1	1	1	1		1	1	1	1	1
2	2	2	2				2		2	2	2	2		2		2	2	2	2	2	2		2	2	2					2	
																								3							
3	3	3	3		3	3	3	3		3	3	3	3	3		3	3	3	3			3		3	3	3	3	3			
1	1	1	1			1	2			1	1	2	2	1		2	2	2	1	1	1	1	2	1	1	2	1	2	2	1	1
1			1	1	2*	1		1	1			1	1	1	1	1	1		1	1			1	1	1	1		1	1		
3	3		3	3		3	3	3	3		3	3	3		3	3		3	3	3			3	3		3	3	3			3
1	1		1	1		1	2	1	1	1		1	1			1	1						1				1		1		1
6			6	6							6					6							6	c		6					
									2			2				2															
									2															2							

5. May receive. 6. Reasonable hour. 7. Advised or recommended.

Comparison of parole regulations (continued)

	Federal Parole	Alabama	Alaska	Arizona	Arkansas	California	Colorado	Connecticut	Delaware	Florida	Georgia	Hawaii	Idaho	Illinois	Indiana	Iowa	Kansas	Kentucky	Louisiana
19. Airplane (or power boat*) license																1*			
20. Report if arrested	3							3											
21. Treatment for V.D.		3							3										
22. Credit on return as P.V.											5								
23. Criminal registration		3																	
24. Church attendance		7							7										
25. Permit home or job visits (search*)		3					3*	3		3	3			3			3		
26. Comply with law	3	3	3		3	3	3	3	3	3	3		3			3	3	3	3
27. Maintain gainful employment (inform employer of parole*)	3	3	3			3	3		3	3	3	3	3	3			3	3	3
28. Return to county (or state*) of commitment							1							1*					
29. Act as informer	2										2								

Key: 1. Must have permission. 2. Prohibited. 3. Compulsory. 4. Allowed but not to excess.
a. 50 miles b. 11:00 p.m. c. 10:30 p.m.

ment in nineteen states. In three of these states (Colorado, New York, and North Carolina) the condition includes approval for search of the parolee's person or his property.[7]

26. *Comply with the law.*—Forty-three states have a condition specifying that the parolee agrees to comply with the law.

27. *Gainful employment.*—Maintenance of gainful employment is a condition in thirty-one states, including Pennsylvania, where the parolee must inform the employer of his parole status.

28. *Return to county or state of commitment.*—In Colorado, the parolee may

[7] See Alexander Holtzoff, "The Power of Probation and Parole Officers to Search and Seize," *Federal Probation,* December 1967, pp. 3–7.

Maine	Maryland	Massachusetts	Michigan	Minnesota	Mississippi	Missouri	Montana	Nebraska	Nevada	New Hampshire	New Jersey	New Mexico	New York	North Carolina	North Dakota	Ohio	Oklahoma	Oregon	Pennsylvania	Rhode Island	South Carolina	North Carolina	Tennessee	Texas	Utah	Vermont	Virginia	Washington	West Virginia	Wisconsin	Wyoming
																1*			1												
3											3	3	3	3																	
																		3													
											5	5	5								5	5									
												3							3												
									3					7																	
3								3			3	3	3*	3*				3	3	3	3					3	3				
3	3	3	3	3	3	3	3	3	3		3	3		3	3	3	3	3	3	3	3	3	3	3	3	3	3	3	3	3	3
		3	3	3		3		3			3	3	3	3	3				3	3*		3		3	3	3	3	3			
									1*										1*												

5. May receive.   6. Reasonable hour.   7. Advised or recommended.

not return without permission to the county where he was convicted; in Idaho, Montana, and Oregon, he may be banished from the state.[8]

29. *Act as informer.*—Only in Hawaii is the parolee specifically barred from serving as a police informer.

The license isssued to a parolee under England's Criminal Justice Act (1967) says he must do these five things:

1. He shall report to an office indicated.

2. He shall place himself under the supervision of an officer nominated for this purpose.

3. He shall keep in touch with his officer in accordance with the officer's instructions.

[8] Brent T. Lynch, "Exile within the United States," *Crime and Delinquency,* January 1965, pp. 22–29.

4. He shall inform his officer at once if he changes his address or loses his job.

5. He shall be of good behavior and lead an industrious life.

Ideally, the movement in the U.S.A. ought to be in the direction of reducing all our parole rules—at least twenty-nine of them and perhaps as many as fifty —to the five listed above and perhaps eventually to only the fifth, which seems to cover everything. Obviously, no single one of our present proliferation of prohibitions is absolutely necessary. Therefore, closer examination should be made and a reorganization effected that recognizes the relationship between the parole officer and his client as more important than a bank of do's and don't's.

32
Interstate Supervision of Parole and Probation

RALPH C. BRENDES

Only two juridical documents have formal and practical application throughout all of our fifty states—the Constitution of the United States and the Interstate Compact for the Supervision of Parolees and Probationers.

Unlike the Constitution, little has been written on the Compact; the *Handbook on Interstate Crime Control,* published by the Council of State Governments, which serves as Secretariat to the Parole and Probation Compact Administrators' Association, is the only published source of information on the Compact. This paper will analyze the present operation of the Compact and discuss problems likely to arise in the future.

The states have collaborated in this form of crime control for two reasons: (1) the ever increasing mobility of the American citizen, which frequently results in his conviction away from his home state, although it is in his home state that rehabilitation is more likely to occur because of the positive influences of family and friends; (2) the need to eliminate "sundown probation"—a procedure whereby a criminal sentence would be suspended if the offender left the state by sundown. To improve protection of communities, each state found it mutually advantageous to supervise its resident probationers and parolees who had been convicted in other states. This combination of humanitarianism and local self-

SOURCE. *Crime and Delinquency,* **14,** July 1968, pp. 253–260. Reprinted with the permission of the author and the National Council on Crime and Delinquency. Copyright, 1968, National Council on Crime and Delinquency.

interest to avoid unregulated and uncontrolled interstate movement of unsupervised probationers and parolees led to the drafting of the Interstate Compact for the Supervision of Parolees and Probationers.

The beginning of the Compact can be traced to the Crime Control Consent Act of 1934,[1] which permitted two or more states to enter into agreements of mutual assistance in the prevention of crime. The operative section of the Act reads:

> The consent of Congress is hereby given to any two or more states to enter into agreements or compacts for cooperative effort and mutual assistance in the prevention of crime and in the enforcement of their respective criminal laws and policies, and to establish such agencies, joint or otherwise, as they may deem desirable for making effective such agreements and compacts.[2]

A national conference called by the United States Attorney General in 1934 to discuss implementation of the Act resulted in establishment of the Interstate Commission on Crime. Representatives of the states and the federal government met in Trenton, N.J., to draft uniform laws designed to improve law enforcement practices and eliminate the infirmities of multijurisdictional authority. The Commission drafted the Compact, which almost immediately was signed by twenty-five states; today, all fifty states, as well as Puerto Rico and the Virgin Islands, are signatories, agreeing to serve as every other state's agent in the supervision of parolees and probationers.

GENERAL PROVISIONS

The Compact provides that (1) any state (receiving state) will supervise a parolee or probationer from any other state (sending state) if he is a resident of the receiving state and has employment there; (2) the receiving state will supervise the sending state's parolee by the same standards used for its own parolees; (3) the sending state may revoke parole or probation in any case and retake the parolee or probationer at its discretion and with a minimum of formality.

To be classified a resident of the receiving state, the parolee or probationer must have been an inhabitant of that state for more than a year before he went

---

[1] Public Law 293, 73rd Congress, 2nd Session; Title 4, U.S.C. 111.

[2] Such consent may not have been required. Article 1, Section 10, of the Constitution says that "No state shall, without the consent of Congress, . . . enter into any agreement or compact with another state . . . "; however, under the doctrine of *Virginia v. Tennessee,* 148 U.S. 503 (1893), such compacts as are discussed in this article may be valid without Congressional consent. In that case the two states had agreed to the exact location of their boundary lines. Virginia later attacked the agreement, requesting the Supreme Court to declare it null and void since it was entered into without the consent of Congress. The Court held that this was not the type of agreement that the clause was intended to cover and that the terms "compact" and "agreement," as used in the Constitution, "were directed to the formation of any combination tending to the increase of political power in the states which may encroach upon or interfere with the just supremacy of the United States." If a compact did not do this, Congressional approval was not necessary.

to the sending state and must have resided within the sending state for less than six months immediately preceding the commission of the crime for which he was convicted. If he fulfills those conditions of residence, the receiving state must accept him, provided his family resides in the state and he is able to find employment there. In all cases the receiving state is given the opportunity, before the parolee or probationer is sent there, to investigate his home and his prospective employment. If he lacks the residence or employment qualifications, he may nevertheless be sent from one state to another if the receiving state consents.[3]

Actual state use of the Compact is impressive. On June 30, 1967, about 10,500 parolees and about 11,000 probationers were under Compact supervision.[4]

States working under the Compact are not bound by any strict rules; they adapt the general terms of the Compact to the specifics of each case.

The Compact has never had an unfavorable court decision. Most courts have construed the Compact liberally. While there has never been a ruling by the United States Supreme Court on the Compact, denials of *certiorari* may indicate the Court's endorsement of the Compact.[5]

Constitutional attacks on the Compact were resolved favorably in *Ex parte Tenner.*[6] After endorsing the principles of the rehabilitative ideal and stressing the importance of interstate cooperation in this regard, the California court said that provision by a state for the compulsory return of parole or probation violators was not unconstitutional. The states were not to be restricted to extradition, the sole method provided in the Constitution. The Compact method does not conflict with or render ineffectual the federal extradition laws, which are always available to a state. The violator still has a right to complain by means of habeas corpus if the authorities do not comply with the law, but he has no right to choose the method a state uses in returning him.

ADMINISTRATORS' ASSOCIATION

Formed in 1946, the Parole and Probation Compact Administrators' Association meets annually to discuss questions of policy and Compact interpretations and develop necessary administrative regulations. The annual meetings, affording opportunities to solve many operating problems by personal contact among administrators, are a significant factor in the successful operation of the Compact.

Some accomplishments of the Association include establishment of regular

[3] Copies of the Compact are available from the Council of State Governments, 36 West 44 St., New York City, as are copies of all Compact materials referred to in this paper. Résumés of some of the major cases dealing with the Compact are printed in the *Handbook on Interstate Crime Control* (Chicago: Council of State Governments, 1966).

[4] Council of State Governments. "The Interstate Movement of Parolees and Probationers under the Parole and Probation Compact," Annual Report, July 1, 1966, to June 30, 1967 (New York: Council of State Governments).

[5] *Handbook, op. cit. supra* note 3. p. 74.

[6] 20 Cal. 2d 670, 128 P.2d 388 (1942), *cert. denied,* 314 U.S. 585, 317 U.S. 597 (1942).

statistical reporting, development of the *Parole and Probation Compact Administrator's Manual,* outlining of standard administrative procedures under the Compact,[7] sponsorship of the *Handbook on Interstate Crime Control,* and development of certain new agreements relating to control of interstate crime.

PROBLEMS SOLVED

Progress Reports

The Compact's regulations call for quarterly progress reports on each case. Many states, however, have changed their own reporting systems to require less frequent reports, maintaining that they need to hear about their men more often only if some problem arises concerning an individual case, and therefore have suggested that this be the procedure under the Compact also. Consequently, an annual meeting of the Administrators decided that any two or more administrators could agree among themselves to send reports less frequently.

Residence and Employment

A second problem arose in the early days of the Compact, when many states required strict adherence to the residence or job requirements. Today, most states will take any man who presents evidence of bona fide residence in their jurisdiction and some likelihood of employment. Many states will even take a man if he fulfills only one of the two requirements. At the same time, most states will not send a man under terms they would not accept themselves. If they have any doubts in the matter, they may ask the receiving state to investigate before they send a man. If a probationer or parolee does not have the necessary residence or employment qualifications, the transfer decision rests with the administrator of the proposed receiving state.

Can a state refuse to supervise a probationer or parolee who fulfills the residence and employment requirements but is considered a poor risk? Though a receiving state may indicate its reluctance to accept such a person, it must undertake supervision if the sending state authorizes transfer. Very few states will force a man on another state, however, even though they have the legal power to do so under the Compact. In any instance where the sending state and the receiving state cannot agree upon the facts of residence and employment, they refer the matter to the Association's Council.

In a few cases, states which consistently refused probationers were persuaded

---

[7] Copies of the forms used as well as other material relating to the Compact's operation are described in the *Parole and Probation Compact Administrator's Manual,* available on loan from the Council of State Governments, New York City.

by the Association that they could not do this.[8] The incidence of states refusing reception of parolees or probationers even in borderline cases is rare.

Apprehension of Violators

A third problem often discussed at Association annual meetings is the apprehension of technical violators by one state for another state. There was some question whether a state which permitted its officers to arrest its own violators without a warrant could allow them to arrest its out-of-state violators without a warrant if that other state required a warrant, and vice versa. The Compact provides that "the same standard of supervision as applies in the receiving state in the supervision of its own parolees shall apply to out-of-state parolees sent there."[9] and the *Manual* reports: "The policy adopted by many states holds that the power to arrest is inherent in the power to supervise since power to supervise is useless without power to apprehend."[10]

Informal Arrangements

A fourth problem involves parolees or probationers who are not sent to what would have been a receiving state under the Compact but who nevertheless move there. Sometimes, without any instructions to do so, they report to an official of the second state, who has no prior knowledge of the case. In such instances, the second state usually requires the supervisee to sign a waiver of extradition.

If one state wishes another to retake a violator who never was under the terms of the Compact, it may do so only if he has waived extradition as a condition of being granted parole or probation:

Since he (the local parolee) has waived extradition on good consideration—*i.e.,* the grant of parole—he personally is barred from objecting to any failure to use formal extradition. . . . He is not paroled under the Compact. Hence, the Compact itself would not apply. On the other hand, since his . . . waiver bars his rights to object to being retaken anywhere by any proper officer of the paroling state, . . . only the authorities of the state where he is arrested, or the authorities of the state which has paroled him, . . . can object to his arrest and return in that manner. Such arrest and return, while not under the

---

[8] In 1961, Oklahoma decided it would not longer supervise out-of-state probationers. The annual meeting discussing the problem pointed out that a state could go to court to force another state to abide by the Compact, but decided that more subtle means of persuasion should be attempted. A resolution sent to the governor and other Oklahoma officials set forth the facts and requested them to take steps to alleviate the situation. Oklahoma complied with the Association's resolution.

A somewhat similar problem arose in Arizona, where the Compact administrator said that his office lacked the facilities to administer probation cases properly. The Association decided, therefore, to distribute to every Compact administrator a list of Arizona's county probation officers so that he could deal with them directly.

[9] *Handbook, op. cit. supra* note 3, p. 12.

[10] *Manual, op. cit. supra* note 7, ch. 2. Sec. 408.4.

Compact, would nevertheless seem practically to be effective, unless the state where he was arrested desired to make trouble for the state which had paroled him.[11]

UNSOLVED PROBLEMS

Several Compact problems have arisen which may require more than action by the administrators at their annual meeting for resolution. These involve detainers, return of violators, and local officer cooperation.

Detainers

A prisoner who has committed crimes in various jurisdictions before being apprehended will often have a number of detainers placed against him. Until these are resolved, it is difficult for the prisoner and his supervisor to make intelligent decisions concerning his future. To alleviate this problem, the Agreement on Detainers has been promulgated by the Association of Administrators and the Council of State Governments.

The Agreement on Detainers [says the Council] makes the clearing of detainers possible at the instance of a prisoner. It gives him no greater opportunity to escape just convictions, but it does provide a way for him to test the substantiality of detainers placed against him and to secure final judgment on any indictments, informations, or complaints outstanding against him in the other jurisdiction. The result is to permit the prisoner to secure a great degree of knowledge of his own future and to make it possible for the prison authorities to provide better plans and programs for his treatment.

Basically, the Agreement provides that a prisoner may, in writing, petition the prosecuting officer for a final disposition of the indictment, information, or complaint which forms the basis of the detainer. In most cases, the prisoner is entitled to a reply, within 180 days after the request, which either initiates a trial or drops the charges. In this way, the prisoner is able to have a clearer view of his future and prison officials have a better chance to bring about his rehabilitation, because definite plans can be made for his eventual release, free from the fear that a trial after his release will result in continued imprisonment.

Drafted in 1957, the Agreement has been passed by twenty states.[12] The intention was to observe its operation in a few states before encouraging uniform ratification, because this Agreement is more complex than the Compact and an experimental period seemed advisable. Experience under the Agreement has been so successful that the Council of State Governments and the Administrators' Association are now actively soliciting all states to join. The Association of Attorneys General has passed a resolution endorsing the Detainer Agreement and urging its enactment.

---

[11] *Id.*, Sec. 501.6.

[12] California, Connecticut, Hawaii, Iowa, Maryland, Massachusetts, Michigan, Minnesota, Montana, Nebraska, New Hampshire, New Jersey, New York, North Carolina, Pennsylvania, Rhode Island, South Carolina, Utah, Vermont, and Washington.

Returning Violators

Another problem which could not be solved by the administrators themselves involves the return of violators, totaling more than 250 probationers and 1,500 parolees annually. Often a supervisee has only a short period left to serve, so there is some question that it is worth the sending state's time and money to retake him; yet, if he is not retaken, some of the strength and leverage of the rehabilitative system is lost. Two plans—the Agreement for the Joint Return of Violators and the Out-of-State Incarceration Amendment—have been worked out by the Council and the Association; a third plan, calling for the posting of a cash bond before the supervisee leaves the state, is being used by Maryland and some other states.

Essentially, the plan for the joint return of violators requires only legislation permitting the deputization of out-of-state agents. Some type of clearing-house system would be used to notify each state when other states intended to transfer violators to or through its state. The state then would deputize the agents of another state to enable them to transfer its violators in their custody at the same time as they took their own. For example, New York might want to bring back a violator from California at the same time that Illinois would want to bring back a violator from New York, and California one from Illinois. The New York agent could be deputized by California and Illinois, and thus one man would do the job of three, saving the states time and money. This plan has not been well received because (1) if a state cannot incarcerate a violator from another state for more than a very short period (and most states cannot or do not), the statistical probability of the above circumstances is not high; (2) communication by a clearing house or any other plan has not been established. In practice, few state administrators feel that the return of violators is a significant enough problem to warrant such a proposal; also, the increased speed and lower costs of transportation may eliminate the need for such arrangements.

The Out-of-State Incarceration Amendment to the Compact is also used infrequently. It provides that the receiving state may put a violator in its own prison to serve the remainder of his term. The sending state would then reimburse the receiving state for the expense involved, thereby saving the expense of bringing the violator back to its own prison. The amendment is applicable only if both states have ratified it. Only eight states have done so, and three of them—New York, New Jersey, and Connecticut—are geographically juxtaposed, so that it is easier to return violators rather than incarcerate them out-of-state. A true test of the agreement has not yet occurred.

The plan independently developed by the Maryland authorities requires a parolee or probationer to post bond sufficient to cover the cost of his return. A number of Maryland's neighbors have adopted this idea and it has apparently worked very well. Because the sending state does not have an obligation under the contract to send a supervisee out of the state, attaching conditions to such action is not illegal. The argument can be made that this bond requirement violates the *spirit* of the Compact by imposing a financial obstacle to placing the

supervisee in the best possible rehabilitative location. The social-policy consideration may outweigh financial considerations. Maryland's approach to the financial
problem has been to permit the supervisee to send payments back to the state on
the installment plan. Furthermore, there is no bond-posting requirement if the
parolee or probationer is sent to a nearby state. Authorities in Maryland are
pleased with the system. Last year, the total cost to the state for returning
violators was under $500.

Local Cooperation

Few major problems have arisen since the inception of the Compact. Some
of them can be traced to the administrative policies of the state. While parole is
everywhere a statewide operation, probation is not. Some states have county-
based probation programs without state-wide coordination or supervision. Other
probation programs may be locally run with an advisor or coordinating central
agency. Often this high degree of local autonomy causes problems of cooperation
between states under the Compact.

Some difficulty results from local officials and judges' ignorance of the Compact. To alleviate this, the Administrators' Association has published a brochure,
detailing the advantages and operations of the Compact, which many states have
distributed to local officials and judges with a good deal of success. Some states
have gone even further in persuading the local probation authorities to operate
under the Compact. Minnesota, for example, has enlisted the assistance of the
state's Judicial Conference in preparing some of the forms to be used, and the
Compact administrator addresses the judges twice a year, stressing the importance of following Compact procedure. A Pennsylvania court has ruled that when
a probationer or parolee is sent out of the state without the use of Compact
procedure, the state loses jurisdiction over him. This decision may help to persuade more people to operate within the Compact, even where judges have been
reluctant to do so in the past.

Recent decisions providing the parolee or probationer with greater rights in
the determination of an alleged parole violation may create administrative problems. The leading case on this subject is *Hyser v. Reed,*[13] in which the court held
that federal parolees charged with parole violation were entitled to an informal
preliminary interview, before being transferred to prison, at a point as near as
possible to the place where the alleged violation occurred and as promptly as
possible after the arrest. The court refused to hold, however, that due process
required the hearing to have the trappings of a trial such as appointment of
counsel to indigents, confrontation of witnesses, cross-examination, discovery,
and compulsory process. Nevertheless, if state courts follow the lead of this case
and preliminary hearings become necessary in cases of parole violation, some
changes will become necessary in Compact operation. The Compact will have to
be amended to enable states to hold a violator in their jails and to conduct

[13] 318 F.2d 225 (1963).

hearings for the sending states. The trend is not yet entirely clear, however, and it may be that procedural changes will suffice. There is a great resistance to changing or amending the Compact in any way. Since it is, aside from the Constitution, the only document accepted in all fifty states, there is a fear that amendment, which would need approval by all states to be effective, might jeopardize the smooth operation of the Compact.

The Compact has been very successful so far and gives every indication of continued success. Effective means of operation have been devised to carry out its administration, and equally effective methods have been provided to enable necessary adaptations to be made should future conditions necessitate them. Annual meetings, increased sophistication of parole and probation authorities, more knowledgeable judges in this area, and an effective Secretariat—these are just a few of the factors that have brought about the Compact's success.

COMMUNITY-BASED CORRECTIONS

The six selections in this Section on community-based corrections clearly indicate the diversity of programmatic activities which have a "community-based" label. The United States Public Health Service has noted that community treatment as a phrase is "used to describe such a wide variety of efforts at every stage of the correctional process (that it) has lost all descriptive usefulness except as a code-word with connotations of 'advanced correctional thinking' and implied value judgments against the 'locking up' and isolation of offenders." Clearly, probation and parole are community-based corrections; so too are the many diversion programs which are emerging nationwide. Prerelease centers, halfway houses, foster and group homes, work and training release, and community treatment centers are also labels that reflect an increasing interest in moving corrections from walled and isolated institutions to more natural community environments.

This section begins with the National Advisory Commission chapter on corrections and the community. The Commission considers community-based corrections "as the most promising means of accomplishing the changes in offender behavior that the public expects—and in fact now demands—of corrections" and notes that "the future lies with community-based corrections." The Commission chapter probes a number of important areas—the definition and significance of community-based corrections, the rationale for this community-based effort and the role of the community itself. It also examines the responsibility of citizens and the correctional systems themselves in community corrections. Finally, the Commission chapter discusses the implementation of community-based corrections. The Standards which evolved from this chapter included the development of plans for community-based alternatives to confinement, marshalling and coordinating community resources, the responsibility of corrections for citizen involvement and inmate involvement in community programs.

The second selection in the section is from a Public Health Service publication. Perhaps the most significant aspect of that report is the observation that " . . . while one may express the opinion that since prisons are not effective (a validated observation), then one *might as well* retain offenders in the community, it cannot be assumed without adequate controlled research that the best *rehabilitative* possibilities are to be found in the community." A major theme of this selection is that a large number of offenders who are candidates for incarceration may instead be retained in the community as safely, as effectively, and at much less expense. The questioning of the emergent doctrine that corrections in the community is "better" is important and it may be that "until alternatives to institutionalization are demonstrated to be more effective than imprisonment in preventing further crime, a major rationale for use of community programs will be that correctional costs can be considerably reduced by handling in the community setting a large number of those offenders normally institutionalized."

Bertram S. Griggs and Gary R. McCune, both experienced correctional administrators, provide the third selection in this section. Their article focuses on programs designed to facilitate the transition of adult offenders from prison to the community through community-based correctional programs. Conducting a survey across the United States, Griggs and McCune trace the development of community-based programs, identify the sources of funding, ascertain the need for legislation, determine the types of programs and populations serviced and conclude that "the question is not one of whether a correctional agency should become involved in community treatment programs, but rather how and when."

Two selections by John M. McCartt and Thomas J. Mangogna on halfway houses and community treatment centers were prepared under contract with the Law Enforcement Assistance Administration. The first of the selections briefly provides a history of the halfway house movement in the United States which dates to the early 19th Century. The purposes of the early houses were to provide, on a temporary basis, shelter, food, clothing, advice and assistance in obtaining employment. Typically separated from the correctional systems of their times, these facilities and their managers were isolated from the criminal justice system. By 1950, a revival had occured; the International Halfway House Association had come into existence, and the role of the halfway house organization and personnel began to merge into the mainstream of corrections in the community.

But even with the emergence of the halfway house/community treatment center as a partner of sorts in the 1950's, a number of issues have been surfaced and addressed, if not resolved. McCartt and Mangogna identify and discuss a number of these issues including the heterogeneity of halfway houses/community treatments centers, the relationship of these community programs with the criminal justice system generally and corrections in particular, the functions of the halfway house/community center as it relates to corrections, and the requirements for evaluation and research.

The final selection is by Richard L. Rachin of the Florida Department of Health and Rehabilitative Services. Rachin surfaces a number of issues related to those identified by McCartt and Mangogna and deals with considerations about size of these community facilities, site selection and community relations.

33

Corrections and the Community — National Standards and Goals

NATIONAL ADVISORY COMMISSION ON CRIMINAL
JUSTICE STANDARDS AND GOALS

Revised public and professional expectations of corrections have brought about a transformation in its means and ends during the last several years. Tradition required institutions merely to hold prisoners until ordered to release them. Now both the public and the correctional staff expect prisoners to be, at least, no worse for the correctional experience and, at most, prepared to take their places in society without further involvment with the law. Tradition required probation and parole merely to provide some form of nominal supervision. Now it is expected that the experience of probation and parole will provide the offender with positive assistance in making a better adjustment to his circumstances. (Probation and parole are discussed in detail in Chapters 10 and 12 respectively.)

These revised expectations have led on an awareness that corrections must be linked to the community in every phase of operations. These links are hard to forge because correctional agencies of all kinds traditionally have maintained an isolation from other human service agencies.

In a sense this entire report is a discussion of what is conveniently referred

SOURCE. *Corrections,* National Advisory Commission on Criminal Justice Standards and Goals, Washington, D.C., U.S. Government Printing Office, 1973, pp. 221–245.

to as community-based corrections. The Commission considers community-based corrections as the most promising means of accomplishing the changes in offender behavior that the public expects—and in fact now demands—of corrections.

Dissatisfaction with incarceration as a means of correction has grown to a point where some States have almost completely abolished incarceration for some classes of offenders. In other States, experimental programs have been successful enough that once-overcrowded prisons and reformatories now are unused. Clearly, the future lies with community-based corrections.

The institution model for corrections has not been successful in curbing potential crime. But at least it exists, with its physical plant and identified processes of reception, classification, assignment, custody, work, academic and vocational training, religion, and recreation.

The substitute models are talked about and are occasionally used. But community-based corrections is not well organized, planned, or programmed. This task is the challenge of the future. Required is a complicated interplay among judicial and correctional personnel, those from related public and private agencies, citizen volunteers, and civic groups. This interplay of the correctional system with other parts of the public sector and greater involvement of the private sector, including civic participation in dimensions not foreseen in the correctional world just a few years ago, requires leadership in the entire criminal justice field to collaborate in the exploitation of all possibilities for successfully changing repression to reintegration. Policymakers must understand the essential elements of a sound community-based correctional system as well as they now understand the orderly management of the prison.

DEFINITION

As used in this chapter, the term "community-based corrections" includes all correctional activities that take place in the community. The community base must be an alternative to confinement of an offender at any point in the correctional process.

At the beginning of his experience as a subject of criminal justice decisionmaking, the offender has not even been defined as such. A police officer decides whether to arrest or give him a summons. A magistrate rules on his eligibility for release on his own recognizance or on bail. Released in either of these ways, he may or may not receive correctional attention. Some communities have court employment projects. Some have informal probation for certain types of juvenile offenders. More have diversion programs for alcoholics and narcotics addicts. Such preadjudication programs are discussed in Chapter 3.

After conviction and commitment to the control of the corrections agency, the now officially defined offender may be placed in the oldest community-based correctional program, supervision under probation. Probation service is described in Chapter 10. This chapter stresses probation as a foundation on which to build a wide range of community-based services.

Most persons confined to custodial control are potential participants in community-based corrections through work- and study-release programs, family visiting furloughs, and reentry programming. Finally, well-established parole services constitute the community-based programming core for offenders released from relatively lengthy custody.

This enumeration of major program components does not exhaust the potential of community correctional services, but the central principle of the definition is clear. Community-based correctional programs embrace any activity in the community directly addressed to the offender and aimed at helping him to become a law-abiding citizen. Such a program may be under official or private auspices. It may be administered by a correctional agency directly or by a noncorrectional service. It may be provided on direct referral from a correction agency or on referral from another element of the criminal justice system (police or courts). It may call for changing the offender through some combination of services, for controlling him by surveillance, or for reintegrating him into the community by placing him in a social situation in which he can satisfy his requirements without law violation. A community-based program may embrace any one or any combination of these processes.

The use of control and surveillance is basic to a sound community corrections system. Both policy makers and the public must understand that the elimination of incarceration does not eliminate control.

SIGNIFICANCE OF COMMUNITY-BASED CORRECTIONS

In this chapter, the significance of community-based corrections will be assessed from three aspects: humanitarian, restorative, and managerial. The criteria of success in each differ markedly.

The humanitarian aspect of community-based corrections is obvious. To subject anyone to custodial coercion is to place him in physical jeopardy, to narrow drastically his access to sources of personal satisfaction, and to reduce his self-esteem. That all these unfavorable consequences are the outcome of his own criminal actions does not change their reality. To the extent that the offender can be relieved of the burden of custody, a humanitarian objective is realized. The proposition that no one should be subjected to custodial control unnecessarily is a humanitarian assertion. The key question is the definition of necessity, which must be settled by the criterion of public protection.

The restorative aspect concerns measures expected to achieve for the offender a position in the community in which he does not violate the laws. These measures may be directed at change, control, or reintegration. The failure of offenders to achieve these goals can be measured by recidivism, and their success is defined by reaching specific objectives set by correctional decisionmakers.

The managerial goals are of special importance because of the sharp contrast between the per capita costs of custody and any kind of community program. Any shift from custodial control will save money. But the criterion of correctional success is not fiscal. A major object of correctional programs is to protect the public. Therefore, any saving of public funds must not be accompanied by a loss of public protection. When offenders can be shifted from custodial control to community-based programming without loss of public protection, the managerial criteria require that such a shift be made. Otherwise public funds will have been spent without satisfying a public objective.

It is necessary here to note that public protection is not always the sole objective of correctional programming. Some kinds of offenders, especially the most notorious, often could perfectly well be released without jeopardizing public safety. But their release will not be countenanced because public demands for retribution have not been satisfied. Offenders in custody should be there predominantly because public protection seems to require it. Decisionmakers must disentangle these objectives to assure that use of community-based correctional programs is not denied for irrelevant reasons.

RATIONALE FOR CORRECTIONS IN THE COMMUNITY

The movement toward community-based corrections is a move away from society's most ancient responses to the transgressor. For thousands of years, society relied mainly on banishment, physical punishment, or the death penalty to accomplish the goals of criminal justice. The world is now too small for any society to eject anyone. Our culture has so changed that we no longer consider imposing capital penalties on the sweeping scale that seemed appropriate to our ancestors.

Out of the realization that the old ways were unacceptable there emerged the prison, a place for artificial banishment or civil death. Nearly two centuries of experience with the penitentiary have brought us to the realization that its benefits are transient at best. At its worst, the prison offers an insidiously false security as those who were banished return to the social scene of their former crimes. The former prisoner seldom comes back the better for the experience of confinement. The effectiveness of the prison as a school for crime is exaggerated, for the criminal can learn the technology of crime far better on the streets. The damage the prison does is more subtle. Attitudes are brutalized, and self-confidence is lost. The prison is a place of coercion where compliance is obtained by force. The typical response to coercion is alienation, which may take the form of active hostility to all social controls or later a passive withdrawal into alcoholism, drug addiction, or dependency.[1]

---

[1] Although these views are too well known to require detailed documentation, those seeking a recent and persuasive brief are referred to Hans W. Mattick, *The Prosaic of Prison Violence,* University of Chicago Law School Occasional Paper, 1972.

Mitigating Damages Done by Prisons

One of the tasks of corrections is to mitigate alienation. For generations this task has been attempted mainly placing some offenders on probation instead of sending them to prison. When offenders have been incarcerated, parole has made it possible for them to serve part of their terms in the community, in the belief that assistance of a parole officer will help them to choose a law-abiding course.

There has been a growing realization that prison commitments for most offenders can be avoided or at least abbreviated without significant loss of public protection[2] If the committed offender eventually returns to the community, it is best that his commitment removes him for as short a time as possible. The principle has evolved: incarcerate only when nothing less will do, and then incarcerate as briefly as possible. The services provided by probation and parole should strengthen the weak, open new channels to the erratic, and avoid openly reinforcing the intimidation that is latent in the relationship between the offender and the state.

The objective is to motivate each offender by the incentives that motivate most citizens toward orderly social life. In large part these incentives derive from an economic philosophy in which a day's pay for a day's work forms a unit in a prospect of lifetime security. Such employment is the necessary, if not sufficient, basis for conventional life in America. Emphasis on the employment of the offender is a response to the common-sense awareness that the unemployed offender is a probable recidivist.

But community-based corrections cannot be limited to the services of an employment office. A man who has committed a crime and been caught and convicted has suffered a blow to his self-esteem that may be masked by bravado or indifference. He has good reason to believe that conventional persons will reject him, and he therefore seeks out the unconventional. In the prison he has no choice; he must associate with the unconventional. In the community, probation and parole resources should make accessible a whole range of social support services as needed.

The difficulty of the task is obvious. Far more is required than the one-to-one contact between probation or parole officer and the offender. The offender's predicament stems from the combination of personal deficits and social malfunctions that produced a criminal event and a social status. Most personal deficits characterizing offenders are also commonly found in nonoffenders. The social malfunctions of unemployment, discrimination, economic inequity, and congested urban living affect most citizens. The offender, like other citizens, must find a way to live with his deficits and with the disorder around him. If corrections is to mitigate alienation, it must mobilize the community services that can make such an outcome possible.

---

[2] See, for example, Heman G. Stark, "Alternatives to Institutionalization," *Crime and Delinquency,* 13 (1967), 323.

To a much larger extent than has been realized, social support services must be given outside the official correctional apparatus and inside the community. Schools must accept and help reintegrate the delinquent instead of exiling him to reform schools. Unions and employers must open doors to adult offenders instead of restricting their employment to the most menial and insecure labor.[3]

Corrections cannot continue to be all things to the offender. The correctional structure must change from a second-class social system consisting of a correctional bureaucracy and a dependent population of offenders subject to official control and service. Although the pattern of the future is not yet clear, it seems to consist of a brokerage service in which the agency opens up to the offender community services where such services exist, or helps create new services for the entire community where none existed before. This enlarged theory of corrections will be unfamiliar to many correctional and community agency personnel, but it offers the only reasonable prospect for dealing more successfully with the serious problem of the recidivist offender.

Community-Based Corrections as Deterrents

There remain two additional public policy considerations in the rationale for community-based corrections: the deterrence or intimidation of the offender who is caught and the deterrence of potential offenders. It may be legitimately argued that the milder punishment aspects of community-based programs will not sufficiently deter either the actual or potential offender.

For the offender who has been under control, deterrence can be measured by whether he commmits further crimes. Current measurements hardly support the contention that incarceration deters. But, regardless of this finding, no one should minimize the deterrent effect of noninstitutional control by the correctional system. Indeed, the deterrent effect of proper control within the community, coupled with realistic opportunities for the offender to make an adjustment there, may be expected to be considerable, not only on the basis of theoretical assumptions but also as indicated by preliminary studies which offer suggestive findings[4] And the experience of simply being under official jurisdiction constitutes a punitive experience for nearly all offenders.

The deterrence of potential offenders has not been supported by evidence. Despite many attempts, especially in the controversies over capital punishment,

---

[3] See Jewett T. Flagg, "A Businessman's Interest in Corrections," *Crime and Delinquency,* 6 (1960), 351, for the employer's views.

[4] See District of Columbia Department of Corrections, *In-Program and Post-Release Performance of Work-Release Inmates: A Preliminary Assessment* (Washington, 1969); and Gordon P. Waldo, Theodore G. Chiricos, and Leonard E. Dobrin, "Community Contact and Inmate Attitudes," unpublished study, Florida State University, Tallahassee, c. 1970. For a tentative assessment of community-oriented programs, see LaMar T. Empey, *Alternatives to Incarceration* (Washington: U. S. Department of Health, Education, and Welfare, 1967).

no one has ever proved that the threat of severe punishment actually deters crime. Indeed, there is evidence that swiftness and certainty have much greater deterrent effect than a long prison sentence.[5] This raises the serious question of how just it is to adhere to a policy that can be supported only by assumption.

But even if we allow that some crime deterred by the criminal justice system, the deterrent potentiality of the prison is grossly exaggerated. The argument should be framed properly in terms of the statistical chances of getting caught. In the case of most crimes other than homicide, the chances are much less than even. In most communities a criminal can reasonably assume that, even with repeated law violations, his chances of getting caught are relatively slight. The prospect of incarceration or other punishment is distant.

Documentation of the foregoing is available, particularly with reference to the failure of imprisonment in primary deterrence; that is, the discouragement of further criminal activity by those punished at least once. Available studies suggest strongly that jurisdictions making extensive use of probation instead of prison do not experience increased recidivism.[6]

Similarly, studies of confinement length do not establish that lengthier prison terms result in decreased recidivism.[7]

Secondary deterrence—the discouragement of first time criminal behavior by persons who may fear punishment—is a more elusive subject. However, the available statistical studies and analyses on varying punishment and prison confinement practices in different localities offer some basis for comparison.

We can conclude that, at the least, there is no established statistical base relating crime rates to the severity of dispositions imposed by court in different locales. Sophisticated studies of this problem are currently being conducted by Solomon Kobrin at the University of Southern California. Using complex mathematical models he has arrayed different jurisdictions according to the degrees of severity of criminal sanctions imposed. The studies also take cognizance of known variables that may be related and that otherwise could account for differences. In general, the summary of the study indicates that again there is no known relationship between severity of punishment and the deterrence of nonoffenders.[8]

[5] See Franklin E. Zimming, *Perspectives on Deterrence* (Rockville, Md.: National Institute of Mental Health, Center for Studies of Crime and Delinquency, 1971), p. 89.

[6] See Frank R. Scarpitti and Richard M. Stephenson, "A Study of Probation Effectiveness," *Journal of Criminal Law, Criminology, and Police Science,* 59 (1968), 361-369; and California Criminal Statistics Bureau, *Superior Court Probation and/or Jail Sample: One Year Followup for Selected Counties* (Sacramento: 1969).

[7] LaMar T. Empey, *Alternatives to Incarceration,* p. 2. See also Carol Crowther, "Crimes, Penalties, and Legislatures," *Annals of the American Academy of Political and Social Science,* 381 (1969), 147–158.

[8] Solomon Kubrin, "The Deterrent Effectiveness of Criminal Justice Sanctioning Strategies," unpublished paper, University of Southern California School of Public Administration, Los Angeles, 1972.

ROLE OF THE COMMUNITY IN CORRECTIONS

The recent shift in our Nation's values—particularly in corrections' views of criminality—helps explain the rationale and current emphasis on citizen involvement and community programs. Within this general context, the various roles citizens play and corrections' responsibility to involve the public can be understood better.

Circumstances of the past decade have had dramatic impact on corrections. The poverty programs of the 1960's, which failed to win the war on poverty but made strong impressions on the Nation, are of particular import for corrections. The ideology underlying those programs suggested that persons of minority origin and low socioeconomic status systematically are denied access to higher status in American society. They thus are persistently overrepresented among those who experience mental and physical illness, educational failure, unemployment, and crime and delinquency.

Programs that attacked such systematic exclusion from higher status used varied techniques. Emphasis on cultural awareness attempted to promote dignity and pride among minority groups, inserted minority history into America's records, and resulted in new group cohesion, political clout, and often militant reactions with newly discovered strength. The "maximum feasible participation" emphasis of poverty programs, although ultimately failing to achieve what it called for, made official the acknowledged but often ignored rights of all Americans to have a say in their own destiny.

The disadvantaged began to assume positions on boards of public and private agencies designed to serve them but formerly run for them by persons of more affluent status. "New careers" provided alternative routes for low-income persons to social and economic mobility through revised employment and training schemes. The pervasive ideology proclaimed to the formerly powerless that "you, too, have power, if you choose to exercise it."

This trend, visible in civil rights concerns, in welfare activism, and in student unrest, has its counterpart in correctional systems, and for the first time the voices of the inmate and the ex-offender are being heard. There are prisoners' unions and racial and ethnic ex-offender groups in all American cities. This as yet undocumented movement offers powerful new allies for correctional reform if professionals in corrections choose to take that view instead of the frequent, defensive reaction to exclude.

Today American prisons contain, for almost the first time in our history, substantial numbers of young persons of middle and upper socioeconomic levels, largely through prosecution of the Nation's youth for drug use. Another new set of allies for correctional reform thus exists today: concerned parents and friends of such youths, along with a vast body of parents who fear that their children might be among those jailed or imprisoned in the future.

This group is perceived by correctional staffs as less threatening than minority group ex-offenders. The reforms they urge may be listened to with greater attention. But coalitions are to be expected. These young persons learn militant and disruptive techniques very quickly and will employ them if they observe that rational discussion does not accomplish the desired reform.

Corrections has a unique opportunity to enlist such potential supporters and to organize their widespread concern into constructive aid for improving the correctional system. This audience is a prime source for volunteers. These citizens have political influence and know-how about influencing policy at local and State levels. The corrections system must design and implement public information systems to present facts and interpretations. If the potential of this group in aiding the correctional cause is to be realized, agencies must inform the public of their needs and welcome participation.[9]

Social Service Agencies

Other social services agencies also have an impact on corrections. As community-based treatment programs increase in number and variety, correctional personnel and offenders will interact increasingly in formal and informal ways with professionals from other human service areas such as welfare, education, health, and employment. As institutional walls disintegrate, figuratively speaking, the boundaries between the various human service areas will disappear as well —and correctional problems will come to be the problems of a range of professionals serving communities.

Another group of allies thus is identified: colleagues in related fields, many of whom have had relatively limited contact with the world of corrections. While there has been some professional mobility between welfare and corrections, or corrections and rehabilitation work, such relationships will become closer and more common as community-based programs develop. Concerns for meeting human needs are shared; common problems are faced in various settings. Social welfare personnel, broadly defined, clearly are allies of corrections. Their special talents and experiences will add enormously to the strength of correctional reform movements.

Education

In a similar vein, greater interest and concern for all correctional issues can be fostered among educators. Corrections is related to education on many levels. Schools are a frequent point of contact for direct services, particularly with juveniles. Universities are training and recruiting grounds for future correctional personnel and increasingly are involved in inservice education. Various high school and college programs are part of the services offered in correctional settings. And, perhaps most importantly of all, the Nation's schools provide citizens with their basic knowledge of the community they live in: its problems, its government, its criminal justice concerns. Correctional personnel should make

[9] This involvement has already begun on many fronts. For a typical report, see "Citizen Involvement." *Criminal Justice Newsletter,* March 13, 1972, p. 46.

conscious attempts to relate effectively to educational personnel to insure that the public is informed fully about correctional issues. Such efforts will be repaid many times over.

A final word must be said about American citizens in general. The Nation recovered from the wartime traumas of the 1940's and entered the 1950's, an era of apathetic affluence, in which many persons thought America finally had realized her goals and could rest on her laurels in comfortable unconcern. The 1960's, however, challenged that assumption and generated a national concern with issues of race, poverty, violence, and international responsibilities. The Nation, now into the 1970's, is bruised and shaken in confidence but hopefully prepared to set its house in order in quieter, more rational ways than in the frenzied 1960's. Few houses require ordering more than the Nation's prisons.

Corrections and Correctional Personnel

In addition to increased public concern, corrections' view of how to solve the problem of criminal behavior has contributed to acceptance of citizen participation and community programs. Since the 1920's, research concerning crime and delinquency has undergone a gradual shift from the individual per se as the object of study to the environment in which he has his origins. Clifford Shaw, who discussed individual criminals from a social point of view in the 1920's and 1930's,[10] and Richard Cloward and Lloyd Ohlin, who provided a sophisticated theoretical framework for the understanding of crime causation in the 1960's,[11] illustrate this shift spanning the last 50 years.

In that period, the view of social as opposed to individual causation of human behavior has come to represent a majority opinion. Crime is conceived as linked more to social factors than to factors in the individual. This concept does not ignore psychological, physical, or other individual characteristics, but considers them as they occur in a particular setting.

This change in concept supports a somewhat different correctional thrust: if the social milieu to a substantial degree causes criminal behavior, the social milieu itself must be attacked and changed. This rationale suggests that the correctional system must involve itself in social reform to control and prevent crime. Further, it requires an understanding that, if behavior is related to events and circumstances in the offender's milieu, changing his behavior in isolation from that world will not solve the problem. Evidence of behavioral change in the isolation of the total institution is meaningless. It is behavior at home, on the job, and on the streets that matters.[12]

---

[10] See, for example, Clifford R. Shaw, *The Natural History of a Delinquent Career* (University of Chicago Press, 1931).

[11] Richard A. Cloward and Lloyd E. Ohlin, *Delinquency and Opportunity* (Glencoe, Ill.: Free Press, 1960).

[12] A consideration of some of the issues raised here from the viewpoint of corrections may be found in Milton Burdman, "Realism in Community-Based Correctional Services," *Annals of the American Academy of Political and Social Sciences,* 381 (1969), 71.

The shift in correctional thought that underlies the change to community-based correctional programming also can be understood by considering empirical evidence as to the effectiveness of current programs in controlling crime and the promise of new patterns. Corrections is a large, uncoordinated set of subsystems, with large gaps in service, irrational resource allocation, inadequate information, and a range of treatment modes that lacks a consistent and workable rationale. The confusion about individual vs. social causation underlies some of the lack of coherence. Contemporary corrections has not integrated its theoretical base and its practice. Despite the shift in social science theory, notions of intervening in community circumstances have not been applied widely. Rather, the emphasis has been on changing the individual—on a "treatment" philosophy that largely ignores the enormous potential of the community as the place for reduction of criminal behavior.

It already seems clear that substantial numbers of offenders can be treated in the community safely, effectively, and at substantially lowered cost to the taxpayer.[13] These are sufficient reasons to justify use of community programs and facilities in preference to institutions with their well-documented personal costs to individuals and social and financial costs to communities. Experimentation accompanied by adequate research and documentation increasingly will aid correctional systems in allocating resources more effectively.

Many correctional leaders feel a sense of optimism regarding the future. Problems of the field are more visible than ever before instead of being hidden behind high walls and locked gates. Some correctional administrators may object to public airing of their problems, but they are aware that old programs are not working and that new insights and methods are needed.

Perhaps the greatest significance of the move toward community corrections is the implicit consequence that communities must assume responsibility for the problems they generate. The failure of prisons to rehabilitate was blamed unfairly on correctional personnel; responsibility for community programs is shared widely. Corrections must be increasingly conceived as part of the larger social system. Problem and person, crime and criminal, are imbedded in community life and must be dealt with there—this is the thrust of corrections for the future.

Community programs have two operating (as opposed to programmatic) objectives: to use and coordinate existing community service agencies offering resources in areas such as family planning, counseling, general social service, medical treatment, legal representation, and employment; and to involve other agencies in the mission of corrections. The varying and changing nature of communities limits the feasibility of setting precise standards for community participation. Implementation of community programs involves consideration of geographic area to be covered, number of individuals required from the com-

---

[13] The final word on costs and effectiveness must await full implementation of community-based correctional variants. See, however, two publications of the District of Columbia Department of Corrections: "Costs, Benefits, Recidivism in Work Release, Prison College Program." *Newsletter,* January-February 1972, p. 2; and *Cost Analysis of the D.C. Work Release Program.*

munity, which persons must become involved, availability of programs from other agencies, etc. A systematic procedure for making these decisions is outlined in Chapter 9, Local Adult Institutions. A general discussion of citizens' varied roles and the correctional administrator's responsibility for involving them should provide overall guidance in assessing what is available and possible.

RESPONSIBILITY OF CITIZENS

In a democratic nation, responsibility for provision of necessary public services is shared broadly by the citizenry. Decisions are made directly by public interest and demand for services, or indirectly by public neglect. In the case of correctional services, as with education, health care, and welfare needs, the decision regarding type and quality of service is determined ultimately by the public's will. An objective, therefore, in considering ways to improve criminal justice standards and goals must be attainment of an informed and concerned public, willing to insist on exercising its right to make informed decisions concerning correctional services.

Historically this objective has not been realized, and a massive public information campaign to bring about citizen involvement will be required to reverse the patterns of the recent past. In an earlier era, the community directly exercised law enforcement and correctional responsibilities: for example, the relegous tribunals of New England, with punishments of banishment, public pillories, and even executions; and the citizen posses of the frontier West, with their "out of town by sunset" sentence or execution by hanging. These are well-documented examples of citizens acting to maintain public order and safety.

As the Nation developed in size and complexity, these functions were delegated to public servants, supposed experts with specialized knowledge and certain personal characteristics. The sheriff's staff and the police force replaced the posse; the court system replaced church tribunals and posse justice; jails, workhouses, and prisons replaced the public pillory, banishments, and summary executions. A professional criminal justice system came into being.

Nowhere in modern times has a public information program to bring about citizen involvement in the criminal justice system been fully implemented and documented. In some areas, however, the involvement of citizens in correctional decisions and community-based experiments has been described by the correctional unit responsible for recruiting and utilizing volunteers.[14]

Over the years, the public has come to feel little sense of responsibility for these services. To a considerable extent it has come to view the criminal justice system as an adversary—an institution to be outwitted and opposed rather than a service controlled by an organized to serve the interests of individual citizens and the general public. One has only to listen as the young discuss the police and their elders talk of circumventing tax laws or traffic regulations to realize the

---

[14] See, for example, Bucks County (Pa.) Department of Corrections, *Citizen Volunteer Program,* Fact Sheet 1–72, p. 2.

extent to which the American public views the criminal justice system as "them" and not as "us."

The citizenry must be involved again, in more constructive ways than in the past, in determining the policies of the entire criminal justice system. The participating public should be able to exert a real influence on the shape of any community program, not only in the planning stages but at all crucial junctures involving actual operations. Because of their representative status, citizens must be considered as a resource on which the eventual success of a program heavily depends. Opinions and reactions of citizen participants can provide a useful index to levels of public tolerance, insights into ways of affecting certain attitudes, and suggestions for new techniques to generate further public participation.

The immediate aim of administrators should be to consult as many public representatives as possible during all stages of a program from planning through operation. This should not be token participation for the sake of appearance, or confined to individuals and organizations representing a single community sector. It is especially important not to limit participation to persons associated with the power centers of the community or with whom corrections officials have closest rapport and can expect to be in least conflict.

The correctional administrator lauching new programs faces a conflict that may be inherent in any effort to offer services for convicted persons: the limit of innovation beyond existing levels of public acceptance. The easiest programs to launch are those that do not require radical adjustment of attitudes toward the offender.

The correctional administrator cannot abdicate his responsibilities for the custody and activities of offenders committed to his care. Nor can he give only lip service to community involvement while actually ignoring public fears and wishes. Complex decisions are required—determinations of initial eligibility, conditions for participation, selection of activities, extent of custody and supervision, revocation proceedings, standards for evaluation, and program changes. These decisions must be made while keeping legal rights of offenders, legitimate community concerns, and administrative prerogatives in balance.

But programs cannot be geared toward existing attitudes with the assumption that attitudes never change. The ability of corrections to make an increasing impact on the problem of crime reduction must not be limited by unwillingness to risk uncharted territory, even when it appears potentially hostile or politically undesirable. Community support or opposition leading to achievement or frustration is related directly to the manager's skills in mediating among the variety of forces represented and his understanding of the varying roles citizens play.

The Community as Policy-Maker

A variety of specialized policymaking roles currently are undertaken by citizens, often at the request of criminal justice officials. In such situations, lay citizens function in task forces or study groups and serve a general advisory role to the government. A by-product, perhaps more important than this advisory objective, is the creation of an ever-larger pool of citizens who have in-depth knowledge of corrections issues. They provide much-needed feedback to corrections, especially regarding lay thought and opinion.

It is important that meaningful roles be assigned without expecting the advisory body merely to rubber stamp the decisions that the correctional administrator has made. Community involvement that is only a facade will be discovered quickly. Therefore, administrators should carefully analyze, in advance of creating citizen committees, the areas in which their input is desirable, if not essential. Decisions to be left to the agency should be specified and communicated to the committee.

Frequently, advisory bodies are comprised of "leading citizens" representing only one element of the community rather than a cross-section. In recent years, the necessity of broad representation has been recognized, and most groups seek appropriate membership of minorities, ex-offenders, women, and special community interest groups.

A somewhat different model is the citizen organization that is not sponsored governmentally but is a voluntary association of private citizens with shared concerns. The State citizen councils on crime and delinquency affiliated with the National Council on Crime and Delinquency are examples of this type of citizen participation. They are characterized frequently by "blue-robbon" opinion leaders, wide membership, and support from voluntary contributions. They usually confront only problems of specifically local concern. Sometimes they provide service functions in the "prisoner's aid" tradition. Frequently such councils have strong, if informal, and mutually supportive links to State correctional systems.

In the past few years, all States have created instrumentalities of one kind or another for developing and administering State plans for utilization of funds from the Law Enforcement Assistance Administration. These agencies have taken a variety of forms, but invariably involve citizen participation, often in concert with professionals from law enforcement, the judiciary, and corrections. This involvement represents another model of citizens serving in advisory roles.

In some cases, special boards have been created with advisory and policymaking objectives for subparts of the criminal justice system, such as juvenile courts, local correctional agencies, or branches of State systems or institutions. At the local level, a broad spectrum of citizenry can be involved, in contrast to the "important person" membership of the State and Federal commissions. No data exist on how widely this mechanism is employed, but where used, as in the county juvenile justice commissions in California, it is viewed as effective in interpreting correctional issues and enlisting local community support.

The Citizen as Reformer

The penal and correctional reform groups springing up in recent years are yet another model of citizen participation. They may have no formal or informal links with the correctional system, may even be organized to oppose correctional programs and to attack current practices. Such groups vary widely in philosophy and are characterized by extremely diverse membership patterns in different areas of the Nation.

Church memberships, radical political entities, a range of ethnic organizations, counterculture youth movements, and ex-inmate associations have taken up the cause of penal and correctional reform. The scope of this reformist movement is undocumented but represents a ground swell to be observed with interest by the public and by professionals in the criminal justice system. In the tradition of the great reform movements of American history, such as abolition of slavery and child labor, penal reform groups of today have ample evidence of wrongs to be righted, of underdogs to be aided, and of inequities to be restored to balance.

This involvement of many citizens in penal reform clearly is an important way in which citizens relate to policymaking for the criminal justice system. The correctional administrator—so long removed from any public scrutiny and vested with unquestioned discretion—probably has great difficulty in responding constructively to some of these groups. For example, some of them oppose any improvements in corrections in the belief that they will serve only to perpetuate an inherently bad system. Yet the goal of the administrator and penal reformer is the same: protection of society through protection of individual rights. With common cause, the efforts of both should be directed toward solution of problems rather than toward quarrels with each other. Professionals in corrections long have decried public apathy and lack of knowledge.

When the public cries out in protest against inadequacies of the system, expressing concern and seeking fuller knowledge, administrators have tended to close the doors more tightly, feeling that criticism reflects personally on them. Correctional personnel react with hostility to accusations, confrontations, and adverse publicity, despite the fact that the reformers are saying only what professionals have said to themselves for decades.

To be criticized publicly is painful. The challenge to correctional administrators is to utilize constructively the public concern lying behind the criticism. Appropriate strategies must be planned and implemented. The almost unprecedented public concern for improving correctional services can be put to constructive use. Dissipating energy and resources by reacting defensively can only delay progress. Courageous and enlightened correctional leaders (with very tough skin) are needed to accomplish this difficult task.

Citizens in Direct Service Roles

Involvement of citizens in direct service roles with correctional clientele is not a new phenomenon but a revived one. All students of elementary criminology and penology know of probation's origins in the goodhearted endeavors of the Boston shoemaker, John Augustus, in the mid-19th century. His willingness to take responsibility for an alcoholic who had been sentenced to incarceration and was released into his care was a first step. Gradually more citizens were enlisted to follow his example, but in time their work was assigned to hired professionals. In the century following Augustus' invention, use of the volunteer in direct service fell away, to be revived only in the mid-20th century.

Use of volunteers in corrections today is massive. Estimates of the National Information Center on Volunteers in Courts suggest that citizen volunteers outnumber professionals four or five to one, and that, exclusive of law enforcement agencies and above the misdemeanant court level, approximately 70 percent of correctional agencies have some sort of volunteer program.[15] The varieties of such programs are impressive, including one-to-one big brothers, pen pals, aviation training for delinquent boys, group programs of many kinds, basic and continuing education offerings, and legal services.

Some of these roles supplement professional responsibilities (teaching services and supervisory roles), while others are roles unique to volunteers (friendship situations). Other citizens play less direct service roles, serving as fund raisers or organizers of needed services, goods, and facilities. In recent years, institution doors that were formerly closed have been opened to groups of citizens in volunteer roles, including Alcoholics Anonymous and other self-help groups, ethnic culture programs, and church organizations. Such programs have the double effect of enhancing citizen involvement with the correctional system and providing needed services to correctional clients.

Correctional administrators must define roles in which volunteers can serve.[16] They must recruit, train, and properly supervise volunteers across the entire range of programs, from intake to discharge, from highly skilled roles to simpler relationships, from group social events to intensive casework, including library work, teaching, legal service, and cultural activities. The range seems endless. It is a mistake to conclude that volunteer services are entirely free. Constructive use of volunteers requires careful analysis of needed tasks, exhaustive searching out of resources, and careful guidance.

Much attention in recent years has been given to the role of the volunteer, and a growing amount of literature is available to aid administrators. The National Information Center on Volunteers in Courts located at Boulder, Colorado; the National Council on Crime and Delinquency, Hackensack, N.J.; the Commission on Voluntary Service and Action, New York, N.Y.; and the National Center for Voluntary Action, Washington, D.C., all further volunteerism. Each has substantial material to assist correctional agencies, such as research information, organization and management aids, training guides, and audiovisual materials. The literature in this area is richer than in most other suggested areas for citizen involvement.

The interested reader should also refer to this Commission's Report on Com-

---

[15] Ivan H. Scheier et al. *Guidelines and Standards for the Use of Volunteers in Correctional Programs* (Washington: Law Enforcement Assistance Administration, 1972), pp. iii, 5.

[16] For one scheme of classifying these roles, see Vincent O'Leary, "Some Directions for Citizen Involvement in Corrections," *Annals of the American Academy of Political and Social Science,* 381 (1969), 99. The paper also presents possibilities for expanding these roles.

munity Crime Prevention. The chapter on citizen action in that report contains an extensive discussion and listing of citizen-initiated and citizen-organized activities in preventing and reducing crime.

Volunteer roles increasingly are played by a wider range of citizens. Formerly a province of the middle or upper-class person desiring to perform useful services for those less fortunate, volunteer services now are provided in increasing amounts by youths, minority groups, organized labor, university students and staff, and local community groups of all kinds.

There are many ways in which community involvement has been elicited or suggested. Some, such as tax credits for employers, require statutory authorization. Trade advisory councils have been formed to oversee training techniques, procure equipment, and establish links between corrections and the public in connection with industrial programs.[17] Volunteer counselors have been used successfully as institutional counselors and parole aides.

Professional persons in education, religion, medicine, psychology, law, and other fields have donated services. University departments have established institutional field placements in which interested students are supervised jointly by correctional and academic officials in work-study programs. (See Chapter 14.) Aid organizations concerned with specialized problems such as alcoholism, drug abuse, family breakdown, and prisoner rights have set up units within institutions.

The two main roles for citizen participation—policymaking and direct service —directly interact with one another, each making the other increasingly effective. The person who works as a volunteer can have a more effective voice in policymaking by his increased understanding, and the informed citizen will be more willing to undertake volunteer activities as he understands the need for bridges between community and correctional client.

RESPONSIBILITY OF CORRECTIONAL SYSTEMS FOR COMMUNITY PARTICIPATION

Correctional systems themselves must assume responsibility for enlisting broad community support for correctional programs. Despite the above descriptions, it still must be said that very little public involvement has yet been permitted or realized.

Agencies generally are responsible to administrative branches of government and only indirectly to the legislature and public. An unconcerned public has been relatively unaware of correctional issues. Correctional agencies have operated with little public scrutiny and in general have enjoyed that autonomy while simultaneously complaining about the lack of public support of their endeavors.

Given the realities of rising community concern and citizen involvement, these circumstances are likely to be altered drastically in the years ahead. It is

[17] Jude P. West and John R. Stratton, eds., *The Role of Correctional Industries* (Iowa City: University of Iowa, 1971), p. 3.

in the general interest of correctional programs for citizens to exercise their prerogatives as participants in a democratic society. The correctional systems of today bear a heavy burden of responsibility for the lack of involvement with the community in past decades and should expend extra effort to make amends.

Corrections' Information and Change Agent Role

Correctional agencies must provide a continuous flow of information to the public concerning issues and alternatives involved in implementing correctional programs, so that citizens may participate intelligently in the major decisions involved. For example, a major difficulty in instituting various types of community-based treatment centers is communities' refusal to have centers located in their territory. Such resistance will not be overcome immediately, but involvement of many citizens can be expected to bring success eventually.[18]

Similarly, experience has shown that simply being able to prove that new techniques can be efficient in reducing crime or costs of crime control does not guarantee their acceptance. Bail reform measures, for example, have been carefully evaluated and have demonstrated beyond question that costs of jail incarceration can be reduced without increasing the risk to society.[19] In addition to such cost effectiveness, bail reform substantially reduces the inequities of a jailing system that systematically discriminates against the poor. Still, release on recognizance projects have been instituted in only a fraction of the Nation's courts.

The information program should go beyond the usual press releases and occasional public hearings. Corrections must assume an educational role, a change agent role, for it is clear that drastic changes are required to bring the community-based correctional process into being.

The change agent role also involves working with private agencies that too often have offered services in a way that favors other groups in the general population over inmates or former inmates. By selectively serving individual clients who are not as problem-ridden or difficult to deal with, these agencies have burdened governmental agencies with a disproportionate number of offenders. It is reasonable and appropriate to seek a redistribution of caseloads, so that the private sector assumes a greater share of responsibility for those with the major social disabilities of conviction and imprisonment.

It goes without saying that corrections officials should also work actively with private agencies and organizations that are concerned with such matters as prisoner aid, police, probation, or parole. These groups usually have specialized units that provide either direct services or access to sources for job placement, treat-

---

[18] See, for example, Marshall Fels, *The Community—Site and Source of Correctional Rehabilitation* (Olympia: Washington Department of Social and Health Services, 1971).

[19] See *The Manhattan Bail Project* (Criminal Justice Coordinating Council of New York City and Vera Institute of Justice, 1970); David McCarthy and Jeanne J. Wahl, "The District of Columbia Bail Project," *Georgetown Law Journal*, 53 (1965), 675; and Gerald Levin, "The San Francisco Bail Project," *American Bar Association Journal*, 55 (1969), 135.

ment for alcoholics and drug users, residential counseling facilities, foster homes, emergency housing, hospitalization, vocational and therapeutic counseling, and similar services.

The change agent model should include massive public education efforts through the communications media and intensive educational-organizational efforts with the many subcommunities—ethnic, racial, special interest groups—for support of general community corrections and specific projects. This concept of correctional responsibility to educate and serve as a catalyst for change requires a sophisticated understanding of society as a system and of criminal justice, including corrections, as an integral part of the larger society.

Perhaps most of all it involves commitment on the part of correctional personnel, from top administrator to line worker, to the new role of change agent. The commitment extends to efforts to change those aspects of society that are related to crime causation—poverty, racism, and other inequities.

However, the step from recognizing a problem to implementing its solution is difficult. For the most part, the community alternatives that have been developed to date simply are minor variations on some older ideas. For example, the phrase "alternatives to incarceration" still is used, reflecting corrections' preoccupation with institutions. As the National Council on Crime and Delinquency points out, the emphasis should be reversed—"imprisonment must be viewed as an alternative to community treatment."[20] Work-release usually is still limited to the last few weeks before release from an institution; some halfway houses resemble small penitentiaries rather than open community residences. Implementation of the fundamentally different set of assumptions implied by community corrections is the challenge for this decade.

IMPLEMENTATION OF COMMUNITY-BASED CORRECTIONS

A basic principle underlying the philosophy of community-based corrections is that all efforts consistent with the safety of others should be made to reduce involvement of the individual offender with the institutional aspects of corrections. The alienation and dehumanization engendered in jails, work-houses, prisons, even probation services, are to be avoided wherever possible. The less penetration into the criminal justice system the better.

A second basic principle is the need for extensive involvement with the multiple aspects of the community, beginning with the offender and his world and extending to the larger social system.

As a final basic principle, it is apparent that community-based programs demand radically new roles for inmates, staff, and citizens. This must be made

[20] National Council on Crime and Delinquency, *Policies and Background Information* (Hackensack, N.J.: NCCD, 1972), p. 15.

explicit in altered job descriptions, new patterns of training, different performance expectations.

The principle implies changes in recruitment. Since corrections needs to relate increasingly with the various facets of the community, its work force must increasingly represent those facets. This means greatly expanded recruitment from minority and economically disadvantaged groups, with all that implies for location of services (such as prisons), for innovative training, and for new kinds of staffing patterns.

Community Alternatives to Confinement

Diversion, probation, and parole—the major community alternatives—and the use of community resources and services that should characterize these programs, are discussed in detail in Chapter 3, Diversion from the Criminal Justice Process, Chapter 10, Probation, and Chapter 12, Parole, and will not be repeated here.

NONRESIDENTIAL PROGRAMS   Structured correctional programs, which supervise a substantial part of an offender's day but do not include "live-in" requirements, are another community-based necessity. The clients are persons who need more intensive services than probation usually can offer, yet are not in need of institutionalization. School and counseling programs, day treatment centers with vocational training, and guided group interaction programs are among the treatment modes used, many with related services to families.

Many such programs are described substantially in corrections literature.[21] Essexfields and Collegefields, community descendants of the Highfields residential program, were based on group dynamics theory and utilized peer group pressures to modify behavior. The Provo experiment in Utah used similar theoretical approaches. The programs, in brief, involved intensive daily programs of work or school and counseling sessions. Essexfields in Newark, N.J., used employment in a county mental hospital; Collegefields, a short-term project, used an academic program adapted for individual student needs, as the heart of the program.

Each of these projects has demonstrated success in treatment outcomes sufficient to warrant further experimentation. Each clearly showed that intensive programs in communities are at least as effective as, and usually somewhat better than, institutionalization and that offenders who otherwise would be in penal settings can be treated safely in the community. To date, these types of programs have been used most extensively with adolescent populations.

FOSTER AND GROUP HOMES   Juvenile judges frequently have felt it necessary to commit youngsters to an institution when circumstances in the parental home were totally unsuitable. Foster home development and more recently the

---

[21] Saul Pilnick, Robert F. Allen, and Neale W. Clapp, "Adolescent Integrity from Highfields to Essexfields and Collegefields," paper presented to the National Conference on Social Work, 1966. See also LaMar T. Empey and Maynard L. Erickson, *The Provo Experiment* (Heath, 1972).

group home, when used for aiding delinquent youths, are attempts to prevent unnecessary institutionalization.

Foster homes, also extensively used to meet child dependency needs, are operated under a range of administrative arrangements, public and private, State and local, court and correctional. A project conducted by the Merrill Palmer Institute[22] of Detroit sought information concerning the nature of supportive services required for successful foster home care of disturbed and delinquent young persons and applied the information on an experimental basis. Particular attention was given to the need for training foster parents, an area usually neglected, and appropriate psychiatric and educational support was developed.

In most jurisdictions, foster care has been far less intensively aided than in the Merrill Palmer experiments. Foster care appears to be considered a less useful tool than the more recently developed group homes. These quasi-institutions often are administered by agencies with house parents as paid staff, in contrast to foster homes where a monthly or daily room and board fee is customarily made to foster parents. The theoretical assumptions underlying the group home are related to child development stages. Most delinquency occurs in adolescence when family ties are loosening as adulthood approaches. Transfer to a new family situation, as in the foster home, is felt to be less desirable than the semi-independence from family that is possible in the group home, along with a supportive environment and rewarding experiences with adults.

The group home model usually has six to ten young people living in a home owned or rented by agencies and staffed by employed "parents" or counselors, supplemented by other necessary professional services obtained mostly through existing community resources. Correctional agencies in Minnesota and Wisconsin use such group homes extensively. California has systematized the use of group homes through a classification related to particular types of youth. A group home variant in Boulder, Colorado, the Attention Home, is supported mainly by volunteer contributions of funds and personnel.[23]

Evaluation of such efforts generally is positive. Costs are high relative to nonresidential treatment, but not as high in most cases as institutional care and, in the case of Boulder where community resources are extensively used, considerably less.

THE COMMUNITY CORRECTIONAL CENTER   The popularity of the "community correctional center" concept in recent years has led to a bandwagon effect with rapid growth of a wide variety of programs. Definition, therefore, becomes increasingly difficult. For purposes of this report, the term is used to mean a

---

[22] "The Detroit Foster Homes Project of the Merrill Palmer Institute," unpublished report.

[23] See John E. Hargardine, *The Attention Home of Boulder, Colorado* (Washington: U.S. Department of Health, Education, and Welfare, 1968); Andrew W. Basinas, "Foster Care for Delinquents," *Social Service in Wisconsin* (1968), 7–9; Niels Christiansen, Jr. and William Nelson, *Juveniles in Group Homes* (Minneapolis: Minnesota Department of Corrections, 1969); John W. Pearson and Ted Palmer, *The Use of Group Homes for Delinquents* (Sacramento: California Youth Authority, 1968).

relatively open institution located in the neighborhood and using community resources to provide most or all of the services required by offenders. The degree of openness varies with offender types, and use of services varies with availability and offender needs. Such institutions are used for multiple purposes—detention, service delivery, holding, and prerelease.

The lines between community-based and institutional programs are blurring substantially. Because of their newness, projects of this nature have generated little evaluation, minimum descriptive material, and few guidelines. They do, however, provide a flexible and theoretically sound design with potential for meeting varied correctional needs.

The Institute for the Study of Crime and Delinquency, Sacramento, California, has undertaken a lengthy study to develop a model community-based treatment program for young adults, with attention to architectural design as well as services and management concerns.[24] The project, originally planned to develop a model prison, eventually came to envision a blurring of lines between institution and community. This was done intentionally to tailor the amount of "freedom" to the needs of each individual. An offender progresses from secure facility to open community residence gradually in systematic phases. Decisions on individual programs are shared by offenders, staff, and citizens. The model represents a kind of amalgam of institution and community-based programs.

A comprehensive project undertaken by the Department of Architecture, University of Illinois, and supported by Law Enforcement Assistance Administration funds, has developed "Guidelines for Planning and Design of Regional Community Correctional Centers for Adults." Its concepts are discussed more fully in Chapter 8 of this report, Juvenile Intake and Detention, and Chapter 9, Local Adult Institutions.

Many types of community correctional centers are in existence today, using such facilities as jails, parts or all of hotels or motels, floors or wings of YMCA's, surplus army barracks, and former fraternity houses. Some are used as alternatives to penal service, others as adjuncts to institutionalization. They serve many types of offenders, usually in separate facilities. An interesting variant in Minnesota is a "restitution" house where offenders live while working to earn funds to compensate victims.

Community Adjuncts to Institutions

The program activities discussed so far have been designed generally to serve as alternatives to the use of the institution. A major assumption throughout this report is that most persons committed to correctional authority can be served effectively and economically in community settings. The implications require a brief review.

It seems obvious that institutional populations will be made up increasingly

[24] See Harold B. Bradley et al., *The Non-Prison: New Approach to Treating Youthful Offenders* (Sacramento: Institute for the Study of Crime and Delinquency, 1970).

of hard-core criminals and persons difficult to control. Prison will become the final resort. However, all but a very small fraction of institutionalized individuals ultimately return to the community, and it is therefore essential that institutional programs also involve the community.

The notion that isolating individuals from the community influences that made them engage in crime and that exposing them to the influences of prison will reform them is no longer accepted.[25] Instead, as this report so often notes, prisons have proved to be criminogenic in themselves. For this reason, administrators have been seeking alternative experiences for inmates.

Many of the programs in use today favor the traditional values of work, training, and education. While reintegration efforts must encompass standards that society accepts and endorses, correctional administrators should not impose their own value systems on the potential range of community programs. To do so may restrict the breadth and innovative character of what is offered.

Instead, the range of activities permitted in the larger community should be considered. For example, some offenders might participate with nonoffenders in private group therapy, consult with their own lawyers, conduct investigations in connection with their own trials, negotiate with community institutions, participate in school activities, attend social functions, and engage in athletics in the community.

Some of these ideas may seem unrealistic and foreign to today's conception of the inmate's role. However, the hypothesis is that the benefit to be derived when an offender's feelings of hopelessness and powerlessness are dissipated by virtue of his having a measure of control over his own destiny will far outweigh administrative anxieties and burdens.

The institutional custodial climate that so clearly separates the keeper from the kept should be replaced in significant measure by one of mutuality as staff and offenders work together in responsible citizen roles that are meaningful to both parties.

The concept of "bridging" is used to denote programs that establish links between imprisoned inmate, institution, and free society, to afford the inmate experiences expressly intended to maximize his reintegration potential. Inmates participate in training, work, education, or other activities that provide as many normal transactions and experiences with community persons and organizations as possible. The number and variety of community resources that can be developed for these purposes is virtually unlimited.

The bridging concept contains the reciprocal notions of inmates relating outward to the community and of opening the institution to community access. As bridging from the prison to the outside is intended to normalize interactions with community resources, so bridging into the prison is intended to transform traditional prison activities into more normal patterns of life. Families and neighbors, employers and teachers, ministers and counselors enter the prison, partici-

---

[25] For a history of this function of the institution, see David J. Rothman, *The Discovery of the Asylum: Social Order and Disorder in the New Republic* (Little, Brown, 1972).

pate in its life, and bring the ongoing community life into the formerly insulated institution.

Bridging activities provide much-needed diversification of options for inmates. Staff and program can be augmented significantly by utilizing more fully the opportunities available outside the walls or by bringing them inside. Inmates have the opportunity to try out socially acceptable roles in a planned transitional process.

The dependence fostered by institutionalization can be reduced. Inmates are allowed to discharge a measure of social and personal responsibility by assuming financial obligations and a larger measure of control over their destinies, thus contributing to their self-esteem and an awareness of their stake in the community.

Citizens who participate in bridging activities become involved in correctional services and decisionmaking. Greater public participation should result in increased understanding of and support for these programs. Such public involvement also will prepare communities for a certain amount of conflict and failure, for bridging concepts imply risk of an unassessed nature. Expectations of total success will lead only to disillusionment, but realistic optimism for potential gains must be retained. (See Chapter 11. Major Institutions.)

WORK RELEASE   Work-release programs began to be used extensively in the 1950's. The practice permits selected inmates to work for pay outside the institution, returning each night. Prisoner employment is not new; the work gang for hire is a well-known feature in penal history. The work-release concept differs markedly, however, in allowing regular civilian employment, under specified circumstances, for selected low-risk inmates. Initially used mainly with misdemeanants, work release now is used widely with felons and youthful offenders.[26] Other versions, similar in intent, provide for weekend sentences, furloughs, and release for vocational training or educational programs. All help to reestablish links to the community for the incarcerated.

In a few instances, commercial manufacturing operations have been introduced into prisons. Honeywell, Inc., has loaned a computer to a Massachusetts prison for use by inmates to do programming and data processing for various departments of State government, an up-to-date version of "state use." Union involvement in such efforts is crucial; it will add a much needed dimension to employment programs and represent a further potential resource for correctional programs.

FAMILY VISITS.   Prisons are attempting in a variety of ways to assist the reintegration of offenders into family circles, as well as the work world. Prison visiting always has been allowed, frequently under less than favorable circum-

---

[26] The problem of predictability in these endeavors may pose specific burdens on the administrator which are not posed by programs confined largely to institutions or others carried on in the community with more control and surveillance. However, some scientific certitude may be introduced into the selection process. See, for example, Isaac Fair, Inc., *Development of a Scoring System to Predict Success on Work Release: Final Report* (Washington: D.C. Department of Corrections, 1971).

stances, with minimum opportunities for privacy and personal communication. Conjugal visits long have been the practice in Mississippi institutions[27] but have not been allowed elsewhere in this country until recently. A relatively new California scheme allows entire families to spend up to two days in cottage-like houses on prison grounds.[28]

Family counseling programs for inmates and families are available in many States. A family life education program in Hennepin County, Minnesota, is used with adult inmates, their families, and with juvenile probation caseloads.[29] Adlerian group counseling methods, with involvement of even very young children, underlie this attempt to assist the offender and his family.

Volunteers of America programs for youth involve families in somewhat similar ways, with special Sunday events such as picnics or parties to which families are invited for socializing.

In the Swedish penal system, where family visitation is taken for granted, some institutions even permit husband and wife to live together if both are institutionalized. Most interesting is their "holiday" policy—inmates, like other citizens, are entitled to a two week vacation at the beach accompanied by families.[30] Such programs seem startling to American observers but are sensible if assisting families through difficult days and preparing them for stable relationships are desirable goals.

EDUCATIONAL PROGRAMS.   An educational bridging program is the Newgate model, in which mini-universities are established within prison walls to serve higher educational needs of inmates. Newgate programs are located across the country in State and Federal institutions.[31] Each uses different procedures, but the common thread is use of education as the major tool.[32] Opportunities for continuation of college on release are arranged, and extensive support given. Evaluation evidence developed thus far is positive; a serious limitation of the program, however, is its very high cost.

Students from Augsburg College, Minneapolis, as part of their regular curriculum attend classes held in the penal institution with inmates and prison

---

[27] Described in Columbus B. Hopper, *Conjugal Visiting at the Mississippi State Penitentiary*, (privately printed), and Hopper, *Sex in Prison: The Mississippi Experiment with Conjugal Visiting* (Baton Rouge: Louisiana State University, 1969). See also *NCCD News*, April 1972, "Conjugal Visits: More to Them than Sex."

[28] See, for example, "The Family Visiting Program at the California Correctional Institute, Tehachapi, July 1968," in *Annual Research Review*, 1970 (Sacramento: California Department of Corrections, 1970), p. 43.

[29] See Richard E. Ericson and David O. Moberg, *The Rehabilitation of Parolees* (Minneapolis: Minnesota Department of Corrections, 1969), p. 42.

[30] *Kriminalvarden, 1968* (Stockholm: Swedish Correctional Administration 1969). Has summary in English.

[31] See William L. Claiborne. "Special Course at American University—Lorton Inmates Learn about Outside Life." *Washington Post*, February 19, 1972.

[32] There remains some disagreement among professionals as to the most effective approaches to be adopted in the educational area. See *New York Times*, March 26, 1972, p. 54, "Prison Officials Back Reform of Education for Inmates but Differ on Details."

officers as fellow students.[33] While a range of courses are taught in this "co-learner" model, the criminology course is of most interest—as a living laboratory with mutual benefits to all students.

ETHNIC PROGRAMS.   In recent years, with heightening cultural and ethnic awareness, various minority consciousness groups have formed in the Nation's prisons, many involving extensive contact with similar groups outside. Enriching in many ways and clearly of potential assistance to the reintegration of inmates with their community, such programs are sensitive issues in correctional circles. Prisons mirror the racial unrest of the Nation in aggravated form associated with the tensions of anxiety and fear, close quarters, lack of privacy, and hours of idleness. Cultural groups, strengthening the individual's awareness of his group identity and raising questions of discrimination, are potential sources of discord. But they are nonetheless vital links to the self-help potential of such groups on the outside.

PRERELEASE PROGRAMS.   The Federal prison system pioneered in the development of prerelease programs in the early 1960's. In several cities small living units were organized, usually in leased quarters, to which individuals could be transferred for the final months of a sentence as part of preparation for release. Special orientation programs and employment assistance were provided, with gradually increasing opportunities to exercise decisionmaking. The purpose was to phase inmates into community life under supervision, with assistance as needed. Such centers are used increasingly in State programs.

The California system has reorganized its services to give its field staff (parole personnel) greater responsibility for inmate programming during the last 6 months of confinement, in essence converting that period into a release-planning phase. Arrangements have been made to permit temporary release at any time in the last 60 days before the official release date, thus permitting more flexible timing as plans are developed. Inmates within 90 days of release may make unescorted trips to home communities on 3-day passes to facilitate release plans, another way of easing into the often difficult postrelease period.[34]

SHORT-TERM RETURN OF PAROLEES.   Related closely to prerelease planning is recent development in many States of programs permitting the short-term return of parolees who have made a misstep that is potential cause for parole revocation and return to the prison. Frequently, prerelease facilities are used for this function. The return to a relatively open institution allows the parolee a breather, more supervision than in the community, and time to plan a new and hopefully more effective reentry into the community. Research indicates that short-term returnees in California do as well on second release as those released after a long period of reimprisonment.[35]

---

[33] Connie Schoen. "Things Volunteers Do," *American Journal of Correction* (1969), 26–31.

[34] Norman Holt, *California Prerelease Furlough Program for State Prisoners: An Evaluation* (Sacramento: California Department of Corrections, 1969).

[35] California Department of Corrections, *Short-Term Return Unit Program* (Sacramento: 1968).

Standard 7.1

Development Plan for Community-Based Alternatives to Confinement

Each State correctional system or correctional system of other units of government should begin immediately to analyze its needs, resources, and gaps in service and to develop by 1978 a systematic plan with a timetable and scheme for implementing a range of alternatives to institutionalization. The plan should specify the services to be provided directly by the correctional authority and those to be offered through other community sources. Community advisory assistance (discussed in Standard 7.3) is essential. The plan should be developed within the framework of total system planning discussed in Chapter 9, Local Adult Institutions, and State Planning discussed in Chapter 13, Organization and Administration.

Minimum alternatives to be included in the plan should be the following:

1. Diversion mechanisms and programs prior to trial and sentence.
2. Nonresidential supervision programs in addition to probation and parole.
3. Residential alternatives to incarceration.
4. Community resources open to confined populations and institutional resources available to the entire community.
5. Prerelease programs.
6. Community facilities for released offenders in the critical reentry phase, with provision for short-term return as needed.

Standard 7.2

Marshaling and Coordinating Community Resources

Each State correctional system or the systems of other units of government should take appropriate action immediately to establish effective working relationships with the major social insitutions, organizations, and agencies of the community, including the following:

1. Employment resources—private industry, labor unions, employment services, civil service systems.

2. Educational resources—vocational and technical, secondary college and university, adult basic education, private and commercial training, government and private job development and skills training.

3. Social welfare services—public assistance, housing, rehabilitation services, mental health services, counseling asistance, neighborhood centers, unemployment compensation, private social service agencies of all kinds.

4. The law enforcement system—Federal, State, and local law enforcement personnel, particularly specialized units providing public information, diversion, and services to juveniles.

5. Other relevant community organizations and groups—ethnic and cultural groups, recreational and social organizations, religious and self-help groups, and other devoted to political or social action.

At the management level, correctional agencies should seek to involve representatives of these community resources in policy development and interagency procedures for consultation, coordinated planning, joint action, and shared programs and facilities. Correctional authorities also should enlist the aid of such bodies in formation of a broadbased and aggressive lobby that will speak for correctional and inmate needs and support community correctional programs.

At the operating level, correctional agencies should initiate procedures to work cooperatively in obtaining services needed by offenders.

Standard 7.3

Corrections' Responsibility for Citizen Involvement

Each State correctional system should create immediately: (a) a multipurpose public information and education unit, to inform the general public on correctional issues and to organize support for and overcome resistance to general reform efforts and specific community-based projects; and (b) an administrative unit responsible for securing citizen involvement in a variety of ways within corrections, including advisory and policymaking roles, direct service roles, and cooperative endeavors with correctional clients.

1. The unit responsible for securing citizen involvement should develop and make public a written policy on selection process, term of service, tasks, responsibilities, and authority for any advisory or policymaking body.

2. The citizen involvement unit should be specifically assigned the management of volunteer personnel serving in direct service capacities with correctional clientele, to include:

    a. Design and coordination of volunteer tasks.

    b. Screening and selection of appropriate persons.

    c. Orientation to the system and training as required for particular tasks.

    d. Professional supervision of volunteer staff.

    e. Development of appropriate personnel practices for volunteers, including personnel records, advancement opportunities, and other rewards.

3. The unit should be responsible for providing for supervision of offenders who are serving in volunteer roles.

4. The unit should seek to diversify institutional programs by obtaining

needed resources from the community that can be used in the institution and by examing and causing the periodic reevaluation of any procedures inhibiting the participation of inmates in any community program.

5. The unit should lead in establishing and operating community-based programs emanating from the institution or from a satellite facility and, on an ongoing basis, seek to develop new opportunities for community contacts enabling inmate participants and custodial staff to regularize and maximize normal interaction with community residents and institutions.

Standard 7.4

Inmate Involvement in Community Programs

Correctional agencies should begin immediately to develop arrangements and procedures for offenders sentenced to correctional institutions to assume increasing individual responsibility and community contact. A variety of levels of individual choice, supervision, and community contact should be specified in these arrangements, with explicit statements as to how the transitions between levels are to be accomplished. Progress from one level to another should be based on specified behavioral criteria rather than on sentence, time served, or subjective judgments regarding attitudes.

The arrangements and procedures should be incorporated in the classification system to be used at an institution and reflect the following:

1. When an offender is received at a correctional institution, he should meet with the classification unit (committee, team or the like) to develop a plan for increasing personal responsibility and community contact.

2. At the initial meeting, behavioral objectives should be established, to be accomplished within a specified period. After that time another meeting should be held to make adjustments in the individual's plan which, assuming that the objectives have been met, will provide for transition to a lower level of custody and increasing personal responsibility and community involvement.

3. Similarly, at regular time intervals, each inmate's status should be reviewed, and if no strong reasons exist to the contrary, further favorable adjustments should be made.

4. Allowing for individual differences in time and progress or lack of pro-

gress, the inmate should move through a series of levels broadly encompassing movement from (a) initial security involving few outside privileges and minimal contact with community participants in institutional programs to (b) lesser degrees of custody with participation in institutional and community programs involving both citizens and offenders, to (c) partial-release programs under which he would sleep in the institution but have maximum participation in institutional and outside activities involving community residents, to (d) residence in a halfway house or similar noninstitutional residence, to (e) residence in the community at the place of his choice with moderate supervision, and finally to release from correctional supervision.

5. The presumption should be in favor of decreasing levels of supervision and increasing levels of individual responsibility.

6. When an inmate fails to meet behavioral objectives, the team may decide to keep him in the same status for another period or move him back. On the other hand, his behavioral achievements may indicate that he can be moved forward rapidly without having to go through all the successive stages.

7. Throughout the process, the primary emphasis should be on individualization—on behavioral changes based on the individual's interests, abilities, and priorities. Offenders also should be afforded opportunities to give of their talents, time, and efforts to others, including other inmates and community residents.

8. A guiding principle should be the use of positive reinforcement in bringing about behavioral improvements rather than negative reinforcement in the form of punishment.

34
Community-Based Correctional Programs: Models and Practices

COMMUNITY-BASED CORRECTIONAL PROGRAMS

For several years theorists and practitioners have argued for community based correction programs if correction is to attain the mission of making law-abiding citizens of convicted offenders and adjudicated delinquents. Community treatment, however, as a term used to describe such a wide variety of efforts at every stage of the correctional process, has lost all descriptive usefulness except as a code-word with connotations of "advanced correctional thinking" and implied value judgments against the "locking up" and isolation of offenders. Although the practice of handling offenders outside the institution is not especially new, the development of "community treatment" as a powerful catchword appears to be fairly recent. As the term has become popularized, and as the phrase is increasingly associated with avant-garde thinking in corrections, the concept has been stretched to include a widening variety of treatment efforts, some of which are "community based" only in that they are less isolated and confining than the traditional prison.

In the literature on alternatives to institutionalization, the descriptive term "community treatment" has been applied to probation and parole (these being

SOURCE *Community-Based Correctional Programs*, Public Health Service Publication No. 2130, Washington, D.C., U.S. Government Printing Office, 1971.

the traditional noninstitutional correction measures); probation alone (parole in this case considered an extension in the community of institutional treatment); aftercare (juvenile parole) and halfway house "bridges" between the institution and free society; community-based institutions (located in the community, with perhaps some use of community resources for health, education, or recreation purposes); noninstitutional boarding arrangments such as foster care, small group homes, semi-institutional or "open" cottage living; forestry, work, or outdoor probation camps; and a number of daycare programs, outpatient clinics, and nonresidential work/group-therapy programs. Occasionally, community treatment is viewed as encompassing efforts which are essentially preventive, such as street work with antisocial gangs or early identification and treatment of "predelinquents." The latter are of necessity community-based because in most cases the formal processes of criminal justice have not been invoked.

This lack of clear delimitation might be at least partly attributed to the phenomenon of "jumping on the bandwagon." Increasing evidence that institutionalization may be more destructive than rehabilitative, and may in fact increase probabilities of recidivism, initiated a trend which emphasizes alternatives to imprisonment or, where institutionalization is felt to be necessary, transitional programs in the community to facilitate reintegration.

Disillusionment with the traditional correctional institution as a rehabilitative tool appears justified. Research evaluating imprisonment has received support from studies which reveal the ineffectiveness of institutionalization not only in correctional but in mental health, child care, and related fields. Following a California study of the effects of institutionalization of mental patients, which found that this experience did not improve the social competence of the mentally ill, a study was made in that state of the deterrent effects of criminal penalties.[1] Penal legislation in California, as in most other States, has been based on the presumed deterrent effect of severe penalties. In this study substantial evidence was found to suggest that lengthy incarceration does not deter crime or recidivism. Recidivism rates of released prisoners were found to be generally consistent for all States despite variations in correctional practice. Specific analysis supporting the general conclusions included studies of attacks on police officers, marijuana offenses, and bad-check writing. In each of these cases, increased penalties did not deter commission of the offense. Reducing incarceration time was found to effect no significant increase in recidivism, and in some cases was associated with a decrease in future offending.

Disenchantment with imprisonment as a corrective measure, however, seems to have led to a less than critical acceptance of noninstitutional alternatives as "more effective." Both classification and evaluation of community correction programs are complicated by this lack of clarity and by the interference of value-laden assumptions. As popular and professional support for incarceration of offenders has declined and as the goals of reintegration, resocialization, and

[1] Carol Crowther, "Crimes, Penalties, and Legislatures," *Annals of the American Academy of Political and Social Science,* 381: 147–158, 1969.

rehabilitation have replaced punishment as primary theoretical concerns, it has become fashionable to label any modification of traditional incarceration as "treatment" and any effort to reduce isolation of the offender as "community-based treatment." As a result it has become extremely difficult to identify actual alternative dispositions for those offenders who are candidates for incarceration or to make realistic judgments of their relative effectiveness. In reviewing practices of "community treatment," one must first determine which programs are in fact noninstitutional alternatives and then attempt to distinguish those evaluative results which are relatively free from the influence of interfering variables, including ideological commitment to program on the part of both project and research personnel.

ALTERNATIVES TO INSTITUTIONALIZATION

Within the range of correctional efforts commonly referred to as community treatment there can be discerned a category of programs which are accurately considered alternatives to institutionalization and which also may be fairly clearly distinguished from regular probation supervision. These might be called *intensive intervention in lieu of institutionalization.* Intensive intervention as an *alternative* to institutionalization would seem to imply exactly that—a means of handling the offender without incarceration. This would not include *post*-institutional measures such as parole or other aftercare, halfway houses for releasees, work furlough, imprisonment at night or on weekends, or any other program or partial or intermittent confinement or of "transitional" management as part of a sentence of imprisonment. Such measures may be favored as improvements over custodially oriented, punitive isolation; they may even be found to effectively rehabilitate. But if the objective is to avoid the negative effects of isolation from the community, the severing of family ties and noncriminal associations, and the institutional culture, then for those offenders for whom institutionalization is neither necessary nor beneficial, the correctional alternative would seem to require that no kind of formal institutionalization be imposed.

The importance of distinguishing a type of disposition discrete from both the institution and probation is pointed up not only by research on the effects of institutionalization; research in probation has suggested that certain offenders do very well with minimal supervision. A survey of probation effectiveness in such states as Massachusetts, California, New York, or in a number of foreign countries presents similar reported results with the modal success rate at about 75 percent.[2]

Empey suggests that, since the majority of offenders now placed on probation can succeed without intensive supervision, many of those offenders now incarcerated might succeed under intensified community supervision. These observations imply that intensive intervention, or specialized treatment in the community

---

[2] Cited by La Mar T. Empey, "Alternatives to Incarceration" (Washington: Office of Juvenile Delinquency and Youth Development, 1967). p. 32.

setting, should be viewed *not as an alternative to probation*—which seems to do fairly well for a large number of the individuals now served—but as an alternative to the institutionalization of those offenders who are seen to require greater control than that offered by regular probation supervision.

In other words, while the probation system could be upgraded by changes in structure and operation, it should not be viewed by even its severest critics as an outdated predecessor of the newer community programs. There is considerable evidence that many offenders do well under regular supervision and there is no reason to subject them to further and more intensive "treatment." Probation and intensive intervention both are viable alternative dispositions, each with distinct advantages and uses. The latter envisions a much greater involvement with the offender than mere supervision and attempts to achieve a sometimes considerable modification of values, attitudes, and behaviors which may extend beyond the prevention of specific violations of the law. Probation should be retained as a separate disposition of low intervention level. Intensive intervention can make possible the management in the community of those offenders who otherwise would be placed in an institution. For those now institutionalized, the alternatives to be considered would be imprisonment or intensive community supervision; for those now on probation the alternative would be regular probation, minimal supervision, or suspended sentence with no supervision.

Varieties of Intensive Intervention

Intensive intervention programs, then, are those which provide the means for retaining in the community those offenders who are eligible for institutional placement because they cannot be placed safely and effectively under probation supervision. Most of the community alternatives which have been developed fall generally into one of three classifications: (1) specialized units of probation and parole agencies (probation "plus," or more intensive involvement and supervision than normal probation); (2) nonresidential intensive treatment (attendance centers, guided group interaction programs); or (3) residential programs and out-of-home placement alternatives. A fourth category may develop from the community correctional center. The distinctions among categories are not always clear. Some specialized units in probation or parole may be so intensive that they are difficult to distinguish from daycare; and some residential programs are so structured and self-contained that they must be classed as community-based institutions, rather than as alternatives to incarceration. The groupings nonetheless may be generally useful in identifying alternative noninstitutional dispositions.

Specialized Units in Probation/Parole

While a valid distinction may be made between regular probation or parole supervision and intensive intervention, much of the most interesting research with relevance for the design and operation of intensive community programs has come from the fields of probation and parole. In recent years, the emphasis of research in these areas has shifted from the question "Is probation effective?" to "Under what conditions is probation effective?" For many years it was believed that if caseloads could be reduced, if officers had more time to devote to each case, then probation (or parole) supervision could more effectively rehabilitate. The 50-unit caseload—and, more recently, the 35-unit caseload—has been repeatedly recommended as the "ideal." Specialized units in probation and parole have developed from the findings of caseload research.

Caseload Research

Despite the appeal of reducing caseloads to improve supervision, research during the past decade has clearly indicated that merely reducing caseload size is not the answer. A parole research project in Oakland, California, began in 1959 to test whether reducing caseloads of parolees in Alameda County, California would improve parole performance.[3] Additional agents were employed and ten experimental 36-unit caseloads were set up, with five 72-unit caseloads as controls. When the project was terminated in 1961 no overall difference was found between parole performance in reduced and in full-size caseloads. It was observed that many parolees required so much service that a modest increase in agent time available for each case had little effect.

The University of California's San Francisco Project has undertaken to study Federal probation and parole and to examine the effects of specific caseload sizes.[4] Individuals placed on probation or parole were randomly assigned to caseloads receiving one of four types of supervision: Minimum, intensive, ideal, or normal. Persons in minimum or "crisis" supervision caseloads were required only to submit a monthly written report to the probation office; no routine contacts occurred except when requested by the offender. Intensive caseloads consisted of 20 units each and contact occurred at least weekly; ideal caseloads were composed of 50 units; and normal caseloads consisted of 100 units per month. It was found that when cases were randomly assigned to different degrees of supervision, offenders in minimum caseloads performed as well as would be expected had they been receiving normal supervision; the minimum and the ideal caseloads had violation rates which were almost identical; and in intensive caseloads, despite 14 times the attention provided the minimum cases, the violation rate not only failed to decline but increased with respect to technical violations. These results were interpreted as suggesting that some offenders will succeed under supervision regardless of the type of service, while others will violate no matter how much treatment they receive; and that with identification of these offenders, officer time could be allocated to give most attention to those whose success depends on the presence of certain types of supervision. It was concluded that the concept of

[3] Bertram M. Johnson, "The Failure of a Parole Research Project" *California Youth Authority Quarterly,* 18 (3): 35–39, 1965.

[4] University of California School of Criminology, San Francisco, Research Reports, Berkeley, 1965.

50-unit (or any other number) caseload is meaningless without systematic classification and matching of offender type, treatment, and officer.

The Special Intensive Parole Unit (SIPU), conducted in California from 1953 to 1964, obtained similar results.[5] Study of parolees released to caseloads of various sizes found no differences in violation rates until parolees were classified according to "risk" categories on base expectancy scores (i.e., estimates of probability of recidivism) and assigned on this basis rather than randomly. It was found that while, regardless of size of caseload, high-risk parolees violated extensively and low-risk parolees seldom violated, the middle-risk cases performed distinctly better in smaller caseloads. The low-risk cases did as well in very large caseloads as in regular caseloads.

As supporting evidence accumulated, the emphasis in research shifted from reducing caseloads to classification of offenders and development of appropriate treatment types. One of the most widely acclaimed experimental/demonstration projects, the California Youth Authority's Community Treatment Project, was established to test the feasibility of substitutimg intensive supervision of juveniles in the community for the regular program of institutionalization plus parole and to develop optimum treatment/control plans for defined types of offenders.

The California Community Treatment Project

The Community Treatment Project (CTP) was instituted in California in 1961. Phase 1, completed in 1965, had the following as its objectives: (1) to determine whether selected Youth Authority wards could be released directly from a reception center to a treatment/control program in the community, and whether communities would be willing to accept the return of wards who had just been committed to the Youth Authority; (2) to compare the effectiveness of a period of intensive supervision in the community with treatment in the regular institutional program; and (3) to develop hypotheses regarding specific treatment plans for defined types of delinquents in specific settings.

During Phase II (1964–1969) the Project continued to develop data relevant to the goals of the first phase, with special emphasis on determining which treatment variables are most related to success on parole for different types of delinquents. Efforts were made to describe program elements in detail to provide a research base for extension of the program, for training correctional staff, and for comparison with other community programs.

In brief, the research procedure consisted of the following. After assessment of eligibility for the project and classification according to I-Level (i.e., a measure of level of interpersonal maturity), male and female Youth Authority wards committed from the juvenile courts of Sacramento, Stockton, San Francisco, and Modesto were randomly assigned to experimental or control status. Experimentals were treated in an intensive community program; controls went into the usual

---

[5] California Corrections Department, Special Intensive Parole Unit, *Reports, Phases I-IV,* Sacramento, 1953–1964, *Also see: National Probation and Parole Association Journal,* 3 (3): 222–9, 1957.

Youth Authority Program. In San Francisco (Phase II) experimentals were randomly assigned to one of two different forms of community treatment: A Differential Treatment Unit or a Guided Group Interaction Unit.

The CTP progress reports have been consistently positive in their evaluation of the experimental program. During Phase I, the program was judged to be feasible in the community and the overall success rate of the project participants was found to be significantly higher than that of youths in the regular Youth Authority program. Differential success rates were reported: certain types of youths appeared to do especially well under the given treatment conditions while others did about as well as they would have in an institution or on parole. Additionally, in terms of psychological test scores, experimentals were observed to have achieved greater positive change and a higher level of personal and social adjustment than control subjects. Throughout Phase II, ongoing followup of study subjects from both phases continued to indicate large differences favoring experimentals over controls. Factors associated with greater effectiveness of the community program have been identified: (1) differential and treatment-relevant decisionmaking: (2) matching of types of offenders with types of workers; (3) intensive and/or extensive intervention by workers made possible by reduced caseloads; (4) ability and perceptiveness of workers; and (5) emphasis on working through of the worker/ward relationship.

Another explanation of these results has been offered. Robinson and Smith have analyzed the findings of the Community Treatment Project in terms of factors which influenced the recidivism rates of experimentals and controls.[6] They explain that recidivism rates can be influenced, within certain limits, by the decision-making authorities, and that in the CTP study, rates were managed in such a way as to make the experimentals appear favorable. Quoting from the seventh Progress Report (1966) of the CTP, they show that 68 percent of control failures and only 29 percent of the experimental failures were accounted for by the agent's recommendation that parole be revoked. Quoting Lerman[7] in a reexamination of the data, the authors explain that when the offense is of low or moderate severity, experimentals are less likely to have their parole revoked; they are treated similarly to controls only when the offense is of high severity. Experimentals, they conclude, were no less delinquent in their behavior than the controls. They suggest that the important point is that an ideological belief in the effectiveness of community treatment apparently altered the experimental results.

Research findings on the relative effectiveness, in terms of recidivism at least, of one major community project are equivocal. Despite the enthusiastic endorsement that the CTP has received from most sources, it appears that the experimental program is not yet established as clearly superior to institutionalization *for reducing the recidivism rate.* While intensive intervention programs generally are less costly and probably less personally damaging than the institutional experi-

---

[6] *See* James Robinson and Gerald Smith, "The Effectiveness of Correctional Programs," in Section One.

[7] P. Lerman, "Evaluating the Outcome of Institutions for Delinquents," *Social Work,* 13 (3): 1968.

ence, evaluative reports of all such projects should be scrutinized for interfering variables which might affect or determine relative success in terms of violation rates.

Community Delinquency Control Project

Another community-based treatment program for young offenders who normally would be institutionalized is the Community Delinquency Control Project (CDCP) of the California Youth Authority Department. This program also offers intensive supervision in the community, makes use of multiple resources, and provides different types of treatment. Both the Community Treatment Project and the CDCP are located in community centers which serve selected offenders released directly on "parole" without prior institutionalization. The main difference between the two projects is that the Community Treatment Project systematically classifies offenders in terms of Interpersonal Maturity and matches types of wards with types of supervising officers.

The Community Delinquency Control Project was begun in 1964 in an effort to reduce overcrowding in Youth Authority Institutions, to determine the feasibility and effectiveness of such a program in the community, and to effect significant and lasting behavioral change in a nondelinquent direction. Three CDCP units were established in Los Angeles and one in Oakland, California. Each unit was designed to supervise 95 wards in the intensive phase (for an average of 12 months) and up to 50 program graduates under less intensive supervision. Wards receiving intensive service are placed in caseloads of 15, with each agent carrying a total caseload of fewer than 25 parolees. The major treatment elements include: increased general supervision, intensive individual counseling, group and family counseling, remedial tutoring, psychiatric and group-work consultation for agents, increased use of subsidized out-of-home (foster home and group home) placements, and activity groups for wards. Originally, wards eligible for CDCP placement were male first admissions to the Youth Authority. Eligibility was later broadened to include both sexes, juvenile court readmissions, and adult-court first admissions.

Two of the project goals were rapidly achieved: commitments to juvenile institutions were reduced and the community and law enforcement officials demonstrated their acceptance of the program. In March 1966 a random experimental design was introduced in two Los Angeles units to determine whether CDCP eligible wards assigned to the program do better than CDCP eligibles assigned to a regular Youth Authority program. The California Youth Authority reports that it is too early to derive any definite conclusions from the Los Angeles study. Their tentative analysis showed that of 187 CDCP male first commitments, 51 had violated parole within six months (27.3 percent) as compared to 29.4 percent of the 102 controls.

A 1968 study of 565 male wards released to the four CDCP units (not including the Los Angeles study population) reported a parole violation rate of 41.6 percent over 15 months, as compared to 47.7 percent for wards on parole statewide. It is suggested that since CDCP eligible were statistically poorer risks (younger and excluding offenders against persons), the difference between the program population and a true control group might be much greater. In July 1969 the four CDCP units were terminated and converted into Community Parole Centers. The program elements of these centers are generally the same as in the CDCP, except that all parolees from the local community will be served, rather than selected wards in lieu of institutionalization.

The Community Delinquency Control Project, like the Community Treatment Project, has not yet provided unqualified support for the thesis that management of offenders in the community is significantly *more* successful in preventing further crime that is institutionalization. However, both programs have demonstrated a more important fact: offenders normally not released to community supervision can be as safely and at least as effectively handled in intensive intervention programs without institutionalization.

Other Programs of Specialized Supervision

Another attempt to test the effectiveness of intensive community intervention was the San Francisco Rehabilitation Project for Adult Offenders, instituted to provide individual offenders with a helping relationship focused on changing patterns of behavior. Its purpose was to replace a jail or prison term with professional counseling in the community. The offender sample of 109 subjects was intended to be broadly representative of the group normally sent to jail and prison, although Robinson and Smith report that project cases tended to be somewhat younger, with fewer minority group members, and a disproportionately high number of property offenders and low number of narcotic offenders. The final report of this project suggested that while the superior results obtained by the community program must be considered tentative, it is safe to conclude that intensive counseling by professionally trained workers can reduce recidivism at least as effectively as imprisonment. It is emphasized that this program can be set up by existing governmental agencies and that its economic returns, in terms of support of the offender and his dependents during treatment, can exceed the costs of treatment.

Most of the programs of specialized supervision that have been instituted in various parts of the United States have not been rigorously evaluated. Assessments of "effectiveness," where they have been attempted at all, frequently are not very useful—no control group is used, the groups are not comparable, or assignment is not random. Many descriptive studies merely report the subjective judgments of staff or the observed changes in arrest patterns over time of the project participants. This means that much of the "community treatment" literature must be guardedly interpreted; but it is still useful in suggesting the variety of intervention alternatives that have been tried and that may be duplicated elsewhere.

A very broad range of services and programs have been provided for the treatment of offenders who require more intensive services than regular supervision; group or family counseling may be offered as a service of the juvenile court; the offender may be referred to a psychiatric clinic for additional treatment; probation officers may meet in frequent sessions of guided group interaction with selected probationers; the juvenile probationer may be required to attend daycare centers or centers providing remedial education and vocational training; or juveniles for whom living with their families is contraindicated because of undesirable home situations may be placed in foster homes, group homes, or in "halfway houses."

The variety of services available as an adjunct to probation has permitted many courts greater flexibility in their disposition of offenders for whom neither probation nor institutionalization is suitable. However, in a large number of jurisdictions the court simply has no available alternatives to imprisonment and many offenders are sent to prison or training school because probation supervision is not felt to be sufficient. The state probation subsidy programs have emerged in an attempt to reduce costs and overcrowding in state institutions by handling more offenders in the local community. Some of the savings resulting from reduced commitments are returned to the county probation departments for purposes of expanding and upgrading probation services.

State Subsidy Programs

In 1965, the California State Legislature passed legislation which provided a State subsidy to county probation departments to set up "special supervision" programs, to increase the degree of supervision of individual cases, and to develop and improve supervisional practices. Reduced commitment rates of offenders to state correctional institutions was made a mandatory condition for the receipt of subsidy monies. The enabling legislation was the result of the recommendation of a 1964 study undertaken to determine how state costs could be reduced while county probation programs were improved. This study found wide variations in the frequency of the use of probation in different counties and determined that 25 percent of the state correctional commitments could be maintained safely and effectively within the county systems if probation facilities were improved. The plan that was ultimately adopted provided for reimbursement by the state to the counties in proportion to the number of cases retained in the county exceeding the existing rate. A sliding scale was developed to avoid penalizing counties that already had a low commitment rate. Since its implementation, the subsidy program has resulted in a reduction of expected institutional commitments by 2,481 in 1967-1968. Forty-seven percent of this number were adults. Of the 36 counties participating in the program, all but two have reduced their expected commitment rates.

Not all state subsidy programs have been used to upgrade or modify probation supervision. In Oregon, state funds were used to develop small-group home facilities, and in Philadelphia a day center was established. The concept of the state subsidy to county probation departments or, as in Oregon, to the public or private agency operating the program, is a flexible tool that could be used not only to finance improvements in probation services or to set up specialized units, but also could provide the means for the development of a wide range of other community programs for offender rehabilitation.

NONRESIDENTIAL INTENSIVE TREATMENT

Guided Group Interaction Programs

Of the various kinds of nonresidential programs that have been experimented with, one group of programs can be distinguished by their common theoretical orientation. These are the guided group interaction (GGI) programs, which are primarily concerned with peer group dynamics and the operation of the peer group in restructuring the youth "subculture" around more socially acceptable norms and values. These programs also depend sometimes to a considerable extent on the involvement of youth in their own treatment. While other nonresidential programs frequently incorporate the group session into the daily program, less emphasis is placed on the peer group as the major treatment resource.

GGI programs involve the delinquent in frequent and intensive group discussions of their own and other members' current problems and experiences. Based on the theory that antisocial youth behavior receives the support and approval of the delinquent values and attitudes also requires the support of the peer group, these programs encourage the development of a group culture and the acceptance by members of responsibility for helping and controlling one another. As the group culture develops and the group begins to accept greater responsibility, the staff group leader allows the group a greater degree of decision-making power. Over time, the group's responsibility may extend to decisions involving disciplinary measures imposed on a member or determination of a member's readiness for release.

Demonstration projects based on the use of peer group dynamics derived their program content from the Highfields project, established in New Jersey in 1949. Highfields was a short-term residential program for a maximum of 20 boys at any given time, ages 16 to 17. The boys worked during the day at a nearby mental institution and participated in guided group interaction sessions in the evening. There were few formal rules. The project was judged to be at least as successful as a training school, in terms of recidivism, and much less costly. The basic principles of Highfields have been applied in nonresidential settings with apparent success. Essexfields, Collegefields, and the Provo experiment are perhaps the best known examples.

Guided group interaction programs are unique in that the group process itself is expected to determine the culture and social system of the entire program. The decision-making authority permitted the group is considerably greater than in traditional group therapy, possibly a crucial factor in the rehabilitation of youth through group influence and support.

THE COMMUNITY CORRECTION CENTER

The term "community correctional center" usually refers to a community-based institution, located in a carefully selected neighborhood in an effort to reduce the isolation from community services and other resources. Most designs do not envision any considerable participation of the offender on the outside. Others are centers for released offenders where services are not provided in lieu of institutional commitment. The community correctional center is perhaps more accurately described as a community-based institution than as a noninstitutional community resource. An institution situated in the locale that supplies the offender population is better able to draw upon the medical, social work, psychiatric, educational, and employment resources of the community and to involve community residents and family members in offender rehabilitation and reintegration. The forms taken by programs based on this model could vary widely in degree of community contact, in the proportions of time spent in custody and living in the community, and in the amount of involvement of the offender in the decision-making process.

"Community Treatment": The Community as Correctional Client

The growing emphasis on the role of the community in the etiology of crime and the rehabilitation of offenders, which undergirds the movement to establish corrections in the community settings, has led to speculation as to the proper goals of community correction programs. If the offender is to be retained in the community in order to facilitate his reabsorption into community life, then the correctional goal is presumed to be the reintegration of the offender. The goal of reintegration, as opposed to goals of punishment, removal from society, or even reform of the offender, implies a dual target: both the offender and the receiving community often must be changed if reintegration is to be achieved. A number of writers have suggested that community corrections involves change in both the offender and his society—that the task of corrections involves the reconstruction or construction of ties between the offender and the community through maintenance of family bonds, obtaining education and employment, and finding a place for the offender in the mainstream of social life.

One writer has suggested that the goal of social change and offender reintegration is not feasible for corrections.[8] First, the community will resist being cast in the role of correctional client and resent the associated stigma. In addition, the global nature of the goal of achieving reintegration prevents the delimitation of the boundaries of correction. If the goal is offender-community reintegration, the sphere of interest and responsibility of the correctional program is unlimited and success or failure cannot be operationally defended or assessed.

---

[8] *See* J. Robert Weber, "Goals of Community Correction: A Redefinition."

This observation has important implications for intensive intervention programs and any other correctional measures involving the community. If, as Weber suggests, the goal of community correction is to provide the means and opportunities for reintegration by directing the offender to community resources and acquainting the community with the needs and skills of the offender, then success may be defined as the appropriate provision of those opportunities. Community corrections, then, could concentrate on helping the offender to link appropriately with the normal community resource channels.

Community correction goals, and the relative weights to be given to treatment *in* the community as opposed to treatment *of* the community, need further attention and clarification to facilitate program evaluation.

CONCLUSIONS

In the California study of the effects of criminal penalties it was concluded that since severe penalties do not deter more effectively, since prisons do not rehabilitate, and since the criminal justice system is inconsistent and has little quantitative impact on crime, the best rehabilitative possibilities would appear to be in the community. This reasoning is fairly typical of much current thinking in correction and it serves to illustrate the kind of cognitive leap on which enthusiasm for "community treatment" is based. If prisons do not rehabilitate, and if the stated goal of correction is to reduce recidivism through integration of offender and community, it seems irresistibly logical that treating the offender without removing him from society will be more effective. Unfortunately, while one may express the opinion that since prisons are not effective (a validated observation), then one *might as well* retain offenders in the community, it cannot be assumed without adequate controlled research that the best *rehabilitative* possibilities are to be found in the community.

The most rigorous research designs generally have elicited the finding that offenders eligible for supervision in the community in lieu of institutionalization do *as well* in the community as they do in prison or training school. When intervening variables are controlled, recidivism rates appear to be about the same.

This is not to derogate community alternatives to institutionalization, for it is a most important finding: a large number of offenders who are candidates for incarceration may instead be retained in the community *as safely, as effectively, and at much less expense.* Additionally, the observed effects of the overcrowded and isolated institution on the personality and social adjustment of the incarcerated individual are avoided. It is unnecessary to demonstrate, as most experimental/research projects appear to feel pressured to do, that recidivism rates are *lower* when offenders are retained in the community. Given the fact that expensive and overcrowded institutions are not doing the job they are intended to do, it is appropriate to suggest that less costly, less personally damaging alternatives be utilized wherever they are at least as effective as imprisonment.

Until alternatives to institutionalization are demonstrated to be more effective than imprisonment in preventing further crime, a major rationale for the use of community programs will be that correctional costs can be considerably reduced by handling in the community setting a large number of those offenders normally institutionalized. Experimental/demonstration projects in intensive intervention have shown that for a large number of institution candidates incarceration is clearly unnecessary. Thus, if society is still determined, in the light of this evidence, to keep these offenders in prison and training schools, it must be willing to pay the price. The central question becomes: are the goals of punishment and custodial control worth the high costs of constructing institutions and maintaining the inmates in the institutions, as well as the observed and the still unknown personal and social costs incurred through exposing individuals to the institutional experience.

The cost of building an institution has been estimated at about $22,000 a bed; maintaining and treating a ward in an institution costs about $400 a month. The cost savings obtained in substituting intensive intervention programs for institutionalization are clearly demonstrated in the concept and operation of the probation subsidy. Following a study that found that 25 percent of state correctional commitments could be maintained safely and effectively in the community, where counties were given the means to improve probation, the California subsidy program was carefully "sold" to the state legislature in terms of a cost reduction. During the 1966-1967 fiscal year, the 31 counties participating in California's subsidy program reduced institutional commitments to the extent that what would have been a 5.8 million dollar expenditure on institutional programs was reduced to 2.4 million for intensive supervision programs. The literature reflects a growing interest in cost-benefit analysis as a means of determining more systematically which correctional procedures actually "succeed" in terms of return on funds invested.

Review of the literature on alternatives to institutionalization leads to one other observation: there is a conspicuous lack of interest in intensive supervision programs for adult prison candidates. While there has been some experience with reduced caseloads and specialized units in probation and parole agencies dealing with adult offenders, these have generally been limited to groupings based on age, sex, or offense category. Alcoholics, narcotic addicts, and misdemeanants are sometimes given special treatment, but it might be argued that such offenders should instead be *diverted from* the criminal justice system. Probation "plus" for adults has included attendance at mental health clinics and group therapy programs.

Adults are more often handled by a *"prison* plus" approach: once confined to prison, selected inmates are then partially released on furlough, to work-release programs, or to halfway houses. Evidence that many adult inmates can be safely released to work in the open community should suggest that most offenders who are eligible for such programs could be safely and effectively retained in the community in the first place.

There would appear to be no factual basis for the assumption that only juveniles are significantly influenced by their peers, that group dynamics function only among the young, or that selected adult offenders could not greatly benefit from involvement in their own treatment and the decision-making process. Placement in a work/training/guided-group interaction program could be offered as an alternative to institutionalization for adults as well. Group homes and "foster family" or single placement boarding homes might even be made available *on a voluntary basis* to adult offenders without family or ties in the community or who need assistance until they are able to establish themselves in a job and neighborhood. Just as probation and the treatment orientation for adult offenders followed the development of these concepts for juveniles, adult correction might now be moved to benefit from the experience of juvenile correction in the community.

A major obstacle to the wider development and use of community alternatives in both adult and juvenile correction may be the widespread rejection of the offender by the community itself and the desire on the part of society to keep the offender "out of sight and out of mind." The task of "social" control has been relegated progressively to a smaller proportion of the social body, while the majority of society refuse responsibility for an increasing variety of behaviors and persons. Isolation and banishment have not "worked." Unless society is willing to keep a very large and growing number of its "offenders" in permanent custody, it must begin to accept greater responsibility in the areas of social control and correction.

The evidence obtained from experimental work in community programs, supported by the results of experience with partial imprisonment and graduated release, the treatment of mental illness, and alternatives to processing by the criminal justice system, clearly indicates that a vast proportion of offenders could be managed in the community at least as effectively, and with much less cost, or diverted from the justice system entirely, thus returning to the community its responsibility for dealing with behavior it defines as antisocial or deviant.

35
Community-Based Correctional Programs: A Survey and Analysis

BERTRAM S. GRIGGS AND GARY R. McCUNE

This article focuses on programs designed to facilitate the transition of adult offenders, male and female, from prison back into the community via community-based correctional programs. An attempt was made (1) to trace the rate of growth and development of community-based programs, (2) to identify the sources of funding, (3) to ascertain the need, if any, for legislation, (4) to determine the various types of programs, (5) to identify the populations serviced, and (6) to review and comment on problem areas.

The basic method of gathering information was by questionnaire and telephone calls to state correctional agencies and state planning agencies (LEAA). Additional information was secured from the International Association of Halfway Houses and the U.S. Bureau of Prisons. Also, onsite visits were made to community-based programs operated by (1) a private agency that contracted for federal prisoners, (2) state programs operated on the grounds of institutions, and (3) state programs operated in the community without the usual prison safeguards.

SOURCE. *Federal Probation,* XXXVI, June 1972, pp. 7–13. Reprinted with permission of the authors and *Federal Probation.*

LIMITATIONS OF THE STUDY

There are community treatment programs for adults and juveniles, for males and females, for felons and misdemeanants, for parolees, probationers, and offenders committed to these centers as an alternative to incarceration. The variety of populations served made it necessary to narrow the scope of this study to adult felons, male and female, who are programmed in the community *prior* to release or parole.

Initially, the focus was to be confined to a survey and analysis of just those persons residing in community-based facilities. It soon became apparent that the focus would have to be expanded to include those housed in local jails and institutions, because they are being programmed in the community for reasons identical to our original target group and are considered by many as being involved in community-based programs despite their residence.

It appears that sometimes these programs are operated out of jails and state correctional facilities primarily for legal considerations and, more often than not, for budgetary considerations. Obviously, programs in local jails or correctional institutions also allow for participation by a larger number of eligible inmates. It is anticipated that as funds become available there will be a shift from jails and prisons to "genuine" community facilities, *i.e.,* hotels, apartments, large boarding homes, etc.

BACKGROUND OF THE STUDY

It is estimated that by 1975 the average daily population in corrections will be 1.8 million.[1] Approximately 98 percent of that population will eventually be released. Most of the offenders will return to the same community, even the same homes. Many will be under some kind of supervision. Will society be ready and willing to accept them? Perhaps even more important, will they, by virtue of their institutional experience, be ready to take their place in society?

It is difficult under our present system to prepare a person confined in prison for months, or years, to make the transition from prison back to the community. Fear, lack of information, distrust, and a variety of other forces combine to cause the releasee to approach the experience with trepidation and a sense of helplessness.

The President's Crime Commission focused on one aspect of the problem when it stated: "Institutions tend to isolate offenders from society, both physically and psychologically, cutting them off from schools, jobs, families, and other supportive influences and increasing the probability that the label of criminal will be indelibly impressed upon them. The goal in reintegration is likely to be fur-

---

[1] *The Challenge of Crime in A Free Society,* 1967, p. 160.

thered much more readily by working with the offender in the community than by incarceration"[2]

The Report further states: "with two-thirds of the total corrections caseload under probation or parole supervision, the central question is no longer whether to handle offenders in the community but how to do so safely and successfully."[3]

Over the years there have been sporadic attempts, mostly by religious and other humanitarian groups, to operate small community and prison institution programs for offenders. These pioneering programs, for the most part met only the bare necessities and did not allow for enough active offender participation in organizing, planning, and day-to-day operations. Borrowing from the experiences of these small, private agencies, government agencies have developed a rationale for residential centers, *i.e.*, community treatment programs. The concept was clearly delineated by the Task Force on Corrections of the President's Crime Commission:

> The general underlying premise for the new directions in corrections is that crime and delinquency are symptoms of failure and disorganization of the community as well as the individual offenders. In particular, these failures are seen as depriving offenders of contact with institutions (of society) that are basically responsible for assuring the development of law-abiding conduct . . .
>
> The task of corrections therefore included building or rebuilding solid ties between the offender and the community, integrating or reintegrating the offender into community life —restoring family ties, obtaining employment and education, securing in a larger sense a place for the offender in the routine functioning of society. . . . This requires not only efforts directed toward changing the individual offender, which has been almost the exclusive focus of rehabilitation, but also mobilization and change of the community and its institutions.

Maximum effort, therefore, will be required of departments of corrections to influence those conditions that will assist the offender to build a solid bridge back to the community. That bridge must enable offenders to participate in work, education, training and other aspects of community life.

Some efforts have been made by a number of states to develop ways to reestablish offenders in the community through the use of community treatment programs. Many such programs focus on offenders after they have been paroled. This approach is more or less traditional, making use of postrelease "halfway houses" operated by state and private agencies.

We are concerned in this article with a more modern trend, *i.e.*, the programming of offenders in the community *prior* to release or parole. Without attempting to evaluate the effectiveness of these programs, we have attempted to determine their extent, rate of growth and the trends that may be developing, and the present status of prerelease community-based correctional programs.

[2] *Ibid.*, p. 165.
[3] *Ibid.*

Results of Study

The responses from the state departments of corrections were excellent—46 out of 51, or 90 percent, completed and returned the questionnaire.[4] Of the 46 responses, 28 departments of corrections (59 percent) have community treatment programs, although as already noted, some of them are operated out of local jails and state institutions.[5]

Presently there are five departments of corrections without programs, but with definite plans to establish programs within the next 2 years.[6] There are 13 departments of corrections without programs and are not presently planning any.[7]

Approximately 4,143 inmates were participating in treatment programs (all categories), ranging from a high of 437 in one state to a low of 10.[8] It is significant that the high of 437 represents less than 2 percent of the state's total prison population. Nine of the state programs are limited to males and 18 have programs serving both sexes, including several that are coeducational to the extent that both men and women are housed in the same building. One state program serves females only. All of the states reporting Frograms service their own clients, and four of the 28 states also handled federal inmates.[9]

The major source of funds came from state budgets, but there were other sources—especially LEAA. Thirteen of the 28 states used state funds exclusively, one was financed totally by Federal funds, and the balance were combinations of state, Federal, and private funds.[10]

Types of Facilities

The study revealed that many types and combinations of physical facilities were used by states in operating their community treatment programs.[11] In those

[4] The 50 states plus the District of Columbia. The Federal Bureau of Prisons is treated separately, see pages 539 and 540.

[5] See table on page 537.

[6] Arizona, Delaware, Missouri, New Hampshire, West Virginia.

[7] Alabama, Arkansas, Idaho, Iowa, Kansas, Kentucky, Mississippi, Nevada, New York, North Dakota, Ohio, South Dakota. Wyoming.

[8] The average length of participation is approximately 90 days. This means a turnover of four times per year or a potential capacity of 16,572 cases. Should the capacity be increased by 70 percent within 2 years, as anticipated, the annual capacity would be over 28,000 cases.

[9] The authors are aware of programs in some states, operated primarily by private agencies, which serve Federal offenders on a contractual basis, but which do not serve state prisoners in the same status. Most of these programs have a combination of Federal prisoners who participate prior to release and state offenders who participate while on parole, or on a postrelease basis. Programs of this nature were not included in the survey data but are covered in the section on Federal programs.

[10] Eight used combinations of state and state LEAA funds; three used combinations of state, state LEAA, and private funds; one each used state and federal funds (*e.g.* Model Cities, Department of Labor, HEW), state and private funds, and state, state LEAA, and Federal funds.

[11] Eight states used noncorrectional facilities only, such as hotels, YMCA's, apartments, etc. Five used state correctional institutions only. One used county jails only. Two used a combination of state

States With Community Treatment Programs for Adult Felons, Male and Female, Prior to Release on Parole

State	Residents			Source of Referrals				Source of Funding				Type of Facility		
	Capacity	M.	F.	State institution	Federal prisons	Courts	Other	State (LEAA)	State (other)	Federal	Private	Hotel or Apt.	Jail	State (institution)
Total	4,143	27	19	27	5	6	1	13	25	3	4	20	9	16
Calif.	437	X	X	X					X			X	X	X
Colo.	60	X		X				X	X					X
Conn.	112	X		X					X	X				
Fla.	150	X	X	X	X			X	X			X	X	
Ga.	138	X	X	X	X			X	X			X	X	
Hawaii	145	X		X					X			X		X
Ill.	60	X	X	X					X			X		X
Ind.	214	X	X	X				X	X			X		X
La.	150	X	X	X				X	X		X	X	X	X
Me.	10		X	X					X		X	X		
Md.	189	X	X	X					X	X		X		
Mass.	72	X	X	X				X	X			X		X
Mich.	125	X	X	X				X	X			X		X
Minn.	70	X	X	X		X		X	X		X	X	X	
Neb.	25	X		X					X			X		
N.J.	30	X	X	X					X			X		
N.C.	151	X	X	X					X			X		X
Okla.	48	X		X					X			X		
Oreg.	183	X	X	X	X	X		X	X			X	X	
R.I.	50	X		X	X	X		X	X			X		
S.C.	311	X		X	X	X		X	X			X		
Tenn.	50	X	X	X				X	X			X		
Texas	350	X		X				X	X			X		
Vt.	298	X	X	X	X	X			X			X		X
Va.	105	X	X	X					X			X	X	X
Wash.	25	X		X					X		X	X	X	
Wis.	250	X	X	X					X					X
D.C.	335	X	X		X	X	X		X	X		X		X

states which have a combination of community-based and institutional or jail-based community programs, the work-study release programs usually preceded the state's involvement in community-based operations. However, in regard to strictly community-based programs (operated out of noncorrectional facilities in the community), only 8 states reported having programs of this type without also operating work-study release out of jails and correctional institutions.

In most states which submitted copies of their work release laws, the legislation was similar and usually required that the inmate be "returned to a penal or correctional institution at night." In those instances, new legislation would be required to permit participation in community programs where the prisoners are housed in noncorrectional facilities. In those states which have only institution or jail-based work-study release, practically all indicated intentions to expand existing programs in the same facilities, as well as plans to establish new community treatment programs.

Program Emphasis

Without exception, each of the 28 correction departments with community treatment programs featured work release or work furlough. Of these 28, 12 also included "school release"—or study release. Most of these programs included one or more of the following: individual and group counseling, prerelease orientation, family counseling, accelerated release for those participating in the program, community involvement and use of volunteers, and maximum use of all community resources. There are also some special programs in cooperation with public and private agencies that provide assistance to individuals with psychiatric, narcotic, and related health and emotional problems.

We were struck by the similarity rather than the difference in the programs described in the information we received. Many departments believe that allowing inmates serving time in prison to go into the community is a unique and giant step in the right direction. Based on the past history of corrections, it is difficult to argue with that. Five or 10 years from now, hopefully that feeling will have changed significantly to one that sees programming in the community as being "routine" and imprisonment, in the traditional sense, the exception.

Problem Areas

Because community treatment programs for inmates still serving sentences are relatively new, it seemed appropriate to provide an opportunity for respondents to our survey to discuss "problem areas." The most sensitive issue for all of the programs was the reaction of the community. Other comments related to lack

---

correctional institutions and county jails. Six used a combination of state correctional institutions and noncorrectional facilities. Three used county jails and noncorrectional facilities. And three used a combination of county jails, state correctional institutions, and noncorrectional facilities.

of funding and the need for statutory and programmatic changes. Some typical comments are the following:

We have encountered problems in preparing the community to accept a house with offenders. It is our experience that a great deal of public relations is necessary before moving into a neighborhood and that if possible the citizens should become part of the policy making of the house.

Correctional centers have both detention and sentenced population. Most problems are related to the inability to segregate the two classes. This requires too high a degree of security for prerelease prisoners. (Our only problem.)

. . . begin actively involving members of the community 1 to 2 years prior to the planned opening of the center . . .

The original legislation is ambiguous and omitted some important items.

Need for a weekend furlough program.

We would anticipate community reaction if we were attempting to establish a house in the community; we have maintained fairly rigid house rules and our experience has been this is preferable to more permissive procedures; we have found a large untreated alcohol problem which surfaces when men are placed in the program and for which a treatment program is needed.

. . . Negative community attitudes to be overcome and the appointment of a blue ribbon committee to study the needs and sites for these problems.

Legislation

Twenty-one of the 28 departments making use of community treatment programs stated that special legislation had been required before they could permit inmates to participate in such programs. Four states indicated that no additional legislation was necessary, and three did not respond to that specific question.

Most of the new laws stated in essence that the directors of corrections may utilize facilities located off the regular institution grounds as community correctional facilities and the director may enter into agreements with city or county jails and transfer inmates to such facilities for purposes of work release or work furlough. A small number of states required only limited modifications of their statutes. In the District of Columbia, Congress had to enact laws authorizing the establishment of community correctional center programs.

The Federal Program

For the purposes of this survey, the community treatment programs operated by the Federal Bureau of Prisons and those programs which serve Federal prisoners on a contract basis are treated separately and summarized in this section. Although the Bureau of Prisons operates work release programs out of most of their institutions, this summary focused only on their community treatment centers and those contract community-based programs where Federal prisoners are sent prior to release. At the present time the Bureau of Prisons operates a total of 14 community treatment centers (CTC) programs. The first CTC was established in Chicago in 1961. The combined capacity of these programs is approximately 350, out of an inmate population of approximately 21,500.[12] A majority of the centers are operated out of hotels or apartment facilities. Over half of them serve both male and female offenders. Although most of these facilities are funded exclusively by the Bureau of Prisons, one is partially funded by both state and the Vocational Rehabilitation Administration and one receives some private funding.

Until recently, the federally operated community treatment centers served prisoners scheduled for release from Federal, and, in some cases, state institutions. However, the passage of Public Law 91–492 in October 1970 now makes it possible for Federal courts to direct a probationer to reside or participate in the program of a CTC as a condition of probation when such facilities are available. Similarly, the U.S. Board of Parole may require a parolee or mandatory releasee to reside or participate in the program of a CTC as a condition of parole or mandatory release.

This "half-way-in" approach to dealing with offenders as an alternative to imprisonment is a major step forward, and one which will necessitate the development of additional facilities. In the Federal program at this time, the actual, as well as projected, populations of the CTC's will consist of approximately 10 percent probationers and parolees and 90 percent inmates scheduled for release.[13] The Bureau of Prisons has plans to expand existing programs by developing more satellite units in the larger metropolitan areas, as well as establishing new centers in areas where they can be justified in terms of referrals from institutions, courts, and the parole board.

The CTC program has undergone substantial expansion, especially during the past 4 years. Possibly even more significant has been the increase in the number of contracts initiated with state, local, and private agencies which provide similar programs to Federal prisoners in areas where the concentration of releasees has been too small to justify a Federal facility. The Bureau currently has contracts with 35 such programs (representing 60 facilities) located in 15 states and the District of Columbia. A significant number of these programs are at least partially funded by private agencies and organizations. A few of them are operated in states such as Massachusetts, where laws now preclude participation of state offenders, except after release or while on parole. One would hope that these programs would serve to demonstrate the value of such a resource to states which are not now using their program for prerelease purposes. The Bureau of Prisons expects to continue expanding its contract programs as more resources become available.

A review of the laws and program policies of those states with community-based programs (including work release) indicates that many were modeled after the Federal program. Although the Bureau of Prisons may not have pioneered in community treatment programs, it has been an important transmitter of this innovation to the state and local systems.

---

[12] As of March 31, 1972.

[13] From February 1971 to February 1972 134, or 9.5 percent, of 1500 CTC residents were probationers or parolees.

Growth and Trends

The period of greatest growth in community treatment programs was during 1968 and 1969, when six states implemented programs during each of those years.[14] The slower growth in 1970 may be explained by the mild recession the Nation experienced. Also, it appears that there has been a shift in emphasis, as reflected in some recent state plans (LEAA), toward development of community treatment programs as alternatives to any imprisonment. It may well be that the rate of growth in these programs will slow down or level off because of the shift in emphasis to the beginning of the correctional process. It should be pointed out, however, that 21 of the states presently involved in community-based programs have specific plans to expand existing programs substantially and/or to increase their community-based facilities within the next 2 to 5 years. These increases would account for an additional 64 units or facilities and 2,891 beds or program spaces. This represents an increase of approximately 70 percent over present level. If these plans materialize, the total program capacity would be approximately 7,000.[15] However, considering the total prison population, and the recognized need to increase the efficiency of correctional programs, the number is relatively insignificant.

Where considering the question of introducing community-based treatment programs into correctional systems that are complex and often under critical attack, one must be aware of the many forces operating in the communities that may determine the programs' effectiveness.[16] As we have seen, the most crucial area, based on the experience of those operating such programs, is *community acceptance* of the idea that inmates serving time would not be a serious risk to the community. Even though over 93 percent of the inmates currently confined will eventually be released, the paramount question continues to be how to do so safely and successfully. Community-based treatment programs offer some hope.

Recommendations

Community treatment programs for offenders due to be released from prison are still in a relatively early stage of development. Before any firm conclusions can be drawn regarding their effect on reducing recidivism, or other criteria of success, considerably more research will be required. However, there is no question but that programs of this type do help facilitate the offender's inevitable reentry into the community by: (1) providing some continuity with education and

---

[14] Before 1968, programs had been implemented in two states in 1963, one in 1964, three in 1965, two in 1966, and four in 1967.

[15] See footnote 8.

[16] LEAA announced in 1971 a grant of $194,544 for the development of a research plan for evaluating community-based correctional treatment programs and analyzing their cost effectiveness, by the Pacific Northwest Laboratory of the Battelle Memorial Institute, Richland, Washington. *Criminal Justice Newsletter,* Vol. 2, No. 8, April 19, 1971.

training programs begun in the correctional institutions; (2) assisting the offender in obtaining adequate employment; (3) increasing utilization of community resources; and (4) providing needed support during this difficult initial period of adjustment. On this basis alone, the question is not one of whether a correctional agency should become involved in community treatment programs, but rather how and to what extent.

At the conclusion of this survey, it became obvious that there is an evolutionary process in the development of community treatment programs. On a nationwide basis, the stages of this process range from states with "no programs—no plans" to states with a variety of progressive programs. Somewhere in between lie the bulk of states which are operating or have recently initiated work release programs in their correctional and detention facility as well as those states which are operating or planning to establish community-based treatment centers. This evolutionary process could be shortened considerably through a greater exchange of information and experience, as well as more efficient use of funding resources and technical assistance. With this in mind, the following recommendations are offered:

(1) The Federal Bureau of Prisons has considerable experience in both the operation of community-based treatment programs and work-study release which is institution-based. Their expertise and leadership in this area is well established. By virtue of the LEAA Technical Assistance Program, the Bureau of Prisons is able to provide direct assistance, including on-site visits, to state correctional agencies. This assistance can include drafting legislation, planning and implementing community treatment programs, and devising methodology for and actually conducting evaluation. It is recommended that the states make use of this excellent resource.

(2) The International Halfway House Association, an affiliate of the American Correctional Association, has as its purpose to "exchange ideas on developing programs and techniques, to provide training programs and organizational assistance to new agencies, and to provide an ongoing program of public information and education. These goals are achieved through issuance of a newsletter, periodic training programs, an annual conference, and other contacts between member agencies." This organization is in an excellent position to serve as a clearinghouse for ideas and information regarding community treatment programs. It is recommended that correctional agencies take advantage of this resource in planning and operating their program.

(3) An increasing number of private agencies and foundations have become involved in operating community-based treatment programs which serve correctional agencies on a contract basis. Many of these programs are excellent. They offer an alternative to states which are unable to establish their own capabilities in this area for reasons of funding, other priorities, or volume of offenders to be served. It is recommended that states explore the use of privately operated programs and cultivate private agency interest in this area as an alternative or as an adjunct to state-operated programs.

(4) Correctional agencies frequently encounter strong resistance in establishing community residential facilities for offenders. This is especially true of programs for offenders who are still serving sentences. Sometimes this resistance is less when community programs are operated out of local or county jails. However, programs in local jails are not as desirable as those in noncorrectional facilities. Since penal and correctional institutions are frequently located in isolated areas, the use of local jails does allow many offenders to be returned to their home community prior to release. It is recommended that states explore the use of local jail facilities as another alternative in establishing community treatment programs.

(5) An additional and important source of funding for correctional programs, including community treatment programs, is the Law Enforcement Assistance Administration (LEAA). From our survey, it would appear that many states have not made use of LEAA funds for prerelease community treatment programs. The reason for this may be the result of other higher correctional priorities. However, it is recommended (1) that LEAA be considered by states in combination with other sources of funding; (2) that LEAA be more active in encouraging the development of plans for community-based programs; and (3) that state planning agencies, in administering LEAA funds, give high priority to community-based programs. In addition, it is recommended that state correctional agencies and state planning agencies (LEAA) develop closer coordination with regard to long-range planning in the area of community treatment programs.

(6) The American Correctional Association in its *Manual of Correctional Standards* has developed a section on standards for community correctional centers. These standards, currently being revised, and upgraded, would serve as an excellent source of information for the operation of community-based programs. It is recommended that states consult this additional source of information.

36
History of Halfway Houses in the United States

JOHN M. McCARTT AND THOMAS J. MANGOGNA

Halfway houses received their first trial in the United States when New York, Pennsylvania and Massachusetts established such facilities in the early part of the Nineteenth Century.[1]

Although there is evidence of early interest in halfway houses by some governmental bodies (a Massachusetts Commission recommended the establishment of such facilities in 1820),[2] the main thrust for the movement came from religious and private volunteer groups.[3] Both groups were composed of idealistic, hardworking, humane and highly dedicated people who all too frequently lacked the requisite skills to administer an agency or to provide a treatment program.

Their purpose, which they met effectively, was to provide such services as a temporary place of shelter, food, clothing, friendly advice and sometimes, efforts

SOURCE. *Guidelines and Standards for Halfway Houses and Community Treatment Centers*, Law Enforcement Assistance Administration, Washington, D.C., U.S. Government Printing Office, 1973, pp. 1–5

[1] *"Halfway Houses: Community-Centered Corrections and Treatment"*, by Oliver J. Keller and Benedict S. Alper; D.C. Heath & Co., p. 7. Also, *"Crime and Its Corrections"*, by John Conrad, University of California Press, Berkeley, Calif., 1965, p. 275.

[2] Keller and Alper, *op. cit.*, p. 7.

[3] *Ibid.*, p. 7.

to assist the ex-offender in securing gainful employment. The public offender usually did not have the above-named services at his disposal upon release from an institution.[4] In addition, they helped cushion the impact of release from an institution to open society and, although no hard data is available (a chronic problem in corrections), it does not seem unreasonable to assume that they had a beneficial effect on their clients.[5]

The early halfway houses were self-contained and relatively isolated from the correctional staff and facilities providing them with releasees.[6] This is one of several factors which may have led to their eventual failure to survive as a permanent part of the correctional system, if indeed they could have been considered part of the system as it existed at that time. From all available evidence, it is not too much to assume that the early halfway houses were not considered a part of the correctional system and, although this may have been a factor in their failure to flourish, it was (in all probability) a factor which was attractive to the ex-offender who needed assistance.

More than forty years after the Massachusetts Commission made its recommendation, a halfway house for women released from institutions opened in Boston in 1864. It remained in operation for about twenty years.[7]

Amidst public indifference and even hostility, a group of Quakers opened a halfway house in New York City, which has survived to the present as the Isaac T. Hopper House. The House of Industry, established in Philadelphia, Pennsylvania, in 1889, also continues to receive parolees from Pennsylvania prisons.[8]

Despite opposition by the American Prison Association, a temporary shelter for ex-offenders was opened in New York City in the late 1890's. In September of 1896, Maud Booth, along with her husband, co-leader of the Volunteers of America, rented a building in the Washington Heights section of Manhattan. The facility, known as Hope Hall, came under such harrassment from the police that Mrs. Booth was forced to appeal directly to Theodore Roosevelt for help.[9]

A second Hope Hall was established in Chicago, Illinois in 1903, and eventually, under the same auspices, halfway houses were established in New Orleans, Louisiana; Columbus, Ohio; Fort Dodge, Iowa; San Francisco, California; Hampton, Florida; and Waco, Texas.[10]

Several of the Hope Halls remained in existence for only a short period of time, while others managed to survive for many years. Eventually, however, they

[4] *"Administration of Justice in a Changing Society",* A Report of Developments in the United States–1965–70, prepared for the Fourth United Nations Congress on the Prevention of Crime and Treatment of Offenders, p. 69.

[5] "Halfway Houses for Reformatory Releasees", by Robert H. Vasoli and Frank J. Fahey, *Crime and Delinquency,* Vol. 16, No. 3, July, 1970, p. 293.

[6] Vasoli and Fahey, *op. cit.,* p. 294.

[7] Keller and Alper, *op. cit.,* p. 7.

[8] *Ibid.,* p. 7. Also see "Halfway Houses: An Historical Perspective", by Edwin Powers, *American Journal of Corrections,* Vol. XXI, July-August, 1959, p. 35.

[9] Keller and Alper, *op. cit.,* p. 7.

[10] *Ibid.,* p. 7.

all ceased operations. It seems ironic that as more such facilities were established, Parole authorities argued increasingly against them. The basic objection used was that association with former prisoners was forbidden by parole regulations.[11]

Although there were many instances of halfway houses being established in the early and middle 1800's, it was not until the close of the Nineteenth Century that enough facilities had been established to assist any sizeable number of ex-offenders.[12]

The founders of the halfway houses in the 1800's were the true pioneers of community treatment centers, but they often were looked upon with contempt or, at most, tolerance, by most professional correctional workers. They met with public as well as official hostility and/or indifference. Their work, in the main, was with the offender released from a penal institution. They also sowed the seed and laid the groundwork that others, who were to follow decades later, were to reap and build upon.

REVIVAL OF THE HALFWAY HOUSE MOVEMENT IN THE UNITED STATES

It was not until the 1950's that the halfway house movement was revived with the founding of such facilities as St. Leonard's House, Dismas House, and 308 West Residence. Acute awareness of the multitude of problems facing the ex-offender released from a penal institution, as well as a growing dissatisfaction with high recidivism rates, helped to spark the revival of halfway houses in general and also served to commence the beginnings of a national halfway house movement.[13]

There are certain parallels between the halfway houses founded over one hundred years ago and those which came into existence approximately fifteen years ago. Both were started by religiously-oriented or volunteer groups. Both lacked professionally trained personnel and dealt primarily with the ex-offender released from a penal institution. Both lacked "programs" as such, but had as their aim the goal to meet the offender's basic needs for survival and re-entry into the community. Treatment, as such, was not an integral part of either the early halfway houses or those founded little less than two decades ago. Both were meant to be a buffer, a halfway step between the highly structured and regimental setting of the traditional correctional institution, to free and constructive life in the community. Both were relatively isolated from the correctional staff and institution providing them with releasees and both met with resistance from the community as well as from some correctional workers.

One factor present in modern day corrections which was absent over one hundred years ago was a century of dismal failure of the traditional correctional system. This factor, the recognition of it by many in the correctional field, and

---

[11] Keller and Alpert, *Op. cit.,* p. 7.

[12] *Ibid.,* p. 8.

[13] *Ibid.,* p. 8.

the renewed advent of halfway houses as a means of assisting offenders released from institutions, all served to create a favorable climate for the "evolutionary development" of the halfway house concept.[14]

As mentioned in the *Introduction,* it was not until 1964, only eight years ago, that some of those involved in the halfway house movement met and formed what is now the International Halfway House Association. Since that time, a host of agencies, private and public, have established community treatment centers to service a wide variety of target populations.

While most halfway houses have and still are serving the general public offender, some are now specializing in the treatment of specific problem areas, such as alcoholism, and here again, private agencies have pioneered and paved the way "as a result of the indifference of professional and governmental agencies".[15]

[14] For a description of the operation of one of the early prototypes of modern-day halfway houses, see "The Lessons of Norman House", by Merfyn Turner, *"Annals of the American Academy of Political and Social Science"*, January, 1969, p. 39.

[15] "Task Force Report: Drunkenness", *The President's Commission on Law Enforcement and the Administration of Justice,* U. S. Government Printing Office, 1967, p. 19.

37

Overview of Issues Relating to Halfway Houses and Community Treatment Centers

JOHN M. McCARTT AND THOMAS J. MANGOGNA

HALFWAY HOUSES—A HETEROGENEOUS CONCEPT

The term *halfway house* or *community treatment center* does not convey a homogeneous meaning. Halfway houses are as varied and different from each other as "closed" institutions such as jails, prison, training schools and mental hospitals vary among and between themselves.

There is no single definition or description which can possibly be devised at this time which would adequately encompass the wide range of facilities which call themselves or which are called halfway houses or community treatment centers.[1]

Intake criteria, length of stay, treatment goals, target population serviced,

SOURCE. *Guidelines and Standards for Halfway Houses and Community Treatment Centers,* Law Enforcement Assistance Administration, Washington, D.C., U.S. Government Printing Office, 1973, pp. 6–34.

[1] *"Halfway Houses: Community-Centered Corrections and Treatment,"* Oliver J. Keller and Benedict S. Alper; D. C. Heath & Co., pp. 11 and 12.

services offered, quantity and quality of staffing, physical plant, physical location, and numerous other factors are so diverse that a unified, capsulized definition is virtually impossible.[2]

For example, there are in existence today, halfway houses or community treatment centers for the psychiatric patient, the neglected child, the delinquent child (the latter two are variously called halfway houses, group homes and even group foster homes), the adult public offender—both misdemeanant and felon—for the homeless adult with social or adjustment problems, and for individuals with specialized problems such as drug abuse, alcoholism and mental retardation.

The point is that each type of halfway house or community center mentioned above differs, often widely, from others which logically could be grouped in the same type.

One reason halfway houses have developed in this manner was to meet varying needs for different target populations and communities. A second, and more valid reason, is that with no standards or guidelines to follow, halfway houses reflected the personal treatment and other philosophies of their founders or directors.[3] To establish a halfway house ten or even five years ago was a formidable task for anyone, whether the facility was privately or publicly sponsored. Those who assumed the responsibility were usually driving, energetic, creative and individualistic. In an area of practice which was very new to the modern correctional field, and which demanded the kind of qualities listed above, homogeneity could not be expected. Indeed, even at this stage of development, diversity—as wide as it is currently—should be viewed as an asset rather than a liability. Differing ideas, programs, goals, treatment modalities, staffing patterns and techniques need to be implemented; however, there is a desperate need for their evaluation. More will be said of evaluation later.

Suffice it to say now that there has been little of it in the halfway house and community treatment center field, as is true of most other areas of corrections.[4] As diverse as they currently are, halfway houses provide a rich and fertile ground for research in the area of community corrections.[5]

In the short period of time that halfway houses have been a part of the correctional scene, many have evolved rapidly into highly sophisticated programs. The evolution probably has taken place more out of necessity to meet ever-increasing demands for services for varying groups of clientele, and the demonstrated need for those services, as well as a change in our correctional approach.[6]

[2] Keller and Alper, *op. cit.,* pp. 13 and 14.

[3] Keller and Alper, *op. cit.,* p. 123.

[4] "The Continuum of Corrections," H. G. Moeller, *Annals of the American Academy of Political and Social Science,* January, 1971, p. 86.

[5] For a broad discussion on the topic of correctional research, see *Crime and Delinquency,* Vol. 17, No. 1, January, 1971, in which the entire issue is devoted to the problem.

[6] *"Administration of Justice in a Changing Society,"* A Report of Developments in the United States—1965–70, prepared for the Fourth United Nations Congress on the Prevention of Crime and Treatment of Offenders, p. 7. C.f. Moeller, *op. cit.,* p. 82.

The halfway house whose average length of stay is thirty days is undoubtedly serving as a "way station" for its clientele, more than anything else. On the other hand, halfway houses whose average length of stay is a year to eighteen months are probably serving groups with specialized problems, such as drug abuse and alcoholism. The first type of house mentioned probably has little or no "program", as such. The second, more often than not, uses various modifications of "therapeutic community" techniques. Most halfway houses, with the exception of those just noted and those serving juveniles, usually have their clients in residence from eighty to one hundred and twenty days.[7]

Some halfway houses and community treatment centers have as few as six to eight residents, while others may have as many as eighty. "A small population is an essential characteristic of the halfway house idea, and is found almost universally." "Most authorities maintain that a population of approximately twenty is close to ideal, permitting informal and close interaction among the residents."[8]

It should be noted that a maximum capacity of twenty residents appears as Standard No. 7 under "Programs" in Chapter 6 of this report. The two exceptions to this standard are those therapeutic community settings whose clients are in residence from nine to eighteen months, and whose orientation is the alleviation of drug abuse, alcohol or psychiatric problems. Therapeutic communities often serve more than forty clients in residence at a given time.

The second exception is juvenile halfway houses, or group homes, where the maximum population is usually twelve or less. Additional rationale is presented with the standard itself.

Qualifications of staff working in halfway houses run the spectrum, from highly trained personnel to those who are virtually untrained.[9] Professionals with graduate degrees or with undergraduate degrees, and an equivalent number of years of experience for a graduate degree, ex-offenders and volunteers, all operate or staff halfway houses. There does seem to be a greater reliance on professionally trained personnel today as compared to the forerunners of modern-day halfway houses.[10]

As noted in the "Standards" of this report, neither an academic degree nor the fact that a person is an ex-offender, in and of themselves, qualifies an individual to operate or to staff a halfway house. The requisite personality and

[7] See Question No. 6 in Appendix F, Section II of the questionnaire sent to halfway houses throughout the United States. It was considered to be "essential" by the majority of respondents that the length of a client's stay should be determined on a case-by-case basis. Therefore, the figures eighty to one hundred and twenty days are not viewed as a recommendation, only as a report of widespread current practice.

[8] Keller and Alper, *op. cit.*, p. 12. *C.f.* U. S. Bureau of Prisons, *"Trends in the Administration of Justice and Correctional Programs in the United States,"* a Report prepared for the Third United Nations Congress on the Prevention of Crime and Treatment of Offenders, U. S. Government Printing Office, Washington, D. C., 1965, p. 34.

[9] Keller and Alper, *op. cit.*, p. 13.

[10] "Halfway Houses for Reformatory Releasees," by Robert H. Vasoli and Frank J. Fahey, *Crime and Deliquency*, Vol. 16, No. 3, July, 1970, p. 294.

temperament for the type of program operated must be present if the individual is to be effective with the target population of the halfway house.

The above is not meant to sidestep a crucial issue in the current halfway house movement. The questionnaire, which is an appendix to this report, addressed several questions as to what the qualifications of professional treatment staff should be, as well as qualifications of para-professional treatment staff. These issues are treated in Nos. 34 and 35, in section II of the questionnaire, and Nos. 1, 3, 4 and 5 under "Personnel" of the "Standards" in Chapter 6 of this report.

For professional treatment staff, minimum qualifications are four years of college plus two years of experience in the social service field, or a Master's Degree in one of the behavioral sciences. For para-professional treatment, personnel, one and one half years of college is preferred, plus one year of experience. "Para-professional" is defined to include the ex-offender and all other indigenous workers who work along with and beside the professional staff. Experience may be substituted for education, but this must be clearly established in the agency's job qualifications.

In most halfway house settings, with the exception perhaps of the Federal Bureau of Prisons and a very few states, staff are underpaid, and this situation does discourage professionally trained workers from entering the community treatment center field.[11]

Furthermore, working conditions in the halfway house setting are usually not the best. Hours are long, arduous, and—due to the intensity of the work—emotionally and physically draining.[12] There would seem to be no dichotomy between hard work, dedication and good pay, but this is not the way it usually works out in practice. Here too, the "Standards" of this report require (No. 2, under "Personnel") that agencies provide competitive salaries and benefits in order to attract and retain competent personnel.

Another issue involving personnel of halfway house programs was addressed by the questionnaire. "Who should conduct halfway house programs? Professional staff only? Indigenous staff only? A combination of the two?" this issue was formulated in questions 24, 25 and 26 in Section II of the questionnaire. A majority of respondents answering question No. 24, that halfway house programs should be conducted by professional personnel only, stated that this was "desirable". A majority of respondents answering question 25, that halfway house programs should be conducted by indigenous staff only, stated that this was "undesirable". However, when question No. 26—which stated that halfway house programs should be conducted by a combination of professional and indigenous personnel—was presented, a majority of respondents stated that this was "essential".

As a result, Standard No. 6 under "Personnel" states that a balance of professionals and para-professionals is the preferred staffing pattern. Additional rationale is given with the standard.

[11] Keller and Alper, *op. cit.*, p. 122.
[12] *Ibid.*, p. 121.

The use of professionals and para-professionals, including ex-offenders, in the same setting, merits attention here as an issue confronting halfway houses or community treatment centers today.

In its current state of social and economic development, the greatest growth occupations in the United States for the foreseeable future will be the service occupations.[13] Because of a shortage of skilled personnel, as well as the recognition of the contribution which can be made by para-professional persons, their use as sources of manpower is growing rapidly in the field of corrections as well as in mental health.[14]

Professionally trained workers are frequently unclear and uneasy about the role and ability of para-professional workers and, therefore, the agency has the responsibility to carefully define that role *before* para-professionals join the staff. This can be accomplished through a variety of means, two of which are formal and informal staff training sessions, in which the tasks and competencies of the para-professional worker are clearly defined. Fears and negative feelings of professional staff can be dealt with at this time.[15]

Laying aside for the moment the issue of manpower shortage, why use para-professionals, including ex-offenders, in treatment capacities? One of the most essential values in their use lies in their capacity to act as a bridge between the often-times middle-class-oriented professional and the target population served, which is often from lower socio-economic groups. Being from the same socio-economic group, and having experienced many of the same problems as the target population, para-professional workers may well have special skills for establishing a special communication with the clientele which the professional may lack. Why? If the para-professional worker is truly indigenous, it means that he has the same socio-economic background as those being served, is from the same neighborhood, shares a common language, ethnic origin, life style and interests as the target population. These are factors which are almost impossible, if not undesirable, for most professionals to acquire or maintain. Therefore, the fact that indigenous workers can more readily establish communication with the target population is based not on what they have been taught, but what they are.[16]

Aside from the factors just noted, which are formidable arguments in favor of utilizing para-professional workers, there is the problem of a shortage of skilled professionals in the area not only of corrections, but social services generally.[17] The use of para-professionals can tremendously increase manpower resources, and as a result, services, in several ways.

[13] *"Administration of Justice in a Changing Society"*, op. cit., p. 4.

[14] "Task Force Report: Corrections," *The President's Commission on Law Enforcement and the Administration of Justice*, U. S. Government Printing Office, 1967, p. 102; and *"The Indigenous Non-professional: A Strategy of Change in Community Action and Mental Health Programs,"* by Robert Rieff and Frank Riesman, Monograph #1, Behavioral Publications, Inc., Morningside Heights, N. Y., 1965, p. 3.

[15] Rieff and Riesman, *op. cit.*, p. 23.

[16] Rieff and Riesman, *op. cit.*, p. 7.

[17] "Task Force Report: Corrections," *op. cit.*, p. 102. *C.f.* Rieff and Riesman, *op. cit.*, p. 3.

First, tasks which are now performed solely by professionals can be redesigned to create viable functions for para-professionals. This will have the effect of freeing professional staff to perform those tasks which only they can effectively carry out. Thus, functions would be reallocated so that para-professional staff with specific training would perform portions of a total task previously performed by one professional. It also would have the reverse effect, in that para-professionals would perform tasks which they can more effectively carry out than can the professional.

Second, new jobs can be developed to provide sorely needed services which are not now offered because of a lack of manpower. There are services that para-professional workers can perform quite effectively.

Third, those who are now functioning as para-professionals can, through appropriate in-service training and college or university work, be upgraded to professional status.[18]

The indigenous worker can more readily identify with the client and thereby bring a totally different perspective to the agency, which can be of invaluable assistance in the rehabilitation process.

As mentioned earlier, however, neither an academic degree nor indigenous or ex-offender status, in and of themselves, qualifies a person to assume a helping role. While personality and temperament are very important, the factor of training is a must.

Orientation and in-service training are considered elsewhere in this report. However, for the purpose of overview, it would be wise to review some general considerations in the training of indigenous workers.

First, continuous on-the-job training should commence as soon as the worker joins the staff. As considerable anxiety could develop with a long period of preparatory training, the para-professional worker should be given tasks as quickly as possible. Initially, assignments should be simple and within the range of the para-professional worker's current skills; as training continues more progressively, complex tasks can be assigned.

Second, rather than take a lecture approach, an activity approach would seem to be more appropriate for para-professional workers, with a heavy emphasis on role-playing.

Third, informal, individual supervision—at any time—either at the request of the worker or the supervisor, should be an essential element. This type of supervision should be supplemented by group discussion and supervision.

Fourth, it should be recognized that concepts and theories which are presented properly are within the grasp of the para-professional worker. Clarity and detail should be emphasized with a teaching style that accents the concrete.

In a small agency, it may be that one person will have the responsibility of training the para-professional worker. In a large agency, perhaps a highly organized, separate component will have responsibility for this task. In either instance,

---

[18] "Task Force Report: Corrections," *op. cit.*, pp. 102 and 103.

good in-service training is essential if the para-professional worker is to be effective and fulfill a meaningful function within the agency.[19]

Other than the fact that they are para-professionals and have the proper personality and temperament, workers must have the capacity and a deep desire to learn and develop as well as a desire to help others.[20]

Practically speaking, suitable candidates for the para-professional positions may be recruited from probation and parole agencies, the population served by the recruiting agency itself, other social service agencies in the community, neighborhood community groups, penal institutions, departments of welfare, and a host of other agencies, public and private, with direct contact with people, who may be able to suggest numerous names of former or present clients who could adequately fulfill the para-professional worker role.[21] Several articles have been written on the use of offenders in various types of correctional settings, both public and private. One such article, which covers a range of roles carried out by the ex-offender, is listed below.[22]

THE HALFWAY HOUSE IN THE CRIMINAL JUSTICE SYSTEM— WHERE DOES IT BELONG?

It was noted earlier in this report that the early halfway houses were relatively isolated from the correctional staff and facilities providing them with releasees. They were not considered a part of the correctional or criminal justice system.[23] Some halfway houses in existence today are still somewhat isolated from the "system" and indeed, prefer to remain so. Some community-based services, such as the Youth Services Bureau concept, as formulated by the National Council on Crime and Delinquency, insist on remaining not only independent of, but apart from, the juvenile justice system.[24]

Vasoli and Fahey note that in comparison to its forebears, the halfway house of today is more frequently closely coordinated with and even a part of the correctional system.[25] It is common knowledge that the criminal justice system as it exists today, and even components within that system, such as corrections, are too fragmented, and thus lose much of their effectiveness. Increasingly, reference is made not to the "system" but to the "non-system". It also has been recognized that there have been histories of barriers between institutional and

[19] Rieff and Riesman, *op. cit.*, pp. 20, 21 and 23. *C.f.* "Task Force Report: Corrections," *op. cit.*, pp. 102 and 103.

[20] *Ibid.*, p. 27.

[21] *Ibid.*, p. 26.

[22] "The Involvement of Offenders in the Prevention and Correction of Criminal Behavior," Albert Morris, *Correctional Research*, Bulletin No. 20, October, 1970.

[23] Vasoli and Fahey, *op. cit.*, p. 293.

[24] Sherwood, Norman, "The Youth Services Bureau: A Key to Delinquency Prevention," *National Council on Crime & Delinquency*, Paramus, New Jersey, 1972, pp. 8, 16 and 17.

[25] Vasoli and Fahey, *op. cit.*, p. 294.

community programs themselves, such as probation and parole, which are frequently administered by different agencies.[26]

As the Task Force on Corrections notes, "It is clear that new community programs must be integrated into the main line of corrections, if they are to succeed and survive."[27] This would seem to support the contention made earlier in this report that the self-containment and isolation of the early halfway houses was one of several factors leading to their failure to survive.

By grants and contracts awarded to both public and private agencies, governmental funding bodies have fostered the phenomenal growth of halfway houses. As a practical stipulation of most grants and contracts, cooperation with other agencies, especially correctional agencies, is required. Such cooperation is an absolute necessity if halfway house programs are to have any measure of success, much less survive. More will be said of cooperative relationships later, but it is noted here to emphasize the fact that halfway houses, no matter who operates them, must have solid ties with other segments of the criminal justice system, and corrections in particular.

Keller and Alper consider halfway houses organizationally related to corrections.[28] Controversy about where halfway houses "belong" in the organizational structure of the system have arisen among and between public agencies as they have become involved in their establishment and operation.[29] The most reasonable viewpoint offered on this controversy seems to be that, "Despite differing views, it probably matters little whether the management of a center falls under the sponsorship of a public or private agency, or in fact, becomes part of the responsibilities of a probation, parole or correctional institution administrator. Of far greater importance are the quality of the programs offered, the competence and integrity of the center's staff and the working relationships between the center and the correctional agencies that use the resources."[30]

The issue, therefore, does not seem to be which agency, public or private, should operate halfway houses, but:

1. Are halfway houses, public or private, a part of the correctional system?

2. If they are a part of the correctional system, what is their function in relationship to that system?

For public agencies, we can be safe in answering the first question in the affirmative. For private agencies, the majority seem to view themselves as part of the correctional system, but this view is by no means unanimous. As a practical matter, those private agencies who wish to remain isolated from the system will find it increasingly difficult, not only to survive as an increasing amount of public funds go to support privately operated programs, but also will find that the

---

[26] "Task Force Report: Corrections," *op. cit.*, p. 6. *C.f.* Moeller, *op. cit.*, p. 87.

[27] "Task Force Report: Corrections," *op. cit.*, p. 44.

[28] Keller and Alper, *op. cit.*, p. 15.

[29] Moeller, *op. cit.*, p. 87.

[30] "The Residential Center: Corrections in the Community," United States Bureau of Prisons, Department of Justice, Washington, D. C.

services they could offer to the offender will be severely restricted because of their isolation. As the early halfway houses did, they will undoubtedly continue to service only those released from institutions. In isolation, they will be unable to participate in the "more positive and dynamic role for community treatment centers" that is "a hopeful substitute for the large prison".[31] Furthermore, they will be unable to assist the offender by offering many services now being delivered by halfway houses over and above the traditional "transitional facility" concept.

If halfway houses, public or private, are truly to be a part of the criminal justice system and serve their clientele most effectively, then strong relationships must be developed with the other components of the system—both at the administrative and line staff levels. This means the whole spectrum of the justice system: chiefs of police and police officers, prosecutors, defense attorneys (especially public defenders), jails, judges, probation and parole authorities (both adult and juvenile), workhouses, houses of detention, prisons and reformatories, training schools and other community treatment center programs in the same geographical area. Here we have spoken only of the relationships which must be developed within the system. Many other community relationships need to be developed also.[32]

At this point, a question should be asked: "Why corrections in the community?" Our communities are conditioned to the "correctional process" taking place elsewhere. Corrections is too frequently equated with prisons. Unfortunately, notions of punishment still underlie much of the community's attitude toward corrections,[33] and the symbol of punishment is prison.

Although most offenders currently incarcerated in our prisons are from large metropolitan areas, the prisons themselves are usually located away from urban areas. The original reasons for establishing these institutions in remote locations were diverse. To a large extent, those reasons are now outdated, i.e., the communities' interest in banishing the offender to a remote locale, the desire of rural legislators to provide public employment for their constituents and the belief that a rural setting was beneficial and salutary for individuals reared in cities, are just a few.[34]

Two factors, of which many unfamiliar with the field of corrections are unaware, however, are that only about one-third of all offenders are in institutions, while two-thirds are already under supervision in the community,[35] and that approximately 95% of all offenders committed to penal institutions are eventually released and returned to the community. Even though two-thirds are in the community under supervision, the treatment afforded them is more illusion than reality.[36]

---

[31] "Administration of Justice in a Changing Society," *op. cit.*, p. 69.
[32] "The Residential Center: Corrections in the Community," *op. cit.*, p. 11.
[33] "Task Force Report: Corrections," *op. cit.*, p. 2.
[34] *Ibid.*, p. 4.
[35] *Ibid.*, p. 1.
[36] *Ibid.*, p. 4.

Crime and delinquency are symptoms of failure and disfunctioning of the community as well as of the individual offender.[37] The community has its share of responsibility to bear for the conditions conducive to crime and as a result must share in the "responsibility to deal with the results of these conditions".[38] With the recognition that traditional penal institutions have not adequately performed their rehabilitative functions, community programs such as halfway houses are being developed in order to reduce the flow of individuals into those institutions.[39] While institutional populations have been showing a decrease in many areas of the country, community-based treatment programs are showing a considerable increase.

The best opportunity for successful integration or reintegration of the offender seems to lie in the community itself.[40]

The field of mental health has paved the way for corrections by establishing community-based programs whose aims are to ease the patient's transition back into the community and to prevent their removal from it in the first place, if possible.[41] Adequately trained personnel and other resources which only the community can offer with any degree of quality or quantity are essential for the rehabilitative process. Physicians, dentists, psychiatrists, psychologists, social workers, para-professionals, including indigenous personnel, teachers, vocational counselors, and other personnel, are not to be found in sufficient numbers in places other than metropolitan areas. Resources such as schools, diverse vocational training courses and employment opportunities, mental health centers, recreational opportunities and not least of all, family and friends, are also located in metropolitan areas.

It was noted earlier that we have spoken only of relationships which the halfway house must develop with other components of the criminal justice system, but that many other community resources and relationships must also be developed. To provide a successful and viable program for its clients as well as to achieve its purpose as a community-based program, a halfway house must develop strong relationship with a host of non-correctional or criminal justice agencies, public and private, as well as various citizen and neighborhood groups.

Vocational rehabilitation agencies, including vocational training centers, public and private, medical and mental health facilities, schools, including colleges and universities as well as centers for adult and juvenile basic education, agencies providing family counseling and recreational facilities, chambers of commerce, labor unions, the news media (radio, television, press), employers, civic and fraternal groups such as the Lions, Rotary Clubs, U. S. Jaycees, citizen groups interested in the criminal justice field such as the Alliance for Shaping a Safer

[37] "Task Force Report: Corrections," *op. cit.*, p. 7.
[38] Keller and Alper, *op. cit.*, p. 108.
[39] *Ibid.*, p. 110.
[40] "The Residential Center: Corrections in the Community," *op. cit.*, p. 1.
[41] Keller and Alper, *op. cit.*, p. 5.

Community, and various neighborhood improvement and association groups, are just a few samples of the type of community agencies, groups and resources with which halfway houses must develop strong relationships.

A key function of corrections today is to help the offenders avail themselves of the variety of services they need in order to take advantage of the opportunity structure which they have previously lacked, or to open doors to services which have been denied them in the past.[42]

Therefore, those who work in corrections must develop the knowledge and skill it requires to see that those services are made available to the offender.[43] The answer to the question: "Why corrections in the community?" should now be obvious. The next issue we need to address is the function and place of halfway houses or community treatment centers in relation to the correctional system.

THE FUNCTION AND PLACE OF THE HALFWAY HOUSE IN THE CORRECTIONAL SYSTEM

Traditionally, the early halfway houses, including those founded fifteen to twenty years ago, served the parolee or mandatory releasee from penal institutions almost exclusively. Some halfway houses or community treatment centers, however, have developed rather sophisticated programs, and have broadened not only the scope of services they offer, but also the target populations being serviced. Corrections is moving away increasingly from traditional methods of confinement, and community-based programs are being utilized in numerous ways as the appropriate alternatives. Halfway houses or community treatment centers are being developed rapidly and as the range of alternatives for courts and correctional officials broadens for the treatment of the public offender, such alternatives will be increasingly utilized in preference to traditional methods.[44]

As corrections becomes increasingly more community-based, the range of possible alternatives available to our courts and correctional officials will offer a flexibility for the treatment of the offender hitherto unknown to corrections, and will allow for the flow of offenders from one alternative to another, as need dictates.[45]

While the place of halfway houses or community treatment centers has not been decided from an organizational standpoint for either public or private agencies,[46] the present and possible future functions of such facilities have become increasingly clear. As indicated above, many halfway houses are serving a much wider target population and are being utilized for many other purposes than just the parolee or mandatory releasee. Starting with the traditional populations

[42] Moeller, *op. cit.*, p. 84.

[43] For a discussion of the availability of community resources in conjunction with correctional agencies, see Mandall, Wallace, "Making Corrections a Community Agency," *Crime & Delinquency,* Vol. 17, July, 1971.

[44] "Administration of Justice in a Changing Society," *op. cit.*, p. 7.

[45] "Task Force Report: Corrections," *op. cit.*, p. 11.

[46] Moeller, *op. cit.*, p. 82.

served by halfway houses, we will list the current uses of community-based residential treatment facilites.

Mandatory Releasee and Parolee

The mandatory releasee or parolee who is in need of a transitional center, and the range of services it offers (see Standards Nos. 10, 11, and 12 under "Program") has always been and still is being served by the community treatment center. The rationale for servicing this population has been to ease their transition back into free society and to buffer the many negative effects of their period of incarceration and isolation from the community.

Until the recent past, parolees were usually received directly upon release from the institution. One innovation, however, recently formalized by Federal law for Federal parolees, is the use of halfway houses for the parolee who is already "on the street", but who is having difficulty in his adjustment and perhaps stands the risk of revocation. Instead of waiting for failure, and sending such an offender back to the institution, the alternative to send him to community treatment centers for more intensive treatment and supervision, while keeping him in the community, is now available. While we are unaware of any state or local jurisdictions which have such formal provisions written into statute or ordinance, parole officers at those levels are using community treatment centers informally for this purpose already. Here is one added alternative to the traditional options of parole or reinstitutionalization.

The Probationer

Many halfway houses are increasingly accepting persons placed on probation. Probationers are referred to a halfway house under two sets of general circumstances: First, the court may consider the individual too much of a risk to simply place them on probation to be supervised by an already over-worked probation officer, who will be unable to give the needed time and attention to the prospective probationer. At the same time, the court may recognize that the individual in question does not need incarceration in the traditional institutional setting. Therefore, the court may choose to stipulate that, as a condition of probation, the individual agree to participate in a halfway house or community treatment center program. This stipulation takes place prior to the time the person is placed on probation. The alternative just described has been practiced informally by courts and probation officers at all jurisdictional levels throughout various parts of the United States for the past few years. Its use has been dependent largely upon the intake policies of a given halfway house and whether they have been willing to accept such potential probationers.

Second, an individual may have been placed on probation already, but like the parolee described earlier, may be experiencing adjustment problems in the community, and running the risk of revocation. Rather than revoke an individual in such a situation, the court or probation officer may refer them to a halfway house. Again, intensity of treatment and supervision is much greater, but the benefits of remaining in the community are maintained. The Federal government has also passed legislation formalizing the procedure for utilizing halfway houses for probationers in the situation just described. This alternative is also being utilized informally by many state and local courts and probation officers.

The Pre-releasee

For several years, Federal law, and more recently, the laws of several states, have allowed for the release of prisoners to halfway houses or community treatment centers prior to their actual mandatory release or release on parole. The period of time for which an individual is released under this provision ranges from thirty to one hundred and twenty days, although some jurisdictions allow for pre-release status for up to six months. While the pre-release of such individuals is considered an administrative transfer from one "institution" to another "institution", the pre-releasee receives the benefit of community-based treatment and supervision *prior* in time to the mandatory release or parole. Therefore, when the pre-releasee reaches mandatory release or parole status, he has had the opportunity of working through many of the problems of adjustment, and utilizing the necessary community resources, such as vocational training, employment placement, psychiatric and medical resources, housing, re-establishing family and other community ties, with which the parolee or mandatory releasee newly released to a halfway house is just beginning to cope. Many halfway houses, public and private, are accepting pre-releasees from Federal and state referral sources.

Study and Diagnostic Services to Offenders

Depending on their level of sophistication, many halfway houses are now capable of offering study and diagnostic services to courts. Such services are rendered prior to final disposition in court. It was mentioned earlier that the court may consider an individual too great of a risk to place on probation and yet recognizes that the individual does not need incarceration and, therefore, stipulates that they enter a halfway house program as a condition of probation. The court may be able to arrive at this conclusion based on information provided by the pre-sentence report.

Study and diagnostic services, however, is a more formalized method of assisting the court to arrive at a final disposition, especially when the pre-sentence investigation cannot provide enough information about special problematic areas facing the offender. In such instances, the court of jurisdiction may place the offender in a halfway house or community treatment center for "study and observation" for a sixty-to-ninety-day period. During this time, a complete battery of psychiatric or psychological tests are administered, as well as psychiatric or psychological interviews with an accompanying assessment; a complete social history is also developed along with an assessment of the offender's prior record, if any; vocational and/or employment history, assessment and potential, and a record of the individual's progress and behavior while at the halfway house. A prognosis and recommendation is submitted to the court for its consideration for final disposition. Upon completion of study and diagnostic services, the individual may be placed on probation and/or possibly required to remain in the community treatment center, either as a condition of probation with the provisions of the "split sentence"* procedure, or sent to a more traditional correctional institution.

While study and diagnostic services have been utilized with community treatment centers primarily by the Federal justice system, there is much promise that such services will be rendered to offenders at the state and local levels if "correctional center complexes" as described in the *Task Force Report on Corrections* are constructed in metropolitan areas.[47]

The Juvenile—Neglected and Delinquent

Halfway houses, or group homes, as they are often called, are being utilized increasingly for the child who is neglected or delinquent. The establishment of such group homes has been increasing at an extremely rapid pace. Many times in the past, the neglected child was placed in detention facilities or training schools along with delinquent children, simply because there were no other resources to draw upon. Without any violation of the Juvenile Code, a child could, in effect, be incarcerated. Not enough foster parents are available to care for these children, and as a result, group homes have been established to meet this pressing need.

Group homes for the delinquent child are serving several purposes. First, they give the court of jurisdiction an alternative to incarceration if the child does not respond to the supervision of his probation officer or social worker. This prevents the child from being sent to training schools, which often are ill equipped to meet the child's needs. A child may be in residence in such a home for well over a year. The child's inability to care for himself, secure gainful employment, and be exclusively responsible for his own welfare, often makes a longer length of stay in a group home necessary.

Second, the group home may be used as a short-term facility for the delinquent child while community resources are brought to bear on the root of his problems, such as family difficulties which may be resolved by intensive counseling in a relatively short period of time.

Third, the group home is also used as a "halfway out" facility for children who have been incarcerated and do not have an adequate home plan.

The group home may be used flexibly as one of many alternatives for the delinquent child. Community correctional centers seem to be approaching reality more quickly for the juvenile delinquent than for the adult offender. Relatively small institutions with greater security but also intensive treatment for the hyper-aggressive child are being established in metropolitan areas, in lieu of "training

---

* That sentence in which the offender is initially committed for a brief period prior to supervision on probation.

[47] "Task Force Report: Corrections," *op. cit.,* p. 11.

schools" located in rural areas. In addition to regular probation supervision, intensive treatment units are being established for children still living in their own homes. Intensive treatment units may have a ratio of one social worker or counselor for every six to ten children. The establishment of group homes in conjunction with the other alternatives listed above will give courts of jurisdiction tremendous flexibility to move the child from one component of the "system" to another as need or progress dictates. It should be noted that all of the alternatives listed above would be based in the community.

Use of Halfway Houses for Individuals with Special Difficulties, such as Drug Abuse, Alcoholism and Psychiatric Problems

Halfway houses or community treatment centers are being utilized for target populations with special difficulties such as drug abuse, alcoholism or psychiatric problems. Due to the nature of the problems being treated, the length of stay in such centers is usually much longer than in those servicing the general offender population, often for as long as eighteen months. Many, perhaps most such centers, utilize one form or another of the therapeutic community technique. Especially in the case of drug abuse and alcoholism, such centers are frequently staffed by individuals who have experienced and successfully worked through the problem. In many such centers, professionally trained personnel who have not experienced the problem being treated, were often excluded from the staffing pattern as a matter of treatment philosophy. However, there is evidence that professionally trained staff are now being accepted more readily as a part of the treatment team. Because of the nature of the difficulties experienced by drug abusers and alcoholics, many of them have passed through our criminal justice system. This has occurred usually as a direct result of their problems.

Use of Halfway Houses for Individuals Released on Bail Prior to Final Disposition

We have been speaking of some of the traditional and more recent uses and functions of the halfway house in relation to the correctional system. What are some other innovative uses which may be made of halfway houses? What other functions may it serve in the correctional system?

Bail reform has been spreading rapidly in the United States. Federal and many state and local jurisdictions have enacted bail reform measures. Although innocent until proven guilty, it is known that most individuals accused of crimes are from lower socio-economic groups,[48] and cannot afford ten per cent of the bail set by the court, which is usually required by professional bondsmen. As a result, the poor remain in jail to await final disposition while those more affluent are able to obtain their release.

To remedy the inequity of this situation, "Recognizance Bond" legislation has

⁴⁸ "Task Force Report: Corrections," *op. cit.,* p. 2.

been and still is being enacted in various parts of the nation. If the individual meets certain criteria, he may be released upon his own signature, promising to reappear in court on the appropriate date. This provision does away with the need for the accused to produce a certain amount of cash or property for his bail.

One of the usual standard requirements is that the individual have roots in the community in which he stands accused, i.e., family, friends, job, etc. Many accused individuals, however, have poor family ties, and poor work histories, which are often the result of educational and cultural deprivation. Not meeting some of the basic criteria, they are excluded from the use of recognizance bond and must await final disposition in jail. The bad effects of this situation have been expounded by governmental commissions, hearings by committees of Congress, and state legislatures, and several publications in professional journals and books.

The halfway house should consider the possibility (and some already have) of providing services to an individual enabling him to become eligible for recognizance bond. At a minimum, this would include providing shelter and supervision prior to final disposition. However, whether the accused is found guilty or not, they are usually in need of a range of services which the halfway house is often in a position to provide, directly or indirectly. Medical, dental, psychological and psychiatric services, individual and group counseling services, vocational evaluation and counseling services, as well as employment placement services, can all be provided to the accused who has not been found guilty, but who is in need of such services. The delays which occur between the time of arrest and final disposition are often lengthy, ranging from six months to a year or more. Even if the process is speeded up, and the time from arrest to final disposition is reduced to two or three months, there is still much that can be accomplished during this period of time.

The next point is obvious: as most halfway houses deliver their range of services between an eighty to one hundred and twenty day period, a question should be asked: Why not intervene on the client's behalf long before final disposition, and why not deliver needed services prior to the final disposition?

If the accused are found not guilty, they are in a much better position after the delivery of these services to pursue a more meaningful and constructive life. In one sense, this approach might be considered crime prevention in the true sense of the word. If the accused is found guilty, a range of services has been delivered already which may well affect the outcome of final disposition, e.g., probation rather than incarceration. In this instance, the halfway house would be in a position to offer valuable information to the court even before a pre-sentence investigation commences. The progress (or lack of it) of the individual found guilty could be reviewed with the court of jurisdiction as well as the investigating probation officer.

Additional or continued treatment plans could be formulated prior to the time of sentencing and if the person is to be placed on probation, made a part of the probation treatment plan. Even if the person is to be incarcerated, the services rendered, progress made, and information obtained need not be wasted, but could be shared with institutional treatment staff to help them formulate a plan for treatment with the client while he is incarcerated. Even if incarcerated, the fact that the individual was willing to avail himself of needed services while on recognizance bond could have a positive effect on how quickly he is released back into the community.

Few halfway houses have experimented in this area, but it seems to be a fertile ground for new uses of the halfway house.

Use of the Halfway House for Diversion from the Criminal Justice System

Halfway houses or community treatment centers can be utilized in the future to divert individuals from the criminal justice system. The question of diversion has been discussed in criminal justice circles for some time. Some that were formerly arrested and convicted repeatedly for an offense such as public intoxication are now being diverted from the criminal justice system in some jurisdictions.

When it is realized that in 1965, one-third of all the arrests in the United States were for the offense of public drunkenness, the magnitude of the problem of processing these individuals through the criminal justice system can be appreciated. The burden on police departments, courts, prosecutors, probation and parole officers and jails, as well as other penal institutions, is tremendous.[49]

The criminal justice system seems to be ineffective to alter the behavior of the chronic alcoholic and to meet his underlying medical and social problems. The "system" only served to remove the publicly intoxicated individual from public view.[50] *The Task Force Report on Drunkenness* states that, "The commission seriously doubts that drunkenness alone (as distinguished from disorderly conduct) should continue to be treated as a crime."[51]

A general trend seems to be developing in the United States to restrict the scope of the criminal sanction by removing those statutes which tend to regulate the private moral conduct of individuals. Channeling through the criminal justice system those who have committed "victimless crimes" gravely dissipates the resources as the command of that system.

Time, energy, manpower, financial and other resources are diverted from coping with the type of offenses that threaten a community most, and affect the quality of life of its citizens, i.e., various forms of violence and theft.[52]

If alternative mechanisms are established to deal with victimless crimes, not only is the individual diverted from the criminal justice system, and relieved of the burden of the lasting stigma which is the result of the formal adjudication process, but a greater opportunity exists for obtaining the desired results of rehabilitation.[53]

[49] "Task Force Report: Drunkenness," *op. cit.,* p. 1.

[50] *Ibid.,* p. 3.

[51] *Ibid.,* p. 4.

[52] "Administration of Justice in a Changing Society," *op. cit.,* p. 10.

[53] *Ibid.,* p. 11.

The Board of Trustees of the National Council on Crime and Delinquency has issued a policy statement in support of abolition of victimless crimes statutes.[54] There are also a substantial number of individuals at both the juvenile and adult offender levels, who could be diverted from the justice system, well before the point of sentencing, to alternative treatment programs.[55] As far as juveniles are concerned, this is certainly the thrust of the Youth Service Bureau as espoused by the National Council on Crime and Delinquency.

Legislation has been enacted already by the Federal government permitting drug abusers, for instance, to commit themselves voluntarily for treatment. Federal legislation also allows drug abusers who have been apprehended to be committed for treatment with the consent of the United States Attorney. If the individual successfully completes treatment, criminal charges against him are dropped.

In some areas of the United States, it is the policy of local police departments to take those who are publicly intoxicated to detoxification centers for treatment, rather than charging them with such petty offenses as disorderly conduct and vagrancy. If the person arrested consents to treatment, charges are not brought against him.

Halfway houses as well as public health facilities can be utilized to divert and treat a substantial number of people such as alcoholics, drug abusers, and petty offenders who are currently being channeled through our criminal justice system. Obviously, not all such persons will want treatment, and in those instances, the mechanisms have been created to protect the individual and the community. With the proper legislation, halfway houses can be the focal point of a whole new direction for the diversion of individuals from the criminal justice system.

To return to an issue raised earlier would now be appropriate: if halfway houses serving the offender (primarily the privately-operated halfway houses) do not consider themselves a part of the correctional system, and if they do not establish cooperative relationships with correctional and other agencies but prefer to remain relatively isolated, they will be limiting the scope of their services and seriously restricting their participation in future innovative programs. We see this as being true for two reasons:

1. Correctional authorities will be increasingly hesitant to refer individuals to a house or center which does not have some type of cooperative relationship with them, especially as the numbers of such centers grow and the authorities have alternative houses or centers to which they may turn.

2. Without such cooperative relationships, which in themselves make a house or center a part of the correctional system, in fact if not by law, public funds will be increasingly difficult to obtain, whether by grant or contract with public agencies. Relying solely on private sources of income, the vast majority of private halfway houses would have extreme difficulty not only in offering a wide range

---

[54] "Crimes without Victims—A Policy Statement," Board of Trustees, National Council on Crime and Delinquency, *Crime and Delinquency,* Vol. 17, No. 2, April, 1971.

[55] "Task Force Report: Corrections," *op. cit.,* p. 22.

of quality services to meet the varying needs of its clientele but also in simply surviving. Those who would suffer most, of course, would be the clientele halfway houses are serving, and the community of which both the client and the halfway house are a part.

EVALUATION AND RESEARCH

The halfway house has the advantage of helping the client cope with stressful situations under real life circumstances as opposed to the isolated and insulated atmosphere of closed institutions. If the client has difficulties with drug abuse, alcohol, acting out, or any other problem, the staff can immediately respond to problem situations as they develop on a day-to-day basis. Even other forms of community based treatment such as probation and parole, do not have the distinct advantage of close supervision and intensive treatment which is a part of the halfway house structure. If a client does not get up for work in the morning, the halfway house staff knows it immediately. The probation and parole officer may find this out after the client has lost his job. If the client is abusing drugs or alcohol, the halfway house staff will know and be able to deal with these situations almost immediately. The probation and parole officer may find this out after the client has been arrested.

If the client is reverting to criminal behavior, the halfway house staff is in the same position of knowing and acting with great speed. No matter what the situation, there does not seem to be any other form of supervision and treatment currently in existence which is as responsive to the clients' needs.

However, the evaluation and research of the halfway house program is a must and was considered essential by a majority of the respondents replying to the questionnaire. As a result, evaluation and research appears in Standards, Nos. 21, 22 and 23, under "Programs". Some halfway houses are involved in gathering quantitative data on the clientele they serve. Such data is usually necessary for annual reports to the governing body or unit of government sponsoring the programs, as well as to other agencies funding the program. There are any number of variables which may be measured quantitatively. However, halfway houses must also commence qualitative research on the effectiveness of their programs. This is necessary both because those in the field of corrections and governmental funding agencies are increasingly inquiring into the quality of such programs, and also because halfway house administrators cannot afford to base programmatic judgments on "cumulative experience" or "intuition". Virtually the whole field of criminal justice has always been in this position. Halfway houses must avoid this vicious circle of perpetuating something which may well be ineffective or not changing a program which is not as effective as it could be.

One word of caution is in order. Virtually all of the criminal justice system has been qualitatively unevaluated, as noted above. In their present forms, halfway houses are relatively new. Sufficient resources and time must be allowed these programs to be evaluated adequately from a qualitative standpoint. By the same token, program administrators must have the objectivity to change and modify programs, once valid qualitative results are available. Because the field of correctional research has been so generally ignored, tools of valid measurement have still to be developed. Halfway houses, along with all other components of the correctional field, must be involved in the process of developing valid measurements. However, halfway houses should not now be held accountable for the current unavailability of valid measurements when the field of corrections as a whole has failed to develop them over a period of decades. A sample of quantitative data collection appears in Appendix I.

It is strongly recommended that, as a program is planned, and implemented, a research design created by competent personnel also be planned and implemented. Funding sources and governmental agencies have a special responsibility to make the resources for such research available.

38

So You Want to Open a Halfway House

RICHARD L. RACHIN

The halfway house is intended to meet a need for client services between highly supervised, well structured, institutional programs and relatively free community living. In its popular function the halfway house has been a kind of decompression chamber through which institutional releases are helped to avoid the social-psychological bends of a too rapid reinvolvement in the "real world." Although increasing numbers of halfway houses include treatment components, many are still limited to providing bed and board, assistance in finding employment, and help in locating more permanent shelter.

The need for short-circuiting unnecessary institutional commitment has led to the development of the "halfway-in" house. Utilized primarily at this time for youth, treatment considerations and responsibility-oriented, reality-bound, programming have been the hallmarks of these facilities. In addition to its traditional function, then, the halfway house can provide a means for diverting people from the institutional mill which, as so many have pointed out, has more often harmed than helped. As we are coming to learn, the need for removing anyone from community living should be confined to persons of legitimate danger to themselves—and how often this has been abused—or others. There are no other sensible reasons for doing this. The halfway-in utilization of the program for delinquents has catalyzed a movement away from the stark, antiseptic, emotion-

SOURCE. *Federal Probation*, XXXVI, March 1972, pp. 30–37. Reprinted with permission of the author and *Federal Probation*.

ally uninvolved, and spiritually suffused programs which traditionally operate under the halfway house rubric. The small therapeutic community has replaced the way station, much to the advantage of people involved. This article discusses the utilization of the halfway house for delinquent youths. The principles, however, are generally applicable to other groups whose need for this type of program are no less apparent.

THE HALFWAY HOUSE: WHAT, WHO, HOW

At one end of the residential correctional spectrum the training school best meets the requirements of relatively large and seriously problem-ridden populations. The institution is designed ideally to be self-contained and largely self-sufficient in its day-to-day operations. Highly structured programming and security considerations are most appropriately met in this setting. The group foster home, at the other extreme, best accomodates children whose remaining in the community is jeopardized primarily by their own poor home situations. Provided with parent surrogates in warm, supportive, home-like settings, children with these needs require little or no planned treatment services.

The halfway house is a versatile program providing meaningful placement alternatives for youths with needs between these extremes. Its utilization can safely hasten release from institutions. It offers practical and realistic opportunities for testing out one's ability to deal responsibly and in a socially acceptable manner with the stresses of the "real world." It improves significantly upon traditional institutional assessments of readiness for parole or unsupervised discharge which frequently bear little relationship to the realities of conventional community living. Youths failing on probation or with needs beyond that of foster or group homes can be placed in a halfway house and helped while still remaining in their own communities. The halfway house can also assist parolees whose behavior indicates the need for closer or more intensive treatment services that they can receive under ordinary parole supervision. In some cases, revocations or recommitments can be made more suitably to a halfway house than to the institution from which a youth was paroled. In effect its utilization is appropriate for a variety of needs within a broad middle-range of the correctional spectrum.

Youths, and not referral sources, should be considered in selecting program residents. It should make no difference whether one is "halfway-in" or "halfway-out" of an institution. Although offense data alone are a poor index of suitability for this type program, heavy emphasis is still placed here both by the public and correctional administrators. The same undue stress seems to have been laid on clinical impressions of personality difficulties. For some, diagnostic impressions have too frequently become self-fulfilling prophecies. With many youths, it has become interesting to speculate which came first, the disorder or the diagnostic impression. More dependable are selection procedures which minimize the past and focus on strengths, motivation, capacity for change, and more productive living.

Halfway house candidates should be mature enough and have the capacity for participation in confrontative, probing, and anxiety-provoking examination of their day-to-day behavior. Equally important, they must express some interest in doing this. It is unimportant how sincere a youth may be in professing his concern about examining the utility of his behavior. Candidates, however, must convey some uneasiness about their lives and indicate at least a willingness to consider the possibility of doing things differently. They should be able to acknowledge an ability to cope responsibly with daily, unsupervised, community living. It should not matter whether they were successful in doing this previously.

The importance of the peer group in influencing and directing behavior should not be neglected. For a treatment-oriented halfway house to operate effectively, residents must be able to concede that others with whom they live can understand their problems and empathize with their feelings, even though they might not agree with their explanations about them.

Much can be gained by house membership which is representative of the "real world" in which residents are usually involved. People must learn to deal with life as they knew it and to which, realistically, they must be expected to return. Homogeneous groupings which therapeutically detour offenders from such "real life" exposures are, at best, apprenticeships from which most offenders must be expected to graduate. Variables such as socioeconomic class, race, clinical impressions of emotional disturbance, offense, and intellectual (nonmentally defective) capacity offer no serious obstacles to effective group participation, interaction, and the development of cohesive group cultures.

Age, however, cannot be discounted in designing group programs for adolescents. A variance of more than 2 or 3 years should be avoided in selecting youths for a halfway house. Program expectations, the kinds of responsibilities placed on residents, and peer pressure toward exacting norm-adhering behavior, require a degree of maturity and impulse control which youths less than 16 years of age do not usually possess. Emotional maturity is a more important consideration, however, than chronological age.

Youths whose behavior appears, both to themselves and others, to be beyond their ability to control, or who genuinely seem unconcerned about responsible decision-making *at the time when interviewed for the halfway house,* should not be admitted. By the same token, the unreliability and questionable validity of diagnoses and conventional personality measures warrant consideration of applicants otherwise ordinarily screened on the basis of their past records alone. While a youth who evinces a *current* inability to control his behavior might make a poor program candidate, nevertheless, his concern about this behavior and what has been happening to his life may be more important considerations.

Rather than establishing exclusionary criteria, a more realistic and productive approach would be to admit youths who possess certain positive characteristics, regardless of other considerations. These attributes should include: (1) a feeling of uneasiness, unhappiness, or discontent with oneself or his life and some concern about doing something to change it; (2) recognition and acceptance that one does or can control what happens to him, even though the past may have indicated he was unable to do much about it; (3) a willingness to examine things about himself with others, even though it may make him angry, unhappy, or embarrassed to do so; (4) a belief that other residents, and the program itself, will benefit from his participation.

A preplacement "peertake" meeting (one's peers take part in selecting youths for the program) is helpful in clearly and forcefully conveying—"the program means something to us" and "we make decisions" nature of the group norms. Residence should be limited to young people who both choose to be involved and are found acceptable by youths in the program. In addition, the newcomer should be required to make his own decision whether he can accept the responsibilities which participation entails.

There are few delinquents who will not opt for what they perceive to be the more desirable of two alternatives placed before them. This does not mean that at the time he makes his decision, a youth should be expected realistically to choose between changing his behavior and remaining a delinquent; rather, in return for being in the community, under near conventional living circumstances, a candidate must at least verbalize his acceptance of group (program) norms, values, and expectations. Of course, many youths will be doing little more than choosing between what they define as something which they want little part of (the halfway house) and something else which they want even less (the training school). Certainly, the more sophisticated youths should be expected to opt for admittance not as a willing challenge to some ingrown delinquent attitudes and values, but rather as a conforming game-playing exercise at which many are quite experienced and adept.

Changes in behavior do not usually occur unless some doubt is perceived about the efficacy of one's present conduct in satisfying his needs and some alternative is identified with which the person can experiment. Enduring changes do not result unless another mode of conduct is experienced as a more certain or desirable means for goal attainment.

It is not important, therefore, that a candidate be truthful in discussing his "wanting," but rather his "willingness" to take a "good hard honest look at himself" and the utility of his behavior. To be accepted into the program, however, should be understood clearly by the newcomer to mean that he will be held to the terms of a "contractual arrangement" to which he must first agree. Stated succinctly, the following must be carefully stressed:

1. Residents will be accepted only after they fully understand what the program involves, what will be expected of them, and providing that their participation is approved by youth and staff with whom they will live. No one can be sent against his will. Everyone makes his own decision to come.

2. A youth cannot "stay the same" and remain in the program. Everyone must be expected to be doing more with himself tomorrow than he did today, and less tomorrow than he will do the day after.

3. Not doing anything "wrong" (irresponsibly) should not be considered an indication of progress and may more properly be interpreted to mean just the opposite. What a person does "right" (responsibly) is what counts.

4. "Good" or "bad" behavior has no meaning. Only responsible kinds of behavior have any value (utility). Everything a youth does or does not do he will be held accountable for from the day he enters the program. Self-defeating, escapist, or excuse-ridden antics should be viewed to be as deviant (irresponsible) as the more customarily recognized, overt, antisocial actions.

5. The halfway house is neither a prison nor a sanctuary. Residents should neither be able to "do time," nor avoid doing the most with the time available to them to complete treatment. Residence should be indeterminate, with the actual length of stay being a decision in which a youth himself, his peers, and staff should participate. No one should be permitted to remain beyond a maximum length of residence (which can vary from program to program) and there should be no fixed minimum period of time required or permitted.

We have conceptualized our halfway house model as a residential treatment alternative for youths whose problems and needs, while beyond that of other community programs, are short of their requiring institutionalization. Our therapeutic community includes as the core of its program, intensive (daily, hour and one-half) responsibility-oriented, reality-bound, group treatment meetings in which the focus is on the "here and now" and the primary change agents are one's fellow program residents.

The self-help treatment model is believed to offer advantages over more traditional treatment approaches in working with young people. Youth are much more responsive to the encouragement and pressure of their peers (with whom they can identify) to change their attitudes and behavior than they are to the ministrations of adult professionals. An atmosphere of trust and concern is required and the emotional involvement of residents and staff far exceeds that customarily expected or found in traditional correctional programs. It is the intensity of everyone's (staff and residents) involvement that distinguishes our treatment model from most others.

The voluntary nature of program participation must be emphasized. Admittance should not be automatic and alternatives to acceptance must be clearly spelled out. It must be stressed with the newcomer that he does not *have* to be in the program but rather has to *want* to be in the program.

Residence of approximately 4 to 6 months may be anticipated in order to accomplish treatment goals. Candidates should clearly understand that residents must believe themselves to be capable of "solving their problems" within this period of time. Program expectations should be made explicit. Progress must be expected each day. The longer a youth is in the program, the less need there should be for his remaining in the program. Responsibilities can and should increase with the length of residence. It should be emphasized that there are no privileges but only added responsibilities which are expected to accrue as one remains involved in treatment. Indeed, the longer a youth is in the program, the more demanding and difficult should his participation become. The expectations which staff have for residents—what they believe them to be capable of accomplishing, and the time in which they feel they can do this—can either enhance or inhibit goal directed behavior.

SIZE CONSIDERATIONS

The size of the program should be limited. An optimum population may range from 20 to 25 youths. Several factors are considered in determing this number:

1. *Per Capita cost which, of course, changes as a variable population numerator is placed over a fairly stable fixed-cost denominator.*—Approximately the same costs will be incurred for certain expenses (staff, utilities, communications, office equipment, building repairs, etc., give or take a range of about 18 to 25 residents).

2. *Developing and retaining the advantages of small group interaction.*—While face-to-face relationships are essential, the number of residents could vary depending on staff skills, architectural considerations, programming content, location, and other site considerations. Nevertheless, it appears that 30 is about the maximum number beyond which the attributes of close peer group interaction become jeopardized. Below 20, cost considerations become a problem.

3. *Not overwhelming a community with large numbers of new residents.*— Community acceptance, which we will discuss later, must be carefully considered and courted. It is not realistic to ignore the very real, if not too legitimate, fears and anxieties which people have when confronted with a halfway house opening in their neighborhood. While there is no simple relationship between program size and the crescendo of community concern, it is wise to assume that the more "threatening" the type of population—that is, the greater its number, the more visible the facility, and the more "problem-ridden" its residents—the more anxious and less tolerant is a community's reaction likely to appear.

4. *Given the many important and different considerations involved in selecting appropriate sites for a halfway house there is an inverse relationship between the size of the population and the available number of desirable sites.*—Site location committees frequently must choose second, third, and even less desirable alternatives, not because of the unavailability of facilities within the preferred area, but because considerations of importance to the local community often have been neglected, if not ignored. A well-planned and meaningfully organized community relations campaign looms large as the most important consideration in planning halfway houses (or other community programs).

Insufficient funding may require changes from an optimum size. At times, this may mean that larger (more than 25), or smaller (less than 20) residents must be considered. The advantages of face-to-face interaction, however, must always be balanced against budgetary concerns.

SITE SELECTION

Site selection is extremely important. As much time as possible should be set aside for this purpose. The time allotted can vary depending on the nature of the program, the particular area being considered, whether the structure is to be built, or leased, and the actual construction or renovation time contemplated. Six months should be a minimum and a year ideal. Plans must be drawn, contracts let, and changes made. An unhurried pace permits careful and important planning.

Community leaders should be contacted early and informed of an agency's plans. This is particularly true when programs are designed for offender groups. To do otherwise is to omit gaining and risk alienating the support of people and agencies whose acceptance and involvement is essential. It makes little sense, and it is unlikely, that efforts to confront a community with a *fait accompli* with succeed. This simply polarizes community resistance and hinders understanding and cooperation.

Site selection requires planning and care. There are few, if any, ideal locations. Both the advantages and disadvantages of a site should be carefully evaluated and weighed against each other. Once a target area is chosen, it is helpful to consider the following:

- Brokers familiar with the area can be engaged.
- If the agency has a field staff in the prospective target area, its assistance should be enlisted.
- Community leaders are well informed about available real estate. Their help in site selection is invaluable. In addition, their involvement makes it more likely that the program will gain recognition as a cooperative, community-agency venture to which all can more easily become committed. The expense in time and cost of site location efforts may be lowered appreciably by the cooperation and assistance of community leaders.
- Public agencies in particular should seek out and contact other governmental agencies in the target area for a discussion and appraisal of the "do's" and "don'ts." Local social agency directors are usually privy to the kinds of information which indigenous leaders may be reluctant to furnish or find it difficult to be objective about. Directors of these agencies are important, therefore, to call upon for an assessment of the community pulse and the likely reactions of local leaders.
- Agency staff, who are residents in the target area, can also provide important leads and information. These people should not be overlooked for other reasons —they can be of assistance, or on the other hand, they may make it difficult to establish positive community relations.

Selecting a site within the target area requires careful attention to several matters:

- The neighborhood chosen must be zoned properly. It is important to have a statement in writing from the zoning board that the use intended for the property is not in conflict with local zoning regulations.
- Public transportation must be accessible and within walking distance of the facility. Residents should be able to travel (to work, school, clinics, recreation, etc.) during most times and days of the week. If possible, locations which offer access to alternative means of public travel are preferable. The office vehicle should not be required to transport residents for any reasons other than emergency trips or group outings.

● Residents should be able to come and go and mix in with the neighborhood as much as possible. Program participants must feel relatively comfortable and safe in the area selected. A racially, culturally, and economically diverse community offers advantages to mixed populations.

● The architecture should be planned to blend in with that existing in the area selected. For example, a 25-bed multistory, ultra-modern building would not be suitably located on a block of modest single family residences.

● Signs, flag staffs, or other official-looking designations should be avoided. The facility will be no stranger to block residents who can, when necessary, quickly direct visitors to the building.

● Offender groups are not readily received in quiet residential communities. Commercial-residential areas or locations adjoining light industrial sections are preferred. Areas in transition also provide good sites in which to locate. The community, however, should not be disorganized or deteriorating, but could be one where this process has stabilized or been reversed.

● Commercial services (barber, shoe repair, snack shops, cleaners, etc.) should be within walking distance of the facility.

COMMUNITY RELATIONS

The halfway house should be designed to make maximum use of local resources including educational, religious, vocational, recreational, and medical services.

Community programs have both an opportunity and obligation to tap in on the skills, counsel, and support of volunteers, local citizen groups, and service organizations. Local colleges are usually willing to develop mutually beneficial relationships.

As community-based programs, halfway houses must be community integrated and involved, and responsive to the concerns, fears, and anxieties of their neighbors. Halfway houses which fail to establish close and effective community relations may expect, at best, suspicion and frequent misunderstandings of their program. Open hostility is equally as likely an occurrence. It is unwise and mistaken to regard the community as a necessary evil into which the facility has been thrust. There are only advantages to be gained from open, regular, and responsive community relations.

Certainly, a careful assessment should be made of a community's probable reaction to a proposed halfway house. There are very few desirable areas to locate where much deliberate and time-consuming planning need not be spent in developing preprogram community relations. Some people and organizations will be antagonistic. Others may be equally as opposed but less open about it. People will be resistive; probably most will be suspicious and uncertain about whether the halfway house will not depreciate property values, result in a crime wave, or simply be a burden on already existing community services.

It is always helpful in the planning stages to meet *individually* with community leaders to discuss the program and their reaction to it. They must be permitted and encouraged to air their questions and misgivings. It is not likely that those who favor the proposal will acknowledge this at large community meetings. The numbers opposed initially are not nearly as important as determing who the opposition is, its following, and motivation.

Community leaders approached individually may be expected to react favorably in most cases. Their positions as community leaders, however, must be considered and recognized as a factor which makes it difficult to gain their open support. Realistically, the problem of enlisting community support lies in assuaging the anxieties of the least informed but potentially most vocal community groups. Community leaders often are placed in the difficult position of reconciling their professional judgments with their roles as the representative voice of their communities. Planning a halfway house requires recognizing the difficult position in which community leaders are placed when their support and assistance are solicited.

Communication is an ongoing and two-way process. It is extremely important to appoint staff early to assume responsibility for building and maintaining positive community relations. Enlisting community support requires recruiting indigenous spokesmen of whom and with whom citizen groups will be much less suspicious and more likely to cooperate. Early consideration should be given to organizing local leaders into a community relations committee. Their involvement serves quickly to establish a positive agency image. The committee's importance later on as a buffer between the program and community should not be ignored. Its value is inestimable in times of crises. A community relations committee can be employed for fund-raising, obtaining special services, and other important purposes. In a nutshell, forming this committee is probably the single most important task facing new program administrators.

Programs that are successful in establishing effective working relationships with local agency and citizen groups have carefully planned and systematically organized their efforts to enlist community support. It pays dividends to meet at least once monthly (once every two weeks before the program opens) with the community relations committee whose advice and assistance should be sought regularly. It must be made clear in the beginning, however, that this is not a policy-setting board.

A helpful sequence for establishing sound community relations is as follows:
● Meet individually with local leaders of government, planning boards, private and public social, health, and welfare agencies, fraternal, church, and neighborhood improvement groups. Local police support is essential. If school-age populations are involved, school authorities should be contacted. This list is not inclusive and is only suggestive of the many important groups to contact.
● A steering committee of local leaders should be formed. It is helpful to have this group meet regularly to permit recognition and assurance of their mutual interest and support for the program.
● The program should be explained honestly. It is inadvisable and mistaken to not discuss the program in all its ramifications—this means difficulties and problems expected, as well as benefits and advantages.

● The assistance of neighborhood leaders, whose support has been enlisted previously, will do much to temper community antagonism and help avoid negative opposition forces from polarizing.

● Regularly scheduled meetings should be held both during the planning stages and after the program opens. It is helpful to think of annual or semiannual community meetings (open houses) to which all who are interested may come to visit, meet staff, and learn of the progress, problems, and needs of the halfway house.

Administrators should realize that there is a relationship between what is "put into the community" and what one expects to "get out of it." The halfway house should not only be able to utilize community resources, but it also should provide some reciprocal measure of service to the community. It is good practice to encourage various community organizations to hold their regularly scheduled meetings occasionally in the facility. The dining room or lounge may be large enough to lend itself for this purpose. Neighborhood block associations, civic improvement clubs, and fraternal organizations are examples of the many groups which could be scheduled periodically. The advantages to this type of community-center involvement far outweigh any inconvenience.

Given a sensitive and community-responsive staff, a halfway house can help strengthen the fabric of community organization and relations. The community should be encouraged to look upon the halfway house as intimately and meaningfully involved in neighborhood affairs—regardless whether the facility is directly affected by particular issues or not.

It is a mistake for community programs not to be concerned about day-to-day neighborhood problems and activities. Communities will not accept halfway houses and offer their support until and unless the agency and its staff can convince local people of their concern and interest in neighborhood affairs. For this reason, it behooves administrators of community programs to avoid isolating themselves or even giving this appearance to their neighbors. It is also unrealistic to expect residents to benefit from halfway house programs in which the administration itself avoids rather than confronts the realities and responsibilities of community involvement.

SPACE REQUIREMENTS

● Two youths to a bedroom is a desirable number. Although some raise questions about sexual problems where two youths share a room, experience would likely demonstrate that staff anxieties and expectations are a more important consideration. When space or economy reasons do not permit two to a room, as many as four youths in a single room could be accommodated.

● The rooms can be small, but should allow enough space for furniture and lounging. It is important that each room have its own window. When more than two youths occupy a room, bunk beds are fine space conservers. Two youths can share a single dresser and one large table (in addition to having space available in some other part of the building) for school work, letter writing, etc. A single closet or clothing bar can be shared to hang garments.

● Steel furniture is a much more practical investment both in terms of its durability and cost. Durable plastic chairs, table tops, etc., are also worth consideration.

● Sleeping two to a room, 12 double and three single rooms would be ideal for 25 youths. The two additional single rooms should be available for emergencies (unexpected visitors, unanticipated admittances, and postponed releases). The single rooms would be multipurpose quarters. Youths for whom some program crisis, illness, or other reason made it important for them to sleep alone, could have this space available. In addition, three larger, single sleeping rooms should be reserved for staff, trainees, and guests. Each of these rooms should also have its own toilet and shower.

● When the sleeping rooms are above the first floor, brick or masonry construction should be preferred. Horizontal construction offers many advantages over vertical designs. The building should permit quick and easy egress in case of fire, especially from sleeping areas. At least three exits from any part of the building should be available.

● Space should be provided for adequate storage of household supplies, clothing, recreation equipment, etc. These rooms should have adequate ventilation and be located in places where access and purpose is considered. Space should also be set aside for combustibles which meets with the approval of the local fire department. It is important to invite the fire marshal to inspect the (plans) building, and make periodic recommendations. Local fire regulations should be complied with and fire drills held regularly.

● Both the dining room and kitchen should be situated in areas that can be closed at times other than when meals are being served. The kitchen should be large enough for a commercial freezer, refrigerator, and stove, as well as offer adequate working space for the cook and helpers. If a building is being constructed, some of the larger pieces of equipment should be delivered before the door-bucks and partitions are installed. Large equipment should not be ordered until all pertinent dimensions are known.

● Conference rooms are intended primarily for the daily group treatment meetings which form the core of our halfway house model. Their use, however, should be multipurpose (staff meeting rooms, classrooms, and quiet study areas). A location should be chosen which is away from the noise and hub of building activities. The offices must also afford some privacy and quiet, but should be easily and readily identifiable to visitors and permit visual control of the main entrance.

● There are many advantages to having a resident superintendent. It is not likely however, that such a job requirement will interest qualified applicants unless salaries are made attractive, and modern, pleasant, living accommodations are provided. If residence is required, it should be made available without cost.

Approximately 9,000 square feet is suggested for a 25-bed halfway house. Construction costs vary but can range from $20 to $30 a square foot in the types of communities discussed. Facilities can also be leased. Per capita operating costs for the halfway house model discussed are about $11.15 per day. Properly planned, halfway houses can still be built for less than half the cost and operated at about two-thirds the amount per bed of traditional institutional programs. Large investments in buildings, time-consuming architectural planning, and relatively long construction periods can be avoided by leasing which also makes it possible to open these programs with comparative ease.

WHERE DO WE GO FROM HERE?

Cost considerations alone should make it necessary to explore alternatives to institutionalizing people. Studied in the light of any fair appraisal of the benefits derived from traditional correctional systems, our weary dependence on institutions would likely evaporate. The bulk of our offender populations (adult and juvenile) do not belong in institutions. An increasing number of legislators and correctional administrators have become aware of this and appear committed to see changes brought about. Our prisons and conventional juvenile institutional programs are as much an anachronism as a social cancer. One of these days we may understand that our horror and fear of crime and criminals is by no means unrelated to our ignorance and apathy as to its causes and our "medicine man" approach to its cure. Unwittingly, criminal behavior has been nurtured and exacerbated by the public's ignorance about the consequences of traditional correctional practices. In this regard, poorly located, punitively designed, and primitively programmed institutions, in which far too many offenders spend time, are monuments to our ignorance.

We are not discovering anything new. As Hans Mattick pointed out in a volume which should be required reading for anyone apprehensive about the failings of our correctional system, some of the same points were made over a century ago.[1] Mattick reminds us that, "The thirty-seven principles enunciated at that time (1870) by the foremost prison administrators in this country touched upon every significant phase of imprisonment and many of the recommendations made still remain to be implemented by most of the prisons existing today."[2] Not too much has happened since Mattick wrote this. There are exceptions, however, where dramatic progress, no matter how long overdue, is being made. The move toward community programs and more socially and psychologically productive living seems to be catching hold.

While institutions have become much more humane in treating offenders, vested interests which many have in jobs, contracts, and payrolls, remain as the most obvious and difficult problems with which reformers must struggle. When

---

[1] Hans Mattick, "Foreword: A Discussion of the Issue," *The Future of Imprisonment in a Free Society*, Volume 2. St. Leonard's House, Chicago. 1965, p. 8.

[2] *Ibid.*

the needs of offenders, as well as the public, are placed above parochial interests and concerns, the use of community programs should increase significantly. Until this happens, halfway houses will remain a sorely needed, underutilized, albeit readily available correctional "Best Buy."[3]

---

[3] Space requirements for halfway houses and budgetary information may be obtained by writing to the author at 311 South Calhoun Street, Tallahassee, Florida 32304.

LEGAL ASPECTS

It is the considered opinion of the editors that too many academic programs in criminal justice, criminology, and related fields of study do not pay adequate attention to the legal aspects of criminal justice.

This is particularly the case with regard to the legal aspects of corrections, notably probation and parole. We have attempted to provide a means for giving more balance in these educational programs by including three relevant items in this Section.

The issues are complex. As our first selection notes, " . . . it is not surprising that, with no consistently stated goal for corrections, correctional agencies grew in a haphazard manner." Legal precedents to some degree have assisted in interpreting statutes and in regulating some practices. However agencies of correctional administration have wide discretion to interpret and translate legislation into practical applications. It is interesting to question whether more legislative control would assist in the attainment of the correctional objectives, whatever these might be. The law has been of value in providing constraints upon the procedures that fall short of the contemporary interpretation of humanitarian principles. The law can also assist in providing some insulation from the day-to-day pressures of political interests in the criminal justice processes.

The too severe limitation of the discretion of correctional and other agencies can be as unsatisfactory or even as damaging as unchecked discretion. It may, indeed, be questioned whether there is any significant meaning to the concept of discretion except in terms of conscious and rational departure from some general standard. The move toward mandatory sentences that characterizes much current legislative thinking is open to challenge on many gounds; some of the material in our first selection, "The Statutory Framework of Corrections," throws some light on this area and provides a basis for informed discussion.

How does the idea of "due process" apply to the treatment of offenders? The two articles by Professor Fred Cohen discuss this important issue. We have not included materials published by various groups advocating legislation regarding prisoners' rights. Students might find it useful to obtain some of the pamphlets published by various forms of prisoners' unions and interest groups and to relate their contents to the materials in this section. There seems little doubt that the immediate future will see much argument and political action addressing the procedures and philosophies of probation, parole, institutions, sentencing, and, in general, the idea of the exercise and control of discretion at all levels in the criminal justice process. The background and history, with the case decisions (including often the dissenting opinions), are important if these issues are to be addressed in a satisfactory manner.

39
The Statutory Framework of Corrections: National Standards and Goals

NATIONAL ADVISORY COMMISSION ON CRIMINAL
JUSTICE STANDARDS AND GOALS

Law is the foundation on which a good correctional system is based. Indeed, it is doubtful whether an effective correctional system could exist without a good statutory foundation. But the reverse is not true. Good law will allow good administration; it will not assure it. If appropriate programs are authorized, but poorly staffed, then little benefit will result.

It is difficult to quantify statutory reform in crime reduction terms. Legislation can authorize or prohibit; it cannot implement. Correctional statutes must seek to authorize an effective correctional system and prohibit the abuse of individual rights.

In developing standards for correctional legislation, it is necessary to bear in mind that correctional "law" has three components in addition to statutes. These are: constitutional enactment, court decisions, and administrative rules and regulations. Thus all three branches of government have a hand in shaping the structure of correctional "law." The first problem in recommending a statutory framework, therefore, is to decide which component can best handle the particu-

SOURCE. *Corrections*, National Advisory Commission on Criminal Justice Standards and Goals, Washington, D.C., U.S. Government Printing Office, 1973, pp. 534–593.

lar issue being considered. If the decision is that the matter should be covered by statute, the question then becomes one of the intent and content of the law.

The narrative of this chapter explains how a legal system for correctional programs should be developed and what "essentially legal" problems arise. The standards developed at the chapter's end are of two varieties, general and specific. Three general standards enumerate what types of issues are appropriate for legislation and general correctional law reform. The remaining standards are specific and deal directly with substantive correctional issues. They provide examples of how certain correctional issues can be resolved by legislation.

CORRECTIONAL CODES AND THE CORRECTIONAL PROCESS

The correctional code includes statutes governing sentencing, probation, incarceration, community based programs, parole, and pardons. These statutes are the foundation on which a criminal corrections system is built. Short of constitutional restrictions, the legislature has wide latitude in determining the nature of the correctional code and its substantive provisions. Seldom, however, has a legislature considered broad questions of the role and limitation of legislation when enacting statutes affecting corrections.

In most States, statutes governing corrections cannot be considered a "code." They are collections of statutes enacted at varying times under varying conditions to solve specific and often temporarily controversial problems. The lack of consistency, comprehensiveness, and direction of these statutes has forced the correctional system to develop in spite of the statutory framework rather than because of it. To some extent the legislature has lost its rightful control over the governmental agencies involved. In other instances, progressive correctional administration has been frustrated by unrealistic and outmoded statutory restraints.

The Purpose of Legislation

Correctional legislation has one essential task—allocation and regulation of governmental power. In the context of criminal corrections the power to be allocated and regulated is substantial. An individual who violates criminal law subjects himself to possible deprivation of those attributes of citizenship that characterize free societies. Allocation and regulation of correctional power is a sensitive undertaking for a legislature in a free society. The potential for abuse of that power is apparent and real; the potential for effective and constructive reform of criminal offenders is less clear.

Authorizing Correctional Power

The ability to exercise control over criminal offenders is dependent on authorizing legislation. The initial decision in enacting correctional legislation is to determine for what purpose and in what manner this power is to be exercised. The legislature has the opportunity and the responsibility, in the first instance, to establish public policy on corrections—the ends sought and the means allowed.

Two possible functions for the correctional system are apparent: (1) punishment of individuals who break society's rules; and (2) reduction of crime. The first may be justified on the basis that rules require effective enforcement mechanisms. Law violations, when sanctions are not properly applied by government, may stimulate private retributive actions. Thus government through the criminal law legitimatizes and institutionalizes private retributive feelings.

The second goal for corrections is reduction of crime. Correctional power may reduce crime in two ways, by deterring potential lawbreakers from criminal conduct or by operating on existing offenders in such a way as to cause them not to commit further crimes.

Difficult questions are posed regarding the means to attain either of these two correctional goals. Satisfaction of community retributive desires involves issues of the intensity of correctional power. What level of punishment is required to assuage public desire for retribution? Is the infliction of human misery and degradation required?

The means available for crime reduction vary. This would again pose questions of the intensity of punishment required.

Rehabilitation of criminal offenders is another corrections approach. Based on the theory that offenders commit crimes at least in part because of a lack of skills, education, or motivation, rehabilitation requires the correctional agency to provide programs to overcome these deficiencies and assist the offenders' reintegration into the free community.

However legitimate each of these ends and means is, not all can be implemented compatibly by a single correctional system. The level of punishment necessary to satisfy some retributive feelings may be counterproductive in reducing recidivism. Conditions that, in theory, would increase the deterrent effect of corrections also may reduce the system's ability to change offenders constructively. More important, the failure to choose which theory is to predominate in a correctional system may result in inconsistent and competing programs that assure failure to attain any goal.

Each of the various punishment theories has been prominent at some time in corrections history. It is, however, difficult to find an instance where the legislature has made the conscious choice of theory. In fact, the thrust of a particular correctional system is generally determined by correctional personnel and shifts as the personnel changes. These basic public policy decisions should be made by the legislature after appropriate public debate. They should not be delegated either consciously or through inaction to administrators.

Legislatures have had some impact on the selection of correctional ends and means. In many States, statutory provisions assume implicitly a particular policy for corrections. However, this assumption is not uniformly applied. Some statutory requirements facilitate rehabilitation programs; other statutes make implementation of such programs difficult. To have an effective correctional system, it is not only appropriate but essential that the legislature (1) establish uniformly and comprehensively the "public policy" on corrections and the general goals and approaches for the exercise of correctional power, and (2) legislate consistently with that declaration.

The Instruments of Correctional Power

The legislature's second major task in legislating for corrections is to create and organize the instruments for correctional decisionmaking. The goals of correctional agencies and the quality of their personnel are decisions only the legislature can make. Only after the correctional system's goals and methodology are determined can the nature of the instruments for their implementation be considered adequately.

ORGANIZATION.   Once a consistent and comprehensive goal for the correctional system is established, the system's organization is dictated by that goal. Comprehensiveness in planning and programming requires a unified organization.

It is not surprising that, with no consistently stated goal for corrections, correctional agencies grew in a haphazard manner. In many States, each correctional institution was created separately, with separate administration. Prison confinement was the predominant response to criminal behavior. Each new reform, generally a reaction to the harsh conditions of incarceration, seemed to require a new governmental agency independent of the prison administration.

Probation developed as an arm of the sentencing court and subject to its control. Persons were not "sentenced to" probation; the sentence to confinement was suspended. The court viewed probation as a device to keep certain deserving offenders out of the correctional system, rather than as a more appropriate and effective correctional technique.

The recognition that institutional confinement has limited utility for the majority of criminal violators makes probation the major sentencing alternative. It should become the standard sentence, with confinement reserve for the dangerous offender. On the other hand, probation staff will draw on institutional resources. The use in several jurisdictions of short-term diagnostic commitments prior to sentencing is one example.

Institutional programming will be required to respond to the failures of probation programs. Judicially imposed sentences of partial confinement, where an offender remains under community supervision during most of the week, with his leisure time spent in a residential correctional facility, will require close cooperation between probation and institutional staff. Coordination and mutual understanding between all correctional personnel will become increasingly important. Continuing court supervision of the probation system inhibits the coordination required.

Sentencing courts do have an interest, however, in maintaining some control over the development of presentence reports, a function now generally performed by probation officers. The presentence report forms the basis for the court's sentencing decision. The report may also contain the sentencing recommendation of the probation officer.

There may be good reasons for separating the presentence investigation function from that of supervision of probationers. Studies indicate that where one officer does both, time-consuming investigations and report writing seriously interfere with his ability to supervise probationers. A person directly responsible to the sentencing court could perform the investigations as well as assist the court in other judicial functions such as bail investigations.

In many States, parole agencies developed independently. To moderate long prison sentences, parole boards were established and given authority to release some offenders from confinement if they agreed to supervision in the community. Parole also was viewed as getting the offender out of the correctional system rather than altering the nature of his correctional program. Parolee supervision in the community was administered in several instances by a board of parole rather than by the correctional agency. It remains under a board in 18 States.

Parole, like probation, is one of several correctional tools. Prison programs should prepare an offender for parole and other aftercare programs—for reintegration into the community. Imaginative use of parole conditions, such as a requirement that the parolee reside at a halfway house, may involve institutional personnel directly. Effective and efficient parole planning and programming require close coordination with other correctional activities.

Juvenile and adult institutions developed independently and remain autonomous in several States. Numerous factors appear to account for this division of correctional organization. The public is more often willing to support new and innovative programs for juveniles than for adults. Proponents of juvenile programs find it politically expedient to retain their autonomy. Different approaches are authorized, at least implicitly, for juveniles.

It is assumed that adults need more punitive measures, provisions for tighter custody, and fewer correctional programs. Juveniles, on the other hand, are more salvageable. The agency designated to administer adult programs is thought to be custody-oriented. Juvenile programs, based more on the welfare model, are envisioned as directed more toward rehabilitation.

In addition, under juvenile court acts juveniles are not "criminals" and thus avoid the stigma of criminal conviction. They are viewed differently from adults who have committed the same offense but are tried as "criminals" rather than "delinquents." To compound matters, juveniles who have committed no criminal offense—those who are neglected, dependent, or in need of special supervision—often are confined with delinquents.

For some, the specter of housing juveniles and adults in the same facility—a common occurrence in some areas—inhibits consolidation of corrections.

Most major reforms in adult corrections are preceded by identical reforms in juvenile corrections. Where appropriate, techniques and programs proved successful for juveniles should be made available for adults and vice versa. For example, because of their delinquency status, juveniles remain eligible for licenses and other citizenship rights that adults lose on conviction of a felony. It is increasingly apparent that these collateral consequences of a criminal conviction are seldom appropriate for adults either. Success in juvenile corrections with group counseling, community-based programs, and imaginative aftercare supervision can be translated easily into similar programs for adults.

Adult and juvenile programs should be administered within a single agency. This would not prohibit the development of specialized programs for juveniles or adults. However, the efficient utilization of scarce resources and the integration of programs into a continuum of correctional processes require unification. In some States, adult and juvenile programs, although autonomous, have developed informal relationships fostering coordination. Where these are operating effectively, the formal unification of programs under one agency in less urgent.

Misdemeanant corrections is an essential component of any integrated correctional system, if only because most offenders convicted of felonies previously have been convicted of a misdemeanor. In a California survey conducted for the President's Commission on Law Enforcement and Administration of Justice (the Crime Commission), 74 percent of those entering a State prison on their first felony conviction had a history of misdemeanant convictions.[1] Thus the State correctional system inevitably must respond to the failures of misdemeanant correctional programs. Coordinated planning and administration will assure a consistent approach toward individual offenders who graduate through the system of corrections from the misdemeanant to the felony level.

Local jails generally are characterized by idleness, hostility, and despair. They are, for the most part, devoid of correctional programs. Except in large metropolitan areas, there are insufficient resources to develop and maintain effective programs. Probation services are minimal or nonexistent. Work-release programs are scarce. Vocational or educational training programs are lacking. Since the jails are operated for the most part by law enforcement personnel, there is little professional correctional expertise. Institutional management and custodial arrangements are often inadequate. (See Chapter 9, Local Adult Institutions.)

The most important, and perhaps the most difficult, step toward unification of corrections will be to integrate local misdemeanant facilities into the State correctional system. Such integration is imperative because, as the Crime Commission remarked, "it is not feasible in most States to expect that advances . . . will be made as long as jails and misdemeanant institutions are administered separately from the rest of corrections."[2]

Corrections, if it is to be effective, can no longer be viewed as a group of separate and diverse entities independently exercising power over a criminal offender. Rather, it must be viewed as a system comprised of various components that must operate in a consistent and coordinated way. These components are

---

[1] President's Commission on Law Enforcement and Administration of Justice, *Task Force Report: Corrections* (1967), p. 72.

[2] President's Commission on Law Enforcement and Administration of Justice, *The Challenge of Crime in a Free Society* (1967), p. 178.

interrelated; the planning and performance of one will affect the others directly.

The correctional code should unify the administration of all correctional facilities and programs under one agency on the State level. That agency should have responsibility for probation, confinement facilities, community-based programs, and parole for adults, juveniles adjudicated delinquent, misdemeanants, and, where appropriate, those confined awaiting trial.

The major problem with total unification of all elements of the correctional system is the board of parole. As community-based programs implemented by institutional staff expand, the board will increasingly act to review institutional decisions. The board must be insulated from institutional pressures and perspectives in order to perform this function.

However, in view of the need for coordination in planning, resource allocation, and evaluation, the board of parole may be administratively part of the unified State corrections system. Where this form of organization is adopted, the board must remain autonomous in its parole decisionmaking functions. Methods for assuring such independence are discussed in Chapter 12, Parole.

PERSONNEL.   Once the elements of the correctional system are merged, the legislature shall act to insure that they are staffed with persons having appropriate qualifications. The qualifications required for a given position will depend primarily on the goal and methodology of corrections as enacted by the legislature. If punitive measures are to be the keystone of the system, then little expertise is needed. However, if reintegration of the offender into the community is the system's goal, then certain professional qualifications become important.

Drafting legislation to assure that programs are staffed with competent personnel is a difficult task in any governmental area. Recruitment and retention of competent staff require legislative action providing for three factors: adequate compensation, appropriate qualifications for those employed, and job security.

In many states, legislatures have set the salaries for top management correctional personnel. This creates a rigid system that precludes negotiation to induce a qualified person to accept a position or to retain one if he is offered additional compensation elsewhere. Legislatures should avoid codifying specific salary levels but should grant flexibility to the appointing officials to compete for the most qualified person within authorized appropriations.

Corrections is a politically sensitive function of government. Good correctional legislation requires that personnel recruitment be insulated from political patronage. However, as an arm of the government, corrections should be responsive to public attitudes. Political patronage is improper to the extent that unqualified persons are appointed. Appointment by the governor with the advice and consent of the legislature is a standard means of striking a balance. Statutory qualifications for a particular office are another.

Legislative attempts to dictate qualifications for correctional staff positions take several forms. Many States provide statutory qualifications for some top management positions including the chief executive officer of the correctional agency, probation or parole director, and the parole board members. Such qualifications range from broad provisions directed toward assuring some minimum professional expertise[3] to specific requirements regarding academic and professional training experience.[4]

Precise statutory qualifications for most positions are difficult to draft. The more specific they become, the more likely that some qualified persons will be ineligible. The system becomes more rigid and less adaptable to changes in the nature of correctional roles. General qualifications alone, without a procedure limiting the influence of political patronage, are meaningless.

Imposition of irrelevant qualifications is undersirable and nonproductive. Height, weight, and residency restrictions clearly do not foster any legitimate correctional goal.[5]

Legislatures also have experimented with negative qualifications—specific conditions automatically precluding a person from employment. These have generally frustrated, rather than assisted, efforts to recruit appropriately trained staff. The tendency to prohibit ex-offenders from occupational opportunities in the criminal justice system generally and in corrections particularly has hindered the utilization of persons who might have special qualifications for working with offenders.

Civil service systems, with their emphasis on promotion and seniority, impede attraction of qualified personnel to top or middle management positions as well as movement of personnel from one agency to another.

Protecting job security by legislation creates a dilemma of its own. Some job security is required to attract qualified professionals and to insulate professional judgments from political pressures. However, job security also creates risks of protecting incompetence.

Three basic systems are possible. In many States, top correctional officials serve at the "pleasure" of the appointing official. This system creates no job security.

In some States sensitive personnel are appointed for a specified term. This gives some security during the term and allows periodic review of the individual's competence. The security provided by the specific term appointment will depend on the causes listed for removal during the term. A standard phase is that the official may be removed for "disability, neglect of duty, incompetence, or malfeasance in office." A hearing where cause for removal is asserted should be required. Political considerations can be minimized by providing terms that overlap that of the appointing official.

In a few jurisdictions a person may be appointed to a permanent position

---

[3] The statutory qualifications for the director of corrections in the South Carolina are: "qualifications and training which suit him to manage the affairs of a modern penal institution." S. C. Code Ann. Sec. 55–299 (1962).

[4] The statutory qualifications for the director of corrections of West Virginia are: "duly qualified by education and experience with a degree in sociology, psychology, social science, or some related field and with a minimum of three years experience in the field of correction or a related field." W. Va. Code Ann. Sec. 62-13-3 (1966).

[5] Tennessee, for example, requires the director of corrections to have resided in the state for 5 years. Tenn. Code. Ann. Sec. 4-603 (1971).

subject to removal for cause. Again, a procedure requiring a hearing should be provided.

The term and permanent appointment schemes strike the balance between security and competence and provide adequate protection from political patronage and influence.

Below top management positions, the legislature should authorize flexibility in procedures for the selection and dismissal of personnel. Although some job security is required to build a strong career service, experimental programs utilizing ex-offenders, lay volunteers, and minority group members in correctional roles should be authorized and encouraged.

Allocation and Regulation of Correctional Power: The Issue of Discretion

The most critical issues facing corrections involve the exercise and control of correctional power. To the extent that correctional programs are to provide an individualized response to criminal offenders, correctional decisionmakers require broad discretionary power. Legislatures generally have conferred such power. Sentencing statutes are delegated without real direction to the sentencing courts. Parole boards are instructed to grant or deny parole in the "interest of the public." This discretion has given correctional administrators vast and often unchecked power over the lives and property of offenders.

Discretion has played, and no doubt will continue to play, an important role in the correctional process. No system of government has been devised that can be operated solely by rules without the exercise of discretion. It has been argued that the existence of discretionary power creates hostility and resentment that undermine reform activities. The exercise of power without restraint certainly can be counterproductive. But the issue facing legislative reform efforts is not *whether* discretion should be granted—for its authorization is inevitable—but *when* and *how much.* Resolution of this issue should be the major objective of legislative drafters. A legislature can have its most constructive and dramatic impact on the correctional process through effective regulation of correctional power.

THE RAMIFICATIONS OF DISCRETION.   Law has always recognized the need for discretion to temper the rigidity of rules. It is impossible to develop rules that will achieve just results in all cases to which they may be applicable. The crime of armed robbery, for example, may be committed by a professional criminal or a teenager responding to a dare from his peers. Unique considerations and varying circumstances require that some discretionary power exist.

The correctional system attempts to individualize programs. Offenders with little education are offered academic opportunities. Those who need skills to increase employability are provided vocational training. Some offenders require substantial custody; others only minimal supervision. These differences have no necessary relation to the offense committed, but rather to the particular offender. To provide individualized programs, discretionary power is needed.

The nature of correctional decisionmaking requires professional expertise.

Professionalization of correctional personnel is a response to the expectation that corrections will do more than confine offenders. Reliance on rules alone makes expertise unnecessary. Discretionary power allows the adaptation and utilization of advances in knowledge throughout the correctional process.

A governmental agency cannot be creative without the flexibility that discretion provides. It is particularly important that corrections maintain its ability to progress. New techniques, new concepts, and new programs require experimentation. Only through discretion can the system both experiment with untested theories and modify its programs and services to reflect advances in knowledge and technology.

On the other hand, unchecked discretion, no matter how beneficently exercised, creates its own hazards. It is particularly susceptible to abuse and to arbitrary and mechanical decisionmaking. Disparity in the treatment of substantially similar offenders may breed tension and hostility toward the correctional staff. If the offender perceives the disparity to be unjustified, he probably will not be receptive to or cooperative with efforts made on his behalf.

Unnecessary power exercised by correctional staff leaves the offender little control over his own life, and he is continually at the mercy of his keepers. Where this occurs, the offender gains little insight into the responsibilities and decisions he will face on release. And the correctional staff loses its ability to perform any function other than custodial. Abuse of discretion destroys any possible constructive relationship between the correctional staff and the offender.

THE CONTROL OF DISCRETION.   The absence of controls on the wide range of discretion conferred on administrative agencies has long produced conflict. Our Constitution and traditions reject the exercise of unbridled power because of its potential for abuse, not because such power inevitably leads to bad decisions or exploitation. The "due process" clauses of both the fifth and fourteenth amendments directly restrain the exercise of discretionary power. Our system of government creates a presumption against the exercise of power, which can be set aside only for the most compelling reason.

In the context of criminal corrections, the thrust of legislation should be to authorize necessary discretion with appropriate restraints and protections against improper use. The legislature can achieve this goal by adapting to corrections certain techniques and procedures that have been tested and proved effective elsewhere.

One method of limiting discretion is through *legislative decisionmaking.* Here the legislature makes some decisions itself through statutory enactment, often in setting policy on matters of importance, such as determining the public policy of corrections. Another example would be a statutory unification of historically independent elements such as local jails and juvenile institutions; this not only requires specific legislative approval but is the type of major public policy decision the legislature should make. However, once the major organizational framework is established and the chains of command are firmly stated, the legislature should grant the administration discretion to make minor adjustments within the basic framework.

Some decisions required to protect an offender from abuse should be legislatively determined. Enactment of a code of rights for offenders removes discretionary action in certain areas. A statutory prohibition against corporal punishment is a noteworthy example; several States have enacted such laws. However, legislatures generally have been reluctant to codify provisions specifically protecting the interests of offenders. The absence of legislative guidance in this area has been a major factor in creating the need for judicial appraisal of correctional practices. Legislative provisions assuring basic freedoms and an acceptable level of humane treatment would have mitigated the need for expensive litigation and reduced the confusion and ambiguities that inevitably result from a judical case-by-case declaration of offenders' rights.

Decisions requiring individualized responses should not be made by the legislature. Elsewhere in this chapter the value of mandatory sentences is questioned. Precluding individuals from various correctional programs because of the offense committed seriously undermines the ability of the correctional process to have a constructive impact on the offender.

Through *statutory criteria* the legislature can delegate a particular correctional decision to a correctional agency and, in addition, provide criteria and guidelines governing the agency's discretion. Most legislative delegations of power include some broad direction for its exercise. However, these are generally ineffective and authorize such wide discretion that it becomes almost impossible to determine whether the direction is followed.

Statutory criteria for decisionmaking should be specific enough so that a review of particular decisions can be effectively undertaken to assure compliance. Such guidance allows sufficient discretion for individualizing justice while assuring some protection against arbitrary or inappropriate decisions.

In corrections, sentencing decisions are particularly susceptible to direction through statutory criteria. These are decisions of direct public interest and have an immediate and substantial impact on the offender. The length of time over which the State exercises control of the offender and the relative degree of liberty or confinement imposed are basic to the correctional process and are critical from the offender's viewpoint.

Two decisions are appropriate for development of detailed statutory criteria. The first is the trial court's selection of the sentencing alternative to be imposed initially on the offender. The broader the range of sentences available, the more important become criteria to protect against disparate results. In most jurisdictions, the major decision for the court is between probation and confinement. Selection 7.01 of the Model Penal Code (discussed later in this chapter) provides a useful model for the development of criteria for this determination. The code first recognizes that for most offenders probation will be the most appropriate alternative, with confinement to be used only as a last resort.

The section requires withholding a sentence of confinement unless the court finds that imprisonment is necessary for protection of the public because:

(a) there is undue risk that during the period of a suspended sentence or probation the defendant will commit another crime; or

(b) the defendant is in need of correctional treatment that can be provided most effectively by his commitment to another institution; or

(c) a lesser sentence will depreciate the seriousness of the defendant's crime.

The section then lists 11 factors to be weighted in favor of withholding a sentence of imprisonment. These include the fact that the defendant's crime did not cause nor threaten serious harm, the defendant acted under strong provocation, the victim induced the commission of the crime, or the defendant's conduct would be unlikely to recur.

The decision to parole is another sentencing decision susceptible to detailed statutory criteria. Section 305.9 of the Model Penal Code illustrates acceptable criteria for this decision. They are fundamentally similar to the criteria for initial sentencing. The code lists 13 factors to be considered in determining whether a particular offender should be paroled. In addition, Section 305.10 lists particular information the parole board must consider, including such items as the presentence report, reports of physical or mental examinations, institutional reports, and the prisoner's parole plan.

These sections provide useful guidelines for development of statutory structure for parole decisionmaking. The proposed structure should minimize the possibilities for arbitrary decisions.

Articulation of these criteria, factors, and data tends to reduce the number of disparate decisions. It provides the offenders some measure of protection against capriciousness. However, the actual effectiveness of the criteria, factors, and data bases will depend on the procedures developed to enforce them.

Statutory criteria structure and confine discretion; they do not abolish it. Much must be left to *administrative rules and regulations.* Although the legislature can guide decisionmakers, it cannot legislate for every conceivable circumstance. Discretion, even though structured and confined, still will play a decisive role within the correctional system.

While research and experimentation are rapidly expanding our understanding of various assumptions, only tentative criteria can be developed. In these areas, flexibility is needed; and continuing review and alteration of professional judgments are warranted and essential.

The legislature should require for these decisions that correctional administrator structure their own discretion through formal adoption of administrative rules and regulations. By announcing in advance the criteria to be employed, the result to be sought, and the factors to be considered in a particular case, the potential for arbitrary action is reduced. When circumstances or new knowledge suggest different approaches, the rules and regulations can be changed quickly without the need for complicated and time-consuming legislative procedures. Legislatures generally have been lax in requiring correctional administrators to adopt rules governing their own actions.

The dramatic increase of administrative agencies during the last few decades has stimulated legislative concern for protecting the public from arbitrary administrative decisions. In 1946, the concern culminated in passage of the Federal Administrative Procedure Act. Shortly thereafter, the National Conference of

Commissioners on Uniform State Laws promulgated a Model State Administrative Procedure Act for regulating State administrative agencies. The Model Act has been adopted in several States and used as a guide in others.

In some States, and on the Federal Level, the General act regulating administrative agencies is equally applicable to the correctional system but often is ignored. These acts provide a rational approach to administrative action through rules and regulations that should be adopted and used by correctional agencies.

The thrust of the administrative procedure acts is to publicize agency action. A major protection against arbitrary or inappropriate decisionmaking in a free society is to require openness and full discussion. Under most acts, major policy decisions by an agency are first announced as proposed rules. Persons affected by a rule have an opportunity to present argument or comment on the rule before it is enacted. Adopted rules are placed on file and made available to the public.

Most correctional decisions not otherwise regulated by statutory criteria are susceptible to some regulation through utilization of this procedure. The flexibility of rulemaking and the ease with which rules can be changed to adjust to changing circumstances would protect against unnecessary interferences with or disruption of correctional programming. The procedure likewise would provide a valuable means of allowing offenders and the public to participate in and influence the formulation of critical correctional policies. Ability of offenders to participate in decisions directly affecting their liberty and property would do much to relieve the hostility and resentment the present system breeds.

Another task for the legislature is to determine whether and when there should be *a review of decisions.* For some decisions, promulgation of criteria or rules and regulations is sufficient assurance of responsible action. For others, some check on the exercise of discretion by a reviewing agency is both useful and necessary. The review, regardless of how it is conducted and by whom, should be designed to answer three questions: Did the decision follow statutory criteria and procedures? Did the agency abide by its own rules regarding both criteria and procedures? Is the decision consistent with constitutional requirements?

A prerequisite to review of any discretionary decision is a requirement that the decisionmaker state the reasons for his decision. Most judicial decisions contain findings of fact and conclusions of law to allow orderly appeals. Similar procedures within administrative agencies would facilitate review. Likewise they would lay greater emphasis on criteria, whether established by legislation or by agency rule.

Most governmental agencies institute internal review procedures to check on subordinates. These usually contemplate review by a superior. Some decisions are made by more than one person, assuring a check on the actions of each. In some agencies review is periodic and informal. In others, there are formalized procedures for reviewing decisions made by correctional staff. These procedures are designed to assure top management that established policies and standards are carried out by the staff. Legislation is not required to authorize this form of review, and rigid legislatively imposed procedures are not essential.

Review of decisions should be extended to all persons affected or likely to be affected by the decision. Specific legislative provisions authorizing offenders or other interested parties to initiate a review procedure should be enacted. Some correctional agencies have been slow to adopt internal mechanisms whereby offenders may challenge staff decisions. There is a natural tendency to support the actions of a staff member over an offender. However, if the offender is to be protected from arbitrary or mistaken actions on the part of the staff, he must have a means of effectively challenging decisions against his interests. He, more than anyone else, has an interest in seeing that established criteria are followed. He is likely to know when decisions are made that are inappropriate or based on findings contrary to fact.

Since it is in the public's and the agency's interest that correctional decisions have a constructive effect on the offender, both should support mechanisms to allow the offender to challenge the factual basis for such decisions. An erroneous or arbitrary decision is not constructive; it breeds resentment and disrespect for society and its institutions.

In formulating a procedure for offender-initiated review of decisions, the legislature and the correctional agency must recognize that the procedure not only must arrive at fair decisions but also must appear to do so from the offender's perspective. Review procedures can vary in formality and extent. A procedure enabling an offender to relay a complaint to a superior of the decisionmaker constitutes a review procedure.

Some institutions may wish to experiment with an ombudsman system in which an official is specifically designated to receive and respond to offender grievances. The ombudsman should be an impartial person who is not officially connected with the correctional administration. More formalized grievance procedures are envisioned where a formal complaint is filed and a hearing is held to resolve a disagreement. Some decisions may be appealed to a mixed board of offenders and correctional staff. The devices available for internal review are varied.

Review of discretionary powers by courts is another alternative. Traditionally, courts were reluctant to consider the appropriateness of correctional decisions and generally abstained from involvement in the internal administration of prisons and other correctional programs. However, as noted previously, in recent years courts have taken an increasing interest in the procedures and practices employed for the care of criminal offenders. Most court decisions have tested inmate complaints against constitutional requirements. However, with the development of statutory criteria and more effective use of rules and regulations, courts also could review discretion not challenged as unconstitutional. They may be appropriate agencies to enforce legislative directives.

The nature of the procedure for review should depend on the importance of the decision to the life, liberty, or property of the offender. Minor decisions need not be subjected to judicial review as long as a simple, informal, and fair internal review procedure is available. Some disciplinary decisions such as temporary suspension of minor privileges would not require judicial intervention. Assignment to a particular cell or dinner shift normally would not raise substantial issues, although regulations announcing how cells are assigned may do so.

On the other end of the spectrum, decisions having a direct bearing on the length of time an offender will serve require great concern for protecting the offender's interest. The initial sentencing decision requires procedural safeguards, including the presence of counsel. Appellate review of sentencing is becoming a reality in many States. The decision to revoke probation requires formal procedures and is amenable to judicial review. The United States Supreme Court recently held in *Morrissey* v. *Brewer,* 408 U.S. 471 (1972), that the Constitution requires certain procedural formalities for revocation of parole.

Some institutional decisions have a direct effect on the sentence of the offender. Disciplinary proceedings that could result in loss of "good time" credits can substantially extend an offender's sentence. Procedural safeguards against arbitrary action should be required, and, in the absence of formal and impartial internal procedures, judicial review seems appropriate.

A number of other decisions indirectly affect the offender's sentence and eligibility for parole. Assignment to a particular institution or selection for certain programs, including community-based programs, may delay his actual parole date substantially. An offender should have some protection from erroneous or arbitrary decisions of this nature.

The Model State Administrative Procedure Act discussed later in this chapter provides a useful illustration of the enactment of judicial review of critical administrative decisions. It provides that in a contested case a person aggrieved, after exhausting internal review procedures, may seek judicial review. Section 15, subsection (g) provides the basis for judicial review which seems appropriate for implementation in correctional decisionmaking.

(g) The court shall not subsitute its judgment for that of the agency as to the weight of the evidence on questions of fact. The court may affirm the decision of the agency or remand the case for further proceedings. The court may reverse or modify the decision if substantial rights of the appellant have been prejudiced because the administrative findings, inferences, conclusions, or decisions are:

(1) in violation of constitutional or statutory provisions;

(2) in excess of the statutory authority of the agency;

(3) made upon unlawful procedure;

(4) affected by other error of law;

(5) clearly erroneous in view of the reliable, probative, and substantial evidence on the whole record; or

(6) arbitrary or capricious or characterized by abuse of discretion or clearly unwarranted exercise of discretion.

The most immediate and substantial impact that a legislature can have in reforming prison conditions and the correctional process generally is to develop and enact a code of administrative justice along the lines just discussed. A consistent and fair approach to structuring and reviewing discretionary decisions will serve the interests of the offenders, the public, and the correctional system. Fair decisions based on adequate procedures and sound factual information are good correctional decisions. Decisions that appear fair to those affected are good correctional decisions. Good correctional decisions are essential if corrections is to have any effect in reducing recidivism and decreasing crime.

PENAL CODES AND THE CORRECTIONAL PROCESS

The penal code includes the statutory provisions that designate an activity as criminal and prescribe the applicable criminal sanction. The penal code has a direct and influential effect on the corrections component of the criminal justice system.

Substantive Provisions

The penal code defines the clientele of the correctional process. It determines in a general way the type of person who will journey through the correctional system. Criminalization of conduct that directly threatens life or property will result in a correctional clientele of young males, the group most prone to commit such offenses. Criminal prohibitions against homosexuality, if enforced, will result in a correctional clientele of homosexuals. Sanctions aginst drunkenness increase the alcoholic offender population.

Those statutes establishing criminal conduct also determine the type of correctional programs required. To the extent that different activities reflect different personality or social defects, making an activity criminal imposes the obligation to insure that a correctional program is available to meet these defects. If alcoholism is made a criminal offense, the correctional system should have programs for alcoholics.

Often the normally prescribed criminal sanctions are inappropriate. For example, there is little use in confining persons guilty of nonsupport, because the family of the offender remains impoverished.

The major impact of the penal code on corrections is in determining the gross number of offenders entering the system. As noted in Chapter 3, criminalization of a wide range of activity in the United States has overburdened the correctional process. The failure to discriminate between categories of conduct and to establish priorities for criminalization has forced the correctional system to spread resources thin among those who either may not need correctional treatment at all or who will be least likely to benefit from it. Inability to concentrate resources on offenders who present a clear threat to lives or property is no help to the preservation of public safety.

In the juvenile area, persons who have committed no criminal offense often are included as correctional clients. In some States, dependent and neglected children are subject to incarceration in institutions for delinquents. Client diversity creates the need for program diversity that may or may not be administered compatibly.

When framing criminal offenses and revising outdated criminal codes, the legislature should consider the following factors: (1) impact on the correctional system; (2) level of correctional resources required and available for the potential violators; (3) assignment of appropriate priority for utilization of correctional resources; and (4) potential for meeting the needs of certain offender types with traditional correctional programs.

Penalty Provisions

Statutes defining criminal conduct generally specify the limits of the sanction that may be imposed for violations. In many States, these limits are phrased in confinement terminology. Thus, a standard clause at the end of a criminal statute reads: " . . . and upon conviction thereof shall be sentenced to imprisonment for not less than one nor more than ten years." Such provisions reflect the assumption that imprisonment is the normative criminal sanction. The increased use of community-based supervision through probation and the development of partial confinement and other alternatives to incarceration recognize that total confinement is unnecessary and inappropriate for many offenders. Maximum and minimum terms thus will take on new significance as they influence and are influenced by changes in the correctional process.

EFFECT OF MAXIMUM SENTENCES ON CORRECTIONS. Most criminal codes, either modern or antiquated, provide varying maximum sentences for various criminal offenses. Establishment of these maximum sentences has a direct bearing on the development and success of correctional programs.

Legislatively imposed maximums establish the length of time for which an offender is subject to correctional power. From a purely correctional standpoint, it could be argued that the legislature should not impose any maximum. The sentence for every offense would be for life with correctional authorities making discretionary decisions terminating their control when an offender's rehabilitation is complete. This model is based on a pure form of individual treatment. Commission of an offense provides the rationale for unlimited treatment. The legislature would not be forced to scale the sanction by the gravity of the offence or to reflect the intensity of retributive feelings in the community. These decisions would be delegated to other agencies, either courts or correctional officials.

In fact, however, society does have a scale of values attributing greater severity to some criminal offenses than to others. This discrimination reflects retributive notions that can be reflected through differing maximum terms. Differentiating the length of the sentence on the basis of the seriousness of the offense reflects societal notions of fairness as well. Retribution aside, it would appear unjust for an individual who shoplifts a $10 watch to be deprived of his liberty for a substantially longer period than an individual who commits armed robbery.

Maximum terms reflect values in addition to correctional policy. Our system of government long has regarded governmental intervention in individuals' lives as an evil to be avoided without good cause. And the government's intention to intervene for the good of the individual rather than for punishment seldom has been found to be sufficient cause to extend the period of intervention. The maximum limit of state control over the individual, reflected in the criminal statutes, places time restraints on correctional programs not related directly to needs of the program or the offender. This would tend to force planning for correctional activities to contemplate concentrated rather than extended programs.

There is a growing recognition of the fact that inequality of sentences directly undermines correctional programs. Offenders who labor under grossly excessive sentences, as compared with other offenders who committed relatively similar offenses, are not receptive to correctional programs. The justification that the sentence is "individualized" generally is not accepted by the offender. Lack of legislatively imposed maximum sentences, graduated in relation to the gravity of the offence, increases the possibility of disparity in sentencing. Legislatively imposed maximum sentences are the first step toward equality of sentencing. To this extent, maximum limits established by law—although limiting the time available for correctional programs—tend to enhance the effect of correctional programming by increasing offender morale.

Most States now provide for maximum sentences other than life imprisonment for most offenses. It is generally agreed. however, that most sentences are far too long. There is, for the vast majority of offenders, no justification for long maximum terms. Studies of the American Law Institute, the National Council on Crime and Delinquency, and the American Bar Association have urged that no maximum sentence be longer than 5 years except for the few offenders who present a serious threat to others. American sentencing statutes now tend to set the maximum for a particular offense with the infrequent offender who represents a continuing threat to the community in mind. Maximums should be established for the vast majority of offenders and authority granted to extend such maximums when the facts warrant.

Long sentences impede correctional programming. An offender who faces a long sentence is not prone to accept and benefit readily from correctional programs. Moreover, valuable resources are consumed in the care and provision of services for many offenders who do not need extended correctional supervision. And finally, no study has yet indicated that, for the majority of offenders, any socially useful benefit is derived from long sentences.

Thus, although legislatively established maximum limits are useful for the development of correctional programs as well as for the equitable administration of criminal justice, the value of such maximums is lost if they are too long. The standards for statutory sentencing provisions, set forth here and in Chapter 5, reflect the need for legislatively imposed maximums of generally short duration with provisions for extended terms where justified. Legislatures should recognize that long sentences when applied to all offenders may adversely affect public safety rather than enhance it.

EFFECT OF MINIMUM SENTENCES ON CORRECTIONS. Legislatively established minimum terms serve a different function. Since the legislature may contemplate only the offense and not the individual offender when setting the limits of criminal, sanction, the promulgation of minimum sentences is unrelated to correctional programming requirements. The diversity, length, and inconsistency of present maximum sentences may account for the present tendency for State legislatures to enact minimum sentences.

The minimum sentence imposed by statute serves only to affect the offender adversely. Since the minimum term generally determines parole elibiligity, it prolongs confinement unnecessarily. This over-confinement results not only in ineffective use of valuable resources that might be allocated more appropriately to other offenders but also may undermine seriously the progress of an offender.

The argument that a statutory minimum of 1 year should apply to all felonies represents the theory that a shorter period of confinement does not allow sufficient time for the development of a correctional program. Assuming that the corrections system cannot effectively operate in less than a year, the question remains as to which agency should make that decision. By imposition of a legislatively imposed 1 year minimum, all flexibility within that year is lost. When the judge makes a mistake in terms of correctional needs, the mistake cannot be rectified.

Whether the judge should be authorized to impose a 1-year minimum is a different question. The sentencing judge is in a position to determine on an individual basis if satisfaction of retributive feelings requires that a minimum be imposed. If imposed for that purpose, then judicially imposed minimums are justifiable, regardless of what effect they may have on correctional programming.

If the 1-year minimum is essential for correctional programming purposes, the wisest course would be to adopt by administrative rule a policy of not paroling individuals within the first year except in unusual situations. Thus, the minimum sentence decision based on correctional programming requirements would be made by those responsible and knowledeable in those programs. This also would allow adequate flexibility for individualized justice.

EFFECT OF MANDATORY SENTENCES ON CORRECTIONS.   There are two important factors in fashioning sentencing provisions: the offender and the offense. The legislature, in enacting a penal code with penalty provisions, can deal only with the offense; the offenders who will be convicted under the provision over the history of its enactment will span the spectrum of guilt. Recently there has been an increase of laws which differentiate between the killing of a policeman and other homicides. The FBI Uniform Crime Reports indicate that persons who kill police officers range from husbands interrupted in the course of a family dispute to deranged persons lying in ambush. No legislature can determine in advance the nature of the offender who will be prosecuted under a particular penalty provision.

In a number of instances, however, legislatures have, because of public reaction to a particular offense, attempted to write mandatory sentences into law. These take the form either of specifying what sanction shall be applied or eliminating certain sentencing or correctional alternatives from consideration. Minimum sentences established by law operate as manadaory provisions since they generally postpone parole.

Legislators should not impose mandatory sentences. They are counterproductive to public safety, and they hinder correctional programming without any corresponding benefit. To the extent that the mandatory provision requires an individual offender to be incarcerated longer than necessary, it is wasteful of public resources. To the extent that it denies correctional programming such as probation or parole to a particular offender, it lessens the chance for his successful reintegration into the community. To the extent that mandatory sentences are in fact enforced, they have a detrimental effect on corrections.

However, mandatory sentences generally are not enforced. The Crime Commission's Task Force on Courts found "persuasive evidence of nonenforcement of these mandatory sentencing provisions by the courts and prosecutors."[6] Prosecutors who find that an unusually harsh sentence in a particular case is unjust will, through plea negotiations, substantially circumvent the provision. Where lengthy mandatory sentences are imposed, undermanned prosecutors may be forced to alter the charge to obtain quilty pleas, since mandatory sentences leave little incentive for the offender to plead guilty.

Mandatory sentences in fact grant greater sentencing prerogatives to prosecutors than to courts. The result increases rather than decreases disparity in sentences and subverts statutory provisions by a system designed to enforce them. The resulting disrespect for the system on the part of both the offender and the public tends to undermine our system of criminal justice.

The Idaho Supreme Court recently held legislatively decreed mandatory sentences in violation of the Idaho constitution. The court noted:

> A judge is more than just a finder of fact or an executioner of the inexorable rule of law. Ideally, he is also the keeper of the conscience of the law. For this reason the courts are given discretion in sentencing, even in the most serious felony cases, and the power to grant probation. We recognize that rehabilitation, particularly of first offenders, should usually be the initial consideration in the imposition of the criminal sanction. Whether this can be better accomplished through the penal system or some other means, it can best be achieved by one fully advised of all the facts particularly concerning the defendant in each case and not by a body far removed from these considerations.[7]

Similar decisions in other jurisdictions would not be unexpected.

EFFECT OF COMMUNITY-BASED PROGRAMS ON CORRECTIONAL CODES

The growing recognition that achieving behavior change among criminal offenders can be enhanced by community-based programs rather than by institutionalization has numerous effects on correctional legislation. Many present statutory provisions were based on the assumption that, unless probation was

---

[6] President's Commission on Law Enforcement and Administration of Justice, *Task Force Report: The Courts.* (1967) p. 16.

[7] *State* v. *McCoy,* 94 Ida. 236, 486 P. 2d 247 (1971).

granted, the sentence of the offender would be served behind walls. A small percentage would be granted "leniency" through early parole.

The judicial sentence generally was structured in terms of confinement to a specific institution for a specific period of time. Since the offender was under a court order of "imprisonment," specific statutory authority was required to effectuate an earlier release. Since "imprisonment" was assumed to mean confinement behind walls, any type of program removing an inmate from the prison required specific statutory authorization. Many States gave authority for the warden to remove the prisoners in case of fire or epidemic. Specific legislation was thought to be required for trusties, for allowing offenders to travel from the prison to a nearby prison farm, and other close custody programs conducted outside the prison walls. The two major community-oriented correctional programs, probation and parole, are encumbered with elaborate statutory provisions.

Statutory Authority

Because of this history, community-based programs emanating from institutions should have specific statutory authority. Many sentencing statutes have been changed recently to provide for sentencing offenders to the custody of the director of corrections. Under these statutes, it could be argued that no further authority is necesary for assignment of an offender to any location, including the community, as his site of custody. However, to allay any questions of authority or responsibility, community-based programs should be authorized by statute.

This does not mean that each type of program need be specified. With increasing knowledge and experience, new and different programs will continually be developed. Essentially, the statute should authorize the director of corrections or other appropriate official to "extend the limits of confinement" of a committed offender for a wide range of purposes. This would authorize work, education, and vocational training release programs and furloughs. Transfer of offenders to community-based halfway houses also would be proper. In juvenile corrections, such broad authority would authorize foster homes and educational and other programs with a community orientation.

Correctional administrators need broad discretion in developing community programs and selecting offenders to participate in them. These programs need the active support of community members. The community's traditional suspicion of offenders makes it necessary to plan carefully and negotiate skillfully to obtain community cooperation and resources. The correctional adminstrator will need flexibility to move into programs as such resources become available. Legislative restraints on the nature or type of community-based programs can impede the development of these programs substantially.

Administrative Discretion

In authorizing community-based programs, the legislature will face a number of questions involving the exercise of adminstrative discretion.

- How best can the public safety be protected by limiting participation in these programs to offenders who represent no threat to the community?
- How best can the legislature assure fairness in the selection of offenders for such programs?
- How best can the legislature assure fairness in the revocation of community-based privileges?

The legislature's response to each of these difficult questions in the long run will influence the level of success of community-oriented programs.

The legislature cannot by statutory edict insure the proper selection of offenders to participate in such programs. Since the legislature has before it only the offense and not the individual offender, any conclusions it might make regarding public safety must be the result of a generalization from the offense itself. Such generalizations cannot enhance public safety; they can only impede it.

Community-based programs are short-run risk taking programs. Lengthy confinement without graduated programs of release creates greater risks. An offender, while confined, represents a lesser risk to the public safety than one living in the community. But the offender who participates in a gradual return to society through a variety of community-based programs represents a lesser risk in the long run than the offender who serves a long prison term and then is released abruptly without supervision.

There is certainly the temptation to exclude persons convicted of certain offenses from participation in these programs, as has been done in the case of probation and parole. All such temptations should be resisted. There are sufficient practical and political restraints operating against the overuse of community corrections.

- As long as resources are scarce, correctional administrators will tend to select the "best risks" for available programs.
- Any correctional administrator will tend toward the conservative use of these programs because, in the last analysis, he personally bears the responsibility for failure.

Requiring fairness in the selection of participants for community programs presents two separate issues.:

1. Where resources are scarce, how is the administrator to select participants from among all of those qualified?

2. Where resources are available, does the offender have an appeal from an administrative decision refusing to place him in such programs?

These two issues are based on assumptions that community-based programs are, from the offender's point of view, preferable to continued total confinement, and that the advantages of such programs are substantial enough to create some legal interest in the manner in which they are allocated. These advantages may include direct pecuniary gain because, at present, offenders participating in work-release programs are paid full market wages, whereas offenders working in institutional industrial programs are paid substantially less.

The first issue, the selection for limited spaces in available programs from similarly qualifed individuals, is one peculiarly appropriate for administrative discretion. The most the legislature can expect to accomplish is to define generally the criteria for determining the class of qualifed individuals. A legislative statement that community-based programs are authorized to facilitate the offender's reintegration would guide the correctional administrator in establishing the offender class from which participants in these programs should come.

The second issue is subject to more legislative control. Institutional administrators often may place excessive value on institutional adjustment. If a committed offender adjusts to prison life without "causing trouble," he is assumed to be ready for more demanding assignments in the community. However, adjustment to the close controls of prison life may have little bearing on adjustment in the free society. Thus there may be offenders for whom community programs are both appropriate and required, who are not assigned to these programs for reasons unrelated to their potential for success.

The legislature can respond to this problem by recognizing the changing role of the parole board caused by the expanding use of community-based programs. Historically, the board of parole was the only agency with statutory authority to release a committed offender before the expiration of his sentence.

Parole Board Functions

As correctional administrators obtain through legislation more discretion in utilizing community resources—particularly the authority to house offenders within the community—the parole board will take on different functions. It will, under these circumstances, act more as a reviewing agency to determine which offenders ought to be participating in community-based programs but are not because of correctional administrator's refusal to assign them to such programs. It would seem proper and advisable to view the parole board in this role. It would require some modification in present statutes establishing the board.

1. The concept of parole eligibility, if it restricts the jurisdiction of the board in all cases, should be restructured to allow the board to act prior to eligibility dates for purposes of approving participation in community-based programs other than parole supervision.

2. The parole board should be given authority to assign offenders to community-based programs other than those historically designated as "parole" programs. Thus, halfway houses, work release, and educational release programs should become available resources for the parole board as well as the director of corrections.

3. A procedure should be authorized allowing an offender not assigned to a community-based program to initiate a review by the parole board. This can be accomplished either by allowing an offender to initiate a hearing before the board for the specific purpose of testing the adminstrator's refusal to assign him to a community-based program or by requiring the board periodically to review the record and history of each offender. The latter would allow a review of not only community-based participation but also parole eligibility.

4. The fourth issue—fairness in revocation of community-based privileges—

lies at the heart of the growing tension between legal requirements and correctional expediency. Probation and parole revocation now require procedural safeguards, including the rights to a hearing, notice of the charges, and an opportunity to present the offender's side of the case.

Due Process Requirement

As the correctional system changes from a confinement/total freedom system to a system of gradual diminishment of governmental restraints through varied community-based programs, the movement toward procedural due process will extend further into the correctional process. When the alternative to confinement was parole supervision, revocation of parole produced a dramatic change in the status of the offender. It was one that called for procedural safeguards against administrative abuse.

With less dramatic import but with similar impact on the offender, the revocation or modification of community-based privileges demands some legal restraints on governmental arbitrariness. If current trends continue, judicial decisions will eventually require the development of such restraints. Case-by-case statement of the nature of such restraints by judicial decisions inevitably results in a transition period of uncertainty and a less than comprehensive solution. The requirements of due process are flexible enough to allow some legislative flexibility in establishing procedures that will protect the offender's interest and at the same time will allow the efficient operation of correctional programming.

An offender should not be removed from a community-based program without good reason. This is a simple enough statement, but it contains difficult implications. The determination of whether there is "good reason" in our society contemplates certain procedural requirements: (1) the offender should know what the reason is; and (2) he should be able to present information to the decision-maker in the event the reason is not founded on fact. Adequate provisions implementing these procedures should be required by correctional legislation.

Use of Community Resources

The assignment of offenders to the community also contemplates that nongovernmental community resources will be utilized as a critical component of the correctional program. Traditionally, governmental functions may be delegated, in whole or in part, to a private agency or individual. Among the ramifications of this for the correctional code are the following:

1. Statutory authorization for the correctional administrator to utilize community resources, generally on a contractual basis, is essential. In some jurisdictions, the right to contract for private services may not be considered an implied power of a governmental agency and thus should be expressly provided for in the statute.

2. Statutory authorization should be conferred for transferring custody in fact if not in law to a private party or organization. It is preferable to have the

offender remain in the custody of the correctional agency as a matter of law for purposes of determining sentence, punishing for escape, maintaining control, and revoking community privileges. However, where private resources are utilized, the offender may be in the actual control and supervision of private individuals. In addition to the ability to transfer custody, the following other legal issues should be resolved by legislation.

● Power of arrest. Does the private agency or individual supervising an offender have the power to arrest him should he violate the conditions under which he was placed in the community? On balance, the distribution of the arrest power to private individuals has serious consequences. Other than the arrest privilege private individuals already have under common law, trained law enforcement officers should be relied upon if arrests become necessary.

● Civil liability. Does the private agency or individual obtain, by performing a governmental function, the immunities and privileges of a governmental officer? For example, if an offender escapes from a community program and injures a third party, what recourse should the injured party have against the agency or individual responsible for the offender's care? Legislation should either establish the standard of care required of private individuals or agencies participating in community-based programs; stipulate that except for intentional misconduct, the government will indemnify the individual or agency against loss; or authorize the corrections agency to contract with regard to the liability issue.

Sale of Goods

In addition to affirmative provisions authorizing community-based programs, some present statutory provisions must be revoked as an undue restraint on the development of such programs. The two major areas where statutory reform is essential are: laws restricting the use of prison labor; and laws restricting the occupational or governmental privileges that may be granted to those convicted of criminal activity.

Most States and the Federal government have specific provisions restricting the sale of prison-made goods. The Federal provision prohibits the transport in interstate commerce of goods or merchandise manufactured in whole or in part by prisoners "except convicts or prisoners on parole or probation."[8] State laws generally prohibit the sale or offer for sale of goods or merchandise manufactured wholly or in part by prisoners "except convicts or prisoners on parole or probation." These statutes were enacted when probation and parole were the only community-based programs envisioned.

Important for consideration is that newly developing work-release programs and other community-based efforts do not fit comfortably under the category of "probation" or "parole." Thus the provisions restricting the sale or transportation of goods manufactured by prisoners indeed may limit severely the type of employment available for offenders under work-release programs. Although the

[8] 18 U.S.C. Sec. 1761.

language is obscure enough to argue reasonably that they do not directly apply to work-release programs, the ambiguity is sufficient to suggest either outright repeal of these provisions or at least modification to exempt community-based correctional programs.

Restrictions Due to Offender Status

Equally restrictive are specific provisions that preclude felons from obtaining governmental licenses of all sorts. In many jurisidictions, restrictions prohibiting those convicted of crimes from entering a given occupation have proliferated far beyond any legitimate occupational or governmental interest. The further extension of licensing provisions that restrict ex-offenders from areas of employment will make correctional programs increasingly more difficult.

Civil death statutes may also have a direct impact on community programs. As the offender becomes more integrated into the community, he will obtain, in addition to the responsibility of citizenship, many of the burdens of societal living. It is to be expected that his need for access to the courts on civil matters arising out of his employment or other community programs will increase and at times may be critical to his success. Statutes that in any way detract from the offender's integration into the community will reduce the effectiveness of community-based programs without serving any societal interest.

MODEL ACTS

The drafting of a comprehensive correctional code of the scope envisioned here is a substantial undertaking. However, a wide variety of model laws generally consistent with the thrust of this chapter are available. Discriminating use of these proposals will facilitate the development of a draft for legislative consideration. Many of the model acts are accompanied by commentaries and references stating the arguments for and against specific provisions and citing secondary material that can be consulted. Thus, much of the preliminary work of code reform has already taken place and is readily accessible.

The most significant models are discussed here briefly. No attempt is made to analyze in detail the specific provisions of each. The discussion is intended to indicate the scope and general thrust of the various proposals.

Model Penal Code

The Model Penal Code, Proposed Official Draft, 1962 is available from The American Law Institute, 101 North 33rd St., Philadelphia, Pa. 19104.

The Model Penal Code, promulgated by the American Law Institute, is the foundation for most other model acts developed since 1962. Although other organizations have added to or modified some provisions, its basic framework and approach have set a standard against which all other proposals are measured.

The Model Penal Code primarily is a proposal for substantive criminal law reform. However, the drafters recognized that the definition of criminal conduct was inextricably linked with the sanction imposed. Thus the code contains articles on the disposition of offenders, the authority of the court in sentencing, and relatively extensive provisions regulating the organization and administration of probation, imprisonment, and parole. It illustrates how the corrections system can be merged into an effective and coordinated response to criminal corrections.

The code's most significant achievement for correctional practices was development of statutory criteria for sentencing decisions. The standards in this chapter urge that comparable provisions be enacted in all jurisdictions.

The Model Penal Code has several deficiencies. In some organizational areas it is too detailed for smaller correctional systems. Moreover, it does not consistently provide procedures for judicial review of critical correctional decisions.

Several recent developments and innovations are not included. Work release, although provided for short-term offenders, is not authorized for felons. There generally are no provisions stating the rights of offenders. The recent expansion of correctional litigation and the courts' new willingness to redress offenders' grievances have occurred since the code was published. Thus, although the Model Penal Code still is an extremely useful tool in correctional law reform efforts, it requires some modifications.

Earlier tentative drafts of the code include commentaries on the various sections and other useful background information.

NCCD Model Acts

Model acts in several fields which have been proposed by the National Council on Crime and Delinquency are available from NCCD at 411 Hackensack Ave., Hackensack, N.J. 07601.

The National Council on Crime and Delinquency has promulgated a number of model acts relating to correctional programs and organization. They generally are modest in scope and directed toward a small part of the entire correctional code. Thus, they do not provide a model from which a comprehensive code can be developed. However, the individual provisions are useful models for particular problems and, in some instances, offer alternatives to the Model Penal Code. The various relevant acts are as follows:

1. Model Sentencing Act (1963). This model covers presentence investigations and sentencing alternatives for felonies. Alternative provisions for sentencing minors also are included. The act does not provide for the organization of any correctional agency but is limited to the actual imposition of sentence. Criteria for each sentencing alternative are very general and do not approach the specificity of the Model Penal Code.

The Model Sentencing Act was promulagated specifically in response to certain features of the Model Penal Code. Where the code requires a 1-year minimum for a sentence to confinement, the act provides for no legislative minimum. While the code provides for a parole term over and beyond the term of confinement, the act rejects the additional term.

The Model Sentencing Act is currently being revised.

2. Standard Act for State Correctional Services (1966). This model provides a basic structure for correctional organization and some modest provisions authorizing correctional programs. Although useful as a model for specific provisions, it is not a comprehensive act. It is inconsistent with some standards proposed in this chapter in that it provides for a lay board of corrections to establish departmental policy.

3. Standard Probation and Parole Act (1955). This proposal provides only a basic framework for a probation and parole system. It does not provide for criteria for probation and parole decisions. Although once an an important model for State legislation, it generally has been superseded by the more extensive and contemporary Model Penal Code.

4. Model Act for the Annulment of a Conviction of a Crime (1962). This act is a useful model provision for annulling criminal convictions to minimize the collateral consequences.

5. A Model Act for the Protection of Rights of Prisoners (1972). This recently promulgated act illustrates possible provisions for protecting offenders from the grossest forms of governmental abuse. Directed toward prison conditions, it provides legislative protection against inhumane treatment, regulates solitary confinement, outlines disciplinary procedural formalities, requires a grievance procedure, and establishes visitation rights. The act also provides enforcement mechanisms including judicial relief.

The act is an excellent model for the issues it covers. However, legislative action regarding a much broader range of what can legitimately be called "offenders' rights" is appropriate and desirable. Provisions implementing various consitutional requirements including freedom of speech, religious exercise, and access to the media should be included. Thus, although the act is a useful model for specific provisions, it should not be considered an all-inclusive statement of the rights of offenders.

Illinois Corrections Code

Illinois Unified Code of Corrections (Tentative Final Draft 1971), promulgated by the Illinois Council on the Diagnosis and Evaluation of Criminal Defendants, is available from the Council, 175 W. Jackson Blvd., Chicago, Ill. 60604.

In June 1972, the Illinois Legislature enacted, in large part, the Illinois Code proposed by the Council on the Diagnosis and Evaluation of Criminal Defendants. Some amendments were included. The code, as enacted with appropriate commentary, is scheduled for publication. When published it will be available from the Council. References throughout this chapter to the Illinois proposal are to the tentative final draft without the legislative changes. It is important to recognize that most of the provisions are now governing Illinois corrections.

The Illinois draft is perhaps the most complete and comprehensive model available for correctional code reform. All major elements of the correctional code are included from sentencing through release. Correctional organizations are included.

The Illinois proposal is also the most detailed of any model act. It provides statutory provisions and standards regulating every facet of correctional administration.

The proposal reflects the increasing concern with protecting the interests of offenders. Procedures are required which provide the offender with substantial opportunities to challenge administrative action where it substantially affects his sentence or treatment.

The Illinois proposal is a useful checklist of appropriate provisions in enacting a comprehensive correctional code, and its basic approach is sound.

Nebraska Acts and Study

The Nebraska Treatment and Corrections Act (Neb. Rev. Stat. Sec. 83–170 et. seq. (Reissue 1971)).

The Nebraska Probation Adminstration Act (Neb. Rev. Stat. Sec. 29–2246 et seq. (Supp. 1971)).

"The Handbook for Correctional Law Reform," unpublished study.

In the Nebraska Treatment and Corrections Act, the Nebraska legislature has enacted provisions patterned after the Model Penal Code. Although some amendments were made, the basic thrust of the code remains intact. Statutory criteria are established for parole decisions. Organization of the correctional agency was unified, with the exception of probation and local misdemeanant facilities.

The Nebraska Probation Administration Act, while retaining judicial control, provides for State level administration of all probation services and provides criteria for sentencing alternatives reflecting the philosophy that probation generally is the most appropriate sanction, with imprisonment to be utilized as the last resort.

The Nebraska provisions in some instances do not adequately protect the interests of offenders, and no system of administrative review or code of offenders' rights is provided.

The Nebraska provisions, other than those governing probation, have been analyzed in the "Handbook for Correctional Law Reform," a study developed for the Law Enforcement Assistance Administration. The provisions are set out with appropriate commentary. The laws of the 50 States are compared to the act, section by section. The Handbook also includes essays on correctional law reform and criticism of existing State statutes.

New Federal Criminal Code

Study Draft of a New Federal Criminal Code, National Commission on Reform of Federal Criminal Laws, 1970, available from the Superintendent of Documents, U.S. Government Printing Office, Washington. D.C. 20402.

The study draft, although directed primarily at the substantive criminal code, does contain model provisions relating to major sentencing decisions, including parole. The draft develops a wide variety of sentencing alternatives and specific criteria governing the imposition of each. The draft is patterned after the Model Penal Code but includes some additions and alterations in the criteria proposed. A procedure is provided for removing disqualifications and disabilities imposed by law as a consequence of conviction.

Uniform State Laws

Proposals of the National Conference of Commissioners on Uniform State Laws are available from the Conference, 1155 East 60th St., Chicago, Ill. 60637.

The Conference has promulgated three acts relating to correctional law.

1. Uniform Act on Status of Convicted Persons (1964). This statute provides a model for removing many of the disqualifications and disabilities imposed by law for conviction of a crime. The act has been adopted by Hawaii and New Hampshire.

2. Model State Adminstrative Procedure Act. This proposed statute, enacted in several States, is a general provision designed to regulate discretion in all State administrative agencies. It provides a useful model for developing a code of administrative justice for the correctional system.

3. Uniform Juvenile Court Act (1968). This proposed act governs primarily the creation, jurisdiction, and procedures of the juvenile court and only indirectly includes provisions related to correctional programs. The act does provide a list of sentencing alternatives as well as provisions for probation and related programs short of incarceration. To the extent that the act authorizes the juvenile court to administer these programs directly, it is in conflict with the standards presented in this chapter.

State Correction Department Act

The State Department of Correction Act promulgated by the Advisory Commission on Intergovernmental Relations, 1971, is available under the title "For a More Perfect Union—Correctional Reform," from the Superintendent of Documents, U.S. Government Printing Office, Washington, D.C. 20402.

Patterned after the NCCD State Correctional Services Act, this act is designed to "provide for a more systematic State-local approach to corrections by expanding State administrative and supervisory responsibilities and by increasing State financial and technical assistance." The proposal governs only the organization and programs of the department of corrections.

Legislative Guide for Juvenile Programs

Legislative Guide for Drafting State-Local Programs on Juvenile Delinquency promulgated by the Youth Development and Delinquency Prevention Administration, U.S. Department of Health, Education, and Welfare is available from the Superintendent of Documents, U.S. Government Printing Office, Washington, D.C. 20402.

The proposed guide is in two parts. The first contains legislation establishing a State-administered program of juvenile delinquency prevention and treatment. It considers many of the issues contained in the standards of this chapter as they relate specifically to juvenile delinquents. Included are provisions for probation, confinement, community-based treatment programs, and parole. This part of the guide is the most detailed model available that is specifically directed at juvenile corrections.

The second part of the guide contains modifications to authorize a program administered in part by the State and partly by local authority. Such a modification would make it inconsistent with the standards proposed herein, which contemplate State control.

Most of the provisions of Part I of the guide are consistent with the standards proposed by this chapter and are useful illustrations of solutions to correctional problems relating to juvenile services.

The guide was designed to mesh with the provisions of an earlier document entitled *Legislative Guide for Drafting Family and Juvenile Court Acts* published by the Children's Bureau of the same department. The latter is available from the Superintendent of Documents under Children's Bureau publication number 472–1969.

STANDARDS FOR CORRECTIONAL LEGISLATION

The standards developed herein relate to improving the statutory framework for the correctional system. The first three standards are of a general nature dealing with approaches and principles. The remainder primarily illustrate application of the first standards to specific correctional issues.

Two prefatory statements are necessary to explain the proposed standards. The historical separation of juveniles and adults has provided, at times, a different rhetoric for correctional agencies and programs. Juveniles are not "convicted" and "sentenced" but rather "adjudicated" and "placed" or "committed." Programs also have varied. In many States "aftercare" for juveniles is granted by institutional staff; adult parole is conferred by a board of parole.

Most of the differences for juvenile offenders result from conditions in adult corrections that are inappropriate for any age group, adult or juvenile. The solution is not to exempt juveniles but to reform the system as applied to all correctional clients. The standards herein, unless they specifically state otherwise, should be applicable to both adults and juveniles.

Not all persons subject to correctional power have been convicted of a criminal offense. Persons awaiting trial frequently are confined in correctional facilities. The confinement often results from defects in release procedures. No reform of bail and other pretrial release, however, contemplates that all offenders will be returned to the community to await trial. Some accused persons will remain confined. Others may be released subject to supervision by correctional personnel.

The development and applicability of standard correctional programs to persons awaiting trial creates some difficulties. The presumption of innocence limits the ability of correctional administrators to require participation. However, correctional programs, particularly those authorizing community-based supervision, should be made available to those not yet convicted.

The standards developed herein do not address specifically the problems arising from persons awaiting trial. The standards protecting convicted offenders from arbitrary power should, in all events, be considered applicable to these persons.

Standard 16.1

Comprehensive Correctional Legislation

Each State, by 1978, should enact a comprehensive correctional code, which should include statutes governing:

1. Services for persons awaiting trial.
2. Sentencing criteria, alternatives, and procedures.
3. Probation and other programs short of institutional confinement.
4. Institutional programs.
5. Community-based programs.
6. Parole.
7. Pardon.

The code should include statutes governing the preceding programs for:

1. Felons, misdemeanants, and delinquents.
2. Adults, juveniles, and youth offenders.
3. Male and female offenders.

Each legislature should state the "public policy" governing the correctional system. The policy should include the following premises:

1. Society should subject persons accused of criminal conduct or delinquent behavior and awaiting trial to the least restraint or condition which gives reasonable assurance that the person accused will appear for trial. Confinement should be used only where no other measure is shown to be adequate.

2. The correctional system's first function is to protect the public welfare by emphasizing efforts to assure that an offender will not return to crime after release from the correctional system.

3. The public welfare is best protected by a correctional system characterized by care, differential programming, and reintegration concepts rather than punitive measures.

4. An offender's correctional program should be the least drastic measure consistent with the offender's needs and the safety of the public. Confinement, which is the most drastic disposition for an offender and the most expensive for the public, should be the last alternative considered.

Standard 16.2

Administrative Justice

Each State should enact by 1975 legislation patterned after the Model State Administrative Procedure Act, to regulate the administrative procedures of correctional agencies. Such legislation, as it applies to corrections, should:

1. Require the use of administrative rules and regulations and provide a formal procedure for their adoption or alteration which will include:

    a. Publication of proposed rules.

    b. An opportunity for interested and affected parties, including offenders, to submit data, views, or arguments orally or in writing on the proposed rules.

    c. Public filing of adopted rules.

2. Require in a contested case where the legal rights, duties, or privileges of a person are determined by an agency after a hearing, that the following procedures be implemented:

    a. The agency develop and publish standards and criteria for decision-making of a more specific nature than that provided by statute.

    b. The agency state in writing the reason for its action in a particular case.

    c. The hearings be open except to the extent that confidentiality is required.

    d. A system of recorded precedents be developed to supplement the standards and criteria.

3. Require judicial review for agency actions affecting the substantial rights of individuals, including offenders, such review to be limited to the following

questions:

    a. Whether the agency action violated constitutional or statutory provisions.

    b. Whether the agency action was in excess of the statutory authority of the agency.

    c. Whether the agency action was made upon unlawful procedure.

    d. Whether the agency action was clearly erroneous in view of the reliable, probative, and substantial evidence on the record.

The above legislation should require the correctional agency to establish by agency rules procedures for:

    1. The review of grievances of offenders.

    2. The imposition of discipline on offenders.

    3. The change of an offender's status within correctional programs.

Such procedures should be consistent with the recommendations in Chapter 2, Rights of Offenders.

Standard 16.3

Code of Offenders' Rights

Each State should immediately enact legislation that defines and implements the substantive rights of offenders. Such legislation should be governed by the following principles:

1. Offenders should be entitled to the same rights as free citizens except where the nature of confinement necessarily requires modification.

2. Where modification of the rights of offenders is required by the nature of custody, such modification should be as limited as possible.

3. The duty of showing that custody requires modification of such rights should be upon the correctional agency.

4. Such legislation should implement the substantive rights more fully described in Chapter 2 of this report.

5. Such legislation should provide adequate means for enforcement of the rights so defined. It should authorize the remedies for violations of the rights of offenders listed in Standard 2.18, where they do not already exist.

Standard 16.4

Unifying Correctional Programs

Each State should enact legislation by 1978 to unify all correctional facilities and programs. The board of parole may be administratively part of an overall statewide correctional services agency, but it should be autonomous in its decisionmaking authority and separate from field services. Programs for adult, juvenile, and youthful offenders that should be within the agency include:

1. Services for persons awaiting trial.
2. Probation supervision.
3. Institutional confinement.
4. Community-based programs, whether prior to or during institutional confinement.
5. Parole and other aftercare programs.
6. All programs for misdemeanants including probation, confinement, community-based programs, and parole.

The legislation also should authorize the correctional agency to perform the following functions:

1. Planning of diverse correctional facilities.
2. Development and implementation of training programs for correctional personnel.
3. Development and implementation of an information-gathering and research system.
4. Evaluation and assessment of the effectiveness of its functions.
5. Periodic reporting to governmental officials including the legislature and the executive branch.
6. Development and implementation of correctional programs including aca-

demic and vocational training and guidance, productive work, religious and recreational activity, counseling and psychotherapy services, organizational activity, and other such programs that will benefit offenders.

7. Contracts for the use of nondepartmental and private resources in correctional programming.

This standard should be regarded as a statement of principle applicable to most State jurisdictions. It is recognized that exceptions may exist, because of local conditions or history, where juvenile and adult corrections or pretrial and postconviction correctional services may operate effectively on a separated basis.

Standard 16.5

Recruiting and Retaining Professional Personnel

Each State, by 1975, should enact legislation entrusting the operation of correctional facilities and programs to professionally trained individuals.

Legislation creating top management correctional positions should be designed to protect the position from political pressure and to attract professionals. Such legislation should include:

1. A statement of the qualifications thought necessary for each position, such qualifications to be directly related to the position created.

2. A stated term of office.

3. A procedure, including a requirement for a showing of cause, for removal of an individual from office during his term.

For purposes of this standard, "top management correctional positions" include:

1. The chief executive officer of the correctional agency.

2. Members of the board of parole.

3. Chief executive officers of major divisions within the correctional agency, such as director of probation, director of parole field services, and director of community-based programs.

This standard assumes a unified correctional system that includes local jails used for service of sentence. In the event that such a system is not adopted, the definition of Item 3 immediately above should include the chief executive officer of each correctional facility including local jails.

The foregoing legislation should authorize some form of personnel system for correctional personnel below the top management level. The system so authorized should promote:

1. Reasonable job security.
2. Recruitment of professionally trained individuals.
3. Utilization of a wide variety of individuals, including minority group members and ex-offenders.

Legislation affecting correctional personnel should not include:

1. Residency requirements.
2. Age requirements.
3. Sex requirements.
4. A requirement that an employee not have been convicted of a felony.
5. Height, weight, or similar physical requirements.

Standard 16.6
Regional Cooperation

Each State that has not already done so should immediately adopt legislation specifically ratifying the following interstate agreements:

1. Interstate Compact for the Supervision of Parolees and Probationers.
2. Interstate Compact on Corrections.
3. Interstate Compact on Juveniles.
4. Agreement on Detainers.
5. Mentally Disordered Offender Compact.

In addition, statutory authority should be given to the chief executive officer of the correctional agency to enter into agreements with local jurisdictions, other States, and the Federal Government for cooperative correctional activities.

Standard 16.7

Sentencing Legislation

Each State, in enacting sentencing legislation (as proposed in Chapter 5) should classify all crimes into not more than 10 categories based on the gravity of the offense. The legislature should state for each category, a maximum term for State control over the offender that should not exceed 5 years—except for the crime of murder and except that, where necessary for the protection of the public, extended terms of up to 25 years may be imposed on the following categories of offenders:

1. Persistent felony offenders.
2. Dangerous offenders.
3. Professional criminals.

The legislation should contain detailed criteria, patterned after Section 7.03 of the Model Penal Code as adapted in Standard 5.3, defining the above categories of offenders.

Standard 16.8

Sentencing Alternatives

By 1975 each State should enact the sentencing legislation proposed in Chapter 5, Sentencing, reflecting the following major provisions:

1. All sentences should be determined by the court rather than by a jury.

2. The court should be authorized to utilize a variety of sentencing alternatives including:

    a. Unconditional release.

    b. Conditional release.

    c. A fine payable in installments with a civil remedy for nonpayment.

    d. Release under supervision in the community.

    e. Sentence to a halfway house or other residential facility located in the community.

    f. Sentence to partial confinement with liberty to work or participate in training or education during all but leisure time.

    g. Imposition of a maximum sentence of total confinement less than that established by the legislature for the offense.

3. Where the court imposes an extended term under Standard 5.3 and feels that the community requires reassurance as to the continued confinement of the offender, the court should be authorized to:

    a. Recommend to the board of parole that the offender not be paroled until a given period of time has been served.

    b. Impose a minimum sentence to be served prior to eligibility for parole, not to exceed one-third of the maximum sentence imposed or be more than three years.

c. Allow the parole of an offender sentenced to a minimum term prior to service of the minimum upon the request of the board of parole.

4. The legislature should delineate specific criteria patterned after the Model Penal Code for imposition of the alternatives available.

5. The sentencing court should be required to make specific findings and state specific reasons for the imposition of a particular sentence.

6. The court should be required to grant the offender credit for all time served in jail awaiting trial or appeal arising out of the conduct for which he is sentenced.

Sentencing legislation should not contain:

1. Mandatory sentences of any kind for any offense.

2. Ineligibility for alternative dispositions for any offense except murder.

Standard 16.9

Detention and Disposition of Juveniles

Each State should enact legislation by 1975 limiting the delinquency jurisdiction of the courts to those juveniles who commit acts that if committed by an adult would be crimes.

The legislation should also include provisions governing the detention of juveniles accused of delinquent conduct, as follows:

1. A prohibition against detention of juveniles in jails, lockups, or other facilities used for housing adults accused or convicted of crime.

2. Criteria for detention prior to adjudication of delinquency matters which should include the following:

    a. Detention should be considered as a last resort where no other reasonable alternative is available.

    b. Detention should be used only where the juvenile has no parent, guardian, custodian, or other person able to provide supervision and care for him and able to assure his presence at subsequent judicial hearings.

3. Prior to first judicial hearing, juveniles should not be detained longer than overnight.

4. Law enforcement officers should be prohibited from making the decision as to whether a juvenile should be detained. Detention decisions should be made by intake personnel and the court.

The legislation should authorize a wide variety of diversion programs as an alternative to formal adjudication. Such legislation should protect the interests of the juvenile by assuring that:

1. Diversion programs are limited to reasonable time periods.

2. The juvenile or his representative has the right to demand formal adjudication at any time as an alternative to participation in the diversion program.

3. Incriminating statements made during participation in diversion programs are not used against the juvenile if a formal adjudication follows.

Legislation, consistent with Standard 16.8 but with the following modifications, should be enacted for the disposition of juveniles:

1. The court should be able to permit the child to remain with his parents, guardian, or other custodian, subject to such conditions and limitations as the court may prescribe.

2. Detention, if imposed, should not be in a facility used for housing adults accused or convicted of crime.

3. Detention, if imposed, should be in a facility used only for housing juveniles who have committed acts that would be criminal if committed by an adult.

4. The maximum terms, which should not include extended terms, established for criminal offenses should be applicable to juveniles or youth offenders who engage in activity prohibited by the criminal code even though the juvenile or youth offender is processed through separate procedures not resulting in a criminal conviction.

Standard 16.10
Presentence Reports

Each State should enact by 1975 legislation authorizing a presentence investigation in all cases and requiring it:

1. In all felonies.
2. In all cases where the offender is a minor.
3. As a prerequisite to a sentence of confinement in any case.

The legislation should require disclosure of the presentence report to the defendant, his counsel, and the prosecutor.

Standard 16.11

Probation Legislation

Each State should enact by 1975 probation legislation (1) providing probation as an alternative for all offenders; and (2) establishing criteria for (a) the granting of probation, (b) probation conditions, (c) the revocation of probation, and (d) the length of probation.

Criteria for the granting of probation should be patterned after Sec. 7.01 of the Model Penal Code and should:

1. Require probation over confinement unless specified conditions exist.

2. State factors that should be considered in favor of granting probation.

3. Direct the decision on granting probation toward factors relating to the individual offender rather than to the offense.

Criteria for probation conditions should be patterned after Sec. 301.1 of the Model Penal Code and should:

1. Authorize but not require the imposition of a range of specified conditions.

2. Require that any condition imposed in an individual case be reasonably related to the correctional program of the defendant and not unduly restrictive of his liberty or incompatible with his constitutional rights.

3. Direct that conditions be fashioned on the basis of factors relating to the individual offender rather than to the offense committed.

Criteria and procedures for revocation of probation should provide that probation should not be revoked unless:

1. There is substantial evidence of a violation of one of the conditions of probation;

2. The probationer is granted notice of the alleged violation, access to official records regarding his case, the right to be represented by counsel including the

right to appointed counsel if he is indigent, the right to subpoena witnesses in his own behalf, and the right to confront and cross-examine witnesses against him; and

3. The court provides the probationer a written statement of the findings of fact, the reasons for the revocation, and the evidence relied upon.

In defining the term for which probation may be granted, the legislation should require a specific term not to exceed the maximum sentence authorized by law except that probation for misdemeanants should not exceed one year. The court should be authorized to discharge a person from probation at any time.

The legislation should authorize an appellate court on the initiation of the defendant to review decisions that deny probation, impose conditions, or revoke probation. Such review should include determination of the following:

1. Whether the decision is consistent with statutory criteria.

2. Whether the decision is unjustifiably disparate in comparison with cases of a similar nature.

3. Whether the decision is excessive or inappropriate.

4. Whether the manner in which the decision was arrived at is consistent with statutory and constitutional requirements.

Standard 16.12

Commitment Legislation

Each State should enact, in conjunction with the implementation of Standard 16.1, legislation governing the commitment, classification, and transfer of offenders sentenced to confinement. Such legislation should include:

1. Provision requiring that offenders sentenced to confinement be sentenced to the custody of the chief executive officer of the correctional agency rather than to any specific institution.

2. Requirement that sufficient information be developed about an individual offender and that assignment to facility, program, and other decisions affecting the offender be based on such information.

3. Authorization for the assignment or transfer of offenders to facilities or programs administered by the agency, local subdivisions of government, the Federal Government, other States, or private individuals or organizations.

4. Prohibition against assigning or transferring juveniles to adult institutions or assigning nondelinquent juveniles to delinquent institutions.

5. Authorization for the transfer of offenders in need of specialized treatment to institutions that can provide it. This should include offenders suffering from physical defects or disease, mental problems, narcotic addiction, or alcoholism.

6. Provision requiring that the decision to assign an offender to a particular facility or program shall not in and of itself affect the offender's eligibility for parole or length of sentence.

7. A requirement that the correctional agency develop through rules and regulations (a) criteria for the assignment of an offender to a particular facility and (b) a procedure allowing the offender to participate in and seek administrative

review of decisions affecting his assignment or transfer to a particular facility or program.

Standard 16.13

Prison Industries

By 1975, each State with industrial programs operated by or for correctional agencies should amend its statutory authorization for these programs so that, as applicable, they do not prohibit:

1. Specific types of industrial activity from being carried on by a correctional institution.

2. The sale of products of prison industries on the open market.

3. The transport or sale of products produced by prisoners.

4. The employment of offenders by private enterprise at full market wages and comparable working conditions.

5. The payment of full market wages to offenders working in State-operated prison industries.

Standard 16.14

Community-Based Programs

Legislation should be enacted immediately authorizing the chief executive officer of the correctional agency to extend the limits of confinement of a committed offender so the offender can participate in a wide variety of community-based programs. Such legislation should include these provisions:

1. Authorization for the following programs:

   a. Foster homes and group homes primarily for juvenile and youthful offenders.

   b. Prerelease guidance centers and halfway houses.

   c. Work-release programs providing that rates of pay and other conditions of employment are similar to those of free employees.

   d. Community-based vocational training programs, either public or private.

   e. Participation in academic programs in the community.

   f. Utilization of community medical, social rehabilitation, vocational rehabilitation, or similar resources.

   g. Furloughs of short duration to visit relatives and family, contact prospective employers, or for any other reason consistent with the public interest.

2. Authorization for the development of community-based residential centers either directly or through contract with governmental agencies or private parties, and authorization to assign offenders to such centers while they are participating in community programs.

3. Authorization to cooperate with and contract for a wide range of community resources.

4. Specific exemption for participants in community-based work programs from State-use and other laws restricting employment of offenders or sale of "convict-made" goods.

5. Requirement that the correctional agency promulgate rules and regulations specifying conduct that will result in revocation of community-based privileges and procedures for such revocation. Such procedures should be governed by the same standards as disciplinary proceedings involving a substantial change in status of the offender.

Standard 16.15
Parole Legislation

Each State should enact by 1975 legislation (1) authorizing parole for all committed offenders and (2) establishing criteria and procedures for (a) parole eligibility, (b) granting of parole, (c) parole conditions, (d) parole revocation, and (e) length of parole.

In authorizing parole for all committed offenders the legislation should:

1. Not exclude offenders from parole eligibility on account of the particular offense committed.

2. Not exclude offenders from parole eligibility because of number of convictions or past history of parole violations.

3. Authorize parole or aftercare release for adults and juveniles from all correctional institutions.

4. Authorize the parole of an offender at any time unless a minimum sentence is imposed by the court in connection with an extended term (Standard 5.3), in which event parole may be authorized prior to service of the minimum sentence with the permission of the sentencing court.

In establishing procedures for the granting of parole to both adults and juveniles the legislation should require:

1. Parole decisions by a professional board of parole, independent of the institutional staff. Hearing examiners should be empowered to hear and decide parole cases under policies established by the board.

2. Automatic periodic consideration of parole for each offender.

3. A hearing to determine whether an offender is entitled to parole at which the offender may be represented by counsel and present evidence.

4. Agency assistance to the offender in developing a plan for his parole.

5. A written statement by the board explaining decisions denying parole.

6. Authorization for judicial review of board decisions.

7. Each offender to be released prior to the expiration of his term because of the accumulation of "good time" credits to be released to parole supervision until the expiration of his term.

8. Each offender to be released on parole no later than 90 days prior to the expiration of his maximum term.

In establishing criteria for granting parole the legislation should be patterned after Sec. 305.9 of the Model Penal Code and should:

1. Require parole over continued confinement unless specified conditions exist.

2. Stipulate factors that should be considered by the parole board in arriving at its decision.

3. Direct the parole decision toward factors relating to the individual offender and his chance for successful return to the community.

4. Not require a favorable recommendation by the institutional staff, the court, the police, or the prosecutor before parole may be granted.

In establishing criteria for parole conditions, the legislation should be patterned after Sec. 305.13 of the Model Penal Code and should:

1. Authorize but not require the imposition of specified conditions.

2. Require that any condition imposed in an individual case be reasonably related to the correctional program of the defendant and not unduly restrictive of his liberty or incompatible with his constitutional rights.

3. Direct that conditions be fashioned on the basis of factors relating to the individual offender rather than to the offense committed.

In establishing criteria and procedures for parole revocation, the legislation should provide:

1. A parolee charged with a violation should not be detained unless there is a hearing at which probable cause to believe that the parolee did violate a condition of his parole is shown.

   a. Such a hearing should be held promptly near the locality to which the parolee is paroled.

   b. The hearing should be conducted by an impartial person other than the parole officer.

   c. The parolee should be granted notice of the charges against him, the right to present evidence, the right to confront and cross-examine witnesses against him, and the right to be represented by counsel or to have counsel appointed for him if he is indigent.

2. Parole should not be revoked unless:

   a. There is substantial evidence of a violation of one of the conditions of parole.

   b. The parolee, in advance of a hearing on revocation, is informed of the nature of the violation charged against him and is given the opportunity to examine the State's evidence against him.

   c. The parolee is provided with a hearing on the charge of revocation.

Hearing examiners should be empowered to hear and decide parole revocation cases under policies established by the parole board. At the hearing the parolee should be given the opportunity to present evidence on his behalf, to confront and cross-examine witnesses against him, and to be represented by counsel or to have counsel appointed for him if he is indigent.

  d. The board or hearing examiner provides a written statement of findings, the reasons for the decision, and the evidence relied upon.

3. Time spent under parole supervision until the date of the violation for which parole is revoked should be credited against the sentence imposed by the court.

4. Judicial review of parole revocation decisions should be available to offenders.

In defining the term for which parole should be granted, the legislation should prohibit the term from extending beyond the maximum prison term imposed on the offender by the sentencing court and should authorize the parole board to discharge the parolee from parole at any time.

Standard 16.16
Pardon Legislation

Each State by 1975 should enact legislation detailing the procedures (1) governing the application by an offender for the exercise of the pardon powers, and (2) for exercise of the pardon powers.

Standard 16.17

Collateral Consequences of a Criminal Conviction

Each State should enact by 1975 legislation repealing all mandatory provisions depriving persons convicted of criminal offenses of civil rights or other attributes of citizenship. Such legislation should include:

1. Repeal of all existing provisions by which a person convicted of any criminal offense suffers civil death, corruption of blood, loss of civil rights, or forfeiture of estate or property.

2. Repeal of all restrictions on the ability of a person convicted of a criminal offense to hold and transfer property, enter into contracts, sue and be sued, and hold offices of private trust.

3. Repeal of all mandatory provisions denying persons convicted of a criminal offense the right to engage in any occupation or obtain any license issued by government.

4. Repeal of all statutory provisions prohibiting the employment of ex-offenders by State and local governmental agencies.

Statutory provisions may be retained or enacted that:

1. Restrict or prohibit the right to hold public office during actual confinement.

2. Forfeit public office upon confinement.

3. Restrict the right to serve on juries during actual confinement.

4. Authorize a procedure for the denial of a license or governmental privilege to selected criminal offenders when there is a direct relationship between the

offense committed or the characteristics of the offender and the license or privilege sought.

The legislation also should:

1. Authorize a procedure for an ex-offender to have his conviction expunged from the record.

2. Require the restoration of civil rights upon the expiration of sentence.

40

The Legal Challenge to Corrections: The Context of Change

FRED COHEN

Until quite recently those who administer our correctional systems could confidently pursue their varied goals by virtually any technique deemed satisfactory to them. True, there existed internal scrutiny and review; legislative committees or citizen groups might ask occasional questions, but the courts rarely interfered and legislative guidelines on basic policy and decision-making criteria either were nonexistent or so vague as to be nonexistent.

This situation has not changed drastically, but there are today some clear signs that the correctional process—the imposition, execution, and relief from criminal sanctions—no longer will remain outside the domain of the rule of law. That this is neither idle threat nor wishful thinking is documented by such factors as the increase in the volume and the variety of challenges to correctional decision-making in the courts, the findings and recommendations of the President's Commission on Law Enforcement and Administration of Justice, the work of the American Bar Association's Project on Minimum Standards for Criminal Justice, the increasing concern about correctional decision-making in legal education and

SOURCE. *The Legal Challenge to Corrections*, Joint Commission on Correctional Manpower and Training (Consultant's Paper), Washington, D.C., March 1969, pp. 1–14. Reprinted with permission of the author and the American Correctional Association.

legal scholarship, even a hint of concern in the legislatures, and, perhaps most significantly, the concern of correctional administrators themselves.

The primary purpose of this work is to describe and analyze legal trends in the area of corrections and to offer some suggestions about how corrections might respond. However, in order to do this properly it is necessary first to broaden the inquiry beyond corrections, indeed beyond the criminal process. To begin with sentencing and then proceed to probation, imprisonment, parole, and restoration of civil rights would perpetuate the false notion that corrections somehow stands apart from the rest of the legal system and is unaffected by change occurring elsewhere.

The correctional process has not suddenly been singled out from the criminal justice system, found wanting, and made the isolated object of legal concern. Quite the contrary. Concern about how public officials make decisions, how the government and public institutions seek to extend their aid or apply sanctions, is occurring on a broad front. Before surveying developments in the criminal justice process, we shall briefly examine four areas of governmental activity that are currently undergoing legal challenge to the existing order. The developments in these areas provide clues for the future development of the broad field of corrections.

PUBLIC WELFARE

The vast public welfare field is being scrutinized for procedural regularity, for rationality and consistency, and for basic fairness in decision-making. The long-obscured issue of "poverty in the midst of plenty" has surfaced, and among the dozens of crucial items competing for attention is a heightened sensitivity to bureaucratic arbitrariness. The cliches of "right" and "privilege" are giving way to a concept of *entitlement,* a concept that implies that those who are to be helped have a legitimate interest, and must have a voice in the protection of *expectations* aroused by government. Perhaps most important is the current trend of asking *what is happening:* who is making and applying what policy and with what effect? The old shibboleths are not dead, but they are being engaged.

Lawyers have involved themselves in the problems of the poor in far greater numbers than ever before. The Office of Economic Opportunity has funded 250 programs employing nearly 1,600 full-time lawyers in 48 states. In addition to providing the needed day-to-day legal assistance to the poor—290,000 cases in fiscal 1967—the Legal Services Programs have achieved some victories of major impact. Perhaps foremost are the five cases that struck down continued residence as a precondition to the receipt of welfare benefits. The issue now is on appeal to the Supreme Court. If the Court affirms, the Office of Economic Opportunity has conservatively estimated it will add about $130 million to the income of poverty-stricken families. Other major judicial successes have included prohibition of the punitive eviction and an injunction against a threatened reduction of medical benefits to indigents in California.

JUVENILE JUSTICE SYSTEM

In many ways the juvenile justice system is more pertinent to corrections than the field of public welfare. To date, the major legal challenges have been aimed at the *adjudicatory* stage of the juvenile process. The intake and custody stages along with the dispositional-correctional stages have not been challenged in so basic a fashion as the process for determining *how* a youngster may be labelled delinquent. Nonetheless, the judicial activity in the juvenile field has some clear messages for corrections.

The major decision is, of course, *In re Gault,* where the Supreme Court held that juveniles had the right to notice of charges, the right to counsel, the right of confrontation and cross-examination, and the protection of the privilege against self-incrimination.

For our purposes, it is more important to emphasize what motivated the Court to take action in a field it had virtually ignored since its inception than to analyze the niceties of the decision. Justice Fortas, writing for the majority of the Court, acknowledged that "the highest motives and most enlightened impulses" led to the creation of the juvenile court movement. However, the gap between expectation and performance, whether caused by inadequate theory or inadequate resources, proved to be so wide as to invoke the Court's power to impress constitutional safeguards on the process. The key factor is the Court's emphasis on the wide gap between what the juvenile system set out to do—provide "help" in a nontraumatic and nonstigmatic proceeding—and what it has been able to do —become, in effect, a criminal process for children offering neither effective help nor procedural safeguards.

Gault speaks to corrections on yet another point. The juvenile process managed to avoid the procedural requirements of the criminal justice process by the rather simple expedient of calling itself a *civil* proceeding. The judge was viewed as a "wise parent" acting only in the best interests of the child and representing the state in its *parens patriae* capacity. Since a child was not charged with or convicted of a "crime" but merely found in the condition of delinquency, and since the state sought only to help and not to punish, the proceedings could be denominated *civil* and the child spared the rigors of the criminal law.

In *Gault,* however, the Court took notice of the fact that delinquency is indeed a stigmatic term and that, call it what you will, the process involves a deprivation of liberty in its most fundamental sense. The Court served notice that labels are not the final determinants of legal safeguards, that the use of such words as *custody* instead of *arrest, detention* instead of *jail,* and *adjudication* instead of *conviction* does not nullify the necessity for basic fairness.

A third lesson is to be derived from *Gault* only by implication or, as some lawyers put it, by a "creative reading" of the case. There appears to be an unarticulated assumption that when laws are enacted to provide help, the basic text of the law must of necessity be quite broad. Juvenile Codes, for example, often include as a condition of delinquency one who "habitually so deports himself as to injure or endanger the morals or health of himself or others; or habitually associates with vicious and immoral persons."

Such broad categories of delinquency have a pervasive effect on the way in which the system is administered. They represent a grant of vast discretion to law enforcement and prosecution, the courts, and the correctional process. The ostensibly legitimate range of choices available to those who invoke, apply, and administer the available sanctions is so great that who is screened in or out of the process becomes a matter of idiosyncratic choice. The point is that such a broad grant of authority permits those who operate within the system to develop their own policy, for good or evil, and also allows them to operate in a random, *ad hoc* fashion and perhaps "discover" policy by looking back to determine what has been done.

While *Gault* does not directly address itself to the problem of statutory ambiguity, at a minimum, it assumes the involvement of more attorneys in the juvenile process, and, as more attorneys begin to represent juveniles, it is inevitable that vague statutes—like those that abound in the area of corrections—will be challenged. Corrections would be well advised to compare the law of its own existence with that of the juvenile process. It will be discovered that in probation and parole the policy and criteria governing the grant, the supervisory period, and termination are so vague as to provide little or no direction to those in authority or to those whose lives are sought to be regulated.

COMMITMENT OF THE MENTALLY ILL

The public mental health field shares many of the characteristics of the correctional process:

1. It holds itself out as a "helping" field.
2. It has available the use of officially sanctioned coercion to achieve its objectives.
3. There is little or no agreement on objectives: "cure," "remission," "resocialization," "protection of the community and/or the individual" all compete for primacy.
4. The field is woefully underfinanced and, as a consequence, is poorly staffed.
5. There is some distrust of law and legal process and an emphasis on relaxed procedures and the "expertise" of the treaters.
6. There is an increasing emphasis on the need for prevention, early diagnosis, and community treatment.

The public mental health field has not experienced the same form of legal challenge as public welfare and the juvenile process. Only recently has legal scholarship turned its attention to the area. The courts, for the most part, have been silent. Curiously, the mental health movement has managed to keep the issues on substance and to bring the debate to the legislative arena, an arena many believe to be more appropriate than the judicial for mental health *and corrections.*

The civil commitment process, however, will not long escape legal challenge. There simply are too many people who are deprived of their liberty for too long by procedures that are at least questionable and who receive "help" that may be little more than custodial and "tranquilizing." The civil commitment process is disturbingly like the juvenile process: "help" is more an expectation than reality, administrators exercise a vast and unreviewable discretion, and labels are used to camouflage actual occurrences.

By highlighting these issues in a work that is concerned with law, there is a natural inference to be drawn that law and lawyers will provide *the* answers. No such implication is intended. Indeed, the author is convinced by observation that lawyers have little notion either of their own role or of how to protect their clients in the civil commitment process. However, the lamentable fact is that if fair and discriminating decisions are not made by those who administer this or any other "helping" system, lawyers and the legal process are the only viable alternative. The basic mission of the legal process is, after all, to perform an *individualizing* function; to translate the generalities of legislation into the specific terms of a case. When the case involves an individual faced with the prospect of a loss of liberty and of the social consequences of the label "mentally ill," we must insist on accuracy and fairness.

STUDENT RIGHTS

Only recently has the term "student rights" begun to acquire any meaning. In the past, no one seriously questioned the power of administrators to expel a student without notice and without the semblance of a hearing. The courts not only expressed a toleration for arbitrary action but approved it. In an early New York case, the state court actually upheld the discipline of a university student because she was found to be not "a typical Syracuse girl." In 1917, a student was not permitted to register for his senior year at Columbia University because of his antiwar and antidraft speeches. The New York court held that he must not be permitted to inculcate "impressionable young men" with the "poison of his disloyalty"; his behavior was characterized as "culpable and cowardly."

Charles Frankel recently stated, "it has finally come to be accepted that American colleges and universities are in trouble." The student movement can hardly be blamed as the cause—to do so is akin to blaming the doctor for the illness he diagnoses—but it surely has exposed the problems and made reform an urgent issue. The movement, however, whether judged successful or not, has succeeded in exposing the inner workings of the university. Student apathy is giving way to activism; the separation of the university from the community is being breached; university students are demanding an end to the *in loco parentis* theory; and administrators and faculty have been forced to confront the reality of their behavior instead of continuing in the comfort of ritualistic adherence to the past.

It was the civil rights movement that first brought the issue of procedural and substantive arbitrariness of university officials into the judicial spotlight. The leading case is *Dixon v. Alabama State Board of Education,* which involved the expulsion of students from a tax-supported college after their participation in civil rights activities. The students were not given notice of the "charges" against them nor were they given any opportunity to explain their conduct. Expulsion was upheld by the district court on the basis that petitioners had no *vested right* to attend the college. The court said that the regulations of the board of education indicated that attendance was based on a contract theory, and that students waived the right to notice and hearing as a condition of attendance.

The court of appeals quoted the pertinent regulation:

Attendance at any college is on the basis of a mutual decision of the student's parents and of the college. . . . Just as a student may choose to withdraw from a particular college at any time for any personally determined reason, the college may at any time decline to continue to accept responsibility for the supervision and service to any student with whom the relationship becomes unpleasant and difficult.

and added its own interpretation:

We do not read this provision to clearly indicate an intent on the part of the student to waive notice and a hearing before expulsion. If, however, we should so assume, it nevertheless remains true that the state cannot condition the granting of even a privilege upon renunciation of the constitutional right to procedural due process.

The court did not allow itself to become enmeshed in the right-privilege distinction that clogs analysis of correctional decision-making. Rather, it held that a student has an "interest" in his continued attendance, described in the following terms:

The precise nature of the interest involved is the right to remain at a public institution of higher learning in which the plaintiffs were students in good standing. It requires no argument to demonstrate that education is vital and, indeed, basic to civilized society. Without sufficient education the plaintiffs would not be able to earn an adequate livelihood to enjoy life to the fullest, or to fulfill as completely as possible the duties and responsibilities of citizens.

Once the court had determined that the petitioners had an interest that had been adversely affected, and had noted that there had been no showing that other colleges were willing to accept petitioners, it followed that the expulsion of petitioners without notice and hearing constituted a denial of due process prohibited by the Fourteenth Amendment.

Beyond the quest for procedural fairness, the student rights movement has come to include a quest for broader participation in the decision-making processes of the university. Students seek to influence the curriculum, the character of the teaching staff, the rules of campus life, the composition of future student bodies—in short, the nature of the university. The pressure for some form of "university democracy," in turn, exerts, pressure on existing administrative structures and the composition of policy-making and administrative bodies, from the trustees to the faculty committees.

It is doubtful if corrections will experience a similar movement from "within." However, the criminal offender and the student join voices in saying that they are not merely objects to be acted upon. The search is for a new identity and, as a consequence, a set of new responsibilities that arise from a set of new relationships. Just as public universities can no longer hand out "education" to benign and grateful students, corrections may find it increasingly difficult to dispense "correction" to the nonperson described by such terms as "felon" or "convict."

INTERRELATIONSHIPS

Our consideration of the developments in public welfare and student rights was designed to illustrate movements of the "disadvantaged" in the direction of establishing new relationships with public institutions and the government as well as a new sense of identity. If public welfare and student rights are somewhat marginal to corrections, the juvenile process and the commitment of the mentally ill are more parallel tracks. The latter areas represent alternatives to the traditional criminal process and, as pointed out, are sufficiently analogous to corrections to view developments there as a barometer for correctional change. The lesson seems clear: persons who are classed in a deprived or dependent status— whether it be welfare recipient, student, juvenile, or mentally ill—are seeking to alter the social and legal consequences of that status. Under particular stress is the notion that when a governmental or public entity seeks to provide help or largess, the grateful recipient has little or no procedural or substantive claims. The quest in these areas is for greater personal autonomy, a voice in the management of these programs, and a demand that decision-makers be accountable. There is no reason to believe that corrections will remain immune from similar challenges. Yet, one detects in corrections no awareness and no concern with legal developments unless they are immediate, direct, and crisis-provoking.

THE CRIMINAL JUSTICE PROCESS AND CONSTITUTIONAL CHALLENGE

One message for corrections is so clear that it deserves mention at the outset without regard to sequence or a detailed foundation. In the late 1950s and early 1960s anyone giving even superficial attention to what the judiciary—the Supreme Court in particular—was saying to law enforcement could hardly misunderstand the message. Time and again the Court reviewed practices that it characterized as "shocking the conscience," "measures flagrantly, deliberately, and persistently violating fundamental principles." Yet agencies of law enforcement and prosecution pressed close to the line of constitutionality as a matter of regular practice and appeared to overstep the line with sufficient regularity to finally move the Court to a series of broad, reformatory rulings.

An instructive example is the Court's treatment of the Fourth Amendment's protection against unlawful search and seizure. Until 1949, the Court's position was that the Fourth Amendment applied only to the federal government and that objections to the "search and seizure" activity of *state* officials would be reviewed, if at all, by the more abstract and *more permissive* standard of "fundamental fairness" embodied in the "due process" clause of the Fourteenth Amendment. In *Wolf v. Colorado,* the Court found that the security of one's privacy against arbitrary intrusion by the *state* police was "implicit in the concept of ordered liberty" and was required by the standard of fairness. This, in effect, made the substance of the Fourth Amendment applicable to the states through the operation of the due process clause.

Now, suppose a state agency did violate the security of one's privacy and seized evidence later used to convict that person of a crime. Did any constitutional rule operate to exclude such evidence from trial or require a reversal if the evidence was admitted and proved to be a factor in the conviction? *Wolf* said no, and thus stopped short of requiring that the states adopt what is known as the "exclusionary rule." The Court in *Wolf* said, in effect, we serve notice that basic rights are involved and while we are aware of the regularity with which they are violated, we prefer that the states act on their own to design methods to effectively control unconscionable police activity.

Twelve years later Justice Clark, a former Attorney General, wrote the historical opinion in *Mapp v. Ohio.* Justice Clark observed that some states had indeed moved to provide procedures that would protect the right of privacy guaranteed in the Fourth Amendment, but that where means other than the exclusionary rule prevailed (e.g., police disciplinary proceedings, civil suits for damages) they have been "worthless and futile." He further stated that once the right of privacy was recognized as enforceable against the states, the Court could "no longer permit that right to be an empty promise"; it could "no longer permit it to be revocable at the whim of any police officer who, in the name of law enforcement, chooses to suspend its enjoyment."

With these words, the Court embarked on a series of decisions that would alter the entire course of federal-state relations in the field of law enforcement. *Mapp* was the opening shot in the battle to reform law enforcement practices. Yet if a positive response from the state legislatures was to be expected, one searches in vain for it. To date, no state has adopted a comprehensive code of prearraignment procedures.

Corrections today appears to be in a position similar to that of law enforcement prior to 1961, that is, prior to *Mapp.* As was indicated earlier, the messages are being relayed from a variety of sources—courts, commissions, scholars—and the question is *how* corrections will respond. Should corrections choose to stand pat—as enforcement agencies did in the period between *Wolf* and *Mapp*—increased judicial intervention in the area is likely. If there is sweeping judicial activity in corrections, it will no doubt precipitate a crisis, as the Court's *Escobedo* and *Miranda* decisions did in the pre-arraignment enforcement process.

That we must often have crisis to stimulate change is a lamentable fact. If corrections is convinced of the need for change, and is able to mobilize itself in the precrisis stage, one can predict that it will be able to control its own destiny to a far greater extent than if it waits. Crisis tends to polarize opinion and to take the decisions away from those who are most directly affected. How corrections properly might react now—and therefore guide its own future—depends largely on an understanding of the requirements of the due process clause of the Fourteenth Amendment, which constitutes the template against which changes in the correctional process must be measured.

DUE PROCESS NORMS

Why is it that lawyers and courts persist in raising challenges to the *manner* in which decisions are reached? Are words of caution, indeed of restriction, offered only to denigrate the motives of those who wish only the best for the people put in their charge? Why should those who seek to help be forced to go over legally imposed hurdles that impede, and at times eliminate, the possibility of help? Even if law and legal process do some good, are they worth the costs involved?

These, of course, are fundamental questions. They require rather complex answers and—as we shall see—where answers are possible, they relate to specific areas rather than to the broad area of social control through law. An effort must be made to deal with these questions because unless the field of corrections has some notion of what is meant by the rule of law and the objectives of legal challenge, there is little possibility for meaningful change.

As the *Mapp* case indicates, the due process clause can serve as a conduit through which specific protections of the Bill of Rights are made applicable to the states. Through the due process clause, the privilege against self-incrimination, protection against illegal search and seizure, the right to a speedy trial, the right to compulsory process, the right of confrontation and cross-examination, protection against cruel and unusual punishment, right to counsel, and the right to a jury trial, all have been made applicable to the states.

But the due process clause is more than a mere conduit; it also has an independent content. Justice Douglas was referring to this independent content when he wrote, "Due process, to use the vernacular, is the wild card that can be put to such use as the judges choose." Thus far, the judges have not often played their wild card in encounters with the correctional process. Those encounters are increasing, and with the "wild card" available it is important that corrections understand what values are sought to be protected by due process norms, to estimate if current procedures achieve those values, and, if not, how best to correct and remodel them.

Perhaps the most basic explanation of the independent content aspect of due process—and clearly the most open-ended—is *fundamental fairness.* From the term "fundamental fairness" flow such concepts as "impartiality," "honesty," "conformity with existing rules," "objectivity," and "proper balancing of competing interests." Although these overlapping concepts give almost no direction on solving a specific problem, they do set a tone; they emphasize the need to seek *normative* guidance as opposed to the most logical or efficient solution. Functionally, due process norms assume that there are and must be limits on the power of government. Where due process has not received specific application, as Justice Douglas has said, it serves as a healthy reminder to officials that power is a heady thing and that there are limits beyond which it is not safe to go.

Much of the work of lawyers and legal tribunals involves the reconstruction of past events—the fact-finding process—as a basic component of the adjudicatory (or dispute-settlement) process. Due process is one of the controls on the ascertainment and the use of facts, and this control has been expressed in terms of assuring *reliability* in fact finding by use of the twin concepts of *notice* and *hearing.* The most fundamental aspect of due process is that no person shall be deprived of life, liberty, or property without an opportunity to *know* and *to be heard.* The right to be informed and the right to challenge—to be a participant in official decisions respecting an individual's interests—is at the core of due process.

By way of contrast, spokesmen for the correctional process often emphasize the *conclusion* (e.g., a "bad risk," "immature," "unfit to remain at large") and the *good faith* or *expertise* of the person making a decision. While facts and conclusions need not be at war with each other, too often this is the case. Conclusions, particularly when couched in diagnostic or legal terms—or when used as manipulative labels—may easily divert our attention from an inquiry into the factual foundation for the conclusion. It is much more convenient to say that a person is "sick" or "dangerous" or "not ready for parole" than to establish the facts and the steps used to arrive at such a conclusion.

It is clear that the fundamental requirements of notice and a hearing and other residual norms, such as visibility and consistency, actually impair efficiency and effectiveness: *and that is precisely what they are intended to accomplish.* Orderliness, the step-by-step development of a case, an active role for counsel and his client, and demands for proof, require more time than an *ex parte* determination of a case. The considerable emphasis, then, that correctional decision-makers place on efficiency, effectiveness, and their expertise and conclusions creates a tension with due process norms. This particular problem pervades every aspect of corrections and legal change and should be kept in mind as we consider in detail the various stages of the correctional process. It should be remembered that due process norms are concerned with values that transcend the essential mission of the criminal law. Society seeks to prevent or, more realistically, reduce criminality and to discover, apprehend, and apply sanctions to those who are not deterred. Due process norms dictate that this be accomplished within a set of rules that assure the dignity of the individual and require that government observe the charter of its own existence.

41

Corrections and Legal Change: Probation and Parole

FRED COHEN

Probation and parole are, of course, not without important distinctions.[1] Probation evolved as an alternative to imprisonment,[2] while parole evolved as an alternative to continued imprisonment. Where probation generally is administered at the local level and as a component of the judicial system, parole is generally administered at the state level and by an administrative agency that is part of the executive branch of government.[3] There are broad differences in the characteristics of probationers and parolees; probationers tend to have committed less serious offenses and exhibit fewer recidivist tendencies.

Despite these differences it is clear that probation and parole "now share

SOURCE. *The Legal Challenge to Corrections,* Joint Commission on Correctional Manpower and Training (Consultant's Paper), Washington, D.C., March 1969, pp. 26–63. Reprinted with permission of the author and the American Correctional Association.

[1] This section will not give special attention to misdemeanor parole or conditional pardon.

[2] Many jurisdictions permit a defendant to be incarcerated prior to the initiation of probation supervision. *See, e.g.,* MODEL PENAL CODE, §301.1(3) (P.O.D. 1962) which provides for a term of imprisonment not to exceed thirty days. Under classical probation theory, this practice is a contradiction in terms.

[3] *See* NATIONAL PAROLE INSTITUTES, A SURVEY OF THE ORGANIZATION OF PAROLE SYSTEMS (1963).

precisely the same goals and use precisely the same techniques . . . "[4] Both devices pursue the goals of rehabilitation, surveillance, and economy; both assist the agencies of law enforcement, prosecution, and institutional confinement; conditions are attached to the grant of either; the community serves as the correctional arena in both; and the individual is in each case under the supervision of someone who has access to coercive authority.[5]

Since we are concerned here primarily with legal issues, and not with issues like appropriate casework supervision, caseload distribution, individual vs. group therapy—that is, correctional strategy[6]—such differences as do exist between probation and parole have little direct relevance. Indeed, as we shall see, the legal issues involved in the granting, supervision, and termination of probation and parole are virtually identical. *The legally relevant situation involves authoritative decision-makers exercising a vast discretion within a broad statutory framework in the regulation of individuals who are convicted of a crime and who either desire their liberty or who seek to retain it.*[7]

DYNAMICS AND COMPONENTS OF DECISION-MAKING

Probation and parole decision-making occurs within a statutory framework that characteristically is vague both as to basic objectives and specific criteria. This is true whether we refer to the supervisory process, the decision to grant or deny, or the decision to terminate. In Texas, for example, probation may be granted "when it shall appear . . . that the ends of justice and the best interests of the public as well as the defendant will be subserved thereby."[8] Parole, on the other hand, may be awarded "only for the best interest of society."[9]

Probation decision-making, which is simply a specific aspect of sentencing, typically will be restricted by statutory exclusions relating either to the nature of the offense, the prior criminality of the offender, or the number of years assessed in the current proceedings.[10] Parole decision-making, on the other hand, is limited

---

[4] NEW YORK STATE, PRELIMINARY REPORT OF THE GOVERNOR'S SPECIAL COMMITTEE ON CRIMINAL OFFENDERS 35 (1968). *See also* President's Commission on Law Enforcement and Administration of Justice, TASK FORCE REPORT: CORRECTIONS 60 (1967), hereafter referred to by title.

[5] The existence of these multiple and often conflicting goals will be discussed at another point. For now let it be plain that the writer is in basic disagreement with the usual rhetoric, "Probation and Parole have as their sole purpose rehabilitation of the offender." Sklar, *Law and Practice in Probation and Parole Revocation Hearings,* 55 JOURNAL OF CRIMINAL LAW, CRIMINOLOGY AND POLICE SCIENCE 175, 196 (1964).

[6] Even the standard works in the field make no basic distinction on "treatment strategies." *See, e.g.,* Newman, SOURCEBOOK ON PROBATION, PAROLE AND PARDONS 205–331 (3d ed. 1968).

[7] Some jurisdictions permit the grant of probation without the entry of a verdict or a judgment of conviction. For an excellent discussion of this practice, *see* Skinker v. State, 239 Md. 234, 210 A.2d 716 (1965).

[8] TEXAS CODE CRIM. P. ANN. art. 42.12 §3 (1966).

[9] TEXAS CODE CRIM. P. ANN. art. 42.12 §15(c) (Supp. 1968).

[10] In Texas, if the jury assesses more than ten years, the judge cannot grant probation.

not only by statute but also by the leeway left after the sentencing authority has acted within legislatively defined limits. In some jurisdictions parole is prohibited for persons sentenced for specific felonies or to a life term.[11] Typically, however, eligibility is based on serving some portion of the sentence—one-third or one-half of the maximum—or on completing a minimum term, usually less good-time credits. In some jurisdictions, the offender is immediately eligible for release on parole.

Once we move beyond the basic eligibility factors and the broad policy statements like those in the Texas Code, the law becomes even more vague. Even on such a fundamental question as whether or not a violation must exist before the grant may be terminated, the absence of legislative standards has created needless conflict and confusion in the courts.[12] Before undertaking a consideration of some specific legal issues in probation and parole decision-making, it would be helpful to analyze several matters that pervade the entire subject: (1) the benevolent purpose doctrine; (2) the theories of privilege, contract, and continuing custody; and (3) distinctions between so-called sentencing (granting) decisions and termination (suspension and revocation) decisions.

Benevolent Purpose

The earlier decision of juvenile justice, the mentally ill, and students' rights illustrated both the use of the benevolent purpose doctrine in other areas and its susceptibility to legal challenge. The doctrine also appears in various guises and is put to a variety of uses by and on behalf of corrections. In the context of probation and parole its most fundamental use may be stated in these terms:

1. No governmental entity is required to establish a probation or parole system; and therefore, should one be established, no individual has an enforceable claim to the grant of supervised freedom.

2. When an individual is granted probation or parole, he receives more largess (or less punishment) then that to which he is entitled and therefore cannot complain about the burdens of supervision or the manner in which the grant may be terminated.[13] Perhaps the most fundamental challenge to correctional decision-making processes relates to the continued reliance on the benevolent purpose doctrine.

---

[11] *See* Workman v. Kentucky, 429 S.W.2d 374 (Ky. 1968).

[12] *See, e.g.,* Kaplan v. United States, 234 F.2d 345, 347–48 (8th Cir. 1956) (Probation).

[13] There are, of course, some problems connected with this use of the benevolent purpose doctrine. There are few activities that a government is *required* to undertake. For example, it is not clear that a government is constitutionally required to adopt a penal code or maintain a system of public education or even maintain a municipal police force. While the affirmative duties of government are few, the undertakings of government are too numerous to describe.

To determine the legitimacy of claims raised about the conduct of government programs by determining whether it is required to undertake a particular program is not only to overlook the reality of govermental activity but also to virtually mandate the answer.

The major correctional consequence of adherence to the doctrine can be understood best from an examination of Justice Black's observations in *Williams v. New York,* an important case dealing with sentencing procedures.[14] Justice Black writes, "Retribution is no longer the dominant objective of the criminal law. Reformation and rehabilitation of offenders have become important goals of criminal jurisprudence."[15] He concludes from this "benevolent purpose" of corrections that due process should not be treated as a device for freezing correctional procedure in the mold of trial procedures. To do so, he states, would impair correctional devices like indeterminate sentences, probation, and parole—a position warmly supported by many spokesmen for corrections.[16]

The operating principle that emerges from the use of the benevolent purpose doctrine, then, is that the goals of corrections can best be obtained by the preservation of maximum discretion on the part of judicial and correctional authorities. Discretion, in turn, is maximized by the reduction or elimination of procedural "obstacles;" minimizing the role of the offender or his representative in the decision-making processes; and the maintenance of a statutory framework that is so broad that virtually any decisions can be smuggled through the mythical borders of legislative intent.

One would think, as a matter of both logic *and* sound legal-correctional policy, that precisely the opposite conclusion should flow from Justice Black's observations. That is, as those in authority are granted more power—more freedom of action over the lives of other individuals—there should be more, not less, judicial concern for procedural safeguards. One need not be steeped in the lore of correctional strategies to label inconceivable the idea that corrections would claim that a reign of absolute authority is a prerequisite for adequately inculcating offenders with noncriminal values. And, for those who are tempted to make that argument, consider Justice Douglas' admonition: "Law has reached its finest moments when it has freed men from the unlimited discretion of some ruler, some civil or military official, some bureaucrat. Where discretion is absolute, man has always suffered."[17]

The most fundamental problem, however, with the benevolent purpose doctrine is its basis: the factual assumption that reformation and rehabilitation are

---

[14] 337 U.S. 241 (1949). The *Williams* decision is often cited as authority for the position that there is no constitutional right to disclosure of the presentence report. Actually, it is authority for a more narrow constitutional ruling: *In the absence of a specific request to do so, due process does not require confrontation and cross-examination of persons who have supplied out-of-court information used in the determination of the sentence.* See Rubin, *Sentences Must Be Rationally Explained,* 42 F.R.D. 203, 216 n.27 (1967).

[15] 337 U.S. at 248.

[16] How this impairment would occur and with what consequences is not made clear. In Powell v. Texas, 392 U.S. 514, 530, Justice Marshall wrote, "This court has never held that anything in the Constitution requires that penal sanctions be designed solely to achieve therapeutic or rehabilitative effects. . . . "

[17] United States v. Wunderlich, 342 U.S. 98, 101 (1951) (dissenting opinion).

important goals for corrections. It may well be that they are important *goals,* but there exists impressive evidence that they remain goals and not achievements.[18] As Sol Rubin puts it:

Probation and parole date from the last century, and neither one has been a real success: they are promising devices, but their promise has yet to be fulfilled.

Despite probation and parole and despite the contribution of psychiatry and casework, the picture we have today is, with slight exception, of steady increase in the use of imprisonment, of institutions that are as large or larger than ever they were and for the most part no less secure, and of men serving terms that are ever increasing in length.[19]

The present allocation of funds and manpower for treatment purposes demonstrates a minimal commitment to the rehabilitative ideal. The national profile of corrections reveals that about 80 percent of all "correctional" costs are expended on institutions, with 14.4 percent of all costs going to probation and only 3.5 going to adult parole.[20] In a recent study of correctional personnel conducted by Louis Harris and Associates for the Joint Commission on Correctional Manpower and Training, it was found that no correctional setting receives a positive rating by a majority of the correctional personnel. There is also relatively high agreement on the low level of correctional accomplishments. The study also confirmed the low level of formal training all groups have had in the corrections and criminology, and for administrators, the low level of training in business or public administration.

It may be argued that to demonstrate that corrections has been unable to achieve the goals of reformation and rehabilitation does not necessarily demonstrate that these are not the primary goals. However, it seems clear that probation and parole are concerned with other goals: goals that are neither latent, indirect, nor unintended.[21] For example, when probation is granted on condition that the probationer cooperate with the grand jury[22] or when it is systematically denied unless the accused pleads guilty, the rehabilitative ideal is far from primary.[23]

Indeed, the judge's freedom on the decision to grant probation and the conditions he may impose is such that he is able to pursue virtually any objective that

---

[18] A review of the outcome of correctional programs in 100 studies conducted between 1940 and 1959 disclosed that those studies in which the greatest care had been taken in the experimental design reported either harmful effects of treatment or, more frequently, no change at all. Bailey, *Correctional Outcome: An Evaluation of 100 Reports,* 57 JOURNAL OF CRIMINAL LAW, CRIMINOLOGY AND POLICE SCIENCE 57, 153–60 (1966). These findings also are reported in TASK FORCE REPORT: CORRECTIONS 12 (1967).

[19] Rubin, *The Model Sentencing Act,* 39 NEW YORK UNIVERSITY LAW REVIEW 251 (1964).

[20] TASK FORCE REPORT: CORRECTIONS 115–212 (1967).

[21] One writer describes probation supervision as more a process of verification of behavior than a process of modification of behavior. Diana, *What is Probation?,* 51 JOURNAL OF CRIMINAL LAW, CRIMINOLOGY AND POLICE SCIENCE 189, 197 (1960).

[22] United States v. Worcester, 190 F. Supp. 548, 556 (D. Mass. 1961).

[23] United States v. Wiley, 184 F. Supp. 679, 684 (N.D. Ill. 1960). *See also* People v. Morales, 252 Cal. App. 2d 537, 544, 60 Cal. Rptr. 671, 678, *cert. denied,* 390 U.S. 1034 (1968), involving the imposition of consecutive sentences because the accused demanded a jury trial and was believed to have interposed a frivolous defense.

suits his fancy. In some cases probation is granted in order to assist law enforcement or the prosecutor;[24] in other cases it is granted to assist local merchants in the collection of debts;[25] in still others, it is used to deter student protests or civil rights activities, to facilitate a guilty plea, or (the most common condition) provide for support of the probationer's family.[26]

In parole, virtually the same situation prevails. The board's discretion is at least as broad as that of the sentencing authority and the board members' accountability just as minimal. Any differences that exist between probation and parole do not affect our general proposition; they merely reflect the fact that parole is an alternative to *continued* confinement. Thus, parole decisions may be based on the exigencies of over-crowding in the prison or, the obverse, the need to maintain a given population level in order to maintain prison industry or to justify the budget. Parole may be denied in order to enforce prison discipline or to avoid the risk of incurring criticism of the system. On the other hand, parole may be granted, despite doubts about reformation, as a reward to an informant.[27]

To sum up, probation and parole suffer alike from inadequate financing, marginal training of personnel, unmanageable caseloads, inadequate research, and inadequate and conflicting theory. It also seems clear that rehabilitation and reformation are not primary or exclusive goals; indeed, the term humanitarianism is probably more descriptive of the best of what corrections does under the label of rehabilitation.[28] Among the other goals are surveillance, economy, and direct assistance to the other agencies of criminal justice.[29] The point of all this is not to discredit probation and parole but to demonstrate the fallacy—engendered by the benevolent purpose doctrine—of drawing conclusions about the need for legal safeguards in corrections from a conceptually inaccurate description of the goals of corrections and from a factually inaccurate description of their accomplishments.[30]

---

[24] *See* Sherman v. United States, 356 U.S. 369, 374 n.3 (1958) for an example of use of the suspended sentence as a device to create government informers. *See also* United States v. Worcester, 190 F. Supp. 548, 556 (D. Mass. 1961), in which probation was used to assist the prosecutor with other cases growing out of a massive conspiracy.

[25] *See, e.g.,* Stover v. State, 365 S.W.2d 808, 809 (Tex. Crim. App. 1963).

[26] *See generally* Best & Birzon, *Conditions of Probation: An Analysis* 51 GEORGETOWN LAW JOURNAL 809 (1963).

[27] *See generally* Dawson, *The Decision to Grant or Deny Parole: A Study of Parole Criteria in Law and Practice,* 1966 WASHINGTON UNIVERSITY LAW QUARTERLY 243.

[28] In many jurisdictions probation and parole officers are invested with the power of peace officers. *E.g.,* IOWA CODE ANN. §247.24 (Supp. 1968). In Texas, for example, it is not uncommon for probation officers to wear a pistol. Indeed, many probation officers in Texas, particularly in the more rural settings, are recruited from law enforcement agencies and continue to view themselves as law enforcement officers.

[29] Absent an agreed upon definition of rehabilitation, it is impossible to engage in any meaningful research to determine whether "it" is accomplished. *See* Sherwood, *The Testability of Correctional Goals* 42, in RESEARCH IN CORRECTIONAL REHABILITATION (Joint Commission on Correctional Manpower and Training, 1967).

[30] *See* discussion on page 3 *supra.*

Privilege, Contract, and Continuing Custody

This section deals briefly with the "holy trinity" of legal rationalizations used to deny legal claims brought by probationers and parolees. These rationalizations have been so thoroughly discredited—although too many courts and correctional administrators seem unaware of the fact—that any extensive treatment here is not justified.[31] However, on the assumption that most readers are not lawyers and thus not familiar with the legal literature, a rather summary treatment of these matters seems appropriate.

The privilege, or act of grace, theory is a more specific way of stating one aspect of the benevolent purpose doctrine. Stated simply, the privilege theory—an inheritance from the sovereign prerogative of mercy—is used to deny the existence of any enforceable claims either to the grant, to the conditions of supervision, or to the manner of termination.[32]

A fundamental problem with this theory is that probation is now the most frequent penal disposition just as release on parole is the most frequent form of release from an institution. They bear little resemblance to episodic acts of mercy by a forgiving sovereign. A more accurate view of supervised release is that it is now an integral part of the criminal justice process and shows every sign of increasing popularity. Seen in this light, the question becomes whether legal safeguards should be provided for hundreds of thousands of individuals who daily are processed and regulated by governmental agencies. The system has come to depend on probation and parole as much as do those who are enmeshed in the system. Thus, in dealing with claims raised by offenders, we should make decisions based not on an outworn cliche but on the basis of present-day realities.[33]

The contract-consent theory, an offshoot of the privilege theory, rests on the notion that an offender is "entitled" only to the maximum prison term allowed by law, and probation or an early release from prison is characterized as a

---

[31] *See, e.g.,* Kadish, *The Advocate and the Expert—Counsel in the Peno-Correctional Process,* 45 MINNESOTA LAW REVIEW 803 (1961); Van Alstyne, *The Demise of the Right-Privilege Distinction in Constitutional Law,* 81 HARVARD LAW REVIEW 1439 (1968); Note, *Judicial Review of Probation Conditions,* 67 COLUMBIA LAW REVIEW 181 (1967); Note, *Parole: A Critique of Its Legal Foundations and Conditions,* 38 NEW YORK UNIVERSITY LAW REVIEW 702 (1963).

[32] The privilege theory appears in appellate decisions far more often than the contract and continuing custody theories. *See, e.g.,* Escoe v. Zerbst, 295 U.S. 490, 492–93 (1935) (probation); Ughbanks v. Armstrong, 208 U.S. 481, 487–88 (1908) (parole).

[33] Outside the area of corrections, the right-privilege dichotomy largely has given way to the doctrine of unconstitutional conditions. Under this doctrine, government cannot extend "benefits" and at the same time withhold or dilute constitutional rights. *See, e.g.,* Speiser v. Randall, 357 U.S. 513, 528–29 (1958), in which the state was prohibited from conditioning a tax exemption upon the signing of a loyalty oath. *See also* Wieman v. Updegraff, 344 U.S. 183, 191–192 (1952), holding that constitutional protections extend to discharge of a public employee although he may have no enforceable right to employment. *See generally* Comment, *Unconstitutional Conditions: An Analysis,* 50 GEORGETOWN LAW JOURNAL 234 (1961).

bargained-for agreement, the terms of which are subject to enforcement by the court or the board. This theory is used most often to justify the imposition of a condition that is alleged to be unconstitutional—for example, consent to search and seizure—and to justify summary revocation based on a "breach of contract."

A contract is a freely bargained-for, mutually acceptable, agreement supported by a valuable consideration and arrived at by parties who possess some equivalency in bargaining power. Even if we assume that the offender has the power to refuse the grant,[34] we must recognize that he will accept virtually anything to gain his freedom.[35] The probation or parole "agreement" handed to the offender, then, bears little resemblance to a contract; realistically, it is a notice of conditions arrived at *ex parte* by the court or parole board and no more. Furthermore, it makes little sense to borrow a concept from the world of commerce and put it to work in an area which involves the regulation of liberty. The important legal problems in corrections will be better handled if the particular question involved is analyzed instead of being obscured by this type of makeweight legalism.

Despite the fact that many parole statutes state that the "prisoner at liberty shall be deemed to be in the legal custody of the board," the continuing custody theory is the most specious of the "holy trinity."[36] The premise of this theory is that a parolee is a prisoner who is not actually at liberty but who rather continues to serve his sentence within ever-expanding prison walls. It thus asserts what our senses deny.

The fact is that parole is a grant of conditional liberty and whether or not the prisoner had an enforceable legal claim to it and no matter how "conditional" it may be, he is not within an institution. Indeed, regulations that may be supportable within the prison—for example, denial of sexual access to the prisoner's wife —would be indefensible if applied to a parolee. If parole is in fact doing time behind invisible walls, how can we justify the common practice of denying credit for "street time" should the parolee be reimprisoned? If prison authorities sought to do something similar, it would clearly be the illegal imposition of an additional penalty.

The point here, as with the other theories discussed, is that we continue to rely on a false and inadequate theory to solve difficult legal questions. One might conclude that an individual who is under probation or parole supervision is and should be without substantive or procedural rights. If so, a far better theory and explanation than any reviewed here is required.

---

[34] *Cf.* Biddle v. Perovich, 274 U.S. 480, 482–83 (1927).

[35] In Mansell v. Turner, 14 Utah 2d 352, 353 n.4, 384 P.2d 394, 395 n.4 (1963), the court stated that if the prisoner does not like the condition imposed—leaving the state—he can simply refuse the offer of parole. Needless to say, the writer takes a dim view of this logic, particularly when it is used to answer a challenge to the legality of banishment as a parole condition.

[36] For a discussion and citation to statutes on point, *see* Note, *Parole: A Critique of Its Legal Foundations and Conditions,* 38 NEW YORK UNIVERSITY LAW REVIEW 702, 711–20 (1963).

Sentencing and Revocation Decisions

In the current debate over appropriate procedures in the peno-correctional process, distinctions are often drawn between *sentencing-type decisions*—disposition after verdict or plea and the grant or denial of parole—and *revocation-type decisions*—suspension or revocation of probation or parole. It is argued that a sentencing-type decision is essentially diagnostic and predictive. A factual base, or "history," is necessary, but only as a prelude to a judgment about future behavior. A revocation-type decision, on the other hand, is said to be oriented toward a finding of fault or violation as a prelude to the imposition of a term of confinement. Although the two decisions are not without distinctions, the present tendency to dichotomize them has generated more confusion than clarity and has led to some unfortunate procedural consequences.[37]

The problem exists with the failure to analyze revocation-type decisions. When the term "revocation" is employed, it tends to be used and understood in its prescriptive sense; that is, it implies both that proper grounds have been established to terminate probation or parole *and,* necessarily, that the appropriate disposition of the matter is to imprison the offender. If the judge or the board were *required* to imprison whenever the authority to do so was found—and no such law has been discovered—then a revocation proceeding would indeed be limited to a determination of fault. But properly viewed, every revocation proceeding contains the basic components of a trial, however merged these components may become in practice. Namely, facts must be produced and measured against a norm of conduct—a parole or probation condition or a penal law—and a conclusion must be reached concerning whether the norm was violated; if it was, then another decision—a sentencing-type decision—must be made. In short, a revocation-type decision is not in itself dispositional, but merely includes within it the possibility of making a dispositional or sentencing-type decision.

What are some of the problems generated by the failure to make this analysis? When a revocation proceeding is equated with a sentencing proceding, as it frequently is, the need to properly acquire the authority to resentence—that is, the need to find fault—is submerged, and the appropriate disposition becomes the only focus of the proceeding. This, in turn, triggers the "no rights" thinking that has dominated correctional legal theory, at least until the recent decision in *Mempa v. Rhay.*[38] From this it follows that the role of legal process and the lawyer become insignificant, since sentencing is a process of diagnosis and prediction and the adversary process, it is said, hardly is appropriate.

---

[37] The author first presented this analysis in Cohen, *supra* note 14, Chapter II at 27–29.

[38] 389 U.S. 128 (1967). For a discussion of *Mempa,* see text accompanying notes 14–17, Chapter II, *supra.*

On the other hand, if revocation-type proceedings are viewed exclusively as an inquiry into violation, as assertion and counter-assertion over facts and norms, then the role of legal process and the lawyer are viewed with more favor. This after all is the adversary model in its most pristine form, and the argument for trial-type proceedings and legal representation seems quite supportable.

It is analytically erroneous and operationally unsound to view a revocation-type proceeding either as though it were exclusively a search for a violation or as though it were simply a sentencing-type determination. Every proceeding that may lead to the loss of conditional liberty contains both issues, and to omit or underemphasize one perpetuates a basic error. The solution, as we shall see, requires the adoption of the procedural format that is best suited to the fair and accurate resolution of the questions both of authority to reimprison and of the appropriate disposition. That may well require a trial-type proceeding for the former and a more relaxed proceeding for the latter—but in the era of *Mempa,* not so relaxed as in the past.

Having developed three themes that lie at the heart of any consideration of legal norms and corrections, we turn now to an examination of specific issues.

THE DECISION TO GRANT PROBATION AND PAROLE

Eligibility and the Right to Fair Consideration

Judicial decisions invalidating the legislative decision to exclude certain classes of offenders from eligibility for probation and parole are virtually nonexistent.[39] However, if a legislature should decide to exclude a class of persons on distinctions that have no reasonable relationship to a legitimate governmental objective—for example, redheads or Negroes—the legislation would be invalid either as a denial of equal protection or as an "unreasonable, arbitrary, and capricious" law violating the due process clause of the Fourteenth Amendment.

A more appropriate avenue of inquiry is to assume that an offender is statutorily eligible for probation or parole and then ask if he has any right to be fully and fairly considered for it. At the outset, it should be made clear that while there has been a significant increase in the volume and variety of judicial challenges to correctional decision-making, the revocation process has undergone far more challenges than the granting process.[40] In the wake of *Mempa,* there are now a few judicial decisions that deal with the granting process, but most of what is said here is based more on the author's speculations than on conclusions drawn from reported decisions.

---

[39] But *see* Workman v. Kentucky, 429 S.W.2d 374 (Ky. 1968), which involved a 14-year-old convicted of rape and sentenced to life without parole. The court, in a most unique holding, found that exclusion from parole eligibility a cruel and unusual punishment.

[40] *See generally* Kimball & Newman, *Judicial Intervention in Correctional Decisions: Threat and Response,* 14 CRIME AND DELINQUENCY 1 (1968).

The right to fair consideration for probation is probably now a reality, since *Mempa* requires the presence and participation of counsel at sentencing, and the decision to grant probation is but an aspect of sentencing. Counsel's role in such proceedings undoubtedly will include the presentation of facts with a rationale favorable to the grant of probation, and he will no doubt scrutinize and challenge the work of the probation staff in an effort to influence the disposition. The participation of counsel in these proceedings assures that they will follow an orderly procedural format, which in turn assures that a request for probation will be given fair consideration.

The issue of procedural safeguards in the parole granting or denial process —best symbolized by the issues of legal counsel and the right to a fair hearing —is among the most difficult issues we shall confront. While almost every jurisdiction provides for some type of hearing when parole eligibility is established, a recent survey of parole boards suggests that the word "interview" may be more descriptive of what actually transpires.[41] Indeed, the present parole hearing process is an excellent example of near-total discretion in operation. The parole applicant generally is not officially informed about the reasons for a denial—and consequently cannot know what he must do to prove worthy—and he is denied the usual procedural tools used to influence the decision and subsequently to challenge it.

Creative lawyers already have begun to argue for procedural rights in the parole granting process and, not unexpectedly, they are seeking a logical extension of *Mempa*. Despite several decisions to the contrary,[42] it is difficult to escape the conclusion that the decision to grant or deny parole is indistinguishable from the judicial sentencing decision and that therefore the right to counsel mandate of *Mempa* applies.

Whether a prisoner is entitled to the assistance of an attorney in preparing for a parole hearing or a lawyer's presence at the hearing may or may not be the most significant aspect of the quest for precedural safeguards—but the issue has

[41] NATIONAL PAROLE INSTITUTES, A SURVEY OF THE ORGANIZATION OF PAROLE SYSTEMS (1963).

[42] For example, in *In re Briguglio,* 55 Misc. 2d 584, 585, 285 N.Y.S.2d 883, 884 (Supreme Court 1968), the state court was asked to hold that the parole hearing required by New York law is analogous to a deferred sentencing proceeding, and since *Mempa* spoke directly to deferred sentencing, the prisoner must, by analogy, be allowed representation by counsel at the hearing. The court, however, although plainly troubled by the logic of the prisoner's argument, denied the request for counsel, relying on a supposed distinction begween *giving* and *taking*. The court reasoned that when probation, and presumably parole, is to be terminated, there is a divestment of something that is possessed—freedom. In the matter of granting, if was stated, freedom already has been denied by due process and there is no additional divestment. *Id.* at 586. 285 N.Y.S.2d at 885.

In a recent federal habeas corpus action, a state prisoner, once again relying on *Mempa,* claimed that he had a right to counsel before the Adult Corrections Commission on review of his sentence to determine his possible release on parole. The court stated that "parole consideration is not a proceeding against a defendant within the meaning of constitutional guarantees." Sorenson v. Young, 282 F. Supp. 1009, 1010 (D. Minn. 1968). *See also* Mahoney v. Parole Board, 10 N. J. 269, 276, 90 A.2d 8, 13 (1952), in which the court held that there was no constitutional right to a hearing on the classification of prisoners despite the fact that classification decision involved the formulation of the time for parole consideration.

unparalleled symbolic value. The point is that eventually a brake must be applied to the mass processing of parole applicants, and there must be some technique to bring visibility and accountability to parole decision-making. Providing for the assistance of an attorney and insisting on a hearing, however informal, is one way to accomplish this. There are, of course, other techniques—provide for sufficient, fully trained board members,[43] adequate institutuional staff and program, and effective post-release programs—but these seem quite remote. And even if such improvements occur, one continues to sense the need for someone standing outside the system, wholly identified with the parole applicant and by his presence exercising a continuing challenge on behalf of the individual client.

In the recent expansion of the constitutional right to counsel, the Supreme Court has reached decisions based on a functional analysis: Is there an important role for counsel at this stage of the proceedings?[44] The clearest case for counsel and a fair hearing exists where the parole decision may turn on disputed facts, perhaps a charge of prison misconduct. If the determination of misconduct is made by administrative fiat and then becomes the pivotal factor in the release decision, not allowing challenge to the earlier decision perpetuates the most arbitrary type of regime. Under such circumstances, no one should be surprised when the establishment's exhortations to lawful conduct fall on deaf ears.

Although fact disputes present the clearest case, it may be misleading to single out that situation leaving the impression that "run of the mill" decisions are not

---

Perhaps the most interesting recent decision involving the grant or denial of parole is Mastriani v. Parole Board, 95 N. J. Super. 351, 231 A.2d 236 (1967). The prisoner was given a parole hearing by the Board, and when parole was denied, he complained that the denial was unfair and based on prejudice. The prisoner requested reasons for the denial, but the Board stated that it was not obliged to do so by law and did not elect to do so as a matter of policy. When Mastriani then appealed to the courts, the Board granted him a second hearing "in the light of a new parole plan," and once again parole was denied. The prisoner, pursuing his judicial appeal, now also argued for the right to inspect the Board's records as well as for a more definite statement regarding the denial.

The court did not grant any of the prisoner's requests, but the interesting aspect of this case is the nature of the demands as a portent of the future. Relying on the outworn "parole is a matter of grace" theory, the court simply disallowed the demand for a statement of reasons, for a transcript, and for inspection of the records. It held in effect, that the only process due the prisoner is that found in the statutes and since there was no proof that the Board failed to follow statutory requirements, the prisoner's arguments necessarily failed.

[43] Judge Skelley Wright recently urged the abolition of politically appointed and politically influenced parole boards. Instead, he would substitute a professional correctional agency. *See* Wright, *The Need for Education in the Law of Criminal Corrections,* 2 VALPARAISO LAW REVIEW 84, 91–92 (1967).

[44] *Compare* Schmerber v. California, 384 U.S. 757 (1966) with United States v. Wade, 388 U.S. 218 (1967). Assuming that counsel has a role in the parole granting process, it is not the essentially negative role—"Don't give any statements"—he has in pre-arraignment proceedings; nor is it quite like the "shepherd's" role he has at a police lineup. We may also fairly reject the flaming oratory, embattled advocate role we tend, often unfairly, to associate with the performance of counsel in the courtroom. Counsel's role in the parole hearing would seem to be eclectic, having some of the characteristics of the "shepherd's" role and a good many of the charcteristics of his role as negotiator in plea bargaining and judicial sentencing.

also in need of increased legal attention. In the later discussion of prisoner's rights, the question of legal services for inmates is dealt with. At this point we need only say that if legal services were systematically available to inmates, then among the services that should be provided are assistance in the preparation for parole and, in some cases, actual representation before the board.[45]

To conclude this section on an affirmative note, an outline of procedural regularity for parole hearings will be offered. At a minimum, every prisoner eligible for parole should be given a full and fair hearing. The procedures need not be formal, although in the case of fact disputes there should be a greater concern for procedural regularity. A verbatim record should be kept, and the board should be required to make written findings of fact and a brief statement supportive of its conclusion.

If the board uses a hearing panel, then the prisoner who is denied release should have an administrative appeal to the entire board. This procedure may be as simple and as expeditious as possible. For an administrative appeal, the prisoner might be given ten days to file a "notice of appeal" which, in turn, would result in the transcript being made available to the entire board. The prisoner should be requested to state the gounds for the appeal but only in the most rudimentary form. A basic premise is that all these procedures should be carefully thought out and articulated in advance.

The prisoner, of course, should have the opportunity to appear before the board in order to state his case and be subject to questions. A decision would then be rendered within a reasonable time. Access to the courts would continue to be available, but in the face of an orderly and reasonable administrative procedure, the courts may well continue their reluctance to interfere. Without some internal procedure, the courts may well see the merit of combining logic and policy to find that parole boards and sentencing judges engage in identical functions in which a judicially imposed procedural framework is a necessity.[46]

The issue of providing legal counsel is more complicated. For example, if one opts for a rule that permits retained counsel to appear before the board, the possibility of an equal protection argument lurks in the background. That is, one might argue that if attorneys appear on behalf of those prisoners who are able to afford them, then presumably they have a function to perform and the factor of indigency cannot be used to determine the exercise of so fundamental a right as legal counsel when liberty is at stake.

In the face of an equal protection challenge, the position might be taken that no attorney should be permitted to appear before the board. This "all or nothing" argument has a certain logical appeal, but somehow we rebel at the prospect of

---

[45] The discussion of sentencing procedures, page 18, need not be repeated here. The similarity of judicial sentencing and parole decisions has been discussed. Thus one need only transpose the discussion of sentencing and ask: To what extent do logic and policy require an identity of procedural safeguards?

[46] Probation is not mentioned at this point because everything said previously about sentencing applies directly. For a complete discussion of sentencing-probation decisions, see Cohen, *supra* note 14, Chapter II.

a total denial merely in pursuit of logical consistency and in the face of a shadowy constitutional argument.

A very practical solution is to encourage the use of attorneys in a limited number of jurisdictions as part of an experimental program providing a full range of legal services to inmates. A carefully designed experimental model should be developed to test the ultimate question: Does an attorney have a useful role to perform in the decision to grant or deny parole?

Parole board members have stated privately that they fear the "wheeler-dealer" attorney who takes a substantial fee and performs no substantial service.[47] There are, of course, some unscrupulous attorneys who will take advantage of clients and attempt to corrupt the system. However, it will be the responsibility of the board to control the performance of counsel, and it remains the responsibility of the bar to improve its disciplinary functions. Law schools are giving increased attention to the area of corrections, and the impact of this training should be felt in the very near future. The hope is that the additional law school training and sensitivity to the issues will create a "new breed" of attorney. But, as a prelude to a system of total availability of counsel, we must at a minimum insist on the right of a prisoner to retain counsel who may appear before the board on behalf of his client.

Conditions

Once the decision is made to grant probation or parole, the conditions attached to the grant become the measure of the individual's freedom and responsibility. Since revocation may be based on the failure to observe a condition, the legal significance of conditions is clear. The symbolic value of the condition is that it makes clear that probation and parole are not grants of absolute freedom. The discretion to fashion conditions, the variety of conditions actually imposed, and the supervisory-enforcement discretion of the field officer are crucial issues in the consideration of additional legal safeguards in corrections.

The basic legal issues associated with probation and parole conditions may be summarized as follows:

1. Conditions often affect such basic constitutional freedoms as religion, privacy, and freedom of expression.

2. Too often they are automatically and indiscriminately applied, without any thought given to the necessities of the individual case.

3. In many instances conditions lack precision and create needless uncertainty for the supervised individual and excessive revocation leverage for those in authority.

4. Some conditions are extremely difficult, if not impossible, to comply with.

---

[47] In Chappel, *The Lawyer's Role in the Administration of Probation and Parole*, 48 AMERICAN BAR ASSOCIATION JOURNAL 742, 745 (1962) the author is very skeptical about the contribution made by counsel in correctional proceedings. Indeed, he suggests that at times the attorney does injury to the cause of his client.

Whether one seeks guidance on basic policy or specific criteria, once again legislative direction is almost nonexistent. Some statutes list the conditions that may be imposed and include a general grant of authority to fashion other conditions, while others permit "such terms and conditions as the court deems best."[48] A proposed variation is to list specific conditions and then permit the judge or the board to fashion any other conditions reasonably related to the rehabilitation of the offender of specially related to the cause of the offense and not unduly restrictive of his liberty or incompatible with his freedom of conscience.[49]

The courts have on many occasions reviewed challenges to the legality of conditions. The standard of review most often employed is: Conditions will be upheld unless they are illegal, immoral, or impossible of performance.[50] It should be noted that the legality of the conditions in this context means, essentially, their constitutional validity. A condition that is somehow outside the scope of the governing legislation—a most unlikely occurrence, given the breadth of existing legislation—or one that is determined to be against "public policy" or "not within the legislative intent" may also be voided.

Any condition that is illegal is, by definition, unenforceable and may not be used either as a basis for the regulation of conduct or as a ground for revocation. The grant of probation or parole and the remaining valid conditions should be considered in full force and effect until lawfully altered.[51] A contrary view, followed in some jurisdictions, leads to the result that a successful challenge to a particular condition results in the withdrawal of the grant and the imposition of a term of imprisonment.[52] This sort of Pyrrhic victory, of course, operates to discourage the legitimate exercise of legal rights.

At this point, we should consider the question whether an offender must accept probation or parole. Although cases can be found on both sides of the issue, the more recent decisions affirm the view that the offender can reject the offer of conditional freedom.[53] Any lingering doubts concerning the power to reject the offer may be traced to the oftcited opinion in *Biddle* v. *Perovich,*[54] where

[48] *See, e.g.*, 18 U.S.C. §3651 (Supp. 1964).

[49] MODEL PENAL CODE §§301.1 (2) (1), 305.13 (1)(j) (P.O.D. 1962). The reference to rehabilitation contained therein is limited to probation conditons. In Mansell v. Turner, 14 Utah 2d 352, 354–55, 384 P.2d 394, 396 (1963), the concurring judge argued that there should be a relationship between the condition—banishment from Utah—and rehabilitation or the protection of society. The chief justice severely admonished his colleage for his "bold view," arguing, in effect, that if a prisoner does not like the condition, he need only reject parole. *Id.* at 353 n.4, 84 P.2d 395 n.4.

[50] *See, e.g.*, State v. Harris, 116 Kan. 387, 389, 226 P. 715, 716 (1924). In Sweeney v. United States, 353 F.2d 10, 11 (7th Cir. 1965), the court determined that it was unreasonable to impose a "no drinking" condition on a chronic alcoholic.

[51] *See* Tabor v. Maxwell, 175 Ohio St. 373, 376, 194 N.E.2d 856, 858 (1963).

[52] *See* Note, *Judicial Review of Probation Conditions,* 67 COLUMBIA LAW REVIEW 181, 195 (1967).

[53] *Compare* Cooper v. United States, 91 F.2d 195, 199 (5th Cir. 1937), holding that probation laws vest a discretion in the court and not the offender, with *Ex parte* Peterson, 14 Cal. 2d 82, 85, 92 P.2d 890, 891 (1939), holding that a prisoner is free to reject parole. For recent confirmation of the right to refuse "position," *see* People v. Miller, 64 Cal. Rptr. 20, 25–26 (Cal. App. 1967) (probation); *In re* Schoengarth, 57 Cal. Rptr. 600, 604, 425 P.2d 200, 204 (1967) (parole).

[54] 274 U.S. 480 (1927).

Justice Holmes took the position that a prisoner could not successfully challenge the commutation of a death sentence to a life sentence. The essential difficulty with using *Biddle* in the probation and parole area is that the case involved the exercise of executive clemency. Whatever may be the contemporary utility of executive clemency, it is an episodic and unsystematic ameliorative device and thus bears little resemblance to the modern institutions of probation and parole.

Most judicial opinions concluding that an offender is free to reject the offer of conditional freedom arise in the context of challenges to a questionable condition. By reasoning that the "offer" of the grant does not become operative until "acceptance," the court dutifully pursue the logic of their position and uphold the challenged condition. Rather than become entangled in the niceties of an inapposite contract analogy, it seems more sensible to deal with the question in terms of the discretion of the court or the board to refuse to make the grant unless the offender indicates his willingness to abide by the proposed conditions.

Adherence to the strained concept of consent merely impairs our ability to deal with the real issue. All of us recognize that probation and parole involve a legal situation where the government, presumably by prior lawful procedures, has the legitimate authority to exercise some control over the liberty of an individual. While the offender should be afforded a more active role and greater procedural and substantive protections, ultimately it is those in authority and not the offender who select between a community or institutional disposition; the offer of freedom, however conditional, normally will be more attractive than the alternative. Thus our major concern should be for determining the appropriate limits on the exercise of authority, and not for a chimerical right of rejection.

CONSTITUTIONAL FREEDOMS.　　It should be clear beyond argument that "no civil authority has the right to require anyone to accept or reject any religious belief or to contribute any support thereto."[55] The authority for this proposition is, of course, the First Amendment. This type of condition rarely is encountered in the reported decisions; the reason, undoubtedly, is the certainty of its unenforceability.[56] However, a very real possibility is that such a condition may be imposed "informally" either by the court or the board or even the field officer. Many prisons encourage inmates to attend religious services regularly, and such attendance is viewed as evidence of "a positive approach to the prison program." To the extent that this questionable practice spills over to probation and parole it should be condemned, and care should be taken to assure that anyone with the temerity to challenge such a practice is not the object of retribution.

Increased reliance on public protest as a means to obtain social and political redress has recently resulted in the use of a probation condition that restrains the probationer from participation in future demonstrations. This type of condition has been used in such instances as the demonstrations at the University of California at Berkeley, civil rights demonstrations in Florida, and failure to

---

[55] Jones v. Commonwealth, 185 Va. 335, 344–45 38 S.E.2d 444, 448 (1946) (a juvenile case).

[56] 2 ATTORNEY GENERAL'S SURVEY OF RELEASE PROCEDURES, PROBATION 222–257 (1939) contains an exhaustive survey of conditions, yet makes no mention of conditions dealing with religious freedom.

register for the draft.[57] If such a condition means no more than a restriction from participation in *unlawful* political protest, then it is simply redundant. Every grant of probation and parole includes a prohibition against unlawful conduct. We must assume, then, that the condition is intended to prohibit otherwise lawful speech and assembly, and we may further assume that it will be used most often against persons who have engaged in political protest.

Unquestionably, this type of restraint on political expression could not be imposed on persons generally through the use of the criminal law.[58] The problem is whether this type of condition avoids the proscription of the First Amendment since it is imposed after conviction and incident to the grant of probation.[59]

One might argue that although political expression is a constitutionally protected activity, given the conviction and the possibility of spending time in prison —where political demonstrations are not "encouraged"—the probationer cannot complain about this condition. The contract-consent argument could also be urged in an effort to preclude a successful challenge to such a condition. But considering the obvious potential for using the condition to prevent political protest, and absent any compelling social needs, it is difficult to find a rationale to support the prior restraint of First Amendment freedoms. The late Alexander Meiklejohn held the view that certain evils that government might want to prevent must nonetheless be endured if the only way of avoiding them is by abriding freedom of speech, upon which the entire structure of our free institutions rest. Meiklejohn's view seems correct, and on that basis, this type of condition is subject to the higher law of the Constitution and is thus an impermissible restraint.[60]

It is not unusual for probation and parole to be conditioned on the waiver of Fourth Amendment rights to privacy. Conditions frequently grant the field officer "permission" to visit the offender's home or place of employment, sometimes qualified by the phrase "at a reasonable time," but never requiring the officer to obtain a search warrant. Again, the question is: Can the grant of conditional freedom be conditioned on the waiver of a fundamental constitutional right?

One way to begin to solve the problem is to ask what interest the offender has in maintaining his right to privacy. Is that interest and our assessment of its social

---

[57] Note, *supra* note 52, at 202.

[58] Few probation cases actually deal with the issue. For example, in Morris v. State, 44 Ga. App. 765, 162 S.E. 879 (1932), the court avoided directly passing on a condition that the offender make no remarks against the sheriff or any other adverse witness.

[59] *See* the discussion in Note, *supra* note 52, at 203–04.

[60] Denying a judge the use of such conditions could, of course, result in arbitrary denials of probation. A judge who finds himself unable to condition probation on a restraint on political activity might deny probation altogether and instead impose a fine or term of imprisonment. If the sentencing procedures previously discussed are adopted and if a successful challenge does not result in voiding the entire grant, then one hopes that arbitrary decision-making will be minimized. However, the prospect of unjustifiable denials of probation must be faced, and a balance struck with the importance of denying judges the power to limit political protest through the use of probation. If public protest reaches the point of clear and present danger to the maintenance of public order, limited use of the condition, analogous to an injunction, during the period of the danger seems desirable.

value sufficient to override the interest of correctional officials in maintaining surveillance without the additional hurdle of obtaining a search warrant?[61]

Under the principle of requiring a reasonable relationship between the condition and the offender's past conduct, we may be able to construct a reasonable accommodation between the conflicting interests. Where the prior offense involves conduct which is not likely to be uncovered without surveillance and a search—drug offenses, gambling, carrying a concealed weapon, the production or receipt of contraband—corrections officials might properly argue that they should not be required to go to the trouble of obtaining a warrant every time they suspect the continuation of the illegal activity; under these circumstances, a condition that permits a warrantless search seems defensible. Repeated use of the condition, however, could be evidence of harassment and, if established, should be grounds for the judicial modification of the condition.

On the other hand, where the prior offense suggests no need for a continuing authority to search, the interest of corrections must give way to the overriding interest in maximizing the individual's interest in privacy. The consequence of placing some limits on the indiscriminate use of this condition is not to withdraw authority to search but merely to place the correctional officer in the same position as the law enforcement officer by requiring either a warrant or that the search be incident to an arrest.[62]

BONDS AND SUPERVISORY FEES   Conditioning eligibility for release on the financial ability to put up a bond or pay supervisory costs raises serious constitutional problems under the equal protection clause of the Fourteenth Amendment. In *Griffin* v. *Illinois*, the Court made it clear that the state cannot discriminate based on poverty either in the trial or the appellate processes.[63] Indeed, long before the resurrection of the equal protection clause, the Attorney General's Survey found that the use of bonds and supervisory fees was at least doubtful.[64] The multiple burdens already imposed on the impoverished need not be increased by practices that, in effect, allow those with resources to buy their freedom and deny it to others.[65]

In a case involving a related problem—whether the costs of prosecution can

[61] Search warrants can be issued only on the basis of "probable cause," and this in turn requires something more than bare suspicion or summary conclusions. *See* Aguillar v. Texas 378 U.S. 108–114 (1964).

[62] The problems associated with searches and seizures when there is no "waiver" will be discussed in the section on Supervision. *See* United States *ex rel.* Randazzo v. Follette, 282 F. Supp. 10, 13 (S.D.N.Y. 1968), in which the court held that the Fourth Amendment by its terms extends to a parolee but reasoned that any search by a parole officer conducted in good faith is reasonable. Although the judge buttresses his opinion by reference to an agreement to search, that issue seems not to have been determinative. *See also* People v. Hernandez, 229 Cal. App. 2d 143, 40 Cal. Rptr. 100 (1964) which, in effect, denies the right of privacy to parolees by using the "what could we do with the offender in prison" approach.

[63] 351 U.S. 12, 17 (1956). *See also* Douglas v. California, 372 U.S. 353, 355 (1963).

[64] 2 ATTORNEY GENERAL'S SURVEY OF RELEASE PROCEDURES, PROBATION 225, 237 (1939).

[65] *See generally* ATTORNEY GENERAL'S COMMITTEE, POVERTY AND THE ADMINISTRATION OF CRIMINAL JUSTICE (1963).

be imposed when sentence is suspended—the Oklahoma Court of Criminal Appeals stated:

The purpose of granting a suspended sentence is to aid in the reformation of the prisoner and to rehabilitate him so that he may make a useful citizen. To extend the terms of the statute so as to confer authority on the court to revoke a suspended sentence upon the failure of the accused to pay costs would place an unfair burden on a poor person. It would deprive a pauper of the equal protection of our laws and punish him because of his poverty.[66]

With regard to the bond, it is obvious that this requirement does not transform a bad risk into a good risk.[67] Indeed, if experience with bail bonds is analogous, then those persons best able to meet the requirement may be the worst risks.[68] In addition, the recent experimentation in the use of release on recognizance demonstrates the invalidity of reliance on a financial deterrent to flight. These same observations apply *a fortiori* to the payment of supervisory costs as a condition precedent to probation.

Distinctions may be drawn between the mandatory and discretionary use of a bond and the payment of supervisory costs. Further, we may distinguish their use as a condition precedent and as a condition subsequent to the grant. The constitutional challenge is ameliorated in the discretionary-condition subsequent situation, particularly if the practice does not tend to exclude the poor. However, as a matter of policy, it would be an extremely rare case—perhaps a well-heeled anti-trust violator or as a condition in support cases[69] —where the use of a bond or costs is justified. The cost issue must be reassessed in the context of a correctional system that deals with an involuntary clientele and under the principle that the system is an assumed responsibility of government.[70]

FINES AND RESTITUTION: PROBATION   Restitution, which is among the most commonly employed conditions, is distinguishable from a fine in that restitution payments are made to the one who is aggrieved by the criminal offense for which probation is extended, while a fine is paid to the government. Restitution may be further distinguished from reparation; the former consisting of reimbursement for property that was misappropriated and the latter consisting of the measure of damages that flow from the criminal event, most often the unlawful operation of an automobile.[71]

---

[66] *Ex parte* Banks, 73 Okla. Crim. 1, 5, 122 P.2d 181, 184 (1942).

[67] In Logan v. People, 138 Colo. 304, 308–09, 332 P.2d 897, 899–900, (1958), the court voided an appearance bond as a condition of probation on the premise that such a bond bore no relationship to the legitimate objectives of probation.

[68] *See generally* Freed & Wald, BAIL IN THE UNITED STATES (1964).

[69] *See, e.g.*, State v. Goins, 122 S.C. 192, 196, 115 S.E. 232, 233 (1922).

[70] *Cf.* Department of Mental Hygiene v. Kirchner, 60 Cal. 2d 716, 720, 388 P.2d 720, 722, 36 Cal. Rptr. 438, 440 (1964) in which the court pointed out that when the state involuntarily detains someone, either in the penal or mental health system, the basic obligation for care, support, and maintenance rests with the government.

[71] *See* Best & Birzon, *supra* note 26, at 826–28.

Fines and restitutionary measures undoubtedly are appropriate sanctioning devices and actually may prove to be rehabilitative in some cases. However, in order to serve legitimate correctional ends, a fine or restitution as a condition should be reasonably related to the probationer's ability to meet the obligation. To impose a financial obligation that either cannot be met or that imposes a crippling burden is to invite noncompliance and may even encourage the commission of a new offense.[72] Indeed, a reasonably good faith effort to meet the financial obligation imposed as a condition should be a valid defense to any effort to revoke for noncompliance.[73]

The legislature should articulate criteria for the imposition of fines and restitution as conditions of probation. Restitution or reparation should be held to the following principles:

1. Payment must be limited to the party actually injured.

2. The amount cannot exceed the damage actually incurred.

3. The amount, of course, cannot exceed the probationer's ability to make the payments.[74]

4. The upper limit for a fine may not exceed the fine that might have been imposed if probation had not been granted.[75]

Procedurally, the amount of the actual loss may be established either by agreement or by an adversary proceeding—not at the whim of the court or the probation officer. If the amount of the loss has been determined in the antecedent criminal proceedings, that would be sufficient. However, if the defendant has entered a plea of guilty and the court is considering probation and restitution as a condition, the sentencing hearing is the appropriate time to establish the actual loss.[76]

---

[72] *See* Donnelly, Goldstein & Schwartz, CRIMINAL LAW 377, 379 (1962), reporting "The Garcia Case—A Case Study in Multiple Jeopardy," in which the probationer committed a bank robbery after being "prodded" about his delinquency in paying a fine.

[73] *See* People v. Marx, 19 A.D.2d 577, 578, 240 N.Y.S.2d 232, 234 (1963). In United States v. Taylor, 321 F.2d 339, 341–42 (4th Cir. 1963), the Court found it an abuse of discretion to revoke probation when there has been a sincere effort to pay the fine and when the failure to pay was a result of poverty. But *see* Genet v. United States, 375 F.2d 960, 962 (10th Cir. 1967), in which revocation was upheld when the probationer was unable to support his family at the required level because he had lost his job and had no way to comply. The judge made clear that he would not have granted probation except to provide for the probationer's large family.

[74] In State v. Summers, 60 Wash. 2d 702, 707 375 P.2d 143, 145 (1962), the court refused to allow "restitution" to run to a former wife of the defendant who was not aggrieved by the present offense.

[75] The existing law in nearly all jurisdictions fails to express any consistent policy with respect to the use of fines. The newly revised NEW YORK PENAL LAW, §80 (1967) allows a fine in a felony case only if the offender gained money or property through the commission of the offense and limits the amount to double the proven gain.

[76] Federal law is quite specific in limiting restitution to the actual deprivation, 18 U.S.C. §3651 (1964). *See* Annot., 97 AMERICAN LAW REPORTS 2d 798 (1964). California follows the questionable procedure of allowing the probation office to determine both the amount of the restitution and the manner of payment. *See* people v. Miller, 256 Cal. App. 2d 377, 64 Cal. Rptr. 20 (1967) which upholds a substantial increase in the amount to be paid on determination of the probation office.

BANISHMENT   Nearly all courts that have considered the question have held that banishment (*e.g.*, return to Puerto Rico and remain there ten years)[77] as a condition of probation or parole is void.[78] The Michigan Supreme Court led the way in this area and without resort to constitutional considerations.[79] It took the highly practical view that if Michigan were to permit the "dumping" of its offenders on other states, the favor would most assuredly be returned.[80]

The use of banishment is yet another example of a supposed correctional measure being used in a punitive and—as the Michigan Court recognized—parochial fashion. The Interstate Compact for Supervision of Parolees and Probationers, adopted by all states by 1951, enables the offender to leave the state of conviction and receive supervision elsewhere.[81] The Compact recognizes the need for mobility and for a change of environment but, unlike banishment, assures the individual and the public that an offender is under supervision.

In concluding this section, we should note that the problem of restricting the offender to the jurisdiction clearly is distinguishable from requiring that he leave. The former restriction obviously is justifiable as an incident to conviction and as an appropriate technique to retain jurisdiction and allow the states' correctional system to operate.

MISCELLANEOUS CONDITIONS AND THE SEARCH FOR PRINCIPLE   Having been left to their own devices, judges and parole boards have devised a rich variety of conditions. At times the condition is just silly—compose an essay on respect for the police;[82] at times the condition violates the individual's basic physical integrity—submit to sterilization.[83] On other occasions the condition is so vague —maintain a correct life[84]—that it cannot be intelligently followed or applied. Some conditions that appear to be irrational—remain out of the motion picture

---

[77] Bird v. State, 231 Md. 432, 437–39 190 A.2d 804, 807 (1963).

[78] People v. Blakeman, 170 Cal. App. 2d 596, 339 P.2d 202, 203 (1959); State v. Doughtie, 237 N.C. 368, 369–71 74 S.E.2d, 922, 923–24 (1953). *Contra Ex parte* Sherman, 81 Okla. Crim. 41, 42, 159 P.2d 755, 756 (1945); *Ex parte* Snyder, 81 Okla. Crim. 34, 39, 159 P.2d 752, 754 (1945). The Utah Supreme Court, however, is an exception and recently put a unique twist on the banishment issue. The court reasoned that although a court cannot impose a banishment, the Board of Pardons could. Why? The Board is given authority to grant parole on certain conditions, but the law, typically, is silent concerning the conditions thay may be imposed. Since the law is silent, the court determined that the Board's authority must be plenary thus even banishment is authorized. Mansell v. Turner, 14 Utah 2d 352, 353, 384 P.2d 394, 395 (1963).

[79] While "public policy" reasons typically are announced as the rationale for voiding the condition, there may also be constitutional issues involved. For example, banishment could be argued to be cruel and unusual punishment analogous to the "loss of citizenship" cases. *See, e.g.*, Schneider v. Rusk, 377 U.S. 163 (1964).

[80] People v. Baum, 251 Mich. 187, 189, 231 N.W 95, 96 (1930). Banishment to an area *within* the state has been held to be illegal as a probation condition. *In re* Scarborough, 76 Cal. App. 2d 648, 173 P.2d 825 (1946).

[81] COUNCIL OF STATE GOVERNMENTS, INTERSTATE COMPACT FOR SUPERVISION OF PAROLEES AND PROBATIONERS (1951). Another very "useful" form of banishment is to delay the trial of a criminal case and to promise dismissal if the accused leaves and remains out of the jurisdiction.

[82] Such a condition was voided in Butler v. District of Columbia, 346 F.2d 798 (D.C. Cir. 1965).

[83] *In re* Hernandez, No. 76757 (Cal. Super. Ct., June 8, 1966).

[84] Morgan v. Foster, 208 Ga. 630, 632, 68 S.E.2d 583, 584 (1952).

business—make more sense when the basis for the underlying conviction, performing oral copulation before a motion picture camera, is learned.[85]

All the problems associated with probation and parole conditions will not be eliminated by sensible legislation, but such legislation certainly could improve the present situation. In the effort to devise sensible legislative policy, however, care should be taken not to overreact to the parade of silly, shocking, and meaningless conditions. If probation and parole are to remain useful correctional devices, there must be enough leeway to allow the conditions imposed to be molded to the individual and the individual circumstances of each case.

The guiding principles for the needed legislation should be:

1. There must be reasonable relationship between the condition imposed and the offender's previous conduct and present condition.[86]

2. Conditions should impose the minimum deprivation of liberty and freedom of conscience.

3. They must be sufficiently specific to serve as a guide to supervision and conduct.

4. Compliance must be possible given the emotional, physical, and economic resources of the offender.[87]

5. There must be an adequate procedural format to permit advocacy on behalf of or in opposition to the conditions, not only at the time of granting but also at revocation proceedings. Challenge of the conditions must also be permitted through appeal or through the expanded use of habeas corpus.[88]

Adherence to these principles in probation and parole would be an important first step in providing both guidance and accountability for those in authority and certainty and reasonableness for those subject to authority.

The extent to which legislation should detail certain specific conditions is the final point to be discussed. The standard conditions—that the offender report regularly, remain within the jurisdiction, and commit no new offense—pose no real problems and might conveniently be set out in the legislation. The problem exists with detailing other conditions and thus inviting their automatic application. Even such regularly used conditions as "carry no weapons" or "do not

---

[85] People v. Bowley, 230 Cal. App. 2d 269, 40 Cal. Rptr. 859 (1964).

[86] When an offender has consistently been in trouble at a time when he is under the influence of alcohol or drugs, it is sensible to impose a condition dealing with this problem. The automatic preclusion of drinking alcoholic beverages, or being in a place where they are sold, however, is generally a good example of no reasonable relationship and of excessive revocation leverage. Another extreme condition is the preclusion of alcoholic consumption when the offender is known to be an alcoholic. *See* Sweeney v. United States, 353 F.2d 10, 11 (7th Cir. 1965), holding such a condition unenforceable.

[87] Economic conditions—fines, restitution, and reparation—should be further limited and perhaps applied in a special category of cases in which their imposition would be meaningful.

[88] This procedure is designed to overcome the position taken in some jurisdictions that probation orders are not appealable and that an effort to appeal is, in effect, a refusal of probation. Implicit in this principle are the presumptions that a probation or parole order is a "final judgment" for appellate purposes, that there is standing to appeal, and that, if successful, the appellant will not be punished by a subsequent revocation.

consort with disreputable persons" would seem to require individualized application and greater clarity.

On the other hand, if the legislation remains at a fairly abstract level, the newly increased opportunities for judicial and administrative appeals invites a case-by-case review of particular conditions. Administrative considerations aside, case-by-case education is not necessarily a negative prospect. Additional principles and further guidance are likely to emerge in the crucible of challenge and counterchallenge; since there is a paucity of authority in this area, it might be well to encourage review, at least for the short run.

SUPERVISION AND THE ABSENCE OF CONDITIONS.   A legislative scheme along the lines of our earlier discussion would greatly aid the court or the board in fashioning conditions, but the task of individualizing and then applying particular conditions remains. Although that task will be aided by a procedural scheme that allows for advocacy and challenge, some situations of concern to those in authority are likely not to be directly covered by either the legislative guidelines or the conditions actually imposed. Indeed, no one seriously argues for legal rules that purport to encompass all interaction between the agents of correction and those in their charge. Having spoken to the question of authority and principle in the imposition of conditions, what remains is a discussion of the supervisory officer's day-to-day power to modify specific conditions, and of the permissible limits of his authority to supervise in the absence of such conditions.

The stated conditions define both the limits of authority and the duty of compliance in the area of behavior covered.[89] But absent a valid condition on point, may a correctional officer conduct a search at will, restrict First Amendment freedoms relating to free speech and assembly,[90] require the supervisee to relinquish the privilege against self-incrimination? A brief discussion of these issues is undertaken not because it is possible to present a summary of existing law—there is practically none—but so that at the level of fundamental constitutional rights we may better understand the implications of conditional freedom and provide some direction for future decision-making.

Where a sensible legislative and procedural scheme exists, then the failure to include a condition that deals with First, Fourth, or Fifth Amendment rights should be regarded as evidence that the condition has been considered and determined to be either *ultra vires* or inapplicable.[91] Linked with this proposition is the suggestion that the probationer or parolee must be regarded as having retained all of the rights and obligations of citizenship that have not been lost by

---

[89] In Cross v. Huff, 208 Ga. 392, 396–97 67 S.E.2d 124, 127 (1951), the court held that when the order of probation was incomprehensible because of ambiguity, no basis for revocation existed. *See also* Lester v. Foster, 207 Ga. 596, 599, 63 S.E.2d 402, 403 (1951), in which the court posits due process as the basis for requiring explicit conditions and proof of their violation as a basis for revocation.

[90] *See* Roberts v. Peppersack, 256 F. Supp. 415 (D. Md. 1966), *cert. denied,* 389 U.S. 877 (1967), for a discussion of the restrictions on free speech while in prison.

[91] If a record is kept and findings are recorded, then no speculation would be necessary.

virtue of provisions in the Constitution,[92] statutes, and, of course, valid conditions.[93]

Absent a valid condition dealing with search and seizure, it is difficult to understand why correctional officers should be in a different position than law enforcement officers. A search and seizure by a correctional officer is not an abstract event; it is conducted to obtain evidence of violation that may be used to terminate the grant. As such, it is analytically indistinguishable from the efforts of law enforcement to obtain evidence that may be used as a basis for conviction and the imposition of penal sanctions. Only if we determine that the nature of the underlying conviction justifies dissolving the protection of the Fourth Amendment can we reach a contrary conclusion.[94]

With some 800,000 persons under probation or parole supervision at any one time, the human dimensions of the issue become clear. In response to the insistent demands of a few of these individuals, three distinct lines of judicial reasoning on this issue are in the early stages of development:

1. There is no protection afforded a probationer or parolee whether the evidence taken is used at a new trial or at a revocation proceeding.

2. The Fourth Amendment protects the individual under supervision, but only where the evidence is sought to be used at a new trial.

3. The individual is protected both at a new trial and at a revocation proceeding.[95]

The Supreme Court made it plain in *Mapp* that it imposed the exclusionary rule on the states because it was deemed the only effective deterrent against lawless police action.[96] Is it desirable to seek to impose a similar deterrent on corrections? The answer would appear to be yes.

While an individual who is placed under supervision in the community concededly does not—and often should not—enjoy all the freedoms of ordinary citizens, our earlier discussions have attempted to establish a principle of imposing on offenders only those deprivations that are consistent with a valid correctional objective and that relate to the offender's prior conduct and present condition. An effort was made to establish that the imposition of some conditions —*i.e.,* requiring observance of religious practices—is beyond the power of the

---

[92] U.S. CONSTITUTION, AMENDMENT XIII, §1 declares, "Neither slavery nor involuntary servitude; except as punishment for crime whereof the party shall have been truly convicted, shall exist. . . . "

[93] Coffin v. Reichard, 143 F.2d 443, 445 (6th Cir. 1944).

[94] The scope of the Fourth Amendment recently has been extended to inspections of residential dwellings, Camara v. Municipal Court, 387 U.S. 523, 528–534 (1967), and inspection of commercial structures, See v. City of Seattle, 387 U.S. 541 542–46 (1967). In neither situation is *liberty* necessarily at stake as it may always be in our situation.

[95] For a thorough discussion of these issues, *see* People v. Hernandez, 229 Cal. App. 2d 143, 40 Cal. Rptr. 100 (1964). The following cases should also be consulted: United States v. Lewis, 274 F. Supp. 184 (S.D.N.Y. 1967); People v. Villareal, 262 Cal. App. 2d 442, 68 Cal. Rptr. 610, (1968); People v. Langella, 41 Misc. 2d 65, 244 N.Y.S.2d 802 (1963).

[96] Linkletter v. Walker, 381 U.S. 618, 637 (1965).

state, regardless of any prospects for successful rehabilitation. As Justice Frank-furter put it, the security of one's privacy against arbitrary intrusion by the police is basic to a free society and implicit in the concept of ordered liberty.

The right of privacy is so basic to our society that it is found not only in the Fourth Amendment but is an aspect of the First, Third, and Fifth Amendments.[97] By now it must be clear that we confront a value choice, and the writer opts for the insulation of probationers and parolees against arbitrary intrusions. In order to deter such intrusions any evidence of misconduct that is obtained without a warrant, not incident to a lawful arrest or not under a permissible condition, must be excluded at any new trial and, by a parity of reasoning, at any further proceed-ings involving the possible termination of the grant. It must also follow that a refusal to consent or cooperate with an illegal search cannot be made the basis of revocation. Obviously, such a proposal increases the risk of undetected viola-tions as well as the burden on field officers. The judgment is that the value of privacy, of personal autonomy while in the community, more than offsets the possible risks.

It must be stressed that such an approach does not eliminate visits or searches but merely requires that before a search is made the field officer must have probable cause to believe that a new crime or a violation has been committed. The facts upon which he bases that belief should be tested before some neutral and detached magistrate.

Having previously concluded that the use of an express condition to restrict First Amendment rights should be outside the scope of judicial or administrative power, it must necessarily follow that the field officer has no discretion to restrict those rights. The difficulty is not so much with explicit restrictions—they appear to be rare and, as previously noted, are most often used by courts to deter unpopular political activities—as with the "gentle hint" that certain political activities are viewed as evidence of a "failure to adjust." For the relatively few individuals to whom such a provision would matter, it must be made absolutely clear that their First Amendment rights remain intact.[98]

Whether or not a probationer or parolee is protected by the Fifth Amend-ment's bar against self-incrimination is a fascinating question. Another way to phrase the question is to ask to what extent can a probationer or parolee be required to assist in a subsequent prosecution or revocation proceeding and to what extent must he be provided with *Miranda*-type protections?

Many, perhaps most, revocation proceedings grow out of an arrest for a new offense.[99] While the probationer or parolee is held in jail, the sheriff's office will

---

[97] Giswold v. Connecticut, 381 U.S. 479, 481–484 (1965).

[98] A fascinating case in point involves Leroy Eldridge Cleaver, the Black Panther leader. Cleaver successfully challenged the effort to cancel his parole by showing that it was his political activity and not any violation which triggered the revocation process. *See In re* Cleaver, No. 5631 (California Superior Court, June 11, 1968).

[99] Much of the descriptive data in the discussion that follows is based on extensive interviews with correctional personnel in the Seattle district office of the Washington Board of Prison Terms and Parole. The cooperation of Mr. William Young, District Supervisor, and his entire staff is gratefully acknowledged.

notify the field officer who, in turn normally will place a "hold" on the prisoner. The hold is designed to accomplish two related objectives: deny the individual the opportunity to make bail and provide the field officer with a convenient opportunity for interrogation.[100] It is in this fairly typical situation that the question of the application of *Miranda* must be confronted.

It seems reasonably clear that an in-custody interrogation by a correctional officer which produces inculpatory or exculpatory statements where no appropriate warnings or opportunity to consult with counsel are given cannot be used in any subsequent criminal proceedings.[101] Is there any valid reason why such information might be used in a revocation proceeding?

The question can be stated more generally: to what extent must the procedural protections on the road to possible revocation parallel those on the road to conviction? The correctional officer normally is in a much better position to elicit information than a police officer. He deals with an individual with whom he has established some sort of relationship, and he is able to use in-custody interrogation in such a way that "I only want to help you" sounds credible. The person under supervision can easily be convinced that failure to cooperate is indicative of a "poor adjustment" and that silence may be converted into grounds for revocation.

As a matter of sound policy, correctional personnel should inform the suspect that he has a right to remain silent, that anything he says might be used in a revocation proceeding, and that *his silence will not be used as a basis for revocation.*[102] This approach, of course, does not rule out a revocation based on the conduct that led to the arrest; it simply requires that those in authority prove the violation by evidence that is not forced from the individual or secured on the basis of ignorance of the right to remain silent.

THE DECISION TO REVOKE PROBATION AND PAROLE

This is the area in which there exists the greatest tension between legal norms and correctional practices. There are almost as many cases dealing with revocation as with all other areas of the correctional process. Wherever there is agitation for reform, there tends to be basic agreement on the need to improve the revoca-

---

[100] Use of the "hold" to deny bail was questioned by the majority of field officers interviewed. At this time, Seattle attorneys successfully use the writ of habeas corpus to obtain release or the setting of reasonable bail. Should pretrial or prerevocation release become common, however, the officers realize that they face serious problems in obtaining the necessary facts to determine whether or not to take action based on the arrest.

[101] Whether or not the interrogator has statutory law enforcement authority is not significant since in these circumstances the correctional officer would be acting as an agent for law enforcement. *See,* *e.g.,* Sherman v. United States, 356 U.S. 369, 373–75 (1958), an entrapment case, in which the actions of an unpaid informer were held attributable to the government.

[102] *Cf.* Garrity v. New Jersey, 385 U.S. 493, 496–500 (1967), in which the Court held that police officers could not be removed from their jobs if they invoked the privilege against self-incrimination during an investigation into the fixing of traffic tickets.

tion process. There is, however, considerable disagreement on the specific changes required and on whether those changes should result from court decisions, comprehensive or permissive legislation, or administrative rules.

The tendency to analyze incorrectly revocation-type decisions and to confuse sentencing with revocation-type decisions already has been discussed. Our use of the term revocation refers to the formal termination of a grant of conditional freedom and the imposition, execution, or reinstatement of a term of imprisonment. Used in this fashion, revocation becomes a shorthand term for both the process of establishing authority and the decision to impose or order the execution of a term of imprisonment.[103] In the discussion of appropriate revocation procedures, the reference is to any proceeding that may result in imprisonment even though the court or agency actually imposes measures short of imprisonment.[104]

The central issues in the revocation process are *the right to counsel* and *the right to a fair hearing*. As was demonstrated earlier, the existing law on revocation procedures reveals a total lack of uniformity and ranges from fairly comprehensive treatment to silence.[105] There is, of course, great variation on the availability of counsel and the right to a hearing.

In *Mempa* v. *Rhay*[106] the Supreme Court determined that a state probationer was constitutionally entitled to counsel "at this proceeding whether it be labeled a revocation of probation or a deferred sentencing."[107] Although there was some confusion on the point, the Court dealt with the case as though the imposition of sentence had been deferred. This is an important point because subsequent decisions that seek to limit the potential impact of *Mempa* seize on this fact and determine that the right to counsel exists only where the revoking authority must determine and impose the original sentence.[108]

---

[103] Where the court has imposed sentence and then suspended its execution and granted probation, the resentencing discretion of the revoking authority is identical with the discretion exercised by a parole board.

Because some jurisdictions allow revocation of probation by the parole board, particularly if sentence has been imposed, revoking authority is the more accurate term. *See* the discussion in John v. State, 160 N.W.2d 37, 43 (N. D. 1968).

[104] The process by which liberty once extended may be taken away provides an excellent opportunity to demonstrate the interrelatedness of all the issues previously discussed. Take, for example, the question of whether a violation must be proved before there exists authority to resentence and imprison. Unless a violation—either a new offense or the breach of a non-penal condition—must be proved, then our concern about the need for a guiding principle about specificity in conditions should be reduced. If probation and parole were primarily, if not exclusively, concerned with rehabilitation, then a determination of "failure to adjust" or "failure to maximize treatment" opportunities, while difficult to prove, would be consistent with the basic objective and thus serve as an adequate basis for revocation. Having previously demonstrated the multiplicity of goals that are inherent in and actually pursued by corrections, there must be considerable doubt about the invocation of the clinical model at the point of termination when non-rehabilitative objectives have been applied in granting and supervising the conditional freedom.

[105] For a fairly detailed treatment of parole revocation procedures, *see* Shelton v. United States Parole Board, 388 F.2d 567 (D. C. Cir. 1967); Hyser v. Reed, 318 F.2d 225 (D. C. Cir. 1963).

[106] 389 U.S. 128 (1967).

[107] *Id.* at 137.

[108] *See, e.g.,* Rose v. Haskins, 388 F.2d 91, 97 (6th Cir.), *cert. denied,* 392 U.S. 946 (1968); John v. State, 160 N.W.2d 37, 43–44 (N.D. 1968).

This clearly is an unduly restrictive reading of *Mempa.* If a distinction is sought to be made, it should not be on the basis of whether the imposition or the execution of sentence was suspended but rather on the amount of sentencing discretion possessed by the revoking authority. One might argue that once the power exists to imprison, and imprisonment is imposed, there is no point to a hearing and the presence of counsel unless the sentencing authority has some choice on the term of years. While there is a ring of credibility to this argument, *Mempa* itself undercuts its acceptability. Under Washington law, where *Mempa* originated, the court is required to fix the maximum prison term of a sentence, and the Board of Prison Terms and Paroles then sets the duration of confinement.[109] Ironically, the Board has more sentencing discretion than the court, and pursuing the logic of their own position should disquiet those who seek to restrict *Mempa* on the basis of sentencing discretion.

Curiously, *Mempa* makes no specific mention of the right to a hearing in a probation revocation proceeding. In order to decide if the states were required to appoint counsel, the Court first had to characterize probation revocation as a critical stage in the criminal process. The marriage of right-to-counsel and "critical stage" is largely based on the assumption that counsel has a meaningful function to perform. Presumably, that function is something more than chatting with the judge or the probationer after a revocation decision has been made. Unless counsel is afforded an opportunity to affect the course and outcome of the proceeding, it is difficult to conceive what it is he is supposed to do.

The format for an effective performance by counsel is a hearing, thus it seems plain that *Mempa's* express requirement of counsel carries with it an implied right to a fair revocation hearing.[110] If this interpretation is incorrect, then *Mempa* overturned an earlier decision, *Escoe* v. *Zerbst,*[111] and without the courtesy of even a footnote reference.

Escoe v. Zerbst: The Right to A Hearing in Probation Revocation

Escoe is an important decision and deserves comment here. *Escoe* involved an interpretation of federal probation law, which then required that, prior to revocation, a probationer "shall forthwith be taken before the court."[112] The probationer had been arrested as a violator; shortly thereafter the federal judge signed an order of revocation, and the probationer was on his way to Leavenworth. By a writ of habeas corpus he then complained that he was entitled to a revocation hearing both under the statute and as a matter of constitutional law.

Justice Cardozo's opinion stated flatly that the statute was mandatory and had

---

[109] WASH. REV. CODE ANN. §§ 9.95.010, –.040 (1961).

[110] There are at least seven jurisdictions that have denied the right to a revocation hearing—three by statute (Iowa, Missouri, and Oklahoma) and four by judicial decision (Arizona, California, District of Columbia, and South Dakota). *See* Sklar, *supra* note 5, at 175.

[111] 295 U.S. 490 (1935).

[112] Act of March 4, 1925, ch. 521, §2, 43 Stat. 1260. The recently amended FED. R. CRIM. P. 32 (f), in effect, codifies the holding in *Escoe.*

inexcusably been violated. The Justice, however, went further and embellished his opinion with what has been termed "a most pernicious dictum":

> Probation or suspension of sentence comes as an act of grace to one convincted of a crime, and may be coupled with such conditions in respect of its duration as Congress may impose.[113]

It is this dictum, that there is no constitutional right to a probation revocation hearing, which *Mempa* appears to have abandoned.

Cardozo's rationale for interpreting the statutory language of "shall forthwith be taken before the court" to mean a mandatory hearing is likely to survive his dictum.[114] The Justice stated that the objective of an appearance before the court must be to enable an accused probationer to explain away the accusation.[115] Although this does not mean a trial in any formal sense, "it does mean . . . an inquiry so fitted in its range to the needs of the occasion as to justify the conclusion that discretion has not been abused by the failure of the inquisitor to carry the probe deeper."[116]

With counsel and a fair hearing viewed as constitutional rights, Cardozo's rationale can provide the broad outline for the requisite hearing: an inquiry that is suited to the occasion and thus one that necessarily will vary. If, for example, facts are in dispute, then a trial-type proceeding—one that includes the summoning of witnesses, the right of confrontation, and cross-examination—is in order. Should counsel and the probationer agree to enter a "plea of violation," then all that is needed is a sentencing-type hearing.

The "judicializing" of probation revocation procedures is not likely to be regarded by corrections as a serious threat. But should the same inroads be made into parole revocation procedures—and that seems inevitable—acquiescence is likely to give way to howls of protest.

For probation officers, the regular use of a hearing and the regular appearance of counsel may produce unanticipated, positive side effects. The roles played by the various participants should be sharpened and clarified. Probation officers need not, and indeed should not, play the roles of prosecutor, defense attorney, and chief witness. Their roles should be limited to the presentation of facts within their personal knowledge on the question of violation and to the presentation of dispositional alternatives on the question of the appropriate sentence. Where prosecutors have not regularly appeared, it is important that they now do so. One of the inevitable consequences of the extension of the right to counsel to one litigant is counsel's appearance thereafter on the other side.

---

[113] 295 U.S. at 492–93.

[114] In Green v. McElroy, 360 U.S. 474, 506–08 (1959), involving the revocation of a security clearance of an employee of a private corporation, the Court held that the employee had a right to confrontation and cross-examination.

[115] 295 U.S. at 493. In Hyser v. Reed, 318 F.2d 225, 237 (D. C. Cir. 1963), Judge Burger wrote, "we do not have pursuer and quarry but a relationship partaking of *parens patriae.*"

[116] 295 U.S. at 493.

The "Difference" Between Parole Revocation and Probation Revocation

Although efforts are made to do so, it seems impossible to satisfactorily distinguish parole revocation from probation revocation.[117] As a New York court put it: that the sentence cannot be altered, that parole can be viewed as no part of the criminal proceedings, creates no vital differences on the question of the right to counsel. When one disposes of all the legal niceties, parole revocation involves the question of liberty or imprisonment. *Gault* and *Mempa* combine to make the right to counsel applicable at parole proceedings.[118]

In *Rose* v. *Haskins,* a majority of the court of appeals for the sixth circuit took a different approach.[119] Rose, a state prisoner, brought habeas corpus in the federal courts and argued that his right to due process under the Fourteenth Amendment was violated when, without a hearing, the parole board declared him a violator.

Rose had asked to be tried for the new offense, child molesting, but the prosecutor took no action. Ohio law required no hearing on revocation and still insulates the parole board to such a degree that it is doubtful if any remedy exists by which to challenge parole revocation.[120] The eclectic majority opinion borrowed from all the theories used to deny procedural rights to a parolee. First, the opinion seemed enamoured of the privilege theory, arguing that Ohio did not have to create a parole system; thus if it chose to do so, it might stipulate its own terms and conditions.[121] Ultimately, however, the court fixed on a version of the continuing custody theory, as announced in *In re Varner.*[122] *Varner* likened the parolee to a "trusty" who may be allowed temporarily to leave the confines of the institution but who obviously remains within the custody and control of the head of the institution.

What apparently escaped their attention is the fact that the liberty of a "trusty," indeed even a prisoner on work-release, not only is conditional but is granted for a limited time and as an aspect of the institutional program. A "trusty," like any other prisoner, is reducing the time left on his sentence every day he remains in that status. Indeed, in most jurisdictions he is earning the maximum good-time credits allowed by law. Parole, on the other hand, is an indefinite grant of liberty and separates the parolee physically and pragmatically

---

[117] *See, e.g.,* Hutchinson v. Patterson, 267 F. Supp. 433, 434–35 (D. Colo. 1967) (denying an alleged parole violator, *inter alia,* the right to an adequate hearing); Johnson v. Wainwright, 208 So. 2d 505 (Fla. App. 1968) (no right to counsel at parole revocation proceeding). In the former case, the judge thought the law might change after *Mempa,* but was unwilling to do it.

[118] People *ex rel.* Combs v. LaVallee, 29 A.D.2d 128, 130–31, 286 N.Y.S.2d 600, 603 (1968). It should be noted that New York law required a hearing before a "parole court," thus this court did not have to begin with the hearing question.

[119] 388 F.2d 91 (6th Cir. 1968).

[120] Revocation decisions are not reviewable by habeas corpus, mandamus, prohibition, or certiorari. It is not clear, however, whether appeal is available. 388 F.2d at 98, n.1 (dissenting opinion).

[121] 388 F.2d at 93.

[122] 166 Ohio St. 340, 346–48, 142 N.E.2d 846, 850–51 (1957).

from the releasing institution. The parolee generally is neither reducing his sentence nor earning "on-the-street" good-time credits.

Of particular interest is the majority's treatment of the well-known decision in *Fleenor* v. *Hammond*,[123] which held that a conditional pardon issued by the governor of Kentucky could not be revoked without a hearing. The hearing was held to be required by the due process clause of the Fourteenth Amendment. The majority distinguished the situation in *Rose* from that in *Fleenor* on the highly questionable ground that Kentucky had no rules governing the issuance of conditional pardons and that, in any event, the pardon vested rights in the prisoner that could not be divested without a hearing.[124] The majority opinion rejects not only the analogy between conditional pardon and parole but also the analogy between probation and parole suggested by *Mempa*. The opinion rather casually brushes off *Mempa,* reading it as a ruling that applies only at deferred sentencing.[125]

Judge Celebrezze, former Secretary of Health, Education, and Welfare, writes a sparkling dissent,[126] an opinion that is likely to serve as a model for those courts that are desirous of finding a constitutional right to a hearing. He gives short shrift to the theories of privilege, contract consent, and continuing custody and emphasizes that parole is an integral part of the criminal justice system. He views the grant, in effect, as a promise of continued freedom provided there is conformity with specified conditions. Revocation, he suggests, rests on a determination that there has been a violation, and that determination cannot fairly be made without a hearing.

Judge Celebrezze does not make the mistake of confusing the procedural problems associated with a decision to grant or deny parole with the problems associated with termination. He concedes an extremely broad discretion in the decision to grant or deny but cogently argues that a different legal situation is created once freedom is extended.[127]

Fears that judicial interference will disrupt the whole revocation scheme are dismissed as supported by nothing more than the untutored intuition of the person expressing them. He reviews all of the commonly expressed fears:

1. Parole boards would become bogged down in needless procedure.

2. Parole boards would become unduly conservative for fear of not being able to expeditiously arrange for reimprisonment.

---

[123] 116 F.2d 982 (6th Cir. 1941).

[124] Because the *Fleenor* court analogized revocation with probation, if the rights referred to by the majority concern restoration of civil rights following a full pardon, the majority simply has misread *Fleenor*. The interesting point is that while *Fleenor* may be correctly decided, the court commited a fundamental error in reaching its conclusion. The *Fleenor* court took a quotation from *Escoe* dealing with the necessity for a hearing as a matter of *statutory construction* and used it in support of a conclusion that due process required a revocation hearing. As we have noted, *Escoe* rejected the argument that a probation revocation hearing was constitutional.

[125] 388 F.2d at 97.

[126] *Id.* at 99 (dissenting opinion).

[127] *Id.*

3. Informers would be reluctant to testify if subjected to confrontation and cross-examination.

4. The increase in cost would make the program prohibitive.[128]

These arguments are either rebutted or considered too slight to be determinative of due process safeguards when liberty is at stake.

The Right to Counsel and A Fair Hearing in Parole Revocation Proceedings

As one might expect, the number of jurisdictions that permit the revocation of parole without a hearing exceeds those that permit the revocation of probation without a hearing.[129] Many jurisdictions will not even permit retained counsel to appear on behalf of the parolee; the right to appointed counsel is almost unheard-of.[130]

The Model Penal Code adopts a format for parole revocation proceedings that goes a long way—although not far enough—toward protection against bureaucratic arbitrariness.[131] The Code requires:

1. A hearing within 60 days of return to the institution as a suspected violator;

2. Notice of the charges filed;

3. A verbatim record of the proceedings;

4. A requirement that the decision be based on substantial evidence; and

5. An opportunity to advise with the parolee's own legal counsel in advance of the hearing.[132]

There are many gaps in the Code's coverage of the revocation process, and some of the policy positions no longer seem supportable. The failure to speak to such issues as the situs of hearings and advice concerning the right to remain silent and to detail specific attributes of the hearing process are examples of important gaps. The denial of the right to counsel and the allowance of revocation for "conduct indicating a substantial risk that the parolee will commit another crime"[133] represent questionable policy positions. Nevertheless, adoption of the Model Penal Code's provisions, adding the right to counsel, would make a substantial improvement in the procedures of most jurisdictions.

The right-to-counsel problem has been challenging even for the more sophisticated courts. One of the most important recent cases involving counsel and

---

[128] *Id.* at 101–02.

[129] There are about 16 jurisdictions that allow parole to be revoked without a hearing. Even where not required, however, hearings may be held in the discretion of the board. *See* Sklar, *supra* note 5, at 175; Annot., 29 AMERICAN LAW REPORTS 2d 1074 (1953).

[130] *See* TASK FORCE REPORT: CORRECTIONS 87 (1967).

[131] MODEL PENAL CODE § 305.15 (P.O.D. 1962).

[132] The Code is more solicitous of the probationer than the parolee. The probationer has been extended the right to be represented by counsel. *Id.* at § 301.4

[133] *Id.* at § 305.15 (2) (b) (ii).

other parole revocation issues is *Hyser* v. *Reed.*[134] *Hyser* continued a process of interpretation of federal law that gives a modicum of procedural protection to federal parolees and mandatory releases.[135]

The appellants in *Hyser* claimed that they were entitled to a hearing before the Board and (1) appointed counsel; (2) specification of charges; (3) confrontation and cross-examination of the Board's informants; (4) the right to examine reports deemed confidential; (5) compulsory process to obtain witnesses; and (6) a hearing held in the district where the alleged violation is said to have occurred.

The District of Columbia Court of Appeals previously had construed the statutory language of "opportunity to appear before the Board" to allow parolees to be represented by retained counsel and to present voluntary witnesses. In the present case, petitioner's claims were based on, *inter alia,* the Sixth Amendment and the due process clause of the Fifth Amendment. The court held those amendments inapplicable to the actions of the Board.[136] The court did, however, broaden the "statutory" protections to require that:

1. The arrest warrant should reveal with reasonable specificity the reasons why revocation is sought.

2. The preliminary interview must be conducted at or reasonably near the place of the alleged violation.

3. It must be held as promptly as is convenient after the arrest.

The field officer or board member who conducts this informal preliminary inquiry is required to hear voluntary witnesses and record a summary or digest of their statements. Additional information also may be tendered to the Board before any final action is taken.[137]

Mempa and its Aftermath

Returning to the basic issues of a hearing and the right to counsel, it should be reiterated that it seems impossible analytically to distinguish probation and parole revocation proceedings to the extent of requiring counsel and a hearing at

---

[134] 318 F.2d 225 (D.C. Cir. 1963).

[135] The mandatory releasee—one who must be released under supervision for the period of his earned good-time credits minus 180 days—and the parolee are generally treated alike by the federal courts. *See, e.g.,* Shelton v. United States Parole Board, 388 F.2d 567, 570–71 (D.C. Cir. 1967).

[136] The protection of the Sixth Amendment was not explicitly urged on the court, but the majority opinion made it plain "that we should not accept the contention." 318 F.2d at 237. The reason offered is that the amendment applies only to "criminal prosecutions." Now that *Mempa* and *Gault* have elasticized the concept of "criminal prosecution," the coverage of the Sixth Amendment must be considered open to further development.

[137] *Id.* at 245. In a separate opinion Chief Judge Bazelon announced that in a controverted case he would require confrontation and cross-examination, inspection of the records, and the appointment of counsel. In addition, because, to his mind, poverty bears no more relation to parole violation than to guilt, he saw a lack of "equal protection" in the practice of allowing only those with money to appear with counsel. *Id.,* at 248–57 (concurring and dissenting). *See* State v. Hoffman, 404 P.2d 644 (Alaska 1965) in which the court used an equal-protection rationale to require appointed counsel in probation revocation proceedings.

one and denying it at another. The decision in *Mempa* may prove to be the springboard for procedural reform although the lower court decisions interpreting *Mempa* indicate either that its implications are not understood or perhaps are understood too well.

Mempa has returned to the State of Washington with a vengeance. A superior court judge recently granted a writ of habeas corpus to a prisoner who, it was held, was denied due process in the revocation of parole.[138] The judge determined that there are no substantial differences between probation and parole revocations, and, given a statute that provides for a hearing, he resorted to due process to determine how the hearing should be conducted. The court held that there is a right of access to the violation report and a right to confront and cross-examine witnesses. The court further held that the hearing must be near the place of the alleged violation in order to facilitate the voluntary appearance of witnesses, that counsel must be appointed, and that there must be a neutral evaluation of the reasons for arrest.

While this judicial development is extremely noteworthy, the recommendations for new legislation prepared by the Washington Board of Prison Terms and Paroles is even more exciting. The proposed revisions go beyond the lower court's requirements in some respects and in others are a bit more restrictive:[139]

a) Conducting the parole revocation hearing at a place reasonably near where the alleged violation of parole occurs;

b) Providing the parolee with proper and timely notice of the alleged violation of the conditions of parole;

c) Providing subpoena power to the Board in order that compulsory attendance of witnesses on behalf of the parolee is available;

d) Providing opportunity for cross-examination and confrontation of witnesses alleging violations of the conditions of parole;

e) Appointing attorneys at state expense for indigent parolees accused of violations of the conditions of parole;

f) Providing that the hearings will be recorded and transcripts be made available only in case of appeal;

g) Providing that no part of the testimony taken in the parole revocation hearing be used in further criminal prosecutions against the parolee;

h) Requring that the parolee answer questions and that if he refuses to answer that in itself is considered sufficient reason for the revocation of parole.[140]

This action suggests that correctional agencies can take the initiative and further that they realize that a comprehensive legislative scheme is far more desirable

[138] *In re* Bailey. No. 57125 (Wash. Super. Ct., May 22, 1968).

[139] The recommendations make no provision for access to the Board's files but do provide for compulsory attendance of witnesses.

[140] Sections (g) and (h) clearly recognize the applicability of some version of the privilege against self-incrimination. Section (g) resembles an "immunity" law and where a person under interrogation is granted immunity from prosecution, he traditionally has been required to testify on pain of being held in contempt. The question here is whether silence can be used to revoke parole even though no prosecution could be had.

than time-consuming court battles that inevitably produce *ad hoc* and perhaps unduly restrictive results.

Rights of A Probationer or Parolee Who Has Been Convicted of a New Crime

The important situation where the probationer or parolee has been convicted of a new crime has not yet been mentioned. A final conviction of a new crime logically may serve as the requisite authority for making the resentencing decision. The proceedings underlying the conviction presumably were replete with more procedural formalities and determined by a more stringent standard than any proposed for revocation.[141]

Let it be clear, however, that the fact of conviction does not obviate the need for a hearing and counsel; it only alters the decisions to be made. Since the court or the board is not required to impose or reimpose a prison term, the individual must have an opportunity to affect the disposition. A parolee or probationer may well be able to argue for the imposition of a concurrent sentence.[142] In any event, he should have the opportunity to force the issue and receive a timely determination rather than be required to serve a prison term facing a violator's warrant lodged as a detainer.

Finally, there may be situations where the field officer believes that an alleged violation is sufficiently serious to bring to the attention of the court or the board but he may also believe that a sanction short of imprisonment is appropriate. The officer, after consultation with his superior, may conclude that a reprimand would be effective, that the burdens of supervision should be increased, or that more onerous conditions be imposed.[143]

Unless the individual's liberty is at stake, a more relaxed procedure seems permissible. The alleged violator should be given notice and an opportunity to appear and tell his story, but it seems unncesssary to require counsel, confrontation, a record of the proceedings, and the like. Should the revoking authority decide that imprisonment may be the appropriate sanction, then (unless the matter has progressed to the point where, for example, uncounselled and damaging admissions have been obtained) the proceeding may be converted into a more formal hearing.

In concluding this section, several matters that previously have been implied or touched upon obliquely should be glorified. The discussion concerning the need for a hearing and the assistance of counsel has assumed that the fault principle —the need to establish a violation—is operative. Yet, at least in probation proceedings, there is no unanimity in the law on this point. Indeed, Judge Bazelon,

---

[141] This point is discussed in Shelton v. United States Parole Board, 388 F.2d 567, 575–77 (D.C. Cir. 1967).

[142] In probation proceedings counsel may often "plead to the violation" in return for dismissal of the criminal charge. On the other hand, he may plead to both if he is assured of concurrent sentences.

[143] *See*, MODEL PENAL CODE §305.16 (P.O.D. 1962).

writing in *Hyser* v. *Reed,* stated, "But no specific violation of probation need be found in order to revoke probation." It has not been satisfactorily explained why this position can be maintained for probation and how a distinction can be drawn between probation and parole.[144]

The approach taken here has been to urge specificity and rationality in the imposition of conditions and to recognize the individual's legitimate expectations of continuity when those conditions are observed. When an alleged breach occurs, it should be regarded as a solemn event to be proved expeditiously, with adequate ceremony, and with basic fairness.

[144] The leading "no need for a violation" case is Kaplan v. United States, 234 F.2d 345 (8th Cir. 1956).

ORGANIZATION, ADMINISTRATION, AND PERSONNEL

This section begins with the chapter from the National Advisory Commission on Criminal Justice Standards and Goals relating to the organization and administration of corrections. The selection itself begins with the observation that "American corrections is a diffuse and variegated system. Its organization and management processes reflect those conditions." The Commission chapter identifies and discusses some of the more basic problems in correctional organizations by examining the organizations themselves, organizational development and analysis, management by objectives and planning responsibility, and management style and organizational climate. The chapter makes it clear that probation and parole operate within organizational and administrative freedoms and constraints.

The second selection in the section is also from the National Advisory Commission and is directed toward manpower for corrections and begins with the observation that "people are the most effective resource for helping other people." The Commission focuses on emerging issues that affect manpower, ranging from disenchantment with prisons through racial strife and political activism among offenders to manpower needs including recruitment, retention, staff education, and development. The selection notes that manpower problems in corrections include shortages of professional personnel, poor working conditions, and poor allocation of both human and fiscal resources.

E. Kim Nelson, formerly Associate Director of the President's Commission on Law Enforcement and Administration of Justice (Corrections), and Catherine Lovell provide perspectives on correctional management, their observations being the product of a special study of correctional administrators made for the Joint Commission on Correctional Manpower and Training. Nelson and Lovell summarize the research on correctional management, examine the evolution of the management function in corrections, and target on corrections and the development of a science of management.

Mark S. Richmond, retired Assistant Director of the United States Bureau of Prisons, identifies and examines major issues related to the concept of the offender as consumer of resources. Urging increased effectiveness of correctional planning and program management, he notes that the problem is two-fold, that the costs of dealing with the offender are both enormous and increasing and there is virtually no evidence that present correctional methods are effective interventions in criminal careers. With insight he addresses the complicated phenomenon of a failure to define and synthesize the goals of criminal justice and corrections.

Finally, the section terminates with the Code of Ethics subscribed to by the United States Probation and Parole Officer, a code generally shared throughout corrections.

42

Organization and Administration of Corrections

NATIONAL ADVISORY COMMISSION ON CRIMINAL
JUSTICE STANDARDS AND GOALS

American corrections is a diffuse and variegated system. Its organization and management processes reflect those conditions. The range includes huge, centralized departmental complexes and autonomous one-man probation offices; separation of corrections from other governmental functions and combination of corrections with law enforcement, mental health, and social welfare; highly professionalized management methods and strikingly primitive ones.

In spite of these differences, there are commonalities. Of special interest are the stubborn problems and dilemmas which run through the whole fabric of correctional organization. These focal problems and concerns will be discussed in the following pages.

SOURCE. *Corrections,* National Advisory Commission on Criminal Justice Standards and Goals, Washington, D.C., U.S. Government Printing Office, 1973, pp. 439–454.

BASIC PROBLEMS OF CORRECTIONAL ORGANIZATIONS

What is the nature of correctional organizations in the United States? What are the attendant problems facing correctional agencies, and how, if at all, are these problems being addressed?

The answer to the first question is made clear by a series of statistical reports recently prepared by the Law Enforcement Assistance Administration.[1] The reports, which provide data on justice services at State and local levels, reveal that we have an almost incomprehensible maze of departments, divisions, commissions, and boards functioning at city, county, and State levels, developed and maintained without the benefit of inter–or intra–governmental coordination. Contributing also to this diversity are the Federal institutions dealing with both adult and juvenile offenders that operate independently from the functions of the State and local governments.

The national summary of the LEAA reports indicates that there were 5,312 corrections facilities in the United States in 1971 (4,503 for adults and 809 for juveniles) and 2,444 probation and parole agencies.[2] While a cursory examination of these figures may not be startling, more detailed evaluation reveals the fact that only 16 percent of the adult and juvenile correctional facilities are operated at the State level, with the remaining 84 percent, consisting predominantly of county and local jails and lockups, dividing among the 3,047 counties in the Nation and an even greater number of cities, townships, and villages.

Dividing correctional activities into the two major divisions, institutions on the one hand and probation and parole activities on the other, provides a clearer understanding of the national corrections picture. For example, LEAA statistics show that approximately 12 percent of adult correctional facilities in the Nation are provided at the State level, while the remaining 88 percent are provided by city and county governments. Juvenile correctional facilities are distributed more equally. Approximately 45 percent of them are provided at the State level, with the remaining 55 percent supported almost exclusively by county governments. With regard to probation and parole agencies, approximately 30 percent are administered by State governments, with the remaining 70 percent at the local level. As in the case of juvenile correctional facilities, the county governments perform the majority of the local functions.

While the statistical description of correctional services confirms claims of fragmentation, isolation, and multiple levels of delivery of services, further insights into the scope of the problem can be gained through an examination of a 1971 report by the Advisory Commission on Intergovernmental Relations, *State-Local Relations in the Criminal Justice System*. The information provided by this

---

[1] These reports, one for each State, were prepared by the Statistics Division, National Institute of Law Enforcement and Criminal Justice of the Law Enforcement Assistance Administration. For explanations of the limitations of the data and definitions see the Appendix of this report.

[2] These figures are provided by the LEAA reports. Percentages and other interpretations were extrapolated from the original figures.

report details the broad spectrum of organizational arrangements that presently characterizes our correctional agencies and reinforces the image of corrections established by the national statistics cited earlier. (See Appendix.)

Major Issues in Organization

The summary of the Advisory Commission's major findings indicates that in the area of organizational and jurisdictional problems, the following major issues have been identified.

All but four States have highly fragmented correctional systems, vesting various correctional responsibilities in either independent boards or noncorrectional agencies. In 41 States, an assortment of health, welfare, and youth agencies exercise certain correctional responsibilities, though their primary function is not corrections.

In over 40 States, neither State nor local governments have full-scale responsibility for comprehensive correctional services. Some corrections services, particularly parole and adult and juvenile institutions, are administered by State agencies, while others, such as probation, local institutions and jails, and juvenile detention, are county or city responsibilities.

More than half of the States provide no standard-setting or inspection services to local jails and local adult correctional institutions.[3]

The States that exercise control over all correctional activities within their systems have become five in number since the report was written. They are: Alaska, Connecticut, Delaware, Rhode Island, and Vermont.

Three basic problems emerge from this analysis of correctional organization in the United States:

● The problem of unifying and coordinating a highly fragmented array of services and programs.

● The problem of shifting fiscal resources from Federal and State levels to local governments, while guiding and assisting localities to improve the quality of their services.

● The problem of changing correctional organizations from closed, hierarchical systems oriented to retribution and restraint into open and flexible systems capable of rehabilitating and resocializing the offenders committed to them.

Coordination is needed not only among correctional agencies, but between them and the other components of the criminal justice system. Moreover, the interrelationships between correctional agencies and other organizations concerned with human problems (e.g., mental health, social welfare, poverty reduction) are of vital importance. Linkages must be established with the private as well as the public sector. Paradoxically, intimate relationships between corrections

[3] Advisory Commission on Intergovernmental Relations, *State-Local Relations in the Criminal Justice System* (Washington: Government Printing Office, 1971), p. 15.

and law enforcement may impede the ability of corrections to develop reciprocities with the health, education, and welfare complex. Thus, coordination and unification are delicate functions, requiring finesse as well as firm use of available sanctions.

The problem of financing correctional improvements is of critical importance. Ironically, the greatest fiscal capability has existed within large and senior government units, while the services most needed are at the level of local government, whose fiscal impotence is known to everyone.

As to the problem of rigid, stratified, and encapsulated forms of correctional organization, it must be remembered that these organizations were in many cases established in the late 18th or early 19th century. Consequently their structures follow the traditional authoritarian model—one that was appropriate to achieve the then-held goals of revenge and restraint. However, correctional organizations have superimposed additional goals since that time—rehabilitation and, more recently, reintegration of offenders into the community. It is probably impossible to achieve these goals in a traditional organizational milieu. The incompatibility of these more recent trends with the traditional physical plant and organizational structures of corrections represents a profound problem in the renovation of correctional systems.

Some Directions for Change

How can the organization of correctional services be redesigned to meet the problems described above? What can be done to overcome fragmentation and duplication of scarce resources? How can existing finances be reallocated and new funds generated? Are there ways of changing closed and hierarchical systems? There are no easy answers, but there are directions that can be taken with the assurance of significant improvement over the present inadequate scheme.

To begin with, there can be a more rational and coordinated distribution of tasks and missions among the various governmental jurisdictions involved. The Federal Government should relinquish most direct correctional services for offenders, retaining only those which cost-benefit analyses indicate are inappropriate for State and local governments.[4]

At the same time, the Federal level should greatly increase its role in providing financing, standard setting, technical assistance, and manpower development to the correctional services carried on locally. Leadership, stimulation, knowledge discovery, information, coordination, and catalytic influence should be key features of the new Federal role. There are encouraging indications that the Law Enforcement Assistance Administration is moving in this direction. It is less apparent that the Federal Bureau of Prisons and Federal probation services are

---

[4] Examples of appropriate activities might be: development of regional Federal facilities for female offenders; and the development of special facilities for "mentally ill offenders," a group which has fallen between psychiatric and correctional institutions.

prepared to divest themselves of major elements of operating responsibility.

The major arena for reintegrative programs is the local community. Administrative power and sanction must be placed there if such efforts are to be strong, well articulated with local resources, and suitably responsive to local needs and problems.

The key to such a redistribution of authority and responsibility lies in the development of new methods of financing correctional services. The probation subsidy program in California is one illustration of a strong effort to strengthen county services and reduce reliance on State institutions. Experimentation with varied subventions, grants, and other forms of intergovernmental assistance will be required. A combination of assistance and regulation—carrot and stick—will be necessary to bring about the needed changes.

There is, moreover, a major opportunity for regional solutions to problems which no single jurisdiction can meet unilaterally. It is essential to have intergovernmental agreements and flexible administrative arrangements which bring offenders to the optimal location for supervision and rehabilitation.

The solution to the traditional reliance of corrections upon hierarchical, authoritarian forms of organization lies in breaking that mold in favor of more creative systems. Instead of large, isolated, custodial institutions operating as self-sufficient baronies, there is a need for small, community-oriented facilities, linked in myriad ways with the resources required for successful reentry to legitimate life.

Instead of jails which operate as appendages of law enforcement and *at best* merely "warehouse" the misdemeanants sentenced to them, the need is for jails which are a part of integrated correctional services, tied closely to probation and parole, and providing such obvious services as medical aid, educational and employment assistance, and attention to the gross, statistically overwhelming problems of alcoholism, drug abuse, and social alienation.

It should be noted that, while the accomplishment of these organizational changes is a formidable task, certain trends and innovations already are taking place. Examples of such activities are provided in the following statement from a previously quoted report of the Commission on Intergovernmental Relations:

Nine States have established regional juvenile detention facilities while regional jails and correctional institutions have been established in at least seven others.

Over ten States provide inspection services for juvenile detention facilities, jails, and local correctional institutions, and a comparable number of States have stipulated minimum standards for jails, local institutions, and juvenile and misdemeanant probation services.

In four States, a single State department administers all juvenile activities; in three States, the same agency is responsible for administering both juvenile and adult correctional services.[5]

---

[5] *State-Local Relations in the Criminal Justice System,* p. 17.

The Commission believes that unification of all correctional programs within a State will allow it to coordinate programs that are essentially interdependent, better utilize scarce human and fiscal resources, and develop more effective programs across the spectrum of corrections. This concept is elaborated in Chapter 16, The Statutory Framework of Corrections, particularly in Standard 16.4, Unifying Correctional Programs.

In this section an effort has been made to examine the organizational arrangements that characterize corrections today. Some general perspectives and directions for change have been noted.

The following sections approach the development and improvement of correctional administration in a broader context. Several recent theories of how to secure organizational growth and change are applied to the problems of the correctional field.

CORRECTIONAL ORGANIZATIONS

Corrections is a "human resource" organization; that is, its material is people, its product, behavior. The unique features of this type of organization complicate its structural design and management and make both a central part of implementing programs discussed in other chapters of this report.

Unlike a manufacturing operation, the "production process" consists of trained specialists operating on intangibles, and so organizational design must consider the added interpersonal dimension of employee-client relationships. Behavioral and attitudinal effects of specialists on the client are interdependent, and the degree to which various functional specialists are integrated into a "team" determines organizational effectiveness. The relation of functional integration to the effectiveness of human resource organizations places a premium on clearly defined and mutually agreed-to objectives whose identification must precede structural design. Too frequently, organization analysis begins with a set of diagrams rather than a detailed analysis of the problem as a description of alternative functional groupings in relation to previously specified objectives.

Managing a human resource organization is probably even more difficult than managing other public agencies because many traditional management tools are not directly applicable. Data describing effects of the correctional process relate to behavior or attitudes and are subject to subjective, frequently conflicting interpretations. The feedback loops necessary for judging the consequences of policies are difficult to create and suffer from incomplete and inaccurate information. There has not been in corrections an organized and consistent relation between evaluative research and management action.

The management of corrections as a human resource organization must be viewed broadly in terms of how offenders, employees, and various organization processes (communications, decisionmaking, and others) are combined into what is called "the corrections process."

ORGANIZATION DEVELOPMENT

Management by objectives (MBO), planning and organization analysis are elements of a relatively new concept called organization development (OD). Bennis defines it as "a response to change, a complex educational strategy intended to change beliefs, attitudes, values, and structure of organizations so that they can better adapt to new technologies, markets and challenges and the dizzying rate of change itself."[6] Demands for innovation, the trend toward integrated services, and disagreement over objectives suggest that OD programs are applicable to the correction field. To specify how this could be done would require a separate book. Hence the discussion here will outline only the interrelations between basic elements of OD and will concentrate on three areas considered to be of top priority in corrections today: organization analysis, management by objectives, and planning. However, ideally and for completeness, any contemplated activity in these areas should not be considered apart from the broader concept of OD.

Organization development is based on two sets of ideas: one relating to groups and organizations, and the other to individuals.[7] Organizational development views organizations as many interrelated subsystems mutually affecting each other. Problem solving, therefore, is interdependent. In corrections, a simple example would be a change in the industrial production schedule that limited the time offenders could spend in counseling programs.

A distinction is made between tasks or functions and the processes used to perform them. A planning function, for example, can be performed by a task force or a planning office, and it may begin at the operating level or the executive level. OD emphasizes *how* things are done, on the assumption that *what* is done will be determined in large part by the process. In turn, the work climate (e.g., the leadership styles discussed later) is a determinant of which processes are selected.

Reflecting OD's social science origins, anonymous questionnaires and interviews are used to collect data on work group interrelationships, employees' attitudes, etc. Findings then are discussed with employee groups to improve their insights into such organization processes as line-staff and executive-staff communications, location of decisionmaking, and perceived roles.

Within the organization, individuals are encouraged to develop mutual trust, be candid, openly discuss conflict, and take risks. A premium is placed on the individual's self-actualization fulfillment of his needs within the organization's overall goals and objectives.

A variety of specific interventions are used to implement these ideas and are

---

[6] Warren G. Bennis, *Organization Development: Its Nature, Objectives, and Prospects* (Addison-Wesley, 1969), p. 2.

[7] Much of the following discussion is drawn from Arthur C. Beck and Ellis D. Hillman, eds., *A Practical Approach to Organization Development through Management by objectives* (Addison-Wesley, 1972).

limited only by the creativity of the change agent. Team building, intergroup problem solving, surveys, reorganization, training in decisionmaking and problem solving, modifying work flows, and job enrichment are examples of the types of techniques frequently employed.[8] An OD program usually involves an outside consultant to begin with, but it is essential to have (or develop) a capability for continuing the program within the organization. Generally, these techniques and processes are used in the work situation—the functions to be performed—to integrate the factors necessary for employee effectiveness (interpersonal skills, individual performance objectives, etc.) with the goals of the organization. OD practitioners feel that this complex process is necessary to relate organization design, planning, objectives, and employee performance.

ORGANIZATION ANALYSIS

Organization analysis and design is a specialty that should not be left to whim, the pressures and forces of the moment, or the experience of individuals whose direct personal knowledge of the organization is limited. On the other hand, the analyst should realize that reorganization may have salutory political effects by giving the appearance of change while everything remains the same.

The historical correctional proclivity for fads should be avoided in organizational design. Calling for simple unification of institutions, parole, and probation into a State department of corrections has become a frequent suggestion. While in some situations this will improve correctional services, it is a delusion to believe that tinkering can, by itself, effect the functional integration desired. Frequently, sub-units of large-scale organizations carve out a functional territory and vigorously guard it against intrusion and change. Organization, although important, is not the panacea for all operational problems; formally redefining roles does not automatically change actual operations.

There are many types of organizational structures and many ways to analyze them. Depending on the assumptions, an organization may be divided on the basis of region, line-staff relationships, functions, or missions. These divisions rarely appear in pure form; for example a regional organization may be subdivided on the basis of functional groupings. In corrections, it is not unusual to base organizations on the sex, age, and offense of the clientele. Regardless of the type chosen, the correctional manager should recognize that the specific structure should be evaluated in terms of its relation to decisionmaking, the objectives of the organization, and the environment in which it operates.

As one organization analyst states, "Among the first things to consider in the organization of work are basic, underlying assumptions. All too frequently work

---

[8] Robert E. Blake et al., "Breakthrough in Organization Development: Large-scale Program That Implements Behavioral Science Concepts," *Harvard Business Review*, 42 (1964), 133–155; and Warner W. Burke, "A Comparison of Management Development and Organization Development," *Journal of Applied Behavioral Science*, 7 (1972), 569–579.

is organized in terms of solutions, practices, even theories; yet basic beliefs about individuals who make up the organization are either ignored, or are merely implied."[9]

Principles of organization analysis are as numerous as the structures they produce. How phenomena are interpreted depends on the way they are analyzed. In one view, the organization is conceived as an "organism," the critical features of which are its ability to (1) test reality, (2) interpret the test, and (3) adapt to changes.[10] Another model focuses on the psychology of the individuals who make up the organization (motivations, desires, gratification, etc.).[11] A sociological view would identify the various groups comprising the organization, the norms governing their interaction, and the prevailing value systems.[12] A more mechanical interpretation of organizations sees subunits as carefully integrated contributors to the production process which perform their assigned duties routinely without regard for the work of other units.

Any reorganization problem should be viewed from all these perspectives to draw out the possible implications or effects of the particular structure being proposed as a solution. The exigencies of the time may require a compromise of specific "principles" of organization. For example, two basic principles frequently violated by correctional organization are "unity of direction" and "equality of authority and responsibility." Interposing a policy board between the State's chief executive and the correctional agency limits the governor's authority over an organization for which he is responsible to the public. Policy authority is divorced from operational authority, even though there may originally have been sound reasons for this departure from "principles."

Similarly, overlapping responsibilities are not, per se, undesirable. In some situations, in fact, they may positively contribute to a stated organizational objective. For example, the Air Force does not have sole responsibility for military air operations. The Marine Corps and the Army also have organizational units providing air services because the prime objective for the Marines is troop mobility and for the Army, air support of ground maneuvers. When visibility is an objective, a program-based organizational unit (e.g., narcotics treatment) may be superimposed on a functional categorization (e.g., education, counseling).

Failure to recommend a specific solution will not satisfy the manager who wants a meal and not a recipe. But there is no single or simple answer. Rather the most appropriate organizational arrangements must be decided after the problem is analyzed from a variety of perspectives and in relation to what the particular structure is ultimately to accomplish.

---

[9] Hugh Estes, "Some Considerations in Designing an Organizational Structure," in Mason Haire, ed., *Organization Theory in Industrial Practice* (Wiley, 1962), p. 15.

[10] Mason Haire, "Biological Models and Empirical Histories of the Growth of Organizations" in Mason Haire, ed., *Modern Organization Theory* (Wiley, 1959), pp. 272–276.

[11] Rensis Likert, "A Motivational Approach to a Modified Theory of Organization and Management" in Mason Haire, ed., *Modern Organization Theory* (Wiley, 1959), pp. 184–217.

[12] Rensis Likert, *New Patterns of Management* (McGraw-Hill, 1961).

The important features in a reorganization are the *actual* changes in employee interrelations and the policies communicated to them, not the arrangement of boxes in an organization chart. Effective work groups and interpersonal relations are not formed and dissolved by policy statements. A reorganization cannot be accomplished solely by pronouncement. It must include a specification of what processes (meetings, group discussions, timing, etc.) will be used to implement it. Management disenchantment with reorganization usually arises because these processes are ignored.

An organization's objectives partially determine its most effective structure. Although offenders are affected, corrections' retribution objective relates primarily to serving society. A rehabilitation or reintegration objective focuses directly on the individual, and consequently organizational arrangements must be different from those focusing on retribution.

The emphasis on opening institutions to the community increases the number of employees whose primary frame of reference is external to the organization.[13] Such "boundary persons" typically have attitudes more congruent with persons outside the organization, a fact which may increase the difficulties of resolving internal conflicts.

The emphasis on offenders' rights implies more than a new office or changed procedures; it will require a more independent organizational subunit and an attitude of negotiation rather than confrontation. The present stress on innovation and the prospects of a continuing demand for change in corrections require flexible organizational arrangements where work groups are viewed as fluid and temporary.

Analysis of Correctional Organization

For many years it has been an almost universal practice in the corrections field to refer to "systems" when considering the corrections process. Earlier, the reference was to "penal systems" or "prison systems." Currently, the phrases "correction systems" or even "criminal justice systems" are favored. This long-term and widespread use of the word "systems" has tended to obscure the fact that most correction jurisdictions are neither designed nor managed as organizational systems.

Correctional services can be described only as nonorganized. Virtually all larger correction agencies have organization charts that presume to depict the flow of authority and accountability among the diverse elements that comprise each specific correction organization. Many such organizations also have policy manuals, job descriptions or position profiles for staff, job specifications, other organizational and personnel documents, and standard operating procedures that reinforce the notion of organization. But the salient characteristic of virtually all correction organizations today is their high degree of inter-and intra-organizational separatism for legal, political, and bureaucratic reasons.

[13] Thomas Mathiesen, *Across the Boundaries of Organizations: An Exploratory Study of Communications Patterns in Two Penal Institutions* (Glendessary, 1971).

In substantial part this organizational fragmentation is the heritage of the legal background from which all contemporary correction organizations have evolved. This legal heritage limited the operational boundaries of "correctional" responsibility to the time span between sentencing to institutional custody and release from institutional custody. What may occur earlier is perceived as the responsibility of legislative bodies, police, courts, and probation. Whatever may occur subsequent to conditional release from institutional custody is perceived as the responsibility of parole.

Among the negative consequences occurring directly or indirectly from the acceptance by most correction managers of the legal frame of reference are these:

• Managerial thinking has tended to become constricted and reactive to the emergence of problems, rather than innovative and anticipatory.

• The boundaries of the corrections field largely have been accepted as statutorily and bureaucratically defined, rather than creatively probed and, where appropriate, professionally challenged. For example, definition and prevention of crime tend to be seen as the responsibility of others. Relatively few correctional administrators have been concerned professionally with the existence of wide disparities in the law and court practice regarding sentences.

• Input of offenders into correction organizations tends to be accepted without demur, the attitude of correctional managers too often being "we take what they send us and do the best we can." This acquiescence frequently has resulted in the sentencing of juveniles to adult institutions, imprisonment of offenders who need psychiatric or other mental health care in institutions that lack competent staff and adequate facilities, and acceptance from the criminal justice process of inordinately large numbers of the black and the poor.

• The focus of correction organizations tends to be institutional, reflecting the emphasis in the criminal justice process on whatever facility is perceived as the "appropriate" extension of the court of jurisdiction: the training school for the juvenile offender, the prison for the convicted adult violator.

Traditionally, the institutional focus has been custodial, whatever may be the philosophic rhetoric of the correction jurisdiction. This orientation too stems from an historic perception of the institution as the "holding" extension of the courts.

The nonorganization of corrections also results from political arrangements. The Federal Government, through the Department of Justice and the judiciary, operates three distinct correctional agencies: the Bureau of Prisons, the Board of Parole, and the Probation Service. As noted earlier in this chapter, each of the 50 States operates a corrections "agency." And, through bureaucratic subdivision, many operate several separate agencies; for example, juvenile corrections, adult corrections, probation, and parole. Local governments present varied organizational patterns, ranging from a relatively complex correctional organization in New York City to simple detention facilities in small city police stations or rural courthouses.

Further separatism is the product of bureaucracy. Even within those States with administratively grouped correctional responsibility, there nonetheless is the tendency to establish bureaucratic subjurisdictions. Administratively these may be divided into probation and parole, juvenile corrections, and adult corrections.

These major categories sometimes are further subdivided on the basis of the individual's offense, age, and sex. Hence, the "organization" of corrections in each political jurisdiction tends to emphasize separate institutions for the adult offender, subdivided in turn into minimum, medium, and maximum security facilities for men and women. Until recently, State correction agencies and local facilities segregated each category of offender on the basis of race, often in separate institutions for each offender category.

Within correctional agencies and specific institutions of such agencies, there is often a philosophic and operational separation of staff members whose duties are principally custodial from those whose responsibilities concern offender programs. Also, like all large-scale organizations, corrections has informal or social organization of staff and of inmates, frequently working at cross-purposes to the formal goals of the organization.

Fragmentation hampers the ability of an organization or a group of organizations to respond to new environmental forces and stress. An organization's ability to achieve specified objectives is contingent on its detection of and responsiveness to changing environmental factors. It first must recognize and accurately assess changes that affect its operations (e.g., public attitudes toward alcoholism) and then develop a response consistent with overall objectives (e.g., treat alcoholism as a medical problem). Similarly, as the general population's education level increased, correctional agencies were required to provide college-level programs for offenders.

The corrections field already is being substantially affected by dramatic changes occurring in American society. The incidence of crime nationwide has risen at an alarming rate, and younger persons comprise a disproportionate amount of this increase. Therefore, it reasonably can be expected that the number of offenders requiring services will rise substantially in the immediate future. Because of the national pattern of high birth rates from the end of World War II into the mid–1960's, the average age of offenders probably will decline somewhat, at least in the immediate future.

There have been perceptible shifts in public opinion regarding correctional operations and their effects on offenders. This has been reflected in growing legislative criticism and demands for reform. The judiciary has extended the application of civil and constitutional rights to almost all aspects of corrections. Professional groups such as the American Bar Association have assumed an active role in advocating reform and direct services to offenders.

The field of corrections faces a period of rapid and dramatic change with a highly fragmented organization and a substantially inappropriate management orientation. Considerable evidence exists to suggest that the organizational arrangements and managerial approaches that largely characterize the corrections field today did not serve well the relatively stable situation of the past. There is every reason to believe that they will serve even less well in the dynamic and fluid environment of tomorrow.

MANAGEMENT BY OBJECTIVES

Management by objectives (MBO) emphasizes a goal-oriented philosophy and attitude. Goal-oriented management focuses on results with less concern for method, as long as it is within accepable legal and moral limits. Traditional management, on the other hand, tends to be task-oriented, with emphasis on task performance without adequate regard for results.

The purpose of management by objectives is to: (1) develop a mutually understood statement regarding the organization's direction and (2) provide criteria for measuring organization and individual performance. The statement is a hierarchical set of interrelated and measurable goals, objectives, and subobjectives. If properly conducted, the process may be as important as the objectives themselves because it improves vertical and horizontal communication and emphasizes interdepartmental integration.

For an MBO system to be implemented successfully, it must be based on a participative management philosophy and fulfill several specific conditions.[14]

First, the full support of top managment is essential. Indeed at each level of management the superior's degree of acceptance of this managerial approach will determine substantially whether or not subordinage accept the system and try to make it work.

A second necessary condition is a goal-oriented management philosophy. The motivational value of an MBO approach depends in great part upon giving each manager and employee responsibility to carry out a job without constant supervision and then assessing him on his degree of accomplishment.

Third, each superior-subordinate relationship should be characterized by the highest degree of cooperation and mutual respect possible.

Fourth, managerial focus should be on any deviations from agreed-upon levels of goal attainment, not on personalities; and the evaluation system should report any such deviations to the manager or employee establishing the goal, not to his superior.

The fifth condition is feedback. If managers are to be evaluated on the results they obtain, they require timely and accurate readings of their progress to take corrective action when necessary. Further they need substantially accurate projections and interpretations of demographic, technical, social, legal, and other developments likely to affect their progress and performance.

Finally, to be successful, an intensive training program must precede organizational implementation. A followup consultative service should be available to organizational members or units requiring assistance in implementing this system.

[14] David Schreiber and Stanley Sloan, "Management by Objectives," *Personnel Administration,* 15 (1970), 20–26.

Implementing MBO

Designing and implementing management by objectives requires the achievement of the following sequential steps:

1. An ongoing system capable of accurately identifying and predicting changes in the environment in which the organization functions.

2. Administrative capability through a management information system to provide data quickly to appropriate organizational members, work groups, or organizational units for their consideration and possible utilization.

3. Clearly established and articulted organizational and individual goals, mutually accepted through a process of continuous interaction between management and workers and between various levels of management. Unilateral imposition of organizational goals on lower echelon participants will not result in an MBO system but another bureaucracy.

4. An ongoing evelution of the organizational and individual goals in the light of feedback from the system. Such feedback and evaluation may result in the resetting of goals.

5. A properly designed and functioning organizational system for effective and efficient service delivery. In such a system, goal-oriented collaboration and cooperation are organizationally facilitated, and administrative services fully support efforts at goal accomplishment.

6. A managerial and work climate highly conducive to employee motivation and sclf-actualization toward organizational goal accomplishments. Such a climate should be developed and nurtured through the application of a participative style of management to be discussed shortly.

7. A properly functioning system for appraising organizational, work group, and individual progress toward goal attainment.

CORRECTIONAL MANAGEMENT'S PLANNING RESPONSIBILITY

It is an unfortunate reality that most correction agencies do not engage in planning in the fullest sense. While many have a general notion of where they are going and some engage in specific aspects of planning such as facilities construction, few are engaged in the full planning process. This process involves development of integrated long-range, intermediate-range, and short-range plans for the complete spectrum of their administrative and operational functions.

Several rationalizations are offered to account for the lack of comprehensive planning. Perhaps the most common is "We can't tell what the legislature is going to do." This "explanation" ignores the fact that what the legislature does (or does not do) often comes about precisely because no practical, planned, and documented alternative has been proposed by corrections management. Also commonly heard is the rationalization, "There is simply not enough time—our organization is already overworked and understaffed." But corrections managment always finds the time and staff resources to deal with crises rising in the system.

Planning, contrary to the opinion of many, is not something new and difficult. To paraphrase the historian Arnold Toynbee, "One of the characteristics of being human is that one makes plans." While the efficiency experts of World War II and the PPB (Planning, Programing, Budgeting) experts of the mid-1960's may lay claim to a large share of the limelight and insight, planning is something that all men engage in to varying degrees. One need only recall the past 50 years to recognize the continuum of changing planning styles that has taken place in the United States:

- Long-range corporate planning from the 1920's to the present.
- New Deal economic planning.
- World War II military operations and production planning.
- Fair Deal, New Frontier, and Great Society full employment and social welfare planning.
- Suburban growth and urban renewal planning.
- Systems planning (PPB and PMS) and application to human resources programs.

Too frequently, planning has been left to an isolated office staffed with technicians, and the organization has received their product with reluctance. Failure to differentiate types of planning (e.g., strategic and tactical) has led to two extremes: either the planning function is considered the total purview of top management, or it is seen as the aggregation of individual plans from many organizational subunits. In fact, it is neither. The planning process should involve input (information, objectives, progress, etc.) from all organizational units, but the major decisions regarding goals and resource allocations are responsibility of top management.

Role of the Planner

The effective planner is not an ivory tower technician, but some unique features of his role should be recognized and supported. His effectiveness depends in part on a sensitivity to the changing conditions under which the organization must operate. Therefore, he is frequently seen as an "outsider" by the rest of the organization because he continually raises questions not immediately impinging on daily operations. The planner is a "devil's advocate" and questions the basic assumptions and operating practices of the organization. In examining alternatives to the status quo for their possible application to the organization, he is placed in the role of an unwanted change agent.

The planner sometimes contributes to his own alienation by not recognizing that large organizations always contain conflicting opinions that must be reconciled by the chief executive. There are pragmatic restrictions on what ideally should be a rational process. Even though managment decisions may be at odds with the "compelling evidence," the planning function should at least make the reasons for the decisions explicit.

The planner should be a participant-observer in the short-term decisionmaking of top management. Only in this way can he be in a position to point out the relationships between daily action and long-range intentions. Planning can be called a manager's technique to invent the future. It can also be thought of as a systematic examination of future opportunities and risks and the strategies to exploit the opportunities and avoid the risks. It would appear, however, that planning more clearly is the rational process of directing today's decisions toward the accomplishment of a set of predetermined short and long-range goals. This process depends upon how problems are identified, broken down into manageable dimensions, related to one another, and resolved through the choice of a number of alternatives.

Planning and Budgeting Systems

The budget expresses in financial terms the correctional manager's plans or goals. Budgeting is an administrative mechanism for making choices among alternative and competitive resource uses, presumably balancing public needs and organizational requirements against available and requested funds. When the choices are coordinated with the correctional organization's goals, the budget becomes a plan.

Like planning, budgeting is something that everyone does including the wealthy. We budget our time, money, food, entertainment, and other requirements with a general view to meeting our personal and family goals. The correctional manager is charged with budgeting his resources to meet organizational, staff, and offender goals.

Operating, annual, capital, or facilities budgets are common differentiations in types of budget. The distinction largely is related to differences in timing (annual vs. long-range), degree of uniqueness (ongoing requirements vs. one-time expenditures), and differentiated financing arrangements (annual tax collection vs. bonded indebtedness).

The distinction between line-item and program budgets is of substantial managerial significance. The line-item budget is input-oriented, focusing on specific, discrete items of expenditure required to perform a service and categorized by organizational units. A program budget is output-oriented, focusing on the function or service performed.

The line-item budget tends to focus the attention of decisionmakers, including legislators, on specifics such as food, supplies, clothing, and books. The program approach tends to elevate the decisionmaking focus to the level of programmatic concern and consideration of alternative courses of action.

The Program Planning and Budgeting System (PPBS), popular in the 1960's is a system-oriented effort to link planning, budgeting, and management by objective processes through programs. Under this sytem an agency or organization first would ask itself: "What is our purpose, and what goals are we attempting to realize?"

Once our purposes or objectives have been determined, action programs to achieve these objectives would be identified or, if nonexistent, designed.

Next, each such program would be analyzed. In existing programs, the analysis would be in terms of the extent to which they were oriented to achievement of the organization's objectives. Reference would be made to the level of effectiveness at which they were functioning toward such attainment. In the case of newly formulated, objective-oriented programs, the analysis would be in terms of their anticipated costs and expected contribution to accomplishment of organizational objectives.

Finally, in terms of the decisionmaking process, existing and new alternative programs would be analytically compared as to their respective costs and anticipated benefits. Should an alternative, on the basis of such a cost-benefit analysis, be deemed preferable to an existing program, the latter would be discarded and the alternative adopted.

Implicit in this management system is a longer-range programming perspective coupled with a continuous process of reevaluation of objectives, programs, and budgetary amounts as circumstances change.

Regardless of how organized and formal an organization's planning, there are six criteria by which managers may judge the comprehensiveness and adequacy of the planning process. These criteria are stated in terms of questions that sould be asked repeatedly with reference to any specific planning approach:

● Has the system's planning process adequately identifed the key influences in development and trends of American society, the region, and the State, and properly evaluated the impact of each such influence on the field of corrections, its functional components, and on the specific correction system itself?

● Have the strengths and weaknesses of the system been assessed accurately?

● Have the capacities and capabilities of different system functions to support the plan been projected far enough ahead?

● Have alternatives been considered and evaluated adequately?

● Is there a realistic timetable or schedule for implementation?

● What provisions have been made for possible future reverses?

The basis of correctional planning must shift from individuals to a group framework, as the concerns of the correctional manager and planner quickly become more universal.

"One of the great challenges facing . . . [the planner] is the necessity of coordinating knowledge, influence, and resources on a scale commensurate with the human problems he is addressing. . . . [These] problems are interrelated, complex and resistant to piecemeal efforts."[15] Clearly, a logical, systematic planning approach is needed that recognizes problem complexity, changing concepts, and changing priorities, and provides a means for developing more effective programs.

The objective of community corrections, for example, is to maximize offenders' access to local resources, not as an alternative to incarceration but as a solution itself. This goal requires more integration of criminal justice components (statewide and within each local area) and coordination with other social service delivery systems. (See Chapter 9.)

---

[15] Robert Perlman and Arnold Gurin, *Community Organization and Social Planning* (Wiley, 1972), p. 238.

Planning for the Future of Corrections

The rate of change in corrections has not reached a pace that makes planning impossible. Many of today's problems are related directly to the failure to anticipate the operational impact of general social and environmental changes. The extension of the range of offenders' rights, for example, was a natural outgrowth of a similar movement involving racial minorities and students.

The need for a more coherent approach to correctional programs long has been recognized. Historically, correctional reform has been limited to minor variations on a discordant theme. Reform can and should be a continuing process, not a reaction to periodic public criticism. The planner's role as a skeptic or devil's advocate regarding underlying concepts and basic assumptions can keep the corrections field from a state of complacency.

Even the best plan, however, is of little value if the organization's climate, structure and employee resistance obstruct its implementation. Employees react negatively to changes imposed from above. So access to decisionmaking is important, even though the chief executive's leadership responsibilities require that innovations cannot always be vetoed by subordinates.

As human resource agencies, corrections must make a special effort to integrate various functional specialities into an organization team that holds mutual objectives vis-a-vis the client not only among its members but also between members and the organization. Accomplishing this organization climate will require a participatory and nonthreatening leadership style in which employee, offender, and the organization needs are met in a compatible way.

MANAGEMENT STYLE AND ORGANIZATION CLIMATE

The administrative climate prevailing in an organization system is substantially the consequence of the management style favored and practiced by the small group of top managers.[16] If these managers are autocrats, the system below them will reflect this fact. If, on the other hand, they are democratic and participative, and consciously share with the men under them the making of decisions and the rewards of organizational accomplishment, the organization likely will become more democratic and participative.

Tradition is, of course, a factor to be reckoned with in organizations. Attitudes and modes of organizational behavior favored by previous administrations carry forward and influence attitudes and behavior in subsequent administrations. Still it is true that new management at the top can significantly alter an organization's climate.

Inasmuch as the managerial style of key decisionmakers determines in a major

---

[16] The following discussion relies heavily upon an unpublished paper prepared by Kenneth Henning, University of Georgia, for the U.S. Bureau of Prisons in connection with its contribution to the National Advisory Commission on Criminal Justice Standards and Goals.

way the climate of an organization or subparts of it, it is appropriate to consider management style and organizational climate simultaneously. Four quite different management styles and organizational climates may be identified: bureaucratic, technocratic, idiosyncratic, and participative.

Bureaucratic Style

The bureaucratic management or organizatinal climate is rule-oriented, position-focused and downward-directed in communication flow.[17] Examples are military organizations and paramilitary systems, such as many corrections agencies are. Dedicated bureaucratic managers perceive their jobs as requiring loyal, unswerving, unquestioning execution of organizational policy.

The bureaucrat's tendency is to avoid development of personal relationships with subordinates in the belief that personal involvement weakens his "authority." Real organizational input in the form of suggestions, ideas, innovations, and danger signals usually is restricted to those few persons in high office. Consequently, reality feedback to the top from operating organizational levels is slow at best. It occurs with considerable difficulty, if at all. Identification of problems and performance monitoring are gained by the top decision group almost exclusively through statistical reports and compilations. These reports may be incomplete, inaccurate, or even deliberately misrepresentative of fact in order to show lower echelons in a favorable light.

The reasonably efficient bureaucracy is an adequate and sometimes excellent action system in the areas to which it is geared. But it is almost universally a poor system for analyzing the need for change, responding to it, and gaining and holding member commitment to its goals, particularly under conditions demanding rapid alteration or modification of goals.

Technocratic Style

A second managerial style is the technocratic, in which the manager views himself as the principal expert in his organization. The technocratic manager largely discounts the importance of hierarchical position or rank, which he associates with "administration" (i.e., paper work), preferring rather to define his role as interpreting technical matters and modifying organization programs to fit the changing needs of the technological situation.

The technocrat performs the management role as the senior in expertise, relating personally with colleagues but striving to remain dominant through his perceived superior technical knowledge and ability to give specific directions on jobs. Within the corrections field, psychologists and social workers frequently are technocratic in their managerial application.

---

[17] Warren G. Bennis, *Changing Organizations* (McGraw-Hill, 1966), pp. 5–10.

Within the larger technical organization where a number of specialities are operating simultaneously (as in mental hospitals), a "pecking-order" of expertise customarily develops, certain types of experts having higher status than other types. Within each speciality, other personnel arrange themselves in descending order of expertise or seniority in accordance with the status model. When certain higher hierarchical positions in the organization are occupied by individuals with lower expert status, functional and communications bypasses develop, significantly altering the designed or intended strutural relationships.

Idiosyncratic Style

The idiosyncratic or "big daddy" manager views his role as administering organizational rules and regulations flexibly to orient them to specific individuals. In the best sense, he manages by attempting to stimulate, guide, and develop individual subordinates to carry out their responsibilites to the best of their abilities. But he may also manage by personal manipulation. The idiosyncratic manager is likely to reserve a substantial amount of decisionmaking to himself and frequently bypasses subordinates in his efforts to influence the behavior of individuals several echelons below in the hierarchy.

This manager's need for information to motivate, influence, or manipulate individuals may cause him to become preoccupied with direct personal contact or minute organizational detail. He usually supposes himself to be adept at the practice of psychology and often believes control over the organization's affairs and its effectiveness as a system depend substantially upon his capacity to deal with differing kinds of personalities or even upon his charm.

Application of this style is likely to result in certain problems, especially in larger organizations. First, like the bureaucratic and technocratic manager, he reserves most decisons for himself. In those areas of little or no personal interest to him, he relegates rather than delegates. Decisionmaking is delayed while subordinates wait for his decisions. Second, the idiosyncratic manager makes his choices more on the basis of personal interest or the personalities involved than on information or the organizational significance of the decision. Third, in the more manipulative applications of this style, the organizational consequences are likely to be either that the organization will lose its more interpersonally skillful subordinates or that it will tend to deteriorate in a pathology of intrigue.

For example, custodial and treatment staff, under the watchful eye of an efficiency-minded administrative officer, begin to vie for position by playing to the manager's idiosyncracies. Rather than assembling and organizing data for a rational argument, they try to shade the issues so that the outcome they prefer appears to be a natural consequence of the decisionmaker's predispositions. A request for more caseworkers, for example, is justified in terms of how counseling may contribute to institutional security and order by providing an outlet for inmate grievances.

Participative Style

The fourth management style or organizational climate is the participative. Such a manager is group-oriented and perceives his managerial role as involving the integration of the work group and its development into an effective team. Toward this end, the participative manager believes he should maintain an informal, friendly relationship with all employees as individuals or, in the larger organization, as groups. Besides sharing information with them, he solicits and respects their opinions about the work sitaution. Sometimes this manager becomes too concerned, even sentimental, about his organization. Since he dislikes conflict and lack of harmony, he may tend on occasion to sacrifice the organization's work requirements in his efforts to gain or hold member acceptance and cooperation.

Classic Styles in Correctional Management

The two management styles most frequently used in the history of corrections, particularly in institutional management, are the bureaucratic and idiosyncratic. But, as specialized intensive treatment institutions more characteristic of juvenile corrections spread to the adult field, the technocratic style may become more prevalent, particularly if the rigid hierarchical features of the bureaucracy are retained. While the idiosyncratic style may result in an effective managerial application in organizations of limited size and both the idiosyncratic and bureaucratic may do so under conditions of substantial stability, neither is ideally suited to the administration of large, complex systems under conditions of rapid change.

The idiosyncratic correctional manager is less insistent on lines of authority than the bureaucrat but retains much of the decisionmaking authority by coopting subordinates informally. He likes to "tour" the institution casually, not to make a grand inspection but to keep in close touch with operations. The general is sacrificed for the specific. He devotes too much time to cases and neglects overall population characteristics and organization progress. Decisions, consequently, are based on anecdotal experiences rather than aggregate data. His "recidivism" statistics are Christmas cards from ex-offenders.

The idiosyncratic manager prides himself on knowing each inmate and has an index with names, pictures, etc., readily available in his office. The bureaucrat's zeal for reports and statistics is replaced by the idiosyncratic manager's error of omission. Some subordinates must indulge the manager's unwillingness to abandon his career specialty. The former food service administrator may have the best kitchen but neglects postrelease job placement of graduates from the bakers' training program.

The control function traditionally assigned to corrections may account in large measure for the prevalence of a bureaucratic organization climate. When coercion is the prime objective, it is efficiently administered by codifying prohibited behavior and making routine the application of sanctions. A more noble objective of "equality" frequently is cited for uniformly following disciplinary procedures that may, for a particular case, be inappropriate. Even a "treatment" purpose implies a limited degree of coercion, because the indiviual has been sent to a corrections unit to endure his "illness." If a deviation from routine is passed to the bureaucrat for decison, he self-assuredly asserts, "Rules are rules, and if we make one exception, everyone will want to do it."

A significant part of corrections' fragmentation can be explained by the pervasiveness of a bureaucratic mentality. Postrelease adjustment is considered the parole board's problem. Probation is a court function. Halfway houses are run by a community services unit.

A bureaucratic management style is particularly inappropriate for a human services organization, because it focuses on organizational processes rather than what is being processed—people. The manager's intentional aloofness from his subordinates is reflected by the sort of inmate-staff relations that view programs as done *for* the offender, not *with* him. The organization has established certain activities to which individuals are assigned, regardless of appropriateness.

Adding behavioral change to corrections' traditional control function requires a structural organizational change to permit integration of more functional specialties. This is almost impossible in an organizational climate that insists on a rigid categorization of functions and the undesirability of shared responsibility. A treatment team composed of different specialists is an attempt to superimpose an interdepartmental procedural arrangement on a functional categorization. Even taking officers out of uniform or allowing the teacher to participate in disciplinary decisions does not obscure the fact that critical judgments regarding their job performance, promotions, etc., are made by their functional supervisors. Under these conditions, the individual's frame or reference probably will be his specialty, which may or may not be consistent with what are perceived as the team's objectives.

It should be noted that these managerial styles seldom appear in their pure form. As pointed out in *Leadership and Exchange in Established Formal Organizations,*[18] the effective manager and his subordinates do recognize their role differentiation but, at the same time, share in the decisionmaking process.

The Ideal Managerial Climate

A well-managed organization is one in which the attitudes and values of the individual members are in substantial agreement with the organization's attitudes and values, and in which organizational positions are matched properly with the personalities and skills of the occupants of the positions. Adequate satisfactions for the needs of its members are provided. Organizational members, voluntarily and willingly, undertake to do what is organizationally necessary. As Douglas

---

[18] T. O. Jacobs, *Leadership and Exchange in Formal Organizations* (Alexandria, Va.: Human Resources Research Organization, 1970).

McGregor emphasizes, "The acceptance of responsibility [for self-direction and self-control] is correlated with commitments to objectives."[19]

This is, of course, an ideal state of affairs. More commonly, the organization's authority system and its informal social system drift or are driven apart. The strains between the two finally become so severe that an "emotional" separation of these two components occurs. Following such division, the lower echelons usually organize, as in the case of a union, and formally represent themselves to the authorities as an opposing organization. Their goals are to redress grievances and bring about a more equitable balance between the burdens the organization imposes and the rewards and satisfaction it offers.

Managerial Requirements of the Future

To function effectively in today's dynamic and fluid environment, correctional organizations must be flexible. If a system knows exactly what it needs to accomplish and how best to accomplish it, and is administered with benevolence and esprit de corps, a bureaucratically managed organization probably is the most efficient delivery system.

Under conditions of rapid environmental change, however, organizations cannot know exactly what needs to be done or exactly how best to proceed. The urgent requirement confronting modern corrections organizations, therefore, is to structure themselves so that they are adaptable, their participants voluntarily embrace the organization's goals as their own, and they have a capability for determining and interpreting forces impacting upon them.[20] This requires effective problemsolving processes, employee participation in setting organizational objectives, access to the decisionmaking process, and mechanisms for testing reality (e.g., avoiding stereotyping).

Employee participation, by increasing the sources of information, will give management a fuller understanding of the altering environment and a better indication of the organizational consequences of such changes. Management receives assessments from a wider range of perspectives in a form allowing personal interaction and discussion. Full commitment by an organization membership also will help develop those strategies that are most appropriate for accomplishment of the organization's goals under rapidly changing conditions.

To meet these contemporary requirements, corrections must replace its older management orientation and organization structure which was predicated upon a set of beliefs about human nature and human behavior labeled by Douglas McGregor as Theory X. This theory assumed that:

· The average human being has an inherent dislike of work and will avoid it if he can. Because of this human characteristic of dislike of work, most people must be coerced,

---

[19] Douglas McGregor, *The Human Side of Enterprise* (McGraw-Hill, 1960), p. 68.

[20] For a discussion of these prerequisities for organizational health, see Bennis, *Changing Organizations,* pp. 52–55.

controlled, directed, and threatened with punishment to get them to put forth adequate effort toward the achievement of organizational objectives.

The average human being prefers to be directed, wishes to avoid responsibility, has relatively little ambition, wants security above all.[21]

McGregor challenged the validty of these assumptions and proposed instead his Theory Y, which held that:

The expenditure of physical and mental effort in work is as natural as play or rest. The average human being does not dislike work inherently.

External control and the threat of punishment are not the only means of bringing about effort toward organizational objectives. Man will exercise self-direction and self-control in the service of objectives to which he is committed. The average human being learns under proper conditions, not only to accept but to seek responsibility. Avoidance of responsibility, lack of ambition, and emphasis on security generally are consequences of experience, not inherent human characteristics.

Commitment to objectives is a function of the rewards associated with their achievement.

The capacity to exercise a relatively high degree of imagination, ingenuity, and creativity in the solution of organizational problems is widely, not narrowly, distributed in the population. Under the conditions of traditional life, however, the intellectual potentialities of the average human being are utilized only partially.[22]

The assumptions of McGregor's Theory Y are being augmented and modified as greater insight into human complexity is gained from research. Students of management today recognize man as more complex than either the traditional view or the Theory Y model assumed him to be. Schein has observed, "Not only is he more complex within himself, being possessed of many needs and potentials, but he is also likely to differ from his neighbor in the patterns of his own complexity."[23] This statement is followed by Schein's summary of the assumptions which underlie the "complex man view of human nature":

Man not only is complex, but also highly variable; he has many motives arranged in some sort of hierarchy of importance to him, but this hierarchy is subject to change from time to time and situation. Furthermore, motives interact and combine into complex motive patterns (for example, since money can facilitate self-actualization, for some people economic strivings are equivalent to self-actualization).

Man is capable of learning new motives through his organizational experience. Ultimately, his motivation pattern and the psychological contract he establishes with the organization is the result of a complex interaction between initial needs and organizational experiences.

Man's motives in different organizations or different subparts of the same organization may vary; the person who is alienated in the formal organization may find fulfillment of his social and self-actualization needs in the union or in the informal organization. The job may engage some motives while other parts engage other motives.

[21] McGregor, *The Human Side of Enterprise,* pp. 33–34.
[22] McGregor, *The Human Side of Enterprise,* pp. 47–48.
[23] Edgar Schein, *Organizational Psychology* (Prentice-Hall, 1965), p. 60.

Man can become involved productively with organizations on the basis of many different kinds of motives; his ultimate satisfaction and the ultimate effectiveness of the organization depends only in part on the nature of his motivation. The nature of the task to be performed, the abilities and experience of the person on the job, and the nature of the other people in the organization all interact to procude a certain pattern of work and feelings. For example, a highly skilled but poorly motivated worker.

Man can respond to many different kinds of managerial strategies, depending on his own motives and abilities and the nature of the task; in other words, there is no single managerial strategy that will work for all men at all times.

Shifts in Managerial Philosophy

The philosophy underlying managerial behavior in certain forward-looking organizations recently has shifted fundamentally because of the demands of contemporary society. The change is reflected most of all in the following three areas:

● A new concept of *Man,* based on increased knowledge of his complex and shifting needs, which replaces the over-simplified, innocent push-bottom or inert idea of man.

● A new concept of *power* based on collaboration and reason, which replaces a model of power based on coercion and fear.

● A new concept of *organizational values,* based on a humanistic, existential orientation, which replaces the depersonalized, mechanistic value system.[24]

The history of recent organizational experience clearly reveals that only those managements that recognize the direction, magnitude, and rapidity of change and that can marshal the fullest employee commitment and effort will be able to design and direct the anticipatory, adaptive, and effective organizational systems required. This organizational climate will be conducive to assessing change, deciding where to go, and selecting a method to get there.

THE UNION AND CORRECTIONAL ADMINISTRATION

Public employment is the fastest growing sector in the American labor force today. It is widely predicted that by 1975 about one out of every five workers will be employed by some governmental agency, Federal, State, or local.

Labor organizations for public employees have grown rapidly since collective bargaining was authorized by States and cities, beginning in 1958.[25] By 1970, one-third of all public employees were members of unions. Indeed, one of the fastest growing unions in the country is the American Federation of State, County, and Municipal Employees, which has organized in many correctional institutions.

---

[24] Bennis, *Changing Organizations,* p. 188.
[25] Anthony V. Sinicropi, "Employee-Management Relations," in *Managing Change in Corrections* (College Park, Md.: American Correctional Association, 1971).

Union growth is reflected in the increase in work stoppages by public employees. In 1958, 15 work stoppages, involving 1,720 workers, resulted in 7,520 lost man days. A decade later, 254 stoppages, involving 201,800 public employees, resulted in 2,545,000 lost man days.[26]

Not only correctional employees are, or wish to be, organized. Demands by inmates for representation by unions in matters of pay, training opportunities, complaints, and grievances are being heard in increasing numbers. It is therefore essential for correctional managers to have some familiarity with the development of public employee unions.

Labor organization in the United States has passed through three distinct periods. The period from 1900 to the mid 1930's saw formation of craft unions. Semi-skilled and unskilled manufacturing unions were formed and became powerful forces spurred by the depression and "New Deal" between the mid-1930's and 1950's. And the 1960's brought the organization of white collar and service employees, with substantial representation of public employees.

During the early 1960's, public employees became aware of their potential power. Urbanization, a service economy orientation, and the emphasis on education increased the demand for their services. The political climate of the time was receptive, and the civil rights movement provided a significant spark. Public employees long had witnessed the effectiveness of private sector unions in making important gains in wages and benefits.

New York State acted in 1958 to recognize public employee organizations, and Wisconsin recognized public employee collective bargaining in 1959. By the end of 1970, 40 States had legislation authorizing some form of union activity by public employees. Eight of the remaining States had no legislation, and two had legislation specifically prohibiting union activity of any kind.[27]

Two recent legislative developments involve provisions for strike and compulsory arbitration when all else fails. The Pennsylvania Public Employee Relations Act of 1970 provides for collective bargaining and the mediation of impasses. Strikes are permitted in procedures for impasse situations are exhausted and if they are not enjoined as a clear and present danger or threat to public health, safety, or welfare. The scope of collective bargaining under this act extends to wages, hours and working conditions. New York City has authorized compulsory arbitration for its municipal employees in the case of deadlocked disputes.

For years it was assumed that public employees would not and could not strike. However, since 1958, public employees have exercised the strike tool (sometimes thinly disguised as "blue flu" or other absenteeism) in many cases, despite specific statutory prohibitions. Such action was necessary, unions said, because public managers (1) fail to consult with unions before adopting policies and procedures that affect them, (2) assert management prerogatives even when

---

[26] Advisory Committee on Intergovernmental Relations, *Labor-Management Policies for State and Local Government* (Washington: Government Printing Office, 1969), p. 24.

[27] Joseph P. Golden, "Public Employee Developments in 1971," *Monthly Labor Review,* 95 (1972), 63.

employee aims are to improve service to clients, and (3) are not responsive unless shocked or driven to action by militant, aggressive public employee behavior.

Collective bargaining traditionally has focused on matters of wages, benefits, and working conditions. Public employees have extended the limits of such bargaining substantially in recent years; and the future appears to hold further surprises for the public manager. Organized professionals seek greater influence in matters of policy, goals, and staffing, previously held to be the province of managers alone. Teachers, for example, are making collective bargaining issues of such matters as the need for teacher aides, reduction of class sizes, elimination of double shifts, textbook selection, and policymaking.

These trends will have an increasing impact on correctional managers in the future. They can choose to follow the course industrial managers followed, resist unionization and end up in a strong adversary relationship. Alternatively, they can adopt a more open stance, reduce the need for employee organizations, and work cooperatively. This latter approach recognizes that employees have needs that the organization may not be able to meet.

43

Manpower for Corrections

NATIONAL ADVISORY COMMISSION ON CRIMINAL
JUSTICE STANDARDS AND GOALS

People are the most effective resource for helping other people. In corrections, as in most other fields, they also are the most underutilized and misappropriated resource.

Manpower problems in corrections include: critical shortage of specialized professional personnel; poor working conditions; and poor allocation of both human and fiscal resources. Women, members of ethnic minorities, ex-offenders, and volunteers are generally underutilized as correctional manpower and in some areas are not used at all.

Problems shared by all areas of corrections—its poor image and conflict among personnel as to its mission—also complicate solution of manpower difficulties.

Manpower problems have been especially crucial because they usually have not been given sufficient recognition by persons responsible for financing and managing corrections. Not until 1965, when Congress passed the Correctional Rehabilitation Study Act, was a major manpower study launched. The results of the study were presented in a summary volume *A Time to Act,* released in 1969 by the Joint Commission on Correctional Manpower and Training.

Originally, the Joint Commission concerned itself with remedies for the man-

SOURCE. *Corrections,* National Advisory Commission on Criminal Justice Standards and Goals, Washington, D.C., U. S. Government Printing Office, 1973, pp. 463–470.

power shortage in corrections. However, this initial concern gave way to the need to address pertinent issues of utilization and training of all personnel, old hands as well as recruits.

Since the conclusion of the study in 1969, some of the problems noted there have been itensified, and new ones have surfaced. This chapter will seek to analyze the current situation in corrections as it bears specifically on manpower and to set forth standards by which solutions may be reached. These standards, building in part on the 1969 study, will set out in detail the steps to effective use of correctional manpower.

A HISTORICAL VIEW

Correctional manpower and training programs have developed haphazardly. There has never been a national manpower strategy, and State and local correctional systems have had few, if any, guidelines. From the beginning, persons working in corrections were there largely by chance, not by choice. Most correctional personnel were used then, as now, in large custodial institutions. Prerequisites for employment were low. For much of this century, the usual way to get a job in corrections was through political patronage. Vestiges of that practice remain today.

Institutions were in isolated rural areas where it was difficult to induce professional staff to locate. Manpower was drawn largely from the local population and thus reflected a rural point of view out of line with that of most offenders, who came from cities.

Historically, corrections personnel resembled military and law enforcement officers. Correctional staff members were used almost entirely in paramilitary capacities, even in the State "schools" for juveniles and youths. Parole officers were more akin to law enforcement officers than to "helping service" personnel. Many carried guns and wore or carried official badges. Some correctional staff still wear uniforms and have military titles, as they did from the beginning. At least half of all job titles in corrections include the word "officer"—custodial officer, parole officer, probation officer, training officer, and the like.

This identification with the military strongly influenced manpower and training policies and practices. Staff members were promoted up the ranks. They were not to fraternize with the inmates, who were to call them "sir." They conducted inspections and kept demerit lists. They were trained in military matters.

In all too many modern correctional institutions, these policies and practices remain. Great conflict is evident as this militaristic system is confronted today by persons urging adoption of modern organizational concepts.

At times, corrections has moved toward rehabilitation. Educational, vocational, and individual and social therapy programs, with attendant staff, have been introduced. As various rehabilitation strategies gained prominence in other fields, they were imported to corrections. The history of correctional management is dotted with treatment fads and cults, among them psychiatric and psychoanalytic programs, religious conversion, Dale Carnegie courses, guided group interaction, transactional analysis, group therapy, psychiatric casework, realty therapy, encounter groups, hypnosis, behavior modification, and operant conditioning. Reviewing staff training programs over the past 30 years is like thumbing through the pages of survey texts in psychology and sociology.

As correctional practice developed haphazardly, so did its goals and philosophy. Every informed observer since Tocqueville has remarked on the confusion and contradictions that exist within the American correctional system. And this confusion has profoundly affected the recruitment and performance of personnel. People who work in corrections—and the public which employs them—are uncertain as to whether the system is supposed to punish lawbreakers or to rehabilitate them, to protect society or to change social conditions, or to do some or all of these things under varying circumstances. Employees who have no clear concept of their roles—and disagree among themselves as to what their roles should be—are unlikely to perform well or to find satisfaction in their work. This state of affairs can only be made worse as the public holds them increasingly accountable for the failures of the system.

It is difficult to plan staff training programs or to recruit personnel from specialized disciplines when conflict over organizational goals and training mission is the rule, rather than the exception. For years, training has been routine and superficial.

Corrections started with closed, secure institutions, then added field services in the form of probation and parole. In efforts to make the institutions corrective in nature, professionals from education, vocational programs, behavioral sciences, medicine, and psychiatry were recruited. In the rush to professionalize, different correctional agencies have followed the beats of different drummers. Professionalization could not be achieved under these circumstances.

As this report has made clear, corrections is a multifaceted field. There are dehumanizing prisons, overcrowded jails, expensive and excessively staffed reception and diagnostic centers, halfway houses, youth industrial schools, experimental community treatment programs, and field services such as probation and parole. Each of these settings requires several types of personnel, and a variety of ways have been used to prepare staff. Often the programs have operated in conflict, internally as well as with each other.

EMERGING ISSUES THAT AFFECT MANPOWER

Out of the changes taking place within the correctional system and within society as a whole have emerged several issues with profound effects, and potential effects, on correctional manpower.

Disenchantment with Prisons

Although institutions house less than a quarter of all convicted offenders, they employ more than two-thirds of all persons working in corrections, and they spend more than 70 cents of each dollar spent on corrections. This gross maldistribution of human and financial resources has strong implications for a restructuring of the corrections system.

Prisons, jails, and juvenile institutions, which are the focal point of public concern about corrections have beee termed a failure by many authorities. In his address to the National Conference on Corrections at Williamsburg, Va., in December 1971, President Nixon said:

> Our prisons are still colleges of crime, and not what they should be—the beginning of a way back to a productive life within the law. . . . Locking up a convict is not enough. We must offer him the keys of education, of rehabilitation, of useful training, of hope— the keys he must have to open the gates to a life of freedom and dignity.[1]

This statement reflects the widespread and growing disenchantment with the ability of closed, security-oriented institutions to "change" offenders, a disenchantment shared by the public, corrections officials, and prisoners. Many are asking why a system that shows such poor results should be allowed to continue.

If, as is to be hoped, institutions play a decreasing role in corrections, there will be corresponding shifts in manpower needs. Moreover, the education and training appropriate for the staff of the developing correctional programs will differ sharply from what was needed in the past.

The Move Toward Community-Based Corrections

As noted many times in this report, the community is recognized today as the rightful site and source for most correctional programs. With the closing of traditional institutions, as the juvenile training schools were closed in Massachusetts in 1972, more offenders will be treated in the community. As probation and parole subsidy programs succeed, as they have in California and Washington, correctional action will center increasingly in the offender's home community. As youth service bureaus are established to meet youth problems in urban areas, new patterns of service delivery emerge.

With these shifts toward community programs, new and different manpower demands will develop. Staff now engaged in helping inmates will do so in community settings. New requirements will bring new persons into the field who may help provide a new image for corrections. The image of the staff member oriented to the military and to law enforcement will give way to that of the community correctional worker. He will be armed with different skills. He will not be preoccupied with custody, control, and regimentation but intent on using community resources as the major tool in his rehabilitative mission.

Less than one-third of all correctional staff members presently are employed in community corrections programs, where they serve three-fourths of all offenders. It is estimated that by 1975 more than 80 percent of all offenders will be

---

[1] *We Hold These Truths,* Proceedings of the National Conference on Corrections (Richmond: Virginia State Department of Justice and Crime Prevention, 1972), p. 5.

served in some type of community-based programs.[2] It is mandatory that existing staff be reallocated and additional staff hired to meet the obvious needs of community correctional programs.

Racial Strife

Emergence of racial strife is a major concern in all correctional programs. Television coverage of the prison disturbances of 1971 and 1972 brought the charge of institutional racism directly into the Nation's homes. Such charges are now being made throughout the correctional system, in community programs as well as institutions. Many adult and juvenile programs are faced with explosive racial situations. Staff members in some States spend more hours of training in riot control than in human communications or organizational development.

Minorities are found disproportionately in the ranks of corrections: overrepresented as clients and underrepresented as staff. Unfortunately, there are no reliable national figures on minority group clients in the correctional system. Estimates place the percentage high but vary with geographical regions and urban-rural distribution of the population. For example, in California almost half of the 20,800 inmates are blacks or Chicanos. In the total New York State system, 56 percent of all inmates are blacks or Puerto Ricans. At least one-third of all Federal offenders are members of minority groups.[3] American Indians are still being arrested and confined in alarmingly high numbers in both Dakotas, in the Southwest, and in Alaska, as they were in 1967.[4]

In most States, the proportion of minority group members confined is much greater than the proportion of such persons living in the State. Urban jails usually hold disproportionately large numbers of minority group members. In many large Eastern and Central Atlantic cities, 50 to 90 percent of the jail inmates are reported to be black, poor, and without jobs. In jails in the Nation's capital, 90 to 95 percent of the inmates are black. Juvenile institutions in the Southwest detain proportionately far more Chicano youths than are found in the general State population. Illinois confines three times more black youths than whites[5] Obviously it is immediately necessary to increase the number of correctional personnel who come from minority groups.

Political Activisim Among Offenders

Prison inmates, parolees, and ex-offenders are organizing to demand correctional reform and to begin to provide the "ingredient for changing people"— giving of themselves to help each other and their families. Offender organizations

[2] Allen F. Breed, statement in *We Hold These Truths*, p. 91.
[3] State and Federal data from presentations at the National Conference on Corrections.
[4] Joint Commission on Correctional Manpower and Training, *Differences That Make the Difference* (Washington: JCCMT, 1967).
[5] Hans W. Mattick, "The Contemporary Jails of the United States: An Unknown and Neglected Area of Justice" in Daniel Glaser, ed., *Handbook of Corrections* (Rand McNally, forthcoming).

are capable of activist efforts, and they are openly testing present policies and practices within the institutions and in the free community. Citizen support for their efforts is growing.

Political organizations are springing up at the local level, but they can be foreseen as a national movement. These challenges are likely to increase. Perhaps no other development has unnerved correctional staff more than politicalization of the offender. Staffs, from wardens down, have been ill-equipped to deal with it. The old training manuals on riot control are totally obsolete in dealing with the sophisticated organizational skills used by many inmate groups.

The first evidence of this politicalization was the prison underground newspaper produced by inmates. In some States, the prison newspapers are not subjected to censorship, and the underground press has surfaced. The content is political in nature, with two primary characteristics: concern with the counterculture (anti-establishment in nature) and racial militancy.

Untapped Manpower Resources

Corrections needs to look at other groups as well as minorities for the additional manpower it needs. More ex-offenders, women, and volunteers should be used. These "new manpower resources," as they are sometimes called, actually are resources that have always been at hand but have not been used effectively by corrections administrators.

While corrections once was an operation to control, hold, survey, and regiment the behavior of its wards, today it is oriented increasingly to behavior modification. When the emphasis was on physical control, physical strength was a primary prerequisite for positions.

This long-cherished tradition has been challented and is giving way. As the social distance between the keepers and the kept has decreased, a push to utilize once-untapped resources has surfaced.

Utilization of ex-offenders, women, and volunteers will introduce different skills, as well as help change the custodial image of the corrections system.

MANPOWER NEEDS

The changing trends in corrections portend a need for dramatic and immediate change in manpower policy—recruiting and keeping staff, training personnel, and allowing them to participate in program and agency management.

Staff Recruitment

Corrections can offer an attractive future for active, innovative persons. As the image of corrections changes, an effective recruitment service will point out the opportunities awaiting those who want to enter a field involved in dramatic change.

In the past, few wanted to enter this work. Among talented, trained persons, it was a second, third, or last career choice. Today it should rank high as a challenging career possibility.

According to a survey made for the Joint Commission, persons working in corrections feel that they help others; participate in changing a system, making it more responsive to society; find rewarding personal satisfaction; and shape new roles in the changing correctional system[6] These rewards should offer more than adequate incentive for entering corrections as a career.

However, the severe personnel shortage that still exists in the field is due in part to corrections' poor public image and in part to the reluctance of some correctional administrators to recruit actively the talented, creative, sensitive, and educated persons needed to meet the challenges of the changing correctional structure.

The Joint Commission found in 1969 that:

> Young people are missing from the correctional employment scene. While other vocations have tried to capture the enthusiasm and vitality of the present generation of students, the Joint Commission was unable to uncover any broadscale effort in corrections. Only 26 percent of correctional employees are under 34 years old, a statistic that is particularly disconcerting in view of the fact that juveniles make up about one-third of the total correctional workload and are being referred to correctional agencies at a greater rate than adults. Generation gap problems between workers and young correctional clients will no doubt increase if efforts are not made to recruit young people into the field.[7]

Staff Retention

Once staff are recruited and prove to be capable employees, the system should try to keep them. Corrections has failed in the past to retain many of its highly trained, young, and creative staff members, particularly those who come from minority groups.

An anticipated outcome in the effort to improve corrections personnel systems is a change in the image of the correctional worker—and this image needs changing. A Louis Harris survey in 1968 revealed that both the public and correctional workers themselves had a relatively poor image of corrections and persons working in the field.

In a public opinion poll conducted in California by the Field Research Corporation, corrections fared somewhat better, but the results were hardly encouraging. Thirty-five percent of the adults queried had no impression of the kind of job being done by probation officers, 43 percent as to parole officers, and 42 percent as to correctional officers. Only 2 percent of the adults thought that any of these correctional workers were doing an "extremely good job." The reaction among teenagers was somewhat more favorable. But of all positions in the criminal

---

[6] Joint Commission on Correctional Manpower and Training, *Corrections 1968: A Climate for Change* (Washington: JCCMT, 1968), p. 33.

[7] Joint Commission on Correctional Manpower and Training, *A Time to Act* (Washington, JCCMT, 1969), p. 31. Publication referred to hereinafter by title.

justice field—district attorneys, judges, police, correctional officers, etc.—teenagers as well as adults felt that the correctional officers were doing the poorest job.

As corrections moves toward community-based programs and the institutions adopt participatory management, the image of personnel working behind bars should change to an image of helping offenders help themselves to return to society successfully.

Staff Education

A critical point in corrections is lack of education among its personnel. The lack of educated manpower in corrections was a primary issue when the Joint Commission conducted its studies from 1966 to 1969. The same issue exists today, relieved only slightly by the Law Enforcement Education Program (LEEP) and the promise of a National Institute of Corrections.

The need for educated personnel increases with the changes in corrections. Educational standards of the 1960's will not suffice in the 1970's.

Several problems block a simplistic solution to the educational problems of corrections. Correctional programs vary widely, ranging from maximum security incarceration to voluntary drug abuse treatment. Educational requirements for personnel to run these programs overlap in some areas, differ significantly in others. Because of this confusion, development of a core discipline that could prepare a person to work in corrections or the broader criminal justice system has been slow.

Corrections has low status in most academic circles, and most faculty members have not encouraged students to seek correctional employment. The field generally has been viewed as a confusing array of services, personnel, clients, and settings that befuddle perceptive researchers, academicians, and employees.

Improving Educational Programs

To improve education for existing and prospective corrections employees, the Joint Commission made the following recommendations:

1. The undergraduate degree should be the standard educational requirement for entry-level work in probation and parole agencies and for comparable counselor and classification positions in institutions. Preferred areas of specialization should be psychology, sociology, social work, criminology/corrections, criminal justice, education, and public administration.

2. Correctional agencies should adopt a career strategy, allowing persons with high school education or less to enter the field and participate in combined work-study programs to work their way up in the system.

3. Community colleges should expand their programs to provide educational opportunities for correctional personnel.[8]

---

[8] *A Time to Act,* p. 30.

Some progress has been made toward achieving these recommendations. The bachelor's degree generally is accepted as the minimum degree for a professional position in corrections. Career ladders have been developed in several systems, and LEEP has provided funds and some direction to community colleges.

Also needed is a criminal justice curriculum to unify knowledge in criminology, social control, law, and the administration of justice and corrections. This will require correctional and educational leaders to agree on a least the basic elements of such a curriculum. It should not include the training content and functions that can be handled more appropriately by the subsystems of criminal justice—police, courts, and corrections. The continued involvement of criminal justice practitioners should be maintained to assure that the theoretical content of the curriculum keeps up with rapid developments in the field.

Clues for the development of a criminal justice curriculum can be taken from the graduate schools of criminal justice which have been established at a number of universities around the country in the past decade. These schools generally offer interdisciplinary programs for persons with bachelor's degrees or first professional degree in social science, law, and related professional fields. Their purpose is to develop a fundamental understanding of basic fields in criminal justice, using background materials in supporting disciplines. They provide opportunities for research. In general, they supply the base for professional advancement to positions of policy determination and agency leadership. Further development of such programs is discussed in the Commission's report on The Criminal Justice System.

When the criminal justice curriculum is refined and established, it should include degree offerings from associate of arts through the doctorate. In addition to criminal justice operational personnel, the curriculum should be required of criminal justice planners so they may achieve the knowledge and skills necessary to assist in charting new directions for the system. Finally, the Law Enforcement Assistance Administration and other funding organizations should furnish financial support for continued program development, faculty, student loans and fellowships, and research.

Financial Assistance

The Joint Commission made many recommendations about financial assistance to educational efforts.

Correctional agencies, community colleges, and colleges and universities involved in the education and training of correctional personnel were urged to seek funds from Federal programs concerned with corrections.

Establishment of a comprehensive financial assistance program in an appropriate Federal agency was urged to provide support for persons in or preparing to enter the field of corrections. Such a program should provide scholarships, fellowships, guaranteed loans, research and teaching assistantships, work-study programs, educational opportunity grants for disadvantaged persons, and forgivable loans to help defray costs of college education and provide incentive for further work in the field.

Prior to establishment of the Law Enforcement Assistance Administration (LEAA), educational programs received meager financial support, and large numbers of correctional workers had never taken a college-level course. Some specific problems included these:

1. Criminology and corrections degree programs were developed erratically and frequently were terminated when once-interested faculty left.

2. Social work graduates rarely chose corrections careers, although the Master of Social Work degree was a preferred credential for probation and parole as well as some institutional positions.

3 Sparse, if any, financial assistance in the form of loans or scholarships was available to preservice or inservice personnel.

4. Institutions of higher education rarely provided more than token assistance to staff development efforts in nearby correctional programs.

The picture has changed considerably since LEAA became operational in late 1968. Thousands of inservice correctional staff have taken advantage of LEEP loans and grants. A smaller number of preservice personnel have participated. The largest number have been line workers studying for an associate of arts degree. After achieving that degree, some have continued work toward the bachelor's degree. Many field service and treatment staff have taken advantage of LEEP loans and grants to pursue master's degrees. Although most LEEP funds at first went to law enforcement staff members, in 1972 the balance was shifting to provide more equitable assistance to correctional manpower.

States are now beginning to consider incentive plans to stimulate correctional employees to undertake relevant academic work. A bill authorizing such a plan was introduced in the Connecticut State legislature in 1971 but failed to pass. When such incentive plans are realized, it will be necessary to insure that personnel departments reclassify on the basis of their recently acquired skills those persons who have undertaken such education.

Staff Development

The Joint Commission survey in 1969 reported a paucity of staff development programs in corrections. Less than 14 percent of any category of workers were participating in an inservice training program at the time of the survey. Most staff training terminated after the orientation effort, and many agencies offered no staff training at all. Only 4 percent of all juvenile agencies and 19 percent of adult agencies had a full-time staff training person.

The quality of training was not measured in that study, but staff ranked it as no more than routine when queried in a Harris survey. At that time, very little Federal funding was provided to support staff development in corrections.

Because educational preparation for various aspects of correctional work is in a confused state, and for most persons in corrections is not even a reality, the importance of staff development cannot be overemphasized. Yet staff development has a very low priority as indicated by lack of commitment of training dollars, training staff, and staff time in most correctional agencies.

An adult correctional institution with a training program that is anything more than a plan on paper is more apt to have training conducted by a correctional sergeant or lieutenant who probably has no background in training methodology or objectives. If he has a program at all, he finds it difficult to get staff together for training because employees are not or cannot be released during regular working hours and overtime is expensive. Thus the barriers against training are great in adult corrections.

In the juvenile institutions field, training usually is the responsibility of the assistant superintendent who also has little preparation for this function. The end result is meager training with unclear objectives. In the Joint Commission surveys, 49 percent of the juvenile institutions reported that they had no training personnel.

Adult and juvenile field service staff get the most training attention, yet many are not provided ongoing programs. Almost all state-operated agencies have orientation training, but local probation and court services have few staff development programs.

This lack of staff development reflects an attitude of indifference about the services that staff provide to the clients of the system. It also suggests to staff that management feels keeping up with the field has low priority.

National Institute of Corrections

The proposed National Institute of Corrections can help redirect staff development efforts. The impetus for the institute came from the U. S. Department of Justice. In December 1971, the Attorney General proposed establishment of a national corrections academy to serve as a center for correctional learning, research, executive seminars, and development of correctional policy recommendations.

The idea of a national correctional center of this type has been expressed over the years by numerous groups, most recently in 1969 by the Joint Commission, which recommended after 3 years of study:

A network of national, and state training programs should be created to develop programs and materials as well as to provide technical assistance and other supportive aids to correctional agencies. Such centers should have manpower development rather than a limited definition of training as their focus, and should develop close working relationships with colleges and universities as well as with private training organizations. Federal and state funds are urgently required for the development and ongoing support of these centers.[9]

---

[9] *A Time to Act,* p. 79.

The National Institute of Corrections still is in the planning stage. But the concept is a very important one, and the fact that it has developed to the point of implementation represents a significant step forward.

Purchase of Services

Frequently large salaries are provided to correctional management to hire a psychiatrist, a clinical psychologist, or an education specialist. Corrections should reassess this practice and move toward purchase of service from such highly specialized manpower. Contracts for specialists would free funds as well as resolve personnel problems frequently associated with keeping highly trained staff in the traditional organizational system of corrections.

Purchasing the services of highly trained professionals will allow corrections to draw upon the best persons available, rather than having to settle for those persons willing to work full-time within the correctional setting. In addition to specialists commonly associated with corrections, a concentrated effort should be made to secure the services, as needed, of persons skilled at handling intergroup relations, community development, public information, and other activities designed to link the correctional agency more closely with the community.

Participatory Management

An appropriate way to accomplish the needed change in manpower utilization is through participatory management. This concept is new and threatening to many managers, but if corrections is to be changed to meet the realities of the 1970's, innovations are inevitable.

Some correctional systems are already experimenting with participatory management. They are bringing together staff, clients, and managers to plan and operate their new organizations. Each is a part of the organization and should have a stake in making it effective. In the past, most staff and clients were not included in decisionmaking or planning organizational operation. As the reorganization of corrections proceeds, many roles for staff, offenders, and managers will change, forcing new trends in manpower development as well as providing a new view of manpower needs. Daniel Glaser predicts, "Within institutions there will be more collaboration of inmates and staff in management, hence more inmate responsibility and less social difference between staff and inmates"[10]

The trends noted portend much for correctional change and reflect dramatic need for changing correctional manpower and training, for both today and the next decade. The example is drawn clearly from higher education. Since 1968, as university administrators began seriously to include students in decisionmak-

---

[10] "Changes in Corrections during the Next Twenty Years," unpublished paper written for Project STAR, American Justice Institute, p. 61.

ing roles throughout the campus structure, student protest has diminished and student commitment to the system emerged. It is ironic that massive violence shook the campus before the prison yard, but lessons must be learned from this phenomenon. A priority in corrections must be participatory management sessions in which managers bring staff and inmates together to chart the future course for all of them.

PLANNING TO MEET MANPOWER NEEDS

Most correctional agencies have been too preoccupied with day-to-day staffing problems to attempt systematic long-range planning to meet manpower needs. Sporadic efforts to remedy pressing difficulties through raising wages, reducing workloads, or other piecemeal actions do not get to the heart of the problems with which this chapter has been concerned.

Elements of effective manpower planning are:
- Assessment of manpower needed to meet the agency's goal.
- Redesigning of present jobs on the basis of task analysis.
- Development of methods to recruit additional manpower needed
- Training and staff development.

These elements must be the responsibility of the State. For only on a statewide basis can real needs for manpower be assessed and measures planned to utilize effectively the manpower now at hand and to secure the additional personnel needed.

Unless there is a basic consolidation to eliminate the present balkanization of corrections, it is unrealistic to expect overall manpower planning. But at least each system—institution, probation, parole, etc.—should be working now toward long-range statewide planning to meet manpower needs. Special needs in manpower planning for probation and parole are considered in Chapters 10 and 12.

44

Perspectives on Correctional Management

E. K. NELSON AND CATHERINE H. LOVELL

This is the report of a special study of correctional administrators made by the University of Southern California for the Joint Commission on Correctional Manpower and Training. Its aim is to clarify the roles correctional administrators play, the problems they encounter, and the theoretical and practical skills they need for successful performance of their demanding duties.

The report should be viewed in the context of two broad movements. The first is the movement of the correctional field away from its isolating, institution-based system of custodial confinement and toward a goal of reintegrating the offender into the fabric of community life. The second is a profound shift in ways of thinking about the role of the administrator in American society. This shift is away from the traditional view of the administrator as one who mechanically performs specified functions in officially prescribed ways within closed organizational systems. The movement is toward a conception of the administrator as a creative and highly skilled professional who works within organizations which are "open" in the sense that they interact dynamically with myriad forces around

SOURCE. *Developing Correctional Administrators,* Joint Commission on Correctional Manpower and Training, Washington, D.C., 1969, pp. 1–11. Reprinted with permission of the authors and the American Correctional Association.

733

them. The convergence of these two movements may well bring about a renaissance of management in correctional programs within the next decade.

In its major report, *The Challenge of Crime in a Free Society,* the President's Commission of Law Enforcement and Administration of Justice described the status quo of American corrections in the following words.

"Corrections," America's prisons, jails, juvenile training schools, and probation and parole machinery, is the part of the criminal justice system that the public sees least of and knows least about. It seldom gets into the news unless there is a jail break, a prison riot, or a sensational scandal involving corruption or brutality in an institution or by an official. The institutions in which about a third of the corrections population lives are situated for the most part in remote rural areas, or in the basements of police stations or courthouses. The other two-thirds of the corrections population are on probation and parole, and so are widely, and on the whole invisibly, dispersed in the community. Corrections is not only hard to see; traditionally, society has been reluctant to look at it. Many of the people, juvenile and adult, with whom corrections deals are the most troublesome and troubling members of society: The misfits and the failures, the unrespectable and the irresponsible. Society has been well content to keep them out of sight.

Its invisibility belies the system's size, complexity, and crucial importance to the control of crime. Corrections consists of scores of different kinds of institutions and programs of the utmost diversity in approach, facilities, and quality. On any given day it is responsible for approximately 1.3 million offenders. In the course of a year it handles nearly 2.5 million admissions, and spends over a billion dollars doing so. If it could restore all or even most of these people to the community as responsible citizens, America's crime rate would drop significantly. For as it is today, a substantial percentage of offenders become recidivists; they go on to commit more, . . . and often more serious, crimes.[1]

In addition to identifying the problems which beset a fragmented and malnourished corrections system, the Commission also stressed the opportunity which now exists for introducing significant changes.

However, there are hopeful signs that far-reaching changes can be made in present conditions. The Commission found, in the course of its work, a number of imaginative and dedicated people at work in corrections. It found a few systems where their impact, and enlightened judicial and legislative correctional policies, had already made a marked difference; a few experimental programs whose results in terms of reduced recidivism were dramatic. A start has been made in developing methods of classification that will permit more discriminating selection of techniques to treat particular types of offenders. But many of the new ideas, while supported by logic and some experience, are yet to be scientifically evaluated. Nevertheless, the potential for change is great.[2]

The report of the President's Commission and the advent of the Joint Commission on Correctional Manpower and Training are parts of a movement which has for the first time brought the needs of the correctional field clearly to the attention of government leaders and to the general public. The public opinion polls conducted for the Joint Commission by Louis Harris and Associates re-

---

[1] President's Commission on Law Enforcement and Administration of Justice, *The Challenge of Crime in a Free Society* (Washington: U.S. Government Printing Office, 1967), p. 159.

[2] *Ibid.*

vealed not only widespread agreement that basic changes are imperative in the American corrections system but also a high level of consensus as to the major goal of change—a strong, diversified, and well-coordinated network of services capable of reintegrating the offender into the legitimate life of the community.[3]

How competent are correctional administrators to serve as the leaders of change? What types of special capability do they require to perform that function? These are the questions which prompted the present study.

RELATED RESEARCH

Researchers have completed a number of instructive studies on the social processes within penal and correctional institutions. These studies help to delineate both the dynamics and the impediments of organizational change in such settings. Starting with the pioneering research of Clemmer at Menard Reformatory, Illinois, in the 1930's,[4] a number of American social scientists have performed increasingly penetrating inquiries into the nature of prisons as examples of organizations which Goffman has typified as "total institutions."[5] No similar analyses have been made of probation and parole organizations although they are responsible for some two-thirds of the offenders under correctional management in the United States today.[6]

A few studies of correctional organizations have particular significance for the management function. In Street, Vinter, and Perrow's comparative study of six institutions for delinquents, the styles of the administrator and the characteristics of the management process were scrutinized. The researchers compared the six institutions through the use of three organizational models constructed on the basis of staff perceptions about the handling of offenders: (1) obedience-conform-

---

[3] *The Public Looks at Crime and Corrections* (Washington: Joint Commission on Correctional Manpower and Training, 1968), pp. 7-10.

[4] Donald Clemmer, *The Prison Community* (Boston: Christopher Press, 1940; reissued New York: Rinehart, 1958).

[5] Erving Goffman, *Asylums* (Garden City, N.Y.: Doubleday, 1961). Some major inquiries are: Donald R. Cressey, ed., *The Prison: Studies in Institutional Organization and Change* (New York: Holt, Rinehart and Winston, 1961), cited hereinafter as *The Prison;* Richard A. Cloward *et al., Theoretical Studies in the Organization of the Prison* (New York: Social Science Research Council, 1960); Gresham M. Sykes, *The Society of Captives* (Princeton: Princeton University Press, 1958); Howard W. Polsky, *Cottage Six: The Social Systems of Delinquent Boys in Residential Treatment* (New York: Russell Sage Foundation, 1962).

[6] A promising study of parole is being conducted by Dr. Elliot Studt, of the Center for the Study of Law and Society at the University of California, Berkeley. Significant studies of probation are being carried on at the School of Criminology, University of California, Berkeley, and at the Youth Studies Center, University of Southern California. For a report on the single major inquiry which has examined a total organizational system including both institutions and parole (the federal prison and parole services), see Daniel Glaser, *The Effectiveness of a Prison and Parole System* (Indianapolis: Bobbs-Merrill, 1964). For a consideration of the interaction between professional and organizational norms, see Lloyd E. Ohlin, Herman Piven, and Donnel Pappenfort, "Major Dilemmas of the Social Worker in Probation and Parole," *National Probation and Parole Association Journal,* II (1956), 213.

ity; (2) reeducation-development; (3) individual treatment. They reached the following conclusions about institutional administrators' predisposition to act as leaders of needed changes or, alternatively, as protectors of the status quo.

In general, the executives seemed to be guided by one of two major orientations. Executives who had the *resigned conservatism* orientation were largely satisfied with current levels of organizational attainment. Demands or expectations of others for higher achievement were regarded as inappropriate because of limitations set by resources and the intractability of inmates. These executives readily proposed concrete improvements which could be undertaken only if resources were increased. Typically, such improvements were additions to present services and contemplated no significant departures from current practices. In this view the executive's obligation was to define the needed resources; the parent organization had the responsibility of obtaining and making them available.

Executives with the *dissatisfied innovation* orientation were far less content with current levels of organizational achievement and sought improvement in directions they already had charted. These executives also cited needs for new resources but did not believe that failure to secure them vitiated all possibility for advance. They accepted responsibility for mobilizing as well as defining needed resources and contemplated somewhat greater innovation if new resources were forthcoming. Within existing circumstances they found many opportunities to enhance operational patterns, and they were interested in new information and techniques.[7]

The research is significant first because of its effort to distinguish change-capable administrators from system-maintainers, and second because it identifies two areas of powerful impediment to change in correctional institutions: those rooted in their social structure, and those derived from theoretical assumptions about the treatment of offenders. The researchers stated that

. . . our data suggest many of the limits upon the capacities of correctional organizations and executives to accomplish major changes, as well as of the treatment model to provide a wholly satisfactory ideal for innovation. All institutions suffered from the tendency toward routinization, the deficit of information on organizational processes and outcomes, and the inability to integrate all staff, particularly the teachers, into the total program. Especially important was the fact that the perspectives of the mental health field from which the treatment model flows induced a concern with emotional problems and two-person therapy that was inadequately addressed to organizational realities and design even in the "milieu" treatment institution. Although the positive results of treatment appeared to require the use of an adaptive approach to inmate social organization, in which the staff fosters positive group relations and informal leadership, staff members in the treatment institutions were only beginning to grasp the general ramifications of this approach.

Most important, none of the institutions was truly successful at producing changes appropriate to the lives the inmates would lead on the outside.

Correctional institutions lack the organizational capacity to handle the provision of post-release services adequately. However, these organizations could profitably seek to specify the changes sought in the inmates from a longer time perspective and to work to

[7] David Street, Robert D. Vinter, and Charles Perrow, *Organization for Treatment* (New York: Free Press, 1966), p. 260.

mesh their programs more fully with processes and agencies involved in reintegrating the inmates into the community. Both in theory and reality there appear to be many alternative opportunities for breaking out of the unilateral strategy by cooperating with community and other agencies to assure a better sequence of resocialization activities.[8]

Another researcher, Richard H. McCleery, has provided important insights concerning correctional administration. He observed the process of organization change in Oahu Prison, Hawaii, as that institution moved erratically (and sometimes violently) from an authoritarian regime toward a more open system of rehabilitating offenders through democratization of staff-inmate relationships.

McCleery describes the movement of the prison system from "the good old days" when all participants knew where they stood, through a period of "multiplying ingratitude" when staff shared influence with the inmates, to a period of unstable equilibrium. He offers a practical demonstration of the problems arising from changes in communication patterns and in the distribution of power. His study vividly illustrates the consequences of discrepancies between expectation and fulfilment when efforts are made to democratize a repressive, authoritarian regime. McCleery states:

> The following analysis of this institutional transition and crisis directs attention to the relationship between power and the processes by which influence is communicated to the centers of agency decision-making. However, it also focuses attention on the notion that the decisions involved in any system of social control are decisions of compliance as well as of command—of consent as well as of coercion. Our general propositions border on truisms: the status of an element within a social system is determined by its capacity to impose its definitions of the situation as premises on the behavior of others; decisions reflect the interests which are communicated most effectively on the organizational level at which they are made . . . Finally, by pointing out the manner in which values and definitions become entrenched in the conventional procedures of an institution, the analysis demonstrates the problems and limits of institutional change. Any social institution is more than a pattern of lines and boxes on a chart. It is a potentially explosive system of human energies in delicate balance, and ill-considered change may generate tensions which even a prison cannot contain.[9]

The research on parole being conducted by Dr. Elliot Studt at the Center for the Study of Law and Society at the University of California, Berkeley, was incomplete at the date of this writing, but discussions with Dr. Studt revealed that her data have clear implications for the correctional management function. By focusing the research effort at the level of everyday interaction among parolees, parole officers, and significant others, the investigators discovered gross disparities between the "public world" of formal administrative norms, policies, and procedures, and the real but "invisible world" of mutual accommodation between the parolees and the officers. The extremely tenuous relationship between ad-

---

[8] *Ibid.,* pp. 281–282.

[9] Richard H. McCleery, "The Governmental Process and Social Control" in *The Prison,* p. 152. For a case study of the pervasive constraints operative in a prison community on efforts to share decisional power with staff and inmates, see Elliot Studt, Sheldon L. Messinger, and Thomas P. Wilson, *C-Unit: Search for Community in Prison* (New York: Russell Sage Foundation, 1968).

ministrative policy and operating reality, and the patterned ways in which the former was dysfunctional to the latter, raise serious questions about the capacity of many correctional systems to sustain (much less bring about) programs for the successful reintegration of offenders into the community.

These illustrations of research which is relevant to the administrative process in corrections should serve to make clear the paucity of systematic inquiry in this area. Existing data and conceptualization help to illuminate the territory to be covered and permit hypotheses to be formed concerning the roles which correctional administrators might play in bringing about needed changes. But little information is available on how well or how badly they play those roles or with regard to the kinds of managerial selection and development which might be expected to increase their effectiveness.

We shall turn next to a brief review of how the management function has evolved and changed in American corrections.

EVOLUTION OF THE MANAGEMENT FUNCTION IN CORRECTIONS

Glaser has summarized the history of corrections succinctly by suggesting that we have passed through three stages, each characterized by a particular emphasis in the handling of offenders: first, *revenge;* second, *restraint;* and finally, *reformation.*[10] Correctional management has mirrored these changing emphases and presently is beginning to reflect the increasing commitment of the system to a fourth goal, that of *reintegrating* the offender in the community.

We must recognize, however, that each new emphasis was superimposed upon the earlier ones. Thus the present network of services is a bewildering combination of all of the functions mentioned. The nation's jails, for example, although primarily serving the function of revenge and restraint, occasionally develop programs for reforming and rehabilitating individual offenders. On the other hand, even the most advanced probation and parole agencies seek to exercise restraint as well as to reform and reintegrate offenders, as evidenced by continuing concern with varied sanctions designed to induce conforming behavior on the part of those under correctional supervision.[11]

The nature of the "mix" between reformation and restraint as correctional management modalities has varied greatly by type of organization. The following diagram indicates some of the major tendencies.

---

[10] Daniel Glaser, "The Prospect for Corrections" (paper prepared for the Arden House Conference on Manpower Needs in Corrections, mimeographed, 1964), pp. 203; see also Clarence Schrag, "Contemporary Corrections: An Analytical Model" (paper prepared for the President's Commission on Law Enforcement and Administration of Justice, mimeographed, 1966).

[11] Sanford H. Kadish, "The Advocate and the Expert-Counsel in the Peno-Correctional Process," *Minnesota Law Review,* XLV (1961), 803; see also Fred Cohen, *The Legal Challenge to Corrections* (Washington: Joint Commission on Correctional Manpower and Training, 1969).

Tendency toward restraint	Tendency toward reformation
Programs for adult offenders	Programs for juvenile offenders
Programs for male offenders	Programs for female offenders
Programs for recidivistic offenders	Programs for infrequent offenders
Programs for "dangerous" offenders	Programs for "nondangerous" offenders
Institution-based programs	Community-based programs (probation and parole)

There are, however, interesting contradictions and reversals of these tendencies. Some forms of intensive individual treatment are not available to offenders until they establish criminal career patterns or commit violent crimes and are institutionalized. Some of the most advanced forms of treatment (e.g., "milieu therapy" in which both staff and inmates are given responsibility for implementing the treatment goal) are found more often in institutions than under probation or parole auspices.[12]

Influence of the Prison

The traditional prison (the archetype of all correctional organizations) was an autocracy. Its single purpose was to maintain custody over the inmates. To accomplish this, it developed a rigid and highly stratified hierarchy along lines made familiar by military organizations. Authority and status were related to rank from the warden to the guard. Staff tended to be highly protective of this structure, holding to the closely defined prerequisites and prerogatives attached by custom to the various positions and levels.

The reorganization of many correctional institutions within the last few decades has added another kind of hierarchy, the noncustodial personnel, to the framework of organization. A deputy warden in charge of treatment, heading a battery of professional and specialized services, was given formal authority and position equal to those of the deputy warden in charge of custody. Business managers, heads of prison industries, and directors of honor camp programs were added according to local needs. The special authority connected with functionalism and specialization was fitted into the structure alongside the traditional authority of rank and seniority held by custodial personnel. These trends led to major redistributions of power and authority in formal organization and resulted in a variety of stresses and adjustments in the informal organization of most institutions.

Simon speaks of an "environment of decision" which conditions the choices

---

[12] See *Offenders as a Correctional Manpower Resource* (Washington: Joint Commission on Correctional Manpower and Training, 1968).

made at various administrative levels within formal organizations.[13] This environment has changed drastically for correctional organizations as they have evolved from the traditional form. In the authoritarian prison, all significant decisions were made at or very near the top of the hierarchy. Moreover, these decisions were made according to simple and well-understood criteria. Such values as good control and safe custody have a concrete quality when compared to such vague prescriptions as "helping each individual to the extent that he is able to help himself" or "individualizing treatment according to the needs and problems of each inmate."[14]

One major effect of adding more complex and nebulous criteria to the administrator's decision-making matrix has been to force the actual making of decisions downward toward the level of operations. The more difficulty administrators have encountered in harmonizing treatment and custodial values in statements of policy and procedure, the more they have left the responsibility for significant decisions to their subordinates.

Even while the prison was establishing itself as the dominant organizational form for adjudicated offenders, other approaches developed. Institutions for juveniles, while strongly influenced by their adult counterparts tended to be smaller, less monolithic, more committed to the goal of individual treatment. Probation and parole organizations, operating in the free community, produced less encapsulated, formal, and hierarchical management structures. Nevertheless, certain characteristics of penitentiaries and reformatories have conditioned the process of management and the style of managers in all correctional settings.

Characteristics of Correctional Management

Three pervasive themes which run through correctional management may be identified.

First, the goals of restraint and reformation have helped to reenforce correctional administrators' perceptions of offenders as morally, psychologically, physically, and educationally inferior human beings. They must be upgraded, and in the meantime they must be controlled. As a result of this perception, correctional administrators focus the resources at their command primarily upon the individual offender.

Because the offender is the major target of organization activity, little effort is made to mobilize and co-opt community resources, a fraction which is the very essence of the reintegration model of correctional intervention. This management posture has many consequences, as, for example, the division of offenders into "caseloads" for purposes of treatment and supervision, recruitment of varied specialists (therapists) whose efforts are seldom coordinated, and, as mentioned above, the scarcity of well-conceived efforts to work cooperatively with such

---

[13] Hebert A. Simon, *Administrative Behavior* (New York: Macmillan, 1958), p. 243.

[14] Elmer K. Nelson, Jr., "The Gulf Between Theory and Practice in Corrections," *Federal Probation,* XVIII (1954), 48.

community institutions as the schools, employment services, and neighborhood centers.

As Cloward points out:

> In order to ease the process of reintegration in the community, we shall have to give much greater attention than we do now to our aftercare [parole] programs. Since the real struggle between conformity and deviance takes place back in the community, the aftercare program is strategic. Yet aftercare tends to be the weakest program in most correctional systems. Somehow correctional administrators are reluctant to allocate funds for aftercare if that means reducing the scope of prestigeful clinical activities within the institution itself. Professional personnel, in turn, tend often to shun aftercare work. Somehow the thought of spending one's time working with families, teachers, and employers in the interests of mobilizing social opportunities for a returning boy seems distasteful; such activities do not carry the same prestige as therapeutic activities. But whatever the reasons, aftercare programs seem to get short shrift in the allocation of personnel and money.[15]

A second persistent attribute of correctional management has been a particularistic approach to program development and change. This approach has been characterized by faddism, a somewhat frivolous subscription to "new" ideas and generally nonrigorous, nonscientific rules of thumb, for determining what to delete from the old system and what to add to it. The predominant conservatism of system managers has militated against deviations from familiar ways and has led to tokenism in the launching of new measures.

Correctional administrators are not so much responsible for this condition as they are the victims of two realities: society's uncertainty about the causes and solutions of the crime problem; and the present inability of social science and research to provide a solid frame of reference for considering alternative courses of action and estimating their consequences. Nevertheless, in any effort to understand how these executives might be effective innovators, it is necessary to confront the difficulties and frustration which currently surround the process of change.

It is important to note that there are numerous small-scale examples of change in correctional organization and programming which run counter to the general pattern described above.[16] Some experimental programs have been firmly supported by theoretical premises and have been evaluated objectively. Some correctional administrators and consultants have addressed the problem of how to make the discovery and refinement of knowledge additive rather than fragmentary.[17] Some executives in the system (as subsequent chapters of this report will document) have attempted to move toward change along relatively rational lines while

[15] Richard A. Cloward, "Social Problems, Social Definitions and Social Opportunities' (paper prepared for the National Council on Crime and Delinquency, mimeographed, New York, April, 1963).

[16] See LaMar T. Empey, *Alternatives to Incarceration,* Office of Juvenile Delinquency and Youth Development Studies in Delinquency (Washington: U.S. Government Printing Office, 1967), p. 7.

[17] President's Commission on Law Enforcement and Administration of Justice, *Task Force Report: Corrections* (Washington: U.S. Government Printing Office, 1967), pp. 13-15 (cited hereinafter by title).

still coping skillfully with a plethora of "irrational" forces in their environments. It is this growing edge of innovation, of improved dissemination of knowledge, and of close connection between discovery and implementation of technique that offers hope for major gains in the near future.

A final theme which has its roots in the "prison culture" of the past and still runs through correctional management today is the syndrome of isolationism and withdrawal. This condition has helped to conceal the realties of life in institutions and probation and parole agencies from the public, and has thus acted to perpetuate stereotypes and myths. Prisons, after all, were designed and located to keep criminals out of the sight and mind of the larger populace. Prison administrators found it functional to honor that mandate. When community-based correctional programs gingerly sought to gain a foothold, their managers seemed intuitively to avoid exposure to public scrutiny and judgment. While the police tend to publicize aggressively their views of crime and punishment, the leaders of corrections tend to avoid public debate, particularly debate centering around controversial issues.[18]

This tendency has had serious consequences. The correctional field has had little success in developing public understanding and support for needed changes. Simplistic or erroneous conceptions of the nature of crime and its treatment have flourished, partly because there has not been effective spokesmen for more sophisticated interpretations, especially at times of "opportunity" when conflict or crisis have awakened the interest of an otherwise apathetic public.

Centripetal Pressures Toward Integration of Services

One of the most important developments in American corrections over the past three decades has been a movement toward centralization and integration of services in some of the more progressive systems. The concept of a coordinated correctional system, possessed of a variety of rehabilitative services and custodial facilities, was in direct contradiction to the historic pattern in which the head of each penal institution reigned almost as a monarch, typically under the large umbrella of a multi-purpose "administrative" board. As McGee pointed out in 1951:

The trend is marked and distinct. Increasing centralization of authority and responsibility is evident incorrectional organizations. The movement is in the direction away from decentralization . . .

The single state department with a professional administration is doubtless the most satisfactory administrative form developed to date. More extensive authority and direction

[18] E. K. Nelson, Jr., "Organizational Disparity in Definitions of Deviance and Uses of Authority: Police, Probation and the Schools' in *Schools in a Changing Society,* Albert J. Reiss, Jr., ed. (New York: Free Press, 1965), p. 30; see also "The Juvenile Gang Debate," editorial, *Los Angeles Times,* April 8, 1963.

over corrollary functions—probation, parole, local jails—reflect the growing unity of correctional administration.[19]

Generally, most of the significant innovations in correctional practice have occurred within professional, centralized administrative systems whose parts were related through a coherent framework of policy and whose programs were implemented through planning, research, and varied staff services.

Yet, while centralization of correctional services within jurisdictions has been a major trend, the correctional services of the nation as a whole remain balkanized. Different levels of government operate duplicative services. There are schisms between services for juveniles and services for adults, between institutional facilities and community-based programs. The jails are more attached to the world of law enforcement than to the corrections establishment. The correctional field is still undecided as to whether a board or a single administrator can provide more effective management for correctional systems and programs. It is still divided, for example, as to whether the administration of field parole services should be controlled by the boards which make release decisions or by the departmental structures which administer institutional services.

The original zeal for centralization of correctional service has been tempered. Correctional administrators now realize that total centralization is impossible as well as undesirable in such a functionally variegated and politically federated field. The corrections task force of the President's Commission on Law Enforcement and Administration of Justice envisioned an idealized correctional system with moderate integration *within* numerous subsystems and strong links *between* those subsystems. Such a system would encourage exchange of information and expertise, financial and technical aid from larger to smaller governmental entities, and flexible, reciprocal use of scarce rehabilitative resources.[20]

The centralization issue raises many subsidiary questions about the consolidation of services. Individual views on these questions are derived from value premises and reflect the educational background and professional "socialization" of those who hold them.

Should juvenile and adult correctional services be fused organizationally? Many leaders in the juvenile field would answer in the negative, pointing to the "better image" of juvenile programs and their demonstrated capacity to secure more generous budgets than their adult counterparts.

Should institutional and parole services be integrated? Although many correctional administrators would answer in the affirmative, the prevailing practice is

---

[19] Richard A. McGee, "State Organization for Correctional Administration" in *Contemporary Correction,* Paul W. Tappan, ed. (New York: McGraw-Hill, 1951), p. 89. For a more recent affirmation and elaboration of the same view, see The American Correctional Association's *Manual of Correctional Standards* (Washington: The Association, 1966).

[20] *Task Force Report: Corrections,* pp. 107-111.

to keep the two in quite separate organizational compartments, with resulting discontinuities in the management of offenders.

Should jails be removed from law enforcement and brought into the correctional systems? Yes, in theory (at least), say many correctional authorities. But there is a reluctance on their part to accept responsibility for such financially and programmatically improverished facilities, and a reluctance on the part of many (although not all) of the politically elected sheriffs to relinquish the patronage opportunities afforded by the operation of the jails.

The question of what functions should be "organized" together goes beyond the confines of those services which are more or less correctional in nature. Some of the most disquieting problems of correctional management concern alternative ways of relating corrections to other systems, e.g., social welfare, mental hygiene, and vocational rehabilitation.

The President's Commission on Law Enforcement and Administration of Justice strongly recommended the close coordination of all of the functions having to do with the administration of criminal justice—the police, the prosecutors, the courts, and the correctional agencies. The Commission asserted that the gaps and the cross-purposes among these services seriously handicap the national effort to contain the burgeoning problems of crime and delinquency. They emphasized their belief that the criminal justice system processes offenders in serial fashion and that differences in strategies and tactics, as well as underlying conflicts of philosophy, act to vitiate the total effort. This argument has particular appeal to correctional administrators because their workload—that is, the ever-moving population of offenders coming into corrections—is subject to the often arbitrary screening decisions of police, prosecutory, and judicial officials.

And yet it seems dogmatic to assume that the partners of correctional agencies of necessity always *must* be the other public agencies which have primary responsibility for those individuals formally defined as criminal or delinquent. Correctional services across the country have formed interestingly different alliances, some with social welfare, some with mental hygiene, and others in idiosyncratic forms which reflect some local attitude toward the role of government in this controversial area.

Certainly there is nothing in contemporary theory or practice to suggest an easy formula for deciding about the organizational content or configuration of corrections. Different administrators playing different roles in different regions and settings will and should arrive at sharply different answers. The important point, from the standpoint of our interest in developing capability for change in correctional managers, is that the answers should reflect a commitment to desirable goals, such as the expansion of community treatment programs, the co-optation of numerous resources needed for offender reintegration, and the perfection of a "strategy of search" in refining the techniques of the field.

Centrifugal Pressures Toward Dispersion of Services

The dispersion of correctional services arises largely from the plethora of governmental and functional interests which have provided auspices for them, and from the generally erratic, unplanned way in which they developed. In recent years, however, a rationale has emerged for purposeful decentralization of services, a development which should have a significant influence on future correctional management strategies.

To some extent this rationale is based on a recognition of the dysfunctional attributes of bureaucracy. Large, hierarchical systems tend to inhibit creative responses to need by the sheer weight of routine.[21] This problem has not been studied adequately in corrections (although Studt's current investigations of bureaucratic process in parole agencies are relevant), but it has been investigated in somewhat similar organizations.

For example, Wooden long ago noted the ways in which the bureaucratic organization of hospitals may interfere with the treatment of individual patients.[22] From an analysis of critical incidents, he pointed out discrepancies between theoretically expressed purposes and actually applied purposes. He suggested that organizations often reflect more concern for operational functions than for patients. There is informal evidence that such problems are even more acute in correctional organizations, where staff can easily rationalize that the offender's access to appropriate treatment is more a privilege than a right (after all, he has violated the law). Pressures for requiring conformity to procedural norms may be given added strength by self-righteous feelings of deprecation toward the least statusful members of the organization; ergo, the multiplication of bureaucratic controls over offenders.[23]

The rationale for dispersion of correctional services, however, goes well beyond a general concern for bureaucratic stagnation and constraint. Correctional authorities now believe that the reintegration of offenders must take place in the community and that it cannot be achieved unless a broad spectrum of community interests are drawn into the task.[24] The successful transition from a predominantly institutional to a predominantly community-based system of corrections will depend upon developing leadership, freedom for innovation, and commitment of human and financial resources close to the locus of action rather than in geographically and hierarchically distant power centers.

We might conclude, in reviewing the relative advantages of integration vs. dispersion of correctional services, that no absolute case has been made on either side. Rather, the reorganization of activities in the future should be guided by analytic judgments which seek to maximize the impact of local programs while providing them with the support and "back-up" made possible by the centralization of some functions. Nor is it necessary to think in terms of the traditional dichotomy which places a given service *either* within *or* outside the administrative control of a parent organization. There is much opportunity for imaginative

---

[21] Edward H. Hempel, *Top Management Planning* (New York: Harper, 1945), pp. 31-32.

[22] Howard E. Wooden, "The System May Come Ahead of the Patient," *The Modern Hospital,* XCI (1958), 102.

[23] Maxwell Jones, "Therapeutic Communities" (paper presented at the Institute on Therapeutic Communities, Youth Studies Center, University of Southern California, October 28-30, 1963).

[24] Elmer K. Nelson, Jr., "Community-Based Correctional Treatment: Rationale and Problems," *Annals of the American Academy of Political and Social Science,* CCCLXXIV (1967), 85-86.

forms of cooperation and reciprocity along the boundaries which separate correctional programs from each other and from related public and private enterprise.[25]

CORRECTIONS AND THE DEVELOPMENT OF A SCIENCE OF MANAGEMENT

As corrections has evolved and changed, producing new styles of management and proliferating new environments for administrators, so also have there been pervasive changes in theories of formal organization and in concept related to administrative leadership and behavior. The evolution of correctional management has moved along pathways which run generally parallel to this larger movement. In fact, there is reason to believe that the generic management sciences have something to learn from correctional administration, which has had to address change within encapsulated systems where the dynamics of power and compliance are highly concentrated and executive mistakes are heavily penalized. But the reverse, of course, also is true, and our perspective on correctional management should include an effort to place it in the context of the larger theoretical movement.

Conceptions of formal organizations and of the roles of their managers have changed radically in the past half-century. Taylors "scientific management" movement portrayed the administrator as a highly skilled technician who insured the smooth operation of such organizational processes as planning, organizing, staffing, directing coordinating, reporting, and budgeting.[26] Seen from this vantage point, the ideal executive is a *rational* individual who manipulates the levers of a human machine, correcting deficiencies by rearranging the span of control, the line of command, or the interrelationships of the structural components. Taylor's emphasis was on the anatomy of the system as symbolized by the organization chart. The pyramidal form, with its built-in caste system of status gradations, was sacrosanct.[27] The basic human tendency not to conform to official specification was ignored, a fact which contributed greatly to the early demise of the scientific management movement.

The so-called "human relations" movement which followed proclaimed somewhat pompously (as it now seems) that the need and predilections of the human participants within formal organizations exert a powerful influence, and management would do well to recognize and accommodate them.[28] Especially, it

[25] See Alvin W. Gouldner, "Reciprocity and Autonomy" in *Symposium on Sociological Theory*, Llewellyn Gross, ed. (New York: Harper and Row, 1959), pp. 241-266.

[26] Frederick W. Taylor, *The Principles of Scientific Management* (New York: Harper, 1911).

[27] L. H. Gulick and L. F. Urwick, *Papers in the Science of Administration* (New York: Institute of Public Administration, 1937).

[28] For a more recent series of papers illustrating and testifying to this point of view, see Robert Dubin, *Human Relations in Administration* (Englewood Cliffs, N. J.: Prentice-Hall, 1951).

was argued, the workers' need to find rewarding *social* satisfactions in their relationships with each other operates as a strong determinant of morale, and therefore of production. Research findings soon reinforced this position.[29]

An undoubted contribution of this school of thought was an elaboration of the idea of "informal organization," which takes account of the myriad ways in which the actual dynamics of status and influence differ dramatically from the static juxtaposition of lines and boxes on an organization chart. The boss's secretary, it was pointed out, may exercise great influence, though she has little formal status, because she can control the access of people and information to her superior.

In recent years, more sophisticated theories and research methodologies have been brought to bear upon the informal side of organization life. Just as penal institutions came to be conceived of as social systems, generic theories of organization began to define all of the systems within which men join together to accomplish work goals as "complex" and "open."[30] It was asserted that such organizations strain toward equilibrium and survival, and that change, far from being easily initiated and controlled, usually results from the cumulative effects of those internal and external forces which produce disequilibrium.

This way of thinking about organizations directed attention to many variables which had not been considered by the earlier, more formalistic theories. The modern systems conception of organization opened a number of new areas for study, such as the communications networks, the processes by which conflict is generated and resolved, the nature of the elites within the organization, the expectations people have of each other, and the sanctions they use in efforts to influence each other.[31]

Concern for the psychological and social ingredients of organization life gave rise to ideas which differed sharply from the mechanistic and authoritarian doctrines of the scientific management era. Increasing emphasis was placed on the responsibility of management to create conditions under which participants could use their capacities fully and creatively.[32] Attention was given to the dilemma of satisfying the legitimate requirements of the individual and the organization concurrently.[33] In contrast to the former preoccupation with hierarchy and the downward flow of authority, modern theorists argue that organizations should be seen as composites of problem-solving groups in which the leaders are primarily concerned with generating wide participation among the members and decisional power is shared genuinely with them.[34]

[29] Fritz J. Roethliesberger and William J. Dickson, *Management and the Worker* (Cambridge: Havard University Press, 1939).

[30] Daniel Katz and Robert L. Kahn, *The Social Psychology of Organizations* (New York: Wiley, 1966).

[31] James G. March and Herbert A. Simon, *Organizations* (New York: Wiley, 1958).

[32] Douglas McGregor, *The Human Side of Enterprise* (New York: McGraw-Hill, 1960).

[33] Chris Argyris, *Integrating the Individual and the Organization* (New York: Wiley, 1964).

[34] Rensis Likert, *New Patterns of Management* (New York: McGraw-Hill, 1961).

MANAGEMENT THEORIES BASIC TO THIS STUDY

Some recent formulations concerning management techniques seem especially applicable to developments in the field of corrections and therefore help to provide a context for the research reported upon here. Schein has pointed out that the work styles of managers reflect the assumptions which they make about people.[35] He sets forth four views or assumptions about the nature of man which seem to have been operative in correctional management.

The first view sees man as *rational* and *economic* in nature, primarily, motivated by materialistic rewards, requiring from management a firm structure of incentives and controls in order to carry out predetermined tasks.

The second view sees man as *social,* primarily motivated by his need for meaningful relationships with others, requiring from management a concern for his feelings and a structuring of work to bring about satifying human interactions and group experiences.

The third view sees man as potentially *self-actualizing.* After satisfying lower-level needs, such as survival, self-esteem, and autonomy,[36] man responds to internal forces in seeking a sense of achievement and meaning in his work. The function of management, under this view, is to facilitate the efforts of organization members to use their energies in creative and productive ways.

The fourth view sees man as *complex* and, while capable of self-actualization, highly varied in his responses to different situations. This view challenges management to develop diagnostic skills and wide flexibility in meeting the needs, and thereby maximizing the contribution, of different organization members under constantly changing circumstances.

Some aspects of all of these views can be found in correctional administration, both historic and contemporary. The staffs of large, routinized institutions have generally been treated by management as rational-economic. Smaller institutions (especially those for juvenile offenders) and community-based correctional programs have moved toward the view that employees are motivated by social as well as economic satisfactions. Some of the most interesting experimental programs (for example, institutional efforts to develop "therapeutic communities," and demonstrations of intensive treatment on probation or parole) have given the staff many opportunities for self-actualization. Some managers, as will be shown in the research reported here, do view their staff as complex and seek to use varied skills and methods in working with them, along the lines suggested by Schein.

We must remember, of course, that correctional administrators have managerial relationships not only with staff but with offenders. Indeed it is the balancing and harmonizing of these two sets of relationships that creates some of the most difficult problems, perhaps because administrators (consciously or unconsciously) adopt one view of man when dealing with staff and another when

[35] Edgar H. Schein, *Organizational Psychology* (Englewood Cliffs, N. J.: Prentice-Hall, 1965).
[36] Abraham H. Maslow, *Motivation and Personality* (New York: Harper and Row, 1954).

dealing with offenders. Consider, for example, the dynamics which might occur in an institution where the management treats staff as motivated by social and economic needs, while viewing inmates as capable of responding only to coercion.

The historic and contemporary picture of correctional management's view of offenders seems even more varied than its views of staff. Many offenders have been, and still are, viewed as responding only to force or threat of force. Both the time-honored penal work programs, which provide opportunities for small earnings on a sliding scale, and the practice of reducing the time of incarceration ("giving good time") for conforming behavior stem from a rational-economic view of inmates.

One of the most significant developments in correctional rehabilitation, the use of small group process to bring about changes of attitude and behavior, seems to rest on the concept that offenders are social men. Other innovations, such as furloughs for work or study, have overtones of both the self-actualization and the complex views of man.

The position implicit in our research is that correctional management will be most effective if it is generally consistent in its view of *all* participants (whether staff or offenders) and if it seeks to develop approaches to them based on the assumption that, while complex, they are capable of self-actualization.

Another formulation from management theory which seems useful in assessing trends in correctional administration is the typology of organization and management styles suggested by Likert.[37] Distinguishing basically between authoritative and participative organizations, Likert posits four approaches to management, each with specified consequences for the motivation of participants, their job satisfaction, communication, decision-making, production, and other variables. The four types, which Likert views as stages of development, from ineffective and pathological to effective and healthy management are: (1) exploitive-authoritative; (2) benevolent-authoritative; (3) participative-consultative; and (4) participative-group.

It appears that aspects of all four approaches are to be found in contemporary correctional organizations. The general trend, however, has been away from type 1, which is illustrated by the traditional prison with its dependence on coercive uses of authority, and into types 3 and 4 through a mixture of benevolently applied authority and limited democratization of the management process. The use of inmate advisory councils, the delegation of case management authority to probation and parole officers, and the involvement of junior staff in long-range planning are examples of the participative-consultative practices adopted in many correctional agencies, particularly those based in or closely tied to the community. The general pattern in corrections, however, seems closer to Likert's benevolent-authoritative type than to any of the other three.

Some progressive correctional programs operate along lines very similar to Likert's fourth type, participative-group. Examples of such an approach can be

[37] Likert, *op. cit.*, pp. 223–234.

found in the New Jersey Highfields experiment,[38] the Pinehills project in Utah,[39] and the California Community Treatment Project.[40] While differing from each other in many ways, these and similar experimental ventures distribute influence and decisional power widely among the staff and the offenders involved and make extensive use of group process in guiding program operation.

The research reported here is based on the assumption that correctional administrators should seek to develop participation at all levels with their organizations. It should be recognized, however, that much empirical research is needed (both in correctional administration and in generic management processes) to refine understanding of how participative techniques may be employed successfully and how they may be adapted to the realities of particular programs. As has already been noted, precipitous efforts to democratize correctional organizations not only tend to be dangerous but are usually destined to fail. The introduction of participative methods into programs which are oriented toward the goals of revenge and restraint requires great sensitivity to the forces at work in the organization and in its environment.

A final theoretical formulation of relevance to the development of correctional administration is Etzioni's typology of organizations (and, implicitly, of management styles) based upon the kinds of power used by administrators and the kinds of compliance or "involvement" exhibited by the "lower participants."[41] Etzioni suggests that there are three major ways in which power may be used: (1) *coercively,* through force or the threat of force; (2) *remuneratively,* through manipulation of economic and related rewards; (3) *normatively,* through the use of symbols (e.g., the goal of reintegrating offenders into the community) to which the lower participants become committed.

Each type of power, according to Etzioni, elicits a distinctive and "congruent" response from those involved. The use of coercive power (as illustrated every day in the authoritarian prison) elicits an alienative response characterized by distrust and psychological distance between the managers and those who are managed. The use of remunerative power (as illustrated by administrative process in a factory producing goods on a piece-work basis) elicits a calculative response in which the commitment of the employees is related to their desire to secure designated materialistic benefits. The use of normative power (as illustrated in a university faculty which is committed to such symbolic norms as "academic excellence") elicits a moral response from participants who conform to organizational requirements because they have a personal commitment to them, rather than because of force or economic incentive.

[38] Lloyd W. McCorkle, Albert Elias, and F. Lovell Bixby, *The Highfields Story: An Experimental Treatment Project for Youthful Offenders* (New York: Holt, 1958).

[39] Empey, *op cit.,* pp. 37–40.

[40] The development of the Community Treatment Project is reported in a series of "Community Treatment Reports' issued by the Division of Research, California Youth Authority, Sacramento, California, 1962–1968.

[41] Amitai Etzioni, *A Comparative Analysis of Complex Organizations* (New York: Free Press, 1961), p. 12.

Applying Etzioni's theory to corrections, again we see a mixed picture. Some prisons, indeed some entire correctional systems, clearly appear to be close to the coercive-alienative mode.[42] Other correctional organizations seek to "purchase" conformity, at least temporarily, by the manipulation of materialistic sanctions. Still other programs, however, seem to be pushing toward the normative-moral pattern by management methods which are designed to gain the commitment of all who are involved to the people-changing goals of the system.

Obviously, there is a great deal of similarity and overlapping among the formulations of Schein, Likert, and Etzioni. All three are reviewed here not only because they are largely consistent but mainly because, taken together, they provide a context for thinking about the general directions of change needed in corrections today. The lines of conceptualization, and the limited research available to support them, suggest that correctional managers should seek to create conditions leading to participative, normative organizations in which all participants are perceived as complex and capable of self-actualizing behavior.[43]

[42] It should be noted, however, that coercive power in the traditional prison in reality is shared by the staff with an elite of prisoners. See Sykes, *op. cit.,* chs. 3, 4. For a useful analysis of the dynamics of power in a youth institution, see Allen F. Breed, "Inmate Subculture," *California Youth Authority Quarterly,* XVI, (1963), 3–16.

[43] While the participative and "normative-moral" models of organization seem most desirable for future correctional organizations, knowledge remains too limited to permit hard, doctrinaire conclusions. For example, some impressive results are now appearing in correctional agencies which use behavior-modification techniques involving various sanctions to reward desired behavior and to penalize that defined as unacceptable. For a description of such a program at the National Training School for Boys in Washington, D. C., *see Task Force Report: Corrections,* p. 53.

45
Measuring the Cost of Correctional Services

MARK S. RICHMOND

From the moment of his arrest, if not before, the offender becomes a consumer of public resources, most of which are tax supported. The cost of his apprehension and booking are the first expenses on the list. Unless he is released immediately on bail or personal recognizance, the taxpayers pay for his confinement in jail until his trial. Add the cost of prosecution (and defense, if he cannot afford to hire counsel) and the expense of trial and related court services. In the event of his conviction, probation or imprisonment and parole will be paid for with tax money. Expenditures for correctional programs and services will include the use of health and welfare services, education and training programs, legal services, and any other resources that may be employed until the offender is discharged from the system.

Twelve years ago the estimated cost of operating criminal and juvenile courts and correction (probation, institutions, and parole) in one state (Massachusetts) was more than $30-million a year. This amounted to about $6.30 for each man, woman, and child who lived in the state. These figures did not include estimates of loss or damage resulting from the commission of offenses; the cost of law enforcement, arrest, or prosecution; capital investments in and maintenance of buildings, facilities, and equipment other than correctional institutions; and any extra-agency costs associated with trial, conviction, and imprisonment. The Presi-

SOURCE. *Crime and Delinquency,* **18**, July 1972, pp. 243–252. Reprinted with the permission of the author and the National Council on Crime and Delinquency.

dent's Commission on Law Enforcement and Administration of Justice estimated that national expenditures for police, prosecution and defense, the courts, and correction exceeded $4-billion for the fiscal year that ended June 30, 1965. These costs are borne primarily by taxpayers at the state and local levels.

But how much does *correction* cost? NCCD conducted a survey for the President's Crime Commission and estimated that the cost of operating state and local correctional services in 1965 was almost $1-billion. About 80 per cent of the total operating cost was allocated for institutions, and more than half of that allocation went to support state adult correctional institutions. It was estimated that the average daily cost per case ranged from $11.15 for juvenile detention to $.38 for adult probation. The daily cost of a juvenile in an institution was ten times that of juvenile probation or aftercare. For adults, state institutional cost was about six times that of parole and about fourteen times that of probation. Construction being planned in 1965 for completion by 1975 in state and local institution systems could increase bed capacity by 24 per cent at a cost of over $1-billion (based on a very conservative estimate of $10,000 per bed).

Another way of looking at the cost of correction is to consider the cost of a criminal career, but this is as difficult as estimating the total cost of crime and delinquency. Records are often incomplete; data relating to one component or jurisdiction may be incompatible with data from another; it is often a matter of personal judgment as to what costs to include; and many costs are frankly unknown.

A partial view of career costs can be gained from applying estimated daily average costs per case to a hypothetical, yet fairly typical, offender. Cost rates in the following illustration are estimated national averages reported to the President's Crime Commission in 1965.[1] This hypothetical offender made his first appearance in juvenile court at the age of sixteen. For twenty-five years he has been in and out of trouble. Now, at age forty-one, he is in prison. When he is released again, the statistical probability is that he will not return to prison, but he will probably continue to consume public resources in other ways.

1. Arrested at age sixteen and placed in a juvenile detention facility. Released on probation. Committed to a state training school for a new offense and violation of probation. Paroled.

14 days juvenile detention @ $11.15 per day	$ 156.
6 months on probation @ $.92 per day	166.
14 months in training school @ $10.66 per day	4,530.
5 months on parole @ $.84 per day	126.

[1] Note that these estimates, are for one year only and have been extrapolated for a hypothetical 25-year history. This introduces a bias by failing to account for actual cost fluctuations over that span of time. For more detailed applications of this kind of cost analysis, see Barbara Cantor and Stuart Adams, *The Cost of Correcting Youthful Offenders* (Washington, D.C.: Department of Corrections, 1968); and Stuart Adams and Calvin C. Hopkinson, *Interim Evaluation of the Intensive Supervision Caseload Project* (Los Angeles: Los Angeles County Probation Department, 1964).

2. Violated parole by committing a new offense. Sentenced to jail instead of being returned as a parole violator. Over the next three years he was in and out of jails awaiting trial on subsequent offenses or serving short sentences.

14 months in local jails @ $2.86 per day	$1,215.

3. Committed a felony offense and placed in jail to await trial. Placed on probation. Violated by committing a new offense and sentenced to a state reformatory. Paroled; violated.

6 months in jail awaiting trial and sentence @ $2.86 per day	$ 515.
4 months probation @ $.38 per day	46.
18 months in state reformatory @ $5.24 per day	3,256.
2 months on parole @ $.88 per day	53.
12 months in reformatory @ $5.24 per day	1,913.

4. Arrested a few months after release for a felony offense. Committed to jail to await trial and sentence. Charges reduced to a misdemeanor; sentenced to jail.

4 months in local jail @ $2.86 per day	$ 343.
5 months served on jail sentence @ $2.86 per day	429.

5. Committed a more serious felony offense. Detained in jail awaiting trial and disposition. Sentenced to state prison. Paroled; violated, and returned to serve remainder of sentence.

8 months in local jail @ $2.86 per day	$ 684.
3 years in state prison @ $5.24 per day	5,737.
4 months on parole @ $.88 per day	106.
2 years in prison @ $5.24 per day	3,301.

6. The commission of a subsequent offense resulted in the same sequence of events. He is still serving his sentence.

5 months in jail awaiting trial, etc., @ $2.86 per day	$ 429.
6 years in prison @ $5.24 per day	11,476.
Total	$34,481.00

If this illustration can be accepted as at least remotely representing the cost of a typical criminal career that can be multiplied by tens of thousands, it has many implications relating to the consumption of resources. The most salient question is, What has been accomplished by the expenditure of these funds? But there are other questions. Is it possible that a greater commitment of resources at the onset of a criminal career like this could have produced better results? Do the astonishingly low daily costs of probation and parole suggest that these are starvation rates which cannot buy actual services and controls? Is it significant that the offender spent a total of 3½ years in local jails in which there were no correctional programs?

GOALS AND ASSUMPTIONS

The foregoing measures of resource consumption are process-oriented rather than goal-oriented. The customary approach to all correction has tended to be process-oriented, the preoccupation with operating procedures and the sequences in which they occur has been almost ritualistic. Decision points in the process have offered little more than the exercise of either-or choices: whether or not to arrest, whether or not to prosecute, whether to place on probation or sentence to imprisonment, whether or not to grant parole.

This situation must no longer be tolerated. Rising costs will eventually outstrip the availability of funds for meeting them. The ineffectiveness of the system is now seen as a major contributor to the alarming increase in the crime rate. Waste and inefficiency cannot be condoned in the competition for tax funds. Programs whose results are unknown and to which evaluations of outcome have not been systematically applied will not be given continuing support. Therefore, since the offender will remain a consumer of resources, ways of insuring better returns on resource investment must be found.

A goal-oriented approach provides the most practical solutions to this problem because it is the only approach in which outcomes carry more weight than processes and programs in the allocation of resources. Goal-setting is a painstaking and difficult process in itself. It begins with defining and formulating broad aims and objectives and obtaining consensus about them. These are supported by specific, measurable goals, whose feasibility and practicality can be considered only in terms of required strategies and possible alternatives. The strategies that are selected are implemented by a series of action steps and checkpoints at which progress can be assessed and subsequent courses of action can be modified as circumstances dictate. Objectives and goals are related to purpose and needs.

What are the objectives of criminal justice and correction? Correction today displays evidence of a number of ideas and practices, some of which are in conflict, each seeking to cope with the difficult problems of punishing, deterring, restraining, and rehabilitating offenders. None has resolved these problems, and change from one to another probably has been more the result of humanitarian concern that the product of rational or scientific process.

Notions of punishment still underlie much of correctional practice today, particularly in popular views of what ought to be done with those who commit criminal acts. These notions satisfy primitive needs for retribution, but the focus is exclusively on the offender, and punishment is measured according to the type and seriousness of offense. As the focus broadens to include concerns for society, punishment is seen as a deterrent to the future behavior of the offender and as an inner control for those who might otherwise be tempted to commit a criminal act. The idea of restraint as a necessary ingredient of correction is associated primarily with the objective of public protection, but this is a relatively temporary means of achieving it. The rationale for rehabilitation is related to humanitarian concerns for the offender and to the ultimate objective of public protection.

Thus the problems of goal-setting in correction are compounded at the outset by uncertain objectives and limited knowledge of the direct causes of criminal behavior. In addition to many unresolved basic issues, other concerns have been growing—questions of due process, equitable treatment of offenders, the efficiency of the criminal justice system, and the cost-effectiveness of correctional efforts. Yet certain assumptions can be made on the basis of facts that are known. In the absence of a better starting point, the following assumptions can be used to assess needs, define purpose, and establish objectives and goals:

1. "The general underlying premise for the new directions in corrections is that crime and delinquency are symptoms of failures and disorganization of the community as well as of individual offenders. . . . The task of corrections therefore includes building or rebuilding solid ties between offender and community, integrating or reintegrating the offender into community life. . . . This requires not only efforts directed toward changing the individual offender, which has been almost the exclusive focus of rehabilitation, but also mobilization and change of the community and its institutions."[2]

2. The task of correction is to intervene in delinquent and criminal careers, through management and control of crises and through programs designed to overcome handicapping deficiencies.

3. The more an offender is plunged into correctional processes and the longer he is locked up, the greater the cost and the improbability of his successful reintegration in the community.

4. An offender's need for control or help should be considered and treated individually, whatever his status in the criminal justice system.

To assess the feasibility of change, one must consider some alternative strategies: improved operations within correctional systems and agencies, mobilization of resources outside correctional systems for the prevention of crime, and increased fairness in the administration of correctional systems.

The first of these may include more efficient procedures to promote a faster flow of people through the system, methods of upgrading personnel, reorganization, and new information systems and management methods. There may be many obstacles to change in these areas, and changes of this kind are unlikely to be achieved unless they are treated as part of a broader approach toward organizational development and renewal.

The second and third alternatives call for new involvement of schools, medical services, welfare agencies, business and industry, labor organizations, civic groups, and legal services. But many of these resources are already inadequate to the tasks they are expected to perform. Action strategies that would funnel

---

[2] President's Commission on Law Enforcement and Administration of Justice. *Task Force Report: Corrections* (Washington, D.C.: U.S. Government Printing Office, 1967), p. 7.

offenders into outside resources must confront the capabilities and interests of the agencies involved. Effective collaboration with other agencies requires them to perceive offenders as legitimate recipients of their services and to give the criminal justice system a visibility and a place of central importance which, for the most part, it now lacks.

THE COST-EFFECTIVENESS APPROACH

While some people have difficulty understanding or accepting theories of criminal behavior, are confused over correctional goals and objectives, or question the purposes of specific correctional programs and procedures, few have trouble understanding the meaning of dollars. Dollar values have a universal appeal to taxpayers when they are expressed as ways of spending less money or getting more for the money spent. Applying the cost-effectiveness approach to goal-setting does not simplify the tasks involved: it merely uses terms and concepts that have instant meaning to everyone.

The obvious starting point is an analysis of existing costs. It has already been said that this can be a major undertaking because of incomplete and incompatible records, unresolved questions of what costs to include, and unknown costs. However, there are ways of making approximations that will suffice for planning purposes. One was illustrated above in spreading the correctional costs of a "criminal career." Take an "average" offender's history and tally known or estimated unit costs for the various programs, services, and procedures in which he has been involved. This computation can be manipulated and projected according to the number of offenders known to have been involved in different programs and procedures. Often the actual costs of programs, services, and procedures are not known, but these too can be estimated closely enough for planning purposes. Fairly accurate figures are available for costs of materials and supplies. The costs of procedures such as supervision, instruction, or counseling can be expressed in man-hours or man-days at estimated rates. Supportive costs, such as utilities, depreciation of equipment or facilities, and transportation can be prorated from known categories of expense. Known or estimated equivalent costs can be applied when necessary.

Identification and Application of Resources

Goal-setting cannot proceed far without much thought being given to the resources that will be needed. These generally consist of money, manpower, materials, and facilities. The resources to deliver the programs and services in question do not have to be provided all at once to all offenders, or even by the agency directly responsible for the activities. The feasibility of programs and goals must be considered in terms of the kinds and amounts of support that may be available from all sources. This will enable priority choices; for example: Shall the greater emphasis be placed on diagnostic work or on expansion of social casework services? The distribution, sequence, timing, and amounts of funding must also be considered.

Process in Relation to Outcome

Traditional line budgeting has virtually dictated that costs must be presented on a per capita basis, as summary amounts of money per offender per day, week, month, or year. There are many accounting difficulties and possible questions of policy in computing *all* costs in these summary amounts, but the major limitations of this budgeting procedure for planning purposes are that (1) the figures have no meaning without reference to total time (man-days served) and (2) there is no reference to outcome. For example, the average per-capita operating cost of one community residential facility (halfway house) amounts to $15 a day if it operates at full capacity all of the time. If the average length of stay is ninety days, the total investment per resident amounts to an average of $1,350. The daily per capita cost of another such facility is about $12. At this facility the average length of stay is eighty-five days. Thus, at full capacity, the total average investment per resident is $1,020. The central question is whether the outcome of one is better than that of the other.

The concept of total process cost in relation to outcome is particularly useful to planners and program managers alike. It not only suggests alternative ways to stretch the budgeted dollar without sacrificing program quality, but also constantly focuses attention on benefits to the offender and society in terms of the total investments made. Thus, correctional goals and objectives assume prime importance. For example, it can be shown in dollars that simple safekeeping or minimal domiciliary care at low per capita rates can be more costly over extended periods of time than intensive treatment at high per capita rates for shorter periods when results of the latter demonstrate a reduced or delayed rate of failure in the attainment of preset goals.

This concept introduces a new dimension of cost analysis in which correctional agencies and programs can be seen as vehicles for the delivery of certain services. A number of related issues must be considered. Foremost among them are offender selection, program evaluation, and management.

Offender Selection

Not all offenders need the same controls and correctional treatment. Failure of the system or of decision-makers to take this into account can be highly wasteful of resources, and it risks more long-range harm than good to offenders who become saddled with processes they do not need. One of the persistent criticisms of the traditional jail, designed for maximum security, is that commitment to such a facility has not been based on differences in need for control and correctional treatment. The result has been that the most expensive kind of facility is used for all offenders when only a small percentage of the persons committed need this degree of control.

Obviously, selection must be based on careful estimates of danger and risk to the community and on offender problems and needs in relation to certain correctional objectives. Ideally, a correctional system should match types of offenders with types of programs geared to meet specific needs. The choices would range from nonsupervisory measures in structured community programs to total incarceration. Greatest flexibility should attend these choices, but we are far from this ideal, both philosophically and practically; diagnostic procedures, when they occur at all, take place *after* many important decisions have been made and sentences have been imposed.

Program Evaluation

The development of a more effective correctional system will require new knowledge and better research. More discriminating criteria are needed for classifying offenders. Whatever the availability of correctional resources, individuals must be differentiated according to the degree of treatment and control they require (intensive, selective, or minimal). There is a continuing need for knowledge for training staff in correctional processes and training offenders in the specific behaviors that are required for successful community adjustment. Research on community-based programs, for example, would contribute much to this knowledge and, at the same time, would enable more sophisticated development of the programs themselves. More must be learned about those types of offenders who can make the most and those who can make the least effective use of various correctional experiences. Questions must be raised about the character of correctional experiences for the offenders involved in them. There is evidence, too, of a need to study the appropriate "dosage" of correction for different types of offenders.

COLLABORATIVE MANAGEMENT

It is clear from the preceding discussion that neither the criminal justice system itself nor its individual correctional agencies can realistically aspire to have all of the resources needed to conduct a broad range of preventive and corrective programs and services. It should be equally clear by now that such an attempt should be avoided.

The programs and services required for the prevention, treatment, and control of crime and delinquency can be viewed as providing for a spectrum of needs. They include preventive measures that can be applied before an offense is committed, alternatives to court procedures and disposition, correctional treatment of convicted offenders, and aftercare services designed to help and control the processes involved in the offender's reintegration for successful community life.

Correctional agencies in any jurisdiction need far more resources than have been available to them until now. But it is no longer necessary or wise for correction to try to be autonomous. Many of the needed resources can be found increasingly outside of the criminal justice system. Specific services for offenders may be purchased from other agencies and organizations, both public and private; they may become available as extensions of an agency's own programs when offenders are added to the target group; or, as in the case of private industry, they may help meet the needs of the organization offering the services. The vast potentials of volunteer services are just now being explored. But the problem is a much larger one than gaining access to resources.

Redesign of Vehicles Delivering Services

The national profile of correction consists of a number of organizational components: juvenile detention, juvenile probation, juvenile institutions, juvenile aftercare, misdemeanant probation, felony probation, local adult institutions and jails, state and federal adult institutions, and parole. Alaska is the only state in which all nine correctional services are organized into a single department. In most jurisdictions the agencies providing these services function autonomously and their relationships to other correctional programs, if not entirely remote, lack the integration that would enable total coordinated correctional effort.

The primary organizational models are local, regional, and statewide, as well as various kinds of collaborative administration. The precedents for these models are deeply imbedded in patterns of governmental organization and traditional ways of doing things. Program managers and planning groups cannot do much about the political and jurisdictional limits imposed on correctional programs. However, from a painstaking examination of the issues involved and from an understanding of the capabilities and mechanisms needed for the eventual delivery of comprehensive, coordinated correctional services, a design can emerge for the eventual attainment of long-range goals.

Who determines priorities? The planning process itself requires choices among alternatives and the identification of priorities with which feasible action steps can be taken. But there is a management aspect of this as well. In these days when correctional program managers are finding a growing abundance of local resources for services to offenders, the problem is the relatively simple one of obtaining commitment, making necessary arrangements, and adjusting operating schedules. The correctional program manager, however, is not the only agency representative laying claim to these services. As more agencies increase their claims, the time will come when the risks of demand exceeding supply will be foreseen by the organizations possessing the services or resources. The competition that ensues will probably have to be resolved in nontraditional ways. There may be a need for local, regional, and state planning and coordinating groups who will be authorized to cut across customary organizational lines to achieve an equitable distribution of available resources among multiple service needs on a priority basis. This will be an increasingly complex task that will have meaning only if consensus is reached on long-range goals and as responsible agency representatives participate in the choice of program and service alternatives.

What are the management implications of decisions within the criminal justice system? Comprehensive planning is really concerned with future effectiveness. While the initial focus may be on programs and services, planners recognize that the difficulties of planning and implementing change may be tactical and strategic as well as substantive. Clearly, an attempt to cope with existing problems on a massive scale risks outrunning available resources and the level of understanding that can be brought to bear on them. If a strategy is adopted that is consistent with limited resources and understanding, the effort may appear inadequate in relation to the magnitude of the problem. The choice of a starting point should reflect an effort that is part of a larger and more significant undertaking.

The very limited traditional view of correction has not yet been abandoned. In this view, one thinks of imprisonment and what happens after guilt has been established as comprising the universe of correction. This paper has taken a broader view. From the point of first contact between an alleged offender and police there can and should be an increasing range of decision points and alternative courses of action, each of which influences and is influenced by the others. A great deal more must be learned about key decision points—what the choices are and who chooses among them—and there is a need for more information that can be used to evaluate the effects of the decisions that are made. Any significant change, whether planned or unplanned, will decidedly alter the existing system. Changes should be planned with full awareness that they will have impact and that their ultimate effectiveness will be measured as contributions to the value of the system in which they occur.

There is no question that the offender is a consumer of resources, nor is there any doubt that the costs he incurs will increase as new and expanded correctional programs and services are developed for his benefit and society's. The central question now becomes, How can greater returns be produced by the resources that are consumed?

The preceding pages have briefly examined some of the difficult issues related to this question. A common approach may be impossible because of the profusion of special circumstances that surround each situation. It is also evident that the question is of such magnitude that there is no single answer; many solutions must be sought.

46

Code of Ethics

FEDERAL PROBATION OFFICERS' ASSOCIATION

Code Of Ethics
Federal Probation Officers' Association

As a Federal Probation Officer, I am dedicated to rendering professional service to the courts, the parole authorities, and the community at large in effecting the social adjustment of the offender.

I will conduct my personal life with decorum, will neither accept nor grant favors in connection with my office, and will put loyalty to moral principles above personal consideration.

I will uphold the law with dignity and with complete awareness of the prestige and stature of the judicial system of which I am a part. I will be ever cognizant of my responsibility to the community which I serve.

I will strive to be objective in the performance of my duties; respect the inalienable rights of all persons; appreciate the inherent worth of the individual, and hold inviolate those confidences which can be reposed in me.

I will cooperate with my fellow workers and related agencies and will continually attempt to improve my professional standards through the seeking of knowledge and understanding.

I recognize my office as a symbol of public faith and I accept it as a public trust to be held as long as I am true to the ethics of the Federal Probation Service. I will constantly strive to achieve these objectives and ideals, dedicating myself to my chosen profession.

September 12, 1960

SOURCE. Federal Probation Officers Association, September 12, 1960.

RESEARCH

The selection of materials in this Section are more *about* research than examples *of* research. There may be debate in some quarters as to whether evaluation is true research; note that in industry, quality control generally is not under the research department. Yet, without doubt, there is need for evaluation and the methods are not well developed. Much of the research relevant to issues and problems in criminal justice is fundamental research normally carried out in other disciplines. However there are problems specific to criminal justice; for example, legal concerns are related to concerns about crime, and concerns about crime are related to concerns about ethics as well as efficiency.

Before we give the viewpoint of the National Advisory Commission on Criminal Justice Standards and Goals, we present an article by Professor Daniel Glaser. He points out some things that are not too often recognized about research. There are fashions in research. These fashions are related to fashions in other sectors. This is, of course, not in itself undesirable, but it is a matter to be recognized. He also notes that the world of research in criminal justice is not so very far removed from political activities.

Professor Glaser, perhaps himself following a fashion, strongly advocates the controlled experiment as a research method in the assessment of variations of procedures in the criminal justice area. Readers may wish to examine the controlled experiment as the ideal in this field and consider whether or not alternatives are more acceptable, if not more powerful.

The next item in the section is from the National Standards and Goals; it discusses research and development, and links these with information and statistics. A number of research findings are concisely summarized. The extract ends with some notes on research priorities.

Dr. Gordon Waldo in the article which follows sets down in elegantly simple form some of the ways in which research and researchers are often misunderstood.

The two articles by Leslie Wilkins are also explanations of research intended more for the intelligent laymen than for the sophisticated researcher. All researchers have had the problem of trying to explain some of the statistical methods they use. The "Problem of Overlap" is an attempt to explain to laymen the kinds of answers derived from multiple regression. The article entitled "Inefficient Statistics" discusses an empirical finding that, in fact, inefficient statistical methods work better than more efficient methods when we are dealing with offender records. Suggestions for further research are made somewhat tentatively, since it appears that all "real life" data bases are dogged by "noise." Methods of analysis and interpretation which are resistant to "noise" seem to be preferable at this stage of development.

Before any enthusiastic researcher goes, or attempts to go, "into the field" with his favorite research design to test his theories, he would be advised to read the last article in this section by Dr. Jerome Rabow. There are different perspectives held by those who play different roles in the criminal justice field. Communication between researchers and those who see their function as treatment is often conflicted. And the researcher is often quite unsympathetic to the viewpoint of the administrator or clinician. Perhaps there should be more cooperative research; rather than research being "carried out on behalf of" the administration, researchers and administrators could become a team with shared goals.

47

Correctional Research: An Elusive Paradise

DANIEL GLASER

The history of correctional research resembles the history of religion. There have been successive periods of discontent, new cults promising simple solutions, and social movements institutionalizing the new approaches in judicial or correctional practice. But discontent recurs, and new movements continually emerge.

SCIENCE AS SALVATION

Commitment to a penal policy has almost always rested purely on faith in its efficacy, or on a selfish interest in it, rather than on empirical evidence proving that it achieves its professed purposes. Yet proponents of each way of treating criminals, whether it be capital punishment or solitary confinement, hard labor or nondirective counseling, have all asserted that their method succeeds, either in changing criminals or in deterring others from becoming criminals. The literature proposing penal standards, from Old Testament injunctions to Beccaria's essay, from Bentham's "felicific calculus" to the latest pronouncements of prison psychiatrists, is replete with empirical claims. But this literature is almost uniformly deficient in scientifically adequate evidence on the validity of these claims.

SOURCE. *The Journal of Research in Crime and Delinquency*, 2, January 1965, pp. 1–11. Reprinted with the permission of the author and the National Council on Crime and Delinquency. Copyright 1965, National Council on Crime and Deliquency.

Successful experience is illustrated or implied for each treatment method, but there is no proof that the cases cited are typical of those to whom the treatment would be directed if a correctional system adopted it; often there is not even adequate evidence that the reformation of cited cases occurred *because of* a particular treatment rather than *despite* it. Indeed, usually the only evidences of change in the criminals are favorable impressions gained by the reporter rather than actual statistics on posttreatment criminality.

With the rise of science in the nineteenth and twentieth centuries, proposals for penal reform at times shifted from specific prescriptions for changing criminals, to demands for institutionalizing scientific research as a guide for penal practice. Research was to be the new Utopia to inspire reform movements, and sometimes it was described in moving exhortations, for it had to compete with other proposals, each generally supported by exaggerated claims. Thus Enrico Ferri, in his *Criminal Sociology*, which had its first Italian edition in 1884, asserted:

> The naturalistic philosophy from the year 1850, impelled by the new data furnished by the experimental sciences, from astronomy to . . . sociology, has completely dissipated the moral and intellectual mists left by the Middle Ages . . . We enter, with the natural study of crime . . . upon a road that the jurists have not yet attempted, and whose difficulties we recognize without fear, because combat was always a condition of victory.[1]

And in 1903, Aschaffenburg, in Germany, insisted:

> Thy system of criminal law . . . must . . . bow to the advance of science . . . Only the natural scientific method . . . can smooth the way that leads to a knowledge of crime and of criminals. Not until then will a sure foundation be laid for the proud structure of legal security.[2]

Professor Ernest W. Burgess, dean of applied sociology, represented the University of Chicago in 1927 on an inter-university commission to evaluate the Illinois sentencing and parole system. Law school professors, representing Northwestern and the University of Illinois, raised legal and administrative questions, but Burgess addressed the behavior prediction problem inherent in sentencing and parole decisions. At this was a scientific matter, he systematically tabulated data on the correlates of parole outcome for 3,000 cases. In this pioneer parole prediction study he proposed that the state regularly improve his prediction tables:

> An expectancy rate should be as useful in parole administration as similar rates have proved to be in insurance . . . Our prisons and reformatories should become laboratories of research and understanding into the causes of the baffling problem of the making and unmaking of criminal carrers.[3]

The ideal of resolving the crime problem by relying on science found its most

---

[1] E. Ferri, *Criminal Sociology* (Boston, Little, Brown, 1917), pp. 566–567.

[2] G. Aschaffenburg, *Crime and its Repression* (Boston, Little, Brown, 1913), pp. 321–322.

[3] A. A. Bruce, E. W. Burgess, and A.J. Harno, *The Workings of the Indeterminate-Sentence Law and the Parole System in Illinois* (Springfield, Ill., Department of Public Safety, 1928), pp. 248–249.

vociferous salesman in Sheldon Glueck, who glowingly set forth the prospect for science in the sentencing process by this conjecture:

> Suppose . . . that a judge had before him separate prognostic tables based on fines, on imprisonment in a penitentiary, on imprisonment in a reformatory, on probation, or even more discriminately on results obtained by different probation officers. And suppose that the judge, on consultation of the prognostic tables, found that Prisoner X according to past experience with other prisoners who in certain pertinent particulars resembled X, had, say nine out of ten chances of continuing in crime if sent to a prison, seven out of ten if sent to a reformatory, five out of ten if placed on probation, and only two out of ten if placed on probation, under Supervisor Y. Clearly, the judge . . . [by] using objectified and organized experience . . . based on hundreds of similar cases . . . would greatly improve his exercise of discretion in imposing sentence.[4]

ABANDONED UTOPIAS

From time to time in the past few decades, research offices have been established in correctional agencies and assigned the task of procuring facts for the guidance of correctional decisions. Like other Utopian colonies, these offices either disappeared quickly or survived only by a metamorphosis in their goals and practices, through which they ceased to be a force for change. The research movement, however, is still with us, and there are signs that it may have a continuing impact on correction. A survey of its recent history can provide source material for new exhortations to mobilize research on the effective handling of criminals. It may also stimulate research on the integration of research with practice.

In the early 1930's Professor Burgess launched an epoch of sociological prediction research (not only in criminology, but also in marriage and other fields). He persuaded the state of Illinois to establish in each of its three major prisons an office manned by civil-service employees entitled "sociologist-actuaries." The assignments of this new kind of correctional official were first, to advise the parole board of the violation probability predicted by the Burgess tables for each parole applicant, and second, to conduct research to improve the prediction tables. This, ideally, would create a cumulatively increasing contribution of science to correctional decision-making.

The three sociologist-actuary offices, now in operation for over thirty years, have been manned by two to four sociologists at all times. These research personnel have served some useful functions, but their contribution to the scientific guidance of policy has been far short of that which Burgess envisioned. Why was this dream unfulfilled? Does its history have lessons for applied research elsewhere?

Illinois had a part-time parole board consisting predominantly of lawyers who were politically appointed, were generally oriented toward reaching their deci-

---

[4] S. and E. Glueck, *After-Conduct of Discharged Offenders* (London, Macmillan, 1946), pp. 68–69.

sions in a minimum of time, and frequently responded precipitously to badgering by the press. They seemed to want to retry each case, so as to assess what would be just punishment. Probably their major social function was the latent one of somewhat equalizing the impact of disparate sentencing policies among the many judges sending men to prison. Some parole board members indicated that in their decisions they took into account the predictions submitted by the sociologist-actuaries, but few understood the derivation of the prediction tables, or their potentialities and limitations.

Over the years the Illinois parole boards solicited longer and longer narrative summaries for each case from the sociologist-actuaries. During the 1940's and 1950's preparation of these reports, based on interviews with the inmates, became almost the sole task of these presumed research personnel. Any improvement of the prediction tables occurred primarily because some sociologist-actuary was interested in parole prediction research for these purposes. When he received his higher degree, he moved to the academic world. What happened, essentially, was that the correctional researchers were coopted to serve the primarily legal and political interests of the parole board, in exchange for which they received job security. As long as the narrative reports seemed to be prepared competently and were ready when the parole board members come to the prison to conduct their hurried hearings, the work of the sociologist-actuaries was approved by those who controlled their salaries. Any actuaries who were concerned with research interacted in a different social and cultural world from all except one or two of the many parole board members who they served in this thirty-year period; there was little communication between these two worlds.[5]

Simultaneously with the employment of actuaries in Illinois, many other state correctional administrations established research positions in their central offices. These were concerned primarily with the compilation of statistics to monitor the effectiveness of the correctional system. Actually, few of these offices compiled the kinds of longitudinal statistics on criminal careers which are needed for an evaluation; some isolated California work was the most notable exception.[6] I have heard reports of other evaluative studies conducted by such offices but suppressed from publication by administrators who considered the findings unflattering or feared that they would be misunderstood. At any rate, these researchers soon were assigned the task of counting the volume of business conducted by the correctional system, as a means of justifying budgets. This so-called "research" mainly produced tables for annual reports which indicated prisoners on hand at the beginning and end of fiscal periods, or received and released during these periods. Again we see the cooptation of researchers by administrators trying to equate correctional research with simple head-counting.

[5] The few years when sociologist Joseph Lohman headed the parole board provided the major exception to this pattern, but his term was too brief to affect drastically the total validity of these generalizations.

[6] State of California, *California Male Prisoners Released on Parole, 1946–49* (Sacramento, California Board of Corrections, 1953).

THE NEWEST JERUSALEMS

A resurgence of research enterprise in correctional agencies has occurred in the past decade. The British Parliament, in the 1948 Criminal Justice Bill, instructed the Home Office to conduct research on the effectiveness of judicial and penal policies. This directive was finally followed in the 1950's by sponsorship of the Mannheim and Wilkins analysis of prediction possibilities in the Borstal youth prisons.[7] A Research Unit was then established in the Home Office with Leslie Wilkins as a senior researcher. By 1959 they could report about 80 research projects under way, all either conducted or facilitated by the Home Office.[8]

In 1957 the Budget Committee of the California legislature, faced with immense increases in correctional costs, insisted that research offices be established in the Department of Corrections and the Youth Authority to assess the effectiveness of treatment expenditures. In an annual correctional budget of approximately 100 million dollars, this state now spends approximately half a million per year for research.[9] Although small as a percentage, the amount far exceeds correctional research expenditures by any other state or national government. In addition, California has encouraged and facilitated much correctional research financed by private foundations or federal research agencies.

In the late 1950's a group of top federal prison officials and outside persons solicited foundation funds to finance university research in federal correctional system. This resulted in the 1958–63 University of Illinois study of federal penal programs, financed by the Ford Foundation.[10] While this was in progress, offices which had previously compiled only routine "head-count" statistics in the U.S. Bureau of Prisons, and in Wisconsin, Minnesota, and other state correctional systems, were expanded. They now performed some types of research which could test the effectiveness of correctional practices, or they engaged others to conduct such research.

It is interesting that so much of the initative for this expansion of correctional research came from outside the correctional administrations. In Britain and California, legislative bodies were the prime movers: elsewhere, prominent citizens and public foundations, both outside the government, provided leadership in what ostensibly were government undertakings. What "cultural base" had Western society reached, which resulted in these recent nearly simultaneous and largely independent expansions of correctional research? Clearly there must have been a conjunction of reduced public interest in punishment, continued public

[7] H. Mannheim and L. T. Wilkins, *Prediction Methods in Relation to Borstal Training* (London, Her Majesty's Stationery Office, 1955).

[8] British Home Office, *Penal Practice in a Changing Society* (London, Her Majesty's Stationery Office, 1959).

[9] Estimate by R. A. McGee, Administrator, California Youth and Adult Correction Agency, in a discussion at the Working Conference on Probation, National Institute of Mental Health. Bethesda, Md., July 8, 1964.

[10] Reported in D. Glaser, *The Effectiveness of a Prison and Parole System* (Indianapolis, Bobbs–Merrill, 1964).

concern with the crime problem, and widespread skepticism about the claims of competing treatment approaches. Such skepticism, obviously, was a potential source of conflict between the researchers and the administrators in correctional agencies.

TERRORS AND TEMPTATIONS

Are the new research establishments any more successful than the older ones at achieving the goal of scientifically guided correctional practice? Do they have any more influence on the treatment of criminals than did the sociologist-actuaries, or the correctional "head-count" statisticians?

To some extent, the developments which vitiated older endeavors have recurred in the new research efforts. One or more researchers in almost every one of the half-dozen correctional systems which conduct the most extensive evaluative research have, at one time or another in recent years, informed me of the suppression of their research reports. In some state correctional systems it is quite evident that research units have been largely coopted into service of the *status quo*, for they have abandoned longitudinal evaluative statistics compilation in favor of "head counts" only.

The reasons for this are quite obvious. Correctional officials procure financial appropriations for their agency by convincing the legislature that their programs protect society, either by incapacitating criminals or by changing them into noncriminals. When research confirms these claims, the officials are happy to promulgate the findings. Frequently, however, research has indicated that added appropriations to make treatment more effective, by reducing caseloads, hiring more psychiatrists, etc., have made no difference in posttreatment criminality or may even have increased it. Time-study analysis of the average hours per week which presumed treatment personnel actually spend in what might be considered treatment activity almost invariably yields a figure which the public would find surprisingly low. These are types of research findings which agency heads are reluctant to release.

There have been two styles of research suppression in correctional agencies. One style not only prohibits release of the report, but cancels further research as dangerous to the agency's "public image," or as the British express it, "embarrassing to the Minister." The real problem usually is that some officials, just above the researchers in a staff hierarchy, feel threatened by negative findings; the Minister or his American equivalent never hears of the research.

A more constructive style of research suppression involves the insistence of higher officials that there be further research before any results are released. This may simply be an enlargment of the sample, often to cover a more recent time period, on the usually spurious assumption that the treatment services studied have been getting better all the time. Frequently it is a reanalysis, perhaps requiring additional data, to permit cross-tabulations, perhaps leading to inferences as to the conditions under which the treatment studied is ineffective and the conditions under which it is effective. Reanalysis of this sort often indicates, roughly speaking, that special treatment services succeed in reducing failure rates appreciably only for "middle risk" cases; the least criminal cases have a low failure rate with or without special services; the highly criminal or unstable cases often fool and exploit treatment personnel or get unrealistic expectations from special training, so their long-run failure rates are higher following some of the special measures than after traditional programs.[11]

In some projects, reanalysis of research has involved an alteration of the criterion by which a program is evaluated. For example, cases given special treatment often compare much more favorably with cases not receiving this treatment if the two groups are evaluated by "total *time* reconfined" during a given period after release, rather than by "*per cent of cases* reconfined."[12] The reason is that special programs often reduce the *speed* with which released offenders get into further difficulty with the law more markedly than they reduce the proportion who eventually get into difficulty.

Occasionally the release of research results is deferred long enough for the officials involved to realize that any results can be interpreted favorably if the program is given multiple goals, such as "treatment" and "control." Under these circumstances, a more rapid return of cases to incarceration is credited to "control," but a less rapid return would have been credited to "treatment." This "heads I win" and "tails you lose" arrangement achieves the gambler's dream, for the state does have this dual objective, although ideally it would achieve control by successful treatment.[13]

Some research reports from correctional agencies are not suppressed, but might as well be, for few officials—or even researchers—can understand them. Most notable among such reports are those which describe the use of various types of multiple correlation or multiple association statistical analysis of case data in administrative records to find guides for correctional operations. These reports are submitted to correctional officials who do not understand the statistical terminology and who feel no urgency to learn to understand it since the researchers share with the operations officials the impression that this statistical analysis has little or no practical value at present. Thus, these researchers operate in a separate world, inadequately linked either with the university social system, which seems to be their reference group, or with the leaders of the correctional system, which they are presumed to serve.

It is statistical maxim, in most behavioral science problems, that with strong

---

[11] *Cf.* J. Havel and E. Sulka, *Special Intensive Parole Unit, Phase Three (SIPU 3),* Research Report No. 3 (Sacramento, California Department of Corrections, March 1962).

[12] *Cf.* S. Adams, "The PICO Project," *The Sociology of Punishment and Correction,* N.B. Johnston, *et al.,* eds. (New York, Wiley, 1962), pp. 213–224; and B.M. Johnson, *Parole Performance of the First Year's Releases, Parole Research Project: Evaluation of Reduced Caseloads,* Research Report No. 27 (Sacramento, California Youth Authority, Jan, 31, 1962).

[13] *Cf.* W. R. Burkhardt and A. Sathmary, *Narcotic Treatment-Control Project, Phases I and II.* Research Report No. 19 (Sacramento, California Department of Corrections, May 1963).

data you can use weak methods; the strong methods (*e.g.*, factor analysis) are useful primarily to squeeze a suggestion of relationship out of weak data. Strong relationshps can be demonstrated adequately with simple tables of percentages. Perhaps the high intelligence and dedicated effort invested in research into statistical methods would be more fruitful to the correctional system if they were employed not so much in seeking new methods of analysis for old types of data (that can be left to mathematical statisticians in the universities, who can be hired as consultants), but preferably in obtaining new types of data, derived from closer study and greater involvement in correctional operations. Furthermore, greater confidence in the reliability of correctional research results generally is gained by obtaining a redundancy of data, by procuring similar findings independently from several correctional situations, and by having several alternative indices of the key variables, than by mere statistical tests which assume the absence of bias in sampling or measurement.

PROGRESS FROM PITFALLS

In the long run, I believe, the paradise lost is most likely to be regained by controlled experiments. In the past two decades we have had many evangelical movements, from Cambridge-Somerville to SIPU and beyond, vainly preaching salvation by experimentation. The earlier sects repeatedly assembled the faithful to await miracles—and then disappointed them. Many of the sins we have been ascribing to correctional research grew out of frustration from experimentation. Yet negative or inconclusive results are but trials by which these pilgrims to the shrines of science are tested. They still may progress toward grace if they recognize past sins and seek salvation through new research design.

The value of experiments, when comparing two ways of handling offenders, is that they reduce the prospect of statistically uncontrolled variables accounting for the findings obtained. As an extreme example, consider a comparison of prison and probation. The higher rate of return to crime following imprisonment may not mean that prison is a more criminalizing experience than release on probation would be, but that most offenders receiving imprisonment are more criminalized when sentenced than are most who receive probation. Even if we compare only prison and probation cases that are matched by every index considered relevant (number of previous arrests, age, employment record, marital status, and so forth), it is possible that within each category of classification by these variables the judges have differentially selected worse risk cases for probation, employing some subjective indices or weights not taken into account by the researchers' categories. Sometimes researchers have reason for inferring that such judicial perspicacity does not prevail, an inference suggested by the superiority of statistical to case study prediction.[14] Nevertheless, judges and top correctional officials

---

[14] *Cf.* H. G. Gough, "Clinical versus Statistical Prediction in Psychology," *Psychology in the Making,* L. J. Postman, ed. (New York, Knopf, 1962), ch. 9.

are not readily convinced by such indirect evidence. Only when they are willing to have an appreciable number of treatment decisions made by purely random selection can we sharply increase everyone's confidence that differences in the subsequent behavior of offenders are due to differences dependent on the correctional treatment to which they were assigned, rather than due to selection variables. But even this is not an easy path to knowledge.

The history of medicine is marked not only by major progress through experimentation, but also great resistance to such experimentation. People refuse to be in a control group if they know this means they are denied a treatment which they presume is helpful, or they refuse to be in an experimental group receiving a treatment whose worth still is unestablished. There are also confounding variables which render experimental results inconclusive. For example, the "placebo effect"—which sociologists know as the "Hawthorne effect"—arises from the fact that the special attention given any group just by their being studied can alter their lives in a more influential way than the treatment being investigated.

These familiar difficulties of medical research recur in correctional research, but often only the physician has checks against them. For example, medical researchers use the double-blind technique of randomly mixing medication with placebos, so that even the persons administering the drugs do not know which is which. In correctional research (as in such medical fields as psychiatry, surgery, and physical therapy), treatments cannot be readily masked. Furthermore, if several programs are provided at one location, both staff and subjects may have strong feelings about alleged reasons for differential treatment of control and experimental cases, and these feelings may have an impact on treatment results. If two programs are operated at different locations, there may be many other uncontrolled situational variables. Experimentation can nevertheless go on, but the prospect that confounding factors affect the results makes the repetition of experiments in many places highly desirable.

In addition to these parallels to problems in medical research, special research problems arise from the extent to which correctional treatment still is administered in a tradition of punishment and adjudication, and frequently in a setting of public hysteria over the crime problem, the latter leading to occasional searches for correctional whipping boys. All these influences have impinged upon the conduct of some experiments. Such problems, and some of their implications as well as solutions, may be illustrated by comparing three widely heralded correctional experiments with counseling centers for youthful offenders: the Highfields Project, the Provo Experiment, and the Sacramento-Stockton Community Treatment Program. These were initiated sequentially, and the design of the second and third was based upon the experience of the preceding project.

Highfields

The Highfields Project, while an innovation, was not truly an experiment, for it had no control group selected by the same process as the treatment group.

However, after Highfields had been in operation for some time the postrelease behavior of its wards was compared to that of a number of offenders from the same counties, matched by age, offense, prior delinquent record, and other variables, who had been committed to the state training school at Annandale. While the Highfields cases had a somewhat better postrelease record than the Annandale youth, serious questions still could be raised about these findings. Was the judicial selection for Highfields, such as to give it cases with better prospects for avoiding future criminality than those of ostensibly similar youth sent to Annandale? After all, Highfields youth were placed on probation by the court, with the stipulation that they go to Highfields for four months. Some of them may have been comparable to cases whom the judge would otherwise have placed on probation in the community, rather than comparable to Annandale cases. Even if one assumes that there were no distorting influences on judicial selection, one can question whether the Highfields youths had better records because the program was different there, or because they were not confined with older and more advanced offenders, as were the youth sent to Annadale.[15]

Provo

The Provo Project modified the Highfields design in three major respects. In the first place, instead of being sent to reside at a small institution devoted to "guided group interaction," the Provo youth resided at home and were required to report daily to the counseling center. Second, the group counseling technique was somewhat altered by an increase in self-government in the group, including powers to discipline their members and even to recommend to the project director that a youth be briefly committed to jail. Third—and most notable for this discussion—the judge, after deciding that a case warranted serious state intervention, was to draw from an envelope a random number which would determine

---

[15] In the research directed by Weeks, in which the data were analyzed independently by several persons, Highfields boys were compared with boys who were received at Annandale at about the same time and who met the Highfields admission criteria with respect to age, lack of prior institutional commitments, and lack of psychosis or feeble-mindedness. See H. A. Weeks, ed., *Youthful Offenders at Highfields* (Ann Arbor, University of Michigan Press, 1958). In the research conducted separately by Highfields staff, an effort was made to control for judicial selection by comparing Highfields cases with boys sent to Annadale in the years just preceding the opening of Highfields, with the two groups matched by the same variables as those used by Weeks, except that a few boys in each group who made a very poor institutional adjustment were eliminated. See L. W. McCorkle, A. Elias, and F. L. Bixby, *The Highfields Story* (New York, Holt, 1958). If Highfields received both boys whom the judges would otherwise have sent to Annandale and boys whom the judges might have placed on probation in the community had Highfields not existed, absence of the latter in the staff's control group of pre-Highfields commitments to Annandale may also impose judicial selection bias. For a highly critical review of Highfields research, see C. C. Sherwood and W. S. Walker, "Some Unanswered Questions about Highfields," *American Journal of Correction*, May-June 1959, pp. 8–9, 25–27.

whether the youth would be released on probation with traditional supervision, would be released on probation with the requirement that he participate in the counseling center, or would be sent to the state reformatory.[16] The difficulty with executing this research design was foreshadowed when I described it to a professor of criminal law. He said that he wished he had as a client some youth sent to the reformatory under this program, since he considered it a violation of the right to due process. Regardless of the possible legal rebuttal to this charge, the research design is not being followed with respect to commitment to the reformatory; the experiment now is primarily a comparison of probation with and without a special counseling program.

Sacramento-Stockton

The Community Treatment Program, operated in Sacramento and Stockton by the California Youth Authority, has benefited by studying the Provo experience. It starts with youth whom courts of these two cities commit to institutionalization under the Youth Authority. The Authority's paroling board immediately screens out those youth whom it considers too emotionally unstable or dangerous for immediate release (so far only 26 percent of the boys and 7 percent of the girls). The remainder is then divided randomly. About half are sent to the court-authorized regular institution program, in which the average stay of youth from these cities in past years has been eight months, and half are paroled immediately, with the special requirement that they attend community treatment centers.

The experimentally released youth in the Sacramento-Stockton program receive intensive supervision by parole agents who have caseloads varying from as little as eight to a maximum of about thirty. (The Authority's average with regular parolees is about seventy cases per officer). The community treatment center conducts a guided group interaction program much like those at Highfields and Provo, in addition to providing individual and group psychotherapy, tutoring, and other special assistance to the delinquents and their families. Most distinctively, this program attempts to offer a different style of supervision for each classification type, using both social and personality, diagnostic variables. Thus, it has primarily supportive relationships for the highly immature, who are viewed as largely unsocialized in any adult role; it has firm, though fair, supervision for youth socialized into delinquent subcultures and manipulative toward officials; it has an open and interpretative approach to those viewed as mature and conventionally socialized but delinquent because of neuroses or situational problems. Still another distinctive feature of this program is that the parole agents may

[16] *Cf.* L. T. Empey and J. Rabow, "Experiment in Delinquency Rehabilitation," *American Sociological Review,* October 1961, pp. 679–696.

confine a youth for from one to thirty days in a local youth detention facility, without returning him to the Youth Authority as a parole violator.[17]

From the standpoint of the evolution of research design, the Community Treatment Program is notable for its accommodation of the conflicting pressures which impinged on prior experimentation in correction. Because the law does not permit incarceration of anyone who does not, by the court's judgment, merit so extreme a denial of liberty (even if it is called "treatment"), this experiment—to compare a program in the community with commitment in traditional institutions—starts with persons adjudicated for incarceration. Because the public insists upon punishment for notorious offenders and blames the parole board if serious new offenses are committed by parolees, this research starts with a pool of cases commmitted to institutions but screened by the parole board to eliminate those whom it is not willing to risk immediately in the community. (This, of course, imposes the research burden of identification of these types of cases denied eligibility for the experiment. Fortunately this group has been relatively small.) Finally, the parole agents can swiftly impose brief arrest on a non-cooperative youth instead of waiting for him to commit infractions sufficiently serious to warrant his return to longer-term incarceration. This breaks down traditional barriers, and the sense of working at cross purposes, between correctional and law-enforcement agencies; it integrates rehabilitation and control, the dual aspects of protecting society from known criminals.

The project has had its difficulties. One law enforcement leader was vociferous about the release of a little so-and-so just after there had been so much trouble catching him. However, this same official now has joined others in loudly praising the program, for it appears to have had impressively successful results. Not only has the percentage of new offenses been smaller for those treated in the community than for the members of the control group (paroled after regular institution commitments), but also, among those who committed new offenses, the community-treated new offenders were apprehended more quickly, and more often by the parole agent than by the police. Finally, the community treatment program, despite all its special services and small caseloads, costs less per man-month than commitment to an institution.

CONCLUSION

The recurrent criminological dream of a correctional system directed through research has not been a prophetic one, since researchers have been either coöpted by administrators or oriented to a monastic world divorced from practice. Yet

[17] M. Q. Warren, T. B. Palmer, and J. K. Turner, *Community Treatment Project,* CTP Research Report No. 5 (Sacramento, California Youth Authority, February 1964); H. G. Stark, "A Substitute for Institutionalization of Serious Delinquents: A California Youth Authority Experiment." *Crime and Delinquency,* July 1963, pp. 242–248.

progress toward this dream of scientific correction has been made, particularly in the past decade and particularly through experimentation.

Experimentation has its pitfalls which often lead to abandonment of the research faith. On the other hand, even when blessings follow experimentation, there is a need for caution. For example, the success of the Sacramento-Stockton project was cited, but would the same type of community treatment program work as well in a large city slum as it has in cities with relatively less severe and less concentrated delinquency? This points up the need for redundancy in the correctional research ritual, and for meeting negative results by new designs.

The discontent which generated the cult of research in correction probably will always be with us. As Durkheim pointed out, even in a society where everyone was what today would be considered saintly, some people would have still higher or different standards of behavior and would be offended by others.[18] Indeed, we have reason to believe that despite some increases in the causes of crime with increased urbanization, there has been a net decrease in the behavior traditionally called criminal[19]; "crime waves" may express not increased violence but only an increase in the intensity of society's reactions to violence.

Most social movements are sustained by the belief of their followers that their cause is right, and that what is right will ultimately prevail. The movement for research in correction is no exception to this rule. In the judicial and correctional areas, so many decisions radically affecting the lives of others are made by vague subjective impressions, untested rules of thumb, and nonrational prejudices, that almost any strengthening of the empirical basis for decision policies inspires the faithful.

Faith in the progressive growth of what Ohlin has called the "routinization of correctional change"[20] also is justified by empirical study of societal trends. For correctional change to occur not just by crisis reaction, but by planned development on the basis of research, would be part of what Moore has called "the institutionalization of rationality."[21] This is a trend in almost all parts of any society undergoing modernization, although it grows most slowly in the more tradition-ridden and subjectively guided components of these societies, such as the agencies of criminal law interpretation.

[18] E.Durkheim, *The Rules of Sociological Method* (Glencoe, Ill., Fress Press, 1950), pp. 67–69.

[19] *Cf.* H. A. Bloch and G. Geis, *Man, Crime and Society* (New York, Random House, 1962), p. 259.

[20] L. E. Ohlin, "The Routinization of Correctional Change," *Journal of Criminal Law and Criminology,* November-December 1954, pl. 400–11.

[21] W. E. Moore, *Social Change* (Englewood Cliffs, N.J., Prentice-Hall, 1963), p. 95.

48

Research and Development, Information, and Statistics

NATIONAL ADVISORY COMMISSION ON CRIMINAL
JUSTICE STANDARDS AND GOALS

Since World War II, a massive empirical attack has been launched on problems inherent in controlling offenders and reducing criminal behavior. Some problems have been solved, others better formulated, because of a succession of studies. Much remains to be learned, but the record of achievement insures that corrections never again can be the same. The impact of research has drastically modified assumptions and changed practice. This record of accomplishment will be used as a foundation for new approaches to the use of information in the disposition of offenders.

Two complementary sources of research are required to meet corrections' continuing needs. First, research must be incorporated as an integral instrument of correctional management. Modern administration depends on the collection and analysis of information as a basis for policy formulation and a guide for

SOURCE. *Corrections,* National Advisory Commission on Criminal Justice Standards and Goals, Washington, D.C., U.S. Government Printing Office, 1973, pp. 496–518.

specific decisions. No information system can replace the decisionmaker, but availability of selected information, carefully interpreted, offers an invaluable aid to his reason and judgment. Every correctional manager should be afforded the tools of research methodology and the degree of objectivity an agency research program can provide.

Second, there is need for research done outside the agency. Not all sources of innovation can be found within the confines of any one agency or system. Continued improvement of corrections can be expected only from the application of new ideas and models derived from basic research and prototype projects. The support of such research by national funding agencies insures contribution of ideas from the private sector, the academic community, and other sources. Also required is a continuing hospitality to the conduct of research in the operating correctional agencies.

Research alone cannot create a new day in corrections. It offers the administrator opportunity to learn from the mistakes of others. The administrator's task in attempting to meet needs as they arise is to utilize all tools with which innovations are forged.

HISTORICAL PERSPECTIVES

Housekeeping, budgeting, and audit have always required managers to maintain accounts and statistics. Students of penal history can find crude data surviving from the early 19th century. For the most part, these statistics were maintained to report on past years and to project future needs. Professional accuracy was neither maintained nor claimed. Analytic techniques were not introduced until concerned administrators saw the need for statistical projection in planning and implementing programs for expanding offender populations.

Statistical analysis raised questions about practice. In the early 1950's, reviews of data in several States suggested that the costs of incarceration might be reduced by increasing the use of probation and parole. Clearly, if experiments of this kind were to be tried, steps would have to be taken to insure that public safety would not be impaired. Results of such innovations would have to be documented and verified. From the first, it has been an accepted principle that significant changes in corrections must be supported by evidence that public protection has not been diminished thereby.

This principle established a continuity of statistical analysis. The effectiveness of correctional programs has been assessed for many years by counting the participants who return to criminal behavior. Thus recidivism has become the ultimate criterion of the success of correctional programs. An agency's capability of carrying on this evaluation is fundamental to operational control. Unfortunately, few correctional agencies are equipped to conduct this kind of analysis. There are serious obstacles to systematic collection of data on recidivism. Most of these obstacles can be traced directly to fragmentation of the criminal justice system. Even the best statistical bureaus are blocked from attaining complete coverage of recidivism.

Statistical analysis of correctional operations has opened questions that cannot be answered by statistics alone. A statistical tabulation will present reality as unsparingly as an unretouched photograph. It will not explain what it presents, nor will it indicate changes that might improve results.

Research and statistics are operationally interdependent. Without the explanatory methods of research, the meaning of the statistics would be lost. Indeed, decisions as to which statistics should be collected must be based on a theoretical judgment of their significance. Existence of a responsible statistical system in an agency will facilitate research. Most successful correctional research is the product of systems in which statistical operations are accepted as part of the administrative culture.

The history of research related to penal problems can be traced from the years immediately after World War I. It is a brief history, but it boasts successes beyond the expenditure of effort and resources. In the twenties and thirties Sheldon and Eleanor Glueck[1] initiated the empirical test of programs by examining the experience of those exposed to them over considerable periods. This theme continues to the present as concern about the effectiveness of programs has heightened interest in their assessment.

Thus, a considerable amount of evaluative research has accumulated. Most of it has examined the usefulness of specific treatment methods in achieving offender rehabilitation. The influence of these studies has played a critical role in development of correctional policy. Few studies have culminated in unquestionable findings, but the absence of significant conclusions has itself been significant. It is especially noteworthy that treatment program tests have been conducted in a wide variety of incarcerative settings without establishing the rehabilitative value of any. The consistency of this record strongly indicates that incarcerative treatment is incompatible with rehabilitative objectives. This conclusion is tentative, but influential. It is responsible for the present wave of interest in developing community-based alternatives to incarceration.

Mounting evidence of the ineffectiveness of correctional treatment programs for confined offenders has led to a new body of opinion about the role of the prison. This consensus holds that use of incarceration should be limited to the control of offenders from whom the public cannot be protected in any other way. It is further held that the changing of offenders into responsible citizens must take place in society, not behind prison walls. Although it is appropriate to provide prisoners with opportunities for self-help, there is no evidence that treatment prescribed and administered by institutional staff has any positive effect.

The impact of this consistent finding in recent correctional research cannot be overestimated. In some States complete reorganization of correctional services has resulted. Many members of the bench and bar have changed their views about the disposition of offenders. The Nation will have to support prisons for many

---

[1] Sheldon and Eleanor Glueck, *500 Criminal Careers* (Knopf, 1930).

years to come, but the reasons for doing so have been altered as a result of examined experience.

BASIC RESEARCH COMPONENTS

Research is the process of acquiring new knowledge. In all science it begins with description of the objects of study. In most social sciences, description calls for measurement of events and processes. Description of a prison, for example, might require discrimination of an enormous number of events comprising the flow of offenders through the process of differential control. As events and processes are accurately described over an extended period, it becomes possible to attempt an explanation of the interaction of persons with sets of events so that outcomes may be predicted.

From this level of understanding, it sometimes is possible to modify the system to obtain a predictably different outcome. Such a modification is called "innovation." In addition, the explanatory procedure facilitates evaluation of process, developing criteria for measuring success in goal attainment.

If evaluative research is the first strand in correctional self-study, experimental research also has produced fundamental change. There has been far too little experimentation in corrections, perhaps because theorists have been slow to recognize the value of the correctional system as a laboratory. Experiments conducted by Warren[2] in California, McCorkle[3] in New Jersey, and Empey[4] in Utah have demonstrated the relative feasibility of various alternatives to incarceration. Each of these innovating researchers based his program assumptions on well-developed behavioral science theory. None of the theoretical positions supporting their innovations survived empirical test without major revision. Nevertheless, each innovation has shown clearly that wide ranges of offenders can be programmed safely for maintenance in the community. Recidivism attributable to community programs has not exceeded results obtained by extended incarceration at vastly greater expense. Program changes based on these findings have been slow in coming, but the impact of these studies on correctional thought is fundamental.

A third strand in the analysis of corrections is reflected by a series of studies of prison communities from widely varying viewpoints. The early work of Clemmer[5] documented the powerful forces that socialize confined offenders to the artificial circumstances of prison life. These observations were followed by the

[2] Marguerite Q. Warren, "The Case for the Differential Treatment of Delinquents," *Annals of the American Academy of Political and Social Science,* 381 (1969), 47.

[3] Lloyd McCorkle, Albert Elias, and F. Lovell Bixby, *The Highfields Story* (Holt, 1958). See also H. Ashley Weeks, *Youthful Offenders at Highfields* (University of Michigan Press, 1958).

[4] LaMar T. Empey and Jerome Rabow, "The Provo Experiment in Delinquency Rehabilitation" in *Proceedings of the 90th Congress of Corrections* (American Correctional Association, 1960). See also LaMar T. Empey and Steven G. Labecic, *The Silver Lake Experiment* (Aldine, 1971).

[5] Donald Clemmer, *The Prison Community* (Rinehart, 1958).

theoretically oriented investigations of Schrag;[6] Sykes and Messinger;[7] Studt, Messinger, and Wilson;[8] and Goffman.[9] These studies have documented the forces inherent in confinement which oppose favorable behavior change. They confirm clinical impressions of much longer standing and support the trend of evaluative research outlined above.

The combined impact of this research on correctional policy has been far-reaching and cumulative. In California it has caused the radical redistribution of offenders from institutional to community programs under the Probation Subsidy Act. Similarly, the deactivation of Massachusetts' juvenile correctional facilities has demonstrated the impact of research on policies that are supported only by tradition.

It is impressive that studies producing such similar effects have been so scattered. To this day, few correctional agencies have organized their own research sections. The notion that research should be an instrument of administration is widely accepted, but its implications have yet to be explored fully.

If research is seen to be a necessary component of sound administration, much correctional research will be done, but its nature will change. It is important to consider the direction of these changes.

A heavy emphasis on studies to improve the quality of management can be expected. Current management theory stresses continuous research for information, verification of results, and projection of future requirements. The work of Drucker,[10] Forrester,[11] and many other management scientists in the context of business administration has demonstrated the gains possible from management by objectives, performance budgeting, and accountability for results. (See Chapter 13.)

The historical role of the correctional agency was to administer punishment. The administrator was not expected to concern himself with results. Addition of industrial, vocational, and educational programs has been incidental to control of offenders. Administrators have seen that maintenance of control and absence of disorder and scandal have constituted the limits of public expectations of correctional service.

There is reason to believe that the situation is changing. The executive and legislative branches of government, the press, and other influential groups are becoming aware of the benefits of the new managerial approach. The essence of this approach is that good management is measured by results. The stress on results requires information to document and verify them. In corrections, this

[6] Clarence Schrag, "A Preliminary Criminal Typology," *Pacific Sociological Review,* 4 (1961), 11–16.

[7] Gresham Sykes and Sheldon Messinger, "The Inmate Social System" in G. A. Grosser, ed., *Theoretical Studies in the Social Organization of the Prison* (Social Science Research Council, 1960).

[8] Elliot Studt, Sheldon Messinger, and Thomas P. Wilson, *C-Unit: Search for Community in Prison* (Russell Sage Foundation, 1968).

[9] Erving Goffman, *Asylums* (Anchor Books, 1961), pp. 1–124.

[10] Peter Drucker, *Managing for Results* (Harper and Row, 1964).

[11] Jay Forrester, *Industrial Dynamics* (MIT Press, 1961).

emphasis will call for a different order of research from that of the evaluative studies and the experiments with innovation mentioned above.

Much attention must be given to design of information systems and creation of meaningful feed-back loops. During the coming decade all large and middle-sized correctional systems in the country can be expected to install information systems to support objective-oriented management. Small agencies must adapt to accommodate this trend.

Research will bring about change in operations. The achievement of a significant internal review of operations requires all administrative functions to undergo a difficult transition. New categories of professional personnel must be introduced into correctional operations. Their criminal justice background will be minimal. They must be familiarized with their new environment before their technical expertise can be useful.

An even more difficult transition must be made by present management personnel. Positions that once called only for intuitive planning and decision-making must be adapted to requirements of a new style. For many executives, continued effectiveness will depend on completion of inconveniently technical retraining.

Hesitance in facing such rapid evolution in management style is understandable. Planning, budgeting, and administering research operations present opportunities for serious mistakes. Errors in personnel decisions are hard to rectify. Acquisition of expensive equipment that does not meet agency needs causes serious waste.

Establishment of standards will not prevent all possible mistakes, but their availability will at least form a basis for intelligent decisions in building research and statistics capability.

INFORMATION AND INFORMATION SYSTEMS

Language is a source of misunderstanding between layman and technician. In ordinary language, the word "information" refers to any knowledge, useful or not, pertinent or not. In research, the term is limited to specific facts that reduce uncertainty in decisionmaking. For computer technology, the term is further limited to data prepared for processing.

The significance of these definitions is obvious. Whereas in everyday life everyone is assailed with vast amounts of information, both relevant and irrelevant to his concerns and decisions, an operational agency must limit information processing to that which is essential to making advantageous decisions. Research must determine the characteristics of information that will increase a system's power to control its future. In this chapter, "information" means items of knowledge with a demonstrable utility in maintaining operational control.

An "information system" includes the concepts, personnel, and supporting technology for the collection, organization, and delivery of information for administrative use. Information divides into two main categories. "Standard information" consists of the data required for operational control. The daily count at a prison, payroll data in a personnel office, and caseload levels in a probation agency are obvious examples of standard information.

In addition, an information system must be capable of supplying "demand information." A manager does not need to know regularly how many prisoners will be eligible for release during the next 12 months by offense, length of term, and month of release, but an information system must be capable of generating such a report when required.

It follows that an information system should be capable of collecting data for statistical use and providing itemized listings for administrative action. Although the capabilities mentioned are conceptually simple, much is gained by organizing for computer operations. Recent studies by Hill[12] indicate the feasibility of a generic model for a corrections information system, despite differences in policy and practice among correctional agencies. Development of such a generic model will aid assimilation of the new managerial ideology of planning and review.

Uses of Information

An information system for corrections must supply data for an enormous number of individual decisions. Decisions about the classification of offenders—their custodial requirements, employment, and training—are common to every correctional agency. In prisons and reformatories, decisions must be made about housing, discipline, work assignments, and control. Many are so routine they hardly seem to be decisions at all, but each action requires certain information for fairness and efficiency.

In virtually all correctional agencies these case determinations now are made on the basis of information from a cumbersome, usually disorganized file. Its use is so clumsy that record study often is supplanted by intuition. Clearly if decision-makers are to benefit from information, a transition from intuition to rationality must be made.

Hill puts the problem aptly: "It is generally recognized . . . that information requirements for management have been difficult to identify. This is not so much because of management reluctance to specify its information needs but rather because management cannot always anticipate what it will need to know."[13] Because Hill was concerned with the information needs of correctional administration, he undertook a survey of claimed and actual requirements. The diversity of needs reported by administrators making the same kinds of decisions would have precluded implementation of any system if only claimed data needs were to be provided. Hill therefore recommends creation of a system in which it it is possible to examine the interrelationships between data used and decisions made.[14]

---

[12] Harland Hill, *Correctionetics* (Sacramento: American Justice Institute, 1972).
[13] Hill, *Correctionetics,* p. 3.
[14] Hill, *Correctionetics,* p. 148.

The process of verifying information requirements will introduce new elements of rationality to the system it serves. Studies of the actual use of information in criminal justice decisionmaking indicate that the number of items required will be surprisingly small.

QUALITY CONTROL. The idea of a formal quality control capability still is new to most correctional administrators. Until now they have relied on informed intuition and spot inspections to guarantee maintenance of operational standards. An information system can assure compliance with standards projected by agency plans and budget. Processing rates can be established for significant periods. For example, the number of presentence investigations in a probation office or boys in a vocational training program can be projected as norms. A later check will determine how close performance was to the norms and can identify some of the causes of discrepancies. When there is close correspondence with projections, routine reports are delivered to the manager. When there is variance beyond established minimum tolerance, exception reports will be furnished to facilitate corrective inquiry.

The importance of quality control capability for the modernization of correctional management hardly can be exaggerated. If accountability for results is to be achieved, the administrator must have the means of knowing how well he is delivering on his commitments. Quality control capability assures that he is among the first to know when discrepancies between promise and performance begin to appear. He will not necessarily know whether the agency is achieving its goals. He will know whether the agency in carrying out programs intended to reach those goals.

EVALUATION. Maintenance of internal quality control by an information system will facilitate evaluation of goal achievement. When program participation and execution are documented objectively, it is easy to assure that evaluation of goal achievement is tied to an operational reality. In the past, there has been reason for concern over the validity of evaluations that lacked certainty as to who participated in which program to what extent, or even whether some element of the program ever really existed. Design of an information system should provide confidence on these points.

Two levels of evaluation can be distinguished. At the first level, the manager needs to determine the statistical achievement of goals. For example, he must know whether a machinist training program is turning out qualified machinists. The individuals trained can be tracked after release to determine how many actually were employed as machinists and how many become recidivists. If the persons trained as machinists commit fewer crimes than others, it may be roughly indicative of the program's value.

At the second level is the explanatory evaluation, in which research instruments are introduced to facilitate statistical comparisons beyond checking expectations against observed outcomes. Each program has special features that must be allowed for if its progress is to be understood. Provision in the system for all the special features of all the programs in an agency will inordinately complicate the system and the reporting requirements that support it. However, the generic problem of correctional evaluation calls for a solution in terms of the classification of the population exposed. The intent of explanatory evaluation is to distinguish (1) those special features of a program that make a difference in outcome and (2) offenders on whom programs are and are not effective.

Design of a Model Correctional Information System

Design details of an information system do not concern the layman. For a comprehensive account of the problems and their solution, see Hill's six-volume study, *Correctionetics,* already cited. Despite the hazards of a little knowledge, administrators should understand the general characteristics of an information system that effectively utilizes all current technological knowledge. Hill's studies specify the following essential capabilities as being both basically required and technically feasible:

- Point-in-time net results.
- Period-in-time reports.
- Automatic notifications.
- Statistical/analytical relationships.

POINT-IN-TIME NET RESULTS   At any point in time, the system should be able to deliver routine analyses of program status. Such analyses depend on having the following information in the data bank:

1. Basic population characteristics such as offense data, age, race, originating jurisdiction, educational status.

2. Program definition and participants.

3. Organizational units, if any; for example, probation district offices, institutions within statewide systems.

4. Personnel characteristics.

5. Fiscal data such as costs and budget projections.

With this information in the system, necessary figures such as population accounting, program participation, and staff coverage at the time the report is submitted can be delivered routinely at intervals selected by the administrator or on his emergency demand. Design of reports of this kind calls for close collaboration of the administrator with the information system manager.

PERIOD-IN-TIME REPORTS.   The point-in-time report freezes the data at some specific time so the administrator will know the status of activities under his jurisdiction on the demand date. The period-in-time report provides a statement of flow and change over a specified period. The movement of a population, the amount and flow of expenditures, and occurrence rates of actions or events can be delivered periodically for review and analysis.

Few administrators attempt to manage operations without such reports, usually prepared manually. The information system assures that the reports will be current, statistically correlated as required, and delivered on demand.

The focus in this aspect of the system is on events: the admission of a new inmate, his transfer, his hearing before a parole board, his release on parole, his transfer from one parole agent to another. When aggregated, data of this kind provide an accounting of a system's movement that is essential to rational planning and control. To maintain such a system, the following kinds of data must be stored:

1. Summary of offender events and results of events, i.e., transfers to alternate control, hearings by the parole board and actions taken by the board, and releases to parole.

2. Personnel summaries, including appointments, assignments, relief from assignments, and separations.

3. Event summaries by population characteristics.

4. Event summaries by personnel characteristics.

5. Fiscal events summarized by programs; for example, expenditures for facilities and equipment and personnel.

A system capable of routine period-in-time reports of these kinds also will be capable of a wide variety of demand information.

AUTOMATIC NOTIFICATIONS.   As suggested above, the information system should generate management exception reports for immediate delivery. Such reports are initiated automatically by conditions that vary from standards previously established for the system. Four kinds of exception reports are of particular value to the manager:

1. Volume of assignments to programs or units varying from standard capacity.

2. Movement of any type that varies from planned movement; for example, number of probation awards granted for a specified period, probation revocations, staff resignations, commitments to jail as a condition of probation.

3. Noncompliance with established decision criteria. If policy prescribes that certain kinds of offenders should not be assigned to maximum security institutions, the assignment criteria can be specified in the system so that assignments in violation can be reported immediately for administrative review.

4. Excessive time in process. A standard time can be prescribed for completion of any process. When an individual is in process too long, a report will be generated. For example, if juvenile offenders are not to be held in detention for more than 30 days before a court hearing, reports can be generated to alert the chief probation officer of the approach and expiration of the time limit.

This automatic notification system can be programmed to include requirements sufficient to inundate the administrator unless care is taken to establish tolerances of deviation from standards. Judicious design of the automatic notification capability will enable the administrator to avoid many kinds of surprises and emergencies. The notification reports also will constitute a useful basis for the researcher in the conduct of program analysis.

STATISTICAL/ANALYTICAL RELATIONSHIPS.   The interrelationships of data are critical to the interpretive process review. Not all interrelationships are significant enough to warrant continuous study, but many analyses should be available regularly for audit and planning. For example, the system should report to the administrator the numbers of probation or parole failures chargeable to given programs. It may be of occasional interest to know how many offenders aged 40 or older violate parole, but a quarterly report on this relationship probably will be unnecessary. Regular reports should be programmed and responses to special queries should be readily retrievable.

The Technology of Information Systems

A system with the capabilities outlined is easily achievable with current information technology. Such a system has been feasible for at least 5 years, but there have been obstacles to its implementation in corrections agencies. The first has been lack of money; the second, failure to preceive the usefulness of an information system.

Benefits to management and research easily justify the considerable capital outlay for equipment and software and the less significant maintenance costs. Correctional agencies cannot be expected to increase their effectiveness or achieve full partnership in the criminal justice system without competent information services. Without adequate information bases, correctional systems are notoriously static in program and planning. It could not be otherwise. Changes of significance cannot be planned intelligently without some empirical identification of need. Unless some statistical basis can be found in system trends and changes, there can be no basis for innovation but opinion. The resistance to change with which correctional personnel are so often charged is partly attributable to the inability of those who propose change to justify it.

The current information explosion profoundly affects the police, prosecutors, courts, and all other local, State, and Federal services. Effective participation of corrections in planning for criminal justice on one hand and for coordinated government services on the other depends on a fully developed capability for information processing.

Data characteristics required by correctional systems for construction of basic information systems are sufficiently generic that statewide systems should be feasible for the larger States. In such systems local and central correctional agencies of all sizes would be included. Regional systems can be established for smaller States, especially where there is a large flow of interstate traffic, as in New England.

The structure of the correctional information system generally lends itself to a uniform model of design, operation, and display. Much will be gained by standardizing correctional information technology for the entire Nation, with suitable provision for the special characteristics of local legislation and practice. For example, a State organized for statewide probation administration will have significantly different bases for input to the system than one that provides for county administration of services. Nevertheless, the processes of probation will be more alike than different. The same information system model can be adapted to both situations.

Problems of Implementation

This chapter has urged participation of correctional personnel in the "information revolution." In historical perspective, there is reason to believe that the information revolution will be as momentous for society as the industrial revolution two centuries ago. Without understanding the drastic changes in management concepts this benign revolution is bringing about, administrators can cripple themselves and their agencies.

Until the advent of the new technology, information tended to be enormously expensive because it had to be processed manually. It was usually incomplete and unreliable when it arrived on the administrator's desk. Now information can be made available to the administrator in enormous quantities and with speed and accuracy heretofore inconceivable. There are three dangers inherrent in this prospect.

The first is that the information will not communicate. The administrator must be equipped to use what he gets. For the most part, he will get what he has asked for, which will be more than he can use unless he has been rigorously selective. He therefore must determine exactly what reports he needs, why he needs them, and in what form they can be most useful to him. Since the potentiality of the information system is more than he requires, he must limit his appetite for its products to those he really needs. He must require his staff to do likewise.

The second danger is that the potential to free management from an unwieldy number of reports will be ignored because available material is interesting and suggestive. The significant service of an information system is that it can free the administrator from analysis of manually processed information. This level of analysis is the characteristic activity of most administrators. With accurate, well-processed reports delivered by computer equipment, the administrator can become free to observe, reflect, and consult. But if he uses the information system to increase his consumption of reports simply because more reports are available, his style of operation is regressive. Use of the information system should reduce drastically the time devoted to report review.

The third danger is that the information system will create a static system of its own with special resistances to innovation. Unless information review creates a basis for innovation in the minds of the staff, the system is not achieving its potential. It should never be implied that desirable changes in program cannot be undertaken because the information system might have to be changed.

ADMINISTRATIVE CONTROLS. Correctional data collection is especially vulnerable to misinformation. Some data must be drawn from unreliable sources. Other data are susceptible to incorrect recording; for example, dates, identification numbers, and special codes. An information system that replaces manual operations without provision for verification and editing will be a dubious asset to administration.

Both concepts and equipment in computer operations lend themselves to the installation of verification procedures. Full advantage should be taken of the opportunity to improve methods of recording information for processing. But while the computer can reduce error by reducing the number of times manual processing of data occurs and by verification procedures, human fallibility will continue to justify utmost vigilance. The administrator's active emphasis on accuracy is the most effective assurance that vigilance will be maintained. Only his insistence on verification processes can keep mistakes to a minimum.

Administrators also must protect the system from unauthorized access. Interfaces with other criminal justice data banks must be maintained. But maintenance of security in handling sensitive materials should discourage interfaces with systems outside criminal justice or response to queries from any but specifically authorized persons and agencies. Precaution should be taken to protect files and equipment from intrusion.

INTERSYSTEM RELATIONSHIPS.   A useful correctional information system will provide for delivery of a large volume of case decision information and specialized management data of no significance outside the agency. As already suggested, the state of correctional information technology supports the development of statewide or regional information depositories. Terminals would serve cooperating agencies. In the interest of national uniformity of statistical reporting, standardization of information formats should be encouraged as far as practicable.

At the same time, development of information systems to serve courts and police is proceeding. The feasibility of creating an information system to serve all criminal justice interests has not been determined. It is not certain whether advantages in service or economy would accrue from such an imposing development.

At this juncture, when necessary design elements of the correctional information system seem reasonably clear, it is possible to define three principles that should govern future strategy.

First, if the correctional information system is to be designed as an independent entity managed by correctional personnel, provision must be made for interface with systems in other States and regions for exchange of information on clients moving from one jurisdiction to another.

Second, an independent correctional information system will draw some data from information systems serving police and courts and will contribute data in return. Whether this requirement is to be served by a basic data bank serving three separate information systems or by interfaces with police and court systems depends on the resolution of problems that seem to be barely defined. But the correctional information system will have to design interfaces for use by courts and police.

Third, if a consolidated criminal justice information system is to be designed, it must be capable of providing full support for both management and case decisionmaking in corrections. A system not capable of meeting these requirements should be unacceptable.

STATISTICS

New concepts and technology for the delivery of information to management have been considered. But research and statistics constitute only two uses to which information must be put. Historically, information for management has been primarily the responsibility of the statistician. Today, the statistician becomes a user, rather than only the processor, of information. It is therefore important to distinguish between the functions of an information system and the professional services of the statistician.

"Statistics" is defined here as a mathematical method of ordering, analyzing, and displaying information and making interpretive inferences therefrom. This method comprises a wide range of procedures used by the statistician. Although many of these procedures can be adapted for the information system, many special analyses should be accomplished individually.

Interpretation of the enormous volume of information contained in the system depends on the application of professional expertise. This kind of skill always should be available in large systems. Mechanization of statistics cannot be expected to ferret out the meaning of unexpected events or to bring relevant and well-defined alternatives into consideration. The statistician benefits from the new information technology. He has not become obsolete. Just as the information system frees the administrator from the personal review of an array of manually produced reports, the statistician is freed from the production of routine compilations that hitherto have required his supervision and individual analysis. He now is able to assist the administrator in such functions as:

- Evaluation of program achievement.
- Determination of workload requirements.
- Projection of future requirements.
- Choice between decision alternatives.
- Construction of special statistical instruments.
- Analysis of problem areas.

Certainly these functions do not exhaust the possibilities of professional statistical services. Nevertheless, they illustrate the range of capabilities that the statistician can provide. Reliance on the information system alone will deny the administrator the depth of analysis needed for an understanding of operations status and effective development.

Evaluation of Program Achievement

Collaborating with operating staff and research social scientists, the statistician should be responsible for installing standard measures of achievements in the information system. Reliability of measurements used by the system should be reviewed periodically. This review will be especially important if predictive devices are installed to facilitate comparison of expectations with observed outcomes.

This evaluation technique is well suited to standardized use by information systems. A standard base expectancy table is established to predict results of programs for groups, using criteria such as recidivism or completion of training. Such a device will be capable of assigning any given subject to a class of like subjects grouped by the statistical weighting of aggregated characteristics. Group expectancy for success or failure as determined by recidivism or other criteria can be expressed in percentiles.

Use of base expectancies for comparison with observed outcomes may be thought of as a "soft" method of evaluation. But its economy, in comparison with the classical control group procedure, is considerable. It eliminates the need for routine management of research controls over extended periods. Comparison of predicted with observed outcome affords a rough estimate of program effectiveness. For example, if the average expected recidivism of a group of offenders exposed to a behavior modification program is 50 percent, but the observed outcome is 25 percent, a prima facie indication of program effectiveness is established.

Such an indication affords the administrator some assurance that a program previously subjected to a controlled evaluation with similar results is continuing to be effective. It also may provide a rough estimate of the value of a program that has not been evaluated under control.

This kind of evaluation has many limitations. The predictive device is valid only to the extent that the group observed is typical of the population used as the basis for the standard. For example, if the group to be studied has been selected by accepting only those who possess a "good attitude toward treatment," comparison with a population containing a substantial number of subjects with a "bad attitude" will be invalid.

A second objection to the use of predictive devices in evaluation rests on the tendency of the predictive bases to deteriorate. The applicability of a prediction under circumstances prevailing in Year One will not necessarily be the same for the circumstances prevailing in Year Ten. Accordingly, it is good practice to audit the accuracy of the predictive device at least every five years.

A third objection is that predictive devices can be used only for global indications of program effectiveness. They cannot tell the administrator anything about a particular individual or his participation in a program. The decisionmaker unfamiliar with the use of predictive devices may be tempted to seek prognosis of individual behavior as a basis for program refinement. It must be emphasized that the type of instrument under discussion cannot provide that kind of information. If it is desired to know whether some clients benefit from a program while others do not, a rigorous evaluation providing for classification of both experimental and control groups must be carried out.

The study of differential effectiveness is a particularly significant requirement in correctional evaluations. Where the differentiations are standard and can be applied to the information system (for example, an age group, an offense category, an educational status), much can be done to assure that evaluations will be differentiated. But some classifications will be experimental aspects of the research. In such cases, statistical procedures unsuited to information systems must be designed and applied.

Despite these considerations, soft comparison can be recommended for discrimination of program effectiveness if provision also is made for analysis and controlled investigation to verify trends. The method should not be attempted without supervision of a professional statistician.

The statistician's participation in controlled research on program effectiveness will be discussed later in this chapter.

Determination of Workload Requirements

Most correctional systems still determine workload requirements by tradition instead of rational analysis. With new management principles, planning and budgeting are based increasingly on analytic concepts such as cost-benefit analysis. Criteria and measurement have not been standardized for any of these concepts. Much experimental work must be done to achieve a commonly acceptable analytic model.

Program budgeting has been an aspiration of many administrators, but it has foundered on technical problems. Most of these problems can be traced to difficulties in defining goals. The multiplicity of goals in corrections and the apparent conflicts among them make resolution of these difficulties improbable.

But even in the present imperfect status of correctional statistics, application of program budgeting concepts to the study of agency policy sheds some light on the best workload distribution. For example, recent statistical studies in California showed that substantial savings could be made by reducing parole time for most classes of offenders from an average of more than two years to a one-year maximum. In this case recidivism rates at the end of one year closely approximated those at the end of two. Statistical analysis of experience over a number of years was necessary to confirm this conclusion. The impact on workload as a result of this policy change obviously was large.

It also is clear that many kinds of differentiation can be made in the correctional workload. Most of these differentiations will have implications for resource allocations as well as treatment. Some offenders require no service at all, even though committed to custody. Others require constant medical treatment, psychiatric supervision, maximum custody, or frequent surveillance. A statistical study of the incidence of special requirements and the resources for meeting them can assure that needs are met without wasting resources. It cannot be said that this level of workload analysis is frequently encountered in correctional administration. The statistical analysis of effort and results still is the exception rather than the rule.

Projection of Future Requirements

The statistician's most elusive goal is projection of future trends and requirements. Because correctional administrators do not have control over intake and outgo, workload prediction is especially difficult. Unexpected intake can result in disastrously over-crowded prisons and jails. No statistician can claim accuracy in forecasting population movement for any period under prevailing conditions in corrections. Nevertheless, much can be done to establish the consequences of defined contingencies.

The study of contingencies is the essence of sound statistical projection. Reliance on straight-line projection is a pitfall for the administrative amateur who assumes that past and present rates of growth or decline will be the best guide to future conditions. This kind of guidance has resulted in dangerously over-crowded conditions in some correctional systems. In others, new institutions have been built, only to stand unused for years for lack of inmates to fill them.

Statistical study of contingencies depends on a sequence of inquiries asking: "*If* this condition, then *what* consequences *when?*" A wide range of conditions must be considered in this projections model. Criminal law may impose harsh or lenient sanctions. The parole board's release policy may alter suddenly in response to increases in some categories of reported crime. Fluctuations in the birth rate 15 years ago or changes in economic conditions must be considered for their impact on the commitment rate. It is a complex model, but it offers advantages in addition to accuracy in projection of requirements. Through consideration of contingencies the statistician can alert the administrator to options for legislative or policy change.

The projection of a 10-year plan for capital outlay is one of the most difficult assignments. Such plans may envisage construction involving many millions of dollars. Working together, statisticians and administrative staff can define contingencies and establish options for various possible outcomes. The plan should provide for systematic annual comparisons of status with expectations, from which changes in the plan can be derived.

Any long-range plan not based on at least this level of statistical sophistication should not be considered a plan at all. The allocation of public funds based on straight-line projection is nothing less than maladministration.

Choice of Decision Alternatives

Most operational decisions are determined by policy rather than information and statistics, but policymaking should depend increasingly on the statistical study of process and outcome. If outcome does not correspond to goals, then modifications of process must be investigated.

It has long been a common procedure for the statistician to estimate the impact of changes in legislation or agency policy. Such estimates must be made in terms of a relatively small number of parameters, disregarding many consequences of administrative significance.

New simulation models and the kinds of analysis they make possible enable the statistician to increase the precision and applicability of his estimates. The decisionmaker is not relieved of responsibility for choice. Few decisions depend on quantifiable information alone. In many cases the imponderables will be more significant than the statistics. For example, it may be assumed that the penalty for a certain offense must be increased because of public opinion. However, statistical study of the consequences of such increase will help determine the true impact of the legislation.

Legislative and policy decisions in corrections have potential impact on two areas. In the fiscal-management area, the impact is direct and easily traced. There can be no excuse for making a policy decision without reference to so easily measurable an impact. The impact on the much less understood area of correctional effectiveness is difficult to measure or predict. It may be learned, for example, that a new policy will require 10 new employees for a particular program. The monetary cost of this decision can be easily determined. The impact of the decision on the program's effectiveness is much more difficult to assess. Provision for statistical study of noneconomic consequences of policy changes will influence development of models by which such measurements can be made reliable.

Construction of Statistical Instruments

Construction of base expectancy tables already has been cited as an example of predictive instruments that can be used in an information system. Explorations leading to more useful predictive devices are under way. Predictive techniques are expected to become much more versatile than the versions of the base expectancy model now in use.

The statistician's role in development and maintenance of these devices is critical. Although the concepts are or can be standard, their application will depend in part on local conditions. A predictive device developed in California would have to be modified for use in New England by a study of the differing characteristics of the two populations. This kind of study requires statistical supervision.

The armory of statistical instruments also should include change indicators. Time-series lines reflecting correctional population movements will aid decision-making. It will be useful to maintain continuties in computing and recording rates of commitment of various correctional programs. They should be standard features of the program audit that should be conducted as part of the planning cycle.

Perhaps the most important instrument to be designed by the statistician is hardly thought of as an instrument at all. An agency's annual statistical report is a handbook of permanent importance to the orderly evolution of policy. It should include: sections on population characteristics, tabulated for given points in time; a recapitulation of population movement for the full year; and an analysis of recidivism by offense and other characteristics. Although the administrator should determine the areas for study, he should be guided by the statistician's recommendations for analysis and display.

Analysis of Special Problem Areas

The information system should be capable of responding to a broad range of special queries. It should be flexible enough to provide for cross-tabulations not included in the routine reporting schedule and to allow for rapid delivery of information in response to many administrative inquiries. The professional statistician's skill is called for when data are needed that have not been incorporated in the information system. This case may result from an experimental program requiring special information processing. It also may result from the perception of a new problem area; for example, the influence of methadone on probation and parole violations.

Although administrators and legislators may generate inquiries surpassing the capability of the information system, the main source of special problem analysis should be the exception reports the system will generate routinely. The report of a variance from expectations that exceeds planned tolerance almost always will require investigation of its causes and consequences. The statistician's responsibility for these studies will facilitate rational response to the situation.

Future of the Correctional Statistician

The information system, once activated, will greatly increase the need for professional statistical services. It also will change the character of these services. The adaptation of the generic correctional information system to the special situation of any correctional agency is a statistical responsibility. The professional staff carrying out that responsibility must be capable of systems analysis and design. These skills will continue to be required when the system is operating. It is essential to the production of useful information that the system be readily adaptable to changing administrative conditions.

The statistician will be freed of the managerial requirements of a manually operated system. The manual system stresses economical generation of the minimum statistics required for effective management. By contrast, in an automated information system the stress is on selecting, out of the enormous range of available data, the reports of greatest use to the administrator. The correctional statistician interprets the abundance of information rather than attempting to find significance in scarcity.

RESEARCH

The term "research" will be used in this discussion to include the *description* and *explanation* of human behavior. These closely related functions obviously are important to the effectiveness of the correctional process. Through documentation of criminal careers and consequences of correctional intervention, a basis is created for the explanation of behavior. Through the processes of confirmation, some explanatory theories are accepted, some rejected. Knowledge acquired through this process forms an empirically supported theoretical base for correctional practice. The key concept is empiricism, the reference of policy to experience as documented by observation. This concept is enlarged by the empirical perception that social change alters the meaning and significance of experience, so that policy decisions based on the experience of 20 years ago will not necessarily be sound today.

Introduction of empiricism for the support of theory is immensely important for the entire criminal justice system. No human institution is more tradition-oriented. The foundations of criminal control rest on unverified and conflicting assumptions about behavior motivation and change. For correctional practice, these assumptions result in decisions made with invalid justifications. For example, to justify incarceration by the expectation that those incarcerated will be rehabilitated thereby is to substitute wishful thinking for realism. To the extent that research has reduced the influence of such expectations on policymaking, both public protection and fairness to the individual have been served. Replacement of assumptions by empirically tested principles has started, but it is far from complete.

Description in Correctional Research

The element of description in correctional research deserves more discussion. The information system will capture a huge amount of detail about individual and group events. The detail can be examined for any individual or any group, but what is available is limited to the system's capability to record routinely. The research investigator must focus on the antecedents or consequences of an event in order to explain it. His role is to draw on his knowledge of similar events to determine what must be known in order to describe and account for the event under study. The system may accurately record the criminal history, demographic characteristics, and sentence of a man convicted of homicide. To make decisions about him and persons like him, much more must be known about his motivations and behavior. Aggregation of these descriptive details for significant categories of offenders is a fundamental task of research.

Similarly, consolidation of information into statistical reports constitutes an excellent picture of the state of a system as a whole, of its experience with the offenders it controls, and of the consequences of its policy and decisions. Such reports cannot provide the administrator with a description of the system in sufficient detail to enable him to explain and innovate. He does not always need such detail. Those elements of the system that are functioning as expected can be left alone. The information system can give him better assurance of satisfactory operations than he ever could have from personal inspection and staff reports. But where change is needed, detail will be required that cannot be obtained from the information system. In assembling these data, the researcher provides for fuller description of the agency's process. His effort is guided by the experience of social scientists in describing similar processes for explanatory purposes.

An example may clarify this principle. The information system may report a sudden increase in the parole violation rate. It may also report that most of this rise can be accounted for by an exceptional number of parole violations in a metropolitan center. The meaning of this change cannot be understood without accumulation of more descriptive detail. The researcher usually will have a good idea of what he is looking for. It may be a sudden change in employment conditions. It may be an excess of zeal by new parole officers. But until more facts are assembled for describing the situation, the explanation must be speculative.

If description is the process of accumulating sufficient information to explain events and processes, then explanation is the use of descriptive information to produce the understanding necessary for modification of policy and practice. Understanding does not depend on the mere accumulation of facts. The researcher can describe events and processes, and he can relate his description to accepted social science principles. He can even establish new principles from his perception of reality. But in the end, understanding is shared. To the explanations he derives from his perception of reality must be added the moral, administrative, and fiscal considerations observed by the administrator. The researcher may account for an increase in recidivism by attributing it to a new parole supervisor's interpretation of policy. He may show that the interpretation is not justified by data. But if the police and courts have urged the new supervisor to "tighten up," reversing the change may not be a simple matter.

This section will focus on the functions of evaluation and innovation. It will show that research is fundamental to both. The statistical comparisons on which evaluative information is generated for administrative review must be derived from accepted principles of measurement. These principles depend on satisfying answers to the questions: "What is an adequate description?" and "What is a sufficient explanation?"

Creation of an information system and management of a comprehensive statistical apparatus are absolutely necessary to the description and explanation of events and processes. They alone are not sufficient for these purposes. The philosopher may convince us that a full description and explanation of anything always will elude our grasp. But criminal justice services constitute a corner of the universe in which certainty can be more closely approached than it is now.

Program Evaluation

The requirement of program evaluation capability within the information and statistics system has been emphasized. Such capability is feasible now, but it far exceeds that available in even the most advanced correctional agency. The effort to achieve this functional level should not mislead the administrator into believing that the ultimate evaluative requirements have been met. Accomplishment of this goal will give him a monitoring service. For control, this service will be a vast contribution to a new level of administrative effectiveness. The administrator will know where corrective action is needed, and how urgently. He will not know the reasons for change in program outcome, nor will the printout tell him what actions he should take. His own inspections and review of operations may suffice for action, but many occasions will arise when evaluative research will be necessary for full understanding of program shortcomings. This use of research staff should be encouraged.

Evaluation is the measurement of goal achievment. It may be macroscopic and measure the agency's achievement of the overall objectives. This type of evaluation, for example, might determine whether an increased period of incarceration reduced the recidivism rate. Such evaluation usually is not concerned with effects on individuals; the concern is to define the benefit of the total program. The value of the indiscriminate macroscopic measurement is limited.

The study of subordinate goals is much more profitable. But whatever the level of goals to be achieved by the system, they must be precisely specified. This requirement seems obvious, but it is not always clear that a program is related to its stated objective. A recent study by Kassebaum, Ward, and Wilner[15] demonstrates the point. These investigators were engaged to study the effectiveness of group counseling in reducing recidivism. A meticulously classic research design was applied to the problem, but no relation between program and recidivism or nonrecidivism could be discovered. The first question asked, however, was whether there was any reason to suppose that such a relationship might exist. The project staff also explored the more plausible proposition that group counseling might produce a better prison adjustment on the part of those exposed. Nothing of the sort could be demonstrated, probably because the program directors had not produced a model consistent enough to study.

It is not enough that the goal be clearly defined and logically related to the program. It also is necessary that the program itself be sufficiently consistent in definition to establish a clear relationship to the objective.

Most evaluation research is adapted from the experimental model in the natural sciences. It is assumed that the population to whom the program under study is to be applied will be defined rigorously. A random selection produces an experimental group, to which the program is administered as an independent variable. All other conditions remaining constant for both experimental and control groups, the program's success is measured by a dependent variable. Almost always in correctional programs this variable will be recidivism. Guttentag[16] has pointed out the discrepancy in the assumption that a social action variable can be controlled in the same sense that a variable in the natural sciences can be maintained within defined limits of consistency. No satisfactory solution to this anomaly has been proposed. Its resolution at this stage seems to depend on classification of the population under study and controlled differentation of program.

The work of Warren[17] illustrates the value of this approach. This project concerned design and test of a comprehensive community-based treatment program for a wide range for delinquents. The test consisted of nine sub-studies comparing treatment variables between comparable and well-defined experimental and control groups. All the experimen-

[15] Gene Kassebaum, David Ward, and David Wilner *Prisoner Treatment and Parole Survival* (Wiley, 1971).

[16] Marcia Guttentag, "Models and Methods in Evaluation Research," *Journal of the Theory of Social Behavior*, (1971), 75–95.

[17] "The Case for Differential Treatment of Delinquents."

tal groups were treated in the community; all the control groups were confined in youth training schools. As a result of this elaborate design, the strengths and weakness of the total program of community treatment could be identified. Without these discriminations, both the positive and the negative findings in the groups treated would have been obscured.

Not all evaluative research lends itself to this kind of design. Nevertheless, it is a good rule to recognize and define the complexity of experience so that something can be learned from it. The virtues of simplicity in research are limited. Generally, the simpler the design, the less will be learned.

Hierarchy of Evaluative Research

A hierarchy of evaluative research illustrates this principle. The best analysis of this hierarchy is to be found in Suchman's authoritative work.[18] Suchman perceived that the utility of evaluation depended largely on the complexity of the measurement criteria. He defined five categories of criterial used in evaluation. A recapitulation of his analysis will illustrate the usefulness of controlled complexity in design.

1. At the most primitive level of evaluation, one merely measures *effort*. These measurements are made in terms of cost, time, and types of personnel employed in the project studies. Information of this kind is essential to the study of a program's economics, but it tells us nothing about its usefulness. An example from correctional practice is a study of effort expended on a reformatory vocational training program. The equipment, personnel, and number of training sessions required to achieve a specified level of vocational proficiency for a varied class of trainees would be documented. This kind of study is not without value to the policymaker. He may not know what the program contributes to achievement of his goals, but he will have a rough idea of whether he can afford it.

2. The second evaluation level is the measurement of *performance*. The question here is whether immediate goals of the program are achieved. In the case of the vocational training program, the success criterion would be the number of trainees reaching the planned level of proficiency within the time allotted. The significance of this simple level of evaluation should not be overlooked. Too many correctional administrators are unable to say how their programs are operating at this basic level. Obviously no highly specialized research apparatus is necessary for this kind of evaluation. Such a comparision can be maintained by the correctional information system.

3. At the third evaluation level, the *adequacy of performance* is determined. This step begins determination of the program's value for offenders exposed to it. In the study of the vocational training program, the number of trainees who achieved the desired proficiency and proved to be employable in a related occupation after release would be determined. Until integration of information systems is much improved from current practice, individual followup of some kind will

---

[18] Edward Suchman, *Evaluation Research* (Russell Sage Foundation, 1967).

be necessary to deliver this level of assessment. The conceptual basis for this research is simple, and its relevance for planning is clear, but few such evaluations of correctional programs have been accomplished.

4. The objective at the fourth evaluation level is determination of *efficiency*. This is the level of assessment that characterizes most evaluative research in corrections. Unfortunately, a shortcut methodology omitting the study of effort and performance has been achieved, thereby reducing the value of the conclusions made. Assuming that effort and performance are documented, much can be learned about whether programs have definable value compared with other programs administered to comparable groups.

In the vocational training program example, it might be discovered that the expected number of trainees reached the specified minimum proficiency level and were employed at their new trade after release. But the planner will have more questions for the researcher. He now wants to know, "Did this employability make any difference? Is it possible that a comparable group of offenders who did not receive this expensive training might have a recidivism rate just as low?" Other, less crucial questions fall into this category. It might be asked whether a lower and less expensively achieved proficiency level might have produced the same number of employable trainees. Could the minimum proficiency level for reliable job placement be reached with a shorter, less costly, more intensive training? The policymaker, the vocational training director, and the researcher, must collaborate carefully in identification and formulation of issues so answers will lead to constructive decisions.

5. Finally, the most elaborate form for evaluative research will include the study of *process*. A research design directed at the links between processes and results also will provide assessment of performance adequacy and efficiency. The purpose is to find out the relative contributions of processes to goal achievement. Although such a study ordinarily will be initiated to settle administrative issues, this kind of analysis often will produce findings of scientific significance.

There are four main dimenstions of study with which process analysis usually must be concerned:

- Attributes of the program related to success or failure.
- Recipients of the program who are more or less benefited.
- Conditions affecting program delivery.
- Effects produced by the program.

The study of process in the vocational education example would begin by considering instructional effectiveness. Is it possible, for example, that not enough time was given to demonstrating the use of tools? Were classes too large for individual attention? Does comparison of the success of the different instructors in conducting the training reveal anything?

The second category of inquiry would call for a study of the trainees. Can factors be found that separate the successful from the unsuccessful? What happens to them after they leave? Did failure in this program have adverse effects on susbsequent conduct?

The third study dimension would require investigation of administrative variables. Did full-time assignment to the program for three months achieve better results than half-time assignment for six months? What was the effect of compulsory assignment to the program? Would better results be achieved by voluntary assignments?

The fourth approach to process study leads to the secondary effects of the program, which, of course, are of great importance to correctional planning. A before-and-after comparison of attitudes toward work and authority would shed light on the usefulness of training for other dimensions of socialization. Another study might be directed to the attitudes of the program failures. Still other studies might examine the influence of the instructors as role models for the trainees.

The structure and requirements of evaluative research in corrections have been discussed at length because of a consensus that much more of it is needed. The costs will be high. The temptation to economize is universal; there is still an inclination to limit evaluation to the opinion of a visiting expert called in late in the day to meet a budgetary requirement for evidence to support the program's value. In such a situation, the most conscientious expert is limited to brief observations, a review of existing data, and perhaps a few interviews with staff and trainees. Sometimes such consultations are of great value, but they should not be mistaken for systematic, empirical evaluations.

In a time of great change, when policy is shaped by evidence, new evaluation standards should be established and maintained. Crude and oversimplified evaluation results in discrediting old programs without creating a basis for evaluation. At this point in correctional history, evaluative research is a dubious investment unless it is designed for the understanding of operations as well as their statistical assessment.

Innovation

In addition to program evaluation, research contributes to the improvement of corrections by facilitating innovation in policy and operations. The scope of innovation in corrections is relatively narrow. What can be done must be related to penal objectives. These essentially are maintenance of control over offenders and reduction of criminal behavior. A limited range of means is available to achieve these goals. Given the present structure of corrections and the underlying assumptions, the room for research maneuver is limited. It is a domain of research in which the number of alternatives provided by theory is relatively small. The challenge to the administrator and the social scientist is to explore existing alternatives in sufficient depth to gain an accurate knowledge of their potentials. A further survey of the issues is much less likely to be profitable.

There is an instructive contrast between the impressive success of innovations in control and the almost negligible success of innovations in behavior change. Diversification of control methods has moved rapidly from conception to implementation. The reduction of criminal behavior through programs administered by correctional agencies has yet to be convincingly demonstrated. The role of research has been decidedly different with respect to these two categories of innovation.

Numerous theoretical issues are involved in effective offender control. The large amount of literature on prison communities documents many of these issues and even suggests the resolution of some. Although numerous modifications have been made during the last quarter century, few have been derived from theoretical propositions. Humanitarian and economic motives have combined to produce alternatives to incarcertaion such as community treatment, work-release, and probation subsidy. The objective of each of these innovations was reduction of the enormous economic waste of incarceration and of some of the needless suffering it imposes on offenders and their families. The principle underlying each of these innovations called for a simple pragmatism in testing. The only requirement was that a less costly control of offenders be imposed without decreasing public safety. Many administrators vaguely hope these relaxed controls will have rehabilitative effects in themselves, but the significant success criterion is a low level of criminal incidents involving program participants. The criterion supporting success is the conservative selection of offenders.

The position of innovation in change of offender behavior offers much less reason for confidence. Theories about change of human behavior by agents that are not supernatural are of recent origin. There is little evidence of their effectiveness in domains other than corrections. Because change is so much to be desired, much effort has been given to adapting the practice of behavior change to the peculiar circumstances of the offender. Most of these attempts have been derived from the limited range of socialization theory. This range consists of three principal groups of theories on which practice can be based.

The first group of theories is grounded on the belief that human behavior is influenced most powerfully by administration of rewards and punishments. This belief is so deeply embedded in the general perception of human nature that our whole system of criminal justice depends on it. Despite popular consensus on the validity of the rewards-and-punishment theory, the punitive measures applied have never achieved predictable successes. The pattern of results from incarceration, fines, and public reprimand shows that, whatever the ultimate value of the theory, we do not know how to punish in a way that consistently achieves desired results.

The renaissance in behavioral psychology and its sociological correlates has indicated new avenues for correctional innovation. The history of corrections promises many interesting points of initiative for influencing behavior. Such applications as programmed learning and token economies are adapted from educational and mental health. Except for some unpromising and unattractive attempts at aversive conditioning and behavior modification by electronic devices, little has been done to develop techniques for behavior modification that are native to corrections.

The second group of theories has generated the most research and probably the most disappointment. These theories are based on the idea that socialization is dependent on acquisition of insight, and on the associated idea that criminal behavior originates in defective socialization. A wide range of applications in counseling and therapy depends on these propositions. So far, conclusions on the value of treatments based on this group of theories have not borne out the hopes held by the clinical professionals. It is beyond the scope of this chapter to consider the reasons in the detail they deserve. The principal factor to which failure can be attributed are the involuntary aspect of treatment, the inapplicability of the technique to the psychological conditions addressed, lack of clarity as to the kinds of insights desired, and the overwhelming adverse social conditions faced by many offenders. Despite their failures and the cogency of the argument that well-defined reasons for failure can be identified, correctional therapy proponents have made a less than sufficient effort to refine theory to accommodate the unfavorable empirical findings.

The third group of theories is the least developed. It comes under the heading of "reintegration," a concept supported by the Corrections Task Force of the President's Commission on Law Enforcement and Administration of Justice.[19] This set of ideas is based on the theory that a change in the nature of the offender's relation to the community, rather than a change in the offender himself, is to be sought. The focus therefore is on the interaction between the offender and his surroundings. The objective is to achieve a better "reintegration" than the integration that existed before the trouble occured. The theory holds that nonoffenders share the same psychological abnormalities as offenders, and attempts at rehabilitation by psychological change are superfluous if the only intent is to reduce recidivism. The task of the correctional apparatus therefore should be to help the offender achieve the level of integration enabling him to choose a law-abiding career regardless of his psychological state.

The difficulty with these theoretical positions is that so far they have not lent themselves to a clearly identifiable operational technique. The a priori logic of the theory is persuasive, so far as it goes, and there should be increasing interest in deriving innovations from it.

The foregoing sketch of theoretical positions by no means exhausts all possible models available to corrections, but it does include those currently influential. Their limited valued for operational use in correctional settings reflects a serious constraint on practical development. Two possible explanations might account for this contraint. First, a theory of sufficient power to support the social restoration of the offender has not been discovered. It is possible that there is no theory or group of theories to support the planned change of offenders, or alternately, to provide for their reintegration without change.

The second explanation is that some attributes of the current correctional experience and setting seem to rule out the possibility of such change or reintegration. A method for resolving these problems has yet to be devised. The importance of achieving a resolution is increasingly clear.

---

[19] President's Commission on Law Enforcement and Administration of Justice, *Task Force Report: Corrections* (Washington: Government Printing Office, 1967), p. 30–31.

MAJOR CURRENT RESEARCH ISSUES

Measurement in Correctional Research—Recidivism

The paradox of correctional measurement is the existence of a criterion variable that is easily recorded, simple to measure, and logically relevant but that also obscures research. Unlike any other social service system, corrections possesses in recidivism a criterion whose salience is universally agreed upon.

There has been considerable variation in the way recidivism has been measured. A standard definition is needed. Three main factors should be considered in developing recidivism statistics: the nature of events to be counted, categorization of the behaviors and degrees of seriousness to be included, and duration of the followup period.

If the objective of the correctional apparatus is reduction of crime by reduction of recidivism, then all criminal acts committed by offenders who are or have been under correctional supervision should be counted as recidivism. But what is a reliable count? The choice is between an arrest reported by the police and a conviction reported by the courts. The police argue for counting recidivism by arrests, on the basis that arrests represent observed behavior whereas the judicial process results in much illegal behavior being excluded from a recidivism count based solely on convictions. Correctional administrators argue that recidivism should be measured by convictions alone because many arrests may represent erroneous attribution of illegal behavior to the highly visible released offender or probationer.

In a integrated criminal justice information system, arrests will be related to prosecutions and convictions or acquittals. Until that time, the use of arrests as the data for recidivism is subject to the objection that neither the behavior of the offender nor its significance has been verified by court action. In a system of law based on presumption of innocence, such verification is essential.

Recidivism should be measured by reconvictions. A conviction is a well-defined event in which a recorded action has been taken by the court. Further, measurement by reconvictions is established practice in corrections. It is desirable to maintain this continuity in statistical practice. This position is not meant to discourage measurement of arrests or a study of the relationship of arrest rates of ex-offender to release rates. The significance of such studies must be assessed in light of a realistic view of the nature and validity of the data used.

Another consideration as to the nature of events to be included relates to technical violations of probation or parole. Technical violations based on administrative action alone should be excluded from a general definition of recidivism because they are not established formally as criminal acts. Rather, they are reflection of administrative practices and may indicate parole policy more than correctional effectiveness (See Chapter 12.) Technical violations in which a sentencing authority took action that resulted in an adverse change in an offender's legal status should be collected but maintained separately from data on reconvictions.

A second major problem in recidivism measurement relates to the degrees of seriousness to be identified and their significance. The recidivist event may vary in seriousness from a booking and dismissal of a minor offense to conviction for a major felony. Many correctional administrators will argue that success should be measured in terms of a reduction in seriousness of an offense pattern or an increase in the period of law-abiding behavior between offenses. This logic is not persuasive. If the objective of the corrections system is to change behavior, or at least establish successful control, nothing in its operation can or should be aimed at converting major offenders into lesser offenders. A program aimed at resocialization or reintegration should be directed at a positive result. An offense above a determined level of seriousness must be charged against the system as a failure because the program has not reduced the burden of crime. The problem lies in prescribing a level of seriousness that separates those criminal acts so minor or nonserious as not to merit public attention from those major or serious enough to be reported.

There are several reasons for not using present offense groupings in a definition of recidivism, First, new groupings of crimes should be specified which divide criminal acts into categories based on the gravity of the offense. (See Chapter 16.) If this recommendation were implemented, it would be a simple matter to decide which of the offense categories should be included in recidivism rates. At the present time, however, there is no commonly accepted categorization. Different bodies utilize various groupings such as misdemeanors and felonies, violent and nonviolent offenses, crimes against property and against persons, or serious and nonserious offenses as defined in the FBI's "Uniform Crime Reports." Furthermore, these terms are used to specify different acts in different jurisdictions.

The second way criminal acts may be grouped for reporting is to differentiate on the basis of sentence received. For example, recidivism sometimes has been defined by criminal acts committed by probationers or released offenders that resulted in conviction by a court a sentence of not less than a certain number of days of confinement (usually 60, 90, or 180 days). Given the trend toward using confinement as the disposition of last resort, however, some fairly serious criminal acts may not result in confinement and would therefore be excluded from such a definition. A mechanism for recording more serious offenses which is not dependent upon confinement must be established.

This is not to say that measurement of recidivism necessarily should be divorced totally from the sentence imposed. Particularly while offense categories and sentencing practices are not standardized and practices such as plea bargaining are used widely, the sentence received may reveal more about the court's perception of the seriousness of the offense than its designation. Ideally, some factor that combines the offense category and the sentence received should be utilized.

The length of time offenders should be followed after their release from the supervision of the courts or the corrections system is the third important element in developing recidivism statistics. Measurement of recidivism should be pursued for three years after the release of the offender from all correctional supervision. This arbitrary figure is chosen because the few recidivism studies that have followed offenders more than three years have not revealed a significant difference between recidivism before and after the three-year point. Arbitrariness of the period is less important than the need to establish a standard measure with a specific time frame so that comparisons among programs and systems will have a consistent base. A figure should be set that will not undermine the ability to get feedback within a useful time frame and take corrective action. This is not meant to discourage reporting over longer periods, which provides valuable control information concerning reconvictions and their occurrence after the three-year period.

A Definition of Recidivism. To sum up the points made here, the following definition should be used.

Recidivism is measured by (1) criminal acts that resulted in conviction by a court, when committed by individuals who are under correctional supervision or who have been released from correctional supervision within the previous three years, and by (2) technical violations of probation or parole in which a sentencing or paroling authority took action that resulted in an adverse change in the offender's legal status.

Technical violations should be maintained separately from data on reconvictions. In addition, it is important to report recidivism so that patterns of change can be discerned. At the minimum, it should be possible to ascertain from the statistical tables the number of recidivists in each annual disposition or release cohort at six-month intervals for the three-year followup period. Discriminations by age, offense, length of sentence, and disposition (probation, jail, prison commitment, etc.) are easy to make and will provide planners with trend lines for adjustment of policy.

The Measurement of Success. The definition of recidivism does not resolve all problems for which use of this variable is responsible. No matter how faithfully the definition is followed, only failure can be measured by using it. When recidivists are subtracted from the total cohort, the remainder are not necessarily to be credited to the system as successes. In rhetoric defending their programs, some administrators make statements to the effect that although 40 percent of their releases failed, 60 percent succeeded. Success is attributed to the system or the program to be defended. The argument is fallacious.

Although the failures of corrections can be differentiated on a wide range from the inevitable to the accidental, they nevertheless are failures. But it does not follow that the program succeeded with those who did not fail. There are several reasons for this paradox.

First, some offenders commit new offenses, but not in a jurisdiction that will report them to the agency that supervised or confined them. This common deficiency may be corrected when a national retrieval of criminal histories becomes an actuality, but not before.

Second, even though no new offense has been committed, the offender may have become a public dependent of some other kind. He may be a client on welfare rolls, a patient in a mental hospital, or an alcoholic on skid row. All these ex-offenders, while not technically correctional failures, can hardly be termed correctional successes.

The third, and by far the most frequent, fallacious inclusion in a success roster is the offender who endured the program without benefit but for various reasons managed to abide by the law or avoid detection in the commission of new crimes for the followup period or who did not require correctional services to begin with. It is easy to claim such individuals as successes, but unless the success can be related to the program in some demonstrable way, the claim is an inflation of fact.

It is not implied that there is no such thing as a correctional success. Some offenders do benefit from programs in which they participate. Their number is not likely to increase unless we study the processes that produced favorable change. To decide that these individuals are statistically identical with the spurious successes will obscure what may be learned from their favorable outcome.

The first problem is that recidivism can tell us only about correctional failures. Inevitably it is linked as the dependent variable in the study of program effectiveness. The logic is compelling. If the object of penal process is reduction of recidivism, then achievement of the reduction determines whether the effort was worthwhile.

The second problem in a study of recidivism is to take into account the heterogeneity of the population. Offenders vary from those without hope of adjusting to those whose prospects preclude a likelihood of a return to criminality. If we are merely comparing the incidence of recidivism from year to year, these distinctions hardly make a difference. But, if the task is to define a correctional program's effectiveness, inclusion of the certain failures and successes without distinguishing them from those with whom an element of chance was involved, the likelihood of proving anything is severely impaired.

The third problem is maintenance of relevance to the experience being measured. Consider again the vocational training program used as an example in an earlier section. The program's logic from the planner's viewpoint will lead to employability. If the offender is employed at the work for which he was trained in the reformatory, he will be motivated to enjoy the benefits of a law-abiding life and less inclined to return to criminality. This is a plausible sequence of assumptions and worthy of test. Unfortunately, documentation is difficult, and follow-up reporting is impractical and costly. Numbers in some groups are likely to be statistically insignificant. The researcher probably will not follow the program's logic to the end. A crude assumption may be made that the program is ineffective if a significant number of those exposed failed to complete it. But the failures may include those who completed the program and obtained postrelease employment as well as those who were inappropriately assigned and dropped out during the first month of training. Unless the study discriminates success and failures at each point, nothing can be learned from whatever success the program may have produced.

A fourth, but closely related, problem is the limited inference that can be made from the study of failure. Much can be learned from unrealized expectations. But preoccupation with failure and its explication obstructs the study of success. Avoidance of failure is not identical by any stretch of logic with promotion of success. No profession ever improved its service through the exclusive study of its failures. Because they are frequent and expected, the failures of corrections are less enlightening than most.

From the foregoing, three rules can be formulated for the measurement of corrections:

1. The study of recidivism as a measure of correctional effectiveness is primarily of administrative use in the determination of whether objectives and expectations have been realized.

2. The study of program success is essential if research is to contribute to increased correctional effectiveness.

3. The discrimination of program failures from expected failures is essential to understanding recidivism. The discrimination of program successes is equally essential, but these successes must be individually verified, not inferred from statistical class.

Improvement of Evaluation

Evaluation is not novel to the correctional administrator. He has endured, or at least observed, a considerable number of assessments placing his professional opinions and judgments in jeopardy. A familiar and accepted evaluation model now exists. Comparison between experimental and control groups, from the latter of which a program has been withheld as an experimental variable, can lead toward assessment of program effectiveness. Depending on the program to be studied, much can be done to complicate this model with classification matrices and differential interventions. Much attention can be given to process, and with useful results.

It will not be argued that this model is anything but valuable and necessary. It has achieved many historic results, some of which have been recounted in this chapter. To learn what will not work, and why, is important in corrections, a field heavily encumbered with ineffective concepts and practices.

What is needed now is an armory of alternatives to the existing structure. Evaluation research no longer should be limited to measuring treatment variables in laboratory tests. The evaluative tools should be used instead to create a model of effective intervention including consideration of the wide range of offender careers with which the correctional apparatus must cope.

The experimental model of evaluation must be elaborated. It is not possible here to specify the nature of this elaboration or its minimum requirements, if only because its design has not been undertaken. The need can be stated, however.

Policy decisions depend on identification of the quantitative results of differential interventions in criminal careers. The characteristics of criminal histories differ widely. Few useful generalizations can be made.

But intervention in any career is the interaction of a finite number of controlled processes (a jail term, an assignment to group therapy, a vocational training agreement) on the life span of a single person. Other processes outside anyone's control also are at work at the same time. So far as possible, all these processes must be defined. The interaction taking place produces events that set new processes in motion. This complexity must be ordered and categorized to determine which combination will lead to the most favorable set of results for the various categories of offenders defined by decisionmakers. The task is difficult and must be approached with utmost caution.

Two reciprocal questions are asked:

Which distinctions among offenders make a difference in combinations of intervention?

And which combinations of intervention processes will lead to what changes affecting categories of offenders?

An example may clarify the inherent difficulties. A mature adolescent boy has been committed to custody for homicide. A second youth, otherwise comparable, has been committed for auto theft. Despite their resemblances, they may need to be included in different programs. The goal is to decide, from a study of a wide variety of program combinations, which will have the most likelihood of success. Under the present research model, researchers tend to aggregate both youths in a high-maturity group in order to study the effectiveness of a program like group counseling.

A new research paradigm stresses discovery of the interactions in the longitudinal careers of these two boys that will bring about the most favorable growth. The outcome of the interaction of all these interventions will be reflected in recidivism. But by the time the reflection is seen in recidivism, a much more profound understanding of what has happened to these two youths and others like them will have developed. From such an understanding comes discovery of the limits of what can be done to resocialize the offender and protect the public.

The rigorous belief in recidivism as the only true criterion of evaluation and in the experimental model as the only acceptable methodology will be increasingly unproductive for evaluative research. The frantic search for escapes from controlled investigations or for meaningless refinements of recidivism will lead only to pointless conclusions. The focus must be on creation of a methodology leading to understanding. This is a challenge requiring support of longitudinal research and a complex and untried methodology. The professional risks are considerable; this work easily can lead the researcher into blind alleys. But the need is imperative.

Study of Treatment

Research has cast doubt on the effectiveness of psychological treatment of offenders. The evidence now on hand indicates that some offenders can be helped by psychotherapy, but there is persistent uncertainty as to which offenders are helped and how much they are helped. The preponderance of the research strongly suggests that most offenders are not coverted to law-abiding ways by psychotherapy.

The emphasis since World War II on programs derived from psychotherapeutic models thus comes into serious question. It is important that perspective be maintained and that research continuity be pursued in that light. Generalizing from the present body of research, the following propositions seem to hold:

1 Involuntary treatment of offenders by individual or group counseling does not produce results reflected in recidivism measurement.

2. Application of the sickness lable to any offender without supporting diagnosis does not increase the effectiveness of the correctional process.

3. There are weak indications that some offenders—those more mature, more intelligent, and more socialized than average—can benefit from psychological treatment, if they are motivated to participate.

This is not an encouraging position. Nevertheless, it has several implications for further research. These findings, being essentially negative, provide a basis for further study. They do not constitute a platform of action. Unless it is concluded that the situation is hopeless, that human beings cannot help each other, exploration of the helping processes must be continued by following the clues presently available. The findings listed herein are drawn from studies using efficiency criteria, as outlined in an earlier section. Until the study of treatment processes is carried out by differentiating categories of offenders and their interactions with specific intervention combinations, correctional administrators will not be in a good position to design innovations.

It therefore is appropriate to examine each of the pessimistically stated tentative conclusions about treatment in terms of the questions they contain. Thus:

If the involuntary element is the obstacle to treatment success, then what kind of treatment, conducted under what circumstances, should be made available? Studies prompted by this question must be initiated at an exploratory level before a procedure is ready for experimental trials.

If the self-concept of sickness is an obstacle to successful treatment for most offenders, what selfconcepts can be expected to contribute to remedial socialization? How can these self-concepts be fostered?

If it is true that some offenders achieve actual gains from treatment, what is the process that produces these gains? Can a theoretical formulation be designed to account for them?

In addition to these issues, and underlying each, is the question of attribution of delinquent behavior to an identifiable psychological state. Conventional psychiatric thought traces delinquency to an ill-defined state designated by such terms as "psychopathy," "behavior disorders," or "sociopathy." No satisfactory accounting for the state has been achieved, nor has guidance been given for successful treatment of the condition. To an extent that must embarass the thoughtful clinician, there is a circularity in a diagnosis that "discovers" that a subject's delinquency is symptomatic of the psychopathy that accounts for his delinquency. This state of affairs cannot contribute to effective rationale for treatment and control.

Behavior Modification Theory and Correctional Applications

The work of Goldiamond,[20] Cohen,[21] and McKee[22] among others, has led to the hope that through behavior modification techniques it will be possible to achieve the remedial socialization of some kinds of offenders. So far, the results of explorations do not produce a clearly favorable picture. One complication has been that most of these explorations were conducted in custodial situations. Use of behavior modification techniques in community-based corrections has been scant.

Most techniques of behavior modification have been generated either in the mental hospital or for educational use. Although their application to the correctional situation is not necessarily inappropriate, sufficient attention has not been given to the nature, scheduling, and limits of the reinforcement repertory available in the correctional apparatus. Thus the use of tokens for behavior reinforcement in a reformatory may or may not be a suitable application of an approach that works well in mental hospitals, where the problems of manipulation for secondary gains are not so prominent.

The explorations conducted so far furnish a basis for continued study of an ancient correctional problem: the usefulness of incentives and punishments in changing behavior patterns. Most of the offender population is now managed in community-based programs, and the proportion will increase. Therefore, future development in operant psychology should be directed toward making behavior modification techniques available (subject to experimental scrutiny) to probation and parole officers and voluntary agencies engaged in the treatment of the offender in the community.

A familiar hazard lurks in this strategy. It is tempting to the correctional policymaker to hope for more than he can get from a promising intervention. Operant psychology will not transform corrections into a success story. Psychologists working in this field should not encourage the hope that all offenders will respond significantly to their approach. Much must be done before it can be certain that any will respond consistently enough for categorization.

Study of Management and Staff Problems

Correctional administration has been relatively unaware of the services of management analysis and operations research. The principal gains from these services are financial savings and better allocation of personnel. Business, commerce, and defense have benefited in these ways, although the substance of service rarely is affected conceptually.

[20] Israel Goldiamond, "Self-Control Procedures in Personal Behavior Programs," *"Psychological Reports,* 17 (1965), 851–856.

[21] H. L. Cohen et al., *CASE II-Model: A Contingency-Oriented 24-Hour Learning Environment in a Juvenile Correctional Institution* (Silver Spring, Md.: Educational Faculty Press, 1968).

[22] John McKee, *Application of Behavior Theory to Correctional Practice* (Elmore, Ala.: Rehabilitation Research Foundation, 1971).

It may be a different matter in corrections. The enormous costs of incarceration have been compared to the modest outlays required by probation and parole. What seems to be a national movement has been generated by this contrast. The Probation Subsidy Act of 1965 in California may have been the first major departure toward the goal of reducing incarceration costs by minimizing prison sentencing. This kind of legislation not only has reduced prison population; it has also focused new attention on improvement of probation practice.

Other illuminations of correctional effectiveness can be expected from management analysis. Such topics as optimal sentencing, custodial supervision patterns, organization of probation services, and management of cost-effective prison industries certainly will respond to operations research. The need for studies of this kind throughout the correctional apparatus is acute. Long years of haphazard planning, pressure on administrators to speed changes toward managerial efficiency, and increasing versality of operations research as a discipline combine to make the study of correctional administration an attractive investment.

Perhaps the most compelling factor favoring management research in corrections is the serious inefficiency characterizing so many operations. This inefficiency wastes money and contributes to program ineffectiveness. Good services cannot be delivered by an inefficient agency.

ORGANIZATION FOR CORRECTIONAL RESEARCH

The Role of Agency Research

Implicit the argument of this chapter is the expectation that correctional management must use research if the necessities of change are to be met effectively. This expectation easily can be misunderstood. Installation of a large scientific capability in every correctional agency is not required. For all but the largest agencies, the necessary research tools will be provided by a modest information and statistics section capable of periodic reports on the consequences of policy and decisionmaking. The need for complex evaluative studies will be occasional and can be satisfied by contract research.

Large agencies will benefit from the establishment of a professional staff capable of designing and executing special assessment studies to amplify and explicate reports generated by the information system. More sophisticated studies of process and innovations can be accomplished with a varied scientific staff.

Effective management requires periodic retrospective reports on the consequences of policies and decisions. These reports will form the basis for informed decisions about action alternatives. The manager's skill in using reports of this kind will determine how extensive his needs for specialized research will be. Manager and statistician should collaborate continously in planning for a usable information system. Its dimensions should never be left solely to the statistician's imagination.

The necessity to defend correctional policy opens the question of the need for research done outside the agency. A legislative committee, a budget or fiscal office, and the press are all interested in the effectiveness of a correctional agency in achieving its goals. This interest may be satisfied by a review of internally generated statistics as interpreted by agency staff. But where major issues are at stake, an external review of findings and methods will always be appropriate. Naturally, such a review almost always will depend on the data the agency can supply. The reviewer's confidence in the integrity of the data will indicate the direction of his analysis.

Some kinds of research are beyond the proper scope of the most amply staffed agency research section. For example, where policy decisions must be made about the redistribution of effort at different governmental levels or among several agencies, it is inappropriate for an intramural research group to perform the supporting analysis. Regardless of the position researched, it would be executed under constraint of the agency's interest. Principles identifying conflict of interest apply to agencies as well as to individuals.

Research Organization in Larger Agencies

The minimum requirement of a research section is management of the information system and preparation of statistical reports. These requirements call for a manager-planner, who will be responsible for creation of the system and its development to meet changing demands. He should be supported by at least one professionally qualified systems analyst to design the structural details, and programers and machine operators needed for the routine operation of equipment.

The statistical service should be integrated with the information system. It should be supervised by a professional statistician competent for the collection, analysis, and display of statistical tables. He should have enough staff to audit information and to take corrective action when error seems to be indicated by anomalies in the data.

The independence of the research staff is essential to its usefulness. The chief should be accountable directly to the agency executive. The relationship of research staff to policy and decision making must be fostered by direct access to the agency executive and to the chiefs of other staff sections.

An almost unique problem in public administration is the relationship of agency information systems to computational services. It is uneconomic for any correctional agency to operate its own computer, although some agencies still have exclusive use of equipment. The trend in most States and large counties is toward the shared use of a computer with other government agencies. The economies achieved by this arrangement are obvious; no correctional agency can occupy the full potentiality of a large computer. As long as the sensitivity of the data is adequately protected, there is no reason to resist a generally beneficial evolution of information technology.

As the concepts of a truly comprehensive correctional information system are seen more clearly, statewide or regionwide information systems become attractive prospects. The concepts and technology are now available, but no concerted attempt has been made to create such a system. An early review of capabilities and requirements should be made to determine whether the benefits would justify implementation.

A completely comprehensive local and regional information system would interface with a national criminal history file. This file, being developed under the auspices of the Federal Bureau of Investigation and the Law Enforcement Assistance Administration, will facilitate orderly management of comprehensive information services. Its usefulness in principle will be great. In practice it will depend on how well participating agencies cooperate in sharing information.

Correctional Research in the Smaller Agency

The preponderance of correctional service is carried out by counties, not by Federal or State governments. Most metropolitan agencies are large enough to maintain information and statistics sections of their own. Smaller agencies should have minimum information-processing capabilities. Separate staffs might not be justified, but with some investment in a computer terminal and some training of administrative staff, a reasonable information and statistics capability can be expected.

This kind of management should be facilitated by State government. The State should store local data with access provided through agency terminals and no loss of local autonomy. Control of the system should be in the hands of representatives of participating agencies. Admission to the system should be voluntary, but benefits should be clear enough to encourage membership. A share of the development costs should be borne by the State or regional consortium. The move toward unified correctional systems also will help alleviate the problem of incorporating small agencies.

The usefulness of this service depends on training and motivating agency personnel. The skeptical sheriff and the overburdened probation officer will not involve themselves, even nominally, unless it is worth their while. The claim that additional staff is needed often will be authentic. Unless they are trained, agency personnel will not benefit from the system, no matter how carefully it is designed. Ways must be found to meet these requirements realistically through grants-in-aid and administrative extension services.

49

Myths, Misconceptions, and the Misuse of Statistics in Correctional Research

GORDON P. WALDO

Now that research has been certified as a legitimate member of the correctional world, everyone agrees that it is not being fully utilized for the advancement of the postadjudicatory treatment system.

The benefits to be derived from comprehensive research in program measurement have only been faintly perceived. A substantial increase in these activities is warranted.[1]

The single most important need in the post-adjudicatory treatment system is the development of a body of knowledge with respect to the effect of its operations upon its objectives.[2]

We need desperately to make our correctional system truly correctional. We must find out through carefully conducted research what works and what does not work to rehabili-

SOURCE. *Crime and Delinquency,* **17**, January 1971, pp. 57–66. Reprinted with permission of the author and the National Council on Crime and Delinquency.

[1] California Youth and Adult Corrections Agency, *Organization of State Correctional Services in the Control and Treatment of Crime and Delinquency* (Sacramento, May 1967), p. 71.

[2] *Preliminary Report of the* [*New York*] *Governor's Special Committee on Criminal Offenders* (Albany, June 1968), p. 316.

tate public offenders. Old and established programs, techniques, and concepts must be re-evaluated in terms of present requirements. Ineffective programs must be discarded. New programs must be developed and tested. Research and demonstration programs will help us reach our goals.[3]

Although correctional research has been hampered by the shortage of both funds and competent personnel, the researchers themselves have, by negligence, contributed to the unhealthy state of affairs. They have permitted a number of correctional myths and misconceptions to go unchallenged, and they have permitted a misuse of statistics to appear in the everyday language and annual reports of correctional systems.

A "misconception" as used here is an idea or belief that is based on inaccurate information; a "myth" is a widely circulated misconception that has proven difficult to eradicate (like a practitioner's view of correctional research). In this paper the terms are almost always interchangeable.

On the other hand, when statistics are misused the reason may be ignorance, or an oversight, or a misinterpretation, or purposeful distortion of the facts—in part by correctional researchers and in part by practitioners as they prepare annual reports and other documents.

MYTHS AND MISCONCEPTIONS

I do not imply that *all* practitioners believe some of the misconceptions concerning research presented below, or that *some* practitioners believe all of them; rather, most of these erroneous notions have been observed frequently enough, either in my personal contacts or in correctional literature, to indicate the need for clarification.

Programs Not Suitable for Evaluation

The first misconception is that while some programs are suitable for evaluation, others are not—a belief that collides with one of correction's primary needs: adequate evaluation of all programs now in existence as well as the new ones being devised.

Those who adhere to the misconception tend to mistake difficulty for unsuitability. It is, of course, normally more difficult to evaluate a program that has been running for some time without a research design having been built into it than one in which the evaluation component is established at the same time as the program itself. But any program, new or old, can be evaluated if the research design is properly conceived and maintained. Some may require more elaborate techniques than others, but virtually all can be evaluated.

---

[3] U.S. Joint Commission on Correctional Manpower and Training, *Research in Correctional Rehabilitation* (Washington, D.C.: Joint Commission, 1967), p. 2.

"Informal" Program Evaluation

The second misconception is that we can obtain a sound evaluation of the effectiveness of a program by examining "informally" the original logic on which the program was based and by gathering the impressions of persons involved in the program.

If the main criterion of effectiveness is reduced recidivism, an "informal" evaluation can be grossly misleading—as it was, for example, in the Cambridge-Somerville project.[4] Interviews with administrators, caseworkers, and program participants indicated that everyone felt the program was accomplishing its goals and being very effective. However, when adequate comparisons were made by proven research methods, the project was seen to have had no measurable impact in reducing delinquency. It now stands beside other classic failures in delinquency prevention.

Invalid Comparisons

The third misconception is that a recidivism percentage by itself is sufficiently informative.

To measure a program's effectiveness we must have a valid base against which it can be compared before we can assess the significance of our findings. Suppose we find that a new inmate treatment program had a recidivism rate of only 12 per cent. This would probably be quite impressive—most correctional systems have considerably higher rates of recidivism[5]—until we discovered that a group of comparable inmates in a regular correctional program had a recidivism rate of only 5 per cent. Rather than relate the 12 per cent figure to an imaginary base of total recidivism, we can now examine a recidivism figure for a similar group of inmates. Having access to the figure for the second group totally changes our interpretation of the first recidivism figure. Our basic conclusion would have to be that the program is doing more harm than good! Though both groups are doing better than the normal prison population, the difference is a result of the selection process, not the program. The inmates who participate in the programs are likely to be different from the other inmates in the system. If all our "good" inmates are selected to participate in the program, obviously they will have a lower recidivism rate than the remainder of the prison population. Thus what is measured is not the effectiveness of the program but simply our success in selecting inmates likely to be less recidivistic than other inmates in the system.

---

[4] Edwin Powers and Helen Witmer, *An Experiment in the Prevention of Delinquency: The Cambridge-Somerville Youth Study* (New York: Columbia University Press 1951). See also William McCord, *Origins of Crime: A New Evaluation of the Cambridge Somerville Youth Study* (New York: Columbia University Press, 1959).

[5] For a discussion of recidivism rates, see Elmer H. Johnson, *Crime, Correction and Society*, rev. ed. (Homewood, Ill.: Dorsey Press, 1968), pp. 644–51; Leslie T. Wilkins, *Evaluation of Penal Measures* (New York: Random House, 1969), pp. 13–15, 41–59.

They would have lower recidivism rates regardless of their participation in the program.

Fear of Random Assignment

The fourth misconception is that "random assignment" of inmates means that they are placed in a particular program without regard to their special qualities and characteristics; in other words, any inmate can be selected for any type of program.

This is what the practitioner fears; it is not what the researcher means by random assignment, which can be an effective evaluative technique.[6] For example, we can use random assignment of inmates after we have established controls for a series of specific characteristics and qualities. If we are about to set up a particular program, we do not randomly select from the total inmate population some persons who will be placed in the program and others who will be placed in the control group. The manner in which we proceed is to select all individuals who would be eligible for the program under the existing set of criteria. If the program calls for a special form of group training for all first offender males under age twenty-one with an IQ of 110 or better, we would select all inmates who meet these criteria. Of those who do, half would be placed in the experimental program and the other half in the control group. If it appears that not enough persons are selected under the criteria to fill the experimental program's resources completely and still provide a control group, perhaps the criteria can be broadened without doing harm; for example, we might reduce the IQ for eligibility from 110 to 100. Or we might raise the age from twenty-one to twenty-four. This not only does no damage to our program but may, in fact, increase its versality, for it enables us to determine which type of inmate is helped more by the new program. In other words, (1) does the program work better for the 19–21 group than for the 22–24 group; (2) is age even a relevant variable in this program?

Perhaps more important than the misunderstanding of randomization is the objection based on the "moral question." Random assignment, say some critics of it, commits a gross injustice against either the inmate or the total institutional system—against the inmate because he is either included or excluded from a particular program, or against the institutional system because of the impact on one part of it or another by the selection process. But "all sorts of injustice," Gilbert Geis reminds us, "prevail in the exigencies of everyday existence . . . as the consequence not of scientific experimentation but of happenstance."

For most of us, it would be unthinkable that a sample of armed robbers be divided into two groups on the basis of random assignment—one group to spend ten years in prison, the second to receive a sentence of two years on probation. Nonetheless, at a recent federal judicial conference, after examining an elaborate presentence report concerning a

---

[6] For a brief statement on the benefits of random assignment, see Daniel Glaser, "Correctional Research: An Elusive Paradise," *Journal of Research in Crime and Delinquency,* January 1965, p. 7.

bank robbery, seventeen judges said they would have imprisoned the man, while ten indicated they favored probation. Those voting for imprisonment set sentences ranging from six months to fifteen years. From the offender's viewpoint, the vagaries of random assignment for experimental purposes might seem preferable to the lottery of exposure to the considered judgment of a member of the judiciary.[7]

The apparent injustice in random assignment is perhaps less onerous than the injustice already present in the criminal justice system. Justice might better prevail through random assignment than it does now through purposeful assignment subject to individual bias and misdirection.

Until a new program has been shown to be more effective than older programs, either assigning inmates to it or not assigning them to it may be considered an injustice. If the program turns out to be not only ineffective but also actually harmful, as many studies have indicated, assigning an inmate to it may be detrimental to him. On the other hand, if it proves to be extremely effective and the inmate has been deprived of the opportunity to avail himself of it, not assigning him to it may be just as detrimental. How, then, can we make the proper decision on assignments? We should be honest about it and admit that, until we have accumulated and analyzed sufficient evidence to guide us in our decisions, we are indeed assigning inmates randomly or—even worse, when we are misdirected by well-meaning but uniformed decision-makers—haphazardly. Leslie Wilkins has stated the issue well in his definition of the correctional treatment process.

We may say that treatment consists of those operations which are intended to benefit the offender through the reduction of the probability that he will offend again and can be shown to have such an effect. In other words, until it can be established that the operation concerned has the consequence of reducing the probability of recidivism, this operation should not be classified as treatment, and we may not know what it is. It may be punishment. . . . What is done may or may not be functional for society as a whole.[8]

Until we are able to show, by using correctional research, that a special program *is* more or less effective than programs currently in operation, we should not say that any new alternative is producing better or worse inmates or is unfair to some.

Either-Or Results

The fifth misconception is that when a research design is used to evaluate a program, the finding is either success or failure—there is no middle ground.

A program may be successful for inmates with certain characteristics or under particular circumstances; it need not be a success for all inmates. We may, for example, be concerned with determining the types of inmates most influenced by a specific program, and the circumstances under which it has the most impact. Does it affect the young inmates more than the older ones? Does it have a greater

---

[7] Gilbert Geis, "Ethical and Legal Issues in Experimentation with Offender Populations," in U.S. Joint Commission, *op. cit. supra* note 3, p. 34.

[8] Wilkins, *op. cit. supra* note 5, p. 19.

impact on inmates who began the program somewhat retarded academically? Does it work better for first offenders than for recidivists?

An adequate research design can help us obtain answers to these sorts of questions. An additional advantage is that a good research design can help us understand some of the dynamics involved in the "failure" of a program. In the preliminary evaluation of a new program, we would likely call it a "failure" if the success rate for the experimental group was no greater than that of the control group. Upon further analysis, however, when we examine the experimental program for differences in success rates between property offenders and personal offenders, for example, we may find that it is a total failure for the former, who actually do much worse than those who are not in the program. At the same time, we may find that personal offenders in the program do much better than inmates who are not in the program. If only overall comparisons are made, clues to situations that are significantly favorable or unfavorable may be concealed; no difference between the two groups would be shown when in reality there might be some very significant differences that would be extremely important to administrators trying to select the proper inmates for the program.

Growth of Correctional Knowledge

The sixth misconception is that correctional knowledge advances in leaps and bounds as a result of major breakthroughs.

Most of the information obtained in any field usually builds upon past knowledge. What we know about a topic grows by slow accretion, not by dramatic discovery through a sudden flash of insight.

Most valuable research is the result of hard work, not the result of a cat (black or otherwise) knocking over a laboratory milk bottle or a similar coincidence. . . . We are, as it were, trying to find stepping stones through the slough of our ignorance, and we cannot take any "great leap forward" from an insecure foothold.[9]

This is not to deny that many ideas and theories have been spawned as a result of brilliant intuitions and serendipitous discoveries, but they are the exceptions, not the rule. For the most part, valid correctional knowledge is obtained by a slow and laborious process in which we apply the scientific method to a problem in an attempt to build a sound base of information. Academicians should not become discouraged and practitioners should not become impatient when the process takes more time and demands more effort than was anticipated. Short of divine revelation, it is the only method we have for enriching correctional knowledge.

Cost of Research

The seventh misconception is that research "costs too much."
The frequently heard statement that "We can't afford good research" should

[9] *Id.,* p. 33.

be completely reversed: we should be saying that we can't afford *not* to have good research in correction. True, good research is expensive; true, starting a program without an evaluation component costs less than one with it—in money, time, and energy—but only in the short run. If we have a long-range plan for the future of a correctional system, the money spent for research will probably prove to be our best investment. It can keep us from wasting money, time and energy on programs that are not achieving the goals of the system.

One rational approach to establishing a new program that includes a research component is to set a trial period limit; after evaluation at the end of that time, we will have a valid basis for continuing, expanding, modifying, or eliminating the program. If we eliminate it we can start a new program, similarly for a trial period, and evaluate it in the same manner.

We should conserve funds by dropping our substantially modifying specific correctional programs which do not appear effective based on research findings. We should expand more aggressively into programs which seem to be most productive based on research findings.[10]

MISUSE OF STATISTICS.   Many fields frequently misuse statistics, and correction is no exception. This portion of the paper deals with some misuses of elementary statistical tools in annual reports, in research projects, and in everyday communication.[11]

The "Average" Inmate

We frequently encounter statements about the "average inmate." What, or who, is an average inmate? When we say that the average inmate "is in the correctional system for the crime of burglary," or "has an IQ of 92," or "has a 2½-year-sentence," what do these statements mean? The word "average" is used rather carelessly at times when we refer to the characteristics of inmates. Part of the problem is that the term can refer to three entirely different statistical measures.

When we say that the average inmate is in the correctional system for the crime of burglary, we are probably using the "mode" as our measure: what we have in mind is that there are more inmates in the correctional system for the crime of burglary than for any other crime. That does not necessarily signify, however, that a majority of the inmates are in the system for burglary.

When we say that the average inmate has an IQ of 92, we are probably talking about an arithmetic "mean." This type of average is derived by dividing the number of inmates in the system into the total of IQ scores for all inmates in the system. This is the more typical form of average that we use.

When we say that the average inmate has a 2½-year sentence, we are probably

---

[10] California Youth and Adult Corrections Agency, *op. cit. supra* note 1, p. 71.

[11] Several of the ideas in this section are adapted from Darrel Huff, *How to Lie with Statistics* (New York: W. W. Norton, 1954). See also Travis Hirschi and Hanan C. Selvin, *Delinquency Research: An Appraisal of Analytic Methods* (New York: Free Press, 1967).

using the "median," which is the score we obtain when we count down into an array of scores and select the one that is exactly in the middle of the distribution.

Obviously it makes a lot of difference whether one or another of these "average" figures is used by the researcher or administrator in describing his population, and it is incumbent upon him to indicate clearly which one he is using. It is also incumbent upon him to use the average that will best describe his population. When the scores are vastly different from one another, he should cite all three figures so that the reader can decide for himself which score best represents the population.

The use of an unspecified score creates a tendency to confuse "average" with "normal" or even "desirable"; not uncommonly, "average" behavior is identified as normal behavior or the most desirable form of behavior.

The term "average" can also be misleading when we try to predict individual behavior through certain instruments successful in predicting group behavior. We can predict perhaps that 75 per cent of the persons in a group having a particular characteristic will respond in a particular manner under a given set of circumstances. What the group instrument cannot determine, however, is who will be in the 75 percent category and who will be in the 25 per cent category.

Samples in Research

If we wish to evaluate a particular program, we can place five inmates in the experimental group and another five in a control group. One of three outcomes is possible: the experimental group may do (1) better than, (2) worse than, or (3) the same as the control group.

If, however, we are unscrupulous, we can produce custom-made results (providing that our procedure is not examined closely) to prove whatever we want to —for example, that inmates in our program do better than inmates not in it. We would place one hundred inmates in the program, divide them into twenty groups of five each, and then compare them with a control group of five inmates. We would very likely find that some of these twenty groups differ significantly from the control group in the desired direction. We then simply throw into the wastebasket all results from those groups that did worse than or no better than the control group, retaining the "the sample" only those groups that show a significant change in the predicted (desired) direction to argue for the success of our program. Probability theory tells us that at least one out of the twenty groups studied should have had the "predicted" outcome simply as a result of chance. We select this one "study," conveniently forget about the nineteen others studies, and fail to mention the number of inmates in those studies. Obviously this is a violation of scientific ethics. The only way we can really be safe in making assumptions about the success of a program is to use a large sample and show that the results are the same in a significant number of studies.

In any scientific endeavor, research findings are based rigorously on a statement of probability. When we say something is true, we are really saying it is true within a certain range of probability. When we say that a particular program is successful, we mean that only one time out of one hundred, or perhaps one time out of twenty, would we find chance factors responsible for the same results we found in our study.[12] But it is always possible that the one study we conduct *is* the "one out of one hundred" that was produced by chance. This is why we need several studies of the same phenomenon before we can be certain of our results, Science is never exact. It always works within a range of probabilities.

"Availability" of Programs

Annual reports of correctional systems often include statements such as "Education is available to three-fourths of our inmates." Aside from the quite different effect obtained if, instead, the remaining fraction is emphasized—"Education is *not* available to one-fourth of our inmates"—the statement is obscure. Does it mean that three-fourths of the inmates are actively participating in educational programs? Does it mean that three-fourths of the inmates are in classification categories eligible for an educational program? Does it mean that three-fourths of the inmates are in institutions which have educational programs? Or does it mean that three-fourths of the inmates are in institutions which allow them to go out and participate in educational programs in the community? This type of statement is meaningless and, what is worse, misleading.

Correlation and Causation

Does the association of two characteristics mean that one has caused the other? Suppose we find that persons who have gone through a particular program have a higher success rate than those who have not: Is the program the "cause" of the higher success rate? The answer, obviously, is that it may, or may *not*, be. That one characteristic caused another is one possibility; there are three other possibilities:

1. The relationship may be a chance correlation—that is, two things occur together simply coincidentally. As mentioned earlier, the probability that a given occurrence can happen by chance alone is one out of twenty. The social sciences are replete with nonsensical chance correlations.

2. Perhaps the causal relationship should be reversed; in other words, it is not participation in the program that causes success but success that causes participation in the program. In this particular case the latter interpretation is not very realistic because the successful adjustment came *after* the program and therefore could not possibly have caused the program. In many cases, however, the chronology is not so clear-cut: what came first is not so obvious. For example, does a particular type of personality "cause" delinquency, or does being a delinquent "cause" a particular type of personality to develop?

3. It is possible that neither of the characteristics causes the other to occur.

---

[12] For a good discussion of probability theory see Solomon Diamond, *The World of Probability* (New York: Basic Books, 1964).

It may not be the program that causes the participant to have a higher success rate, and obviously it is not the higher success rate that causes the participants to be in the program. Instead, a good selection process for the program draws the best candidates; thus, a third variable causes both of the characteristics and leads to the higher rate of success.

The confusion over recidivism figures is directly related to this blurring of causation. If a parole department, for example, says it has a 90 per cent success rate while inmates released at expiration of sentence have only a 40 per cent success rate, what do these figures mean? They do *not* indicate that parole is more successful than release at expiration; they may indicate merely that the parole board is successful in *selecting* for parole those persons who are likely to have a lower recidivism rate. And they also indicate that the selection criteria are probably too rigid because the success rate is *too* high; in short, the criteria are excluding from parole many persons who could profit form this experience.

The same criticism applies to probation departments and institutional correction at both the adult and juvenile levels. Whenever the success rate for a program becomes exceedingly high, we should make a critical examination of our selection criteria and determine whether this procedure is excluding many individuals who could profit from the program. A higher success rate is not *always* a good sign.

VALIDITY OF RESEARCH FINDINGS.   If you're about to say now that statistics can't be trusted and that Disraeli was right[13]—don't. The statistics are valid; it's some of the people who use them that we can't trust. But how are the practitioners and administrators to know when research findings are valid? Whom can you trust?

The easy answer is to say: Learn more about research and statistics. But we can't all be researchers and statisticians. A better approach is to ask yourself several questions when you come across some interesting statement or finding:

1. *Identify*—What are the credentials of the person uttering the statement? Is he qualified by training and experience to make the statement? Is he affiliated with a reputable organization?

2. *Vested interests in the findings.*—Does he have something to gain or to lose by obtaining a particular finding? Does he have a job that is dependent on the success of the program?

3. *Misconceptions and misuses of statistics.*—What are the data on which the findings are based? How was the sample obtained? How large is the sample? Are valid comparisons made between people in a program and those not in the program? Are other possible explanations for the findings considered and eliminated?

You do not need to know very much about research methods to ask yourself these questions. If you can answer them and other related questions favorably, you can place considerable confidence in the findings.

---

[13] "There are three kinds of lies: lies, damned lies, and statistics." As cited in Huff, *op. cit. supra* note 11.

50

The Problem of Overlap in Experience Table Construction

LESLIE T. WILKINS

Every individual makes predictions of the likely behavior of those other individuals with whom he comes into contact. Without such predictions life would be impossible. Some persons may be more inclined than others to "do their own thing"—that is, they may be more eccentric—but, nonetheless, much common behavior is predictable within varying limits. In ordinary life we use our general experience to make statements about the likely behavior of others. In business we may use statistical tables or actuarial estimates of probabilities based on certain mathematical assumptions. Some of the methods which have a basis in the calculus of probabilities have been worked out for certain behaviors of offenders. It is in relation to these methods that some peculiar results have been recently observed. It seems that the reasons for these results may be traced back to factors in the operational aspects of the criminal justice system.

Let us try to discuss these rather indigestible statistical problems with some light-hearted examples. Suppose you had a "computer date." You had asked to be put in touch with a girl (we will not specify age) of below average height. You

SOURCE National Council on Crime and Delinquency, Parole Decision-Making Series, Supplemental Report Three, Davis, California, 1973, pp. 1–18 (mimeo.) Reprinted with permission of the National Council on Crime and Delinquency.

might think it wiser to specify "below average height" rather than "below average weight," since you hope to be friendly when you meet! You will, of course, realize that height and weight tend to go together (positively correlated), and although you may be unlucky and get a girl who is both short and heavy, this is a risk you may have decided to take. Whether this is a wise decision or not we may at this stage leave to the imagination. (How much time are you prepared to waste either in obtaining more data or in meeting dates who turn out unsuitable?)

But to continue our specification, which we are attributing to you, let us say that you add "dark, black hair; straight, small nose; mild manners." Let us suppose that the computer dating service says that it has found a girl who fits this specification.

Now consider that you are to meet her at either Tokyo or Stockholm airport! You will appreciate that at Tokyo almost every girl (having left age unspecified) who steps from an aircraft has dark, black hair, and so on; and you would have great difficulty in finding your friend without some other details. Alternatively, suppose you prefer blondes, tall, with fine figures; you would have no difficulty in identifying your friend at Tokyo, whereas in Stockholm the situation would be very different.

The point of this is, of course, to make it obvious that information in one setting is useless as a means of discrimination, while in another setting the same information is quite useful and may well isolate a particular individual from the mass of others. In this example we have used Tokyo and Stockholm locations, but the same thing would apply if the location were in the form of another item of information. It is a feature of the addition of items of information that when we have any one item—say, the first item whatever it might be—we are usually able to make a better than chance guess as to what the second item might be. In terms of our girls, the specification of "black hair" makes it almost unnecessary to specify "dark eyes"; and, similarly, the specification of "blonde" makes it almost certain that we shall meet a blue-eyed girl. If we have strong feelings about the eye color and we object to blue eyes while preferring blondes, we are going to be a little difficult to satisfy!

We see that, given one piece of information, another piece of information *in addition* to that we already possess has a different value from that which it has when it stands alone. This is a case of one and one not making two, except in a few situations where the first and second items of information are uncorrelated. There is, however, one further point which we may identify in our example— namely, that the value of the information can be tested only by reference to some utility. It was assumed that we wanted to identify the girl and to meet her at an airport. If we had had other intentions, equally honorable, of course, the value of the information would have been differently assessed. Thus, we can claim that whether a particular item of data is or is not "information" depends upon how well it assists us in arriving at a rational decision. Or, more generally, as mathematicians are apt to say, information is that which reduces uncertainty. An item —or an addition of an item—which does not reduce or reduce further, our uncertainty is not information. What may be information regarding the likelihood of recidivism may or may not be information about amenability to a form of training. Whatever may reduce your uncertainity with respect to the identification of the girl may or may not reduce your uncertainty as to whether you might marry her at some time. Thus, there is no general "information" in this meaning of the term. To put the case within our own particular framework, it may be information for the policeman concerned with identification that a suspect has "blue eyes," but it is not information for the judge who is considering sentence. Now, clearly, we can assess our uncertainty only about one thing at a time; and, hence, we can only assess the power of information with respect to one thing at a time.

We now have two requirements which we can state about information when we are concerned with more than one item singly, and with respect only to one external activity, namely: (1) to qualify as "information" data must reduce uncertainty and (2) the reduction of uncertainty can relate only to one factor at a a time.

Now it may seem obvious that so long as the information we consider is "relevant to the decision," the more of it we can consider, the better should be the decision. But it is not so simple as that. Any item of information (in the lay meaning of the term) may be highly relevant when it stands on its own—that is to say, it is correlated with the criterion. But the same information item may not remain significant when taken into consideration with other items because anything we may have learned about the criterion may already have been covered by the item or items already considered.

From the argument we have stated so far, we may have proved our previous claim—that, when adding items of information, one and one do not make two. If this is so, then we need some other convention for addition which will assist us in the use of cumulative information because we want to make the best use of all that we might know. Statisticians have developed methods for this form of addition.

It is possible to examine a large body of data and find the one piece of information which on its own is the most useful in predicting a paticular criterion. This would be that item which was most highly correlated with the criterion. Clearly we can select only one criterion at a time because the item which is most highly correlated with one criterion may not be that which is most highly correlated with another criterion. When we have identified the most powerful item of information, we can search the field of information for another item which, *given the first item,* is *then* most highly correlated with the criterion. It is, of course, necessary to find a means for taking out of the reckoning the power of the first item before we add the second or even attempt to assess its contribution to the prediction of the criterion. This is usually termed the problem of "overlap." If two items of information are highly correlated with each other, then, when we have taken the first into consderation, the second will have lost almost all of its power. In the same way we can go along searching for a third item which, in the presence of the previous two items, adds something new to our ability to predict the criterion. It is not usually long before it becomes very difficult to find items which, *in the presence of those already included,* add anything new to the prediction. The process described is, of course, known as "step-wise regression."

Step-wise regression is one of a family of similar techniques for combining information. All of these methods require an external criterion. That is to say, the information about the individual is divided into two distinct parts, one being the collection of information about him which is used in order to make statements about the other one single item, namely, the "external" criterion (e.g., reconviction, return to prison, or other mesurement or classification). But there is a different family of techniques which do not begin with the idea of using a body of information to make statements or predictions about an event, classification, or measurement external to the information so used. These methods ask only about the differences between persons or information where it is treated as all alike and not separated into two parts (information and criterion sets).

If we have a large collection of information, it is possible to ask how it may be divided up. It can be divided up in terms of two different considerations. We may say that we require similar information to be put together or that we require *similar persons* to be put together. In these methods we use the data to determine its own subdivision according to certain rules. This family of methods is usually known as "taxonomic analysis." Again, there are several ways in which the mathematical methods may be applied; and, again, they have a similarity. Instead of examining the body of information in the light of the question, which item is most powerful in prediction of the criterion, we examine the data and ask either (a) which person, in the light of the information about himself and all other persons, is the *most unlike* all others (a sort of leader of the opposition!); or (b) which information, in the light of *all* the information, separates the set into parts with the greatest efficiency. If we follow (a) once we have identified the person who is "most different" from all others, we may set him aside and search the remaining persons "set" for persons who are more like him than others. We then "transfer," as it were, the identified individuals until such a time as the differences *between* the groups are maximized and the difference within the groups are minimized. A similar procedure can be used for items of information.

When the "taxonomic analysis" is completed (without reference to the criterion of reconviction or other such measure), we may examine the different classes of persons identified either by the "person" subdivision or the "information" subdivision to see how well the method discriminates an external criterion such as those who become recidivists from those who do not. At this stage in this project, this is the matter of concern.

Perhaps these methods seem sophisticated and reasonable. Certainly, statisticians have advocated methods of these kinds; and the power of the methods has been demonstrated in many fields of operational research, business, and economic analysis. The argument is convincing both in theory and by example that these methods must be superior to the simple allocation of weights without reference to any of the statistical theory of regression or taxonomy. But convincing as is the theory and sound as are the examples from other fields of application, the fact remains that in the field of criminological predicition these methods do not work too well. We must, of course, define what we mean by "working well," but perhaps this may be deferred for a moment while we look at some cruder methods of adding information together.

There is a time-honored system of adding information used in the marking of examination papers. Each question assessed as correct is given a mark of one point, and the "score" is the simple sum of the number of correct answers. another system assesses some questions as more difficult than others and gives weights according to the difficulty which is believed to attach to the questions.

One of the earliest, if not the first, prediction table for the use of parole boards was constructed by Burgess. He used the simple weighting system, giving one point for each item of information about an offender which was associated with later success and one point with a negative sign attached for each item which was negatively associated with success. Items which did not show any correlation with later success or failure were omitted. This is called the "Burgess system" of weighting. It is, without doubt, the simplest possible system of adding information. It makes no allowance for the overlap factor.

Another name associated with parole and other criminological prediction table construction is that of the husband and wife team, Sheldon and Eleanor Glueck. Their method of weighting was to consider the percentage differences between the successes and the failures and to give weights accordingly. Again, there was no consideration of the overlap between items of information.

Both the Burgess system of weighting information and the Glueck system may be used for any number of items of informtion. However, while Burgess used a large number of items, the Gluecks tried to make the best "prediction" possible with as few items as possible. There is no statistical theory to support either the Glueck or the Burgess system of weighting. It may, however, be expected intuitively that the Burgess system, if used with a large number of items, would be less likely to be in error than that of the Gluecks with a small number of items and with large weightings given to some two or three facts or assessments.

Prediction tables are constructed by the use of experience of the past. Any method of weighting of information, for the purpose of testing methods for its addition, can be constructed only upon the basis of data from a sample. The sample which is used for "construction" of the tables is, not surprisingly, called "the construction sample." Whether the tables work for the construction sample or not is unimportant to those who wish to use them for the future. Of course, it is unlikely that a good table could be constructed without its fitting the construction sample; but the test of the table is not how well it fits *the data upon which it is based* but rather how it fits other (i.e., future) data. This would seem to be an obvious fact of considerable simplicity.

Testing the tables on other samples is known as "validation," and the samples upon which it is so tested are termed "validation samples." It might seem surprising that very few prediction tables have been tested on validation samples, but such is the case. Where there are exceptions, of course, it has been noted that the power to predict success or failure on the basis of information (added together by any means preferred by the constructors of the tables) is considerably less for the validation sample than it is for the construction sample.

The difference between the power to separate successes from failures (or any other external criterion) in the construction and in the validation sample is termed "shrinkage." Since hindsight is always more correct than foresight, the power of prediction is always some degree smaller in the validation sample. Correlations between the "scores" (calculated for individuals by the addition of items of information about them) and the criterion are used as measures of the power of the tables, and the differences between the correlations measure the shrinkage. Despite the fact that everybody must have expected shrinkage to take place between construction and utilization or validation, very few of those who have built "prediction tables" have actually tested them in any prediction situation. Moreover, it is only within the last year or two that studies have appeared which have tested the degree of shrinkage which occurs with different methods of building tables. Statisticians have, it seems, been convinced by the theoretical support for the principles of optimal estimation, while others were not concerned with statistical sophistication and did the best they could with rather simple and intuitively satisfying procedures.

From studies in different countries and with very different sets of data derived from various sectors of the correctional processes, there are now sufficient data to make it clear that, when tested against the hard reality of utilization in a prediction situation, the most efficient statistical methods suffer considerable shrinkage. Often the shrinkage is greater for the more "powerful" methods than for the simple methods of addition, such as that employed by Burgess nearly half a century ago. The several studies which have been published, together with our own data in the present project, may be summarized as follows: the more powerful and efficient the statistical procedures for the addition of information into a prediction score, the better the score fits the "construction" sample; however, when a variety of possible methods are used on one set of data and tested on validation samples, the less powerful methods shrink less and may (indeed, usually do) end up in practice better than the sophisticated techniques.

It was in the light of these results that it was decided to prepare for the use by federal parole board under this project a broadly-based experience table, where the addition of items of information was carried out by means of the simple Burgess weighting system.[1]

There is no doubt that the simple methods have been shown to be trustworthy, while the complex methods of weighting have not. There can be no doubt, too, that the statistical theory is correct. These two statements seem to be in direct conflict. It must be remembered, however, that the statistical theory is based on

[1] Wilkins, L. T., Gottfredson, D. M., Hoffman, P. B., Pasela, G. E., and Brown, W. H., *Development of Experience Tables: Some Comparative Methods, Report Number Twelve,* Davis, California: Parole Decision-Making Project, National Council on Crime and Delinquency Research Center, June, 1973.

assumptions about the basic data upon which the calculations are made. The phenomenon observed, which may be summarized as "inefficient statistics are best," is true only in respect of data which do not satisfy the assumptions which are made in statistical theory. The peculiar finding does not suggest that there are factors concerning *offenders* (about whom data are collected) which give rise to this odd result, rather the nature of the data *as they are collected, recorded, and classified* must provide the clue. Statistical efficiency assumes quality data, and this assumption is not satisfied with respect to the information recorded regarding offenders in the penal system.

Any major advance in the development of prediction methods—and all those other techniques which could be marshalled by research workers through modern technology—must await better quality data. Data of the kind necessary can only be obtained of they are honest at source, carefully recorded, and efficiently transmitted throughout the processes concerned. It is interesting to note that a very considerable amount of money is spent on auditing accounts—even down to trivial detail; but statistics, upon which equally important decisions are based, are subject to no audit or monitoring function. The recording of statistical information is often relegated to the lower levels of clerical worker, and those who would suffer serious pangs of conscience to enter a few pennies under the wrong heading in accounts feel quite free to "adjust" statistical data as seems reasonable to them.

Doubtless some persons concerned with the correctional management system will regard this finding as a blinding glimpse of the obvious. Everybody, it may be claimed, who is closely connected with the processing of offenders knows that the recording of information is not treated with any great respect; and that in some establishments the offenders themselves have some responsibility for some of the recording procedures. To arrive at this result the research workers, as usual, have gone the long way around and have introduced plenty of inconsequential theory! Perhaps the poor quality of the basic data is obvious to some persons, but those persons presumably use the information recorded or some of it to make their decisions regarding disposition of offenders, provisioning, or transportation and other questions. Therefore, it must be assumed that the quality of the information generally has been regarded as "good enough" for its purpose and that any investment of money to increase the quality of data was unjustified—which, as shown, is clearly not the case! As a temporary measure to accommodate poor quality data, we may apply poor quality methods to the utilization of it because this strategy provides a better result than that which we can obtain by the use of higher grade methods. There is some analogy with extraction of minerals: high quality ore is needed if powerful methods of extraction are to be used; poor quality ore can be used in rougher methods of extraction. But data are not natural products over which we have no control; data about offenders are generated within the criminal justice system. The criminal justice system is the "consumer" of these data; and the same system is concerned (or should be) with the quality of the product. The products generated out of data are decisions. Decisions cannot be better than the data upon which they are based, no matter what techniques of handling the data may be employed. The conflict of statistical theory with experience in the practical world of decision-making in criminal justice has revealed a fundamental problem of the quality of the raw material, and it has shown beyond all reasonable doubt that the quality of the basic information is not inconsequential.

51
Inefficient Statistics

LESLIE T. WILKINS

The problem of estimating the probability of recidivism of offenders by the use of data available at different points throughout the criminal justice process has been referred to many times in this series of reports. It has been noted that the "Burgess" system of providing "weights" has, thus far, proved more robust than more sophisticated methods, when the tables so calculated have been applied to samples drawn later than those upon which the initial information was based.[1]

It has been shown that information recorded about offenders is not without error. There is a possibility that errors in the data-base (upon which prediction tables have been calculated) may be an explanation of the inefficiency of "efficient" statistics, and this has been explored to some degree. The results to date give some support to this.

It is clear, also, that those of us who have concerned ourselves with the building of prediction tables have not been as flexible in our thinking as we might. We have tended to use those few methods which we thought were "best" (being perhaps a little too easily convinced by theory), and we have not explored the several hundreds of possible combinations and permutations of methods which may be developed from the known mathematical models. While we should, perhaps, take the blame for being persuaded to look only at a few methods (and usually those which had been tried before in the field!), we must plead that money

SOURCE. National Council on Crime and Delinquency, Parole Decision-Making Series, Supplemental Report Six, Davis, California, 1973, pp. 1–36 (mimeo). Reprinted with permission of the National Council on Crime and Delinquency.

[1] Singer, Susan M., Gottfredson, D. M., *Development of a Data Base for Parole Decision-Making, Report Number One,* Davis, California: Parole Decision-Making Project, National Council on Crime and Delinquency Research Center, June, 1973.

for "merely playing" with different forms of equations has not been forthcoming to criminal justice research.

DO WE NEED EFFICIENT PREDICTION TABLES?

To ask whether efficient prediction tables are needed may seem like the beginning of a heresy, or a capitulation to those who have always claimed that decision-makers did not need any assistance of this kind. Heresy it may be, but capitulation it is not. If "prediction tables" are to be superseded, then they must be replaced by something which "does the job" better. The problem, of course, is in what is meant by "the job" and "better." Perhaps we should first clear up a few points of terminology. Without a doubt, regression equations and related techniques will always be required for appropriate purposes in research designs. When we have mentioned "prediction tables," we have had in mind more than the research utilization of estimates of probabilities and research operations with various forms of equations. Rather, we have had in mind the provision of "tables" which may be referred to by decision-makers. That is to say, the use of the provided estimates (of whatever form) is not seen as confined to the making of inferences in terms of research results, but in some decision by persons other than the research workers themselves. Statistical methods must be assessed in terms of appropriateness to the *research* questions. When we consider a *more general purpose* instrument in the form of a prediction table, a different question of utility arises. The provision of different kinds of instruments can be assessed only in terms of the user requirements, and the users of prediction tables are not primarily research workers. If different users are using an instrument, then, presumably it will have differing functions. If designers of prediction tables have shown some rigidity in their thinking about data and the means for adding it together, perhaps this rigidity has also infected their thinking about the kind of instruments which other kinds of users should find useful? We should examine our methodologies —which have been expanded very considerably in recent years—to see what we have in our tool kit that might be more appropriately developed to provide instruments of value to decision-makers in the criminal justice process. It has been said that if a man can make a better mouse trap then anyone else, a path will be beaten to his door. There is an implicit suggestion here that improvements are better than innovations! Perhaps we should not devote too much attention to "making better mouse traps"!

Whether we look for the construction of instruments which will satisfy different needs, or whether we look for different ways of providing for the needs which we believe (or believed!) were met by the provisions of prediction tables, it is still important to know where we stand about the problems of prediction. At the moment we do not have very firm ground upon which to stand; and we need firm ground from which to make any leap forward. So, before departing from the general area of prediction tables, let us consider the present state of the art or science.

Sequential methods have not been used in criminal prediction. This means that a large area of mathematical model building is still unexplored, even though it seemed highly attractive as a means for increasing the score utility and precision of prediction equations. There is, of course, still considerable hope that sequential methods might be developed. Perhaps as an interim measure, we should now also examine a related area which has not been explored in the criminal justice field, namely, the use of "dynamic coding." A few studies have shown that this method has considerable promise; but beyond that, the research workers have not been able to go. The difficulty has been that the kinds of projects which are concerned with the exploration of models do not commend themselves to fund granting agencies who find the level of abstraction too high and do not define this work as within their area of support. Perhaps a word or two might be appropriate at this stage to fill in some details of what is meant by "dynamic coding" and to note other possible improvements.

POSSIBLE IMPROVEMENTS IN PREDICTION TABLE BUILDING

Dynamic Coding

In coding data about offenders we have usually noted such things as, say, that he had previously served time on probation and that he had served a term in local jail. However, we have not coded the *sequence* of these events. Is a period in jail which *follows* a period on probation *the same thing* as a period on probation which *follows* a period in jail? Our methods of data handling have usually *assumed* that this is so. This is, of course, only one example of a sequence which is ignored in the usual forms of coding of data about offenders. If the data are not coded, the information is not included in the building of prediction equations. In addition to the sequence of "treatment" factors, it may be thought that the sequence of offenses is important. Is a person who reveals a "rake's progress" not different in some way from a person who seems to commit different types of crimes almost at random? There seems to be some probability of our picking up some previously unexplained variance by looking at the time factor and incorporating some aspects of sequence into the code for the information. Now, clearly, if we utilize sequence in respect of all items where sequence could be used, we are expending "degrees of freedom" at a fast rate. (It is doubtful at what rate!) However, the few studies which have looked at this kind of issue have found that there are "lines of aggregation" in terms of sequences.

Sequential Methods

Dynamic coding of data from the past is of similar form to the use of "sequential" factors. However, it is possible to look at sequences in a somewhat different way. It is possible to take the individual as "his own control" and to consider factors about him as variants of his prior behavior rather than, or in addition to, variants of behavior on the part of persons in general. Instead of the "norm" being that of the sample of offenders, the "norm" in this model is that of the individual person who deviates from his own "norm" from time to time and in different ways. This is usually termed "ipsative" scoring. Again, this kind of use of data has not been explored. We will look further into this method later (see pp. 13–19).

Nonclinical Orientation

In the usual coding of data for input to multiple regression analysis, we have sought quick and simple methods. The main reason for this strategy has been its relative economy in terms of computer programming time and the emphasis on quick, practical results, rather than development of mathematical models "in their own right." The basic data have been taken in most of their original form and coded into categories. The processed data has resembled closely the case files and the ways in which information has been considered by the clinical decision-maker. Indeed, much of our thinking about what now appear to be statistical problems has been conditioned by the clinical viewpoint. We have fallen into the cognitive bind in which others in the field have already become confined. It would have been possible from the start to take the statistical viewpoint and to reject any clinical reference bias. It may be that more power could have been achieved from the equations if this kind of approach had been taken. This must now be examined. Further, there is no need to stay with either approach; we can work for a while, with certain data, as though the clinical viewpoint did not exist, and later (with other data) we can take up again the clinical reference. The utility of any model is in terms of how well it works; it is not dependent upon the theory upon which it is based. Indeed, theory has a way of following successful demonstration, as well as sometimes leading it!

Multiple Coding and Free Scales

If we free ourselves from the clinical reference and the ways in which such a reference set relates to the ways in which we perceive classifications, we can substitute for clinical kinds of categories, categories which are determined by assumptions of probabilities. There is no reason to expect (unless we are tied to some theoretical framework) that the scales of variables will be monotonic. There is no essential ordering of the classifications except in terms of some theory. We loosely use the term "higher level occupations" for those which are highly regarded or are paid more or paid less frequently; but these are not necessarily the same kinds of scales, nor are the values necessarily positively correlated. If we were to classify occupations in terms of the concept of psychological stress, we would have a very different ordering from that which we might obtain if we had some other concept as our reference. Thus, the ordering of the input variables is usually determined in terms of some theory or preceptual set. There has been a tendency in the classification of input data for prediction tables to use those sets which are commonly found in the field of criminal justice, namely the sociological or psychological reference set. If the purpose of the building of "prediction tables" were to *test* psychological or sociological theory, this might be more appropriate than it is now. We are not proposing to *test* existing theory. We are using methods in relation to a decision framework where the criterion is not how right or wrong some particular theorist was, but how well the particular method of handling the data carries out some function. We can specify this function in terms of the behavior of offenders and of decision-makers in the criminal justice process. Our reference can be independent of constraints suggested by any theory of crime.

Constraints of some kind must, of course, be accepted. Indeed, the nature of the constraints in any model is a matter for research design, as in any other aspect of research methodology. But we may develop models which fit different forms of constraints and test each in turn against experience and observations of behavior. The reference used in such models may be that of statistical probability and decision theory. If this is accepted, we see that we can regard all variables for our purposes (including those which relate to measurements such as "intelligence" or other scales) as free from constraints as to the intervals or even the direction of the initially proposed scales. We may examine the relationships between various "cuts" in the continua with a view to estimation of the "odds" for such division being associated with recidivism or as relating to any other category which we wish to predict.

Stable Predictors

There is no particular reason to expect that items of information which accord with theory will be more stable over time or over groups in our association with criteria of interest to us than items for which there is no plausible theory. What constitutes plausible theory at this time is wholly or mainly derived from observations of the past. Many of the observations were based on biased samples and the observers were influenced to look for factors which fitted their prior theoretical reference set.

If items of information are to be used in prediction equations, these items should tend to be stable over time as well as resistant to variation due to coding errors or errors of observation and recording. It has generally been assumed that if the samples of individuals were drawn according to sound statistical procedures, the variance of the factors measured would fit statistical theory—the normal curve (Gaussian), the binomial distribution, the Poisson distribution, and the like could be assumed to apply. However, such assumptions may be expected to hold only where the population sampled is homogeneous with respect to time (or place). It is not reasonable to assume that incarcerated populations are so stable or homogeneous. It is known that prediction tables worked out for one sample do not work on other samples of different populations of offenders. In our case, while the California Base Expectancies worked well for the adult Federal offenders, the California Youth prediction tables did not work for the younger Federal offenders. Often there is no expectation that tables should "work" for different populations. However, we do expect the same prediction equations to hold for similar populations over time. While there are certain uses to which prediction tables can be put, even where they relate only to construction samples, it is usually assumed that what was "good" in the construction sample will be "good" in the validation sample and in other samples, i.e., neither the construction nor validation sample. Some criminologists have defined what they mean by a "cause" as that which remains a predictor at different periods of time and at different geographical locations. Ignoring such philosophical irrelevance, we can agree that items of information which continue to be predictive despite location and time differences are, in many ways, *to be preferred* to those which do not display this invariance. It has usually been assumed that statistical tests of significance provided a means for the sorting out of items which should withstand changes from those which might be more liable to vary. Thus, prediction tables have, conventionally, been built from items of information which have a high chi-squared, high correlation, or other such measure.

It is probable that items of information which, in one sample, show correlations with a criterion such that there is only a small probability that this was due to chance, should, in other independent samples, reveal a similarly significant correlation. However, it is probable that some of the variance between samples may be underestimated by the use of within sample variance. Estimates of variance are dependent upon the extent to which the data are normally distributed. It may be possible to obtain better measures for the probability of correlations to remain stable by use of "Monte Carlo" methods. In any event such methods would be worth exploration.

SOME NEW METHODS

Evolutionary Processes

The coding of the sequence of events in the case history, in addition to the nature of those events, we have termed "dynamic coding." We wish to reserve the term "sequential" for a different kind of operation. Our methods, so far as we are aware, and all other methods used in the criminal justice area, relate each individual to a general norm. We classify each individual in terms of the information we have about him and the general pattern of that information in the population of offenders studied. It is possible to describe as many norms as we may wish, and to describe individuals in terms of their conformity with, or departure from, these norms. It is, of course, expected that within different samples, there will be different norms. It is partly for this reason that we do not expect prediction tables constructed for one population (base for norms) to apply to another population (probably different norms).

It is possible to describe a person's body temperature in terms of some measure of magnitude of departure from 98.6° (the general population norm being taken as an arbitrary zero). It is also possible to describe a person's body temperature as now measured, as a departure of a certain magnitude from the reading when his temperature was *last* taken. Any arbitrary point of origin could be selected as the reference; such as, say, when a person is received into the Reception Center at the first medical examination. But one reading, taken at initial examination, does not usually provide any better basis for making statements about the individual's characteristics than the readings taken at any other time. If we are to use the *individual's* norms as the control (arbitrary zero) for our measurements, we need some "sample" of such readings. In a very interesting paper several years ago, G. P. Box suggested a statistical model and method which he termed "evolutionary processes." The method we now propose in relation to methods for prediction is essentially similar to this, except in regard to the nature of the construction of the data and the inferences to be drawn. Box noted that "nature," in order to "decide" how to evolve, had to make use of information, and that this information was obtained in the very process of evolution itself. He applied his model to the chemical industry. Information about the output of the product was obtained *in the course of production of the product,* and this information provided the basis for determining whether changes should be made in such variables as time or temperature. Certain values for such variables as time and temperature were held constant for sufficient time to generate information about output, then another set of values was chosen and similarly held constant while information was generated. The whole system was thus "hunting"[2] for an optimal output. With each iteration of the process, under stable conditions, it was closing in on the optimum value for all the variables in terms of the output. In our case the method would draw some analogy between personal development and evolutionary processes models. What happens when an individual departs from his "norm" for a particular variable and in any particular direction? If we can establish norms for individual persons, we can discuss departures from these norms by persons. Thus, we might take sufficient measures of a person's body temperature to establish that his norm was, say, 98.3° (there are apparently such persons who are quite healthy). A temperature of 98.6° would represent for such a person a departure in an upward direction, although, presumably, of insignificant magnitude. In a similar way, if it were possible to obtain the basic information; the changes in an offender's career; his reactions to "treatment"; and many other kinds of data could be analyzed in this form. The availability of computers makes it possible to contemplate the development of such methods. It means, of course, that almost as much computational effort will have to be put into one individual case as is currently put into a whole sample.

A new approach to *kinds* of data which may be useful is also called for. We are now interested in finding "stable correlates," and hence we look for *measures* which are also stable. We prefer to measure whatever we measure only once and to hope that that measure is not only correct for that time, but that it is sufficiently correct for the person for almost all time. If the sequential methods are to be put to best use, we shall have to look specifically for behaviors, measures or symptoms which we *expect to change,* and preferably to change frequently. If we can relate

---

[2] This term refers to cybernetic theory, not big game hunting!

the changes to theories, which in turn relate to decision-making, this will also suggest interesting developments.

If one of the factors in which penal treatment has an investment can be termed "the adjustment" of the offender, then it might be expected that changes which indicate a trend towards "adjustment" would be noticeable, and hence recordable and measurable. The sequential method would be appropriate as a method for interpreting these kinds of data. Whether sequential measures would best be keyed into "prediction" remains doubtful. The question is not one of the use of prediction methods, but rather the major question we must face is related to the nature of decisions and the value of kinds of data to decision-makers who are concerned with various kinds of tasks. There are kinds of decisions which are made frequently, and each decision-maker makes many such decisions. There are kinds of decisions which are made rarely by any one decision-maker, but frequently by people generally. And there are decisions which very few people ever have to make. The decision regarding what to order from the lunch menu, the decision to get married, and the decision of a king to go to war would typify each of these three broad classes. Most management decisions concern events which fall into the first class, and many decisions are made which have considerable similarity to other decisions. This is the class of decisions within which the decisions of parole board members falls. Each case is unique, but each case has considerable similarities with other cases, and many decisions are made by board members. It would be absurd to discuss the parole board's decision regarding the time to hold an offender in the same terms as though it were the decision to get married or to declare war! How much information and what type of information is useful for board members to have in making decisions *about defenders?* That is the central issue. This cannot be answered in ideal terms, but only in operationally relevent terms.

Let us consider the present "state of the art" of prediction; examine what improvements seem likely to be achieved if they are sought; test each case against the hard test of utility in respect to parole board decisions.

Better or Different?

A well-known mouse trap manufacturer may be expected when challenged regarding the efficiency of his product to claim that he could make a better mouse trap. It is hardly to be expected that he would recommend that the inquirer to go a dispenser of poisons. The authors of this and related reports are usually regarded as "mouse trap makers" (prediction/base expectancy/prior probabilities and variants thereof). We are inclined, therefore, to think that we could make better prediction tables. We have set down, thus far, some possible means which might work towards this end, namely:

    1. "Dynamic" coding of information: using sequence of events to a greater degree than has been done to date;

    2. Use of "probits" or "logits" and other related measures to assess individual items of information and their contribution to any summed information;

3. A search for "stable predictors," perhaps by the use of Monte Carlo methods, rather than a reliance on coefficients of variation and measures of significance as found in construction samples or in subdivisions of a sample (split-half);

4. Sequential, ipsative measures of change could be explored and a different form of instrument developed.

But do we need a better "mouse trap"? Or do we need a modified "mouse trap"? Have we thought of the best ways in which to deploy the prediction methods we already have? Should we consider predicting other factors or estimating other kinds of criteria? Is the major problem *how* to predict, or *what* to predict? Perhaps we could profitably devote some attention to rethinking what it is we should be predicting, if, indeed we should be predicting at all. We may make up equations which are more resistant to poor quality data by working with "noise"; we may produce equations which account for larger proportions of the variance in outcome, and so on; but are these the things which are most needed?

It may seem obvious that base expectancy tables are needed. We have shown in this series of reports that when parole board members are given estimates of the probability of reconviction, they reveal differences in their decisions about the cases concerned. Thus, it may seem the board "needs" such tables. However, we also know that if board members are asked to provide subjective estimates of the probabilities of reconviction, their decisions also vary.[3] There is some evidence that a significant part of the decision-making process is concerned with estimation of probabilities (or the related concept of degrees of belief).

Different Kinds of Prediction?

It is not possible to say by how much prediction could be improved if and when it becomes possible to examine the various suggestions made in the preceding paragraphs. It is reasonably certain that a fair degree of improvement could be expected. However, such improvements would require a sound data base. Let us assume that the data base can be repaired and that much more powerful prediction statements could be made, given the necessary investment. Would it be desirable to give such investment? Should the work concentrate on those forms of predictive statements which have been made (however poorly) in the past? Before the idea of prediction is dismissed, let us consider two variations of the present theme and ask about their possibile utility in parole decision-making.

Conditional Probability Statements

Instead of providing a general statement of the probability for an individual to be reconvicted (or other criteria), it would be possible (given adequate base data) to make estimates in conditional terms, such as the following examples:

[3] Hoffman, P. B., Gottfredson, D. M., Wilkins, L. T., Pasela, G. E., *The Operational Use of an Experience Table, Report Number Seven,* Davis, California: Parole Decision-Making Project, National Council on Crime and Delinquency Research Center, June, 1973.

$P\ r/a =$ if offender is released and goes to his old address, his chance of reconviction is x%.

$P\ r/m =$ if offender is released and goes into the Armed Forces, his chance of reconviction is y%.

and so on for $P\ r/\ .\ .\ .\ .\ .$ (the probability of r given a variety of other factors as assumed). It is unlikely that there will be sufficient data for many such statements to be made; however, it should be possible to consider some factors. Perhaps we could examine those items for which it was more important to be able to make these kinds of conditional statements. Of course, there must be experience of the particular conditions $(a)\ .\ .\ .\ .\ .\ (m)$; theoretical estimates relating to hypothetical considerations are outside the scope of this kind of analysis.

Predicting the "Predictors"

In addition to estimates of conditional probability and to some extent related to this method, it would be possible to consider the calculation of predictors for those factors which themselves predict reconviction. How many such predictions might be of utility cannot at this time be estimated. The factor predicted would, presumably, best be an item about which some action could be taken and which was reasonably strongly associated with criminal activity. Thus, for example, we know that "drunkenness" is a predictor of reconviction; we could examine the data to ascertain whether, and if so to what degree, drunkenness was "predictable" in terms of other factors, and how much of the variation was "unique" to this item of information.

It is obvious that at this point, if not well before, we have moved from an area of concern for the provision of instruments which can be used by decision-makers in individual cases in the course of their own decisions to research analysis to answer specific questions. It is equally obvious that multiple regression, discriminant function analysis, numerical taxonomies, partial differential equations, and many more related and unrelated methods can be used to investigate a large number of issues. However, investigation of issues is not the same as the *provision of instruments* to be used in decision processes. The work of administering a parole system is not the same as the work of research into parole aspects of criminal behavior. Research workers have tended to assume that those results which they found interesting and useful for purposes of research should also be found interesting and useful by others whose main concerns were with different aspects of social control. Early prediction workers assumed that the probability of reconviction was the rational basis for the parole decision. They could not understand why parole boards did not make use of the instruments they had provided. It is easy to fall into the trap (mouse trap?) of thinking that the provision of other forms and more powerful versions of prediction methods will provide the answers. It is necessary to devise a strategy of operations which divides the research effort from the operational effort in such a form that the two components can compliment each other. It may be important for research to be devoted to the construction of instruments which are not themselves used for research but are designed specifically for providing assistance to operational decision-makers. It may also be important for research to concentrate on specific problems. It is certainly inappropriate to assume that both kinds of tasks can be achieved by the same means.

Design and Use of Instruments Vs. Research Investigations?

There are interesting examples in the physical sciences of the relationship between the development of instruments (enabling and facilitating measurement) and "discoveries." Any analogous relationship which may be postulated to apply in the social science is of doubtful validity. The measurement of "intelligence" is the measurement of what intelligence tests measure and what they measure is not independent of the methods of construction and analysis. In some psychophysical methods the relationship is closer and the analogies hold reasonably well, but as we move towards the socio-psychological, the analogies with the measurement by "instruments" becomes extremely strained. In particular, attitude measurement is often no more than the construction of an intervening variable of undemonstrated utility. The research worker may construct means for measurement or devise other forms of comparison in order to consider the reasonableness of his inferences. The public decision-maker is not so much concerned with inferences from his observations as he is with how others will see his decision—will they (i.e., his public critics) regard them as reasonable, fair, expedient or unfair? In a word, the assessment of a public decision-maker is in terms of a *value* system, not a *rational* system. Whether a rational system is also moral is not a question which scientific methods can arbitrate.

If this line of reasoning is sound, then there is clearly a difference between "instruments" which satisfy a "scientific purpose" (whatever that may be), and an instrument which will prove useful to public decision-makers who are proposing to use it to facilitate individual decisions. It appears that the means whereby estimates of probability may be made (prediction tables) alone do not qualify as useful instruments in the latter category. It seems also to be clear that the improved prediction methods and the prediction of other factors as suggested earlier in this report are not of themselves sufficient to transform the prediction table into a generally useful instrument for parole decision-making. The point is that the parole decision is a complex decision. The prediction table provides a one-dimensional assessment—that is what it is designed to do. The parole board decision-maker is required by society to provide a "best" decision in terms of a balancing of several important considerations and to resolve these several dimensions into a one-dimensional answer. The one-dimensional answer is, of course, to be in terms of whether and when to release an offender from incarceration—the dimension is that of *time*. The one-dimensional estimate of probability is not sufficient in itself to transform into the one-dimensional (answer), time. How do we know this? This is no proof; indeed, we could take up a moral position which declared that probability *should be* the only factor to be transformed into time in the parole decision case. This is, of course, a claim to a value, and the question at issue is who has the right or duty to declare such values. If we can accept the authority of the church, the church through its officials would be expected to give guidance as to the moral relationship between a statement of probability and our rights or duties to other humans.

Scientists cannot avoid taking a moral position. Nonetheless, it is possible to utilize our methodologies to insulate our observations and inferences from any interaction between our values and our reasoning. Such insulation is, of course, never complete; social science research will usually reveal some value positions —the stronger where the methodology is weaker![4] If we are looking for expressions of *values* in regard to parole decisions, we can look to *parole boards*. It is clear that parole boards have not made the transformation from *probability* into *time;* this is another way of saying, as we did many pages earlier, that parole boards have not used prediction tables! They may well have been right in this! Moreover, the failure to use such tables has not, it seems, been only due to their lack of power since they have been shown to be more powerful than other means for estimation of probability.[5] In this study the very close cooperation between the research workers (methodologists) and the parole board (public policy interpreters) has enabled communication considerable depth. Each viewpoint has examined the other and attempted to translate what was seen into its own language. We have learned that the probability of reconviction is certainly one of the items of information or belief which is taken into account is determining the time an offender is to be held. It is not the only factor.

Of Models and Simulation

It is not necessary to reject the idea of prediction of reconviction (or other criteria); it is necessary to *go beyond* this concept and to furnish parole boards with *more complex* models of the decision process. (It does not follow that a model which takes into account more of the complexities of a situation is itself more complex to use!) Improved, expanded, and refined prediction methods will be *one component* of these models, but other components will also be necessary. One of these other components is the assessment of the seriousness of the offense for which the offender is serving his time in prison. Another consideration of parole board members is the behavior of the offender in the institution, perhaps, with somewhat more emphasis on recent violations of prison rules. This third item may be seen rather as a constraint than as a variable. Thus, we can now assemble together three items of information or estimates: (1) seriousness of offense; (2) probability of reconviction; (3) institutional adjustment. These can be related to time served or to be served. Another factor may be the probable seriousness of any recidivism. In some way this may be seen as (although difficult

---

[4] "Metfessel, M., and Lovel, C., "Recent Literature on Individual Correlates of Crime," *Psychological Bulletin,* 39: 133–164, 1942.

[5] Meehl, P. E., *Clinical Vs. Statistical Prediction,* Minneapolis: University of Minnesota Press, 1954.

to visualize as), a four-dimensional model of the decision process. It has been shown that a model of this kind may fit the present decision processes fairly closely. Perhaps further sophistication of models could increase the closeness of the "fit" of the model to the decision process.

It may be thought that this procedure of research is merely trying to find ways of replacing the human decision-maker by a formula. This is only partly true. The objective is to remove from the decision-maker some elements of his decision processes in order to permit his concentration upon other elements of the decision. Some elements of the decision can be simulated, and we can consider in what ways the simulation might be varied to accommodate more preferred values. If a decision-maker were prepared to specify the function $P \alpha T$ (probability proportional to time), he could be replaced by a prediction table. Thus, the decision as to whether a decision-maker can or cannot be replaced by an equation is *his* decision, or more precisely, *is determined by the nature and quality of his decisions.* A rational decision-maker would presumably desire that as much of his decision-making as possible should be "taken over" by mechanical means, since then he could develop more of his ability as a human person of greater complexity than the machine.

If, then, easy-to-operate complex models of decision processes can be developed, the decision-maker could first examine the decision suggested by the model. If he had reason to adjust the model *in terms of its parameters,* his modification could be an improved decision. However, if the decision-maker believes that his subjective estimate of the *the probability* of reconviction is more accurate than the objectively ascertained estimate of *that probability,* he is quite likely to be incorrect. If the human decision-maker disagrees with the implied *values* of the model, then he may well be correct. It will be necessary to sort out what types of work are best done by "models" and which activities must be the focus of human value assessments and human imagination and daring. At present we must (as it were) tell the computer *the values,* and we do not design computers to be either imaginative or daring! In even the ideal case, policy and ethics are human inputs, but these inputs may be more effectively applied to suggesting changes in "scales" than in attempts to fit in an individual case. Thus, if a model shows that seriousness, probability of reconviction and institutional misconduct are treated equally in a representational "map" of decisions, the human decision-makers may suggest that this implied policy is incorrect; that, say, institutional conduct should receive less consideration than the other two variables. Such decisions are related to *values,* and hence are essentially human decisions, and such kinds of decisions can *more effectively* be put into operation by the use of models than by attempts to deal with individual cases.

Moreover, we have noted that models are not restricted to general norms. The sequential methods open up a different kind of approach. The generalized norm models provide a different kind of "map" from those provided by ipsative scoring. The individual varies from time to time about his own norm, and his norm varies from the general norm of the population. There are, as it were, two sources of variance—within individual and between individuals. The variance between individuals has conventionally been utilized in social measurements, and the variance within individuals has conventionally been regarded as "error." Perhaps, an analogy for the kind of approach we now consider to be most worth developing in future research may be given. Maps of a given area often have insets of more detailed maps of particularly significant areas, such as the centers of cities. The detail is not required in the surrounding rural areas (except for a small and specialized group of users), and the provision of such detail would inhibit the utility of the maps for the general user. If all maps were of one-inch-to-the-mile detail, we should almost certainly have many more motorists lost! Perhaps there is a case for considering certain periods in an offender's career as requiring a "close up" of the trajectory at that point. Or, to stay with the previously used analogy, the larger scale maps may require "insets" for specific localities.

The significance of these considerations is that the provision of intruments for use by the decision-making body (in this case the United States Board of Parole) is seen as involving a different set of research operations from the undertaking of general research in relation to parole and the criminological field of inquiry. The provision of instruments to facilitate decisions must be able to reflect complex processes and to make clear the underlying value postulates upon which the models rely so that board decisions may be related to such policy or value considerations. Fact finding and other research operations should continue and feed into the model building so that the instruments which are provided are soundly based. The provision of "prediction instruments" as single dimension estimates of probability of reconviction is not the goal of "computer assisted decision-making," rather it is a section of work which is necessary *in order* to build models which are more closely related to the complex goals of parole and, of course, as a basic tool in research analysis.

Pure and Applied Research?

The kind of division proposed may seem like the common classification of research into "pure" and "applied." This is not exactly the case, rather it is a matter of the level of obstraction at which it is necessary to attempt solutions to problems which are equally "applied" or "relevant." It is clear that there is a need for fundamental research and that some of the questions which it may be appropriate for such kinds of research to address emerge from operations research. And operations research requires a very close cooperative effort between the research workers and the decision-makers at the level which has characterized this project. It may be that we are now beginning to see rather more clearly the roles which may be played by the *different forms of research strategies.* The present stage of this project provides some examples. In the current study it was noted that "inefficient statistical methods" for adding together items of information stood up better to "shrinkage" than the preferable "efficient" methods. This is a problem which will require "fundamental research" methods as, for example, in the addition of "noise" to basic data and the study of the effects on the behavior of forms of equations. The methods for the analysis of information search procedures (or types of decision-makers) may also take us into forms of research which require the application of methods usually classified as "fundamental research." (As an incidental point, information search strategies and many other related issues raised in these notes require the study of branching networks which fall within the area of "stochastic processes.")

We have, then, to consider a strategy of research and cooperation between fundamental and operational research on the one hand and, on the other, the development of operational instruments and their utilization. Of practical significance in the immediate future is the funding of such diverse kinds of research which could be integrated only in their field of application. Grant awarding agencies interested in crime control will not find it easy to justify funding a research into "branching networks," "stochastic processes" or "subjective probability"; and it is not clear what agencies would consider such a mixture of abstraction and application.

52
Research and Rehabilitation: The Conflict of Scientific and Treatment Roles in Corrections

JEROME RABOW

The contribution any rehabilitation program can make to a field of knowledge is determined not by impressionistic evidence that can be gathered in favor of the program but by scientifically adequate evidence that places the program within the context of a sound research design. By this means a program can be evaluated rigorously in comparison with other treatment approaches. Nevertheless, the urgent need for sound research in corrections has, as yet, not been met on any wide scale by social scientists. As Ohlin has pointed out "the creation of a realistic

SOURCE. *The Journal of Research in Crime and Delinquency,* 1, January 1964, pp. 67–79. Reprinted with the permission of the author and the National Council on Crime and Delinquency. Copyright 1964, National Council on Crime and Delinquency.

design for evaluative research would unquestionably do more to speed the development of a science of penology than any other single contribution."[1]

Although some factors, such as the difficulties involved in setting up controlled experiments in correctional facilities, are discussed in the literature,[2] some of the main reasons for the paucity of sound research are unarticulated. One important aspect of this lack of articulation is not intrinsic to the difficulties associated with setting up and describing well designed programs, but is inherent in an ideological gulf separating those persons responsible for treatment from those responsible for treatment evaluation.

This gulf, which has been described as an "age old split,"[3] has created many difficulties in corrections. In certain instances, historical arguments between professionals in the behavioral sciences have proved to be important for scientific advancement; members of opposing groups were willing or pressured to reexamine and revise concepts, assumptions and premises, and occasionally procedures. The arguments between treatment and research groups in corrections have not, as yet proved especially fruitful.

While both groups agree that knowledge about treatment is important, in practice, their disagreements seem to belie their common orientation. Perhaps this is because the disagreements are inherent in the present division of labor with respect to treatment. The treatment group focuses on *practical* problems of a "here and now" nature, while researchers are more concerned with the abstract problems of setting up research so that there might be some *ultimate* evaluation.

The resulting differences between the two have been akin to political debates in which the debaters tend not only to utilize different facts to support their points of view, but disagree with the interpretation of the facts which they have in common. Thus, typically, the clinician says, "Recidivism is not a good criterion of success because it overlooks those who are 'better adjusted' and whose offenses, therefore, are 'less serious'."[4] The researcher counters with, "You may be right, but what empirical evidence do you have that the success rate might not have been just as high for those who received no treatment whatsoever or perhaps received a different kind of treatment?"

This paper will focus on some of the sources of conflict between scientific and

[1] Lloyd E. Ohlin, *Sociology and the Field of Corrections*, New York: Russell Sage Foundation, 1956, p. 52.

[2] Joseph Zubin, "Design for the Evaluation of Therapy," *Psychiatric Treatment*, Baltimore: The Williams and Wilkins Co., 1953, XXXI, pp. 10–15: Eli A. Rubinstein and Morris B. Parloff, eds., *Research in Psychotherapy*, Washington, D.C.: American Psychological Association, 1959; Elizabeth Herzog, "Some Guide Lines for Evaluative Research," Washington, D.C.: U.S. Department of Health, Education, and Welfare, 1959, pp. 64–71.

[3] Benjamin Kotkov, Chapter 19, "Research," in *The Fields of Group Psychotherapy*, ed. by S. R. Slavson, New York: International Universities Press, Inc., pp. 316–317. Kotkov describes experimental contributions without emphasizing the dysfunctions of the division. Paul E. Meehl in *Clinical* v. *Statistical Prediction*, presents a precise but detailed examination of the more general conflict existing between clinicians and actuarialists, University of Minnesota Press, Minneapolis, 1959.

[4] Donald R. Cressey, "The Nature and Effectiveness of Correctional Techniques," *Law and Contemporary Problems*, Vol. 23 (Autumn, 1958), pp. 754–771.

treatment personnel as well as the dysfunctions created by those conflicts for the field of corrections. Specifically the researcher-evaluator role and the clinician-therapeutic role are under examination. It should however, become clear to the reader that the description of the problems described in this particular case study and the suggested solutions have a much broader application to the difficulties generated by contact of the practitioner, be he teacher, social worker, or administrator, with the researcher. The obvious similarities to other areas will be ignored and the focus will be upon the conflicts as they manifest themselves in the corrections field.

HISTORICAL PERSPECTIVE FOR THE SEPARATION

This ideological separation between clinician and researcher is part of the age old split between men of socially planned action and men whose lives are devoted to the abstract problem of cultivating and formulating knowledge.[5] The men of action have undertaken rehabilitation, educational training and settlement house work, all with the very practical problems of having to do something. Traditionally their idea has been that the effectiveness of the methods they used could be based upon common sense and testimony as to their efficacy.

This kind of humanitarian approach is obvious in many American correctional practices today. Any techniques which make the offender's life more comfortable or his surroundings more home-like are embraced and considered helpful. They are considered beneficial because they seek both to reduce deprivations resulting from impoverishment or incarceration and to produce the warm emotional environment of which many offenders were supposedly deprived in earlier years.

But, in addition to humanistic values, such treatment approaches also include many middle class values,[6] some residues of a punishment philosophy and an admixture of Freudian Psychology and social science information. From a researcher's point of view, this amalgam is an evaluative nightmare. The *potpourri* of humanistic and middle class values which form the foundations for many practices, because they have been viewed as absolutes, have not been subjected to evaluation. In a similar way many clinical practices are viewed as an art in which any evaluation must be intuitive and subjective[7] rather than empirical and objective.

As a consequence, treatment practices are accepted *a priori* and the men who

[5] Robert K. Merton, *Social Theory and Social Structure*, Glencoe: The Free Press, 1957, p. 209.

[6] Donald R. Cressey, "Limitations on Organization of Treatment in the Modern Prison," *Theoretical Studies in Social Organization of the Prison*, New York: Social Science Research Council (March, 1960), pp. 92–93.

[7] Reik contends that most insights and understanding in psycholnalysis spring from the therapist's and the patient's unconscious. Any attempts to categorize treatment in a "systematic, orderly, consistent" manner will result in drivel. Theodor Reik, *Listening With the Third Ear*, New York: Grove Press, Inc., 1948, pp. 440–441.

hold them tend to proceed with unbounded faith in what they are doing, apparently feeling that any problems are due to a failure to apply what is known rather than to evaluate that which is in progress. They are more concerned with pointing out the need for "professional treatment" than in defining the precise way in which such treatment is applied or is successful in changing people.

On the other hand, the traditional position of the evaluator might best be compared to that of an "unattached intellectual"[8]—an individual who has little commitment to the system he is examining: economic, emotional, or otherwise.

The researcher can continue to be adamant in abiding by his suggestions and findings since he is not intimately involved in translating them into action. Consequently he often fails to recognize the multifarious problems which must be borne by administrators and clinicians who are responsible for treatment.[9]

The traditional arguments and counter-arguments by both treaters and researchers have been latently functional in that they have served as ideologies which have given each group a sense of identity, meaning, and purpose. But the manifest functions for which each group supposedly exists, i.e., to improve and apply treatment successfully, has been lost in the effort of each to maintain its own vested interest. Any possibilities for treatment to be viewed as a dynamic and creative phenomenon has been stifled because latent functions have become ascendant. But just as the question of federal aid to education may not be *effectively* resolved by the clash between vested interests, the question of improved treatment likewise may not be effectively resolved on the merits of latent arguments designed to protect existing patterns.

Instead, the dysfunctions of these latent positions must be demonstrated, any virtues residing in them must be brought out, and new alternatives explored which might make possible an inventive approach to treatment. The remainder of the paper is devoted to this task.

SOME BASIC QUESTIONS AND A RESEARCH MODEL

Scientifically selected treatment and control groups are imperative for any realistic evaluation of treatment. Yet, only rarely have such groups been systematically compared. But to add complexity to an already difficult problem, it should be noted that a comparison of groups, whether on the basis of recidivism rates, personality tests, or other characteristics, is only one dimension of evaluation. In the absence of supporting information, significant statistical differences among groups do not necessarily justify attributing these differences to one treatment method or the other. In many cases differences might not be a direct function of treatment, but due to the effect of other variables which the statistical comparison does not reveal.

Before differences can be attributed to the utilization of a particular treatment

[8] Merton, *op. cit.*, p. 211
[9] *Ibid.*, pp. 218–219.

approach, evaluation would have to be seen as occurring in a series of stages in which answers to several important questions were available. The following are possible stages.

Stage I is concerned with the population of offenders from which treatment and control groups will be selected. Answers for such questions as the following are needed:

1. How is the population of offenders from which groups will be selected defined with respect to age, record of offenses, geographical location, or any social or personality characteristics thought to be important?
2. How is selection carried out in order to eliminate bias—by random means or some matching process?
3. When, and by whom is selection carried out? What are the mechanics?
4. What steps are taken to demonstrate the lack of bias in selection?

Stage II is concerned with the treatment process and the need to understand what is involved in it:

1. What is the theory of causation upon which treatment is proceeding?
2. What is the intervention strategy utilized in treatment by which the causation variables will be modified?
3. Can a logical relationship between causation variables and intervention strategy be demonstrated?
4. Can it be demonstrated that the treater is fulfilling role requirements specified by the intervention strategy?
5. Assuming that treatment role requirements are being fulfilled, can it be demonstrated that variables cited in the theory of causation are being modified?
6. How shall any change in the variables be measured?

Stage III involves the actual comparisons of groups subsequent to treatment and is concerned with such questions as:

1. What are the goals of treatment: that is, how shall success be defined—in terms of recidivism, attitudinal change, new social relationships, personality modification?
2. How is measurement of these characteristics carried out?
3. Over what period of time are comparisons to continue?
4. How is cooperation of subjects obtained?

Other Variables

In addition to the variables in each of these stages, there are others—race, class, marital status, job status, etc.—which can also affect treatment results. Because these variables are not a direct function of treatment, efforts must be taken to control them or they can result in misleading and unexplained differences.

Figure 1 sums up graphically the stages just described. It might be viewed as a research model highlighting the need for a systematic integration of research and treatment.

The necessity of having information for each stage of evaluation becomes

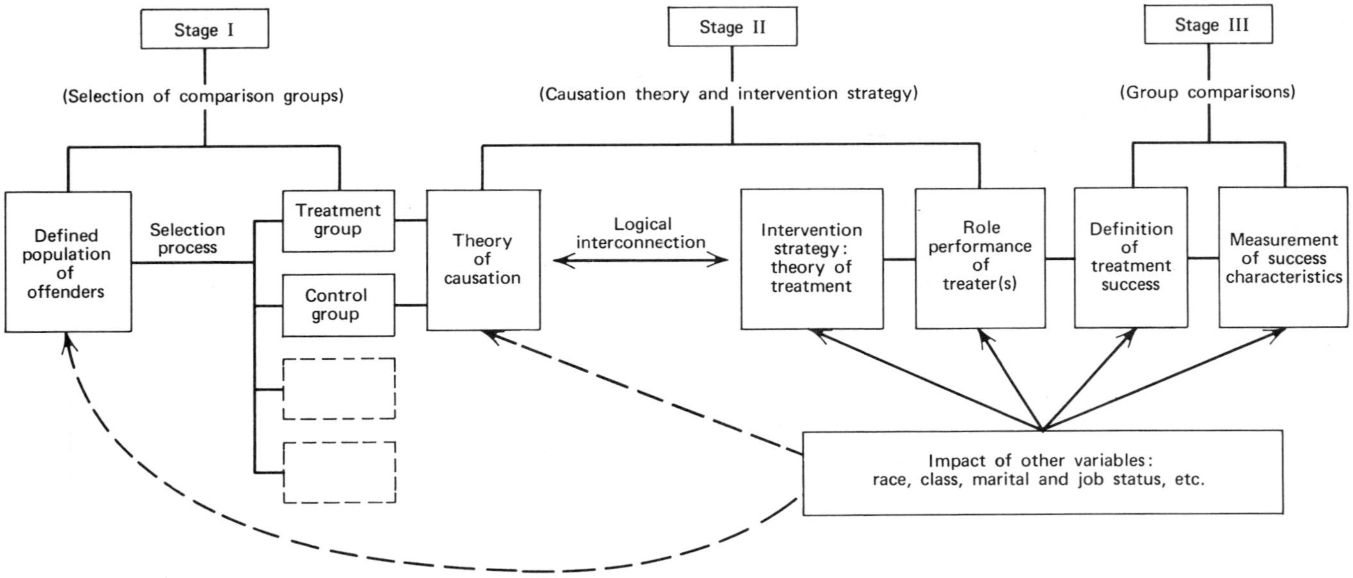

Stage I
(Selection of comparison groups)
Stage II
(Causation theory and intervention strategy)
Stage III
(Group comparisons)
Defined population of offenders
Selection process
Treatment group
Control group
Theory of causation
Logical interconnection
Intervention strategy: theory of treatment
Role performance of treater(s)
Definition of treatment success
Measurement of success characteristics
Impact of other variables: race, class, marital and job status, etc.

Figure 1

manifest when one considers a few of the ways in which it can affect the statistical comparisons. Suppose, for example, a statistical comparison of treatment and control groups reveals no differences among them. Without further knowledge it is difficult to assess such findings. But if a careful analysis of Stage II (causation theory and intervention techniques) indicates that the causation variables though most important were successfully altered, then it is possible that methods for selecting the groups were biased (Stage I) or that treatment has been concentrated on the wrong variables. In either case, one has better information on where to search for answers.

On the other hand, if the statistical comparison of groups revealed that there were significant differences in favor of the treatment group, and that causation variables were successfully altered, then it would be more reasonable to assume that causation and intervention theory had an important effect on rehabilitation —providing, of course, that other important variables such as race, marital status, etc., were controlled.

Finally, in a more complex way, suppose the analysis revealed that, although significant statistical differences occurred between groups, important causation variables were not actually altered. In attempting to discover what had caused the differences, one would have to investigate several problems: Was there bias in the method of selecting treatment and control groups (Stage I)? Is causation theory correct (Stage II)? Was the comparison carried out over a long enough period of time (Stage III)? Were outside variables sufficiently controlled?

Since answers to these questions form the foundation for knowledge about treatment programs, any examinations of the arguments between clinician and researcher should be analyzed in the light of them. In this way it might be possible to pinpoint present difficulties. It should be kept in mind, however, that this paper is not concerned with all of the difficulties which inhibit effective treatment and evaluation. It focuses instead upon the manner in which the bifurcation of treatment and research roles permits treatment to proceed without scientific validation.

DYSFUNCTIONS PERPETUATED BY THE TREATMENT GROUP

The Dearth of Research on Treatment Techniques

Most professionals in corrections, or otherwise, seem to feel that some evaluation of treatment methods is warranted, although, as Goode points out, the few evaluations of such techniques as psychotherapy that have been made do not meet "minimum canons of research design."[10] But most clinicians are either unwilling or unaware of the need to subject themselves and their techniques to the various stages of evaluation by which statistical comparisons can be made meaningful.

[10] William J. Goode, "The Profession: Reports and Opinions," *American Sociological Review*, 25 (Dec., 1960), p. 912.

One of the greatest obstructions is the tendency for existing treatment theories and methods to be accepted virtually on an *a priori* basis. For example, many people have assumed that since "the effectiveness of psychotherapy has long since been established,"[11] it can be applied effectively to the treatment of criminals. Yet *neither* assumption is empirically validated.[12]

The psychotherapist's role has seldom, if ever, been examined since many clinicians feel that research on it is superfluous. In their opinion all of the necessary rules of conduct in therapy are known.[13] Yet, most descriptions of the clinical role are derived from different schools of thought and are generalized rather than specific in nature.[14] Thus, the assumption that all therapists follow a recognized and shared treatment role is highly questionable and merits examination.

If the treatment role remains unarticulated and unevaluated, results such as those obtained in the Cambridge-Sommerville Study will continue to occur.[15] In that project, statistical comparisons revealed that the number of offenses for the treatment group was greater than those for the control group, while counselors felt that therapy was effective with two-thirds of the treatment group. This discrepancy highlights the importance of having information on the treatment procedure (Stage II). Counselors in that study had the opportunity before they

[11] Rubinstein and Parloff, *op. cit.*, p. 278. These authors do not assume the effectiveness of psychotherapy but mention those who do.

[12] Hans J. Eysenck, "The Effects of Psychotherapy: An Evaluation," *Journal of Consulting Psychology*, 16 (1952), pp. 319–324: Karl R. Schuessler and Donald R. Cressey, "Personality Characteristics of Criminals," *The American Journal of Sociology*, 55 (March, 1950), pp. 476–484; LaMay Adamson and H. Warren Dunham, "Clinical Treatment of Male Delinquents: A Case Study in Effort and Result," *American Sociological Review*, 21 (June, 1956), p. 320. Davidson goes so far as to suggest that the "psychiatric" approach does not work with delinquents. Henry A. Davidson, "The Semantics of Delinquency," *The Welfare Reporter*, New Jersey State Department of Institutes and Agencies, XI (July, 1960), p. 135.

[13] Hans-Lukas Tueber and Edwin Powers, "Evaluating Therapy in a Delinquency Prevention Program." *Psychiatric Treatment*, Baltimore: The Williams and Wilkins Co., XXXI (1953). p. 145.

[14] Gisela Konopka, "The Role of the Social Group Worker in the Psychiatric Setting," *American Journal of Orthopsychiatry*, 22 (1952), pp. 176–185; Rudolf Kaldeck, "Group Psychotherapy by Nurses and Attendants," *Diseases of the Nervous System*, 1950–1951, 12 (February, 1951), pp. 138–142; Margaret Hagan and Marion Kenworthy, "The Use of Psychodrama as A Training Device for Professional Group Workers in the Field of Human Relations," *Group Psychotherapy*, IV (April–August, 1951–1952), pp. 23–40; Henrietta T. Glatzer and Helen E. Durkin, "The Role of the Therapist in Group Relations Therapy," *The Nervous Child*, 4 (April, 1945), pp. 243–251; S.H. Foulkes and E.J. Anthony, *Group Psychotherapy: The Psycho-Analytic Approach*, Penguin Books (1957); Rudolph Ekstein and Robert S. Wallerstein, *The Teaching and Learning of Psychotherapy*, New York: Basic Books, Inc., 1958, *passim*: Robert G. Hinkley and Lydia Hermann, *Group Treatment in Psychotherapy: A Report of Experience*, Minneapolis: University of Minnesota Press (1951), *passim*. One recent exception is a publication by Henry L. Lennard and Arnold Bernstein, *The Anatomy of Psychotherapy*, New York: Columbia University Press, 1960, *passim*.

[15] Tueber and Powers, "Evaluating Therapy in a Delinquency Prevention Program," *op. cit.*, pp. 138–146. See also Edwin Powers and Helen Witmer, *An Experiment in the Prevention of Delinquency: The Cambridge-Somerville Youth Study*, New York: Columbia University Press (1951).

began treatment to define the "helping" role, to indicate their goals, and how they expected to achieve these goals. However, because they failed to do so, it is impossible to know what led to the results obtained: whether they were due to the theory of treatment utilized, the failure of counselors to fulfill roles derived from treatment theory, or to other variables. Thus, treatment, as the independent variable, cannot be taken for granted. It must be subjected to scrutiny.

Likewise, the way in which personality disorders might relate to criminality have not been empirically demonstrated.[16] Yet, treatment methods based upon the idea of their importance have flourished. Until it can be shown that there is a clear relationship between any transformed personality charcteristic and a lower recidivism rate, the theory must be subject to question. At present we have neither the evidence to accept or reject it.

The Treatment Potpourri

Another treatment problem contributing to research difficulties lies in the extent to which correctional facilities, as part of their general treatment programs, include a great variety of treatment practices. Each of these practices might be viewed as a separate treatment technique and evaluated as such. Yet, the entire host of procedures is also often considered as a single entity for which evaluation is asked. For example, Gersten describes how interview group therapy, directive and nondirective therapy, handicrafts, films, and psycho-drama were employed in a single treatment program. Although the program was judged successful by several criteria, it is difficult, if not impossible, to tell which specific techniques of the program contributed to its success.[17]

Before legitimate examination can be made of any total treatment program, steps must be taken by which to assess the merits of specific treatment practices in the total picture. Obviously this is a difficult task, but there are at least two principles whose adoption might maximize a solution to the conundrum of relative effectiveness.

First, treatment personnel might pay greater attention to the need for establishing logical integration among the treatment techniqes they utilized. The ideal would be to devise a treatment program around specific and logically integrated theories of causation and intervention. Only those techniques shown to have relevance would be included. A *potpourri* of unrelated activities could, and probably would, set up conflicting goals. For example, if one theorized that delinquency is primarily a peer group phenomenon, he might then want to test this theory by concentrating on techniques designed to change peer relationships. Attempts on his part to utilize individualized as well as group techniques, each of which is

[16] Schuessler and Cressey, *op. cit.*; see also Henry D. McKay, "Differential Association and Crime Prevention: Problems of Utilization," paper read at the annual meetings of the American Sociological Society, Chicago, September 2–5, 1959.

[17] Charles Gersten, "An Experimental Evaluation of Group Therapy for Juvenile Delinquents." *International Journal of Group Psychotherapy*, I (1951), pp. 18–33, pp. 318–331.

derivable from different intervention theories, could easily destroy his efforts to make a systematic evaluation of his causation and treatment theories.

The second principle would involve the integration into any program, means by which specific segments of that total program could be examined and evaluated with respect to their contribution to successful rehabilitation. Later evaluation of the total program as a single entity might then have greater meaning. The corollary, and ideal result, would be the development of a self-correcting system capable of discarding those techniques which are inadequate and promoting those which are of value.

Professional Canonization

Treatment personnel who have the practical problem of dealing daily with inmates cannot be expected, any more than the general medical practitioner, to create many new and revolutionary approaches to treatment. Nevertheless, the efforts of some schools of treatment to maintain their vested interests go beyond the necessity to train treatment personnel. Their efforts are dysfunctional for a scientific penology because they place an undue emphasis on the canonization of new inductees at the expense of determing the validity of their own treatment methods.

Current training procedures seldom emphasize skepticism and creativity as an approach to treatment, but instead concentrate upon the steps necessary for certification. Concern over the latent function of maintaining professional stature and prestige tends to outweigh the manifest need for improved treatment techniques. As a consequence, the treater role is circumscribed with a whole series of prerequisites which can be obtained only under the observation and supervision of those already canonized.[18]

It is difficult to take exception to the idea that treatment personnel should be well trained. But all too often the techniques, and the process of learning them, become ends in themselves. The resulting effect on the trainee is to provide him with an efficient set of blinders—blinders which enable him to misperceive or ignore programs whose rehabilitative efforts do not include techniques consistent with the standards which he has been taught to accept.

---

[18] These prerequisites emphasize personality characteristics as well as training. In some schools, personality requirements include: the therapist's ability to deal effectively with his own anxieties: to be comfortable with certain types of emotional behavior; (Morris B. Parloff, "Some Factors Affecting the Quality of Therapeutic Relationships," in *Group Psychotherapy,* ed. by William F. Hill, Utah State Hospital, Provo, 1961, pp. 179–187) and to have come from a background with a wide variety of personal experiences. (S. R. Slavson, "Qualifications in Training of Group Therapists," *Mental Hygiene,* XXXI (1947), pp. 386–391; Gisela Konopka, "Group Therapy; Knowledge and Skills of the Group Therapist," *American Journal of Ortho–Psychiatry,* XIX (1949), pp. 56–60). Training includes observation, practiced application, supervision and often stresses individual therapy for the candidate. Aichhorn stressed the later point in 1925. August Aichhorn *Wayward Youth,* New York: The Viking Press (1935). p. 9.

The Anxiety of Evaluation

The canonization of treatment personnel, and the institutionalization of treatment techniques, introduce problems of evaluation which are unrelated to the tremendous methodological difficulties involved. Besides clinicians, administrators and board members concentrate more upon lending credence to already accepted methods than to an objective, unbiased appraisal of the techniques used. This approach again is analogous to the debater who seeks mainly for evidence to support his previously accepted proposition rather than to the scientist who refrains from making any conclusion until he examines both sides of a question. The debater presents only those data which support his viewpoint and discards the remainder. The scientist must draw his conclusion from the total mass of data.

Because many people are committed to *particular* treatment approaches, any objective evaluation is viewed with anxiety. As a result, the evidence presented in favor of a program by treaters is usually anecdotal in which striking examples of success are illustrated, but in which failures are rarely mentioned, or, if mentioned, are explained with a series of complex rationalizations. Thus, we may hear: "The technique is effective enough, but it is not designed for this particular individual (failure)," or, "This study doesn't really invalidate our approach. It just points up the need for a much longer experimental study," or, "Our program may be a statistical failure, but how can you judge a program by its failures! If one man was saved from a life of crime, then I consider it worthwhile."[19]

By hiding behind such rationalizations those responsible for treatment are seldom required to define their goals or to attempt to relate them systematically to their intervention techniques. Consequently, treatment may often pursue ends which may not be directly associated with lawbreaking, e.g.. personality adjustment, educational achievements, or the learning of handicraft or athletic skills. Perhaps this is what occurred in the Cambridge-Sommerville Study when the treatment group seemed to benefit in ways unrelated to lawbreaking. The recidivism rates of offenders were not appreciably changed, but certain qualititive adjustment differences occured.

If greater efforts were expended in the direction of carefully defining treatment goals and in attempting to show how they relate to lawbreaking, research might then be able to indicate: (1) whether important goals were actually realized; and (2) whether, if they were realized, they helped to lower the recidivism rate. But, again, a systematic articulation and examination of goals depends upon the extent to which treatment is a function of logically integrated causation and intervention strategy. A conglomeration of unrelated activities is functional in maintaining vested interests because there is something in it for everyone. But it also makes a careful definition of goals difficult and effective evelation impossible.

[19] Cressey, "The Nature and Effectiveness of Correctional Techniques," *op. cit.*

DYSFUNCTIONS PERPETUATED BY THE RESEARCHER

Research personnel have also perpetuated dysfunctions with regard to effective treatment evaluation. The following are some of the more important ways in which they have done this.

The Emphasis on "Pure" Research

It has become traditional among many social scientists to question the scientific objectivity of any individual who becomes involved in an action program.[20] This tradition is not without some validity. William Grahams Sumner pointed out, early in the development of American sociology, the difficulty of discussing and criticizing any social system of which one is an intimate part.[21]

But this tradition is dysfunctional for scientific penology in at least three ways: (1) It does not take into account advancements in such fields as Anthropology, Psychology, and Sociology, which give the modern social scientist considerable insight into social-psychological mechanisms and the relativity of any approach to treatment, (2) It separates the researcher from intimate contact with the subjects of his study, and, while he may have contributed to an understanding of the causes for delinquency, he is dependent upon the intuitive interpretations of the clinician for information regarding both the usefulness of his theory and its application in the treatment process, (3) It removes him from the process of planning and evaluating the early stages of any research project—that is, he is seldom involved in helping to integrate logically the intervention strategy with the theory of causation, with helping to define and examine the treatment role, and with defining treatment goals in such a way that they can be evaluated. Thus, he usually enters the picture late in the process in an attempt to evaluate a program that he knows relatively little about. His principal recourse is to make a statistical comparison of groups or to do post-mortem interviews with treaters and subjects. However, as suggested above, such techniques may be notoriously inadequate.[22]

In the absence of specific information about the treatment process, the researcher is incapable of determining the errors or strengths in the intervention strategy or errors or strengths in the way the strategy is applied. Consider the following example from the author's own experience.

---

[20] See the discussion of Max Weber by Harry E. Barnes and Howard Becker, *Social Thought From Lore to Science,* New York: D. C. Health & Co., 1938, II. pp. 896–898; and Donald R. Cressey, "Changing Criminals: The Application of the Theory of Differential Association," *The American Journal of Sociology,* 61(July, 1955), p. 116, who says " . . . Sociology is essentially a research discipline . . . " For opinions to the contrary see Robert S. Lynd, *Knowledge for What,* Princeton University Press, 1939; and Edward A. Shils, "Social Inquiry and the Autonomy of the Individual," in *The Human Meaning of the Social Sciences,* ed. by Daniel Lerner, New York: Meridian Books, Inc., 1959.

[21] William G. Sumner, *Folkways,* Boston, 1907, pp. 97–98.

[22] See also Tueber, *op. cit.,* p. 141, who discusses the weaknesses of interviewing with delinquents.

An offender, two months after release from the Provo Experiment in Delinquency Rehabilitation,[23] burglarized a home with his younger brother and stole $380. Yet, at the time of his release there was little question in anyone's mind that this boy would be a success. The therapist in charge of the boy's daily therapy group, as a part of the research evaluation, predicted that the boy would be a success. Likewise, the interviewer who gave him his release interview was impressed with his acuity and perceptiveness. He was able to verbalize well about the treatment system: The stages of development through which his group had gone, the importance of his own ability to help other boys and be helped in return, the changes in his friendship and familial relationships, and his feelings about himself. After he had gotten into trouble, however, a careful look at the treatment process was in order. Fortunately, some data were available.

The following is one example of the types of information that were revealed. One of the basic assumptions for treatment in the program was never utilized as a part of the boy's treatment experience. This assumption involved anxiety and suggested that because most habitual delinquents are affectively and ideologicaly dedicated to the delinquent system, they must be made anxious about the ultimate utility of that system for them. Several things revealed, however, that this boy had never really been made uncomfortable in his entire stay in the program. It seemed likely that he had never been forced by a feeling of necessity to examine himself deeply or to evaluate realistically the implications of continued delinquent behavior. In summary, it appeared that the role of the therapist had not been adequately filled.

Such a finding does not, by itself, constitute a complete answer as to why the boy failed. It does suggest, however, at least two important things: (1) that so long as the therapist does not perform consitently with the theory of intervention, treatment technique designed to test that theory will not be adequately examined; and (2) that if the program had relied solely on the therapist's subjective interpretation or upon the researcher's statistical analysis this and other factors contributing to an understanding of the boy's failure would have remained undetected. An emphasis on "pure" research at the expense of an intimate surveillance of the treatment process leaves too many unanswerable questions.

Inadequate Knowledge of Treatment for Predictive Purposes

The greater portion of research in penology has concentrated upon "objective" variables—work reports, length of stay, job prospectus, etc.—as a means of measuring success or failure on parole. In terms of the ideological conflict between researcher and treater, this concentration is the counterpart of the treater's resistance to a rigorous evaluation of the treatment process *per se*. Although "objective" variables are important because of their impact on the offender, they

---

[23] Lamar T. Empey and Jerome Rabow, "The Provo Experiment in Delinquency Rehabilitation," *American Sociological Review*, 26 (Oct., 1961), pp. 679–696.

can be seen, when viewed in terms of the theoretical scheme mentioned earlier, as variables which *impinge* upon treatment but are not always a function of it. Therefore, predictions based upon them do not include any information on, or evaluation of, the very variables—i.e., those which *are* a direct function of some treatment technique, which, according to the treater, are most important in changing people. Consequently, most predictions are based on a segment of variables which affect the offender, not upon a total configuration.[24]

Any prediction based upon the results of a particular treatment process can only follow a systematic articulation and understanding of that treatment process. But the researcher seems to have accepted the clinician's premise that therapy, like true art, consists, of the "concealment of all of the signs and efforts of the art."[25]

Treatment, the clinician asserts, is an ongoing process: It is a dynamic and subjective experience for everyone involved. How, therefore, can it be systematically codified and articulated? Furthermore, the relationship between counselor and counselee is a subtle but indispensable variable which is of value in and of itself. These delicate but important variables, he maintains, cannot be evaluated except intuitively. Consequently, any predictions based upon them must likewise be intuitive.

Apparently, it has been functional for the researcher to accept this point of view. But, as a result, he and the clinician have ended up using two different frames of reference in evaluating treatment. The researcher uses statistical data and "objective" variables whwich are not always shown to have a clear connection with the treatment process. And the clinician has utilized subjective interpretations based upon his feelings for what has occurred in therapy. By contrast, there are research findings in the behavioral sciences which suggest that if treatment techniques, *per se*, were productively analyzed, predictions could be based on them *and* "objective" variables as well. The two would constitute a larger body of empirical data from which to make predictions. For example, in addition to controlling such "objective" variables as marital status, job outlook, length of stay, etc., the total treatment setting might be examined as a social system in which participants develop and are guided by a shared set of values, norms, status-roles, and sanctions; the types of treatment interaction thought most productive could be defined and the actual behavior during treatment sessions analyzed to see whether interaction conforms to these standards; or "stimulated recall"[26] might be conducted on subjects following treatment sessions as a means

[24] The importance of having descriptive information on particular types of populations has been cited recently by Paul Meehl and Edward Rosen. See "Antecedent Probability and the Efficiency of Psychometric Signs, Pattern or Cutting Scores," *Psychological Bulletin,* 1958, pp. 199–211.

[25] Merton, *op, cit.,* p. 14.

[26] Eugene L. Gaier, "When They're Not Talking," *Adult Leadership,* I, No. 10 (March, 1953), pp. 28–29; Eugene L. Gaier, "Memory Under Conditions of Stimulated Recall," *The Journal of General Psychology,* 50 (1954), pp. 147–153; B. S. Bloom, "The Thought Process of Students in Discussion," in *Accent On Teaching,* ed. by Sidney J. Flinch, Harper and Bros., 1954, Chap. 1.

of understanding their reactions—whether for example, they are actually experiencing treatment in the way the treater thinks they are experiencing it.

Many things might be done, but so long as the researcher prefers to examine variables traditionally defined as "objective," and leaves predictions based upon the treatment process to the subjective interpretations of the therapist, his behavior will be dysfunctional for the development of a scientific penology.

SUMMMARY AND CONCLUSION

The foregoing analysis suggests that a successful bridging of the ideological gulf between researcher and treater might contribute significantly to the development of a scientific penology. It is recognized, of course, that efforts to eliminate this gulf in ongoing penal systems will not be simple. In those systems where punitive methods are still in practice, research poses as much a threat to those in control as it does to the clinician in treatment-centered systems. However, since the primary purpose of this paper has been to point out the dysfunctions which are perpetuated by the gulf, it would be hoped that future analyses could be devoted to defining, in detail, steps by which a new research-treatment role might be implemented in both types of systems.

A summary of that which has been emphasized in this paper would seem to include two important points:

Research Model

An effective analysis of any treatment system requires an integration of research and treatment efforts. At the very onset this would require a union of researcher and treater on theoretical matters. It would seem impossible to conduct effective evaluation unless the researcher participated intimately with the treater in defining goals in terms of a logical integration of causation theory, intervention strategy, and treatment roles. Therefore, cooperation between these two parties would permit the treater to enter into the problems associated with Stages I and III of the Research Model (the selection and comparison of treatment and control groups) and would permit entry of the researcher into problems associated with State II (the actual treatment process). The researcher could help to operationalize treatment techniques and goals, and the treater could illustrate some of the complexities of the treatment process.

Statistical findings on the success or failure of any program (Stage III) could best be understood if data were available by which to establish whether the causation theory or the actual treatment techniques used (Stage II) were responsible for any differences that were found, or whether one must look to other variables impinging upon treatment for explanations. Such differences could be due to variables which are not a direct function of treatment. If this is the case they must be discovered.

Communication and the Avoidance of Anxiety

The second point in bridging the gulf between treater and researcher has to do with the importance of maintaining treater-researcher communication and responsibility regarding research findings.

The goal would be two-fold: (1) to approach current techniques with a disciplined skepticism—that is, any treatment technique would be viewed as an hypothesis to be examined rather than a method based upon absolute knowledge; and (2) to give both parties a greater stake in the development of new knowledge about treatment techniques rather than in the perpetuation of traditional vested interests.

A new and shared vested interest, based upon a desire for new knowledge, would help to reduce anxiety on the treater's part over any results which discredit his technique. Instead of threatening him with economic and prestige problems as though his practices were of an all-or-none variety, he, along with the researcher, would be called upon to revise techniques or develop new ones.

This, of course, would not eliminate anxiety, only modify it. Now, however, both could be more concerned with the dimension of discovery; that is, with the problem of knowing what is really happening to inmates as a result of treatment practices rather than with the maintenance of power in the correctional structure. The latter type of anxiety could only be reduced by a scientific approach to the understanding and improvement of rehabilitative techniques.

The field of corrections is now at a stage where the humanitarian concern for the welfare of prisoners by professionals needs to be at least partially supplanted by a disciplined, scientific orientation. The alternatives open to society and those working with offenders are limited. What can be done with hard-core offenders except to: destroy them, incarcerate them permanently, or rehabilitate them? The tendency among most people has been toward the latter alternative. However, so long as the vested interest of research and treatment personnel continue to pursue divergent goals, it will be difficult to establish a scientific penology by which reliable answers can be discovered On the other hand, the welding of research and treatment roles might constitute one step towards a comprehensive understanding of, and fruitful approach to the problems involved.

The exclusive focus on the field of corrections in this paper is a function of the author's experience in that area. I suspect, however, that the problems described above occur in such diversified fields as education, social work, administration and governmental planning. The prerequisites of organizational maintenance seem to necessitate these conflicts and problems. The solution would seem to be not only to call for the development of closer, working relationships, but to institutionalize the training and organization of individuals who can work effectively within both organizational contexts.

Index

865